KEEPER OF THE LOST CITIES

LODESTAR

Also by Shannon Messenger

KEEPER
OF THE
LOST CITIES
LODESTAR

SHANNON MESSENGER

SIMON & SCHUSTER

For Katie and Jo,
who bring new meaning to the words
"above and beyond"

First published in Great Britain in 2020 by Simon & Schuster UK Ltd

First published in the USA in 2016 by Aladdin, an imprint of
Simon & Schuster Children's Publishing Division

3 5 7 9 10 8 6 4 2

Simon & Schuster UK Ltd
1st Floor, 222 Gray's Inn Road
London
WC1X 8HB

www.simonandschuster.co.uk
www.simonandschuster.com.au
www.simonandschuster.co.in

Simon & Schuster Australia, Sydney
Simon & Schuster India, New Delhi

A CIP catalogue record for this book is available from the British Library.

PB ISBN 978-1-4711-8945-6
eBook ISBN 978-1-4711-8946-3

Printed and bound by CPI Group (UK) Ltd, Croydon, CR0 4YY

PREFACE

THIS IS WHAT THEY WANT.

The words tumbled through Sophie's mind as she raced up the spiral staircase, counting her steps, trying to guess which door to take.

The first handle she tried was locked.

Another opened into darkness.

A third revealed a path that glowed with eerie blue balefire sconces.

The floor shook as she hesitated and threads of dust slipped through the ceiling, scratching her throat and making it hurt to breathe.

She followed the flames.

Back and forth the halls snaked—a careful maze, designed to deceive. Swallow. Separate.

The tremors grew with every step, the shifting subtle but unmistakable.

And too far away.

No one else would feel the ripples swelling, like waves gathering speed.

They were too focused on their celebration.

Too caught up in their imagined victory.

Too trusting.

Too blind.

Too late.

The ground rattled harder, the first fissures crackling the stones.

This is what they want.

ONE

THIS IS A SECURITY NIGHTMARE!"
Sandor grumbled, keeping his huge gray hand
poised over his enormous black sword.

His squeaky voice reminded Sophie more of
a talking mouse than a deadly bodyguard.

Several prodigies raced past, and Sandor pulled Sophie
closer as the giggling group jumped to pop the candy-filled
bubbles floating near the shimmering crystal trees. All around
them, kids were running through the confetti-covered atrium
in their amber-gold Level Three uniforms, capes flying as they
caught snacks and bottles of lushberry juice and stuffed tinsel-
wrapped gifts into the long white thinking caps dangling from
everyone's lockers.

The Midterms Celebration was a Foxfire Academy tradition—hardly the impending doom Sandor was imagining. And yet, Sophie understood his concern.

Every parent roaming the streamer-lined halls.

Every face she didn't recognize.

Any of them could be a rebel.

A villain.

The enemy.

Sandor watched Sophie tug on her eyelashes—her nervous habit, back in full force. "Nothing is going to happen," he promised, tucking her blond hair behind her ear with a surprisingly gentle touch for a seven-foot-tall goblin warrior.

It definitely helped having Sandor back at her side—especially after almost losing him during the battle on Mount Everest. And Sandor wasn't the only goblin at Foxfire anymore. Each of the six wings in the main campus building had been assigned its own patrol, with two additional squadrons keeping watch over the sprawling grounds.

The Council had also added security throughout the Lost Cities.

They had to.

The ogres were still threatening war.

And in the three weeks since Sophie and her friends had returned from hiding with the Black Swan, the Neverseen had scorched the main gate of the Sanctuary *and* broken into the registry in Atlantis.

4

Sophie could guess what the rebels had hoped to gain from the elves' secret animal preserve—they obviously didn't know that she'd convinced the Council to set the precious alicorns free. But the registry attack remained a mystery. The Councillors kept careful records on every elf ever born, and no one would tell her if any files had been altered or stolen.

A bubble popped on Sophie's head, and Sandor caught the box of Prattles that had been hovering inside.

"If you're going to eat these, I should check them first," he told her.

Sandor's wide, flat nose scented no toxins in the nutty candy, but he insisted on examining the pin before handing them over. Every box of Prattles came with a special collectible inside, and in the past, the Black Swan had used them to send Sophie messages.

He fished out the tiny velvet pouch and Sophie caught herself clutching her allergy remedy necklace. She still kept the silver moonlark pin that Calla had given her attached to the cord—a reminder of the friend she'd lost, and a symbol of the role she needed to figure out how to play.

"Looks like we're good," Sandor said, handing her the small boobrie pin—a strange black bird with bright yellow tail feathers. "Can't imagine *that* means anything important."

Sophie couldn't either. Especially since the Black Swan had been annoyingly silent.

No notes. No clues. No answers during their brief meetings.

Apparently they were "regrouping." And it was taking forever.

At least the Council was doing *something*—setting up goblin patrols and trying to arrange an ogre Peace Summit. The Black Swan should at least be . . .

Actually, Sophie didn't know what they should be doing.

That was the problem with having her friend join the enemy.

"There you are!" a familiar voice said behind her. "I was starting to think you'd ditched us."

The deep, crisp accent was instantly recognizable. And yet, the teasing words made Sophie wish she'd turn and find a different boy.

Fitz looked as cute as ever in his red Level Five uniform, but his perfect smile didn't reach his trademark teal eyes. The recent revelations had been a huge blow for all of her friends, but Fitz had taken it the hardest.

Both his brother and his best friend had run off with the Neverseen.

Alvar's betrayal had made Fitz wary—made him doubt every memory.

But Keefe's?

He wouldn't talk about it—at *all*.

Not that Sophie had many chances to bring up the subject. Only a handful of people knew the truth. The rest believed the Black Swan's carefully crafted lie, and thought Keefe was taking time away to mourn his mother's disappearance. Even the

Council had no inkling, and Sophie hoped it would stay that way. The less everyone knew, the easier it would be for Keefe to come home.

If he came home.

"You okay?" Fitz asked, making her realize she'd forgotten to say hello. "I hope you're not worrying about your tests. There's no way you didn't pass."

"I don't know . . ."

Her photographic memory *helped*—but lately she'd struggled to concentrate during her school sessions. Honestly, though, she'd barely given her midterms a second thought. She wasn't the same girl she'd been the year before, who thought failing out of Foxfire would be the end of the world. Now she'd been kidnapped, presumed dead, banished from the Lost Cities, and helped stop a plague from killing off the entire gnomish species. She'd even snuck into the ogres' capital and helped destroy half the city—which happened to be why the Council was struggling to negotiate a new elvin-ogre treaty.

"Relax," Fitz said as her mind spun to nightmares of lumpy-faced ogres tearing through the elves' glittering streets. "We're supposed to be celebrating."

His cheer sounded forced. But she knew Fitz was trying.

That's what they did now.

Try.

Wait.

Hope.

"Just let me grab my thinking cap," she told him, heading for her locker. The long floppy hat was required during midterms, designed to restrict Telepaths and preserve the integrity of the tests—not that anything could block Sophie's enhanced abilities. But after the exams, the hats became present sacks, and everyone filled them with treats and trinkets and treasures.

"I'll need to inspect your presents before you open them," Sandor warned as he helped Sophie lift her overstuffed hat.

"That's perfect," Fitz said. "While he does that, you can open mine."

He pulled a small box from the pocket of his waist-length cape and handed it to Sophie. The opalescent wrapping paper had flecks of teal glitter dusted across it, and he'd tied it with a silky teal bow, making her wonder if he'd guessed her favorite color.

She really hoped he couldn't guess why. . . .

"Hopefully I did better this year," Fitz said. "Biana claimed the riddler was a total fail."

The riddle-writing pen he'd given her last time *had* been a disappointment, but . . .

"I'm sure I'll love it," Sophie promised. "Besides. My gift is boring."

Sandor had declared an Atlantis shopping trip to be far too risky, so Sophie had spent the previous day baking her friends' presents.

She handed Fitz a round silver tin and he popped the lid off immediately.

"Ripplefluffs?" he asked, smiling his first real smile in days.

The silver-wrapped treats were what might happen if a brownie and a cupcake had a fudgey, buttery baby, with a candy surprise sunken into the center. Sophie's adoptive mother, Edaline, had taught her the recipe and helped her invent two flavor combinations.

"How did you know that chocolate and mint is my favorite?" Fitz asked, peeling off the silver wrapper and devouring the whole fluff in one bite.

"I didn't," Sophie admitted. "If I had, I wouldn't have given you any of the butter toffee ones."

"Those look amazing too," he said, then frowned at his present. "Aren't you going to open it?"

"Shouldn't I wait until we're with the others?"

"Nah. It'll be better if it's just the two of us."

Something about the way he said it made her heart switch to flutter mode, even though she knew Fitz didn't think of her that way. Her mind raced through a dozen theories as she carefully tore the shimmering paper. But she still wasn't prepared to find . . .

"Rings?"

"They go on your thumbs," Fitz explained. "It's a Cognate thing."

She wasn't sure what thumb jewelry had to do with their

rare telepathic connection. But she noticed Fitz was wearing an identical set. Each ring had initials stamped into the verdigris metal. *SEF* on the right—Sophie Elizabeth Foster—and *FAV* on the left.

"Fitzroy Avery Vacker."

"Your full name is Fitzroy?" she asked.

"Yeah. No idea what my parents were thinking with that one. But watch this. Try opening your thoughts to mine, and then do this."

He held his hands palm-out, waiting for her to do the same.

As soon as she did, the rings turned warm against her skin and snapped their hands together like magnets.

"They're made from ruminel," Fitz said, "which reacts to mental energy. It doesn't change anything, but it'll show us when our minds are connected, and I thought it would help us concentrate and . . ." His voice trailed off. "You hate them, don't you?"

"Of course not!"

She liked them a little too much, actually.

She was just trying not to show it.

There were a lot of kids staring at them.

And whispering.

And giggling.

Fitz twisted his palms, breaking the rings' connection. "I guess I should've gone with the necklace Biana showed me. You just have so many necklaces—and the last one you got . . ."

He didn't finish the sentence.

It would've meant mentioning Keefe.

"I'm glad you got me these. Seriously. They're my fave." She pointed to the "FAV."

That earned her another smile, and Fitz brushed his dark hair off his forehead. "Come on, I'm sure Dex and Biana are getting sick of waiting for us."

"Where did Grizel go?" Sandor asked as they turned to leave. "She's supposed to stay by your side."

"I'm right here," a husky female voice said as a lithe gray goblin in a fitted black jumpsuit seemed to melt out of the shadows. Fitz's bodyguard was just as tall as Sandor, but far leaner—and what she lacked in bulk she made up for in stealth and grace.

"I swear," she said, tapping Sandor on the nose. "It's almost too easy to evade you."

"Anyone can hide in this chaos," Sandor huffed. "And now is not the time for games!"

"There's always time for games." Grizel tossed her long ponytail in a way that almost seemed . . . Was it flirty?

Sandor must've noticed too, because his gray skin tinted pink. He cleared his throat and turned to Sophie. "Weren't we heading to the cafeteria?"

She nodded and followed Fitz into the mazelike halls, where the colorful crystal walls shimmered in the afternoon sunlight. The cafeteria was on the second floor of the campus's five-story glass pyramid, which sat in the center of the courtyard framed by the U-shaped main building.

Sophie spent most of the walk wondering how long it would take Dex to notice her new accessories. The answer was three seconds—and another after that to notice the matching rings on Fitz's thumbs.

His periwinkle eyes narrowed, but he kept his voice cheerful as he said, "I guess we're all giving rings this year."

Biana held out her hand to show Sophie a ring that looked familiar—probably because Sophie had a less sparkly, slightly more crooked, definitely less pink version on her own finger.

"I also made one for you," Dex told Fitz. "It's in your thinking cap. And I have some for Tam and Linh, whenever we see them again. That way we'll all have panic switches—and I added stronger trackers, so I can home in on the signal even if you don't press your stone. Just in case anything weird happens."

"Your Technopath tricks aren't necessary," Sandor told him, pointing to their group of bodyguards—four goblins in all.

"But it's still good to have a backup plan, right?" Biana asked, admiring her ring from another angle. The pink stone matched the glittery shadow she'd brushed around her teal eyes, as well as the gloss on her heart-shaped lips. Biana reminded Sophie of the dolls her human parents had tried to get her to play with as a kid—too beautiful and stylish to be real.

"Thank you again," Biana told Dex. "I'm never taking it off!"

Dex's cheeks turned the same color as his strawberry-blond hair.

Sophie smiled, glad to see Dex and Biana getting along so well—especially after all the years Dex had spent resenting the Vackers. He used to call Fitz "Wonderboy" and claimed their legendary family was too snobby and perfect.

Nobody thought that anymore.

In fact, both Fitz's and Biana's thinking caps looked emptier than they'd been the previous year. Their parents had decided not to let the Black Swan cover for Alvar's disappearance like they'd done for Keefe. Alvar had lied for more than a decade and used his position in the nobility to spy on his father and the Council—and helped kidnap Sophie and Dex. He didn't deserve protection, even if it brought undeserved shame on the family.

Awkward silence settled over their table and Sophie tried not to look at the empty chairs. Not only was Keefe missing, but Jensi had chosen to sit with his old friends. He'd reconnected with them during the months that Sophie and the others had lived with the Black Swan, and he seemed reluctant to come back, like he was worried they'd abandon him again. Marella was avoiding them too—though she also wasn't at Stina Heks's table, like Sophie would've expected. Marella sat by herself in the farthest corner, while Stina sat with Biana's former best friend, Maruca.

Stina caught Sophie watching her and didn't return her

smile—but she didn't offer her usual glare either. Apparently that was as nice as Stina was going to get, now that her dad was working with the Black Swan.

"Here," Dex said, placing a white box into Sophie's hands. "Made this for you—and sorry it's not wrapped. Rex and Bex used up all the ribbon tying Lex to a chandelier."

Dex's younger triplet siblings were notorious troublemakers. Sophie had a feeling the loudest shouting on the other end of the cafeteria was coming from them. And she'd expected to open the box and find another Dex-ified gadget. But his gift reminded her that he was also an amazing alchemist.

"You made me Panakes perfume?" she asked, shaking the fragile crystal bottle and watching the pinkish-purplish-bluish petals swirl through the shimmering syrup.

She twisted open the top and closed her eyes as she inhaled the rich, sweet fragrance. Instantly she was back in the Havenfield pastures, standing under the swaying branches of Calla's tree. A Panakes only grew when a gnome willingly surrendered their life and shifted into their final tree form. Calla had made the sacrifice for her people, to let her healing blossoms end the deadly plague the ogres had unleashed.

"I'm sure you smell them all the time," Dex said, "but I know how much you miss her. And this way, when you wear the perfume, you're keeping a small part of her with you everywhere you go."

Sophie's voice failed her, so she grabbed Dex and hugged him

14

as tight as she could—but she *might've* held on a bit too long. When she let go, Dex was redder than Fitz's school uniform.

They were saved from the awkwardness by the doors to the cafeteria bursting open.

Despite her earlier calm, Sophie's palms turned clammy as she searched the flood of parents for Grady and Edaline. She spotted Grady's tousled blond hair first, and as soon as his bright blue eyes met hers, his chiseled features curved with an enormous smile.

"Passed with flying colors," he and Edaline both shouted as Sophie raced across the room to meet them.

She threw her arms around both her parents. "Even linguistics?"

That had been her iffyest subject—by far. Being a Polyglot made her naturally understand languages, but after the trick Keefe had pulled, Sophie refused to practice mimicking voices. Plus, her relationship with her Mentor was . . . complicated. Lady Cadence had a special affinity for the ogres, and was *not* happy with Sophie for helping flood the ogre capital.

"That was your lowest score," Edaline admitted, shaking a piece of her wavy amber-colored hair out of her eyes. "But you were still well within passing range."

"And your highest score was inflicting," Grady added. "Councillor Bronte said you've been incredibly dedicated during your sessions. In fact, he said you've now reached his most advanced level of training."

"Is that bad?" Sophie asked, not missing his raised eyebrow. She didn't *like* inflicting pain—but the ability had saved her life. And training at least gave her *something* she could do to prepare for the next time she faced off with the Neverseen. "I just want to make sure I can defend myself—and I know I have Sandor. But it's not like he's invincible. Isn't it smart to plan for the worst-case scenario?"

"It *is* smart," Grady agreed. "But I also think you and I should talk later. Okay?"

Sophie gave him half a nod. The last thing she wanted was another "with great power comes great responsibility" lecture. But she was pretty sure it was unavoidable.

"Do you guys want to go?" she asked, knowing her parents weren't fans of crowds. Before she'd moved in with them, Grady and Edaline had spent sixteen years hiding away, mourning the death of their only daughter. Jolie had been killed in a fire they'd recently discovered was set by her fiancé, Brant—a secret Pyrokinetic, and a leader of the Neverseen.

"We're fine," Grady promised, squeezing Sophie's hand. "And we can't leave until Magnate Leto makes his final announcement."

He said the name so easily, without tripping over it the way Sophie tended to. Now that she knew his secret identity, her brain always wanted to call him *Mr. Forkle*.

Sophie scanned the room to check for her friends and found them smiling and celebrating. Even Alden and Della—Fitz and Biana's parents—looked happier than she'd seen them in weeks. She was on her way to say hi when the lights dimmed and Magnate Leto's face projected across the glass walls.

"You kids did an excellent job on your midterms!" he said, starting his speech with his two favorite words.

No matter how many times Sophie studied his slicked dark hair and sharp features, she still couldn't see the bloated, wrinkled face of the Black Swan leader behind them. But she'd watched Mr. Forkle's ruckleberry disguise fade right before her eyes.

"I realize this is usually the point where you're dismissed for a six-week break," Magnate Leto continued, "but in light of recent events, the Council has elected to do things a bit differently. I won't go into further details—the Council will be sending out official scrolls after the weekend. But I wanted to mention it now so you'd be prepared. In the meantime, enjoy the rest of the celebration. And remember, change can be a powerful, inspiring thing when we keep an open mind."

Murmurs turned to a roar as his projection flashed away, leaving everyone debating possibilities.

"Do you have any idea what he's talking about?" Grady asked Sophie.

She didn't—and that made it even more frustrating. After all the debates she'd had with the Black Swan, all her endless pleas for them to include her and trust her, they still insisted on keeping her at arm's length.

"Looks like everyone's heading home," Grady said, offering to gather up Sophie's gifts while she returned her thinking cap to her locker.

The atrium was empty when she arrived—just Sophie and Sandor and a few forgotten candy bubbles. She left her hat on the middle shelf of her locker and was about to walk away when she noticed a white envelope bearing a familiar curved black symbol on the top shelf.

"Finally," she whispered, ripping the thick paper right through the sign of the swan.

Inside she found a short note—and a gift.

She slipped the long necklace around her neck, not bothering to inspect the pendant's swan-neck shape, or the round piece of glass set in the center. The Black Swan had given her the same monocle when she swore fealty to their order, and she was glad to have a replacement for the one Brant had destroyed.

"What does the note say?" Sandor asked, reminding her that she would not be sneaking off for secret assignments without him.

She handed him the paper, which was more direct than the Black Swan's usual clues:

Principal's office.
Now.
Come alone.

"I don't like this," Sandor mumbled.

"You never do."

He followed her without further comment as she made her way back to the glass pyramid. Sophie kept her eyes down as she walked, relieved when she reached the apex without running into her friends. If they'd known about the note they would've *insisted* on joining her.

"You may come in, Miss Foster," Magnate Leto's deep voice called through the heavy door before Sophie could even knock. "But I'd like Sandor to keep watch outside. This conversation cannot tolerate eavesdroppers."

Sandor's sigh sounded like a snarl. "I'll be *right* outside— and if you leap away without me, there will be *consequences*."

"Close the door behind you," Magnate Leto told her as she entered, the words echoing around the glass office.

Afternoon sunlight streamed through the windows, turning the triangular room blindingly bright. The sloped glass walls had mirrors set into every other pane, remnants from the days when Councillor Alina—Sophie's least favorite Councillor— was principal of Foxfire.

"I'm glad you came," Magnate Leto said from the other side of his huge swiveling desk chair. He was turned toward the windows, hidden behind the stiff winged-back cushion. "Sorry my note was so hasty. Next time I'll make sure it rhymes."

The last few words sounded higher pitched, and Sophie was

trying to figure out why when the chair slowly spun around to face her.

Instead of the dark-haired elf she'd been expecting, she found a boy dressed all in black, with artfully styled blond hair and an infamous talent for mimicking voices.

"Keefe?" she whispered.

He smirked. "Did you miss me?"

TWO

W

HOA, THAT IS AN EPIC wave of emotions you're hitting me with," Keefe said, fanning the air between them. "It feels like you either want to hug me or strangle me—and personally, I'm rooting for the hug."

He leaned back in the chair, stretching his arms wide open.

"You're really going to joke about this?" Sophie asked, trying to keep her voice low. She didn't want Sandor bursting in until she'd gotten some answers.

"Don't come any closer," she warned as Keefe stood to approach her. "I've been practicing inflicting. A *lot*."

One hand moved to her stomach, rubbing the knot of

emotions lodged under her ribs. Bronte was teaching her to tie them away, ready to unravel whenever she needed a burst of furious power.

Keefe's smile faded. "Are you *afraid* of me?"

"You're the Empath."

The words hung there for several seconds, turning heavier and heavier.

Keefe sank back into his chair. "Wow . . . I didn't expect that."

"What *did* you expect? You ran off with the Neverseen! You realize those are the people trying to kill me, right? The same people who killed Kenric and Jolie, and almost killed all of the gnomes and—"

"I *know*," Keefe interrupted. "But you know me, Foster."

"I thought I did."

"You *do*. I'm still the same guy. All I'm trying to do is end this nightmare. If I can figure out what they're planning—"

"Nope," Sophie jumped in. "Worst idea ever. Playing both sides never works. Sooner or later they're going to make you *commit*."

Keefe shifted in his seat. "I realize that what I'm doing is risky—"

"And stupid," Sophie added. "And dangerous. And—"

"I still have to do it. And it'll be fine. It's all about keeping the right balance."

"There's no *balance* when it comes to the bad guys, Keefe. They're bad. It's that simple."

"You and I both know it's *never* simple. In fact, I seem to remember you telling me that the villains are never *all* bad."

"I didn't say that because I wanted you to join them! I said that's what makes them so scary!"

"I know. But . . . I have a plan. I have to stick to it."

His ice-blue eyes met hers, pleading for understanding.

She shook her head. "We can beat them together. Team Foster-Keefe, remember?"

"And how many times will you almost die in the process?" he asked. "How many emergency physician visits will there be? And what if Elwin can't fix you?"

"What if Elwin can't fix *you*?"

"I . . . don't matter."

And there it was.

Keefe's *guilt*.

The most dangerous emotion an elf could feel.

Most were crippled by it. Alden's sanity had once shattered because of it. But for some people it made them *reckless*.

"It's not your job to protect me," she told him.

"Maybe not. But if something happens . . ."

She waited for him to say the rest—the real reason he felt so responsible. When he didn't, she said it for him.

"I know you blame yourself for what your mom's done—"

"This isn't about her!"

But it was.

Sophie knew him too well.

Keefe's family life had always been miserable, thanks to his stiff, insulting father. But he'd been on a downward spiral ever since he'd discovered that his mom was one of the leaders of the Neverseen. She'd even erased some of his childhood memories and hidden a tracker in his family crest pin so he'd lead the Neverseen straight to his friends. But that was all before the Neverseen left her to die in an ogre prison as punishment for allowing one of her cohorts to be captured.

Keefe kept claiming he didn't care. But Lady Gisela was still his mom—and he'd joined the Neverseen right after he found out they might be willing to help him rescue her.

"Please," Sophie begged. "We can do anything they can do. Just come home—before it's too late."

"It's already too late."

His voice was the same flat tone he'd used before, when he'd told her *I can't pretend I'm who you want me to be anymore.*

"So this is about the Lodestar Initiative, then?" she asked.

She'd only heard the mysterious project mentioned twice—once from the Neverseen and once in Keefe's mind, in a memory his mother had tried to erase. It seemed to be the Neverseen's grand plan. And Keefe believed he was a part of it.

Keefe stood to pace the small room, keeping a careful space between them.

"What *is* the Lodestar Initiative?" she pressed. "And what other lost memories did you recover? You said there were more."

"It doesn't matter."

"Obviously it does."

Keefe tilted his head toward the ceiling, his eyes focused on the highest point. "All you need to know is that I'm not like you, okay? The Neverseen aren't going to give me a choice."

Sophie was part of a project too—the Black Swan's Project Moonlark. They'd genetically enhanced her abilities and filled her mind with important secrets for reasons they'd still never fully explained. But Mr. Forkle had always made it clear that any further involvement was up to *her*.

"There's always a choice, Keefe."

"Yeah—I'm going to find a way to end this on *my* terms. *That's* my choice."

Silence swelled between them, and Sophie played with the monocle pendant he'd included with the note. "Was this the one that Brant ordered you to brand me with?"

Keefe cringed. "No. That one's mine. I stole it back."

"What happens when they notice it's gone?"

He shrugged.

She sighed. "This is never going to work, Keefe. Brant and Fintan are crazy—but they're not stupid. Neither is Alvar. One of them is going to figure out what you're doing, and then who knows how they'll punish you? Just quit now and we'll come up with a new plan together."

She offered him her hand.

Keefe stared at it for so long Sophie's arm muscles began to ache.

"That's it?" she asked when he turned away. "You'd rather keep hurting the people who care about you?"

"I'm helping you!"

"And hurting us. Do you know what Fitz did when I told him you left?"

Keefe ran his hands through his hair, wrecking his careful style. "I'm guessing yelling was involved."

"That's what I'd been hoping for. But he didn't even raise his voice. He just looked away so I wouldn't see him crying. So did Biana. Even Dex teared up."

Seconds ticked by. Maybe minutes. It felt like forever before Keefe whispered, "What about you?"

"I cried harder than any of them," she admitted. "And then I got angry. You stole Kenric's cache from me. You mimicked my voice!"

The marble-size gadget held seven Forgotten Secrets—information deemed too dangerous for even the Council to know. Each Councillor had their own cache, and Kenric had asked Oralie to entrust Sophie with his when he died. Sophie had vowed to protect the cache with her life, and if she didn't get it back before the Council discovered it was missing . . .

"I also helped you escape," Keefe reminded her.

"Yeah, but you only made me one special bead. So what happens the next time the Neverseen find me? Or Dex? Or Fitz? Or Biana?"

"I'll find another way. I'm already working on a few things. And I only rigged one bead because I knew the Neverseen wouldn't fall for the same trick twice."

"I love how you keep talking about them like you're not one of them now."

"I'm *not*."

"Are you sure?"

She pointed to the patch on the sleeves of his long black cloak, the same symbol that kept haunting her nightmares—a white eye set in a circle.

"This is just a costume," Keefe insisted.

"Even if it is, the things you're doing are *real*. That cache could destroy everything. And you handed it over like it was no big deal—"

"Because it wasn't! They can't open it. They've had all their Technopaths working on it, and they can't break through the security."

"And when they finally figure it out?"

"I'll steal it back long before that happens. I can handle this, Sophie. It's my *legacy*."

"What does that mean?"

"I'm still putting all the pieces together. But I know enough to know I have to do this. And my plan is already working. Every day they're trusting me a little bit more."

"Why is that?" she snapped. "What horrible things are they making you do to prove yourself?"

Keefe tried to pace again, but she blocked his path. "Did you help them break into the registry?"

"Of course not."

"Because they didn't ask you? Or because you told them 'no'?"

His fidgeting made her wish she didn't have to ask her next question.

"What about the Sanctuary?"

The Neverseen had spent months trying to break into the animal preserve to steal Silveny and Greyfell—the only known alicorns, who also happened to be Sophie and Keefe's friends.

"You were there, weren't you?" she asked when he moved away from her. "You helped the Neverseen burn the gate?"

"All I did was keep watch."

She shook her head. "How could you be a part of that?"

The Neverseen were willing to risk anything to steal Silveny. They'd even broken one of her wings. All because the elves believed that allowing a creature to go extinct would throw off the delicate balance of the entire planet. Whoever controlled the last two alicorns—and their unborn baby—could blackmail the Council. They'd also prove to the world how little the Council could do to protect something it cherished, and fuel the unrest threatening to boil over.

"I knew Silveny and Greyfell weren't there anymore," Keefe argued. "That's the only reason I agreed. And in case you're wondering, I haven't told the Neverseen *anything*."

"*Yet*," Sophie corrected. "Even if you don't tell them, they can use a Telepath to fish out all of your secrets."

"They don't have a Telepath right now. Gethen was their only one, and the Council has him locked away—thanks to *us*. I'm telling you, I've thought this through. I just need you to trust me."

She wanted to.

She really did.

She'd even done her best to convince Fitz, Dex, and Biana to not give up on him.

But she could still hear the Neverseen telling Keefe: *Surely you've realized that switching sides means betraying your friends.*

"Please," Keefe begged. "I promise, I'm still me. And I can do this."

He took a cautious step toward her.

Then another.

And another.

Until he was right in front of her, his lips curling with the world's saddest smile.

"Back to nervous habits, huh?" he asked as he brushed a fallen eyelash off her cheek.

"It's been a rough few weeks," she whispered.

"Yeah. It really has."

He blew the eyelash away and she wondered if he'd made a wish—until she remembered that elves didn't have silly superstitions like that.

She probably shouldn't either, but she went ahead and sent a silent plea into the universe.

"You're not still afraid of me, are you?" he asked. "You trust me?"

She honestly didn't know. So she offered him a shaky hand. "You tell me."

Keefe's fingers curled around hers and his brow creased as he closed his eyes.

"Thank you," he whispered, his lips stretching into a glorious smile. "I knew I could count on you, Foster."

"Don't make me regret it."

"I won't. That's why I came here today—I had to find a way to warn you. The Neverseen are planning something big. I don't know any specifics yet, but I know it involves Grady and Edaline and—whoa, easy there." He steadied her when her knees wobbled. "It's going to be okay. See why I'm doing this? I can stop things *before* they get bad."

Sophie took a slow, deep breath, trying to remind herself that Grady's ability as a Mesmer gave him an incredible advantage. She'd seen him make all twelve Councillors smack themselves in the face. He'd even made Brant burn off his own hand.

But the Neverseen were ruthless.

And clever.

And always ahead of the game.

Which made her realize . . .

"You can't go back there, Keefe. Today was probably a test. I bet they gave you that information to see if you'd sneak away to warn me. They could be tracking you right now—what?" she asked when she noticed how hard he was biting his lip.

"It's not a test. They . . . *sent* me here."

"Why would they do that?"

Keefe's eyes returned to the ceiling. "Probably because I suggested it. I needed a way to warn you—and they needed me to prove my loyalty. This was the best solution I could come up with."

Cold chills washed through Sophie as he removed two items from his cloak pocket—a flat golden triangle and a blue pendant with a single facet.

"This next part is going to be rough," he whispered. "But if you cover your face, I promise you'll be safe. And just in case . . ." He unfastened his cloak and wrapped it around her shoulders, pulling the hood up over her head. "I'll tell them I lost this in the chaos."

"What chaos, Keefe? What are you doing?"

"I'm helping you. Sometimes things have to get worse before they get better."

Sophie tried to shout for Sandor, but Keefe covered her mouth with one hand and flung the golden triangle toward the ceiling with the other. One of the points stuck to the center of the apex and the gadget flashed green.

"That means we have ten seconds." Keefe said. "Just get down and cover your face—everything is going to be okay.

Sandor will be safe. Goblins have super-thick skin—just trust me, okay?"

He pulled his hand back, but Sophie was shaking too hard to scream. She dropped to her knees and pulled the hood against her head.

"Please don't hate me," Keefe begged as he held his blue crystal up to the light to make a path. "Tell everyone I'll be back as soon as I finish this. And remember—I'm on your side."

He glittered away right as the green gadget turned red and a high-pitched squeal blasted from the ceiling, sending a rippling sound wave rushing down the walls.

Shattering all of the glass.

THREE

"IT'S NOT AS BAD AS IT SEEMS."

Magnate Leto had said the words a dozen times—and Sophie wanted to believe them. But all she could see were the slivers of glass glinting in his hair.

She was covered in them as well, but they were mostly stuck to Keefe's thick cloak. She'd been spared any cuts or scratches, just like he'd promised.

The glass pyramid hadn't been so fortunate. Magnate Leto's office was in shambles, its walls now empty metal frames. And while the rest of the pyramid had simply crackled and splintered, all of the glass would have to be replaced.

At least no one had been hurt—and the other buildings on

campus had been spared. But that didn't change the fact that the Neverseen had now attacked Foxfire.

And it had been Keefe's idea.

All twelve Councillors had visited the school to assess the damage, and questioned Sophie thoroughly. Then Magnate Leto had followed her home to get the *real* story.

The fading twilight glow seeped through Havenfield's glass walls, painting the elegant white décor of the main room in shades of purple, gray, and blue. Even with the soft shimmer from the twinkling chandeliers, Sophie felt like the whole world had been bruised.

"Truly, Miss Foster," Magnate Leto said as he plopped next to her on the plush sofa. "I've been meaning to redecorate my office since I took over as principal. I've never been a fan of my reflection—especially in this form."

Sophie shook her head. "You know this is about more than broken mirrors."

"She's right," Grady agreed, stalking down the curved staircase in the center of the room with Brielle—his svelte goblin bodyguard with tight curly hair—in tow. "This is about That Boy! I know he used to be your friend—"

"He *is* my friend," Sophie corrected.

And he was working with her enemies.

Grady crouched in front of her. "Whatever he is or isn't to you doesn't change the things he's doing." He plucked an especially jagged shard of glass off of her sleeve.

The razor-sharp edges would've shredded her skin if Keefe hadn't given her his cloak.

Then again, she wouldn't have needed it if he hadn't blown up the place.

She reached for Grady's hands. "I'm fine. And Keefe did this to warn us."

"That doesn't make destroying Foxfire okay!"

No, it didn't . . .

"Technically, he only destroyed my office," Magnate Leto argued. "And my own foolishness is partially to blame. I should've suspected something the moment I was called to the Level Five atrium to remove a pair of gremlins from the lockers. Causing havoc has always been one of Mr. Sencen's specialties. As is breaking into the principal's office."

"You're seriously going to equate this with one of his pranks?" Grady asked. "Like it's just another Great Gulon Incident?"

If the vein in Grady's forehead hadn't been so bulgy, Sophie would've asked someone to *finally* share the story of Keefe's legendary triumph.

"It's all a rather dark shade of gray," Magnate Leto admitted. "But that's a color all of us are familiar with, aren't we? Wouldn't you use it to describe your behavior when you confronted Brant about what he did to your daughter? Or Miss Foster, when you drugged your human family so you could be erased from their lives? And surely the Council would apply it to most of my actions. After all, I helped form an illegal organization. Experimented with the genetics of an innocent child. Secreted her away in the Forbidden Cities to be raised by humans. Erased two of her memories without her permission—"

"We have a bigger problem," Sophie interrupted, not needing any more reminders of how weird her life had been. "I'm sure Oralie knew I was lying when I said I didn't see who triggered the sound wave. I was way too emotional to fool an Empath."

"Councillor Oralie has always been your loyal supporter," Magnate Leto assured her.

"Okay, but Councillor Alina looked suspicious too—and she hates me. All it takes is one of them to figure out that it was Keefe, and he'll never be able to come back."

"Not necessarily," Magnate Leto said. "Questionable actions can be forgiven when they're done with good intentions. Think of the Ancient Councillors' reasons for not warning the gnomes that the ogres possessed the plague. With time, most have come to understand their complicated motivations."

The key word in that sentence was "most."

In Keefe's case there'd be many who'd see a notorious troublemaker graduating to a new level of mayhem. Or worse: a loyal son stepping into the role his mother designed for him.

Sophie sank back into the sofa's cushions, trying to disappear into the fluff—anything to avoid having to figure out what to do or think or—

"I know this is all very overwhelming," Magnate Leto said. "But that's only because you're trying to interpret Mr. Sencen's actions with your head. You have a very good head, Miss Foster. Very logical and clever and strong. But do you know what's even more powerful?"

He pointed to her heart.

"Which means what?" Grady asked. "We're relying on *teenage feelings?*"

"I wouldn't be so quick to dismiss them. Miss Foster understands Mr. Sencen in ways the rest of us simply cannot. I watched them most carefully during their time in Alluveterre. He opened up to her. Leaned on her. Trusted her. So"—his eyes met Sophie's—"what does your heart tell you?"

Sophie crossed her arms over her chest, wishing she could reach in and pluck out the answer. Instead, her head kept taking over, flooding her consciousness with memories:

Keefe crying on her shoulder the day she'd had to tell him that his mom might be dead.

The window slumber parties they'd held so they wouldn't have to face the tougher nights alone.

His room covered in notes and crumpled bits of paper as he desperately tried to piece together the truth hidden in his past.

A much younger Keefe, sitting and waiting in Atlantis for a family that didn't care enough to remember him.

Over and over the scenes replayed, until another image slowly replaced them.

Keefe, in the Healing Tent in Exillium, his humor and confidence stripped away, revealing the scared, angry boy he kept hidden underneath.

The memory didn't tell her anything. But it made her heart ache—made her wish she could wrap her arms around him and make everything okay.

Magnate Leto nodded, as if he'd been eavesdropping on her thoughts. Which made her wonder . . .

"When we were in Alluveterre, did you ever read his mind?"

Telepaths weren't supposed to invade anyone's privacy without permission—but Magnate Leto had never been one to follow rules.

"You're asking if I knew he was going to join the Neverseen?" he asked. "I knew he was considering it. But the idea was incredibly tentative. It didn't truly take shape until you were heading for Ravagog—and even then, he still seemed undecided. But I can tell you that he saw it as a necessary evil to right the wrongs his mother caused."

"'Evil' is right," Grady muttered. "And if That Boy comes anywhere near you again, I want you to drop him with the full weight of your inflicting."

"Grady!" Edaline gasped.

She'd been standing by the farthest wall next to Cadoc—her hulking new bodyguard, who almost made Sandor look skinny—staring so silently at the pastures of grazing dinosaurs and other crazy creatures that Sophie had forgotten she was there.

"Need I remind you that Keefe's doing the same thing our daughter tried to do?" Edaline asked him.

The words knocked Grady back a step.

They hit Sophie pretty hard too.

Jolie had tried to infiltrate the Neverseen, and the plan had been working—until they ordered her to destroy a human nuclear power plant to prove her loyalty. A few days after she refused, she was dead.

Grady moved to Edaline's side and wrapped his arm around her waist. "I'm sorry. I guess I have some trust issues, after Brant."

He said something else, but Sophie didn't catch it, her mind too stuck on the huge reality Keefe was facing.

As much as she'd worried and fretted and stressed, she'd never truly imagined the impossible choices he'd have to face—or the worst-case scenario:

A tall, lean tree with blond shaggy leaves and scattered ice-blue flowers growing on a grassy hill in the Wanderling Woods—the elves' version of a graveyard.

Each Wanderling's seed was wrapped with the DNA of the person it had been planted to commemorate, and it grew with their coloring and essence.

"He's going to get himself killed," Sophie mumbled as the knot of emotions under her ribs twisted a million times tighter. "We need to get him out."

"How do you propose we do that?" Magnate Leto asked.

Sophie wished she had suggestions. But she didn't even know where Keefe was. She'd been trying to track his thoughts for weeks, like she used to do when she played base quest. But all she could tell was that Keefe was very far away.

"He'll come home when he's ready," Magnate Leto told her. "In the meantime, I suggest we make use of the information he's gone to such lengths to bring us." He turned to Grady and Edaline. "I trust that you'll allow your new bodyguards to do their jobs?"

"Brielle and Cadoc are some of our regiment's best," Sandor added.

"Do you think the Neverseen will guess that Keefe warned us if Grady and Edaline suddenly have goblins following them around?" Sophie had to ask.

"I'm sure Mr. Sencen has a plan for that," Magnate Leto promised.

"Uh, we're talking about the same Keefe, right?" Sophie asked.

"It doesn't matter," Grady told her. "I don't need a bodyguard."

Brielle cleared her throat. "With all due respect, Mr. Ruewen, there's a reason the elves rely on goblin assistance. Are you truly prepared to kill if the need arises?"

Grady looked more than a little green as Brielle unsheathed her sword and slashed it with a deadly sort of grace. The elvin mind couldn't process violence. Their thoughts were too sensitive—their consciences too strong. It was why the Never-seen were so unstable—though Fintan held his sanity together far better than Brant.

"What if we stay here?" Edaline suggested. "The Council hasn't given Grady an assignment in weeks, and we have plenty to keep us busy with the animals. We can pass Cadoc and Brielle off like they're additional guards for Sophie—which shouldn't seem strange after what happened."

"*That,*" Magnate Leto said, "is a brilliant solution."

"Except it puts us on house arrest," Grady argued.

"Isn't it worth it to be safe?" Sophie countered.

"Hey—that works both ways, kiddo," Grady reminded her. "If I agree to this, I need you to agree that there will be no more one-on-one meetings with anyone associated with the Neverseen—especially That Boy."

Sophie groaned. "His name is Keefe!"

"Not right now, it isn't. He has to earn that back. And if he's really on our side, he won't mind you having your bodyguard around as backup. Understood?"

Sophie agreed, mostly because Sandor would clobber her if she didn't. "What do you think the Neverseen want with you guys?"

"I suspect this is primarily a power play," Magnate Leto said quietly. "Much like their attempts to capture the alicorns. If they possess something you love . . ."

"They can control me," Sophie finished.

Magnate Leto nodded. "I'm betting that they—like myself—assume Kenric would've known his cache is far more valuable to you if you have a way to access the information inside. This could be their plan to force you to open it for them."

"Oh good—so the thing That Boy stole is putting all of us in more danger," Grady muttered.

"If it weren't that, it would be something else," Magnate Leto assured him. "They've been after Miss Foster from the beginning. And honestly, the more valuable they see her as, the safer she is—relatively speaking."

"I don't even know how to open the cache," Sophie reminded everyone—though *technically* she'd never tried. She had enough crazy information stored in her head. The last thing she wanted was to fill it with secrets even the Council couldn't handle.

Still, Magnate Leto's theory raised other questions—the kind that made her voice get thick and squeaky.

"I know you don't want to tell me who my genetic parents are—"

"Wrong," Magnate Leto interrupted. "I *can't* tell you."

Sophie glanced at Grady and Edaline, trying to decide if she should leave the conversation at that. She rarely mentioned her genetic parents around them—or her human family. It was complicated enough having three different moms and dads—especially since one pair no longer remembered her, and another was a complete mystery.

But she needed to know.

"Was Kenric my father? He was a Telepath. And he was always so kind to me." Her throat closed off as she remembered his bright smiles.

The red-haired Councillor had been one of Sophie's strongest supporters, right up until the day she'd lost him to Fintan's inferno of Everblaze.

Magnate Leto reached for Sophie's hand, tracing a finger across the star-shaped scar he'd accidentally given her when he healed her abilities. "Kenric wasn't involved with Project Moonlark. And that's *all* I can tell you. Some secrets must remain hidden. Besides, we have much more pressing matters to discuss, like the other significant piece of information we learned from Mr. Senccn. Did he really say that Gethen was the Neverseen's only Telepath?"

"Why docs that matter?" Sophie asked.

"Because telepathy is generally considered to be our most vital ability. We'd never have known the humans were plotting to betray us all those millennia ago if our Telepaths hadn't overheard their schemes. That's why there are more Telepaths in the nobility than any other talent. So either the Neverseen have failed to recruit any others—which could tell us something about their method of operating. Or there's a reason they're avoiding the talent. Either way, it means I should press the Council about allowing a visit to Gethen."

Sophie's eyes narrowed. "I've been saying that for weeks!"

"I know. And I've been stalling—partially because I promised to bring you with me, and I still believe Gethen intends to harm you if you try to search his mind. But mostly because I wanted to see exactly what role Mr. Sencen was going to play before choosing our next step."

"Well, now we know," Grady muttered, holding up the shard of glass again.

"I know you look at that and see violence and destruction," Magnate Leto told him. "But I see a boy willing to do anything to tear the Neverseen's organization apart. And I for one am going to believe in him—especially since he may have unwittingly given us another advantage. May I have that cloak, Miss Foster?"

"I'm sure there's a hidden tracker," Sandor warned as Sophie handed it over.

"That's what I'm hoping for. Perhaps if we move it somewhere *interesting*, we can lure them out of their little hiding places."

"You want to meet with them?" Grady asked.

"I want to send a message. Can I borrow a dagger?"

Brielle whipped a jagged silver knife from her boot and handed it to Magnate Leto. He sliced open the cloak's hem along the bottom edge, revealing two disks—one gold and one black—sewn between the folds of thick fabric.

Sandor frowned. "The gold one's the tracker—but I've never seen anything like the black. It's not even made of metal."

"Indeed it's not," Magnate Leto said, severing the threads securing the black disk to the lining. "And it's not magsidian, either."

The rare dwarven mineral changed properties depending on how someone carved it, and it was often used as a form of security authorization.

"Careful," Sophie warned as he held the disk up to the grayish light. "I'm sure that's covered in aromark."

The powerful ogre enzyme wouldn't hurt him. But it could only be removed through an *unpleasant* process.

"I've only seen aromark on metal," Magnate Leto murmured. "And this symbol . . ."

He traced his finger over the thin white etchings across the top—a line decorated with dashes, sandwiched between two different-size circles.

"Do you know what it means?" Sophie asked.

"Sadly, no," Magnate Leto admitted. "But I've seen it before—along with other similar markings—on a shard of memory I recently recovered."

"From who?" Sophie asked.

Magnate Leto sighed, letting several seconds crawl by before he told her, "From Prentice."

FOUR

PRENTICE," SOPHIE REPEATED, NOT sure if she felt relieved or furious. "The same Prentice you've been telling me isn't strong enough to have me search his mind?"

"That would be him," Magnate Leto agreed, and with that, Sophie's fury won.

Prentice used to be a Keeper for the Black Swan, in charge of protecting their most crucial secrets. And he'd allowed his sanity to be broken to prevent the Council from discovering Sophie's existence. He'd spent years locked away in the elves' underground prison, needing her abilities to grow strong enough to heal him. But when Sophie was finally ready—and the Council had freed him from Exile—his consciousness disappeared, leaving him an empty shell.

Nothing had seemed capable of bringing him back—until a few weeks earlier, when Prentice woke up. Sophie had assumed the news meant he'd made a major recovery, but sadly, his mind was still badly broken. She'd been begging the Black Swan to let her heal him, and each time she'd been told that Prentice's mind was too weak, too fragile, too unstable.

"Why would you lie to me?" she snapped as Edaline placed a calming hand on her shoulder.

"I didn't," Magnate Leto promised. "I told you he wasn't ready to be *healed*—not *searched*."

"And I thought my enhanced abilities made me the only one strong enough to search a broken mind," Sophie argued.

"You are. I paid dearly for my attempt. But I had to see if I could figure out why he called swan song."

The Black Swan used the words as a code, to warn each other when they were in extreme danger. Prentice had given the signal right before the Council arrested him, almost like he'd known it was coming.

"Why didn't you let me help you search his mind, then?" Sophie asked.

"Because . . . I didn't trust myself not to beg you to heal him. You have no idea how much it pains me to leave him in darkness. But his mind needs to grow stronger before we bring him back to full consciousness. He has far too much to bear—and if his sanity collapses again, I fear there won't be enough left for you to attempt another repair."

The crack in his voice deflated a bit of Sophie's anger.

The rest faded when she admitted she shared the same worries.

A lot had changed in Prentice's life since he'd sacrificed his sanity. His wife, Cyrah, had died in some sort of light leaping accident. And his son, Wylie, had grown up barely knowing his father. That was a tremendous amount of grief for a weakened mind to process.

"You could've at least told me what was going on," Sophie grumbled.

"I know. When it comes to Prentice, I never seem to follow the course of wisdom. I suppose I feel too responsible."

"How do you think I feel? He's broken because of me!"

"Careful, Sophie," Grady warned. "You saw what thoughts like that did to Alden."

Alden's guilt over his role in Prentice's capture—even though he hadn't known Prentice was one of the good guys at the time—had shattered his sanity. If Sophie hadn't found the strength to heal him, he'd still be lost to the madness.

She took a steadying breath and pointed to the black disk. "We need to find out what that symbol means. And the best way to do that is to take me to see Prentice—just to search his mind for additional memories. Not to heal him."

Magnate Leto's jaw set and Sophie braced for him to argue.

But when he spoke, he told her, "I suppose I can arrange to bring you tomorrow."

"Why not now?" Sophie pressed.

"Probably not a good day to sneak away," Grady reminded her, pointing to the crystal dangling from her choker-style registry necklace. The pendant monitored her location—and while a Technopath could cheat the signal, after what happened at Foxfire the Councillors would likely be watching her much too closely.

"Do you think it'll be safe to slip away tomorrow?" Edaline asked.

"It will with careful arrangements." Magnate Leto tucked the black disk into his cape pocket. "I'll test this for enzymes tonight, just to be safe. I'll also see if I can figure out what it's made of. And we should get rid of this."

He handed Keefe's cloak to Brielle.

"Do you want me to salvage the tracker?" she asked.

"No, I think it's best we avoid the Neverseen's attention until we better understand the significance of the disk. I'd prefer that they believe we destroyed the cloak without discovering its secret."

Brielle headed for the door, her curls bouncing with every step. "Will fire be enough?"

"As long as the tracker melts completely." He turned to Sophie. "I'll be back to pick you up at dawn, along with Mr. Vacker. I think it would be wise for you to have your Cognate on hand. He won't be able to enter Prentice's mind, but he can boost your mental energy."

Sophie's stomach soured. "Does Fitz know that Keefe was behind what happened today?"

"If he doesn't already, he will soon. His father hailed me before I left campus, and I promised to get back to him with details. I suspect he fears his eldest son was involved. Why? Is that a problem?"

"It might be. Fitz has been weird about Keefe. It's like he wants to pretend they were never best friends."

"Sometimes that's easier," Edaline said quietly. "Missing someone can hurt too much. It's safer to be angry."

Anger definitely was Fitz's default. But his reaction to Keefe felt different.

Less angry. More . . . afraid.

"Well, if there's one thing I have no doubt of," Magnate Leto said as he reached for his pathfinder—a slender wand with an adjustable leaping crystal on one end—"it's that you know how to help your friends through their struggles. Perhaps you can help Mr. Vacker tomorrow. In the meantime, try to get some rest. I'll need you in top form to face Prentice."

They watched him glitter away, leaving behind a silence that felt itchy.

"I think I'm going to shower and get in bed early," Sophie decided, kissing each of her parents' cheeks before heading upstairs, where her bedroom suite took up the entire third floor.

"Do you think you'll be able to sleep?" Edaline called after her.

"Probably not."

But no one offered her any sleeping aids. They knew how much Sophie hated sedatives, after all the times her enemies had drugged her. Even Sandor said nothing as he completed his nightly security sweep of her bedroom. But his check was more thorough than usual—inspecting every corner and closet and cranny—despite the fact that none of the petals in the flowered carpet showed even the slightest trace of a new footprint.

"All clear," he announced after peeking under her giant canopied bed. "And I'll be right outside if you need me."

As soon as he closed her door, Sophie jumped straight in the shower to let the warm, colored streams wash away the last flecks of glass. They looked insignificant as they swirled down the drain. But her brain wouldn't stop repeating what Keefe had told her.

Sometimes things have to get worse before they get better.

Emotions swelled with each reminder. Fear. Doubt. Dread.

She closed her eyes and imagined each as a solid thread—then twisted them into the knot under her ribs the way Councillor Bronte had taught her. The tangle burned as she worked, and she pressed her hands against her skin, taking deep breaths until the feelings cooled.

Worry can bring power, Bronte had told her. *Better to embrace it than ignore it.*

But as she crawled into bed and clung tightly to Ella—the bright blue stuffed elephant she couldn't sleep without—new threads of fear kept flaring up. Even when Iggy—her tiny pet imp—flitted to her pillow and snuggled his blue furry body up next to her, his squeaky purring couldn't make her relax. Only one thing might help—the thing she'd been too scared to try before.

Her enhanced telepathic abilities allowed her to stretch her consciousness impossibly far and transmit to people and creatures on the other side of the world. She mostly used the talent to communicate with Fitz—or for her regular check-ins with Silveny to make sure everything was going safely with the alicorn's pregnancy. But that night, there was someone she needed to talk to so much more.

Keefe?

She sent the thought spiraling through the deep black nothingness, shoving the call with her full mental strength. She'd never pushed her limits to communicate with someone who wasn't a Telepath—which was the excuse she'd been using for why she hadn't tried this before. But really, she'd been afraid she couldn't trust him.

Or that he would ignore her.

Keefe? she called again, repeating the word over and over. He wouldn't be able to transmit back to her, so she'd have to connect directly to his thoughts.

She pressed her consciousness lower, imagining she was

aiming for his mind like an arrow slicing through the night. A rush of warmth flooded her head when she finally hit the mark, along with a single, shaky thought.

Foster?

Yes! she transmitted—a bit too loudly. She lowered her mental voice before asking, *Can you still hear me?*

DUDE. This wins for freakiest mind trick ever!

Sorry! Did I scare you?

You think? How does Fitz not pee his pants every time you do this—or wait, DOES HE?

Don't be gross.

I'm not. I'm keeping it real. And, um . . . does this mean you're searching my memories right now?

She didn't actually know if she *could* from so far away—but it didn't matter. She'd paid the price for violating the rules of telepathy too many times.

Besides—if she was going to trust Keefe, she had to *trust* him.

I'm keeping my mind focused on what you're saying, she promised—though his loudest thoughts buzzed in the back of her consciousness like a TV in the background. So she could hear how relieved he was to know that she was safe—and even more so that she was still talking to him. He also sounded very worried that someone would catch them communicating.

Is this a bad time? she asked.

No. But I'm glad Ruy and Alvar are heavy sleepers. There was definite squealing and flailing when I first heard your voice.

The idea of him being so close to one of her kidnappers—and the Psionipath who'd attacked her and Biana—made Sophie shiver. *Can you go somewhere we can talk?*

I'm not allowed to leave my room without one of them with me. But I should be fine here, as long as I stay still. So . . . what's up? Did something happen?

Aside from you destroying part of Foxfire?

Hey, it was my turn to blow up the school. You've been hogging all the fun.

This isn't a joke, Keefe.

It can be if we make it one. We just have to commit!

Sophie sighed, letting her frustration ripple through her mind.

Nobody was hurt, right? he asked.

You got lucky this time, she agreed.

Luck had nothing to do with it. I planned it perfectly.

That's exactly the kind of overconfidence that's going to get you killed.

Not necessarily. I know you don't want to hear this—and believe me, I'm not happy about it either—but . . . I'm kind of important to their plans. At least, I think I am. I'm still working it all out. But I can tell they want me here. I just have to convince them they can trust me before they'll tell me why—and I made some serious progress today. Fintan totally looked ready to join Team Keefe when I met him at the rendezvous point so he could bring me to the hideout.

Every part of that made Sophie sick to her stomach. But she reminded herself that he was doing this for a reason—the same reason she'd reached out to him.

If you're really going to stay there, you need to let me help. You can't keep sneaking away—sooner or later they'll catch you. So I'll reach out to you like this every night and you can tell me anything you've learned.

That's actually not a bad idea, he admitted. *Though it does mean I won't get to use my brilliant plan for my next escape. It didn't have any explosions, either. Just a LOT of selkie skin.*

Sophie felt her lips smile, even if she probably shouldn't.

I'm not going to be able to tell you everything, though, his mind added quietly. *I can only leak so much without getting caught.*

I know. Sophie tried not to wonder how much he was already hiding. *Are nights safer to reach you? Or would mornings be better?*

Definitely nights. My training starts early—and I'm sure you're probably imagining all kinds of scary things, so just know the stuff they've been having me do isn't a big deal.

That'll change once they really trust you.

Yeah. Probably.

It was his cue to tell her he had a brilliant plan for that, too. But his mind had gone achingly silent.

I really hope you know what you're doing.

I do. I can't promise I won't have to be a part of some more shady things. But I know where the hard lines are, and I won't cross them.

She could feel the threads of his conviction, like roots digging deep. But whether they would hold him steady through the coming storms, she couldn't tell.

She'd have to keep an eye on him.

Is this the best time to reach out to you each night? she asked.

Yep—it's a date. Tell your boyfriends not to be jealous.

She wished she had a way to roll her eyes in a mental conversation. *I don't have any boyfriends.*

I dunno. I can think of a few dudes who might not be fans of all this Keefoster time.

Keefoster?

Sounds way cooler than Sophitz or Dophie, right? And don't even get me started on Bangs Boy. By the way—don't think I didn't notice those new rings on your thumbs today. The Fitzster has a matching set, doesn't he? I bet they look so cute when you guys are holding hands and staring deep into each other's eyes.

We don't stare into—why are we talking about this?

Would you rather hear about how loud Ruy snores? Or how this room smells like rotting toenails? Or Alvar's crazy theories for who the Forklenator is?

The last question reminded her that Keefe had already run off before the Magnate Leto–Mr. Forkle reveal happened.

You found out another one of his identities, didn't you? Keefe guessed.

I did. But I don't think it'd be good to tell you. You already have enough secrets to protect.

There you go, ruining all the fun with your logic.

I guess that's my job.

That doesn't mean you have to be so good at it—though it is kinda nice having someone look out for me.

You don't make it easy.

Another thing you and I have in common.

His floating thoughts made it clear how determined he was to protect her. It made her heart somehow both light and heavy at the same time.

Have you learned anything else I should know? she asked.

I wish. They haven't let me meet any of the other members of their order yet. And this run-down shack I'm in is where they bring all new recruits because there's nothing worth finding. They won't give me my own crystal or pathfinder—and the ones they let me borrow always leap to neutral meeting places.

They trusted you enough to let you help at the Sanctuary, she reminded him.

Only because that mission was about causing chaos. They knew they wouldn't get inside the preserve. They just wanted to make the Council look bad and keep people on edge.

Is that what the registry was about too?

No, they were super secretive about that, so I'm betting there was more to it. It's on my list of things I'm trying to find out.

What else is on that list?

Not gonna lie—it's a LOT. But I'm trying to focus on details that will tell me how to shut them down.

Well . . . I know one thing that might be worth looking into. Her mind filled with the symbol from the black disk they'd found in his cloak.

Am I supposed to know what that is? Keefe asked.

You've never seen it before?

Nope. Why, where did you find it?

If you don't know, I don't think I should tell you. It might be something they're trying to keep hidden from you. Just keep an eye out for it, okay?

Done. Anything else?

That's all I can think of for now.

Awesome. Then it's my turn to ask you a question. He paused, like he was gearing up for something incredibly important. *How'd Dizznee react to your new rings?*

Sophie shook her head, refusing to dignify the question with a response.

You can ignore it all you want, Foster, but sooner or later you're going to have to solve the triangle. Or should we get real and call it a square?

I have no idea what you mean.

I'm pretty sure you do. I bet if I were there I could feel your mood shifting.

Right, because I'm trying to figure out if it's possible to strangle you with my thoughts!

There you go, rocking the whole adorable-when-you're-angry thing. I think that's what I've missed about you the most.

She knew he was only teasing—but she still found herself transmitting, *I miss you, too.*

His thoughts went quiet for a second. And when he came back, his mental voice sounded heavier.

Well, he told her, *I should probably get some sleep. Gotta rest up for another day of playing nice with the bad guys—and no need to tell me to be careful. I've got that one down.*

She doubted that. "Careful" wasn't a word that described Keefe Sencen.

Fine, she said. *But before I go, I need you to promise me something.*

Yes, I will call you Lady Lectures-a-Lot every time you transmit to me.

That's definitely not what I meant.

What about Little Miss Heartbreaker?

Keefe!

Okay, fine, we'll stick with the Mysterious Miss F. Deal?

Deal, she agreed. *And can you focus for one second?*

I suppose I can try. . . .

I need you to promise that if this gets too tough, you'll walk away. No matter how close you are to what you're trying to learn.

Edaline had once made Sophie give her a similar promise, after admitting she should've said the same thing to Jolie.

It's not going to come down to that.

Then promise me anyway.

Endless seconds slipped by before he told her, *Okay, fine, I promise. Now get out of my head, Miss F. I need my beauty sleep.*

FIVE

YOU KIDS WOULD SLEEP THE DAY away if I'd let you," a wheezy voice grumbled, dragging Sophie out of her tangled dreams.

She rubbed the crustiness from her eyes and waited for her vision to adjust to her still-very-dark bedroom. "I thought you said dawn—and whoa. You're back to the Forkle disguise?"

She hadn't seen the heavyset figure standing in her doorway since the day he'd revealed his other identity. But there he was, looking wrinkled and puffy and reeking with the dirty-feet scent of ruckleberries.

Strangely, Sophie liked him better that way.

This was the face she'd known her whole life. The nosy

next-door neighbor who'd kept watch over her while she'd lived among humans. The elf who'd healed her abilities after they'd been damaged by a failed light leap, and fought at her side on Mount Everest. The elf who'd driven her crazy with his riddles and secrets—but who seemed to know her better than anyone.

"As I told you before," Mr. Forkle said, "it's easier for me to compartmentalize my life. When I'm in the Lost Cities, I rely on my established identities. But today we're going to the Stone House."

The name launched sparks through Sophie's nerves.

She'd only been to the isolated cottage twice, and neither were happy memories. One was the day they'd first brought Prentice home—when they'd discovered how severely his condition had deteriorated. And the other was when Calla had brought her there to deliver devastating news about the gnomish plague.

"You know, the last time I was there, you weren't in Forkle mode," she reminded him.

She probably should've figured out his secret identity right then. But Magnate Leto had given her some story about how the Black Swan had brought him along to help cover for Tiergan and Wylie's visit.

Sometimes it was better if she didn't think about how good he was at lying.

"That was for young Mr. Endal's benefit," Mr. Forkle told her. "He's unaware of my other identities—and I'd prefer it stay that way for the time being."

"Will Wylie be there today?"

"Are you hoping to avoid him?"

Seeing Wylie tended to be unpleasant—he'd spent the majority of their conversations blaming her for every horrible thing that had happened to his dad.

But their last talk hadn't been *as* awkward.

"I just want to be prepared," she said. "I'm sure he's wondering why I haven't healed Prentice yet."

"Actually, Wylie came to us after his father woke, begging us not to perform the healing until we understand why Prentice slipped away. He's terrified of undoing what little progress his father has made. So remember: You and Mr. Vacker are going there to retrieve, not heal."

"Wait—Fitz is here?"

She scrambled to cover her frumpy pajamas and accidentally launched poor Iggy off the bed. He flapped his black batlike wings and shook his tiny blue arms as he flew to the top of her canopy and glared down at her.

"Mr. Vacker's waiting downstairs," Mr. Forkle said, snapping his fingers to turn on her lights, "and your imp looks like he's plotting revenge. So I'll leave you to get ready. But do try to hurry. I'd prefer to get out of here before sunrise."

Sophie tried not to think about how early that meant it was—or how little she'd slept—as she stumbled out of bed and threw on a simple tunic and pants.

"You might want to consider using a hairbrush," Sandor

warned as she passed him on her way to the stairs.

Sophie rarely gave much thought to her appearance, but Sandor's twitching smile sent her rushing to the nearest mirror.

A tiny face appeared in the corner and immediately burst into laughter.

"What'd you do—get zapped by a Charger?" Vertina asked, swishing her silky dark hair.

Sophie glared at the spectral mirror, wishing she could tell Grady and Edaline to get rid of the obnoxious piece of technology. But the mirror had once belonged to Jolie. And Vertina had occasionally proven herself useful.

Plus, her hair *did* look like the top part of a pineapple.

"You're making it worse," Vertina said as Sophie tried brushing out the tangles. "Go grab a box of hair pins and let me save you from this impending disaster."

Sophie was tempted to ignore her—Vertina would disappear the second she stepped out of the mirror's range—but she let Vertina walk her through pulling her hair into some sort of sleek, twisty ponytail.

"Aren't I a genius?" Vertina asked as Sophie tucked the final strand.

"You actually are," Sophie begrudgingly admitted.

"Okay! Now for your makeup. Go get—"

Sophie stepped out of range, done with primping.

"Whoa," Fitz said as she made her way down the stairs. "I didn't recognize you for a second."

"Bad hair day," she mumbled, fidgeting with the end of the ponytail.

"No—it looks good," he promised. "It really draws attention to your eyes."

She knew Fitz probably meant it as a compliment. But she'd never gotten used to being the only brown-eyed elf.

Why couldn't the side effect of her tweaked genes have been green eyes?

Or purple?

"You should do that more often," Grizel said, emerging from her hiding spot in the shadows. "It'll drive the boys wild."

"Um, maybe."

Attention made Sophie sweaty and fidgety. Especially attention from Fitz.

He was studying her so closely she finally had to ask, "What?"

"Just . . . checking for cuts or scratches. Making sure he didn't hurt you."

"You mean Keefe?"

Fitz cringed at the name. His hands also curled into fists—the knuckles turning white from the pressure.

Sophie turned to Mr. Forkle. "Can we have a minute?"

Mr. Forkle nodded and led Sandor and Grizel to the other side of the room.

Sophie motioned for Fitz to take a seat next to her on the sofa and decided it'd be easiest to talk telepathically. She gave him permission to enter her mind—he and Mr. Forkle were the only ones who could—and he effortlessly slipped past her mental blocking. Apparently she had a point of trust, and if someone transmitted the right thing, it worked kind of like a mental password. But it all happened subconsciously, so she had no idea what they said.

Okay, Sophie thought, sitting on her hands so she couldn't tug on her eyelashes. *We have to talk about Keefe. I know you don't want to. But the more we ignore it, the more it's going to affect our ability to work as Cognates.*

All of their training focused on being open with each other. Their ultimate goal was supposed to be *no secrets at all.*

Are you sure it's a good idea? Fitz asked. *We both know I say stupid stuff when I'm angry.*

Are you angry? she asked. *I know you are at Alvar—and I'm with you on that. But are you sure that's what you're feeling toward Keefe?*

Uh—did he or did he not destroy part of Foxfire yesterday?

Yeah, but it wasn't like how you're picturing.

In his mind, Keefe looked like a proper villain, laughing as the glass rained down.

Just watch, okay? She rallied her concentration and replayed what actually happened, from the moment she stepped into Magnate Leto's office, to the final shattering seconds. Her photographic memory painted the scenes in perfect detail, and she left nothing out.

Okay, so maybe it's not as bad as I thought, Fitz reluctantly admitted. *But I still think you should've Sucker Punched him as soon as he spun around in that chair.*

I thought about it, Sophie admitted, tracing her finger across the wide bracelet Dex had given her to make her punches stronger. *But I'm glad I heard him out.*

Fitz sighed. *I guess that's why he went to you instead of me.*

Does that bother you?

No.

There was a strange prickliness about the thought, though.

What would you have done if he'd left the note for you instead of me? Sophie asked.

Fitz flopped back against the pillows and stared at the cascading crystal chandelier. *I have no idea.*

Are you sure? Sophie pressed. *I can feel the words bubbling in the back of your mind. Just let them out—I can take it.*

Fitz chewed his lower lip. *Fine. I . . . don't trust Keefe. I know you want me to—and I know I probably should, since he's my best friend and he's been through a ton of hard stuff. But he also has a LOT in common with my brother. Shoot—he used to call Alvar his hero.*

Keefe didn't know Alvar was with the Neverseen when he said that.

Maybe not. But it still makes me sick. Did you know that Alvar went to your planting in the Wanderling Woods? After he'd drugged you and tied you up and staged the cave to make everyone think you'd drowned? Then he stood there with his hand on my shoulder and offered to let me borrow his stupid handkerchief. And later that night, he snuck back to the Neverseen's hideout and helped them torture you.

The skin on her wrists stung, phantom pain left from the interrogation.

Brant was the one who questioned me, she reminded him quietly.

Yeah, but Alvar let it happen. He knew what they were doing. Probably heard you screaming.

He punched one of the fluffy pillows so hard, bits of feather swirled through the air.

You're right, Sophie said as the fluff slowly settled. *But that was Alvar. You can't keep lumping him together with Keefe. Your brother is . . . I don't even know. I don't understand why he would turn his back on his family, or do such unimaginably awful things. But Keefe really is trying to help us. He's in over his head, and his plan is probably full of holes, and I'm betting we're going to have to save him before this is over—but . . . his heart is still in the right place. I have to believe that.*

Fitz shook his head. *How do you stay so trusting after all you've been through?*

It's not always easy. Her hand moved to rub the emotions tangled under her ribs. *Did I ever tell you what happened with Councillor Bronte? Remember how much he used to hate me?*

Yeah, I used to hear my mom and dad whispering about what they'd do if Bronte got you expelled or banished.

He tried really hard. And when the Council made him my inflicting Mentor, I was pretty sure that would do it. It got so bad that Kenric had to be there to make sure Bronte wasn't hurting me during the lessons. But then, Bronte made me teach him how I inflict positive emotions. And the happiness I blasted into his mind caused this weird mental shutdown. I still don't know how to explain it. But I had to pull his consciousness back, and his head was seriously one of the scariest places I've ever been.

She shuddered just thinking about it.

After that, I figured things would get way worse between us, she continued. *But somehow Bronte ended up becoming one of my only supporters on the Council. I didn't know what caused the change until after the whole ability restrictor nightmare. Bronte sent me a message through Magnate Leto. He told me, "It takes a special person to see darkness inside of someone and not condemn them." But the funny thing was, I had condemned him. I'd decided he was a traitor. I'd even asked Keefe to go all Empath-lie-detector on him to see if we could find proof that he was leaking confidential information from the Council. So . . . now I try to be the person Bronte thinks I am. Which is why I'm not ready to give up on Keefe. Not yet.*

I guess that makes sense. But—

I'm not trying to change how you feel. In fact, maybe it's better this way. I'll be the believer and you can be the skeptic and we'll keep each other in check—but that only works if you're honest with me and actually talk about stuff.

He sighed. *There you go being all practical and wise.*

Hey, one of us has to be.

He laughed at that—and reached over to give her ponytail a playful tug.

She moved to block him and their rings snapped their hands together—which would've been startling enough without Mr. Forkle asking, "I take it the hand-holding means you've worked things out?"

"I think so," Sophie mumbled, not looking at Fitz as she pulled her palm free.

"Very good, because we really do need to get going. The window of time that we can be away is closing by the minute."

"And you have your Imparter in case you need me?" Grady asked Sophie as he strode in from the kitchen.

Sophie showed him the square silver gadget she'd tucked safely in her pocket. Imparters were the elves' much sleeker voice-commanded version of a videophone.

"All will be fine," Mr. Forkle assured Grady. "We're going to a secure location."

Grady strangled Sophie with a hug anyway. "I keep thinking it's going to get easier, sitting back and letting you take risks," he told her. "But every time, I want to drag you back upstairs and barricade you in your room."

"That makes two of us," Sandor said. "But I'll keep an eye on her."

"And *I'll* keep an eye on both of them," Grizel said. "Show them how it's done."

Grizel tossed her long hair—which she'd let hang loose that day—as Mr. Forkle pulled a pink pathfinder out of his cloak, making Sophie wonder how many types of leaping crystals the elves actually used. Blue went to the Forbidden Cities. Green went to the ogres. Pale yellow to the Neutral Territories. And clear to the Lost Cities. She'd also seen the Black Swan use purple crystals. But this was the first time she'd seen pale pink—and its hundreds of facets sparkled with different colors, like a diamond.

"Please tell me this isn't going to be like leaping with the unmapped stars," Sophie begged. She'd experienced that particular misery several times, and really didn't have the energy to endure it again.

"No, the hint of opalescence is simply an added security measure," Mr. Forkle assured her. "Now everyone lock hands."

Their group formed quite a chain, with Sophie, Fitz, Mr. Forkle, Sandor, and Grizel.

"You ready for this?" Fitz asked.

"Of course she is," Mr. Forkle answered for her. "This is what she was made for."

SIX

PRENTICE'S NORMALLY RICH BROWN skin had a grayish tint, and shiny streams of sweat trickled down his forehead and soaked his tangled dreadlocks.

But he was awake.

His cloudy blue eyes kept darting blankly around the room.

Even his mumble-gurgle sounds were a huge improvement from his previous deathly silence.

Still, Sophie understood Mr. Forkle's reasons for keeping her away.

Watching the string of drool hanging from Prentice's lips made her want to dive into his mind and call him back to reality. He deserved to be *truly* awake—not strapped to a bed so that his flailing limbs wouldn't send him crashing to the cold silver floor.

All in good time, Mr. Forkle transmitted. *And I'm not reading your mind, in case you're worried. I know you well enough to know that your thoughts echo mine. But we must be strong.*

"Everything okay?" Fitz asked as Sophie gave Mr. Forkle a reluctant nod.

She forced a smile and tried to look anywhere but at Prentice.

The house was exactly as she remembered it. Sleek and sterile and sparse—and small. Sandor and Grizel chose to patrol the moorish grounds to escape the low ceilings.

The only pieces of furniture were the neatly tucked cot Prentice was resting on and a medicine-strewn table next to it. The rest of the space was floor-to-ceiling apothecary shelves and one narrow counter under the room's only window, covered in an elaborate alchemy setup.

"Isn't someone watching him?" Sophie asked, studying the beakers on the burners, which were bubbling with some sort of smoky magenta liquid.

"Of course," a ghostly voice said from the loft hidden above.

Seconds later, Wraith's silver cloak came swishing down the narrow corner staircase. *Just* his cloak—though his invisible body was clearly moving underneath the slinky fabric. He used a trick called partial vanishing—hiding his body, but not his clothes—to keep his true identity secret.

All five members of the Black Swan's Collective had crazy nicknames to match their even-crazier disguises. So far Sophie and her friends had only learned who two of them actually were. They knew Mr. Forkle was both Magnate Leto and Sir Astin—though he'd admitted that he still had other identities they'd yet to uncover. And they knew . . .

"Granite!" Sophie said as a bizarre figure struggled up the narrow staircase from the cramped basement below. He looked like a cracked, unfinished statue come to life, thanks to the chalky indurite powder he ingested for his disguise. Sophie knew him better as Tiergan, her telepathy mentor at Foxfire—and she still couldn't believe she'd trained with him for more than a year and never guessed he was secretly involved with the Black Swan.

"Squall already left," Granite told Mr. Forkle. "And she won't be able to return for our evening meeting."

Mr. Forkle nodded. "I'd suspected that might occur."

Squall used her ability as a Froster to crust herself with ice and obscure her identity—and whoever she was in real life seemed to make it very difficult for her to sneak away from the Lost Cities for long.

"Blur should be here momentarily," Granite added.

Almost on cue, a smudged-looking figure passed through the solid wood of the cottage's front door. As a Phaser, Blur could break down his body and walk through anything—but he only let himself partially re-form, in order to hide what he looked like. All Sophie could see were splotches of color and shadow in a vaguely elflike shape as he turned back to open the door for two familiar figures.

"You know, you could use the door like a normal person," Tam said as he stalked into the room.

"Where's the fun in that?" Linh asked, trailing behind her brother.

She'd opened her mouth to say something else when she spotted Sophie and Fitz. Then there was a whole lot of hugging—while Tam settled for a nod-shrug-wave from the doorway.

The twins looked a lot alike—especially with their silver-blue eyes, and the silver tips they'd added to their jet-black hair. But personality-wise, they were night and day.

"I wish I'd known you'd be here," Linh mumbled. "I was so happy to leave the house, I didn't bother changing out of my training clothes." She fussed with the sleeves of her simple blue tunic, which were wet along the edges. She must've been practicing hydrokinesis.

"You look beautiful," Sophie promised.

Linh always did.

All elves were inherently gorgeous, but Linh was especially striking with her soft pink cheeks and lips contrasted against her dramatic eyes and hair. Tam was just as handsome, but with more edge to his style, thanks to his jagged bangs and ultra-intense stare.

"Why aren't you letting Tam and Linh leave Alluveterre?" Sophie asked Mr. Forkle.

"The same reason we haven't let you visit," he told her. "Far too many people would love to find that hideout."

Tam and Linh lived in the same tree houses that Sophie and her friends had stayed in while they were banished from the Lost Cities, hidden deep under the earth in a subterranean forest only the Black Swan knew how to access. They could've returned home when their banishment was lifted, but they chose to stay away from their family—not surprising, considering their parents let them spend more than three years scrounging for food and living in tattered tents instead of standing by Linh's side as she adjusted to the strength of her ability.

"Does that mean you're not going to Exillium anymore?" Fitz asked the twins.

"No, they let us out for that," Tam told him, "but only with our dwarven stalkers."

"Bodyguards," Blur corrected. "And they'll only surface if they hear trouble."

"King Enki assigned four of his royal brigade to Tam and Linh's charge," Granite clarified as he made his way over to check on Prentice, who seemed completely unaware of the noise around him. "The goblins have been spread a bit thin, between the forces they've stationed outside Ravagog and the patrols in the Lost Cities. And honestly, it's better for Tam and Linh to have a discreet form of cover at Exillium."

"How's it going there, by the way?" Sophie asked.

Linh smiled. "It keeps getting better—thanks to you."

Sophie shrugged, not sure she should be given credit for the changes. All she'd done was tell Councillor Oralie what life was truly like at the neglected school. Oralie had arranged the improvements herself.

"I never thought I'd miss that place," Fitz said. "But some of the skills they taught were pretty awesome."

"We miss you guys even more," Sophie added. "Dex and Biana are going to be so jealous that we got to see you."

"Seriously," Fitz said, "Biana was already super sulky that she couldn't come with us this morning, so when I tell her we saw you guys she's going to flip."

"All four of them have been nagging me to let them visit you two for weeks," Mr. Forkle added. "I'd wager they've broken Mr. Sencen's record for Most Visits to the Principal's Office to plead their case."

The name drop might as well have dragged a giant woolly mammoth into the room.

Tam cleared his throat. "So . . . have you heard from him?"

"You could say that," Fitz said, glancing at Sophie.

"I saw him yesterday." She hoped Tam would leave it at that. But of course he didn't.

"I'm guessing there was drama?"

"Mr. Sencen has chosen a very challenging path," Mr. Forkle said carefully. "But we're still hoping for the best. And I want you all to know that we are not trying to keep you separated from each other. But we have to protect Alluveterre. The Council is watching your pendant feeds *very* closely, and while they may not be actively working against our order, we also cannot truly count them on our side."

"I'm sure Dex could cover us sneaking away for a few hours," Sophie argued.

"Mr. Dizznee's talents are especially creative," Wraith agreed. "But the Council's new measures are cleverer than you might expect. It took our Technopath most of last night to set up the false feed we're using right now. And it's only for a limited time."

"Besides, we need Dex concentrating on other things," Blur added.

"Like what?" Sophie asked, surprised that Dex hadn't mentioned anything.

Mr. Forkle shot Blur a look that seemed to say, *That was top secret information!* before his voice filled her head.

We've given Mr. Dizznee access to all of the eldest Mr. Vacker's registry records, hoping he'll be able to determine why the Neverseen went to such lengths to destroy the files.

Is that why they broke in to the registry? Sophie asked.

In part. The investigators were unable to determine if any additional files were accessed. But all of Brant's, Fintan's, Ruy's, and Mr. Vacker's records were erased. It's quite fortunate we'd made our own copies before the break-in. And I'm sure you can understand why we asked Mr. Dizznee to keep this project quiet.

"I know you're talking about me," Fitz said when Sophie's eyes darted his way. "And you know I can eavesdrop on what you guys are saying, right?"

"But you won't," Granite told him. "Because you respect Sophie too much to violate the rules of telepathy."

Tam snorted. "Telepaths are weird."

"Said the guy who won't trust anyone until he's read their shadowvapor," Linh teased.

Tam was a Shade, which meant he could manipulate shadows—including the inner darkness everyone hid in their minds. He claimed he could tell whether someone was trustworthy simply by sensing how much shadowvapor he felt when he took a reading—and it seemed to be true. Tam had doubted both Alvar and Keefe because they'd refused to submit to the test. Sophie was still waiting for the *I told you so.*

"Just tell me what's going on," Fitz said, and Sophie could hear the desperation hidden in his voice.

She sighed. "Dex is investigating your brother, trying to see if he can learn anything about the Neverseen. And they didn't tell us because . . ."

She pointed to his hands, which were fisted so tightly, his thumb rings were cutting into his skin.

It took Fitz six painful seconds to relax his grip, and when he did, he turned to Mr. Forkle. "I want to know what he's found."

"Nothing at the moment—another reason we've waited to

78

tell you. If you don't believe me, you're welcome to speak to Mr. Dizznee directly."

"I will," Fitz assured him—and Sophie made a mental note to be there in case the conversation turned into an epic disaster.

"Now, can we focus on the reason we're all here?" Mr. Forkle asked. "Mr. Song—"

"I've told you I don't want to be connected with my parents' name," Tam interrupted.

"Right. My apologies. Mr. *Tam*. Did Blur explain the plan?"

"He said something about having me lift another veil. And I've been hoping I misunderstood. You remember what happened last time."

"I do," Mr. Forkle said. "Prentice finally woke up."

"Right—but after that," Tam pressed. "I'm never going to forget those screams."

"Why was Prentice screaming?" Sophie asked as Linh reached for her brother's hand.

"It only lasted a few minutes," Mr. Forkle assured her—which was hardly reassuring. "And I suspect it was from the influx of jagged memories released by the veil."

"Anyone else confused?" Fitz asked.

"Very," Sophie said. In all the times she'd been in people's minds, she'd never felt any veils.

"Shadowvapor forms in layers," Tam explained. "Only Shades can sense them. And I like to think of them as veils, since they usually feel thin and wispy—and they're always covering the things we're trying to hide. That's why I can learn so much from reading someone's shadowvapor. The more you have, the more secrets you have. But the veils of darkness in Prentice's mind felt like they were made of solid metal. It took all my energy to lift one, and when I did, his consciousness surged back as it released the memories hidden underneath."

"All the years of Exile and madness must've buried him in darkness," Granite said quietly. "I just wish I understood what caused the final avalanche."

"We'll figure it out," Mr. Forkle promised. "But today, we need to focus on peeling back another veil—which should be lighter now that we've lifted the layer that smothered him. The piece of memory I recovered was tethered to something else—something weighed down by darkness. Hopefully if we remove the veil, Miss Foster can find it."

"But what if this makes Prentice worse?" Sophie whispered.

"Believe me, I've asked that question a thousand times," Granite told her. "But last time, the process made him significantly better. So it stands to reason that lifting another veil might actually help him."

Out of everyone in the room, Granite had the strongest connection to Prentice. He'd resigned from Foxfire after Prentice's Memory break, and despised the Vacker family for years because of Alden's involvement with what had happened. He'd also adopted Wylie and raised him as his own son.

So if Granite thought it was worth the risk, it had to be a good sign.

"Have you told Wylie we're doing this?" Sophie asked.

Mr. Forkle nodded. "He gave us his blessing."

"Then why isn't he here?" Fitz asked.

"Knowing something is the right decision doesn't make watching it any easier," Granite reminded him. "But he trusts me to protect his father—and I *will*."

"As will I," Mr. Forkle said. "As I'm sure you will as well, Miss Foster. And you, Mr. Tam. We all have the same goal."

Tam sighed. "What memory are we even trying to find?"

"The remaining portion of a symbol. I found one piece during my ill-advised search, and we've now found part of it etched onto a disk connected with the Neverseen—which, by the way, tested negative for any enzymes, in case you were worrying," he told Sophie. "It's made of a stone called duskitine, which is neither rare nor valuable. But it does react to starlight, which may be a clue to its purpose—though at the moment, I'm still at a loss for what it could be. Perhaps once we have the rest of the symbol all will become clearer."

"Can I see the full piece of memory you already found?" Sophie asked.

He shuffled to her side and placed two fingers on each of her temples, sending a scrap of jagged darkness surging into Sophie's mind. The chill made her shiver as the memory emerged from the shadows: white symbols glowing through the dark—three diagonal lines, each decorated with different patterns of dashes before they ended in open circles. The line in the center matched the disk from Keefe's cloak.

"It's possible we're missing more than one piece," Mr. Forkle warned.

"How will I know if I've found them all?"

"Send anything you find to me," Fitz offered. "I'll piece them together and let you know when you're done. And if you need an energy boost, just squeeze my fingers."

He offered her his hand, and after all their months of working together, relying on Fitz felt like putting on a pair of comfy running shoes.

"Are we ready?" Mr. Forkle asked.

Everyone turned to Tam.

He shook his bangs out of his eyes and let go of his sister. "I really hope we don't regret this."

"As do we all," Granite whispered.

Tam's shadow sprang to life, crawling slowly across the room until it fell across Prentice's face and sank into his mind.

SEVEN

TAM HAD BEEN RIGHT ABOUT Prentice's screams.

Sophie would never forget his eerie wails—the sound of someone caught between pure terror and overwhelming despair.

Each second was an eternity.

Each breath a knife in her throat.

And then, as quickly as it started, it was over.

Prentice's mouth snapped shut and his head lolled to the side as Tam stumbled back, his shaky legs collapsing underneath him. Linh lunged to catch him, easing Tam's trembling body to the cold floor as she gathered the moisture in the air into some sort of floating forehead compress.

"Wow," Fitz breathed, the same way he always did when he saw Linh's Hydrokinetic tricks.

Sophie was impressed too—especially with Linh's control. Linh had come a long way since her days of being the Girl of Many Floods and causing so many catastrophes that she'd ended up banished.

"I'm fine," Tam managed to mumble. "How's Prentice?"

"Strong," Mr. Forkle promised.

Sophie turned to check for herself, relieved to see how clear Prentice's eyes looked. The cloudiness she'd noticed earlier had lifted, and his gaze was focused and steady. Even his thrashing had calmed, and his mumbles had dulled to whispers.

"What happened?" Linh asked her brother, shifting his water compress with him as he sat up. "You weren't this affected last time."

"Yeah, well, last time the veil wasn't that heavy." Tam turned to Mr. Forkle. "Your theory about the next layer being lighter was *way* off. It was like trying to lift a big, blubbery whale."

"That's quite the mental picture," Mr. Forkle noted. "And that should give you extra pride for the strength and skill it took to lift it."

"Yeah . . . about that." Tam curled his arms around his knees. "It felt like he helped me."

All four members of the Collective crouched around him.

"What does that mean?" Granite asked.

"It's hard to explain," Tam mumbled, reaching though

84

Linh's water compress to tug on his bangs. "But I was running out of strength, and I thought . . . maybe it'd help if Prentice knew I was on his side. So I used my shadow to send a message—which won't mess with his consciousness at all, I swear," he added quickly.

Tam had used the same trick when he was first getting to know Sophie. Exillium had strict rules about Waywards communicating with each other, so their first conversations had happened entirely in her head. Whenever his shadow crossed hers, it opened a channel between them, allowing him to whisper directly inside her mind.

"Anyway," Tam continued, "I told him I was working with the Black Swan, and that I needed to move the darkness so that Sophie could search his memories. And as soon as I said her name, the resistance lessened and the veil started budging."

Granite whispered something Sophie didn't catch as he rushed back to the cot and grabbed both of Prentice's hands. "Prentice—can you hear me?"

Everyone stopped breathing.

Waiting.

Wondering.

And . . . nothing.

"It's for the best," Mr. Forkle said quietly, before turning to Sophie. "If Prentice responds to your name, I'd be wary of using it when you're in his mind. And speed must be of the essence. In fact, I think we should set a timer."

He fumbled in his cape pocket and pulled out a shimmering crystal hourglass.

"Do you always carry that around?" Sophie asked.

"A wise leader is always prepared. You'll have ten minutes. I don't think you should be in his mind any longer than that."

The lump in her throat blocked Sophie's voice. But she did her best to look confident as she approached Prentice's bed. Fitz moved behind her, taking her hand to help steady her nerves.

"Squeeze my fingers if you need me," he told her. "I'll also randomly send a few bursts of energy just in case."

Sophie nodded, taking one last look at each of the worried faces of her friends before she focused on the only one that mattered.

"I'm not going to hurt you," she promised Prentice.

Then she pressed her consciousness into his mind.

Down, down, down she sank—through darkness and shards of memory that battered against her mental barriers. Her stomach plummeted with the rush, even though she knew her body wasn't actually moving.

The farther she fell, the more the blackness faded.

First to gray.

Then to white.

Then to something . . . else.

A color too bright for her mind to name.

It was all colors in one—blindingly perfect in its purity. And as her consciousness slowly adjusted, other images took shape.

Fractal patterns.

Flecks of rainbows.

Everything opalescent and swirly.

And standing amid all of that beauty was a figure.

A young woman in a pale purple gown, with long blond hair and a dazzling smile.

"Hello, Sophie," Jolie whispered. "I knew you'd come back to see me."

EIGHT

SOPHIE KNEW JOLIE WASN'T ACTUALLY there—but that didn't make the vision any less real. Prentice had conjured up Grady and Edaline's daughter in perfect vibrant detail, right down to the wispy, frilly gown in Jolie's favorite color. He'd used the same projection once before, to guide Sophie out of his madness when she'd first tried reading his mind. But this time, instead of a meadow, they were nestled in a pocket of space among all the shimmer and sparkle.

"I'd thought your mind would feel more familiar," Jolie said. "But it's different somehow. Stronger."

You remember me? Sophie transmitted.

"Sometimes I do, and sometimes I don't. Reality is relative."

Jolie's turquoise eyes focused on her slender fingers, wiggling them, like she was checking to see if they really belonged to her. "Am I right? Has something changed?"

Last time my powers were broken, Sophie told her. *They had to fix me before I could come back. And then you were gone.*

"I had to go away," Jolie whispered. "I don't remember why. But I'm here again—and it's so much brighter this time!"

She raised her arms and twirled, her featherlight skirt floating around her.

Why do you use Jolie to communicate with me? Sophie had to ask. *Did she mean something to you?*

"You're still looking for reason. The mind is a funny thing. Logic doesn't always run things the way it should. So often it's feelings." Jolie reached out and caught a green fractal pattern floating by, and it turned blue and swelled large enough to surround them.

"I make you feel safe, don't I?"

Yes.

Sophie had never met Jolie, but she knew that if she had, she would've liked her. Everyone who knew her had loved her. Even the person who'd killed her.

"You remind me of her," Jolie said, flipping the ends of her golden hair. "And it's easier this way. I've lost such track of myself, I don't know how to be me."

But I am talking to Prentice right now? Sophie asked, needing to be sure.

Jolie's smile faded. "Prentice is everywhere and nowhere. *He* can't help you. Though rumor has it, you can help him."

I can, Sophie said, her heart thundering so loud, she wondered if the whole room could hear it. *But it might not be safe yet. He—or, I guess I should say* you—*need to get stronger.*

The fractals shifted again, flickering through so many colors it felt like standing in a disco ball. Jolie's image flickered too, her features growing vague and smudged. "It's strange. Sometimes I feel so sane. And other times . . ."

The light shattered.

Icy splinters jabbed Sophie's consciousness, screeching like nails on a chalkboard as she plummeted. She tried to squeeze Fitz's hand for help, but her body felt disconnected.

No strength.

No power of her own.

Blackness crashed around her, so thick it felt tangible—and then it *was* tangible as the shadows twisted into—

A swan?

"Sorry," Jolie said from somewhere behind her as Sophie struggled to get a firmer grip on the soaring bird's slender neck.

Jolie's arms wrapped around her waist and the touch felt warm and soft—despite the blizzard they were flying through. A storm of blurry fragments that seemed determined to send them careening again.

"I'm trying to hold it together," Jolie told her. "Black Swans always keep me centered."

I wasn't supposed to talk to you, Sophie admitted. *They're afraid I'll make you worse.*

"Nothing could be worse than where I've been."

I'm so sorry.

The words were never enough—but Sophie didn't have anything else to offer.

Where are we going? she asked, trying to figure out if they were flying forward or backward or sideways.

"Somewhere. Nowhere. Everywhere. It's all the same here. Always now but never then. Always then but never now."

That doesn't make a whole lot of sense.

"Welcome to my world. I'd love to say you get used to it, but . . ."

The swan started spinning loop-di-loops, tossing Sophie's stomach around with it. She wondered if she could throw up in someone else's head.

"You're looking for something, aren't you?" Jolie asked. "That's what the voice in the shadows told me before you came."

That was Tam. He's a friend.

"I'm glad I didn't drag him under, then."

You do that?

"Sometimes. Not always by choice."

So . . . sometimes you do it on purpose?

"If I did, would that scare you?"

A little. But I trust you.

"Does that mean you'll come back?"

Of course I will, Sophie promised. *But right now, I'm only allowed to stay for a few more minutes. Can you help me find the memory I need before I have to go?*

"I can try," Jolie said as the swan tucked its wings and plunged. "But the memories here aren't what they used to be."

On and on they sank, until they reached a fog of glowing shards all scrambled up and flipped around and crashing into each other. Some had images painted across them. Others moved like fragments torn from a movie. And others held only a cacophony of noises.

"Everything that once was, is gone," Jolie said sadly. "All that's left is fractured and fragmented."

I'm only looking for a piece—or maybe a few pieces.

Sophie projected the image Mr. Forkle had sent her and it flared in front of them like a hologram.

"That doesn't look familiar," Jolie murmured.

Mr. Forkle found it the last time he was in here.

Jolie's arms tensed. "Someone else visited?"

You don't remember?

"I hear voices sometimes. But I can never tell if they're echoes. I hope I didn't hurt him."

He was able to get out—but only barely. That's why he sent me.

"You're the moonlark," Jolie whispered. Her arms clung so tightly that Sophie had to fight to breathe.

Or maybe the pain in her chest came from Jolie's next question.

"How long has it been since I was me?"

I'm probably not supposed to tell you.

"But you're old now, aren't you? Far older than my son was when . . ."

Don't think about it, Sophie said. *There's a lot that needs to be explained—but we have to wait until you're strong enough to handle it.*

"That doesn't sound like good news."

It is and it isn't. There are a million reasons to keep fighting. But it's probably not going to be easy.

The shards trembled and tightened.

"I think I'm slipping away," Jolie warned.

A burst of energy flooded Sophie's senses—probably Fitz sending backup—and Sophie wrapped it around Jolie's fading form.

Please—if you can't stay for me, do it for Wylie.

"Wylie," Jolie repeated. She kept murmuring the name as she waved her arms and made another glowing bubble around them, spinning the shards like leaves in a windstorm. "I still don't see what you're looking for."

It has to be there. I'm pretty sure this is one of the memories you were protecting. Maybe even the reason you called swan song.

The bubble burst at the words.

"I don't know what that means," Jolie said as they sank

into the glittering oblivion. "But the phrase has a pull, like an anchor dragging me toward . . . I don't know."

Down they went again—so far that Sophie wasn't sure she'd ever be able to claw her way back up. But it was worth the fall when Jolie whispered, "There."

She waved her arms and the fragments parted, revealing three blindingly bright pieces. "Those are what you need. I . . ."

Jolie's image vanished into the dark.

Sophie had just enough strength left to wrap her mind around the gleaming shards and transmit a call for Fitz's help.

He sent a tidal wave of heat, launching everything up, up, up—through softness and sludginess and pain and relief until she was back in her body, shivering in a pair of warm arms that held her close and careful and wouldn't let her fall.

"Shhhh," Fitz whispered. "You're back. You're safe."

"How's Prentice?" she asked as Mr. Forkle pressed two fingers against her temples to check her memories.

"Same as before," Fitz promised. "Why? What happened in there?"

"Incredible things," Mr. Forkle whispered. Tears streamed down his wrinkly cheeks as he cleared his throat and added, "I'll explain later. Right now we must focus. Mr. Vacker— perhaps you could ensure I'm assembling these memories properly?"

Fitz slipped into Sophie's mind and she watched as the bits of symbol snapped together. The three diagonal lines from the original image converged with other lines bearing similar circles and dashes, all meeting in a central point and fanning out like rays from the sun.

The symbol was abstract, of course, but it reminded Sophie of an asterisk.

Or a star.

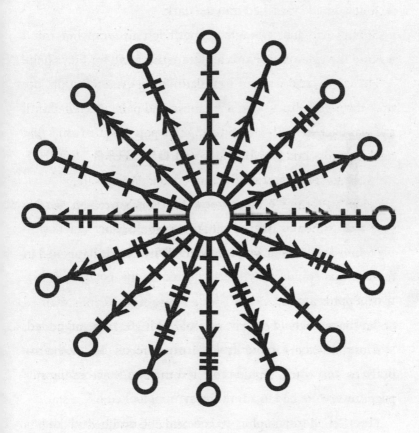

NINE

THE SYMBOL IS A LODESTAR," SOPHIE whispered. "Isn't it?"

"We don't know that for sure," Mr. Forkle said. "Technically, the word 'lodestar' refers simply to any kind of star that can be used as a guide."

"But this could easily be connected to the Lodestar Initiative," Sophie argued.

"Perhaps it would help if we could see?" Granite suggested.

Blur retrieved a memory log from one of the apothecary drawers, and when Sophie projected the image across the stiff pages, everyone had to admit the symbol looked like a star.

"Even if the symbol *is* a Lodestar," Granite said after a moment, "we're still a long way away from understanding what it means. All those dashes and circles have to be significant. I'm assuming you saw nothing that could help us translate while you were in Prentice's mind?"

"I wish. It seemed like Prentice didn't even remember that he'd seen the symbol before. But . . . he only found it after I mentioned swan song. So the two must be connected."

They all tilted their heads and squinted at the star from different angles, as if the explanation would pop out at them if they just stared hard enough.

"Soooooo," Tam eventually said, "anyone want to explain why lodestars are so important? Or are you going to keep acting like Linh and I aren't here?"

"Didn't they tell you?" Fitz asked, glancing at the members of the Collective.

"I told them Keefe joined the Neverseen," Blur said. "I didn't get into why."

"Care to clue us in now?" Tam asked, not sounding happy to have been kept in the dark.

Mr. Forkle explained what little they knew about the Lodestar Initiative and how Keefe's mom seemed to have created it.

"And the Initiative had something to do with what happened to the gnomes?" Linh whispered, tugging nervously on the silver ends of her hair.

"*That* is unclear," Mr. Forkle emphasized. "Fintan implied a connection when he first threatened the Council with the plague. And he made the Initiative sound as though it's the

Neverseen's grand plan. But he also admitted to eliminating Mr. Sencen's mother so he could take over the project, so it's highly possible he's made his own amendments."

"Does Keefe know what the plan is?" Tam asked.

"He says he's still piecing it together—but I know there's something he isn't telling me," Sophie said quietly. "Maybe he'll be more willing to share when I show him the whole symbol."

"I assume that means you've found a way to transmit to him?" Mr. Forkle asked.

Sophie nodded. "We're going to check in every night."

"You are?" The tightness in Fitz's voice made Sophie realize she'd forgotten to mention that detail when they talked.

"It'll be safer this way," she explained. "He can update me on anything he's learned without having to sneak away."

"Or feed you a bunch of lies," Tam pointed out. "Hey—don't look at me like that. You have to admit it's possible."

"*Anything* is possible," Sophie argued. "All I know is that if I'd been brave enough to try transmitting to Keefe sooner, he wouldn't have had to destroy part of Foxfire to warn me."

"Whoa—back up," Tam said. "*He destroyed part of Foxfire?!* Okay, seriously, am I really the only one who thinks trusting this guy is a bad idea?"

"No," Wraith said, folding his invisible arms under his cloak. "Some of us are a bit more reluctant."

"I'm not," Blur jumped in.

"Well, Squall is just as torn as I am," Wraith said. "So is Granite."

"You are?" Sophie asked.

Granite had seemed so supportive when he first heard about Keefe. He'd even decided to reveal his true identity to help reassure her that she shouldn't be afraid to trust people. But now he shifted his hefty weight, filling the small space with the crunch of his crystallized joints. "I don't doubt that Mr. Sencen left with good intentions—but we can't ignore the possibility that he might become corrupted. He's immersed in the Neverseen's world—training in their methods, being exposed to their teachings and theories. There's no telling how that might influence him."

"Exactly," Tam agreed. "You're with me on this, right?" he asked Linh.

Linh shook her head. "Remember how people have doubted us? Their murmurs and snipes about the strength of our powers. Their outrage when you left with me after I was banished. Not to mention the mistrust because we're twins. They had reasons for their feelings. Did that make them right?"

"No—but their reasons are stupid," Tam argued.

Multiple births were rare in the elvin world, and for some reason that bred judgment and scorn. Sophie would never understand how the elves could be so brilliant and sophisticated and still have so many strange prejudices. They didn't care about skin color or money or appearance. But they condemned anyone without a special ability, or anyone with unusual genetics.

"And you think that's the same as joining the enemy?" Tam asked.

"No, I think it means we shouldn't pass judgment until we see how things play out. Actions never tell the whole story. Good can be done for the wrong reason. And bad can be misunderstood."

"Fine," Tam grumbled. "But if he comes anywhere near me, I'm siccing the dwarves on him until he lets me take a reading. And you guys should be keeping us way better updated about this stuff," he told the Collective.

"The incident at Foxfire was only yesterday," Mr. Forkle explained. "But I realize you're both feeling very separated— and that's because you are."

"Maybe it would be easier if we returned to the Lost Cities," Linh told her brother.

"You really want to go back to Choralmere?" he asked. "You want to deal with Mom panicking that you're going to flood the house every time you gaze at the ocean? You want to hear Dad constantly lying about us, like our very existence brings him shame?"

"Of course not," Linh told him. "I just—"

"I might have a solution for you," Mr. Forkle interrupted. "I've been in talks with the Council about a new arrangement that would allow you to visit the Lost Cities regularly. But nothing is official yet, so I'm going to need you—"

"Let me guess," Tam jumped in, "You want us to be patient?"

Mr. Forkle smiled. "I know I ask for that a lot. I also demand it of myself. I've often said that it seems we're attempting to drain the ocean with a leaking spoon. But even if that's the case, we can either give up, or we can continue taking it one dripping spoonful at a time. And *this*"—he pointed to the symbol Sophie had projected—"is a pretty important spoonful. We need to find out what it means."

"I can ask Keefe," Sophie offered. "Though he didn't recognize the black disk or the symbol when I showed it to him last night, so I doubt he'll be much help."

"I can think of someone who might know more about the symbol," Fitz mumbled. "But . . . you're not going to like it."

Sophie was about to ask who when she figured it out on her own.

She groaned. "Please tell me you're not asking us to trust Lord Cassius."

TEN

WOW," LINH WHISPERED, staring at the stark crystal sky-scraper looming over them. "*This* is where Keefe grew up?"

"It explains a lot, doesn't it?" Sophie mumbled.

Mr. Forkle hadn't been sure if it would be wise to bring the twins on this excursion—but Sophie had insisted. Maybe it would help Tam understand where Keefe was coming from.

Their feet crunched on the gravelly ground as they crossed under an intricate arch with the word CANDLESHADE woven into the iron. Lord Cassius answered the golden door before Mr. Forkle finished knocking, looking pristine in his intricately embroidered blue cape. He reminded Sophie far too much of his son—same blond hair and ice-blue eyes. Same handsome features. But he was the version where all the fun had been squeezed out and only the sour was left.

Even his smile was creepy—oily and insincere as he said, "Why, Miss Foster. I almost didn't recognize you with your hair back. But it's always a pleasure to see you. And you as well, Mr. Forkle. And Mr. Vacker." His eyes flicked past Sandor and Grizel without acknowledging them and settled on Tam and Linh. "And who might our surprise guests be?"

"This is Tam and Linh Song," Mr. Forkle told him, ignoring Tam's scowl at the use of his last name.

"Song?" Lord Cassius repeated. "You're Quan and Mai's children?"

"Their *twins*," Tam corrected.

Tam's father had tried to convince people that Tam and Linh were a year apart in age, but they refused to play along.

"I see the resemblance now," Lord Cassius said, studying the twins more closely. "I know your father well. He was a Level ahead of me at Foxfire, but we often studied together. We still meet for drinks in Atlantis sometimes."

Tam glanced sidelong at Sophie. "I suppose I shouldn't be surprised to hear that."

"Do your parents know you've joined the Black Swan?" Lord Cassius asked.

"I don't see why they would," Tam told him. "And for the record, we haven't sworn fealty."

"Yet," Linh added quickly.

"I know the feeling." Lord Cassius had volunteered to join the Black Swan himself—which made Sophie want to vomit on his jewel-encrusted shoes. She didn't care that he'd been searching his wife's possessions for clues to her Neverseen activities. Finding a bunch of maps and a leaping crystal kit would never make up for the way he'd treated his son.

"Oh my," Lord Cassius said, fanning his face, "I always forget how intense your emotions are, Miss Foster. It's such a strange sensation to feel them wafting through the air. A bit like static electricity, only pricklier."

Most Empaths needed physical contact to take a reading, but for some reason Keefe and his father were different—at least when it came to Sophie.

"Well," she said, hoping he could feel the massive waves of disgust she was sending his way, "some things give me a stronger reaction than others."

Abuse came in all forms—and while Lord Cassius had never hit his son, his constant belittling criticism had done plenty of damage.

Not surprisingly, he didn't bother asking for an update on Keefe as he stepped aside to let them in. The sparse foyer felt as cold and welcoming as a morgue—black floor, sleek walls glinting with sparks of blue balefire, and a silver staircase that spiraled all the way up to the two hundredth floor.

"You said you needed my help with something when you hailed," Lord Cassius prompted.

"Indeed. We're looking for any information you might be able to provide us about this symbol." Mr. Forkle removed the memory log from his cape pocket and handed it over.

Lord Cassius's eyes widened. "Lodestar."

"So that *is* what the symbol means?" Sophie asked.

Lord Cassius frowned, turning the memory log to study the symbol from different angles. "It's strange. The word clicked when I looked at the image, but I have no idea why."

Memories could do that sometimes—especially memories that had been erased. Some triggers only dragged certain details back. Others unleashed the entire scene in a dizzying rush. Sophie knew the feeling well, thanks to the secrets the Black Swan had planted in her brain. It was also why she wasn't allowed to ever visit her human family, in case seeing her made them remember.

"I feel like there's something I'm missing," Lord Cassius said, scratching his head and messing up his immaculate hairstyle.

"The mind is a tricky thing," Mr. Forkle told him, taking the memory log back. "If you remember anything else, you know how to reach me."

"Of course. Though I don't see why you need *me*. Surely you realize there's someone who could be infinitely more helpful."

Sophie was about to ask who when realization dawned, spreading goose bumps across her skin. "You . . . want us to ask your *wife* about the Lodestar Initiative?"

"Why not?" Lord Cassius asked. "Isn't this whole thing her mess? Who better to solve the problem than the one who created it in the first place?"

"Uh, maybe someone who's not locked away in an ogre prison?" Fitz suggested.

For the briefest glimmer of a moment, Lord Cassius's expression faltered and he looked like a grieving husband and a crushed father, standing all alone in his cold, empty tower.

Then he blinked and it was gone, replaced with his dripping smile. "Where there's a will, there's a way."

"Not in this instance," Mr. Forkle told him. "If we express interest in Lady Gisela, we turn her into an ogre bargaining chip—one that would come at far too high a cost."

"Diplomacy so rarely yields results," Lord Cassius agreed. "But that's why I've grown so passionate for your order. Rumor has it, the Black Swan staged a rather successful raid on Exile a few months back. Why not pull the same trick again?"

"Because we've gained wisdom," Mr. Forkle told him. "And experience."

Their adventures in Exile hadn't exactly gone as planned, between Fitz nearly dying and the Council almost arresting everyone. And yet, Sophie couldn't help finding Lord

Cassius's suggestion *tempting*. Not only could Lady Gisela teach them all the things Keefe was so determined to learn from the Neverseen, but Keefe also wouldn't need Fintan to rescue his mom.

No, Mr. Forkle interrupted. *A jailbreak in an uncharted prison run by a particularly violent species will never be a worthwhile risk—especially considering that Lady Gisela may no longer be alive.*

Dread hit her stomach with a thud. *But Fintan told Keefe—*

Yes, I know what he promised. I also know he gave Mr. Sencen that information when he was trying to lure him into joining their order. And even if the report was accurate, it's been weeks since then—and Lady Gisela was badly wounded at her arrest. Or if she is alive, it's also incredibly likely that they erased her mind before they sent her away.

You've put a lot of thought into this, Sophie noted.

Of course. The Collective and I have discussed it at length. I never mentioned it because I know how you struggle to ignore possibilities.

Or maybe it was because your first instinct is to say no to everything. You realize that ninety percent of the time, you give me a big speech on all the reasons why an idea is too dangerous, and then a few weeks later we end up doing it anyway?

A rueful smile curved his lips. *And in each of those instances, it was only because the situation grew especially desperate. Thankfully, we're not there yet. There are avenues we haven't yet explored—like*

showing the symbol to Gethen when we meet with him and seeing if
we can trick some answers out of him.

I guess that's true, Sophie hated to admit.

She'd been expecting him to offer his usual less-than-help-
ful solutions, like "read a bunch of really long books" or "practice telepathy with Fitz."

Gethen . . . might actually work.

Good—it's settled, Mr. Forkle told her as he turned to their
group. "Forgive our moment of distraction."

Lord Cassius nodded. "I'm sure we're all used to Telepaths.
Have you at least come to a decision?"

"Only that we'll be focusing on alternate plans. But thank
you for the suggestion. I wonder if I could trouble you with
one further request. I'd love to take a look around before I
leave. Perhaps my fresh eyes might turn up a clue your wife
left behind."

"Where would you like to search?" Lord Cassius asked.
"There are *quite* a few places."

Talk about an understatement.

Sophie doubted an army of gnomes would be able to search
the massive estate in less than a week—and gnomes were
the most efficient, industrious creatures she'd ever met. Still,
Keefe had stayed at Candleshade the night before he ran off
with the Neverseen. And while he was there, *something* must
have changed.

When he'd left Sophie's house he'd seemed upset—but nothing like the mess he'd been the next day.

Something had triggered new memories—memories that made him believe he was part of the Lodestar Initiative.

So maybe if she searched his room, she could find what made him remember.

ELEVEN

"H UH," FITZ SAID. "SO THIS IS KEEFE'S room."

Sophie blinked. "That's right—you've never been here."

"Uh, have *you*?"

"I'd like to know that answer as well," Tam said.

She shook her head. "Keefe told me he didn't like to have friends over to his house. But I've seen it in a few of his memories."

The memories weren't happy memories, though, so she hadn't paid much attention to the scenery. The room took up three stories, and was one of the fanciest places Sophie had seen—sparkling crystal walls, swirling chandeliers, and tons of ornate furniture in shades of black, white, and gray.

"This place reminds me of our old room," Linh mumbled. "We weren't allowed to decorate it either."

"You guys shared a room?" Fitz asked.

"It was our punishment for telling people we were twins." Tam rolled his eyes.

Linh hooked her arm around him. "Too bad I liked sharing a room better."

"And yet you ditched me the first second we got to Alluve-terre."

"Hey, what girl is going to pass up her own private tree house?" Linh asked.

"Definitely not me," Sophie said, trying to figure out where to start their search. Everything seemed so un-Keefe, it was hard to imagine him touching any of it.

"What exactly are we looking for?" Tam asked. "Keefe doesn't hit me as the Dear Diary type—though if we find one, I call dibs."

"No you don't," Sophie told him. "We're not here to *snoop*. I just figured we should look around and make sure there's nothing important."

"Well, this place is huge," Fitz said. "So maybe we should split up—some of us upstairs and some of us downstairs and meet in the middle?"

"New game!" Grizel jumped in. "Girls versus boys. Losers owe the others a favor. GO!"

"Bring it on!" Fitz said, sprinting for the stairs.

Grizel beat him there and bolted downstairs, so Fitz raced up.

"Looks like we have closet and bathroom duty, guys!" he shouted.

"I'm going on record right now and saying I'm not getting within ten feet of Keefe's underwear!" Tam shouted back.

Sandor heaved a sigh as he turned to follow the boys. "If you care about me at all, Miss Foster, *lose* this silly game. Do whatever you have to do."

Sophie and Linh shared a look before they made their way downstairs, where Grizel was already busy flipping though one of the notebooks piled on an enormous gilded desk. "Either of you want to give me a hand with these?"

Linh grabbed one. "Wow. The whole first page is just *'bored bored bored'* written over and over."

"He also makes some rather entertaining notes about his Mentors in the margins," Grizel said. "But none of that is particularly useful, so we'd better get moving. We're winning this thing! And when we do, Sandor is taking me dancing."

"Dancing?" Sophie repeated, trying to picture that.

Nope.

Her brain couldn't compute.

"Does dancing mean something else to goblins?" Linh asked.

"I don't know—does it mean this?" Grizel hummed a silky beat and shook her hips in a move that reminded Sophie of belly dancing, only with less arm waving and more head bopping.

"You really think Sandor's going to do *that*?" Sophie asked.

"He will if you help me force him. Think of the favor you could demand from that pretty boy up there. And I bet our little Linh would love to force her brother to do something especially embarrassing."

Linh grinned. "How do we win? You never explained the rules."

"Of course I didn't. How else can I change them? Now get to work!" Grizel pointed across the room—which seemed to be some sort of study, complete with oversize armchairs and walls of bookshelves. From a distance, anyone would think a model student lived there—or maybe a snooty professor. But as Sophie looked closer, she could spot glimmers of Keefe in the details. Like the subtitles he'd scrawled on the spines of the books:

688 pages that don't actually tell you anything.

Does anyone honestly care this much about fungus?

I tore a page out of the middle somewhere—good luck trying to find it!

"Think this is significant?" Grizel asked, pulling a silver Imparter from one of the desk drawers.

"I'm betting he left that so no one could track him down," Sophie said "But you're welcome to compare it to mine to see if there's something unique."

She handed over her Imparter, and Grizel studied them from every angle. "Ugh, I guess you're right. These look identical—oh, what's that?"

Linh showed them the notebook she'd been flipping through, where Keefe had drawn a detailed map of Foxfire and marked several places with "Hide gulon here."

Grizel snorted. "I'll give the boy this—he's definitely creative."

"That's true," Sophie realized, trying to see the room through Keefe's eyes. "We need to search beyond the obvious places. He'd want to be clever—hiding stuff in plain sight where no one would suspect. He'd also enjoy damaging things his father cared about, like the walls or the floor or . . ."

Sophie squatted to find the *S* section on the bookshelf. Specifically: *The Heart of the Matter* by Lord Cassius Sencen.

Keefe's father had published his theory that elves generated emotions in both their minds and their hearts, and believed the heart was where the purer emotions lived. Sophie actually found the idea fascinating—and it synced with certain things she'd experienced during her inflicting training. But Keefe's subtitle was: *I'd rather gouge my eyes out with a Prattles pin.*

She flipped back the cover and found that Keefe had glued all the pages together, then cut out their center, creating a hollow space he'd packed with vials of elixirs.

"Victory is ours!" Grizel shouted, handing Sophie back her Imparter.

"It's not about who finds something first—it's about who finds the most!" Sandor snapped back. But Sophie could hear him yelling at Fitz and Tam to work faster.

"I'm not sure this stuff is actually important," Sophie warned, holding up two of the vials—Burp Blaster and Pus Powder. "I think it's Keefe's pranking supplies."

"Maybe some of it," Grizel said, fishing out a silver forklike gadget from the bottom. "But this is an effluxer—also known as an ogre repeller. One of my favorite inventions you guys make, by the way."

"Yeah, but Keefe uses those for pranks," Sophie argued. "One time he tried hiding them in the grounds at Foxfire, so they'd go off right as the principal walked by."

"No wonder he and my brother don't get along," Linh said. "They're basically the same person."

Practically on cue, Tam shouted from the bathroom above, "Dude—this guy uses more hair products than I do!"

"Well," Grizel said, tucking the effluxer next to her sword, "I'm still counting this as a find. The rules never said it had to be related to the Neverseen."

She winked.

"But we're not done searching yet," she added. "I don't just want to win. I want to crush them like a sanguillisk."

"Do I want to know what that is?" Sophie asked as she followed Grizel back upstairs.

"Depends on how you feel about bugs," Linh told her.

"Imagine a roach and a mosquito having a ten-pound flying baby."

"And . . . now I'm never going to sleep again."

Grizel laughed as she and Linh got busy searching under the bed and between the mattresses.

Sophie studied the space, trying to think like Keefe again. "Where's Mrs. Stinkbottom?"

"Am I going to regret asking what that is?" Grizel asked.

"She's a green gulon stuffed animal that Elwin and I gave Keefe to help him sleep. He didn't have a satchel when he left, so she should be here."

They checked under the bed again, and under the decorative pillows piled on top, before making their way upstairs.

"This is our territory," Sandor growled, blocking them from entering the humongous bathroom, complete with mirror-lined walls and a swimming pool–size bathtub.

Grizel stroked his cheek. "Are we making you nervous?"

Sandor flinched out of the way, not saying a word as Sophie and Linh made their way into the closet. They found Fitz and Tam sorting through the racks of clothes—*so* many clothes. Enough to last Keefe a decade or two.

"Anyone see any stuffed animals?" Sophie asked. "I can't find Mrs. Stinkbottom."

Tam snickered.

"Hey, all the cool kids are sleeping with stuffed animals these days," Fitz informed him.

"I take it that means you have a Mrs. Stinkbottom of your own?" Linh asked.

"*I* have a Mr. Snuggles."

"Wow." Tam said. "Just . . . wow."

Grizel clapped her hands. "Enough about stuffed animals. Did you boys find anything?"

Sandor's smile was undeniably smug when he showed her the two stashes of pranking elixirs they'd found in Keefe's shoes—plus a rather terrifying container labeled MIXED FECES that had been hidden behind a rack of tunics.

"We also found my favorite bramble jersey," Fitz added. "I *knew* he stole it."

"That doesn't count," Grizel told him.

Sandor shrugged. "Either way, we're still winning. And I already decided on my favor."

"Yeah, well, don't go counting on it yet," Grizel warned. "Girls—help the boys with this closet. I'm sure they've missed something."

Sandor was busy assuring her they hadn't when Linh noticed the edge of a silver chest in the shadows of the highest shelf.

Sophie floated the trunk down using her telekinesis. "Looks like more pranking supplies—another effluxer, a few empty medicine vials, and a bottle of Drooly Dew."

The bottle was wrapped in crumpled green paper, and when she spotted an opened card underneath it, Sophie realized she was looking at the gift she'd given Keefe for midterms the year before. He'd teased her mercilessly about the detention dance lesson she'd been forced to share with Valin—nicknamed one of the "drooly boys" by Marella—so she'd decided to get back at him. In the card she'd written, "Now you can be drooly too!"

She couldn't believe he'd kept it.

"All right, back to searching," Grizel said. "I'm not settling for a tie. You boys found three stashes, and we found two, and learned that Mrs. Fartbottom is missing."

"Stinkbottom," Sophie corrected. "And honestly, I'm starting to think we're wasting our time. If Keefe left something for us, he probably would've asked me if I found it. And if he had something to hide, he probably would've taken it with him."

Grizel shrugged. "Either way, we still need a winner. Did you boys already check all of the cape pockets?"

"Some of them," Fitz said.

Grizel clicked her tongue and rushed over to a rack of cloaks. "Clearly I need to teach you some dedication. But we'll do that *after* I destroy your lazy butts with the find of the night. Come on, Sophie and Linh, let's crush these boys!"

"Not if we crush you first!" Sandor shouted, charging into the cape-pocket showdown.

"Are all goblins this competitive?" Sophie asked, deciding to watch from the sidelines as Sandor and Grizel tried to shove their meaty hands into the narrow pockets.

"It's just *her*," Sandor squeak-growled.

"Nothing wrong with a girl who goes after what she wants,"

Grizel argued. "And what I want is a whole night of you wearing those silver pants I know you still have and sashaying around the dance floor."

Sophie giggled. "Can I be there?"

Sandor tore through the capes even faster. "No, because it's not happening!"

"Oh, sweetie, I hate to break it to you—but BAM!" Grizel pumped one fist while she used the other to wave a sealed envelope under Sandor's nose. "Would you like do the honors, Sophie—even if you don't deserve it, after you chose to be Too Cool for the Cape Hunt?"

Sophie caught herself holding her breath as she took the envelope from Grizel, slid her finger under the flap, and removed a folded, crumpled paper.

"Did Keefe draw that?" Fitz asked, peeking over Sophie's shoulder at the photo-real sketch of Lady Gisela looking elegant and aloof—but with a hint of her son's smirk.

"I think so," Sophie said.

She'd seen the same sketch in a memory Keefe had shown her, of his father screaming at him for drawing during his Foxfire sessions. Lord Cassius had torn all the pages out of Keefe's notebook and stormed off. But after he was gone, Keefe's mom had retrieved one drawing.

Sure enough, when Sophie turned the portrait of Lady Gisela over, she found a note in loopy writing.

Signed: *Love, Mom.*

TWELVE

"THE ENVELOPE WAS STILL SEALED," Fitz said, taking the drawing from Sophie to study it closer. "So that means Keefe never saw this."

"But why would Lady Gisela hide it somewhere Keefe wouldn't look for it?" Sophie asked.

The note gave them the answer.

Dear Keefe,

You may think you understand what you saw today on the mountain. But there's so much more that needs to be explained.

I think you're ready for the truth. But it's going to be confusing.

I need you to trust me.

I've left a way for you to find me.

And I know you're smart enough to figure it out.

This is your legacy. All it takes is a leap of faith.

I'll see you soon.

Love, mom.

81 / 34 / 197

"Lady Gisela must've written this right after the battle on Mount Everest," Sophie mumbled, rubbing her knot of tangled emotions. "After she phase-shifted off the cliff, she must've come here and left it for him."

"But Keefe didn't come home," Fitz added. "We all went to my house—and then we left to find the Black Swan. So he never found it."

"I wonder what he would've done if he had," Sophie whispered.

Would it have stopped him from joining the Neverseen?

Or would it have made him run away sooner?

More important: What had Lady Gisela planned to tell him?

"It sounds like there are a bunch of stories you haven't shared," Tam said, reading the letter over Fitz's shoulder. "But I guess that's how it goes for the new kids in the group."

"We'll try to catch you up," Fitz promised.

Linh pointed to the digits under Lady Gisela's signature. "Do you guys know what those numbers mean?"

"I'm guessing that's what she meant about leaving Keefe a way to find her," Sophie said. "But I have no idea how three numbers would help."

The only theory she could come up with was latitude and longitude coordinates. But those were always in pairs, and they usually had decimal points.

"What's the sparkly stuff?" Linh asked, pointing to the glints on the edge of the paper.

Sophie had been wondering the same thing. They were too small to be temporary leaping crystals, and there were more inside the envelope, like Lady Gisela had added in a pinch of microglitter before she sealed the letter.

But why would she bother—especially since it seemed like she'd been in a rush? Her writing looked much sloppier than the other time Sophie had seen it.

"Well," Grizel said, "while you guys ponder all of that, let's not forget that girls win!"

"Forget it!" Sandor snapped. "It's not happening."

"What isn't?" Mr. Forkle asked from the top of the stairs. Lord Cassius loomed behind him.

Grizel grinned and shook her hips. "Dancing. Sandor's going to be doing a *lot* of it."

"I . . . think I've missed something." Mr. Forkle's eyes were on Sophie, and she was pretty sure his piercing stare meant he'd noticed the not-so-subtle way Fitz had flailed to hide the note behind his back.

Lord Cassius must've noticed too.

"I'm assuming you found something," he said.

Before Sophie could figure out a good lie, Tam grabbed the jar of feces from Keefe's stash and tossed it to him. "We did. Isn't it awesome?"

Lord Cassius grimaced and stalked over to one of the bathroom sinks to wash his hands, even though he'd only touched the container. "We both know that's not what I was referring to."

"We also know that anything Keefe hid in here was because he didn't want *you* finding it," Tam said. "So do you really think we're going to tell you about it?"

Lord Cassius raised one eyebrow. "I see why your father struggles."

All the shadows in the room seemed to stretch.

Lord Cassius let out a sigh. "No need for dramatics. Keep your secrets. I'm done trying to control willful teenagers."

Sophie breathed a sigh of relief, even as Mr. Forkle's voice filled her head.

As soon as we get back to Havenfield, you're showing me that letter.

Out loud he said, "Can someone at least explain why Grizel keeps dancing?"

"Because it's *happening*," Grizel told him.

Sophie explained the specifics of their game.

"And let's not forget that Pretty Boy owes you a favor too," Grizel reminded her. "And Twinny is at his sister's mercy."

"I'm betting this means we're getting a pet," Tam mumbled.

Linh nodded. "As soon as we're able to leave the house more, you're taking me to Claws, Wings, Horns, and Things."

Lord Cassius whistled. "Either your control has improved significantly or you enjoy flooding Atlantis."

Linh didn't reply, but she formed a small bird out of water, letting it soar around the room before splashing Lord Cassius's shoes.

"Whoa," Fitz breathed, blinking several times before turning to Sophie. "What about me? What's my punishment?"

"I'm . . . still narrowing it down," she hedged, her mind screaming with too many possibilities.

"That's fine," he said. "But I think we need to set a time limit so you can't hold this over me forever. Let's say: If you don't call in the favor within a month, it becomes mine."

Sophie agreed, not sure why the deal made her nervous. Worst-case scenario, she'd just rattle off whatever lame idea she came up with off the top of her head.

"Anyway," Mr. Forkle said, "we shouldn't impose on Lord Cassius's hospitality any longer."

"One thing before you go," Lord Cassius said as Mr. Forkle reached for his pathfinder. "I know you saw my son yesterday," he told Sophie. "And that he was behind the damage at Foxfire.

I wanted to thank you for keeping that information private."

"I didn't do it for you," she said.

"That doesn't stop me from appreciating it. I've always valued your friendship with my son. If anyone can guide him along this challenging path he's chosen, it's you. I also assume he'll be contacting you again—and if so, I hope you'd be willing to give him a message."

Sophie steeled herself for some sort of cruel threat. Instead, Lord Cassius told her, "Please let him know that no matter what happens, he will always have a room here at Candleshade. I realize my son and I do not get along. I'll even own that it's primarily my fault. But regardless of our differences . . . Keefe and I will always be family. And no matter where he goes or what he does, he can *always* choose to come back home."

It definitely wasn't the kind of speech that left Sophie feeling warm and snuggly. But Lord Cassius was offering his son more than Tam and Linh's parents had done for their children.

"I'll let him know," she promised.

Lord Cassius nodded. And with that, they leaped back to Havenfield.

Mr. Forkle gave them ten seconds after their group arrived in the creature-filled pastures before he held out his pudgy hand. "Show me the letter."

Fitz obediently passed it over.

"Well," Mr. Forkle said when he'd finished reading, flipping the note over to study the drawing. "Mr. Sencen is a remarkable artist."

"That's it?" Sophie asked as Tam groaned. "What about the note? And the numbers?"

"And the sparkles," Linh added.

"Excuse me for wanting to give proper praise to Mr. Sencen's talent. Look at those details! Do we know how old he was when he drew this?"

"He was a Level Three at Foxfire," Sophie said. "And now you're stalling,"

"I am," Mr. Forkle agreed. "But only because I know you're all going to start shouting at me in a few seconds—even Sandor and Grizel."

"Why would we do that?" Fitz asked.

"Because . . . I know what the numbers mean."

"YOU DO?" six voices shouted in unison.

Mr. Forkle rubbed his temples. "Just as I expected. And now . . ."

He pointed to the path that led to the T. rex pasture, where Grady came sprinting toward them covered in neon green dinosaur feathers.

"Is everything okay?" Grady asked. "I heard shouting while I was bathing Verdi."

"We're fine," Mr. Forkle said. "But by all means, please join this conversation. It'll save me from having to explain a second time."

Mr. Forkle handed Grady the note from Keefe's mother and pointed to the line under the signature. "Eighty-one, thirty-four, one hundred and ninety-seven. I'm surprised none of them could guess after seeing the crystal powder."

Grady sighed. "Path angles."

Mr. Forkle nodded. "For those who've never made a temporary leaping crystal before, the beam is made by three facets that converge to a single point, and then collapse in on each other once the leap is done. In this case, the crystal that Lady Gisela is instructing her son to carve has an eighty-one-degree angle, a thirty-four-degree angle, and a one-hundred-and ninety-seven-degree angle. She also provided the crystalline powder he'd need in order to form it, so he could take the leap of faith and meet her."

"So we can do the same thing, right?" Sophie asked, hoping she hadn't lost any of the powder when she opened the letter.

"I assumed that would be your next question," Mr. Forkle said. "And I'm sure all of you are now imagining rather dramatic scenarios that involve storming a secret Neverseen hideout and solving everything with an epic showdown."

"That'd be nice," Tam said.

"Though I'd be even happier if they surrendered without a fight," Fitz admitted. He rubbed the spot on his chest where he'd been impaled during their Exile prison break.

"*We* are the only ones who will be storming anything," Sandor assured him, pointing to himself and Grizel.

127

"That won't be necessary," Mr. Forkle interrupted. "And no, Miss Foster, I'm *not* saying that because my first instinct is to deny things. I happen to know where this particular crystal will lead, and it's nowhere we need to be visiting. I used the same angles the day I came to rescue you and Mr. Dizznee from the Neverseen."

THIRTEEN

THE FLASHBACKS HIT SOPHIE HARD.

No visuals. Only sounds.

Ghostly laughter. Haunting threats. Questions with no answers.

"Are you okay?" Fitz asked as Sophie dug her fist under her ribs, trying to keep the tangled emotions from unraveling.

"I'm fine," she promised—then cleared her throat and tried again without the definitely not-fine squeak. "I just don't have good memories of that place."

"Neither do I," Mr. Forkle mumbled. "Seeing you blistered and drugged and strapped to a chair . . ."

Everyone shuddered.

Sophie didn't have the same memories. Her blindfold had prevented her from seeing the hideout. And the cloyingly sweet-scented drugs had dulled the rest.

All she remembered was pain.

And panic.

And scattered random details, like the weight of her bonds, the rush of the elevator they'd used during their escape, and the endless minutes as Mr. Forkle had carried her and Dex through the halls. Then she'd woken up on the streets of Paris with new abilities and three vague clues to help them find their way back to the Lost Cities.

"Just so I'm understanding this right," Tam said, "you guys actually know where one of the Neverseen's hideouts is?"

"An abandoned one, yes," Mr. Forkle said. "They managed to destroy the entrance in the brief time it took me to treat Miss Foster's and Mr. Dizznee's wounds—and by the time I found a new way in, they'd removed all trace of themselves. Which is probably why Lady Gisela chose it for her rendezvous point. If the note fell into the wrong hands, all anyone would find are a few empty underground rooms—and even then, only if they knew exactly how to find them."

"Does that mean the numbers in the note are a dead end?" Fitz asked.

"Unfortunately, yes. I'm sure any lookout Lady Gisela posted there is long gone now that she's in prison. And we monitor the area. No unusual activity has ever been reported."

Fitz's shoulders slumped. "Just when I thought we were getting somewhere."

"We *are* getting somewhere," Mr. Forkle said. "This note is not the only discovery we made today. All we need—"

"I'd like to see it," Sophie interrupted. "The hideout, I mean."

"That would be very unwise, Miss Foster. Reliving all the trauma—"

"I can relive the trauma anytime," Sophie interrupted. "I'm doing it right now."

Grady pulled her close.

"Really, I'm fine," she promised, glad her voice matched the words. "All I'm trying to say is that it's not like I'll ever forget what happened to me."

"Maybe not." Grady kissed her forehead. "But you could trigger additional flashbacks."

"That could be a good thing," Sophie argued. "We might learn something important."

"I can assure you, Miss Foster, that whatever miniscule truths you might glean from those dark flashbacks won't be worth the additional stress they'll cause. Your mind and sanity are far too precious to take such a risk."

"I can handle it," she insisted.

It'd been months since her kidnapping, and she'd never once considered going back. But to stand in a Neverseen hideout—even just the shell of it . . .

Maybe it would help her get inside their heads.

"We know way more about the Neverseen now than we did when I was taken," Sophie reminded them. "Back then, we didn't know the name of their organization, and we hadn't seen the creepy white eye symbol on their cloaks. We'd also never heard anyone mention the Lodestar Initiative. So it *is* possible you missed something when you were there. We have to at least check. I promise it won't be too hard for me, and you already said it won't be dangerous—"

"Funny, I don't remember saying that," Mr. Forkle interrupted.

"You said there's been no unusual activity," she reminded him. "Same difference."

"Just because we've seen no sign of the Neverseen doesn't mean it's safe to go sneaking off to a Forbidden City—especially with the Council watching your registry feed so closely."

"We're following an important lead," Sophie argued. "I'm sure the Council realizes that finding the Neverseen is going to require us bending a few rules—and if they don't, who cares? We've never let that stop us before."

Mr. Forkle sighed so hard it made his pudgy cheeks flap. "Can we at least let this idea sit for a few days?"

"What will that accomplish?" Sophie asked. "Besides wasting time we can't afford to lose? If we have a shot at learning something, why not learn it *now*?"

"I'm with Sophie on this one," Tam jumped in.

"Me too," Linh said.

"You kids are getting too smart for your own good," Mr. Forkle muttered. "Fine. Let me reach out to Blur."

He stepped away to whisper into his Imparter, and Grady shifted so Sophie was facing him. "Are you sure this is a good idea, kiddo?"

"I'm never sure of anything," Sophie told him. "But I've been back to the cave they grabbed me from, and it didn't cause a breakdown."

"This will be much harder," Grady warned. "And you've already had a long, tough day. You've been up since before dawn."

"I know." Sophie yawned just thinking about it. "But we both know I'm never going to sleep until this is done."

"I doubt you will afterward either," he said sadly. "Just . . . promise you won't be afraid to admit if it gets too hard and you need to leave. There's no shame in saying *I can't.*"

Sophie promised as Mr. Forkle returned looking equal parts determined and resigned.

"Blur sent two of our gnomes to inspect the area," he said. "As long as they give the all clear, I'll take you for a quick look— but the emphasis must be on 'quick.' Understood?"

"And you mean all of us, right?" Fitz jumped in.

"I leave that up to Miss Foster. She may well prefer to keep this a private moment."

The idea of bringing an audience to her torture chamber felt *strange.*

But facing it alone sounded worse.

"Just . . . don't freak out if I start bawling, okay?" Sophie asked.

Tam and Linh nodded, and Fitz patted his shoulder. "Ready to cry on if you need it."

"What about Dex?" Grady asked.

The question had a weight to it, pressing on Sophie's heart as she imagined how furious Dex would be if she left him out.

But could she watch him relive the horrors—knowing they happened because of *her*?

"I think the smaller the group, the better," she whispered.

"I agree," Sandor said. "It will be easier for me to protect you."

"*You're* going?" Tam asked.

"I go where Sophie goes."

"And I go where he goes," Grizel said, grabbing Fitz's arm.

"But you guys are seven feet tall and gray," Tam argued.

Sandor was unmoved. "I went with Sophie to visit her former home."

"Yeah, but that street's almost always empty," Sophie reminded him. "Paris is one of the humans' most popular cities. There will be people everywhere, taking pictures and videos. And hilarious as your old-lady disguise was, it was *not* convincing."

"Hang on—old-lady disguise?" Grizel asked, cracking up when Sandor flushed.

134

Even Mr. Forkle was smiling as he said, "No disguises should be necessary. We'll be mostly underground. And I always keep one of these with me for emergencies."

He showed them the obscurer hidden in his pocket—a small silver orb that bent light and sound to hide their presence.

"Some of us won't need your gadgets," Grizel said as she moved into the shadow of a nearby tree. She pressed herself against the trunk and held so still, Sophie lost sight of her.

Sandor coughed something that sounded a whole lot like "show-off" as Mr. Forkle's Imparter flashed with what must've been the equivalent of a text message.

"The gnomes feel the hideout is empty," he said. "And they've agreed to stay nearby in case we need them. So I suppose this is happening."

He pulled a handful of crystals from his pocket and chose one that was pale blue and pear shaped. "I had a permanent crystal cut once I knew the hideout existed."

"You don't think you should change into human clothes before you go?" Grady asked.

"The gnomes are reporting rain in the city," Mr. Forkle said. "Which will clear the streets and make our capes appear far more normal should someone somehow spot us beyond the protection of the obscurer. This mission may seem hasty, but I assure you, I would *not* make it if I foresaw any dangers—no matter how grumpy it might make your daughter."

Grady cracked a smile at that, strangling Sophie with a hug

before Mr. Forkle removed the hourglass from his pocket and handed it to him.

"That will last twenty-five minutes," Mr. Forkle explained.

"I thought it was ten," Sophie said.

"It lasts however long I need it to. Is everyone ready?" He offered Sophie his hand, and she tried not to tremble as Fitz took her other hand and the rest of their group formed a tight circle.

"I'll be waiting," Grady said, holding the hourglass ready to flip.

Mr. Forkle nodded. "We'll be back by the final grain of sand."

FOURTEEN

THE GNOMES WERE RIGHT ABOUT
the rain. In fact, "downpour" would've been
a better word. The fat, sloshy drops fell so
fast they blurred the scenery, bouncing off
the gravelly ground and soaking Sophie's group from both
above and below.

She could feel the dirty water seeping through her boots
when Linh waved one arm back and forth, twisting the rain
into thin, gurgling streams and weaving a weblike bubble
around them. She pulled her other arm into her chest, drawing the moisture out of their hair and clothes.

"Seriously," Fitz told her. "You're amazing."

Linh's cheeks flushed a deeper pink. "My ability makes it easy."

"I wouldn't sell yourself short," Mr. Forkle corrected. "This is remarkable control."

"He's right," Fitz said, unable to take his eyes off Linh.

"Shouldn't we keep moving?" Sophie asked, sounding grumpier than she meant to.

"We should," Mr. Forkle said. "Just let me get my bearings."

They'd leaped to the edge of some sort of garden, where neat rows of trees led toward an extravagant palace surrounded by flowers and benches and statues and a lake-size fountain. The place was probably a huge tourist trap on a clear day, but for the moment it was empty, save for one couple clinging to their cheap umbrellas as they scurried around looking for better shelter.

"Relax," Mr. Forkle said as Sandor and Grizel clutched the handles of their swords. "The obscurer will do its job."

Linh kept the rain away as they headed toward a narrow gate in the iron-and-gold fence, but her legs were shaking from the strain by the time they reached a main street.

"It's fine," Tam told her. "Getting wet isn't going to kill us."

"But the water smells like pollution. Besides. If I could hold back a tidal wave in Ravagog, I can hold back a little rain."

"I seem to remember us having to carry you while you did that," Tam reminded her.

"Well, this time I've got it covered." But she nearly tripped as they ran through the puddled crosswalk.

"How much longer until we're there?" Sophie asked as Fitz wrapped his arm around Linh's waist to keep her steady.

The city looked familiar—narrow streets, stone buildings with iron balconies, charming cafés with bright awnings, and tiny cars that looked more like toys than actual transportation. But she didn't recognize anything. No sign of the Eiffel Tower. Or Pont Alexandre III, with its fancy lanterns. She couldn't even see the Seine.

"We're close," Mr. Forkle promised, ducking down a street that felt more like an alley. Cars were parked right on the sidewalk.

"I've always wondered what it would be like to drive around in these things," Fitz said.

"Did you ever ride in one?" Tam asked Sophie.

"Pretty much every day," she said.

"Wow—was it scary?" Linh asked.

Mr. Forkle said "yes" at the same time Sophie said "no,"

"*You* drove?" Sophie asked.

"Of course not. But occasionally I was unable to avoid being a passenger—and there is nothing quite so terrifying as putting your life in the hands of a distracted human who's operating a piece of deadly machinery they only marginally understand and can hardly control. It's a wonder any of them survive the process."

A siren blared in the distance, making a different wail than the police cars Sophie was used to hearing, followed by screeching tires and a whole lot of honking.

"Case in point," Mr. Forkle told them, turning down an even narrower alley lined with trash cans.

"Lovely place the Neverseen chose," Tam grumbled as Mr. Forkle dropped to his knees in front of a gunk-encrusted manhole cover.

"It gets worse," Mr. Forkle warned.

"Is that their symbol?" Fitz pointed to the curved markings etched along the grimy circle of metal—and he was right. The whole pattern was made of the Neverseen's round eyes.

"See?" she told Mr. Forkle. "Bet you didn't notice that last time."

"I did not," Mr. Forkle admitted as he twisted the cover and lifted it free.

Dread clawed around Sophie's stomach as she stared at the ladder descending into the darkness. "Wasn't there an elevator?"

"They collapsed that tunnel to stop me from coming back. Took me a whole day to find this back entrance—and it's not a direct access point. We still have a journey underground."

"I'll go first," Sandor said, already lowering himself onto the ladder. "And I'll scout the path ahead."

"You might want to duck when you're down there," Mr. Forkle warned. "I remember the ceilings being rather low. You'll also need this."

He removed a long necklace and breathed on the crystal pendant, letting the heat reignite the blue balefire dormant inside.

"Got any more of those?" Fitz asked as Sandor disappeared into the darkness.

"Unfortunately, no," Mr. Forkle said. "So hopefully you remember your Exillium training. You covered night vision, right?"

"Yeah, but I wasn't good at it," Fitz mumbled.

"You were probably overthinking it," Linh told him. "There's always *some* light present. If you make your mind believe that, it will amplify it for you."

"Precisely. Trust your mind, not your eyes. And if all else fails, remember that you have other valuable senses to guide you. I'll see you at the bottom." Mr. Forkle's hefty girth barely squeezed into the cramped tunnel as he shuffled down the ladder.

"I'll go next," Tam said, already crouching to reach for the top rung. "Maybe I can thin some of the shadows and make it brighter for you guys."

"I should go last," Grizel decided. "To make sure no one follows."

"Then I'll go next to last, to keep the rain away," Linh said.

Which meant it was Sophie or Fitz's turn.

"What would be easier for you?" Fitz asked. "I can be a few steps ahead, or right behind you. Either way, I'll be close."

"I'll go first."

She gave herself five deep breaths—wishing they didn't taste like putrid, rotting trash—before she lowered herself onto the ladder. The metal felt cold and scratchy under her fingers, and she cursed the ruined elevator as she climbed down into the stale darkness.

Her mind was racing way too fast to focus on her night vision, so all she could see were smudges and vague outlines. But she could hear shaky breaths and scraping shoes and feel the vibration in the ladder, proving she wasn't alone. She counted the rungs to keep calm, and had just reached number one hundred and thirty-four when her foot touched solid ground.

"Over here," Tam said, taking her hand. "The floor's uneven, so be careful."

She still managed to trip. Several times.

Sandor returned from his sweep of the passage, and his balefire pendant cast a murky blue glow around the cavern, bouncing off the low ceiling and rough stone walls.

"Where are we?" Fitz asked as he climbed down behind her.

"I believe the humans call it the Catacombs," Mr. Forkle told him.

"I was really hoping you weren't going to say that," Sophie mumbled. "You know there are dead bodies down here, right?"

Linh froze on the ladder. "There are?"

"Yes, Miss Linh—I stumbled through several of the mass graves the day I found this passage. But they're quite far away."

"Still. Mass *graves*?" Linh shuffled up a couple of rungs. "Why would humans have something like that?"

"It's what happens when you have a species with a very short lifespan," Mr. Forkle explained. "As I understand it, they ran out of space to bury all of their bodies. So they moved them down to these old mine tunnels. Some of the bones were even arranged into patterns and decoration. Incredibly morbid, but I suppose some would see it as a tribute."

"So, how many bodies are we talking about?" Grizel asked as she forced Linh to finally climb down. Linh walked on her tiptoes, like she was afraid of stepping on bones.

"I remember reading that there were about six million," Sophie said.

"SIX MILLION?" Tam's too-loud voice echoed off the walls. "Sorry. That's just a *lot*."

"And that's only the dead from one city, right?" Fitz asked.

"Also from a specific time period," Mr. Forkle agreed. "Humans have buried billions of their species throughout the centuries. Their population size was one of the reasons the Ancient Councillors chose to leave the bulk of the world to them—if only they put it to better use. But we can lament their missed opportunities another time."

Sandor used the balefire crystal to illuminate a narrow gap in the far wall and motioned for everyone to follow him. They had to walk single file, so they stuck with their same order, and Fitz kept one hand on Sophie's shoulder in case she tripped.

She counted her steps, trying to keep her mind distracted. But the memories made her wrists burn with every pulse.

"Okay," Mr. Forkle called as she took step one hundred and sixty-four. "Ahead is a series of sharp curves, which will lead to what your eyes will tell you is a dead end. It's an illusion. There's a weak spot in the stones for us to slip through."

"What do you mean by 'weak spot'?" Sophie asked, imagining cave-ins.

"They must've had a Fluctuator alter the stones' density. You'll understand once you feel them. And try to hurry. This is all taking much longer than I wanted."

Sophie's knotted emotions pulsed with every step as she followed the zigzagging path to what looked like a very solid wall of rock. Tam ran his hands over the stones until he found the right spot—then pushed his arm straight through the wall. Sophie flinched, waiting for the stones to crumble, but somehow everything held strong.

"You ready for this?" Fitz asked Sophie as Tam shoved the rest of his body through. "If not, I'll turn back with you."

"I'll go too," Linh offered.

"I'm not a fan of this place either," Grizel said. "I could bring you back to the surface while the others search."

Sophie was tempted to take them up on it.

Very tempted.

But . . . she had to face this.

Before she could change her mind, she aimed for the same patch in the wall she'd seen Tam use and shoved her shoulder through the rocks.

144

FIFTEEN

SOPHIE COULD FEEL THE STONES ROLL across her skin—kind of like walking through one of those ball enclosures she used to play in as a kid. And when she emerged on the other side, it felt like she'd stepped into another world.

Gone were the rough walls and low ceilings. The hallway was sleek and metal and bright, lit by thousands of tiny flames of balefire glowing in the glass walls. Fitz stepped through the stones behind her, and Linh and Grizel followed right after.

"This is the hall you carried us through, isn't it?" Sophie whispered.

Mr. Forkle nodded. "Mr. Dizznee was kept over here."

His steps echoed off the metal floor as he led them down

the hall. Fitz held Sophie's hand, tightening his grip when Mr. Forkle slid a panel in the wall aside, revealing a small, dusty room.

A line of thick black bars divided the space in half, but otherwise the room was empty.

Mr. Forkle pointed to the cage's far corner, where a black scorch mark on the floor made Sophie shudder. "They'd left him tied up over there. He was lying so painfully still when I saw him, I feared he might be . . ."

"They burned him when he moved," Sophie whispered, tears brimming in her eyes. "I can't believe I had to *force* you to take him with us."

"I wasn't going to leave him," Mr. Forkle promised. "I simply thought it would be faster to carry you one at a time. And it would've let me hold you a gentler way. You both had raw burns—I was trying to make you as comfortable as possible."

When she turned away, his voice filled her mind.

I can see the doubt in your eyes—and I suppose I deserve it after the times I've failed to protect you. But you have to know that I would sooner die than allow harm come to any of you.

"Everything okay?" Fitz asked.

Sophie nodded and walked away from Dex's grim little cell. "Where did you find me?"

Mr. Forkle sounded like the world's most depressing tour guide as he asked her to follow him to a room on the opposite side of the hall with no bars, no furniture—just silver walls

146

and a pile of splintered wood. Sweetness swam through the air, or maybe it was Sophie's mind playing tricks on her as her thoughts fuzzed and her eyes glazed over.

"I've got you," Fitz said, holding her steady.

Tam and Linh took her hands. Even Sandor huddled close, resting a meaty palm on her shoulder.

"This is it?" Sophie asked. "I wasn't in a cell?"

"They had you restrained to a chair." Mr. Forkle kicked a piece of the jagged wood, revealing thick black cords in the pile.

Sophie bent to touch the rope, remembering the feel of its thick fibers against her skin. The pieces of wood were heavy and solid. Unrelenting.

She picked up a piece that looked like the arm of the chair, gasping as she turned it over.

"Scorch marks," she whispered.

The wood slipped from her hand as the nightmares took over.

You're safe, Fitz transmitted, filling her mind with a soft thread of warmth. Their thumb rings snapped together as he pulled her gently away from the pile of wood.

"I told you this would be a bad idea," Mr. Forkle said, kicking a broken board into the wall.

"I'm fine," Sophie promised. "I just . . . need to get out of this room."

Fitz helped her wobble back to the hall and she sank to the floor, putting her head between her knees to stop the spinning.

Want me to carry you out? Fitz offered.

NO!

The thought was so loud he jumped.

Sorry. I . . . I don't want to be carried out of here again, like some helpless little girl.

No one would ever call you helpless. But I get what you mean. Is there anything I can do?

You're here.

He tightened his hold on her hands.

"Are we ready to go?" Mr. Forkle asked.

Sophie closed her eyes, focusing on tying the threads of panic away with her other emotions. The knot in her chest swelled so huge, it felt like it was pressing on her heart. But after a few slow breaths, she could bear it.

"There's still more to the hideout, isn't there?" she asked.

"Only the old entrance," Mr. Forkle said. "But it's nothing worth seeing. Just an empty room with a collapsed tunnel."

"I still think we should check it. We've come this far."

Fitz helped her to her feet and Sophie was glad to walk on her own. But she was grateful for the hand to hold on to.

"Okay, so I have a question," Tam said, breaking the silence. "And this might be one of those stories you need to catch us up on. But . . . how did you get past the Neverseen while you were here? I haven't seen a single hiding place."

"They must've let down their guard after they learned of the plantings in the Wanderling Woods, thinking no one would

148

come searching for two children who'd been declared dead," Mr. Forkle told him. "So when I triggered my distraction, *all* of them left their posts to investigate."

"Why didn't you stage an ambush?" Fitz asked. "You could've captured the Neverseen and ended this."

"We considered it," Mr. Forkle said. "But there were too many unknown variables, and we couldn't risk that our ambush would lead to further harm to Miss Foster or Mr. Dizznee. I honestly wasn't sure if a rescue was even possible—that's why I didn't have a fully formed plan for returning them to the Lost Cities, and why I had to trigger Miss Foster's abilities and leave the two of them to find their own way back. I tried to comfort myself with the knowledge that Miss Foster was well prepared for such adventures, but . . . not a day goes by that I don't regret the decision. I'm very aware of how lucky we are that you had the strength and foresight to call for aid," he told Sophie, "and that Mr. Vacker found you before you'd completely faded away. This whole nightmare was a huge wake-up call for our order. None of us ever imagined our enemies would dare be so bold."

The saddest part was, their kidnapping seemed rather tame compared to the awful things the Neverseen had done since.

But Sophie was trying not to think about that.

She was trying not to think at all.

Trying to focus on breathing.

And walking.

One foot in front of the other. Until the hall ended in a round, empty room.

Half the curved wall had shattered, leaving a pile of jagged glass and twisted metal that looked ready to slice off the legs of anyone who dared to climb it.

"I take it that was the elevator?" Fitz asked.

Mr. Forkle nodded. "They were very thorough in their efforts to leave no trace."

Even the ceiling was crackled in the center, like they'd ripped out a chandelier.

"I can't believe there's *nothing* useful here," Sophie whispered.

"The Neverseen aren't fools," Mr. Forkle told her.

"Maybe not," Tam said. "But I don't think they understand how shadowprints work either. See this?" He kicked a dusty shard out of the center of the floor and pointed to what looked like a smudge underneath. "If the same light hits the same crystal in the same place enough times, it casts a shadow inside the facets. Most people would never notice them. But if you darken them up . . ."

He waved his hands, grabbing every shadow in the room and pulling them to the center of the floor, the smudges turning blacker and blacker as a shape slowly formed.

"Whoa," Fitz breathed as everyone stepped back to study the pattern. "Is that . . . ?"

Sophie nodded. "It's the Lodestar."

SIXTEEN

EVERYONE ELSE SEES THE SYMBOL, right?" Sophie whispered. "I'm not imagining it?"

"Oh, it's definitely there," Fitz said. "Though I don't remember this."

He pointed to one of the rays, where the open circle at the end had thin lines running through the center.

Linh circled the symbol, moving to the part closest to the rubble. "This is the angle they would've seen it from when they first entered from the elevator, right? If you look at it from here, that new mark looks like two runes that spell out . . . Alabestrine."

"The star?" Sophie asked.

Fitz grinned. "I keep forgetting you have the stars memorized."

"You do?" Tam and Linh asked, their jaws falling in unison when Sophie nodded.

"Wow, what must it be like to live in your head?" Tam asked.

"It's very complicated." Sophie squinted at the rune. "So does this mean the symbol is some sort of constellation?"

"If it is, it's none that I've heard of," Mr. Forkle told her. "My memory is far inferior to yours, but as I recall, Alabestrine is what we call a solo star—one that's not connected to anything else."

"Are there a lot of those?" Sophie asked.

"Millions. No idea why this one would be special." Mr. Forkle wandered the symbol several times, turning his head this way and that. "The problem is, even if this *is* a constellation they've created, we'd need to know more of the stars before we'd be able to match it up. And if we did . . . I'm not certain what that would tell us."

Sophie didn't know either.

But it had to mean *something*.

"Just to be sure that I'm understanding this correctly," Mr. Forkle said, turning to Tam, "you were able to create this mark because the symbol was projected here?"

Tam pointed to the damaged ceiling. "I'm betting there used to be a gadget right there that flashed the symbol across the foyer."

Mr. Forkle scratched his chin. "I don't understand why I didn't see it during the rescue. Mind you, I had a lot to consider in that moment—but I can't believe that I would overlook a glowing mark projected across the floor."

"Maybe they didn't keep it lit up all the time," Linh suggested.

"But it would've had to be on a *lot* in order to leave this strong of a shadow impression," Tam reminded her.

Sophie had a much bigger, much more terrifying question.

"Do you think this means that my kidnapping was part of the Lodestar Initiative?"

She knew the Neverseen had taken her, but she'd thought it was because they wanted to learn why the Black Swan created her. She'd never considered it might've been part of some sort of bigger *plan.*

Mr Forkle sighed. "I figured you might be worrying about that—and before you panic, remember that it's possible this hideout was chosen for its convenience or availability. In fact, that could explain why the symbol wasn't illuminated while I was here."

"Maybe," Sophie said. "But those bars in Dex's cell were permanently installed, weren't they? So even if it wasn't built for me, it was built to hold *someone.*"

"And therein lies the problem of only having pieces of information," Mr. Forkle told her. "It raises more questions than it answers. Which means we need to focus our efforts on learning as much about this symbol as possible—and *try* not to worry about the possibilities in the meantime. Have you memorized the details of this shadowprint? I'll need you to project it for me when we return to Havenfield. And speaking of which, I believe we're already past the timeline I gave your father."

They were.

And Grady was *not* happy.

"I was five minutes from hailing the Council and begging them to track your pendants!" he told them as Sophie made her way over and squished him with a hug. "Missed you too, kiddo. Everything all right?"

It wasn't.

But it felt better knowing she was home.

"Did you find anything?" Grady asked.

Mr. Forkle explained about the symbol.

"Wow," Grady whispered, hugging Sophie tighter. "I guess it's a good thing you went."

"It appears so," Mr. Forkle said, handing Sophie the memory log.

She projected the shadowy symbol on the opposite page from where she'd recorded Prentice's memory. The marks were the same except for the runes.

The design had sixteen rays with sixteen circles—so if each one was linked to a star, that meant they had a *lot* of secrets to discover.

"Speaking to Gethen has taken on a new level of priority,"

Mr. Forkle told her, "so use this time to start working on a plan for how to trick him into cooperating. We'll need something clever to get his attention, beyond showing him this symbol. It's always a game with him, and we cannot face him until we know how to win."

Sophie handed him back the memory log. "How long do you think it'll be before the Council lets us meet with him?"

"I'm on my way to Eternalia right now to find out. Mr. Ruewen, do you have any gnomes who might be willing to bring Mr. Tam and Miss Linh to the Alluveterre for me?"

"Lur and Mitya live here now," Grady suggested.

"Perfect. In fact, it might be wise to see if they know anything about the symbol," Mr. Forkle said.

Lur and Mitya had been the ones to discover the hideout in Paris. If it weren't for them, Sophie and Dex wouldn't be alive.

"So that's it?" Tam asked. "You're sending us home to wait?"

"Only because the next step falls squarely on my shoulders," Mr. Forkle told him. "I'll have more specific assignments once I secure the meeting with Gethen."

"Are you going to see the Council looking like that?" Grady asked, pointing to his Forkle disguise.

"Of course. This is the only identity the Councillors are allowed to know. And, if I'm being honest, it also makes the whole process of haggling with them much more entertaining. Councillor Emery looks so delightfully frustrated as he tries to push past my mental blocking. And Councillor Alina loves to pretend like she *almost* recognizes me. I'm certain she'll fall out of her chair when she realizes they nearly elected me instead of her."

"I've been wondering about that," Grady said. "What would you have done if you'd been voted in?"

"I truly had no idea. In all my years with the order, it never crossed my mind that any of my identities might be considered for the Council. It stirred *quite* the controversy among the Collective. Personally, I didn't fret too much, since I assumed I'd never win. But if I'd been wrong, I would've accepted the position. The same means that allowed me to live among humans for twelve years would surely have allowed me to be both Black Swan *and* Councillor."

"And you still won't tell us how you pulled that off?" Sophie asked.

"Perhaps someday. Now, if you'll excuse me, I must be off. And while I'm away, I trust that you four"—he pointed to Fitz, Sophie, Tam, and Linh—"will be responsible members of the order and await further guidance before doing any of your own investigating?"

"Linh and I aren't members of the order," Tam reminded him.

"Yes, and that's something you might want to reconsider. I'm not trying to rush you, of course. But you do push rather hard to be included in all of our happenings."

Tam tugged on his bangs. "I'm sure I'll take the oath soon. I just have . . ."

"Trust issues," Mr. Forkle finished for him. "Not something I blame you for. But keep in mind that there may also be times when something needs to be restricted to those who are officially in our order."

"Do we have to swear fealty together?" Linh asked.

"Of course not. You're each welcome to make your own decision. And speaking of decisions"—he turned to Sophie—"are you planning on telling Mr. Sencen about our discoveries today?"

Her eyelashes turned itchy. "Should I?"

"I . . . would be careful with the specifics," he said. "As I remember, the last time he found a note from his mother, he took the news quite hard."

"Hard" was putting it mildly.

Keefe had tried to run away to Ravagog to take on King Dimitar all by himself. But part of the reason for his recklessness had been that Sophie kept the note secret.

"Let me know how it goes," Mr. Forkle said before he leaped away.

Tam and Linh left with Lur and Mitya a few minutes later.

"Need me to stay while you talk to him?" Fitz asked.

Sophie shook her head. "I'm sure it'll be okay."

It wasn't.

Keefe's mind exploded with angry flashbacks, and he seemed especially fixated on the word "legacy."

Should I not have told you? she asked.

No—it's . . . whatever. I should be used to it by now.

Do you have any idea what she wanted to tell you?

I wish I did.

He also didn't recognize the Lodestar symbol.

You're sure? Sophie pressed. *Look at it really carefully.*

I am. The only part that's familiar is the piece you already showed me. And I have no idea why my idiot dad would think it's connected to the Lodestar Initiative.

Doesn't that scare you? Sophie asked.

A little, he admitted. *But I learned something super important today. Did you know Fintan has a cache—and not the one I stole from you and gave to him? He has one from back when he was a Councillor. Alvar told me. He asked me how I'm holding up after the Foxfire incident, making sure it wasn't affecting my sanity and getting all big-brothery about it—*

Gross, Sophie interrupted.

I know. But I was able to ask him how Fintan's mind didn't shatter after what he did to Kenric. He told me Fintan knows how to wipe his own memories, and locks anything dark-but-crucial away in his cache before he purges it from his mind so he doesn't have to live with it.

Do you think that's why he hasn't recruited any other Telepaths? Sophie asked. *Because he doesn't need them?*

Maybe—I don't know. But don't you realize what that means? His cache is probably filled with everything we need to know about the Neverseen.

Only if we can open it, Sophie reminded him. *Plus, it can't hold any of their current plans. Otherwise how could he work on them if he doesn't remember them?*

Either way, Keefe said. *That cache is my new target. I'm betting he keeps it with the other one. And I'm going to find a way to steal them both.*

SEVENTEEN

Y OU'RE ALIVE!" SOPHIE SAID AS Sandor helped her shove through the crowd to where Dex stood with his lanky female bodyguard—Lovise—in the purple grass of Foxfire's expansive main field. "I'd started to worry."

A gleaming silver stage had been set up in the center of the field, awaiting the arrival of the Council for some sort of official announcement. Scrolls had been sent out that morning, instructing at least one representative of every family to gather.

"Sorry," Dex mumbled. "I know I haven't been around much."

"Much? I haven't seen you since midterms!" Sophie's eyes strayed to the damaged pyramid in the background, hidden under a bright orange tarp bearing the Foxfire seal.

A week had passed since Keefe set off the sound wave, and, other than that first day—when Sophie had gone to see Prentice and the Neverseen's hideout—it'd been an endless week of nothing, nothing, and more nothing. All Sophie had heard about Gethen was "We're waiting for an answer from the Council." And Alden and Della had asked Fitz and Biana to stay at Everglen for "family time." Even Keefe's nightly check-ins had been unhelpful. He was still trying to figure out if Fintan hid his cache the same way the Councillors did—tucked away in the void of nothingness that only Conjurers and Teleporters knew how to access. If it was—and Keefe could figure out Fintan's secret verbal command—he could steal it the same way he'd stolen Kenric's cache from Sophie. But so far, Fintan and Alvar weren't giving him any clues.

So Sophie had spent the week distracting herself by having lots of telepathic conversations with Silveny, making sure the alicorns were safe and happy and keeping themselves hidden. Silveny was still in the first trimester of her eleven-month pregnancy, and was happy to share more details than Sophie really wanted to know about preggers life—especially the morning sickness.

Spoiler alert: Apparently, alicorn vomit was just as sparkly as their poop.

Silveny's maternal instincts also seemed to be kicking in, and she kept making Sophie promise that she'd call for her if she ever found herself in danger. It was nice to know that

Silveny cared—but Sophie would never do anything to risk the safety of the baby alicorn, no matter how many times Silveny assured her she wasn't as fragile as Sophie feared.

The rest of the time, Sophie spent trying to learn whatever she could about Alabestrine—but she didn't find much in the library of Grady's office. The only slightly interesting detail was that Alabestrine was isolated from other stars, so its white glow was considered "pure" because no other light ever touched it.

But lots of stars were "pure." And pure light didn't seem to do anything special—though reading up on it did remind Sophie that there was a mirror called the Lodestar. The Silver Tower for the elite levels had a round room called the Hall of Illumination, lined with mirrors that were unique—each meant to teach the prodigies a different lesson about themselves.

The Lodestar mirror reflected pure light, and Sophie kept thinking that had to mean *something*. But . . . the mirror was centuries old.

She'd still asked Mr. Forkle about it, and he'd reminded her that the Neverseen didn't invent the word "lodestar." It still seemed like a strange coincidence, though.

"So what have you been up to?" Sophie asked Dex. "I tried hailing you a bunch of times but you didn't answer."

Dex patted his cape pockets and frowned. "I must've left my Imparter at Slurps and Burps. But I've had it with me every day and it never gave me any alerts. I've been trying to help my dad keep up with all the orders at the store. Everybody's been stocking up on medicines. I think people are worried that the next time the Neverseen attack, someone's going to get hurt."

Sophie was worried about that too—and even more worried that Keefe would somehow be involved.

"What about your *other* project?" she asked, keeping her voice low—though no one seemed to be paying them any attention. "The one the Black Swan told you to keep secret?"

Dex's ears turned red. "You know about that?"

"Blur mentioned it. And don't worry, I'm not mad. I know how hard it is to have a secret assignment from the Black Swan. But now it's my turn to be the one saying: *I want to help.*"

"So do I," Biana said, appearing in the space between them.

As a Vanisher, Biana had a special gift for sneaking up on people. It made her goblin bodyguard Woltzer's job a million times harder.

Sophie could see him now, using his skinny-for-a-goblin arms to shove his way over from the opposite end of the crowd. As soon as he made it, Sandor launched into an epic lecture about keeping track of his charge.

Biana gave Woltzer an apologetic smile before turning back to Sophie and Dex and leaning in to whisper. "Whatever you're planning, count me in—and don't even think about visiting any more secret hideouts without me."

Dex straightened. "What is she talking about?"

"I don't think—"

"Sophie went with Fitz, Tam, and Linh to the abandoned hideout where Mr. Forkle rescued you guys," Biana interrupted, not letting Sophie change the subject.

The color drained from Dex's face

"Please don't be mad," Sophie begged. "It was just a weird, long day where one thing kept leading to the next."

"If it makes you feel any better," Biana told him, "they left me out too. Maybe we should start our own group. Team Bianex!"

Dex sighed. "That's . . . not the best name."

"It isn't," Biana agreed. "What about Dizznacker? Or Vackiznee?"

"I don't know what you guys are talking about," Fitz said as he and Grizel joined their group. "But I vote for Dizznacker."

"Traitors don't get a vote," Biana informed her brother.

"You're still on that?" Fitz asked. "Seriously—aren't you forgetting that you and Sophie snuck off with Calla and had a big showdown with the Neverseen's Psionipath without the rest of us? How was that any different?"

"Because you guys went to the place where *I* was held prisoner without me." Dex kept his voice low, but Sophie could see a few people glancing their way.

You're right, she transmitted, making Dex jump. *I made a selfish decision. I'm sorry. I didn't want to see the hurt in your eyes as you walked those hallways, knowing that every flashback you had was my fault. But it wasn't fair to leave you out. Please don't hate me.*

Dex bit his lip. "Is there anything else you haven't told me?"

Sophie nodded and transmitted a quick explanation about the Lodestar symbol, the note from Keefe's mom, the shadow on the floor of the abandoned hideout, the rune for Alabestrine, and Keefe's new plan to steal Fintan's cache.

"I was going to tell you everything," she promised. "That's why I kept hailing you."

"Stupid Imparter," Dex grumbled. "I bet it has a loose wire."

"Does that mean I'm forgiven?" Sophie asked.

"Only if you promise that from now on, you'll include me no matter what."

"Hey, that works both ways," Fitz whispered, glancing over his shoulder at the crowd, who'd thankfully gone back to ignoring them. "I want to know what you've learned from my brother's records."

"Me too," Biana said. "And I want to help."

"But you realize what I'm trying to do, right?" Dex asked. "The Black Swan are hoping I'll find a way to track your brother's movements and find him. And if that happens, best-case scenario is he gets sentenced to Exile. Or there could be way worse punishments."

Fitz shrugged, his eyes like teal ice. "No one forced him to do what he's doing."

"That won't make it any easier when it all goes down," Dex said quietly. "I know you're mad, but . . . he's still your brother. Are you sure you're up for it?"

"If I start to feel sorry for Alvar, I'll just think about how many times I've found my parents sobbing these last few weeks," Biana mumbled. "That's why they're not here now. They weren't up for all the stares and whispers—especially if the announcement has to do with the Neverseen."

"And I'll think about what he did to you and Sophie," Fitz added. "I saw the scorch marks on the floor of your cell, and the burned chair Sophie had been strapped to."

Dex rubbed his side, where Sophie knew he hid a thumb-size scar from the ordeal.

"I've tried to understand my brother," Biana whispered. "I've spent weeks researching my family history, hoping I'd figure out what he meant about the Vacker legacy. But so far I don't see anything wrong—or any reason why he thought *I* would understand and not Fitz. And I've decided it doesn't matter. I know our world isn't as perfect as I used to think it was—so I won't be surprised if my family turns out to be the same way. But nothing justifies doing the kinds of horrible things Alvar's doing. Someone has to stop him. I know it's not going to be easy, but . . . please let us help?"

"I guess you can try," Dex said. "But all the records are in tech code, so I doubt you'll be able to read them."

"Then *you* read them, and I'll help find the best dates to look," Biana suggested. "I can think of lots of times I saw Alvar sneaking away and never thought to ask where he was going."

"Same here," Fitz said.

166

"If that's what you guys want," Dex said. "Just warning—it's *beyond* boring. I thought nothing could be worse than searching that Lumenaria database, but at least with that I got to build the Twiggler to help sort the records. This is literally just reading scroll after scroll of dates and times and tiny coded numbers. I'm going cross-eyed."

"It's on paper?" Sophie asked.

"Yeah—it's easier to spot glitches that way."

"Well, that still sounds better than all the awkward family time I've been having with my parents," Biana told him.

"You guys okay?" Sophie asked.

"We're fine," Fitz said. "My parents definitely have their bad days. But they kept us home because they seem to want to know *everything* about us. It's like they're doubting themselves after not seeing what Alvar was up to."

"My dad even had the world's most awkward conversation with me about boys," Biana said with a shudder.

"Actually, *that* was pretty awesome," Fitz teased.

Biana rolled her eyes. "No, what was awesome was when they asked *you* about girls. You should've seen him squirm," she told Sophie. "They went through this long interrogation about which girls he might be interested in—way worse than the one they put me through. And then they took him to see the matchmakers."

EIGHTEEN

W AIT—WHAT?" SOPHIE ASKED,
wishing she hadn't sounded *quite* so
horrified.

But seriously . . . *what?*

"You went to see the *matchmakers?*" she asked

Fitz glared at his sister. "It's not like I got my first list or anything. All I did was pick up my packet—which every Level Five does after midterms, so we'll have time to fill it out by the end of the school year."

"It's a huge packet," Biana said, miming several inches of thickness. "Honestly, I had no idea it was that in-depth. And the questions are *crazy.*"

"How would you know?" Fitz asked.

"Um, I can turn invisible. Did you really think I wouldn't sneak into your room and read it? Your answers so far have been *adorable*."

"I hate you so much right now," Fitz said.

It took all of Sophie's willpower not to press for details. "I still can't believe you have your packet already. It seems so . . . early."

"It's really not," Biana said. "By Level Five, everyone knows if they're going to get a special ability or not, which is the most important detail for the match. And once they turn the packets in, the matchmakers take a whole year to work through all the information. Your first list isn't ready until you finish Level Six."

"That still feels very soon," Sophie mumbled—though she probably should've realized that was how the process worked. Edaline had told her that Jolie received her matches before she signed up for the elite levels.

Sophie had just never really thought about how young Jolie would've been.

The elite levels started at seventeen.

"It's not like anyone gets married right then," Biana told her. "Well, I guess a few people might. But most only get their lists so they can start considering their options. It takes a while to get to know everybody, you know? There are a hundred names—and that's only one list. It's kind of daunting when you think about it."

"Not everyone picks up their list right away, either," Fitz added. "I know I'm planning on waiting for a bit."

"You are?" Sophie and Dex asked at the same time.

"Yeah. I figure I'll wait at least a year or two."

"Why?" Biana asked. "Aren't you dying to see who's on it?"

"A little. But the thing is . . . you can only get five lists."

"Don't most people find someone on their first list?" Sophie asked.

"Not always. Sometimes it takes a while for the matchmakers to figure out who you're really compatible with. Plus, the longer you wait, the more people have registered, so . . . I want to make sure I have the best selection."

Dex and Biana looked stunned. Sophie, meanwhile, was trying to work out the math.

If she was a Level Three, and couldn't register until she was a Level Five . . .

"Oh, don't act so surprised," Fitz told his sister. "Look at what happened with Dad. You heard that story, right?" he asked Sophie.

"I don't think so." Sophie knew that Councillor Alina tried to break up Alden and Della's wedding, but that was about it.

"My dad is about a hundred years older than my mom, so she definitely wasn't on his first list. In fact, I don't think he actually dated any of his first matches. And after he finished the elite levels, he got super busy with his career. So he didn't ask for his second list for years."

Sophie remembered Edaline explaining that Jolie had been forced to wait at least a month between requesting each of her additional lists. But she'd never considered that people might choose to wait longer.

"And *that* was the list that had Councillor Alina on it," Biana jumped in. "Which was how they ended up dating. But she was too smothering, so they broke up, and after a little while, my dad asked for a new list—and that time, my mom was his number one match."

"So if my dad hadn't waited," Fitz finished, "Biana and I wouldn't exist."

"Wow." Sophie couldn't imagine Alden and Della *not* being together. They were one of the sweetest couples she'd ever known.

But it was hard to wrap her mind around the timeline Fitz and Biana were describing. It was *so* different from the things she'd seen growing up. Most humans married people who were within a few years of their own age, since a thirty-year-old and a ninety-year-old were practically a different species. But it didn't seem to be that way for elves.

In fact, Edaline had once explained that *that* was why the elves did matchmaking. Their indefinite lifespan—and ageless appearance—made courting extra tricky. If they weren't careful, someone could end up marrying a distant relative without realizing and . . . ewwwwwwwww.

Still, the matchmaking thing felt like a mountain of awkward looming on the horizon. The whole process sounded arbitrary and unromantic—especially since the matchmakers focused on things like *ideal genetic diversity*. And it was a *big* deal. If you married someone who wasn't on your list, the relationship was branded a bad match and the scorn would follow you—and your children—for the rest of your lives.

Sophie had seen the kind of hurt and problems the system caused, and it gave her a sour stomach.

"Well," Biana told her brother, "you're welcome to be boring if you want. But I know *I'm* getting my list the first second I can—right, Sophie?"

The best answer Sophie could give was a shrug.

She was torn between hoping the elves would see the flaws in their system and decide they were done with the whole matchmaking thing before she ever had to face it, and *really* wanting to know who would be on her lists.

"What about you?" Biana asked Dex.

He took a deep breath. "I'm still deciding if I'm going to register."

Biana's eyebrows shot up so fast they practically launched off of her face. "But . . . that would guarantee you'd be a bad match."

"So? It worked out fine for my parents."

Kesler and Juline did seem very happy—but they'd had to deal with a lot of drama over the years. Edaline had told Sophie that they'd even been nervous to have children, since they knew their kids would face a ton of judgment. And Sophie had heard some of the teasing Dex had endured—and it had to be a million times worse for the triplets.

"It's just . . . look at the mess matchmaking has made," Dex mumbled. "Brant wouldn't have joined the Neverseen if he and Jolie hadn't been ruled a bad match. If they want to give recommendations, that's one thing. But it shouldn't be mandatory."

"I guess I get where you're coming from," Biana said. "But you can always choose to ignore your lists if you don't like the names on them, right? So why not at least give it a chance? You might find the perfect person is part of your match and save all the hassle."

Dex stared at his hands. "Maybe. It just feels like . . . if I register, I'm saying it's okay. That everything that's happened to my family was fair—and it wasn't. I guess the good news is, I don't have to decide for a few more years."

"Right," Sophie said, deciding to change the subject to something that didn't make every part of her feel twitchy. "So what time should we come over to go through Alvar's records?"

"Oh, you want to come to my house?" Dex asked.

"Isn't that where all the stuff is? Why? Is that bad?" Now that Sophie was thinking about it, he'd never invited her over. Not even when they were practicing alchemy all the time—though that could've been because he was afraid she'd burn down his room.

"Would you rather come to my house?" she offered.

"No, my house is fine. But the triplets will be there." He pointed through the crowd, to where his mom was fighting to keep two boys who looked like mini-Dexes and a red-haired girl from tackling each other. "That's them on good behavior."

Biana giggled. "What are their names again?"

"Rex, Bex, and Lex. My dad's not nearly as funny as he thinks he is."

"Aw, I think it's cute that you guys rhyme," Biana said.

"That's because you don't have to be named Bitz," Dex told her.

"Ohhh, I should start calling you that!" Fitz said, grinning at his sister.

"If you do, I'll start calling you Fiana."

Sophie laughed. "Be glad Keefe's not here or those would be your names from now on."

The teasing screeched to a halt.

For one awkward second, they all just stared at each other. Then Biana whispered, "I miss him."

"Me too," Dex agreed.

"Maybe that's his real plan," Fitz told them. "Make us forget how annoying he can be so we let him be twice as obnoxious when he comes home. Though Sophie's still stuck with him. How are the check-ins going, by the way?" he asked her. "Learn anything useful?"

"Not yet. I'll tell you his plan once we're at Dex's house. Should we head over after we're done here?"

"Actually, I can't today," Dex said. "I promised my dad I'd help at the store as soon as I could. But we could meet up tomorrow morning. Not sure how you guys will get there, though. Rimeshire isn't on a lot of Leapmasters. And the Vackers and the Dizznees don't exactly run in the same circles."

"Well . . . they should." Biana pointed to the ring he gave her. "Go Team Vackiznee!"

"I should've known I'd find you arranging some sort of scheme," a whispery voice said behind them.

They all did a double take when they turned to find Sir Astin with his long blond hair and nearly translucent skin.

"How come you're here as him?" Sophie whispered. "Won't the Council be expecting to see Magnate Leto today?"

"Actually, Magnate Leto is off doing a favor for them. But I wasn't about to miss the big announcement."

"Does that mean you know what's coming?" Fitz asked.

"Most of it. Lately the Council has been full of surprises."

"Is the rest of the Collective here too?" Biana asked, turning to study the crowd.

"You're wasting your time trying to find them," Sir Astin warned. "If you haven't guessed their identities already, I daresay you never will."

"So that means we know them," Sophie said.

"Some of them, yes. Now please act normal—we do not need to create a spectacle. And dare I ask what you all were planning as I approached?"

He seemed relieved to hear they were only making plans to study Alvar's records together—though that didn't stop him from giving a lecture on how anything they uncovered was not to be investigated without checking in first.

"Any update on Gethen?" Sophie whispered.

"Not the news I was hoping for," he admitted. "They're saying Lumenaria is closed for visits of any kind, which is . . . surprising. I'm in the process of seeing if they'll reconsider."

"Is the Council late?" Fitz asked, pointing to the still-empty stage. "It feels like we've been standing here for a really long time."

Sir Astin glanced at the sky. "I was expecting them a few minutes ago. But I'm sure they'll be here any second."

"Did you guys notice that the scrolls the Council sent out said sending one representative from each family today was *mandatory*?" Biana asked. "I've never seen that before."

"Neither have I," Fitz said. "I asked my dad about it, and he said the last time was when the Council canceled the human assistance program."

"Seriously?" Sophie asked, turning to survey the crowd. It did seem larger than normal—easily several thousand people. But could it really represent *every* elvin family?

Sir Astin must've known what she was thinking. "The first wave of the announcement applies to those with family members attending Foxfire," he explained. "From there, it will ripple through the rest of our society as the new program progresses."

"So this is a big change," Sophie confirmed.

"It is. The Council is taking a very brave step. But, as Magnate Leto reminded you, change can be a powerful, inspiring thing."

He'd made his voice sound like his alter ego, and Sophie was still trying to wrap her head around the weirdness of hearing Sir Astin sound like Magnate Leto when two lines of heavily armed goblins marched through the crowd and formed a perimeter of swords and muscle.

"Brace yourselves," Sir Astin said as fanfare rang across the field and all twelve Councillors glittered onto the stage. "This should be very interesting."

NINETEEN

SEVEN DAYS AGO, OUR WORLD SUF-
fered an attack," Councillor Emery said as he
strode to the center of the silver stage. "Though
I suppose it would be more accurate for us to say
'*another* attack.' Such events are supposed to be unheard of.
And yet this was the third incident in as many weeks. And it
comes on the heels of the disgusting plague unleashed upon
the innocent gnomes. Surely you also remember the inferno
of Everblaze that stole the life of our beloved Councillor Kenric
and destroyed much of our beautiful capital. In fact, over the
last year, our world has experienced evils we can hardly begin
to process. And as a result, we've been forced to add goblin
police to our cities and armed guards to our schools."

He paused there, his sapphire blue eyes shining against his dark skin while he studied the crowd shuffling nervously around him.

Councillor Emery served as the spokesperson for the Council primarily because of his ability as a Telepath. He mentally mediated all of the other Councillors' internal discussions to ensure that—out loud—they always presented a united front. But there was also something in the way he carried himself that demanded attention. Maybe it was the rigid line of his posture. Or the dramatic sweep of his shoulder-length black hair. Whatever it was, the longer Sophie watched him, the more she found herself holding her breath.

Eventually she glanced away, focusing her attention on the other Councillors, who'd formed two neat lines on either side of the stage. They each wore a different color, with matching jewels glinting across their capes and circlets. Their posture was stiff and regal—heads held high. Shoulders squared.

But there were thin creases in their brows and cheeks, and their lips were pressed tightly together. Sophie had faced the Council many times—more than she ever would've chosen—and it was rare to see them looking so nervous.

She concentrated on her three most loyal supporters—Bronte, Oralie, and Terik—searching their faces for clues to what news might be coming. But Bronte was his usual scowling, pointy-eared, ancient self. Oralie was equally hard to read.

Her pink cheeks and soft blond ringlets always gave her a serene, ethereal air about her. And Terik was . . .

. . . staring right at Sophie.

His cobalt blue eyes held hers, almost like he was taking another stab at her reading. He was the elves' only Descryer, which meant he could sense people's potential. He'd tried to read Sophie once already, and had been unable to understand what he was feeling. The best he could tell her was that he'd felt "something strong."

"Our world has changed," Councillor Emery continued. "The safety and peace we've enjoyed for millennia is fading. But we will not let it disappear! The rebels' strength is an illusion. Soon all of this will be nothing more than a brief chapter in our long history—a chapter that will testify to our adaptability and reinvention—but we'll get to that in a moment. First, we want to assure you that anything damaged during these growing pains will be rebuilt. Councillor Darek, if you please . . ."

One of the Councillors Sophie didn't know moved toward the back of the stage. His skin had a warm brown tone and his shiny black hair curled at the ends. He reminded Sophie of a bullfighter, probably because of his bright red cape, which made a dramatic swish as he raised his arms toward the pyramid.

Sophie thought he might be a Guster as the tarp fluttered and rippled—but the air remained perfectly still as the thick fabric slowly rose from the center, almost as though a giant invisible hand were lifting it like a handkerchief.

The tarp hovered above the pyramid, casting the structure in deep shadow—which was why it took Sophie a second to notice the more important reveal.

The glass pyramid had been repaired.

Each pane had an opalescent sheen, reflecting swirls of color across the courtyard. And when Darek dropped the tarp and let the sunlight hit the glass, it shimmered and twinkled in every color of the spectrum, as though the pyramid were built from fireworks.

"Yes," Councillor Emery said as the crowd erupted with applause. "Thanks to the tireless—and generous—efforts of our gnomish and dwarven allies, we have brought our illustrious academy to a new level of magnificence. Even the interior of the pyramid has been completely redone with remarkable improvements."

"You'd think they might have consulted the principal before redecorating his office," Sir Astin muttered under his breath.

"Did you not know the pyramid had been fixed?" Sophie whispered.

"I knew they were working on it. Not that they were finished. And I'd heard nothing of the interior being altered."

"Let this be a lesson to those afraid," Councillor Emery said, "as well as to those who might view our world as vulnerable. Any efforts to make us weak will only make us stronger. Our resilience and resourcefulness are what have made our kind what we are. We are elves. We live to dream and inspire. And when we need to, we regroup. We rebuild. At times, we even change—but only when such changes are for the better of our people. And the time has come for one of those changes. Perhaps you've already noticed."

He paused, and the crowd started calling out suggestions.

"Yes, Timkin," Councillor Emery said, pointing to his left. "That's exactly it."

All heads swiveled toward the Heks family, who stood several inches taller than the other families around them. Stina and her mother were practically glowing as Councillor Emery asked Timkin, "Can you repeat that for everyone to hear?"

Timkin's puffed-out chest made Sophie wish she could tell everyone that when he helped the Black Swan, he spent his days as Coiffe, swathed in head-to-toe white curls like a giant two-legged poodle.

"Councillor Darek raised the tarp using telekinesis," Timkin shouted.

Emery nodded. "I suppose I shouldn't be surprised that you were the one to notice, given your background. And yes, Darek moved the tarp with his mind. It turns out, he has the greatest telekinetic strength out of all of us on the Council. We had our own Splotching match of sorts to test it out before we came here today—but that's a story for another time. The point is: Instead of having Councillor Liora snap her fingers and conjure the tarp away, or having Councillor Zarina disintegrate it with one of her electric charges, or even having Councillor

182

Clarette call a flock of birds to carry it away in their talons—we chose to let Councillor Darek use telekinesis—a skill, not an ability. And we did so to remind you of the underutilized arsenal that each and every one of us possesses. That's the beauty of skills. There are no *haves* and *have-nots*."

"Are you trying to tell us that skills are better than abilities?" someone in the crowd shouted.

"It's not a matter of *better*. It's a matter of missed opportunities," Emery told them. "We've been neglecting our skills for far too long. Somehow we've let ourselves become complacent about such opportunities and limited our focus to academics and abilities."

"But you just told us they could've done the same thing with their abilities," another voice yelled.

"Yes, but what would an Empath or a Telepath or a Vanisher do?" Emery asked. "I do not mean to devalue any talent—we all know the vital role that each special ability plays. But they also are limited to only a specific purpose, whereas our skills cast a much wider advantage—far wider than I suspect any of you realize. We brush on some of them in our physical education sessions at Foxfire, but it's a far cry from the proper training such gifts should be given. So from now on, we'll be correcting this—and before any of you protest"—he raised his arms to silence the fresh wave of murmurs—"keep in mind the precarious position we're currently in. It's no secret that elves are not warriors. Our minds shatter from the violence and gore. And that has led some to the mistaken conclusion that we're also defenseless. There are even those who believe that if we were to be separated from our goblin protectors, our world would crumble—and while that's obviously not the case, it does still raise a concern. How many of us could truly protect ourselves if the need ever arose? I'd wager only a small portion, which is unacceptable! And fortunately, we already have a system in place to help us train."

"Oh," Sophie breathed.

Sir Astin smiled. "I believe you're beginning to guess the shift that's coming."

That didn't make Councillor Emery's next words any less shocking.

"All of this is why, starting next week, the Exillium campus will be stationing itself right where we're standing, and we'll all begin a program of specialized skill training with their Coaches."

TWENTY

THEY'RE SENDING EVERYONE TO Exillium?" Sophie asked, turning to the rest of her friends. "As in *everyone*?"

The crowd around them seemed to be shouting the same question.

"Yes, I do mean all of us," Councillor Emery called over the din. "Young, old, and Ancient—*all* will participate in this new program, because *all* of us possess these vital skills. We're in the process of designing a schedule to accommodate this rather large undertaking. But those of you here—and your families—will be the first wave. We'll be dividing you into groups that will then be assigned to a specific day and time for training each week. The schedules will be finished by the weekend and sent out to each household. Training will begin on Monday."

Biana grinned. "I wonder if they'll make everyone wear the crazy uniforms."

"Or go through a dividing," Dex added.

When Sophie and her friends had first arrived at the Exillium campus they'd found themselves snared by thick ropes and left dangling upside down from a high metal arch while all the other Waywards watched. The method they found to escape was analyzed to determine which of the three Exillium Hemispheres they belonged to—the Left Hemisphere for those who favored logic and reason, the Right Hemisphere for those who were impulsive and creative, and the Ambi Hemisphere for those who used elements of both approaches.

"Let's just hope no one starts any fires," Biana said. "Right, Sophie?"

"Hey, if I hadn't started that fire, we might not have become friends with Tam and Linh," Sophie reminded her.

"Plus, a school isn't a school until Sophie tries to destroy it," Fitz teased.

"Uh, I think Keefe has taken over that role," Biana whispered. "I can't decide if that means she's the bad influence—or he is."

"I think they're mutually troublesome." Sir Astin gave Sophie a papery smile. "And much as it would delight me to see some of our particularly sheltered elves endure the kind of creative initiations Exillium specializes in, the Coaches have arranged a much faster, much less invasive dividing process. Everyone will also be provided with simple capes to wear with their tunics, pants, and boots. And in case you're wondering, you will be participating as well. So will all of the Exillium Waywards."

"Is this what you meant when you told Tam and Linh that you were working on something to keep them less isolated?" Sophie asked.

Sir Astin nodded. "They will now be coming to Foxfire twice a week—and should the experiment go well, I've been in talks with the Council about establishing a permanent connection between the schools. I envision an exchange program once a week, to allow both schools to interact and benefit from the other. But the first focus will be on self-defense training."

Dex pointed toward the grumbling crowd. "Doesn't sound like everyone's excited by the idea."

Sophie wasn't surprised. Most of the elves were snobs about Exillium—believing the school existed only for the *hopeless cases*. All the Waywards had been banished from the Lost Cities, and very few had done what Timkin Heks did and earned their way back.

Councillor Emery held out his hands, demanding silence. "Clearly this idea will take some getting used to," he told them. "But it is a *necessary* change."

A fresh round of shouts disagreed, and Bronte stepped from his place at Emery's side.

"Would you honestly rather risk your lives than train to use your skills?" he shouted.

"No, we'd rather you do your job and exile these black-robed idiots," someone yelled back, triggering an eruption of cheers.

Sophie couldn't hear what Bronte said in response, but the set of his jaw was pure disgust.

"If you don't calm yourselves," Councillor Emery shouted, "I will let Noland call for silence. And you all know the headache a Vociferator can trigger."

Most of the crowd obeyed—though Sophie caught a few grumblings about the hypocrisy of threatening them with someone's special ability.

"Regardless of how you may feel about this decision," Emery told them, "keep in mind that this arrangement is not optional. Anyone who refuses training will face a number of consequences."

"Like what?" Sophie whispered to Sir Astin. "They wouldn't exile people, would they?"

"Honestly, I'm not certain," he admitted. "But there is never a shortage of manure to shovel at the Sanctuary."

"And what about the ogres?" a female shouted from somewhere off to the side.

Sophie recognized the voice even before the crowd parted to let her linguistics Mentor march toward the stage. Lady Cadence's dark gray gown looked as tight as the twisted bun in her dark hair and paired well with her stormy glare.

"Why am I not surprised you've decided to interrupt these proceedings?" Emery asked.

"Probably because you've ignored all my requests for a private meeting," Lady Cadence said smoothly. "And I'm hardly the only dissenter. I'd wager you could hear the shouting all the way in the Forbidden Cities. And while most of their arguments are weak and biased, that doesn't change the fact that your plan is deeply flawed. Improving our skills won't do a drop of good in the face of an ogre warrior—and we cannot afford to make them our enemy. When it comes to pure, brute strength, nothing can best them."

Every goblin in the audience snorted.

"Laugh all you want," she told them. "Goblins are powerful in your own way—and you have held your own in many battles. But you survive primarily because of clever battle tactics—tactics that can't rival the ruthless rage I've seen ogres manifest in the heat of a fight."

"The ogres are formidable adversaries," Councillor Emery agreed. "But King Dimitar is wise enough to avoid starting a war that he knows he would lose."

"Are you certain of that?" Lady Cadence asked. "Hasn't he ignored all of your requests for a Peace Summit?"

Councillor Emery glanced at the rest of the Councillors. Several seconds passed as he rubbed his temples, before he nodded and raised his eyes to the crowd.

"We'd been planning to deliver this announcement through

coordinated scrolls, that way everyone would be notified at once. But . . . in light of these apprehensions, it seems prudent to set your minds at ease now, and we'll notify the rest of the populace this evening. King Dimitar *has* agreed to meet for a Peace Summit. We're in the process of arranging the gathering in Lumenaria now. The exact date will not be shared—for obvious security reasons. But we expect to reach a satisfying resolution in the very near future."

The cheer that followed sounded mostly like a collective sigh of relief.

"Did you know about that?" Sophie whispered to Sir Astin.

"No," he admitted. "But it explains why I've received such pushback for our visit to Gethen. I'm not sure if we'll be able to get anywhere near Lumenaria until the summit is over. They'll have everything on lockdown to prepare their security."

"And there's no way to sneak in?" Fitz asked.

"Definitely not. Lumenaria—in many ways—is more secure than Exile."

"So then . . . it probably would've been good if we'd met with Gethen before the ogres agreed to the summit," Sophie said.

"Yes, Miss Foster. The power of hindsight strikes again. Though in all fairness, we wouldn't have known to ask him about the symbol, so there's no telling how useful that meeting would've been."

"I still wish we'd done it," Sophie mumbled.

"As do I. But I wish for many things. . . ." He stared into the distance, tempting her to violate the rules of telepathy and see what he was thinking.

"Does that satisfy your concern?" Councillor Emery asked Lady Cadence, snapping Sophie back to the present.

"Actually, I find it even more concerning," Lady Cadence told him. "King Dimitar is many things—but a fool is not one of them. He will not enter into a treaty lightly. I have no doubt he's monitoring our world very closely. And when he hears that every elf is being given special combat training? He'll assume we're forming an army."

"An army with children?" Councillor Alina asked, not bothering to wait for Councillor Emery to speak for her.

"Ogres begin military training from the moment their children can walk," Lady Cadence explained. "Their entire culture is built around defense and strategy. And I guarantee that if King Dimitar believes we're preparing for battle, it will alter any plans for a peaceful resolution."

"And how is it safer for them to see us as an easy target?" Alina countered.

"When dealing with a daunting opponent, it's far better to be underestimated than overestimated," Lady Cadence retorted. "The more the ogres doubt our strength, the less prepared they'll be should they choose the foolish course in the end."

"Valid as your concerns may be," Councillor Emery said, "they can't justify leaving our people defenseless. The ogres are not the only threat we're facing."

"Then why not focus our efforts on making it easier for people to flee?" Lady Cadence suggested. "I've long wondered why we don't wear emergency rings—crystals we'd always have easily on hand that leap to the same designated safe house at an undisclosed location. I'm sure the dwarves could help you set something up in a matter of days."

"That . . . is something we will take under consideration," Councillor Emery said. "But we must also ensure that we do not become a people ruled by fear. Our authority is being threatened from both without and within—and it's imperative that we prove our strength to everyone daring to challenge us. Spending a few years living with ogres doesn't prepare you for the complexities of ruling this world."

"No—but I know far more about our so-called enemies than you ever will," Lady Cadence argued. "Either you ignored the reports I sent, or that traitor you trusted made sure they never saw the light of day."

Fitz and Biana slouched as grumblings about their brother washed through the crowd.

"The insights I've gained could've prevented many of our current problems," Lady Cadence added. "So you would be wise to heed my counsel now if you want any hope of a successful treaty negotiation."

"Any information you see fit to provide we'd be happy to hear," Councillor Emery told her. "But in a proper, scheduled meeting. And just to be clear"—he turned to the crowd—"*nothing* is going to halt our plans for this program of skill training. We do not bow to fear and speculation or flee to avoid confrontation."

"We have in the past," Lady Cadence reminded him. "Our Ancient Councillors opted to sink Atlantis in order to convince the humans that we had died—and turned our species into a bunch of silly myths and legends—because they knew that was the smarter alternative to involving ourselves in a war."

"Those were different times," Councillor Bronte told her. "We were a small, scattered race, still getting a handle on the different worlds we'd unwittingly become responsible for. I would know. I was there." He tapped the points of his ears as proof of his Ancient standing. "We made the best decision we could—but it has also proven to be our most controversial. In fact, one of the ogres' greatest grievances with us is that we've allowed humans to continue living in relative freedom—and I've heard some in this very audience make the same complaint. I'm not saying it was the wrong decision. But times have also changed, and now is the time for strength. And confidence. And providing a ready reminder of why we found ourselves in charge of this planet in the first place. We didn't choose to rule the world. The world chose us, because our abilities and skills make us uniquely qualified—and yes, I *am* putting both on the same level. I don't know how we, as a race, became so shortsighted about the value of our skills. I myself have even been guilty of such judgments. But it's time we open our minds and start accepting their value."

Lady Cadence stalked closer to argue, then stopped and dipped an especially stiff curtsy.

"Very well," she said. "You've clearly made up your minds. I hope, for all of our sake, that these skills are as powerful as you say. We'll need them when we're dragged into war."

TWENTY-ONE

DO YOU THINK SHE'S RIGHT?" SOPHIE asked Grady and Edaline after she'd caught them up on the afternoon's drama. "Do you think the Council should've listened to Lady Cadence's warning?"

"I think there are degrees of rightness," Grady said, arranging a dozen empty silver buckets into a row. "Our days of easy answers are long past us."

"Did those ever exist?" Edaline asked. "I remember my elvin history sessions teaching about quite a few averted catastrophes."

"You may be right," Grady said. "Though I don't remember

having to worry this much when *I* was a kid—or even when Jolie was Sophie's age."

They both fell silent, lost in their own memories as Edaline snapped her fingers and conjured up a waist-high pile of swizzlespice. It was feeding time in the Havenfield pastures, which could be quite an adventurous process. The animals that Grady and Edaline cared for were transitioning to a vegetarian diet.

Part of the elves' conservation efforts included relocating any species that humans thought were "extinct" or "mythical" to their special animal preserve to ensure the creatures' continued survival. But the process only made sense if there were no predators in the Sanctuary. So they'd developed methods to quell the animals' hunting instincts and fed them a diet of gnomish produce, since the gnomes grew many things that tasted like meat.

"I will say," Grady added, dropping handfuls of shriveled tubers into each of the buckets, "I'm sure Lady Cadence is right about the ogres keeping tabs on what we're doing. And I wouldn't be surprised if the training did add tension to the treaty negotiations. But I can't imagine it'll lead to a violent retaliation. The ogres have never attacked the elves directly."

"What about the plague?" Sophie asked.

The ogres had tried to force the gnomes into servitude in Ravagog, knowing the Lost Cities would fall apart without them. The elves and gnomes had a uniquely symbiotic relationship, with each species relying heavily on the other. Gnomes were too defenseless to hold their own among the fiercer species that inhabited the planet. They also craved work and loved to garden, and were much more plantlike than animal, requiring very little food or sleep because they absorbed their energy from the sun. So in exchange for protection and shelter among the elves, the gnomes shared their excess produce and helped with any tasks that interested them. Sophie hadn't realized just how vital the gnomes were until she'd seen the withering plants and overall disorganization in the Lost Cities when the gnomes were sick.

"That was definitely the boldest move the ogres have made," Grady told her. "But I doubt they would've made it without the Neverseen's urging. They sat on the plague for millennia, and only acted when Fintan suggested it. And let's not forget that making that threat didn't exactly work out well for them."

"Thanks to you," a female gnome with plaited hair and a dress woven from straw said to Sophie as she hauled over more empty buckets. The stack was twice as tall as her child-size body. "I wish I could've been there to see the flood that you and your friends caused. I hope it washed all the filth out of Serenvale."

Most gnomes still referred to Ravagog by its original name, since it had been their homeland before the ogres ran them out, tore down all the trees, and contaminated the water and ground.

"Here are the cravettels," another gnome said—a male this

time, in a shirt sewn from leaves the same earthy tone as his skin. He dragged a huge bag of what looked like bright blue peanuts, flashing a green-toothed smile as he left it at Grady's feet. "There's plenty more where that came from if you need it—and I bet you will. I've never seen a T. rex who didn't gobble these up by the ton."

"Well, you've never met Verdi," Grady said. "Her picky eating is a big part of why we call her our permanent resident. But I can't wait to test them out."

The gnome waved and trotted away, and Sophie realized she didn't know his name. Just like she didn't know the female gnome helping Edaline fill the buckets with swizzlespice.

It wasn't *totally* her fault—they'd had dozens and dozens of gnomes move to Havenfield to be close to the Panakes tree. But ever since she'd lost Calla, Sophie found it too painful to get to know any of them. Staring into their huge gray eyes felt like opening a fresh wound.

"Personally, I'm proud of the Council for making this stand," Edaline said. "It's nice to see them focused on protecting *everyone*—especially the Talentless. And it'll be interesting to see how powerful our skills can truly become when we train ourselves properly."

"That might be a problem," Cadoc said from the shadows. "If either of you leave this house, Brielle and I will have to go with you, and everyone will know we're your bodyguards."

"But the Council said the training is mandatory," Sophie

reminded them. "So if they stay home, that could tip the Neverseen off too."

"Easy solution," Grady said. "You trust that we can take care of ourselves."

"Imagine what you would say if your daughter tried that argument," Brielle told him.

"Right, but she can't do this." Grady narrowed his eyes at Edaline, and her arms shot up on each side and started flailing about like an angry octopus.

"What have I told you about using your power on me?" Edaline snapped, smacking him with her thrashing appendages.

"I know—I'm sorry! I just figured you'd rather I proved the point with you instead of with Sophie."

He calmed Edaline's flailing and she snapped her fingers, conjuring a pile of dinosaur fluff above him and showering him in bright orange feathers. "Now we're even."

"I suppose we are," he said. "And I'm glad you went with feathers and not manure."

"Next time," Edaline warned.

"See," Grady told Sophie. "Strong abilities have consequences. Which reminds me—you and I still need to have that talk about your inflicting. So why don't you come with me to test these cravettels on Verdi and we'll chat as we work?"

"Verdi drool *and* a lecture?" Sophie whined. "Are you trying to punish me?"

"Far from it. I could really use your help. Maybe if you

transmit to Verdi, you can convince her how much she's going to like these new seeds."

Easier said than done. The fluffy green T. rex took one whiff of the cravettels and made a gag-snort-snarl. Then she spun around and knocked her trough over with her tail.

"Aw, come on," Grady said as he righted the silver basin and filled it with more of the seeds. "At least give them a try."

I hear all the other T. rexes love them, Sophie transmitted, adding images of happy dinosaurs gobbling them up.

The snort that Verdi gave them practically dripped with disgust.

"You know how this works," Grady warned. "If you won't try it, I'm going to have to make you."

Verdi threw back her enormous head and let out a defiant *ROOOOOOOOOOOOAAAAAAAAR.*

"All right then, you brought this on yourself." Grady unhooked one of the silver lassoes strapped to his belt, whipping the shimmering rope in wide circles over his head before letting it fly in one swift motion.

ROOOOOOOOOOOOOOOOOOOAAAAAAAAAAAAAAAAR!

"That's not hurting her, right?" Sophie asked as Verdi tried to claw at the cord around her neck with her tiny T. rex arms.

"Her feathers are so thick I doubt she even feels it," Grady promised, digging in his heels to keep his footing. "And don't worry—animals always fight what's good for them."

He had a point. Sophie once helped her human mom give

medicine to their cat, and the amount of yowling that followed made it sound like they were force-feeding him boiling poison.

Grady dragged Verdi toward her trough. "Okay, girl—time to try something new."

ROOOOOOOOOOOOOOOOOOOAAAAAAAAAAAAAAAR!

He took advantage of Verdi's open mouth and jerked the lasso hard, face-planting her into the seeds. Cravettels scattered everywhere—but some must've hit their mark because the next second Verdi was crunching.

"See?" Grady asked. "I hear they taste like pterodactyl."

Verdi crunched some more.

And . . .

SPIT!

"Wonderful," Grady said, shaking off the slimy blue bits he'd been sprayed with. "Can you give me a hand?" he asked Brielle as Verdi tried to drag him into her pasture.

Brielle grabbed him around his waist and together they pulled Verdi back to the trough.

ROOOOOOOOOOOOOOOOOOOAAAAAAAAAAAAAAAR!

Crunch.

SPIT!

And so the feeding went.

But somewhere around bite number ten—paired with a head full of Sophie's calming transmissions—Verdi swallowed and . . .

. . . licked her chops.

"If you would've trusted me from the beginning, you wouldn't have wasted half your dinner!" Grady grumbled as Verdi wolfed down the remaining blue seeds. "But let's hope this means we've found something she *loves*—and that it quells her urge to hunt. A flock of seagulls flew a little too close to her enclosure last week and a couple of them became Verdi snacks."

Sophie shuddered. "I bet you wish you could Mesmer her."

"That would be nice—and what a perfect transition for our important conversation!"

"Ugh, I already know what you're going to say."

"And what's that?" Grady asked, wrapping the lasso around his palm and elbow to coil it back up.

"You're going to tell me that inflicting is a dark power and that I have to be careful about how much I use it because it'll make people afraid of me, just like people were afraid of you after you manifested. And then I'll assure you that I'm just trying to fix a few weak spots. Biana and I had a run-in with the Neverseen's Psionipath a few months back, and my abilities wouldn't work through his force field. He was right there in front of us—and there was nothing I could do. I can't let that happen again. Fitz thinks our telepathy would've been strong enough if we'd worked together as Cognates. But inflicting comes down to me—and if I'd trained harder, I might've been able to stop Ruy from getting away. So see? As Alden would say: *There's no reason to worry.*"

"Actually, that's not what I was going to say—though I appreciate the Alden quote. And I get where you're coming from. I remember testing my ability against a Psionipath once, and it was incredibly unsettling. But you have to understand that there's a cost to training. I learned that the hard way—and almost let my power ruin me."

"Ruin?" *Now* he had her attention.

"You've seen how Fintan was led astray by his craving for flame," Grady said quietly. "I . . . let myself get just as out of control. I didn't kill anyone—but I started using my ability for any passing whim. If someone was slowing me down when I was in a hurry? I'd *motivate* them to clear out of my way. Or if I needed something and didn't have time to go get it? I'd *motivate* someone to bring it to me. The real low point was when the Council refused to grant my request to investigate an issue with the trolls. They didn't think I had enough evidence to justify the drastic measures I was proposing, and I was positive I'd find more than enough if they'd allow me to conduct the search. So I mesmerized Bronte into signing the scroll."

"Did he catch you?" Sophie asked.

"Of course. And if he'd wanted to, he could've had me exiled. At the very least, he could've hit me with the full force of his inflicting. Instead he sat me down and shared how he almost fell into the same trap with his ability. He told me that after years and years of training, he reached a point where the slightest aggravation or annoyance would flare his temper, and he'd unleash his rage. His low point was when he lashed out at his mother."

"So . . . what are you saying?" she asked. "I can't use my ability? Why would the Council order me to train in it, then?"

"Because the only thing worse than overusing an intense power is not learning how to control it. It comes down to moderation. Inflicting is an incredibly valuable ability—and I'm glad you have it. But don't let it take over your life. Bronte said he built up so much anger and frustration that he has to keep it all tangled up in a knot deep inside of him—a constant pressure he fights every day to keep from unraveling. And he told me he's had to teach you the same technique because of all the emotions you're battling."

"Aren't I allowed to be angry about the things that have happened?"

"Of course. And I know you want to protect yourself and your friends. I also know that you feel a tremendous responsibility to be the moonlark—whatever that even is. And those are much more noble reasons to push yourself than anything that motivated me. But that doesn't mean the training isn't eating away at you. Don't think I don't know what you're doing there."

He pointed to her hand, which was massaging the spot under her ribs.

"It's not just a knot of emotions," she told him. "It's power I can draw on when I need it."

Grady sighed and pulled her close. "I know. Just promise

me you'll try to let at least *some* of it go. If you hold on to every-thing, it'll tear you apart."

Sophie nodded, telling herself it wasn't a lie.

She *would* try to let it go.

But not until she felt ready.

Right now, she had too many enemies—too many questions—too many worries.

Keefe gave her another huge one that night when she stretched out her consciousness for their nightly check-in.

FINALLY! his mind screamed. *I was about an hour away from switching to my emergency plan.*

Why? What's happening?

I don't fully know. Something huge is going down tomorrow. No one will tell me any specifics—but based on what I overheard, I'm pretty sure they're going to Havenfield to snatch Grady and Edaline.

TWENTY-TWO

NO ONE SLEPT THAT NIGHT.

Havenfield was a blur of activity as the goblins and gnomes snuck around to prepare.

Everything needed to *look* normal, so that it wouldn't give away that Keefe had leaked the warning. But they still found plenty of ways to increase their security.

Booby traps were set. The Black Swan sent dwarven reinforcements to hide deep underground, ready to pop out at the first sign of trouble. And Grady and Edaline were each given melders—elvin weapons that caused temporary paralysis—and were planning to station themselves outside in the pastures that housed the most dangerous animals.

Sandor had originally suggested they stay inside, but the

last thing anyone wanted was to give Brant a chance to start another deadly house fire.

As for Sophie . . .

"No way!" she said, adding a foot stamp for emphasis. "You're not sending me away like a little kid!"

"Age has nothing to do with this," Grady told her, pulling her in for a hug. "It's about protecting the things that matter."

"I don't need protection."

"*Everyone* needs protection—why do you think we're taking so many precautions? But we have everything covered. You don't have to worry."

"Actually, that's exactly why I *should* be worrying," Sophie argued. "We thought we had everything planned out for the ambush on Mount Everest, and the Neverseen somehow knew we'd be there and showed up with ogres and dwarves."

She'd never forget the feel of those beefy ogre arms grabbing her through the ceiling of their cave and dragging her through ice and stone. If Sandor hadn't come after her, she never would've gotten away—and Sandor had ended up tossed off a cliff for his efforts.

"And we didn't have to deal with the two Pyrokinetics," she reminded him. "Brant and Fintan will try to burn this place to the ground."

Grady brushed her hair off her forehead. "That's why I've been keeping a supply of quicksnuff on hand. Alden also got us some frissyn, after my battle with Brant. So we're ready to extinguish any flames—even Everblaze."

The news *helped*.

But it still didn't feel like enough.

Frustration and anger bubbled up and she knotted them under her ribs, adding to her arsenal. "If you won't let me stay—come *with* me."

Grady shook his head. "I'm not letting them chase me out of my home. And I'm not going to pass up a chance to see if we can catch one of them. That's how you tackle problems like this. You take the organization down one person at a time."

"Then let me help," Sophie begged.

"You've risked your life enough times. Now it's my turn."

"That's stupid."

"It might be. But I'm willing to be stupid if it keeps you safe."

"And *we'll* keep *him* safe," Brielle promised, raising her sword and slashing it with a whip-fast spin that sent her curls flying. "Your father is my charge. No harm will come to him."

"Your mother will be safe with me," Cadoc added. "And Sandor is planning to stay as well."

"You are?" Sophie asked, turning to face her bodyguard.

"I assumed it's where you'd prefer that I be," Sandor told her. "But I'm only willing to separate *if* you stick to your original plan and go to Mr. Dizznee's house. Lovise will protect you there. She's an excellent warrior."

"But—"

"Think of the larger picture," Grady interrupted. "Where can you do the most good? Here? Wasting the day waiting for someone to pop out of the shadows? Or with your friends, working on one of your projects?"

"All we were planning to do is sort through a bunch of registry records," Sophie grumbled.

"Those records still need to be checked," Grady told her. "And I wouldn't be surprised if you guys learn something crucial. Think about all the problems you've solved together."

"We've also survived plenty of battles," Sophie reminded him.

He kissed her forehead again. "I know. But this one isn't your fight. So go pack an overnight bag. You're not coming home until this threat is over."

"Already got you packed," Edaline said, rushing down the stairs with Iggy's cage in one hand and Sophie's purple backpack in the other. Sophie had used the same bag to leave her human life behind—and again when she'd had to flee to the Black Swan's hideout.

She despised using it again to hide.

"Kesler and Juline know you'll be staying the night," Edaline told her. "I also hailed the Vackers and it sounded like Alden and Della were heading over here. I explained the risks, but they're not missing a chance to speak to Alvar. They'll be sending Fitz and Biana to stay the night at Dex's."

"Oh sure, send the kids off for a slumber party," Sophie grumbled.

Edaline smiled. "You can be mad at me if you want. But I'm always going to take any chance to keep you safe. Mother's prerogative."

"*Parents'* prerogative," Grady corrected. "I can survive a lot of things. But if something happened to you . . . ?"

He hugged Sophie again, and Edaline joined in.

"Please don't fight this," Edaline begged, kissing Sophie's cheek. "Let us protect you the way we couldn't protect . . ."

She didn't finish the sentence, but Sophie knew how it ended—and playing the Jolie card was a dirty trick.

"Fine," she said through a sigh. "But only if you promise that if it gets too intense here, you'll leap to safety."

"Deal." Grady tightened his hug before he finally let her go. "And thank you."

Sophie planned to give her best death glare as she slung her backpack over her shoulder and picked up Iggy's cage. But it hit her then that—if something went wrong—this *could* be the last time she ever saw her parents.

"I love you guys," she whispered.

"We love you too," they both said.

"Stay safe," she begged.

Grady wiped his teary eyes. "We'll see you soon."

TWENTY-THREE

SOPHIE COULD HEAR THE SCREAMING and shouting the second she glittered into the otherwise quiet valley, where puffy white clouds hung low around the snow-capped mountains.

"THAT'S MY BOX OF PRATTLES!"

"NOT ANYMORE!"

"MOOOOOOOOOOOOOOOOOOOOM—REX STOLE MY CANDY!"

"DAAAAAAAAAAAAAAAAAAAAD—BEX SMELLS LIKE DRAGON POOP!"

"SO DOES REX!" another voice added.

"STAY OUT OF THIS, LEX!"

"NO WAY—THOSE PRATTLES ARE MINE!"

A whole lot of squealing and crashing—plus a "KNOCK IT OFF!" from Dex—followed the declaration.

"Welcome to Rimeshire," Kesler said, and Sophie spun around to find him standing next to Juline on a wide silver-stoned path. The smile he flashed looked exactly like his son's.

Kesler and Dex both shared the same dimples and strawberry-blond hair and periwinkle eyes. The only difference was time—and several inches of height.

"You'll get used to the noise," he promised as another shriek echoed across the valley.

"No you won't," Juline warned.

Juline was Edaline's sister—which technically made Sophie and Dex cousins by adoption—and they both had the same turquoise eyes and amber-toned hair. But Juline always looked rumpled and exhausted.

"Don't worry," she told Sophie, wrapping a flyaway hair back into her messy bun and securing it with a chewed-on pencil. "I have a trick to keep them under control this afternoon."

"We say that every day," Kesler teased. "I'm still waiting for it to be true."

Lots more squealing and stomping filled the air, along with an "OW—THAT'S MY ARM, YOU JERK!"

"It's okay," Sophie told them. Growing up a Telepath around humans had given her a high tolerance for noise. Plus, her main plans for the day involved obsessively checking her Imparter as she waited for news from her family.

She could do that with or without screaming kids in the background.

"Bet you're glad you're wearing long sleeves, huh?" Juline asked as an icy breeze whipped through Sophie's hair.

Rimeshire was definitely the chilliest place Sophie had visited in the Lost Cities—aside from the entrance to the Sanctuary in the Himalayas. Even the architecture of the Dizznee's house reminded Sophie of an ice castle. All the walls were built from blue cut glass and fitted together into sharp, dramatic angles. And the five swirling towers looked like upside-down icicles. But there was still something inherently warm about the place. Maybe it was the bright light glowing through the walls. Or the curls of white smoke coming from the spiral chimneys.

The house was also massive—probably bigger than Everglen. And the grounds were just as expansive. The landscaping was simpler, but it matched the stark valley: twisted evergreen trees lining each of the silver-stoned paths, and wide plains of jade green grass leading into the rolling foothills.

"You can say it," Kesler told her. "I'm guessing this isn't what you'd been imagining?"

"Well . . . no," she admitted.

She'd been in the Lost Cities long enough to know that social standing didn't affect wealth. Everyone was given the exact same birth fund—which contained more than enough money to live lavishly for the whole of their long existence. But she'd pictured Dex's house looking like Slurps and Burps, with topsy-turvy architecture and colorful walls that belonged in a Dr. Seuss book.

Rimeshire was . . . understated.

Elegant.

Impressive.

"We're only quirky in public," Kesler told her, "because it's fun to mess with the snobby nobles. Deep down, we're disappointingly normal."

"Not disappointing at all," Sophie insisted.

Juline beamed. "I'm so glad you like it. Dex was terrified to have everyone come over. He's in there right now, desperately cleaning his room, even though you'll be camping out in the solarium tonight."

"And don't worry," Kesler said. "The triplets have offered up their sleeping bags—and the gnomes already gave them a good wash."

"Sounds perfect," Sophie told him, even though she'd never considered that Dex, Fitz, and Biana might all be sleeping in the same room. Talk about potential for awkward . . .

But sleep was probably going to be a lost cause anyway.

She checked her Imparter for news from her family.

Nothing.

Not surprising—but it didn't help her antsy-ness.

"Are Fitz and Biana already here?" she asked, having to raise her voice over the triplets' latest shouting match. It sounded like Bex had stolen Rex's favorite jackalope toy and was threatening to tear off its antlers.

"No," Kesler said. "So you're welcome to wait in the house if you want."

Inside, something crashed and shattered into a million pieces.

"Waiting out here sounds good," Sophie decided.

Kesler laughed. "Probably a good call. And let's hope that sound means they finally destroyed the horrendous crystal yeti statue my brother gave us for a wedding present. I moved it to the entryway a few years ago, since the triplets love tearing through there like a pack of dire wolves. But I swear they spare it just to spite me."

"You have a brother?" Sophie asked.

"Actually, I have three. And two sisters."

"Wow, your mom had *six* children?"

Even for humans that was a ton of kids—and for elves it was practically unheard of.

"I see my son talks about his family a lot," Kesler said.

"No he—"

"I'm just kidding," he promised. "You guys have had way more important things to talk about than Dex's estranged relatives."

They definitely had. But Sophie still felt like the world's worst best friend. Sometimes she didn't pay as much attention to Dex as she should.

"Anyway," Kesler said, "my parents were definitely not concerned about the whole 'optimal genetic purity' nonsense."

"That's another recommendation from the matchmakers," Juline explained. "They believe our strongest, purest genetics go to our first child, and after that, our genes grow increasingly diluted. That's why so many families stop after one kid."

"That *can't* be true, can it?" Sophie asked.

"It's hard to say for certain," Kesler said. "I know some pretty incredible second and third children—though my existence tends to verify it. I'm the youngest, and the only one in my family who didn't manifest."

Juline reached for his hand. "I still married the best Dizznee."

"Ha—that's not what your match lists said!"

Sophie wondered if that meant that Juline had been matched with one of Kesler's brothers. She was tempted to ask, but didn't know if that would be rude.

Before she could decide, Fitz and Biana leaped into the valley.

"Wow," Biana breathed as she took in the scenery. "I can't believe Dex lives here."

"And why is that?" Kesler's voice had sharpened along the edges.

Biana didn't seem to notice as she made her way over and flashed her brilliant smile. "I can't believe you live in the Gloaming Valley! My mom told me this is where the Alenon

River connects to the ocean. That's where the wild kelpies live, right? I've always wanted to see them."

Kesler's shoulders relaxed slightly. "Well . . . we're actually on the other side of the mountains. But I'm impressed that your mother knows so much about this place. It's not an area many pay attention to."

"They should," Biana told him. "I hear there's nothing quite like watching the kelpies come ashore."

"There isn't," Juline agreed. "If you visit again, we'll have to make a trip over to the beach. I'd take you today, but Dex's bodyguard is insisting we all stay close to the house so he can keep a better eye on you."

"How you holding up?" Fitz asked Sophie as she checked her blank Imparter again.

"Oh . . . you know. People I care about are in danger, and none of the adults want my help. Same old, same old."

"Right there with you," he mumbled.

"So your parents did go to Havenfield?" she asked. "Is that why Grizel and Woltzer aren't with you?"

Fitz nodded. "Woltzer didn't want to leave us, but Grizel talked him into it when she found out Sandor was at Havenfield. I tried to convince them to let me go too, but my mom gave me a long speech about how she didn't want us getting hurt."

"The nerve of parents these days," Juline said, "trying to keep their kids safe."

"I'm not saying I don't get it," Fitz said. "But, come on. We took on an army of ogres—I think I can handle my *brother*."

"We don't know that Alvar will be there," Biana said, swallowing hard, like there was a lump in her throat. "And if he is . . . Dad deserves to be the one to face him. Besides—we were planning to come here today anyway, right? Is it really so bad?"

Fitz sighed and turned to Kesler and Juline. "No, it's not bad at all—sorry if that sounded rude. Thank you for letting us stay here. My dad wanted me to tell you that Everglen is always available if you ever need him to return the favor."

"Does that offer include babysitting the triplets?" Kesler asked. "Because I'd be happy to drop them off anytime. But somehow I don't think he'd enjoy having them tearing through his historic halls."

Biana shrugged. "We could put them in Alvar's room and let them break all his stuff. And wait—is that Iggy?" she asked as Sophie shifted the cage she was holding.

Iggy greeted Biana with a cage-shaking fart.

Biana coughed. "Whoa, smells like someone ate too many sludgers last night. Clearly we need to work on your diet."

"Yeah, good luck with that," Sophie told her. "The last vegetables I gave him ended up plastered all over my ceiling."

"Aw, he'll eat some for me—won't you, boy?" Biana asked. "I'll give you an extra-long tummy rub—and save you the softest spot on my pillow."

"*You're* going to sleep with the imp?" Kesler asked.

"Of course! We shared a pillow every night at Alluveterre. I still miss his rumbly snore."

Biana nuzzled Iggy's nose through the bars and Sophie noticed Kesler studying her like he was seeing her for the first time. She might look like a pampered princess, but that definitely didn't make her a delicate flower—despite the fact that she'd packed *two* overnight satchels.

"Can I help you with your bags?" Kesler offered. "They look heavy."

"They are," Fitz said, holding up his own half-full bag as a comparison. "I think Biana packed enough for twenty people."

"He teases me now," Biana said. "But when it's time to do his hair in the morning he'll totally be sneaking a bit of my LovelyLocks."

An earsplitting howl cut off Fitz's retort, followed by what sounded like a pack of galloping brontosaurs as the door to Rimeshire burst open and the triplets sprinted down the path.

Bex was in the lead, her red hair flapping against her cheeks as she waved a stuffed bunny with antlers.

"GIVE IT BACK!" one of the boys shouted as he lunged to grab her arm.

Bex pivoted out of his grasp. "NOT UNTIL HARRY GETS A MUD BATH."

"DO IT! DO IT! DO IT!" the other boy chanted.

"IF YOU RUIN HARRY I'LL—"

All three of them screeched to a halt when they noticed Sophie, Fitz, and Biana.

"HEY, DEX," Bex shouted toward the house. "YOUR GIRL-FRIENDS ARE HERE—AND THAT GUY WHO'S WAY COOLER THAN YOU ARE!"

"You'll have to excuse our daughter," Kesler said, glaring at Bex. "She's developed a gift for figuring out the most embarrassing thing she can possibly say and then saying it. We're working on it."

"If she bothers you," one of the boys told Biana, "let me know and I'll take care of it."

"Dude, she just saw you crying over your stuffed Jackalope!" the other boy snorted.

"I WASN'T CRYING!"

"That's because Harry hasn't gone mud-diving yet!" Bex waved the Jackalope under his nose and took off toward the trees.

"So," the other boy said as his brother chased after Bex. "Now we can all see who the cool one is."

He winked at Sophie and Biana.

"You guys are *the worst*," Dex groaned as he stomped outside to join them, shadowed by his bodyguard. "Can't I have Lovise tie them up somewhere?"

"I don't think I have strong enough rope," Lovise warned.

"He's just jealous," the boy told Biana. "He knows the ladies like me better."

"Okay," Kesler said, grabbing the boy's arm before he could wrap it around Biana's waist. "Looks like we need to have another talk about appropriate behavior around girls, Lex. Rule number one—we do not touch them without their permission."

"And by the way," Dex told his brother, "she's way too good for you."

"YEAH WELL THEY'RE BOTH TOO GOOD FOR YOU!" Bex and Rex shouted as they circled back.

Dex turned pleading eyes to his mom. "You *promised* you'd keep them away."

"I will," Juline said. "I was just waiting until everyone was here." She closed her eyes and raised her arms, sweeping her hands back and forth in broad, graceful motions.

"Are you a Froster?" Biana asked as tiny flecks of white formed all around them.

It felt like they were standing in the middle of a shaken snow globe, and the flakes swirled in the same pattern as Juline's wispy movements.

The triplets stopped fighting to watch as their mom gathered the bits of ice into a cloud that grew and stretched until their whole property was covered. Then, with a whoosh of breath, Juline dropped her arms and let the snow fall, turning their yard into a winter wonderland.

"Amazing," Sophie whispered.

But something about it felt wrong.

"Didn't you tell me that being a Froster is a stupid talent?" she whispered to Dex. "After the day they made you test for it in ability detecting?"

"I probably did," Dex mumbled. "And it's *not* my favorite talent. But . . . I think I was grumpy because I didn't manifest. I'd figured that was my best shot, y'know?"

Biana seemed to be asking herself much bigger questions. She glanced between Juline and the snow—back and forth. Then her eyes widened. "It's you, isn't it?"

"I don't know what you mean," Juline said—but there was a tightness to her voice that said otherwise.

"No one else sees it?" Biana asked, turning to Sophie, Fitz, and Dex. "Try really looking at her—and think about her voice."

"Really, I think you have me confused with someone else," Juline insisted. "And maybe we should—"

"Wait," Fitz interrupted. "I think I see it."

"See what?" Dex asked.

"Nothing," Juline said quickly.

"You're really not going to tell him?" Biana asked.

"Tell me *what*?" Dex snapped, his eyes narrowing at everyone.

"I don't know what's going on," Kesler jumped in, "but if you're accusing my wife of something—"

"I'm not *accusing*," Biana interrupted, focusing on Juline. "If you don't want me to say anything I won't."

Juline smiled sadly. "I think we're well past that."

222

Her fingers scratched nervously at her neck as she watched the triplets disappear into the trees, lobbing snowballs at each other the whole way. "And I suppose it's overdue. I've been putting this off, hoping I'd find a perfect moment."

"What are you talking about?" Kesler asked.

"It's . . . probably easier if I show you."

Juline took a slow breath and held up her arms, letting the snow gather around her again. But instead of whipping into a storm, she pulled the flakes in close and let the frost coat her skin.

Layer by layer, the ice grew thicker, until her whole body was encased in a frozen shell.

"See?" Biana said as Sophie sucked in a breath.

Dex's jaw dropped as far as his lips could stretch.

"Will someone please tell me what's going on?" Kesler asked.

It took Dex a few seconds to mumble, "She's . . . Squall."

TWENTY-FOUR

SQUALL?" KESLER REPEATED, GRAB-
bing Juline's frozen hands. "Who is Squall?
Wait—you're one of *them*? Like the guy who eats
all the ruckleberries?"

"The Black Swan," Juline corrected, keeping her voice low
as she glanced over her shoulder to check for triplets. They
were still among the trees, screaming and shouting through
their snowball fight. "I'll have to figure out how much I can
trust them to know. I should've prepared better for this—I just
didn't expect anyone to notice. It's not like I'm the only Froster
in our world!"

"Sorry," Biana mumbled. "The whole time I've been here,
I kept thinking your voice sounded familiar. So when I saw

the snow, it clicked. I think it's because Squall—or I should probably say 'you'—was the member of the Collective I was the most curious about. I actually thought you were someone on the Council who was secretly a Froster, because you were always having to race back to the Lost Cities."

"That would've been a more interesting anecdote," Juline said, twirling a few times to shed her icy disguise. "Really I'm just the only member of the Collective with a family living at home who would notice my absence. Wraith was also concerned that Dex would recognize me."

Dex laughed—dark and thick and definitely not because he found anything funny. "Guess he was wrong. Apparently I'm an idiot."

"No, you're not," Sophie promised.

"She's right," Kesler said. "There's nothing idiotic about trusting your mother not to lie to you."

"I haven't *lied*," Juline said quietly. "But yes, I have kept secrets. I had to—those who know the truth have to be involved, and that required risks and sacrifices that I wasn't about to let any of you suffer."

"What if I wanted to be involved?" Kesler asked. "You know I have no warm feelings toward the Council."

"I know." She reached for his hand, and for a second it looked like he might pull away. But he sighed and let Juline twine her fingers with his. "If both of us were part of an illegal rebellion, it would've put our whole family at risk. Who would've cared for our children if we'd been discovered and captured?"

"Okay, but what about me?" Dex asked. "I'm *part* of the Black Swan. How could you stand there in Alluveterre after I swore fealty and not tell me?"

"It was the Collective's decision—though I did support it." She reached for him, but unlike his father, Dex *did* pull away. "I'm so sorry, sweetheart. I know how huge this must feel. But I had to protect our organization. We'd never planned to let any of you join—"

"Not even me?" Sophie interrupted.

"Not this early, no. But if we've learned anything over the years, it's that we have to adapt in order to survive. So we let the five of you swear fealty—but we also took measures to minimize our risk. And one of those measures was to keep our identities anonymous until each of you had proven that you could protect our secrets. As it turned out, that was a wise decision, given what Keefe has done."

The frustration in her voice reminded Sophie that Wraith had included Squall in the not-trusting-Keefe camp.

"Okay, fine," Dex said. "But Forkle and Granite showed us who they are a few weeks ago—you could've come clean then!"

Juline stared at the ground, where tiny crystals of ice swirled around her feet. "I could give you a thousand excuses, but none of them will change the fact that I handled this wrong. I should've told you before your friends caught me."

Biana slouched lower. "Sorry again."

"It's not your fault," Juline told her. "If anything, it's a valuable reminder of why none of us should ever underestimate the four of you."

"You mean the three of us." Dex said, kicking the snow. "I'm the jerk who didn't recognize my own mom."

"Hey, my brother was spying on my family for most of my life, and I never noticed," Fitz reminded him. "At least your mom is one of the good guys."

Dex shrugged. "I dunno. The Black Swan have done some pretty shady stuff—don't even try to deny it."

"I won't," Juline said. "It's yet another reason I didn't want to involve my family. I've never done anything I didn't believe in—but that doesn't mean I haven't crossed hard lines."

Sophie remembered the nightmares she'd had after she'd learned that Squall would be freezing off Gethen's fingernails to remove whatever enzyme kept allowing the Neverseen to track him. Squall had assured her the process was painless, but . . .

"See?" Dex said when she shuddered. "Sophie gets it."

"I do," Sophie said. "But I also think we *all* know the hard choices we have to face for this cause. You don't defeat a group of murderers with rainbows and candy."

"I know," Dex mumbled. "It's just . . . weird."

"Aren't you always telling people you like weird?" Juline asked.

She reached for Dex again and this time he stayed put. He didn't even flinch when she brushed the back of her fingers against his cheek.

But he didn't stop scowling, either.

"Am I allowed to know how long you've been with the Black Swan?" Sophie asked.

"Not as long as you're probably thinking. Project Moonlark was well under way by the time I swore fealty. In fact, you'd already been born."

"So when was it?" Kesler pressed.

Juline bit her lip. "A few months after I had the triplets."

"The *triplets*?" Kesler and Dex repeated.

"Are you talking about us?" Bex shouted from somewhere among the trees.

"I'm sharing stories about when you were babies. Want to join us?"

Juline's answer was perfect—not a lie, but all three shouted, "NO WAY!"

Kesler kept his voice low as he said, "You've been with the Black Swan for *eleven years*?"

"Closer to ten," Juline corrected. "But yes, it's been a long time. And it wasn't something I planned. I was at the birthing center, and I kept holding my three innocent, adorable babies and thinking about how horribly our world was going to treat them. I could already see it happening. My physicians kept ending every sentence with 'for triplets,' like they automatically had low expectations. *The babies are healthy 'for triplets.' Their speaking skills are normal 'for triplets.' Their intelligence is strong 'for triplets.'* It broke my heart and made me want to cry and punch people in the throat and pack up our lives and leave the Lost Cities."

Kesler closed the space between them, wrapping his arm around her shoulders. "Why didn't you tell me that was happening?"

"Because I didn't want you to blame yourself. Sometimes you act like you ruined my life by marrying me—and I hate that. I *love* you. I've never regretted my decision for one second. But it's also helped me to see that our world is deeply flawed. That's why I was so grateful to find Physic."

"*Physic* recruited you?" Sophie asked, sharing a look with Fitz.

Physic was the physician who came to Alluveterre to save Fitz's life after he'd been injured in Exile.

Juline nodded. "When I left the birthing center, I asked Elwin for a list of pediatric physicians who would be more . . . open-minded."

"Does that mean Elwin knows who Physic is?" Biana asked.

"Knowing and realizing are two different things. But I'm sure Physic will reveal herself soon. She's not a fan of subterfuge. In fact, she never made any attempt to hide what she was from me. When she came to the house for the first checkup, she asked why I wasn't at the birthing center, and when I gave a vague answer, she flat-out asked if I ever worried that the Council was blind to our world's prejudices. After that, whenever she'd come for a checkup, she wouldn't stop pushing until I'd admitted any callous things people had said or done. A few months later, she asked me, 'If you could change our world, would you?' And when I said yes, she asked if my answer would be different if the only way to change the world involved breaking rules. I was surprised to admit that it wouldn't matter. That's when she told me about the Black Swan and asked me to join. I swore fealty a few weeks later and started out as a simple information channel. But over time, they trusted me more. Eventually, when Physic stepped down from the Collective, she suggested me as her replacement—and I accepted the position."

"Physic was part of the *Collective*?" Fitz asked. "Why did she step down?"

Juline glanced at Sophie.

"It was because of my allergy, wasn't it?" Sophie guessed.

One of the memories the Black Swan had stolen from her—the one they hadn't yet given back—was from when she was nine and woke up in the hospital after a severe allergic reaction. Her human doctors couldn't figure out what had triggered it, but once she moved to the Lost Cities, she discovered she was allergic to limbium—an *elvin* substance. So an *elf* must've given her something that made her sick. But the who and the how and the why were all a big blank.

"I'm guessing you're not going to tell me what happened?" Sophie asked.

"I think we've unearthed enough secrets today," Juline said. "And honestly, Forkle and Physic never told us the whole story. But it did make her decide to focus on medicine again. So she nominated me to take her place in the Collective, and by that time the triplets were in their daily tutoring sessions, and Dex was helping at the store, so I had a few extra hours to devote to the cause."

"And you couldn't have told me *then*?" Kesler asked.

"I thought about it. But I was terrified. I couldn't bear the thought of you hating me."

"I could never *hate* you," Kesler promised.

"But you're still mad at me."

"Well, I think I'm allowed to be a little upset that my wife lied to me for ten years."

"I didn't lie," Juline insisted. "I was very careful about it. If I said I was going somewhere, I really did go. I just . . . took a detour along the way. It's not ideal, I know. But I don't want you thinking you can't trust me. Everything about the life we've shared is real."

"Is it?" Dex asked. "What about when Sophie first showed up at Slurps and Burps and I told you about meeting her? You acted surprised."

"I *was* surprised! I'd had no idea she'd be living with Grady and Edaline. The last I'd heard, she was supposed to live with

Alden and Della. But things were changing minute by minute. We'd planned for a much longer timeline before we brought Sophie into our world. But the Neverseen sparked the white fires and we had to get her somewhere safe." Juline turned to Sophie. "I can't imagine how confusing those days must've been for you. And I'm so sorry we had to uproot you that way. But I'll always be grateful that you ended up with my sister."

"Me too." Sophie's eyes burned with the words, and she had to check her Imparter again.

Still no hails from anyone.

"Are you going to tell your parents about me?" Juline asked.

"Do you not want me to?"

"I think . . . it would be better if I tell them. I'm sure they'll have lots of questions."

"So do I," Dex jumped in. "'Cause I see a lot of things that don't add up. Like, what happened when I was kidnapped? Why would you do a planting in the Wanderling Woods if you knew the Black Swan were still searching for me? And why was Forkle the one who came to rescue us?"

"The days after you were taken were the worst days of my life," Juline whispered. "None of us could piece together what happened, and there were too many conflicting reports for me to feel any hope. I also had a family that needed closure—and a world that expected me to grieve a certain way. So I went along with the planting. I didn't know what else to do. And Forkle went to save you because his mental blocking is stronger than mine, and we weren't sure if he'd have to confront your kidnappers. But if I'd known he was going to leave you both alone in Paris, I never would've let him go without me. When he came back empty-handed, I slapped him so hard he had my handprint on his cheek for three days."

It wasn't the right moment to smile—but Sophie felt her lips twitch anyway.

"This . . . is a lot to take in," Kesler said quietly.

"I know," Juline told him. "This is why Councillors aren't allowed to have families. And the Black Swan used to follow the same policy. They amended their rule for Tiergan—but he was already a member of the Collective when he adopted Wylie. The real reason they agreed to appoint me was because they believed our family could handle it. And we can. I just need you to trust me."

"I need to know something first," Dex said, not quite meeting her eyes. "Did you bring me to Havenfield that first day because you wanted me to spy on Sophie? Like Keefe's mom did with him and Fitz?"

Juline took him by his shoulders. "I promise, Dex. I brought you there because you asked. That's it. And honestly, I was reluctant to do it. I could feel my worlds colliding. But you were so excited to meet Sophie, and I wanted so badly for you to have a friend. I didn't want you spending another year eating lunch in your alchemy session."

"You ate in your alchemy session?" Biana asked.

Shame burned Dex's cheeks as he nodded.

Biana's blush looked even brighter as she whispered, "Sorry. I was really stupid back then."

"Me too," Fitz said.

Juline smiled sadly. "We all make mistakes. The only thing we can do is try to move past them. Can we do that?"

She seemed to hold her breath as Kesler and Dex looked at each other.

"I think we can," Kesler decided.

Dex nodded.

Juline pulled them close, kissing Dex's cheek before she kissed Kesler a whole lot longer.

"EWWWWWWWWWW," the triplets shouted as they raced out of the tree line. "YOU GUYS AREN'T SUPPOSED TO DO THAT WHERE WE CAN SEE YOU."

"Deal with it," Kesler said, kissing Juline again before scooping up an armful of snow and flinging it at his kids.

"Well," Juline said as the triplets retaliated, sending slushy balls of ice whizzing past everyone's heads. "I think that's our cue to get out of the battle zone."

She took Iggy's cage from Sophie and grabbed one of Biana's bags before she marched toward Rimeshire.

Fitz and Biana followed, but Sophie noticed Dex lagging behind.

"You okay?" she asked him.

He kicked more snow. "Would you be?"

"I don't know. It's a lot to get used to. But . . . I keep thinking about the oath we made when we swore fealty. Do you remember it?"

"*I will do everything in my power to help my world,*" Dex said quietly. "It wasn't nearly as fancy as I'd been expecting."

"Same here. But it's actually kinda perfect for what we're all trying to do. Sometimes we hide things. And sometimes it hurts. And sometimes the adults send us away instead of letting us fight alongside them. But . . . we're all just trying to do everything we can to help people."

Dex's sigh lasted several seconds.

"If it helps, I wouldn't have cared why you came to Havenfield that day," she added. "I'm just glad you did. I needed a friend too. And I got the best friend ever."

"GROSS—ARE YOU GUYS GOING TO KISS?" Bex shouted.

"IGNORE HER," Kesler called, scooping up another huge armful of snow and dropping it over the triplets' heads. They squealed and ran into the trees with Kesler right behind.

Dex's face looked so red it was basically purple. "Siblings are the worst."

"They can be," Sophie agreed.

She still missed the human sister she'd grown up with, though. They'd fought all the time. But that's what sisters did.

"Anyway, don't worry," she said. "I know she's giving you a hard time. It's not like . . ."

"Yeah." Dex's brow scrunched, and he opened his mouth like he wanted to say something else. Then he shook his head and his lips shifted to a different word. "Come on, let's go inside. I'm losing feeling in my toes."

Fitz and Biana were waiting by the door, ready with generous amounts of encouragement and support. And amazingly enough, Dex seemed like he was actually glad they were there. They'd come a long way as a group—and had some crazy, impossible, scary, frustrating things happen.

But they also had each other. And *that* was something special.

TWENTY-FIVE

EX'S HOUSE WAS EVEN MORE beautiful on the inside. Everything looked blue and gray and shimmery, with swirls of white like waves in the ocean.

Kesler was right, though—the crystal yeti in the entryway definitely needed to be destroyed. Its jaggedly carved fur looked like some sort of demented, oversize porcupine. And once again, the triplets seemed to have spared its life. Instead, they'd shattered what must've been a vase filled with glass marbles. The white stone floor was covered in the clear glass orbs.

"Walk very carefully," Juline warned.

Sophie made it about ten steps before her foot rolled on a

marble and sent her flying backward like a cartoon character slipping on a banana peel. She would've been in for some killer bruises if Fitz hadn't caught her.

"Maybe I should carry you," he said when she slipped again on her next step.

His teasing smile made it extra hilarious when he fell a second later, landing on his butt with a loud "Oof!"

Biana laughed so hard she nearly fell over too—but Dex was able to catch her by her shoulders.

"Perhaps I should carry all of you," Lovise offered, making it look easy as she helped them back on their feet. "The trick is to slide your steps, so nothing gets underneath you."

She was right—though they all looked like the world's most uncoordinated ice skaters.

"You okay?" Sophie asked when she noticed Fitz rubbing his tailbone.

"He's fine," Biana answered for him. "I knock him down way harder than that in tackle bramble all the time. And by the way—he told me about the favor he owes you. If you need ideas for how to torture him, I have *lots* of suggestions."

"See, Dex?" Fitz asked. "You're not the only one with annoying siblings."

"Trade you!" Dex offered.

"Only if you take Alvar as part of the deal."

The name killed everyone's smiles and had Sophie checking her Imparter again.

"Do you think it's a bad sign that we haven't heard anything?" she whispered.

"We've barely been gone an hour," Biana reminded her.

"Ugh—is that really all?" Sophie asked. "This day is going to take forever."

"I know." Biana twisted the panic switch on her finger. "I think we need to stay busy so we don't go crazy."

They'd made it to the main room by then, where the plush gray carpet was blissfully marble-free, and the clear ceiling let in warm rays of sunlight. Five curved staircases broke up the space, each leading to one of the towers. And all the gray-blue furniture had been arranged around a giant glass cloche in the center. Silver flames tipped with blue flickered under the dome, shimmering with each spark and crackle. Sophie had seen many types of fire since she'd moved to the Lost Cities, but she'd never seen any that were quite so beautiful.

"You okay?" Fitz asked her. "I know you don't like to be around flames."

"I don't," Sophie agreed. "But for some reason these don't bother me."

"Probably because they're a hologram." Juline snapped her fingers and the glowing flames morphed into a black orb of the night sky filled with twinkling stars. "This is one of Dex's inventions."

"That's amazing," Biana said, snapping again and creating a sphere of sunset. "You seriously made this?"

Dex shrugged. "It wasn't hard. All I did was tweak a fire emulator."

Biana shook her head. "You don't give yourself enough credit."

"Sophie's just as bad with compliments," Fitz said. "Look at how red they're both turning right now."

"They really are adorable, aren't they?" Biana asked.

Sophie sighed. "Who invited the Vackers?"

"That one's on you," Dex said. "But at least we have someone to prank now. As soon as they fall asleep—"

"Sleep?" Biana interrupted. "Only lame people sleep during slumber parties. Besides, we all know Sophie's going to keep us up sending telepathic messages to Keefe. Or wait—you don't think he'll go to Havenfield, do you?"

"I . . . don't know if they'll give him a choice," Sophie mumbled. "But Keefe would *never* hurt our families."

"What happens if they tell him he has to?" Fitz asked.

"We hope he has a plan to get out of it," Sophie said. "Like how he had a plan to save me with that bead."

"And if he doesn't?" Fitz pressed.

Sophie didn't have an answer.

"Come on," Juline said, breaking the suffocating silence. "The solarium is this way."

She led them toward the back of the house, into a giant glass bubble of a room that made it feel like they were standing in a life-size fishbowl. A thin row of plants lined the round space, and Sophie noticed that their emerald green leaves shimmered with a thin layer of hoarfrost. The rest of the room was mostly empty—just a few topiaries scattered around and a pile of four rolled-up sleeping bags.

The real focus was the view: a wide stretch of garden filled with flowering vines, gleaming silver fountains, and the most lifelike ice sculptures that Sophie had ever seen—a mix of spring and winter only a Froster could have at the same time.

The woolly mammoth had been carved to scale, and somehow its icy fur looked soft and silky. And the saber-toothed tiger's eyes gave Sophie chills.

"They're amazing," Biana whispered.

Juline's cheeks reddened at the praise. "Thank you. Our lives are too chaotic for pets, so this is my compromise with the triplets. They get to decide which creatures I carve every week. And speaking of pets, is your imp going to need a bathroom spot? We can set up some sort of box if you don't want him out in the cold."

"Or we could give him a way fluffier fur coat!" Biana jumped in. "Maybe change his color, too! Do you have any elixirs, Dex? I'm thinking purple this time—or maybe green."

"I'll check my room," he told her.

Biana clapped. "Yay—first makeover of the night!"

"You mean the *only* makeover," Fitz corrected.

"Aw, come on—you and Keefe let me do it once before!" Biana whined.

"Seriously?" Sophie asked. "Now *that's* a story I have to hear."

Dex snorted. "Me too."

"Aren't we supposed to be searching Alvar's records?" Fitz asked.

Biana shrugged off her satchel. "I can't imagine that's going to take *all* night."

"It might," Dex warned. "There are a *lot* of scrolls. I'll need help carrying them down."

Fitz volunteered, and Biana pouted as the boys headed for the stairs.

Juline handed Biana her other bag and gave Sophie Iggy's cage. "For the record, I hope you guys have a little fun tonight. I know you're worried about your parents. And I know how hard you all work trying to solve everything. But I speak for all of us when I say that we want you to enjoy being normal teenagers."

"But we *aren't* normal teenagers," Sophie reminded her. "Or I'm not, at least."

Juline took her hand. "Yes, you are. Even after everything you've been through. Even with everything you have ahead. You're still a fourteen-year-old girl who deserves to relax and have fun with her friends."

"So what you're saying," Biana said, "is I have your permission to give Dex a makeover?"

Juline laughed. "I'll leave that up to Dex."

She winked and left them alone, and they got to work setting

242

up the sleeping bags—which turned out to be a much trickier job than it should've been. The all-in-a-straight-row concept felt super awkward. But the round room made it impossible to go to separate corners. Eventually they settled on an X shape. That way their heads would be close enough to talk to each other, but they'd each still have as much space as possible.

"Keefe is going to pout so hard when he finds out he missed this," Biana said, claiming the sleeping bag closest to the room's entrance. "We could've all scooted over and put his sleeping bag right here."

Sophie tried not to notice that the arrangement would've looked like a star.

"You know what I hate?" she said, moving her backpack to the sleeping bag on the left of Biana's. "If the Neverseen really do attack Havenfield today—and everyone stays safe—they'll probably know that Keefe warned us. We tried to make it look like all the security was stuff they'd have set up in order to protect me. But *I'm* not there."

"Right, but it's not like you never leave the house," Biana reminded her. "And Keefe's a quick thinker."

"Also a good liar," Sophie mumbled.

But talk didn't mean much to the Neverseen.

If they got suspicious, Keefe would have to do something to prove himself again. And it would have to be even bigger than what he already did at Foxfire. . . .

"You know what *I* hate?" Biana asked, pulling a tab on the

side of her sleeping bag and making it plump up like a pillow.

Sophie copied her, and when she sat down, it felt like sinking into a giant stretched-out marshmallow.

"I hate wondering how many times I should've figured out what my brother was doing," Biana whispered.

"That's why Edaline told me hindsight is a dangerous game," Sophie reminded her.

"I know. But it feels so *obvious*. Like, I remember after my dad's mind broke, Alvar decided to stay the night at Everglen because my mom had a super-rough day. And I couldn't sleep, so I got up to wander the halls. I heard him in my dad's office, talking to someone on his Imparter—but I figured he was trying to help finish one of my dad's projects."

"Do you remember anything he said?"

"Bits and pieces. I should've paid better attention. I heard him say something about changing the timeline. And he asked about test subjects. I also remember him using the word 'criterion' a couple of times. But I don't know what any of that means."

Sophie pulled Ella from her backpack and leaned her cheek on the elephant's pillowy belly. "You know what I miss? Back when I first moved to the Lost Cities—and the Black Swan were running my life from the shadows—I'd know I was on the right track because I'd hear a word and it would trigger new memories. Now it seems like everything we learn is stuff that even the Black Swan don't know."

"Do you think that means they were preparing you for the wrong thing?" Biana asked.

"Ugh—I do now!"

Just when Sophie thought she'd reached maximum worrying capacity.

What if the role she'd been designed to play wasn't even the right one?

Could Project Moonlark be . . . a fail?

TWENTY-SIX

U H-OH, DID SOMETHING HAPPEN?"
Fitz asked as he stumbled into the solarium carrying a black trunk that looked like it weighed as much as he did. "You haven't heard from Grady and Edaline, right?"

Sophie double-checked her Imparter. "Nope. Still nothing."

Fitz set the trunk down in the center of the *X* and took the empty sleeping bag closest to Sophie. "Then why do you look like you want to tug on your eyelashes?"

Sophie sighed. "Biana told me about a conversation she overheard Alvar having. I'm trying to figure out what it could mean."

"What conversation?" Dex asked as he brought an equally enormous trunk and set it down next to the one Fitz brought.

Biana repeated the story while Dex sank onto the only empty sleeping bag, between the two Vackers.

"So . . . you're worried that Project Moonlark is a bust?" Fitz guessed.

Sophie couldn't look at him as she nodded.

"Okay, but even if it is," Fitz said, "haven't you hated feeling like you're some sort of puppet?"

"Yeah, but it's way scarier thinking there's no safety net," Sophie mumbled. "I didn't like feeling controlled—but I *did* like thinking the good guys had a plan."

"I don't know, wouldn't it be kinda weird if the Black Swan knew all these horrible things were going to happen and didn't do anything to stop them?" Fitz asked.

"And just because parts of their plans have changed doesn't mean all of them have," Biana added. "You still have crazy powerful abilities. *And* you have us. We've got this!"

"I guess," Sophie said. "I just wish we had *any* idea what the Neverseen are planning, or what the Lodestar Initiative actually is. I mean, why would your brother be talking about 'test subjects' and 'criterion'? That sounds like some sort of experiment."

Dex sucked in a breath. "Okay—this is going to sound crazy—but hear me out. What if the Lodestar Initiative is the Neverseen's version of Project Moonlark?"

"I'm not sure I know what that means," Biana told him.

"I do," Fitz said. "And please tell me you don't actually think they're trying to build another Sophie."

"Why not?" Dex asked. "They've known she exists for a while. Don't you think they'd try to do something to counter her?"

"They did," Fitz argued. "They tried to find her. And capture her. And now they're trying to control her."

"Maybe," Dex said. "But they could do all of that *and* try to re-create her."

"Can everyone stop talking about me like I'm Dr. Frankenstein's monster?" Sophie grumbled.

"Is that a human thing?" Biana asked.

"Yeah, it's this big scary guy with bolts in his neck, who's pieced together from dead things," Fitz said. "I remember seeing pictures of it one of the times I visited the Forbidden Cities. I think it was a movie?"

"And a book," Sophie mumbled.

"Sorry," Dex said. "I didn't mean it like that. But . . . it would explain what Alvar meant by 'test subjects.' I've also heard the word 'criterion' used with DNA and genetics and stuff."

Sophie hugged Ella so tight all the stuffing bulged in the elephant's head.

"Hey," Biana said, patting Sophie's shoulder. "Even if he's right, it doesn't change anything about *you*—or Keefe."

"I don't think he's right," Fitz added. "Keefe's mom helped create the Lodestar Initiative, and she's definitely not a scientist. And don't even try to convince me Keefe's their version of Sophie. He's older than she is. And he wasn't raised by humans. And he only has one ability. And he's not nearly as awesome."

He grinned at Sophie, but she was too busy panicking to return it.

"He does have a photographic memory, though," Biana said—which did *not* help. "And his empathy is more powerful than other Empaths. Do you think his mom could've had his genes tweaked somehow after he was born?"

"I guess we could ask Forkle about it," Dex said.

"And he'll tell us we're being ridiculous," Fitz assured him.

"Maybe. But they did for sure mess with Keefe's memories," Dex argued. "So maybe all they did was plant secrets in his head, like the Black Swan did with Sophie. You have to admit it's at least possible."

Sophie wasn't going to admit anything.

It was too weird.

Too wrong.

Too . . . no.

Just *no*.

She tried to bury the theory deep—lock it away with all the other Things She Didn't Want to Think About.

But the idea had already dug its claws in deep.

So had the bigger, scarier question it raised, echoing around her head on autorepeat.

If Dex was right, and the Lodestar Initiative was the Never-seen's version of Project Moonlark . . . did that mean Keefe was meant to be her nemesis?

TWENTY-SEVEN

"YOU WERE MADE TO BE THE HERO," Sophie mumbled. "I was raised to be something . . . else."

"What?" Fitz, Biana, and Dex all asked.

"That's what Keefe told me. At the Lake of Blood. When he ran off with the Neverseen. Do you think he meant . . . ?"

She couldn't finish the question.

"Hey," Fitz said, scooting next to her on her sleeping bag. "I don't think it means what you're thinking it means. Brant and Fintan were there—and Keefe needed to convince them he was joining for real. He had to sound like a guy trying to explain to his friend why he was betraying her—and remember, I'm saying that as someone who still has trust issues with Keefe."

"I guess," she said quietly. "But *you* think it proves your theory, don't you, Dex?"

"I don't know," Dex said. "I mean . . . it could. But I *am* also just guessing."

"Exactly," Biana jumped in. "All we really know is that we *don't* know anything."

Somehow, that was the most depressing thought of all.

Sophie flopped onto her back, rubbing the knot under her ribs and trying to tie all the complicated things she was feeling into it. She stared at the sky through the curved glass ceiling, wishing she could stretch out her consciousness to Keefe and pummel him with questions. But it was still early in the day—way too soon for their check-in. And she probably didn't want to know what he was doing anyway.

"Okay," Fitz said. "I think we need a subject change before Sophie's brain explodes."

"He's right," Biana agreed. "Maybe if we figure out where Alvar used to sneak off to, it'll help us understand what that conversation *actually* meant."

Dex scooted over to the trunks and popped both lids open, revealing so many tightly coiled scrolls that Sophie wondered if there was any paper left in the world.

"I told you this is going to be boring," Dex reminded them as Biana unrolled a scroll and gaped at the thousands of tiny black numbers printed across it. "This part you'll probably be able to read"—he pointed to the narrowest column on the left of the scroll—"that's the time stamp, telling you the date, year, and time in hours, minutes, and seconds. But the rest is all code. Some of it has obviously been altered, and I've been trying to figure out which parts, but so far I haven't been able to find a pattern."

"Have you checked the days you were kidnapped?" Biana asked. "That's the one time we know that Alvar wasn't where his records said he was—*and* we know exactly where he was."

"I haven't," Dex admitted. "The triplets got in my room and got into the trunks and . . . let's just say I'm currently brewing a very special elixir for payback."

Fitz sighed. "So all of these are in random order? That's going to take forever."

"Maybe not," Biana said. "Now we have four of us working on it. Okay, so Sophie and Fitz—you guys work on putting the scrolls back in order while Dex and I focus on trying to find the dates from the kidnapping. And once we find one, Dex will switch to checking the tech code part to see if he can find the pattern we need."

"You're assuming they altered Alvar's feed the same way every time," Dex reminded her.

"I know—but isn't that what you'd do?" she asked. "If you knew something was working, wouldn't you keep doing it?"

"I suppose."

"All right then," Biana said. "We have a plan!"

They did.

But the process was *sloooooooooooooooooooooow*. It took them hours before Biana found the first scroll from the time frame they needed.

"I think I'll need at least three to really be able to compare," Dex warned as he squinted at the numbers.

Hours later, Sophie found scroll number two.

"So we only need one more, right?" Biana asked.

"Assuming I can find the pattern," Dex said. "And assuming the pattern actually applies to the other days he snuck away. And assuming I can figure out what the pattern even means."

"That's a lot of assumptions," Fitz noted.

"It is," Biana agreed. "But Dex found secret information about the plague by digging through a database that spanned *centuries*. I'm sure we can find what we're looking for in a couple of trunks of scrolls."

When she put it that way, it didn't sound so daunting. But they still hadn't found the third scroll by the time Juline brought them dinner—which looked like blue french fries and tasted like nachos with extra cheese.

"Still at it?" Juline asked. "And I'm assuming you haven't heard from anyone at Havenfield?"

Sophie shook her head. "I've been checking my Imparter every few minutes. It's driving me nuts."

"Your Imparter *is* working, right?" Biana asked. "Weren't you having a problem with it?"

"I thought the problem was Dex's Imparter," Sophie said.

Dex pulled the silver gadget out of his pocket. "I ran every test I could think of, and they all came back normal. Have you tried hailing me again?"

Sophie held her Imparter to her mouth and told it, "Show me Dex Dizznee."

Dex's Imparter stayed blank.

"That doesn't make sense," Dex said. "Fitz—can you try hailing me?"

Fitz did, and Dex's screen immediately flashed with Fitz's face.

"Hmm. Maybe yours is the one with the loose wire," Dex said. "Give me a sec."

He ran upstairs to get tools, and Sophie stared at her finicky gadget.

"Do you think I should check on my family with your Imparter?" she asked Fitz. "What if they've been trying to hail me?"

"My parents are there too," Fitz reminded her, "and they haven't tried to reach me."

Dex raced back into the room with a kit of the world's tiniest screwdrivers. Within minutes he had the whole Imparter disassembled and hundreds of paper-thin gears scattered across his sleeping bag.

"See anything weird?" Sophie asked as he picked up an especially tiny gear.

Dex shook his head. "Everything was exactly where it should be. I just don't . . ."

His voice trailed off and he leaned closer, squinting at one of the cog's teeth.

"Is that grease?" Biana asked, peering over his shoulder.

Dex said nothing as he fished his monocle pendant out from underneath his tunic and used the magnifying glass to examine a speck of black.

"Whoa," he whispered—then covered his mouth.

"What is it?" Fitz, Biana, Sophie, and Juline all asked at once.

"I . . . think some dirt got into the mechanism and clogged it," he said. "Can someone get me a pen and paper so I can make a note of which cog needs to be replaced?"

Juline pulled the pencil from her hair and Biana flipped one of the scrolls over for Dex to write on the back.

"So it's just a normal malfunction?" Sophie asked.

"Should be."

But Dex's note told a different story.

His left hand shook as he held it to his lips and made the universal *Shhh* sign before he showed them what he'd written.

Someone might be listening.

TWENTY-EIGHT

HE GOOD NEWS IS, YOUR IMPARTER
still works," Dex said, adding another sentence
to his note.

We need to act normal.

"Once I put it back together, it should connect to everything
except my Imparter," he added. "I forgot that I added a safety
protocol to mine, blocking it from communicating with any
abnormal tech."

He amended his sign again.

Can we talk telepathically?

Juline grabbed the note and added:

ALL of us!

Lovise snatched the scroll and wrote: *I expect updates as well.*

Sophie nodded and turned to Fitz, who offered her his hand. Their thumb rings snapped together as the mental energy hummed between them and they opened their minds to Dex, Biana, and Juline.

Okay, Sophie transmitted while their mental voices flooded her head. *I think we're doing what Councillor Emery does when he mediates the other Councillors—and wow, it's LOUD.*

Yeah it is, Fitz said, rubbing the sides of his forehead.

Sophie tried to think around the questions being shouted at her, but it was too much too fast.

Okay, so here's how this needs to work, Fitz said. *Sophie and I can hear all of you guys, but you can't hear each other. So you need to take turns, and then we'll transmit what you said to the rest of the group so everyone can hear it.*

Dex first, Sophie said. *What do you mean someone might be listening? And why aren't we smashing that gear to stop them?*

Because, if they don't know that we've found it, they won't destroy their end of the signal. And that might give me a chance to trace it back to the source. But first I have to get the Imparter reassembled.

His hands were already busy fitting all the tiny cogs back together.

Fitz relayed the information to the others—even jotted down a brief update for Lovise—and transmitted Biana's question: *Who else would it be besides the Neverseen?*

It could be the Council, Fitz told her. *Mr. Forkle said they're keeping close tabs on us.*

Can they hear everything we say? Sophie asked. *Or only when the Imparter's in use?*

I can't tell yet, Dex said. *That's why I don't want us talking, just in case.*

But won't they get suspicious of all this silence? Fitz asked. *Especially since they would've heard that we were disassembling the Imparter?*

That's actually a good point, Dex admitted.

I need you guys to start talking again, Fitz told Juline and Biana.

Biana rustled some of the scrolls. "I think I need a break, guys. All the numbers are turning into a big black blur."

I need to update the rest of the Collective, Juline thought as she told them, "I'm going to make you guys some mugs of cinnacreme. It's always my favorite thing on a cold night."

"Ohhhh, that sounds amazing!" Biana launched into a long explanation of what it tasted like—and it *did* sound delicious. But Sophie was more focused on Dex.

How long do you think they've been listening? she asked.

I'm guessing it's pretty recent. I've had that safety protocol on my Imparter for a while, and it never used to block you. That's why I didn't think of it at first. But now it makes total sense. My Imparter shuts out any signals that aren't secure.

So someone must've tampered with yours, Fitz said to Sophie.

But when? It's always with me. Or it's in my room, and if someone had been in there, Sandor would've known—wouldn't he?

Hasn't Brant fooled Sandor's senses before? Dex thought. *Using ash or something?*

But wouldn't he still have left footprints in the flowered carpet? Sophie asked.

Unless he levitated, Fitz said.

She hated him for being right—hated even more what the possibility meant.

I had my Imparter with me the day Keefe visited Foxfire, she transmitted. *If it was broadcasting, that means the Neverseen might know Keefe's betraying them.*

Her mind flashed through visions of Keefe being dragged to the ogres' prison, bleeding and begging for mercy like his mom.

Hey, Fitz said, tightening his hold on her hand. *Try not to think about that stuff until we know what we're dealing with, okay?*

I'm close to tracking the signal, Dex told them. *But I think we've gotten too quiet again.*

Fitz told Biana to start talking again, and she fumbled for something to say.

Wait—I know! she thought. "Makeover time! Who wants to go first?"

"I think it should be Dex," Sophie told her.

Uh, I'm a little busy here, Dex argued.

I know—but if they think you're getting a makeover, they'll be less suspicious about what you're doing to the Imparter.

Dex sighed. "Fine—but *no* makeup!"

"Duh," Biana told him. "All I'm going to do is fix your hair."

"What's wrong with my hair?"

"Let me show you the many things." Biana dug through one of her overnight bags and pulled out a pink sparkly pouch filled with pots of different colored gels. She chose a yellowish concoction and unscrewed the lid.

"That better not have pee in it," Dex told her.

"Don't be gross. And don't be such a baby."

Fitz snickered. "Now you see what I live with."

How's it going? Sophie transmitted to Dex.

Good. I'm just setting up some aliases to shield my search signals and—

"Ahh! What are you doing?" he shouted.

Biana had scooted closer and was running her fingers through his hair.

"Relax—I'm just making it so your hair isn't plastered to your forehead anymore. Hold still." She dipped her fingers in the yellow goop and reached for him again.

Sophie had never seen Dex so red.

"This style will draw way more attention to your eyes," Biana said. "And the flecks of gold in the gel will bring out the blond undertones in your hair."

She handed him a mirror from her bag. "See? It's awesome, right?"

Dex's grin was so huge it practically caved in his cheeks.

Sophie shifted to get a better look. "Wow. That's . . . *wow*."

Who knew a new hairstyle could make such a difference?

Not that Dex hadn't been cute before—he was an elf, after all. But there'd been something about him that always felt *young*.

Not anymore.

Aren't we supposed to be dealing with the fact that someone might be eavesdropping on us right now? Fitz transmitted. *Or are you trying to bore them to death with all this hair talk?*

Biana smirked. "I think Fitz should be my next makeover. His style has gotten a little helmety lately."

"It has not!" Fitz said. But Sophie noticed he reached up and mussed his hair a bit.

Okay, Dex thought. *I'm ready to track the signal—we have to make sure we keep talking.*

Out loud, he added, "If Fitz is being a baby, how about we give Iggy a new look?"

Biana squealed happily as he handed her a vial filled with a cloudy liquid, and she scooted over to Iggy's cage, waving the elixir near his furry lips. Iggy sniffed the milky serum once before downing it in one giant slurp. He'd barely finished licking his chops when he sneezed and his fur poofed out in every direction, turning him into a ball of blue fluff with only the tips of his ears, hands, wings, and nose sticking through.

"Isn't he going to change color?" Sophie asked.

"Give it a second," Dex said, and sure enough, Iggy's fur started to shimmer as it shifted to a bright purple.

"Awwww, just when I thought he couldn't get more adorable!" Biana cooed.

Iggy bounced up and down and flapped his fluff-buried wings.

"Who's ready for cinnacreme?" Juline asked, sweeping into the room with a tray of four steaming mugs. She froze midstep when she spotted Dex's hair.

"Like it?" Biana asked.

Juline looked a little misty-eyed.

"Ugh, why are parents so embarrassing?" Dex grumbled.

"It's our job." Juline handed everyone mugs of cinnacreme—which tasted like melted snickerdoodles.

What did the Collective say? Sophie asked her.

I was only able to reach Wraith. He's tracking down the others as we speak.

Do you think—

Sophie's question was cut short by a white light flashing from her Imparter.

Dex frowned and tapped the screen a few times.

Something wrong? Sophie asked.

Not necessarily. It looks like I have good news, bad news, and weird news. The good news is: I'm pretty sure no one's listening to us right now. The signal doesn't seem to be reaching anything—which is the bad news. I can't track where it's going. The receiver's either been turned off or destroyed.

So what's the weird news? Fitz asked.

Dex handed the gadget to Sophie. *This isn't your Imparter.*

TWENTY-NINE

WHAT DO YOU MEAN IT'S NOT *my Imparter?* Sophie asked. *I brought it from home.*

I know, Dex told her. *But I just checked the activity log. And unless you hailed yourself a ton of times—which I don't even think is possible—it has to be someone else's. Someone who also hailed Fitz a lot, and made a few very brief hails to Lord Cassius.*

Sophie's eyes widened. *This is Keefe's Imparter?*

Dex nodded.

Why would you have Keefe's Imparter? Fitz asked. *Did he slip it to you the day he blew up Foxfire?*

Wouldn't I have two, then? Sophie asked.

Unless he swiped yours, Fitz said. *Maybe when he put his cloak around you?*

Sophie replayed the moment, but all she remembered were Keefe's hands near her shoulders.

I guess it's possible, she admitted. *But I don't see why he would do that. And I don't think he would've been able to hide that from me during our check-ins. I can see enough of his fleeting thoughts to know what stuff he's worrying about.*

Then where else would you get his Imparter? Dex asked.

No clue. Actually, wait. Grizel found an Imparter in Keefe's desk when we were searching his room, and I gave her mine so she could compare the two. She might've accidentally mixed them up before she gave it back.

I guess that makes sense, Fitz said. *And you know what? I bet this Imparter is how the Neverseen knew about our ambush on Mount Everest. Keefe's mom probably rigged it so she could eavesdrop on Keefe's conversations, and heard us arranging the trap.*

Sophie cringed. *As if hiding a tracker in his family crest pin wasn't disgusting enough.*

HEY GUYS—REMEMBER ME? Biana thought, waving her arms to get their attention. *I'd like to know what's going on too!*

Fitz caught her up on the newest discoveries, then updated Juline and Lovise.

Does that mean it's safe for us to talk? Biana asked.

Dex squinted at the Imparter. *I think we should still be careful—unless you want me to disassemble it again.*

I hate to do that, Juline said after Sophie relayed the info. *Every time we tamper with it, we risk undoing whatever they did, and we might still be able to learn something from it.*

Guess that means we're in for more makeover talk, Sophie transmitted as Juline left to see if Wraith had made contact with the rest of the Collective.

"We could play truth or dare," Biana suggested with an evil smile.

"No way—that got *weird* last time," Fitz told her.

Biana tossed her hair. "I don't know what you're talking about."

"Yes you do—just like you totally knew what you were doing when you turned your head at the last second."

Sophie was about to ask for details, when she remembered Keefe admitting that he'd kissed Biana once on a dare. He'd described it as "mostly on the cheek."

"How about we work on the scrolls again?" she said, deciding that games were too risky. Truth or dare was definitely out, and the only other game she could think of was spin the bottle—which would be a *very* bad idea.

Biana pouted. "I suppose that's the smart thing to do."

And so the hours went, filled with lots of squinting at tiny black numbers on endless scrolls. Their only breaks were for quick checks of their still-silent Imparters.

"Brought you a refill," Juline said, carrying a fresh tray of cinnacreme mugs into the solarium. *And I finally heard from Mr. Forkle. He was over at Havenfield.*

HE WAS? Sophie and Fitz both transmitted together.

Did something happen? Sophie asked.

No—it's still quiet. And it's after midnight, so technically the day is over.

Do you really think the Neverseen care about technicalities? Sophie asked.

I don't know what the Neverseen care about, Juline admitted. *All I know is, for the moment, everyone is safe and I'm going to be grateful. They'll stay on alert for the rest of the night, of course. But we're all cautiously optimistic that the threat has passed. And Mr. Forkle agreed that we should keep avoiding important conversations around the Imparter until he can retrieve it in the morning. So why don't you four try getting some rest?*

"We're getting so close," Biana said after Sophie passed along the message. "We might as well finish."

And they did. And Dex scowled at the final scroll. "I don't know who their Technopath is—but they're *good*. I can't figure out the point of these numbers."

Any chance you're just saying that for the benefit of the Imparter? Fitz asked him.

I wish. This is the code I found hidden in Alvar's records from the days we were kidnapped. He scribbled on the back of the nearest scroll:

0-11-<<-1-1-1-0*

Sophie studied it from a few angles. *Okay, yeah, that doesn't make any sense.*

It really doesn't, Dex agreed. *The most basic digital code—the kind that's so basic, even humans use it—is made of ones and zeroes. But I have no idea what those other symbols are supposed to mean, or how they work.*

Well . . . I'm guessing the asterisk is for Lodestar, right? Fitz asked.

Maybe. But some of the normal registry codes use asterisks too. Plus, the asterisk switches sides sometimes on the other codes I found hidden in Alvar's records. Like this, which I'm pretty sure is from the day Sophie saw The Boy Who Disappeared.

*0-1->-1->-111-0

And I found these during the days that Alden's mind was broken:

*0->-111->>>-1-0
0-<<-1-1-11-<-0*

I'm assuming the sequences are different because each one stands for a different place Alvar went, Dex said. *But no matter how long I stare at it, I still don't understand how to read the numbers and symbols and AARRGGGRRHHH!*

He made the same noise out loud and collapsed backward onto his sleeping bag.

Biana flopped back too, and Sophie and Fitz did the same.

It's still progress, Sophie transmitted. *Remember, this is how it always goes. It's always piece by piece, and it feels like we're never going to figure it out—and then we find another clue and it all comes together.*

I just wish we could skip to the it-all-comes-together part, don't you? Fitz asked as he yawned.

Biana yawned too. "I can't believe I'm about to say this, but I'm exhausted. So I propose a truce. No one pranks anyone, and we all get to sleep. Is that proof that I'm becoming lame?"

"It's proof that we have a lot going on," Fitz told her. "And we'll handle it better if our brains are actually working in the morning. So how about this—if anyone breaks the pact, we make them brush their teeth with reekrod."

"Deal," Dex said. "I'd rather save my prank elixirs for the triplets anyway."

"I'm in," Sophie agreed.

Biana called Iggy to her pillow, and within seconds his squeaky purr filled the room. Dex's soft snores followed, and everyone seemed to still.

Are you trying to reach out to Keefe? Fitz transmitted, nearly making Sophie yelp. *Sorry—didn't mean to startle you.*

It's fine. And . . . I think I'm going to skip tonight's check-in.

Because you're afraid of putting him in danger? Or because you're afraid he's doing something you don't want to know about?

Both, she admitted, hugging Ella tighter.

I wish I knew what to say to help.

I don't think those words exist.

What Keefe was doing was a complicated, impossible mess.

If it makes you feel any better, Fitz told her, *I'm keeping my Imparter right by my head. That way, if my parents hail me I'll be sure to hear it.*

You'll wake me up if they do?

You really think you're going to be able to sleep?

No idea.

Well, you can borrow Mr. Snuggles if you want.

Sophie smiled. *Nah, I couldn't bear to keep you two apart. But thanks.*

Anytime.

His mind went quiet, and Sophie figured he'd dozed off with the others. But right as her mind started to drift, he added, *I'll always be here if you need me.*

THIRTY

SOFT CONVERSATION FLOATED THROUGH
Sophie's mind, the words blurring with her
dreams—until one question caught her attention.

Aren't they cute?

The voices sharpened into focus and she realized there
were a *lot* of sappy adults watching her sleep. But she was too
relieved to be annoyed about it.

"Mom?" she asked, scooting out of her sleeping bag and
waiting for her eyes to focus. "Dad?"

"We're here," Edaline said as both her parents smothered
her with a hug.

"Sorry we woke you, kiddo," Grady said. "Juline told us you

guys were up half the night, after a pretty eventful day. You must be exhausted."

She was. Somehow getting only a little sleep always felt worse than getting no sleep—but she didn't care about that right now. "You guys are safe?"

"For now," Edaline said, squeezing her tighter. "And don't worry, we'll be back on house arrest this afternoon. I just needed to talk with my sister in person. She's been filling me in on . . . everything."

Sophie followed Edaline's gaze to a fidgety Juline—who stood with Wraith, Blur, and Mr. Forkle, clearly making no attempt to hide her involvement with the Collective.

Alden and Della were there too—and Sandor and Brielle and Cadoc and Woltzer and Grizel and Lovise and Kesler. Everyone except Granite and the triplets.

"Wow." Biana mumbled from her sleeping bag. "That's a lot of faces to wake up to."

"It is," Della said, blinking in and out of sight as she crossed the room to hug her daughter. "Did you forget to pack pajamas?"

Biana looked down and blushed when she saw she was still in yesterday's clothes. "No, we forgot to get changed. Ugh, and I forgot to brush my teeth."

She covered her mouth, trying to spare the world from her morning breath.

"So what happened yesterday?" Sophie asked. "Did the Neverseen really not show up?"

"Not at Havenfield," Grady said. "We spent the whole day jumping at shadows—unlike you guys. Why am I not surprised that you had a way more productive day than we did?"

Are we still supposed to be quiet around the listening device? Fitz transmitted as he sat up and stretched.

Mr. Forkle held up a thin black box. "Mr. Sencen's Imparter is in here for the moment. Our Technopath put a small speaker inside to broadcast the sound of normal conversation until she can take a closer look and check for anything Mr. Dizznee could've missed."

"Speaking of Dex," Biana said, pointing to where he lay twisted up in his sleeping bag. "Shouldn't we wake him?"

"Be my guest," Kesler told her. "And good luck. Waking Dex is like waking a hibernating bear. The only thing worse is waking the triplets, who are thankfully still conked out upstairs."

Biana tried nudging Dex's shoulder. And flicking his ear. And kicking his leg. Nothing worked—until she put Iggy on Dex's pillow. One good Iggy burp in the face and Dex was sputtering and coughing and looking very disoriented.

"Hey," Biana told him. "Thought you might not want to miss this."

She pointed to the crowd of adults—who were trying very hard not to laugh.

"Thanks," Dex told her, sitting up and rubbing his eyes. "So . . . what's the bad news?"

"What makes you think there's bad news?" Juline asked.

"Please—there's no way you'd all be here if you didn't have something bad to tell us."

The adults shared a look.

"Why don't we wait until you've all had some breakfast?" Kesler suggested. "The Vackers brought over these amazing pastries. They're like eating a sweet, buttery cloud."

"Uh-uh," Sophie said, ignoring the gurgle in her stomach. "Tell us what's going on."

Mr. Forkle opened his mouth, but his voice didn't seem to cooperate.

"At the moment, we're still piecing the details together," Alden said quietly. "But . . . it appears the Neverseen did have a mission yesterday, like Keefe suspected—but the target wasn't Grady and Edaline. It was—"

His voice caught and he turned away.

Sophie's mind ran through worst-case scenarios, but none felt as shocking—or heartbreaking—as when Della told them, "The Neverseen attacked Wylie."

THIRTY-ONE

WYLIE?" BIANA REPEATED. "Prentice's son?"

Shadows darkened Mr. Forkle's eyes as he nodded. "He suffered an extensive interrogation."

Sophie rubbed her wrists as the ghosts of old wounds haunted her again. "Will he . . . ?"

"Physic is treating him as we speak," Juline promised. "But he'll need to remain sedated for several days."

"Days," Sophie repeated.

She'd only needed *days* of treatment when she'd almost died.

Red rimmed her vision and the knot in her chest begged to

unravel as she sucked in deep breaths, trying to calm the rage bubbling under her skin.

"It's okay," Grady whispered, tightening his hug. "Don't give them this power."

Sophie gritted her teeth, using the anger to bind everything back together.

"Does Physic think Wylie will recover?" Fitz asked.

"She seemed pretty confident," Blur said. "She thinks we caught the injuries early enough that he won't have any scars—physically at least. Psychologically is anyone's guess."

"Granite's with him now, searching his mind to piece together the details of what happened," Mr. Forkle added. "Then we'll decide how many memories to erase."

Normally Sophie wasn't a fan of altering people's memories. But she could see how it might be for the best in this case.

"How's Granite holding up?" Biana asked.

"No one can prepare for such evil to happen to their family," Wraith told her.

"He's barely said ten words since we found Wylie in a crumpled heap on the Stone House's porch," Blur added. "Wylie must've crawled for the door with the last of his strength, after whatever desperate measures he used to escape."

"He still had bonds on his feet—and partial bonds on his wrists—and he reeked of sedatives," Wraith finished sadly.

"Do you know where he escaped from?" Sophie asked.

Mr. Forkle cleared the thickness from his throat. "Unfortunately, no. At the moment, all we know is that he was taken from his room in the Silver Tower."

"How?" Fitz asked. "Aren't there goblins patrolling the campus?"

"Not as many as there should've been," Mr. Forkle admitted. "We're between terms, so most of the fleets have been reassigned to Lumenaria to prepare for the Peace Summit. And the one remaining patrol has been focusing its efforts on securing the newly arrived Exillium tents."

"But even if they got past the patrol, how did they get into the tower?" Dex asked. "The security in the elite towers is supposed to be legendary. My technopathy mentor went on and on about how it was designed the same way they did the insane security at Lumenaria, with a team of anonymous Technopaths each building only one small piece. That way no one would know the full scope, or how all the levels of security actually fit together."

"Truthfully?" Mr. Forkle said, "I have no idea how they got in. I've already accessed the security logs, and there were no unauthorized visitors. In fact, the records show that Wylie is the only prodigy who remained in the tower for the break—with no evidence that the files were altered. And since I'm sure you're going to ask about the Lodestar mirror"—he paused to let everyone react to the name—"let me assure you that it was the first place I checked. Nothing in the Hall of Illumination had been disturbed. There was no trace of a fingerprint or a footprint. No way to remove the mirror from the wall and access behind it. The mirror is just a mirror, designed to teach the elite prodigies to see that the purest version of themselves comes from power, not appearance."

"Could a Phaser have walked through the walls to get in?" Biana asked.

"The tower is impervious," Blur said. "Trust me. I've tried."

"Then they must have someone who has access to the tower who let them in," Fitz said.

"That was my thought as well," Mr. Forkle told him. "But as I said, all the logs show Wylie being alone. I also watched the prodigies quite closely during my time as the tower's Beacon, and none of them ever did anything to suggest a connection to the Neverseen."

"Neither did Alvar," Della said quietly.

The name hung heavy in the air.

"If he was a part of this," Alden whispered. "If he . . ."

Sophie had been thinking the same thing about Keefe. He'd said he wouldn't cross the hard lines—but would he count Wylie as one of them? Or would it be one of those "shady things" he was willing to do in order to keep playing the game?

Wraith's sleeves moved toward Alden, reaching for him with invisible hands. "*You* are not responsible for your son's actions."

"But if we'd noticed—"

"Please don't go down that path," Edaline begged. "We cared for Brant for sixteen years and never suspected either."

"It's one of the biggest regrets of my life," Grady said. "But I'm learning to divide the blame. Yes, I should've paid closer attention and asked more questions. But everything else was Brant's choice. Brant's actions. Brant's wickedness. And the same goes for Alvar."

"I'll try to remember that," Alden told him.

"Try to *believe* it," Grady insisted.

"So where is Wylie now?" Dex asked. "Still at the Stone House?"

"No, we had Physic move him to Alluveterre once he was stable enough for a leap, since we're assuming they'll come after him," Blur said. "The fact that he escaped probably means they hadn't gotten everything they wanted from him."

"What *do* they want?" Kesler asked. "Does anyone know?"

"I can't even hazard a guess," Mr. Forkle mumbled. "And so far, his mind has been too clouded by the trauma for us to recover much."

"He's not broken, right?" Sophie asked.

"Thankfully, no. The Neverseen not having a Telepath worked in our favor—though I suspect that's also why Wylie's injuries were so extreme. Their only means of interrogation was torture."

Everyone shuddered, and Mr. Forkle handed the packaged Imparter to Blur. "I trust you'll take care of getting that to our Technopath? I should get back to Alluveterre."

278

"I want to go with you."

Sophie didn't realize she'd said the words out loud until everyone turned to her.

"No one will be able to search Wylie's memories better than I will," she argued.

She left out her other reason—it was too terrible to admit. But she needed to see Wylie's memories for herself and make sure Keefe wasn't there.

She could forgive him for shattering glass and burning gates—but standing by while someone was tortured?

She had to be *sure*.

"You really think you can handle it?" Edaline asked her. "Wylie probably looks awful."

"'Awful' is not a strong enough word," Wraith warned.

Sophie swallowed hard. "I handled Paris, right?"

"Not the same, even in the slightest," Mr. Forkle told her.

"Doesn't matter," Sophie said. "Wylie needs my help."

"For what it's worth," Blur chimed in, "I think she's right. I think you should take her."

"Take *us*," Fitz corrected. "This has Cognates written all over it."

"If they go—Dex and I are going too," Biana added.

Mr. Forkle rubbed his temples. "Wylie is not up for visitors."

"Then we'll wait outside," Biana pressed. "But we should be there. You might learn something we need to know. Or Sophie and Fitz might need moral support."

The members of the Collective turned to each other, probably conferring telepathically.

"Very well," Mr. Forkle eventually said through a sigh. "But I have a favor to ask." His focus shifted to Sandor. "I need you to separate from your charge for the day. Miss Foster will be well protected by the fleet of dwarves stationed at Alluveterre. We have need of your exceptional senses in the Silver Tower. Perhaps you'll catch something we've overlooked."

"If you're looking for powerful senses," Grizel jumped in, "You should have me go with him. Sandor lacks a certain . . . shall we say, sensitivity?"

"If you feel comfortable separating from Mr. Vacker, we'd be happy to have your assistance," Mr. Forkle told her. "The more thorough we are, the greater our chances of solving this mystery."

"One condition," Sandor said, fixing a stern gaze on Sophie. "*Swear* you will go nowhere beyond Alluveterre and home."

"Are we even sure Havenfield is safe?" Sophie asked. "The Neverseen may still be planning something."

"We've left most of yesterday's precautions intact," Brielle assured her. "And Cadoc and I will not leave their side. You can trust us to protect your family the same way you trust Sandor with your life."

That seemed to settle things, and Sophie and her friends rushed to get dressed in fresh clothes, none of them saying a word as they hugged their parents and locked hands for the leap.

"Brace yourselves," Mr. Forkle said as he created a path to Alluveterre. "Nothing I say can properly prepare you for what you're about to see."

THIRTY-TWO

S OPHIE HADN'T SET FOOT IN Alluveterre's subterranean forest since the day she and her friends left for their mission to Ravagog. And the scenery was as lush and beautiful as ever. But her memories blanketed everything in shadow.

Everywhere she looked, she could see signs of Calla's former presence. Earth Calla had walked. Trees she'd touched. Roots she'd called to transport everyone underground for their various adventures. Even the air seemed to carry the faintest whispers of Calla's songs—though Sophie knew she was probably imagining it.

"This way," Mr. Forkle said, leading them up a winding stairway that wrapped around and around a massive tree, bringing them to one of the mansion-size tree houses. Each step felt like swallowing lemon juice mixed with something spicy, and it coated Sophie's insides with a sour kind of burn.

Mr. Forkle had chosen the western tree house, where the boys lived during their months there, and the inside looked exactly the same as they'd left it. Same hammocks swinging from the ceiling. Same flickering fire pit in the center. But this time the boy reading on one of the boulder-shaped beanbag chairs had silver-tipped bangs.

"Hey," Tam said as he glanced up from his book. "They moved Wylie to the other house. I guess one of the bedrooms has some special plant growing in it that might keep him calm?"

"The reveriebells," Sophie whispered.

Calla had hybridized the flowering vine especially for her, training it to grow across the canopy of her former bed. The blossom's sweet scent had given her some of her most peaceful nights of sleep ever.

"Has he gotten worse?" Mr. Forkle asked.

"Not *worse*," Tam told him. "But I don't think he's getting better as quickly as Physic wants. And Granite—or Tiergan—or whatever I'm supposed to call him, is worried that Wylie's mind is getting darker. He asked me to try lifting a veil—but Wylie's shadowvapor is fine. He had less than I would've expected, given all the awful things he's been through."

Mr. Forkle closed his eyes. "Sounds like you were right to insist on coming, Miss Foster. I suppose we should head over."

"You might want to stay here," Tam warned Dex and Biana. "Physic's being super strict about who she's letting in the room. And at least over here you don't have to stay quiet."

"I guess that makes sense," Biana said. "Plus, I haven't seen you in forever."

Tam's lips twisted into a shy smile. "I hear we'll be seeing more of each other soon."

Sophie had forgotten all about the Exillium training. She wondered if Wylie's attack would delay things.

"Aren't you coming?" Mr. Forkle asked from the doorway.

Sophie and Fitz hurried to follow, but Dex stayed put. She figured that meant he wanted to stay with Biana and Tam, but as they reached the arched bridge connecting the two tree houses, Dex came racing up.

"I know I'm not a Telepath," he mumbled, "but I've been through what Wylie's been through. Maybe I can help."

Sophie reached for his hand, holding on to Fitz with her other as they made their way across the creaky bridge connecting the two houses. Sophie swore she could smell Calla's starkflower stew when they passed through the gazebo in the center. The dish had been Calla's specialty, and even though she'd taught Sophie the recipe, it never tasted the same without Calla.

"Wow," Dex and Fitz breathed as they entered what used to be the girls' tree house.

"Linh's been busy," Sophie mumbled.

The waterfall in the center—which used to be only a misty

trickle—now thundered with torrents of cascading water. The falls splashed hard into the shallow basin, but instead of spilling over and soaking the floor, the water ricocheted up and split into individual streams that arced toward the glass ceiling and fanned out before crashing back down into pots of flowers.

"Wait here," Mr. Forkle told them, pointing to the shrubbery-shaped chairs, which were speckled with glittering dew. "I'm going to let Physic know I've brought you."

The room felt way too quiet after he left.

"Where's Linh?" Dex whispered.

Sophie ducked under a stream of water as she looked down the empty hallway. "She must be in with Wylie."

"How bad do you think he's going to look?" Fitz asked. "Like . . . worse than I looked after Exile?"

The black barb jutting from Fitz's chest—and the swirls of black venom under his skin—had definitely been one of the most gruesome sights Sophie had ever seen. But she had a horrible feeling it had nothing on the pain and suffering Brant and Fintan would be willing to cause in order to get what they wanted.

"I think we need to prepare ourselves for something pretty awful," she said.

She'd flicked three loose lashes away before a familiar woman strode into the room, followed by an ashen Mr. Forkle. Physic's Mardi-Gras-style mask was red this time, with a rim of gold glitter that had showered bits of sparkle across her dark skin.

"You're still wearing your disguise?" Sophie asked.

"I didn't want the focus to be on me." Physic twisted one of her skinny braids around her finger, making the red beads woven through shimmer. "I'm glad you guys are here. Wylie's vitals are improving, but Tiergan's afraid his mind is deteriorating. I don't see any physical proof of that, but I want you two to make a *very* thorough check. And when we go in there, *try* to keep in mind that healing starts on a cellular level. Right now, most of the change is something only I can see—and only with special light and special lenses. But he's honestly recovering faster than I could've hoped for, in large part thanks to Linh. She has him wrapped in a cold-water cocoon to draw out any latent heat while I brew a fresh batch of my burn ointment."

"Do you need help?" Dex asked. "Or need me to get any supplies?"

"I'm low on a few things," Physic admitted, "but they're not the kind of ingredients you'd be able to get from your dad's store."

"Try me," Dex said.

She raised an eyebrow. "Okay, how about jaculus venom?"

"Clear or cloudy? We keep both in my dad's 'extreme collection.'"

"Interesting," Physic said. "Nice hair, by the way."

Dex's cheeks turned the same color as Physic's mask.

"Aren't jaculuses those flying, blood-sucking snake things?" Sophie asked, remembering the first day she'd met Grady, when she'd watched him pull one out of Verdi's feathers.

"They are," Physic agreed. "And their venom has a powerful anticoagulant, which turns into an even more powerful tissue regenerator when I mix it with a few drops of Phoenix sweat."

"We have that, too," Dex said. "And Bennu tears. I'm guessing you also need Pooka pus? If so, we have solid and liquid."

"Okay, now I'm legitimately impressed," Physic said.

"Meanwhile I'm pretty sure I'm going to throw up," Fitz told them.

Physic shrugged. "It's either this or yeti pee—and trust me, yeti pee is way harder to wash off."

Sadly, Sophie knew that firsthand.

"All right," Physic told Dex, "I'll give you my recipe and we'll see what you can find at Slurps and Burps. Take Forkle with you, so you'll have a way to leap back—and so I won't have to watch him wring his hands anymore. He's going to disjoint all his fingers, and I really don't need another patient."

Sophie had almost forgotten that Mr. Forkle was there. He hadn't said a word, and his skin had a sweaty sheen.

"If you think he looks bad," Physic said, "wait till you see Tiergan. I can't get him to let go of Wylie's hand. Even when Linh started with the water stuff, he stood there and got soaked. It might be the saddest thing I've ever seen. But somehow the sweetest, too. You guys ready?"

Sophie didn't trust her voice not to crack. So she nodded, letting Fitz take her hand as they followed Physic down the hall to her old room.

"Remember, he's on some crazy pain medicine *and* a sedative," Physic warned. "So if you can't make sense of his thoughts, don't be afraid that it means anything's permanently wrong. He's just drugged up."

Fitz tightened his grip on Sophie's hand as Physic pulled open the door and the three of them made their way into the bedroom. Sophie inhaled the calming scent of Calla's reverie-bells as she studied her surroundings, avoiding the figure on the bed as long as she could.

Tiergan stood with his back to them—though parts of him were still Granitized, like he'd been standing so long at Wylie's side that his indurite-powder was slowly wearing off. His left shoulder was jagged and rocky, and his neck was white-gray instead of its usual olive tone. Even his pale blond hair had bits of dust and gravel tangled in it.

On the other side of the bed, Linh leaned against the edge with her eyes closed, lips parted as she whispered softly to herself. Her hands were raised over the bed, and Sophie forced herself to look down, and . . .

. . . gagged.

Fitz choked too, and they clung to each other.

Sophie had thought she was prepared—thought the water Linh had swirling around him would muffle the gore. But the giant welts and blisters marring Wylie's arms and legs were too huge and red and violent to be ignored.

And they were shaped like hands.

I'm so sorry they did this to you, Sophie transmitted, digging her fist under her ribs to keep control of her emotions. *I wish I knew how to stop them. I wish I knew what they want.*

Let's find out, Fitz transmitted back, and their thumb rings snapped together as the mental energy rushed between them.

They moved closer to the bed and Sophie put her hand on Tiergan's rocky shoulder. "You can take a break. We're here to help now."

Tiergan didn't seem to hear her.

"You need to let go," she whispered. "Let me try for a minute."

Eight endless seconds passed. Then Tiergan blinked and turned her way.

"He won't talk to me," he whispered. "His mind only gives me cold darkness."

"Should we wait, then?" Sophie asked. "I don't want to force Wylie if he's not ready."

"I . . ." Tiergan spun back to the bed and pressed the fingers of his free hand against Wylie's temples.

"Is everything okay?" Fitz asked.

"I don't know." Tiergan's expression was the strangest mix of relief, disappointment, and fear as he turned to Sophie and told her, "He's asking to talk to you."

THIRTY-THREE

I'M ON MY WAY, SOPHIE TRANSMITTED TO Wylie as she pressed two fingers against his right temple. Fitz did the same on his left, and Linh's water shell splashed their hands as they pressed their consciousness into Wylie's mind.

The blackness felt almost solid—like it had hardened into a wall. But when Sophie transmitted *It's me,* the barrier liquefied, letting them drop down deep into the shadows.

Wylie's mind grew colder as they fell, his thoughts an icy blur, until they landed in a pool of warm light hovering in the nothing. A form emerged from the shadows, growing arms and legs and features and slowly morphing into a boy.

"Hello," he said, offering a shy wave.

His twitching hands fiddled with the pin clasped through his light blue cape—a jeweled sun with rays in yellow and orange and red. His face was rounder than Wylie's, his dark hair longer, crowning his head in a neat Afro. But she could recognize him through the features.

How old are you right now? Sophie transmitted.

Wylie scratched his chin. "Six."

Why is he talking to us as his six-year-old self? Fitz transmitted to Sophie.

I think it's a defense mechanism. I'm pretty sure he was seven or eight when his dad's mind broke, so I bet he's reverting to a safer, happier time.

"I knew you'd understand," six-year-old Wylie told her. "You know how it feels to have a before. And an after."

He shuddered with the words, and the tremors triggered a growth spurt, stretching his body taller and broadening his shoulders as his chin squared and his hair shrank to a short crop.

He looked like a surly teenager—but his eyes looked far older. This was the Wylie who'd lost his father *and* his mother.

I doubt I'll ever understand everything you've been through, Sophie told him. *But I'm here to help.*

"*Can* you help?" he asked.

I'll try. Will you tell me what happened?

Wylie's hands shook so hard, his pin ripped off his cape, vanishing into the darkness.

If you're not ready, we can—

"No," he interrupted. "It's never going to be easier."

He buried his face in his hands, and Sophie noticed red blotches forming.

What are you thinking about? Fitz asked him.

"All the things I shouldn't." Wylie scratched at his arms until they streamed with red.

I think we're going too fast, Sophie said as he morphed into the present-day Wylie she'd seen lying unconscious on her old bed—bloody and blistered and thrashing with the agony of his wounds. *Is there a way to bring back the six-year-old-you?*

Wylie took a shaky breath and closed his eyes, humming a song that sounded like a lullaby as his wounds closed, his body shrank, and his face rounded out.

"Is this better?" six-year-old Wylie asked.

You tell me, Sophie said. *Does it hurt right now?*

"It feels funny. But not, like, 'ha-ha' funny. More like an itchy tingle. I think I can live with that."

I know this is hard to believe, Sophie told him as he stared at his arms. *But the pain only exists in your memories. When you wake up, everything will be healed, and you'll look exactly the same as before.*

"I won't *be* the same, though. Will I?"

She couldn't lie. *Part of the pain will never go away. But you're a survivor, right?*

"Not by choice."

It never is, Fitz told him. *But that only proves how strong you are.*

"I should've been stronger," Wylie whispered. "I shouldn't have let them take me."

You couldn't have stopped them, Sophie promised. *I tried my hardest, and I couldn't.*

Wylie nodded slowly. "I didn't give them what they wanted, either."

What did they want? Fitz asked.

"If I talk about it . . . the other me's will take over."

We can handle them, Sophie promised.

And we can help you hold on, Fitz added as their pocket of space grew brighter and warmer. *I just gave you some extra energy to boost your strength. See how strong you are now?*

Wylie flexed his skinny six-year-old arms, patting the small curve of biceps that shifted. "Okay. I'll try."

"You'll do great," Sophie told him. "Think of it like you're telling us a story. Start at the beginning. How did they find you?"

"I don't know. I was reading in bed when the door burst open and my room swelled with a tornado."

So one of them was a Guster? Fitz asked.

"Must've been. The wind pinned me to the floor. And then I heard people rush in."

Did you see them? Sophie asked. *Or recognize their voices?*

"I couldn't hear much over the wind. And the one who

jumped on me must've been a Vanisher, because I couldn't see him as he ripped off my registry pendant."

Fitz's whole body shook as he transmitted. *That was my brother.*

Sophie tightened her hold on his hand, wishing she had time to properly comfort him. But they had to focus. *What else do you remember?* she asked Wylie.

"I remember kicking and punching and clawing and scratching. But then this white light wrapped around me, and I couldn't move anymore."

That means Ruy was there, Fitz transmitted. *He's a Psionipath. He must've wrapped you in a force field.*

"It shocked me if I touched it," Wylie said. "And it trapped me with the drugs. When I breathed, everything went blurry."

So it was just the three of them? Sophie asked. *No one else?*

"Actually, I think there were four. They said someone was keeping the path open."

Could they have meant the Guster? she asked.

"I don't think so. They made it sound like the path was somewhere else. But everything was far away at that point. I remember someone grabbing my feet and dragging me. I don't know how long or how far. Then warmth pulled me away. After that I couldn't see. My ears were ringing. Everything smelled too sweet. I wanted to throw up, but I couldn't tell if I was actually awake. Is that how it was for you?"

Sort of, Sophie thought quietly. *I was gone for a lot longer than you.*

"How long was I missing?"

We're not totally sure, Fitz said. *But it was less than a day. Do you know what time they grabbed you?*

"No. But I hadn't had breakfast yet." He clutched his middle as his stomach growled.

Do you want Physic to wake you up so you can eat? Fitz asked.

Wylie shook his head. *Awake sounds . . . hard.*

It will be at first, Sophie told him. *But it'll get easier every day. Take the time you need to recover. You'll wake up when you're ready.*

Is there anything else you remember that might help us? Fitz asked.

"Just the interrogations. And my head stayed mushy for those. The only thought I could hold on to was *wait*. I knew they'd make a mistake, and when they did, I'd have to move. It took hours and hours—but they finally burned one of my bonds. It didn't sear all the way through, but it let me shift my hands just enough that I could wiggle my fingers into the secret pocket in my sleeve where I keep the crystal that takes me to see my dad. I think I broke my thumb trying to grab it—I heard a snap." He held his hand up, frowning as the thumb seemed to work perfectly. "But it was worth the pain because as soon as I had the crystal in my hand I sparked a ball of light and leaped out of there."

Sparked? Sophie thought. *Are you a Flasher?*

"Yeah. Same as . . ."

Who? Sophie asked when he started trembling. *Same as who?*

Wylie scratched hard at his neck. "They kept asking the same question over and over, no matter how many times I told them I didn't know. Everything was about her."

Sophie was about to ask, *Her who?* when she figured it out on her own.

Your mom?

Wylie shifted back to surly teenager form.

What did they want to know about her? she asked.

"They thought I was with her when she made her last leap. I kept telling them I wasn't, but they kept burning me over and over and telling me it would stop when I stopped lying. They didn't get it. She died because I found her too late."

Tears streamed down his cheeks as he shifted to the present-day Wylie, screaming through the pain as his wounds reappeared.

Fitz tried sending more warmth and energy, but it didn't help, so Sophie tried inflicting. She couldn't find any happiness, but she gave him a soft wave of hope, and Wylie's breathing slowed to raspy breaths.

"Sorry," he told her. "I guess I'm not as strong as you thought."

You're stronger, Sophie promised. *You've been through so much.*

"Too much," Wylie said. "I don't know if I can take any more."

Maybe you won't have to. Mr. Forkle and Granite are planning to erase the worst memories—

"NO! They can't!"

I know it's weird to imagine them rooting around in your head—but why live with the nightmares?

"Because there might be something important! You can't let them erase anything, Sophie. Promise me you'll stop them."

Okay, she said when he kept repeating the plea. *I promise.*

"You have to stick to that," Wylie begged as he shifted back to six-year-old form. "You owe me."

I know, Sophie said. *And maybe you should rest now. I think your mind could use the break.*

He faded into the shadows. "I'll try. But I need you to do something for me. I need you to look into my mom's death. I don't think it was an accident anymore."

THIRTY-FOUR

THIS HAS EVERYTHING WE KNOW about the day Cyrah faded away," Mr. Forkle said, holding up a golden orb the size of a gumball. "All the evidence we gathered suggested her death was nothing more than an unexpected tragedy."

He spun the top and bottom in opposite directions until they clicked like a combination lock, then handed it to Dex.

Sophie and Fitz had brought everyone back to the boys' old tree house to make sure their conversation wouldn't disturb Wylie—and so Biana and Tam wouldn't miss the update. Only Physic had stayed behind, wanting to run additional tests to triple-check that the pain they'd seen Wylie battling truly lived only in his memories.

"Do you always carry that with you?" Sophie asked Mr. Forkle, wondering how he fit so much in his pockets—and why she'd never noticed him carrying so many weird things before.

"Of course," he said. "It's similar to the Councillors' caches, except it holds the things I need to remember, not the secrets I want to forget."

"So then, there's probably all kinds of info about Sophie on here, right?" Dex asked.

"There are files on all of you—and before anyone gets any ideas, let me assure you that I'm the only one capable of accessing that information. So can we focus on the fact that young Mr. Endal has given us an urgent project?"

"Right," Dex said, squeezing the top and bottom of the sphere to make a hologram flash from the center.

Everyone scooted closer to squint at the projection, which started with a family picture.

Prentice looked like he'd been midlaugh, his eyes focused on his wife—whose auburn hair glowed wild and red where it caught the sun. Between them was the same six-year-old boy Sophie had spoken to in Wylie's memories, and now she could see what an even mix he was of both of his parents. He had his mom's smile and a dash of her creaminess to his skin, and his dad's hair and eyes and nose.

"They were so happy," she whispered.

"They were," Tiergan said, wiping his eyes.

Dex twisted the gadget again, revealing a single document. "This isn't much to go on."

"I know," Mr. Forkle said. "Cyrah was alone for her final leap. Wylie found her sometime after, and it was impossible to tell how long she'd been there. She was unconscious. Barely breathing. Wylie hailed Elwin for help, but the damage was beyond anyone's skills. By the time Elwin called Alden to search Cyrah's memories, her mind had grown too weak to recover anything. The last of her form faded not long after. All they could do was watch."

Sophie blinked back tears as she imagined it.

In order to light leap, their bodies had to break down into particles small enough to be carried by the light. And the only way to re-form was to hold the pieces together, either with a bracelet-style gadget called a nexus—which all younger elves were required to wear until their mental strength reached a proven level—or with the power of their own concentration. If you lost too much of yourself . . .

There were worse ways to die, of course. In fact, out of all of Sophie's brushes with death, fading had been the most pleasant. It started with shocking pain—but the agony soon eased, replaced with an irresistible rushing warmth that pulled like a gentle breeze, begging her to follow it to a world of shimmer and sparkle and color and freedom.

But it was a death all the same.

"Wylie tried to reach me after it happened," Tiergan said,

300

turning to stare out the windows. "He hailed me four times before he gave up and let Elwin hail Alden. Maybe if I'd answered, we could've recovered something from Cyrah's mind."

"Do we know where Cyrah leaped from?" Sophie asked.

"She told Wylie that she was going back to Mysterium—which matched what her registry pendant recorded," Mr. Forkle said. "She went to take inventory of her stall."

"Cyrah had a small sidewalk booth where she sold custom hair ribbons," Tiergan explained. "It wasn't as fancy as the boutique she'd had before Prentice was arrested. But very few nobles wanted to support the wife of a criminal, so she'd moved to a working-class city."

"I went to that stall," Biana said. "My dad took me when I was little—I still have the combs he bought. And I remember being surprised we went to Mysterium instead of Atlantis."

"Alden was always trying to find small ways to assist Cyrah," Tiergan muttered. "As if buying hair clips could make up for destroying her family!"

The words sliced through the room, too dull to draw any blood. But Fitz and Biana winced all the same.

"I'm sorry," Tiergan told them. "I just hate having to think about this again. Wylie's been through so much—and I keep *trying* to make it up to him. But no matter what I do . . ."

He pounded his fist against the window.

Sophie crossed the room and rested a hand on his arm. Tiergan wasn't a touchy-feely kind of person, but . . .

He placed his hand over hers.

She wished she could guarantee that everything would be okay—that they'd find a way to solve all of this. Instead she told him, "Wylie's strong."

"He is. He has to be. Just like you." He squeezed her hand tighter before slowly pulling away. "I suppose the one small relief is that Prentice is unconscious through all of this."

"I've been thinking the same thing," Mr. Forkle said. "We cannot bring him back to a life where his son is in danger and his wife's murder unsolved. He'd never survive it."

"Am I the only one who doesn't understand how murder by light leap is possible?" Tam asked. "An accident, I get. But aren't we the ones in control of our consciousness?"

"That's what I thought too," Sophie admitted. "Otherwise, wouldn't we wear nexuses our whole lives?"

"We remove our nexuses because technology should never replace the natural power of our mind," Mr. Forkle told them. "And because we're supposed to belong to a society where people would never violate the safety of another. But the sad truth is, if someone were to cause Cyrah severe pain right as she was leaping, it could've broken her concentration during the crucial transformation."

"Or if someone shined a secondary light in her path," Tiergan added, "her consciousness would've divided without her realizing. Part of her would've followed one beam—the rest, the other. And she wouldn't have had enough of herself left in either place."

Linh curled her arms around herself. "That's really scary."

"It is," Mr. Forkle agreed. "Safety is an illusion. It exists only when we, as a society, agree to enforce it. But theoretically, any situation could turn violent if someone decided to treat it that way. During my time with humans, I witnessed many horrors that were the result of one individual—or a small group—choosing to violate the trust we all put in each other. The time is coming when we as a species will have to decide if we're going to stray down the same dark path. But I think I've gotten off track. My point is that, yes, sadly, murder by light leap—and many other unimaginable means—is possible."

"Okay, but . . . the streets in Mysterium are always crammed with people," Dex reminded them. "Wouldn't someone have noticed something weird going on when Cyrah leaped?"

"People rarely notice things they don't expect to see," Tiergan told him. "They're too distracted by their own perception of reality."

"Did anyone see her final leap happen?" Sophie asked.

"Not that I could find," Mr. Forkle said.

"So then she could've wandered to a more isolated place before she leaped away," Sophie pointed out. "Maybe she had a secret meeting in the area where the Council stores my human family's old things. It seemed pretty deserted when Councillor Terik took me."

"Or she wasn't in Mysterium at all," Fitz added. "We all know registry feeds can be altered. Did anyone actually see her there?"

"They did," Mr. Forkle said. "Several people saw her sorting stock in her stall."

"This list at the end here," Dex jumped in. "Is that the people who saw her?"

"Yes," Mr. Forkle said. "Why?"

"Marella's mom is on it." He pointed to the name *Caprise Redek*, glowing among a dozen other names.

"Caprise was one of my more memorable interviews," Mr. Forkle said quietly. "She seemed to be struggling quite a bit that day."

Marella's mother had suffered a traumatic brain injury a few years earlier, and despite Elwin's best efforts, she'd battled unstable emotions ever since. She took elixirs to manage the condition, but sometimes they weren't enough.

"What did she say?" Sophie asked.

"Mostly she kept mumbling that Cyrah should've been more careful. I assumed she meant careful during leaping."

That *did* make sense, but . . .

"Now that we know her death might not have been an accident, do you think she could've meant something else?" Sophie asked.

"If it were anyone other than Caprise Redek, I might be ready to wander down that path," Tiergan told her. "But I've seen Caprise on her bad days. It's not her fault—and she tries her best. But reason and rationality abandon her. And when you consider that she would've been saying these things after hearing the devastating news about Cyrah, I think it needs to be taken with an especially potent grain of salt."

"I still wonder if Cyrah went somewhere after Mysterium and her feed was altered," Fitz mumbled. "It just seems too random that she went to count hair ribbons and ended up dead."

"But who would've altered the feed?" Tiergan asked. "We know it wasn't us. And Cyrah was a Flasher, not a Technopath. And if the Neverseen were involved with her death, why would they need to interrogate Wylie?"

"Maybe she was working on something important for them, and they were hoping she might've shared certain key information with him before she died," Tam suggested.

"But then why go after him *now*?" Dex asked. "Why not interrogate him right after it happened?"

"They might not have wanted anyone to know that Cyrah's death wasn't an accident," Linh said.

"Or, it could have something to do with whatever they're planning through the Lodestar Initiative," Biana mumbled.

"We can debate theories all day," Mr. Forkle told them, "But it won't bring us any closer to the truth."

"So what's your plan?" Sophie asked.

"I . . . have no idea." He sounded more tired than Sophie had ever heard.

"Gethen might know something about all of this, right?" Fitz asked.

"That's true!" Sophie realized. "And after Wylie's attack, I'm sure the Council is going to be *very* motivated to find out what happened, so—"

"We're not going to tell the Council about this," Mr. Forkle interrupted. "They do not make wise decisions when they're frightened. And learning that one of their citizens was captured and brutalized—from one of our world's most secure buildings—will send them into a frenzy. The last time that happened, they declared *us* their number one enemy, instead of focusing on the Neverseen. And let's not forget about the ability-restricting circlet they ordered Miss Foster to wear."

Dex winced. The circlet had been his invention—but he'd never thought the Council would use it on Sophie.

"Working against the Council hasn't gone well for us either," Sophie reminded him. "And if Gethen—"

"Gethen is not the grand solution you believe him to be!" Mr. Forkle snapped. He turned away, tearing his hands through his grayed hair. "I know you want to believe—"

"*You* said he was a priority," Sophie interrupted.

"I did. But circumstances have changed. Now our priority must be protecting Wylie—and that includes sparing him the stress of becoming a public spectacle. Surely you remember what it felt like to be The Girl Who Was Taken. Would you wish that on him? After everything he's been through?"

"I'm sure the Council would keep this quiet if we asked," Biana said quietly.

"All we can be *sure* of, Miss Vacker, is that we *can't* be sure of how the Council will respond. So we must err on the side of caution. We must regroup and strategize. And we must wait to act until we have a plan that is in Wylie's best interest."

Sophie glanced at Tiergan. "You really think we should waste time sitting around, lying and hiding things?"

Tiergan turned to the windows, staring at the gently swaying trees. "I think our next course should be up to Wylie. He's the one who will endure the consequences."

Sophie headed for the door. "Okay, I'll ask him."

Mr. Forkle blocked her. "We will *not* be troubling him with these questions until he's fully recovered."

"But that could be *days*."

"In the grand scheme of things, that is a very small amount of time." His tone left no room for arguing.

"We have to do *something*," Sophie insisted.

Sneaking into Lumenaria without the Council's permission sounded impossible—especially with how little they knew about the security in the fortress. And she couldn't imagine she'd be able to communicate telepathically with Lady Gisela in the ogre prison—or that Lady Gisela would actually tell her anything if she could.

So where did that leave them?

"Keefe's trying to steal Fintan's cache," she said after a few seconds. "Do you think it might have any information on it about Cyrah?"

"If it does, why would they need to go after Wylie?" Fitz asked.

"And while we're talking about Keefe," Tam jumped in, his silver eyes focusing on Sophie, "I know you're going to get mad at me for saying this. But before we keep trusting him, we need to find out what he knows—and I don't just mean the little bits he tells you during your nightly flirt sessions."

"That's *not* what they are," Sophie snapped.

"Maybe not for you. But I doubt the guy who calls himself the president of the Foster Fan Club is going to have a bunch of private convos with you and not use that chance to try to keep winning you over."

"Winning me—what?" Sophie asked. "That's not—I—what?"

"Not important," Tam said. "But you know what is? Making sure he's not involved with horrors like this. Can you honestly tell me you're not worried he was somehow part of what they did to Wylie? Or that his whole 'warning' about the danger to your family was actually a lie to keep everyone distracted from what was really happening?"

Sophie rubbed the knot under her ribs. "I know you don't trust Keefe—"

"And I know you do," Tam interrupted. "I get that you two are really, really close—"

"They're not *that* close," Fitz mumbled.

"Uh . . . sure . . . ," Tam said. "All I'm saying is, we need to know exactly who we're dealing with—and not just what he says. We need to know what he's thinking, and hiding, and planning."

"You want me to search his mind," Sophie guessed.

Tam nodded. "I know Telepaths have rules, but Wylie deserves protection *way* more than Keefe deserves privacy."

"But I don't actually know if I can search his mind from far away," Sophie argued. "Having a telepathic conversation is different from probing memories. For that, I usually need physical contact."

She *had* been able to search Prentice's memories through the walls of his cell in Exile—but there was a big difference between stretching her mind to someone a few feet away and searching someone who was probably on the other side of the planet.

"You'd have a better chance if I help," Fitz reminded her.

"Can I be there too?" Biana asked.

"I'm pretty sure all of us want to be there," Tam told her. "You're all welcome to crash here tonight, if that makes it easier."

"Unfortunately, that's not an option," Mr. Forkle informed them. "Those with registry pendants need to get back to the Lost Cities quite soon. I've had our Technopath scrambling our feeds, but it's a slapdash cover at best, and if we stay too much longer, the Council might be able to track us to this hideout. Besides, if you decide to follow this plan, Miss Foster and Mr. Vacker are going to need the full weight of their concentration to have even the slightest chance of achieving this rather impossible task. I'm sure they'll be happy to provide a full report when they're finished."

"I don't have an Imparter," Sophie reminded him.

"I'll get you another," Mr. Forkle said.

And with that, the matter seemed to be decided.

All that was left to do was head home.

And wait.

And hope Keefe didn't let them down.

THIRTY-FIVE

FITZ WENT WITH SOPHIE BACK TO Havenfield, so they could work through Cognate exercises to prepare, while Biana and Dex went to Rimeshire to see if Dex could hack the registry for Cyrah's records. They knew it was a long shot, but they wanted to see if her feed had been altered the day she faded.

"Do you think this is a mistake?" Sophie asked Fitz when they leaped into the surprisingly quiet, empty pastures. Cadoc and Brielle must've made Grady and Edaline stay inside.

"Checking on Keefe?" he asked.

Part of her wanted to say yes—she still felt scrambled up about their plan. But she had bigger worries at the moment.

"It feels like we're wasting time on the wrong things.

Especially since we don't have any actual plans. I mean . . . what is the Collective doing right now—besides shutting down all our ideas and telling us to wait?"

"I know. I think what happened to Wylie really shook them up."

"It shook me up too—but that doesn't mean it's a good idea to sit around doing nothing. I know I'm not as close to him as the Collective is—but maybe that's a good thing. Maybe that makes me able to see what really needs to be done."

"Which is what?" Fitz asked.

Sophie looked away, tugging out an itchy eyelash before she asked, "Do you have a pathfinder?"

"Not with me," Fitz said, "Why? Where do you want to go?"

Somewhere she didn't want anyone knowing—and she needed to do it now, before she changed her mind. They had no bodyguards for the moment. No one even knew they were home. If they were going to sneak away, this was the time.

But how?

Making it up to the fourth-floor Leapmaster without Grady and Edaline spotting them was probably impossible. And teleporting created quite the spectacle, between the whole jumping-off-the-cliff thing, and the booming thunder as they slipped in and out of the void.

They needed something subtler, like maybe . . .

She ran toward Calla's Panakes, hoping to find Lur or Mitya

tending to the majestic tree. But the only gnome she found was the plaited-haired female she'd seen helping Edaline when they tested the cravettels on Verdi.

"Did you need something?" the gnome asked, setting down the garland she'd been weaving from the fallen pink, purple, and blue flowers.

Sophie bit her lip. "Never mind."

"Are you sure?" the gnome pressed. "I'm here to help. Especially *you*, Miss Foster."

Sophie's cheeks burned. "But . . . I don't even know your name."

"Well, there's an easy way to fix that, isn't there?" She flashed a green-toothed smile. "I'm Flori. What can I do for you?"

"Don't look at me," Fitz told Flori when Sophie hesitated. "I'm just as confused as you are."

Flori tilted her head to study Sophie. "Perhaps that means you've come to me as the moonlark?"

Sophie sucked in a breath.

"And if that's the case," Flori continued, "I'm *happy* to help. No questions asked. No need to be shy. Please let me assist you, Miss Foster. It would be my honor."

Sophie closed her eyes, inhaling the sweet scent of Calla's blossoms to fuel her courage as she whispered, "If I needed to go somewhere right now, would you take me?"

"Anywhere," Flori promised.

Sophie nodded, mentally running through her plan one

more time before she turned to Fitz. "You're going to think I'm crazy."

He grinned. "I usually do. But I *also* think you're brilliant— and have solved way more problems than anyone else has. So I'm in."

He offered his hand and she took it, turning back to Flori. "I need you to take us to Eternalia."

THIRTY-SIX

LORI USED THE ROOTS FROM THE Panakes to carry them to the elvin capital city, and somehow that made it feel like they had Calla urging them along their journey.

Sophie closed her eyes, listening to the fragile sound of Flori's voice as she sang to the roots, pushing them faster and faster through the narrow, musty tunnel in the earth.

"I'll be waiting right here," Flori promised when they'd come to a stop and she'd opened a hole for them to climb to the surface.

"Actually, I have my home crystal," Sophie told her, squinting as her eyes adjusted to the sunlight streaming in. "That way you won't have to worry about being gone too long."

"I'm not worried," Flori said. "And either way, I'll still stay here, keeping an ear to the ground until I know you've leaped safely away."

Sophie's voice sounded thick as she thanked her and turned to climb out of the tunnel. Before she reached the top, she spun back and met Flori's soft gray eyes. "I'm sorry it took me so long to talk to you."

Flori smiled. "Time is a relative thing, especially when grief is involved." She patted the roots at her feet. "Someday we can share stories about my aunt. But only when you're ready."

"Wait—you're Calla's niece?"

"I think the proper term is great-great-grandniece. But she always told me the greats meant I was the best."

"She was right," Sophie told her. "And . . . I'd like that."

"Me too," Flori whispered. "Now go, be the brave moonlark you were born to be."

"So are you going to clue me in to what you're planning?" Fitz asked as they emerged from the root-lined tunnel and faced the twelve crystal castles glittering in the afternoon light.

Sophie led him behind one of the towering, palmlike trees that purified the air with enormous fan-shaped leaves.

"It's called *I'm sick of being patient*," she whispered. "So I'm going to talk to Oralie."

She'd expected him to freak out. But all he said was, "Do you know which castle's hers?"

"I wish. The only castle I've been in was Councillor Terik's."
She pointed to a castle toward the center of the row. That left
them with eleven other choices.

Fitz shielded his eyes, squinting into the distance. "Well,
that one near the end over there has pink flowers lining the
path to the door. Think that might mean it's hers?"

Oralie *did* love the color pink—and Sophie couldn't come up
with a better guess.

"What are we going to say if I'm wrong?" Fitz asked as they
bolted down the golden path. "Especially if Councillor Alina
opens the door?"

"I'm *really* hoping that won't happen," Sophie admitted.
"And that I'll come up with a brilliant excuse if it does. I guess
we'll know soon enough."

She knocked the moment she reached the door, not giving herself a chance to wimp out. Each second felt like fifty
lifetimes before the door swung open and Oralie's bright
eyes widened.

"Sophie?" she whispered, her blond ringlets brushing her
cheeks as she pulled Sophie and Fitz into the twinkling foyer
and shut the door behind them, latching it with five heavy silver bolts. "Let's hope Alina didn't see you. She's in the castle
next door."

"Ugh. Worst. Neighbor. Ever," Fitz grumbled.

"Yes. She is."

The sadness laced through the words made Sophie realize . . .

Councillor Alina had probably moved into Kenric's old castle. And Sophie had long suspected that Kenric and Oralie had secretly been in love, but couldn't act on it because they would've had to step down as Councillors.

So imagining them living side by side—and knowing Oralie was now alone—choked off Sophie's voice as she said, "Well, I'm guessing Alina would be banging on the door by now if she'd noticed us."

"I'm sure she would," Oralie said, checking the bolts again. "And I'm assuming the fact that you're here unannounced, without bodyguards, and with soil in your hair means that no one knows you're here."

Sophie bit her lip. "The gnome who brought us here does."

"Hmm" was all Oralie said to that as she reached for Sophie's cheek.

Sophie assumed Oralie was going to brush dirt off her face. But Oralie's fingers lingered, and she closed her eyes, her forehead crinkling as she read Sophie's emotions.

"Looks like it would be wise for me to sit down," she said when she let go. She led them down a crystal hall without another word and into a diamond-shaped sitting room with overstuffed pearl-trimmed pink armchairs, pink chandeliers, and pink crystals cut into the walls in floral patterns.

"This is pretty much Biana's dream room," Fitz said as he sank into one of the throne-size chairs and propped his feet on the jeweled footstool.

"She's welcome to visit anytime," Oralie told him, taking the chair across from Sophie.

"Wow, really?" Fitz asked.

"Why not?"

"Because . . . you're a Councillor. I didn't think you guys were open for visitors."

"Most of us aren't. I've gotten many lectures about my lack of constant security, and how I leave myself too vulnerable. But I think it's important that we make ourselves available to our people. After all, we never know what we're going to learn."

She raised one eyebrow in Sophie's direction and Sophie took the cue, choosing her words carefully.

"We . . . need you to set up a meeting with Gethen. And I know he's in Lumenaria, and that it's on lockdown because you're prepping for the Peace Summit. But we *need* to talk to him."

Oralie frowned. "You weren't hoping to meet with him *today*?"

"Is that possible?" Fitz asked.

"No, definitely not."

"What about soon, then?" Sophie pressed.

"I . . . don't know." Oralie's jeweled heels clicked across the crystal floor as she moved to the room's furthest corner and stood silhouetted by the sunlight, looking so elegant and regal in her pink ruffled gown that it made Sophie wish she'd shaken the dirt out of her hair before she'd come inside.

"I assume you won't tell me why there's such urgency?" Oralie asked.

Sophie glanced at Fitz.

"Your call," he said.

"You . . . might want to sit down again," Sophie mumbled.

Oralie lowered herself onto the arm of the nearest chair and nodded for her to continue. So Sophie did—telling Oralie the whole story, right down to the ogres searching the Silver Tower, Wylie's fears about his mother, and Mr. Forkle's decision not to tell the Council.

"Please don't make me regret telling you," she begged when she'd finished.

Oralie cleared her throat. "I won't. And . . . I'm so deeply sorry to hear about Wylie. Does he need anything?"

"Yeah," Fitz said. "He needs us to find out what happened."

Oralie smoothed the ruffles on her gown. "I fear you're over-estimating my power. I'm only one vote of many—and hardly a popular one at that."

"You were the one who fixed Exillium," Sophie reminded her. "And you did that without getting the support of the other Councillors."

"Yes, but that was a problem I could solve with money. *This* is something else entirely."

"I know," Sophie said. "But there has to be a way."

"Not without my telling the rest of the Council—and I do not believe that would be wise. I'm sure some of my fellow

Councillors would call for my circlet for saying so, but fear has inspired some of our worst decisions. And there are some who feel drastic measures are the only solution."

"Drastic how?" Fitz asked.

"You've already seen the beginning of it. Policing in our cities. Defense training for our citizens. I'm not saying those are bad things. Sadly, they're incredibly necessary. But where do they lead? Stricter crystal restrictions to further regulate where and when people can leap. Curfews. Much more invasive monitoring of our registry pendants. When rulers stop trusting their citizens, freedom is always the cost. And I can think of several Councillors who will see what happened to Wylie as proof that control is the answer."

"And what do *you* see as the answer?" Sophie asked.

Oralie sighed. "I honestly don't know. But . . . I think it starts with people like you. People asking hard questions and taking risks and never letting anything stop them—not because they want power or glory. Because they know it's the right thing to do."

It was a prickly sort of compliment. The kind that made Sophie want to throw her arms around Oralie to thank her— or run away screaming, *I don't need that kind of pressure.*

She settled for staying focused. "Does that mean you'll help us?"

"It means I'll *try*. But it's going to take time. I understand your haste—but this is not something I can snap my fingers and make happen overnight. Please don't let the passing days convince you that I've changed my mind. You have my word that I'll do all I can to help Wylie. His life—and the nightmares he's endured—is proof of my many failings. He deserves a much safer world than the one I've given him."

"It's not your fault," Sophie told her.

"No. But I'm not blameless, either."

Oralie's eyes met Sophie's, so bright and blue it took Sophie a second to realize they were welling with tears.

"I also need you to promise me you'll notify me if Wylie has any further problems."

"That may be tricky," Sophie said. "The Imparter you gave me before we fled to the Black Swan was conveniently missing from my bag when they sent home my things."

"That sounds like them," Oralie said, half a smile curving her lips. "But I can authorize any Imparter. Do you have yours with you?"

"Can we use mine?" Fitz jumped in, pulling the silver gadget from his pocket. "Sophie's is . . . well, it's kind of a long story."

Oralie took the Imparter and held her finger in the center of the underside. "I suspect you both have quite a few long stories that never make it to the ears of the Council."

A green light flashed and she held the gadget close to her lips, whispering, "Permission granted," and making the Imparter flash blue.

She handed it back to Fitz. "Perhaps this will allow us to keep each other better updated on many things. I'm not asking for all of your secrets. But there is one thing I need to know." She turned to Sophie, taking one of her hands as she whispered, "Where's Keefe?"

Sophie's mouth went dry and Oralie must've felt the fear seeping out of her skin.

She nodded, tightening her hold. "I can't tell you if you should go with your doubt or your faith, Sophie. But either way, don't let him make Kenric's mistake."

"What mistake was that?" Sophie managed to whisper.

Oralie let her go and turned away. "He underestimated Fintan. We all did. Don't let Keefe pay the same price we paid."

THIRTY-SEVEN

"EVERYTHING OKAY?" GRADY ASKED
as Sophie and Fitz tried—and failed—to sneak
upstairs before anyone noticed they were back
at Havenfield. They'd barely made it five steps
into the living room before everyone spotted them.

Sophie was still grasping for the best lie when Fitz proved
he was way ahead of her and told both of her parents the revelations about Cyrah to keep them distracted.

"Did you know her?" Sophie asked when Grady turned as
white as the couch.

"Not as well as we should have," Edaline said, sinking down
on a cushion beside him. "We'd crossed paths over the years, but
never spent much time together until Prentice's memory break.

She reached out to us afterward, despite how antisocial we'd become. Said it was hard to find others who understood loss."

"We didn't see her much," Grady added quietly. "But she'd come to visit from time to time. Until she was gone."

"The Council actually asked us if we'd be willing to adopt Wylie," Edaline whispered. "But it was too soon. That's why we didn't go to her planting. I knew I'd never get through having to face Wylie after turning him down. I don't know if he realizes. But . . ."

"Tiergan was a far better guardian than we could've ever been back then," Grady reminded her.

"Wow," Fitz said as Sophie wrapped them both in a hug. "I don't think I realized any of that."

"I doubt your father knew, given his complicated relationship with the Endals," Grady told him. "It's strange, though, isn't it? How small our world truly is? There are always so many subtle connections between everyone and everything."

"I know—try keeping up with it all as the new kid in town," Sophie mumbled.

No matter how much she learned, how many stories people shared, it felt like she'd never actually catch up.

Grady hugged her tighter. "You're doing great, kiddo. Plus, I think it's *good* that all of this is new for you. Fresh eyes hold incredible value. In fact, I think I'll hail Alden and see if he can send me his notes on the day Cyrah died. Maybe I'll notice something he didn't."

Grady headed upstairs to his office and Edaline frowned as she turned back to Sophie. "Is there dirt in your hair?"

Sophie almost smacked herself as she fumbled to remove it. Fitz did the same.

Edaline's frown deepened. "I thought you went to Alluveterre."

"Yeah," Sophie mumbled. "But you know how muddy underground forests can be."

It might've been the lamest excuse in the entirety of elvin history. But Edaline let it go.

"Well," she said, "I'm assuming the odds of me convincing the two of you to relax for the rest of the afternoon are fairly slim. So I won't waste my time. But I *will* make a fresh batch of ripplefluffs. And I'm going to *insist* you take a break and eat them."

"You won't have to tell me twice," Fitz said, flashing his famous grin. "And I'll make sure Sophie takes a break too."

"If anyone can, it's you." Edaline's teasing tone seemed to add meaning to the words, but Sophie didn't feel like riddling out what she was implying.

"So," Fitz said, breaking the silence as they headed up the stairs to her room. "You're still up for some trust exercises, right?"

"I guess."

Fitz laughed. "You know, you'd dread them a lot less if you'd just tell me that secret you were going to share that time Keefe interrupted our training. Don't think I've forgotten."

Sophie kept her face forward, hoping it hid her blush. For one very brief lapse in judgment, she'd almost told Fitz about her silly crush on him. Thankfully, she'd been spared the humiliation.

"I wonder if I could guess," he said as they passed the second floor.

"I doubt it."

His obliviousness was both reliable *and* annoying.

"Oh really?" He scooted past her, blocking her from the next step up. "Want me to try?"

"I . . ." It was the only word she could get out before her voice dried up and crumbled away.

Fitz grinned. "Maybe it would make it easier. That way you wouldn't have to *say* it—assuming I guess right."

Easier.

Harder.

Possibly one huge disaster . . .

Sophie swallowed, trying to choke down the lump that had wedged itself in her throat—but her voice still refused to rise past it.

Maybe he saw the panic in her eyes.

Or maybe he really did guess her secret.

Either way, he backed up a step. "Sorry. It's not fair to rush you—especially after everything we've been through today."

"Yeah," she mumbled, nudging her way past him and trying not to wonder if she'd just been rejected—now was not the time for such petty distractions.

But her eyes still stung and her chest had a heavy, stretched-out feeling.

"Hey," Fitz said, catching up with her at the doorway to her room. "Did I say something wrong? It feels like I did—and I swear I didn't mean to."

She turned toward her room, trying to find anything to trigger a subject change. And that was when she noticed the crushed parts in her flowered carpet.

"Are those . . . ," Fitz asked.

"Footprints," she whispered.

Coming from her open window.

Sophie ducked away from the door, pressing her back against the wall to stay out of sight and wishing Sandor was there to charge in with his deadly sword.

Since he wasn't, she stretched out her mind to search for nearby thoughts. "I don't sense anyone else here, do you?"

"No, it's pretty quiet," Fitz whispered.

Almost too quiet—but that could be her paranoia getting the best of her. She could feel her fear straining against the knot under her ribs, and she slowed her breathing to keep control.

"Wait—where are you going?" Fitz asked as she squared her shoulders and turned to march through her doorway.

"How else are we going to find out why they were here?" she asked, proud of how steady her voice sounded.

Nothing looked out of place—her desk drawers were still closed tight. Her clothes neatly hung in her closet. She followed the trail of footsteps to her bed, sucking in a breath when she took a longer look at her pillow.

"I'm guessing Keefe made that," Fitz said as she reached for the midnight blue bead that had been left in the center.

She nodded, tracing her finger over the silver moonlark rendered in perfect detail.

No one else could've painted it so intricately.

And the eye shimmered with a temporary leaping crystal.

If Sophie had any doubt about Keefe's intentions, it was erased when she noticed two tiny words painted on the silver bird's wings.

Meet now.

THIRTY-EIGHT

I'M GOING," SOPHIE SAID IN THE SAME breath that Fitz asked, "What if it's a trap?"

"It's not a trap—Keefe had to take a huge risk to come here and leave this." She rolled the bead in her hand, feeling the cool weight of it.

"The Neverseen could've made him do it," Fitz argued. "We're supposed to be finding out how far they're pushing him. Pretty sure that means we shouldn't be going along with a super-dangerous—and kinda creepy—command. I mean, who breaks into someone's room and leaves a bead on their pillow, telling them to meet up without even explaining what's going on?"

"Someone who didn't have a lot of time," Sophie said—though

secretly she did admit the whole thing had an evil-tooth-fairy vibe going on.

"He couldn't have left a note?" Fitz asked.

"A note's a lot harder to explain if anyone found him sneaking out with it. And maybe he didn't want to waste time rummaging around my room for paper and a pen. All that matters is, he wouldn't have gone to this kind of trouble if he didn't have something important to tell me. *Or* he's in danger and needs my help. Either way, I know it's risky. I know I won't find anyone who'll tell me this is a good decision. But I'm going. And I understand if you don't want—"

"No *way* am I letting you go by yourself," Fitz interrupted.

"*Letting* me?"

"Whoa—easy on the glaring. All I meant is, if you're doing this, so am I. I'll cling to your ankle as you leap away if I have to. But you realize we *will* get caught this time, right? Your parents know we're here."

"Yeah . . . I should probably leave a note, that way they won't freak out."

"I'm pretty sure the freak-out will be epic no matter what," Fitz told her. "But I guess it's still better to give some explanation."

Sophie dug a notebook and a pen from her Foxfire satchel and stared at the blank paper.

What was she supposed to say?

Found a leaping crystal from the Neverseen and decided to use it—don't know where I'm going or when I'll be back!

That should go over *really* well.

She brainstormed for another second, then went for short and sweet.

> Found a message from Keefe.
> Don't worry—we're being careful.

"I guess that covers it," Fitz said. "Though you should probably add, '*Please don't ground me for the rest of eternity.*'"

"Last chance to change your mind. I can handle myself."

"Oh, I know. I'm planning on hiding behind you if we end up facing anything scary. But we're Cognates. We're stronger *together*."

He flashed the initials side of his rings as he offered her his hand.

She took it, leaving the note on her bed as she held Keefe's bead up to the light and formed a wispy ghost of a path. "Any guesses where we're going?"

"My money's on somewhere stinky."

The joke made it easier.

So did reminding herself that they were going to see a friend.

But Sophie's knees still shook as she took the crucial step into the light, leaving their lives in Keefe's hands.

"I knew it," Fitz said, plugging his nose and glaring at his feet, which had re-formed in a puddle of oily black swirled with iridescent blue. "Selkie skin. It liquefies as they shed it."

Sophie gagged.

The sour-cheese smell coated her tongue, and the salty ocean air made it ten times worse. The whole beach was covered in the gunk—a maze of sludgy pools and slimy black rivulets trickling toward the white-capped waves. Jagged rocks jutted out of the frothy water, blanketed with sleek black creatures that looked part seal and part snake, with whiskered faces and long, coiled bodies.

"I take it those are selkies?" Sophie asked as one of the bigger beasts raised its head and let out a barklike grunt.

"Yep. I'm betting we're in Blackwater Bay," Fitz said. "Though I don't remember the cliffs being this tall when my tutor brought me here. Or this green."

"That's because this is Inktide Island," a voice behind them corrected. "Which is much more private. Or it's supposed to be. I didn't realize I'd be getting Foster-plus-one."

They spun around to find Keefe wearing another long black cloak, leaning against a clump of weathered rocks in the middle of the beach. The white eye symbol on his sleeves was almost as troubling as his casual smirk.

"So does this mean you guys are a *thing* now?" Keefe asked. "The inseparable Sophitz? Or did you decide to go with Fitzphie?"

"Dude, this is so not the time for jokes," Fitz said.

"Huh, that's pretty much what Foster told me when she first saw me at Foxfire. Do you finish each other's sentences now too?"

"Keefe—we're serious," Sophie said.

"Oh, I know. Fitz is giving me his 'I'm so serious' scowl. And you're hitting me with a whole mess of emotions." He waved his hands through the air and his smile faded. "You're back to not trusting me again? I know I was wrong about my warning—but wasn't that a good thing?"

"You think it's *good* that someone got tortured?" Fitz snapped.

All the color drained from Keefe's face. "Wait . . . what?"

"You don't know?" Sophie asked.

"No—I swear. Was it Dex? Please tell me it wasn't Dex. Or Biana? Or Linh?"

His voice cracked with each name.

"They're all fine," Sophie said. "It was—"

"We're not telling you anything until we search your memories," Fitz interrupted. "We need to make sure you weren't involved."

Keefe rolled his eyes. "Would I be here if I was?"

"Yeah, if this is a trap," Fitz said.

"Right, I forgot." Keefe turned to shout at the empty beach. "They're on to us, guys. Go ahead and attack."

Silence—aside from barking selkies.

"Oh, that's right—there's no one here except me! And do you have any idea how hard it was to get away?"

"How'd you do it?" Sophie asked.

"Don't let him sidetrack you," Fitz jumped in. "We need to stick to the plan. Like Tam said—"

"Ugh, I should've *known* Bangs Boy was part of this," Keefe interrupted. "Let me guess, he's still bitter because I wouldn't let him take that stupid reading?"

"Uh, have you seen what you're wearing?" Fitz asked.

Keefe gripped his sleeves, trying to cover the Neverseen symbols. "It's. A. *Costume*."

"Prove it," Fitz said.

"And what happens if I say no? Are you planning to go all *Cognate power* on me?"

"Just give us five minutes," Sophie begged. "Five minutes to make sure we know what's really going on. If you'd seen what they did to Wylie . . ."

Keefe fell back a step. "They hurt *Wylie*?"

"'Hurt' is putting it nicely," Fitz said. "They drugged him, dragged him out of his room, and burned him over and over."

Gulls circled high above as Keefe watched the sky. "He'll be okay, right?"

"Physic is working on him now," Sophie whispered. "She can heal all of his wounds. Not so sure about the mental trauma."

Keefe looked green as he turned to pace. "Did they let him go? Or did he get away?"

"He got away," Sophie said.

"Wow—someone's going to be in *big* trouble."

"*That's* what you care about?" Fitz asked, shaking sludge off his shoes as he stalked closer.

"Hey—I have to think about what it's going to be like

when I go back there. You would too, if you were in my position."

"I would never be in your position," Fitz argued.

"Yeah, you're better at taking the easy way."

"What does *that* mean?"

"Nothing. It's . . . whatever." Keefe's eyes made their way back to the sky. "Did Wylie see who grabbed him?"

"Sorta," Sophie said. "He felt an invisible hand tear off his pendant, and he got trapped in a force field, so that has to be Alvar and Ruy. But he also suspected there were two others."

"I'm assuming you thought one of them was me?"

"Can you blame us?" Fitz asked.

"You? No." Keefe's eyes focused on Sophie. "But I told you, I won't cross the hard lines."

"You never said what the lines are, though," she whispered. "And I know how desperate you are to make this work."

"So you thought . . ." He choked back the rest of the words.

"If you'd known they were going after Wylie," Fitz said, his voice barely audible over the rolling waves, "would you have stopped them?"

"I would've told you guys, so the Black Swan could handle it. Just like I did with Grady and Edaline."

"But what if we couldn't get to him?" Fitz pressed. "Would you have blown your cover?"

Keefe hesitated—only a second, but it was enough.

"You don't get it," he argued. "These are people who torture someone just because they want something! People who infect an entire species with a disease just to get their way! They have a network that stretches way farther than you could ever imagine. I've only seen a tiny piece of it, and it's seriously terrifying. I can't fight it without making some hard calls!"

"Well, I hope it's worth it," Fitz snapped.

"So do I." Keefe's shoulders slumped with the confession, like his body wanted to retreat.

Salty wind whipped around them, and Sophie choked down the selkie stink. "Do you have any idea who the other two kidnappers would've been? Wylie thought one was a Guster. And he heard them say the other was keeping the path open."

Keefe brushed sand out of his hair. "The Guster would be Trix. So that probably means the other was Umber, since I got the impression that she and Trix work together a lot. Those aren't their real names. I met some of the members a few days ago, but no one would tell me who they really are—and they all kept their hoods up so I couldn't see them."

"So they still don't trust you," Sophie noted.

"Not completely. But Fintan doesn't trust anyone completely. Everyone only gets to know a tiny piece of his plans, and he only gives each person a single task for every mission. That way, everyone's expendable."

"That's pretty terrifying," Sophie mumbled, "considering what he did to your mom."

Keefe shrugged.

"Are they making any progress on their promise to rescue her?" she asked.

"Don't know, don't care. I assumed they were lying when they offered that. Look at how they've abandoned Gethen. He's been a prisoner for how many months now? And do you see them trying to get him back?"

"They tried at first," Sophie reminded him. "Until Squall froze off his fingernails. And now he's in Lumenaria, which is apparently impossible to break into."

"Maybe, but I've never once heard them talk about getting him back. And when I asked Alvar about it, he said, 'Gethen is where he belongs.'"

Fitz and Sophie shared a look.

"What? Are you guys planning to visit him again?"

"We're working on it," Sophie said.

"Well . . . I wouldn't get my hopes up. They want him locked away. I'm guessing that means he's useless."

"I hope you're wrong," Sophie said quietly. "He's pretty much the only plan we have."

"Uh, hello—you have me. I know I got a few details wrong yesterday—but I'm still working on getting Fintan's cache. I *will* get him to trust me."

"That's what I'm worried about," Sophie mumbled. "Trust never comes free."

"Maybe not. But I know what I'm willing to pay. I have my limits. I won't push them."

"That'd be a lot easier to believe if you'd show us what you're doing with them every day," Fitz said.

Keefe opened his mouth to argue, then focused on Sophie. "You really need to know, don't you?"

She nodded.

A wave crashed against the rocks, making the selkies bark so loudly it nearly drowned out Keefe's next words. "I'll give you five minutes to look around my memories—but Wonderboy has to sit this one out."

"Since when do you only trust her?" Fitz asked.

"Since she doesn't look ready to punch me. So that's the deal." He offered his hand for a handshake.

Sophie stepped forward to take it, scowling when her shoe splashed in one of the inky puddles. "Lovely place you picked, by the way."

"Hey, I told you my next plan for sneaking away involved lots of selkie skin."

"You did. I just didn't realize you were serious."

"I'm always serious, Foster. Especially when you think I'm teasing." He cleared his throat, not quite holding her stare. "Remember—five minutes. Then we drop this."

She reached for his temples and he flinched at her touch.

"Dude, are you blushing?" Fitz asked.

"Only because I can feel what Foster's feeling," Keefe snapped back.

Sophie rolled her eyes. "I'm not feeling *anything*."

Or maybe she was feeling too much.

Fear and dread and doubt and worry. But also hope.

She gave herself three seconds to steady her nerves and let the sounds of the waves wash away the other distractions. Then she closed her eyes and took a cold, salty breath before she pushed her consciousness into Keefe's mind.

THIRTY-NINE

KEEFE'S HEAD WAS FULL OF CITIES.

Places Sophie recognized.

Some she didn't.

But they all had one thing in common.

Why are you visiting humans? she transmitted.

Not for the reason you're thinking.

You don't know what I'm thinking.

Actually, I do. Your emotions are so intense, you might as well hold up a sign saying, "I'm worried about THIS." But I'm just there to study people. It's part of my empathy training—and yep, working with the Neverseen is just as annoying as it is with the Black Swan. It's either this, chores, or hardcore skill lessons that make the stuff we did at Exillium look easy.

The scene shifted again, and for a second Sophie thought she was looking at Paris, until she realized the Eiffel Tower-esque structure was white and orange.

When did you go to Tokyo?

Yesterday. If you look at the signs, you can probably find the date somewhere. Now do you believe me when I say I had nothing to do with what happened to Wylie?

You get why we had to make sure, right?

It's still not awesome knowing you guys sat around talking about how you don't trust me.

You don't make it easy.

In his memory, she could see Keefe standing on a rooftop next to Fintan. She wasn't sure she could do that without shoving Fintan off the edge.

Hey, I'm just as disgusted with him as you are.

Quit reading my emotions!

Can't help it. You're impossible to ignore. And believe me, I get the same nauseating fury every time I look at him. He doesn't deserve to be alive after what he did to Kenric.

No, he doesn't.

If it helps, I'm not around him that much. Alvar supervises me during chores. And Ruy's the one in charge of the skill lessons. All Fintan does is take me to crowded places and make me isolate each person's feelings.

Why humans? she asked as the city scene shifted again, showing a street full of life and movement and color—and people. *So*

342

many people. Rich and poor. Young and old. Locals and tourists. Talking, laughing, shouting—selling food and trinkets. Some wore saris and turbans, which meant Keefe was probably in some part of India—but Sophie couldn't tell which city.

Well, for one thing, the Neverseen can't exactly go hopping around the Lost Cities, Keefe reminded her. *But I can also feel most human emotions through the air without needing contact. Plus, humans fascinate Fintan. He hates them, but he's also obsessed with knowing everything about them.*

The next city was London, right in the heart of Piccadilly Circus, where people seemed to be gathering around a weird statue and watching a bunch of ads on the giant screens.

So this is all you do? she asked. *What about during the skill lessons?*

Those are just Ruy showing off. He must've been Exillium's star student, and I'm pretty stinktastic at everything, so the lessons usually end with him calling me useless.

Sophie could feel the sting the word triggered, after all the times his dad had hurled the same accusation. But she was glad he wasn't excelling at the Neverseen's training.

And that's it? she asked. *You don't do anything else?*

Pretty much. There are lots of nasty chores. And there's been the occasional mission, like the day they stormed the Sanctuary—but I had NOTHING to do with Wylie. I swear I didn't even know it was happening. I'm actually glad you guys told me, so I can prepare before I head back.

Will you be safe?

Sure—why not? I wasn't part of the botched mission. In fact, some people might get demoted.

You say that like it's a good thing.

It is a good thing. It'll make Fintan use me more.

But for what?

I can't worry about that, Foster. I can't think about what-ifs or maybes. I can only take it one day at a time—one assignment at a time—and fight my way through.

In the memory, Fintan smiled at something Keefe said, and Sophie's insides twisted.

I hate that he's the one training you. He's not even an Empath.

I know. But all the one-on-one time I'm getting with him is crucial if I'm going to steal his cache. Plus, there aren't any other Empaths to train me. I asked him why, and he said, "It's rare to find those who are open to new sensations."

He made his mental voice sound like Fintan, and the knot of emotions under Sophie's ribs pulled so tight, it hurt to breathe.

Sorry. I guess it's probably pretty hard to hear that after the awful times you've been in his head, Keefe mumbled.

I don't know how you stand it. It makes me want to claw my ears off—or claw his lips off, or I don't know—I just want to claw something.

I know. I'm super glad you're not clawing me. And fortunately, he doesn't talk much. Mostly he says, "Tell me what they're feeling" and points to some random person in the crowd. It only gets weird

at the end. Before he brings me back to the hideout, he always asks,
"If you could only save one of these people, who would you save?"

That's . . . terrifying.

I know. I totally thought he was going to burn down the city,
and I had no idea what I'd do if he did. But he just scratched his
chin and asked why I chose the person. He always writes down my
answer in this little notebook he keeps in his pocket. Most of the time
he tilts it up so I can't see what he's writing. But a couple of days ago
it was windy and the pages kept flipping, so he held it at a different
angle and it looked like he's making a list—but I have no idea of
what. The label at the top said: "CRITERION."

FORTY

I'M GUESSING THERE'S A REASON YOU JUST *gasped,* Keefe said as the city in his memories shifted again, to a colorful barrio filled with music and dancing.

Sophie bit her lip. *Biana overheard Alvar talking to someone on his Imparter at Everglen a few months back. And he used the word "criterion." He also talked about "test subjects."*

She let that sink in before she asked, *Do you think that means they've been planning to train you like this for a while?*

Probably, Keefe said, disgust laced through every syllable. *I keep trying to tell you—I'm not the guy you want me to be.*

I don't want you to be anyone except you. *Whatever the Lodestar Initiative is—it doesn't define you any more than Project Moonlark defines me. Especially since I'm starting to think their plans aren't even working. I can't remember the last time the Black Swan were ahead of all the crazy stuff going on—and it seems like the Neverseen are scrambling too. These groups may have created the game. But that doesn't mean we have to play by their rules. And if there's one thing you and I are both good at, it's making things up as we go along.*

I guess I can live with that, Keefe thought as his memory changed to a quaint village-style city, with a long wooden bridge spanning the peaceful river in the center. Enormous snowcapped mountains loomed in the distance, and Sophie assumed that meant they were somewhere like Austria or Switzerland.

So . . . what are your criteria for deciding which person you would save? she asked.

It depends. I mostly look for whoever feels the happiest, since I figure they'd appreciate getting to live. Or I pick one of the kids. They're so cute and small and innocent and wow, that's a huge wave of sappy mushiness you're hitting me with.

What do you expect? You're talking about saving kids!

And ten minutes ago you thought I was Wylie's fourth kidnapper. Remind me to thank Bangs Boy for that the next time I see him. And the Fitzster.

If you could've seen Wylie's injuries, you'd understand why we had to be sure. She had to clamp down on her memories to stop herself from picturing it. *Besides, seeing you in that robe . . .*

Yeah, I can feel how much you hate it.

"Hate" isn't a strong enough word. I want to rip it to shreds.

Well, don't. I'm not wearing anything underneath.

He snort-laughed when she scrambled back a step.

I'm kidding—though your gross-out is noted. And FYI, the reason I'm still wearing it is because I can't risk losing another one. Fintan flipped out when I came back from Foxfire without it, probably because he couldn't track me or something.

That's not the only reason.

Oh?

Yeah.

Seconds passed.

Aw, come on, Foster. I'm the cute guy who chooses to save the kids, remember? How can you resist me?

Who said anything about cute?

It totally goes without saying. Don't even try to deny it.

She couldn't.

And he knew it.

And she hated it.

If I tell you, I want something in return, she decided.

Isn't my eternal devotion enough?

Not even close.

That hurts, Foster.

That's the game. If I tell you what we found in your cloak, I want a secret in return. I want to see whatever memory you got back that freaked you out and made you run away.

His mind seemed to squirm.

Come on, Keefe. Sooner or later you're going to have to tell me anyway.

See, but "later" sounds way better than "sooner."

You think it does, because hiding stuff always sounds easier. But all it really means is that you're stuck carrying the burden all alone.

That's better than dumping it on you.

But I'm asking you to—and I promise, it's not going to change anything.

Oh, it changes everything. *You'll see.*

Does that mean we have a deal?

She heard him sigh. *Fine. But you go first.*

Fair enough.

She explained about the disk in his cloak, and how Prentice's memory of the symbol seemed to be connected to him calling swan song, and how they found the shadowprint of the symbol on the floor of the abandoned hideout in Paris. And while she was at it, she told him about the listening device in his old Imparter.

Your turn! she finished.

Whoa, hang on—you can't just dump all of that on me and not give me a second to process. There was a listening device in my old Imparter? How did you even have it?

Yours accidentally got switched with mine the day we searched your room and found your mom's note. Dex couldn't track the signal, but we're assuming it went to the Neverseen, and that's how they knew about our ambush on Everest and had time to prepare.

Mom of the year strikes again. His mind seemed to darken as thick clouds of anger swirled through his consciousness. *I don't know why I even get surprised anymore.*

Because you haven't let her break you—and I hope you never do.

She watched him gather the words, tucking them away somewhere safe before he asked, *So the disk you found in my cloak—was it a kind of tracker?*

Sandor and Mr. Forkle didn't think so. It wasn't covered in any enzymes, and it's made of something called duskitine, which is apparently a type of stone that reacts to starlight. We have no idea why it has a piece of the symbol carved on it, but it can't be a coincidence. And you haven't seen the symbol anywhere?

Nope. But I'm still at their stupid "new recruit" house. I bet I'll find it once I get to a real hideout. And in the meantime, maybe I need to lose this cloak and see what happens. . . .

Bad idea—especially after you took such a risk to meet with us today.

There you go again with your logic. It's really cramping my style.

Well then, why don't you stop me by showing me that memory?

Are you sure you wouldn't rather lecture me a little longer?

Tempting, but no.

When he still hesitated, she added, *Come on, Keefe, haven't you stood by me through all the weird things in my past? Let's not forget I'm the girl with the alicorn-inspired DNA.*

Yeah, but that lets you teleport—and communicate with Silveny—so it's a total win. How are she and Greyfell doing, by the way?

They're good. If they were here, Silveny would tell you to stop stalling.

Pretty sure she'd be chanting KEEFE! KEEFE! KEEFE! As everyone should be when they see me.

There you go, changing the subject again.

Caught that, huh? You're a quick one, Miss F. And I'm pretty sure I've given you way more than five minutes, so—

Nope. You're not getting out of this. We made a deal, and I'm holding you to it.

See, and I'd kinda like to find out how you'll punish me if I don't.

She was tempted to snap back with a long list of incredibly creative forms of Keefe torture. But then she'd be giving him the distraction he wanted.

Please? she tried. *I'm tired of wondering about that memory. I'm tired of worrying what side of the line you're on every time things get weird. I'm tired of having Dex tell me he thinks you're my nemesis and—*

Whoa—back up. Dizznee thinks I'm your what?

Well, he didn't actually say "nemesis"—but he implied it. We were trying to guess what the Lodestar Initiative is, and he wondered if it's the Neverseen's version of Project Moonlark, which would basically mean they made you to stop me.

Wow. That's just . . .

He burst into a fit of snorty giggles.

I'm glad you find this so amusing.

You don't? Don't tell me you actually believe him.

I don't want to. But what else am I supposed to think? You told me when you ran off that you were meant to be something other than the hero. And just a few minutes ago, you told me you're not the guy I want you to be.

Ugh. I guess you do need to see that memory, don't you?

Yeah, I really do.

Okay. The word felt sluggish, like his mind was dragging its feet. But after several seconds, a new flashback began.

FORTY-ONE

IT WAS DARK IN KEEFE'S BEDROOM. SO black he could barely make out the silhouette of his mother leaning over his bed, as her arms shook him from his dreamless sleep.

"Mom?" he asked. "Is something wrong?"

His voice was squeakier than Sophie was used to hearing it. She guessed that meant he was more like nine or ten years old.

"Everything's fine," Lady Gisela told him as she yanked back his covers.

A whoosh of cold air rushed around him and he curled up tighter, shivering in his overstarched pajamas.

"None of that," she said, grabbing his wrist to stop him from reaching for his blanket. "Put this on. It's even colder where we're going."

She tossed a thick black cloak at him as he slowly sat up.

Sophie squinted through the dim memory, half expecting to find the white eye symbol staring back at her from the sleeves. But the cloak was plain, and the coarse fabric seemed to swallow Keefe's skinny frame as he stumbled to his feet, his knees still shaky with sleep.

His eyes slowly adjusted to being awake, letting him see more of his mom, who looked as immaculate as ever. Despite the middle-of-the-night time, her lips were glossed, her heavy black cape glittered with flecks of onyx, and her shiny blond hair was twisted into an intricate updo.

She clicked her tongue as he stood there gaping at her.

"Honestly, Keefe. You can't figure out that you need to put on your shoes?"

Keefe stared at his bare feet.

Lady Gisela rolled her eyes and dropped to her knees, grabbing a pair of soft black boots from the foot of the bed.

"No socks?" Keefe asked, clinging to her shoulders as she ordered him to step into the left shoe. "And shouldn't I change first?"

"We won't be gone that long." She pulled the other boot on and adjusted the collar of his cloak, securing the fabric higher up on his neck. "There. Good enough."

"Where are we going?" Keefe asked as she strode across the

room and pulled back the curtains covering his windows. Only a sliver of moon lit the lonely night sky. "Why isn't Dad coming with us?"

"Because. This is our special secret. You like secrets, right?" She offered half a smile as he gave an enthusiastic "Yes!"

"Good. Then let's get going." She reached for the back of her head and pulled a long silver hairpin out of her twisted style. Her hair fell around her face in silky waves, softening her features. But the look in her eyes was hard as iron as she held the pin up to the window, letting the pale silver light illuminate the smooth stone set among the swirled pieces of metal.

"Is that crystal glowing?" Keefe asked, pointing to the pin's white-blue aura.

"It's not a crystal. It's a rare starstone—which is important. Someday I'll need you to remember that. But not tonight. Tonight I just need you to take my hand."

He did, his fingers looking so much smaller than hers as they twined together. A wide golden nexus covered his left wrist, glittering with dozens of diamonds.

"Concentrate," Lady Gisela said as they stepped into the starstone's glow and let the cold rush sweep them away.

The memory shifted then—picking up after the leap, at a gleaming silver door surrounded by shadows and snow. Elvin runes had been carved into the metal, forming words that looked like gibberish to Sophie.

"Where are we?" Keefe asked as an icy breeze prickled

his ears. He dropped his mom's hand and pulled his arms against his chest, trying to preserve what little warmth he could.

"It doesn't matter yet," Lady Gisela told him. "Someday this place will be the solution our world needs. But for the moment, we're just here for security. Better keep your hands out of those sleeves. It'll be easier if your fingers go numb."

"Why?"

"You'll see. And relax," she added, tapping the frown on his lips. "It'll be over fast."

"What will?"

"So many questions. Don't you trust me?"

Keefe nodded, but his eyes were focused on the way she was holding her hairpin—more like a dagger than a fashion accessory. It drew his attention to the fact that the pin had a long, twisted stem with a needle-sharp point.

"Oh please," she said as Keefe flinched back a step. "Did I raise you to be a coward?"

"No," Keefe mumbled.

"Then give me your hand."

"What are you going to do?"

"I'm going to ensure your legacy. And that kind of gift comes with a price. Now. Give. Me. Your. Hand."

"What if I don't want a legacy?"

"Everyone wants a legacy. Or would you rather prove that your father's right about you?"

356

The words lit a fire inside him, a burning need to meet the challenge.

"Good boy," she said as Keefe held out his shaky left hand. "Though clearly we're going to have to work on toughening you up."

"I'm tough."

"I'll believe it when I see it."

The words echoed around Keefe's mind as his mom uncurled his fingers. Sophie could see how much he wanted to pull away. But his mom's insults had done their job. He wanted to please her more than he wanted to stop her. So he held perfectly still as she pressed the point of the hairpin against the soft pad of his thumb, lingering only a second before she sliced a thick cut from the joint to the tip.

Keefe gritted his teeth through the pain as warm red pooled from the gash.

"Let it bleed for a second," she told him. "I want a pure sample."

All Keefe could do was nod. Wooziness was setting in—he'd never seen so much blood before. And the nerves around the cut stung like he'd touched acid.

"I know what you're thinking," his mom said. "You're wondering why I can't just use your DNA, like we do for everything else."

The elves normally found anything that drew blood to be barbaric.

"Blood is our life force," Lady Gisela told him. "The deepest essence of our being. Without it, our bodies would grow still and cold. And therein lies the power. Anyone can offer up their DNA—it doesn't take guts to lick a sensor. But to paint it with blood? Now *that's* something special. Don't you feel powerful?"

All Keefe felt was hurt. And confused. And he couldn't put a finger on the other emotion, but Sophie could.

He felt betrayed.

He didn't say that, though. He nodded like the brave, obedient son he knew his mom wanted him to be, letting her pull him closer to the door.

"Last step," Lady Gisela said, stretching his hand toward a clear rectangle set into the metal, right next to the handle.

Sophie expected the door to swing open as Keefe smeared his blood across the smooth panel. But a metallic click echoed through the dark instead.

A lock clicking into place.

Lady Gisela stepped back, shaking her hair out of her eyes. "Finally done."

The blood on the panel steamed, filling the air with the unsettling scent of barbeque as the red turned to ash and then crumbled away, leaving no trace.

"This is your future, Keefe," his mother told him, stretching her arms wide and gazing at the door with obvious awe. "Your legacy. Safe and secure. Until our world is ready to change."

"Change to what?" Keefe asked, cradling his wounded thumb, which was still streaming red down his wrist.

Of course his mother hadn't thought to bring him a bandage.

She didn't answer him either.

She just grabbed his elbow and held her hairpin up to the midnight sky, leaping them both back to Keefe's room.

"Starstones," she told him, twisting her hair back into its sleek style and pinning it in place, "always remember the path back to where they've been. You'll need to know that someday."

Keefe didn't care about someday.

He cared about *now*.

And now . . . his hand really hurt.

And his limbs ached from the cold. And his stomach was queasy with fear and pain.

All he wanted to do was curl up under the covers in a little ball and cry.

"So ungrateful," his mom said as she watched him stumble toward his bed. "And so melodramatic. But I suppose that's to be expected, given your age. Give me that cloak before you sit."

Keefe tossed it to her, kicking off his boots, too. He left a bloody handprint on his blanket as he pulled the covers tightly around his neck.

Lady Gisela crinkled her nose. "I'll have to find an ointment to stop that—and something to clean up that stain before your father notices."

"Whatever," Keefe mumbled, keeping his wounded hand tight to his chest.

He squeezed his eyes shut as his mom pulled out a silver Imparter.

The last thing he remembered was her brushing his hair off his forehead and whispering, "Don't worry, Keefe. The Washer will be here soon."

FORTY-TWO

SOPHIE DROPPED HER HANDS FROM Keefe's temples, severing their mental connection. But the horrible scenes kept replaying in her mind.

"Keefe, I . . ."

There were no words.

She threw her arms around his shoulders, hugging him as tight as she could. Maybe if she never let go, she could hold the broken pieces together.

"I'm pretty sure you just ruined your shoes in a huge puddle of selkie skin," Keefe told her.

"I don't care. And you don't have to do that. You don't have to make this into a joke."

"Yes, I do."

The crack in his voice splintered through her heart, and she buried her face against his shoulder, feeling tears leak onto his cloak.

"Sorry," she mumbled. "I'm not supposed to be the one crying."

"Neither of us should. It was just a stupid cut. It didn't even leave a scar."

She leaned back to look at him. "We both know it did."

Keefe turned away, watching the waves crash onto the beach. "I don't want you feeling sorry for me."

"I can't help it. But it's not pity. It's . . . I don't know what the word for it is. I'm too conflicted."

Keefe sighed. "You always are when it comes to me."

"Well, right now I mostly want to blast my way into that ogre prison and punch your mom as hard as I can in her snobby face. And then, when the blood's streaming from her nose, I want to give her some stupid speech about our life force and ask her if she feels powerful."

"Wow, who knew you had such a dark side?"

"Certain things bring it out. And this?" Her whole body trembled as her knotted emotions stirred—a monster ready to burst from her chest.

Keefe held her steady. "I appreciate the fury, Foster. But seriously. It's not worth it."

She knew he really meant *I'm not worth it.*

362

She hated that most of all.

"Someday I'm going to make you see how wrong you are," she promised.

"I'm just glad you're not shoving me away."

"You really thought I would?"

"Sometimes I think you'd be better off."

He tried to pull back but she refused to let go.

"I'll only be better off when you come home and I know you're safe," she whispered.

He didn't agree. But he didn't argue, either, both of them deciding to leave it at that.

"What made you remember this?" she asked.

"I didn't find her hairpin, if that's what you're thinking—and believe me, I *tried*. The memory flashed back while I was looking for that beaded necklace I gave you. She had a bunch of hairpins in her jewelry box, and one of them pricked my finger and the whole thing rushed back. After that I searched everywhere I could think of, but she either hid the pin really well, or got rid of it—or took it with her. I even endured a conversation with my dad to ask if he remembered it, but he called starstones 'plain' and said he'd never give my mom something so drab. I'm guessing that means she bought it herself."

"She probably had it custom-made. In the memory she called it a 'rare starstone.' And I'm guessing you don't know where that door she brought you to is, or what's behind it?"

"Nope. The weird thing is, I don't think the Neverseen do either. I'd figured they'd drag me there the second I joined and make me open that door. But they've never even asked me about it. So either my mom didn't tell them, or they don't realize my blood is the key."

"Or they're waiting for the right time," Sophie said.

"Why do you think I'm still with them? You get that now, right? Whatever's on the other side of that door—whatever my mom planned—she made me a part of it. And I have to believe that means I can stop it."

"What do you think is in there?"

"No idea. But nothing good ever comes from my mom."

"One thing did," she said. "One of my favorite things."

The cold, stinky wind rushed between them as he pulled away. "I hate to break it to you, Foster, but you have terrible taste in friends. You saw how I acted in that memory. What kind of loser goes along with something like that without demanding answers?"

"A boy who's been bullied and manipulated his entire life. That's how verbal abuse works. It drains you bit by bit, until there's not enough energy left to keep fighting."

"Yeah, well, I also knew she was erasing the memory—did you catch that at the end? I was nine when that happened. I definitely knew what Washers were by then. I knew what was going to happen. And I didn't stop it because I wanted to forget. I *chose* to be oblivious."

"I would've done the same thing," a crisp, accented voice said behind them.

Sophie's cheeks burned. She'd gotten so lost in the memories, she'd forgotten Fitz was watching them.

"Sorry," he mumbled. "I didn't mean to butt in. But seriously, Keefe. You make it sound like nine years old is so grown up. You were just a kid. And you know what kids do? They trust their parents—even when part of them knows that something feels off—because our parents are our world. And what do you think would've happened if you'd told your mom no? Do you think you would've gotten out of there without giving up some of your blood?"

"I take it this means you were eavesdropping on Foster's thoughts this whole time?" Keefe asked.

"Not at first. But then Sophie gasped—and when I asked if you guys were okay, you didn't respond. So I slipped past her blocking just to make sure nothing weird was happening, and . . . I couldn't stop watching. The whole time I kept asking myself how I'd feel if I'd remembered something like that—what I'd do if I knew I was part of something that feels so ominous. And I'm pretty sure the answer is, *I'd do whatever I had to do to stop it.*"

Keefe blinked hard, and Sophie didn't think it was from the sandy wind.

"Joining the Neverseen was the only thing I could think of that might help," he whispered. "I know I've made some mistakes—and I know it's going to get messier and messier. But this *is* working. I *am* learning things. That's why I had you meet me here. I won't be able to talk tonight, and I didn't want to lose a whole day. Your parents are still in danger—don't let them drop their guard. I don't know when Fintan will make his move, but I know he still has plans for them. And I found out something else this morning—something *big*. Fintan's been trying for weeks to get the ogres to meet with him to reconcile. And last night, King Dimitar finally agreed."

FORTY-THREE

ARE YOU SURE DIMITAR'S NOT agreeing to the meeting so he'll have the perfect chance to slice off Fintan's head with his extra-scary, extra-spikey sword?" Fitz asked. "Because if I were him, that's what *I'd* want to do after the way the Neverseen's plague plan backfired on him. And I'd be good with that. They're welcome to take out Alvar, too."

"I wouldn't mind if the ogres finished off Brant, either," Sophie added, trying to scrape the selkie slime off her shoe. "Same goes for anyone else that helped attack Wylie."

"Don't worry, they'll be in huge trouble for letting him get away," Keefe promised.

"Do you know how they'll be punished?" Fitz asked.

"I know it won't be fun. Alvar told me that when Brant realized Sophie actually *was* the girl they'd been looking for—and that Alvar messed up the day she saw him disappear—he locked Alvar in a room and set everything on fire except one square of floor in the middle. He left him roasting in there for a whole day."

"Good," Fitz said. "I hope they do even worse for this."

"That's . . . pretty dark, dude."

"So is what he let them do to Wylie."

Sophie reached for Fitz's shaky hand, wishing she knew how to peel back some of his building anger. Fury was always his mask, but if he hid too far behind it, he might lose himself.

She also couldn't stop imagining Keefe trapped in a room, surrounded by smoke and flames. "If they find out you came here . . ."

"They *know* I'm here," Keefe told her. "There's an ogre enzyme that stinks like the entire world is rotting, and I may have *accidentally* knocked a vial of it into the laundry basin while I was washing Fintan's favorite cloaks. It can only be removed with selkie skin, so they sent me to get what I need to clean up my mess."

"He's making you do his laundry?" Sophie asked.

"It's one of my chores. That's what happens when you join an organization that attacks the gnomes. We're stuck doing everything ourselves."

"And he won't be able to tell you went to Havenfield before you came here?" Fitz asked.

"Nope. I found a way to hide five seconds from my tracker. I'm pretty sure Dex would think it's the stupidest trick ever. But it works. And I used those five seconds to drop off the bead before I headed here. It was perfect."

"But all it takes is one mistake," Sophie told him. "Especially now that the ogres are back in the picture. King Dimitar will remember you from Ravagog, and I'm sure he'll try to convince Fintan that you're a traitor."

Keefe had been their distraction during the mission in the ogres' capital, pestering the king with questions and misleading information while Sophie and Fitz searched his memories.

Keefe shrugged. "I won't be getting anywhere near King Dimitar—and not just because I sometimes have nightmares about that metal underwear he walks around in. He demanded to meet with Fintan alone."

"That sounds like a really good way for Fintan to get killed by an angry ogre," Fitz noted.

"I dunno. If the meeting unravels, I think we'd have fire-roasted ogre long before we'd have a headless Fintan," Keefe told him. "*But*, I also think this is one of those 'the enemy of my enemy is my friend' kind of deals. Or is it 'my enemy isn't my enemy if they're also my enemy's enemy'?"

"You lost me," Sophie admitted.

"Yeah, the logic's kinda wonky. What I mean is, the Neverseen and the ogres both want the Council gone. And now that King Dimitar's being forced into treaty negotiations, he must be feeling pretty desperate. He *has* to know his only chance of beating the Council is with help from the Neverseen. I'm sure the Councillors have all kinds of secret defenses that Fintan knows about, since he used to be one. And Fintan has also realized that he needs the ogres' help to pull off his plans. So my guess is, he's going to offer to share his secrets with the ogres—and provide elvin backup—*if* King Dimitar works with him to overthrow the Council. I'm sure they'll turn on each other afterward, and there's no telling who would win. But it won't matter because by then everything would already be ruined."

"But didn't the ogres and the Neverseen already try teaming up for the plague?" Fitz asked. "It didn't go well."

"Right, but they didn't really *commit*, either," Keefe reminded him. "The Neverseen sat back and let the ogres do all the dirty work, and the ogres thought the plague would be enough. If they teamed up for a *real* attack, I think it would be a whole other story."

"You really think the Council could fall?" Sophie whispered.

"Yeah, I do," Keefe said. "Don't get me wrong—the Councillors are freakishly powerful. I was a little stunned at how prepared they were to stomp us when we broke in to Exile. But they're also too slow. Too blind to a lot of our problems. Too reluctant to make the hard choices. Look at how they handled the plague. They investigated a bit, called a few assemblies, and . . . that was it. *We* had to stop it—and Calla had to give up her life."

Sophie locked her arms at her sides so she wouldn't pull on her eyelashes as the Councillors' faces filled her mind. Some good. Some cruel. Some annoying. Some she didn't even know.

None of them deserved to die.

And Oralie . . .

Imagining the ethereal Councillor in the hands of the ogres—or the Neverseen—made her want to leap back to Eternalia and beg the Council to go into hiding.

But would that really keep them safe?

And what message would that send the rest of the world?

Then again, what would happen if the Council fell?

"We have to stop it," Sophie said.

She didn't know *how*. But . . . they never knew what they were doing, and somehow they always made it work.

"There's the confident Foster we all know and love!" Keefe cheered. "I bet your head is already filling up with brilliant plans."

"Not yet," she admitted. "Warning the Council seems pointless. They'll just tell us they can handle themselves."

Or worse—they'd use it as an excuse to enact some of those restrictions that Oralie had been worried about.

"Maybe the Black Swan will have some ideas," Fitz said.

"Because they had so many awesome ideas for what to do about Wylie?" Sophie countered.

"Any chance you've manifested some new abilities that could solve all of our problems in one fell swoop?" Keefe asked Sophie.

"No—and I don't know why you keep thinking I'm going to. Wouldn't the Black Swan have triggered it when they triggered my other ones?"

"Uh, this is the Black Swan we're talking about," Keefe argued. "They take a million years to do anything—and just so you know, I'm rooting for Phaser. Think of how much havoc you could cause if you could walk through walls."

"Shouldn't we be trying to come up with an actual plan?" Fitz asked. "Instead of putting all the pressure on Sophie?"

"But Foster's always the one who figures it out. You just gotta give that fancy brain of hers a second to work."

"That's not true. I . . ." Sophie's words trailed off as an idea started to take shape.

Keefe grinned. "Go ahead, Foster. Amaze us."

She stared at the black sludge trickling across the sand. "It's not a full plan yet. But the ogres and the Neverseen already have a precarious relationship, right? So what if we do something to push it over the edge, and make sure they never trust each other again?"

"See?" Keefe said. "Told you she'd solve it. Maybe we'll get our wish and they'll destroy each other in the process. So what are you thinking? Convince Dimitar that Fintan told everyone Dimitar's butt looks dimply in those metal undies? Or maybe we fill Fintan's bedroom with those nasty ogre plants Lady Cadence used to make us peel in detention—what were they called? Curdleroots?—and he'll be like, 'Oh no Dimitar didn't—it's *on!*'"

"Do you even know where any of the Neverseen's other hideouts are?" Sophie asked.

"Wait," Fitz said. "Are you actually considering those plans?"

"No, they're totally insane. But if we're going to come up with something better, we need to know what we have to work with, like who we have access to, and how much time we have. Do you think you can find out when and where King Dimitar and Fintan are going to meet?" she asked Keefe. "Because if we can cause something to go wrong during that meeting, they'll each think the other set a trap."

"I . . . don't know. One thing I've learned as New Kid in the Evil Rebellion—it's not a good idea to ask too many questions. And I've been trying to save them to find out how to steal the caches."

"The caches *are* important," Sophie said. "But this has a bigger time crunch. It sounded like the Peace Summit is coming up quick, and I'm assuming they'll be meeting before then."

"Yeah, I guess that makes sense," Keefe said, shaking the sand off his cloak. "I'll see if I can find a way to bring the ogres up during my next empathy lesson. Maybe the fact that Fintan's going to be angry at everyone for botching the Wylie thing will make him a little more willing to open up to me."

"Be careful," Sophie begged, still imagining fiery punishments. "None of this is worth what they'll do to you if they figure out you're helping us."

"I got this," Keefe said, ducking behind the rocks he'd been leaning on when they arrived. He returned carrying a sludgy, stinky bucket. "I'd better get back. I'm sure the person meeting me at the rendezvous point is there by now."

"I think we should check in more than once a day from now on," Sophie told him as he fished out a simple blue crystal. "That way you won't have to try to slip away again. Is there another time that's safe to talk?"

"I get a breakfast break around sunrise, and a dinner break around sunset, so we could go with either of those times. Or both. But no check-ins tonight. I'm supposed to have a special skill lesson with Ruy—and even if that's changed, I should probably lie low."

"Tomorrow morning, then," Sophie said, trying not to think about how early she'd be waking up from now on.

"Woo-hoo for bonus Keefoster time! Try not to get jealous, Fitzy. She still likes you better than me—but someday I *will* wear her down. I'm sneaky like that."

"Not sneaky enough!" a voice growled behind them.

Sophie's panic mixed with dread when she realized the voice was high-pitched and squeaky.

Sure enough, when she turned around, she found Sandor, Grizel, Alden, and Grady glaring at them.

"Uh-oh—that's my cue," Keefe said, his eyes on his feet as he moved his crystal to the light and disappeared through the path.

Grady's lips pressed into a rigid line, parting enough to only release one word.

"Grounded."

Alden added, "For the rest of eternity."

FORTY-FOUR

GRADY MADE GOOD ON HIS THREAT, sending Sophie to her room the second they got back to Havenfield and informing her that she wouldn't be leaving the house again until her ears turned pointy.

Even after she'd warned him about the alliance between the Neverseen and ogres.

Even after she'd explained the plan they were working on to prevent it.

Even after she'd shared Keefe's darkest memory to help prove he was trustworthy.

Reasoning with Grady was sometimes like giving Verdi something new to eat.

And from the look in Alden's eyes as he dragged Fitz back to Everglen, she had no doubt Fitz was meeting the same fate—though Grizel's lecture would surely be less brutal than Sandor's. Sandor's stretched on for an hour and seventeen minutes—and yes, Sophie counted. He ranted for so long, her butt went numb—and she was sitting on her very soft, very comfortable bed.

Apparently Alden had come to Havenfield after Grady told him about Cyrah, and they'd gone upstairs to ask Sophie a few follow-up questions. Cue massive chaos when they found her note on the bed. They'd hailed Sandor to have him find her through the emergency trackers hidden in her clothes, and Grizel had insisted on coming along, since Fitz was her charge.

"Don't tell me you were careful," Sandor ordered when his speech finally wound down. "If you were careful, you would've waited for me. After what just happened to Wylie—"

"Keefe wasn't a part of that," she interrupted. "And they needed you at Foxfire, trying to figure out how the Neverseen got into the Silver Tower—not wasting time on me."

"Protecting you will *never* be a waste of time. You've also proven that you can't be left without supervision, so Lur and Mitya are taking over the search at the tower. Gnomish senses aren't quite as keen, but they'll be able to work much faster. And you will not leave my side from this moment forward—I don't care what any cute boys leave on your pillow."

Sophie's cheeks burned. "It wasn't about *that*. He—"

Sandor held up his hands. "Whatever your reasons, the answer will forever remain, *I go where you go.*"

"Which means you'll be seeing a lot of these walls," Grady said as he stalked into the room with Edaline. Sophie opened her mouth to argue, but he held up his hand. "We'll discuss it in the morning. Right now, I want you to eat some dinner and go to sleep."

Edaline snapped her fingers, conjuring up a tray of something neon orange and gloopy. Fortunately, elvin food always tasted better than it looked.

Sophie sighed as they each kissed her on the cheek and closed her in her room with Sandor guarding the door. If they were freaking out this much about her sneaking off to meet with Keefe, she couldn't imagine what they'd do if they found out she'd *also* visited Eternalia. . . .

You okay? she transmitted, stretching out her mind to Fitz after she'd eaten and showered and climbed into bed.

Yeah. I'm good. Though Grizel says I'm now required to participate in Sandor's dancing humiliation. There was lots of talk of matching silver pants.

Sophie giggled. *Maybe you and Sandor can work out some choreography.*

Hey—if I have to dance, you are SO dancing with me. In the frilliest, sparkliest gown Biana can find in her closet. And heels.

She knew Fitz was only teasing—but the idea sounded . . . interesting. Well, the dancing part—not the stupid dress.

What about you? he asked. *How bad is the punishment?*

I'm still awaiting sentencing.

Yikes. Waiting's the worst. Sorry.

No—I'm sorry. I'm the one who got you into this.

Nah, I chose to go. And I'm glad I did. I think I finally get where Keefe's coming from. That memory . . .

I know. I'm pretty sure I'll be having nightmares about it for a while. Though that's still less terrifying than imagining what'll happen to him if he gets caught.

Seriously, I think you were right when you told me that we're probably going to have to figure out a way to save him by the end of this. I mean, this isn't the kind of thing he can just walk away from. If he tries to leave, they will *come after him—and that's assuming he gets out before they figure out what he's doing.*

Sophie reached for Ella. *How do we save him when we don't even know where he is?*

No idea, Fitz admitted. *But . . . Keefe is dead-on about one thing. You do always find the solution.*

Gee—no pressure there.

I know. I promise, I'll do everything I can to help. I just meant . . . try not to stress about it too much. If we really need to help him, you'll figure it out.

How can you be so sure?

She could almost feel the warmth of his smile radiating through the connection between them as he told her, *Because you're Sophie Foster. That's what you do.*

"Well, at least you obeyed one thing I told you," Grady said, startling Sophie awake. "I think this is the latest you've slept as long as you've lived here—without sedatives, at least."

Sophie rubbed her eyes. "What time is it?"

"Lunchtime."

"LUNCHTIME?" Sophie groaned as he opened her shades, flooding the room with sunlight. "Ugh—I slept through my check-in with Keefe."

"Good," Grady said.

"No—not good. Now I can't make sure he's okay until dinnertime."

"You should be more worried about *you*. We need to discuss your punishment."

Sophie sighed and sat up, twisting her Sucker Punch bracelet. "I'm sorry I worried you. But . . . Fitz and I weren't actually *in* danger."

"Every minute you spend with That Boy is dangerous," Grady insisted. "If he wants to risk his own life—that's his choice. But I'm not letting him drag you—or Fitz—down with him."

"He's not dragging us down—he gave us crucial information. Why can't you see that?"

"Actually, I can. I was up late giving Mr. Forkle a thorough update on everything you told me. He's asked you to record all of your memories—especially the one about that door. And the whole Collective will be brainstorming ways to prevent this new alliance from forming. They think your plan to sabotage Dimitar and Fintan's meeting is very clever. But none of that changes the fact that you met up with a member of the Neverseen without permission and without protection—that's never going to be okay."

"Neither is grounding me for meeting with a *friend*," Sophie argued. "Especially since I left a note!"

"Yeah, let's talk about that." Grady scooted her lunch tray closer. "Your mom and I were right downstairs. You could've told us what you were doing. But you chose to scribble a hasty message and sneak away. Why do you think that is?"

Sophie hated when he made good points.

"I didn't have time to deal with anyone trying to stop me," she mumbled. "I know you guys want to keep me safe—but Keefe is putting his life on the line to help us. So . . . if he gives me instructions, I'm going to follow them—grounding or no. Same goes for whatever plan we come up with to ruin the ogre–Neverseen meeting—and if the Black Swan need me to search more of Wylie's memories, or to check on Prentice, or meet with Gethen, or—"

"I'm aware that you might find some extenuating circumstances," Grady interrupted. "In fact, I've already assured Mr. Forkle that if something urgent comes up, all he has to do is hail me. I'd prefer he bring the problem here, but if he can't, I'll allow you to go *with Sandor*."

"And I will ensure that you come home immediately after," Sandor said from the doorway.

"I'm also still going to let you have *this*"—Grady handed her a wrapped parcel—"so that you'll have a way to stay connected to your friends and the Black Swan."

Sophie peeled back the thick paper and found a new Imparter along with the black case Mr. Forkle had put Keefe's Imparter in.

"It's still in there," Grady explained. "The Black Swan's Technopath couldn't trace the signal either."

Her shoulders slumped.

"Yeah, I know. I was hoping we'd learn something from it too. But try to remember that a dead end is better than any of the awful things that could've happened if that listening device had still been active. The Black Swan locked the case so you can't open it. You're welcome to throw it away, or smash the whole thing into itty-bitty pieces—"

"I'd be *happy* to crush it for you," Sandor offered. "But Mr. Forkle suspected you'd want to hang on to it."

She did—even though she knew it was silly. Somehow knowing the Imparter still existed made it feel like she might someday discover a secret from it.

"I'm not going to put any restrictions on who you're allowed to contact," Grady added. "And I'm willing to let you have your friends visit to work on projects. Despite what you may be thinking, I'm not grounding you because I'm angry. I'm just trying to protect you—even if it means being annoying. I know you're the moonlark. I'd like to think I've been pretty support-ive. Didn't I let you fly off with Silveny to get your abilities fixed? And didn't I let you run away to join the Black Swan? If you think any of that was easy for me, you overestimate my inner calm. Most days, I want to grab you and Edaline and find somewhere safe to hide until all of this is over. But I know that's not what you want—and I'm proud of you for being so ready to accept your responsibilities. I just need you to remember that you're also my daughter, and I'd like to keep you alive."

"Okay, but . . ."

"But what?" Grady asked, when she didn't finish.

Sophie stared at the crystal stars that dangled over her bed. "If I hadn't gone to meet with Keefe, would you have gotten so angry?"

"I'm not sure what you're getting at, kiddo."

"I *mean*, if I'd snuck out with Dex or Biana to do something for the Black Swan—or if Fitz and I had left to do some Cog-nate training—would you have grounded me like this?"

"Of course," Sandor said.

Grady didn't look as sure. "That's not a fair question. None of them are actively involved with our enemies. And none of them have ever sent you home in a panicked, sobbing heap after betraying you."

"Uh, Biana and I had that huge fight at Foxfire a few months back, remember? I ran home crying and went to the cave to be alone and ended up getting kidnapped—not that Biana had anything to do with *that*. And Fitz blamed me for what happened to Alden and said all kinds of mean things that made me cry. And that ability restrictor Dex made for the Council was one of the most painful, humiliating things I've ever been through."

"So you want me to be mad at all of your friends?" Grady asked.

"No—I want to know why you're so much harder on Keefe. Now that you know what he's been through . . . why won't you cut him some slack?"

Grady let out a sigh that seemed to drain all the air from his body. "Okay, if you want to have this conversation, I guess we can."

"What conversation?" Sophie asked.

Grady raised an eyebrow. "About boys."

FORTY-FIVE

BOYS?" SOPHIE REPEATED, TRYING TO come up with any other meaning for the word besides the one Grady's raised eyebrow implied.

"Yeah, it's always awkward to talk about this stuff with your parents," he told her. "But remember, I went through this with Jolie. I know it's not easy dealing with . . . feelings."

"He means crushes," Sandor clarified, just to add the final nail to her coffin of misery.

"Ugggggggggggghhhhhhh—seriously, *why* are we talking about this?" Sophie asked, wondering if she could slip past Sandor if she sprinted for the door.

Sandor and Grady shared a look.

"We're talking about it because you asked why I'm harder on That B—on *Keefe*," Grady said.

"He seems to be *special* to you," Sandor added. "And he also happens to be a very good-looking boy—for an elf."

"THIS IS THE WORST EVER!" Sophie shouted, flopping back on her bed and pulling her hair over her face to hide.

"I'm right there with you, kiddo. If I had my way, you wouldn't get your match lists until you're at least a hundred. *But* even if I got my wish on that, I also know that feelings . . . happen."

"Well, they're not happening here. He's. My. *Friend.*"

"That's often how it starts," Sandor said. "And then the friendship turns to teasing and the teasing turns to flirting and—"

"Yeah, but this is Keefe," Sophie interrupted. "In case you haven't noticed, he teases *everyone*. It doesn't mean anything. Especially with me."

"You really believe that, don't you?" Grady asked, glancing at Sandor when she nodded.

"If you guys look at each other like that again I'm going to punch you," Sophie warned. "And I'm still wearing my Sucker Punch!"

"Look at each other like what?" Sandor asked.

"Like . . . *Isn't she cute?*"

"You *are* cute." Grady took both of her hands and pulled her back to a sitting position. "And you're sure there's nothing you want to tell me? I promise I won't freak out."

"Kinda sounds like you would. *Not* that it matters, but aren't

386

you basically telling me that you don't approve of Keefe? Isn't that why I'm grounded?"

"You're grounded because you nearly gave me a panic meltdown," Grady told her. "And it's not about *approval*. This is your life. You'll get to choose who you share it with. But I will say this: *Anyone* who wants to be special to you should have to prove that they deserve you. Not just Keefe—though he'll definitely have more of an uphill battle. I'd be saying the same thing if we were talking about someone else. Like . . . oh . . . I don't know. Dex? Or Fitz?"

Sophie buried her face in her hands. "Someone please kill me now."

"Uh-oh, that doesn't sound good," Edaline said as she crossed the bedroom to join them. "Do I want to know what you guys are talking about?"

"Boys," Sandor and Grady said at the same time.

"That's what I was afraid of." Edaline sat on Sophie's other side and patted her knee. "If it helps, he drove Jolie just as crazy. You should ask Vertina to share some of the horror stories."

"There's nothing wrong with making sure Sophie knows that we have high expectations for anyone she chooses," Grady said. "Another thing to keep in mind, kiddo: Whenever you start to narrow it down, I *will* be having a loooooooooooooooong conversation with him."

"Please tell me he's joking," Sophie whined to Edaline.

"Don't worry, we'll come up with a plan of attack before your first Winnowing Gala," Edaline promised.

"I have a feeling I'm *really* going to regret this question," Sophie mumbled. "But . . . what's a Winnowing Gala?"

Edaline smiled. "Whenever you pick up a new match list, it's customary to hold a party and invite everyone on the list to come, so you can start narrowing down who you might actually be interested in. We never held one for Jolie, because her mind was already made up. But if you're less decided, the gala can be a fun way to start figuring it out. I know all of this probably feels huge and embarrassing, and I promise we don't have to talk about it any more for now. But I do want to make sure you know that Grady and I will support whoever you choose."

She glared at Grady until he agreed.

"And now, we'll change the subject to something that won't make you want to tug out all of your eyelashes," Edaline said, handing Sophie a thin curled-up scroll. "This is your schedule for the Council's new skill training program. Looks like you're part of the Wednesday morning group, so you'll get a break from your grounding at least once a week. And my sister told me that Magnate Leto made sure all of your friends are in the same group."

"What group are you guys in?" Sophie asked.

"None for the moment. Our house arrest continues." She kissed Sophie's cheek before she stood and straightened the fabric of her simple blue-and-white gown.

"Are you heading out?" Grady asked.

Edaline nodded. "The gnomes told me they'd have dinner waiting for you in the kitchen, since I'll probably be home late."

"Wait, you're leaving?" Sophie asked. "I thought you just said you're on house arrest."

"I am. But I'm sneaking out to Alluveterre, where there's plenty of security to protect me. Juline made the arrangements. She didn't want to at first, but she's feeling very guilty for all the things she's hidden from me over the years."

"As she should," Grady grumbled.

Edaline took his hand. "We both know we spent the majority of that time misunderstanding the Black Swan and their role in what happened to our daughter."

Grady had once believed that the Black Swan killed Jolie to punish him for resisting their efforts to recruit him.

"Why are you going to Alluveterre?" Sophie asked.

"I need to visit Wylie. I owe it to Cyrah to try to help her son. I owed her that years ago and wasn't strong enough to fulfill it. But I'm hoping it's better late than never."

"If there's anything I can do . . . ," Sophie said.

"I promise I'll let you know." She kissed Sophie's cheek before she left with Grady, the two of them heading upstairs to the Leapmaster.

"And where do you think you're going?" Sandor asked as Sophie made her way across the room.

She pointed to her bathroom. "Am I supposed to stay in my pajamas forever?"

"I suppose not. I'll give you privacy to use the bathroom and get changed. But otherwise, consider us joined at the hip."

"Well," Sophie said, flashing her most mocking smile, "at least that means I'll get to be there for all the dancing."

Sandor grumbled under his breath as she swung her hips like Grizel.

"I think she likes you," she called through the door after she'd closed it in his face. She'd expected Sandor to deny it, but he let out a squeaky sigh.

"Grizel has gone to dramatic lengths to make that abundantly clear. She and I grew up together, and everyone assumed we'd someday settle. I'm fairly certain I'm the reason Grizel joined the elvin regiments, even though she'd been offered a position in our queen's royal guard."

The idea of a goblin queen was *almost* enough to distract Sophie—but not quite.

She finished changing and left the bathroom. "So . . . I take it that means you're not interested?"

"Interest has nothing to do with it."

"Does that mean you are? Because I actually think you two could be super cute together!"

"I can assure you, we wouldn't be," Sandor said, shadowing her as she retrieved her memory log from her desk and headed for her bed. "And I love how you're suddenly the expert on all things romantic. Moments ago you proved yourself exceptionally clueless."

"I'm not clueless. I'm . . . realistic."

"As am I. The reality is that I have no time for a companion, nor do I have need of one. I'm far better suited as a warrior than a husband. I've told Grizel as much—several times. And *that* is the end of any discussion of my love life."

"I can't believe you *have* a love life," Sophie admitted. "Talk about a mind blow."

"And why is that?" Sandor huffed. "I'll have you know that among my species I am *quite* the specimen."

Sophie giggled. "Man, I wish Keefe had been here to hear you say that."

"Interesting that he was the first boy you thought of."

"Only because he'd start calling you Specimen Sandor. I'll be sure to tell him during our next check-in."

"I'm sure you will," Sandor said. "And on that note, I'll leave you to record your memories. But I'm *right* outside should you have the slightest notion of leaving."

He marched to his usual post, and Sophie slipped under the blankets and opened her memory log. Alden had given her the familiar teal book with the silver moonlark on the cover after she'd discovered that the Black Swan had hidden secrets in her brain, so she'd have a way to keep track of any that triggered. And as she flipped through the pages, it was crazy to see how long it'd been since she'd recorded any of those kinds of discoveries. For months, everything she'd projected were clues and secrets she'd found on her own.

She closed her eyes and slowly projected everything Keefe had shown her, zooming in on the details that seemed most important, like Lady Gisela's hairpin. The silver-white stone was smooth and oval, but when the light hit it, thin veins of blue shot through in an asterisk pattern.

"Dinnertime!" Grady said, making her jump as he crossed her room carrying a tray with a bottle of lushberry juice and a bowl of what looked like pink spaghetti.

"Already?" Sophie glanced out her windows and sure enough, the sun was setting. "Ugh—I almost missed my check-in with Keefe. These are going to be hard to remember."

"I think I'll sit right here, in case you learn anything important from him," Grady told her, plopping down next to her on the bed and setting the tray in her lap.

Sophie was positive his real motive involved a whole lot of spying. But she closed her eyes and pretended he wasn't there as she stretched out her mind.

Really bad time right now, Keefe told her.

You're okay, though, right?

Yeah, I just need to pay attention.

She could feel his mind trying to close down and concentrate, so she didn't ask any more questions. But a sour taste coated her tongue.

"He can't talk right now," she told Grady as she pushed the tray of food away.

"If he was in danger, I'm sure he would've told you," Grady

said, nudging her dinner back into her lap. "At least try a few bites. Flori told me it's a rare fruit called threadleens, and she grew them especially for you. When did you guys start talking?"

Sophie stirred her dinner, hoping Grady wouldn't notice that she didn't answer. "Did you know she's Calla's niece?"

Grady nodded. "I swear the Panakes sprouts twice as many blossoms every time Flori sings."

Sophie smiled as she pictured that, and she took a small bite of the pink strings—and while it definitely wasn't as delicious as starkflower stew, it tasted spicy and tangy and made her want to keep eating.

Grady scooped up her memory log as she took another forkful. "Is this the pin Keefe's mom cut him with?"

"Yeah—any idea where Lady Gisela would've bought it?"

"Not really. Lots of places make hairpins with starstones—though I'm pretty sure the stones usually flash with green veins."

"She told Keefe it was rare."

"Well, I'll ask some of the jewelers I know in Atlantis, but I'm betting whoever made it won't admit it. See how there aren't any etchings on the metal? Most artists leave a craftsman mark, like a signature."

He flipped to the next page, which showed a wide view of the door—the cold metal surrounded by snow and shadows.

"The star only rises at Nightfall," he mumbled, pointing to the runes carved into the doorframe. "That's what these say."

Sophie repeated the phrase. "Do you think it's a riddle?"

"Riddles usually lead to a *What am I?* But I'm sure the word 'star' isn't a coincidence."

"Could it be a quote from something, then? Like how the Black Swan used 'follow the pretty bird across the sky' from that old dwarven poem?"

"If it is, I've never heard it before. But I'm definitely not an expert on those kinds of things. Maybe the Collective can show it to their dwarves to see if it sounds familiar."

Sophie hoped they would—though she was pretty sure she could guess at least part of the meaning.

Whatever Lady Gisela had built.

Whatever she'd locked away with Keefe's blood.

It was going to make the world a much darker place.

FORTY-SIX

PLEASE TELL ME YOU'VE LEARNED *something we can use,* Sophie transmitted as soon as the first rays of dawn sliced through her bedroom.

Well, good morning to you too, Keefe thought. *Is this how these extra check-ins are going to be? No 'hello'? No 'I missed you'? No 'I can't stop thinking about you'?—and don't even try denying that last one.*

Sadly, she couldn't—but not for the reason he was teasing. He'd told her during their final check-in the night before that he'd heard Fintan get an urgent hail on his Imparter and use the word "escaped" during the conversation. But when she'd asked if that meant they were planning something for Wylie, Keefe had to go because Alvar and Ruy were fighting.

You're so cute when you worry, he told her.

Sophie grit her teeth. *Be very glad I haven't figured out how to mentally smack you. It's on my list of goals.*

Fine. Forgive me for trying to have a little fun after yesterday's drama. I guess Fintan's blaming Ruy and Brant for Wylie's escape, since Brant burned one of Wylie's bonds, and Ruy was the one who was supposed to clear out all of Wylie's pockets. Brant doesn't seem to care, but Ruy's flipping out because Fintan's threatening to change their role in some big project coming up—and no, I don't know what the project is. So Ruy spent most of last night trying to convince Alvar to say that all four of them share the blame for what happened, and Alvar won't.

No honor among criminals, huh?

Nope, Alvar's all about watching his own back. So Ruy left to try to talk Trix and Umber into it. I'm assuming that means I was right and Umber was the fourth kidnapper.

Did you ever tell me what her ability is?

I probably forgot. She's a Shade. A freakishly powerful one. She puts Bangs Boy to shame—and she doesn't have stupid hair.

I thought she always hid under her cloak.

She does. But as the crowned king of good-hair land, I can tell when I'm talking to one of my rightful subjects.

That might be the most ridiculous thing you've ever said.

Doesn't mean it's not true. How else would I know that you have an adorable case of bed hair right now?

I do not!

But when she patted her hair, she was pretty sure the whole pineapple-head situation was back. She burrowed deeper under her covers. *Did you learn anything else?*

Just that it's a bad time to be asking questions. But after everyone went to sleep, I tore open the seam in my cloak and found another black disk right where you said it would be.

Did it have a different piece of the symbol on it?

Nope, it's the same marking. And I snuck out of bed and checked all the doors to see if I could figure out what the disk does. But so far no luck.

So basically . . . we lost a whole day and learned nothing.

Whoa—when did you become Little Miss Negativity?

I'm just sick of all these vague bits of information. You're sleeping under the same roof as the enemy, and we still have no idea what they're planning.

I know. I'm working on it. We just have to be—

If you say "patient," I'm ending this conversation.

Yeah, I sound like the Forklenator—and don't go into shock, but . . . I think I'm starting to understand what he means. Look at what happened with Wylie. The Neverseen made their move, and they botched it. And now the Black Swan will make sure they never get another shot at it.

Uh . . . isn't that good?

For us, yeah. But not for the Neverseen. That's the thing—if Fintan gets too suspicious of me, I'll ruin my chance and that'll be it. So I have to make sure I wait until the time is right.

Wow, who are you and what have you done with Keefe Sencen?

Is all of this wisdom killing my cool cred?

A little. But . . . wise Keefe has a way better shot of getting out of this alive.

Oh, I'm getting out of this—unless the food here kills me. These kernalfruits we just harvested taste like banshee droppings. Next time I fake-join an evil organization, remind me to choose one that hasn't angered the gnomes, okay?

She could see the shriveled green fruit in his mind, and it looked like a cross between a pomegranate and an ear of corn—which wouldn't have been *that* bad, if the grains of fruit hadn't been coated in a black powder that looked way too much like mold.

How about you go get something good from the kitchen and describe it as you eat it? he asked.

Yeah, I'm not going to do that.

Aw, come on, Foster—I'm starving here!

He spent the rest of their conversation recounting the horrible things he'd had to eat over the last few weeks.

The whining resumed that night, during their dinner check-in—though Sophie couldn't blame him. Keefe's meal consisted of slimy, withered leaves that tasted like sneeze.

I'll keep snacks in my pocket, she promised. *That way if we meet up again, I can share.*

As if I needed another reason to wish you were here.

Shouldn't you be wishing you were here—*where the food is good and there aren't any crazy murderers running free?*

That does sound nice. But the crazy murderers are useful. I learned something from Fintan today—not what I was hoping to find out, but it's still important. He started venting about Brant and Ruy, and how frustrating it is to work with people who disappoint him again and again. And then he said he's counting on me to live up to my potential.

Potential for what?

He didn't say. But I took a chance and asked if he wanted me to do the Empath-lie-detector thing when he meets with King Dimitar. I told him I was worried the ogres were going to double-cross us, and he seemed impressed that I was thinking about things like that. He said it's good to see that I care so strongly about his vision—and of course he didn't say what his vision is. But he draped his arm around my shoulders—

UGH!

Yeah—I wanted to shove him away, trust me. But I held still and listened while he told me he's worried about the ogres too. And then he said that he gave King Dimitar an assignment to prove they can work together—kind of like a test.

Sophie sat up straighter. *That's perfect! We need to find out what that test is and make sure the ogres fail!*

Working on it, Keefe promised. *But I'm assuming whatever the ogres are up to will involve someone getting hurt, so no ditching Gigantor, okay?*

Like I could. Did I mention you got me grounded? I've been stuck in my room all day with nothing to do except stare at my memory log. And Sandor's standing next to me right now, telling me he wants to know everything you're saying.

Aw, give him a kiss for me—and I'm not saying that to be a brat. I'm seriously glad he's there to protect you. Everyone else has a bodyguard, right? Fitz? Biana? Dex? Grady? Edaline? Alden? Della?

Everyone except Alden and Della. But they rarely leave their house, so they're safe.

I don't know. The gates at Everglen are designed to block people from light leaping in. That won't stop ogres from popping out of the ground.

She closed her eyes, trying to squeeze out the nightmare scene Keefe had just painted. *I'll ask the Collective to send some additional guards for the Vackers—maybe dwarves, so the Neverseen won't notice any changes if they're watching. I swear, at this rate, our group has more security than the Council. Seems unfair, doesn't it?*

What do you mean?

I don't know. It's just . . . we spent hours prepping Havenfield to keep my family safe—and while we were doing that, the Neverseen snatched Wylie out of his room and tortured him.

I'm so sorry I messed that up. I'd heard them talk so much about your family that when Fintan said we were ready to shift to the next phase, I thought—

The next phase of what? Sophie interrupted.

400

The Lodestar Initiative.

Wait. Whatever they're planning to do to my family is part of the Lodestar Initiative? I thought the Neverseen only wanted to take them so they could control me.

That's probably part of it. But it's starting to feel like they're doing some sort of . . . gathering. It's almost like Fintan has this list of people and information he needs, and he's checking them off one by one.

Sophie's mind flashed to the cell Dex had been held in at the Paris hideout.

Was this what the room had been meant for?

You okay over there? Keefe asked. *You've gone quiet on me.*

I'm just trying to think. Is Wylie's kidnapping—and maybe his mom's death—also part of the Lodestar Initiative?

That's what I'm assuming.

He made it sound so obvious—and maybe it was. But Sophie hadn't considered the connection. Her brain throbbed under the weight of a thousand new questions.

How's Wylie doing by the way? Keefe asked.

About the same. Edaline saw him yesterday and said his wounds looked healed, but his thoughts were still so dark that they're going to keep him sedated for at least another day.

And they don't want to erase his memories?

Wylie told us not to. He wants to make sure we don't get rid of anything that could help us find out what happened to his mom.

That's . . . very brave.

Keefe's mind flashed to his nine-year-old self, curled up in a ball under the covers as he waited for the Washer to come erase his memories.

You can't compare the two, Sophie told him.

He didn't agree. But Keefe stuffed the memory away, his mind practically forcing a smile as he told her, *Fintan's supposed to come to this hideout tonight for a strategy meeting, so it's probably not a good idea to do another check-in until tomorrow morning. And be prepared for some breakfast whining. We harvested something called yolksnips today—and they smelled exactly like Iggy farts.*

Apparently they tasted like them too. But Keefe barely mentioned them when Sophie connected with his mind at daybreak. He was too excited to share his news.

He still hadn't learned anything about the test for the ogres, or Wylie, or the plan for Grady and Edaline, or Brant and Ruy's punishment, or Fintan's cache, or any of the things that had kept Sophie up most of the night.

BUT, Keefe said, his mental voice so loud, it echoed around her head. *I've finally been granted clearance to move into one of their other hideouts. You're now talking to a fully initiated member of the Neverseen!*

FORTY-SEVEN

DOES THAT MEAN KEEFE SWORE an oath?" Fitz asked, careful to keep his voice low in the crowded Foxfire field. "Like we did when we were accepted into the Black Swan?"

"I was afraid to ask," Sophie admitted.

She glanced around, relieved to find everyone too distracted by the proceedings to pay attention to her group of friends—and their bodyguards. Still, she huddled closer to Fitz, Dex, Biana, Tam, and Linh as she added, "He said he'll be settled at the new hideout this afternoon."

The crowd surged forward as another batch of people moved to take their test, halting their conversation. It was the first day of their Exillium skill training, and while Sophie and her friends already knew their Hemispheres, everyone else was being sorted by a written exam before being given a black cape marked with a colored handprint on the back.

Red for the Left Hemisphere, blue for the Right, and purple for the Ambis.

The three Exillium tents bore the same colors. And after so many years of scorn and judgment, it seemed strangely reassuring to have the vibrant canopies stationed proudly around the glass pyramid.

Still, Sophie found her eyes constantly drifting to the twisted gold and silver elite towers. The Black Swan had stuck to their plan and kept Wylie's assault a secret, so no one around them had any idea about the added danger. Even with dozens of goblins stationed among the crowd—even with a fleet of dwarves secretly positioned under their feet—Lur and Mitya had yet to figure out how the Neverseen had gotten inside the tower. So the rebels still had a secret way to invade the campus.

"Maybe the Neverseen use a vague oath," Linh whispered when the crowd settled again. "Like the one the Black Swan had us say."

"Hopefully," Biana said. "And wait—does that mean you guys swore fealty?"

Both twins revealed the swan-shaped monocle pendants they'd tucked under their tunics.

"I was sick of Linh nagging me," Tam said, earning an eye

roll from his sister, and a sudden splash of water to the face. "Oh, it is *so* on later."

"Ready any time you are," Linh told him, tossing another sphere of water back and forth from palm to palm.

"Wow," Fitz whispered, as Dex leaned closer.

"Are we sure this is a good thing?" he asked. "Not the part about you guys joining the Black Swan—that's *awesome*. But the whole 'Keefe going to one of their serious hideouts' thing. Is he sure they won't lock him away like they did to his mom?"

"I asked him the same question," Sophie said. "And he promised he's keeping a close read on everyone's emotions. He said he'll bail if he senses anything suspicious."

"But *how* does he bail?" Biana asked. "They're not going to let him walk away now."

Fitz shared a look with Sophie. "We may have to help him get out of there—but we can't come up with a plan until we know more about where he is. So right now, we're just hoping he's being careful."

Tam snorted. "Zero chance of that."

"Probably," Sophie whispered. "But he's taking this crazy risk to help us. So we need to get the most out of it that we can."

"You told him to watch for shadows on the floor of the hideout, right?" Tam asked. "To see if they use an illuminated symbol like the one in Paris?"

Sophie nodded. "Keefe has a photographic memory. So I

told him to make sure he takes a good look at *everything*. Then he'll share it with me and I'll project it all on paper so you can check the shadows. But you'll have to come to Havenfield to see it. I'm still grounded."

Biana grinned. "So is Fitz. My dad told him he's not allowed to go anywhere until he finishes his matchmaking packet."

"Too bad for him, I finished it yesterday," Fitz said smugly.

"You did?" Sophie, Biana, Dex, and Linh asked at the same time.

Fitz shrugged. "It's not like it's hard. I just had to answer some personal questions."

"A *lot* of them," Biana said. "Aren't you worried that if you rush through, you won't give very good answers?"

"Nah. I know what I like. Besides, the questions aren't what you'd think they'd be. Sure, they ask what you find attractive, and what personality traits you like and stuff. But then it gets into all kinds of things about your genetics and abilities, and finishes with a ton of questions that are just . . . *deep*. It's like they're trying to get to know you on another level—which I guess makes sense, since we fill out the packets when we're sixteen. Our likes and dislikes are probably going to change, so they're trying to figure out the *real* us."

"You're sixteen?" Linh asked.

Dex mumbled something about Fitz being super old as Biana turned to Tam. "I don't think you guys ever told us how old you are."

Both twins had to think for a second.

"Pretty sure we're fifteen," Linh said. "It's hard to remember, thanks to my father. He was always trying to convince us that we had our inception date wrong."

"Good old Dad," Tam muttered, scanning the crowd, like he was checking to make sure his parents weren't there. "Uh, do you guys know that girl off to the right? She's staring at us pretty hard."

All of their goblins reached for their swords.

"Relax—it's just Marella," Sophie told them, dropping her voice before she added, "She's the one whose mom saw Cyrah the day she faded."

"And she's not staring at *us*," Biana corrected. "She's checking out Tam."

Tam's eyebrows shot up, and he stole another glance. Marella tossed her long blond hair—which always had a few tiny braids woven in—and gave him her flirtiest smile.

"Huh," he said.

"That's all you have to say?" Biana pressed.

"I don't know." Tam blushed brighter than Sophie would've thought possible, given his general surly demeanor. "What am I supposed to say?"

"She's not his type," Linh jumped in. "He likes brunettes."

"Gross, why do you know that?" Tam asked.

Linh smirked. "Because you're not as sly as you think."

"Is anyone else wondering why Marella's not hanging out

with Stina anymore?" Sophie asked, rescuing Tam with a subject change.

"Stina's the tall girl over there," Biana explained to the twins, tilting her head to where Stina's unruly curls stuck out above the crowd. "Her dad works with the Black Swan, so you'd *think* she'd be nice. But she still thinks she's better than everybody. And ugh, looks like she's in the Left Hemisphere. Guess that means Fitz and I get to watch her try to show off all day."

"Who's the other girl she's with?" Linh asked. "She's staring at Sophie too."

"Really?" Sophie asked, waiting before she turned to see who Linh meant. It took her a second to recognize the pretty black girl beside Stina—especially with the blue streak she'd added to her straightened hair. "That's Maruca."

"There's a Marella and a Maruca?" Tam asked. "Yeah . . . I'm never going to be able to keep that straight."

"You probably won't have to," Biana said. "Marella's been avoiding us for a while. And Maruca and I haven't talked in months—ever since I told her I couldn't trust her. She blabbed a bunch of my secrets to get back at me for becoming friends with Sophie."

Tam whistled. "Girls and your drama."

"Right—because you and Keefe get along so well." Linh flicked his bangs. "And maybe I'm just imagining this but . . . doesn't Maruca look sad?"

Sophie had to agree. Maruca's turquoise eyes were glassy, and her full lips were pressed into a tight line.

And she was still staring at them.

"Think we should go over to her?" Sophie asked.

Biana shook her head. "If she needs to talk to us, she can come over here."

Maruca didn't.

But she didn't stop staring, either.

The whole thing felt very unsettling, and Sophie was relieved when a deep voice boomed above the crowd, directing everyone's attention to where Magnate Leto hovered above them. His levitation was wobblier than he probably wanted—and his feet nearly grazed the crowd's heads—but he managed to hold himself steady despite the strong breeze that kept whipping his long black cape—marked with a purple handprint—around his legs.

"Welcome to your first round of skill training!" he said. "A momentous step in our world's history! I'll be practicing along with you, so I'm turning this session over to your talented Coaches. Everyone, please show them how much we appreciate their efforts."

Scattered applause greeted three figures as they rose from the tents and floated to where Magnate Leto had just been hovering—one wearing a long red cape, another in a long blue cape, and the third in a long purple cape. The Coaches' levitation was flawless—so smooth, they might as well have been standing on solid ground.

"Those in the Left Hemisphere will be training with me," the red Coach said, her voice even raspier than Sophie remembered it. Her auburn hair was cropped into a sleek, angled bob, and she had thick black eyeliner rimming her pale blue eyes, giving her words an air of drama as she told them, "All of you are welcome to call me Coach Wilda."

"I'm Coach Bora," the blue Coach added, his high, nasal voice a strange contrast to his slicked blond hair, olive tone, and sharply angled features. "I'll be working with the Right Hemispheres over there." He pointed to the blue canopy.

"Which of course means that all of you Ambis are with me," the purple Coach said with a smile. Her long black hair was so shiny it seemed to glow against her cinnamon-toned skin. "I'm Coach Rohana. And yes, for those wondering, it *is* essential that you train with your designated Hemisphere, regardless of where your friends or family might have been sorted. All three groups will be practicing the same skills, but you've been separated by your learning style so that we'll be able to tailor your lessons for maximum efficiency."

"It's important that you not let yourselves get frustrated if you don't immediately succeed at what we're teaching," Coach Wilda added. "The Council has asked us to focus on a particular skill—one that, for most of you, will be an entirely new way of using your mind."

"The lessons will be grueling," Coach Rohana promised. "At times they may even be confounding. But this process is about

410

stepping-stones and building blocks that piece together with time and patience to achieve a new kind of strength."

Each Coach removed a tennis-ball-size glass orb from their cloak pockets and held the clear spheres in front of them.

When they narrowed their eyes, all three orbs exploded into a million glinting fragments.

"What you've just witnessed is one manifestation of a skill we call outward channeling," Coach Wilda shouted over the gasps. "It harnesses a power limited only by our concentration and commitment. For instance . . ."

Coach Bora pulled a metal orb from his pocket and held it in front of him.

The orb exploded, sending flakes of metal raining like confetti—or maybe "shrapnel" was a better description.

"Nothing can be spared from the will of a skilled mind," Coach Bora told them. "Not crystal. Not metal. Not stone. Not even flesh and bone."

"Did . . . they just admit they're training us to kill?" Sophie whispered to her friends.

"Sure sounded like it," Fitz mumbled.

"Indeed it did," Sandor said, glancing at the other bodyguards.

Their expressions were hard to read. Nervous? Angry?

"We sense your unease," Coach Rohana told the crowd. "And applaud you for it. Fear breeds restraint and responsibility. But it will not change the fact that this is a skill we each possess naturally. Saber-toothed tigers have claws and fangs. Peluda dragons have poison quills. Even the fragile flitterwings have venom in their tiny teeth. They do not fear these gifts. Yes, some creatures use such things to hunt and others to defend themselves. But either choice doesn't change the fact that the power exists."

Sophie could see the logic behind her reasoning. But it still felt like giving everyone guns and hoping they didn't shoot each other.

And then she remembered Keefe telling her that his Never-seen training included hardcore skill lessons . . .

Were *they* mastering outward channeling?

"It's also important to note that power is not a new feature of our world," Coach Wilda reminded them. "Many of our special abilities could cause tremendous damage should we choose to use them for such. That doesn't mean we shy away from ability training, does it?"

"Our goals here are simple," Coach Bora added. "We want you to understand your strength and to be able to call on it should you need it. And together, we want to show the world that—whether they like it or not—*we* are the strongest creatures. We do not need weapons or armor. Only the strength of our mind and the discipline and determination to master it."

Murmurs rose among the crowd—most sounding like agreement. But Sophie kept remembering Lady Cadence's warnings to the Council.

Maybe the elves would be proving their strength. Or maybe they were about to throw a match in a room full of kindling.

"You look . . . concerned," she whispered to Sandor as the Coaches instructed everyone to head to their assigned tents.

"I am. I'm not sure how I'm supposed to protect you from an attack of this nature—especially one to flesh or bone. And if crystal and stone are also vulnerable, what's to stop someone from exploding the ground we're standing on, or shattering a building around us?"

"Our own natural limitations," Magnate Leto said, sneaking up beside them. "There's a reason the Coaches chose small orbs for their demonstration. The larger the object, the more energy it takes to destroy it. And while our minds can hold an incredible amount of energy, we also drain most of it through normal daily activities. There are ways to build reserves, of course, but they take a tremendous amount of time and discipline. Very few have such skill or patience. So for most, this power will be saved for an especially desperate moment. Nothing more. And now, I must mingle among the other Ambis, lest someone suspect I have favorite prodigies."

He winked as he walked away, heading for the far side of the purple tent.

Sophie followed Tam and Linh to the back, where they used to train when they all went to Exillium together.

Halfway there, Tam and Linh froze, their widened eyes fixed on two figures.

A couple with jet-black hair and silvery eyes.

Tam and Linh's parents.

FORTY-EIGHT

"WELL," TAM'S FATHER SAID, fidgeting with his cloak pin—two silver-and-black dire wolves craning their necks in a graceful howl. "This is unexpected."

"It is and it isn't," Tam said, his eyes scanning the crowd until he found Magnate Leto, who looked . . . slightly guilty. "But I'll make it easy."

Tam took Linh's hand and turned to walk away.

Their mother grabbed his arm. "Please. Maybe we should—"

Tam jerked free of her hold. "No. We shouldn't."

She dropped her eyes to the ground—her slender fingers still lingering in the air as her husband reached for her. There was tenderness in the gesture. A soft gentleness in the way he cradled his wife's shaky hand, tracing his thumb across her palm.

The love between them was obvious. Even a little sweet.

But it made the tight fist of his other hand so much more heartbreaking as he glared at his children.

"Apologize to your mother. And stop making a scene!" He glanced nervously over his shoulder at the other Ambis watching.

Tam shook his head. "It's always about appearances with you."

"Please," their mother begged as they turned away again. "I never asked for the situation that was handed to me. I've never claimed I handled it well."

"That's what we are now?" Linh whispered. "A situation?"

Her mom cleared her throat. "What do you want to be?"

"Nothing," Tam said. "Absolutely nothing."

"Then you're doing a good job," his father told him, frowning at Tam's silver bangs. Both of the twins had melted their registry necklaces and dipped their hair in the molten metal as proof that they didn't need the family that left them to fend for themselves.

Tam pulled the silver over his eyes. "You like the look?"

His father shook his head. He didn't have the arrogance of Lord Cassius, or the unsettling smile or stare. All he looked was tired.

"Children are supposed to respect their parents," he said quietly.

Linh pulled Tam away. "Respect has to be earned."

"Wait," their mom begged. "Just wait."

Linh glanced over her shoulder. "We waited for more than three years."

"I know," her mother whispered. "You look so much older."

"That's what happens when you leave your kids alone with nowhere to live and nothing to eat," Sophie snapped, no longer able to bite her tongue. She knew this moment fell into the none-of-her-business category. But she'd already watched one friend unravel because of his horrible family. She wasn't going to let it happen to Tam and Linh.

"Whatever excuses you've given yourselves," she told the Songs, "whatever lies you've let yourself believe—this is the truth, right in front of you. You have two incredibly talented, smart, powerful kids who don't need you anymore. And if you ever want them in your life again, you have to earn it."

"How?" both of the Songs asked.

Sophie shrugged. "You have to figure it out for yourselves or it won't mean anything. Come on," she told Tam and Linh, taking their hands. "We have better places to be."

"I can't believe you said that," Linh whispered as they moved to a spot in the front of the tent and Sandor stood behind her, creating a wall of muscle between them and the Songs.

Sophie lowered her eyes. "Sorry if I shouldn't have interfered."

"No—you absolutely should have," Tam said.

Linh nodded. "The look on my father's face—that was the greatest gift you ever could've given me."

"I wish I could do more." It didn't seem fair that Sophie had been given *two* loving families, when so many of her friends hadn't even gotten *one*. And for all she knew, her genetic parents were also awesome—though that was a little harder to believe, given the whole never-meeting-their-daughter-and-letting-her-be-experimented-on thing.

"Dude," a voice said behind her. "Am I in the same Hemisphere as the Great Sophie Foster? Never thought that would happen!"

Sophie turned and found a familiar face grinning at her near one of the tent poles.

"Guys, this is Jensi. And Jensi, this is Tam and Linh," Sophie introduced.

"Cool!—I love your hair!" Jensi practically shouted. "Is that real silver?—And wait—are you from Exillium?—Is that where you met Sophie?—What's it like there?"

Jensi had a way of talking like he'd drunk a dozen bottles of caffeinated soda. Tam and Linh were naturally overwhelmed.

"Jensi was one of the first people to help me find my way around Foxfire," Sophie explained. "Though I haven't seen him around much lately."

Jensi's round cheeks flushed, and he ran a hand through his messy brown hair. "Sorry—you're just always so busy—and I figured I fit in better with the Drooly Boys, anyway."

"You fit in wherever you *want*," Sophie told him. "Though, for the record, I've never seen a drop of drool on your chin."

Coach Rohana strode into ·the tent before Jensi could respond, carrying a big bag of purple splotchers. The Ping-Pong-ball-size orbs were like squishy paintballs, and had Sophie hoping the day's exercise would give her a chance to hurl a few at Tam and Linh's parents.

"Outward channeling requires a different understanding of your power," Coach Rohana said, rolling a splotcher around the palm of her hand. "The method you've all learned for telekinesis taught you to gather energy from deep within your core and then thrust it out with your mind, controlling the force as though the energy were an extension of your existing limbs. But you need to stop thinking of the energy as *core* energy. It's simply *your* energy—and it does not need to remain connected to you in order for you to manipulate it. In fact, it's far more powerful when you bury it in other things. For instance"—her eyes narrowed at the splotcher in her hand—"you can hide it here, letting it swell and surge until . . ."

The splotcher erupted, splattering her with purple.

"It's a bizarre concept, I realize," she said, wiping the paint off her cheeks. "And it will take time for your minds to accomplish it. In fact, I'd wager that most of you will not burst any splotchers today. We're providing them mostly to give you a goal—a first stepping-stone to strive for. But there's nothing wrong with needing several baby steps before you get there. Try to trust your instincts. Also don't be surprised if you find the process exhausting. Please take breaks if you need them. Everyone ready?" She handed the bag of splotchers to Jensi.

He grabbed enough for Sophie, Tam, and Linh before he passed the bag along and plopped next to Sophie on the purple grass. "Maybe I can absorb some of your awesomeness," he said, then told Tam and Linh about Sophie's performance during the Ultimate Splotching Championship. "Flung herself and Fitz into the wall and knocked them out cold!"

Linh laughed. "Sounds like Sophie's caused almost as many disasters as I have."

"You should come to Foxfire!" Jensi said. "You two could have a Chaos Competition—it would be epic!—Or wait—*can* you come back to Foxfire?"

Linh glanced over her shoulder at her parents. "When we're ready."

"Let's get started!" Coach Rohana called. "Place your splotcher on the ground in front of you and clear your head. I won't be giving you any specific pointers, because it's far better for you to find your own natural trick. But try to understand that your body is not an impermeable vessel holding a well of energy. It's a stake in the ground, marking the epicenter of your own personal energy cloud."

"Does Exillium training always sound this loony?" Jensi asked. "Or is this extra weird?"

"It's extra weird," Tam said.

"I don't know. I kinda get it." Linh furrowed her brow as she stared at her splotcher. "It's like how water is both without and within."

"Uh, sure . . . ," Jensi said.

Tam laughed. "Don't worry. I don't understand half the stuff my sister says."

Sophie was just as confused. But she tried to imagine her energy like a seed, and pictured herself planting it in the center of the splotcher. She hummed a song in her head to make it grow, letting the energy spread through the paint like roots through soil and . . .

. . . the splotcher burst with a squish of purple.

Jensi pumped his fist. "Told you she'd kick our butts!"

"Telepaths tend to catch on faster at this," Coach Rohana said, handing Sophie a cloth to wipe the paint off her face. "Their minds naturally hold a much larger reserve of energy, which can make it easier to transfer—though this could be a new record."

Sophie glanced at Magnate Leto, and he offered an unsurprised smile.

"Normally I'd tell you to rest, since most would find their energy depleted," Coach Rohana added. "But after such an effortless display, I'm curious to see if you can continue."

She handed Sophie a new splotcher, making her promise to take a break if she got a headache. But Sophie felt fine.

And when she planted another "seed," the splotcher splattered purple everywhere.

Coach Rohana tilted her head. "I suspect you could bring down a mountain if you sat in solitude long enough."

"Why solitude?" Tam asked.

"No distractions or activities to drain her reserve." Their Coach offered Sophie a third splotcher, and—while it took significantly longer—Sophie still managed to burst it like the others.

Only two other Ambis burst their splotchers before the end of the lesson: Magnate Leto and—surprisingly—Jensi.

"I think my osmosis theory worked," Jensi said, bouncing on the balls of his feet. "Unless this means I'm going to manifest as a Telepath—which would be *awesome!*—though I'd kinda been rooting for Phaser—like my brother—or maybe a Charger—or . . ."

He continued naming abilities, but Sophie had stopped listening, too aware of everyone watching her.

"I know what you're feeling," Linh whispered. "I've often wondered if I have more power than I should. But I stopped worrying about it after I flooded Ravagog."

"Whoa—that was you?" Jensi butted in.

Linh nodded. "First time I've ever been glad to hold so much power. And you'll do far greater things with yours," she told Sophie.

Sophie thanked her, not sure why she felt so . . . ruffled. This definitely wasn't the first time she'd discovered that her mental powers were a little too close to the scary side of the line.

But something about this skill felt *wrong*—like the elves were setting aside everything they'd believed in and going darker.

And there she was: the poster child for the New Darkness.

Jensi bounded off to brag to the Drooly Boys as soon as the Coaches dismissed them, and Sandor agreed to let Sophie stay to say goodbye to her friends. Tam and Linh lingered with her—until they noticed their parents heading over. They leaped away with seconds to spare.

The Songs were too intimidated to approach Sophie, especially when Fitz and Biana—and their bodyguards—joined her. Fitz seemed especially bummed to hear about Sophie's three-splotcher session. The most he'd accomplished was making his splotcher quiver.

Sophie was giving him a few pointers when a smug voice behind them asked, "Waiting for Dizznee?"

Sophie fought off a sigh as she turned to find Stina—and Maruca. "Why do you care?"

"I don't," Stina said. "But I figured *you* might—especially since I saw him pull Marella aside after the lesson. They've been whispering ever since. Jealous, Foster?"

Sophie rolled her eyes. "Since when are you and Marella back to being friends?"

Stina's smug expression faltered. "We never stopped. She's

just . . . having a hard time now that I manifested as an Empath."

"Oh."

Sophie wasn't sure if it was her, Fitz, or Biana who'd said it—but they had to all be thinking it. Stina had a long history of Empaths on her mother's side of the family, so the news wasn't unexpected. But poor Marella had been trying for years to trigger the ability, in the hopes that she might be able to help her mom better control her emotions.

"That's rough," Sophie mumbled.

Stina nodded. "I wish she'd manifest already—even if she doesn't get the ability she wants. It's a million times harder with all the constantly wondering *What if?*, you know?"

Sophie did know. And before she could think of what to say, she realized Maruca had gone back to staring at her.

Stina elbowed her friend. "Just say it, already. That's why you made me come over here."

Maruca nodded.

She cleared her throat so many times it almost sounded painful. Then she told Sophie, "I need you to take me to see Wylie."

FORTY-NINE

NO ONE'S GOING ANYWHERE," Sandor said, placing a heavy hand on Sophie's shoulder. Grizel and Woltzer held on to Fitz and Biana as well.

Sophie dragged Sandor with her as she moved closer to Maruca, hoping her glare hid her lie as she whispered, "I don't know why you're talking to me about this."

"Yes you do." Maruca waited for a nearby group of Left Hemispheres to wander further away before she added, "Stina told me the Neverseen attacked Wylie, and that the Black Swan have him hidden away."

"Don't look at me like that," Stina told Sophie. "I overheard my dad whispering about it—and Wylie is Maruca's family. She deserved to know what was happening."

"Wylie's your family?" Biana asked.

Maruca nodded. "I never said anything because there was so much weirdness with him and your dad. But he's my second cousin—and my mom used to take me to visit him all the time. She's freaking out right now—"

"Wait, you told your *mom*?" Stina interrupted. "You promised you wouldn't tell anyone!"

"That was before I knew what the secret was," Maruca told her. "I can't hide this from my family—no matter what I said."

She had a point. Some problems were too important to worry about breaking promises.

But Sophie still couldn't help her.

"I'm not allowed to talk about this," she whispered. "Maybe you should ask Stina's dad."

"Oh please, you know my dad's not going to tell us anything," Stina argued. "He'll just ground me for eavesdropping."

"You should've thought of that before you did it," Fitz told her.

Stina snorted. "Like you've never listened to your dad's secret conversations."

"Oh, I have," Fitz said. "But I'm always prepared to be busted if I get caught."

"Who cares about getting caught?" Maruca asked—her voice more hiss than whisper. "My mom is ready to go to the Council—"

"She can't do that!" Sophie interrupted. She checked to make sure Magnate Leto was deep in conversation with the Coaches on the other side of the field before she whispered, "The Black Swan don't want the Council to know this happened."

"Then bring us to see him," Maruca said.

"Is that a threat?" Biana asked.

Maruca shrugged, tucking her blue strip of hair behind her ear. "If that's what it takes to see Wylie."

"But you're threatening the wrong person," Sophie told her. "I don't have a crystal to get to the place where they're keeping him."

"Even if that's true, if anyone can make it happen, it's *you*," Maruca insisted. "You're their suncatcher—or their boobrie—or whatever weird bird they call you."

"It's a moonlark," Fitz told her. "Though now I'm kinda wishing they'd called it Project Boobrie."

Sophie was too stressed to smile. "You're overestimating how much the Black Swan listen to me," she told Maruca. "They shoot me down *all* the time—and they've been especially difficult about Wylie."

Maruca bit her lip. "All I'm asking is for you to try. Please. I know you don't know me—and that I haven't been very nice to you. But I need to see him. I need to know for sure that he's okay—that they haven't finally broken him."

The catch in her voice crumbled Sophie's resolve.

"Fine. I'll hail the Collective when I get home and see if they'd be willing to arrange something."

"Why not hail them now?" Maruca pressed.

Sophie pointed to the groups of kids hanging out all around them. "Because we shouldn't even be talking about this at *all* right now."

"Then let me go to your house with you," Maruca begged. "I'm not saying I don't trust you. I just might be able to help you convince them."

"She is pretty pushy," Fitz said. "It might be kind of fun to sic her on the Collective."

Sophie rubbed her temples. "If they say no, you have to promise you'll leave it at that, okay? Or find someone else to hassle about it."

Maruca nodded and Sophie pulled out her home crystal.

Stina looped her arm through Sophie's. "I'm going with you guys."

"So am I," Fitz said.

"What about Dex?" Biana asked. "He'll be sad if we all go without him."

"Then why don't you stay here," Fitz suggested. "I'll meet you back at Everglen as soon as we're done and we can trade stories."

"Yeah, I want a full update," Sophie told Biana, pointing to where she'd spotted Dex and Marella talking.

Marella had her face turned away, so it was a little hard to tell.

But Sophie could've sworn she was crying.

Sophie couldn't hail Mr. Forkle, since he was still in Magnate Leto disguise at Foxfire. So she reached out to Granite.

"Whoa," Maruca whispered when Sandor and Grizel opened the door to let Granite in. "That's a *crazy* disguise."

"It is," he said, his limbs cracking as he followed them into the living room. "And I'm trusting you not to tell anyone you've seen me like this."

"Why?" Maruca asked. "It's not like I know who you are."

"We still prefer the public know as little about our organization as possible." He turned to Sophie. "Where are your parents?"

"Out with the new stegosaurus that arrived this morning. Why—did you need them?"

"Not at the moment. I'm just glad to hear they're well and safe. And I need all of you to understand that ordinarily I would never agree to a meeting like this. The only reason I did is because I know how much your family matters to Wylie," he told Maruca. "And as it happens, Physic will be easing Wylie off the sedatives tomorrow. We've sheltered him as long as we can, but it's time for him to begin returning to reality. And it might be helpful for him to have a few familiar faces there when he wakes up—if you think you and your mother would be up for it."

"We are," Maruca assured him, wiping away a few tears. "We'll do whatever he needs. What time and where should we meet and how—"

"I'll send instructions to your house as soon as I've spoken with Physic," Granite interrupted. "Keep an eye out for a scroll tomorrow morning."

"Can I go too?" Sophie asked.

"I think it's best that we not overwhelm him," Granite said. "Plus, I fear that once he sees you, he'll grow too fixated on the favor he requested."

"What favor?" Stina and Maruca asked.

"*That* is classified," Granite told them. "As is tomorrow's meeting. No one can know that it's happening, aside from your immediate families. And speaking of which"— he stalked closer to Stina— "in the future, I hope you'll pay more respect to your father's privacy. Overhearing something does not give you the right to repeat it to others."

To her credit, Stina kept her head held high as she told him. "Maruca needed to know."

"Then you should've informed your father and let him handle the matter through proper channels. We are an *order*, Miss Heks, and there are rules and protocols that must be followed."

"Is that what you say to Sophie?" Stina snapped back.

"Miss Foster has received her fair share of lectures. She's also a very special circumstance, so I would not make the mistake of putting you—or your father—in the same category. If we have reason to view your family as a security risk, we'll have no choice but to release your father from his oath. Is that what you want?"

Stina tried for a careless shrug. But Sophie could see her tremble.

Granite must've noticed too, because he nodded, promising Maruca he'd see her the next morning, before he leaped away.

"You . . . have a very weird life," Maruca told Sophie as she stared at the cloud of gravelly dust he'd left in his wake.

"Tell me something I don't know," Sophie mumbled.

And things got even weirder after Maruca and Stina left. Fitz was just getting ready to head home when they heard another knock on the front door and found Councillor Oralie standing on the porch, dressed in full regal garb.

"Is this about Gethen?" Sophie asked.

Oralie smiled. "It's nice to see you too."

"Sorry," Sophie said, realizing how rude she was being to a Councillor. She dipped one of her embarrassingly ungraceful curtsies. "How can I help you?"

"You can call for your parents," Oralie told her as Sophie stepped aside to let her in. "We have much to arrange. And yes, it's about Gethen."

FIFTY

YOU GOT US A MEETING?" SOPHIE
asked, for what had to be the fifth time. But it
was such a relief to hear it.

Oralie smiled as she smoothed her already
perfect ringlets. "Yes. I've been given clearance to escort you
and Mr. Forkle into the Lumenaria dungeons next week. I'm
still waiting to find out the exact day, but it will most likely be
Friday. And we'll only have fifteen minutes with Gethen, so
you'll need to plan your time accordingly."

"What about me?" Fitz asked.

Oralie took his hand. "I realize that you're Cognates—and that
you could be a valuable asset to the meeting. But the clearance is
limited to Sophie, Mr. Forkle, and myself. No exceptions."

"Aside from her bodyguard," Sandor corrected.

"You'll be able to escort her to the main gates of the fortress," Oralie told him. "Lumenaria's guards will take it from there."

Sandor stalked closer. "Miss Foster was assigned to *my* charge."

"Yes, I'm aware. In fact, I'm the one who recommended you for the assignment. But no one can enter the castle and view the security measures being put into place for the summit— even someone as well respected as you. As it is, Sophie and Mr. Forkle will be blindfolded during the walk to the dungeon."

"Seriously?" Sophie asked. "Do you really think we're going to tell someone about anything we see?"

"It has less to do with actuality and more to do with potential. The thing you must understand is that the leaders of every intelligent species will be present for the summit—and we don't allow them to bring their own guards, lest any be spies or traitors. But that means we can't use our regular bodyguards, either. A wholly new set of guards has been gathered, vetted, and trained specifically for the summit—after enduring a rigid approval process through the leaders of each world. We also guarantee that no one who isn't a guard—or an attendee of the summit—will set so much as a toe inside the castle now that we've begun organizing our security, in order to ensure that no one has any opportunity to plan a raid."

"Then how can you bring Sophie and Mr. Forkle to see Gethen?" Fitz asked.

"That's why I needed to talk to you," Oralie said, turning to where Grady and Edaline stood near the staircase, each covered in purple dinosaur feathers. "Sophie's presence has been requested at the summit."

Sophie felt her jaw fall open. Grady, Edaline, and Fitz did the same—and Sophie was pretty sure every goblin in the room sucked in a sharp breath.

"I know—I was just as surprised as all of you," Oralie told them. "But Sophie's unique role in many of our world's most recent challenges has aroused a certain curiosity about her among the other leaders—King Enki of the dwarves and Queen Hylda of the goblins especially. And King Dimitar has asked that he be allowed to cross-examine her regarding the events in Ravagog."

"All the more reason I should be there," Sandor argued.

"I can assure you, Sophie will have an abundance of security," Oralie promised. "*And*, because of her age, she'll be escorted by a parent or guardian."

"And you chose Mr. Forkle over us?" Grady asked.

"No, Mr. Forkle has been invited to represent the Black Swan. The order has made a name for itself in recent months, and the world leaders have requested to hear its thoughts on the negotiations as well. Miss Foster's guardian will be Miss Ruewen, if she's willing."

"Me?" Edaline asked as Grady shook his head.

"My wife is an incredible force to be reckoned with—but

of the two of us, I'm able to offer Sophie far better protection."

"Possibly," Oralie said. "But the leaders won't tolerate a Mesmer in their presence. I'm sure you can understand their reasoning."

"So you're asking me to send my wife and daughter into fraught treaty negotiations?" Grady asked.

"Actually, I'm asking Sophie and Edaline if they'd be willing to participate in a world-changing event, which will have more security than anyone could ever imagine," Oralie corrected. "And they will be the ones deciding if they will accept."

Grady scowled but didn't argue as he turned to Edaline. "You think this is crazy, right?"

"I do," she said, nervously snapping her fingers and making a Panakes blossom appear and disappear in her palm. "But I don't think I should be the one deciding. What do you think, Sophie?"

It felt like all of Sophie's insides were crawling up her throat. But she managed to mumble, "I think we have to go."

"Doesn't this technically mean that Edaline could go with you to see Gethen, then?" Fitz asked, breaking the silence that followed.

"I suppose it does," Oralie said. "But I wouldn't recommend it. I visited Gethen yesterday as I arranged the meeting with his guards, and he's far too eager to face Sophie again. Having anyone else she cares about in the room will only give him further ammunition."

"Oh yeah, I'm feeling *really* good about this visit," Grady grumbled.

"Same here," Sandor snarled.

"I've had enough encounters with Mr. Forkle to feel confident that he can handle Gethen," Oralie told both of them. "And I will provide any help I can."

"I can also handle myself," Sophie reminded everyone.

"No one is doubting your strength," Oralie told her. "It's what makes you Gethen's target."

"And Forkle's really okay with all of this?" Grady asked.

"I'm sure he will be once I inform him," Oralie said. "I have a meeting with him later this afternoon."

"Wait—he doesn't know?" Edaline asked. "How can that be?"

Oralie stole a glance at Sophie.

Sophie sighed, realizing it was time to come clean. "I . . . went to see Oralie and asked her to set up the meeting with Gethen, because I was worried that the Black Swan were missing an important opportunity. And, um, I also told her about Wylie."

The air shifted with the confession, taking on a charge that burned Sophie's throat.

"When did you and Oralie have this little heart-to-heart?" Grady asked.

Sophie fussed with her Sucker Punch. "Right before you grounded me."

Sandor's squeaky growl made the hairs on her arms prickle.

"So that means you went with her," Edaline said, turning to Fitz, who slunk back a couple of steps when Sandor growled again—along with Grizel. "Is that why you both had dirt in your hair?"

Sophie nodded. "Flori took us. And please don't be mad at her—or Fitz. It was all my idea."

Grady pinched the bridge of his nose. "I knew going through the teenage years again was going to be tricky. But I never prepared for *this*."

"*This* is me trying to stop the Neverseen from hurting people," Sophie snapped. "It's not like I'm sneaking around just for fun."

"Well," Oralie said, standing and removing a pink-wanded pathfinder from her cape. "Family debates aren't really my area of expertise. But I do hope you won't go too hard on Sophie. She was perfectly safe in my castle. And she was wise to come to me."

Grady didn't agree. As soon as Oralie left, he sent Fitz home to confess to Alden and sentenced Sophie to a week of Verdi pedicures. Which was why Sophie was elbow deep in T. rex toe jam when Mr. Forkle leaped into the pasture.

"I'm assuming you can guess why I'm here," he said quietly.

Sophie wiped her hands on her tunic. "I know what you're going to say—"

"I'm not sure you do." He cleared his throat several times before he told her, "I came here to thank you."

"You're right. *That* wasn't what I was expecting."

Tiny smile lines crinkled around his eyes. "I'm not saying I want you kids regularly disobeying my advice or sneaking away without your bodyguards—and just because everything worked out this time doesn't mean you should feel free to act on such whims whenever you feel them. *But* . . . in this case, you made the right decision."

"That doesn't get you out of pedicure duty!" Grady called from the next pasture over.

Mr. Forkle smiled. "And thus we have the cost of rebellion. Being right doesn't spare the consequences of breaking rules. But I'm happy to know you're ready to stand up for your convictions."

He stayed a few minutes longer, giving her a long lecture on the need for them to create a clear plan for the meeting with Cethen.

"We have a week," he told her. "And I'm counting on you to figure it out. You're finally stepping into the role we imagined for you. Now let's see what you can do."

FIFTY-ONE

GET READY TO WISH YOU COULD hug me, Keefe said as Sophie watched the first rays of dawn paint across the murky sky. *Actually, I'm pretty sure this is good enough news that you're going to want to kiss me—and I'm happy to accept an IOU, by the way.*

Just tell me what you learned, Sophie ordered, too tired to joke around.

Keefe had skipped both their dinner and before-bed check-ins the night before, because there was another huge argument going on with the Neverseen. So she'd been up most of the night worrying—and failing to come up with a plan to rescue him.

Fine—but you should at least have to write an epic poem in my honor. Here—I'll help you. "Ode to Keefe Sencen—that brave, lovable nut. He may not have teal eyes, but he has a really cute—"

KEEFE!

All right, fine. But I'm calling you Foster Grumpypants for the rest of this conversation. And brace yourself because I'm about to blow your mind. Are you ready for it?

I've been ready for the last five minutes.

You think you're ready. But there's no way you possibly can be.

JUST TELL ME.

Okay. Just don't say I didn't try to prepare you. Fintan gave me another cloak when he moved me to this new hideout. And by the way, it's WAY nicer over here. I actually have my own room—and it doesn't smell like rotting toenails!

If that's the only news you have, I'm never talking to you again.

Wow, you ARE Foster Grumpypants. Sheesh. Everything okay?

Yeah, I'm fine. I just get nervous when you tell me the Neverseen are arguing. The last time Brant lost his temper, he killed Jolie.

Jolie's name seemed to demand a moment of silence.

I'm being careful, he promised. *And Brant's actually not the one fighting. It's all Ruy, making a big fuss about his punishment for letting Wylie get away. It's been hard to get details. But Fintan's definitely changing their roles for that big project, and Ruy thinks his new assignment is unnecessary and demeaning.*

And I'm assuming you still don't have any ideas about what the project is?

Sadly, no. Just like I haven't gotten any more info about the ogres' test, or King Dimitar's meeting with Fintan, or Fintan's cache, or any of the things I can't get anyone to talk about—but before you get all Doom and Gloom, remember, I still have huge, kiss-worthy news!

If you start talking about cloaks or rotting toenails again . . .

But that's how it started! Well, not the toenails—but whatever. Fintan made a big deal about how I needed to wear my new cloak the whole time I'm here, and I figured it had to do with the black disk you found. So last night I opened the bottom seam and yep— another disk, with a different piece of the symbol.

He shared his memory of the etching, and the pattern of dashes breaking up the line matched a ray on the opposite side of the Lodestar symbol.

Is that it? Sophie asked.

Of course not—what kind of amateur do you take me for? I also found where the symbol projects on the floor, just like Bangs Boy wanted. It wasn't there when I first got here, but it popped up when Fintan was getting ready to leave. I'm guessing it's their funky version of a Leapmaster, since the projection comes from a crystal sphere mounted to the ceiling. But I couldn't figure out how it worked, and when Fintan caught me studying it, he said I'll never be able to understand the symbol—or how to use it—without know-ing the key. And THAT is the mind-blowingly awesome revelation.

It is?

Think about it—what needs a key besides a lock?

440

Um . . .

Wow, you really must be tired.

Yeah, thanks to you.

She tried to think of any phrases that used the word "key." And then it clicked.

Is the symbol a map?

BOOM! Admit it, I just blew your mind.

He kinda had.

But a map of what? she asked, trying to picture all the circles and rays and dashes. *Their hideouts?*

That's what I'm assuming.

His mind shifted to his memory of the symbol glowing across the dark stone floor. The ray that matched the disk in his new cloak had something extra in the end circle.

It has new runes, Sophie said.

Yep. And in case you can't read them, it says Gwynaura.

Another star.

Right again, you little star-memorizing show-off.

She ignored his teasing, letting her mind sort through the star maps she'd memorized, hoping to spot anything that might make Gwynaura unique.

It wasn't a particularly bright star. But it had a pure white glow, just like Alabestrine.

Do you think the map is based off a constellation they created? she asked.

It might be. But the stars could also just be guides. That's what lodestars are, right? So maybe Gwynaura leads to the hideout I'm at. And Alabestrine leads to Paris. And each of the other hideouts has a star and a rune to guide you to them.

But I don't understand how that actually works, Sophie told him. Light needs a crystal to bend the path where we want to go. So it's not like we can just bottle the starlight and magically end up at a Neverseen hideout.

I'm guessing that's what Fintan meant about me needing the key. But remember, a gadget projects the symbol. So I'm hoping Dizznee's Technopath brain will be able to put all the pieces together—especially since Fintan gave me one more clue to play with. He seems to want to see if I'm smart enough to figure this out, so he told me, "All you need to know is that the code is simple."

FIFTY-TWO

THE CODE IS SIMPLE," DEX MUMBLED, staring at Sophie's memory log, where she'd projected everything Keefe had shown her. "What code?"

"No idea," Sophie admitted. "Keefe was hoping you'd be able to figure that out."

"Great." Dex flopped back on her bed, repeating the clue over and over.

Fitz, Biana, and Dex—and their bodyguards—had met Sophie at Havenfield that morning to brainstorm, while Tam and Linh stayed in Alluveterre to see how Maruca's visit with Wylie went.

"So there's a symbol that's also a map, projected by a

gadget," Dex said, "and we need a key that's probably related to a code that's simple."

"Wow, my brain hurts just trying to follow that sentence," Biana said, blinking in and out of sight as she paced across Sophie's flowered carpet. "*But*, if Alvar can understand this, I'm sure we can too."

"Yeah, but they probably *gave* Alvar the key," Fitz reminded her as he slumped into Sophie's desk chair and petted Iggy through the bars of his cage. "We're stuck guessing. And don't forget there are also runes and star names and black disks hidden in cloaks and—"

"Okay, so we need to work on this piece by piece," Sophie decided, trying to massage away the headache she could feel forming. "Keefe seemed to think the gadget part was crucial, that's why he wanted me to talk to Dex."

She flipped to the page in her memory log where she'd recorded Keefe's memory of the crystal sphere. "Notice anything that might help us?"

"Maybe if I had the gadget in front of me and could open it up and see all the inner workings," Dex told her. "But I can't tell much from a picture. The only thing that stands out is this line." He traced his finger over a glowing strip of purple down the center of the crystal sphere. "That *could* be some sort of scanner."

"And what would a scanner do?" Fitz asked.

"Well, the obvious answer is 'scan stuff,'" Dex said, "which might fit, since scanners usually scan *codes*. So maybe there's a code hidden in the symbol? And the gadget scans it, and that somehow tells it to make a light path—maybe using the light from the corresponding star?"

"I guess that does make sense," Fitz said. "But, dude, couldn't they just use a Leapmaster or a pathfinder?"

"Maybe they think this method is more secure," Dex said, "since crystals can get lost or stolen, and this would only work for people they train. *Or*, maybe the Technopath who designed it wasn't very good."

"I thought you said their Technopath was super talented," Biana reminded him. "When we went through Alvar's registry records you seemed super impressed."

"They did do a lot of crazy tricks I never would've thought of," Dex admitted. "So maybe this was designed by a different Technopath. Or . . ."

"Or?" Fitz prompted when Dex didn't finish.

"Hang on. I need to think for a second," Dex said, sitting up and flipping back through the memory log until he found a page showing the symbol.

One second turned into two—then three and four and five and on and on, until Sophie got tired of counting.

"While he does that"—she turned to Biana—"did Dex ever tell you what he and Marella were talking about yesterday?"

"Oh! That's right, I only told Fitz. I guess Dex decided to

ask Marella if we could talk to her mom about the day Cyrah faded—and she freaked out. Partially because he wouldn't tell her why. But mostly because her mom can't handle that kind of stress. She told him her mom's gotten so bad lately that she won't even leave the house, and Marella thinks it's because she's heard about the awful things the Neverseen have been doing. So she can't risk freaking her out more by talking about painful memories."

"That makes sense," Sophie said quietly. "And must be so hard for her."

"I know. Dex said she cried. Makes me feel super guilty for not checking on her sooner—but now if I try, she'll think I'm just trying to get information about Cyrah."

"Probably. But there has to be *something* we can do," Sophie said. "Maybe if we—"

Dex jumped to his feet. "Do you remember those number chains I uncovered in Alvar's registry records well enough to project them?" he asked Sophie.

"Of course."

She took the memory log back and recorded the four chains of ones and zeroes, plus all the extra dashes and symbols and asterisks.

$$0\text{-}11\text{-}<<\text{-}1\text{-}1\text{-}1\text{-}0*$$
$$*0\text{-}1\text{-}>\text{-}1\text{-}>\text{-}111\text{-}0$$
$$*0\text{-}>\text{-}111\text{-}>>>\text{-}1\text{-}0$$
$$0\text{-}<<\text{-}1\text{-}1\text{-}11\text{-}<\text{-}0*$$

Dex stared at the numbers for so long that Sophie was about to turn back to her Marella conversation.

But before she did, Dex laughed and pumped his fist, shouting, "I know what the clue means!"

FIFTY-THREE

THE NUMBERS AREN'T NUMBERS!" Dex said. "Well, I guess they kinda are—it's the symbol that's not really a symbol. Or maybe it's both, depending on which way you're looking at it."

He sighed when they gave him nothing but blank stares.

"Okay, let's try this another way," he said. "Can I get something to write with?"

Sophie gave him one of her school notebooks and a pencil and he flipped to a clean page.

"Biana, can you read me the first sequence of numbers we found in Alvar's records—and give me all the dashes and symbols and stuff too?"

"Sure. It's zero, hyphen, one, one, hyphen, less than, less than, hyphen, one, hyphen, one, hyphen, one, hyphen, zero, asterisk."

Dex grinned as he stared at what he'd written. "See what happens when I convert the whole thing to pure symbols?"

He held up his drawing.

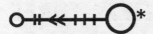

Everyone sucked in a breath.

The markings looked exactly like one of the rays in the Lodestar symbol—and not just any ray. The ray they'd connected to the Paris hideout—which happened to be where Alvar was when his registry pendant had given that code.

"And you can do the same thing with all four of the codes I found," Dex added. "The asterisk tells you which zero is the center. See?"

He drew the three remaining codes and held them up, each one matching a ray of the symbol perfectly.

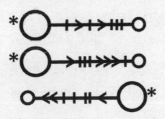

"Wow, how did you figure that out?" Fitz asked.

"It was Fintan's clue," Dex said. "I remembered whining

about how using a code made of ones and zeroes was too simple. And the really crazy part is, this isn't simple at all. It's a seriously brilliant system. The code is hidden but not hidden, still useable and scannable in both forms, *and* it keeps perfect track of their locations. See? This top one? That's the hideout that Alvar went to when he was The Boy Who Disappeared."

Sophie's stomach soured. "That's the same hideout they just moved Keefe to."

It shouldn't surprise her—and it shouldn't make her so nervous. But it really did.

"So those other two rays are hideouts Keefe hasn't seen yet, right?" Biana asked. "Does that mean we know how to find them?"

"*Technically*, yes," Dex said. "We should be able to find any of the hideouts we want, but—"

"I'd like to take this moment to make it clear that *none* of you will be leaving this house," Sandor interrupted, reminding their group that they had four goblins eavesdropping on their conversation from the hallway.

"Don't worry, we can't," Dex told him. "The only way this works is if we have one of their special gadgets to scan the code and convert it into a path for us—assuming I'm even right and that's what that gadget does."

"Can you build one?" Fitz asked.

"Not without having one to study," Dex said. "Though maybe if I play with a scanner and—"

"Again," Lovise interrupted. "No one will be building any gadgets to sneak away to see the enemy."

Dex rolled his eyes. "Just because I build it doesn't mean I'm going to use it."

All four goblins snorted a laugh.

"Yes," Sandor said, "because the four of you are known for your restraint."

"Well, you can't stop me from trying," Dex told him. "Though, honestly, I'm probably not going to be able to pull it off. The intricacy of this system is *crazy*, so the odds of me duplicating it without having something to copy are pretty much zero. Especially since I'm still not sure how the star runes fit in. The gadget could be channeling their light—but the Paris hideout was underground, so I don't know how that would work. And the stars *could* just be the names of their hideouts—but that seems too easy."

Sophie sighed. "So once again, we've learned a ton of things, but we still basically know nothing. And I don't even see a plan for what to do now."

"I guess we could tell Keefe all of this," Biana said, "and when everyone's asleep, he could sneak out of bed and—"

"Bad idea," Sophie interrupted. "I bet if he goes to another hideout without the matching black disk in his cloak, the Neverseen will know they have an intruder."

"Yeah, you're probably right," Biana mumbled. "Ugh—this whole so-close-but-so-far thing is super frustrating. Are we missing something?"

The minutes ticked by as they all stared at the symbol.

Sophie was about to give up when Biana made a weird squeaky sound.

"What if this gadget is how the Neverseen got into the Silver Tower?" she asked. "If they hid one inside somewhere, it could've let them leap in, couldn't it?"

"It depends on how the gadget works," Dex said. "The tower has tons of defenses to block people from leaping in, but maybe it uses light a different way?"

"But wouldn't someone have found the gadget during their search?" Fitz asked.

"Not if the Neverseen took the gadget with them when they left," Biana argued. "Why not have Tam search the tower to see if he can find a shadowprint, like the one in Paris?"

"That'll take *forever*," Dex warned.

"It will," Fitz agreed. "But it's better than nothing. And he could start with the Lodestar mirror, since I still think that's a weird coincidence."

"It's worth a try," Sophie decided. "And Fintan will probably be impressed when Keefe pretends he figured all of this out."

"And you can ask Gethen about it," Fitz added. "I still can't believe you're doing that without me—what's the point of being Cognates if they don't let us work together?"

"It's *almost* as ridiculous as assigning her a bodyguard and then not allowing him to accompany her on dangerous missions," Sandor shouted from the hallway.

"I'll be *fine*," Sophie told both of them. "I've handled Gethen before."

She was more worried about the fact that they were only giving her fifteen minutes. In that short time, she'd be lucky if she coaxed *one* piece of information out of him.

"What's the most important question," she said, "out of all of our questions?"

"What do you mean?" Fitz asked.

"I mean, what's the one thing we absolutely have to know—more than anything else? I'm trying to figure out what I need to focus on during the conversation."

The last time, they'd needed to learn anything they could about the gnomish plague and what might've happened to Keefe's mother. But this time the threat came in so many fragments and pieces and mysteries.

Should she ask what the Neverseen wanted with Grady and Edaline? Or about Keefe's legacy and the mysterious door into the mountain? Or should she try to get specifics about the Lodestar Initiative, and what it had to do with "test subjects" and "criterion" and Keefe's theory about a "gathering."

All of those were crucial—but were they crucial enough to be her one play in this crazy, confusing game?

The more her mind tossed the question around, the more

she realized the Neverseen had tipped their hand. It didn't matter what *she* thought was important. It mattered what they cared about—what they'd wanted so desperately that they'd taken a tremendous risk.

Which meant she needed to ask Gethen what the Neverseen wanted from Wylie.

FIFTY-FOUR

THE TRICK WITH GETHEN IS TO MAKE him think we're interested in one thing, so he doesn't have his guard up around the stuff we really need," Sophie told Fitz as they both stared at the page she'd not-so-creatively titled: *Plan for Tricking Gethen*.

The rest of the paper was blank.

And had been blank for days.

Sophie was starting to worry it would be blank for the rest of eternity.

Six days had already passed since Councillor Oralie told her they'd be visiting Lumenaria—and since the meeting was still scheduled for Friday, that meant they only had two days left to figure it out.

The most logical option—in Sophie's opinion—was for everyone to stop babying her and let her use her genetically enhanced telepathy. But the suggestion had been unanimously voted as the Worst Idea in the History of Bad Ideas. No one was willing to give the Neverseen's only Telepath a chance to mess with Sophie's head. So Mr. Forkle would be doing all the dangerous mental searching, and Sophie would once again be relegated to the role of "distractor."

"This isn't going to work," she mumbled, leaning back against the side of her bed. Her legs were going numb after so many hours of sitting on the floor, attempting to brainstorm ideas with Fitz. "Keefe and I were the distraction last time, so Gethen will be ready for that play—especially since he knows everyone's super overprotective of me."

"Then make the distraction so big he can't ignore it," Fitz said.

"Okay, but *how?*"

Annnnnnnd . . . they were back to where they'd been stuck for the last six days.

Overall, their group had made almost zero progress.

Keefe's updates had morphed into super-short answers before he'd tell her "gotta go—try not to worry" and turn his attention away. He *had* managed to tell Sophie that Fintan gave him an important assignment as a reward for solving the symbol's riddle—but everything after that had been "yes," "no," and "*relax*, Foster."

Dex, meanwhile, had made several attempts to build a version of the Neverseen's gadget. But so far, all he'd done was burn a hole in the floor of his bedroom. And Tam's search for a shadowprint of the symbol at the Silver Tower was going slooooooooooowly. The Lodestar mirror had nothing significant, so now he was stuck going room by room by room.

Linh chose to spend her days at Alluveterre with Wylie. He'd woken up when Maruca and her mom visited, but hadn't talked to anyone since. The only things he responded to were Linh's Hydrokinetic tricks. She'd even earned half a smile when she'd shaped the water into a graceful dancer and let it splash and twirl all over the room. But it wasn't enough to stop everyone from worrying about Wylie's sanity.

And Biana might've chosen the most impossible project of all, deciding it was time to fix their friendship with Marella—even though she knew Marella would be suspicious of her motives. So far, the only words Marella had said to her were, "I liked it better when you guys had forgotten about me."

Even their latest skill lesson with the Exillium Coaches had been more exhausting than educational. They were supposed to channel their energy into the ground and cause a tremor. But Sophie was the only one in her Hemisphere who'd pulled it off—and her mighty earthquake had lasted two whole seconds. The feat seemed especially embarrassing when she compared it to the way the dwarves could crack the earth with a single stomp of their hairy feet. And it made Sophie wonder if the whole skill-training program was going to be a waste. Maybe over time the elves would learn to impress. But at the rate they were going, it would take *years*.

Even the Coaches seemed disheartened. Coach Rohana had told Sophie, "Half the battle is getting the mind to *commit*— but everyone still thinks these skills are 'common' and would rather go back to training in their abilities."

At least Grady and Edaline had found a useful way to spend their days. They'd arranged regular meetings with Lady Cadence to learn as much as they could about the ogres before the Peace Summit. Their conversations usually focused on the complicated politics between the species. But when Sophie and Fitz headed downstairs for a snack, they found the adults in an intense discussion on how best to manage King Dimitar's temper.

"You're overcomplicating it," Lady Cadence told Grady and Edaline. "All you have to do is treat him like an intelligent equal. Ogres are different from us, but they're still sophisti-cated, complex creatures with their own culture, their own wants and needs—"

"Who've tried to murder the entire gnomish species," Sophie interrupted. "Twice. Also stole the gnomes' homeland. And tried to cripple the Lost Cities by forcing the gnomes into slavery. And allied with the Neverseen. And—"

"I'm not saying the ogres haven't made mistakes," Lady Cadence said, earning snorts from all the goblin bodyguards.

"I'm saying that doesn't erase the good in them—especially considering that the elves are not blameless either. We've compounded the tensions between our species by refusing to take any time to understand them. Instead, we try to force them to set aside fundamental elements of their society. Who are we to decide how they should live? Who are we to micromanage other societies and species?"

"When those societies want to wage war with other species in order to steal their land, I'd say they need to be micromanaged," Sandor argued.

"No, they need to be *managed*," Lady Cadence corrected. "The fighting needs to stop—but that doesn't mean we can't find better compromises. I met with King Dimitar and—"

"*What?*" everyone simultaneously interrupted.

"Oh, don't sound so horrified. Dimitar and I have a long history, and when I heard he agreed to the summit, I asked if he'd let me visit his city."

"*You* went to Ravagog," Grady clarified.

"To what's left of it." Shadows aged Lady Cadence's prim features as she fiddled with her Markchain—a necklace King Dimitar had given her to keep her safe during her years living with the ogres. "I do not fault anyone for the destruction. But it hurts my heart that no one has taken the time to consider what the ogres have suffered. Why do you think Dimitar agreed to meet? I'm one of the few elves willing to listen, willing to open my eyes—"

"Unless you count the Neverseen," Sophie reminded her. "Did he tell you about that? How he'll be meeting with Fintan? And how Fintan assigned him a test to prove they could form another alliance?"

"Actually, he did tell me about that. And I strongly advised him against it. You have to understand—Dimitar sees no other option. Many of the restrictions the Council hopes to impose through this new treaty will force the ogres to change their very ways of being."

"And that gives him the right to form an alliance with murderers?" Fitz asked.

"Of course not, Mr. Vacker. Which is what I told Dimitar. I tried to help him find a different path. I'm still hoping the Council can create a treaty that brings peace to all of our worlds while still granting the ogres the freedom to remain who they are. But if that's not possible, I hope the king will turn to something other than violence."

"Like that'll ever happen," Sophie snorted.

Lady Cadence clicked her tongue. "You disappoint me, Miss Foster. I'd hoped you might bring a bit of compassion to this summit. After all, you're willing to excuse humans from the many grievances held against *them*, aren't you? And when it comes to violence, the humans have no rival. Yes, the ogres must learn to share this planet peacefully. And yes, they need to face the consequences for what they did with the plague, and any other species they've harmed. But if we insist on restricting them to a set of laws that would disrupt their very ways of being, we're sealing our own fate. King Dimitar values elvin guidance—but only from those who treat him as a friend."

"Yeah, well, I don't want to be King Dimitar's friend," Sophie told her.

Lady Cadence let out a slow sigh. "And that is a mistake. One I very much hope you'll reconsider, before it's too late."

"I wouldn't hold my breath," Sophie said, stalking back upstairs. "Can you believe her?" she asked Fitz as soon as they were back in her room. "She wants me to be friends with someone who's tried to kill me at least two different times—someone who's the reason Calla had to sacrifice herself!"

Fitz let out a long sigh as he sank back to the floor. "If it helps, I doubt she meant you should invite him to your Winnowing Gala."

"Ugh, now *there's* a mental picture I didn't need," Sophie grumbled, imagining King Dimitar standing among her long line of matches.

Then again, the idea of a long line of matches felt equally terrifying.

"I think her point," Fitz said quietly, "is that the ogres would cooperate more if we didn't treat them like they're our enemy. And that *does* make sense. If the Council walks into the Peace Summit planning to boss the ogres around and put them in their place, it's only going to make King Dimitar dig in his heels that much more."

"Don't ruin my pouting with your logic," Sophie mumbled.

Fitz laughed. "That sounds like something Keefe would say."

"Does it? Ugh, he must be getting in my head."

"Not too much, I hope." Fitz's tone was teasing. But there was a heat in his eyes that made her cheeks feel warm, even when he added, "I'm not sure the world can handle more than one Keefe Sencen."

Sophie's heart was pounding so loudly, she only caught the last word of his next question.

"What did you say?" she asked.

He picked up their still-blank plan for tricking Gethen. "I said, what if friendship is the answer? Instead of treating Gethen as your adversary when you meet with him, what if you made him think you came there because you want to be friends?"

"I'd never be able to pull that off," Sophie told him. "Remember, this is the guy I Sucker Punched in the face."

"Oh, believe me, I'm never going to forget that. But I'm not talking about becoming BFFs. What if you asked Gethen to be our ally? Reminded him that the Neverseen have left him rotting in that cell for months and have no plans of rescuing him? And then offer a trade?"

"The Council will never cut a deal—and I wouldn't want them to."

"I know," Fitz said. "But we're only aiming for a distraction, remember? And what could be more distracting than getting offered a chance at freedom? Tell him about Wylie. Tell him we're ready to do *anything* to stop something like that from happening again. If he makes other demands, pretend to consider them. You'll have a Councillor with you—get Oralie to back you up. It doesn't have to be real. Just convincing enough to make him think. Because the more he thinks, the more he'll let his guard down, and Mr. Forkle will be able to sneak in and learn what you need. Think it'll work?"

"I think . . . you're a genius."

Fitz's grin curled wider at that, and his eyes sparked with that same hint of heat, making Sophie's cheeks blush again.

"Not a genius," he said, tracing his fingers over his Cognate rings. "But we make a great team. Don't we?"

Sophie nodded. "The best."

FIFTY-FIVE

I CAN'T BELIEVE YOU GUYS WERE SERIOUS about the blindfold," Sophie grumbled as she clung to the rough hands of the goblins guiding her through Lumenaria. Descending a stone spiral staircase without falling to her death was hard enough when she could see where she was going.

She'd already tripped so many times, there'd been serious discussion about carrying her piggyback. And they'd barely begun their journey to the dungeon.

Sandor had escorted Sophie to the island at dawn, per the instructions Oralie had sent them, and they'd found Mr. Forkle and the golden-haired Councillor waiting on the rocky shore. Dark waves crashed in the distance, and the glowing castle sat silhouetted against the gray-pink sky as a dozen heavily armed goblins had marched out to greet them.

The guards had patted everyone down, taking any weapons, gadgets—even jewelry—before leading Sophie, Oralie, and Mr. Forkle into the main courtyard. The gates clanged closed behind them, sealing them in the fortress, and the last thing Sophie saw was Sandor's I'll-be-waiting-right-here stare before the guards covered her eyes with the starched blindfold.

Two sets of hands had pulled her forward then, one stumbling footstep after another. The air shifted as they walked. Sometimes hot, sometimes cold, sometimes sweet or salty scented, depending on the room. The staircase they were currently tackling was damp and sour. The only sound was the echoey thud of footsteps, which swelled louder in the tighter spaces.

Sophie counted every step, trying to create a mental map of the mazelike fortress. It seemed like the kind of information she might be glad to have someday—though with so many twists and turns, she hardly got an accurate picture.

"You'll be able to see again once we reach the main dungeon," the goblin holding her left hand told Sophie. She wasn't allowed to know any of the goblins' names, so she'd decided to call her guards Lefty and Righty.

Lefty caught her as she tripped again, and Sophie used the opportunity to steady herself against the wall. The surface felt wooden this time, and creaked with the impact.

Another door.

The fourth door she'd felt in the last few minutes—though there could've been others in the interim.

"We're almost there," Righty promised, her voice hoarse and wheezy. "Just a few more hallways and a final descent."

"That doesn't sound like 'almost,'" Sophie noted. "I knew this place was huge, but it didn't look *this* massive."

"Another part of the security," Oralie explained. "Lumenaria's dungeon was designed to house diplomatic prisoners—those who hold too much value to be stashed in the center of the earth in Exile. But it had to be just as unreachable."

"How many prisoners are there?" Sophie asked.

Oralie seemed to hesitate before she admitted, "I'm not certain."

"There are two," Righty told them.

"I assume your ignorance means the other prisoner belongs to a Forgotten Secret?" Mr. Forkle asked.

"It must be," Oralie said quietly.

"If it's a Forgotten Secret," Sophie asked, "how do the guards know?"

"Because we have to care for the prisoner," Lefty told her. "And because we need to know all possible threats and dangers. But we are under strict orders not to divulge any specific details, even to the Council. This way."

He pulled Sophie into a hallway that felt wider than the others. The darkness seemed thinner, fuzzing with gray.

Sweat trickled down Sophie's spine as they navigated

several more twists and turns before her guards pulled her to a stop.

"I'm going to carry you for the last part," Lefty said as he lifted her by the waist and draped her over his shoulder like a sack of potatoes. Sophie could feel her feet brushing against cold metal, and Lefty's shoulder muscles straining under her stomach as they dropped slowly down. The air smelled damp and rusty, so she assumed they were descending a ladder.

"We can take the blindfolds off now," Righty said when Lefty set her back on the ground, "but I'd recommend opening your eyes slowly."

Sophie took her advice—but the vivid white glow still sliced across her corneas like a hot blade. She'd been expecting a shadowy stone room with iron bars and other dungeony clichés. Instead, the room they stood in was round, clean, and every silvery-white stone glowed like it had been carved from the sun.

The only thing her eyes could focus on were six arched silver doors lining the room, none of which had any visible locks or handles.

Three of the goblins who'd escorted them placed both of their palms against one of the metal doors, making some sort of combination panel appear.

"Do you know the code they're entering?" Sophie asked Oralie.

"Not at the moment. The codes change three times a day,

and are passed along to the Councillors in a random order to make it impossible for anyone to predict who will have access at any given moment."

"Clever," Mr. Forkle said.

"You have no idea," Righty told him.

"Your fifteen minutes will begin as soon as they open the door," Lefty said. "And there will be no extensions."

"Don't worry," Righty added. "He won't be able to get near you. You'll have a force field that will shift as you move."

"I still want you to stay by my side," Oralie told Sophie, taking her hand. "I'd like to keep contact so I can monitor your emotions."

"And remember," Mr. Forkle added, "do not, under *any* circumstances, attempt to read his mind. No matter how much he may goad you."

"I know the plan," Sophie told him.

And it was a good one. She just had to commit.

Please let it work.

She squared her shoulders, counting to three for courage before she tightened her hold on Oralie and said, "Let's do this!"

FIFTY-SIX

SOPHIE HAD REHEARSED WHAT SHE'D say to Gethen at least a hundred times. And yet, when she stepped into his too-bright, freezing cell, the first words that came out of her mouth were, "Is that the sword in the stone?"

"Glad to hear we haven't crushed that earnest curiosity—yet," Gethen purred from the center of the floor. He sat with his head bowed and legs crossed, as if he'd been meditating—but his wrinkled gray clothes and greasy blond hair betrayed his peaceful composure. And while his bruise had healed, his nose looked permanently crooked from Sophie's punch.

He seemed thinner, too.

Paler.

Wilder.

Behind him, a waist-high stone pillar provided the round room's only ornamentation, with a gleaming silver sword jutting from the center.

"I'm not sure what you mean by *the* sword," Oralie told Sophie, "but each cell has a blade trapped permanently in stone."

"It's my entertainment," Gethen said, his piercing blue eyes studying them one by one. "Though I suspect it's mostly for the guard's enjoyment. I'm sure they've placed bets to see how long I'll keep trying. I always thought I'd be able to resist, but . . ." He held out his right hand, revealing blisters in the same pattern as the diamonds on the sword's hilt. "Sometimes I can't resist a challenge."

"It's not a challenge," Oralie told him. "It's an ever-present reminder that any power you once had is now as useless as that blade."

"So you say. But wouldn't it be ironic if someday I used that blade to chop off your pretty head?"

He jumped to his feet and grabbed the sword, sending Sophie stumbling back.

Oralie didn't blink. "The blade isn't going anywhere."

"Are you sure?" Sophie whispered. Humans had a legend about a sword in a stone, and the sword totally ended up killing people. She wondered if this was where the story came from. Lumenaria did have a Camelot-esque feel.

470

Gethen gave the hilt a halfhearted tug before brushing one finger down the inch of exposed blade, slicing a thin line of red into his pale skin. "Better hope I never find a way to crack this stone."

"I won't be losing any sleep over it," Oralie told him.

"No, you Councillors never do. Tell me—how'd that work out for Kenric?"

Oralie's grip tightened on Sophie's hand, stopping her from lunging for Gethen's throat. "He's not worth it."

"How can you say that?" Sophie asked, desperate to see if her inflicting was strong enough to batter Gethen through the force field.

But her fury faded when Oralie whispered, "Because Kenric would've wanted me to."

Gethen smiled. "Clearly this meeting is going to be worth the energy I'm using—though if you think I don't feel you in my head, you're a bigger idiot than I thought," he told Mr. Forkle. "If you truly want to learn something, you should let the moonlark give it a go."

The hunger in his eyes was enough to convince Sophie that everyone had been right when they told her not to search his mind.

"I only came here to talk," she said, trying to get back to the script.

"Well, then I assume this is the part where you try to distract me?"

"Actually, it's the part where I ask you for help," Sophie corrected.

One of Gethen's eyebrows shot up, and he leaned casually against the curved wall. "Something big must've happened, then—not sure I can guess what. The timeline's been reset so many times, it could be nearly anything."

Sophie bit her lip, steeling her nerves before delivering the next line. "They took Wylie."

"My goodness—they're *full* of surprises lately" was all Gethen had to say. "And a little bit desperate, if they're back to Cyrah."

"Desperate for what?" Sophie asked.

Gethen tapped his chin with his bleeding finger, stippling it with red. "Same thing we all are. Fintan just has a different approach. Gisela was all about cause and effect. Strategy and patience. Fintan's driven by impulse—not that either affects me way down here."

"Doesn't that bother you?" Sophie asked. "Don't you hate that they're carrying on with their plans while they leave you rotting in this cell?"

"Oh, I'd hardly say I'm rotting. The food is far tastier than anything the Neverseen grew, and the guards bring me a squishy pillow every night to sleep on. And who would complain about having so much time to rest and recharge?"

"You really expect us to believe you don't mind being here?" Sophie asked.

"Why not? You expect *me* to believe the offer you're about to make is real."

"I don't have an offer," Sophie said. "I came here hoping I'd find a shred of decency left."

He sucked his bleeding finger. "Sorry to disappoint. And nice trick, Forkle. You might've had me there a few weeks ago, but all this rest made me so much stronger. Good to know that's the information you're interested in, by the way. I assume that means they snatched Wylie from the Silver Tower? What's the matter—can't figure out how they got in?"

"We're working on it," Sophie snapped.

"I'm sure you are. But if you haven't figured it out already, I don't imagine you will. And even if you did, you'd need an ability you don't have to make it work. Seems shortsighted of you," he told Mr. Forkle. "If you gave her extra powers, why not give her one of everything?"

"More isn't always better," Mr. Forkle told him. "Sometimes it's simply *more*. But I wouldn't expect you to understand."

"I might, if you take the time to enlighten me." Gethen sank to the floor again, staring up at the curved ceiling. "Go ahead. Tell me a story."

"Never mind," Sophie said, turning to Mr. Forkle. "Save your energy. He's never going to help us rescue Wylie."

This was the turning point in their plan.

Gethen could either let them walk away, or . . .

"Are they holding the boy hostage?"

Sophie nodded, letting the memory of Wylie's wounds turn her eyes teary—selling the lie. "He's been missing for over a week."

"You don't approve," Mr. Forkle noted when Gethen cursed.

"Not that it matters, but no, I don't. I think it's a horrible play—sloppy and reckless and will surely end as well as Sophie's kidnapping. But that doesn't mean I'm going to help you."

"Why not?" Sophie asked.

"The Council would be prepared to show their gratitude," Oralie added.

"Yes, I'm sure they'd be happy to unlock this cage and let me go free. Maybe they'd pull that sword from the stone and give it to me as a souvenir."

"They'd be willing to offer you an *improved* situation," Oralie corrected. "There are other places you could be held. Places where it's possible to feel the passing of time." She tapped her toe against the glowing stone floor. "The lumenite keeps your world an endless day."

"Really? I hadn't noticed."

"Yes you have," Mr. Forkle said. "I can see the twitch in your eye. I bet you have no idea how long you've been in here. Maybe you should've thought to count the seconds."

"Well, Miss Foster still has that fresh-faced bloom of youth about her, so I'm guessing it hasn't been *that* long. Besides, each time they bring me a pillow it's a dead giveaway."

Oralie smiled. "They never bring the pillow at the same time. It's part of their instructions. Sometimes they go days before they cue you to sleep again. Sometimes only hours. Meals are just as scattered. Haven't you noticed how sometimes the hunger pains feel like they might tear you apart, or morning comes only minutes after you close your eyes?"

"Our bodies run on rhythm and routine," Mr. Forkle added. "Without it, we deteriorate."

"Lovely picture you both paint." Gethen cleared a catch from his voice. "But I'm still quite happy where I am."

"Then why is your mind frantically trying to guess the date?" Mr. Forkle asked. "Perhaps you're starting to realize just how long you've been abandoned?"

"They're not going to rescue you," Sophie pressed. "Oralie's offer is the best chance you have. And all you have to do is tell us where you think they would've brought Wylie."

"It won't do you any good. You'll never be able to find the hideout."

"Actually, we will." Sophie glanced at Mr. Forkle, needing his reassuring nod before she rattled off everything they'd pieced together about the Lodestar symbol. It was a risk, giving away how much they'd learned. But they needed to make an impression.

Gethen rubbed his temples. "This is what happens when you capture people. It lights a fire in their loved ones that burns wilder than Everblaze. Always a losing game."

"So take the win for yourself," Oralie told him. "One piece of information in exchange for a much more comfortable life."

Gethen stood to pace. He'd made several circles around the room before his eyes locked with Mr. Forkle's. "*Very* clever. You almost had me there—but I'm onto you now, so you can get out of my head." He turned to Sophie. "And I'll take my chances here, thank you very much. They're better than you think."

Mr. Forkle's fisted hands made it clear that Gethen wasn't lying about blocking him. And they were out of games. Out of options. Out of time.

Sophie couldn't decide if she wanted to cry or kick something.

"You honestly thought you'd beat me, didn't you?" Gethen asked as their group turned to leave. "Sorry, Miss Foster—I've been playing this game far too long. *But* you raised an interesting question. So I'm willing to make you an offer. Truth for truth. One from me. One from you."

"It's a trick," Oralie said.

"I can assure you it's not."

"How will I know you're not lying?" Sophie asked.

"You won't. But I won't know if you're lying to me, either. That's the game."

"Do I get to choose my own question?"

"Yes—but I get to go first."

Sophie glanced at Mr. Forkle. "Deal."

"Good decision. And here's my question. Has the Peace Summit already occurred?"

Sophie considered lying—but he'd probably be able to tell. And that would guarantee he'd lie with his answer.

"No," she said. "It hasn't happened."

"But it will soon?"

"That's a separate question. Now it's my turn. What was Cyrah's connection to the Neverseen?"

Gethen's eyebrows shot up. "I thought you wanted to know where they're keeping Wylie."

"I did," Sophie said. "But now I want to know this more."

"Interesting."

"That's not an answer."

"It is, actually. Her connection was interesting. You never specified that I had to give details. Just like I didn't specify a better idea on timing. We both chose our questions poorly."

Sophie sighed. "Fine. The Peace Summit will be happening soon. Now tell me what made Cyrah's connection to the Neverseen so interesting."

He sat quiet long enough to convince her he wouldn't answer. Then he told her, "Starstones."

FIFTY-SEVEN

DO YOU THINK HE WAS LYING? Sophie transmitted to Mr. Forkle as their group of goblins led them—blindfolded again—back up the winding staircase. The journey felt twice as endless as it had the first time, and her muscles burned from the incline.

It would be a strange lie to tell, Mr. Forkle said. *Nowhere in the conversation did we mention Lady Gisela's hairpin. Cyrah also worked with many different gems. She specialized in ribbons, but she did sell other hair accessories. And she was a Flasher, so it's possible she did some sort of light treatment to make Lady Gisela's stone flash blue.*

But why would she help the Neverseen? Sophie asked. *She knew her husband sacrificed himself for the Black Swan.*

I honestly have no idea. It's possible she was angry with us for not protecting Prentice. Or Lady Gisela could've ordered the pin without telling Cyrah its purpose. Or she could've been coerced. The Neverseen certainly aren't above blackmail, and a single mother facing the scorn of our world would be especially vulnerable. I'll have to see if Wylie knows anything that could help us narrow down the possibilities. And I'll need to do more research on starstones.

Unless this whole thing is a lie to waste our time, Sophie thought quietly.

Also a possibility. But there's too much potential to ignore it.

What about all that stuff he said about getting into the Silver Tower? Sophie asked. *Do you think the ability he hinted at was a Shade?*

That would be nice, since we're already having Mr. Tam search the tower. But Wylie's assaulters included a Shade, a Vanisher, a Guster, and a Psionipath—all abilities you do not possess. And Gethen did a brilliant job of blocking me from his memories. The energy in his mind felt different. So much stronger and purer. All this idleness must be building his reserves.

"I'm assuming the anxiety I'm feeling from both of you is related to whatever secret conversation you're having?" Oralie asked, reminding them they weren't alone. "And I'm not foolish enough to expect you to tell me what you're discussing. But I'm hoping you might be willing to answer a few simple yes-or-no questions."

"We'll do our best," Mr. Forkle promised.

"Thank you. So first, I'm guessing you've uncovered some sort of clue with starstones, and that's why the word triggered such a strong reaction?"

"Yes," Mr. Forkle said. "We recovered a memory."

"From whom?" Oralie asked.

"That's not a yes-or-no question," Sophie pointed out.

"I suppose it's not. This is going to be harder than I thought," Oralie admitted. "Okay. Do I know the person?"

"Yes," Mr. Forkle said. "But the rememberer is less important than the remembered. In the memory, Lady Gisela used a hairpin set with what she called 'a rare starstone' to light leap to a Neverseen hideout we've currently been unable to locate. And she implied that the stone would be able to guide any user to the same location. But as of this moment, the hairpin is missing."

"Thank you for not making me pry that out of you through yes-or-no questions," Oralie told him. "Does this mean you might be open to answering a few others?"

"I'll answer anything you ask," Mr. Forkle said. "But know that I'm speaking to you as my ally, not as a Councillor."

"I assume that means you don't want me to share the information with the rest of the Council?"

"My instinct is to say yes—but I might be willing to be persuaded if you gave me good reasons why they can be trusted. Our order is not secretive because we enjoy shadows and games. Merely because it was necessary to avoid certain hindrances."

480

"Fair enough," Oralie said. "It's definitely my hope for our groups to work freely together. But until we reach that point, I accept the need for discretion. And so you know, every guard here is well aware that anything they've seen and heard today can never be shared."

"We swore an oath," Righty chimed in, and the other goblins murmured their agreement.

"Thank you," Mr. Forkle told them.

"Back to questions, then," Oralie said, letting several seconds slip away before she spoke. "Do you believe Lady Gisela killed Cyrah?"

It was the question Sophie had been trying not to ask, and she stopped breathing as she waited for Mr. Forkle's answer.

"If Gethen wasn't lying, it *is* a possibility," Mr. Forkle said quietly. "*But* . . . if starstones are important to the Neverseen, it's also logical that Lady Gisela wasn't the only member who utilized them. And it's important to note that Gethen said 'starstones,' plural, and the memory we recovered only displayed one. So for the moment, we have no proof of anything."

"And all those things that Sophie told Gethen during their conversation," Oralie said, "about a symbol that's also a map of the Neverseen's hideouts, as well as some sort of secret code. I'm assuming that was true?"

"Mostly," Sophie mumbled. "I exaggerated how much we understand. Dex thinks he knows how the system works, but we won't be able to tell for sure until we find one of the gadgets and test it out. Tam is looking to see if there's one hidden in the Silver Tower—or at least proof that the Neverseen used one—so we'll know how they got in."

"I'd like to see the symbol," Oralie said. "And I'd like to show it to Councillor Velia. She's an expert on maps and may notice something important. She's also not the type to ask questions, and will keep everything between us. Would you be okay with that?"

"If you believe Velia would be useful in this regard, I'm willing to take you at your word," Mr. Forkle told her. "I'll send a record of the symbol as soon as I return to my office."

"And which office is that?" Oralie asked. "In one of your hideouts? Or maybe somewhere closer to home?"

"Am I to infer that you have a theory as to my identity?" Mr. Forkle asked.

"I've had *many* theories," Oralie said as they reached the top of the stairs. "But this one feels right."

"This is a trap, isn't it?" Mr. Forkle asked. "Pique my curiosity so that I'll be tempted to slip into your head to check your theory, and if I do, my emotions would give you your answer."

"I suppose that would work out rather well," Oralie told him. "But I'd prefer to wait until you're ready to tell me. And don't think I haven't noticed how quiet you're being, Sophie. I'm assuming that means you're already in on the secret."

"*Secrets*," Sophie corrected. "I know two of his identities. Still trying to figure out the others."

"And *that* is enough about me," Mr. Forkle told them. "Did anyone else find Gethen's interest in the Peace Summit to be concerning?"

"Yes," Oralie admitted. "Even without physical contact, I could feel how desperate he was for information."

"Any idea why?" Sophie asked.

"From the glimmers I caught in his mind," Mr. Forkle said, "I suspect the Neverseen once had a plan in the event of an ogre summit, and he believes it will allow him a chance to escape."

All of the goblins laughed.

"Don't underestimate the Neverseen," Sophie warned them.

"Don't underestimate *us*," Lefty told her. "We have security beyond anything anyone could prepare for."

"But perhaps it might be wise to add a few additional measures," Oralie decided.

"Are you allowed to tell us when the summit is?" Sophie asked.

"No—but I suppose it would be wise for you to prepare. The summit is scheduled for two weeks from tomorrow. You'll receive official notice a week prior."

The goblins spent the rest of their trek discussing ways to reorganize their patrols. And soon enough, they'd reached the main courtyard.

"I expect a *thorough* update," Sandor told Sophie after her blindfold had been removed, her belongings returned, and they'd regrouped outside the castle's gates.

"I will," she promised. "But let's wait until we're back at Havenfield. That way I can explain it to everyone at the same time."

"I'll update the Collective," Mr. Forkle told her. "And perhaps we should regroup tomorrow to discuss the best course of action from here?"

"Please keep me in the loop," Oralie told them. "And I'll be sure to do the same. This is a time when working together is in all of our best interests."

"Indeed," Mr. Forkle said, offering a quick bow before raising his pathfinder to the sunlight and leaping away.

"Thank you again for arranging this meeting," Sophie told Oralie.

Oralie gave her a weak smile. "I only hope it was worth it."

Sophie made the same wish as she took Sandor's hand and leaped them both back to Havenfield.

"So should we—"

"STOP!" Sandor snapped, pulling her behind him. He unsheathed his sword and spun around, sniffing the air. "Something's wrong. *Very* wrong."

Sophie had no idea what could have him so freaked out.

And then she saw it.

Streaks of red in one of the pastures. Splashes of it in another.

Fresh blood.

FIFTY-EIGHT

SANDOR COVERED SOPHIE'S MOUTH and hefted her over his shoulder to prevent her from running away.

But she *had* to find Grady and Edaline. What if they—

"You must stop struggling and do *exactly* as I say," Sandor ordered, charging toward the grove where the gnomes lived. "I need to get you somewhere safe so I can search the grounds for your family. And I need you to be quiet, because I can't tell what we're dealing with."

He kept his sword raised, moving so fast the scenery blurred. Sophie tried to keep calm, telling herself the blood belonged to one of the animals—until Sandor slowed and uttered a string of goblin curse words.

She strained to follow his gaze and found a bloody ogre sprawled across the grass.

Dead.

She screamed and twisted in Sandor's arms.

He was no match for her adrenaline-fueled panic, and she took off into the pastures shouting her parents' names as red rimmed her vision while she ran. Her thudding heart pounded almost as hard as the rage pulsing inside her, straining against the tangled threads she'd knotted around it. She pressed her hands against her ribs, willing the emotions to hold steady. She needed to save them for whatever was coming.

She passed another dead ogre in the next clearing. Then two more.

The next body she found was a goblin with long curly hair.

Grady's bodyguard.

Sophie's voice turned into a ragged wail as she collapsed to her knees, unable to get back up—until someone grabbed her shoulder and instincts took over.

Her knotted emotions ripped free, and she shoved the darkness out of her in sickening waves, pummeling her attacker over and over. She could've raged forever, but strained, squeaky words brought her out of the frenzy.

When her vision cleared, she found Sandor collapsed on his side, teeth gritted, his body shaking from her inflicting.

"It's okay," a soft voice said behind her. "The ogres are gone."

Sophie spun around and found Flori standing with a sack of Panakes blossoms.

"I'm so sorry," she whispered. "They told me to wait for you to make sure you didn't panic. But I thought I'd have time to gather more medicine."

Sophie couldn't get her brain to form words as Flori moved to Sandor's side, placing a blossom on his chest and humming a soothing melody while she mopped the sweat off his brow with the edges of her long hair.

Sandor's features relaxed as Flori worked, the pain fading from his eyes.

"Where are they?" Sophie managed to whisper.

Flori knew who she meant. "They're safe. I'll bring you to see them as soon as Sandor's ready."

She said other things, but Sophie's brain was on never-ending repeat.

Safe. Safe. Safe. Safe. Safe.

Seconds crawled by—or maybe it was minutes. Eventually Sandor raised his shaky head.

"At least I know you *can* protect yourself," he told Sophie, offering a weak smile.

Sophie struggled to apologize, but Sandor waved the words away. "My only concern is your safety," he promised, his watery eyes focused on something in the distance.

Sophie didn't have to turn to know he was looking at Brielle's broken body.

"Come on," Flori said, taking Sophie's hand. "I'll bring you to the others."

She sang an entrance into the ground, and Sandor and Sophie followed her into the earth. The tunnel was damp and dark and pleasantly warm as Flori tangled their feet in the roots.

"Brace yourselves," she warned, shifting the cadence of her melody.

The roots obeyed her command, carrying them faster, faster, faster—far away. Into the darkness. Flori filled their journey with soothing songs, trying to keep Sophie calm and steady. But the icy terror didn't thaw until they emerged in a small hollow surrounded by towering red-barked trees.

Grady and Edaline were there—dirty and bloody, but strong enough to throw their arms around Sophie as she crashed into them, holding on with all the strength she had left.

The sobs hit then, wringing out the rest of the fear clouding her mind and unleashing a tidal wave of questions: "What happened? Are you hurt? Has someone called Elwin? Where are we? How did you get away? What's going on? WHY WERE THERE OGRES?"

"We're going to be fine," Grady promised as she reached up to wipe a scratch on his cheek. "Edaline and I were very lucky."

He glanced at something behind her, and Sophie whipped

around to find a dozen gnomes crouched around two more bodies. Flori was busy working with them, smearing their wounds with crushed Panakes petals.

"They're going to be okay," Edaline whispered, holding Sophie tighter as they studied the unconscious, blood-streaked faces of Cadoc and Lady Cadence. "Lur and Mitya went to get Elwin. They should be back any minute."

"Did you sedate them?" Sandor asked, crouching next to Cadoc and checking the pulse point at the goblin's bruised throat.

"No, that's from the shock and the blood loss," Edaline told him. "But their breathing is strong. And their hearts are holding steady. They just need medicine. And lots of rest."

Sophie nodded blankly, trying not to look at all the red. "I saw Brielle."

Grady turned away to wipe his eyes. "She saved me. Took on four ogres at once so I could get to Edaline. Three of them fell by her sword, but the fourth was faster."

Something cracked behind them.

Sophie turned and found Sandor clutching his bleeding fist, and a giant dent punched into one of the trees.

"Keefe was right about his warnings," Edaline mumbled. "The Neverseen finally came after us."

"You saw them?" Sophie asked.

She'd never forgive Keefe if he'd been there. Ever. Not even if he'd stood on the sidelines.

"No," Grady said. "But one of the ogres shouted, 'The Pyrokinetic is waiting.' I don't know if they meant Brant or Fintan, but it doesn't matter. What matters is, their plan failed."

Sophie repeated his last words, trying to find comfort in them.

But all she could think was, *This isn't over.*

FIFTY-NINE

THE OGRES HAD *ALMOST* WON.

Somehow they'd seemed to know that Sandor wouldn't be there. They'd also positioned themselves throughout the pastures to make sure no one had anywhere to run. And they'd known to wait for the afternoon feeding, when everyone would be carrying buckets instead of weapons. They'd even prepared for Grady's ability, blocking his mesmerizing with special ogre-size versions of the thinking caps they used at Foxfire during exams. And when Edaline tried to conjure up weapons from their stockpile, the ogres had been ready to disarm her, as if they'd known exactly what she would do during the battle.

Brielle and Cadoc had fought bravely and ferociously. But there had been *ten* ogres.

Within minutes Brielle was dead, Cadoc and Lady Cadence seriously injured, and Grady and Edaline were preparing themselves to be taken.

"Verdi's the one who saved us," Grady said, his lips twitching with a dark smile. "She charged though her pasture's fence, grabbed one of the ogres with her teeth, and trampled another. The remaining ogres rushed to help and . . . I'll spare you those details, but let's say Verdi got herself a nice taste of ogre meat. And she didn't enjoy it."

"And she's okay?" Sophie asked. "They didn't . . ."

"She took some hard blows," Grady admitted. "She'll probably limp from now on. She also lost a few teeth. But several gnomes stayed at Havenfield to care for her, and I was able to get pressure on her wounds as soon as the final ogre fled."

"Coward," Sandor spit, squeezing the handle of his sword so hard, the skin on his fingers looked ready to rip.

"I know," Grady said. "And it was the ogre who murdered Brielle. He'll have a scar across his chest from her final attack. If I ever see him again . . ."

"You won't," Sandor promised. "We have hunters who will find him and shred him."

Sophie tried not to picture it—but her imagination ran wild.

Elwin saved her from the nightmares when he crawled out of the earth carrying two overfilled satchels. His tousled hair and crazy glasses gave him a bit of a mad-scientist air, but within minutes, his remedies had color flooding back into Lady Cadence's cheeks and Cadoc's eyes fluttering awake.

"I'll need to move them to the Healing Center at Foxfire to clean them up and set a few broken bones," he told Lur and Mitya. "Can you guys rig something to help us transport them through the earth? I'm afraid they might be too weak for a light leap."

The gnomes got to work, weaving fallen branches into nest-like cots. While they built, Elwin turned his attention to Grady and Edaline. They each needed a dozen elixirs—and Grady had two cracked ribs—but Elwin promised Sophie they'd make a full recovery.

"I'm fine," she told him as he snapped his fingers and flashed a blue orb around her face. "I wasn't here."

"I'm checking for signs of shock. You're borderline, so I want you to take these." He handed her two vials filled with a thick lime green syrup. "Not sedatives, I promise."

"And not that weird happy elixir you gave me after Alden's mind broke?" she checked.

"Nope. Think of these as a security blanket for your nerves. They'll take away some of that chill"—he traced a finger down the goose bumps on her arms—"and slow your heart to its normal rate. That's it."

Sophie chugged them, barely registering the honeylike taste as warmth rippled through her.

"Want me to check on Verdi?" Elwin offered.

"If it won't affect Cadoc and Lady Cadence's treatment," Edaline told him.

"And only if you can handle being around a few dead bodies," Grady added.

Elwin cringed. "How many are there?"

"Nine ogres," Edaline whispered. "And Brielle."

Everyone bowed their heads at the name, and Sandor punched the tree again.

"Here," Elwin said, reaching for Sandor's bleeding knuckles.

"Do you have an Imparter with you?" Grady asked him. "I need to hail the Council and let them know what happened."

"I can't believe they had thinking caps," Elwin mumbled. "And that the caps blocked mesmerizing."

"The Neverseen must have designed them," Edaline whispered.

Elwin nodded. "No one knows how to take down an elf better than another elf."

"Which is why you're no longer safe in the Lost Cities," Sandor announced, clenching his newly bandaged hand. "Dimitar won't accept failure—especially for this. This had to be his test to secure his new alliance."

"I wouldn't be so sure," Lady Cadence rasped from her newly made stretcher. "None of these were members of his personal guard—and none of them wore Markchains."

"So he distanced himself from the attack," Sandor snarled.

494

"That's not proof of innocence, only foresight. His next attack will come swiftly. Ogres are expert trackers. We need to move you somewhere even Dimitar would never dare go."

"Where are you suggesting?" Edaline asked.

Sandor's voice seemed to deepen as he said, "The best option is Gildingham. The ogres know that entering our capital city would be a declaration of war."

"Would Hylda approve our visit?" Grady asked as he rejoined them. "I thought she preferred to keep outsiders to a minimum."

"She would never turn away an elvin family in need— especially one as important as yours. I'll contact her now and make the arrangements." Sandor pulled a triangular gadget from his pocket and moved to the edge of the clearing to speak with his queen.

Sophie, meanwhile, was wondering why no one seemed to be addressing the much scarier question.

Now that the ogres had sent ten soldiers to directly attack an elvin family within the boundaries of the Lost Cities—did that mean the ogres and the elves were at war?

SIXTY

"LEAVE THE DIPLOMACY TO THE COUN-
cil," Mr. Forkle ordered when Sophie hailed him
on her Imparter and explained the afternoon's
tragedies.

"I think we're well beyond diplomacy," she mumbled.

"I wouldn't be so sure. Given what Lady Cadence noted
about her attackers, I have no doubt King Dimitar will claim
that anyone involved acted without his permission—which
may even be true."

"You're serious?"

"Are the Neverseen acting with the Council's permission?"
he countered. "I know you're angry and afraid—and justifiably
so. But we cannot let ourselves be controlled by fear or fury,

or rush into any actions that will only cause further death and destruction. Not without gathering evidence. So let the Councillors investigate. And try not to be surprised if they opt to proceed with the Peace Summit."

Sophie's grip on her Imparter tightened. "You really think a treaty is going to stop the ogres from killing innocent people? Or coming after my family again?"

"It depends on who's giving the orders. It's also important to keep in mind that if Dimitar was behind this incident, in some ways that's an advantage. We've been working to prevent the ogres and Neverseen from aligning, and this guarantees it. Fintan will be livid that the ogres failed. And King Dimitar will be furious over losing so many warriors."

The words would've been much more comforting if Sophie weren't picturing Brielle's bloody, broken body.

"Right now, the most important thing is to get you and your family to safety," Mr. Forkle added gently. "I agree with Sandor that Gildingham is the wisest option. Do you need me to bring you a crystal to leap there?"

"Queen Hylda has already sent her chariot," Sandor said over Sophie's shoulder. She'd forgotten he was eavesdropping. "The drivers will be here as soon as they retrieve Brielle."

His voice faltered on the name.

"My deepest sympathies," Mr. Forkle told him. "Brielle was an incredible warrior."

"One of the best," Sandor agreed, looking desperate to punch something again.

"When will she be presented in the Hall of Heroes?" Mr. Forkle asked.

"Aurification will begin as soon as she's brought to Gildingham. The presentation should be tomorrow."

"I'll let the Council know to release their goblin regiments for the ceremony," Mr. Forkle promised.

"Actually, Queen Hylda will be ordering them to remain with their assignments," Sandor told him. "She believes it would be unwise to leave the Lost Cities vulnerable. Dimitar could take advantage."

Mr. Forkle blinked. "That's incredibly generous of her."

"It is," Sandor said. "But now more than ever, we must work as allies."

Sophie wasn't familiar with some of the terms they'd been using, but she assumed they'd been talking about the goblin's version of a funeral.

"Can I go to the presentation?" she asked. "Or is it a goblins-only thing?"

"Presentations are generally only attended by our people," Sandor told her. "But Brielle is the first in the elvin regiments to be lost in a battle, so it might be good to show the public that the elves do not take her sacrifice for granted. I'll raise the matter with the queen."

"We'd like to go as well," Grady called from across the clearing, where he sat with Edaline, both of them so weary they could barely move.

"I'll ask Della to include something gold for each of you to wear when she packs up the satchels we'll be sending," Mr. Forkle told them. "Would you like us to send your imp to keep you company, Miss Foster?"

"No, I think it'd be easier for Iggy to stay with Biana."

Sophie doubted the goblins wanted a tiny purple poof causing havoc in their city.

"Please let me know once you're settled in Gildingham," Mr. Forkle told her. "And I'll keep you updated on any developments. And Miss Foster?" He touched the screen of his Imparter, like he was trying to reach across the distance between them. "I'm so relieved that you and your parents are well. Please keep it that way."

His image flashed away, and Sophie stared at the blank screen, trying to figure out what to feel—what to do.

She was on her way to sit with Grady and Edaline when the ground started to rumble.

"Don't be nervous," Sandor said as she jumped back, preparing for another ogre attack. "It's just Twinkle."

With a name like Twinkle, Sophie definitely wasn't prepared for a fifty-foot snake to burst out of the ground—especially a fifty-foot snake strapped to some sort of golden harness lined with hundreds of golden wheels. The contraption ended in a carriage that looked like a giant golden egg, covered in intricate patterns and symbols.

The snake's scales shimmered with flecks of gold, silver, and pink as it slithered into a tight coil, coming to rest with the egg carriage right in front of them.

"Twinkle is a titanoboa," Sandor explained. "And she's been trained to guide the royal chariot through the Imperial Pathways. Queen Hylda wanted to ensure that Brielle returns to Gildingham with proper honor."

In her head, Sophie's brain was screaming, *YOU CHOSE TO TAKE ME IN THE GIANT SNAKE CARRIAGE OF DOOM WHEN WE COULD'VE LIGHT LEAPED?!*

But she'd caught what he said about Brielle arriving with proper honor. If a monster-size snake offered any sort of tribute for Brielle's sacrifice, she would ride in the carriage all day, every day, without complaint.

A small whimper *did* slip through her lips, though, when Sandor led them past Twinkle's enormous head. The massive snake could've swallowed her whole without needing to unhinge her jaw, and her forked tongue kept flicking around Sophie, like she was trying to take a taste.

A seamless door in the carriage slid open, and two goblins greeted Sandor with a solemn nod as Sophie and her parents climbed in. There were no seats inside. Just a massive golden coffin and narrow spaces to stand on either side.

"Hold on to this," Sandor said, grabbing one of the golden ropes tied to the top of the carriage and handing it to Sophie. Grady and Edaline copied him, coiling the rope around one of their wrists and clinging to Sophie with their other hands as the two new goblins shouted a command to get Twinkle moving.

The carriage had no windows—the only light came from a glowing golden orb set into the ceiling—and the ride was so smooth and steady, it almost felt like they were floating. A low rumble reverberated through the silence, and Sophie counted the passing seconds, surprised when they came to a stop after only five hundred and thirty-nine.

"I didn't realize we were so close to Gildingham," Sophie said.

"We weren't. A team of Technopaths helped engineer Twinkle's chariot to allow her to move at supersonic speeds. We'll disembark after they carry out Brielle."

One of the goblins they'd traveled with slid open the door, flooding the carriage with buttery sunlight as he and the other goblin lifted the coffin.

Sophie focused on the view—her first glimpse of the goblin city, where intricate gilded buildings had been built across the rolling green foothills. The architecture had an almost fragile feel, with so many arches and pillars and windows and balconies that they looked ready to float away on a breeze. A golden lake shimmered in the distance, flowing into a river that shone like the sun. And at the top of the highest peak, a golden step pyramid loomed against the horizon.

501

"That's Queen Hylda's palace," Sandor said, following Sophie's gaze. "And once we're out of the carriage you'll see the Hall of Heroes, where we'll be going for Brielle's presentation tomorrow. The queen invited you to have dinner with her tonight, but I asked her to give you the night to settle in before facing any formalities."

"She wasn't offended, was she?" Grady asked.

"If anything, she was relieved. Generally the night a soldier is lost is a night of reflection for our queen. She only offered because she didn't want to seem an unfriendly hostess."

Edaline smiled sadly. "Then thanks for declining. We're going to have to rely on you for proper goblin diplomacy."

"I'll do my best. For instance, as we step out of this carriage and you see the crowd gathered below, it would be considered proper to offer a solemn wave."

"Crowd?" Sophie asked as Sandor slowly exited. Sure enough, when she followed, she could see that Twinkle had brought them to a level of the city halfway up one of the rolling hills, and the golden streets below were lined with goblin warriors who'd gathered to see them. Some were shirtless with black pants and weapons, like Sandor always wore, but most were adorned in gleaming golden armor.

"This way," Sandor said after Sophie gave the crowd what she hoped counted as a "solemn wave." He pressed his palm against a flat panel in the center of golden door set into the mountain. "Don't worry, my house is much bigger on the inside."

He wasn't wrong.

Not only was the house at least ten bedrooms—but everything was designed for someone seven feet tall. All the doorknobs were closer to Sophie's shoulder height, and she had to stand on her tiptoes in order to climb onto any of the chairs. And it was so *fancy*. Shimmering rugs. Tasseled curtains. Intricately carved furniture, all in the same warm yellow tone.

"I'm assuming there's a reason everything's gold," Sophie said.

Sandor nodded. "Gold is a weak metal. But *we* are strong. We don't build houses or walls for protection. We build them to have a place that inspires awe—a place *worth* defending."

"Well, it's incredible," Edaline told him. "I'd heard stories of the golden city, but I'd never pictured it quite this spectacular."

Sandor wandered to one of the windows. "I wish you could be here under better circumstances. But I suppose it's nice to be home. Della should be here with your clothes and things soon. In the meantime, I'll show you to your rooms."

Grady and Edaline were given their own suite at the end of the longest hall, and Sophie grabbed one more hug before following Sandor to where she'd be staying, in a room with a gilded four-poster bed covered in golden linens. She knew she should probably rest. But as soon as she was alone, she did something much more important.

I don't care if this is a bad time, she transmitted. *We need to talk. NOW.*

She repeated the call at least a dozen times before Keefe's voice rushed into her head.

Are Grady and Edaline okay?

Fury churned as fast as the queasiness in her stomach. *I take it that means you knew?*

Not until a couple of hours ago, when Fintan got a hail from King Dimitar.

So the king is behind this? She rubbed the spot under her ribs, where her tangled emotions used to be. She'd released them when she inflicted, leaving her chest cold and empty.

I don't know, Keefe said. *All Fintan told us is that Dimitar will not be our ally. I've been trying to find a way to reach you ever since. I'm so sor—*

Don't! Sophie interrupted. *Brielle's dead. Sorry isn't going to change that.*

Okay, I don't know who Brielle is, but—

She was Grady's bodyguard. THAT'S how close the ogres came to catching him. And you were supposed to warn us!

I did warn you. I just didn't know the specifics.

I know. But that's the thing neither of us have wanted to admit. If you can't give the specifics, everything you're doing is worthless.

The words hit him harder than she'd expected. But she wasn't taking them back.

I'm doing the best I can, he told her.

Maybe. But it's not enough. Half the time you can't even talk during our check-ins. This isn't working.

I know it feels like that—but I'm seriously SO CLOSE.

Even if that's true—you know what? We're getting close too. We've already figured out what the symbol means, and Gethen gave us a big clue on how to use it.

What are you saying?

I'm saying, we're coming after the Neverseen with everything we have.

Bad idea, Foster. Seriously, so bad.

I don't care. They tried to take my family from me, and I'm not going to sit back anymore. So you better find a way to get out now, Keefe. Before you get caught in the cross fire.

SIXTY-ONE

KEEFE WASN'T GOING TO LISTEN.

Sophie could tell.

He thought she didn't have a plan, and that everything she'd said was just an angry rant.

And a small part of her worried that he was right.

The other part knew they *had* to find a way to fight harder, before she lost anyone else she cared about.

But that included Keefe.

So if he wasn't ready to leave on his own, they'd have to plan a rescue—for real. No more waiting for inspiration and hoping a plan would come together. They needed to sit down and figure it out and make it happen, just like when they'd snuck into Ravagog.

Between their abilities and their skills and the information they'd gathered, there had to be a way to—

A knock at Sandor's front door interrupted her scheming.

Sophie crept to her doorway, relieved when she recognized Grizel's voice. It sounded like Grizel had brought their clothes from the Lost Cities, and Sophie made her way down the hall to pick up her satchel.

But when she turned the corner, she caught a quick glimpse of Grizel clinging to Sandor and sobbing against his shoulder as he wrapped his arms gently around her.

Sophie ducked back, not wanting to interrupt such a private moment.

"I'm sorry," Grizel whispered, her voice thick. "When the news first came through, all anyone could tell me was that a soldier was down at Havenfield. And I thought . . ."

"I don't deserve your worry." Sandor's voice was choked with fury. "I wasn't there when Brielle and Cadoc needed me. I was pacing in front of Lumenaria like a fool."

"Staying with your charge doesn't make you foolish," Grizel told him. "I would've done the same thing."

"Which proves we're both blindly stubborn beyond all reason, not that it was the right decision."

Grizel laughed softly. "The *stubborn* I'll agree to. But the *blind* part might fall squarely on you."

"I'm . . . not as blind as you think."

The shift in his tone made Sophie wonder if she should stop

listening and give them some privacy. But she couldn't seem to make her legs carry her away.

"I couldn't stop you from being assigned to Fitz," Sandor whispered. "But have you ever wondered why I assigned Brielle to watch over Grady?"

"I . . . figured it was because she was an incredible soldier," Grizel said carefully.

"She was. But we both know that charge should've gone to you. Given the rarity of Grady's talent, he needed our strongest warrior. I should've assigned you to protect him and moved Brielle to Everglen. But"—he cleared the catch from his throat—"I worried what would happen if we lived in such close quarters."

"Afraid I'd play too many games?"

"Afraid you'd win."

The confession was so soft, Sophie almost wondered if she'd imagined it.

"Is that really so frightening?" Grizel whispered.

Sandor cleared his throat again, drawing out the moment. "I chose the life of a soldier. And soldiers are strongest when they have nothing distracting them—nothing slowing their hand or forcing caution when the battle calls for risk."

"See, and I always thought the strongest soldiers were those with something worth fighting for. Something to come home to. Something they can't bear to lose that makes them refuse to surrender."

"I don't know," Sandor whispered. "But I can't stop imagining what I'd do if it were you in that coffin. How lost I'd feel."

The silence that followed was so charged, it had Sophie mentally chanting, *Kiss, kiss, kiss!* But real life never seemed to be as romantic as it was in human movies, and the moment slipped away.

"Well," Grizel said. "I suppose I should be getting back to Everglen. Queen Hylda gave me a long list of preparations to make for tomorrow."

The door had started to creak closed when Sandor said, "I haven't forgotten that I owe you a dance."

"Neither have I," Grizel whispered. "But I won't force you."

"You aren't," Sandor breathed. "I can't promise much. But I might be able to handle . . . slow."

"Slow," Grizel repeated, and the hope in her voice made Sophie steal a peek around the corner. She watched Grizel take Sandor's hands and whisper, "I'd be good with slow."

Sandor reached up to brush Grizel's cheek, and she leaned into his palm, closing her eyes and taking a deep breath. Endless seconds slipped by, neither of them seeming to mind. And when she pulled away, a shy smile curled her lips.

"Be safe," Sandor whispered.

"Always," she told him.

She was halfway through the doorway when she turned back with a teasing wink. "This won't get you out of wearing those silver pants."

Sandor sighed. "I suppose that's the least of my worries."

She left without another word, and Sandor waited for the lock to click before he turned to Sophie and said, "I knew you were listening."

"I figured," Sophie told him, too giddy to feel guilty. "And just so you know, I think you made the right decision. You guys are so—"

"Keep in mind that any comments you make about my love life give me permission to talk to you about boys," Sandor interrupted. "I'd also appreciate your discretion. Now is not the time for such things to become known."

"Done," Sophie said, dropping the conversation. "I just want to see you happy. Especially after all the sacrifices you make for me. I'm sorry again for inflicting on you. Next time I'll keep a tighter hold until I'm sure I'm fighting a threat."

Sandor shook his head as he brought over her purple backpack. "How about instead we focus on making sure there isn't a next time?"

Sophie had planned to cry at Brielle's funeral—or presentation—or whatever the goblins called it. She'd even stuffed several hand-kerchiefs into the pockets of her long golden gown. But sadness wasn't the theme of the ceremony. It was about bestowing honor and celebrating Brielle's accomplishments.

The Hall of Heroes itself was a massive acropolis-style structure lined with twisted golden columns and filled with golden statues that reminded Sophie of the terra-cotta warriors she'd seen in human encyclopedias—row upon row of gleaming goblins in heroic battle poses.

It seemed like a beautiful tribute, until they unveiled Brielle's statue and Sophie realized the figure was a little *too* lifelike— every detail perfect, down to the very last curl.

"Is that *her*?" she whispered, fighting off a gag when Sandor nodded. Grady and Edaline didn't look *as* horrified—but they'd definitely gone pale.

"Her body's been aurified," Sandor explained. "It's a process the elves helped us perfect. It transmutes every cell to gold, leaving no flesh or blood behind. Only a powerful likeness to remember our soldiers by." He frowned when he noticed Sophie was cringing. "Honestly, how is it that different from wrapping your DNA around a seed and letting the tree grow with some of your characteristics?"

When he put it like that, it didn't sound *as* creepy. And it wasn't Sophie's place to judge another species' culture anyway.

But she still wouldn't have wanted to be alone in the Hall of Heroes at night—and she was pretty sure she was going to have a more than a few golden mummy nightmares.

She fought hard not to let any of her discomfort show on her face, since the queen had given their group seats on an elevated platform, in plain view of the entire audience.

"It was wise for you to attend," Sandor told them when everyone stood to leave. "I can tell it meant a lot to my people to see that the elves care about the soldiers who protect them."

"It did indeed," a deep, throaty voice said behind them, and Sandor immediately dropped to one knee.

"Your Highness," he mumbled. "I didn't see you there."

"That's because I snuck up on you," Queen Hylda said, tossing her intricately plaited hair. She smoothed the golden lapels of her military-style jacket as her gray eyes focused on Sophie, Grady, and Edaline. "Please, no need for such formalities," she told them as they hurried to bow as well. "You are not my subjects."

"We still owe you our respect," Grady said as he straightened. "You and your warriors have been invaluable allies."

"Well, the elves' knowledge and innovation have been equally precious for our world," Queen Hylda said. "I consider the whole arrangement to be a crucial partnership. Which is why I was hoping I might borrow young Miss Foster for a few minutes. The Council has informed me that she'll be attending the Peace Summit. And if that's the case, I have a favor to ask."

SIXTY-TWO

YOU HAD A PRIVATE AUDIENCE with the goblin queen?" Biana asked, sharing a look with Dex that seemed to say, *Why are we even surprised anymore?*

"We didn't talk for long," Sophie mumbled, checking to make sure no one around them was eavesdropping. "Queen Hylda just wanted to ask me for a favor."

Biana grinned. "Of course she did."

Despite the attack on Sophie's parents—which the Council had revealed to the public to honor Brielle's sacrifice—Mr. Forkle had managed to convince Sandor to bring Sophie to her weekly skill lesson at Foxfire. The Coaches were ramping up the training now that people finally seemed scared enough to commit to it. And it made a difference—by the end of the lesson, almost half of Sophie's Hemisphere had achieved the day's skill and cracked small stress fissures in their stones.

Sophie had shattered hers completely.

The process had left her drained—but it was a good kind of exhaustion. Far better than the five restless days she'd spent pacing around Sandor's house, brainstorming elaborate Rescue Keefe plans and then rejecting them for having too many Things That Would Get Everyone Killed. And her check-ins with Keefe now followed a repetitive pattern of her begging him to leave the Neverseen and him promising, "Soon."

Hopefully, if her group of friends worked together, they'd be able to come up with something that had a chance of success. But getting them all in the same place was proving challenging—especially Tam and Linh. The twins had even skipped the skill lesson that day. Tam was using every spare second to search the Silver Tower, desperate to find whatever last piece they needed to make everything they'd learned about the symbol come together. And Linh had been nervous to leave Wylie alone.

Mr. Forkle had felt obligated to tell Wylie what they'd learned from Gethen about his mother's death and starstones—though he left out any mention of Lady Gisela, deciding to wait until they had a better idea of precisely how she'd been involved. But hearing that his mom had likely helped the Neverseen had knocked Wylie to a new low. Granite had even brought Maruca and her mom back to see him, and all Wylie said during the visit was, "Is anyone who they say they are?"

"What kind of favor are you supposed to do for a goblin queen?" Fitz asked, dragging Sophie out of her dreary thoughts.

She waited for a group of nearby Right Hemispheres to wander away before she whispered, "She wants my support during the summit. She gave me a list of all the things she wants added to the new treaty, and asked me to decide which ones I'll vote in favor of."

"Isn't that cheating?" Biana asked. "Colluding before the summit?"

"Why would it be?" Fitz asked. "It's not a test."

"Your brother is correct," Sandor told her. "The summit is a negotiation. And the best negotiators do their homework ahead of time. I'm sure everyone is determining their allies."

"Anyone else stunned the ogres are still going through with the summit?" Dex asked. "I mean . . . they have to know everyone is going to side against them."

"King Dimitar has no choice," Grizel said, and Sophie noticed she was standing a little closer to Sandor than she truly needed to. "He's claiming innocence in the attack, insisting it was done by a band of rebels. He even sent Queen Hylda a letter offering his condolences. But he knows no one will believe him if he's not also working closely with the Council toward 'achieving a peaceful resolution.'"

She put the last words in air quotes, almost like she no

longer believed they were a possibility. But Sophie was clinging hard to the last shreds of her hope.

Sure, part of her wanted to march into Ravagog and stomp the ogres into the ground for what they'd done to her family. But another part kept thinking about the eerie golden bodies in the Hall of Heroes.

How many more goblins would have to be aurified if the elves and ogres went to war?

How many new trees would be added to the Wanderling Woods?

If there was any chance they could solve this without further violence, they had to try for it.

"So what kinds of things are on Queen Hylda's list?" Dex asked.

"Exactly what you'd expect," Sophie whispered. "She wants the ogres to turn over all their weapons and agree to stop any sort of offensive—or defensive—training, wants them to surrender the borderlands they share with the goblins, and wants King Dimitar to turn over the ogre who killed Brielle. There were a bunch of things that had to do with the previous treaty too. But I didn't understand a lot of that, so I gave copies to Mr. Forkle and Oralie to see if they can help me."

"Are you going to support her list?" Biana asked.

Sophie shrugged.

She understood why Queen Hylda was drawing such a hard line. But she kept thinking about what Lady Cadence had tried to tell her, about how the new treaty would destroy fundamental aspects of the ogres' culture. She had zero sympathy for King Dimitar, but she knew thousands and thousands of innocent ogres would be affected—including the children she'd seen running around during her time in Ravagog.

"Let's just say I'm glad I still have some time to decide," she mumbled, wishing it were longer. The Council was sticking with their scheduled date, so she only had about a week and a half left. "I swear, this whole thing is way more involved than I realized. Did you guys know that summits last multiple days? I got this, like, *packet* saying Edaline and I will have our own room in the castle, and luggage isn't allowed, so we both had to send the Council our measurements and they'll provide several changes of clothes."

"Ohhhh," Biana breathed. "I bet they'll make you the most gorgeous dresses! Will you get to keep them?"

"If I do, they're yours," Sophie promised.

"And here I thought you guys would be discussing *important* stuff," Marella said, rolling her bright blue eyes as she shoved her petite frame into the center of their group. "But apparently we're standing in a suspicious-looking circle surrounded by goblins so we can discuss *clothes*?"

"Does this mean you're talking to us again?" Biana asked.

"It means I'm talking to you *today*," Marella corrected. "And only because I realized you guys were never going to leave me alone until you got what you wanted. So"—she checked over her shoulder and lowered her voice—"since my mom was actually having a pretty good day yesterday, I thought, *Fine, I'll ask her about Cyrah and prove she doesn't know anything.* Only . . ." Her eyes dropped to her feet, kicking at her scuffed shoes. "I guess she does remember something."

"And that something is?" Dex prompted.

Marella twisted one of her braids around her finger. "I'll tell you what I know *if* you do something for me."

"You know that's blackmail, right?" Fitz asked. "Or maybe it's extortion? Either way, it's super shady."

Marella shrugged, unconcerned.

"Why don't we find out what she wants before we get mad?" Biana suggested.

"Clearly you're the smart Vacker," Marella said. "And what I want shouldn't be a big deal. I just want to meet with this mysterious Mr. Forkle guy you're always talking about."

"Why?" Sophie asked.

"That's between him and me."

"Not if you want me to set up a meeting," Sophie argued. "He'll never agree without knowing the reason."

Marella sighed, twisting her braid tighter. "He's the one who triggered all of your abilities, right?"

"Most of them," Sophie corrected—and she had a sinking suspicion she knew where Marella was going with this.

Marella confirmed it a second later when she crossed her arms and arched an eyebrow. "Then I want him to trigger mine."

SIXTY-THREE

"THIS IS NOT HOW THIS PROCESS WORKS," Mr. Forkle told Marella as he closed the door to Alden's circular office. He'd chosen Everglen as a meeting point, since Havenfield felt too vulnerable, and the Vackers had been generous enough to offer their home.

He'd also made Marella wait a day for the meeting, since he'd had a number of appointments forcing him to stay in Magnate Leto mode the day before. And the delay seemed to have made Marella fidgety.

Or maybe it was the hard look in Mr. Forkle's eyes as he told her, "And I don't simply mean that triggering abilities this way is unnatural. Important information about a possible murder should *never* be a bargaining chip."

"I know," Marella mumbled, sinking into one of the plush armchairs that faced the room's floor-to-ceiling aquarium. Dex, Fitz, Biana, and Sophie leaned against the windowed wall behind her, while Sandor, Woltzer, Grizel, and Lovise waited outside to give them more space. "But I've tried *everything* else," she whispered. "And I knew you'd triggered Sophie's abilities—"

"Miss Foster is a very special case," Mr. Forkle interrupted.

"Yeah, I'm aware. But I figured . . . if it doesn't work, at least I'll know I did everything I possibly could. And here, you can see I'm good for the information part." She pulled a thick, sealed envelope from the pocket of her wrinkled cape and set it on the edge of Alden's massive desk. "The secret my mom gave me is in there. If you want to open it first, that's cool."

"That won't be necessary," Mr. Forkle said, even though Sophie was ready to snatch it and tear it open. "Perhaps this will prove that you need not resort to such drastic measures, should you ever seek my help in the future."

He stepped closer, and Marella flinched. "Have you changed your mind?"

"No!" Marella straightened in her chair. "I was just wondering if it will . . . um . . . hurt?"

"Having an ability triggered can be a strange sensation—but not an unpleasant one. It's also important to keep in mind that hardly anyone manifests immediately. It will only take

520

me a few moments to send mental energy into the portions of your brain where abilities develop—but you might not notice a change for several hours or days. Or your mind may still not be ready."

"Is there a way to specifically trigger empathy?" Marella asked.

"No. Our abilities stem from our genetics. Whatever you will or won't be has already been decided—and might I add that oftentimes nature is far smarter than we are. We may want a certain ability, only to discover that what we manifest is far better suited."

"That'd be easier to believe if it weren't coming from the guy who handpicked a billion abilities for Sophie," Marella mumbled.

"As I said, Miss Foster is a special case—though for the record, I did let her genetics guide me. Not every ability she has is one I would've chosen."

"Which ones aren't?" Sophie asked. "Besides teleporting?"

"That's irrelevant information," Mr. Forkle told her. "They're a part of you either way."

"Does she have abilities she hasn't manifested?" Dex asked.

"Let's not get sidetracked," Mr. Forkle said. "Are you ready now, Miss Redek?"

Marella took a deep breath before she nodded.

"Very well. Hold still." Mr. Forkle reached for her face, pressing two fingers against each of her temples as he closed his eyes. "I'll start in three . . . two . . . one."

"Whoa—you were right about it being strange," Marella said, scratching the top of her head. "It's super tingly—and it keeps getting warmer."

"Try to clear your mind," Mr. Forkle told her. "It's best not to focus on the process. I'm trying to trigger your instinct, not your active mind."

"Right," Marella said. "Sorry."

The seconds ticked by and Sophie found herself holding her breath, wishing with everything she had for Marella to manifest. Like Stina had said, even if Marella didn't get the ability she wanted, it would help her *so* much just knowing the issue was settled.

"One last push," Mr. Forkle said, scrunching his brow.

Marella gripped the arms of her chair and let out a tiny squeak before Mr. Forkle stumbled back and leaned against the desk. A sheen of sweat glistened across his face, and his breathing sounded like he'd just run up ten flights of stairs.

"Whoa, it's all spinny and flippy in my head right now," Marella mumbled.

"I'm not surprised. I gave you every bit of mental energy I could spare," Mr. Forkle told her. "I'll leap you home as soon as your head clears—and then you need to rest. Let me know when you feel ready."

"I might need a few minutes," Marella warned, waving her fingers in front of her eyes like her vision had blurred.

"So can we open the envelope now?" Fitz asked, already reaching for it.

"Up to you," Marella said. "Oh, but I should probably explain." She swallowed hard, rubbing her temples as she said, "I asked my mom why she'd told Cyrah she needed to be more careful, and she told me it was because Cyrah was messing with things she didn't understand. So I asked her what *that* meant and she got up and walked away. I figured she was done with the conversation, but—whoa, it's really spinny right now. Hang on."

Marella leaned her head between her knees. "Think this is a sign that it's working?"

"We'll know soon enough," Mr. Forkle told her.

She nodded carefully. "Anyway, my mom came back down and gave me the thing I put in that envelope—but only after I promised her I'd never try to use it. She told me she found it in Cyrah's stall. It doesn't look dangerous to me, but maybe I just don't know what it is."

The four friends huddled close as Fitz tore open the envelope and poured the single item into his clammy palm.

A smooth, oval starstone.

And when Fitz held it up to the light, it flashed blue.

SIXTY-FOUR

WE NEED TO FIND OUT WHERE it takes us," Sophie said, pointing to the blue beam of light that the starstone cast on the floor.

Right on cue, the door burst open and all four bodyguards rushed in, shouting the many reasons none of them would be going anywhere.

"Wow, is this how it always is for you guys?" Marella asked, rubbing her forehead.

"Pretty much." Sophie raised her hands to get everyone's attention. "I know you don't want us to do this. But starstones remember the last place they've been, so we *have* to find out where this one goes. And since goblins can't light leap without elves, some of us are going to have to go. So how about we pick a small group—two elves, two goblins—and make a quick leap? We can keep our crystals right in our hands, that way we're ready to leap away the second we re-form if there's any trouble. And I'm sure Alden and Della have some crystals we can use to make sure we end up back here and everyone knows we're safe."

"Of course," Della said, blinking into sight on the far side of the room—making Sophie wonder how long she'd been eaves-dropping.

The goblins debated a couple of minutes more, and eventually admitted that Sophie's argument was solid. Which brought them to the bigger question.

"How do we decide who goes?" Fitz asked.

Of course everyone nominated themselves—and the adults did their usual adult thing and tried to claim it should be them instead of "children." Round and round it went until Grizel slipped her fingers in the corners of her mouth and destroyed everyone's eardrums with a high-pitched whistle.

"If anyone tries to start another shouting match, I will do that again," she warned. "And I won't stop until everyone has a migraine. So let's try logic instead, shall we? We already agreed that two goblins will be part of the mission—and of the four of us, those ranked the highest are Sandor and myself. And since neither of us can separate from our charges—and we all know there's no way Sophie's not going to be a part of this—that means we'll be bringing Sophie and Fitz, and they will stand behind us and do *exactly* what we say. We go. We look. We leave. It'll be five minutes, tops."

"Works for me," Fitz said, grinning at Biana when she pouted.

"Wow," Marella said. "I've never seen people fight because they all *want* to do the crazy, dangerous thing."

"Welcome to my world," Sophie told her. "Still mad at me for not dragging you into it?"

Marella shook her head. "Starting to think I'm not cut out. You're really going to blindly follow a random beam of light, knowing full well it could leap you into a room full of killers?"

"It's not even the scariest thing we've done," Fitz told her.

Mr. Forkle sighed. "I should go with you. There can just as easily be five to the group, instead of four."

"If we go with that slippery reasoning, there can just as easily be six or seven or eight," Grizel argued. "But the smaller the group, the faster and more discreet we'll be. Besides, you're looking a little wobbly."

She was right—the color still hadn't returned to Mr. Forkle's features.

"And you're supposed to be helping Marella home," Sophie reminded him. "And maybe—if Caprise is up to it—you could ask her some follow-up questions."

"My mom *is* having another kinda-okay day," Marella admitted. "She might be up to talking for a few minutes."

Mr. Forkle looked anything but thrilled with this plan, but seemed to swallow back his protests. "Very well. Make sure you leave the starstone here." He held out his hand, waiting for Sophie to pass it over. "You can just as easily step in to a path created by someone staying here, and that way we have a way to find you if we need to."

"They also have their panic switches," Dex reminded everyone.

Sandor unsheathed his sword. "We won't need them."

Grizel drew her weapon as well, with an especially impressive flourish.

Della gathered Fitz and Sophie into a hug, promising that she and Alden would be waiting for them at Everglen's gates. Biana joined in the embrace, pulling Dex along with her.

"Wow," Marella mumbled. "You guys are huggers."

"We'll be fine," Sophie said as she pulled away—though her voice was slightly scratchier than she wanted it to be.

Fitz reached for her hand, and Sandor and Grizel completed the circle as Mr. Forkle created the starstone's dim path. They each took a second to steady their nerves before together, they let the starstone's blue glow carry them away.

It wasn't the coldest leap Sophie had ever experienced. But it felt strangely turbulent, like the light was part of a windstorm whipping them around, trying to send them scattering. She rallied her concentration and wrapped it tighter around

Sandor and Grizel, refusing to lose a single particle as the world rushed back and they reformed in . . .

. . . a bedroom.

A very fancy bedroom.

Everything was velvet and silk in shades of red and black, with a bed big enough to sleep ten people.

"This isn't what I was expecting," Fitz whispered as Sandor and Grizel sniffed the air.

"Think it's Fintan's room?" Sophie asked, staring at the twinkling balefire chandelier that cascaded from the ceiling. "It wouldn't be Brant's—he can't stand to be around kindling."

"No idea," Fitz said. "I'm just glad it's empty."

The bed wasn't made, and a lump under the blankets caught Sophie's attention. She tiptoed over and peeled back the covers and found . . .

"Mrs. Stinkbottom?"

The fluffy stuffed gulon stared back at her with its glassy eyes.

"So is this Keefe's room?" Fitz asked. "I thought he didn't take Mrs. Stinkbottom with him."

"He didn't," Sophie mumbled. "So maybe . . ."

She wandered to the wall of windows and peeled back one of the curtains. Far below she could see a stark courtyard with an iron arch over the main pathway.

"We're not in a Neverseen hideout," she whispered. "We're in . . . Candleshade."

Her brain was still figuring out what to do with the idea of Lord Cassius cuddling with Keefe's favorite stuffed animal, when Fitz connected all the dots to the much more disturbing implication.

"This proves Cyrah made the starstone in Lady Gisela's hairpin, doesn't it?" he asked.

"It's worse than that," Sophie said, taking a moment to add her dread to the knot of emotions she'd been rebuilding.

She glanced around the room, making sure Lord Cassius wasn't around to hear her before she whispered, "I think it proves for sure that Lady Gisela killed her."

SIXTY-FIVE

I HAVE TO TELL YOU SOMETHING, SOPHIE
transmitted, rubbing the growing tangle under her ribs
as she pushed the call out into the night.

Fitz tightened his hold on her hand, snapping their
thumb rings together.

Once she'd realized they *had* to tell Keefe about his mom,
she'd asked if she could stay the night at Everglen so she
wouldn't be alone. Fitz would be eavesdropping on the conversation, helping her gauge Keefe's reaction—that way she
wouldn't be the only one deciding if he'd reached a danger
zone of guilt and recklessness.

Sandor hadn't been thrilled with the sleepover arrangement,
since he needed to return to Grady and Edaline in Gildingham.

But Grizel had teased him into trusting her to protect both of their charges. If Sophie had known a girlfriend was all it took to get Sandor to relax a little, she would've tried fixing him up months ago.

"Has he said anything yet?" Biana asked, blinking in and out of sight as she wandered Everglen's upstairs guest bedroom.

Sophie had stayed in the cozy-yet-elegant room several times since she'd moved to the Lost Cities, and it always seemed to happen when things got hard.

"What do we do if he doesn't respond?" Dex asked.

"Wait until morning and try again," Sophie mumbled, knowing it would mean a long, sleepless night—though sleep was a lost cause anyway. She hadn't realized how many hopes she'd rested on the slim excuses Mr. Forkle had given for why Lady Gisela might not be Cyrah's murderer, until they'd been ripped away.

Is this going to be another one of those nights where you spend the whole time yelling at me to come home? Keefe asked, making her sit up straighter as his thoughts filled her head. *Because as much as I love it when you get all feisty on me, now's really not a good time.*

Why? Are you with other people? Sophie asked.

Nope. But I'm working on something that's kinda time-pressed. And no, I can't tell you what it is. I don't want to get your hopes up until I know for sure if this is going to work. So let's save the lecture for tomorrow.

It's not a lecture, she transmitted. *It's . . .*

Her hands shook, and Biana and Dex scooted closer, offering support.

Hmm, Keefe said. *This sounds serious.*

It is. I'm really scared it's going to be too much. But I don't think you'd want me to keep it secret, so I don't know what to do.

I take it this means you know about my mom, Keefe thought quietly.

Sophie's and Fitz's eyebrows shot up. *You know?* she asked.

His thoughts felt a little fidgety as he told her, *Yeah. Fintan told me a couple of days ago. I didn't mention it because you've been so mad at me. Plus, I was still trying to figure out how I feel about it.*

How do you feel about it? Sophie asked.

I still don't really know. I smashed a few things—and that felt good. And I did a little sulking. But the thing is, it doesn't actually change anything. I was already done with her long before this.

I guess . . . , Sophie thought, studying Fitz's expression.

He looked as wary as she felt.

Could Keefe truly be this calm? Or was he a ticking time bomb?

So, she said, scooting away from Dex and Biana, who were elbowing her and Fitz, wanting updates on what was happening. *Are you okay with me telling Wylie about this? I promised I'd keep him updated, but I'll wait if you aren't ready to have him know.*

Why did Wylie ask for updates about my mom?

He didn't. He asked for updates about his *mom.*

So what does my mom have to do with his mom?

Sophie frowned. *Isn't that what we've been talking about?*

I . . . don't know anymore.

Sourness pooled in her stomach. *What exactly did Fintan tell you about your mom?*

Why don't you tell me what you were going to say first?

Fitz squeezed her hand for support as Sophie told Keefe everything they knew about the starstone Marella gave them, and where her mother had found it, and how it had leaped straight into his parents' bedroom. She even told him about his dad sleeping with Mrs. Stinkbottom at night. And each new fact rumbled around his brain like a thunderstorm.

So she killed her, Keefe said. His mental voice was flat. His mind gray, like the storm was taking over.

It looks that way, Sophie admitted. *But technically we still don't—*

Forget it, Foster. You don't have to make pretend excuses. We both know there's no way it's a coincidence that someone found a super-rare starstone leaping straight to my parents' bedroom at the place where someone died—especially since Gethen knew something about it. And it's fine. I'm fine. It's . . . whatever. I'm over it.

No you're not, she pressed.

No. But I can't deal with it right now. I'd rather focus on destroying everything she's built, piece by piece.

An understandable goal. Also a super-reckless one. And proof that the only way they'd ever get Keefe to come home would be to drag him there, kicking and screaming.

So, was that it? he asked. *Because I really do need to concentrate.*

Sophie was about to let him go when she realized he'd yet to clear up the misunderstanding. *What did you think I was going to tell you about your mom?*

His mind thundered again, darkening the space between them. *I thought you were going to tell me that no one knows where she is anymore. Dimitar went to check on her at the prison, and she'd escaped.*

SIXTY-SIX

I'M ASSUMING NO ONE KNOWS HOW SHE escaped, or if someone helped her," Mr. Forkle said, watching a stringy-looking creature floating in the dimly lit aquarium. Alden had been kind enough to loan them his office again to talk privately.

Mr. Forkle had been at the Redeks' house when Sophie hailed him with the latest news—resting after giving Marella a second burst of mental energy, since she still hadn't manifested.

"Who would help her?" Sophie asked.

The Neverseen were the ones who'd locked Lady Gisela away, and there weren't exactly a lot of other people in the Lost Cities who knew how to pull off an ogre-prison break.

"Has anyone been keeping an eye on Keefe's dad these last few weeks?" Fitz asked.

"You think *Lord Cassius* pulled this off?" Biana countered.

"I don't know. He's not really a get-his-hands-dirty kind of guy," Fitz said, which was a *tremendous* understatement, "but he did suggest a prison break when we talked to him. Plus . . . she's his wife. Is it so hard to believe he might try to save her?"

"*Trying* isn't the same as succeeding," Biana argued. "Am I really the only one who thinks it sounds impossible?"

"The implausibility of a theory rarely negates its possibility," Mr. Forkle told her. "Especially since Lord Cassius is quite capable of securing allies. I'll have our Technopath dig into his registry records and see if he can shake out anything interesting."

"I can help," Dex offered.

"Only if it becomes necessary. I don't want any of us giving this too much of our energy. It's an unexpected turn of events—even an intriguing one. But not particularly urgent, either."

"Are you sure?" Sophie asked. "Now we're not just fighting the Neverseen and the ogres, we're fighting Lady Gisela and her mysterious supporters too."

"We don't even know that she *has* supporters," Mr. Forkle reminded her. "For all we know, she slipped out of that prison by her own accord. And if she is part of some new, rising order, for the moment, they share our enemies."

"It still feels like this whole mess just got a whole lot more complicated," Sophie mumbled, sinking into one of the office's overstuffed armchairs.

Mr. Forkle took the chair across from her. "You may be right, Miss Foster. These challenges have turned out to be far more intricate than anything I'd originally imagined. And I'll confess that ever since Miss Redek's request earlier today, I've been wondering if I've prepared the four of you as fully as I should have."

"What do you mean?" Sophie asked.

He steepled his fingers and gazed through the wall of windows. Outside, a pair of moonlarks drifted across a small shimmering lake, their long silvery tails rippling the glassy water. "I mean perhaps it's time to stop holding back. I've hinted before that you might have another ability waiting to manifest—"

"I knew it!" Fitz interrupted, sporting a superbly smug grin.

"Is it cool?" Dex asked as Biana said, "Are you going to trigger it?"

"That is a decision I leave up to Miss Foster."

Sophie gripped the arms of her chair—realizing it was the same chair she'd sat on for so many other huge revelations.

Good news. Bad news. Weird news.

She couldn't tell which category this would fall into.

"All abilities come with responsibility," he said quietly. "But some are heavier than others. I told you earlier that your abilities were not all hand selected. Some were a natural result of the various tweaks I made to your genes. And this one gave me a serious amount of pause when I realized it would be part of your makeup—not because there's anything wrong with the ability. It's an incredibly valuable asset. But it's also one that could be taken advantage of."

He reached into his cloak pocket and pulled out a thin package wrapped in velvet. "I've been carrying these since the day I triggered your other abilities. I wanted to be ready in case this talent also broke through. But so far, it's remained dormant—which could mean the talent will never manifest on its own. So keep that in mind when you make this decision. You're fourteen now, growing increasingly close to the time when the manifesting window closes, so it's very possible that if we leave you be, you may never face this responsibility. And no one—including myself—will judge you for whatever you choose. It's entirely your decision."

He handed the parcel to Sophie, and she unwrapped the soft fabric, revealing two wrist-length black silken gloves.

"Am I supposed to know what these mean?" she asked, glad to see Fitz, Biana, and Dex looking just as confused. "Wait—I'm not going to be like Rogue, right?"

"I'm assuming that's a human?" Mr. Forkle asked.

"Sort of. She's a character in these comics my sister loved, where some people have genetic mutations that give them superpowers. Hers makes it so she can't ever touch anyone without absorbing their power—and if she touches them too long, she'll kill them."

"Humans and their wild imaginations," Mr. Forkle said with a small smile. "No, you'll be nothing like this *Rogue*. In fact, it's quite the opposite. Nothing will affect *you*. But you'll be able to empower others with the touch of your hands. It's a rare ability called an Enhancer."

Dex's eyes widened. "I've heard of that! Won't it mean that even being around her will make all of us more powerful?"

"To a very small extent, yes," Mr. Forkle said. "But it's something most won't ever notice. The true boost comes from the touch of your fingertips," he told Sophie. "Your body will store energy there, ready to transfer on contact. Hence the gloves—though they're not a full solution. More a temporary buffer, to ensure you don't accidentally enhance someone, and to buy a few precious seconds for you to break away should anyone try to take unwanted advantage. Still, I'm sure you can imagine how Fintan or Brant might abuse this ability should they discover it."

She definitely could. "And there's no way to turn it off? Like how I shield my mind from people's thoughts?"

Mr. Forkle shook his head. "This ability is more like being a Polyglot. You don't tell your mind to translate the other languages. It just *does*. The energy will gather in your fingertips the same way. Covering your hands or avoiding contact are the only ways to prevent it."

Sophie traced a finger across the silky gloves, trying to imagine wearing them all the time. It made her hands feel hot and itchy and—

"If it helps," Fitz said, squatting next to her chair, "the gloves won't feel like what you're thinking. I wore human gloves once—they were awful. I felt like my hands couldn't touch or grab anything. Our gloves are like a second skin. Try them on, you'll see."

After a slight hesitation, Sophie slipped her fingers into the cool, thin fabric. It seemed to suction against her skin, feather-light and almost undetectable as she flexed her grip a few times.

Fitz reached for her hand, and she still felt the heat of his palm and the smoothness of his skin and the stupid flutter in her heart.

"I'm sure you could wear your Cognate rings on top if you want," he told her.

"Same goes for your panic switch," Dex added helpfully.

"Actually, that will make removing the gloves far trickier when she wants to enhance someone," Mr. Forkle reminded them. "Better to wear as she is, with accessories underneath."

"And I'll really have to wear them all the time?" Sophie asked.

"It will depend on the situation," Mr. Forkle said. "When you're home, or safe among friends, the gloves will not be necessary. But at school or running errands—or certainly whenever you take any risks—you will want to ensure that you're protected."

"And does the ability do anything to benefit *me*?"

"Yes and no. Your own abilities will remain unaffected. But

those around you will become stronger, which *is* an advantage—especially since you've chosen to surround yourself with a group of incredibly talented friends. Imagine how much more they could accomplish if you enhanced their power. The downside is, you could do the same for your enemies."

Sophie rubbed her head, trying to build a mental pros-and-cons list. "What would you do?" she asked Fitz. "If you were the one having to make this choice?"

He brushed his hand through his hair and stared out the window. "Honestly? I don't know. I'm sure it would take our Cognate powers to a whole other level—but I would never want to put you in more danger just for that."

"I feel like there has to be a gadget I could make that would give you more control than a pair of gloves," Dex mumbled. "I wonder what would happen if I made some tweaks to two nexuses—one for each wrist."

He started mumbling to himself, switching to a techie language no one else understood as Sophie focused on Biana. "What about you?"

"I think . . . if you do it, that means it's on us to step up," she said quietly. "We're the ones who get stronger, so we need to work harder to protect you."

"And I know I speak for your currently absent bodyguard," Grizel said, slinking out of the shadows, "when I say that—should you choose to take on this ability—you must make every effort to keep it secret."

"I agree," Mr. Forkle said. "But the decision is still yours, Miss Foster. And we will support whatever you decide."

Sophie stared at her hands, trying to imagine all the crazy ways being an Enhancer would change everything.

Then she thought about Wylie.

And Brielle.

And Kenric.

And Jolie.

And all the nights she'd lost sleep, worrying about her friends and family. All she'd wanted was to keep them safe—and here was a new, important way.

"Trigger the ability," she whispered. "I can handle it."

SIXTY-SEVEN

"LAST CHANCE TO CHANGE YOUR mind," Mr. Forkle told Sophie as he held his fingers a hairsbreadth from her temples.

She took a deep, calming breath as her friends squeezed her hands.

"Do it."

The second his fingers pressed down, warmth flooded into Sophie's head. The sensation felt strange—like sunshine tickling her brain—but also soothingly familiar, taking Sophie back to the other times she'd had her abilities triggered. She'd barely been conscious during those moments, so she'd never experienced the moment when the talent *clicked*—like someone flipped a switch, sending new currents of energy pulsing from head to toe. Her heart raced just as fast, her breaths shallow and frenetic—until the rush settled into her hands and turned warmer. Threads of heat seemed to weave together under the skin of her fingers, forming a thin layer that felt inherently *right*. She hadn't realized how empty her hands had been without it. But now she was exactly as her body meant her to be.

"Feels like it already worked," Mr. Forkle said as he backed away, sinking into the chair and rubbing his sweaty temples. "But perhaps we should test it to be sure?"

Sophie offered Fitz a hand. "Care to try it out, Captain Cognate?"

Fitz beamed his movie-worthy smile. "I'd be honored—though I'm not sold on that nickname."

He reached for her hand, his touch as warm and gentle as ever. Their fingers twined together and . . .

"Whoa. It's like . . . having all the fog shoved out of my mind—which is extra weird because I never thought my concentration was cloudy." He let go of Sophie's hand and creases settled across his brow. "Ugh. And now it's all fuzzy again." He took her hand and his face relaxed. "Wow, this is going to make me want to hold your hand all the time."

Biana rolled her eyes. "Easy now, big brother. Let go of my friend or I will drop you like we're playing bramble."

Fitz blushed and did as Biana ordered.

Sophie was sure her cheeks couldn't get any redder as Biana grabbed her hand and instantly turned invisible.

"This is *so* crazy," Biana's disembodied voice whispered. "I don't even have to *try* to keep the light away. It just glides through me like I'm made of glass."

"My turn!" Dex said, rushing closer as Biana reappeared.

"Perhaps we shouldn't treat Miss Foster like she's our shiny new toy," Mr. Forkle warned.

"Right," Dex mumbled. "Sorry."

"Don't be," Sophie said. "I'm curious too. And who knows, maybe you'll suddenly know how to build one of those Lodestar symbol gadgets. Or those special nexuses to replace the gloves like you'd been talking about."

"Oh, that's true!" Dex's palm felt a little sweaty as he wrapped his fingers around hers and closed his eyes. "Wow, my brain feels like it's working on a hundred things at once. It's . . . I can't keep up with it all—owww."

"Are you okay?" Sophie asked as he stumbled back, rubbing his head.

"Yeah, just info overload. I bet it would've been different if I'd been holding whatever gadget I wanted to work on, since my ability always focuses on something specific. Instead I got this random mix of, like, memories and blueprints and . . . I don't even know. *So* many good ideas—I'm afraid I'm going to forget them all."

"Here," Biana said, handing him a notebook and pen from one of Alden's desk drawers. "Maybe make some notes?"

"Good idea!" Dex dropped into a chair and scribbled furiously.

"It doesn't hurt when you're passing the power to us, right?" Fitz asked Sophie.

"No. All I get is a tingle in my fingers. And it doesn't feel like it drains me either—but that might change if you hold on for a long time."

"Your body will give you cues to let you know if you're pushing yourself too hard," Mr. Forkle assured her. "Though I do think you should try to rest now. Triggering an ability is an exhausting process—and you've had a very long, very challenging day."

Sophie wanted to protest, but as soon as she stood, her head felt twirly. And by the time she'd made it back to the guest room, she barely managed to change into her pajamas and grab Ella before she collapsed into the giant bed.

It was a dreamless, dead-to-the-world kind of sleep, and she might've kept it up forever if someone hadn't shaken her awake.

When she opened her eyes, she was staring into the face of a stuffed sparkly red dragon.

"Mr. Snuggles is always the best thing to see when you first wake up," Fitz told her—and Sophie almost blurted that his glittering teal eyes were even better, but managed to spare herself the humiliation.

Biana laughed from the doorway. "You two are ridiculous—has anyone told you that? Now get dressed." She tossed a very long, very fitted, very red tunic onto Sophie's bed.

"Don't scowl at me like that—it's camouflage," Biana told her. "The fancier your clothes are, the more people won't wonder about your new gloves. *And* you look awesome in red. All you need is a white blouse and some black leggings—you have those, right? Oh—and a killer pair of boots. In fact, I have the perfect ones!"

Sophie sighed as Biana raced off. "She's going to turn me into her little doll."

"Probably," Fitz agreed. "But at least she's right." Sophie figured he was referring to Biana's camouflage-the-gloves strategy—which *was* pretty brilliant, despite how annoying Sophie was sure it was going to be.

But Fitz gave her his most charming smile and added, "Red is definitely your color."

If she were a cartoon character, Sophie's eyes would've turned into little hearts.

"Hurry up and get dressed," Biana shouted from down the hall, saving Sophie from having to come up with a coherent response.

"Why, are we going somewhere?" Sophie called after her.

"Yep." Biana rushed back into the room, proudly holding up a pair of boots with alarmingly tall wedge heels. "While *someone* was getting their beauty sleep, I went to the Silver Tower with Tam to see if having a Vanisher with him made a difference. And we finally figured out how the Neverseen got in!"

SIXTY-EIGHT

I THOUGHT WE'D RULED OUT THE LODE-star mirror," Sophie said as she stood in the center of the Hall of Illumination, surrounded by a circle of twenty mirrors reflecting their group from every angle.

Dex, Fitz, Linh, Alden, Della, Mr. Forkle, *and* Sandor, Grizel, Lovise, and Woltzer had all come with them to see what Biana and Tam had discovered.

"We *have* ruled it out," Tam told Sophie. "Believe me, I've stared at that thing so long, I've gone cross-eyed. All it does is reflect pure light and make me tear up from the glare."

"Then, um . . . why are we here?" Dex asked.

"Because I'm a genius," Biana informed him. "I knew the Neverseen wouldn't be obvious enough to have the actual mirror be the answer. But I kept thinking the name couldn't totally be a coincidence. So I spent way too long staring at my reflection." She ignored Fitz when he coughed, *"What else is new?"* and several in their group laughed. "And that's when I thought to ask: What do lodestars do?"

"Guide people?" Sophie guessed.

Biana nodded. "They show you the way. So what do you see when you look in the mirror—besides your really bright reflection?"

Mr. Forkle sucked in a breath. "You see the mirror directly across from it!"

Everyone rushed to the other mirror, stepping on toes and knocking elbows as they crushed closer.

"It's the Cimmerian," Alden said, tracing a hand down the smooth glass. "One of the hardest mirrors to understand the meaning of."

"It really is," Mr. Forkle said, "I've always suspected it's because many are too distracted by the disruption to their appearance."

"Can't say I blame them," Della mumbled, glaring at the heavy shadows in her reflection. "This mirror is the only thing that ever makes me feel haggard."

"But I still don't understand," Grizel said. "How does it give the Neverseen access to the tower?"

"Because they brought a Shade," Biana said, nudging Tam forward. "Go on. Show them how cool you are."

Tam flushed, squaring his shoulders as he approached the glass. "This is hard to explain. But the mirror multiplies shadows, so I decided to see what'd happen if I messed with them."

He stretched his hand toward the glass and pulled his fingers into a fist, dragging every shadow from their reflections into the center of the mirror like a big black hole.

"And don't ask me why," Tam said, "but my instincts told me to do this."

He spun his wrist in a tight circle, and the shadows followed—curling into a spiral that seemed to sink in on itself as the pattern spun round and round and round.

"What exactly are we looking at?" Mr. Forkle asked.

"I'm not totally sure," Tam admitted. "At first I thought it was just an optical illusion. But then I did *this*"—he shoved his hand through the center of the spiral, making his arm disappear up to the elbow and earning a chorus of gasps—"and I realized it's a gateway. Something about the shadowvapor moving through the glass changes its density."

He pulled his arm back and wiggled his perfectly healthy, normal fingers.

"Just don't ask me to explain the crazy science behind it, okay?" Tam said, "But this is how the Neverseen got into the tower. Maybe they levitated once they were inside so they wouldn't leave a scent trail. But they came from here."

He pushed his whole body through the mirror, disappearing

into the glass. Everyone yelped when he peeked his head back from the other side—and all four goblins drew their swords.

"It's a pretty tight space, so if you want to check it out, you'll have to take turns," he told them. "Probably no more than two or three at a time. But basically, I'm in a secret room hidden somewhere between the towers."

"Someone needs to make sure the space is truly secure before any more of us go through," Sandor decided, blocking Sophie as he pushed forward.

Grizel jumped in front of him, placing a hand in the center of his chest. "I'm smaller *and* my senses are sharper."

Sandor's jaw twitched—ready to argue—but when Grizel leaned in and whispered something, he nodded and took a slow step back.

Tam disappeared through the mirror to clear the path as Grizel tapped Sandor's nose and turned to study the glass. She skimmed her fingers across the swirling shadows before she shrugged and leaped through like a gazelle.

"Do you think they have security telling them we found the hidden room?" Fitz asked.

Dex frowned. "I don't feel any tech or signals."

"And wouldn't someone have come to check it by now?" Biana asked. "Tam and I found this over an hour ago, before we came back to wake up Sophie and get you guys."

Sophie's cheeks flushed. "Sorry I overslept."

"Yes, how dare you take a few hours to recover after manifesting a new ability?" Biana scolded.

"What new ability?" Linh and Sandor asked at the same time.

Sophie held up her gloved hands. "Enhancer."

Linh nearly knocked Della over as she scrambled back. "Sorry." She hugged her arms around herself. "It's not you. It's just still such a struggle for me to maintain control. I can't imagine what kind of flood I'd cause if someone enhanced my ability."

"Yeah, that would *not* be a good idea," Tam said, peeking his head through the glass again. "Not unless we want to wipe out a couple of cities."

"Why does this sound like an ability that's going to increase the challenge of protecting you?" Sandor asked Sophie.

"Because it will." Mr. Forkle explained about the gloves, and how they'd do everything they could to keep the ability secret. But how it was a part of Sophie now. Always.

Grizel peeked her head through the mirror, locking eyes with Sandor. "Don't blame me. We all know Sophie would've triggered the ability even if you'd been there."

"Still, I leave you my charge for *one* night," he grumbled.

"So what's it like on the other side of the mirror?" Sophie asked, eager for a subject change.

She'd expected Tam to answer, but Biana jumped in. "It wasn't at all what I'd imagined. I was rooting for creepy furniture and crazy gadgets and all kinds of cool villainy things. But it's just a cramped, empty stone room that looks like it's been there since they built the tower."

"Does that mean the Neverseen have been around for thousands of years?" Linh asked.

"I suppose it's possible," Mr. Forkle said. "But most likely the room once served some other long-forgotten purpose, and Fintan or Brant—or maybe their Shade—stumbled across it and made it their own."

"Either way, it's definitely how they got in," Grizel said, climbing back out through the mirror. "Their scent is everywhere—but it's also stale, so I don't think they've been back since they took Wylie."

"Am I the only one who still doesn't understand how they actually get into the tower?" Dex asked. "So . . . they get *here*"—he pointed to the floor in the Hall of Illumination—"by coming through *there*"—he pointed to the swirling Cimmerian mirror—"where there's another secret room. But how do they get in *that* room?"

Biana grinned. "Go see for yourself."

Dex didn't need to be told twice, practically sprinting through the mirror.

"*Ohhhhh, it has one of the Lodestar symbol gadgets!*" he breathed.

That was all the invitation Sophie needed to go charging after him, shivering from the waves of cold that rippled across her skin as she passed through the glass. Fitz was right on her heels, and they nearly tripped over each other in the claustrophobic space.

"I'm fine," she told Sandor as his head peeked through the mirror, which looked like a swirling black square on the other side. "Better wait for me out there—we can barely move."

She couldn't imagine how the Neverseen managed to fit Alvar, Ruy, Trix, Umber, *and* Wylie's unconscious body within the narrow, musty walls. But they must have. The Lodestar symbol glowing across the floor proved it.

"It has runes," Fitz said, stepping back to uncover the letters in another circle at the end of one of the rays. "Looks like it says Pallidrose. I'm guessing that's another star."

"Another solo star," Sophie agreed as her mind connected with the memory. "It also glows with pure white light, so those definitely seem to be their criteria. But how does this thing work? I'm assuming we have to *do* something?"

"We're hoping Dex can figure it out," Biana called through the mirror.

"I'll have to get a closer look at the gadget." Dex levitated up to the ceiling and traced his finger along the curved edge. "Weird—I don't feel a lot of mechanisms in this thing. I can't even figure out where it opens."

"I wonder if Tam has to do something," Sophie said. "Or maybe Biana. Gethen made it sound like it relied on someone using their abilities, and they're the only ones that match."

"We already thought about that earlier," Biana said. "I tried everything I could think of."

"So did I," Tam admitted.

554

"Do you think it would help if you enhanced them?" Fitz asked Sophie.

"I . . . don't know." The ability was so new, she hadn't even thought of it. But she peeled off her right glove and offered Tam her hand, wondering if her stomach would always feel this churny whenever she went to touch anyone now.

Tam looked just as nervous as he curled his fingers around hers and the shadows sprang to life on the floor, creating a thick black outline around the glow of the Lodestar symbol.

"That's so crazy," he mumbled. "I couldn't feel that darkness before."

He tightened his grip on Sophie, pulling her with him a few steps as he followed the shadows to one of the rays they had yet to discover the rune for.

"I think this is how they left," he whispered. "See how the shadows are gathering?"

The bits of darkness were puddling together, like rivers of selkie skin flowing into the empty circle.

The darkness rippled like water, parts of it rising up with a rune.

"I think maybe . . ."

"Wait," Fitz said, lunging to grab Sophie's arm as Tam stepped down on the pool of shadows. His fingers connected with her skin right as an arctic rush blasted up and tangled around the three of them, dragging them into the darkness and blasting them away.

SIXTY-NINE

OKAY, *WHAT* JUST HAPPENED?" Fitz asked, still clinging to Sophie as she and Tam fought to regain their balance on the mossy, uneven floor.

The symbol glowed under their feet—the only light in the damp, murky room they'd somehow been transported to. Something dripped in the distance, and their breaths clouded the air. The bitter cold clawed through Sophie's clothes, and she silently thanked Biana for insisting she add a thick black cape to her outfit to match her gloves.

"I . . . think I just leaped us using starlight absorbed by a shadow," Tam whispered. "I didn't even know I could do that. But when I touched Sophie's hand, my instincts took over."

"So this is another hideout?" Sophie asked, slipping her glove back on. She pointed to the new rune illuminating the ray of the symbol under Tam's shoes.

"Valkonian," Fitz whispered. "I'm assuming that's another white-light star?"

Sophie nodded.

Her eyes were adjusting to the murk, letting her pick out more details as she crept forward to get a better view. The moss made the stones slippery, and uneven cracks tried to trip her stupid heeled boots. But she could see brighter light ahead, and carefully tiptoed over.

"It looks like we're in some sort of human ruin," she whispered, brushing a hand across one of the damp, crumbling walls.

She'd never been to Scotland, but something about this place reminded her of it an old, decaying castle, complete with cracked, cut-glass windows leaking rays of gray-blue light. Thick vines covered the ancient stones, and the air smelled of earth and sea. "I don't hear any thoughts around here, do you?"

Fitz shook his head. "How much do you think they're freaking out back at Foxfire?"

"Sandor's probably tracking me as we speak—actually, wait." Sophie ran her hands down her red tunic. "These are Biana's clothes. I doubt they have trackers."

"Dex could hack into our registry feeds," Fitz said. "Or maybe our panic switches."

"We might need them to," Sophie realized. "I'm not wearing my home crystal, since I'm not supposed to go back to Havenfield until the gnomes finish installing the extra security."

Fitz patted his pockets and cursed under his breath. "I didn't bring my pathfinder, either."

"Good thing you have me." Tam pulled a purple-tinted pendant out from under his cape. "It only goes to Alluveterre, but the gnomes can take us from there."

"Wait," Sophie said as he held the crystal up to catch the faint rays of light. "Shouldn't we look around before we go? Isn't this where they brought Wylie?"

"It's where they went when they left the Silver Tower," Tam said. "I know that's why the shadows called to me. But I can't imagine this is where they held him hostage. There's no cell—not even any totally solid walls. And I don't see any rope."

"Can you do that shadow trick again to the symbol here, and see if they went somewhere else?" Fitz asked.

"But why would they bother coming here in the first place?" Sophie asked. "The symbol in the Silver Tower could've taken them to any of their hideouts, right?"

"It felt like it," Tam agreed.

"So then there has to be a reason they chose *here*," Sophie said. "Maybe this part is just the facade to disguise the real hideout, and the shelter's underground? We should fan out and see if we can find a hidden staircase or door or something."

"I'm with you on everything except the fanning-out part,"

Fitz told her. "I think we should stay close so we don't get separated."

"But that's going to make the search take way longer," Sophie argued. "If I'm right about why Keefe's cloak had those disks hidden in it, we've probably triggered some sort of alarm already."

"All the more reason to stay together," Tam said. "I'll keep my crystal in my hand, and we should all hang on to each other—that way if we need to leap away fast, we can."

Sophie couldn't argue with that logic, and did her best to keep a hold on Fitz. But a strange pattern in the cut-glass windows caught her attention.

She let go to take a closer look—just for the briefest second.

And the distance saved her from being caught by the first burst of blinding white light.

The beam of searing energy curled into a wall around Fitz and Tam, trapping them in a narrow force field that shocked them as they pressed against the inner side, fighting to escape.

"It's about time you decided to come and play," Ruy shouted from somewhere in the shadows as he launched another force field toward Sophie. She dove and rolled to avoid it, the edge of the energy clipping her shoulder and stinging with tingles that burned like acid-coated needles.

She gritted her teeth through the pain and crawled behind a crumbling pillar, tucking herself into the darkness to wait him out. She couldn't strike until she had a clear lock on his location.

In the meantime, she let the fury build, stewing with her unraveling emotions, rimming her vision with red. She'd only have one chance at this—one moment to drop Ruy before he caged her in his trap.

A scrape of shoe on stone gave her the direction she needed, and she leaped from the shadows, arms raised, ready to blast Ruy with the full force of her wrath.

But there were four black-cloaked figures waiting for her— and even with their hoods raised, she could see enough of their faces to recognize them.

Ruy.

Brant.

Alvar.

And Keefe.

SEVENTY

Y OU?" SOPHIE BREATHED, FEELING
the fight whoosh out of her as the reality of
fighting Keefe kicked her in the stomach.

The panic in his eyes made it clear he was
just as horrified to see her.

"Don't!" Brant shouted, his scarred features twisting as he
grabbed Ruy's arms with his only hand. "If you shield her, she
can't burn."

A thread of white flame sparked to life at the stumpy end of
Brant's other arm, twisting into fingerlike tendrils.

"She can *inflict*," Ruy reminded him.

"But she won't." Brant released his hold on Ruy and pulled
Keefe close, waving the flames under Keefe's chin. "She still

cares about this one. And she knows I'll melt his face off if she misbehaves."

"He's one of us!" Alvar shouted.

"*That's* still up for debate. But he can prove it now." Brant's scarred lips curled into what little smile they were able to form as he moved his flame-fingers closer to Keefe's throat. With his real hand, he reached into his cape and withdrew the Ruewen crest pin he'd stolen from Sophie months and months ago. "I think I've held on to the past long enough, don't you?"

Sophie knew what was coming, even before Brant shoved Keefe toward her and held the small eagle pin in the searing white flame. The jewels crusting it sparked and crackled, and the pin turned into a red-hot brand.

But he pressed it into Keefe's palm, instead of hers.

Keefe thrashed and screamed, eyes watering, teeth gritted in agony.

"Now," Brant told Keefe, pulling the pin away. "Show her that same pain. And in case you're having trouble following along, Sophie, here's how this is going to work. You tell us where you're keeping Wylie, and I'll have lover boy here put the scars somewhere only you can see them. Try to resist, and he'll give you the same makeover you gave me. And if you fight me," he told Keefe, "I'll melt off parts of your body one by one. Starting with your fingers."

Desperation screamed through Sophie's head as her brain scrambled for a plan.

Somewhere through the chaos she realized there was another voice in the mix.

Sophie, can you hear me?

Fitz?

His thoughts were muffled and staticky, but she was stunned he could reach her at all.

Tam's breaking down the force field with darkness, he explained, *and he says he'll be able to slip his shadow through the cracks and cloud Brant's mind. It'll blind him for a few seconds. Will that be long enough for you to drop him with your inflicting before he burns Keefe?*

It probably would—but only if she was willing to drop *all* of them.

Keefe's too close to Brant, she warned. *I'll have to take out everyone.*

I don't see any other option, do you?

She glanced at the flames under Keefe's nose, and the oozing blister on his hand.

Tell Tam to do it! she transmitted as she reached deep inside, gathering every last emotion and fueling them with any dark thoughts she'd ever had.

Brant flinched, dropping his flames, and Sophie took Tam's cue, letting the cold waves pour out of her, their jagged edges tearing across everything within reach.

Seconds stretched into eternity and reality vanished into pure, pulsing power—and rage.

So.

Much.

Rage.

She wanted to bathe in it, drown in it, let the anger take control until she'd punished anyone and everyone who'd ever hurt her. But she'd held on to one thread of good through the barrage—one wisp of a thought that tethered her to who she needed to be.

Keefe.

The name peeled back the dark curtain and let in a blistering, blinding rush as she dropped to her knees, her hands feeling for shaking limbs across the cold stones. She found him right as her eyes shifted back into focus, and she pulled him into her lap.

If you can hear me, Keefe, try to fight through the darkness, she transmitted. *The pain's not real. Shove it aside and come back to the surface.*

"Tam broke the force field," Fitz said behind her, making her jump. "And he's stamping out Brant's flames. The stones are damp, so the only thing that caught was his cloak. How can I help?"

"Find something to restrain the Neverseen. When this wears off . . ."

"On it," Fitz said.

He turned to leave—then pivoted back. "Stop looking so guilty, Sophie. You did this to save him. Like he said, sometimes things have to get worse before they get better."

She focused on a happier promise. "It's almost over."

And it was, wasn't it?

This was a *huge* victory.

In one afternoon, they'd caught Alvar, Ruy, and Brant—three of the most prominent players in the Neverseen. And now that they knew how to use the gadget and the symbol, they had a way to track down sixteen hideouts.

And they had Keefe.

She craned her neck to watch Tam and Fitz work—stripping each shaking figure of their cloak and shredding the fabric into makeshift rope to bind their hands and feet and cover their mouths and eyes.

"We need to get out of here," Tam said. "Some of their buddies will probably wonder what's taking so long. And these guys could wake up any minute."

Fitz punched his brother in the face. "That should keep him knocked out longer."

"He's not the one I'm worried about," Tam told him. "If that Psionipath wakes up, he'll trap us in two seconds."

Fitz sighed and left Alvar in a bound heap so he could pull Ruy into a choke hold.

Tam held Brant the same way. "I'm keeping his mind clouded with shadow so he can't start any more fires. But I'll feel a lot better when he's locked up in a fireproof cell."

"Me too," Sophie said. "But I don't think it's safe to leap Keefe until he's out of the daze."

"Leap . . . where?" Keefe grunted between labored breaths.

Sophie hugged him tighter. "I'm so sorry—I couldn't take them down without hurting you."

He grit his teeth into a pained smile. "Admit it . . . Foster . . . you're enjoying this . . . a little."

"Never." She rubbed her eyes with her gloved fingers, trying to fight back sobs.

"It's not that bad," he promised, and when she met his eyes, she could see the haze of pain slowly fading.

It crashed right back when he tried to uncurl his blistered, blackened hand. The metal pin seemed to have fused with his skin. "Remind me to kick Brant in the junk a few times once he's awake."

"Only if I get a turn," she said. "Physic has lots of burn salve at Alluveterre. I'm sure she'll get you fixed up."

"Physic?" Keefe asked. "Why not Elwin?"

"Tam's the only one who has a leaping crystal with him, and he's been living at the hideout. We kinda came here by accident—it's a long story. I'll tell you once we're back in the Lost Cities."

"He has a crystal to Alluveterre?"

"Yeah. Why?"

Keefe closed his eyes.

"What's wrong?" she asked. "Is it hurting?"

"No, it's . . ." He took a slow breath and pulled himself up, cradling his singed hand. "I *can't* go with you guys. I know you think this fixes everything—but Fintan's vision is *huge*. And all of this will only be a small setback. We still need someone on the inside—"

"Do you really think Fintan will trust you after you let everyone else get captured?" Sophie interrupted. "Think of what he did to your mom, and she only cost him one prisoner. Look at what Brant just did to you!" She grabbed his wrist, forcing him to see his oozing wound. "Would they do that if they trusted you?"

Keefe turned away, not quite fighting off his shudder. "That's why you have to let me take Alvar."

"Yeah, that's never happening," Fitz practically growled.

"It has to. I know it's brutal—but think of the bigger picture. If I bring Alvar back, I'm the hero who saved one of the team. And Alvar's the safest one for me to take. He's always believed in me—you heard him defend me when Brant sparked the flames! And he's never killed anyone—"

"No, he just kidnaps people and watches them be tortured," Sophie snapped.

"Believe me, I'll make him pay for that—but right now we have to play this smart. Ruy and Brant are part of Fintan's big plan, so take them, lock them up, and have Forkle interrogate the crud out of them until we find out what they know. But they'll only know a piece, so I'll use Alvar to keep my 'in' and learn the rest. I'll be safe. Fintan . . . likes me."

"Dude, save your daddy issues for another time," Tam

ordered. "Fintan doesn't care about you. He doesn't trust you. And if you go back to him, he'll destroy you."

Keefe's eye roll was epic. "Don't you need to go fix your bangs or something?"

"You can hate me all you want," Tam told him. "It won't mean I'm not right. Admit that now, and you might still have a chance to fix what really matters. Or you can wait until you've lost her. It's your call."

"Lost who?" Fitz asked.

Tam shook his head. "We need to go."

"Tam's right," Sophie said, her legs shaking as she stood. "Come on, Keefe. You're never going to get another chance like this. I've tried for weeks to figure out how to get you away from them, and this is it. You're safe. You'll be long gone before they realize what happened. And we'll hide you somewhere until we shut down every single one of their hideouts connected to the symbol. And that'll be the end of it."

"But it won't be," he mumbled. "That's what I'm trying to tell you. There's still so much more to do."

"Then do it *with* us."

She offered him her gloved hand, and her eyes pleaded with him to take it this time.

After a breathless second, he did.

He let her pull him to his feet, leaning on her to stay steady. "I know what matters, Foster," he whispered. "And it's *all* that matters."

The intensity of his stare turned everything floaty and fluttery. But it all crashed back down when he lunged for Tam and snatched the Alluveterre crystal from his hand.

"What are you doing?" Fitz shouted as Keefe bolted to Alvar and hefted him over his shoulder.

"I bet I can trade this for the information I need to steal the caches. And I'd stay back if I were you," he told Fitz and Tam. "You don't want those guys waking up if you jostle them around too much, do you?"

"Then drop him with your inflicting," Tam shouted at Sophie.

But Sophie had drained all her pent-up emotions when she took down the others. All she had left was shock, and a sickening sadness.

"Please don't do this," she begged. "If you leave here with that crystal, you'll trap us—and you'll compromise Alluveterre."

"The Black Swan can sacrifice one hideout for what this will get me," Keefe said. "And you can teleport. There has to be a cliff around here you can jump off to get the momentum."

"Are we supposed to haul two bodies with us as we try to find it?" Sophie argued.

"Use your telekinesis. You're the amazing Sophie Foster. You'll figure it out."

"And you're making a seriously huge mistake," Tam warned.

"Maybe. I'm pretty good at that—but I'm even better at fixing things. That's still what I'm trying to do here. Trust me."

"How?" Sophie's voice cracked along the edges. "After all the times you've lied or ignored us or betrayed us? How do we ever trust you again?"

"I don't know," he whispered.

"And I don't know if I can forgive this one," she whispered back.

Keefe swallowed hard, eyes focused on his feet as he nodded. "Yeah . . . I can feel that. And if you needed proof that I'm not doing this for me—that's it, okay?"

It definitely was not okay.

Nothing about this was okay.

"I'm sorry," Keefe whispered. "You have no idea how much. I'm also guessing this means no more check-ins. So please, please, *please* be careful. Keep your bodyguards close and know that I *will* end this."

It did feel like an end as he stepped onto the glowing Lodestar symbol. She just didn't know what it was the end of.

"Oh—I forgot to tell you," he mumbled. "I finally know how the black disks work. If you have the one you need, and you give the right command . . ."

He moved to a circle at the end of one of the rays and whispered, "Gwynaura."

The ray flashed so bright, Sophie had to look away.

By the time the glow faded, Keefe and Alvar were gone.

SEVENTY-ONE

S O ... THAT HAPPENED," TAM MUMBLED.
"You guys okay?"

Fitz looked like he wanted to stab *many* things.

"Fine," Sophie said, pressing her shaky hand against the glass to steady it. She'd moved to the cracked window, staring at the long grassy field swaying in the wind. "Just trying to figure out how to get out of here. We could be wandering a long time trying to find a cliff."

"And my levitation's not strong enough to lift a whole other person," Tam said. "Especially since it sounds like we need to be pretty high up if we're going to teleport. So weird that you need to free-fall."

"I guess we could press our panic switches," Fitz suggested.

"I thought of that," Sophie said, "but it seems like something about this place must be interfering with the signal—otherwise wouldn't Dex have already brought in the cavalry? He said the stronger trackers could be traced anytime, remember?"

"So what does that leave?" Tam asked. "A telepathic call to Forkle?"

That could work. But the suggestion gave her a better idea. She wasn't ready for another big dramatic scene. And Silveny had made her promise to call for help if she ever needed her.

She only sent the transmission twice before a giddy *SOPHIE! SOPHIE! SOPHIE!* blasted into her brain.

But Silveny picked up on her mood almost immediately. *SOPHIE NEED HELP?*

Yeah, Sophie told her. *I don't know where I am, but—*

FIND! FIND! FIND!

The alicorn's voice flashed away and Sophie barely had time to race outside before thunder cracked the sky and two shimmering alicorns—both gleaming silver, but one bigger, with blue-tipped wings—soared out of the void and circled around the gray, restless clouds.

SOPHIE! FRIEND! HELP!

Both alicorns tucked their wings and dove, slowing their fall at the last second and touching down in the long grass. Clearly Sophie's ability to track thoughts to their locations came from her alicorn-inspired DNA.

"Thank you," Sophie whispered, taking a cautious step forward. She knew Silveny trusted her—but Greyfell was always warier, especially now that he was going to be a daddy.

His deep brown eyes flickered to hers, and then to the empty field, his fur bristling, hooves stamping.

I don't like it here either, Sophie told him. *We'll be quick. We just need to load up.*

"Leave it to you to have our world's most valuable creatures at your beck and call," Tam said behind her as he dragged Brant over.

"And I'm risking their lives by doing it—if the Neverseen show up . . ."

She socked Brant in the face to make sure he stayed unconscious.

Fitz did the same to Ruy.

BAD PEOPLE? Silveny asked.

The worst, Sophie transmitted.

Silveny's thoughts darkened. *BITE THEM?*

Maybe once we get back. Right now, can you and Greyfell lean down so it's easier to load them?

"I'm staying with Brant," Tam said as Sophie and Fitz helped him hoist the limp body onto Greyfell's back. "Can you two both fit on the other alicorn, *and* hold Ruy?"

"We'll make it work," Fitz said, "But I want you to sit behind me," he told Sophie. "That way I can be a buffer between you and Ruy."

"I don't need you to protect me," she argued.

"I know. But *I'd* prefer knowing you're safe. Please? You have no idea how hard it was standing in that force field, watching them attack you. Just thinking about it . . . " He flung Ruy over Silveny's neck and climbed on before offering Sophie a hand. She let him pull her up, blushing when she wrapped her arms around his waist. They had to sit so close, she doubted a piece of paper could've been squeezed in between them.

READY? Silveny asked.

FLY! Sophie told her, and with a majestic flap, both alicorns launched into the sky.

The cold wind whipped her hair and cheeks, turning everything numb—and numb was good. Sophie could use a lot more numb in her life.

Silveny tried to distract her with a quick update on Operation Alicorn Baby—which was thankfully all good news. Then they reached a high enough altitude to dive.

"Hold on tight!" Sophie warned Tam. "And it's okay to scream during this next part."

"I'll be fine," Tam promised—but Sophie heard a fair amount of squealing and yelping as the alicorns zipped toward the ground.

Right when it looked like they'd be splattering all over the grass, thunder cracked and the void split the space in front of them, swallowing them in black.

"Remind me never to lose my leaping crystal again!" Tam

groaned as they drifted through the dark nothingness. "You know how to get us out of here, right?"

Sophie nodded.

She just wasn't quite ready to head back to reality—especially a reality where Keefe had betrayed them *again*.

Fitz must've noticed her hesitation, because he leaned back and whispered, "Whatever happens next, I'm right here with you. You know that, right?"

"I do."

The best part was, she actually believed him.

"Ready?" she asked.

"Sorta. I have to keep reminding myself we're bringing home prisoners."

So did Sophie.

They'd landed a huge win.

But she had a feeling they were both thinking about what they'd lost.

"Okay," she said, tightening her hold. "Here goes nothing."

Her head filled with a clear image of the Silver Tower as white light cracked through the void, blasting them back to Foxfire.

SEVENTY-TWO

SOPHIE HAD BRACED FOR TEARS AND
screaming and lectures—and her friends and
family definitely delivered the second they arrived.
Silveny and Greyfell were kind enough to circle
over the campus a few times to let everyone get the brunt of it
out of their systems, before they swooped in for a gentle landing in the lush purple grass.

Everyone sprinted to meet them, and Sophie realized their
welcome party had grown, now including Elwin, all twelve
Councillors, Grady and Edaline, Kesler and Juline, Granite,
Wraith, and Blur, and—maddeningly—Tam and Linh's parents, all surrounding them in a massive circle.

Questions were shouted. Explanations were demanded. But

it all screeched to a halt when everyone spotted the Neverseen prisoners draped across the alicorns' backs.

Sandor took charge then, ordering everyone to stay back as Woltzer and Lovise hauled Brant and Ruy to the ground and stood guard over their unconscious forms. Edaline conjured up the thickest rope from their supply shed at Havenfield, and Sandor and Grizel bound the prisoners more securely before Elwin poured his strongest sedative down their throats.

"What are you going to do with them?" Grady asked, the words as shaky as his hands. His eyes stayed locked on Brant, and he positioned himself in front of Edaline and Sophie.

"Let us handle it," Mr. Forkle told him.

"*We'll* handle it," Councillor Emery corrected, his deep voice triggering a silence that seemed to still even the wind. The other Councillors gathered around him, their gleaming circlets testifying to their authority as they focused on the members of the Collective. "The Neverseen's crimes stretch well beyond your order."

"Very well," Mr. Forkle said. "What is *your* plan for the prisoners?"

"*That* is to be determined." Emery closed his eyes and turned away to moderate a telepathic debate with the other Councillors.

Everyone else swarmed closer to Sophie, Tam, and Fitz.

"You smell like smoke," Elwin noted, trying to flash an orb of red light around Sophie—even though Edaline was busy strangle-hugging her.

"I'm fine," Sophie promised, not letting her eyes stray to the glass pyramid in the distance. "Tam and Fitz helped me take them down before things got out of control."

"We're fine too," Fitz said as his parents and Biana practically crushed him. "Thank goodness Tam's shadows could break us out of Ruy's force field."

"Is that true?" Tam's mother asked. "You're a hero?"

"Still not ready," Tam said, raising a hand to halt his parents as they approached. Instead, he wrapped his arm around Linh, and she buried her face in his shoulder.

"You guys have a *lot* of explaining to do," Dex told them. "Do you know you trapped me in that room? The mirror sealed shut the second Tam vanished. Sandor had to smash the glass."

Biana begged for the whole story, and Sophie was grateful Fitz had the energy to tell it. He kept it short and sweet, focusing on their victories.

There's clearly more you're not saying, Mr. Forkle transmitted.

See for yourself. Sophie's nails dug into her palms as her mind replayed the whole showdown, from the moment the Neverseen arrived, to Keefe's latest betrayal. *You need to move Wylie out of Alluveterre—now. And Tam and Linh can't go back.*

No, they can't.

Mr. Forkle's eyes flicked to Granite, and Granite scrambled for his pathfinder.

"Excuse me," he told the Councillors. "I must check on my son."

"Your son?" Councillor Terik asked, catching Granite's slip.

"Yes, I have a son, and another life behind this disguise. Surely that doesn't come as a surprise. And hopefully someday you'll learn to cooperate with us and I won't have to hide. But until then . . ."

Granite leaped away, and Blur and Wraith followed.

"One of our hideouts has been compromised," Mr. Forkle explained. "Fortunately, it sounds like the Neverseen are facing the same dilemma."

"On a *way* larger scale, right?" Biana asked. "If Tam does that shadow trick again, won't that take you to all of their hideouts?"

"Any that are connected to the symbol," Tam said. "Not sure if that's all of them."

"Then shouldn't we get moving on that?" Alden asked. "We don't want to give them a chance to clear out."

"We also don't want to be hasty," Councillor Emery said. "First let's handle the prisoners in our custody. We've voted to move them to Lumenaria, where we're already holding their co-conspirator. We'd been hoping to send a message during the summit that this worthless rebellion will soon be a thing of the past. And what better way to do so than to present them with three defeated prisoners? We'll arrange a viewing on the first night."

"I'm assuming you'll also be performing a memory break?" Mr. Forkle asked.

"Not until after the summit."

"That might be too late." Sophie squared her shoulders as all eyes focused on her. "We have reason to believe the Neverseen have a larger plan in the works—a plan that both Ruy and Brant were involved with. Interrogating them is our only chance to learn how to stop it."

"And what is your reason for believing this?" Councillor Emery asked.

Sophie thought she was ready to throw Keefe to the wolves. But . . . her voice wouldn't cooperate.

When Tam and Fitz didn't chime in either, she went with a different tactic.

"You're really going to doubt us—after everything we've uncovered? You don't think this proves we might know a little more than you?"

"When it comes to the dirty schemes of this refuse," Councillor Emery said, sneering at Brant and Ruy, "perhaps you are ahead of us. But *we* must think beyond this simple rebellion. We're trying to send a message to the other species of this world that they should fear and respect our power—and showing them a group of drooling, mindless wastes is not an image we're willing to present. We must *always* appear strong—always superior—even when it comes to our prisoners. Let them see we faced and stopped a worthy foe. And when the Summit is over, we will shatter and squeeze every shred of truth out of these disgraces. But only after we ensure they do not diminish the respect for our kind."

"That doesn't mean we can't interrogate them," Mr. Forkle reminded the Council. "With cleverness, we might be able to glean a few crucial truths."

"Perhaps," Councillor Emery said. "The matter will be taken under consideration *after* the prisoners are properly secured, and *after* we've searched every last one of these hideouts you claim to be able to lead us to. It's about knowing what deserves priority."

Please don't argue any further, Mr. Forkle transmitted as Sophie opened her mouth. *I'll raise the issue again tomorrow, once a few more things are settled. For the moment, it is wise to focus on storming the hideouts.*

Fine, Sophie told him. Out loud, she asked the Council, "Are you going to let us help with the raids on the hideouts?"

"It sounds like we'll require young Mr. Song's assistance," Councillor Emery said, ignoring Tam's scowl at the use of his family name. "The remainder of you should return to your homes."

"It's not that we don't value your assistance," Oralie jumped in. "It's that you've risked your lives enough. I wish we could spare Tam the responsibility as well, but his talent—and the nature of this gadget—make him crucial. I have no doubt we'll need your assistance for many things in the days ahead. So please, take this time to rest."

"I'm not opposed to keeping you safe," Edaline told Sophie gently, wrapping an arm around her shoulders.

The other parents agreed, and that seemed to settle it—except Linh, who insisted on staying with her brother.

"I think it would be wise if you all stayed together," Mr. Forkle told Sophie and her friends. "That way it's easier to reach you with updates and questions."

Alden and Della offered up Everglen, and that became the plan.

"Oh, and Miss Foster?" Councillor Terik said as the Councillors prepared to leap away. "Thank you for bringing the alicorns for a visit. It's good to see they're both healthy and thriving. Let's hope it remains that way."

The last words reminded her that Silveny and Greyfell probably shouldn't linger.

She made her way over and stroked Silveny's velvety nose.

SOPHIE OKAY?

Thanks to you, Sophie told her.

Silveny's deep brown eyes seemed to peer right through her, and the motherly alicorn searched Sophie's emotions until she landed on the one subject Sophie had been hoping to avoid.

KEEFE?

He . . . isn't here.

Silveny nuzzled Sophie's side. *GOOD,* she said. *KEEFE! FRIEND! GOOD!*

I hope so, Sophie told her, breaking eye contact before she ended up a sobbing mess.

She'd cry for Keefe later. Right now, she had to focus.

You and Greyfell should get somewhere safe—and get some snacks. Remember, you're eating for two.

Silveny nudged Sophie's hand. She trotted closer to Greyfell and both alicorns dipped their heads, almost in a bow as Sophie told them she'd check on them soon.

SOON! Silveny agreed as she and Greyfell floated into the sky.

Right before they teleported away, Silveny sent one final transmission.

KEEFE GOOD SOON!

"Wylie has been moved. As has Prentice—to be safe," Mr. Forkle told them after he'd arrived at Everglen that night. Despite the late hour, everyone was still wide awake, gathered in Everglen's glittering dining room—a room Sophie hadn't been in since the day Oralie, Bronte, and Kenric had tested her for Foxfire. The thronelike chairs, sweeping chandelier, and silk-draped windows looked far too grand for such an exhausted group, and no one had touched the platters of food Della had set out—even the mallowmelt. "They've been set up in a secure cabin high in the mountains, where they'll be able to recover together," he added. "Neither seemed strained at all by the sudden move. If anything, they seemed more relaxed than ever."

"What about Tam and Linh?" Biana asked. "Where will they live now?"

"We're setting up a secure residence for them here in the

Lost Cities. That way they'll no longer feel so isolated. Blur has offered to serve as their guardian, and the Council will be assigning them goblin bodyguards. And they've been granted permission to attend Foxfire, once the term resumes again."

Sophie tried to focus on the good news, and the hopeful hints in his tone. But . . . "You'll never be able to use Alluveterre as a hideout again, will you?"

Fitz had spent the last few hours sharing the heartbreaking details about Keefe stealing Tam's crystal and helping Alvar escape. No one except Grady—who'd had quite a few choice comments about *That Boy*—had known what to say. Especially Alden and Della.

"Never is a long time," Mr. Forkle told Sophie. "Most things tend to be much more temporary. And while it's a regrettable setback, it's nothing compared to what the Neverseen have lost this evening. That's another thing I'm happy to report. With the help of Mr. Tam—and a loyal contingent of goblins and dwarves—the Council has now raided all sixteen of the hideouts connected by the Lodestar symbol. Some had long been abandoned, but the others had very recently been sacked."

"So they were empty?" Fitz asked.

"Stripped and scorched, yes," Mr. Forkle admitted. "I'll give them credit for speed and efficiency—it must've been a mad, destructive scramble. And please try not to look so distressed by this news. Gathering more prisoners and evidence would've been nice—but either way, this is a significant victory in our favor. We've now shut down the majority of their network."

"But you don't think we got it all?" Biana asked.

"I think that Fintan's too clever to not have a few emergency evacuation areas. Plus, none of the hideouts had a silver door marked 'The star only rises at Nightfall.'"

Sophie rubbed the new knot forming under her ribs.

So Keefe's legacy was still out there, waiting for him.

She wondered what his mom would say if she'd seen what her son had done that day. Would she have been proud he'd chosen the Neverseen over his friends? Or furious he'd remained with the people who'd imprisoned her?

"I think that's all we can do for tonight," Mr. Forkle said, standing and reaching into his cloak for a pathfinder. "Blur will be bringing Tam and Linh here soon—and then I hope you'll all go to bed and *try* to sleep."

"Wait!" Dex said. "I almost forgot—do you still have Keefe's old Imparter?"

"I returned it to Miss Foster, to do with as she wished," Mr. Forkle told him. "Why?"

"I can't stop thinking about it, ever since Sophie did that enhancing thing to me. I think there's something we missed. Do you have it, Sophie?"

"It should still be at Havenfield," she said.

"I'll retrieve it for you tomorrow," Sandor promised as he stood to bring Grady and Edaline back to the safety of

Gildingham. Before he left, he gave Sophie a *long* lecture on how she was not to leave Grizel's sight even for a second—or trigger any more abilities.

And true to his word, Sandor returned to Everglen the next day, holding the black case he'd collected from her room.

"Is it okay for us to talk around the Imparter?" Biana asked as Dex popped open the case and slid his finger across the silver screen.

"Yeah it's a different kind of signal than I realized." He tapped the screen in each of the corners. "Hmm, it's being fussy again." He glanced at Sophie. "Would it be weird if I asked to hold your hand?"

Tam smirked. "Smooooooooth."

Sophie rolled her eyes. "I know what he meant."

She pulled off her glove, and the second their fingers touched . . .

"Whoa," Dex breathed. "That is such a rush!"

The seconds slipped by, and he tapped the screen a few more places before telling the Imparter, "Bypass."

The gadget beeped and went dark.

"Was that supposed to happen?" Linh asked.

"I don't know." Dex flipped the Imparter over, tapping a few more places.

The silence shifted from tense to restless to *endless*. Then a voice blared from the screen.

"Password?"

SEVENTY-THREE

WHAT'S THE PASSWORD?" Biana whispered.

"No idea," Dex admitted. "And I don't feel a way to hack it. That same crazy-smart Technopath who built all the stuff with the Lodestar symbol must've been the one who designed this."

"Okay," Linh said. "Anyone have any guesses?"

"With Keefe it could seriously be anything," Fitz reminded them.

Tam smirked at Sophie. "I have a theory."

"So do I," she said. "His mom's the one who rigged the gadget, right? So what would *her* password be?"

"But she didn't make it for herself—she wanted Keefe to

find this, didn't she?" Fitz asked. "Didn't the note she left for him kinda hint at it? So she would've picked something she hoped Keefe would guess."

He made a good point. Sophie reread the note in her mind.

"What about 'legacy'?" she asked.

"Access granted," the Imparter chirped, and Sophie felt ice ripple across her nerves.

"Access to what?" Biana whispered.

The screen stayed blank.

"Shouldn't it be doing something?" Fitz asked.

"It is," Dex said. "It opened a private line."

"So it's hailing somebody right now?" Sophie asked.

Dex nodded and they all leaned closer, watching the ominously silent screen.

"Are we sure this is a good idea?" Fitz asked after what felt like an eternity but was probably less than thirty seconds.

"Better to know than wonder, right?" Biana said. "But here's what I don't get. It took Dex's Technopath skills—*enhanced* Technopath skills—to get to the place where you entered the password, right? Wouldn't that mean Keefe never could've gotten there on his own?"

"It's only that difficult for *us*," Dex said, "because I had to bypass the primary sensor, which is what Keefe could've used to gain access. I'd actually noticed that there was a weird, two-tone gear the last time I took the Imparter apart. But I didn't realize it meant the sensor read different things on different sides until I got the boost from Sophie."

"So what else does it read?" Sophie asked.

"Blood."

Everyone squirmed.

"Is it still hailing?" Tam asked.

Dex nodded. "But I doubt anyone's going to answer. His mom probably set this up before they imprisoned her, so I'm sure her Imparter got taken or destroyed."

"How much longer should we wait?" Biana asked.

"Maybe give it another minute?" Sophie said. "Just in case."

She counted the passing seconds, and at around seventy-five Dex told everyone, "I guess that's it."

He swiped a finger across the screen, frowning when the Imparter flashed pale blue. "Wait—was it not actually hailing yet?"

"How would we know?" Fitz asked.

"Ugh, this thing makes no sense! It's like—"

"Hello?" a crackly, garbled voice blared from the Imparter. Even with the distortion, the sound was unmistakable.

Lady Gisela.

They all leaned back in case she could somehow see them. But the Imparter's screen stayed silver, keeping the conversation limited to their voices.

"Keefe?" Lady Gisela asked. "Is someone there?"

Fuzzy static.

"It's you, isn't it, Sophie?"

"Yes." The word slipped out before Sophie could think it through.

"Where's my son?" Lady Gisela demanded.

Sophie glanced at her friends for help, but they only offered blank stares.

"He's . . . where you planned for him to be," she mumbled.

Lots of crackles and static flooded the connection, and when Lady Gisela's voice came back it sounded like the end of a sentence. All Sophie caught was "run things."

"Can you repeat that?" Sophie asked.

"I said it was never my plan to let that idiot run things."

"You mean Fintan?"

Static was her only answer.

"Are you still there?" Sophie asked.

More crackles. Then Lady Gisela said, "I asked if anyone else has been captured."

"Why would I tell you that?"

"Because you have no idea what you're dealing with. And I do."

"And I'm supposed to believe you're going to help me?"

"Exactly," Lady Gisela said. "Because you care about my son. And I don't have a lot of options. So we're both going to suffer through this miserable truce."

Sophie glanced at her friends for guidance, and their expressions all seemed to be unanimously screaming *DON'T YOU DARE TRUST KEEFE'S MOM*. And Sophie had no intention of doing so. But that didn't mean she couldn't try to learn something from her.

"I'll ask you again," Lady Gisela said. "Where's my son? Is he with Brant and Fintan?"

Sophie bit her lip, deciding one tiny piece of information was worth the risk. "He's with Fintan."

"Does that mean Brant's been captured?"

"Tell me why it matters."

"You don't need to know. Who else was taken? Ruy?" When Sophie didn't respond, Lady Gisela said, "I'll take that as a yes. And I need you to listen very carefully. You have to do exactly as I say, or you'll regret it."

"Is that a threat?"

"It's a warning—based on truths and hard realities I don't expect you to understand."

"You know what I don't understand?" Sophie asked. "What you did to Cyrah Endal."

Lady Gisela's voice darkened. "Whatever you think you know is one small, twisted piece of a much larger, much grander whole."

"That sounds like a fancy way of trying to justify a murder."

"Murder," Lady Gisela repeated. "Believe what you want. You may not trust me, Sophie. And you may not like me. But right now, we both care about the same thing. Which means you need to listen to me. Get my son far away from the Neverseen."

The demand was so ironic, Sophie couldn't quite choke back her laugh.

"I take it that means you've tried?" Lady Gisela asked.

"Yeah, and there's pretty much no reasoning with him. He has this desperate need to try to make up for all the creepy things you've done."

"Don't blame this on me. This is what they want. *Their* vision."

"That would mean a lot more if you'd tell me what you're talking about."

"But it would also distract you from what matters. You can't stop this, Sophie. Don't try. It's been in place for too long. So get my son back before it all comes crashing down, and contact me when it's done. And next time, make sure you hail me using his blood."

SEVENTY-FOUR

I'M ASSUMING MR. DIZZNEE TRIED TRACK-
ing the signal," Mr. Forkle said as he studied the now
silent Imparter sitting on Everglen's dining room table.
His eyes were red rimmed and shadowed, and he wore
the same clothes from the day before—and Sophie couldn't
decide if it was the thronelike chair, or if his ruckleberries were
wearing off, but he looked smaller.

"I tried everything," Dex said, "Even with Sophie enhancing
my ability, I got nowhere."

Mr. Forkle nodded. "And I'm *also* assuming that you're not
going to tell Mr. Sencen about this?"

"Doesn't seem like a good idea," Sophie said. "If we couldn't
get him to leave the Neverseen when he had the perfect chance

and the perfect reason, how is telling him that his mom *wants* him to leave going to help? Besides, for all we know Lady Gisela's using us to get Keefe back so she can grab him and force him into his *legacy*."

"Oh, I'm certain her motives are selfish," Mr. Forkle said. "If I'm understanding this correctly, it sounds like this 'vision' Fintan has may be separate from the Lodestar Initiative that Lady Gisela created, and she fears it will wreck her own plans."

"Shouldn't we let it, then?" Dex asked.

"Ah, but that's a risky game. Blindly choosing between two evils could backfire far too easily. For all we know, Lady Gisela could truly be the safer path."

"But she probably killed Wylie's mom," Linh argued.

"And Fintan definitely killed Kenric," Sophie reminded her.

"Yeah . . . they're both horrible options," Biana said. "I want to take them both down."

"Hard to do when we don't actually know what either of them are planning," Fitz mumbled. "After all our investigations into Lodestar, we *still* don't know what the Initiative actually entails. And Fintan's *vision* is even more vague."

"I feel like Keefe is the key," Sophie said quietly.

"Ugh, if he heard you say that, there'd be no living with him," Tam grumbled.

Sophie smiled. It was strange that she could miss Keefe *and* want to bash his face in. "I just meant that there has to be a reason both Fintan and Lady Gisela want him on their side.

It might be because they need him to open that door in the mountain. But then why wouldn't Fintan have made Keefe do that right away?"

"It feels like we're missing something," Biana said. "Doesn't it?"

"When aren't we?" Sophie mumbled, replaying the conversation with Lady Gisela in her mind. There had to be deeper meanings to her vague warnings and advice.

"I guess all we really need to know," she said quietly, "for the moment, at least, is whether Keefe is safer where his mom wants him to be, or safer where he's at?"

"He's safest when he's not in the dark about that decision," Mr. Forkle told her. "And can choose based on knowledge, and not his own misguided reasoning."

The logic hit home.

"I guess I'll tell him what his mom said and see what he does," Sophie decided. "The rest is up to him."

"Try to make it quick," Mr. Forkle told her. "We have lots of other things to discuss when you're done."

"You want me to tell him now?" Sophie asked

"Why put off the inevitable?"

"Uh, who are you and what have you done with the guy who's always telling us to be patient?" Tam asked.

A sad smile curled Mr. Forkle's lips. "Perhaps I'm learning to see the folly in delay. Haste can be dangerous too, of course. But there's a difference between caution and hesitation. Plus, I need Miss Foster's mind free of distraction for what's coming next."

"What's coming next?" Sophie asked.

"One thing at a time, Miss Foster. First settle things with Mr. Sencen."

Sophie sighed, not sure she was ready to have this conversation—especially in front of an audience. But she closed her eyes and transmitted Keefe's name.

Foster? He responded immediately. *What's wrong? I thought you weren't talking to me.*

I wasn't, she admitted. *Is this a bad time?*

Um . . . give me a second.

His mind went silent for a beat—long enough for Sophie to tug out an itchy eyelash.

Okay—I told everyone I had to poop, he said a little too proudly. *That should keep them away for a few minutes.*

Ugh, TMI.

You realize I'm not actually pooping, right? I mean, I know we've shared a lot of things, but I don't think poop should be one of them—unless it's sparkly and from an alicorn. Or blasting like a geyser out of a gulon.

Stop talking about poop!

She shook her head, trying to knock those lovely mental images away and regain her focus. *I have to show you something, and you might want to sit down for it.*

The only way to do that involves a less-than-awesome-smelling

596

toilet—this new hideout is miserable. *Everything is sweaty and sticky—and we're all crammed into this tiny room.*

How many of you are there?

Just me, Trix, Alvar, and Umber. Fintan moved everyone else to a different place. And it's starting to feel like they're my babysitters—they never let me out of their sight.

That . . . doesn't sound like a good sign.

She'd expected him to deny it. But his mind dimmed a little, before he changed the subject. *So what did you need to tell me?*

Right. Brace yourself. This is going to be tough to see. She gathered her concentration and replayed what Lady Gisela had told her word for word.

That . . . complicates things, he mumbled. *And it could all be a trick.*

It definitely could.

But you think I should do what she said and get out?

It doesn't matter what I think. It's not like you listen to me.

The thought had a snap to it, and Sophie could see Keefe's mind sting. But she wasn't going to apologize.

I think a better question is, CAN you get out? she asked.

It'll be rough, he admitted. *But my escape plan will still work. If I use it, though, it'll destroy every single thing I've been working toward.*

I guess you'll have to decide what's most important, then.

His mind seemed to ripple with a sigh. *What happens if I leave?*

What do you mean?

I mean . . . doesn't everyone hate me?

Sophie glanced at her friends, each watching her silently from their fancy chairs. *You have some serious apologizing to do,* she said. *But I don't think any of us can actually hate you—even when we really, really, really want to.*

I could've done without that third "really."

Maybe. But you deserve it.

I do. He replayed his mom's words again before he told her, *I'd better get back—but that's not my decision. I need more time to think.*

Think away, Sophie told him. *You know where to find me.*

"Actually, you won't be here if Mr. Sencen decides to come home in the next few days," Mr. Forkle warned after she'd closed down the mental conversation. "That's why I needed you to focus. I received a scroll this morning—as I'm sure your mother did as well—informing me that the envoy will be retrieving me at five o'clock this evening to bring me to Lumenaria. The Councillors finally agreed that it's imperative we interrogate Ruy and Brant as soon as possible. So they're moving up the Peace Summit, starting tonight."

SEVENTY-FIVE

SOPHIE AND EDALINE'S ENVOYS ARRIVED at Sandor's house at five o'clock sharp, and Sophie was relieved one of them was a familiar face—Righty, the goblin who'd helped guide her when she'd visited Lumenaria. Apparently, Righty had been assigned as Sophie's personal guard for the course of the summit, and the other envoy would be guarding Edaline.

Sandor gave both goblins a long list of procedures and instructions—along with a few threats of violence and dismemberment if anything went wrong.

"We've been well trained," Edaline's guard assured him.

Sophie decided to call her Bunhead. It matched her hairstyle, and her graceful movements as she crossed the room, handing them black tunics, pants, slipperlike shoes, and gloves to change into.

"The simple garb is just until you clear security," Righty explained. "Once you're settled into your rooms you'll find more proper attire for the summit."

"Will our rooms be near each other?" Edaline asked.

"You'll have your own double suite," Bunhead told her.

That was, unfortunately, the only good news. The rest was a whole lot of yuck, starting with the fact that Sophie wasn't allowed to bring Ella. No jewelry was allowed either, except their registry pendants, so Sophie had to leave behind her Cognate rings, panic switch, and Sucker Punch.

"Be safe," Grady whispered as he strangle-hugged his wife and daughter. "And here's hoping this will be a quick summit."

"What's the longest one has ever gone?" Sophie asked, regretting the question when Edaline told her, "A little over three months."

The words kept repeating in Sophie's mind as she endured the security searches at Lumenaria's gates—and the dread grew much louder during the lecture on castle rules. The basic gist was: *If you aren't in an assigned meeting or gala, you'll be locked in your room for your own safety.* It was hard to decide what sounded scarier—the locked-in-her-room part, or the *gala*.

And it could stretch on for *months*.

Even the walk to her room felt endless. No blindfolds that

time, not that it made the journey any clearer, considering how twisty the halls were, and all the identical staircases and doors.

"Your rooms will not have a view," Bunhead warned. "The Council wanted you in the underground quarters, where the security is easier for us to control."

"So basically, they're locking us in the dungeon," Sophie said.

Righty smiled. "I'm sure you'll find the accommodations much more pleasant."

Their rooms *were* beautiful—marble floors, and walls broken up with intricate tapestries and paintings. Ornate chandeliers cast a warm pink light, and all the furniture was overstuffed and draped in luxurious fabrics. The décor was elegant and tasteful—the colors lush and regal. But the lack of windows still made it feel like a cell.

Their door also had two locks—one to keep anyone from getting in. The other to prevent them from leaving.

"We'll let you get changed for the introductory dinner," Bunhead told them. "Knock four quick times when you're ready to go and we'll open the door."

The lock clicked, and Sophie's misery was sealed when she checked her new wardrobe. Her "day gowns" had so many ruffles and gathers they made Cotillion dresses look plain. And her "evening gowns" had just as many frills—with fun bonuses like sweeping trains and corseted bodices and all kinds of other things that were clearly meant to destroy her.

"Remind me what any of this has to do with negotiating a peace treaty?" Sophie asked as Edaline helped her fasten the hundreds of tiny buttons that secured the silky teal gown she'd chosen. The color was her favorite, and the skirt wasn't *as* puffy as a lot of the others. But the drop-waist bodice was so fitted, she wondered how she would sit. And the neckline scooped and squeezed in ways that made her cheeks blush.

"This summit is about more than making King Dimitar sign his name on a piece of paper," Edaline told her. "It's about reminding the world of the sheer magnificence of our culture. Displaying our wealth, beauty, and confidence all work to create the ideal impression."

"Yeah, well, if they wanted me to be confident, they should let me wear shoes I can actually walk in," Sophie grumbled, holding up her impossibly slender heels.

"I guess you'll have to settle for looking beautiful—and so grown up! If any of your boys were here . . ."

Edaline didn't finish the sentence—or name the boys—and for that, Sophie gave her a hug.

"And you understand what's going to happen at the dinner?" Edaline asked as she knocked to let their guards know they were ready.

Sophie fussed with her teal gloves. "I'm going to try not to cause an interspecies incident when I'm introduced to the other leaders. Then we're all supposed to eat fancy food in a stuffy room while everyone pretends they're not secretly wishing they could kill each other."

Edaline smiled, looping her arm through Sophie's as they started the long trek to where dinner would be held. "Not *everyone* hates each other. The animosity exists mostly between the goblins, ogres, and trolls. The dwarves and gnomes are generally content to live and let live, so long as everyone extends that courtesy to them."

"Then let's hope we're seated next to them," Sophie mumbled. "And that none of the food requires knives."

"I'm sure it won't. Did you notice they didn't even give us any hairpins?"

After seeing the damage Lady Gisela had done with one, Sophie wasn't surprised.

"Are we going a different direction than the way we came?" Sophie asked as they started up a winding staircase. "I can't get my bearings."

"And you won't," Bunhead explained. "The paths are intentionally ambiguous to ensure that no one will ever find their way through unless they've been trained."

"Or get really lucky," Righty added.

"Don't be nervous," Edaline told her when they finally reached a set of embossed golden doors. "All you have to do is smile and act natural."

Sophie felt anything but natural as she took in the splendor of the room. The elves were never shy with their displays of wealth, but this? This was something else entirely. The space had the feel of a moonlit terrace garden, but they were still very much indoors, and every fragile flower, every graceful tree, every cascading vine, and every sweeping balustrade—even the stars winking across the swirled black ceiling—had been intricately carved from jewels or cast from precious metals. It was the perfect marriage of nature and craft—a new level of mastery—and everyone in the room could only stare in wonder.

Well, everyone save for one.

King Dimitar couldn't have looked more bored as he leaned his gorilla-size body against the trunk of a tree—a Panakes tree, Sophie realized, which made her wish she still wore her Sucker Punch. He wore his usual metal diaper—though the waistline had been rimmed with glittering black jewels, which matched the stones set into his earlobes—and idly traced a clawed finger along the tattoos crowning his bald head.

"A child in a Peace Summit," he said as Sophie tried to hurry past him. "And yet they criticize my people for training our children to defend themselves."

"If it were only for defense," Councillor Alina said, swishing over in an iridescent gown that shifted from green to purple with every motion, "I doubt anyone would have a problem."

"And yet the greatest defense is a strong offense, isn't it?" Dimitar countered, smiling to show his pointed teeth.

"Is that what you'd call the warriors you sent to capture my family?" Sophie asked, ignoring the warning squeeze Edaline gave her arm.

King Dimitar straightened, his bulging muscles flexing with the motion. "If *I'd* planned that mission, your mother would not be standing at your side—though I'm not convinced your family was even the target. Not everything revolves around you, Miss Foster."

He stalked away, leaving Sophie to drown in the fresh wave of questions.

If Dimitar wasn't lying about the attackers being unsanctioned rebels—which she was far from ready to believe—who else would they have been after?

Lady Cadence? She was one of the ogres' most loyal supporters.

"There you are, Miss Foster," Councillor Bronte said behind her, drawing her back to the present. Sophie turned to find him standing with Councillor Oralie and Councillor Terik, all looking resplendent in their suits, gowns, and capes in the same jeweled tones as their circlets.

Edaline had been right about the elves screaming wealth, power, and confidence. It was like having the prom kings and queens milling around the room.

"Empress Pernille was just telling me she hadn't had the privilege of meeting you," Bronte told Sophie. "Perhaps you'd be willing to let us make the introduction?"

Sophie nodded, letting the Councillors lead her away. But

her mind was still so stuck on the idea of Lady Cadence being the target that she nearly trampled a small, strange creature that looked like a cross between a sloth, a pot-bellied pig, and a small child, with fuzzy skin, an upturned nose, and a short chubby body dressed in a purple tutu.

"Empress Pernille," Councillor Oralie said, dipping a graceful curtsy. "Forgive us for not seeing you."

The creature chirped a reply, and it took Sophie's Polyglot skills a moment to realize she was listening to the ruler of the trolls.

"I'm so sorry," Sophie said, fumbling through a curtsy. "I should never be allowed to wear something this huge—it will only end in disaster."

Empress Pernille blinked her round, yellow eyes. "Rarely do I ever hear an elf address me in my own language—and with such a precise accent."

Sophie stared at her gloves. "I wish I could take credit. But my ability made the shift unconsciously."

"Intelligent, talented, and humble—I see why I hear often of your influence," the Empress said, before turning to Oralie. "Perhaps we could have a word?"

Oralie motioned for the Empress to follow her through an arch lined with cut amethyst flowers, to a more secluded corner of the room.

As soon as Bronte and Terik had wandered away, Sophie whispered to Edaline, "*That's* what trolls look like?" She'd seen images of them as fierce beasts with lots of claws and muscles—meanwhile Empress Pernille could've easily been mistaken for a Muppet.

"The trolls age in reverse," Edaline whispered. "Their bodies shrink with time, rather than growing. And their features soften."

"Does that mean the ancient trolls look like babies?" Sophie asked.

"Not quite that extreme. Sorry, I suppose I should've warned you."

"Anything else I should be prepared for?" Sophie asked.

"I can't think of anything. Actually, yes I can. King Enki is bald."

She pointed across the room, and Sophie did a double take.

Dwarves normally had long, scraggly fur and squinty, pointed facial features that reminded Sophie of oversize talking moles. But the king looked like a plucked chicken, his textured skin a mottled pattern of peach, brown, and black—which looked extra strange considering his pants were made of soft white fur.

"Is that what happens when dwarves age?" Sophie asked.

"No, it's a statement," Edaline said. "The dwarves view it a sign of power and strength for their king to wax himself bare. I've never really wanted to know why."

Sophie did her best not to stare, focusing instead on the king's heavy crown—a thick ring of carved, opalescent shell.

She'd gotten up close and personal once with the giant-sand-crab-like creatures the shell had come from, and still found it strange the king would want any part of its body curled around his head.

He caught her looking and tapped his feet as he offered a bow.

The rest of the introductions were more what Sophie had prepared for. Queen Hylda looked fierce and statuesque in her gleaming golden armor. And a gnome Sophie had seen around Havenfield—now wearing a suit woven from Panakes petals—had been selected to represent his kind, which had no ultimate leader.

"You're handling yourself very well," Mr. Forkle told her, emerging from the shadows he'd been lurking in. "Far better than I could've ever planned."

"Is this what you designed me for?" she asked, raising an eyebrow.

Mr. Forkle smiled. "I designed you to be something new, Miss Foster. Something to get people's attention. And above all else, to be *you*."

The compliments weren't particularly sappy—but the way he said them turned her throat thick.

"Thank you," she whispered.

"For what?"

"For giving me this life—crazy and confusing as it always is."

It was Mr. Forkle's turn to look away, swiping at his eyes.

When he turned back to say something else, the words were drowned out by loud fanfare.

All twelve Councillors gathered in the center of the room to announce that it was time for dinner, and Councillor Liora snapped her fingers and made a U-shaped table appear before them, covered in flowers and candles and dome-covered plates at every place setting. The Councillors took the seats in the center, while the other leaders were stationed along the sides. Sophie was relieved to be seated between her mom and Mr. Forkle.

They feasted on several kinds of gnomish fruit, thinly sliced and artfully arranged. Some tasted like steak and lobster and other fancy things. Others were richer and earthier. No one cleared their plate, but everyone found their favorites and seemed happy when Liora conjured the dishes away.

"It's always refreshing to see our worlds gather in the pursuit of peace," Councillor Emery said as he stood to address his guests. "And to have this rare opportunity for enlightened interchange and mutual benefit. The real work begins tomorrow, but we wanted to end this first night with something we hope you'll find heartening. As many of you know, the complex problems of our modern world have led to the rise of certain groups within the Lost Cities. And while the Black Swan have proven themselves to be both resourceful and reasonable—which is why they're represented here at this Summit—the Neverseen have unfortunately caused incredible chaos. Halting their efforts has proven a challenge, but we finally have proof of our inevitable victory."

Three holograms flashed to the center of the U shape: Brant, Ruy, and Gethen—live projections of each of the prisoners in their blindingly bright cells. They sat in nearly identical poses—backs straight, legs crossed, eyes closed—looking more like meditating monks than warmongering villains.

And yet, as Sophie watched, the faintest whiff of a smile curled Gethen's lips, reminding her how desperate he'd seemed for information about the summit.

They're up to something, she thought, right as a pair of goblins burst into the room and whispered a breathless message to Councillor Emery.

"Is something wrong?" King Dimitar asked.

"'Wrong' is not the word I would use." Councillor Emery glanced at the other Councillors, waiting for each to nod. "I've just received word that the current leader of the Neverseen—an elf named Fintan Pyren—is outside the gates of this castle demanding to be admitted to the proceedings."

SEVENTY-SIX

WHY AREN'T THEY ARREST-*ing him?* Sophie transmitted to Mr. Forkle as the various leaders shouted questions at the Council. *They should be dragging Fintan to one of those cells to join his co-conspirators!*

Diplomacy is rarely as straightforward as it may seem, Mr. Forkle told her. *Both Queen Hylda and Empress Pernille are requesting that Fintan be allowed to participate in the Summit's proceedings. Haven't you been listening?*

She hadn't. Her mind had been too busy piecing scarier things together.

Fintan's arrival.

The fact that none of the prisoners had looked particularly upset about being in their cells.

Lady Gisela telling her "this is what they want."

Even the plan Keefe had mentioned—the one he'd said Brant and Ruy were ordered to take part in, which Ruy had considered unnecessary and demeaning.

Could it have involved letting themselves get captured?

They're up to something, she transmitted. *Probably a jailbreak. It's perfect. They'd get to humiliate the Council, impress or scare the world leaders,* and *get Gethen back, all in one go.*

You may be right, Mr. Forkle said. *And in case you are, I think it would be quite unwise to allow Fintan anywhere near those cells, don't you?*

He stood, clearing his throat as he waited for the room's attention. "For the record, I think Fintan should be heard during the proceedings as well."

At least half the room gasped—Sophie included—even though she knew what Mr. Forkle was trying to do.

"You honestly want to jeopardize the security of these proceedings?" Oralie asked, ignoring the protocol of letting Councillor Emery do the speaking.

"No. I want him to be placed under heavy guard in the small storage outbuilding in the main courtyard," Mr. Forkle said calmly. "And he can remain there until the morning negotiations, in which case he'd be brought into the meeting. Keep as many guards on him as you like—and lock him back in the outbuilding when the proceedings are over. There's no reason for him to attend the galas or dinners."

"There's no reason for him to attend anything at all!" Alina argued. "He's a Pyrokinetic."

"Yes, and lumenite doesn't burn," Mr. Forkle reminded her. "Isn't that why the Ancient Councillors chose it when they built this fortress?"

Oralie stood, her fragile hands gripping the end of the table. "I can't believe anyone is considering this. That lunatic is bent on destroying everything we hold precious. What can we possibly gain from allowing his voice to be heard?"

"Perspective," Empress Pernille told her. "For millennia we've been told there's one way—the elvin way. And now, it appears the elvin way is divided. I find it hard to believe I'm the only one who'd like to know what these other elves have to say—especially since one alternate elvin perspective is already being presented by the Black Swan. Why not hear the other?"

"Because he's a murderer!" Oralie shouted.

"So am I, by elvin standards," Queen Hylda said. "So are most of us. Death goes hand in hand with war."

"*You're* in favor of Fintan joining us?" Councillor Bronte asked the goblin queen. "After his involvement in what happened with Brielle?"

"It's *because* of his involvement in Brielle's death that I would like to hear him out. I'd like to understand what her life was taken for."

"None of us are saying we'll agree with his logic," King Enki added. "We'd simply like to hear what that logic *is*. Isn't it our responsibility to consider the issues from every possible side before we render a decision?"

Sophie was surprised to realize King Dimitar was staying silent during the debate. And he glared at those supporting Fintan's admission with a murderous sort of rage.

The Councillors looked just as disgusted. But—ever the diplomats—they put it to a poll, making it clear that the Council's vote would only count for one. Mr. Forkle was given a vote, since he was a leader of his order. Sophie and Edaline were excluded as observers. The final verdict: four to three in favor of letting Fintan attend.

"Well," Councillor Emery said, massaging his temples. "It appears we have some adjustments to make. So we ask that you please return to your rooms—and understand that you will not be able to leave them for the rest of the night. We need to ensure everyone's safety as we drastically amend our protocols."

Righty and Bunhead shuffled Sophie and Edaline away from the crowd, leading them through a set of balefire-lit halls into the bowels of the fortress.

As soon as the door closed to their suite, Edaline pulled Sophie close. "It looked like you and Mr. Forkle were having a telepathic conversation while everyone argued. Please tell me what's going on. I promise I'm strong enough to handle it."

For most of the time Sophie had spent with her adoptive

family, Edaline had been the fragile one, broken by her grief over losing Jolie. But there was no weakness in Edaline's voice or any tremors in her hands as she rubbed Sophie's back.

So Sophie leaned closer and whispered, "We think the Neverseen are going to attempt a prison break, and we're trying to figure out how to stop them."

Edaline nodded slowly. "And I'm assuming Mr. Forkle didn't ask the Councillors to move the prisoners, because you're worried that's what the Neverseen want?"

"Actually, I think he just knew the Council would never go along with it," Sophie admitted. "But your reason is important too."

"So what does Mr. Forkle want us to do?"

"No idea," Sophie admitted, not missing the way Edaline had included herself in their planning. "It's so hard to strategize when we don't have any idea what they're thinking. Everything we do could play right into their hands."

"Do you think Keefe will have any insights?"

"If he does, they'll probably be super vague and warn us about the wrong thing," Sophie grumbled. But on the off chance, she decided to reach out to him.

Just the girl I wanted to talk to, Keefe told her.

No time for banter, Keefe—Fintan just talked his way into the Peace Summit. I'm pretty sure he's planning to break Ruy, Gethen, and Brant out of the dungeon. In fact, I'm betting Brant and Ruy are a part of it.

Keefe's mind unleashed a bunch of words she'd get in trouble for using.

I take it that means we're guessing right? she asked.

You might be. I know Fintan's off on a mission right now—and Alvar told me they've been building toward it for a while. He said it would make the world lose all faith in the Council.

Sophie's stomach did a twist-flip move that made her really wish she hadn't eaten so much dinner.

Ugh, I'm the biggest idiot on the planet if that nightmare at the Pallidrose hideout was a ploy to get them captured, Keefe mentally grumbled. His thoughts strayed to his burned hand, and Sophie could tell the nerves still hurt him, even though the skin had healed.

It was probably her cue to tell him he wasn't an idiot—but he *had* done some pretty idiotic things.

Then again, so had she.

If getting arrested was part of their plan, we all played right into it. All we can do is hope we've caught our mistake with enough time to stop them.

And I'm assuming you're at the summit? he asked. *Never mind, of course you are. You're probably right where it's most dangerous.*

I am, Sophie said. *And so is Edaline.*

More inappropriate words pounded through his head. *Why would the Council let Fintan in? Didn't they learn after what happened to Kenric?*

It wasn't their decision. Some of the other leaders wanted to hear what he had to say. And Mr. Forkle figured it was safer than letting Fintan anywhere near the cells.

I guess I can see that. But I have a bad feeling about this, Foster.

So do I. Is there anything else you can think of that will tell us what we're dealing with?

Not much. I heard Alvar and Fintan debating about whether or not someone was going to "deliver." So that might mean there's another person who needs to bring them something. Maybe King Dimitar?

Maybe. But he looked pretty furious when Fintan showed up.

Edaline was still rubbing Sophie's back, and Sophie tried to focus on the feeling—tried to keep her head clear so she could think instead of panicking.

It's not too late to beat this, Keefe thought, his mind humming with a new sort of momentum. *Keep your head down and your eyes open, and don't go anywhere without Sandor.*

Sandor's not here. Lumenaria has its own security force.

Can you trust them?

I don't know. My guard seems nice.

Nice isn't good enough. If there is another person helping Fintan, it would make sense that they'd be part of the security. So don't hesitate to unleash that Foster rage on anyone who feels like a threat, okay? I'll be there as soon as I can.

You will? How?

617

Still figuring that out. I don't know if I'll be able to get inside the castle, but I'm sure there's somewhere on the island I can hide.

Sophie doubted that, but she had a more pressing question. *What about your babysitters?*

Already working on it. That's what I was trying to tell you when you first reached out to me. I decided I'm leaving the Neverseen. Tonight.

SEVENTY-SEVEN

SOPHIE PULLED AWAY FROM EDALINE as the crush of emotions hit her. She couldn't decide if she wanted to laugh or cry or shred a few of her bed's fancy tasseled pillows.

On the one hand—Keefe was leaving the Neverseen!

On the other: WHY COULDN'T HE HAVE FIGURED IT OUT BEFORE HE FREED ALVAR, AND STOLE THE CACHE, AND THE ALLUVETERRE CRYSTAL, AND WHEN IT WASN'T SUPER DANGEROUS FOR HIM TO ESCAPE, AND ARRRRGGGGGHHHHH!

Hey, Keefe said, reminding her that their thoughts were still connected. *I don't blame you for the rage-fest, Foster—but I promise I'm going to make it up to you. All of it. Starting tonight.*

She sank onto her bed, deciding sitting was a good idea. *I know you want to help—but coming to Lumenaria is a bad idea. The island is nothing but a cold, rocky beach, and I'm sure there are goblins patrolling it. And Alvar and the others might expect you to go there. I think you should head to Sandor's house in Gildingham. That's where Grady is. They'll keep you safe.*

Uh, I'm pretty sure the most dangerous place I could be right now is alone in a room with your dad and Gigantor.

Flashes of the torturous "boys" conversation raced through Sophie's mind. *Hmm, you might have a point there.*

So it's settled, then, Keefe said. *I'll be outside Lumenaria as soon as I bust out of here. I don't care if there are patrols, I'll find a way to evade them. I want to be close—that way if you need me, I can help.*

Sophie could think of a thousand reasons why that was a horrible plan. But there were other things to worry about.

How are you going to get away from everyone at the hideout? she asked. *You said it was going to be rough.*

It probably will be. And I know everything I've done lately has been made of epic fail. But this is different. I'm back to playing my own games. And Team Foster-Keefe is going to win!

"You both look tired," Mr. Forkle noted as Sophie and Edaline took their seats at the formal summit breakfast.

Tired was an understatement. They'd stayed up late discussing Keefe—and then Sophie's brain had spent the rest of the night churning out nightmares.

620

But she could tell King Dimitar was listening to their conversation, so she told Mr. Forkle, "They wouldn't let me bring Ella. How do people sleep without stuffed animals? I didn't know where to put my arms."

Queen Hylda and Empress Pernille laughed at her joke, and Sophie was glad she'd made it. She hadn't noticed they were also eavesdropping.

Now is not a wise moment for secrets, Mr. Forkle transmitted as Sophie picked halfheartedly at one of the pastries, getting chocolate on her silky gloves.

She told him what Keefe had decided and added, *I've tried checking on him a few times and he hasn't responded.*

There's nothing the Neverseen can do to stop you from communicating with him. If he's ignoring you, it's only because he needs to concentrate.

Technically, there was *one* way the Neverseen could silence Keefe forever—but she was *not* letting her mind go there. Nope. Nope. Nope.

I wish he wasn't coming here, she told Mr. Forkle. *It's way too risky, and he's only doing it because he feels like he needs to make everything up to me.*

He does need to make it up to you. Haven't you realized that yet? That's why you and Mr. Sencen work so well together. You both push each other to believe in yourselves. Don't go easy on him now because you're afraid he's too fragile. The more you let him prove himself, the more he'll realize he's still worthy.

Their conversation ended when a fleet of goblins marched into the room and announced that they'd be escorting everyone to a room called The Circle. It was a long trek, and Sophie cursed her stupid heels—and her much-too-poofy silver-blue gown—as they trudged through a dozen different halls and then up an endless winding staircase.

The Council was waiting for them in the highest room in the tower, at a glowing round table that Sophie was sure had been the inspiration for King Arthur's legend. Twenty-one chairs circled the table at evenly spaced intervals—twelve for the Councillors, three for Sophie and Edaline and Mr. Forkle, one for each of the other intelligent species' leaders, and one that remained empty—until the entire circular wall had been lined shoulder to shoulder with goblin soldiers. Then four additional guards marched into the room, surrounding a figure who rattled with every step.

"Sorry I'm late," Fintan said, waving a chained hand as he clanked into his seat. "The security here is *murder*."

Oralie's cheeks turned as green as the simple gown she wore. Sophie wondered it the outfit was a tribute to Kenric. The elves always wore green to plantings—the color of life.

Councillor Emery cleared his throat as he stood. "As some of you know, this room is designed to remind us that we're all equals. Debate is expected. Emotions will surely run high. But that doesn't mean we can't listen to and respect each other. We all share the same goal: a united world where our people can

coexist peacefully, with a proper balance of freedom and structure to maintain order—"

"And there we have the greatest lie of the elves," Fintan
interrupted, struggling to stand with his clunky chains. "We
talk of freedom and equality—but demand authority and supe-
riority. And why shouldn't we? Simply put: We're better, on
every level. Smarter. More powerful. With talents and skills
none of you can even comprehend."

Angry shouts erupted from the other rulers, and Sophie
slouched in her chair.

She'd heard the elves refer to themselves as superior many
times—and it had always made her uncomfortable. But to
broadcast it so boldly in front of the other species was both
uncalled-for and insulting.

"There's no need to be offended," Fintan called over them,
resting his chained hands on the glowing table. "Being superior isn't all it's cracked up to be. We're stuck solving all of
your problems, trying to keep millions of people with different
wants and needs and challenges satisfied with their lives. Why
do you think we're here?"

"Before you start shouting again," Councillor Bronte interrupted, "remember that you're the ones who voted that Fintan
be allowed to attend. Perhaps now you see why we've been
working so hard to silence him."

"But I *won't* be silenced!" Fintan shouted. "Because the old
ways are failing—and have been failing for centuries. This

world doesn't need diplomacy. It needs quick, decisive leadership from someone who offers actual solutions. Someone not afraid of making the hard choices. Someone willing to make changes. Let's be honest—how many of you fully expect to have most of your demands ignored during these negotiations?"

"And how many would prefer to suffer the consequences of ill-conceived plans?" Councillor Emery countered.

"You look confused," Mr. Forkle whispered to Sophie.

"I don't understand why they're letting Fintan go on like this," she whispered back.

"Because they take the 'equals at the round table' concept very seriously. And they're probably also hoping he'll wear himself out."

"But shouldn't they at least insist he talk about the ogre treaty?" Sophie asked. "Isn't that why we're here?"

"We are indeed," Mr. Forkle said, rising from his seat and addressing the other leaders. "What you're witnessing is the folly of the Neverseen. They don't offer solutions. They shout and wail and stir up unrest, and make everyone lose focus on what actually matters. Let's not forget that we're here today because one leader"—he pointed to King Dimitar—"decided to violate the treaty his people signed, in large part because he was listening to the advice of the Neverseen. Surely you've heard of the disgusting plague they unleashed on the gnomes in a pitiful attempt to force the species into slavery. And the betrayals sadly haven't ended there. Only a handful of days ago, a small band of ogres attacked an innocent elvin family, killing one of the loyal goblins who was there to protect them."

"The latter incident was done without my permission," King Dimitar argued, turning to address Sophie and Edaline. "I cannot force you to believe me—nor will I apologize for something I'm not responsible for. But I will offer you what little I know. The Neverseen proposed an alliance, and spoke of a different test to verify my commitment."

"Which was?" Sophie asked.

Dimitar glared at Fintan. "That is irrelevant. What matters is I decided not to participate—and I did so after receiving sound advice from one of your own. The same someone who happened to be present during the attack at Havenfield."

"Lady Cadence?" Sophie confirmed.

"Seems rather coincidental, don't you think, that a group of ogres rebelling against *my* resolve to separate from the Neverseen would involve themselves in an assault that includes the very person who encouraged me to reject Fintan's offer?"

"My goodness," Fintan said. "Who knew the ogres were such excellent story spinners?"

He was the picture of nonchalance, except for the subtle twitching of his jaw.

Meanwhile Dimitar's expression was hard as iron—no sign of doubt or remorse. Sophie would never be foolish enough to trust the ogre king. But that didn't mean he never spoke the truth.

And the idea of two ogre threats—one from the King and one from this emerging rebellion—opened a whole new realm of horrors.

"Either way," Mr. Forkle said, taking back command of the floor. "Rebels or not, it does not change the fact that the ogres have turned violent, unruly, and willfully disobedient. And if they want the freedom of sharing this planet, they must agree to behave. *That's* what we're here to discuss—not whatever madness this fool is trying to distract everyone with. He's here only to stir up trouble and flatter himself." He flicked an arm at Fintan in a dismissive wave.

"Isn't it ironic to hear such speech coming from someone who is himself the leader of a rebellion?" Fintan asked. "Someone who trusts the Council so little he won't stand in front of them under his true identity. Someone who relies on fake names and false appearances and works on his projects in the shadows. He may like to believe he's better than me, but in all the ways that matter, we are very much the same. And we've both earned the power we've acquired because the people of this planet—regardless of their species—are desperate for the guidance and direction needed to survive the coming crisis. Our world has far greater issues than rebellious ogres—in fact, I happen to know that a primary reason King Dimitar was initially open to my suggestions is something you all grow more frustrated with every day. And if you think this Council is ever going to offer you a solution, get ready to be severely disappointed. They'll hem and haw and return to their glittering castles—maybe even erase the problem from their minds and pretend it no longer exists."

"And what exactly is this problem you speak of?" King Enki asked

Fintan's eyes focused on Sophie, his lips curling into a smile that gave her prickles. "The problem is humans."

SEVENTY-EIGHT

WHAT DO WE DO," FINTAN asked, "with a species that's clever enough to build and create, and yet foolish enough to design its own ruin? Creatures so violent, they're always at war—but with others of their own kind? Creatures that destroy everything they touch, including this planet we're all forced to share? Creatures so prolific, they've consumed the majority of the productive lands, and yet even the Councillors themselves refuse to classify them as intelligent? Creatures we hold to no treaties—no codes of honor—and no laws except their own flawed logic? Creatures that don't even know we exist?" His eyes roved around the table, before coming to rest again on

Sophie. "To them, we're nothing more than silly stories and legends. We're magical. Mythical. Credited to their own fanciful imaginations. And should they discover our existence, their only response would be violence. And yet what has our Council done about it?"

"Another clever way of distracting us from the actual issues at hand," Councillor Emery said. "At this rate, the summit will stretch on indefinitely."

"We can't have that," Fintan told him. "I have a timeline to stick to."

"A timeline for what?" Queen Hylda asked.

"The realization of my vision."

Laughter shattered the silence, mixed with slow, mocking applause. Sophie was surprised to realize it was coming from King Dimitar as he stood to address the table.

"I must say, that was a far more impassioned performance than he gave me when he first mentioned his vision—which at the time, he was calling his Lodestar Initiative."

"Yes, I had to streamline things after you failed so spectacularly," Fintan informed him.

"I suppose I did." King Dimitar turned to the representative of the gnomes. "We all know I let myself be coerced into unleashing the plague. Call it cruel if you like, but I was assured it would be in the best interests of everyone in the long run. I have since come to realize that the Neverseen's promises are no more useful than the Council's blatant refusal to acknowledge anyone's concerns. Don't make my mistake and be fooled by his pretty lies. He'll offer the sun and the moon—so long as you do his bidding. In the end, you'll have nothing to show except grief and ruin. And the same applies to the things you'll hear from all of the elves at this table. Any of these new elvin orders only benefit themselves. Why else would they be focusing their talents and skills on deadly actions and altering their children to make them into weapons?"

"I'm not a weapon!" Sophie snapped when he shot her a glare.

"I don't know what you are, Miss Foster. But I no longer care. You and your friends destroyed half my city and received full pardons instead of punishment. You invaded my mind—twice—and suffered no lasting consequences. Isn't your very existence a violation of the most fundamental elvin laws? And yet here you are, in top-level treaty negotiations, with an equal seat among the leaders of entire worlds. I don't fear the Council—I fear what they'll let you grow to become. And more than that, I fear what lengths he'll go to"—he pointed to Fintan—"in order to stop you. And I want no part of it."

"So what are you saying?" Councillor Emery asked him.

"I'm saying I've looked long and hard for the so-called benefits I've gained from the leadership of the elves. And I can't find any. But I'm also not naïve enough to believe I can stand against you—nor will I align myself any longer with self-serving rebellions. I've spent weeks watching my people suffer the consequences of the trust I put in lunatics. I won't let them suffer any further. All I want—all I came to this summit to achieve—is a treaty that allows my people to remain separate. Leave us our lands and let us be, and I guarantee you'll never see or hear from us again. Draft a treaty that specifies that and I'll sign in a heartbeat."

The discussion that followed seemed even more circular than the table, and after a dozen times around, King Dimitar laughed. "I offer to disappear—and essentially give you everything you want in the process—and still you argue and hesitate?"

"I think," Councillor Emery said carefully, "that things are moving quite quickly in a rather unexpected direction. So I propose we take a brief recess to allow a moment to process."

Righty and Bunhead rushed Sophie and Edaline back to their locked rooms, and Mr. Forkle convinced the goblins to let him tag along.

"I don't understand what's happening in there," Edaline said, collapsing onto a settee in their sitting room.

Mr. Forkle took one of the armchairs. "I think . . . Dimitar spent much of his life believing ogres were actually the superior species, and planning to someday use the plague to take power. It's why he fell for Fintan's lies—and now that he's been properly humbled, he's trying to cut his losses and protect his people. Which has nothing to do with you, Miss Foster. Everything you brought upon Ravagog was provoked and necessary."

"I know," Sophie mumbled.

But it still didn't feel good being called a monster—especially by one of the creepiest people she'd ever met.

Then again, the Dimitar speaking in the Circle wasn't the bloodthirsty beast she'd come to expect. He was articulate. Logical. Clearly concerned for his people. Much more like the king Lady Cadence had described. And the thought that Sophie had played any role in convincing him the best course of action was total isolation made her glad she hadn't eaten any breakfast.

"Did either of you notice how many of the leaders nodded along when Fintan went into his tangent about humans?" Edaline asked quietly.

"Everyone but King Dimitar," Mr. Forkle said. "And I suspect that's simply a refusal to agree with Fintan. Humans truly are quite the conundrum—creatures we're forbidden to help, with weapons powerful enough to destroy the whole planet."

"But what's the solution to that?" Sophie asked.

"Ours is a work in progress," Mr. Forkle admitted.

"And Sophie plays a part in it?" Edaline pressed.

"*That* will be up to her. She's running her own life now. Has been for quite some time."

"Unless Fintan pulls off his 'vision,'" Sophie mumbled, her nerves knotting up just thinking about it.

This is what they want.

Had Lady Gisela meant those words for this potential prison

break—assuming they were right about that threat? Or for some much grander, much darker scheme?

"Perhaps you should use these moments to check on Mr. Sencen," Mr. Forkle suggested. "Rather than worrying yourself sick with unanswerable questions."

He made a good point—though Sophie's heart seemed to lodge in her throat as she transmitted her call with Keefe's name.

If he didn't answer . . .

'Bout time you reached out, Foster.

Tears burned Sophie's eyes and she had to blink them back. Edaline pulled her into a hug to keep her from wobbling.

You're safe? she asked.

I'm better than safe. I'm free! And FREEZING. I had to ditch all my cloaks—and this cave is not blocking the wind like it's supposed to. I mean, it's an ocean cave—it has one job to do!

Does that mean you're here?

Yep. The security patrols don't seem to know this cave exists. So if you need me, I'm close. Call me and I'll find a way to reach you. In the meantime, I'll be practicing my body temperature regulation and hoping nothing with lots of teeth and fangs also calls this cave home.

How did you escape? Was it as rough as you thought it would be?

A little better. A little worse. But I made it. What about you—how's it going at the summit?

Super weird.

She'd just started to tell him about the strange speeches by both Fintan and King Dimitar when Righty and Bunhead knocked to notify them the recess had ended.

King Dimitar was the last to return to the Circle, and refused to take his seat. "I've said my piece," he told everyone. "And have no further reason for debate. I've named the terms I'll agree to for this treaty. You should all find them more than reasonable."

"And you truly wish to withdraw your people from the rest of the intelligent species?" Councillor Emery asked.

Dimitar nodded. "So long as you will leave my people in peace."

"And how do we know this isn't a ploy to remain unsupervised, so you can build your weapons and train for a large-scale invasion?" Queen Hylda asked.

"If the lack of supervision is the issue, I'm happy to grant access to Lady Cadence whenever she wants. Will that satisfy your concerns?"

"It does for me," King Enki voted first.

"And me," Empress Pernille agreed.

Queen Hylda acquiesced next, followed by the gnomish leader whose official name seemed to be Thales the Sower.

"I suppose it works for us as well," Councillor Emery said. "What about you?" he asked Mr. Forkle.

"I believe it's a strange decision," he said. "But I see no objection. And I'd suggest adding language that makes for a simple process to renegotiate should the ogres someday change their minds."

"What about me?" Fintan asked, "I get an equal vote in these proceedings. And this is madness. Sheer, hasty madness. Surely we should take the night to sleep on it."

"My people need me," King Dimitar argued. "And honestly, if I have to suffer through another day of this nonsense I'll be tearing out my teeth just so I have something sharp to throw at you. As I understand it, this does not call for a unanimous vote, only a majority, which I clearly have. Draft the treaty."

"As you wish," Councillor Emery said, rolling up the sleeves of his silver tunic and taking the clean scroll Councillor Liora conjured. "Looks like we're in for a late night."

"Not if you write fast," Dimitar told him. "I'll make this simple. No confusing legalese. No loopholes and amendments. All we need are simple lists of 'I will' and 'I won't.' For example, I *won't* act against any other intelligent species if you *will* allow my people to keep ourselves separate."

And so it went, with King Dimitar mapping out simple, clear demands that none of the other leaders had issue with, and Councillor Emery furiously scribbling it all down. It would've been a relief—if Fintan hadn't looked so stressed. Even Mr. Forkle seemed to notice.

The third time Fintan requested the time, Mr. Forkle asked, "In a hurry?"

"Quite the opposite," Fintan assured him. But he noticeably

paled when Councillor Emery marked the end of the treaty lists with an intricate flourish.

"Would you like to check it over before you sign?" he asked Dimitar.

"No." King Dimitar took the pen and scratched his name. "Done."

One by one, the other leaders added their signatures, and Sophie watched Fintan the whole time. He kept his features composed—and didn't ask for the time again. But tiny beads of sweat trickled down his brow.

"Take this to the records room and have it sealed," Councillor Emery told one of the goblins, handing him the signed scroll. "And ring the bells to mark the official end."

"And take Fintan to the dungeon," Oralie added, sending ten guards swarming around him. "Having a seat at this table does not excuse you of your crimes. You will be held here until a tribunal can determine your final sentencing."

Fintan rolled his eyes. "How predictable of you."

Earth-shaking bells rang through the castle, vibrating the walls.

"Does that mean we're free to leave?" Edaline asked as Sophie tried to keep up with how fast everything was moving.

Could they really have arrested the leader of the Neverseen *and* secured an ogre peace treaty in less than five minutes?

Apparently they had, because Councillor Emery nodded. "Though I hope you'll stay to celebrate at the gala."

"The *gala*," Fintan whispered, so softly he probably thought no one could hear him.

Sophie did. She was watching him so intently, she missed the part where Edaline agreed they'd stay. But she didn't miss the relief in his eyes.

Or the way he smiled at her and said, "Sounds like you'll be celebrating all night," as the goblins dragged him away.

"I think you should leave," Sophie said, as soon as she and Edaline were back in their rooms. "Fintan looked way too happy. And he's down in the prison, where he wanted to be. And he's no longer worried about time. I bet he needed to keep the leaders here up until the hour they'd arranged. And that's why he seemed so stressed when King Dimitar rushed the process— but now he knows everyone will be staying for the gala."

This is what they want.

"And how does getting rid of me change any of that?" Edaline asked.

"Because I'll know you're safe while I figure out what to do."

Edaline took Sophie's gloved hands. "I'm not leaving without you, so let's not waste time debating that. Do you think we should tell the Council what you're thinking?"

"I doubt they'll listen. They'll go on and on about all the security and how impossible it would be for anyone to breach it."

"The security here *is* amazing," Edaline noted. "But I know how sharp your instincts are. If you think there's a problem, we can't ignore it. I just wish I were as good at planning things as you are. The best I can come up with is to go to the gala and talk to Oralie. She made the meeting with Gethen happen— she might be able to sway the Council again."

"I guess that's true," Sophie said, heading for the door.

Edaline grabbed her hand and pulled her back. "Actually, I'd prefer you wait here. If Fintan's planning something, there's a good chance it includes *you*. I saw the way he watched you during the negotiations—like a prize he'd so desperately love to collect. Which means you should stay behind a locked door, where he can't get anywhere near you. Please, Sophie. Use the time to brainstorm backup plans. Or chat with Keefe. Or both."

"Fine," Sophie reluctantly agreed. "But if you're not back in fifteen minutes, I'm coming after you."

She kissed Sophie's cheek and tucked a strand of hair behind Sophie's ear. "I love you so much, sweetheart. Thank you for trusting me."

SEVENTY-NINE

EVERY SECOND FELT LIKE AN HOUR—
and by the time eight minutes had passed,
Sophie was ready to bang her head against the
marble walls.

She'd used two of those minutes to ditch her stupid dress
and change into the simple black clothes she'd been wearing
when she arrived. The rest she'd spent pacing and thinking.

Whenever there were this many unanswered questions, it
always meant they were missing something. And the one that
bothered her the most was: *How were the Neverseen planning to
get out of their cells?*

She'd seen the sturdy locks.

The heavy metal doors.

And lumenite didn't burn, so Fintan's power was useless.

She tried to figure out what she would do if she were trapped, and her mind kept circling back to her recent skill training.

The splotchers she'd exploded.

The stone she'd shattered.

She traced her hand across the cold stones around her door Coach Rohana had told her, *I suspect you could bring down a mountain if you sat in solitude long enough*. Was *that* why Gethen had seemed so content in his cell? Had he been taking the time to rest and build his reserves to break through the doors?

A faint tremor shook the floor, and Sophie tried to tell herself her mind was playing tricks on her. But then she realized the crystals on the chandeliers were swaying.

The motion was so subtle, she wouldn't have noticed it if she hadn't been paying attention.

But she *was* paying attention.

And as she watched, a tiny rustle made the crystals quiver again.

Someone could be walking on the floor above her. Or the wind could be strong enough to shake the castle. Or . . .

Four dangerous prisoners could be breaking out of their dungeon cells.

But why now?

If this was just about embarrassing the Council in front of the other leaders, why not escape the second the summit began?

This is what they want, Lady Gisela had told her—but she'd also told her something else. Something Sophie had thought was just metaphor or hyperbole. But maybe it had been another warning.

Get my son back before it all comes crashing down.

Keefe had told her that Fintan wanted to take out the Council. And here they were all under one roof—the same roof as Gethen. And Gethen had had *months* to build his reserves.

Gethen is where he belongs.

The perfect inside man, hidden in the one place they wouldn't have been able to access any other way. Maybe the person they'd been counting on to *deliver.*

But . . . if Gethen brought down the castle—wouldn't they all be crushed in the rubble?

Fintan had known the Council would arrest him—he'd said as much to Oralie. He'd also stalled the proceedings, making sure it all happened on his timeline. And he wasn't suicidal, so why would he want to be down in the dungeon when it happened? Why would he order Brant and Ruy to get themselves captured?

Ruy.

A powerful Psionipath could shield them under a force field. Keep them alive. Make sure they survived.

It was sickening how perfectly they'd planned everything—and even worse how many clues she'd missed. The warning signs had been there all along, and she hadn't paid close enough attention.

The floor shook again, telling her the time to wonder was over. This was happening.

And the tremors were only beginning.

KEEFE! she transmitted. *If you can hear me, make sure you stay away from the castle. Gethen is going to knock it down. THAT's Fintan's vision.*

She sent the same transmission to Mr. Forkle, begging him to start evacuating. Then she pounded on her door, demanding her guards let her out.

When no one answered, she gathered her mental strength and imagined singing the energy into the lock and the stones around it. Deeper and deeper the power sank, coiling so tight it felt like a wound-up spring. All she had to do was let go.

The explosion knocked her back, but she caught herself on a nearby table, her whole body shaking as she stared at the rubble around her now-open door.

If she could cause that much destruction with so little practice or energy . . .

This is what they want.

She bolted down the hallway as the floor rumbled again, trying to figure out the best plan. She could fight her way to the dungeon—but it would be four against one. And she might not get there in time.

The next tremor was sharper, sending dust swirling through the air. Too strong to be ignored, but too weak to be felt by anyone else—especially a bunch of people higher up at a party, nibbling treats and admiring the splendor and congratulating themselves on the day's victory.

And somewhere among them was Edaline.

Sophie changed direction, her goal clear as she doubled her speed, ducking down halls at random. The maze felt alive, stretching and spreading and shifting, anything to prevent her from getting where she needed to be.

A staircase looked familiar, but most of the doors it led to were locked. She finally chose a path through a hall lined with blue flames, hoping the light was a good sign.

The longer she ran, the more the tremors grew, until she could see cracks fissuring through the stones. The dust made her chest throb and her eyes water—or maybe that was the panic—as she started screaming Edaline's name.

More doorways. More stairs. More halls. More quakes gaining momentum—like distant thunder rolling in with the storm.

She tried to track Edaline with her mind, but her fear shattered her concentration. She'd nearly broken down when she recognized a new sound.

Footsteps.

"EDALINE?"

"SOPHIE?" Mr. Forkle shouted.

She sprinted toward the sound, taking a flight of stairs three at a time before she crashed hard into his bloated belly.

"Is Edaline with you?" she gasped.

"No—she went looking for you. Oralie ordered all the goblins to the dungeon after she talked to your mother. But none of them have made it back, and then the shaking started."

That explained why there'd been no guard outside her door. She couldn't think about what that might mean for poor Righty and Bunhead.

"The Councillors are trying to clear the castle," Mr. Forkle said, grabbing her arm and spinning her around. "I'll show you the fastest way to the exit."

Sophie jerked out of his grip. "Not until I find Edaline."

"Hopefully that's where she's waiting for you. I'd told her that if I found you, I'd send you there."

But there was no sign of Edaline at the exit.

"I'll find her," Mr. Forkle promised. "Get to the beach and go as far as you can. It's hard to know where the rubble will fall."

"I'm not leaving without my mom!"

He blocked her from charging past him. "We both know that's not what she would want. Go somewhere safe. I'll find her and get her out."

"How can you be so sure?"

"I found you, didn't I?"

Technically, *she'd* found *him*—but this wasn't a time for technicalities. It was a time for action. And hope. And trust.

So she did as he asked, and made her way to the courtyard. But when she looked at the once-gleaming castle—now dulled,

644

with wavering walls and light leaking through the cracks—she couldn't walk away.

She couldn't risk a lifetime of wondering *What if I'd stayed?*

She turned and raced back in, keeping her left hand on the wall, hoping it'd help her find her way out when she needed the exit. Faster and faster she ran as the dust and pebbles pelted her, the ground splitting beneath her feet.

Her balance mostly held, but one particularly hard jolt knocked her over and she cried out as her knees crashed into the sharp ground.

"Sophie?" Edaline shouted. "Is that you?"

Just like that, she was on her feet again, coughing as she ran, lungs burning, hair flying—and then there was Edaline. Dusty and panting, her once-lovely gown now filthy and shredded.

She threw her arms around Sophie, hugging her even as she dragged her back the way she'd come. "We have to go."

They ran as fast as they could.

But it wasn't fast enough.

They'd just reached one of the widest halls when the floor collapsed beneath them, whipping their hearts into their throats as they plummeted.

They crashed into the next level down, stones raining all around them—one piece big enough to crush and kill.

Sophie watched it fall, trying to knock it back with her telekinesis. But it had too much momentum. It would've landed right on top of them if Edaline hadn't snapped her fingers, conjuring it away.

"Whoa, that's intense," Edaline said, shaking from the effort. "I've never dumped something that big in the void. But it worked. Come on—this place is coming down fast."

They'd only gone a few steps when a tremor split the wall, sending more stones hurtling toward them.

Edaline snapped her fingers and conjured them each away. But the effort took a huge toll.

"Here," Sophie said, ripping off her gloves. "It'll make you stronger."

Edaline pulled her close. "We'll get through this. I promise."

"Together," Sophie told her as she led Edaline forward.

Step by fumbling step, they made their way through the maze, and Edaline used her enhanced strength to conjure away anything that tried to crush them. Eventually, they spotted a crack that offered a teasing glint of the ocean. It wasn't wide enough to fit through, but Sophie sang the last of her energy into the stones, blasting their way outside to the cold, misty air.

With the final dregs of their energy, they scrambled over the glowing destruction and kept crawling and clawing until they reached a sandy clearing where the waves drowned out most of the noise.

"I think we'll be safe here," Sophie whispered, curling closer to Edaline to keep warm.

646

Edaline tangled her arms around her, quietly sobbing onto Sophie's shoulder. Sophie held her tight, promising it was almost over as she watched the dark waves roll across the shore.

She was about to close her eyes when she spotted four figures crossing the beach in long black cloaks.

When she blinked, they were gone.

EIGHTY

THERE YOU ARE," A CHOKED VOICE said, and Sophie slowly forced herself back to consciousness.

It hurt to focus through all the grit and dust crudding up her poor, dry eyes. But after a few seconds the world sharpened and she found a beautiful blond boy leaning over her.

Keefe's smile was somehow both breathtaking and heartbreaking, but it faded as he stroked her cheek and whispered, "When you and Edaline weren't with the survivors . . ."

"Edaline!" Sophie gasped, and blood flooded her brain as she sat up too quickly. She breathed through the head rush, searching the clearing until . . .

"She looks okay," Keefe said, squatting beside Edaline and using his dirty tunic to wipe some red off her bruised cheek. Edaline stirred at the touch, but not enough to wake up, and Sophie decided to let her sleep.

"Did everyone else make it out?" she whispered.

"Um . . . I know Councillor Terik's hurt pretty bad. I guess he might lose part of his leg—or maybe he lost it already? I couldn't tell. I saw the blood and I bolted so I wouldn't hurl all over everybody. But Elwin was working on him, so hopefully he'll be okay. Physic's here too. Most of the injuries looked pretty minor—just cuts and scratches. Broken bones. Nothing life threatening. Though I heard a lot of the goblins were down in the dungeon when it happened, and so far none of them have come back out."

Sophie shuddered.

The motion made her cough—she was pretty sure she'd be coughing up lumenite forever—and Keefe scooted closer, patting her back until the fit calmed.

She leaned against him, soaking up his warmth. "How bad do I look?"

"You could never look bad. But, um . . ." He brushed a finger across her forehead and showed her the red. "Want me to take you to Elwin?"

"No, he should work on the urgent cases first. Is Grady here? Or Fitz and Biana?"

"The island's on lockdown, even for friends and family,

until the dwarves stabilize the ruins—though Biana managed to sneak over for a couple of minutes. *Vanishers*. She was looking for you guys and totally tackled me when she saw me. I guess she didn't realize I'd already left the Neverseen, so there was a lot of threatening and punching. But I deserved it. I deserve so much worse." His throat closed off, and it took several tries to clear it. "All those months with them, thinking I was playing everything perfectly. I bet they were onto me the whole time. Just like my mom said. And they were planning this."

He punched the sand, sending it spraying around them.

Sophie held him tighter. "This is *not* your fault, Keefe. None of us realized what they were up to."

"Yeah, but I was *living* with them. Helping them. And all I have to show for it is this."

He reached into his pocket and pulled out two clear glass marbles. One with seven colorful tiny crystals set inside. The other with nine.

"You stole the caches?" Sophie whispered, watching them roll around his palm.

Together, the two gadgets contained sixteen Forgotten Secrets.

"It was the only thing that went right with my escape. And I was so smug about it. But who cares? I mean, seriously—who cares about a bunch of dusty old secrets when people can do *that*?" He gestured behind her, to the ruined castle.

"It's still huge," Sophie promised. "I know it doesn't feel like it—but the secrets in those caches have to be important. That's a victory!"

"A pretty weak one," he grumbled, trying to look away.

She reached up and turned his chin back, waiting for him to meet her eyes. "You have to let this go. Don't let this ruin what we have here."

"What do we have?"

She ignored the darkness shredding his tone. "We have a new start. A new lead. A new weapon in this fight."

Also a new world.

At the thought, Sophie forced herself to finally look back at the destruction. The majestic castle was nothing more than a few jagged pieces. When she squinted at it, she could almost imagine it was a giant gnarled hand, reaching out of the ground as the beast it belonged to tried to claw its way to freedom.

It also looked like a message. The Neverseen had just told the whole world that they were the ones to be feared.

"You should probably transmit to Fitz that you're okay," Keefe said quietly. "I hadn't found you when I saw Biana." He looked away again, swiping at his eyes. "If you hadn't been okay—"

"But I *am*," she assured him.

She closed her eyes, picturing Fitz's handsome face as she transmitted, *I'm okay, and so is Edaline. Please tell Grady for me. I promise I'll let you know more soon.*

"Okay, I let Fitz know," she told Keefe. "Have you seen Mr. Forkle?"

Keefe flinched at the name.

"What?" she asked.

The anguish on his face told her everything she needed to know.

"Hey," Keefe said holding her steady as she struggled to stand. "He's not dead, okay? He's just . . . missing."

"But he's missing because of me! I made him go back to find Edaline—and then I went back and found her anyway!"

"Deep breaths, Foster. Try to remember that you were 'missing' a few minutes ago, and yet you're fine. There's a lot of beach to search. A lot of debris to sort through."

She tried to see it like that, but the nausea wouldn't fade.

"Is anyone else missing?" she asked, trying to prepare herself for the worst.

But she definitely wasn't ready for him to whisper, "Oralie."

The world spun upside down and inside out. "We have to find them."

She was half crying, half hyperventilating as she stumbled forward—and immediately collapsed.

"Okay, how about you lean on me and we'll start searching the beach?" Keefe offered.

She shook her head. "We can't afford to waste time. If they're hurt . . ."

She closed her eyes, letting her concentration brew and

bubble before she stretched her mind across the space of the island. She could feel a ton of people on the beach—but no one she was looking for, so she fanned her thoughts toward the ruins and . . .

"I think I feel something! It's weak, but it's *there*."

"Can you isolate it? We can tell the dwarves and as soon as they've secured the structure they'll go in—"

"What do you mean 'as soon as they've secured the structure'?"

"King Enki said it's not safe for anyone to go in right now. All the parts that are still standing have big cracks compromising their integrity, so there's no way to know if the whole thing is going to come down—especially in this wind. He said he'd have it secured by sunset."

"That's too long," Sophie said. "They have to be hurt. Otherwise why aren't they here?"

Keefe tore his hand through his hair, shaking loose dust and sand. "What are the odds of me talking you out of this?"

"Definitely none."

"Then I guess I'm coming with you." He glanced at Edaline, who was still sleeping restlessly. "She's going to freak when she wakes up alone."

Sophie nodded and wrote, *I'm okay—went to find Forkle* in the sand, hoping this note would cause less trouble than her last one.

Then she headed for the rubble.

"Not that way," Keefe said, grabbing her hand and dragging

her into the shadows. "The dwarves are working just around that bend. If they spot us, they'll make sure we don't get anywhere near the castle. We'll have to sneak around the back and find another way in."

They didn't talk as they walked; Sophie was too busy trying to hold on to whatever weak connection she'd found to guide them.

"That looks pretty sturdy," Keefe said, pointing to an arched doorway half blocked by a fallen pillar. "Think you can run for it? We'll want to make sure we're not seen."

"Yeah, just give me a second." She took a couple of breaths and channeled some extra energy to her legs. "Okay."

Keefe nodded, peeking around the corner. "I think we're clear. Ready, go!"

The ground seemed to shift under their feet, but the entrance held steady as they ducked inside, into a dark, dusty hallway.

"We need to find a way up," Sophie whispered, trying not to think about the tightness in her chest. Seeing the cracked walls and floor dredged up flashbacks of the collapse. "It feels like they're above us."

Keefe squeezed her hand. "You okay?"

"Yeah." But she was glad he didn't let go as he took the lead, carving out a precarious path through the maze.

The staircase they found was too crumbling to trust.

"What if we levitate?" Keefe asked, pointing to where the center of the stairs had caved in. "It might be our best shot—but only if you're up for it."

"I'm up for it," Sophie said, rallying her concentration again.

Keefe held tight as they floated, and she had a feeling he was carrying her more than she was lifting herself, but she still fought to push against gravity as hard as she could.

"We need to stop here," she whispered. "It's this level."

She pointed left and Keefe took the lead again.

"So, quick question," he said as they picked their way through an especially dark hallway. "Is there a reason I keep getting this crazy rush every time I touch your hand?" He cleared his throat when he realized how that sounded, "What I mean is, your emotions always feel strong. But now they're on another level."

"It's because I manifested as an Enhancer. I'm supposed to wear gloves, but I took them off to help Edaline."

She figured he'd pick his most creative *I told you so* and gloat about knowing she'd manifest another ability. Instead, all he said was, "So that rush was an even clearer reading of your emotions?"

"Probably. Why?"

"No reason." But when she stole a glance from the side of her eye, she could see a glint of a grin in the dim light.

She was deciding whether to ask him about it, when a strained voice called, "Is someone there?"

"Oralie?" Sophie shouted, racing toward the sound. She hurdled bits of wall and furniture until she reached a crushed golden doorway. Inside was a disaster zone of toppled tables and cracked jeweled trees and twisted balustrades and fallen chunks of starry sky. The air was heavy with the scent of dusty stone and spoiling food and something decidedly iron.

"Over here," Oralie called, and they found her in the clearest corner leaning over a dark shape. Her hands looked glossy and red and they were pressing on . . .

"NO!" Sophie shouted, wobbling so hard, Keefe had to keep her from collapsing.

The shape beside Oralie moved, lifting its head and confirming Sophie's horrible suspicion.

"You kids really shouldn't have come," Mr. Forkle wheezed.

EIGHTY-ONE

WE HAVE TO GET YOU TO Elwin," Sophie said, dropping to her knees and trying to make sense of what she was seeing.

There was so much red—dripping from his mouth, streaming down his arms and forehead. But the real problem was his abdomen.

Oralie was doing her best to keep pressure on the wound, but the gash was so wide and so deep—and near so many important organs.

"Elwin can't help," Mr. Forkle said. "Trust me, I know enough about these things. Sometimes there is no fix. Even for elves. This is my swan song."

Sophie shook her head, grabbing a tablecloth off one of the fallen tables. "Help me lift him, Keefe, and then go get Elwin. If I tie this around his waist, it should hold enough pressure on the wound to give you guys time to get here. Bring Physic too. And a couple of goblins to carry him. And—"

"Miss Foster, this is one time when your stubbornness isn't going to make a difference," Mr. Forkle interrupted. "I've had this same conversation with Oralie. You have to let me go."

"NO!" Tears leaked down Sophie's cheeks. "No—they don't get to do this. They don't get to take you."

"It won't be as bad as you think." His voice had a horrible gurgle to it, but Sophie ordered herself not to think about it.

"I don't understand his wound," she told Oralie. "It almost looks like he's been stabbed."

Oralie looked away.

"It's okay, I'll tell her," Mr. Forkle said, reaching for Sophie's hands. They were so cold and slick—and red—it made it hard to listen as he said, "This is mostly my fault. You kept trying to tell me Gethen was important. And I kept stalling. Focusing on the wrong things. I should've been at his cell every day, fighting my way into his mind."

"I don't understand—did Gethen . . ."

Oralie nodded. "The sword."

That was all she could get out. But it was enough.

As Gethen broke the castle apart, he must've freed the sword in his cell.

But wouldn't it be ironic if someday I used that blade to chop off your pretty head?

"He came to make good on his threat," Mr. Forkle wheezed. "But I blocked him with a clever mind trick—the same one, incidentally, I used to make him back off that day at your human home, when he was dressed as a jogger and tried to take you away. And then I took out Brant. Gethen didn't like that. So he got me back."

"Wait—you took out Brant?" Keefe asked, his eyes widening when Oralie pointed to a cloth-wrapped lump in the corner. Definitely body-size.

"Mr. Forkle shoved him away from me right as a huge chunk of ceiling fell," Oralie whispered, pressing a fresh part of cloth over his oozing wound.

"And you're sure Brant's really . . . ," Keefe asked. "After Fintan . . ."

Oralie nodded. "His skull was crushed completely. Gray matter everywhere."

Something felt wrong with this new information—but Sophie couldn't piece it together. All she could hear were Mr. Forkle's labored breaths growing slower and wetter and heavier.

It was hard to see past the blood, but his body seemed to be in a strange in-between state. Like the ruckleberries were wearing off, but hadn't completely.

"I need the three of you to promise me something," he

rasped. "I need you to remove my body from here. Don't let anyone see it. And you must promise you won't do a planting in the Wanderling Woods. No one can know."

"Won't they have to know, though?" Sophie asked. "When the other yous disappear?"

"The Collective has always had a contingency plan. You'll see it soon enough. And don't worry—they'll make sure you still get the answers I owe you. Secrets never die." He pressed something cold and round into her palm, and Sophie realized it was the gadget where he stored the things he wanted to remember. "Give that to Granite." He turned to Councillor Oralie. "And make me a seed. Coil it with my hair, and bring it to Miss Foster to keep safe. She'll know when and where to plant it."

"How?" Sophie asked. "And why are we talking about this—you're not dying!"

"Yes, I am. But it's okay. I've done far more with this life than I ever could've imagined. I've lived five lives. I'm ready to surrender them. But before I do, I need you to promise you won't let this change you. Don't fall down the bitter, angry hole that death opens up inside of us. It's not a productive place to be. And there's no reason for it. I promise, I've made my peace. I've won more times than I've lost. I can be happy with that. Please be happy with me."

His eyes begged Sophie to assure him, but she couldn't make her mouth form the words.

It was too much.

Too hard.

Mr. Forkle grabbed Keefe's hand. "She needs you now more than ever. Don't let this break her."

"I won't," Keefe promised.

Mr. Forkle nodded, closing his eyes as he reached for Oralie. "Take care of my moonlark."

"No," Sophie said, shaking his shoulder. "Don't give up. Just hold on a little longer."

"Time is a funny thing. Once it's gone, it's gone. But then it passes to someone else. You'll do great things with it, Sophie. Wonderful, incredible things. I'm sorry I won't be there to see them. But don't let that stop you from living them. Dream. Fight. Love. Take risks. Allow yourself to be happy."

"There has to be something we can do," Sophie argued.

"You've already done it," he said. "Thank you for being brave enough to find me this one last time. You gave me the gift of goodbye."

He coughed again, a horrible rattly sound, and Sophie was crying too hard to hear him take his final breath.

But she saw his chest fall still.

Felt Keefe's arms wrap around her, letting her fall apart on his shoulder as he held on tight, keeping her together.

EIGHTY-TWO

ORALIE KEPT HER PROMISES, somehow making Mr. Forkle's body disappear from Lumenaria—and Brant's as well—before the dwarves arrived to help them out of the rubble. And a few days later she visited Sophie at Havenfield and gave her the Wanderling seed, tucked inside a golden locket for Sophie to wear.

Now that the new security measures had been completed— gates even higher than those at Everglen, plus a whole host of underground defenses—Sophie was back living at home, trying not to feel haunted by memories.

"You know what the worst part is?" she whispered as Oralie turned to leave. "I don't even know which 'him' this tree will be."

Oralie hesitated a second, then stepped close and pulled Sophie into a hug.

"I bet that's why he gave you the seed," she whispered. "When the time comes, it'll be one final secret you share together."

"Maybe," Sophie mumbled. "Most days, all I can think about is that he'll never see me heal Prentice. After all the years he waited."

Oralie cleared her throat, slowly pulling away. "Any word from the Collective on their contingency plan?"

"Not yet." She'd passed Mr. Forkle's gadget along to Granite, but as far as she knew, he hadn't tried to access it. "They're being super vague—but I guess I should be used to that."

Oralie smiled sadly. "Sometimes it's good when things don't change."

"And sometimes they have to."

Change was definitely a theme in the elvin world.

It was too early to tell if the attack at Lumenaria would bring all the leaders closer or farther apart. For the moment, they were working together to help the Council rebuild and recover. Elwin and Dex were collaborating on a prosthetic leg for Councillor Terik. And the dwarves and gnomes were still cleaning up the rubble. But nothing would ever be the same.

Sophie spent most of her time at home, hiding under the swaying branches of Calla's Panakes tree, listening to the gentle songs of the leaves and trying not to wonder if things would've been different if she'd thought to carry some of the healing blossoms with her.

Her friends visited, of course—Keefe more than any. He seemed to be taking his promise to Mr. Forkle very seriously. He wouldn't tell Sophie where he was staying—claiming it was safer if she didn't know. But he assured her that the Collective had set him up somewhere the Neverseen—and his mom—wouldn't be able to find him.

His new goal was "never ignore anything," and he'd started making long lists of things he'd remembered, either from his past or from his time with the Neverseen. It wasn't accomplishing much. But it made him feel better. And Sophie wanted to be as prepared as possible before they contacted Keefe's mom to find out what she wanted from her son.

Fitz was also a frequent visitor, and he kept his visits more casual, usually showing up to bring a thoughtful little gift to make her smile. That day he outdid himself, bringing her a sparkly red dragon charm he'd named Mini Snuggles.

"Biana thought she remembered you having a charm bracelet," he told her as he placed the tiny dragon in her gloved hand.

"I do." Grady and Edaline had bought it for her when they'd believed she was dead, as a way to commemorate their visits to her Wanderling. And Mr. Forkle had used it to sneak her secret messages a few times. But Sophie decided it was probably better not to share any of those less-than-cheerful memories and tarnish his amazing gift.

He sat down beside her, leaning against Calla's tree and studying the image she'd been staring at in her memory log.

Four black cloaked figures leaping away from the destruction of Lumenaria.

Four.

She was positive she hadn't imagined it.

Fintan.

Ruy.

Gethen.

And . . . who?

She'd assumed it was Brant, but now she knew he'd been dead by then. So who else could it have been?

It was possible that Alvar had met up with them. But Sophie had a much more terrifying theory. The goblins had told her there was another prisoner in that dungeon—connected to a Forgotten Secret.

And no other bodies had been found in the rubble.

When she'd told Oralie her theory, the pink-cheeked Councillor had blanched and made Sophie promise not to tell anyone. But Sophie would always share things with her friends.

None of them had been happy to hear they might be facing a mysterious new enemy, but Keefe had been quick to point out that the caches could hold the prisoner's identity. Dex was already working hard, trying to break through the caches' security, and Sophie had no doubt he'd figure it out.

"You know, I've been thinking," Fitz said, silencing her

thoughts as he closed the memory log and set it aside for the day. "You owe me a favor."

"I do?"

"Yep! We made a deal—remember? If you didn't call in your favor from me in one month, the favor became mine. And I hate to break it to you, but it's been way more than a month."

Sophie sighed. "I knew that deal was going to come back and haunt me. I should've just made something up and gotten the favor over with."

"You probably should have. But you didn't, so . . . I win!" He shook his hair, flashing his most adorably confident smile, "And I gotta say, I kinda get why you hesitated with this. It's a *big* decision. I mean, on the one hand, I could go for the obvious and make you share whatever secret you keep almost telling me."

Sophie's mouth turned to sandpaper.

"So that still freaks you out, huh? That might be proof that it needs to happen."

His eyes locked onto hers, refusing to let her look away. And when she swallowed, it was so loud, she was sure the entire world heard it.

"Or," he said. "We could skip the talking."

"And do what?" she asked, hating her voice for cracking.

"Any ideas?"

He was so close now, she could feel his breath warming her cheeks.

He leaned a tiny bit closer and someone cleared his throat—*very* loudly.

"Am I interrupting something?" Keefe asked. He'd raised one teasing eyebrow—but he wasn't smiling. And he was fidgeting. A *lot*.

Fitz leaned back against the tree again, his casual posture not matching his scowl. "Just finding new ways to drive Sophie crazy. I had to step up my game while you were gone. What about you?"

"Is that another list?" Sophie asked, pointing to the paper in Keefe's hands.

Somehow the question made Keefe look even more miserable, and he twisted the page so tightly, it looked ready to shred.

"Okay—this is just a theory, so . . . try not to freak out until we really think it through," he said carefully. "I almost don't want to tell you, but I don't want to find out I was right and regret it later."

"Yeah, you're definitely freaking me out," Sophie told him.

He took a deep breath. "Fine, here goes. You told me King Dimitar thinks the ogres who attacked Havenfield were actually after Lady Cadence. And I couldn't figure out why that bugged me. But I realized today that if Dimitar's right and that attack wasn't about Grady and Edaline, then that means the Neverseen never went after your family. And I *know* I heard them talk about it. A *lot*. That's what this whole list is—eleven different times where they mentioned a plan for your family."

"So what are you saying?" Fitz asked.

Keefe closed his eyes, looking a little green when he spoke again. "The thing is, when you look at this list, I wrote down verbatim what I remember them saying. And . . . they never once said 'Grady and Edaline.' They always said 'family.' I just assumed, since you live with them—and Grady's so powerful—that it had to be them. But . . . they're not your only family."

Everything turned cold as Sophie jumped to her feet. "You think they meant my human family?"

"I'm just saying it's *possible*. But you check on them pretty regularly, right? So—"

She shook her head, rubbing the knot under her chest to keep her panic at bay. "I haven't in a while. There's been so much going on, I forgot and . . ."

She ran inside, with Fitz and Keefe right behind her as she sprinted up the stairs and dug her round silver Spyball out of her desk drawer.

"Show me Connor, Kate, and Natalie Freeman," she whispered, using her family's new names.

The Spyball flashed warm in her hands, before red letters blazed across it.

Two terrifying words.

Not Found.

EIGHTY-THREE

BREATHE," KEEFE SAID, AND IT TOOK
Sophie a second to realize she wasn't.

She sucked in a sharp breath, coughing as
her chest tightened. "Why would the records not
be found?" she whispered.

"It could mean lots of things," Fitz promised. "Maybe their
names were changed. You weren't supposed to know them,
right? So maybe the Councillors found out you did, and
changed them. Or maybe my dad changed them after the
Neverseen broke in to the registry, since it was hard to tell
which files they'd accessed."

Or maybe finding out where her family had been hidden was the
reason the Neverseen broke in to the registry in the first place. . . .

"I'll hail my dad to see what he knows. Hang on." Fitz ducked into the hall, and Sophie could hear him whispering into his Imparter as she clung to Keefe, staring blankly at the Spyball.

"Okay—I was kinda right," he said, stalking back into the room a couple of minutes later. "Their names weren't changed—but their registry files were deleted after the break-in, just to be extra safe. And Spyballs pick up registry feeds, so that's why it's saying 'not found.' There's no feed if there's no record to match it to. Make sense?"

Sophie nodded, taking lots of slow, deep breaths and trying to convince herself that the crisis was over.

But it didn't feel over. And it wouldn't. Not until . . .

"I need to see them," she said. "Can you get their address from your dad? I don't care if he gets mad. I *need* to see them."

"Yeah, one sec," Fitz said, slipping back into the hall again for a longer conversation.

"It's going to be okay, Foster," Keefe promised, brushing a rebellious tear off her cheek. "Whatever this is, we'll figure it out and fix it."

"My dad can't give me the address," Fitz said as he returned, "but he has a leaping crystal that goes there. And he'll take you right now for a quick check, if you're ready."

"I am," Sophie told him, already untying her cape. Her tunic, pants, and gloves still looked a little elfy, but she wasn't going to waste time changing.

"I'm coming with you," Fitz said, throwing his cape on the bed next to hers.

"Ditto," Keefe said, doing the same.

"As am I," Sandor announced as he melted out of the shadows. Now that he and Grizel were spending more time together, she'd been teaching him to improve his stealth.

"I'm in as well," Grizel said, appearing at Sandor's side.

Sophie didn't have the energy to argue. "Fine—just try not to look so gobliny."

"Gobliny?" Sandor repeated as Sophie raced downstairs to answer the door.

"Really, Miss Foster, I'm positive you have no reason to worry," Alden assured her as he pulled her in for a hug. "Ready to go?"

Sophie felt anything but ready—but she grabbed Alden's hand as the rest of them linked into a circle, and they all stepped into the beam of bluish light and zipped away.

The house was bigger than Sophie had expected. Small by elvin standards, but at least triple the size of her old house in San Diego. Tudor-style, so it looked like it belonged in a fairy tale—especially butted up against the thick evergreen forest. They weren't in a neighborhood, so there were no other houses around. But there were two cars parked in the driveway and lights on in a bedroom upstairs.

"See?" Alden said. "All is calm and peaceful."

"Maybe," Sophie said. "But I need to see them."

Alden grabbed her shoulder to stop her. "*That* would be very bad. You know how memory wipes work—the Washers can't possibly get every memory. And all it takes is the right trigger and . . ."

He snapped his fingers.

"I didn't say I'm going to let them see me," she argued. "Some of the windows have the curtains open. I just need to take a quick peek. Make sure they're really in there. I promise they'll never know I was here."

Alden sighed. "Be *careful*—and do not be seen."

Sophie nodded and sprinted across the grass, with Fitz and Keefe keeping pace beside her, and Sandor and Grizel on alert a few steps back.

Everyone almost had a heart attack when a dog started barking from the backyard—a deep, husky howl that could probably be heard for miles around.

"Think that'll make them come outside?" Fitz asked as they ducked under the front bay window and hid among the bushes.

"If they do, we'll leap away as soon as I hear the front door," Sophie promised, holding up her home crystal to prove it.

She hadn't realized how hard she was shaking—though she shouldn't have been surprised. She hadn't been this close to her family in more than a year—closer to two years, actually.

And much as she understood why she couldn't let them see her, she also had to admit she didn't want to—not because she was afraid they'd remember her.

Because she knew how much it would hurt if they *didn't*.

"Deep breaths," Keefe said, hooking his arm through hers and pulling her closer to the window.

"It sounds quiet in there," Fitz whispered. "Think it's safe to peek?"

Sophie nodded, doing a silent countdown in her head.

Three . . . two . . . one.

She popped up on her knees, careful to only raise herself up high enough to peer through the spotted glass.

"Everything okay?" Fitz asked when she didn't duck back down.

Sophie frowned. "The house is a mess. *Way* messier than my mom would ever allow it to be."

"People change," Keefe said, popping up to see for himself.

"I guess." But Sophie was starting to learn that when dread pooled up inside her, it was because her instincts were a couple of steps ahead.

Two cars in the driveway.

Dog barking early in the morning with no one shushing it.

Messy house.

Too quiet.

Not found.

This wouldn't end well.

"I have to get inside," Sophie said, ignoring Sandor's protests as she marched over to the door and tried the handle.

It was locked, but her parents still kept a spare key under the smallest flowerpot.

Before she could change her mind, she unlocked the door and slipped inside.

Her heart sank with every step, every new detail her eyes picked up. Dirty dishes in the sink that had to be at least a week old. Papers strewn all over the tables and floor.

"Seems pretty quiet," Keefe said behind her.

"Too quiet," she whispered. No human thoughts blaring into her brain—though human minds did quiet down while they were sleeping.

The stairs creaked as they climbed, but no one startled awake. And the master bedroom was empty. Bed unmade. Lights still on.

"Maybe they're on vacation," Fitz said, offering whatever weak hope he could.

It was Sandor who finally crushed it, calling from downstairs. "The yard smells like ash. As does the house."

Sophie closed her eyes and nodded, letting the tears she'd been fighting slip down her cheeks.

The Neverseen used ash to disguise their scent.

"They were here," she whispered. "They took them. Why would they take them?"

This couldn't just be about controlling her. If that were all it was, they'd have let her know the second they had her family. Instead they'd kept quiet. Letting her discover it all on her own. Maybe even hoping she wouldn't.

Keefe took her by the shoulders, his expression fierce, determined. "I don't know what's going on. But we'll find them, okay? We'll get them back. I *promise*."

"But we don't even know where they are—where to start," Sophie reminded him. The sobs were coming fast and furious now, but she didn't fight them back.

She was so tired of fighting.

Tired of losing.

"There has to be a clue," Fitz said. "We'll take this whole place apart if we have to. Then we'll find them and we'll bring them back and we'll make sure they're happy and safe and that nothing bad ever happens to them again, okay?"

No—it wasn't okay.

It would never be okay.

The Neverseen had her family!

"Does 'Nightfall' mean anything?" a shaky female voice said behind them, eliciting quite a few gasps. "That's what they said. They didn't know I was hiding here—one of them had talked about listening for thoughts, so I let my mind go dark and silent. And I heard them say, 'Take them to Nightfall.'"

"Nightfall?" Keefe repeated as Sophie spun around, following the trail of panicked human thoughts to the voice.

There.

On the wall behind them, a door was open just a crack. Probably a closet or a bathroom.

"It's okay to come out," Fitz promised. "We're here to help."

Several seconds passed before the door swung open and a young girl stepped slowly out.

She was taller than Sophie remembered. Thinner. Her curly brown hair cut short. But even with all those changes, Sophie would've recognized her little sister anywhere.

Her sister's eyebrows pressed together, like she was straining extra hard to figure out what to say.

When their eyes met, she whispered, "Sophie?"

ACKNOWLEDGMENTS

Yay—you're still here! That means you're still speaking to me!

(Or perhaps you're still clinging to the hope that I wouldn't be cruel enough to pause the story there. But after what I did to you at the end of *Neverseen*, surely you know better. *Mwaha-hahahaha.*)

I know these game-changer endings are a severe test of your patience—and I promise I don't do them to torture you! (Though the torture *is* a fun bonus.) Each book in a series is really more like a chapter in a much longer story—so the good news is, this means there are more books ahead!

And you guys are the reason this series keeps growing. If you weren't reading Sophie's story and doing all of the fan-tastic things you do to spread the word, I would've had to cut things short long ago. So thank you, thank you, thank you!!!

I also could *not* have gotten through the rather stressful process of writing this book if it weren't for the support of an incredible group of people.

Mom and Dad, I definitely owe you a trophy for Best Promoters Ever for championing my book to basically everyone you talk to for longer than five seconds, and for baking hundreds of cupcakes for my launch parties.

Laura Rennert, you deserve the SuperAgent trophy—as does everyone at Andrea Brown Literary and the Taryn Fagerness Agency—for all of the tireless ways you keep my career on track.

Liesa Abrams Mignogna, your trophy is shaped like a Batmobile because you really are the Batgirl of all editors. Thank you for not strangling me for falling so behind schedule, and for continuing to believe in Sophie and crew. I also want to give the Most Awesome Publisher trophy to everyone at Simon & Schuster, especially Mara Anastas, Mary Marotta, Jon Anderson, Katherine Devendorf, Julie Doebler, Emma Sector, Carolyn Swerdloff, Catherine Hayden, Tara Grieco, Jennifer Romanello, Jodie Hockensmith, Faye Bi, Lucille Rettino, Michelle Fadlalla, Anthony Parisi, Candace McManus, Matt Pantoliano, Amy Bartram, Mike Rosamilia, Christina Pecorale, Gary Urda, and the entire sales team. And the Most Gorgeous Cover trophy goes to Karin Paprocki and Jason Chan. I don't know how you guys keep upping your game, but I adore you for it.

Cécile Pournin and everyone else at Lumen Editions deserve the Undeniably Awesome French Publisher trophy for their unfailing enthusiasm and care for this series. And Mathilde Tamae-bouhon earns the Translator of the Year trophy for bravely tackling my insanely long books. I also want to give the Outstanding International Fans trophy to my French readers, who wait so patiently for the translated editions.

Kari Olson, I owe you the Ultimate Brainstormer trophy for helping me puzzle out this plot and constantly talking me off the "I'll never not be writing this book" ledge. And Victoria Morris, I give you the Fabulous Beta Reader prize for reading so quickly and chiming in with encouragement right when I need it most.

And the Best Support Group trophy goes to Erin Bowman, Lisa Cannon, Christa Desir, Debra Driza, Nikki Katz, Lisa Mantchev, Sara McClung, Ellen Oh, Andrea Ortega, Cindy Pon, CJ Redwine, James Riley, J. Scott Savage, Amy Tintera, Kasie West, Natalie Whipple, and Sarah Wylie. (And to anyone I've forgotten, here's the Most Forgiving Friend trophy for understanding how deadline brain constantly fails me.)

I also have to give the Ultimate Champions trophy to all of the teachers, librarians, bloggers, and booksellers who've done so many tremendous things to keep this series growing, especially Mel Barnes, Alyson Beecher, Katie Bartow, Lynette Dodds, Maryelizabeth Hart, Faith Hochhalter, Heather Laird, Katie Laird, Kim Laird, Barbara Mena, Brandi Stewart,

Kristin Trevino, Andrea Vuleta, and so many others. If I listed you all, this book would double in thickness, which might cause serious back injury to my poor readers. So I'll just give every single one of you a round of applause.

applauds

And now, I'll stop rambling and get back to writing. On to book six!

Turn the page for a sneak peek at

KEEPER
OF THE
LOST CITIES

Book 6: **NIGHTFALL**

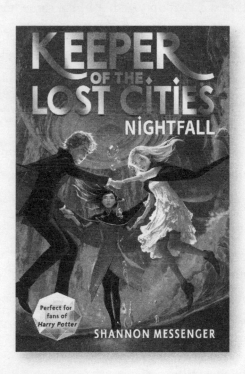

Y OU REMEMBER ME?"

The question slipped from Sophie's lips before she could stop it, and the weighted words seemed to hit the floor of the messy bedroom with a thud.

The wide-eyed, trembling girl standing in front of her slowly nodded, and Sophie's heart swelled even as it plummeted into the sour pit of her stomach.

Her little sister *shouldn't* remember her.

Technically, she wasn't even her sister—at least not genetically. Sure, they'd grown up together in the same house in San Diego, California, both believing they had the same parents—despite the fact that Sophie's blond hair and brown eyes didn't match her family of light-eyed brunettes.

But that was *before*.

Now they were in the *after*.

A world where elves were real creatures—and nothing like the silly stories that humans had invented about them. They were beautiful. Powerful. Practically immortal. Living across the globe in hidden glittering cities. Ruling the earth from the shadows.

And Sophie was one of them.

Born from humans—but *not* human—as part of a rebel group's secret genetic experiment called Project Moonlark. Her DNA had been tweaked. Her abilities enhanced and manipulated. All to mold her into something special.

Something powerful.

Something she still didn't fully understand.

And after years of feeling out of place—even among the family she loved—the elves finally showed Sophie the truth about her life and brought her to the Lost Cities. They'd planned to fake her death to cover her disappearance, but she'd begged to be erased instead, to spare her parents the grief of losing a child. So her family's minds had been "washed" by specially trained Telepaths, to make them forget that Sophie had ever been born. And they'd been relocated to a new city and given new names, new jobs, even the fancy new Tudor-style house that Sophie now stood in, with its quaint windows and wood-paneled walls.

But erased memories were never *truly* gone. All it took was the right trigger and . . .

"I don't understand," her sister whispered, rubbing her eyes like it would change what she was seeing. "You . . . shouldn't be here."

Major understatement.

Sophie wasn't supposed to know her family's new names or where they lived—and she definitely hadn't been allowed to visit them—to ensure that something like this *never* happened. And yet, here she was, raising a mental shield to block her sister's chaotic thoughts as they pounded through her consciousness like stampeding mastodons. Human minds were more open than elvin minds, and they broadcast everything like a radio station on full blast.

"Listen, Amy—"

"That's not my name!"

Sophie kicked herself for the slip. "Right, I meant—"

"Wait." Her sister mouthed the name a few more times, as if her lips were remembering the feel of it. "It is, isn't it? I'm ... Amy Foster?"

Sophie nodded.

"Then who's Natalie Freeman?"

"That's ... also you."

Amy—Natalie—whatever Sophie was supposed to call her—groaned and pressed her fingers against her temples.

"I know how confusing this must be," Sophie told her. Triggered memories tended to flash back in scattered bits and pieces, leaving lots of holes. "I promise I'll explain, but—"

"Not right now," a crisply accented voice finished for her.

Sophie flinched. She'd almost forgotten they had an audience for the Most Stressful Family Reunion in the History of Family Reunions.

"Who are you?" her sister asked, backing away from the guys standing slightly behind Sophie.

"That's Fitz," Sophie said, pointing to a dark-haired boy whose teal eyes flashed as he offered a smile that would put any movie star to shame. "And that's Keefe."

Keefe gave her sister his famous smirk, reaching up to smooth his expertly tousled blond hair. "Don't worry—we're all in the Foster Fan Club."

"They're my friends," Sophie clarified when her sister

shrank back another step. "You can trust them."

"I don't even know if I can trust *you*." Her eyes narrowed at Sophie's outfit: a fitted purple tunic with black leggings, boots, and wrist-length black gloves. Fitz and Keefe also wore tunics and pants, and while none of the outfits were *that* elf-y, they definitely stood out next to her sister's jeans and TARDIS T-shirt.

"You trusted us enough to stop hiding, right?" Keefe asked, pointing to the still-open closet door.

Sophie's sister turned toward the dark nook she'd emerged from, where most of the clothes had been heaped into a pile on the floor. "I only came out because I heard you guys say you'd get my parents back."

And there it was. The reason Sophie had broken all the rules and raced to the Forbidden Cities to check on her family. She'd spent months protecting her adoptive elvin parents, believing they were the ones that Keefe had warned her were in danger. But they'd both forgotten she had another family to worry about—a family without powerful abilities and bodyguards to keep them safe.

"Can you really find Mom and Dad?" her sister whispered, giving Sophie the cue to tell her, "Yes, of course we will! Everything is going to be okay!"

Sophie wanted to. But ... the Neverseen were behind this.

The same villains who'd kidnapped Sophie, tortured her, and killed people she dearly loved. And no matter how hard Sophie fought to stop them, they always seemed to be ten steps ahead.

Keefe reached for Sophie's shaky hand. "We'll get them back safe. I *promise*."

His tone was pure determination. But Sophie could see a shadow darkening his ice-blue eyes.

Guilt.

A few months earlier, Keefe had run away to join the Neverseen, planning to be a double agent and destroy the wicked organization from the inside out—but they'd played him the whole time, tricking him into leading Sophie and her friends down the wrong paths.

Part of Sophie wanted to shove Keefe away, let him shoulder the blame for every terrible thing that had happened. But deep down she knew he wasn't the only one who'd missed the warning signs. He'd also been working every day to make up for his mistakes. Plus, it was dangerous to let him feel guilty. The elvin conscience was too fragile for that kind of burden.

So Sophie squeezed his hand, twining their fingers together as she turned back to her sister. "It'll help if you tell us everything you can about the people who took Mom and Dad."

Her sister wrapped her arms around her stomach, which wasn't as plump as Sophie remembered. She looked taller now too. And her curly brown hair was cut shorter. In fact, everything about her seemed so much older than the hyper nine-year-old she'd been when Sophie had left—and it hadn't even been two full years.

"I don't remember much," her sister mumbled. "Dad was

helping me with my homework when we heard strange voices downstairs. He told me to stay quiet while he went to see what was going on, but I snuck out to the landing and ..." She swallowed hard. "I saw four people in the living room wearing long black cloaks with these creepy white eyes on their sleeves. Mom was passed out over one of their shoulders, and another had a cloth pressed over Dad's mouth. I wanted to run down and help—but there were so many of them. And Dad stopped moving a couple of seconds later. I tried to crawl to a phone to call the police, but then I heard them say something about searching the rest of the house, so I ducked into the nearest closet and buried myself in clothes."

Sophie shuddered as she imagined it, and her nose burned with a sweet scent, remembering the smell of the cloying drugs the Neverseen favored during their abductions. "Did you see any of their faces?"

"They had their hoods up the whole time. But one of them ..."

"One of them what?" Sophie pressed.

"You're not going to believe me."

"Try us." Keefe said. "You'd be surprised what we can believe after hanging around this one."

He elbowed Sophie gently in the ribs, and Sophie knew he was trying to break the tension. Humor was Keefe's favorite coping mechanism.

But she didn't have the energy to joke around. Especially

when her sister whispered, "One of the guys kept disappearing somehow. Like with quick flashes, fading in and out of sight."

Fitz muttered something under his breath. "That was Alvar."

"You know him?"

"He's done a lot of awful things," Sophie jumped in, shooting Fitz a please-don't-say-he's-your-brother look. She doubted it would help her sister trust them.

"How did he disappear like that?" her sister whispered. "It almost looked like . . ."

"Magic?" Sophie guessed with a sad smile. "I remember thinking that too, the first time I saw it. But he's what we call a Vanisher. All he's doing is manipulating light."

"What about the mind reading thing?" her sister asked. "One of them said he was listening for nearby thoughts as he searched the house, so I thought about darkness and silence just in case."

"That was really smart," Sophie told her, stunned her sister had managed to pull that off.

Her sister shrugged. "I've seen a lot of movies. But . . . could he really do that?"

"If he was a Telepath," Fitz said. "Which means it was probably Gethen."

The name sent Sophie spiraling into nightmares of crumbling castle walls and jagged mazes of rubble. Screams echoed in her ears as the world turned red—partially with her rage, but mostly with the memory of a wound that cut too deep for her to stop the bleeding.

A slow breath cleared her head and Sophie concentrated on her churning emotions, imagining her anger, fear, and grief as thick threads before tying them into a knot under her ribs. She'd learned the technique from her inflicting mentor, a way of storing the power as a reserve. Embracing the darkness to let it fuel her later.

"Are you okay?" Keefe asked, tightening his hold on her hand.

It took Sophie a second to realize he was *also* talking to her sister, who'd turned so pale her skin had a greenish sheen.

"None of this should be real," her sister whispered. "These things you're telling me. These weird names you keep saying. Mom and Dad being taken. And then you show up out of nowhere and it feels like ... like you should've been here this whole time. And now my name feels wrong. And this house feels wrong. *Everything* feels wrong."

Sophie hesitated before moving to her sister's side and wrapping an arm around her shoulders. They hadn't been touchy-feely sisters back when they'd lived together. In fact, they'd spent most of their time bickering.

But after a second, her sister hugged her back.

"Where have you been, Sophie? And how do you know these scary people?"

Sophie sighed. "There's a really long, really complicated story I need to tell you. But right now, we need to stay focused on finding Mom and Dad, okay? Did you hear anything else that might be useful?"

"Just the part I already told you, about taking them to Night-fall. Do you know what that means?"

Sophie glanced at Fitz and Keefe.

They'd only seen the word once, in one of Keefe's recently recovered memories—an inscription carved in elvin runes across a mysterious silver door set into a mountain:

The star only rises at Nightfall.

They didn't know what the phrase meant, or where the door led, or even precisely where the door was. But they knew it unlocked with Keefe's blood, and that his mom—who'd been one of the leaders of the Neverseen before getting trapped in an ogre prison—had declared it to be his "legacy."

If that door leads to Nightfall, Sophie transmitted to Keefe, sending her thoughts directly into his head, *wouldn't the Never-seen need to have you with them in order to get inside?*

Keefe focused on the floor. *They would, if they didn't already have some of my blood.*

WHAT?

Yeah . . . not-so-funny story: I traded some for part of the secret I needed to steal the caches.

ARE YOU KIDDING ME?

Caches were marble-size gadgets the Councillors used to store Forgotten Secrets—information deemed too dangerous for anyone to keep in their memory. Councillor Kenric had given Sophie his when he died—and Keefe had stolen it from her to buy his way into the Neverseen. But he got it back before he fled—and he also took the cache that belonged to Fintan, their leader. Dex was now trying to use his ability as a Technopath to hack into the gadgets. But even if they learned something important, Sophie *never* would've told Keefe to trade his blood for the caches.

I know, Keefe told her. *It wasn't my most brilliant idea. I thought I was so close to taking the Neverseen down that it wasn't going to matter. So, when Fintan asked for my blood, I told him he needed to prove that I could trust him by answering one question. And once he did, I had to hold up my end of the deal.*

But I thought you were going to trade Tam's leaping crystal for that information, Sophie reminded him. *Wasn't that why you left me stranded in one of the Neverseen's hideouts?*

Keefe cringed.

Of all the mistakes he'd made during his time with the Neverseen, that one had been the hardest for Sophie to forgive.

That was my plan, Keefe admitted. *But Fintan interrogated me when I got back, and I had to use the crystal to convince him not to burn off my arm.*

Ice rippled through Sophie's veins. *You never told me that part.*

I know.

His shadowed eyes made her wonder what other nightmares he'd secretly endured. But she'd have to save those worries for another time. At the moment, they had much more complicated problems.

Do you really think Fintan would help you steal the caches if they're actually important?

Yeah, Foster. I do. Because he had no idea that he gave me the other piece of the code phrase weeks earlier, after he had too much fizzleberry wine. Trading my blood was a bad call. But I SWEAR the caches are still a score. And I should've told you—I was planning on it, and then everything happened in Lumenaria and I forgot.

Sophie closed her eyes, wishing she could stop her mind from flashing to crumbling walls. But the memories refused to be ignored.

In one night the Neverseen had destroyed the elves' magnificent glowing castle while Sophie, the Council, and the leaders of all the intelligent species were inside for the ogre Peace Summit. Most of the leaders made it out with only minor injuries—and Lumenaria was already being rebuilt. But nothing could erase the message the Neverseen sent that day, or bring back the prisoner that had escaped from the dungeon, or the lives that had been stolen away.

I'll fix this, okay? Keefe promised. *I'm going to fix everything.*

You mean "we," Sophie corrected. *WE are going to fix this.*

If they'd learned one thing from all the disasters over the last few months, it was that none of them should be working alone. It was going to take *all* of their abilities, all of their ideas—and a scary amount of luck—to get through whatever this was.

Does that mean you don't hate me? Keefe asked. His mental tone sounded softer—almost timid.

I told you, I'm never going to hate you, Keefe.

But I keep giving you new reasons to change your mind.

Yeah, you really need to stop that. She offered him half a smile and he gave her the same when she added, *But we're in this together.*

Team Foster-Keefe IS pretty awesome.

And team Vacker-Foster-Keefe is even better, Fitz transmitted, making Sophie wonder how long he'd been eavesdropping.

Fitz was one of the only Telepaths who knew how to slip past Sophie's impenetrable mental blocking. Actually, he was the *only* one, now that Mr. Forkle was . . .

Sophie shut down the devastating thought, not ready to tear open the still-too-fresh wound.

Don't worry, she told Fitz. *We're going to need all the help we can get.*

Though we need a WAY cooler name, Keefe jumped in. *How about Team Foster-Keefe and the Wonderboy?*

Fitz rolled his eyes.

"Why are you guys staring at each other like that?" her sister asked, reminding them they had someone watching their rather lengthy mental exchange.

"We're just trying to figure out where Nightfall could be," Sophie told her.

She'd have to reveal her telepathy eventually—as well as her other special abilities—but she wanted to give her sister more time to adjust before she dropped the *I can read minds and teleport and inflict pain and speak any language and enhance other people's powers* bombshells. "Can you think of anything else that might be important?"

"Not really. After they said the thing about Nightfall, the house got super quiet. I waited another couple of minutes to make sure it was safe, and then I ran for Mom's phone and called 911. I was scared the police would take me if they knew I was here alone, so I said I was walking by the house and saw men dragging two people away. I hid in the trees when the cops showed up—but maybe that was a bad idea. I heard them say they thought my call was a prank, since there were no signs of robbery. One of them said something about following up in a few days, but so far, I haven't seen them."

"How long ago was that?" Fitz asked.

Her chin wobbled. "Five days."

Keefe looked like he was trying hard not to swear. Sophie felt like doing the same—or punching the walls and screaming as loud as she could.

"You don't think it's too late, do you?" her sister whispered. "You don't think they're ... ?"

"No." Sophie let the word echo around her mind until she believed it. "The Neverseen need them alive."

"Who are the Neverseen?" her sister asked. "What do they want with Mom and Dad?"

"I wish I knew," Sophie admitted. "But they won't kill them."

At least not yet.

The Neverseen had been trying to control Sophie since they'd first learned she existed, so she was sure they'd use her parents as the worst sort of blackmail. But there had to be more to it. Otherwise they would've let her know the second they had their prisoners.

At least the Neverseen didn't know her sister heard them say they were going to Nightfall. All they had to do was find that door—and Sophie was pretty sure she knew how to do that.

She just wished it didn't involve trusting one of their enemies.

"I know what you're thinking," Keefe told her. "And I'm in. All the way."

"Let's not get ahead of ourselves," Fitz said, pointing toward the windows, where the sky was fading to twilight. "First, we need to get out of here. They probably have someone watching this place, waiting for us to show up."

Sophie nodded to her sister. "Go pack a bag as quick as you can. You're coming with me."

"Uh, that's *way* too dangerous," Fitz warned. "If the Council found out—"

"They *won't*," Sophie interrupted. "As soon as we get back, I'll hail the Collective."

The Black Swan—the rebel organization that created Sophie—had an extensive network of secret hideouts. And they'd always come through when Sophie needed their help.

Then again, that was before Mr. Forkle was . . .

This time, she couldn't stop her brain from finishing the sentence with "murdered."

She pressed her palm over her chest, feeling for the new locket under her tunic, which held the last task Mr. Forkle had entrusted her with before he took his final breaths.

When an elf passed away, they coiled their DNA around a Wanderling seed and planted it in a special forest. But Mr. Forkle had asked Sophie to hold onto his seed, claiming she'd somehow *know* when and where to do the planting. He'd also asked that his body be removed from the rubble before anyone saw it, which meant only a handful of people knew he'd been killed. But the rest of their world would find out soon enough. The Council had extended Foxfire's midterm break in light of the tragedy in Lumenaria—but school was scheduled to restart in less than two weeks. And one of Mr. Forkle's secret alter egos had been principal of the academy.

Keefe moved closer, leaning in to whisper, "I'll take care of your sister, Foster. The place I'm crashing in is small—and it smells like sasquatch breath mixed with rotting toenails. But I guarantee no one will find us."

Keefe had been living on the run ever since he'd fled the Neverseen—and his offer wasn't a horrible suggestion. But Sophie wasn't letting her sister out of her sight.

"She's coming with me to Havenfield. We'll figure out the rest once we get there."

"Uh, I'm not going anywhere with a bunch of strangers," her sister informed them.

The last word stung more than Sophie wanted to admit, but she did her best to shrug it off. "Do you really think you're safe here? Even if the Neverseen don't come back, the police might. Do you want to end up in foster care?"

Her sister bit her lip, leaving indentations in the soft flesh. "What about Marty and Watson? Who's going to feed them?"

Sophie's eyes prickled. "You still have Marty?"

The fluffy gray cat used to sleep on her pillow every night, and it had broken her heart to leave him behind. But she'd figured her family would need him more than she would.

And Watson must've been the dog she'd heard barking when they'd first arrived. Sophie had asked the elves to move her family somewhere with a yard big enough to allow them to finally get the puppy her sister had always wanted.

"I guess we'll bring them with us," Sophie decided. "Get Watson on a leash and put Marty in his carrier."

"Okay, seriously, we can't do this," Fitz said, reaching for Sophie's hands to force her to listen to him. "You don't understand how dangerous this is."

"It'll be fine," Sophie insisted. "The Black Swan will keep her hidden."

"The Black Swan," her sister whispered. "Wait. I think ... I think they said something about that. Everything was happening so fast, it's hard to remember. But I think one of them said, 'Let's figure out why the Black Swan chose them.'"

Sophie shared another look with her friends.

"I take it you guys know what that means?" her sister asked.

"It ... might be about me," Sophie said. "It's part of that long story I have to tell you—but we should get out of here first."

She tried to reach for her home crystal, but Fitz wouldn't let go of her hands.

"You're not understanding what I'm saying," he told her. "Do you have any idea how risky it is to light leap with a human?"

He'd kept his voice low, but her sister still snapped, "What do you mean *a human*?"

"Exactly what you think he means," a slightly deeper, even crisper voice said from the doorway.

Everyone whipped around to find the three others who'd insisted on joining Sophie, Keefe, and Fitz on this hastily planned—and highly illegal—excursion to the Forbidden Cities. Fitz's father, Alden, who looked like an older, more regal version of his son. And Sandor and Grizel, who instantly triggered a massive amount of screaming.

"It's okay," Sophie promised. "They're our bodyguards."

That only seemed to make her sister scream louder.

To be fair, both Sandor and Grizel were seven feet tall and gray, with flat noses and massive amounts of rock-hard muscle—plus gigantic black swords strapped at their sides.

"Wh-what are th-they?" her sister stammered.

"Goblins," Sandor said in his unexpectedly high-pitched, squeaky voice.

"And we mean you no harm," Grizel added in her huskier tone.

A hysterical laugh burbled from her sister's lips. "Goblins. Like from the bank in Harry Potter?"

Fitz grinned. "She sounds like Sophie did when I first told her she was an elf."

The word triggered another round of hysterical laughter.

"Okay, so two things," Keefe jumped in. "One: How is she understanding us? I just realized we've all been speaking the Enlightened Language, and she has too."

"I gave her—and her parents—a basic understanding of our language before we relocated them," Alden explained. "In case something like this ever happened. Communication can be a powerful weapon, and an essential defense."

"What is he talking about?" her sister shouted. *"WHAT DID YOU DO TO MY BRAIN?"*

"That's the second thing," Keefe said, fanning his arm the way he always did when he was reading emotions through the air. "I'm betting your sister is about three minutes away from a meltdown of epic proportions."

"I'd wager it'll be sooner than that," Alden said through a sigh. "This is exactly the kind of worst case scenario I hoped we'd never have to face. Fortunately, I came prepared."

"What are you doing?" Sophie asked, yanking her hands free

from Fitz as Alden reached into the inner pocket of his long blue cape. She'd been afraid he'd pull out a vial of sedatives. But the round silver disk he tossed at her feet was much more terrifying.

Sophie had used the same gadget the day she'd drugged her family so the elves could erase her. And as the world spun to a blur, she realized she should've held her breath the second the disk hit the floor.

"Please," she begged when her sister collapsed. "She's going to need me. You can't erase me again."

Keefe lunged to help Sophie, but only lasted a second before he went down. Fitz followed a second after that.

Sophie's knees gave out, but she crawled for her sister, pleading with Alden to change his plan. He'd always been so kind to her—a loyal, trustworthy advisor. Almost a father figure. But his face was sad and serious as he released the breath he'd been holding. "Don't fight the sedatives, Sophie. You can't beat them."

He said something else, but she couldn't understand him. Her ears were ringing, and the light kept dimming.

She hated this feeling—hated Alden for putting her through it. But she couldn't focus enough to rally any of her defenses.

"Please," she said again as her face sank against the carpet. "Please don't take my sister away from me. Not again."

Through her hazy eyes she saw Alden crouch beside her, his lips mouthing, "I'm sorry."

Then darkness swallowed everything.

INDEX TO USEFUL REFERENCES

Manufacturing Engineering and Technology

Fourth Edition

Serope Kalpakjian
Illinois Institute of Technology

Steven R. Schmid
The University of Notre Dame

Prentice Hall International
London New York Toronto Sydney Tokyo
Singapore Madrid Mexico City Munich
Paris Capetown Hong Kong Montreal

Acquisitions editor: LAURA CURLESS
Editorial/production supervision: ROSE KERNAN
Vice-president of editorial development, ECS: MARCIA HORTON
Copy editor: PAT DALY
Cover designer: BRUCE KENSELAAR
Vice-President of production and manufacturing: DAVID W. RICCARDI
Managing editor: DAVID A. GEORGE
Executive managing editor: VINCE O'BRIEN
Manufacturing manager: TRUDY PISCIOTTI
Interior designer: ROSE KERNAN
Art director: JAYNE CONTE
Marketing manager: DANNY HOYT
Editorial assistant: LAURIE FREIDMAN

©2001 by Prentice-Hall, Inc.
Upper Saddle River, New Jersey 07458

The authors and publisher of this book have used their best efforts in preparing this book. These efforts include the development, research, and testing of the theories and programs to determine their effectiveness. The authors and publisher make no warranty of any kind, expressed or implied, with regard to these programs or the documentation contained in this book. The authors and publisher shall not be liable in any event for incidental or consequential damages in connection with, or arising out of, the furnishing, performance, or use of these programs.

Reprinted with corrections November, 2000.
Printed in the United States of America

10 9 8 7 6 5 4 3

ISBN 0-13-017440-8

Prentice-Hall International (UK) Limited, London
Prentice-Hall of Australia Pty. Limited, Sydney
Prentice-Hall Canada Inc., Toronto
Prentice-Hall Hispanoamericana, S.A., Mexico
Prentice-Hall of India Private Limited, New Delhi
Prentice-Hall of Japan, Inc., Tokyo
Pearson Education Pte. Ltd., Singapore
Editora Prentice-Hall do Brasil, Ltda., Rio de Janeiro
Prentice-Hall, Inc., Upper Saddle River, New Jersey

To

Granddaughter
Carissa Ann Kalpakjian

and

Shelly Petronis

Contents

Part IV: Material-Removal Processes and Machines   **531**

Part V: Joining Processes and Equipment   771

Part VIII: Manufacturing in a Competitive Environment   1019

Preface

The field of manufacturing engineering and technology continues to advance rapidly, transcending disciplines and driving economic growth. This challenging and broad topic has continued to incorporate new concepts at an increasing rate, making manufacturing a dynamic and exciting field of study. In preparing this fourth edition, our most important goal throughout has been to provide a comprehensive state-of-the-art textbook on manufacturing, which also encompasses the additional aims of motivating and challenging students.

As in previous editions, the text presents topics with a balanced coverage of relevant fundamentals and real-world practices, so that the student develops an understanding of the important and often complex interrelationships among the many technical and economic factors involved in manufacturing.

This new edition basically follows the same introductory nature, format, organization, and balance as the third edition. It has retained its emphasis on (a) the influence of materials and processing parameters in understanding manufacturing processes and operations; (b) design considerations, product quality, and manufacturing cost factors; and (c) the domestic and global competitive context of each manufacturing process and operation, highlighted with illustrative examples.

STUDY AIDS

- Presentation of each topic within a larger context of manufacturing engineering and technology, using extensive schematic diagrams and flowcharts.
- Emphasis on the practical uses of the concepts and information presented.
- Analogies, discussions, and problems designed to stimulate the student's curiosity about consumer and industrial products and how they are manufactured.
- Extensive reference material, including numerous tables, illustrations, graphs, and bibliographies.
- Numerous illustrative examples and case studies to highlight important concepts and techniques.
- Tables comparing advantages and limitations of manufacturing processes.
- A summary, list of key terms, and concise description of current trends at the end of each chapter.

WHAT IS NEW IN THIS EDITION

- Several new examples and case studies have been added.
- There are now a total of almost 2,200 questions and problems, about a quarter of them new to this edition.
- Summaries at the end of each chapter have been completely rewritten and expanded.
- The bibliographies at the end of each chapter have been thoroughly updated.

- More cross-references have been made throughout the text to other sections and chapters in the book.
- New or expanded topics include the following:

Topic	Section	Topic	Section
Abrasive belts; microreplication	25.10	Micromachining	26.12
Atomic force microscope	31.5	Nanofabrication	26.11
Biodegradable plastics	7.8	Nanomaterials	6.15
Bundle drawing	15.11	Nanopowders	17.2
Carbon foam	8.6	Octree representation	39.4
Chemical mechanical polishing	25.10	Overmolding	18.3
Coatings	21.6	Plastics, common trade names	7.6
Compliant end effector	38.7	Porous aluminum	6.2
Conductive graphite fibers	9.2.1	Product liability examples	37.6
Deburring	25.11	Pulsed electrochemical machining	26.3
Diamond-like carbon coating	33.13	QS 9000 standard	36.4
Die failures	14.12	Rapid prototyping	Ch. 19
Die manufacturing methods	14.11	Reflow soldering	30.3
Electrically conducting adhesives	30.6	Robustness	36.6
Friction stir welding	28.4	Rotary ultrasonic machining	25.9
Hexapod machine tools	24.3	Superconductor processing	17.13
ISO 14000 standard	36.4	Taguchi loss function	36.6
Joining plastics	30.6	Thermal effects in machine tools	24.3
Laser interferometry	35.5	Titanic: brittle fracture example	2.10
Laser peening	33.2	Total productive maintenance	38.2
Linear motor drives for machine tools	24.3	Transfer/injection molding	18.12
Microencapsulated powders	17.21	Water-jet peening	32.2
Micrograin carbides	21.11	Wave soldering	30.3

In response to comments and suggestions by numerous reviewers, several major and minor changes have also been made throughout the text. A page-by-page comparison with the third edition will show that literally thousands of changes have been made for improved clarity and completeness.

AUDIENCE

As in the previous editions, this fourth edition has been written for students in mechanical, manufacturing, industrial, aerospace, and metallurgical and materials engineering programs. It is hoped that by reading and studying this book, students will come to appreciate the vital nature of manufacturing engineering as an academic subject that is as exciting, challenging, and important as any other engineering and technology discipline.

ACKNOWLEDGMENTS

This text, together with the first three editions, represents a total of almost ten years of effort; it could not have been written and produced without the help of many colleagues and former students. It gives us great pleasure to acknowledge the assistance of the following in the preparation and publication of this fourth edition.

We are very grateful to Marcia Horton, and Laura Curless, Prentice Hall, for their enthusiastic support, and to Rose Kernan for her supervision of this revision.

We gratefully acknowledge the following reviewers for sharing their knowledge with us and for their constructive criticisms and suggestions:

Our colleagues at the Illinois Institute of Technology: John Cesarone, Ali Cinar, Marek Dollar, Donald Duvall, Jerry Field, Craig Johnson, Marvin Levine, Keith McKee, Satish Parulekar, Mohamed Tarabishy, Bharat Thakkar, and Calvin Tszang.

Our colleagues at other organizations: Subrata Bhattacharyya (formerly at the IIT Research Institute), J T. Black (Auburn University), Theodore Lach (Lucent Technologies), Blaine Lilly (Ohio State University), and James Wingfield (Triodyne Inc.)

Students at the Illinois Institute of Technology: Brian Bosak, Kevin Jones, Milan Savic, John Stocker, and Kristopher West

We are also happy to present below a cumulative list of all those individuals who, in one way or another, made significant contributions to various editions of this book:

B.J. Aaronson	R.L. French	J. Nazemetz
S. Arellano	B.R. Fruchter	E.M. Odom
R.A. Arlt	R. Giese	J. Penaluna
V. Aronov	P. Grigg	M. Philpott
A. Bagchi	B. Harriger	J.M. Prince
E.D. Baker	D. Harry	W.J. Riffe
J. Barak	R.J. Hocken	R.J. Rogalla
J. Ben-Ari	E.M. Honig, Jr.	A.A. Runyan
G.F. Benedict	S. Imam	G.S. Saletta
C. Blathras	R. Jaeger	M. Salimian
G. Boothroyd	J. Kamman	W.J. Schoech
D. Bourell	S.G. Kapoor	J.E. Smallwood
N.N. Breyer	R.L. Kegg	J.P. Sobczak
C.A. Brown	W.J. Kennedy	L. Strom
R. G. Bruce	B.D. King	K. Subramanian
T.-C. Chang	J.E. Kopf	T. Taglialavore
R.L. Cheaney	R.J. Koronkowski	K. Taraman
A. Cheda	J. Kotowski	R. Taylor
S. Chelikani	S. Krishnamachari	S.A. Schwartz
S.-W. Choi	K.M. Kulkarni	L. Soisson
R.O. Colantonio	L. Langseth	B. Strong
D. Descoteaux	B.S. Levy	T. Sweeney
P. Demers	X.Z. Li	W.G. Switalski
R.C. Dix	D.A. Lucca	A. Trager
D.A. Dornfeld	L. Mapa	J. Vigneau
P. Cotnoir	R.J. Mattice	G.A. Volk
H.I. Douglas	C. Maziar	G. Wallace
D. R. Durham	T. McClelland	K.J. Weinmann
S.A. Dynan	L. McGuire	R. Wertheim
J. ElGomayel	K.P. Meade	J. Widmoyer
M.G. Elliott	R. Miller	G. Williamson
E.C. Feldy	T.S. Milo	B. Wiltjer
G.W. Fischer	S. Mostovoy	P.K. Wright
D.A. Fowley	C. Nair	
	P.G. Nash	

Finally, many thanks to Jean Kalpakjian for her help during the editing and production of this book.

Serope Kalpakjian
Steven R. Schmid

About the Authors

Professor Serope Kalpakjian has been teaching at the Illinois Institute of Technology since 1963. After graduating from Robert College (with High Honors), Harvard University, and the Massachusetts Institute of Technology, he joined Cincinnati Milacron, Inc., where he was a research supervisor in charge of advanced metal-forming processes. He has published numerous papers and is the author of several articles in encyclopedias and handbooks; he has also edited various volumes and serves on the editorial boards of several journals and the *Encyclopedia Americana*.

He is the author of three additional manufacturing books, two of which received the M. Eugene Merchant Manufacturing Textbook Award. He is a Life Fellow of the American Society of Mechanical Engineers, Fellow and Life Member of ASM International, and Fellow of the Society of Manufacturing Engineers, and is a full member (Emeritus) of the International Institution for Production Engineering Research (CIRP). He is a founding member and a past president of the North American manufacturing Research Institution.

Professor Kalpakjian has received several awards: Citation by the Forging Industry Educational and Research Foundation for best paper (1966); Citation by the Society of Carbide and Tool Engineers (1977); the "Excellence in Teaching Award" from the Illinois Institute of Technology (1970); the "Centennial Medallion" by the American Society of Mechanical Engineers (1980); the International "Education Award" by the Society of Manufacturing Engineers (1989); and the Albert Easton White Distinguished Teacher Award by the American Society for Metals International (2000).

Dr. Steven R. Schmid is an Associate Professor in the Department of Aerospace and Mechanical Engineering at the University of Notre Dame, where he teaches and conducts research in manufacturing, machine design, and tribology. As the Director of the Manufacturing Tribology Laboratory at the university, he oversees industry and governmentally funded research on a wide variety of manufacturing topics, including tribological issues in rolling, forging and sheet metal forming, polymer processing, medical device design and manufacture, and nanomechanics.

He received his Bachelor's degree in Mechanical Engineering from the Illinois Institute of Technology (with Honors) and Master's and Ph.D. degrees, both in Mechanical Engineering, from Northwestern University. Dr. Schmid has received numerous awards, including the John T. Parsons Award from the Society of Manufacturing Engineers (2000), the Newkirk Award from the American Society of Mechanical Engineers (2000), and the Kaneb Center Teaching Award (2000). He is the recipient of a National Science Foundation (NSF) CAREERS Award (1996) and an ALCOA Foundation Award (1994).

He is the author of over thirty technical papers in various journals, has edited three conference proceedings, has co-authored "Fundamentals of Machine Elements," and has contributed two chapters to the CRC "Handbook of Modern Tribology." He serves on the Tribology Division Executive Committee of the American Society of Mechanical Engineers, and has held officer positions in the Society of Manufacturing Engineers and the Society of Tribology and Lubrication Engineers. He is a registered Professional Engineer and a Certified Manufacturing Engineer.

General Introduction

I.1 WHAT IS MANUFACTURING?

As you begin to read this Introduction, take a few moments and inspect various objects around you: your pen, watch, calculator, telephone, chair, and light fixtures. You will soon realize that all these objects had a different shape at one time. You could not find them in nature as they appear in your room. They have been transformed from various raw materials and assembled into the shapes that you now see.

Some objects are made of a single part, such as nails, bolts, wire or plastic coat hangers, metal brackets, and forks. However, most objects, such as aircraft jet engines (invented in 1939; Fig. I.1), ball-point pens (1938), toasters (1926), washing machines (1910), air conditioners (1928), refrigerators (1931), photocopiers (1949), all types of machines, and thousands of other products are constructed by the assembly of a number of parts made from a variety of materials, as the following list indicates. All of the products mentioned are made by various processes that we call manufacturing.

1

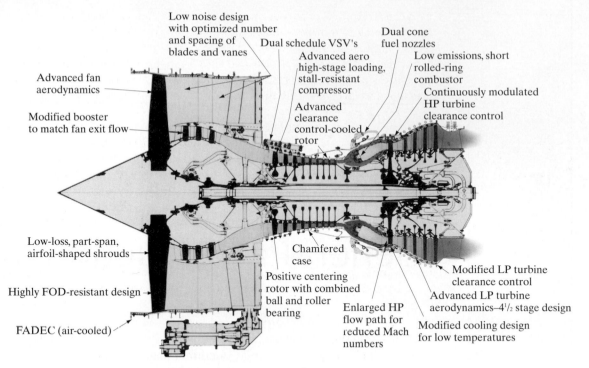

Advanced fan aerodynamics

Modified booster to match fan exit flow

Low noise design with optimized number and spacing of blades and vanes

Dual schedule VSV's

Advanced aero high-stage loading, stall-resistant compressor

Advanced clearance control-cooled rotor

Dual cone fuel nozzles

Low emissions, short rolled-ring combustor

Continuously modulated HP turbine clearance control

Low-loss, part-span, airfoil-shaped shrouds

Chamfered case

Highly FOD-resistant design

Positive centering rotor with combined ball and roller bearing

Enlarged HP flow path for reduced Mach numbers

Modified LP turbine clearance control

Advanced LP turbine aerodynamics–4½ stage design

Modified cooling design for low temperatures

FADEC (air-cooled)

FIGURE I.1   Cross-sectional view of a jet engine, showing various components. Many of the materials used in this engine must maintain their strength and resist oxidation at high temperatures. *Source*: Courtesy of General Electric Company.

Product	Number of parts
Rotary lawn mower	300
Grand piano	12,000
Automobile	15,000
C-5A transport plane	>4,000,000
Boeing 747–400	>6,000,000

Manufacturing, in its broadest sense, is the process of converting raw materials into products. It encompasses (1) the design of the product, (2) the selection of raw materials, and (3) the sequence of processes through which the product will be manufactured.

Manufacturing is the backbone of any industrialized nation. Its importance is emphasized by the fact that, as an economic activity, it comprises approximately 20% to 30% of the value of all goods and services produced. A country's level of manufacturing activity is directly related to its economic health. Generally, the higher the level of manufacturing activity in a country, the higher the standard of living of its people.

Manufacturing also involves activities in which the manufactured product is itself used to make other products. Examples of these products are large presses to shape sheet metal for car bodies, machinery to make bolts and nuts, and sewing machines for making clothing. An equally important aspect of manufacturing activities is the servicing and maintenance of this machinery during its useful life.

The word *manufacturing* is derived from the Latin *manu factus*, meaning made by hand. The word manufacture first appeared in 1567, and the word manufacturing appeared in 1683. In the modern sense, manufacturing involves making products from raw materials by means of various processes, machinery, and operations, through a well-organized plan for each activity required. The word *product* means something that is produced, and the words product and production first appeared sometime during the 15th century.

The word *production* is often used interchangeably with the word manufacturing. Whereas **manufacturing engineering** is the term used widely in the United States to describe this area of industrial activity, the equivalent term in other countries is **production engineering**.

Because a manufactured item has undergone a number of processes in which pieces of raw material have been turned into a useful product, it has a **value**—defined as monetary worth or marketable price. For example, as the raw material for ceramics, clay has a certain value as mined. When the clay is used to make a ceramic cutting tool or electrical insulator, value is added to the clay. Similarly, a wire coat hanger or a nail has a value over and above the cost of the piece of wire from which it is made. Thus manufacturing has the important function of *adding value*.

Manufacturing may produce **discrete products**, meaning individual parts, or **continuous products**. Nails, gears, balls for bearings, beverage cans, and engine blocks are examples of discrete parts, even though they are mass produced at high production rates. On the other hand, a spool of wire, a sheet of metal or plastic, and lengths of tubing, hose, and pipe are continuous products, which may be cut into individual pieces and thus become discrete parts.

Manufacturing is generally a complex activity involving a wide variety of resources and activities, such as the following:

• Product design	• Purchasing	• Marketing
• Machinery and tooling	• Manufacturing	• Sales
• Process planning	• Production control	• Shipping
• Materials	• Support services	• Customer service

Manufacturing activities must be responsive to several demands and trends:

1. A product must fully meet **design requirements** and **product specifications** and **standards**.

2. A product must be manufactured by the most **environmentally friendly** and **economical** methods.

3. **Quality** must be *built* into the product at each stage, from design to assembly, rather than tested in after the product is made. Furthermore, the level of quality should be appropriate to the product's use.

4. In a highly competitive environment, production methods must be **flexible** enough to respond to changes in market demands, types of products, production rates, production quantities, and on-time delivery requirements.

5. New developments in **materials**, **production methods**, and **computer integration** of both technological and managerial activities in a manufacturing organization must constantly be evaluated with a view to their appropriate, timely, and economical implementation.

6. Manufacturing activities must be viewed as a large **system**, the parts of which are interrelated. Such systems can now be modeled, in order to study the effect of factors such as changes in market demands, product design, and materials. Various other factors and production methods affect product quality and cost.

7. A manufacturing organization must constantly strive for higher levels of **quality** and **productivity** (defined as the optimum use of all its resources: materials, machines, energy, capital, labor, and technology). Output per employee per hour in all phases must be maximized. Zero-based part rejection (and consequent reduction of waste) are also an integral aspect of productivity.

I.1.1 A Brief History of Manufacturing

Although it is difficult to be more precise, manufacturing dates back to about 5000–4000 B.C. It is older than recorded history, because primitive cave or rock markings and drawings were dependent on some form of brush or marker using a "paint," or a means of notching the rock; appropriate tools had to be made for these applications. Manufacturing of products for various uses began with the production of articles made of wood, ceramic, stone, and metal (Table I.1). The materials and processes first used to shape products by casting and hammering have been gradually developed over the centuries, using new materials and more complex operations, at increasing rates of production and at higher levels of quality.

TABLE I.1 Historical Development of Materials and Manufacturing Processes

	Period	Casting processes	Forming processes
Egypt: ~3100 B.C. to ~300 B.C. / Greece: ~1100 B.C. to ~146 B.C. / Roman empire: ~500 B.C. to ~476 A.D. / Middle ages: ~476 to 1492 / Renaissance: 14th to 16th centuries	Before 4000 B.C.	Gold, copper, meteoritic iron	Hammering
	4000–3000 B.C.	Copper casting, stone and metal molds, lost wax process, silver, lead, tin, bronze	Stamping, jewelry
	3000–2000 B.C.	Bronze casting	Wire by cutting sheet and drawing; gold leaf
	2000–1000 B.C.	Wrought iron, brass	
	1000–1 B.C.	Cast iron, cast steel	Stamping of coins
	1–1000 A.D.	Zinc, steel	Armor, coining, forging, steel swords
	1000–1500	Blast furnace, type metals, casting of bells, pewter	Wire drawing, gold and silver smith work
	1500–1600	Cast iron cannon, tinplate	Water power for metalworking, rolling mill for coinage strips
Industrial revolution: ~1750 to 1850	1600–1700	Permanent mold castings, brass from copper and metallic zinc	Rolling (lead, gold, silver), shape rolling (lead)
	1700–1800	Malleable cast iron, crucible steel	Extrusion (lead pipe), deep drawing, rolling (iron bars and rods)
	1800–1900	Centrifugal casting, Bessemer process, electrolytic aluminum, nickel steels, babbitt, galvanized steel, powder metallurgy, tungsten steel, open-hearth steel	Steam hammer, steel rolling, seamless tube piercing, steel rail rolling, continuous rolling, electroplating
WWI	1900–1920		Tube rolling, hot extrusion
WWII	1920–1940	Die casting	Tungsten wire from powder
	1940–1950	Lost wax for engineering parts	Extrusion (steel), swaging, powder metals for engineering parts
	1950–1960	Ceramic mold, nodular iron, semiconductors, continuous casting	Cold extrusion (steel), explosive forming, thermomechanical treatment
Space age	1960–1970	Squeeze casting, single crystal turbine blades	Hydrostatic extrusion; electroforming
	1970–2000	Compacted graphite, vacuum casting, organically bonded sand, automation of molding and pouring, rapid solidification technology, metal-matrix composites, semisolid metalworking, rheocasting	Precision forging, isothermal forging, super-plastic forming, dies made by computer-aided design and manufacturing, rapid prototyping, net-shape forming

Source: After J. A. Schey, C.S. Smith, R.F. Tylecote, T.K. Derry, T.I. Williams, and S. Kalpakjian.

The first materials used for making household utensils and ornamental objects included metals such as gold, copper, and iron, followed by silver, lead, tin, bronze, and brass. The production of steel in about 600–800 A.D. was a major development. Since then, a wide variety of ferrous and nonferrous metals have been developed. Today, the materials used in advanced products such as computers and supersonic aircraft include engineered or tailor-made materials with unique properties, such as ceramics, reinforced plastics, composite materials, and specially alloyed metals.

Until the Industrial Revolution, which began in England in the 1750s, goods had been produced in batches, with much reliance on manual labor in all aspects of production. Modern mechanization began in England and Europe with the development of textile machinery

Joining processes	Tools, machining, and manufacturing systems	Nonmetallic materials and composites
	Tools of stone, flint, wood, bone, ivory, composite tools	Earthenware, glazing, natural fibers
Soldering (Cu-Au, Cu-Pb, Pb-Sn)	Corundum	
Riveting, brazing	Hoe making, hammered axes, tools for ironmaking and carpentry	Glass beads, potter's wheel, glass vessels
Forge welding of iron and steel, gluing	Improved chisels, saws, files, woodworking lathes	Glass pressing and blowing
	Etching of armor	Venetian glass
	Sandpaper, windmill-driven saw	Crystal glass
	Hand lathe (wood)	Cast plate glass, flint glass
	Boring, turning, screw cutting lathe, drill press	Porcelain
	Shaping, milling, copying lathe for gunstocks; turret lathe; universal milling machine; vitrified grinding wheel	Window glass from slit cylinder, light bulb, vulcanization, rubber processing, polyester, styrene, celluloid, rubber extrusion, molding
Oxyacetylene; arc, electrical resistance, and Thermit welding	Geared lathe, automatic screw machine, hobbing, high-speed steel tools, aluminum oxide and silicon carbide (synthetic)	Automatic bottle making, Bakelite, borosilicate glass
Coated electrodes	Tungsten carbide, mass production, transfer machines	Development of plastics, casting, molding, PVC, cellulose acetate, polyethylene, glass fibers
Submerged arc welding		Acrylics, synthetic, rubber, epoxies, photosensitive glass
Gas metal—arc, gas tungsten—arc, and electroslag welding; explosive welding	Electrical and chemical machining, automatic control	ABS, silicones, fluorocarbons, polyurethane, float glass, tempered glass, glass ceramics
Plasma arc and electron beam, adhesive bonding	Titanium carbide, synthetic diamond, numerical control	Acetals, polycarbonates, cold forming of plastics, reinforced plastics, filament winding
Laser beam, diffusion bonding (also combined with superplastic forming)	Cubic boron nitride, coated tools, diamond turning, ultraprecision machining, computer integrated manufacturing, industrial robots, flexible manufacturing systems, untended factory	Adhesives, composite materials, optical fibers, structural ceramics, ceramic components for automotive and aerospace engines, ceramic-matrix composites

and of machine tools for cutting metals. This technology soon moved to the United States, where it was developed further, including the important advance of designing, making, and using **interchangeable parts**. Prior to the introduction of interchangeable parts, a great deal of hand-fitting was necessary, because no two parts were made exactly alike. By contrast, we now take for granted that we can replace a broken bolt of a certain size with an identical one purchased years later from a local hardware store.

Further developments soon followed, resulting in numerous products that we cannot imagine being without, because they are so common. Since the early 1940s, major milestones have been reached in all aspects of manufacturing. For example, note from Table 1 the progress made during the past 100 years, and especially during the last two decades with the advent of the computer age, as compared to that during the long period from 4000 B.C. to 1 B.C.

Although the Romans had factories for mass-producing glassware, manufacturing methods were at first very primitive and generally very slow, with much manpower involved in handling parts and running the machinery. Today, with the help of **computer-integrated manufacturing** systems, production methods have been advanced to such an extent that, for example, holes in sheet metal are punched at rates of 800 per minute and aluminum beverage cans are manufactured at rates of 500 per minute.

I.2 EXAMPLES OF MANUFACTURED PRODUCTS

In this section we review briefly the planning and procedures involved in designing and manufacturing some common products. Our purpose is to identify the important factors involved and, with specific examples, to show how intimately design and manufacturing are interrelated.

I.2.1 Paper Clips

The paper clip as we know it today was developed by a Norwegian, Johan Vaaler, who received a U.S. patent in 1901.

Assume that you are asked to design and produce paper clips. What type of material would you choose to make this product? Does it have to be metallic or can it be nonmetallic, such as plastic? If you choose a metal, what kind of metal? If the material that you start with is wire, what should be its diameter? Should it be round or have some other cross-section? Is the wire's surface finish and appearance important, and, if so, what should be its roughness?

How would you take a piece of wire and shape it into a paper clip? Would you do it by hand on a simple fixture, or, if not, what kind of machine would you design or purchase to make paper clips? If, as the owner of a company, you were given an order for 100 paper clips versus one for a million clips, would your approach to manufacturing be different?

The paper clip must meet its basic functional requirement: to hold pieces of paper together with sufficient clamping force so that the papers do not slip away from each other. It must be designed properly, especially in shape and size. The design process is based partly on our knowledge of the strength of materials and of the mechanics of solids.

The material selected for a paper clip must have a certain stiffness and strength. For example, if the stiffness (a measure of how much it deflects under a given force) is too high, a level of force uncomfortable to or inconvenient for users may be required to open the clip, just as a stiff spring requires a greater force to stretch or compress it than does a softer spring. If the stiffness is, on the other hand, too low, the clip will not exert enough clamping force on the papers. Furthermore, if the yield stress of the material (the stress required to cause permanent deformation) is too low, the clip will bend permanently during its normal use and will be difficult to reuse. Therefore, the choice of the basic material is important.

The stiffness and strength depend also on the diameter of the wire and on the design of the clip. Included in the design process are considerations such as style, appearance, and surface finish (or texture) of the clip. Note, for example, that some clips have serrated surfaces, for better clamping.

After finalizing the design, a suitable material has to be selected. Material selection requires a knowledge of the **function** and **service requirements** of the product, and it leads to choosing materials that, preferably, are commercially available, to fulfill these requirements at the lowest possible cost. The selection of the material also involves consideration of its corrosion resistance, because the clip is handled often and is subjected to moisture and other environmental attacks. Note, for example, the rust marks left by paper clips on documents stored in files for a long period of time.

Many questions concerning the production of the paper clips must be asked. Will the material selected be able to undergo bending during manufacturing, without cracking or breaking? Can the wire be easily cut from a long piece, without causing excessive wear on the tooling? Will the cutting process produce a smooth edge on the wire, or will it leave a burr (a sharp edge)? (A burr is undesirable in the use of paper clips since it may tear the paper or even cut the user's finger.)

Finally, what is the most economical method of manufacturing this part at the desired production rate, so that it can be competitive in the national and international marketplace and the manufacturer can make a profit? A suitable manufacturing method and suitable tools, machinery, and related equipment must then be selected to shape the wire into a paper clip.

I.2.2 Incandescent Light Bulbs

The first incandescent lamp was made by T.A. Edison (1847–1931); it was lit in 1879. Many improvements have since been made in the materials and manufacturing methods for making bulbs. The components of a typical light bulb are shown in Fig. I.2. The light-emitting part is the filament, which, by the passage of current through its electrical resistance, is heated to incandescence, that is, to temperatures between 2200 °C and 3000 °C (4000 °F and 5400 °F). Edison's first successful lamp had a carbon filament, although he and others had also tried

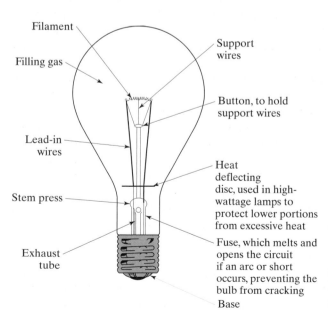

FIGURE I.2   Components of an incandescent light bulb. *Source*: Courtesy of General Electric Company.

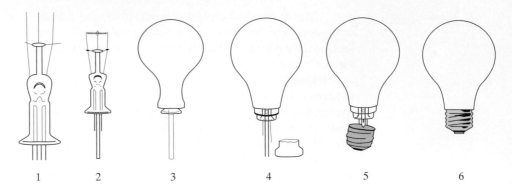

1   2   3   4   5   6

FIGURE I.3 Manufacturing steps in making a light bulb (see text for details).
Source: Courtesy of General Electric Company.

various other materials such as carbonized paper, osmium, iridium, and tantalum. However, none of these materials has the strength, high-temperature resistance, and long life of tungsten (Section 6.8), which is now the most commonly used filament material.

The first step in manufacturing a light bulb is making the glass stem, which supports the lead-in wires and the filament and connects them to the base of the bulb (Fig. I. 3). These parts are positioned, assembled, and sealed while the glass is heated by gas flames. The filament is then attached to the lead-in wires. These and other operations in the making of bulbs are performed on highly automated machines at rates of 1000 a minute or higher.

The completed stem assembly (the mount) is then transferred to a machine that lowers a glass bulb over it. Gas flames are used to seal the rim of the mount to the neck of the bulb. The air in the bulb is exhausted through the exhaust tube (an integral part of the glass stem), and then the bulb is either evacuated or filled with inert gas. For bulbs of 40 W and above, the gas is typically a mixture of nitrogen and argon. The exhaust tube is then sealed off.

The last production step consists of attaching the base to the bulb, using a special cement. The machine that does the attaching also solders or welds (Part V) the lead-in wires to the metal base for electrical connection.

The filament is made by first pressing tungsten powder into ingots and *sintering* it (heating without melting; Section 17.4). The ingot is then shaped into round rods by swaging, and the rods are drawn through a die, in a number of steps, into thin wire (Section 15.10). The wire is coiled to increase the light-producing capacity of the filament. The wire diameter for a 60-W, 120-V lamp is 0.045 mm (0.0018 in.), and it must be controlled very accurately. If the wire diameter is only 1% less than that specified, the life of the lamp may be reduced by as much as 25%. The spacing between coils must also be very accurate, in order to prevent localized heat concentration and possible shorting.

Lead-in wires are usually made of nickel, copper, or molybdenum, and support wires are made of molybdenum (Section 6.8). The portion of the lead-in wire embedded in the stem is made of an alloy of iron and nickel, coated with copper, and has essentially the same coefficient of thermal expansion as does the glass (Chapters 3 and 8). In this way, thermal stresses that otherwise might cause the stem to crack are not developed. The base is generally made from aluminum, specially lubricated to permit easy insertion into the socket.

The glass bulbs are commonly made by blowing molten glass into a mold (Section 17.10). Several types of glasses are used, depending on the kind of bulb desired. The inside of the bulb is either frosted, to reduce glare and diffuse the light better, or plain. The filling gas should be pure; otherwise the inside surfaces of the bulb will blacken. For example, just one drop of water in the gas used for half a million lamps will cause blackening in all of them.

I.2.3 Jet Engines

Compared with the preceding examples, designing and manufacturing a jet engine (Fig. I.1) is a much more challenging and demanding task. We present this figure merely to point out the complexity of this important product, which—depending on its size and capacity—costs up to many millions of dollars and constitutes approximately 20% of the cost of a typical commercial aircraft. Selection of materials and processes, inspection and testing, and quality control are particularly critical for this engine because of the need for very high reliability. Failure of any of the major components in this engine can be catastrophic.

The diverse examples described above show us that each of the manufacturing operations requires thought processes that are common to all manufacture. In the following sections, we present an overview of the important interrelationships among product design, material selection, and manufacturing processes. The end result should be a product that:

a. meets the customer's quality standards and expected service requirements,

b. can be produced with zero-based rejection and waste, and

c. is economical to produce in an increasingly global and competitive marketplace.

I.3 THE DESIGN PROCESS AND CONCURRENT ENGINEERING

The design process for a product first requires a clear understanding of the **functions** and the **performance** expected of that product. The product may be new, or it may be a revised version of an existing product. We all have observed, for example, how the design and style of radios, toasters, watches, automobiles, and washing machines have changed.

The market for a product and its anticipated uses must be defined clearly, with the assistance of sales personnel, market analysts, and others in the organization. Product design is a critical activity because it has been estimated that 70% to 80% of the cost of product development and manufacture is determined by the decisions made in the initial design stages.

Traditionally, design and manufacturing activities have taken place sequentially rather than concurrently or simultaneously (Fig. I.4a). Designers would spend considerable effort and time in analyzing components and preparing detailed part drawings; these drawings would then be forwarded to other departments in the organization, such as materials departments, where, for example, particular alloys and vendor sources would be identified.

The specifications would then be sent to a manufacturing department, where the detailed drawings would be reviewed and processes selected for efficient production. While this approach seems logical and straightforward in theory, it has been found in practice to be extremely wasteful of resources.

In theory, a product can flow from one department in an organization to another and then directly to the marketplace, but in practice there are usually difficulties encountered. For example, a manufacturing engineer may wish to taper the flange on a part to improve its castability or may decide that a different alloy is desirable; such changes necessitate a repeat of the design analysis stage, in order to ensure that the product will still function satisfactorily. These iterations, also shown in Fig. I.4a, certainly waste resources, but, more importantly, they waste time.

There is a great desire, originally driven by the consumer electronics industry, to bring products to market as quickly as possible. The rationale is that products introduced early enjoy a greater percentage of the market and hence greater profits, and that they have a longer life before obsolescence (clearly a concern with consumer electronics). For these reasons, **concurrent engineering**, also called **simultaneous engineering**, has come to the fore.

(a)   (b)

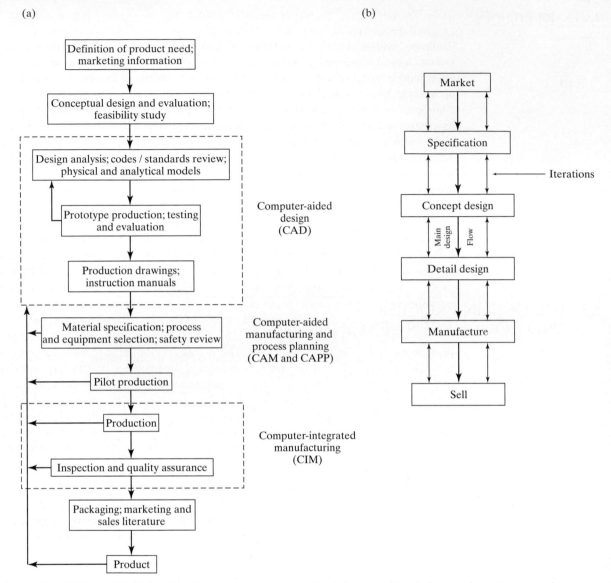

FIGURE I.4   (a) Chart showing various steps involved in designing and manufacturing a product. Depending on the complexity of the product and the type of materials used, the time span between the original concept and the marketing of a product may range from a few months to many years. (b) Chart showing general product flow, from market analysis to selling the product, and depicting concurrent engineering. *Source*: After S. Pugh, *Total Design*. Addison-Wesley, 1991.

A more modern product-development approach is shown in Fig. I.4b. While it still has a general product flow from market analysis to design to manufacturing, it contains deliberate iterations. The main difference from the older approach is that all disciplines are involved in the early design stages, so that the iterations which by nature occur result in less wasted effort and less lost time. A key to the new approach is the now well-recognized importance of *communication* between and within disciplines. That is, while there must be communication between engineering, marketing, and service functions, so too must there be avenues of interaction between engineering sub-disciplines—for example, design for manufacture, design recyclability, and design for safety.

The design process begins with the development of an original product concept. An innovative approach to design is highly desirable at this stage—even essential—for the product to be successful in the marketplace. Innovative approaches can also lead to major savings in material and production costs. The design engineer or product designer must be knowledgeable about the interrelationships among materials, design, and manufacturing, as well as about the overall economics of the operation.

Concurrent engineering is a systematic approach integrating the design and manufacture of products, with a view toward optimizing all elements involved in the **life cycle** of the product. Life cycle means that all aspects of a product, such as design, development, production, distribution, use, disposal, and recycling, are considered simultaneously. The basic goals of concurrent engineering are to reduce changes in a product's design and engineering and to reduce the time and costs involved in taking the product from its design concept to its production and its introduction into the marketplace.

The philosophy of life-cycle engineering requires that the entire life of a product be considered in the design stage: The design, production, distribution, use, and disposal/ recycling must be considered simultaneously. Thus a well-designed product is functional (design), well-manufactured (production), well-packaged (so that it arrives safely at the end user or customer—distribution), durable (functions effectively for its intended life) and maintainable (has components which can be easily replaced, maintained, or repaired—use), and resource-efficient (can be disassembled so that components can be recycled—disposal).

Although this textbook emphasizes the production aspects of a product's life cycle, the need for integration of multiple disciplines in product development pervades the life-cycle. For example, disposal is best addressed during product development, by selecting materials that are easily recyclable. Further, each of these requirements demands new skills from the product development team, and so each demands the application of concurrent engineering.

Although the concept of concurrent engineering appears to be logical and efficient, its implementation can involve considerable time and effort when those using it either do not work as a team or fail to appreciate its real benefits. It is apparent that, for concurrent engineering to succeed, it must:

   a. have the full support of the upper management;

   b. have multifunctional and interactive teamwork, including support groups; and

   c. utilize all available technologies.

There are numerous examples of the benefits of concurrent engineering. One automotive company, for example, has reduced the number of components in one of its engines by 30%, and as a result has decreased that engine's weight by 25% and cut its manufacturing time by 50%. The concurrent-engineering concept can be implemented in companies both large and small, an applicability particularly noteworthy in view of the fact that 98% of U.S. manufacturing establishments have fewer than 500 employees.

For companies both large and small, product design often involves preparing *analytical and physical models* of the product, as an aid to studying factors such as forces, stresses, deflections, and optimal part shape. The necessity for such models depends on product complexity. Today, constructing and studying analytical models is simplified through the use of **computer-aided design (CAD), engineering (CAE), and manufacturing (CAM)** techniques.

Computer-aided design (Section 39.4) allows the designer to conceptualize objects more easily without having to make costly illustrations, models, or prototypes. CAD systems are now capable of rapidly and completely analyzing designs, from a simple bracket to complex structures. The two-engine Boeing 777 passenger airplane, for example, was designed completely by computer (*paperless design*), with 2000 workstations linked to eight design servers. Unlike previous models, the airplane is constructed directly from the CAD/CAM software developed, and no prototypes or mockups are built.

Using **computer-aided engineering**, the performance of structures subjected to static or fluctuating loads and to varying temperatures can now be simulated, analyzed, and tested more efficiently, accurately, and quickly than ever. The information developed can be stored, retrieved, displayed, printed, and transferred anywhere in the organization. Designs can be optimized, and modifications can be made, directly and easily, at any time.

Computer-aided manufacturing (Section 39.5) involves all phases of manufacturing, by utilizing and processing further the large amount of information on materials and processes collected and stored in the organization's database. Computers now assist manufacturing engineers and their associates in organizing such tasks as: programming numerical control of machines; programming robots for material handling and assembly; designing tools, dies, and fixtures; and maintaining quality control.

On the basis of the models developed using the foregoing techniques, the product designer selects and specifies the final shape and dimensions of the product, its dimensional accuracy and surface finish, and its component materials. Often, the selection of materials is made with the advice and cooperation of materials engineers, unless the design engineer is also experienced and qualified in this area. An important design consideration is how a particular component is to be assembled into the final product. Lift the hood of your car and observe how hundreds of components are fitted into a limited space.

The next step in the production process is to make and test a **prototype**, that is, an original working model of the product. An important recent development is **rapid prototyping** (**RP**; Chapter 19), which relies on CAD/CAM and on various manufacturing techniques (using metallic or nonmetallic materials) to produce prototypes rapidly, in the form of a solid physical model of a part, and at low cost. For example, prototyping new automotive components by traditional methods such as shaping, forming, and machining costs hundreds of millions of dollars a year; some components may take a year to produce. Rapid prototyping can cut these costs (and the associated development times) significantly. These techniques are being advanced further, so that they can be used for low-volume economical production of actual parts.

Tests of prototypes must be designed to simulate as closely as possible the conditions under which the product is to be used. These conditions include environmental factors (such as temperature and humidity) and the effects of vibration and of repeated use (and misuse) of the product. Computer-aided engineering techniques are now capable of performing such simulations comprehensively and rapidly.

During testing of prototypes, modifications in the original design, materials, or production methods may be necessary. After this phase has been completed, appropriate process plans, manufacturing methods (Table I.2), equipment, and tooling are selected, with the cooperation of manufacturing engineers, process planners, and others involved in production.

Overdesign.   Surveys have indicated that many products in the past have been overdesigned—that is, they were either too bulky, made of materials too high in quality, or made with precision and quality unwarranted for the intended uses. Overdesign may result from uncertainties in design calculations or from concern by the designer and manufacturer about product safety, in order to avoid user injuries or deaths and resulting product-liability lawsuits. Many designs are based on past experience and intuition, rather than on thorough analysis and experimentation.

Overdesign can add significantly to a product's cost. It must be pointed out, however, that this entire subject is somewhat controversial. From the consumer's standpoint, an automobile, washing machine, or lawnmower that operates satisfactorily for many years without needing repairs or part replacement may be a good product despite a high initial price.

TABLE I.2 Shapes and Some Common Methods of Production

Shape or feature	Production method
Flat surfaces	Rolling, planing, broaching, milling, shaping, grinding
Parts with cavities	End milling, electrical-discharge machining, electrochemical machining, ultrasonic machining, casting
Parts with sharp features	Permanent-mold casting, machining, grinding, fabricating, powder metallurgy
Thin hollow shapes	Slush casting, electroforming, fabricating
Tubular shapes	Extrusion, drawing, roll forming, spinning, centrifugal casting
Tubular parts	Rubber forming, expanding with hydraulic pressure, explosive forming, spinning
Curvature on thin sheets	Stretch forming, peen forming, fabricating, assembly
Openings in thin sheets	Blanking, chemical blanking, photochemical blanking
Cross-sections	Drawing, extruding, shaving, turning, centerless grinding
Square edges	Fine blanking, machining, shaving, belt grinding
Small holes	Laser, electrical-discharge machining, electrochemical machining
Surface textures	Knurling, wire brushing, grinding, belt grinding, shot blasting, etching, deposition
Detailed surface features	Coining, investment casting, permanent-mold casting, machining
Threaded parts	Thread cutting, thread rolling, thread grinding, chasing
Very large parts	Casting, forging, fabricating, assembly
Very small parts	Investment casting, machining, etching, powder metallurgy, nanofabrication, micromachining

In an expanding global and competitive marketplace, manufacturers are sensitive to the public image of their products. In fact, some products that require infrequent repair, such as washers, dryers, and automobiles, have been advertised in the public media as having that characteristic. Many manufacturers believe, nonetheless, that if a product functions well for an extended period of time, it may have been overdesigned. In such cases, the company may consider downgrading the materials and/or the processes used.

I.4 DESIGN FOR MANUFACTURE, ASSEMBLY, DISASSEMBLY, AND SERVICE

As we have seen, design and manufacturing must be intimately *interrelated*; they should never be viewed as separate disciplines or activities. Each part or component of a product must be designed so that it not only meets design requirements and specifications, but also can be manufactured economically and efficiently. This approach improves productivity and allows a manufacturer to remain competitive.

This broad view has become recognized as the area of **design for manufacture (DFM)**. It is a comprehensive approach to production of goods, and it integrates the design process with materials, manufacturing methods, process planning, assembly, testing, and quality assurance. Effectively implementing design for manufacture requires that designers have a fundamental understanding of the characteristics, capabilities, and limitations of materials, manufacturing processes and related operations, machinery, and equipment. This knowledge includes such characteristics as: variability in machine performance, in dimensional accuracy, and in surface finish of the workpiece; processing time; and the effect of processing method on part quality.

Designers and product engineers must be able to assess the impact of design modifications on manufacturing-process selection and on assembly, inspection, tools and dies, and product cost. Establishing quantitative relationships is essential in order to optimize the design for ease of manufacturing and assembly at minimum product cost (a concept called *producibility*).

Computer-aided design, engineering, manufacturing, and process-planning techniques, using powerful computer programs, have become indispensable to those conducting such analysis. New developments include **expert systems**, which have optimization capabilities and so can expedite the traditional iterative process in design optimization.

After individual parts have been manufactured, they have to be assembled into a product. **Assembly** is an important phase of the overall manufacturing operation and requires consideration of the ease, speed, and cost of putting parts together. Also, many products must be designed so that **disassembly** is possible, in order to enable the product to be taken apart for maintenance, servicing, or recycling of its components.

Because assembly operations can contribute significantly to product cost, **design for assembly (DFA)** as well as **design for disassembly** are now recognized as important aspects of manufacturing. Typically, a product that is easy to assemble is also easy to disassemble. The latest trend now includes **design for service**, the goal of which is that individual parts or sub-assemblies in a product be easy to reach and service.

Methodologies and computer software have been developed for DFA, utilizing 3-D conceptual designs and solid models. By their use, subassembly and assembly times and costs are minimized while product integrity and performance are maintained; the system also improves the product's ease of disassembly. The trend now is to combine design for manufacture and design for assembly into the more comprehensive **design for manufacture and assembly (DFMA)** which recognizes the inherent interrelationship between the manufacturing of components and their assembly into a final product.

There are several methods of assembly (for example, by using fasteners or adhesives, or by welding, soldering, and brazing), each with its own characteristics and each requiring different operations. The use of a bolt and nut, for example, requires preparation of holes that must match in location and size. Hole generation, in turn, requires such operations as drilling or punching, which take additional time, require separate operations, and produce scrap. On the other hand, products assembled with bolts and nuts can be taken apart and reassembled with relative ease.

Parts can also be assembled with adhesives. This method, which is being used extensively in aircraft and automobile production, does not require holes. However, the surfaces to be assembled must match properly, and they must be clean, because joint strength is adversely affected by the presence of such contaminants as dirt, dust, oil, and moisture. Unlike components mechanically fastened, adhesive-joined components and those that are welded are not usually designed to be taken apart and reassembled; hence, they are not suitable for the important purpose of recycling individual parts in the product.

Parts may be assembled either by hand or by automatic equipment and robots. The choice depends on factors such as the complexity of the product, the number of parts to be assembled, the protection required to prevent damage or scratching of finished surfaces of the parts, and the relative cost of labor compared to that of the machinery required for automated assembly.

1.5 SELECTING MATERIALS

An ever-increasing variety of materials is now available, each having its own characteristics, applications, advantages, and limitations (Part I). The following are the general types of materials used in manufacturing today, either individually or in combination:

- **Ferrous metals:** carbon, alloy, stainless, and tool-and-die steels (Chapter 5).
- **Nonferrous metals:** aluminum, magnesium, copper, nickel, titanium, superalloys, refractory metals, beryllium, zirconium, low-melting alloys, and precious metals (Chapter 6).

- **Plastics:** thermoplastics, thermosets, and elastomers (Chapter 7).
- **Ceramics, glass ceramics, glasses, graphite, diamond, and diamond-like materials** (Chapter 8).
- **Composite materials:** reinforced plastics, metal-matrix and ceramic-matrix composites (Chapter 9). These are also known as **engineered materials**.
- **Nanomaterials, shape-memory alloys, amorphous alloys, superconductors,** and various other new materials with unique properties (Chapter 6).

As new materials are developed, the selection of appropriate materials becomes even more challenging. Aerospace structures and sporting goods have been at the forefront of new-material usage. The trend has been to use more titanium and composites for the airframes of commercial aircraft, with a gradual decline in the use of aluminum and steel. There are continually shifting trends in the usage of materials in all products, trends driven principally by economic considerations, but also by other considerations, as will be described.

I.5.1 Properties of Materials

When selecting materials for products, we first consider their **mechanical properties**: strength, toughness, ductility, hardness, elasticity, fatigue, and creep (Chapter 2). The strength-to-weight and stiffness-to-weight ratios of materials are also important, particularly for aerospace and automotive applications. Aluminum, titanium, and reinforced plastics, for example, have higher such ratios than steels and cast irons. The mechanical properties specified for a product and its components should, of course, be appropriate to the conditions under which the product is expected to function.

We next consider the **physical properties** of materials: density, specific heat, thermal expansion and conductivity, melting point, and electrical and magnetic properties (Chapter 3). **Chemical properties** also play a significant role, both in hostile and in normal environments. Oxidation, corrosion, general degradation of properties, toxicity, and flammability of materials are among the important factors to be considered. In some commercial airline disasters, for example, many deaths have been caused by toxic fumes from burning non-metallic materials in the aircraft cabin.

The manufacturing properties of materials determine whether they can be cast, formed, machined, welded, and heat-treated with relative ease (Table I.3). The method(s) used to process materials to the desired shapes can adversely affect the product's final properties, service life, and cost.

I.5.2 Cost and Availability

Cost and availability of raw and processed materials and of manufactured components are major concerns in manufacturing. The economic aspects of material selection are as important as technological considerations of the properties and characteristics of materials (Chapter 40).

TABLE I.3   General Manufacturing Characteristics of Various Alloys

Alloy	Castability	Weldability	Machinability
Aluminum	E	F	G–E
Copper	F–G	F	F–G
Gray cast iron	E	D	G
White cast iron	G	VP	VP
Nickel	F	F	F
Steels	F	E	F
Zinc	E	D	E

Note: E, excellent; G, good; F, fair; D, difficult; VP, very poor.

If raw or processed materials or manufactured components are not available in the desired shapes, dimensions, and quantities, substitutes and/or additional processing will be required, and they can contribute significantly to product cost. For example, if we need a round bar of a certain diameter, and it is not available in standard form, then we have to purchase a larger rod and reduce its diameter by some means (perhaps machining, drawing through a die, or grinding). It should be noted, however, that often a product design can be modified to take advantage of standard dimensions of raw materials and thus avoid extra manufacturing costs.

Reliability of supply, as well as demand, affects cost. Most countries import numerous raw materials that are essential for production. The United States, for example, imports most of the amount that it uses of each of the following raw materials: natural rubber, diamond, cobalt, titanium, chromium, aluminum, and nickel. The broad political implications of reliance on other countries may be negative.

Different costs are involved in processing materials by different methods. Some methods require expensive machinery, others require extensive labor, and still others require personnel with special skills, a high level of education, or specialized training.

I.5.3 Appearance, Service Life, and Recycling

The appearance of materials after they have been manufactured into products influences their appeal to the consumer. Color, feel, and surface texture are characteristics that we all consider when making a decision about purchasing a product.

Time- and service-dependent phenomena such as wear, fatigue, creep, and dimensional stability are important. These phenomena can significantly affect a product's performance and, if not controlled, can lead to total failure of the product. Similarly, compatibility of materials used in a product is important. Friction and wear, corrosion, and other phenomena can shorten a product's life or cause it to fail prematurely. An example is galvanic corrosion between mating parts made of dissimilar metals.

Recycling of or proper disposal of component materials at the end of a product's useful service life has become increasingly important as we have become increasingly conscious of the need for conserving resources and for maintaining a clean and healthy environment. Note, for example, the use of biodegradable packaging materials and of recyclable glass bottles and aluminum beverage cans. The proper treatment and disposal of toxic wastes and materials is also a crucial consideration.

Example: Material Selection for U.S. Pennies

The materials used by the U.S. Mint to make pennies have undergone significant changes throughout history, mainly because of material shortages and the cost of raw materials. Billions of pennies are minted each year. The following table shows a chronological development of material substitutions in pennies:

1793–1837	100% copper
1837–1857	95% copper, 5% tin and zinc (bronze)
1857–1863	88% copper, 12% nickel (nickel-bronze)
1864–1962	95% copper, 5% tin and zinc (bronze)
1943 (WW II years)	Steel (plated with zinc)
1962–1982	95% copper, 5% zinc (bronze)
1982–present	97.5% zinc, plated with 2.5% copper

Obviously, these materials, or their combinations, need to impart appropriate properties to the pennies during their circulation.

Example: Material Selection for Baseball Bats

Baseball bats for the major leagues are generally made of northern white ash because of its high dimensional stability, elastic modulus, strength-to-weight ratio, and shock resistance and low density. The bats are made on semiautomatic lathes and then subjected to finishing operations. The straight uniform grain required for such bats has become increasingly difficult to find, particularly when the best wood comes from ash trees that are at least 45 years old. Consequently, consideration is being given to using other materials for bats.

For the amateur market, aluminum bats (top portion of Fig. I.5) have been made for some years by various metal-forming techniques, although at first their performance was not as good as that of wooden bats. The technology has been advanced such that aluminum bats are now made from high-strength aluminum tubing and possess desirable weight distribution, center of percussion, and sound and impact dynamics. They are usually filled with polyurethane or cork for sound damping and for controlling the balance of the bat. However, aluminum bats can be sensitive to surface defects due to use, and they usually fail from fatigue due to cyclic loading.

New developments in bat materials include composite materials consisting of high-strength graphite and glass fibers in an epoxy resin matrix (Chapter 9). The inner woven sleeve (lower portion of Fig. I.5) is made of Kevlar fibers, which add strength to and dampen vibrations in the bat. These bats cost about $125 and perform and sound much like wooden bats. *Source*: Mizuno Sports, Inc.

FIGURE I.5
Cross-sections of baseball bats made of aluminum (top portion) and composite material (bottom portion).

I.6 SELECTING MANUFACTURING PROCESSES

Many processes are used to produce parts and shapes (Table I.2), and there is usually more than one method of manufacturing a part from a given material. The broad categories of processing methods for materials are as follows, referenced to a particular part in this text and illustrated with a simple example for each:

    a. Casting: Expendable mold and permanent mold (Part II); Fig. I.6.
    b. Forming and **shaping:** Rolling, forging, extrusion, drawing, sheet forming, powder metallurgy, and molding (Part III); Fig. I.7a-d.

Part

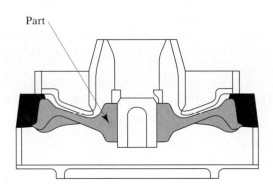

FIGURE I.6   Schematic illustration of a casting operation for a railroad wheel.

FIGURE I.7   Schematic illustrations of various forming processes.

(a)   (b)

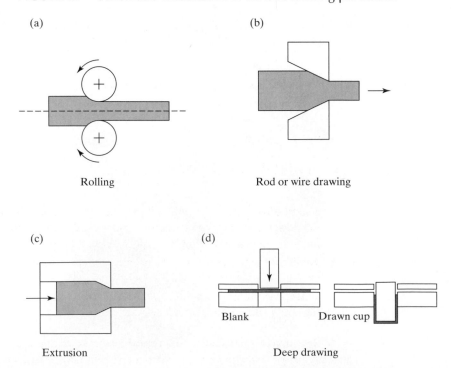

    Rolling   Rod or wire drawing

(c)   (d)

Blank   Drawn cup

    Extrusion   Deep drawing

(a)

Turning

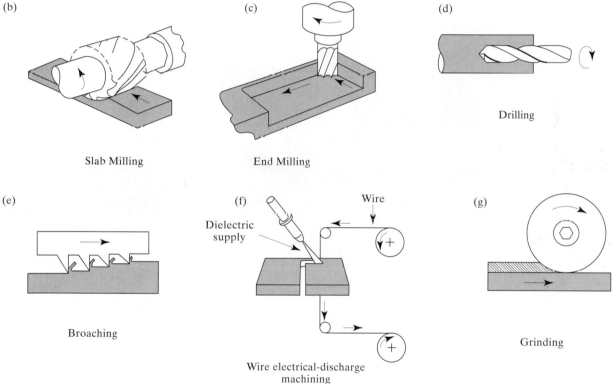

(b)

Slab Milling

(c)

End Milling

(d)

Drilling

(e)

Broaching

(f)

Dielectric
supply

Wire

Wire electrical-discharge
machining

(g)

Grinding

FIGURE I.8   Schematic illustrations of various machining processes.

    c. Machining: Turning, boring, drilling, milling, planing, shaping, broaching, and grinding, ultrasonic machining; chemical, electrical, and electrochemical machining; and high-energy beam machining (Part IV); Fig. I.8a-g.

    d. Joining: Welding, brazing, soldering, diffusion bonding, adhesive bonding, and mechanical joining (Part V); Fig. I.9a-b.

    e. Finishing: Honing, lapping, polishing, burnishing, deburring, surface treating, coating, and plating (Chapters 25 and 33).

    Selection of a particular manufacturing process, or of a sequence of processes, depends not only on the shape to be produced but also on many other factors pertaining to material

(a)

Lap joint

(b)

Butt joint

Joining

FIGURE I.9   Two types of welded joints: (a) lap joint; (b) butt joint.

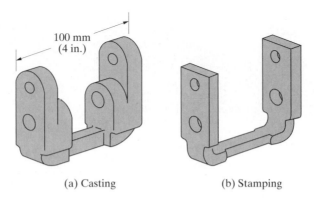

100 mm
(4 in.)

(a) Casting

(b) Stamping

FIGURE I.10   Schematic illustrations of a steel mounting bracket that can be manufactured by casting processes or by stamping processes.

properties (Table 3). Brittle and hard materials, for example, cannot be shaped easily, whereas they can be cast or machined readily by several methods. The manufacturing process usually alters the properties of materials. Metals that are formed at room temperature, for example, become stronger, harder, and less ductile than they were before processing.

Two steel mounting brackets are shown in Fig. I.10, one made by casting, the other by stamping of sheet metal. Note that there are some differences in the designs, although the parts are basically alike. Each of these two manufacturing processes has its own advantages and limitations, as well as production rates and manufacturing cost.

Manufacturing engineers are constantly being challenged to find new solutions to manufacturing problems and cost reduction. For a long time, for example, sheet metal parts were cut and fabricated by traditional tools, punches, and dies. Although the latter are still widely used, some of those operations are now being replaced by laser-cutting techniques (Fig. I.11). With advances in computer technology, we can automatically control the path of the laser, thus increasing the capability for producing a wide variety of shapes accurately, repeatedly, and economically.

Example: Manufacturing a Salt Shaker and Pepper Mill

A commonly used household product is a salt-shaker-and-pepper-mill set. The one shown in Fig. I.12 contains metallic as well as nonmetallic components and is made by various manufacturing processes. The main bodies are made by injection molding (Section 18.3) of a thermoplastic, such as acrylic (Chapter 7), which has transparency and other desirable

FIGURE I.11   Cutting sheet metal with a laser beam. *Source*: Courtesy of Rofin-Sinar, Inc., and *Manufacturing Engineering Magazine*, Society of Manufacturing Engineers.

characteristics and is easy to mold. The top of the salt shaker is made of sheet metal (Chapter 16) and is plated for appearance (Chapter 33). The knob on top of the pepper mill is made by machining (Part IV) and is threaded on the inside to allow for screwing and unscrewing.

A square rod, connecting the top portion of the pepper mill to the two pieces shown at the bottom of the figure, is made by rolling (Chapter 13). The two grinder components are made of 410 stainless steel by powder-metallurgy techniques (Chapter 17); casting or machining them would have been too costly. Note that the materials and processes involved are chosen so as to minimize the cost of these products while still fulfilling design and service requirements.

FIGURE I.12   A salt-shaker-and-pepper-mill set. The two metal pieces (at the bottom) for the pepper mill are made by powder-metallurgy techniques. Reproduced with permission from *Success Stories on P/M Parts*, Metal Powder Industries Federation, Princeton, NJ, 1998.

I.6.1 Dimensional Accuracy and Surface Finish

Size, thickness, and shape complexity of the part have a major bearing on the manufacturing process selected to produce it. Flat parts with thin cross-sections, for example, cannot be cast properly. Complex parts cannot be formed easily and economically, whereas they may be cast or else fabricated from individual pieces.

Tolerances and surface finish obtained in hot-working operations cannot be as good as those obtained in cold-working (room temperature) operations because dimensional changes, warpage, and surface oxidation occur during processing at elevated temperatures. Some casting processes produce a better surface finish than others, because of the different types of mold materials used and their surface finishes.

The sizes and shapes of manufactured products vary widely. For example, the main landing gear for the twin-engine, 400-passenger Boeing 777 jetliner is 4.3 m (14 ft) high, with three axles and six wheels; it is made by forging and machining processes. At the other extreme is the generation of a 0.05-mm (0.002-in.) diameter hole at one end of a 0.35-mm (0.014-in.) diameter needle, using a process called electrical-discharge machining (Section 26.5). The hole is burr-free and has a location accuracy of ± 0.003 mm (0.0001 in.).

Another small-scale manufacturing example is given in Fig. I.13, which shows gears as small as 100 μm (0.004 in.) in diameter. These gears have such possible applications as in microrobots for repairing human cells, in microknives for surgery, and in camera shutters for photography. The gears are made by a special technique involving the electroplating and x-ray etching of metal plates coated with a polymer film. The center hole in these gears is so small that a human hair cannot pass through it. Such small-scale operations are called **nanotechnology** and **nanofabrication** ("nano" meaning one billionth).

Ultraprecision-manufacturing techniques and machinery are now being developed and are coming into more common use. For machining mirrorlike surfaces, for example, the cutting tool is a very sharp diamond tip and the equipment has very high stiffness; it must be operated in a room where the temperature is controlled to within 1 °C. Highly sophisticated techniques such as molecular-beam epitaxy and scanning-tunneling engineering are being implemented to obtain accuracies on the order of the atomic lattice (0.1 nm; 10^{-8} in.).

Human hair

FIGURE I.13 Microscopic gear with a diameter on the order of 100μm, made by a special etching process. *Source*: Courtesy of Wisconsin Center for Applied Microelectronics, University of Wisconsin-Madison.

I.6.2 Operational and Manufacturing Costs

The design and cost of tooling, the lead time required to begin production, and the effect of workpiece material on tool life and die life are major considerations. Depending on a product's size, shape, and expected life, the cost of tooling can be substantial. For example, a set of steel dies for stamping sheet-metal fenders for automobiles may cost about $2 million.

For parts made from expensive materials, the lower the scrap rate, the more economical the production process will be; thus, every attempt should be made toward **zero-base waste**. Because it generates chips, machining may not be more economical than forming operations, all other factors being the same.

Availability of machines and equipment and of operating experience within the manufacturing facility are also important cost factors. If they are not available, some parts may have to be manufactured by outside firms. Automakers, for example, purchase many parts from outside vendors, or they have them made by outside firms according to their specifications.

The number of parts required (quantity) and the required production rate (pieces per hour) are important in determining the processes to be used and the economics of production. Beverage cans or transistors, for example, are consumed in numbers and at rates much higher than are telescopes and ship propellers.

The operation of machinery has significant environmental and safety implications. Some processes adversely affect the environment, such as the use of oil-based lubricants in hot-metalworking processes. Unless properly controlled, such processes can cause air, water, and noise pollution. The safe use of machinery is another important consideration, requiring precautions to eliminate hazards in the workplace.

I.6.3 Consequences of Improper Selection of Materials and Processes

Numerous examples of product failure can be traced to improper selection of material or of manufacturing processes or to improper control of process variables. A component or a product is generally considered to have failed when:

- It stops functioning (e.g., broken shaft, gear, bolt, cable, or turbine blade).
- It does not function properly or perform within required specification limits (e.g., worn bearings, gears, tools, and dies).
- It becomes unreliable or unsafe for further use (e.g., frayed cable in a winch, crack in a shaft, poor connection in a printed-circuit board, or delamination of a reinforced plastic component).

Throughout this text, we will describe the types of failure of a component or product that result from design deficiencies, improper material selection, material defects, manufacturing-induced defects, improper component assembly, and improper product use.

I.6.4 Net-shape Manufacturing

Since not all manufacturing operations produce finished parts, additional operations may be necessary. For example, a forged part may not have the desired dimensions or surface finish; as a result, additional operations such as machining or grinding may be necessary. Likewise, it may be difficult, impossible, or economically undesirable to produce a part with holes using just one manufacturing process, and so a subsequent (additional) process, such as drilling, may be required. Furthermore, the holes produced by a particular manufacturing process may not have the proper roundness, dimensional accuracy, or surface finish, and so they may create a need for an additional operation, such as honing.

Finishing operations can contribute significantly to the cost of a product. Consequently, the trend has been for **net-shape** or **near-net-shape manufacturing**, in which the part is made, in the first operation, as close to the final desired dimensions, tolerances, surface finish, and specifications as possible. Typical examples of such manufacturing methods are near-net-shape forging (Chapter 13) and casting (Chapter 11) of parts, stamped sheet-metal parts (Chapter 16), injection molding of plastics (Chapter 18), and components made by powder-metallurgy techniques (Chapter 17).

I.7 COMPUTER-INTEGRATED MANUFACTURING

The major goals of automation in manufacturing facilities are to integrate various operations so as to improve productivity, to increase product quality and uniformity, to minimize cycle times, and to reduce labor costs. Beginning in the 1940s, automation has accelerated because of rapid advances in control systems for machines and in computer technology.

Few developments in the history of manufacturing have had a more significant impact than computers. Computers are now used in a very broad range of applications, including control and optimization of manufacturing processes, material handling, assembly, automated inspection and testing of products, inventory control, and numerous management activities. Beginning with computer graphics and computer-aided design and manufacturing, the use of computers has been extended to **computer-integrated manufacturing** (**CIM**). Computer-integrated manufacturing is particularly effective because of its capability for making possible:

- responsiveness to rapid changes in market demand and product modification;
- better use of materials, machinery, and personnel, and reduction in inventory;
- better control of production and management of the total manufacturing operation; and
- the manufacture of high-quality products at low cost.

The following is an outline of the major applications of computers in manufacturing (Chapters 38 and 39):

a. **Computer numerical control (CNC).** This is a method of controlling the movements of machine components by direct insertion of coded instructions in the form of numerical data. Numerical control was first implemented in the early 1950s and was a major advance in automation of machines.

b. **Adaptive control (AC).** The parameters in a manufacturing process are adjusted automatically to optimize production rate and product quality and to minimize cost. Parameters such as forces, temperatures, surface finish, and dimensions of the part are monitored constantly. If they move outside the acceptable range, the system adjusts the process variables until the parameters again fall within the acceptable range.

c. **Industrial robots.** Introduced in the early 1960s, industrial robots (Fig. I.14) have been replacing humans in operations that are repetitive, boring, and dangerous, thus reducing the possibility of human error, decreasing variability in product quality, and improving productivity. Robots with sensory-perception capabilities are being developed (*intelligent robots*), with movements that simulate those of humans.

d. **Automated handling of materials.** Computers have made possible highly efficient handling of materials and products in various stages of completion (*work in progress*), such as when being moved from storage to machines or from machine to machine and when at the points of inspection, inventory, and shipment.

FIGURE I.14   Automated spot welding of automobile bodies in a mass production line. *Source*: Courtesy of Ford Motor Company.

e. **Automated** and **robotic assembly systems** are replacing costly assembly by human operators. Products are designed or redesigned so that they can be assembled more easily by machine.

f. **Computer-aided process planning (CAPP).** This tool is capable of improving productivity in a plant by optimizing process plans, reducing planning costs, and improving the consistency of product quality and reliability. Functions such as the estimating of cost and the monitoring of work standards (time required to perform a certain operation) can also be incorporated into the system.

g. **Group technology (GT).** The concept of group technology is that parts can be grouped and produced by classifying them into families, according to similarities in design and similarities in the manufacturing processes employed to produce the part. In this way, part designs and process plans can be standardized, and families of like parts can be produced efficiently and economically.

h. **Just-in-time production (JIT).** The principal of JIT is that supplies are delivered just in time to be used, parts are produced just in time to be made into subassemblies and assemblies, and products are finished just in time to be delivered to the customer. In this way, inventory-carrying costs are low, part defects are detected right away, productivity is increased, and high-quality products are made at low cost.

i. **Cellular manufacturing**. Cellular manufacturing involves workstations, called *manufacturing cells*, usually containing several machines controlled by a central robot, each machine performing a different operation on the part.

j. **Flexible manufacturing systems (FMS).** This methodology integrates manufacturing cells into a large unit, all interfaced with a central computer (Fig. I.15). Flexible manufacturing systems have the highest level of efficiency, sophistication, and productivity among manufacturing systems. Although very costly, they are capable of efficiently producing parts in small runs and of changing manufacturing sequences on different parts quickly; this flexibility enables them to meet rapid changes in market demand for various types of products.

FIGURE I.15   A general view of a flexible manufacturing system, showing several machines (*machining centers*) and an in-line transfer system moving along the aisle. *Source*: Cincinnati Milacron, Inc.

k. **Expert systems.** These are, basically, complex computer programs. They are rapidly developing the capability to perform tasks and solve difficult real-life problems much as human experts would.

l. **Artificial intelligence (AI).** This field involves the use of machines and computers to replace human intelligence. Computer-controlled systems are becoming capable of learning from experience and of making decisions that optimize operations and minimize costs. **Artificial neural networks**, which are designed to simulate the thought processes of the human brain, have the capability of modeling and simulating production facilities, monitoring and controlling manufacturing processes, diagnosing problems in machine performance, conducting financial planning, and managing a company's manufacturing strategy.

m. **Shared manufacturing.** Although large corporations can afford to implement modern technology and take risks, smaller companies generally have difficulty in doing so with their limited personnel, resources, and capital. More recently, the concept of shared manufacturing has been proposed. This would consist of a regional or nationwide network of manufacturing facilities with state-of-the-art equipment for training, for prototype development, and for small-scale production runs, and it would be available to help small companies develop products that compete in the global marketplace.

In view of these advances and their potential, some experts have envisioned the **factory of the future**. Although highly controversial, and viewed as unrealistic by some, this is a system in which production will take place with little or no direct human intervention. The human role is expected to be confined to the supervision, maintenance, and upgrading of machines, computers, and software.

The implementation of some of the modern technologies briefly outlined above requires significant technical and economic expertise, time, and capital investment. Some of the high technology can be applied improperly, or it can be implemented on too large or ambitious a scale, one involving major expenditures with questionable return on investment. In consequence, it is essential to perform a comprehensive assessment of the real and specific needs of a company and of the market for its products, as well as of whether there is good communication among the parties involved, such as the vendors, the suppliers, the technical personnel, and the company's management.

Example: Application of CAD/CAM to Make a Mold for a Plastic Blender Jar

The metal mold used for injection molding of plastic blender jars is made on a CNC milling machine, by use of a ball-nosed end mill, as illustrated in Fig. I.16. The jar is about 230 mm (9 in.) high, and it has a maximum diameter of 127 mm (5 in.). First, a 3-D wire-frame model of the mold is made, as is seen in the photograph on the left, and it is viewed and inspected for various geometric features (see also Section 39.4).

Next, an offset is added to each surface to account for the nose radius of the end mill; the result determines the cutter path, that is, the center of the machine spindle. The NC programming software then executes this cutting program on the CNC milling machine, thereby producing the die cavity with proper dimensions and accuracy. Electrical-discharge machining can be used to make this mold; however, it was found that EDM was about twice as expensive as machining the mold and had less dimensional accuracy. *Source:* Mold Threads Inc., and *Manufacturing Engineering Magazine*, March 1991, Society of Manufacturing Engineers.

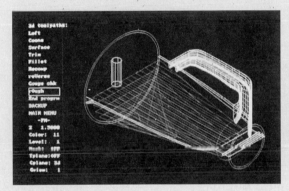 

FIGURE I.16

I.8 QUALITY ASSURANCE AND TOTAL QUALITY MANAGEMENT

We all have used terms like "poor quality" and "good quality" in describing a product. What do we mean by quality? In a broad sense, **quality** (Chapter 36) is a characteristic or property consisting of several well-defined technical (hence objective) and aesthetic (hence subjective) considerations. The general public's perception is that a high-quality product functions reliably and as expected over a long period of time.

Product quality is one of the most important aspects of manufacturing, because it directly influences the marketability of a product before its sale and customer satisfaction afterwards. Traditionally, quality assurance has been obtained by inspecting parts after they have been manufactured. Parts are inspected to ensure that they conform to a detailed set of specifications and standards such as dimensions, surface finish, and mechanical and physical properties.

However, quality cannot be *inspected into* an individual unit of the product after it has been made. The practice of inspecting products after they are made has, therefore, been replaced rapidly by the broader view that *quality must be built into a product*, from the design stage through all subsequent stages of manufacture and assembly. Because products are made by using several manufacturing processes, each of which can have significant variations in its performance even within a short period of time, the control of processes is a critical factor in product quality. Thus, the objective should be to *control processes, not products.*

Producing defective products can be very costly to the manufacturer, creating difficulties in assembly operations, necessitating repairs in the field, and resulting in customer dissatisfaction. Contrary to general public opinion, low-quality products do not necessarily cost less to manufacture than high-quality products do.

Although it can be described in various terms, **product integrity** is a term that can be used to define the degree to which a product (a) is suitable for its intended purpose, (b) fills a real market need, (c) functions reliably during its life expectancy, and (d) can be maintained with relative ease. Product integrity has also been defined as the total product experience of the customer, or as the totality of qualities needed to conceive, produce, and market the product successfully.

Total quality management (TQM) and **quality assurance** are now the responsibility of everyone involved in designing and manufacturing a product. Our awareness of the technological and economic importance of built-in product quality has been heightened further by pioneers in quality control, primarily Deming, Taguchi, and Juran. They pointed out the importance of management's commitment to product quality, of pride of workmanship at all levels of production, and of the use of powerful techniques such as **statistical process control (SPC)** and **control charts** (Chapter 36) for on-line monitoring of part production and for rapidly identifying sources of quality problems.

The major goal is to prevent defects from occurring, rather than to detect and reject defective products after they are made. For example, we now have the capability of producing computer chips in such a way that only a few parts out of a million may be defective.

Important developments in quality assurance include the implementation of **experimental design**, a technique in which the factors involved in a manufacturing process and their interactions are studied simultaneously. For example, variables affecting dimensional accuracy or surface finish in a machining operation can be readily identified by the use of this tool, and that knowledge can make it possible for appropriate preventive actions to be taken.

The major trend toward global manufacturing and competitiveness has created a need for international conformity in the use of and for consensus regarding the establishment of quality control methods. This need has resulted in the International Organization for Standardization *ISO 9000* series on Quality Management and Quality Assurance Standards, as well as *QS 9000* (Chapter 36).

A company's registration for this standard, which is a *quality process certification* and not a product certification, means that the company conforms to consistent practices as specified by its own quality system. ISO 9000 and QS 9000 have permanently influenced the manner in which companies conduct business in world trade, and they have become the world standard for quality.

I.9 GLOBAL COMPETITIVENESS AND MANUFACTURING COSTS

The economics of manufacturing have always been a major factor, and it has become even more of one as the international competition (**global competitiveness**) for high-quality products (**world-class manufacturing**) and low prices have become a simple fact in worldwide markets.

Beginning with the 1960s, the following trends developed which have had a major impact on manufacturing:

- Global competition increased rapidly, and the markets became multinational and dynamic.
- Market conditions fluctuated widely.
- Customers demanded high-quality, low-cost products and on-time delivery.
- Product variety increased substantially and became technically complex.
- Product life cycles became shorter.

To respond to these needs while keeping costs down is a constant challenge to manufacturing companies and an issue crucial to their very survival. The **cost** of a product is often the overriding consideration in its marketability and in general customer satisfaction with it. Typically, manufacturing costs represent about 40% of a product's selling price.

The concept of design for manufacture and assembly and of concurrent engineering, described in Section 4, also includes design principles for economic production:

- The design should make the product as simple as possible to manufacture, assemble, disassemble, and recycle.
- Materials should be chosen for their appropriate manufacturing characteristics.
- Dimensional accuracy and surface finish should be specified as broadly as is permissible, in order to minimize manufacturing costs.
- Secondary and finishing operations on parts should be avoided or minimized, because they can add significantly to cost.

The **total cost** of manufacturing a product consists of the costs of materials, tooling, and labor, the fixed costs, and capital costs. Several factors are involved in each cost category. Manufacturing costs can be minimized by analyzing the product design to determine whether the part size and shape are optimal and whether the materials selected are the least costly ones that possess the desired properties and characteristics. The possibility of substituting one material for another is an important consideration in minimizing costs.

Tooling costs depend on the complexity of part shape, on the materials involved, on the manufacturing process, and on the number of parts to be made. Complex shapes, difficult-to-machine materials, and stringent dimensional-accuracy requirements all add to the cost of tooling.

Direct labor costs are usually only a small portion of the total cost, typically ranging from 10% to 15% of it. The trend toward increased automation and toward computer control of all aspects of manufacturing helps to minimize labor involvement and so to reduce direct labor costs, which continue to decline steadily as a percentage of total cost.

Fixed costs and capital costs depend on the particular manufacturer and plant facilities. Computer-controlled machinery, which constitutes a capital cost, can be very expensive. Economic analysis indicates, however, that, more often than not, such an expenditure is warranted in view of its long-range benefits. In mass production of products, such as automobile engines, specialized machines are arranged in various product-flow lines. These machines, too, require a major capital investment, yet the high production rate makes the cost per part competitive.

I.10 LEAN PRODUCTION AND AGILE MANUFACTURING

The trends we have described thus far have led to the concept of **lean production** or **lean manufacturing**. Although not a novel concept, it basically involves a major assessment of each of the activities of a company: the efficiency and effectiveness of its various operations, the possible dispensability of some of its operations and managers, the efficiency of the machinery and equipment in the operation, and the number of personnel involved in each particular operation. It continues with a thorough analysis of the costs of each activity, including those due to productive and to nonproductive labor.

This concept requires a fundamental change in corporate culture as well as an understanding of the importance of *cooperation and teamwork* between management and the work force. Its results do not necessarily require cutting back on resources; rather, it aims at continually improving the efficiency and the profitability of the company, by removing all waste from the operations (zero-base waste) and by dealing with problems right away, including environmental issues.

Agile manufacturing is a term that has been coined to indicate the use of the principles of lean production on a broad scale. The principle behind agile manufacturing is ensuring agility, hence **flexibility**, in the manufacturing enterprise, so that it can respond quickly to changes in product demand and in customer needs.

This flexibility is to be achieved through people, equipment, computer hardware and software, and sophisticated communications systems. As an example, it has been predicted that the automotive industry could configure and build a car in three days and that, eventually, the traditional assembly line will be replaced by a system in which a nearly custom-made car will be produced by connecting individual modules.

These approaches require that a manufacturer **benchmark** its operations; this method entails understanding the competitive position of other manufacturers with respect to its own and then setting realistic goals for the future. From that perspective, benchmarking becomes a *reference* from which various measurements can be made and to which they can be compared.

I.11 ENVIRONMENTALLY CONSCIOUS DESIGN AND MANUFACTURING

In the United States alone, nine million passenger cars and 285 million tires are discarded each year; about 100 million of those tires are reused in various ways. More than 5 billion kilograms of plastic products are discarded each year. Every three months, industries and consumers discard enough aluminum to rebuild the country's commercial air fleet. Furthermore, in Germany, 800,000 metric tons of old TV sets, radios, and computer equipment are discarded each year.

How do we recycle, treat, or dispose of this waste? What are the side effects of the waste and of how we deal with it? In manufacturing operations specifically, we may cite various examples. Lubricants and coolants are often used in machining, grinding, and forming operations. Various fluids and solvents are used in cleaning manufactured products. Some of these fluids pollute the air and waters during their use.

Many by-products from manufacturing plants have for years been discarded: sand containing additives used in metal-casting processes; water, oil, and other fluids from heat-treating facilities and from plating operations; slag from foundries and from welding operations; and a wide variety of metallic and nonmetallic scrap, produced in operations such as sheet forming, casting, and molding.

The present and future adverse effects of these activities, their damage to our environment and to the earth's ecosystem, and ultimately their effect on the quality of human life are by now well recognized by the public, as well as by local and federal governments. Consider the effects of water and air pollution, acid rain, ozone depletion, the greenhouse effect, hazardous wastes, landfill seepage, and global warming.

In response to these major concerns, many and diverse laws and regulations have been promulgated by local, state, and federal governments and by professional organizations, both in the United States and in other countries. These regulations are generally stringent, and their implementation can have a major impact on the economic operation and financial health of industrial organizations.

Much can be gained by careful analysis of products, their design, the materials used in them, and the manufacturing processes and practices employed in making them. Certain guidelines can be followed in this analysis:

- reducing waste of materials at their source, by refinements in product design and by reducing the amount of materials used;
- conducting research and development into environmentally-safe products and into manufacturing technologies;
- reducing the use of hazardous materials in products and processes;
- ensuring proper handling and disposal of all waste;
- making improvements in recycling, in waste treatment, and in reuse of materials.

Major developments have been taking place regarding these matters, and the term **environmentally-conscious design and manufacturing** has now become common usage in the industry, a development that indicates the broad scope of the problem. A major emphasis is on **design for the environment (DFE)** or **green design**. This approach anticipates the possible negative environmental impact of materials, products, and processes, so that it can be taken into account at the earliest stages of design and production. The main objectives now are preventing pollution at the source and promoting recycling and reuse in place of disposal. These goals have led to the concept of **design for recycling (DFR)**.

In the U.S. automotive industry, for example, about 75% of car parts, mostly metals, are now recycled, and there are plans to recycle the rest as well, including plastic parts, glass, rubber, and foam. The time required to disassemble a car for recycling is another factor that is being studied, in view of its economic impact. Volkswagen, for example, has developed a methodology for stripping down a car in only 20 minutes. The benefits of recycling are also evident from a study showing that obtaining aluminum from scrap, instead of from bauxite ore, costs only one-third as much and reduces energy consumption and pollution by more than 90%.

Cartridges for copiers and printers are now returnable by the customer to the manufacturer, which repairs and replaces some parts and then resells the cartridge. This means that the cartridge had to be designed for replacement of worn parts and for ease of disassembly (such as by the use of snap fits instead of screws).

Japanese and German automobile companies now collect replaceable plastic bumpers for recycling and reuse. BMW's new "3" series uses 81% recycled materials. Automotive plastic parts weighing more than 100 grams are stamped with codes to identify them for sorting and recycling. In the United States, plastic soft-drink bottles are now recycled at a rate of 42%, and this rate is increasing. Some of the recycled plastics are used for making signposts, curbing, and park benches. The woven polyester sailcloth of a full-scale replica of an eighteenth-century British frigate is made of 100% recycled plastic from car fenders and soft-drink bottles.

I.12 PRODUCT LIABILITY

We are all familiar with the consequences of a product's malfunctioning and possibly causing bodily injury (or even death) and financial loss to a person or organization. This important topic is commonly referred to as **product liability** (Chapter 37). Because of the related technical and legal aspects, in which laws can vary from state to state and from country to country, this is a complex subject that can have a major economic impact on the parties involved.

Designing and manufacturing safe products is an important and integral part of a manufacturer's responsibilities. All those involved with product design, manufacture, and marketing must fully recognize the consequences of product failure, including failures occurring during possible misuse of the product. There has been a proliferation of product-liability claims made against manufacturers of consumer and industrial equipment, particularly in the United States, claims with varying degrees of merit.

The following is a typical example of a claim made against a manufacturer and its outcome: A manufacturer of a straight miter saw was sued by the operator, who was injured (while attempting to remove a piece of cut wood) when his hand touched the bottom of the rotating circular blade. The lower half of the saw blade was protected by a gravity-actuated guard. The operator alleged that the guard was inadequate and that the saw should have been equipped with a blade guard.

The jury decided in favor of the saw manufacturer, on the grounds that the guard could not reasonably be expected to protect the user from all types of injuries but did prevent most types of blade-contact injuries. The operator testified that the accident took place in an instant, so the jury agreed that the presence of a brake could not have stopped the saw blade quickly enough to prevent the injury.

Numerous other examples of products that could involve liability can be cited, such as: (a) a grinding wheel that shatters and blinds a worker, (b) a cable that snaps, allowing a platform to drop, (c) brakes that become inoperative because of the failure of a component, (d) machines with no guards or inappropriate guards, and (e) electric or pneumatic tools without proper warnings.

Human-factors engineering and **ergonomic** considerations (human-machine interactions) are important aspects of the design and manufacture of safe products. Examples include (a) an uncomfortable or unstable workbench or chair, (b) a mechanism that is difficult to operate manually, causing back injury, and (c) a poorly designed keyboard that causes pain to the user's hands and arms after repetitive use.

I.13 ORGANIZATION FOR MANUFACTURE

The various manufacturing activities and functions that we have described must be organized and managed efficiently and effectively in order to maximize productivity and minimize costs while maintaining high quality standards. Because of the complex interactions among the various factors involved in manufacturing (materials, machines, people, information, power, and capital), the proper coordination and administration of diverse functions and responsibilities is essential.

Manufacturing engineers traditionally have had several major responsibilities:

- They plan the manufacture of a product and the processes to be utilized. This function requires a thorough knowledge of the product and of its expected performance.

- They identify the machines, the equipment, the tooling, and the personnel to carry out the plan. This function requires evaluation of the capabilities of machines, of tools, and of workers, so that proper functions and responsibilities can be assigned.

- They interact with design and materials engineers to optimize productivity and minimize production costs.

- They cooperate with **industrial engineers** when planning for plant-floor activities, on such topics as plant layout, machine arrangement, selection of material-handling equipment, time-and-motion study, production methods analysis, production planning and scheduling, and maintenance. Some of these activities are carried out under the name *plant engineering*, and some are interchangeably performed by both manufacturing and industrial engineers.

Manufacturing engineers, in cooperation with industrial engineers, also are responsible for evaluating new technologies and how they can be applied and implemented. In view of the rapidly growing amount of technical information, this task in itself can present a major challenge. Gaining a broad perspective on computer capabilities, applications, and integration in all phases of manufacturing operations is important. This knowledge is particularly crucial for long-range production-facility planning, in view of constant changes in market demand and product mix.

There have been important trends in the operational philosophy of manufacturing organizations, particularly in the United States. Traditionally, the emphasis was on top-down communication in the organization and on strong control by management, with priorities for quick financial return (**profits first**) and growth and size (**economy of scale**). However, the trend is now toward broad-based communication *across* the organization.

Corporate strategies in the United States have traditionally emphasized the business and financial aspects of a company, keeping manufacturing subordinate to the overall marketing plan. With **global competition** as a reality and **world-class manufacturing** for multiple markets now a necessity, corporate strategies have been undergoing major changes. Manufacturing has become an integral part of long-range business planning for companies that want to maintain their competitive positions and increase their market share.

These are complex issues because they involve a broad range of considerations such as product type, company size, unions, shareholder attitudes, changing markets, laws and practices in different countries, tariffs and import restrictions, and geopolitics.

In order to respond to these major changes, it is essential in a manufacturing organization to:

- view the **people** in the organization as important assets;
- emphasize the importance and need for **teamwork** and involvement in problem solving and in *decision-making* processes in all aspects of operations;
- encourage **product innovation** and improvements in **productivity**;
- relate product innovation and manufacturing to the **customer** and the **market**; the product must be seen as *meeting a need*;
- increase **flexibility** of operation for faster response to product demands, in both the domestic and the global marketplace (**economy of time**);
- encourage efforts for **continuous improvement in quality** (**quality first**);
- ultimately and most importantly, focus on **customer satisfaction**.

Example: Wheelchair Design as a Multidisciplinary Endeavor

A modern manual wheelchair with significant improvements over its predecessors is shown in Fig. I.17. In many ways, the design attributes of this wheelchair have been determined by the unique desires and needs of the users. Among others, the following disciplines and views have contributed to the design and manufacture of this product:

1. *End Use*. Wheelchair users were directly consulted from the beginning of the product development cycle, and their evaluations and recommendations were incorporated throughout the design process. The chair is designed to facilitate transfer to automobiles and toilets and to allow easy storage.

2. *Nursing*. Nurses were brought in as consultants during the design stage; they emphasized the difficulties that occur when they must lift patients over the arm rests or when patients must lift themselves over the arm rests, in order to transfer into and out of the chair. The arm rests are removable on this wheelchair, because of this input from nurses.

3. *Biomechanics*. The design of the seat is strongly influenced by biomechanics research. The main concern is the elimination of pressure sores, which result from poor blood flow through the lower extremities of the person. Through contouring and through the use of layers of different types of foam, a more uniform pressure distribution on the user is obtained, and the severity of this problem is reduced.

4. *Structural designers*. Because a wheelchair user must, from time to time, lift and move the chair, a lightweight design, fabricated from composite materials and lightweight metals, was adopted.

5. *Mechanical designers*. Quiet, high-performance bearings have been selected, and efficient brakes are utilized. The drive wheels have been tilted towards the user to make pushing easier, and the wheelbase is made narrower for cornering in hallways or maneuvering behind desks. The frame is adjustable to fit the dimensions of the individual user.

6. *Marketing*. Wheelchair users, just like bicyclists and car drivers, care very much about appearance. Surveys of users led to the use of vibrant colors and of a sleek look.

It is very difficult for one person to bring all of these insights into the concept design. This example illustrates the importance and benefits of multidisciplinary efforts in the design of products.

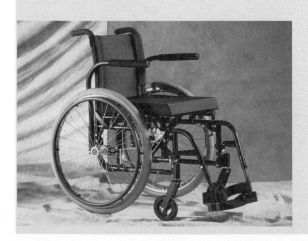

FIGURE I.17   A wheel chair. Illustration courtesy of Sunrise Medical Equipment Co.

SUMMARY

- In this general introduction, we have presented a broad outline of the important aspects of manufacturing engineering and technology, including a wide range of topics (often with overlapping boundaries) and how they interact with each other. The important trends in global manufacturing and in competitiveness were also introduced.

- Because they have become major issues, world-class manufacturing, environmentally-conscious design and manufacturing, lean and agile manufacturing, product quality, and customer satisfaction were also emphasized.

- The inherent complexity of these manufacturing concepts and technologies may lead to controversy over their individual merits, controversy involving differing viewpoints from people having various backgrounds and experiences in significantly different areas. Timely implementation of these concepts and technologies, taken in totality and with their appropriate cost-benefit assessment, has become a major priority in corporate strategy and planning in today's increasingly competitive global marketplace.

KEY TERMS

Adaptive control
Agile manufacturing
Artificial intelligence
Artificial neural networks
Automated materials handling
Benchmark
Cellular manufacturing
Computer-aided design, engineering, and manufacturing
Computer-aided process planning
Computer-integrated manufacturing
Computer numerical control
Concurrent engineering
Continuous products
Design for manufacture, assembly, disassembly, and service
Design for recycling
Design for the environment

Discrete products
Economy of scale
Environmentally conscious design and manufacturing
Experimental design
Expert systems
Flexible manufacturing systems
Global competitiveness
Green design
Group technology
Interchangeable parts
Just-in-time production
Lean production
Life cycle
Manufacturing
Manufacturing engineering
Nanofabrication
Nanotechnology

Net-shape manufacturing
Numerical control
Overdesign
Producibility
Product integrity
Product liability
Production engineering
Quality assurance
Rapid prototyping
Shared manufacturing
Statistical process control
Total quality management
Ultraprecision manufacturing
Value added
World-class manufacturing
Zero-base waste

PART I
Fundamentals of Materials: Their Behavior and Manufacturing Properties

Part I of this text begins by presenting the fundamental properties and applications of materials. Their behavior and engineering properties are explained throughout the following nine chapters, as well as the characteristics, advantages, and limitations that influence the choice of materials in the design and manufacture of products.

In order to emphasize the importance of the topics that are to be discussed, let's use the automobile as an example of a common product that contains a wide variety of materials (Fig. I.1). These materials were selected because, out of all the materials that possess the desired properties and characteristics for the intended functions of specific parts of the automobile, these were the ones that can be manufactured at the lowest cost.

Steel was chosen for much of the body because it is strong, easy to form, and inexpensive. Plastics were used in many components because of characteristics such as a wide choice of colors, light weight, and ease of manufacturing into various shapes at low cost. Glass was chosen for the windows not only because it is transparent, but also because it is hard, easy to shape, easy to clean, and resistant to scratching.

We can make similar observations for each component of an automobile, which typically is an assemblage of some 15,000 parts, ranging from thin wire to bumpers. As stated in the General Introduction, selection of materials for individual components in a product requires an understanding of their properties, functions, and costs. Note that by saving just one cent on the average cost per part, such as by selecting a different material or manufacturing technique, the manufacturer could reduce the cost of an automobile by $150. The task of manufacturing engineers thus becomes truly challenging, especially with the wide variety of materials now available (Fig. I.2).

In this Part, the fundamentals of materials are presented, so that the reader can understand and explain their behavior and take full advantage of their capabilities. A general

FIGURE I.1   Some of the metallic and nonmetallic materials used in a typical automobile.

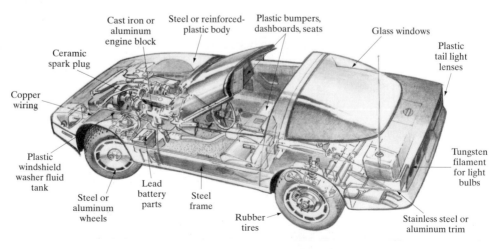

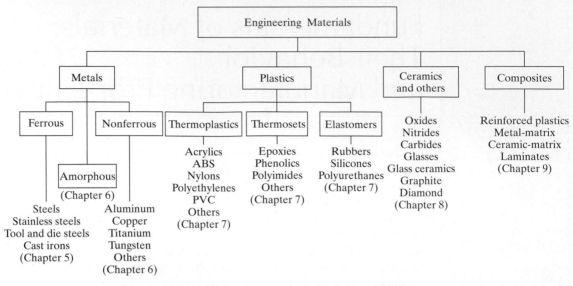

FIGURE I.2   An outline of the engineering materials described in Part I.

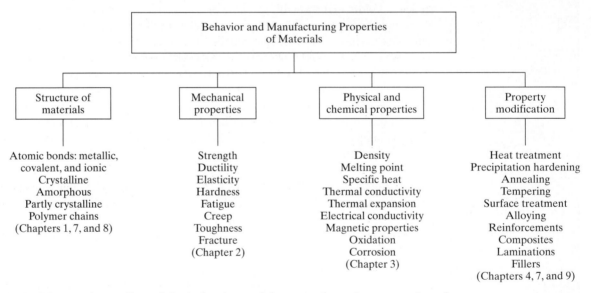

FIGURE I.3   An outline of the behavior and the manufacturing properties of materials described in Part I.

outline of the various topics presented is given in Fig. I.3. The fundamental knowledge presented in Part I about the behavior, properties, and characteristics of materials will help the reader understand the manufacturing processes described in Parts II-IV of this book. This knowledge will also make it possible to analyze the often complex relationships among materials, manufacturing processes, machinery and tooling, and the economics of manufacturing operations.

1

The Structure of Metals

1.1 INTRODUCTION

Why are some metals hard and others soft? Why are some metals brittle, while others are ductile and can be shaped easily without fracture? Why is it that some metals can withstand high temperatures, while others cannot? We can answer these and similar questions by studying the **structure** of metals—that is, the arrangement of the atoms within metals. The structure of metals greatly influences their behavior and properties.

A knowledge of structures guides us in controlling and predicting the behavior and performance of metals in various manufacturing processes. Understanding the structure of metals also allows us to predict and evaluate their **properties**. This helps us make appropriate selections for specific applications under particular external and environmental conditions such as force and temperature.

In addition to atomic structure, various other factors also influence the properties and behavior of metals. Among these are the composition of the metal, impurities and vacancies in the atomic structure, grain size, grain boundaries, environment, size and surface condition of the metal, and the methods by which metals and alloys are made into useful products.

The topics covered in this chapter and their sequence are outlined in Fig. 1.1. The structure and general properties of materials other than metals are described in Chapter 7 (polymers), Chapter 8 (ceramics), and Chapter 9 (composite materials). The structure of metal alloys, the control of their structure, and heat-treatment processes are described in Chapter 4.

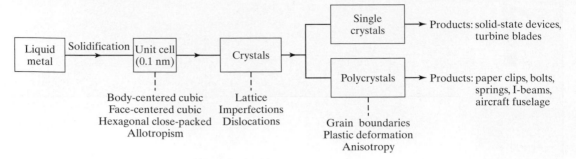

FIGURE 1.1   An outline of the topics described in Chapter 1.

1.2 THE CRYSTAL STRUCTURE OF METALS

When metals solidify from a molten state, the atoms arrange themselves into various orderly configurations, called **crystals.** This arrangement of the atoms in the crystal is called **crystalline structure**. The smallest group of atoms showing the characteristic **lattice structure** of a particular metal is known as a **unit cell.** It is the building block of a crystal, and a single crystal can have many unit cells.

Here are three basic atomic arrangements and some of the metals that use each:

1. **body-centered cubic (bcc)**—alpha iron, chromium, molybdenum, tantalum, tungsten, and vanadium;
2. **face-centered cubic (fcc)**—gamma iron, aluminum, copper, nickel, lead, silver, gold, and platinum;
3. **hexagonal close-packed (hcp)**—beryllium, cadmium, cobalt, magnesium, alpha titanium, zinc, and zirconium.

These structures are represented by the illustrations given in Figs. 1.2–1.4. Each sphere in these illustrations represents an atom. The order of magnitude of the distance between the atoms in these crystal structures is 0.1 nm (10^{-8} in.). The models are known as **hard-ball** or **hard-sphere** models; they can be likened to tennis balls arranged in various configurations in a box. The way in which these atoms are arranged determines the properties of a particular metal. We can modify these arrangements by adding atoms of some other metal or metals, known as **alloying**; it often improves the properties of the metal (Chapter 4).

FIGURE 1.2   The body-centered cubic (bcc) crystal structure: (a) hard-ball model; (b) unit cell; and (c) single crystal with many unit cells. *Source*: W. G. Moffatt, et al., *The Structure and Properties of Materials,* Vol. I, John Wiley & Sons, 1976.

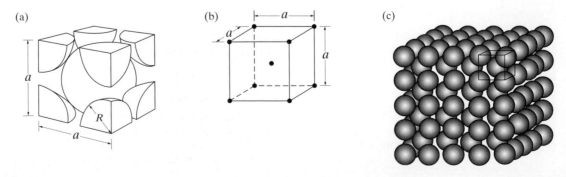

(a)

(b)

(c)

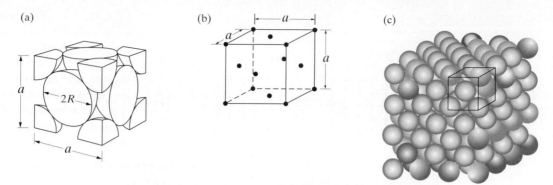

FIGURE 1.3   The face-centered cubic (fcc) crystal structure: (a) hard-ball model; (b) unit cell; and (c) single crystal with many unit cells. *Source*: W. G. Moffatt, et al., *The Structure and Properties of Materials,* Vol. I, John Wiley & Sons, 1976.

As shown in Fig. 1.2, each atom in the bcc structure has eight neighboring atoms. Of the three structures illustrated, the fcc and hcp crystals have the most densely packed configurations. In the hcp structure, the top and bottom planes are called **basal planes**.

The reason that metals form different crystal structures is to minimize the energy required to fit together in a regular pattern. Tungsten, for example, forms a bcc structure because that structure involves less energy than other structures do. On the same grounds, aluminum forms an fcc structure. At different temperatures, however, the same metal may form different structures, because of a lower energy requirement at that temperature. For example, iron forms a bcc structure (alpha iron) below 912 °C (1674 °F) and above 1394 °C (2541 °F), but it forms an fcc structure (gamma iron) between 912 °C and 1394 °C.

The appearance of more than one type of crystal structure is known as **allotropism** or **polymorphism** (meaning "many shapes"). Because the properties and behavior of a metal depend greatly on its crystal structure, allotropism is an important factor in the heat treatment of metals and in metalworking and welding operations (Parts III and V).

1.3   DEFORMATION AND STRENGTH OF SINGLE CRYSTALS

When a crystal is subjected to an external force, it first undergoes **elastic deformation**—that is, it returns to its original shape when the force is removed. An analogy to this type of behavior is a helical spring that stretches when loaded and returns to its original shape when the load is removed. However, if the force on the crystal structure is increased sufficiently,

(a)

(b)

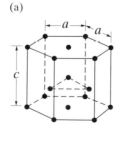

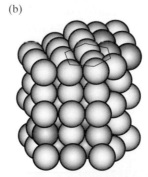

FIGURE 1.4   The hexagonal close-packed (hcp) crystal structure: (a) unit cell; and (b) single crystal with many unit cells. *Source*: W. G. Moffatt, et al., *The Structure and Properties of Materials*, Vol. I, John Wiley & Sons, 1976.

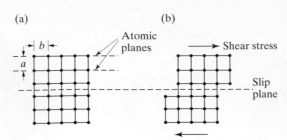

FIGURE 1.5   Permanent deformation (also called plastic deformation) of a single crystal subjected to a shear stress: (a) structure before deformation; and (b) permanent deformation by slip. The size of the *b/a* ratio influences the magnitude of the shear stress required to cause slip.

the crystal undergoes **plastic deformation** or **permanent deformation**—that is, it does not return to its original shape when the force is removed.

There are two basic mechanisms by which plastic deformation may take place in crystal structures. One is the slipping of one plane of atoms over an adjacent plane (**slip plane**, Fig. 1.5a) under a **shear stress** (Fig. 1–5b). Shear stress is the ratio of the applied shearing force to the cross-sectional area being sheared. The deformation of a single-crystal specimen by slip is shown schematically in Fig. 1.6a. This situation is much like the sliding of playing cards against each other.

Just as it takes a certain amount of force to slide playing cards against each other, so a crystal requires a certain amount of shear stress (**critical shear stress**) to undergo permanent deformation. Thus, there must be a shear stress of sufficient magnitude within a crystal for plastic deformation to occur.

The shear stress required to cause slip in single crystals is directly proportional to the ratio *b/a* in Fig. 1.5a, where *a* is the spacing of the atomic planes and *b* is inversely proportional to the atomic density in the atomic plane. As *b/a* decreases, the shear stress required to cause slip decreases. We can therefore state that slip in a crystal takes place along planes of maximum atomic density or, in other words, that slip takes place in closely packed planes and in closely packed directions.

Because the *b/a* ratio is different for different directions within the crystal, a single crystal has different properties when tested in different directions. We say that a single crystal is **anisotropic**. A common example of anisotropy is woven cloth, which stretches differently when we pull it in different directions, or plywood, which is much stronger in the planar direction than along its thickness direction (it splits easily).

The second mechanism of plastic deformation is **twinning** (Fig. 1.6b), in which a portion of the crystal forms a mirror image of itself across the plane of twinning. Twins form abruptly and are the cause of the creaking sound ("tin cry") that occurs when a tin or zinc rod is bent at room temperature. Twinning usually occurs in hcp metals.

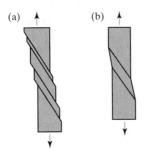

FIGURE 1.6
(a) Permanent deformation of a single crystal under a tensile load. Note that the slip planes tend to align themselves in the direction of the pulling force. This behavior can be simulated using a deck of cards with a rubber band around them. (b) Twinning in a single crystal in tension.

Slip Systems. The combination of a slip plane and its direction of slip is known as a *slip system*. In general, metals with slip systems of 5 or above are ductile, whereas those with slip systems below 5 are not.

1. In **body-centered cubic** crystals, there are 48 possible slip systems. The probability is therefore high that an externally applied shear stress will operate on one of these systems and cause slip. Because of the relatively high *b/a* ratio in the crystal, however, the required shear stress is high. Metals with bcc structures generally have good strength and moderate ductility.

2. In **face-centered cubic** crystals, there are 12 slip systems. The probability of slip is moderate, and the required shear is low because of the relatively low *b/a* ratio. These metals generally have moderate strength and good ductility.

3. The **hexagonal close-packed** crystal has 3 slip systems, and so it has a low probability of slip. However, more slip systems become active at elevated temperatures. Metals with hcp structures are generally brittle at room temperature.

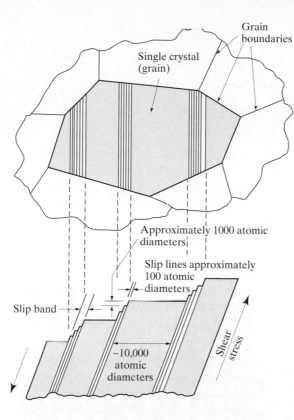

FIGURE 1.7   Schematic illustration of slip lines and slip bands in a single crystal (grain) subjected to a shear stress. A slip band consists of a number of slip planes. The crystal at the center of the upper illustration is an individual grain surrounded by other grains.

Note, in Fig. 1.6a, that the portions of the single crystal that have slipped have rotated away from their original angular position toward the direction of the tensile force. Note, also, that slip has taken place only along certain planes. With the use of electron microscopy, it has been shown that what appears to be a single slip plane is actually a **slip band**, consisting of a number of slip planes (Fig. 1.7).

1.3.1 Imperfections in the Crystal Structure of Metals

The actual strength of metals is approximately one to two orders of magnitude lower than the strength levels obtained from theoretical calculations. This discrepancy has been explained in terms of **defects** and **imperfections** in the crystal structure. Unlike the idealized models we have described, actual metal crystals contain a large number of defects and imperfections, which are categorized as follows:

- Line defects, called **dislocations** (Fig. 1.8);
- Point defects, such as a **vacancy** (missing atom), an **interstitial atom** (extra atom in the lattice), or an **impurity** (foreign atom) that has replaced the atom of the pure metal (Fig. 1.9);
- Volume or bulk imperfections, such as **voids** or **inclusions** (nonmetallic elements such as oxides, sulfides, and silicates);
- Planar imperfections, such as **grain boundaries** (Section 1.4).

Mechanical and electrical properties of metals, such as yield, fracture strength, and electrical conductivity, are adversely affected by these defects; these are known as **structure-sensitive** properties. On the other hand, their physical and chemical properties such as melting point, specific heat, coefficient of thermal expansion, and elastic constants (e.g., modulus

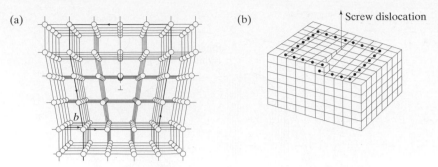

FIGURE 1.8   Types of dislocations in a single crystal: (a) edge dislocation; and (b) screw dislocation. *Source*: (a) After Guy and Hren, *Elements of Physical Metallurgy,* 1974. (b) L. Van Vlack, *Materials for Engineering,* 4th ed., 1980.

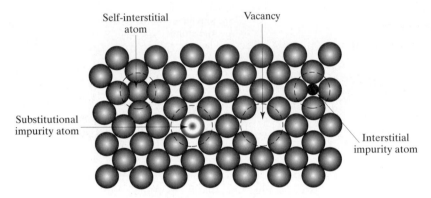

FIGURE 1.9   Schematic illustration of types of defects in a single-crystal lattice: self-interstitial, vacancy, interstitial, and substitutional. *Source*: After Moffatt et al.

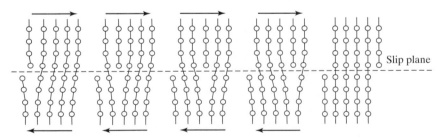

FIGURE 1.10   Movement of an edge dislocation across the crystal lattice under a shear stress. Dislocations help explain why the actual strength of metals is much lower than that predicted by theory.

of elasticity and modulus of rigidity) are not sensitive to these defects; these are known as **structure-insensitive** properties.

    Dislocations.   First observed in the 1930s, **dislocations** are defects in the orderly arrangement of a metal's atomic structure. They are the most significant defects that help explain the discrepancy between the actual and theoretical strength of metals. A slip plane containing a dislocation (Fig. 1.10) requires less shear stress to allow slip than does a plane in a perfect lattice.

There are two types of dislocations: **edge** and **screw** (Fig. 1.8). One analogy used to describe the movement of an edge dislocation is the earthworm, which moves forward by means of a hump that starts at the tail and moves toward the head. Another analogy for an edge dislocation is moving a large carpet by forming a hump at one end and moving it to the other end. The force required to move a carpet in this way is much lower than that required to slide the whole carpet along the floor. Screw dislocations are so named because the atomic planes form a spiral ramp.

1.3.2 Work Hardening (Strain Hardening)

Although the presence of a dislocation lowers the shear stress required to cause slip, dislocations can:

1. become entangled and interfere with each other; and
2. be impeded by barriers, such as grain boundaries and impurities and inclusions in the material.

Entanglements and impediments increase the shear stress required for slip. Entanglement is like moving two humps at different angles across a carpet: where they cross, the two humps interfere with each other's movement, and their combined effect is to make it more difficult to move the carpet.

The effect of an increase in shear stress that causes an increase in the overall strength of the metal is known as **work hardening** or **strain hardening**. The greater the deformation, the greater the number of entanglements, hence an increase in the metal's strength. Work hardening is used extensively for strengthening metals in metalworking processes at ambient temperature. Typical examples are producing sheet metal for automobile bodies and aircraft fuselages by rolling (Chapter 13), making the head of a bolt by forging (Chapter 14), and strengthening wire by reducing its cross-section by drawing it through a die (Chapter 15).

1.4 GRAINS AND GRAIN BOUNDARIES

Metals commonly used for manufacturing various products consist of many individual, randomly oriented crystals (**grains**). We are, therefore, dealing with metal structures that are not single crystals but **polycrystals**, ("many crystals").

When a mass of molten metal begins to solidify, crystals begin to form independently of each other at various locations within the liquid mass; they have random and unrelated orientations (Fig. 1.11). Each of these crystals grows into a crystalline structure or grain. The number and size of the grains developed in a unit volume of the metal depends on the rate at which **nucleation** (the initial stage of formation of crystals) takes place. The number of different sites at which individual crystals begin to form (seven in Fig. 1.11a) and the rate at which these crystals grow are both important influences on the median size of the grains developed.

If the crystal nucleation rate is high, the number of grains in a unit volume of metal will be large; consequently, grain size will be small. Conversely, if the rate of growth of the crystals is high (compared to their nucleation rate), there will be fewer grains per unit volume, and their size will be larger. Generally, rapid cooling produces smaller grains, whereas slow cooling produces larger grains.

Note, in Fig. 1.11d, how the growing grains eventually interfere with and impinge upon one another. The surfaces that separate these individual grains are called **grain boundaries**. Each grain consists of either a single crystal (for pure metals) or a polycrystalline aggregate (for alloys). Note that the crystallographic orientation changes abruptly from one grain to the next across the grain boundaries. Recall, from Section 1.3, that the behavior of

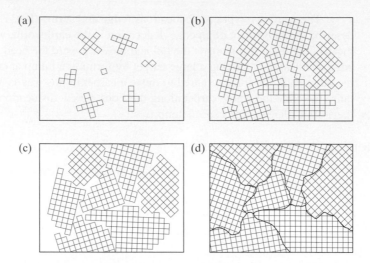

FIGURE 1.11   Schematic illustration of the stages during solidification of molten metal; each small square represents a unit cell. (a) Nucleation of crystals at random sites in the molten metal; note that the crystallographic orientation of each site is different. (b) and (c) Growth of crystals as solidification continues. (d) Solidified metal, showing individual grains and grain boundaries; note the different angles at which neighboring grains meet each other. *Source*: W. Rosenhain.

a single crystal or a single grain is anisotropic. The ideal behavior of a piece of polycrystalline metal is thus **isotropic** because its grains have random crystallographic orientations, its properties do not vary with the direction of testing.

1.4.1 Grain Size

Grain size significantly influences the mechanical properties of metals. At room temperature, a large grain size is generally associated with low strength, low hardness, and low ductility. Large grains, particularly in sheet metals, also cause a rough surface appearance after the material has been stretched (*orange peel*, see Section 1.6).

Grain size is usually measured by counting the number of grains in a given area, or by counting the number of grains that intersect a length of a line randomly drawn on an enlarged photograph of the grains (taken under a microscope on a polished and etched specimen). Grain size may also be determined by comparing it to a standard chart. The ASTM (The American Society for Testing and Materials) grain size number, n, is related to the number of grains, N, per square inch at a magnification of 100X (equal to 0.0645 mm^2 of actual area) by the formula

$$N = 2^{n-1}. \tag{1.1}$$

Because grains are generally extremely small, many grains can occupy a typical unit volume of metal (Table 1.1). Grain sizes between 5 and 8 are generally considered fine grains. A grain size of 7 is generally acceptable for sheet metals for making car bodies, appliances, and kitchen utensils (Chapter 16). Grains can be so large as to be visible with the naked eye, such as those of zinc on the surface of galvanized sheet steels.

TABLE 1.1   Grain Sizes

ASTM No.	Grains/mm^2	Grains/mm^3
−3	1	0.7
−2	2	2
−1	4	5.6
0	8	16
1	16	45
2	32	128
3	64	360
4	128	1,020
5	256	2,900
6	512	8,200
7	1,024	23,000
8	2,048	65,000
9	4,096	185,000
10	8,200	520,000
11	16,400	1,500,000
12	32,800	4,200,000

1.4.2 Influence of Grain Boundaries

Grain boundaries have an important influence on the strength and ductility of metals. Because they interfere with the movement of dislocations, grain boundaries also influence strain hardening. These effects depend on temperature, deformation rate, and the type and amount of impurities present along the grain boundaries.

Grain boundaries are more reactive than the grains themselves, because the atoms along the grain boundaries are packed less efficiently and are more disordered. As a result, they have higher energy than the atoms in the orderly lattice within the grains. For this reason, a polished and etched surface can become rougher. (See, also, *end grains in forging*, in Section 14.8.)

At elevated temperatures, and in materials whose properties depend on the deformation rate, plastic deformation also takes place by means of **grain-boundary sliding**. The **creep** mechanism, that is, elongation under stress over a period of time, usually at elevated temperatures, results from grain-boundary sliding (Section 2.8).

Grain-boundary embrittlement. When brought into close atomic contact with certain low-melting-point metals, a normally ductile and strong metal can crack under very low stresses. Examples are (a) aluminum wetted with a mercury-zinc amalgam or liquid gallium; and (b) copper (at elevated temperature) wetted with lead or bismuth. These embrittling elements weaken the grain boundaries of the metal by **embrittlement**. The term **liquid-metal embrittlement** is used to describe such phenomena, because the embrittling element is in a liquid state. However, embrittlement can also occur at temperatures well below the melting point of the embrittling element, this phenomenon is known as **solid-metal embrittlement**.

Hot shortness is caused by local melting of a constituent or an impurity in the grain boundary at a temperature below the melting point of the metal itself. When subjected to plastic deformation at elevated temperatures (*hot-working*), the piece of metal crumbles and disintegrates along the grain boundaries. Examples are antimony in copper, leaded steels (Section 20.9.1), and leaded brass.

To avoid hot shortness, the metal is usually worked at a lower temperature in order to prevent softening and melting along the grain boundaries. Another form of embrittlement is **temper embrittlement** in alloy steels, which is caused by segregation (movement) of impurities to the grain boundaries.

1.5 PLASTIC DEFORMATION OF POLYCRYSTALLINE METALS

If a piece of polycrystalline metal with uniform *equiaxed* grains (having equal dimensions in all directions, as shown in the model in Fig. 1.12a) is subjected to plastic deformation at room temperature (*cold-working*), the grains become deformed and elongated. The deformation process may be carried out either by compressing the metal, as is done in forging to make a turbine disk (Chapter 14), or by subjecting it to tension, as is done in stretching sheet metal to make a car body (Chapter 16). The deformation within each grain takes place by the mechanisms described in Section 1.3 for a single crystal.

During plastic deformation, the grain boundaries remain intact, and mass continuity is maintained. The deformed metal exhibits greater strength, because of the entanglement of dislocations with grain boundaries. The increase in strength depends on the amount of deformation (*strain*) to which the metal is subjected; the greater the deformation, the stronger the metal becomes. Furthermore, the increase in strength is higher for metals with smaller grains, because they have a larger grain-boundary surface area per unit volume of metal.

Anisotropy (Texture).   Figure 1.12b shows that, as a result of plastic deformation, the grains have elongated in one direction and contracted in the other. Consequently, this piece of metal has become *anisotropic*, and its properties in the vertical direction are different from those in the horizontal direction.

Many products develop anisotropy of mechanical properties after they have been processed by metalworking techniques (Fig. 1.13). The degree of anisotropy depends on how uniformly the metal is deformed. Note (from the direction of the crack in Fig. 1.13a), for example, that the ductility of the cold-rolled sheet in the transverse (vertical) direction is lower than that in its rolling (longitudinal) direction. (See also Section 16.5.)

Anisotropy influences both mechanical and physical properties of metals. For example, sheet steel for electrical transformers is rolled in such a way that the resulting deformation imparts anisotropic magnetic properties to the sheet. This arrangement reduces magnetic-hysteresis losses and improves the efficiency of transformers. (See, also, *amorphous alloys*, Section 6.14.) There are two general types of anisotropy in metals: *preferred orientation* and *mechanical fibering*.

Preferred Orientation.   Also called **crystallographic anisotropy**, preferred orientation can be best described by reference to Fig. 1.6a. When a metal crystal is subjected to tension, the sliding blocks rotate toward the direction of the pulling force. As a result, slip planes and slip bands tend to align themselves with the direction of deformation. Similarly, for a polycrystalline aggregate with grains in various orientations, all slip directions tend

(a)   (b)

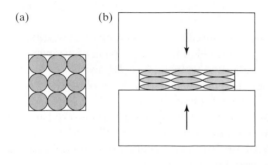

FIGURE 1.12   Plastic deformation of idealized (equiaxed) grains in a specimen subjected to compression (such as occurs in the rolling or forging of metals): (a) before deformation; and (b) after deformation. Note the alignment of grain boundaries along a horizontal direction; this effect is known as preferred orientation.

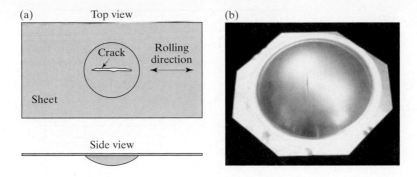

FIGURE 1.13   (a) Schematic illustration of a crack in sheet metal that has been subjected to bulging (caused by, for example, pushing a steel ball against the sheet). Note the orientation of the crack with respect to the rolling direction of the sheet; this sheet is anisotropic. (b) Aluminum sheet with a crack (vertical dark line at the center) developed in a bulge test; the rolling direction of the sheet was vertical. *Source*: J.S. Kallend, Illinois Institute of Technology.

to align themselves with the direction of pulling force. Conversely, slip planes under compression tend to align themselves in a direction perpendicular to the direction of the compressing force.

Mechanical Fibering.   Mechanical fibering results from the alignment of impurities, inclusions (**stringers**), and voids in the metal during deformation. Note that if the spherical grains in Fig. 1.12a were coated with impurities, these impurities would align themselves generally in a horizontal direction after deformation. Because impurities weaken the grain boundaries, this piece of metal will be weak and less ductile when tested in the vertical direction. An analogy is plywood, which is strong in tension along its planar direction, but peels off easily when pulled in tension in its thickness direction.

1.6 RECOVERY, RECRYSTALLIZATION, AND GRAIN GROWTH

We have shown that plastic deformation at room temperature causes the deformation of grains and grain boundaries, a general increase in strength, and a decrease in ductility; it causes anisotropic behavior also. These effects can be reversed, and the properties of the metal can be brought back to their original levels, by heating the piece in a specific temperature range for a period of time. This process is generally called **annealing** (Section 4.11). The temperature range and the amount of time depend on the material and on other factors. Three events take place consecutively during the heating process:

1. **Recovery.** During **recovery**, which occurs at a certain temperature range below the **recrystallization temperature** of the metal, the stresses in the highly deformed regions are relieved. Subgrain boundaries begin to form (a process called **polygonization**), with no appreciable change in mechanical properties such as hardness and strength (Fig. 1.14).
2. **Recrystallization.** The process in which, at a certain temperature range, new equiaxed and strain-free grains are formed, replacing the older grains, is called **recrystallization**.

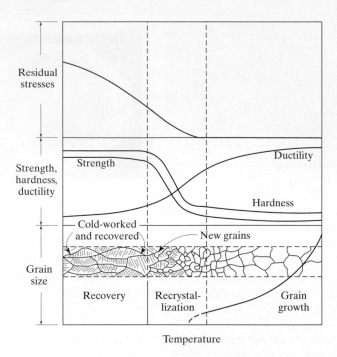

FIGURE 1.14
Schematic illustration of the effects of recovery, recrystallization, and grain growth on mechanical properties and on the shape and size of grains. Note the formation of small new grains during recrystallization. *Source*: G. Sachs.

The temperature for recrystallization ranges between approximately $0.3T_m$ and $0.5T_m$, where T_m is the melting point of the metal on the absolute scale.

The recrystallization temperature is generally defined as the temperature at which complete recrystallization occurs within approximately one hour. Recrystallization decreases the density of dislocations, lowers the strength, and raises the ductility of the metal (Fig. 1.14). Lead, tin, cadmium, and zinc recrystallize at about room temperature; as a result, when cold-worked, they do not work harden.

Recrystallization depends on the degree of prior cold work (work hardening): the more cold work, the lower the temperature required for recrystallization to occur. The reason is that, as the amount of cold work increases, the number of dislocations and the amount of energy stored in dislocations (**stored energy**) also increase. This energy supplies the work required for recrystallization. Recrystallization is a function of time because it involves **diffusion**—movement and exchange of atoms across grain boundaries.

The effects on recrystallization of temperature, of time, and of reduction in the thickness or height of the workpiece by cold working are as follows:

a. for a constant amount of deformation by cold working, the time required for recrystallization to occur decreases with increasing temperature;

b. the more the prior cold work, the lower the temperature required for recrystallization;

c. the greater the amount of deformation, the smaller the grain size becomes during recrystallization—this effect is a common method of converting a coarse-grained structure to one having a finer grain and, hence, improved properties;

d. anisotropy due to preferred orientation usually persists after recrystallization. To restore isotropy, a temperature higher than that required for recrystallization may be necessary.

3. Grain growth. If we continue to raise the temperature of the metal, the grains begin to grow, and their size may eventually exceed the original grain size. This phenomenon is known as **grain growth**, and it affects mechanical properties (Fig. 1.14). Large grains produce a rough surface appearance on sheet metals, called **orange peel**, when they are stretched to form a part, or when a piece of metal is subjected to compression (such as in forging operations).

1.7 COLD-, WARM-, AND HOT-WORKING

Cold-working refers to plastic deformation that is usually, but not necessarily, carried out at room temperature. When the deformation is carried out above the recrystallization temperature, it is called **hot-working**. "Cold" and "hot" are relative terms, as we can see from the fact that deforming lead at room temperature is a hot-working process, because the recrystallization temperature of lead is at about room temperature. As the name implies, **warm-working** is carried out at intermediate temperatures. Thus warm working is a compromise between cold- and hot-working.

The temperature ranges for these three categories of plastic deformation are given in Table 1.2 in terms of a ratio, where T is the working temperature and T_m is the melting point of the metal, both on the absolute scale. Although it is a dimensionless quantity, this ratio is known as the **homologous temperature.** In Part III we will describe the important technological differences in products that are processed by cold-, warm-, and hot-working.

TABLE 1.2   Homologous Temperature
            Ranges for Various Processes

Process	T/T_m
Cold working	< 0.3
Warm working	0.3 to 0.5
Hot working	> 0.6

SUMMARY

- There are three basic crystal structures in metals: body-centered cubic (bcc), face-centered cubic (fcc), and hexagonal close-packed (hcp). Grains made of these crystals are not perfect; they contain various defects and imperfections, such as dislocations, vacancies, impurities, inclusions, and grain boundaries. Commonly used metals are polycrystalline—that is, they are composed of many crystals or grains in random orientations.

- Plastic deformation in metals takes place by a slip mechanism. Although the theoretical shear stress required to cause slip is very high, actual stresses are much lower, because of the presence of dislocations (edge- or screw-type). Dislocations become entangled with one another or are impeded by barriers such as grain boundaries, impurities, and inclusions. As a result, the shear stress required to cause further slip is increased; consequently, the overall strength and hardness of the metal is also increased (an effect called work hardening or strain hardening).

- Grain size has a significant effect on the strength of metals. The smaller the size, the stronger is the metal.

- Grain boundaries have a major influence on metal behavior. They can undergo embrittlement, which severely reduces ductility at elevated temperatures (an effect called hot shortness); they are also responsible for creep, which is due to grain boundary sliding.

- Metals can be plastically deformed (worked) at room, warm, or high temperatures. Their behavior and workability depend largely on whether deformation takes place below or above the recrystallization temperature. Deformation at room temperature (cold-working) results in higher strength but reduced ductility of the metal. It generally causes anisotropy (preferred orientation or mechanical fibering), a state in which the properties are different in different directions.

- The effects of cold-working can be reversed by annealing the metal: heating it in a certain temperature range for a period of time and thereby allowing successive processes of recovery, recrystallization, and grain growth to take place.

KEY TERMS

Allotropism	Grain size	Recrystallization
Anisotropy	Hexagonal clos.-packed	Shear stress
Basal plane	Homologous temperature	Slip band
Body-centered cubic	Hot shortness	Slip plane
Cold-working	Hot-working	Slip system
Creep	Lattice structure	Strain hardening
Crystals	Mechanical fibering	Structure-insensitive
Dislocations	Orange peel	Structure-sensitive
Elastic deformation	Plastic deformation	Twinning
Embrittlement	Polycrystals	Unit cell
Face-centered cubic	Polygonization	Vacancy
Grains	Polymorphism	Warm-working
Grain boundaries	Preferred orientation	Work hardening
Grain growth	Recovery	

BIBLIOGRAPHY

Ashby, M.F., and D.R.H. Jones, *Engineering Materials*, Vol. 1, *An Introduction to Their Properties and Applications* (2d ed.) 1996; Vol. 2, *An Introduction to Microstructures, Processing and Design*, 1986. Pergamon Press.

Askeland, D.R., *The Science of Engineering Materials* (3d ed.). PWS Pub. Co., 1994.

Callister, W.D., Jr., *Materials Science and Engineering* (5th ed.). Wiley, 2000.

Flinn, R.A., and P.K. Trojan, *Engineering Materials and Their Applications* (4th ed.). Houghton Mifflin, 1990.

Shackelford, J.F., *Introduction to Materials Science for Engineers* (5th ed.). Prentice Hall, 2000.

Smith, W.F., *Principles of Materials Science and Engineering* (3d ed.). McGraw-Hill, 1995.

REVIEW QUESTIONS

1.1 Explain the difference between a unit cell and a single crystal.

1.2 In tables on crystal structures, iron is listed as having both a bcc and a fcc structure. Why?

1.3 Define anisotropy. What materials can you think of other than metals that exhibit anisotropic behavior?

1.4 What effects does recrystallization have on properties of metals?

1.5 What is strain hardening, and what effects does it have on the properties of metals?

1.6 Explain what is meant by structure-sensitive and structure-insensitive properties of metals.

1.7 Make a list of each of the major kinds of imperfection in the crystal structure of metals, and describe them.

1.8 What influence does grain size have on the mechanical properties of metals?

1.9 What is the relationship between the nucleation rate and the number of grains per unit volume of a metal?

1.10 What is a slip system, and what is its significance?

1.11 Explain the difference between recovery and recrystallization.

1.12 What is hot shortness, and what is its significance?

1.13 Explain the differences between cold-, warm-, and hot-working of metals.

1.14 Describe what the orange peel effect is.

1.15 Why can't some metals such as lead become stronger when cold worked?

1.16 Describe the difference between preferred orientation and mechanical fibering.

1.17 In microscopy, it is common practice to apply a chemical etchant to a metal in order to highlight grain boundaries and microstructures. Explain why.

1.18 What is twinning? How does it differ from slip?

QUALITATIVE PROBLEMS

1.19 Explain your understanding of why we should study the crystal structure of metals.

1.20 What is the significance of the fact that some metals undergo allotropism?

1.21 Is it possible for two pieces of the same metal to have different recrystallization temperatures? Is it possible for recrystallization to take place in some regions of a part before it does other regions of the same part? Explain.

1.22 Describe your understanding of why different crystal structures exhibit different strengths and ductilities.

1.23 A cold-worked piece of metal has been recrystallized. When tested, it is found to be anisotropic. Explain the probable reason.

1.24 Explain the advantages and limitations of cold-, warm-, and hot-working, respectively.

1.25 Two parts have been made of the same material, but one was formed by cold-working and the other by hot-working. Explain the differences you might observe between the two.

1.26 Do you think that it might be important to know whether a raw material for a manufacturing process has anisotropic properties? What about anisotropy in the finished product? Explain.

1.27 Explain why the strength of a polycrystalline metal at room temperature decreases as its grain size increases.

1.28 Describe the technique you would use to reduce the orange-peel effect on the surface of workpieces.

1.29 What is the significance of the fact that such metals as lead and tin have recrystallization temperatures at about room temperature?

1.30 As we know, temperature corresponds to the amplitude of vibration of individual atoms. Explain why high temperatures are needed for grain growth.

1.31 It has been noted that the more a metal has been cold-worked, the less it strain hardens. Explain why.

1.32 Is it possible to cold-work a metal at temperatures above the boiling point of water? Explain.

1.33 One form of surface treatment of a metal part involves cold-working the surface layer—for instance, by impacting it with small beads. (See, also, Section 33.2). How does this process affect the hardness of the material? Why would this process not work with (a) lead and (b) magnesium?

QUANTITATIVE PROBLEMS

1.34 Plot the data given in Table 1.1 in terms of grains/mm² vs. grains/mm³, and state your observations.

1.35 If the ball of a ball-point pen is 2 mm in diameter and has an ASTM grain size of 10, how many grains are there in the ball?

1.36 By cold-working, a strip of metal is reduced from 40 mm in thickness to 20 mm; a similar strip is reduced in a similar way from 40 mm to 30 mm. Which one of these cold-worked strips will recrystallize at a lower temperature? Why?

1.37 A paper clip is made of wire that is 6 in. long and 1/32-in. in diameter. If the ASTM grain size is 9, how many grains are there in the paper clip?

1.38 The unit cells shown in Figs. 1.2 through 1.4 can be represented by tennis balls arranged in various configurations in a box. In such an arrangement, *atomic packing factor* (APF) is defined as the ratio of the sum of the volumes of the atoms to the volume of the unit cell. Show that the packing factor is 0.68 for the bcc structure and 0.74 for the fcc structure.

1.39 Show that the lattice constant a in Fig. 1.3(a) is related to the atomic radius by the formula $a = 2\sqrt{2}R$, where R is the radius of the atom as depicted by the tennis-ball model.

1.40 Show that for the fcc unit cell, the radius r of the largest hole is given by $r = 0.414R$. Determine the size of the largest hole for the iron atoms in the fcc structure.

1.41 A technician determines that the grain size of a certain etched specimen is 8. Upon further checking, it is found that the magnification used was 180x instead of the 100x that is required by the ASTM standards. Determine the correct grain size.

1.42 If the diameter of the aluminum atom is 0.5 nm, how many atoms are there in a grain with ASTM grain size 5?

SYNTHESIS AND DESIGN

1.43 By stretching a thin strip of polished metal, as in a tension-testing machine, demonstrate and comment on what happens to its reflectivity as it is stretched.

1.44 Draw some analogies to mechanical fibering—for example, layers of thin dough sprinkled with flour or butter between each layer.

1.45 Draw some analogies to the phenomenon of hot shortness.

1.46 Obtain a number of small balls made of plastic, wood, marble, and so forth, and arrange them with your hands or glue them together to represent the crystal structures shown in Figs. 1.2-1.4. Comment on your observations.

1.47 Take a deck of playing cards, put a rubber band around them, and slip them against each other to represent Figs. 1.6a and 1.7. If you repeat the same experiment with more and more rubber bands around the same deck, what are you accomplishing as far as the behavior of the material is concerned?

2

Mechanical Behavior, Testing, and Manufacturing Properties of Materials

2.1 INTRODUCTION

In manufacturing operations, many parts are *formed* into various shapes by applying external forces to the workpiece by means of tools and dies. Typical operations are forging a turbine disk, extruding various parts for an aluminum ladder, and rolling a flat sheet to be processed into a car body. Because deformation in these processes is carried out by mechanical means, an understanding of the behavior of materials in response to externally applied forces is important. Forming operations may be carried out at room temperature or at elevated temperatures and at a low or a high rate of deformation.

The behavior of a manufactured part during its expected service life is an important consideration. For example, the wings of an aircraft, the crankshaft of an automobile engine, and the gear teeth in an automotive transmission are all subjected to static as well as fluctuating forces. If they are excessive, fluctuating forces can lead to cracks and can cause total failure of the components through a mechanism called *fatigue*.

Similarly, a turbine disk and its blades in the jet engine of an aircraft are subjected to high stresses and temperature during flight. Over a period of time these components undergo

55

TABLE 2.1   Relative Mechanical Properties of Various Materials at Room Temperature, in Decreasing Order. Metals are in their Alloy Form.

Strength	Hardness	Toughness	Stiffness	Strength/ Density
Glass fibers	Diamond	Ductile metals	Diamond	Reinforced plastics
Graphite fibers	Cubic boron nitride	Reinforced plastics	Carbides	Titanium
Kevlar fibers	Carbides	Thermoplastics	Tungsten	Steel
Carbides	Hardened steels	Wood	Steel	Aluminum
Molybdenum	Titanium	Thermosets	Copper	Magnesium
Steels	Cast irons	Ceramics	Titanium	Beryllium
Tantalum	Copper	Glass	Aluminum	Copper
Titanium	Thermosets		Ceramics	Tantalum
Copper	Magnesium		Reinforced plastics	
Reinforced thermosets	Thermoplastics		Wood	
Reinforced thermoplastics	Tin		Thermosets	
Thermoplastics	Lead		Thermoplastics	
Lead			Rubbers	

creep, a phenomenon in which the components elongate permanently under applied stresses; creep may eventually lead to failure.

As noted in Fig. 1.2, a wide variety of metallic and nonmetallic materials are now available, and they have an equally wide range of properties, as shown qualitatively in Table 2.1. This chapter covers those aspects of mechanical properties and behavior of metals that are relevant to the design and manufacture of parts, including commonly used tests employed in assessing the various properties of materials.

2.2   TENSION

The **tension test** is the most common test for determining such *mechanical properties* of materials as strength, ductility, toughness, elastic modulus, and strain hardening. The test first requires the preparation of a **test specimen**, typically as shown in Fig. 2.1a. In the United States, the specimen is prepared according to ASTM specifications; it is prepared to the specifications of the appropriate corresponding organization in other countries. Although most tension-test specimens are solid and round, some are flat-sheet or tubular.

FIGURE 2.1   (a) A standard tensile-test specimen before and after pulling, showing original and final gage lengths. (b) A typical tensile-testing machine.

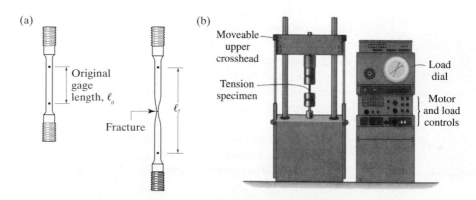

Typically, the specimen has an original **gage length**, l_o, generally 50 mm (2 in.), and a cross-sectional area A_o, usually with a diameter of 12.5 mm (0.5 in.). The specimen is mounted between the jaws of a tension-testing machine. These machines are equipped with various controls so that the specimen can be tested at different rates of deformation and temperature.

2.2.1 Stress–Strain Curves

A typical sequence of deformation of the tension-test specimen is shown in Fig. 2.2. When the load is first applied, the specimen elongates in proportion to the load. This effect is called **linear elastic behavior**. If the load is removed, the specimen returns to its original length and shape, in an elastic process similar to stretching a rubber band and releasing it.

The **engineering stress**, or **nominal stress**, is defined as the ratio of the applied load P to the original cross-sectional area A_o of the specimen:

$$\text{Engineering stress, } \sigma = \frac{P}{A_o}. \tag{2.1}$$

The **engineering strain** is defined as

$$\text{Engineering strain, } e = \frac{(l - l_o)}{l_o}, \tag{2.2}$$

where l is the instantaneous length of the specimen.

As the load is increased, the specimen begins, at some level of stress, to undergo **permanent (plastic) deformation**. Beyond that level, the stress and strain are no longer proportional, as they were in the elastic region. The stress at which this phenomenon occurs is known as the **yield stress**, Y, of the material. The term **proportional limit** is also used to specify the point where the stress and strain cease being proportional. The yield stresses and other properties for various metallic and nonmetallic materials are given in Table 2.2.

FIGURE 2.2   A typical stress–strain curve obtained from a tension test, showing various features.

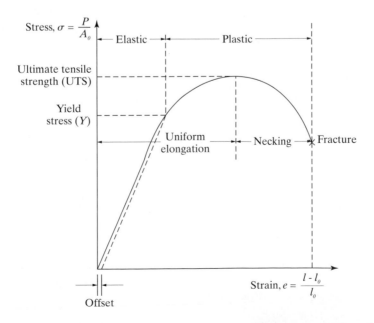

TABLE 2.2   Mechanical Properties of Various Materials at Room Temperature

Metals (Wrought)	E (GPa)	Y (MPa)	UTS (MPa)	Elongation in 50 mm (%)
Aluminum and its alloys	69–79	35–550	90–600	45–4
Copper and its alloys	105–150	76–1100	140–1310	65–3
Lead and its alloys	14	14	20–55	50–9
Magnesium and its alloys	41–45	130–305	240–380	21–5
Molybdenum and its alloys	330–360	80–2070	90–2340	40–30
Nickel and its alloys	180–214	105–1200	345–1450	60–5
Steels	190–200	205–1725	415–1750	65–2
Titanium and its alloys	80–130	344–1380	415–1450	25–7
Tungsten and its alloys	350–400	550–690	620–760	0
Nonmetallic materials				
Ceramics	70–1000	—	140–2600	0
Diamond	820–1050	—	—	—
Glass and porcelain	70–80	—	140	0
Rubbers	0.01–0.1	—	—	—
Thermoplastics	1.4–3.4	—	7–80	1000–5
Thermoplastics, reinforced	2–50	—	20–120	10–1
Thermosets	3.5–17	—	35–170	0
Boron fibers	380	—	3500	0
Carbon fibers	275–415	—	2000–3000	0
Glass fibers	73–85	—	3500–4600	0
Kevlar fibers	62–117	—	2800	0

Note: In the upper table the lowest values for E, Y, and UTS and the highest values for elongation are for pure metals. Multiply gigapascals (GPa) by 145,000 to obtain pounds per square in. (psi), megapascals (MPa) by 145 to obtain psi.

For soft and ductile materials, it may not be easy to determine the exact location on the stress–strain curve at which yielding occurs, because the slope of the straight (elastic) portion of the curve begins to decrease slowly. Therefore, we usually define Y as the point on the stress–strain curve that is **offset** by a strain of 0.002, or 0.2% elongation. This simple procedure is shown on the left side in Fig. 2.2.

As the specimen continues, under increasing load, to elongate beyond Y, its cross-sectional area decreases **permanently** and **uniformly** throughout its gage length. If the specimen is unloaded from a stress level higher than the yield stress, the curve follows a straight line downward and parallel to the original slope (Fig. 2.3). As the load is further increased, the engineering stress eventually reaches a maximum and then begins to decrease (Fig. 2.2). The maximum engineering stress is called the **tensile strength** (or **ultimate tensile strength** (**UTS**)), of the material. Values for UTS for some materials are given in Table 2.2.

If the specimen is loaded beyond its ultimate tensile strength, it begins to **neck**, or *neck down*. The cross-sectional area of the specimen is no longer uniform along the gage length and is smaller in the necked region. As the test progresses, the engineering stress drops further and the specimen finally fractures at the necked region. The engineering stress at fracture is known as **breaking** or **fracture stress**.

The ratio of stress to strain in the elastic region is known as the **modulus of elasticity**, E, or **Young's modulus** (after T. Young, 1773–1829):

$$\text{Modulus of elasticity, } E = \frac{\sigma}{e}. \tag{2.3}$$

This linear relationship is known as **Hooke's law** (after R. Hooke, 1635–1703). The modulus of elasticity is essentially a measure of the slope of the elastic portion of the curve and hence the **stiffness** of the material. Note in Eq. (2.3) that, because engineering strain is

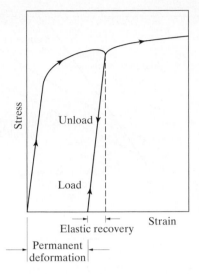

FIGURE 2.3 Schematic illustration of the loading and the unloading of a tensile-test specimen. Note that, during unloading, the curve follows a path parallel to the original elastic slope.

dimensionless, E has the same units as stress. The higher the E value, the higher the load required to stretch the specimen to the same extent, and thus the stiffer the material. Compare, for example, the stiffness of a piece of metal with that of a piece of rubber or plastic, when you try to stretch them to the same extent.

The elongation of the specimen under tension is accompanied by lateral contraction; this effect can be observed by stretching a rubber band. The absolute value of the ratio in the specimen of the lateral strain to the longitudinal strain is known as **Poisson's ratio** (after S. D. Poisson, 1781–1840); it is denoted by the letter ν.

2.2.2 Ductility

An important behavior observed during a tension test is **ductility**, that is, the extent of plastic deformation that the material undergoes before fracture. There are two common measures of ductility. The first is the **total elongation** of the specimen:

$$\text{Elongation} = \frac{(l_f - l_o)}{l_o} \times 100, \tag{2.4}$$

where l_f and l_o are measured as shown in Fig. 2.1a. Note that the elongation is based on the *original* gage length of the specimen and that it is calculated as a percentage.

The second measure of ductility is the **reduction of area:**

$$\text{Reduction of area} = \frac{(A_o - A_f)}{A_o} \times 100, \tag{2.5}$$

where A_o and A_f are the original and final (fracture) cross-sectional areas, respectively, of the test specimen. Reduction of area and elongation are generally interrelated; this effect is shown in Fig. 2.4, for some typical engineering metals.

Thus, the ductility of a piece of chalk is zero, because it does not stretch at all or reduce in cross-section; by contrast, a ductile specimen, such as a piece of clay or of chewing gum, stretches and necks considerably before it fails. Tensile reduction of area has been shown to predict the bendability (Section 16.5) and spinnability (Section 16.11) of metals.

2.2.3 True Stress and True Strain

We have seen that the engineering stress is based on the original cross-sectional area A_o of the specimen. We know, however, that the instantaneous cross-sectional area of the specimen becomes smaller as it elongates, just as the area of a rubber band does. Thus, engineering stress does not represent the *actual* stress to which the specimen is subjected.

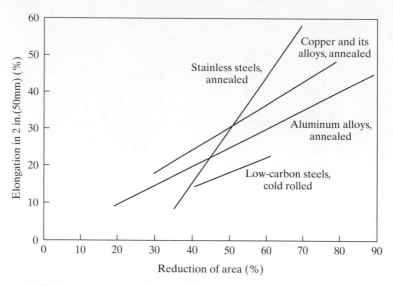

FIGURE 2.4   Approximate relationship between elongation and tensile reduction of area for various groups of metals.

True stress is defined as the ratio of the load P to the actual (instantaneous, hence true) cross-sectional area A of the specimen:

$$\text{True stress, } \sigma = \frac{P}{A}. \tag{2.6}$$

For true strain, we first consider the elongation of the specimen in increments of instantaneous change in length. Then, using calculus, we can show that the **true strain** (*natural* or *logarithmic strain*) is calculated as

$$\text{True strain, } \varepsilon = \ln\left(\frac{l}{l_o}\right). \tag{2.7}$$

Note from Eqs. (2.2) and (2.7) that, for small values of strain, the engineering and true strains are approximately equal. However, they diverge rapidly as the load increases. For example, when $e = 0.1$, $\varepsilon = 0.095$, and when $e = 1$, $\varepsilon = 0.69$.

Unlike engineering strains, true strains are consistent with actual physical phenomena in deformation of materials. Let's assume, for example, a hypothetical situation: A specimen 50 mm (2 in.) in height is compressed between flat platens to a final height of zero. In other words, we have deformed the specimen infinitely. According to their definitions, the engineering strain that the specimen undergoes is −1, but the true strain is −∞. Clearly, true strain describes the extent of deformation correctly, since in this case the deformation is indeed infinite.

2.2.4 Construction of Stress–Strain Curves

The procedure for constructing an engineering stress–strain curve is to take the load-elongation curve (Fig. 2.5a; also, Fig. 2.2), and then to divide the load (vertical axis) by the original cross-sectional area, A_o, and the elongation (horizontal axis) by the original gage length, l_o. Because these two quantities are divided by constants, the engineering stress–strain curve obtained (shown in Fig. 2.5b) has the same shape as the load-elongation curve shown in Fig. 2.5a. (In this example, $A_o = 0.056$ in.^{2} and $A_f = 0.016$ in.^{2}.)

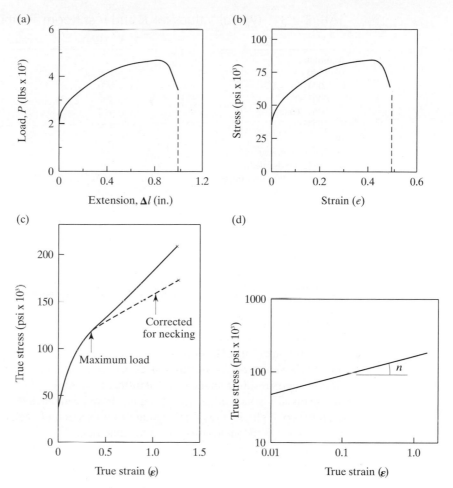

FIGURE 2.5   (a) Load-elongation curve in tension testing of a stainless steel specimen. (b) Engineering stress–engineering strain curve, drawn from the data in Fig. 2.5a. (c) True stress–true strain curve, drawn from the data in Fig. 2.5b. Note that this curve has a positive slope, indicating that the material is becoming stronger as it is strained. (d) True stress–true strain curve plotted on log–log paper and based on the corrected curve in Fig. 2.5c. The correction is due to the triaxial state of stress that exists in the necked region of a specimen.

True stress–true strain curves are obtained similarly, by dividing the load by the instantaneous cross-sectional area, with the true strain being obtained from Eq. (2.7). The result is shown in Fig. 2.5c. Note the *correction* to the curve; this reflects the fact that the specimen's necked region is subjected to three-dimensional tensile stresses, as described in more advanced texts. This state gives higher stress values than the actual true stress; to compensate, the curve must be corrected downward.

We can represent the true stress–true strain curve in Fig. 2.5c by the equation

$$\sigma = K\varepsilon^n, \tag{2.8}$$

where K is known as the **strength coefficient** and n as the **strain-hardening** (or **work-hardening**) **exponent**. The values for K and n for several metals are given in Table 2.3.

If we plot the corrected curve shown in Fig. 2.5c on a log–log graph, we find that it is approximately a straight line (Fig. 2.5d). The slope of the curve is equal to the exponent

TABLE 2.3   Typical Values for K and n at Room Temperature

	K (MPa)	n
Aluminum		
1100–O	180	0.20
2024–T4	690	0.16
6061–O	205	0.20
6061–T6	410	0.05
7075–O	400	0.17
Brass		
70–30, annealed	900	0.49
85–15, cold-rolled	580	0.34
Cobalt-base alloy, heat-treated	2070	0.50
Copper, annealed	315	0.54
Steel		
Low-C annealed	530	0.26
4135 annealed	1015	0.17
4135 cold-rolled	1100	0.14
4340 annealed	640	0.15
304 stainless, annealed	1275	0.45
410 stainless, annealed	960	0.10

n. Thus, the higher the slope, the greater the strain-hardening capacity of the material—that is, the stronger and harder it becomes as it is strained.

True stress–true strain curves for a variety of metals are given in Fig. 2.6. (When they are reviewed in detail, some differences between Table 2.3 and Fig. 2.6 will be noted; these discrepancies result from the fact that different sources of data and different test conditions are involved.) Note that the elastic regions have been deleted, because the slope in this region is very high. As a result, the point of intersection of each curve with the vertical axis in this figure is the yield stress, Y, of the material.

FIGURE 2.6   True stress–true strain curves in tension at room temperature for various metals. The curves start at a finite level of stress: The elastic regions have too steep a slope to be shown in this figure, and so each curve starts at the yield stress, Y, of the material.

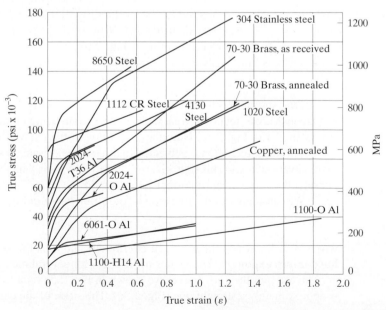

The area under the true stress–true strain curve is known as the material's **toughness**, that is, the amount of energy per unit volume that the material dissipates prior to fracture. Toughness, therefore, involves both the height and width of the stress–strain curve of the material, whereas strength is related only to the height of the curve and ductility is related only to the width of the curve.

2.2.5 Strain at Necking in a Tension Test

As we have noted, the onset of the necking of the specimen in a tension test corresponds to the ultimate tensile strength of the material. Note that the slope of the load-elongation curve at this point is zero, and it is at this point that the specimen begins to neck. The specimen cannot support the load because the cross-sectional area of the neck is becoming smaller at a rate that is higher than the rate at which the material becomes stronger (strain-hardens).

The true strain at the onset of necking is numerically equal to the strain-hardening exponent, n, of the material. Thus the higher the value of n, the higher the strain which a piece of material can experience *uniformly* throughout before it begins to neck. This observation is important, particularly in regard to sheet-metal forming operations that involve the stretching of the workpiece material (Chapter 16). We can see in Table 2.3 that annealed copper, brass, and stainless steel have high n values; this means that they can be stretched uniformly to a greater extent than can the other metals listed.

Example: Calculation of Ultimate Tensile Strength

This example will show that the UTS of a material can be calculated from its K and n values. Assume that a material has a true stress–true strain curve given by

$$\sigma = 100,000\varepsilon^{0.5} \text{ psi.}$$

Calculate the true ultimate tensile strength and the engineering UTS of this material.

Solution: Because the necking strain corresponds to the maximum load and the necking strain for this material is

$$\varepsilon = n = 0.5,$$

we have, as the *true* ultimate tensile strength,

$$\sigma = Kn^n = 100,000(0.5)^{0.5} = 70,710 \text{ psi.}$$

The true area at the onset of necking is obtained from

$$\ln\left(\frac{A_o}{A_{\text{neck}}}\right) = n = 0.5.$$

Thus,

$$A_{\text{neck}} = A_o \varepsilon^{-0.5},$$

and the maximum load P is

$$P = \sigma A_{\text{neck}} = \sigma A_o e^{-0.5},$$

where σ is the true ultimate tensile strength. Hence,

$$P = (70,710)(0.606)(A_o) = 42,850 A_o \text{ lb.}$$

Since UTS $= P/A_o$,

$$\text{UTS} = 42,850 \text{ psi.}$$

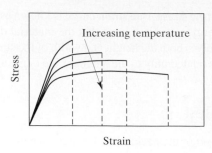

FIGURE 2.7   Typical effects of temperature on stress–strain curves. Note that temperature affects the modulus of elasticity, the yield stress, the ultimate tensile strength, and the toughness (area under the curve) of materials.

2.2.6   Temperature Effects

Increasing temperature generally has the following effects on stress–strain curves (Fig. 2.7):

a. It raises ductility and toughness, and
b. It lowers the yield stress and the modulus of elasticity.

Temperature also affects the strain-hardening exponent of most metals, in that n decreases with increasing temperature. The influence of temperature is, however, best described in conjunction with the rate of deformation.

2.2.7   Rate-of-Deformation Effects

Just as we can blow up a balloon or can stretch a rubber band at different rates, we can shape a piece of material in a manufacturing process at different speeds. Some machines, such as hydraulic presses, form materials at low speeds; others, such as mechanical presses, form at high speeds. To simulate such differences, the specimen can be strained at a rate corresponding to that which it will experience in the actual manufacturing process.

Deformation rate is defined as the speed at which a tension test is being carried out, in units of, say, m/s or ft/min. The **strain rate**, on the other hand, is a function of the specimen length. A short specimen elongates proportionately more during the same time period than does a long specimen.

For example, let's take two rubber bands, one of 20 mm and the other of 100 mm gage length, respectively, and elongate them both by 10 mm within a period of 1 second. The engineering strain in the shorter specimen is $\frac{10}{20} = 0.5$; that in the longer is $\frac{10}{100} = 0.1$. Thus, the strain rates are $0.5 \ s^{-1}$ and $0.1 \ s^{-1}$, respectively, with the short band being subjected to a strain rate five times as high as that for the long band, although they are both being stretched at the same deformation rate.

Deformation rates typically employed in various testing and metalworking processes, and the true strains involved, are given in Table 2.4. Note the considerable difference in magnitudes. Because of this wide range, strain rates are usually stated in terms of orders of magnitude, such as $10^2 \ s^{-1}$, $10^4 \ s^{-1}$, and so on.

The typical effects that temperature and strain rate jointly have on the strength of metals are shown in Fig. 2.8. We note that increasing the strain rate increases the strength of the material (**strain-rate hardening**). The slope of these curves is called the **strain-rate sensitivity exponent**, m. The value of m is obtained from log–log plots, provided that the vertical and horizontal scales are the same (unlike those in Fig. 2.8). A slope of $45°$ would, therefore, indicate a value of $m = 1$. The relationship is given by the equation

$$\sigma = C\dot{\varepsilon}^m, \tag{2.9}$$

TABLE 2.4   Typical Ranges of Strain and Deformation Rate
in Manufacturing Processes

Process	True strain	Deformation rate (m/s)
Cold working		
Forging, rolling	0.1–0.5	0.1–100
Wire and tube drawing	0.05–0.5	0.1–100
Explosive forming	0.05–0.2	10–100
Hot working and warm working		
Forging, rolling	0.1–0.5	0.1–30
Extrusion	2–5	0.1–1
Machining	1–10	0.1–100
Sheet-metal forming	0.1–0.5	0.05–2
Superplastic forming	0.2–3	10^{-4}–10^{-2}

where C is a **strength coefficient**, similar to, but not to be confused with, the strength coefficient K in Eq. (2.8). The constant C has the units of stress; $\dot{\varepsilon}$ is the true strain rate, defined as the true strain that the material undergoes per unit time.

Note, in Fig. 2.8, that the sensitivity of strength to strain rate increases with temperature; in other words, m increases with increasing temperature. Note, however, that the slope
is relatively flat at room temperature—that is, m is very low there. This condition is true for
most metals, but not for those that recrystallize at room temperature, such as lead and tin.
Some typical ranges of m for metals are as follows:

Cold-working: up to 0.05.

Hot-working: 0.05 to 0.4.

Superplastic materials: 0.3 to 0.85.

The magnitude of the strain-rate sensitivity exponent, m, significantly influences necking in a tension test. With increasing m, the material stretches farther before it fails, so in-

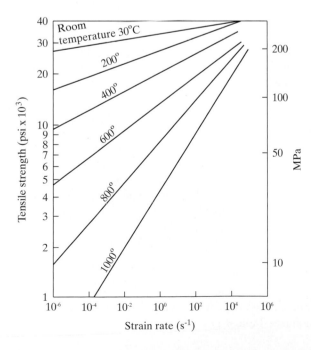

FIGURE 2.8   The effect of
strain rate on the ultimate
tensile strength for
aluminum. Note that, as
the temperature increases,
the slopes of the curves
increase; thus, strength
becomes more and more
sensitive to strain rate as
temperature increases.
Source: J. H. Hollomon.

creasing *m* delays necking. Ductility enhancement caused by the high strain-rate sensitivity of some materials has been exploited in **superplastic forming** of sheet metal (Section 16.12).

Superplasticity. The term **superplasticity** refers to the capability that some materials have to undergo large uniform elongation prior to necking and fracture in tension. The elongation may be on the order from a few hundred percent to as much as 2000 percent. Common materials exhibiting superplastic behavior are bubble gum and glass (at elevated temperatures) and thermoplastics. As a result, glass and thermoplastics can successfully be formed into complex shapes such as beverage bottles and lighted advertising signs.

Among metals exhibiting superplastic behavior are very fine-grain (10 to 15 μm) titanium alloys and alloys of zinc–aluminum; when heated, they can elongate to many times their original length. Superplastic behavior has been exploited in superplastic forming of metals.

2.2.8 Hydrostatic Pressure Effects

Various tests have been performed under hydrostatic pressure to determine the effect of hydrostatic pressure on mechanical properties of materials. Test results at pressures up to 3.5 GPa (500 ksi) indicate that increasing the hydrostatic pressure increases the strain at fracture substantially, both for ductile and for brittle materials.

This beneficial effect of hydrostatic pressure has been exploited in metalworking processes, particularly in hydrostatic extrusion (Section 15.7) and in compaction of metal powders (Section 17.3).

2.2.9 Radiation Effects

In view of the use of many metals and alloys in nuclear applications, extensive studies have been conducted on the effects of radiation on mechanical properties. Typical changes in the properties of steels and other metals exposed to high-energy radiation are increased yield stress, tensile strength, and hardness, and decreased ductility and toughness. Radiation has similar detrimental effects on the behavior of plastics (Chapter 7).

2.3 COMPRESSION

Many operations in manufacturing, particularly processes such as forging, rolling, and extrusion (Part III), are performed with the workpiece subjected to compressive forces. The **compression test**, in which the specimen is subjected to a compressive load, gives information useful for these processes.

This test is usually carried out by compressing a solid cylindrical specimen between two flat dies (platens). Because of friction between the specimen and the platens, the specimen's cylindrical surface bulges; this effect is called **barreling** (see Fig. 14.3). Friction prevents the top and bottom surfaces from expanding freely.

Because the cross-sectional area of the specimen now changes along its height, being maximum in the middle, obtaining stress–strain curves in compression is difficult. Furthermore, friction dissipates energy, so the compressive force is higher than it otherwise would be, in order to supply the work required to overcome friction. With effective lubrication, friction can be minimized, and a reasonably constant cross-sectional area can be maintained during the test.

When the results of compression tests and tension tests on *ductile* metals are compared, the true stress–true strain curves for the two tests coincide. This comparability does not hold true for *brittle* materials, which are generally stronger and more ductile in compression than in tension (see Table 8.1).

P

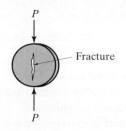

Fracture

P

FIGURE 2.9   Disk test on a brittle material, showing the direction of loading and the fracture path.

When a metal with a certain tensile yield stress is subjected to tension into the plastic range, and then the load is released and applied in compression, the yield stress in compression is lower than that in tension. This phenomenon is known as the **Bauschinger effect** (after J. Bauschinger, who reported it in 1881), and it is exhibited in varying degrees by all metals and alloys. Because of the lowered yield stress in the direction opposite the original load application, this phenomenon is also called **strain softening** or **work softening**.

Disk Test. For brittle materials such as ceramics and glasses, a **disk test** has been developed, in which the disk is subjected to compression between two hardened flat platens (Fig. 2.9). When the material is loaded as shown, tensile stresses develop perpendicular to the vertical centerline along the disk, fracture begins, and the disk splits in half vertically. The *tensile stress* σ in the disk is uniform along the centerline and can be calculated from the formula

$$\text{Tensile stress, } \sigma = \frac{2P}{\pi dt}, \tag{2.10}$$

where P is the load at fracture, d is the diameter of the disk, and t is its thickness. In order to avoid premature failure at the contact points, thin strips of soft metal are placed between the disk and the platens. These strips also protect the platens from being damaged during the test. The fracture at the center of the specimen has been utilized in the manufacture of *seamless tubing* (Section 13.6).

2.4 TORSION

In addition to tension and compression, a workpiece may be subjected to **shear** strains (Fig. 2.10), such as in the punching of holes in sheet metals (Section 16.2) and in metal cutting (Section 20.2). The test method generally used for determination of properties of materials in shear is the **torsion test**. In order to obtain an approximately uniform stress and strain distribution along the cross-section, this test is usually performed on a thin tubular specimen.

The torsion specimen usually has a reduced cross-section, in order to confine the deformation to a narrow zone. The **shear stress** can be calculated from the formula

$$\text{Shear stress, } \tau = \frac{T}{2\pi r^2 t}, \tag{2.11}$$

where T is the torque, r is the average radius of the tube, and t is the thickness of the tube.

FIGURE 2.10   A typical torsion-test specimen; it is mounted between the two heads of a testing machine and twisted. Note the shear deformation of an element in the reduced section of the specimen.

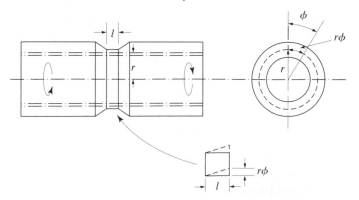

The **shear strain** can be calculated from the formula

$$\text{Shear strain, } \gamma = \frac{r\phi}{l}, \tag{2.12}$$

where l is the length of tube subjected to torsion and ϕ the **angle of twist** in radians.

The ratio of the shear stress to the shear strain in the elastic range is known as the **shear modulus**, or **modulus of rigidity**, G, a quantity related to the modulus of elasticity, E.

The angle of twist ϕ to fracture in the torsion of solid round bars at elevated temperatures is also useful in estimating the forgeability of metals. The greater the number of twists prior to failure, the greater is the forgeability (Section 14.8).

2.5 BENDING (FLEXURE)

Preparing specimens from brittle materials, such as ceramics and carbides, is difficult because of the problems involved in shaping and machining them to proper dimensions. Furthermore, because of their sensitivity to surface defects and notches, clamping brittle test specimens for testing is difficult. Improper alignment of the test specimen may result in nonuniform stress distribution along the cross-section of the specimen.

A commonly used test method for brittle materials is the **bend** or **flexure test**. It usually involves a specimen that has a rectangular cross-section and is supported at its ends (Fig. 2.11). The load is applied vertically, at either one point or two; as a result, these tests are referred to as **three-point** and **four-point** bending, respectively. The longitudinal stresses in these specimens are tensile at their lower surfaces and compressive at their upper surfaces.

These stresses can be calculated using simple beam equations described in texts on mechanics of solids. The stress at fracture in bending is known as the **modulus of rupture**, or **transverse rupture strength** (see Table 8.1). Note that, because of the larger volume of material subjected to the same bending moment in Fig. 2.11b, there is a higher probability that defects exist in this volume than in that in Fig. 2.11a. Consequently, the four-point test gives a lower modulus of rupture than the 3-point test.

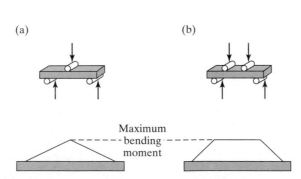

(a)   (b)

Maximum
bending
moment

FIGURE 2.11   Two bend-test methods for brittle materials: (a) three-point bending; (b) four-point bending. The areas on the beams represent the bending-moment diagrams, described in texts on mechanics of solids. Note the region of constant maximum bending moment in (b); by contrast, the maximum bending moment occurs only at the center of the specimen in (a).

2.6 HARDNESS

Hardness is a commonly used property; it gives a general indication of the strength of the material and of its resistance to scratching and to wear. More specifically, **hardness** is usually defined as *resistance to permanent indentation*. Thus, for example, steel is harder than aluminum, and aluminum is harder than lead. Hardness is not, however, a *fundamental* property, because the resistance to indentation depends on the shape of the indenter and on the load applied.

2.6.1 Hardness Tests

Several methods have been developed to measure the hardness of materials, using different *indenter* materials and shapes. Commonly used hardness tests are described below.

Brinell Test.   Introduced by J. A. Brinell in 1900, this test involves pressing a steel or tungsten-carbide ball 10 mm (0.4 in.) in diameter against a surface, with a load of 500 kg, 1500 kg, or 3000 kg (Fig. 2.12). The Brinell hardness number (HB, formerly BHN) is defined as the ratio of the load P to the curved surface area of the indentation. The harder the material to be tested, the smaller will be the impression, so a 1500-kg or 3000-kg load is usually recommended in order to obtain impressions sufficiently large for accurate measurement.

Depending on the condition of the material, one of two types of impression develops on the surface after the performance of a Brinell test (Fig. 2.13) or of any of the other hardness tests described in this section. The impressions in annealed metals generally have a rounded profile; in cold-worked metals they usually have a sharp profile (Fig. 2.13b). The correct method of measuring the indentation diameter, d, is shown in the figure.

The indenter, which has a finite elastic modulus, also undergoes elastic deformation under the applied load. As a result, hardness measurements may not be as accurate as expected. One method for minimizing this effect is to use tungsten-carbide balls; because of their high modulus of elasticity, they distort less than steel balls do. Carbide balls are usually recommended for Brinell hardness numbers greater than 500.

FIGURE 2.12   General characteristics of hardness-testing methods and formulas for calculating hardness. The quantity P is the load applied. *Source*: H. W. Hayden, et al., *The Structure and Properties of Materials*, Vol. III (John Wiley & Sons, 1965).

Test	Indenter	Shape of indentation Side view	Top view	Load, P	Hardness number
Brinell	10-mm steel or tungsten carbide ball			500 kg 1500 kg 3000 kg	$HB = \dfrac{2P}{(\pi D)(D - \sqrt{D^2 - d^2})}$
Vickers	Diamond pyramid	136°		1-120 kg	$HV = \dfrac{1.854P}{L^2}$
Knoop	Diamond pyramid	$L/b = 7.11$ $b/t = 4.00$		25g-5kg	$HK = \dfrac{14.2P}{L^2}$
Rockwell A C D	Diamond cone	120° $t = $ mm		kg 60 150 100	HRA HRC HRD } $= 100 - 500t$
B F G	$\frac{1}{16}$ - in. diameter steel ball	$t = $ mm		100 60 150	HRB HRF HRG } $= 130 - 500t$
E	$\frac{1}{8}$ - in. diameter steel ball			100	HRE

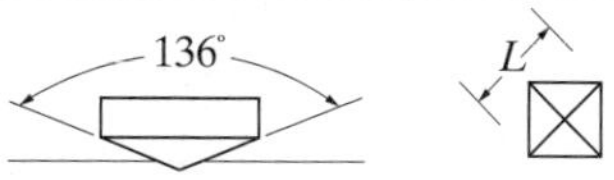

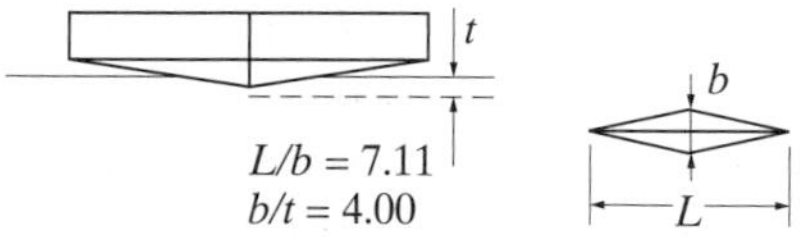

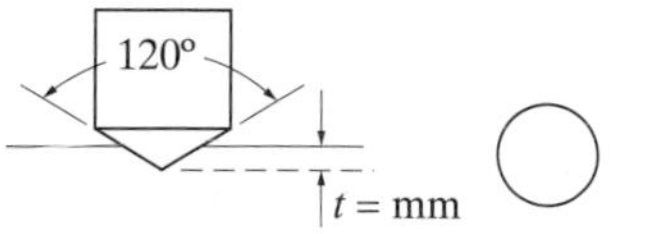

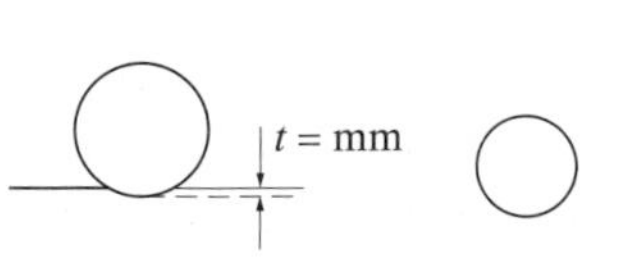

(a)

(b)

(c)

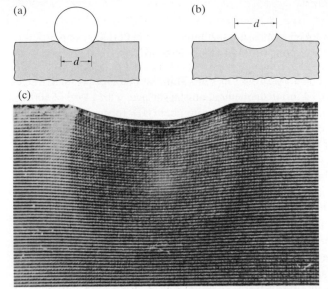

FIGURE 2.13   Indentation geometry in Brinell testing: (a) annealed metal; (b) work-hardened metal; (c) deformation of mild steel under a spherical indenter. Note that the depth of the permanently deformed zone is about one order of magnitude larger than the depth of indentation. For a hardness test to be valid, this zone should be fully developed in the material. *Source*: M. C. Shaw and C. T. Yang.

Rockwell Test.   Developed by S.P. Rockwell in 1922, this test measures the *depth* of penetration instead of the *diameter* of the indentation. The indenter is pressed onto the surface, first with a minor load and then with a major load. The difference in the depths of penetration is a measure of the hardness of the material.

Some of the more common Rockwell hardness scales (and the indenters used) are shown in Fig. 2.12. Rockwell **superficial hardness** tests have also been developed using the same type of indenters but lighter loads.

Vickers Test.   The *Vickers hardness test*, developed in 1922 and formerly known as the *diamond pyramid hardness* test, uses a pyramid-shaped diamond indenter (Fig. 2.12) and a load that ranges from 1 kg to 120 kg. The Vickers hardness number is indicated by HV (formerly, DPH). The impressions obtained are typically less than 0.5 mm (0.020 in.) on the diagonal. The Vickers test gives essentially the same hardness number regardless of the load and is suitable for testing materials with a wide range of hardness, including heat-treated steels.

Knoop Test.   The *Knoop test* (developed by F. Knoop in 1939) uses a diamond indenter in the shape of an elongated pyramid (Fig. 2.12), with applied loads ranging generally from 25 g to 5 kg. The Knoop hardness number is indicated by HK (formerly, KHN). Because of the light loads that are applied, it is a **microhardness** test. Therefore, it is suitable for very small or very thin specimens and for brittle materials, such as carbides, ceramics, and glass.

This test is also used for measuring the hardness of the individual grains and components in a metal alloy. The size of the indentation is generally in the range from 0.01 mm to 0.10 mm (0.0004 in. to 0.004 in.); consequently surface preparation is very important. Because the hardness number obtained depends on the applied load, Knoop test results should always cite the load used.

Scleroscope.   The *scleroscope* (from the Greek skleros, meaning hard) is an instrument in which a diamond-tipped indenter (hammer) enclosed in a glass tube is dropped onto the specimen from a certain height. The hardness is related to the *rebound* of the indenter: the higher the rebound, the harder the material. The impression made by a scleroscope is very small; consequently it is often used for such plated surfaces as rolls for metal rolling and hydraulic rams. The instrument is portable, and it is simply placed on the surface of the part; therefore, it is useful for measuring the hardness of large objects that otherwise would not fit into the limited space of conventional hardness testers.

Mohs Hardness.   Developed in 1822 by F. Mohs, this test is based on the capability of one material to *scratch* another. The Mohs hardness is based on a scale from 1 to 10, with 1 being the measure for talc and 10 that for diamond (the hardest substance known). A material with a higher Mohs hardness number always scratches one with a lower number. Soft metals have a Mohs hardness of 2 to 3, hardened steels about 6, and aluminum oxide (used for cutting tools and as an abrasive in grinding wheels) of 9. Although the Mohs scale is qualitative and is used mainly by mineralogists, it correlates well with Knoop hardness.

Durometer.   The hardness of rubbers, plastics, and similar soft and elastic non-metallic materials is generally measured with an instrument called a *durometer* (from the Latin *durus*, meaning hard). This is an empirical test, in which an indenter is pressed against the surface and then a constant load is rapidly applied. The *depth* of penetration is measured after one second; the hardness is inversely related to the penetration.

There are two different scales for this test. Type A has a blunt indenter and a load of 1 kg; it is used for softer materials. Type D has a sharper indenter and a load of 5 kg; it is used for harder materials. The hardness numbers in these tests range from 0 to 100.

Hot Hardness.   The hardness of materials at elevated temperatures (see Fig. 21.1) is important in applications in which higher temperatures are involved, such as the use of cutting tools in machining and of dies in hot-working and casting operations. Hardness tests can be performed at elevated temperatures with conventional testers, with some modifications, such as enclosing the specimen and indenter in a small electric furnace.

2.6.2 Hardness and Strength

Because hardness is the resistance to *permanent* indentation, we can liken it to performing a compression test on a small volume in a block of material (Fig. 2.13c). Studies have shown that (in the same units) the hardness of a cold-worked metal is about three times its yield stress, Y; for annealed metals, it is about five times Y.

A relationship has been established between the ultimate tensile strength (UTS) and the Brinell hardness (HB) for steels. In SI units, the relationship is

$$\text{UTS} = 3.5(\text{HB}), \tag{2.13}$$

where UTS is in MPa. In traditional units,

$$\text{UTS} = 500(\text{HB}), \tag{2.14}$$

where UTS is in psi and HB is in kg/mm^2, as measured for a load of 3000 kg.

2.6.3 Hardness–Testing Procedures

For a hardness test to be meaningful and reliable, the **zone of deformation** under the indenter (see Fig. 2.13c) must be allowed to develop freely. Consequently, the *location* of the indenter (with respect to the *edges* of the specimen to be tested) and the *thickness* of the specimen are important considerations. Generally, the location should be at least two diameters of the indenter from the edge of the specimen, and the thickness of the specimen should be at least 10 times the depth of penetration of the indenter. Successive indentations on the same surface of the workpiece should be far enough apart so as not to interfere with each other.

Moreover, the indentation should be sufficiently large to give a representative hardness value for the bulk material. If hardness variations need to be detected in a small area, or if the hardness of individual constituents in a matrix or an alloy is to be determined, the indentations should be very small, such as those in Knoop or Vickers tests using light loads.

While *surface preparation* is not critical for the Brinell test, it is important for the Rockwell test and even more important for the other hardness tests, because of the small sizes of the indentations. Surfaces may have to be polished to allow correct measurement of the impression's dimensions.

The values obtained from different hardness tests, on different scales, can be interrelated, and they can be converted using Fig. 2.14. Care should be exercised in using these charts, because of the many variables in material characteristics and in the shape of indentation.

FIGURE 2.14   Chart for converting various hardness scales. Note the limited range of most scales. Because of the many factors involved, these conversions are approximate.

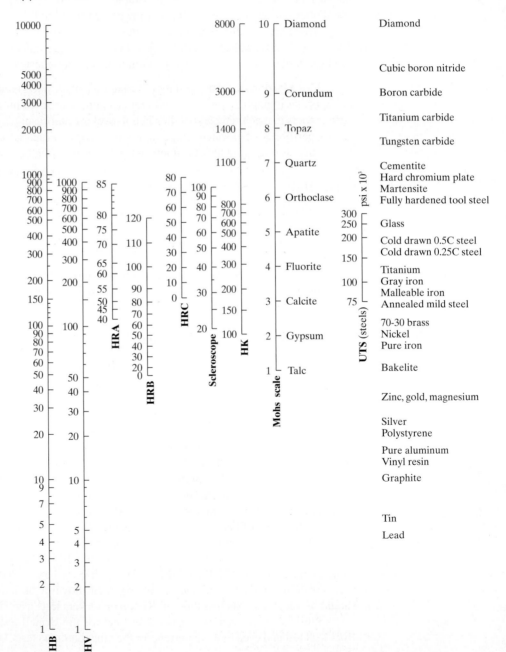

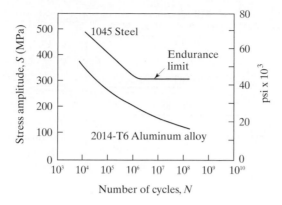

FIGURE 2.15   Typical *S–N* curves for two metals. Note that, unlike steel, aluminum does not have an endurance limit.

2.7 FATIGUE

Various structures and components in manufacturing operations, such as tools, dies, gears, cams, shafts, and springs, are subjected to rapidly fluctuating (cyclic or periodic) loads, in addition to static loads. **Cyclic stresses** may be caused by fluctuating mechanical loads, such as on gear teeth, or by thermal stresses, such as on a cool die coming into repeated contact with hot workpieces. Under these conditions, the part fails at a stress level below that at which failure would occur under static loading. This phenomenon is known as **fatigue failure**, and it is responsible for the majority of failures in mechanical components.

Fatigue *test methods* involve testing specimens under various states of stress, usually in a combination of tension and compression in torsion. The test is carried out at various *stress amplitudes* (*S*); the number of cycles (*N*) it takes to cause total failure of the specimen or part is recorded. *Stress amplitude* is defined as the maximum stress, in tension and compression, to which the specimen is subjected.

A typical plot, known as **S–N curves**, is shown in Fig. 2.15. These curves are based on complete reversal of the stress—that is, maximum tension, then maximum compression, then maximum tension, and so on—such as that imposed by bending an eraser or a piece of wire alternately in one direction and then the other. The test can also be performed on a rotating shaft with a constant downward load. The maximum stress to which the material can be subjected without fatigue failure, regardless of the number of cycles, is known as the **endurance limit** or **fatigue limit**.

Although many metals, especially steels, have a definite endurance limit, aluminum alloys do not have one, and the *S–N* curve continues its downward trend. For metals exhibiting such behavior, the fatigue strength is specified at a certain number of cycles, such as 10^7. In this way, the useful service life of the component can be specified. The endurance limit for metals can be approximately related to their ultimate tensile strength (Fig. 2.16). For carbon steels, the endurance limit is usually 0.4–0.5 times the tensile strength, although particular values can vary.

2.8 CREEP

Creep is the permanent elongation of a component under a static load maintained for a period of time. It is a phenomenon of metals and of certain nonmetallic materials, such as thermoplastics and rubbers, and it can occur at any temperature. Lead, for example, creeps under a constant tensile load at room temperature. For metals and their alloys, creep of any significance occurs at elevated temperatures, beginning at about 200 °C (400 °F) for aluminum alloys and at about 1500 °C (2800 °F) for refractory alloys. The mechanism of creep at elevated temperature in metals is generally attributed to **grain-boundary sliding** (Section 1.4).

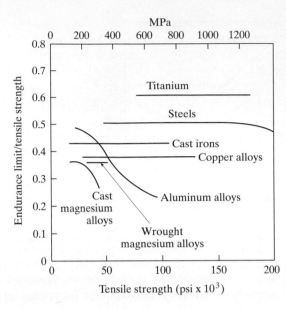

FIGURE 2.16   Ratio of endurance limit to tensile strength for various metals, as a function of tensile strength. Because aluminum does not have an endurance limit, the correlations for aluminum are based on a specific number of cycles, as is seen in Fig. 2.15.

Creep is especially important in high-temperature applications, such as gas-turbine blades and similar components in jet engines and rocket motors. High-pressure steam lines and nuclear-fuel elements also are subject to creep. Creep deformation can also occur in tools and dies that are subjected to high stresses at elevated temperatures during hot-working operations, such as forging and extrusion.

The creep test typically consists of subjecting a specimen to a constant tensile load (hence, constant engineering stress) at a certain temperature and of measuring the changes in length at various time increments. A typical creep curve usually consists of primary, secondary, and tertiary stages (Fig. 2.17). The specimen eventually fails by necking and fracture, called **rupture** or **creep rupture.** As expected, the creep rate increases with temperature and the applied load.

Design against creep usually involves a knowledge of the secondary (linear) range and its slope, because the creep rate can be determined reliably only when the curve has a constant slope. Generally, resistance to creep increases with the melting temperature of a material; that fact serves as a general guideline for design purposes. Stainless steels, superalloys, and refractory metals and alloys are commonly used in applications where resistance to creep is required.

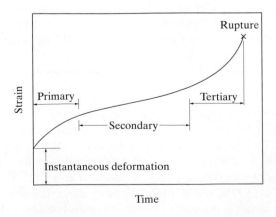

FIGURE 2.17   Schematic illustration of a typical creep curve. The linear segment of the curve (secondary) is used in designing components for a specific creep life.

Stress Relaxation.   Stress relaxation is closely related to creep. In **stress relaxation**, the stresses resulting from a loading of a structural component decrease in magnitude over a period of time, even though the dimensions of the component remain constant. An example is the decrease in tensile stress of a wire in tension between two fixed ends; other examples include rivets, bolts, guy wires, and similar parts under tension, compression, or flexure. This phenomenon is particularly common and important in thermoplastics (Section 7.3).

2.9 IMPACT

In many manufacturing operations, as well as during the service life of components, materials are subjected to **impact** (or *dynamic*) **loading**—for example, in high-speed metalworking operations such as drop forging (Section 14.9). A typical impact test consists of placing a notched specimen in an impact tester and breaking it with a swinging pendulum.

In the **Charpy** test, the specimen is supported at both ends (Fig. 2.18a); in the **Izod** test it is supported at one end like a cantilever beam (Fig. 2.18b). From the amount of swing of the pendulum, the energy dissipated in breaking the specimen can be obtained. This energy is the **impact toughness** of the material. Unlike hardness-test conversions (Fig. 2.14), no quantitative relationships have yet been established between Charpy and the Izod tests.

Impact tests are particularly useful in determining the ductile–brittle transition temperature of materials. (See Section 2.10.1.) Materials that have high impact resistance are generally those that have high strength and high ductility, and hence, high toughness. Sensitivity to surface defects (**notch sensitivity**) is important; it significantly lowers impact toughness.

2.10 FAILURE AND FRACTURE OF MATERIALS IN MANUFACTURING AND IN SERVICE

Failure is one of the most important aspects of material behavior, because it directly influences the selection of a material for a certain application, the methods of manufacturing, and the service life of the component. Because of the many factors involved, failure and fracture of materials is a complex area of study; this section focuses only on those aspects of

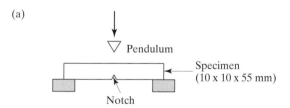

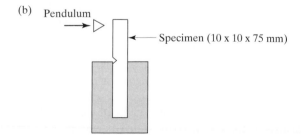

FIGURE 2.18   Impact test specimens: (a) Charpy; (b) Izod.

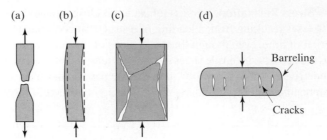

FIGURE 2.19 Schematic illustration of types of failures in materials: (a) necking and fracture of ductile materials; (b) buckling of ductile materials under a compressive load; (c) fracture of brittle materials in compression; (d) cracking on the barreled surface of ductile materials in compression.

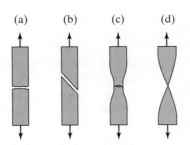

FIGURE 2.20 Schematic illustration of the types of fracture in tension: (a) brittle fracture in polycrystalline metals; (b) shear fracture in ductile single crystals—see also Fig. 1.6a; (c) ductile cup-and-cone fracture in polycrystalline metals; (d) complete ductile fracture in polycrystalline metals, with 100% reduction of area.

failure that are of particular significance to selecting and processing materials. There are two general types of failure:

1. **Fracture** and separation of the material, through either internal or external cracking—fracture is further subclassified into two general categories, *ductile* and *brittle* (Figs. 2.19 and 2.20).
2. **Buckling** (Fig. 2.19b).

Although failure of materials is generally regarded as undesirable, some products are designed in such a way that failure is essential for their function. Typical examples are (a) food and beverage containers with tabs (or entire tops) which are removed by tearing the sheet metal along a prescribed path and (b) screw caps for bottles.

2.10.1 Ductile Fracture

Ductile fracture is characterized by *plastic deformation* which precedes failure of the part (Fig. 2.19a). In a tension test, highly ductile materials such as gold and lead may neck down to a point before failing (Fig. 2.20d). Most metals and alloys, however, neck down to a finite area and then fail. Ductile fracture generally takes place along planes on which the *shear stress is a maximum*. In torsion, for example, a ductile metal fractures along a plane perpendicular to the axis of twist; that is the plane on which the shear stress is a maximum. Fracture in shear, by contrast, is a result of extensive slip along slip planes within the grains; see Fig. 1.7.

Upon close examination of the surface of a ductile fracture (Fig. 2.21), we can see a *fibrous* pattern with *dimples*, as if a number of very small tension tests have been carried out over the fracture surface. Failure is initiated with the formation of tiny *voids*, usually around small inclusions or preexisting voids, which then *grow* and *coalesce*, developing into cracks which grow in size and lead to fracture.

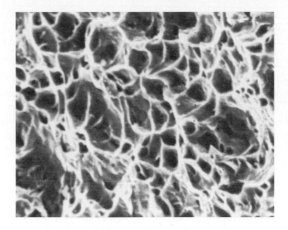

FIGURE 2.21   Surface of ductile fracture in low-carbon steel, showing dimples. Fracture is usually initiated at impurities, inclusions, or preexisting voids (microporosity) in the metal. *Source*: K.-H. Habig and D. Klaffke. Photo by BAM Berlin/Germany.

In a tension-test specimen, fracture begins at the center of the necked region, as a result of the growth and coalescence of cavities (Fig. 2.22). The central region becomes one large crack, as can be seen in the mid-section of the tension-test specimen in Fig. 2.22d; this crack then propagates to the periphery of the necked region. Because of its appearance, the fracture surface of a tension-test specimen is called a **cup-and-cone fracture**.

Effects of Inclusions.   Because they are nucleation sites for voids, *inclusions* have an important influence on ductile fracture and, consequently, on the workability of materials. Inclusions may consist of impurities of various kinds and of second-phase particles, such as oxides, carbides, and sulfides. The extent of their influence depends on such factors as their shape, their hardness, their distribution, and their fraction of total volume. The greater the by-volume fraction of inclusions, the lower will be the ductility of the material. Voids and porosity developed during processing, such as ones resulting from casting (Section 10.3.6), reduce the ductility of a material.

Two factors affect void formation:

a. the strength of the bond at the interface between an inclusion and the matrix—if the bond is strong, there is less tendency for void formation during plastic deformation;

b. the hardness of the inclusion. If it is soft, such as one of manganese sulfide, it will conform to the overall change in shape of the specimen or workpiece during plastic deformation; if the inclusion is hard (for example, carbides and oxides—see also Section 8.2), it could lead to void formation (Fig. 2.23). Hard inclusions, because of their brittle nature, may also break up into smaller particles during deformation.

FIGURE 2.22   Sequence of events in necking and fracture of a tensile-test specimen: (a) early stage of necking; (b) small voids begin to form within the necked region; (c) voids coalesce, producing an internal crack; (d) the rest of the cross-section begins to fail at the periphery, by shearing; (e) the final fracture surfaces, known as cup- (top fracture surface) and cone- (bottom surface) fracture.

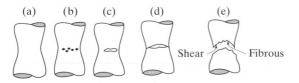

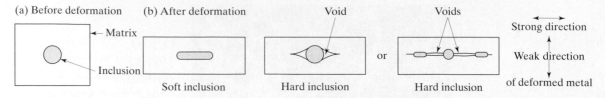

FIGURE 2.23   Schematic illustration of the deformation of soft and hard inclusions and of their effect on void formation in plastic deformation. Note that, because they do not comply with the overall deformation of the ductile matrix, hard inclusions can cause internal voids.

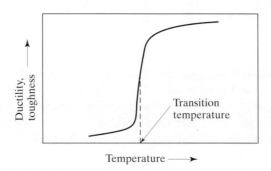

FIGURE 2.24   Schematic illustration of transition temperature in metals.

The alignment of inclusions during plastic deformation leads to **mechanical fibering** (Section 1.5). Subsequent processing of such a material must, therefore, involve considerations of the proper direction of working for maximum ductility and strength.

Transition Temperature.   Many metals undergo a sharp change in ductility and toughness across a narrow temperature range called the **transition temperature** (Fig. 2.24). This phenomenon occurs in body-centered cubic and in some hexagonal close-packed metals; it is rarely exhibited by face-centered cubic metals. The transition temperature depends on such factors as the composition, the microstructure, the grain size, the surface finish and shape of the specimen, and the deformation rate. High rates, abrupt changes in shape, and surface notches raise the transition temperature.

Strain Aging.   **Strain aging** is a phenomenon in which carbon atoms in steels segregate to dislocations, thereby pinning them and, in this way, increasing the resistance to dislocation movement. The result is increased strength and reduced ductility. Instead of taking place over several days at room temperature, this phenomenon can occur in just a few hours at a higher temperature; it is then called **accelerated strain aging**.

An example of accelerated strain aging in steels is **blue brittleness**, so named because it occurs in the blue-heat range where the steel develops a bluish oxide film. This phenomenon causes a marked decrease in ductility and toughness and an increase in the strength of plain-carbon and of some alloy steels.

2.10.2 Brittle Fracture

Brittle fracture occurs with little or no gross plastic deformation. In tension, fracture takes place along the crystallographic plane (**cleavage plane**) on which the normal tensile stress

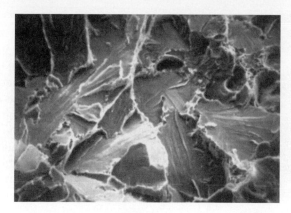

FIGURE 2.25   Fracture surface of steel that has failed in a brittle manner. The fracture path is transgranular (through the grains). Magnification: 200X. *Source*: Courtesy of B. J. Schulze and S. L. Meiley and Packer Engineering Associates, Inc.

is a maximum. Face-centered cubic metals usually do not fail in brittle fracture, whereas body-centered cubic (and some hexagonal close-packed) metals do fail by cleavage. In general, low temperature and a high rate of deformation promote brittle fracture.

In a polycrystalline metal under tension, the fracture surface has a bright *granular* appearance, because of the changes in the direction of the cleavage planes as the crack propagates from one grain to another (Fig. 2.25). Brittle fracture of a specimen in compression is more complex; it may even follow a path that is theoretically at an angle of 45° to the direction of the applied force.

Examples of fracture along a cleavage plane are the splitting of rock salt and the peeling of layers of mica. Tensile stresses normal to the cleavage plane, caused by pulling, initiate and control the propagation of fracture. Another example is the behavior of brittle materials, such as chalk, gray cast iron, and concrete; in tension, they fail in the manner shown in Fig. 2.20a. In torsion, they fail along a plane at an angle of 45° to the axis of twist (Fig. 2.10)—that is, along a plane on which the tensile stress is a maximum.

Defects.   An important factor in fracture is the presence of *defects*, such as scratches, flaws, and pre-existing external or internal cracks. Under tension, the sharp tip of the crack is subjected to high tensile stresses, which propagate the crack rapidly because the material has little capacity to dissipate energy.

The presence of defects is essential in explaining why brittle materials exhibit such weakness in tension (when it is compared to their strength in compression); see Table 8.1. The difference is on the order of 10 for rocks and similar materials, about 5 for glass, and about 3 for gray cast iron. Under tensile stresses, cracks propagate rapidly, causing what is known as *catastrophic failure*.

In polycrystalline metals, the fracture paths most commonly observed are **transgranular** (transcrystalline or intragranular); that is, the crack propagates *through* the grain. **Intergranular** fracture, where the crack propagates *along* the grain boundaries (Fig. 2.26), generally occurs when the grain boundaries are soft, contain a brittle phase, or have been weakened by liquid- or solid-metal embrittlement (Section 1.4).

Fatigue Fracture.   Fatigue fracture typically occurs in materials of a basically brittle nature. Minute external or internal cracks develop at pre-existing flaws or defects in the material; these cracks then propagate, and, eventually, they lead to total failure of the part. The fracture surface in fatigue is generally characterized by the term **beach marks**, because of its

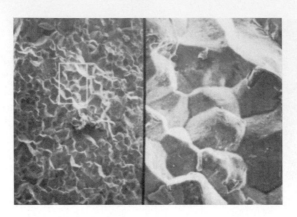

FIGURE 2.26   Intergranular fracture, at two different magnifications. Grains and grain boundaries are clearly visible in this micrograph. The fracture path is along the grain boundaries. Magnification: left, 100X; right, 500X. *Source*: Courtesy of B. J. Schulze and S. L. Meiley and Packer Engineering Associates, Inc.

appearance (Fig. 2.27). Under high magnification (typically more than 1000X), a series of **striations** can be seen on fracture surfaces, each beach mark consisting of several striations.

Improving Fatigue Strength.   Fatigue life is greatly influenced by the method of preparation of the surfaces of the part or specimen (Fig. 2.28). The fatigue strength of manufactured products can be improved overall by the following methods:

   a. inducing compressive residual stresses on surfaces—for example, by shot peening or by roller burnishing (Section 33.2);

   b. surface (case) hardening by various means (Section 4.10);

   c. providing a fine surface finish and thereby reducing the effects of notches and other surface imperfections;

   d. selecting appropriate materials and ensuring that they are free from significant amounts of inclusions, voids, and impurities.

Conversely, the following factors and processes can reduce fatigue strength: decarburization; surface pits (due to corrosion) that act as stress raisers; hydrogen embrittlement; galvanizing; and electroplating.

Stress–Corrosion Cracking.   An otherwise ductile metal can fail in a brittle manner by **stress–corrosion cracking** (also called **stress cracking** or **season cracking**). Parts

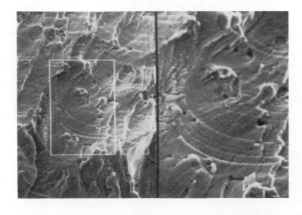

FIGURE 2.27   Typical fatigue-fracture surface on metals, showing beach marks. Magnification: left, 500X; right, 1000X. *Source*: Courtesy of B. J. Schulze and S. L. Meiley and Packer Engineering Associates, Inc.

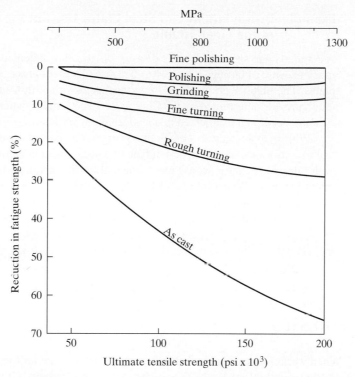

FIGURE 2.28   Reductions in the fatigue strength of cast steels subjected to various surface-finishing operations. Note that the reduction becomes greater as the surface roughness and the strength of the steel increase. *Source*: M. R. Mitchell.

free from defects may develop cracks, either over a period of time or soon after being manufactured into a product. Crack propagation may be either intergranular or transgranular.

The susceptibility of metals to stress–corrosion cracking depends mainly on the material, on the presence and magnitude of *tensile residual stresses*, and on the environment. Brass and austenitic stainless steels are among the metals that are highly susceptible to stress cracking. The environment could include corrosive media such as salt water or other chemicals. The usual procedure to avoid stress–corrosion cracking is to *stress-relieve* the part just after it is formed. Full annealing may also be done, but this treatment reduces the strength of cold-worked parts.

Hydrogen Embrittlement.   The presence of *hydrogen* can reduce ductility and can cause severe embrittlement and premature failure in many metals, alloys, and nonmetallic materials. This phenomenon is known as **hydrogen embrittlement**, and it is especially severe in high-strength steels. Possible sources of hydrogen occur during melting of the metal, during pickling (removing of surface oxides by chemical or electrochemical reaction), and during electrolysis in electroplating; others are water vapor in the atmosphere and moist electrodes and fluxes used during welding. *Oxygen* can also cause embrittlement, particularly in copper alloys.

Example: Brittle Fracture of Steel Plates Used in the Construction of the Liner Titanic

A detailed analysis of the *Titanic* disaster in 1912 has indicated that the ship sank not so much because of hitting an iceberg as because of structural weaknesses in the ship's steel plates. The plates were made of low-grade steel with a high sulfur content; it had little toughness (as determined by the Charpy test, Section 2.9) when chilled (as it was in the Atlantic ocean) and subjected to an external impact loading.

With such a material, a crack that starts in one part of a welded steel hull can propagate rapidly and completely around the hull and cause a large ship to split in two. A plate with higher toughness would have reduced the fracturing and allowed the ship to stay afloat longer and flood more slowly.

Although *Titanic* was built with brittle plates, as we now know from physical and photographic observations of the sunken ship, not all ships of that time were built with such low-grade steel. Furthermore, better construction techniques could have been employed, among them better welding techniques (Part V), to improve the structural strength of the hull.

2.11 RESIDUAL STRESSES

When workpieces are subjected to deformation that is not uniform throughout the part, they develop **residual stresses**. These are stresses that remain within a part after it has been formed and has had all external forces removed. A typical example is the bending of a piece of metal (Fig. 2.29).

The bending moment first produces a linear elastic stress distribution (Fig. 2.29a). As the external moment is increased, the outer fibers in the part reach a stress level high enough to cause yielding. For a typical strain-hardening material, the stress distribution shown in Fig. 2.29b is eventually obtained, and the part has undergone permanent bending.

FIGURE 2.29   Residual stresses developed in bending a beam having a rectangular cross-section. Note that the horizontal forces and moments caused by residual stresses in the beam must be balanced internally. Because of nonuniform deformation during metalworking operations, most parts develop residual stresses.

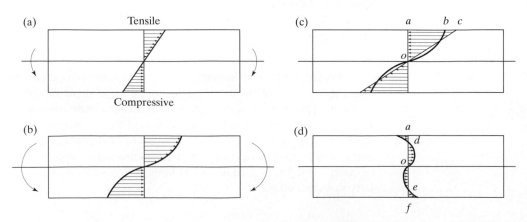

Let's now remove the external moment on the part; this operation is equivalent to applying an equal but opposite moment. Consequently, the moments of the areas *oab* and *oac* in Fig. 2.29c must be equal. Line *oc*, which represents the opposite moment, is linear, because all unloading and recovery is *elastic* (see Fig. 2.3). The difference between the two stress distributions gives the residual stress pattern within the part, as is shown in Fig. 2.29d. Note the compressive residual stresses in layers *ad* and *oe*, and the tensile residual stresses in layers *do* and *ef*.

Because there are no external forces applied, the internal forces resulting from these residual stresses must be in static equilibrium. Although this example involves only residual stresses in the longitudinal direction of the beam, in most cases in manufacturing operations these stresses are three-dimensional.

The equilibrium of residual stresses in Fig. 2.29d may at some time be disturbed by the removal of a layer of material from the part. The beam will then acquire a new radius of curvature, in order to balance the internal forces. Such disturbances of residual stresses lead to **warping** of parts (Fig. 2.30). The equilibrium of residual stresses may also be disturbed by *relaxation* of these stresses over a period of time (see below).

Residual stresses can also be caused by *temperature gradients* within a body, such as occur during cooling of a casting or a forging. The local expansion and contractions caused by temperature gradients within the material produce a nonuniform deformation, such as is seen in the permanent bending of a beam.

Tensile residual stresses in the surface of a part are generally undesirable, because they lower the fatigue life and fracture strength of the part. These conditions result because a surface with tensile residual stresses cannot sustain additional tensile stresses from external forces as high as those that a surface free from residual stresses can.

This weakening is particularly characteristic of brittle (or less ductile) materials, in which fracture takes place with little or no plastic deformation beforehand. Tensile residual stresses can also lead, over a period of time, to *stress cracking* or to *stress–corrosion cracking* of manufactured products.

Compressive residual stresses on a surface, on the other hand, are generally desirable. In fact, as we stated earlier, in order to increase the fatigue life of components, compressive residual stresses are imparted to surfaces by techniques such as shot peening and surface rolling (Section 33.2).

Reduction and Elimination of Residual Stresses.   Residual stresses can be reduced or eliminated either by *stress-relief annealing* or by a further *deformation* of the part, such as stretching it. Given sufficient time, residual stresses may also diminish at room temperature, by relaxation of residual stresses. The time required for relaxation can be greatly reduced by raising the temperature of the workpiece.

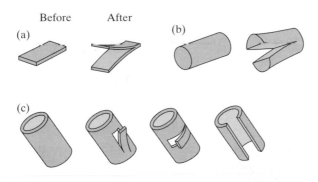

FIGURE 2.30   Distortion of parts, with residual stresses, after cutting or slitting: (a) flat sheet or plate; (b) solid round rod; (c) thin-walled tubing or pipe.

2.12 WORK, HEAT, AND TEMPERATURE

Almost all the mechanical work of deformation in plastic working is converted into **heat**. This conversion is not complete, because a portion of this work is stored within the deformed material as elastic energy. This residual work is known as **stored energy** (Section 1.6), and it is generally 5% to 10% of the total energy input; in some alloys, however, it may be as high as 30%.

In a simple frictionless process, assuming that work is completely converted into heat, the theoretical (adiabatic) *temperature rise*, ΔT, is given by

$$\Delta T = \frac{u}{\rho c}, \tag{2.15}$$

where u is the **specific energy** (work of deformation per unit volume), ρ is the density, and c is the specific heat of the material. It can be seen that higher temperatures are associated with large areas under the stress-strain curve and with smaller values of specific heat. It should be noted that such properties as specific heat and thermal conductivity also depend on temperature, and they must be taken into account in the calculations.

The temperature rise for a true strain of 1 (such as occurs in a 27 mm-high specimen when it is compressed down to 10 mm) can be calculated to be as follows: aluminum, 75 °C (165 °F); copper, 140 °C (285 °F); low-carbon steel, 280 °C (535 °F); titanium 570 °C (1060 °F). In actual operations, heat is lost to the environment, to tools and dies, and to any lubricants or coolants used.

If the process is performed very rapidly, these losses can be relatively small over that period. If the process is carried out slowly, the actual temperature rise will be only a small portion of the calculated value.

Example: Calculation of Temperature Rise

Calculate the specific energy and the theoretical temperature rise for an element in the necked area of a tension-test specimen, using the data given in Fig. 2.5.

Solution: The specific energy of an element in the necked area (at fracture) is the area under the (corrected) true stress–true strain curve in Fig. 2.5c. This area is estimated to be 155,000 in. $\cdot$ lb/in^3. The theoretical temperature rise is obtained from Eq. (2.15). Assuming that the specimen is made of stainless steel with $\rho = 0.29$ lb/in.^{3} and $c = 0.12$ Btu/lb $\cdot$ °F, we have

$$\Delta T = 155,000/(0.29)(0.12)(778)(12) = 477\ °F = 247\ °C.$$

Note that the actual temperature rise will be lower, because of the heat loss, during testing, from the necked zone to the rest of the specimen and to the environment.

SUMMARY

- Many manufacturing processes involve shaping materials by plastic deformation; such mechanical properties as strength (yield, strength Y, and ultimate tensile strength, UTS), modulus of elasticity (E), ductility (total elongation and reduction of area), hardness, and the energy required for plastic deformation are, therefore, important factors. These properties, in turn, depend on the particular material and on its condition, temperature, deformation rate, surface condition, and environment.

- Tensile tests are ones the most commonly used to determine mechanical properties; from these, true stress–true strain curves are developed that are important in determining the strength coefficient (K), the strain-hardening exponent (n), the strain-rate sensitivity exponent (m), and the toughness of materials.
- Compression tests are subject to inaccuracy due to the presence of friction and to resultant barreling of the specimen. Torsion tests are conducted on tubular specimens subjected to twisting. Bending or flexure tests are commonly used for brittle materials, to determine the modulus of rupture or the transverse rupture strength.
- A variety of hardness tests are used to determine the resistance of a material to permanent indentation or scratching. Hardness is related to strength and to wear resistance, but it is, itself, not a fundamental property of a material.
- Fatigue tests indicate the endurance limit or fatigue limit of materials—that is, the maximum stress to which a material can be subjected without fatigue failure, regardless of the number of cycles.
- Creep is the permanent elongation of a component under a static load maintained for a period of time. The specimen eventually fails by rupture (necking and fracturing), as it does in a tension test.
- Impact tests determine the energy required to rupture (completely break) the specimen; this energy is called the impact toughness of the material. Impact tests are also useful for determining the ductile–brittle transition temperature of materials.
- Residual stresses are those which remain in a workpiece after it has been plastically deformed and then has had all external forces removed. Surface tensile residual stresses are generally undesirable; they may be reduced or eliminated by stress-relief annealing, by further plastic deformation, or by relaxation over a period of time.
- Failure and fracture is an important aspect of a material's behavior when it is subjected to deformation in manufacturing operations. Ductile fracture is characterized by plastic deformation preceding fracture, and it requires considerable energy. Brittle fracture can be catastrophic because it is not preceded by plastic deformation; it requires much less energy than ductile fracture. Impurities and inclusions play a major role in the fracture of metals and alloys.

TRENDS

- Testing equipment is being designed and manufactured with computer controls for better accuracy and efficiency of operation.
- New hardness testers have been developed to measure the hardness of coatings as thin as ten nanometers.
- The influence of flaws, of impurities, of inclusions in raw materials, and of various other factors continues to be studied, with a view toward improving the quality and the reliability of manufactured products.
- Reliable test methods for brittle materials such as ceramics and carbides continue to be developed.

KEY TERMS

Bauschinger effect	Creep	Elongation
Blue brittleness	Deformation rate	Engineering strain
Buckling	Disk test	Engineering stress
Compression	Ductility	Fatigue

Fatigue failure
Fracture
Hardness
Impact loading
Inclusions
Microhardness
Modulus of elasticity
Modulus of rigidity
Modulus of rupture
Poisson's ratio

Reduction of area
Residual stresses
Rupture
Shear
Shear modulus
Strain aging
Strain-hardening exponent
Strain rate
Strain-rate sensitivity exponent
Strength coefficient

Stress–corrosion cracking
Superplasticity
Tension
Torsion test
Toughness
Transition temperature
True strain
True stress
Ultimate tensile strength
Yield stress

BIBLIOGRAPHY

Ashby, M.F., *Materials Selection in Mechanical Design* (2d ed). Pergamon, 1999.

Ashby, M.F., and D.R.H. Jones, *Engineering Materials*, Vol. 1, *An Introduction to Their Properties and Applications* (2d ed.), 1996; Vol. 2, *An Introduction to Microstructures, Processing and Design* (2d ed.), 1998; Vol. 3, *Materials Failure Analysis: Case Studies and Design Implications*, 1993. Pergamon.

ASM Handbook, Vol. 8: *Mechanical Testing*. ASM International, 1985.

Boyer, H.E. (ed.), *Atlas of Stress–Strain Curves*. ASM International, 1986.

Budinski, K.G., *Engineering Materials: Properties and Selection*, (5th ed.). Prentice Hall, 1996.

Chawla, K.K., and M.A. Majers, *Mechanical Behavior of Materials*. Prentice Hall, 1998.

Courtney, T.H., *Mechanical Behavior of Materials*. McGraw-Hill, 1990.

Davis, H.E., G.E. Troxell, and G.F.W. Hauck, *The Testing of Engineering Materials* (4th ed.). McGraw-Hill, 1982.

Dieter, G.E. *Mechanical Metallurgy* (3d ed.). McGraw-Hill, 1986.

Dowling, N.E., *Mechanical Behavior of Materials: Engineering Methods for Deformation, Fracture, and Fatigue.* (2d ed.). Prentice Hall, 1999.

Hardness Testing. ASM International, 1987.

REVIEW QUESTIONS

2.1 Distinguish between engineering stress and true stress.

2.2 Describe the events that occur when a specimen undergoes a tension test. Sketch a plausible stress–strain curve, and identify all significant regions and points between them. Assume that loading continues up to fracture.

2.3 What is ductility, and how is it measured?

2.4 In the equation $\sigma = K\varepsilon^n$, which represents the stress-strain curve for a material, what is the significance of the exponent n?

2.5 What is strain-rate sensitivity, and how is it measured?

2.6 What test can measure the properties of a material undergoing shear strain?

2.7 What testing procedures can be used to measure the properties of brittle materials, such as ceramics and carbides?

2.8 Describe the differences between brittle and ductile fracture.

2.9 Explain the difference between stress relaxation and creep.

2.10 Describe the difference between elastic and plastic behavior.

2.11 Explain what uniform elongation is in tension testing.

2.12 Describe the difference between deformation rate and strain rate. What unit does each one have?

2.13 Describe the difficulties involved in making a compression test.

2.14 What is Hooke's Law? Young's Modulus? Poisson's ratio?

2.15 What is necking?

2.16 What is the reason that a yield strength is defined as a 0.2% offset strength?

2.17 Why does the fatigue strength of a specimen or part depend on its surface finish?

2.18 If striations are observed under microscopic examination of a fracture surface, what do they suggest regarding the mode of fracture?

2.19 Explain the difference between transgranular and intergranular fracture.

QUALITATIVE PROBLEMS

2.20 Using the same scale for stress, the tensile true stress–true strain curve is higher than the engineering stress–engineering strain curve. Explain whether this condition also holds for a compression test.

2.21 With the aid of a simple sketch, explain whether it is necessary to use the offset method to determine the yield stress, Y, of a material that has been highly cold-worked.

2.22 Explain why the difference between engineering strain and true strain becomes larger as strain increases. Does this difference occur for both tensile and compressive strains? Explain.

2.23 If a material does not have an endurance limit (for example, aluminum), how would you estimate its fatigue life?

2.24 Which hardness tests and scales would you use for very thin strips of metal, such as aluminum foil? Why?

2.25 Which of the two tests, tension or compression, requires higher capacity of testing machine, and why?

2.26 List and explain briefly the conditions that induce brittle fracture in an otherwise ductile metal.

2.27 List the factors that you would consider in selecting a hardness test and in then interpreting the results from this test.

2.28 Using Fig. 2.6 only, explain why you cannot calculate the percent elongation of the materials listed.

2.29 If you pull and break a tension-test specimen rapidly, where would the temperature be highest, and why?

2.30 Comment on your observations regarding the contents of Table 2.2.

2.31 Is a rubber band an example of brittle or ductile material, when tested at different temperatures?

2.32 Will the disk test be applicable to a ductile material?

2.33 What hardness test is suitable for determining the hardness of a thin ceramic coating?

2.34 An increase in surface roughness leads to reductions in fatigue strengths. On a steel surface, a shot-peening operation leads to an increase in fatigue strength, even though the surface roughness increases. Explain this paradox.

2.35 Wire rope consists of many wires which bend and unbend as the rope is run over a sheave. A wire-rope failure is investigated, and it is found that some of the wires, when examined under a scanning electron microscope, display dimples, while others display transgranular fracture surfaces. Explain these observations.

2.36 A statistical sampling of Rockwell C hardness tests are conducted on a material, and it is determined that the material is defective because of insufficient hardness. The supplier claims that the tests are flawed because the diamond-cone indenter was probably dull. Is this a valid concern? Explain.

2.37 In a Brinell hardness test, the resulting impression is found to be an ellipse. Give possible explanations for this result.

2.38 Some coatings are extremely thin—some, as thin as a few nanometers. Explain why even the Knoop test is not able to obtain reasonable results for such coatings. Recent research has attempted to use highly polished diamonds (tip radius around 5 nanometers) to indent such coatings in atomic force microscopes. What concerns would you have regarding the appropriateness of the results?

QUANTITATIVE PROBLEMS

2.39 A paper clip is made of wire 1.2 mm in diameter. If the original material from which the wire is made is a rod 18 mm in diameter, calculate the longitudinal engineering and true strains that the wire has undergone during processing.

2.40 A strip of metal is 200 mm long. It is stretched in two steps, first to 350 mm and then to 400 mm. Show that the total true strain is the sum of the true strains in each step—that is, that true strains are additive. Show that, in the case of engineering strains, the strains cannot be added to obtain the total strain.

2.41 Identify the two materials in Fig. 2.6 that have the lowest and the highest uniform elongations. Calculate these quantities as percentages of the original gage lengths.

2.42 If you remove the layer of material *ad* from the part shown in Fig. 2.29d—for instance, by machining or grinding, which way will the specimen curve? (*Hint:* Assume that the part shown in sketch *d* in the figure is composed of four horizontal springs held at the ends. Thus, from the top down you have compression, tension, compression, and tension springs.)

2.43 Percent elongation is always described in terms of the original gage length, such as 50 mm or 2 in. Explain how percent elongation varies as the gage length of the tensile specimen increases. (*Hint:* Recall that necking is a local phenomenon, and think of what happens to the elongation as the gage length becomes very small.)

2.44 Make a sketch showing the nature and distribution of residual stresses in Fig. 2.30a and b, before they were cut. (*Hint:* Assume that the split parts are free from any stresses; then force these parts back to the shape they had before they were cut.)

2.45 You are given the K and n values of two different metals. Is this information sufficient to determine which metal is tougher? If not, what additional information do you need?

2.46 A cable is made of two strands of different materials, A and B, and cross-sections as follows:

For material A: $K = 70,000$ psi, $n = 0.5$, $A_o = 0.6$ in^2.

For material B: $K = 25,000$ psi, $n = 0.5$, $A_o = 0.3$ in^2.

Calculate the maximum tensile force that this cable can withstand prior to necking.

2.47 On the basis of the information given in Fig. 2.6, calculate the ultimate tensile strength (engineering) of annealed copper.

2.48 In a disk test performed on a specimen 1.25 in. in diameter and 3/8 in. thick, the specimen fractures at a stress of 30,000 psi. What was the load on it?

2.49 A piece of steel has a hardness of 350 HB. Calculate the tensile strength in MPa and in psi.

2.50 A material has the following properties: UTS = 50,000 psi and $n = 0.3$. Calculate its strength coefficient, K.

2.51 A material has a strength coefficient $K = 100,000$ psi and $n = 0.2$. Assuming that a tensile-test specimen made from this material begins to neck at a true strain of 0.2, show that the ultimate tensile strength of this material is 59,340 psi.

2.52 *Modulus of resilience* is defined as the area under the elastic region of the stress-strain curve of the material; it has the units of energy per unit volume. Derive an expression for the modulus of resilience in terms of the yield stress and modulus of elasticity of the material.

2.53 What is the modulus of resilience for a highly cold-worked piece of steel having a hardness of 260 HB? For a piece of highly cold-worked copper with a hardness of 100 HRB?

2.54 Using only Fig. 2.6, calculate the maximum load in tension testing of a 304 stainless steel specimen with an original diameter of 7 mm.

2.55 Plot the true stress–true strain curves for the materials in Table 2.3.

2.56 The design specification for a metal requires a minimum hardness of 75 HRA. If a Rockwell test is performed and the depth of penetration is 75 μm, is the material acceptable?

2.57 If a material has a target hardness of 400 HB, what is the expected indentation diameter?

2.58 A material is tested in tension. Over a 1-in. gage length, the engineering strain measurements are 0.01, 0.02, 0.03, 0.04, 0.05, 0.1, 0.15, 0.2, 0.5, and 1.0. Plot the true strain versus engineering strain for these readings.

SYNTHESIS AND DESIGN

2.59 List and explain the desirable mechanical properties for (a) an elevator cable, (b) a paper clip, (c) a leaf spring for a truck, (d) a bracket for a bookshelf, (e) piano wire, (f) a wire coat hanger, (g) a gas-turbine blade, and (h) a staple.

2.60 When making a hamburger, have you observed the type of cracks shown in Fig. 2.19d? What can you do to avoid such cracks? (*Note*: Test hamburger patties by compressing them at different temperatures and observe the crack path, i.e., through the fat particles, the meat particles, or their interface.)

2.61 An inexpensive claylike material, called "Silly Putty," is often available in stores that sell toys and games. Obtain some, and do the following experiments. (a) Shape it into a ball, and drop it onto a flat surface. (b) Put the re-rounded ball on a table, and place a heavy book on it. (c) Shape it into a long cylindrical piece, and pull it apart—first slowly, then quickly. Describe your observations, and refer to the specific sections in this chapter where each particular observation is relevant.

2.62 Make individual sketches of the mechanisms of testing machines that, in your opinion, would be appropriate for tension, for torsion, and for compression testing of specimens at different rates of deformation. What modifications would you make to include the effects of temperature on material properties?

2.63 In tension testing of specimens, mechanical and electronic instruments are used to measure elongation. Make sketches of instruments that would be suitable for this purpose. Comment on their accuracy. What modifications would you make to include the effects of temperature on material properties?

2.64 In Section 2.6.1, we described the Mohs hardness test. Obtain small pieces of several different metallic and nonmetallic materials, including stones. Rub them against each other, observe the scratches made, and order them in a manner similar to the Mohs numbering system.

2.65 Demonstrate stress relaxation by tightly stretching thin plastic strings between two nails on a long piece of wood. Pluck the strings frequently, to test the tension as a function of time and of temperature. (Alter the temperature by placing the fixture in an oven set on "low.")

2.66 Demonstrate the impact toughness of a round piece of chalk by first using a triangular file to produce a V-notch, as shown in Fig. 2.18a, and then bending the chalk to break it.

2.67 Using a large rubber band and a set of weights, obtain the force–displacement curve for the rubber band. How is this different from the stress-strain curves shown in Figure 2.5?

3

Physical Properties of Materials

3.1 INTRODUCTION

In addition to the mechanical properties described in Chapter 2, **physical properties** should also be considered in the selection and processing of materials. Properties of particular interest are density, melting point, specific heat, thermal conductivity and expansion, electrical and magnetic properties, and resistance to oxidation and corrosion.

Why, for example, is electrical wiring generally made of copper? Why are metals such as aluminum, stainless steel, and copper so commonly used in cookware? Why are their handles usually made of wood or plastic, while other types of handles are made of metal? What kind of material should we choose for the heating elements in toasters? Why are commercial airplanes generally made of aluminum and some titanium, and why are some airplane components being replaced gradually with ones made of reinforced plastics?

This chapter describes the importance of strength-to-weight and stiffness-to-weight ratios, particularly for aircraft and aerospace structures, and the importance of density will be explained. For example, high-speed equipment, such as textile and printing machinery and forming and cutting machines, require lightweight components to reduce inertial forces. Several other examples of the importance of physical properties are also discussed. Each physical property is presented from the viewpoint of material selection and manufacturing and its relevance to the service life of the component.

3.2 DENSITY

The **density** of a material is its mass per unit volume. Another way to express a material's density is in relation to that of water; this quantity is known as **specific gravity**, and it has no units. The range of densities for a variety of materials at room temperature, along with other properties, is given in Tables 3.1 and 3.2.

Weight saving is particularly important for aircraft and aerospace structures, for automotive bodies and components, and for other products where energy consumption and power limitations are major concerns. Substitution of materials for the sake of weight savings and economy is a major factor in the design both of advanced equipment and machinery and of consumer products, such as automobiles.

A significant role that density plays is in the **specific strength** (*strength-to-weight ratio*) and **specific stiffness** (*stiffness-to-weight ratio*) of materials and structures. The table below shows the ratio of maximum yield stress to density for a variety of metal alloys. Note that titanium and aluminum are at the top of the list; consequently, and as

TABLE 3.1   Physical Properties of Selected Materials at Room Temperature

Metal	Density (kg/m^3)	Melting point (°C)	Specific heat (J/kg K)	Thermal conductivity (W/m K)
Aluminum	2700	660	900	222
Aluminum alloys	2630–2820	476–654	880–920	121–239
Beryllium	1854	1278	1884	146
Columbium (niobium)	8580	2468	272	52
Copper	8970	1082	385	393
Copper alloys	7470–8940	885–1260	377–435	29–234
Iron	7860	1537	460	74
Steels	6920–9130	1371–1532	448–502	15–52
Lead	11,350	327	130	35
Lead alloys	8850–11,350	182–326	126–188	24–46
Magnesium	1745	650	1025	154
Magnesium alloys	1770–1780	610–621	1046	75–138
Molybdenum alloys	10,210	2610	276	142
Nickel	8910	1453	440	92
Nickel alloys	7750–8850	1110–1454	381–544	12–63
Tantalum alloys	16,600	2996	142	54
Titanium	4510	1668	519	17
Titanium alloys	4430–4700	1549–1649	502–544	8–12
Tungsten	19,290	3410	138	166
Zinc	7140	419	385	113
Zinc alloys	6640–7200	386–525	402	105–113
Nonmetallic				
Ceramics	2300–5500	—	750–950	10–17
Glasses	2400–2700	580–1540	500–850	0.6–1.7
Graphite	1900–2200	—	840	5–10
Plastics	900–2000	110–330	1000–2000	0.1–0.4
Wood	400–700	—	2400–2800	0.1–0.4

TABLE 3.2   Physical Properties of Materials, in Descending Order

Density	Melting point	Specific heat	Thermal conductivity	Thermal expansion	Electrical conductivity
Platinum	Tungsten	Wood	Silver	Plastics	Silver
Gold	Tantalum	Beryllium	Copper	Lead	Copper
Tungsten	Molybdenum	Porcelain	Gold	Tin	Gold
Tantalum	Columbium	Aluminum	Aluminum	Magnesium	Aluminum
Lead	Titanium	Graphite	Magnesium	Aluminum	Magnesium
Silver	Iron	Glass	Graphite	Copper	Tungsten
Molybdenum	Beryllium	Titanium	Tungsten	Steel	Beryllium
Copper	Copper	Iron	Beryllium	Gold	Steel
Steel	Gold	Copper	Zinc	Ceramics	Tin
Titanium	Silver	Molybdenum	Steel	Glass	Graphite
Aluminum	Aluminum	Tungsten	Tantalum	Tungsten	Ceramics
Beryllium	Magnesium	Lead	Ceramics		Glass
Glass	Lead		Titanium		Plastics
Magnesium	Tin		Glass		Quartz
Plastics	Plastics		Plastics		

described in Chapter 6, they are among the most commonly used metals for aircraft and aerospace applications.

The range for specific strength and stiffness at room temperature for a variety of metallic and nonmetallic materials is given in Fig. 3.1. Note the positions of composite materials, as compared to those of metals, with respect to these properties; these advantages have made

Alloy	(Maximum yield stress)/density (in. $\times 10^3$)
Titanium	1250
Aluminum	800
Steels	750
Magnesium	675
Nickel	550
Copper	500
Tantalum	375
Molybdenum	215
Lead	5

composites become among the most important materials. (See Chapter 9.) At elevated temperatures, specific strength and specific stiffness are likewise important considerations, because of the temperatures at which certain components and systems operate, such as automotive and jet engines and gas turbines; typical ranges for a variety of materials are given in Fig. 3.2.

Density is an important factor in the selection of materials for high-speed equipment; note, for example, the use of magnesium in printing and textile machinery, many components of which usually operate at very high speeds. To obtain exposure times of 1/4000 s in cameras without sacrificing accuracy, the shutters of some high-quality 35-mm cameras are made of titanium.

The low resultant mass of the components in these high-speed operations reduces inertial forces that otherwise could lead to vibrations, to inaccuracies, and even, over a period of time, to part failure. Because of their low density, ceramics are now being used for components in high-speed automated machinery and in machine tools.

On the other hand, there are applications where weight is desirable. Examples are counterweights for various mechanisms (using lead or steel) and components for self-winding watches (using high-density materials such as tungsten).

(a)

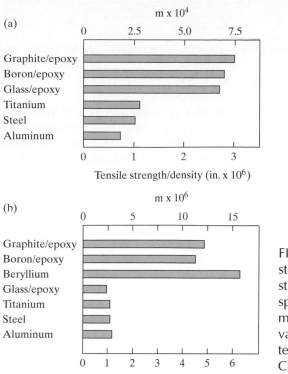

m x 10^4

Tensile strength/density (in. x 10^6)

(b)

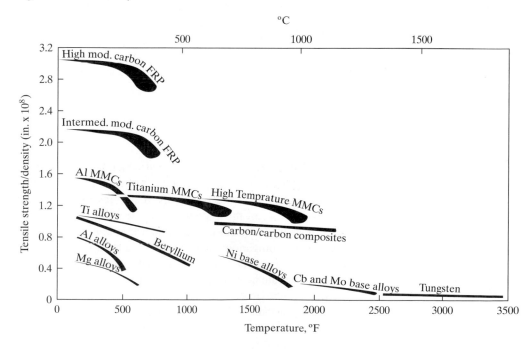

FIGURE 3.1   Specific strength (tensile strength/density) and specific stiffness (elastic modulus/density) for various materials at room temperature. (See also Chapter 9.) *Source*: M.J. Salkind.

FIGURE 3.2   Specific strength (tensile strength/density) for a variety of materials as a function of temperature. Note the useful temperature range for these materials and the high values for composite materials.

3.3   MELTING POINT

The **melting point** of a metal depends on the energy required to separate its atoms. As Table 3.1 shows, the melting temperature of an alloy can have a wide range, unlike that of a pure metal which has a definite melting *point*. The melting points of alloys depend on their particular composition (See, also, Chapter 4).

The melting point of a metal has a number of indirect effects on manufacturing operations. The choice of a material for high-temperature applications is the most obvious effect, applications such as in jet engines and furnaces—any where heat occurs or is generated.

Because the recrystallization temperature of a metal is related to its melting point (Section 1.6), operations such as annealing, heat treating, and hot-working require a knowledge of the melting points of the materials involved. This factor influences, in turn, the selection of tool and die materials in manufacturing operations.

Another major influence of the melting point is on the selection of the equipment and of the melting practice in casting operations (Part II). The higher the melting point of the material, the more difficult the operation becomes. In the electrical-discharge machining process (Section 26.5), the melting points of metals are related to the rate of material removal and of electrode wear.

The temperature range within which a component or structure is designed to function is an important consideration in the selection of materials. Plastics, for example, have the lowest useful temperature range, while graphite and refractory-metal alloys have the highest useful range.

3.4   SPECIFIC HEAT

A material's **specific heat** is the energy required to raise the temperature of a unit mass of it by one degree. Alloying elements have a relatively minor effect on the specific heat of metals.

The temperature rise in a workpiece, resulting from forming or machining operations (Parts III and IV), is a function of the work done and of the specific heat of the workpiece material. Temperature rise in a workpiece, if excessive, can decrease product quality by adversely affecting its surface finish and dimensional accuracy, can cause excessive tool and die wear, and can result in adverse metallurgical changes in the material.

3.5   THERMAL CONDUCTIVITY

Thermal conductivity indicates the rate at which heat flows within and through a material. Metallically bonded materials (metals) generally have high thermal conductivity, while ionically or covalently bonded materials (ceramics and plastics) have poor conductivity (Table 3.2). Because of the large difference in their thermal conductivities, alloying elements can have a significant effect on the thermal conductivity of alloys, as can be seen (in Table 3.1) by comparing the metals with their alloys.

When heat is generated by plastic deformation or friction, the heat should be conducted away at a rate high enough to prevent a severe rise in temperature. For example, the main difficulty experienced in machining titanium is caused by its very low thermal conductivity. Low thermal conductivity can also result in high thermal gradients and, in this way, cause inhomogeneous deformation in metalworking processes.

3.6 THERMAL EXPANSION

The **thermal expansion** of materials can have several significant effects. Generally, the coefficient of thermal expansion is inversely proportional to the melting point of the material. Alloying elements have a relatively minor effect on the thermal expansion of metals.

Shrink fits utilize thermal expansion and contraction. A part with a hole in it that is to be installed over a shaft, such as a flange or a lever arm, is heated, and then it is slipped over a cool shaft or spindle. When it is later allowed to cool, the part shrinks and the assembly becomes effectively integral.

Other examples in which relative expansion or contraction is important are electronic and computer components, glass-to-metal seals, struts on jet engines, and moving parts in machinery that require certain clearances for proper functioning. The use of ceramic components in cast-iron engines also requires consideration of their relative expansions.

Improper selection of materials and assembly can cause **thermal stresses** and resultant cracking, warping, or loosening of components in the structure during their service life. Thermal conductivity, in conjunction with thermal expansion, is what plays the most significant role in causing thermal stresses, both in manufactured components and in tools and dies. This consideration is particularly important in, for example, a forging operation during which hot workpieces are consecutively placed over a relatively cool die, making the die surfaces undergo thermal cycling. To reduce thermal stresses, a combination of high thermal conductivity and low thermal expansion is desirable.

Thermal stresses can lead to cracks in ceramic parts and in tools and dies made of relatively brittle materials. **Thermal fatigue** results from thermal cycling and causes a number of surface cracks, especially in tools and dies for casting and metalworking operations (*heat checking*). **Thermal shock** is the term generally used to describe development of cracks after a single thermal cycle. Thermal stresses may be caused both by temperature gradients and by **anisotropy of thermal expansion**, which we generally observe in hexagonal close-packed metals and in ceramics.

To alleviate some of the problems with thermal expansion, a family of iron–nickel alloys with very low thermal-expansion coefficients has been developed; they are called **low-expansion alloys**. The low thermal expansion characteristic of these alloys is often referred to as the **Invar effect**. The thermal coefficient of expansion is typically in the range of from 2×10^{-6} to 9×10^{-6} per °C. Invar itself typically has a composition of 64% iron and 36% nickel; other materials involve iron-nickel-cobalt alloys.

These alloys also have good thermal-fatigue resistance and good ductility; as a result, they can easily be formed into various shapes. Applications include (a) bimetallic strips consisting of a low-expansion alloy metallurgically bonded to a high-expansion alloy—the strip bends when subjected to temperature changes; and (b) high-quality glass-to-metal seals in which the thermal expansions are matched.

3.7 ELECTRICAL, MAGNETIC, AND OPTICAL PROPERTIES

Electrical conductivity and the dielectric properties of materials are of great importance not only in electrical equipment and machinery, but also in such manufacturing processes as the magnetic-pulse forming of sheet metals (Section 16.15) and the electrical-discharge machining and electrochemical grinding of hard and brittle materials (Chapter 26). The units of electrical conductivity are mho/m or mho/ft, where *mho* is the reverse of *ohm*, the unit for electrical resistance.

The influence of the type of atomic bonding on the electrical conductivity of materials is the same as that for thermal conductivity. Alloying elements have a major effect on the electrical conductivity of metals; the higher the conductivity of the alloying element, the higher the conductivity of the alloy.

Conductors. Materials with high conductivity, such as metals, are generally referred to as **conductors**. **Electrical resistivity** is the inverse of conductivity. Materials with high resistivity are referred to as **dielectrics** or **insulators**.

Dielectric strength. A material's **dielectric strength** is its resistivity to direct electric current. It is defined as the voltage required per unit distance for electrical breakdown, and has the units of V/m or V/ft.

Superconductors. **Superconductivity** is the phenomenon of almost zero electrical resistivity that occurs in some metals and alloys below a critical temperature. The temperatures involved often are near absolute zero (0 K, –273 °C, or –460 °F); the highest temperature at which superconductivity has been exhibited to date is 150 K (–123 °C, –190 °F), but advances continue to be made. These developments indicate that th21e efficiency of such electrical components as large high-power magnets, high-voltage power lines, and electronic and computer components can be markedly improved.

Semiconductors. The electrical properties of **semiconductors**, such as single-crystal silicon, germanium, and gallium arsenide, are extremely sensitive to temperature and to the presence and type of minute impurities. Thus by controlling the concentration and type of impurities (**dopants**), such as phosphorus and boron in silicon, electrical conductivity can be controlled.

This property is utilized in the semiconductor (solid-state) devices used extensively in miniaturized electronic circuitry (Chapter 34). They are very compact, very efficient, and relatively inexpensive; they consume little power; and they require no warmup time for operation.

Ferromagnetism and Ferrimagnetism. **Ferromagnetism** is a phenomenon characterized by high permeability and permanent magnetization that are due to the alignment of iron, nickel, and cobalt atoms into domains. It is important in such applications as electric motors, electric generators, electric transformers, and microwave devices. **Ferrimagnetism** is a permanent and large magnetization exhibited by some ceramic materials, such as cubic ferrites.

Piezoelectric Effect. The **piezoelectric effect** (*piezo* from Greek, meaning to press) is exhibited by some materials, such as quartz crystals and some ceramics, in which there is a reversible interaction between an elastic strain and an electric field. This property is utilized in making transducers, which are devices that convert the strain from an external force into electrical energy. Typical applications are force or pressure transducers, strain gages, sonar detectors, and microphones.

Magnetostriction. The phenomenon of expansion or contraction of a material when it is subjected to a magnetic field is called **magnetostriction**. Some materials, such as pure nickel and some iron–nickel alloys, exhibit this behavior. Magnetostriction is the principle behind ultrasonic machining equipment (Section 25.9).

Optical properties. Among various other properties, color and opacity are particularly relevant to polymers and glasses. These two properties are discussed in Sections 7.2.2 and 8.4.3, respectively.

Example: Electric Wiring in Homes

Because of the increased cost of copper, aluminum electric wiring was widely used in homes built in the United States between 1965 and 1973. It was alleged, however, that aluminum wiring can be a potential fire hazard because its use may cause more resistance heating at junctions in switches and outlets that the use of copper would. Oxidation of the aluminum wire causes loosening of the wire at the terminals and thereby increases its electrical resistance and promotes resistance heating.

This condition can be detected by noting (a) that the areas around switches and outlets have become warm or hot to the touch, (b) that there is an odor of burning plastic insulation, (c) that smoking or sparking occurs, (d) that lights flicker, and (e) that switches, outlets, and circuits fail.

Electrical terminals have since been redesigned to accommodate aluminum as well as copper wiring, by serrating the surfaces of contact. This modification improves contact (reduces electrical resistance) between the wire surface and the terminals. These devices are marked CO–ALR, meaning "copper–aluminum, revised." Labels also state whether a particular switch or outlet is to be used with copper wiring only or may be used for either copper or aluminum wiring.

3.8 CORROSION RESISTANCE

Metals, ceramics, and plastics are all subject to forms of corrosion. The word **corrosion** itself usually refers to the deterioration of metals and ceramics, while similar phenomena in plastics are usually called **degradation**. Corrosion resistance is an important aspect of material selection for applications in the chemical, food, and petroleum industries, as well as in manufacturing operations. In addition to various possible chemical reactions from the elements and compounds present, environmental oxidation and corrosion of components and structures is a major concern, particularly at elevated temperatures and in automobiles and other transportation vehicles.

Corrosion not only leads to deterioration of the surface of components and structures but also reduces their strength and structural integrity. The cost of corrosion to the U.S. economy alone is estimated to be $200 billion per year.

Resistance to corrosion depends on the particular environment and on the composition of the material. Corrosive media may be chemicals (acids, alkalis, and salts), the environment (oxygen, pollution, and acid rain), and water (fresh or salt). Nonferrous metals, stainless steels, and nonmetallic materials generally have high corrosion resistance. Steels and cast irons generally have poor resistance and must be protected by various coatings and surface treatments (Chapter 33).

Corrosion can occur over an entire surface, or it can be *localized*; the latter is called **pitting**. It can occur along grain boundaries of metals as **intergranular corrosion** and at the interface of bolted or riveted joints as **crevice corrosion**.

Two dissimilar metals may form a **galvanic cell** (after L. Galvani, 1737–1798)—that is, two electrodes in an electrolyte in a corrosive environment including moisture—and cause **galvanic corrosion**. Two-phase alloys are more susceptible to galvanic corrosion, because of the physical separation of the two different metals involved, than are single-phase alloys or pure metals; as a result, heat treatment can have an influence on corrosion resistance.

Corrosion can act in indirect ways. **Stress-corrosion cracking** is an example of the effect of a corrosive environment on the integrity of a product that, as manufactured, had residual stresses in it. Likewise, cold-worked metals are likely to contain residual stresses, so they are more susceptible to corrosion than are hot-worked or annealed metals.

Tool and die materials also can be susceptible to chemical attack by lubricants and by coolants. The chemical reaction alters their surface finish and adversely influences the metalworking operation. One example is that of carbide tools and dies having cobalt as a binder (Section 21.5), in which the cobalt is attacked by elements in the cutting fluid (**selective leaching**). Thus, compatibility of the tool, die, and workpiece materials with the metalworking fluid under actual operating conditions is an important consideration in the selection of materials.

Chemical reactions should not be regarded as having adverse effects only. Advanced machining processes such as chemical machining and electrochemical machining are indeed based on controlled reactions (Chapter 26). These processes remove material by chemical action, in a manner similar to the etching of metallurgical specimens.

The usefulness of some level of **oxidation** is exhibited in the corrosion resistance of aluminum, titanium, and stainless steel. Aluminum develops a thin (a few atomic layers), strong, and adherent hard-oxide film (Al_2O_3) that better protects the surface from further environmental corrosion. Titanium develops a film of titanium oxide (TiO_2). A similar phenomenon occurs in stainless steels, which, because of the chromium present in the alloy, develop a protective film on their surfaces.

These processes are known as **passivation**. When the protective film is scratched and exposes the metal underneath, a new oxide film begins to form.

Example: Selection of Materials for Coins

There are five general criteria in the selection of materials for coins.

1. The *subjective factors*, such as the appearance of the coin, its color, its weight, and its ring (the sound made when striking). Also included in this criterion is the *feel* of the coin. This term is difficult to describe, because it combines many human factors. It is similar in effect to the feel of a fine piece of wood, of polished stone, or of fine leather.

2. The intended *life of the coin* is a consideration. This duration will reflect resistance to corrosion and to wear (Chapter 32) while the coin is in circulation. These two factors basically determine the span over which the surface imprint of the coin will remain identifiable and the ability of the coin to retain its original luster.

3. The *manufacturing of the coin* includes factors such as the formability of the candidate coin materials, the life of the dies used in the coining operation (Section 14.3.2), and the capability of the materials and processes to resist counterfeiting.

4. Another consideration is the *suitability of the coin for use* in coin-operated devices, such as vending machines, turnstiles, and pay telephones. These machines are generally equipped with detection devices that test the coins: first, for proper diameter, thickness, and surface condition; and, second, for electrical conductivity and density. The coin is rejected if it fails these tests.

5. A final consideration is the *cost* of raw materials and processing and whether there is a sufficient *supply* of the coin materials.

SUMMARY

- The physical and chemical properties of materials can have various important effects on manufacturing and on the service life of components. These properties and characteristics should be considered during material selection because they affect design, service requirements, and compatibility with other materials, including tools, dies, and workpieces.

- Thermal conductivity and expansion are major factors in the development of thermal stresses and of thermal fatigue and shock, effects which are important in tool and die life in manufacturing operations. Low-expansion alloys (such as Invar) have unique applications.

- Electrical and chemical properties are important in many advanced machining processes such as electrical-discharge, chemical, and electrochemical machining.

- Chemical reactions, including oxidation and corrosion, are important considerations in material selection, design, and manufacturing, as well as on the service life of components. Passivation and stress-corrosion cracking are two important phenomena.

- Some physical properties are utilized in manufacturing processes and their control, such as the magnetostriction effect (for ultrasonic machining of metals and nonmetallic materials) and the piezoelectric effect (for force transducers and various other sensors).

TRENDS

- Greater strength-to-weight and stiffness-to-weight ratios of materials, particularly in fiber-reinforced systems and those using plastic, ceramic, and metal matrices, are being developed.

- Further progress is being made in developing materials with improved and special physical properties for a variety of electronic and computer applications.

- Because of its major economic impact, corrosion resistance of materials and the design of components to promote corrosion resistance continues to be an important area of research.

- Stress-corrosion cracking of aging aircraft and their inspection have become important considerations.

- New alloys are being developed which display superconductivity at higher and higher temperatures.

KEY TERMS

Corrosion
Degradation
Density
Dielectrics
Electrical conductivity
Electrical resistivity
Ferromagnetism
Galvanic corrosion
Invar effect

Heat checking
Magnetostriction
Melting point
Oxidation
Passivation
Piezoelectric effect
Selective leaching
Semiconductors
Specific heat

Specific stiffness
Specific strength
Stress-corrosion cracking
Superconductivity
Thermal conductivity
Thermal expansion
Thermal stresses

BIBLIOGRAPHY

Callister, D.C., Jr., *Materials Science and Engineering* (4th ed.). Wiley, 1997.

Mark, J,E., A. Eisenberg, and W.W. Graessley, *Physical Properties of Polymers.* American Chemical Society, 1993.

Pollock, D.D., *Physical Properties of Materials for Engineers* (2d ed.). CRC Press, 1993.

Schweitzer, P.A., *Encyclopedia of Corrosion Technology.* Marcel Dekker, 1998.

Shackelford, J.F., *Introduction to Materials Science for Engineers* (4th ed.). Macmillan, 1996.

Talbot, D., and J. Talbot, *Corrosion Science and Technology.* CRC Press, 1997.

REVIEW QUESTIONS

3.1 List reasons why density is an important material property in manufacturing.

3.2 Why is the melting point of a material an important factor in manufacturing processes?

3.3 What adverse effects can be caused by thermal expansion of materials?

3.4 What is the piezoelectric effect?

3.5 What factors lead to the corrosion of a metal?

3.6 What is passivation? What is its significance?

3.7 What is the difference between thermal conductivity and specific heat?

3.8 What is stress-corrosion cracking? Why is it also called season cracking?

3.9 What is the difference between a superconductor and a semiconductor?

QUALITATIVE PROBLEMS

3.10 Describe the significance of structures and machine components made of two materials with different coefficients of thermal expansion.

3.11 Which of the properties described in this chapter are important for (a) mechanical pencils, (b) cookie sheets for baking, (c) rulers, (d) paper clips, (e) door hinges, (f) beverage cans? Explain your answers.

3.12 You will note in Table 3.1 that the properties of the alloys of metals have a wide range as compared to the properties of the pure metals. What factors are responsible for this?

3.13 Does corrosion have any beneficial effects in manufacturing? Explain.

3.14 Does thermal conductivity play a role in the development of residual stresses in metals? Explain.

3.15 What material properties are desirable for heat shields, such as those placed on the space shuttle?

QUANTITATIVE PROBLEMS

3.16 If we assume that all the work done in plastic deformation is converted into heat, the temperature rise in a workpiece is (1) directly proportional to the work done per unit volume and (2) inversely proportional to the product of the specific heat and the density of the workpiece. Using Fig. 2.6, and letting the areas under the curves be the unit work done, calculate the temperature rise for (a) 8650 steel, (b) 304 stainless steel, and (c) 1100-H14 aluminum.

3.17 The natural frequency, f, of a cantilever beam is given by $f = 0.56EIg/wL^4$, where E is the modulus of elasticity, I is the moment of inertia, g is the gravitational constant, w is the weight of the beam per unit length, and L is the length of the beam. How does the natural frequency of the beam change, if at all, as its temperature is increased? Assume that the material is steel.

SYNTHESIS AND DESIGN

3.18 From your own experience, make a list of parts, components, and products that have corroded and have had to be replaced or discarded.

3.19 List applications where the following properties would be desirable: (a) high density, (b) low density, (c) high melting point, (d) low melting point, (e) high thermal conductivity, (f) low thermal conductivity.

3.20 Give several applications in which specific strength and specific stiffness are important.

3.21 Design several mechanisms or instruments based on utilizing the differences in thermal expansion of materials, such as bimetallic strips that develop a curvature when heated.

3.22 For the materials listed in Table 3.1, determine the specific strength and specific stiffness. Describe your observations.

3.23 The maximum compressive force that a lightweight column can withstand before buckling depends on the ratio of the square root of the stiffness to the density for the material. For the materials listed in Table 2.1, determine (a) the ratio of tensile strength to density, and (b) the ratio of elastic modulus to density, and comment on the suitability of each for being made into lightweight columns.

3.24 Describe possible applications and designs using alloys exhibiting the Invar effect of low thermal expansion.

4

Metal Alloys: Their Structure and Strengthening by Heat Treatment

4.1 INTRODUCTION

The properties and behavior of metals and alloys during manufacturing and their performance during their service life depend on their composition, structure, and processing history and on the heat treatment to which they have been subjected. Important basic properties such as strength, hardness, ductility, and toughness, as well as resistance to wear and scratching, are greatly influenced and modified by alloying elements and by heat-treatment processes. Improvements in non-heat-treatable alloy properties are obtained by cold-working operations, such as rolling, forging, and extrusion (Part III).

The most common example of property improvement is *heat treatment*; it modifies microstructures and thereby produces a variety of mechanical properties that are important in manufacturing, such as improved formability and machinability. These properties also enhance service performance of the metals when used in machine components (such as gears, cams, and shafts; Fig. 4.1) and in tools and dies. Heat treatment requires an un-

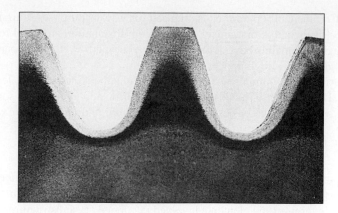

FIGURE 4.1   Cross-section of gear teeth showing induction-hardened surfaces. *Source*: TOCCO Div., Park-Ohio Industries, Inc.

derstanding of several concepts, including the fundamentals of the crystal structure of metals and alloys.

This chapter follows the outline shown in Fig. 4.2, presenting the effects of various alloying elements, the solubility of one element in another, phases, equilibrium phase diagrams, and the influence of composition, temperature, and time. The properties of most nonferrous alloys and stainless steels are also enhanced by heat-treatment techniques, involving mechanisms that are different from those for ferrous alloys.

This chapter also discusses methods and techniques of heating, quenching, tempering, and annealing and the characteristics of the equipment involved. These are important methods for avoiding distortion and cracking of the part during heat treatment due to microstructural changes and to thermal stresses. Nonuniform properties can also develop in the heat-treated part because of differences in the rate of cooling.

4.2 STRUCTURE OF ALLOYS

When describing the basic crystal structure of metals in Chapter 1, we noted that the atoms are all of the *same* type, except for the presence of rare impurity atoms. These metals are known as **pure metals**, even though they may not be 100% pure.

FIGURE 4.2   Outline of topics described in Chapter 4.

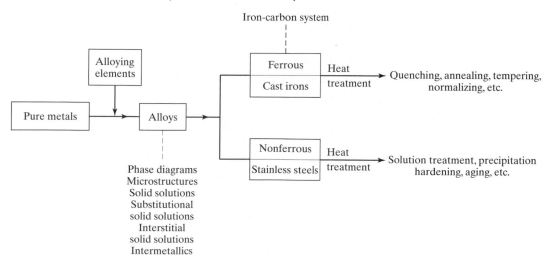

Commercially pure metals are used for various purposes: aluminum for foil, copper for electrical conductors, nickel or chromium for plating, and gold for electrical contacts. Although pure metals have somewhat limited properties, these properties can be enhanced and modified by alloying.

An **alloy** is composed of two or more chemical elements, at least one of which is a metal. The majority of metals used in engineering applications are some form of alloy. Alloying consists of two basic forms: *solid solutions* and *intermetallic compounds*.

4.2.1 Solid Solutions

Two terms are essential in describing alloys: **solute** and **solvent**. Solute is the minor element (such as salt or sugar) that is added to the solvent, which is the major element (such as water). In terms of the elements involved in a metal crystal structure, the solute (composed of solute atoms) is the element that is added to the solvent (composed of *host* atoms). When the particular crystal structure of the solvent is maintained during alloying, the alloy is called a **solid solution**.

Substitutional Solid Solutions.   If the size of the solute atom is similar to that of the solvent atom, the solute atoms can replace solvent atoms and form a **substitutional solid solution** (see Fig. 1.9). An example is brass (Section 6.4), an alloy of zinc and copper, in which zinc (solute atom) is introduced into the lattice of copper (solvent atoms). The properties of brasses can thus be altered over a range by controlling the amount of zinc in copper.

Two conditions (known as *Hume–Rothery rules*, after W. Hume–Rothery, 1899–1968) are generally required to form complete substitutional solid solutions:

1. The two metals must have similar crystal structures.
2. The difference in their atomic radii should be less than 15%.

If these conditions are not satisfied, complete solid solution will not be obtained, and the amount of solid solution formed will be limited.

Interstitial Solid Solutions.   If the size of the solute atom is much smaller than that of the solvent atom, each solute atom can occupy an *interstitial* position; such a process forms an **interstitial solid solution**. There are two conditions necessary for forming interstitial solutions:

1. The solvent atom must have more than one valence.
2. The atomic radius of the solute atom must be less than 59% of the atomic radius for the atom.

If these conditions are not met, limited interstitial solubility may take place—or even none.

An important family of interstitial solid solutions is **steel** (Chapter 5), an alloy of iron and carbon, where carbon atoms are present in interstitial positions between iron atoms. The atomic radius of carbon is 0.071 nm, and that is less than 59% of the 0.124 nm radius of the iron atom.

As we shall see, the properties of carbon steels can be varied over a wide range by controlling the proportion of carbon in the iron. This controllability is one reason that steel is such a versatile and useful material with a wide variety of properties and applications; inexpensiveness is another.

4.2.2 Intermetallic Compounds

Intermetallic compounds are complex structures consisting of two metals in which solute atoms are present among solvent atoms in certain proportions. Some intermetallic compounds have solid solubility. The type of atomic bond may range from metallic to ionic.

Intermetallic compounds are strong, hard, and brittle. Because of their high melting points and their strength at elevated temperatures, their good oxidation resistance, and their relatively low density, they are candidate materials for advanced gas-turbine engines. Typical examples are the aluminides of titanium (Ti_3Al), nickel (Ni_3Al), and iron (Fe_3Al).

4.2.3 Two-Phase Systems

We have seen that a solid solution is one in which two or more elements in a solid state form a single homogeneous solid phase in which the elements are uniformly distributed throughout the solid mass. Such a system is limited by some maximum concentration of solute atoms in the solvent-atom lattice, just as there is a solubility limit for sugar in water. Most alloys consist of two or more solid phases and may be regarded as mechanical mixtures. We call a system with two solid phases a **two-phase system**.

A **phase** is defined as a physically distinct and homogeneous portion in a material; each phase is a homogeneous part of the total mass and has its own characteristics and properties. Let's consider a mixture of sand and water as an example of a two-phase system. These two different components have their own distinct structures, characteristics, and properties.

There is a clear boundary in this mixture between the water (one phase) and the sand particles (a second phase). Another example is ice in water—in this case, the two phases are the same chemical compound of exactly the same chemical elements (hydrogen and oxygen), even though their properties are very different.

A typical example of a two-phase system in metals occurs when lead is added to copper in the molten state. After the mixture solidifies, the structure consists of two phases: one having a small amount of lead in solid solution in copper, the other having lead particles (roughly spherical in shape) *dispersed* throughout the structure (Fig. 4.3a).

The lead particles are analogous to the sand particles in water that we described above. We now find that this copper–lead alloy has properties that are different from those of either copper or lead alone. Lead is also added to steels to obtain leaded steels, which have a greatly improved machinability (Section 20.9.1).

FIGURE 4.3   (a) Schematic illustration of grains, grain boundaries, and particles dispersed throughout the structure of a two-phase system, such as a lead–copper alloy. The grains represent lead in solid solution in copper, and the particles are lead as a second phase. (b) Schematic illustration of a two-phase system consisting of two sets of grains: dark, and light. The dark and the light grains have separate compositions and properties.

(a)

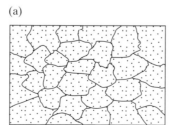

(b)

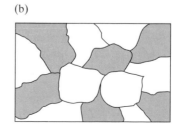

Alloying with finely dispersed particles (**second-phase particles**) is an important method of strengthening alloys and controlling their properties. In two-phase alloys the second-phase particles present obstacles to dislocation movement and thus increase strength.

Another example of a two-phase alloy is the aggregate structure shown in Fig. 4.3b. In this alloy system, there are two sets of grains, each with its own composition and properties. The darker grains may have a different structure from the lighter grains; they may, for example, be brittle, while the lighter grains are ductile.

Defects may appear during metalworking operations such as forging or extrusion (Chapters 14 and 15); such flaws may be due to the lack of ductility of one of the phases in the alloy. In general, two-phase alloys are stronger and less ductile than solid solutions.

4.3   PHASE DIAGRAMS

Pure metals have clearly defined melting or freezing points, and solidification takes place at a *constant* temperature (Fig. 4.4). When the temperature of the molten metal is reduced to the freezing point, the energy of the **latent heat of solidification** is given off while the temperature remains constant. Eventually, solidification is complete and the solid metal continues cooling to room temperature.

Unlike pure metals, alloys solidify over a *range* of temperatures (Fig. 4.5). Solidification begins when the temperature of the molten metal drops below the **liquidus**; it is completed when the temperature reaches the **solidus**. Within this temperature range the alloy is in a mushy or pasty state; its composition and state are described by the particular alloy's phase diagram.

A **phase diagram**, also called an **equilibrium** or a **constitutional diagram**, shows the relationships among the temperature, the composition, and the phases present in a particular alloy system under equilibrium conditions. **Equilibrium** means that the state of a system remains constant over an indefinite period of time.

The word **constitutional** indicates the relationships among the structure, the composition, and the physical makeup of the alloy. As described in detail below, types of phase diagrams include: (1) complete solid solutions; (2) eutectics, such as cast irons; and (3) eutectoids, such as steels.

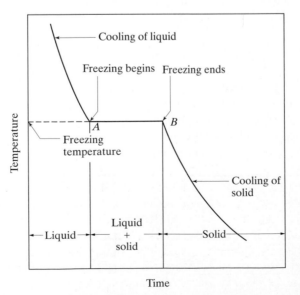

FIGURE 4.4   Cooling curve for the solidification of pure metals. Note that freezing takes place at a constant temperature; during freezing the latent heat of solidification is given off.

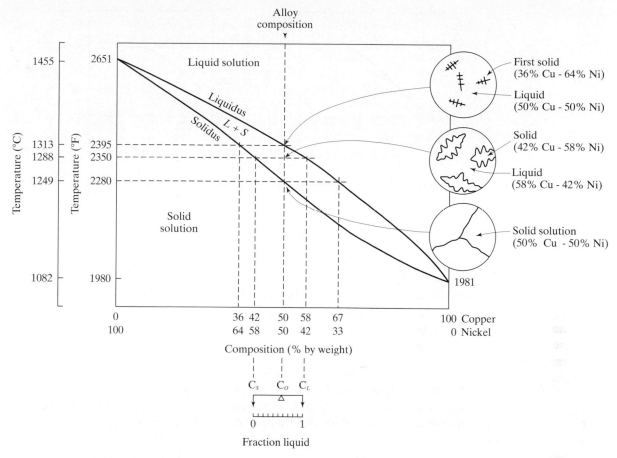

FIGURE 4.5   Phase diagram for nickel–copper alloy system obtained at a slow rate of solidification. Note that pure nickel and pure copper each has one freezing or melting temperature. The top circle on the right depicts the nucleation of crystals. The second circle shows the formation of dendrites (see Section 10.2). The bottom circle shows the solidified alloy, with grain boundaries.

One example of a phase diagram is shown in Fig. 4.5 for the copper–nickel alloy. It is called a **binary phase diagram**, because there are two elements (copper and nickel) present in the system. The left-hand boundary of this phase diagram (100% Ni) indicates the melting point of nickel; the right-hand boundary (100% Cu) indicates the melting point of copper. (All percentages in this discussion are by weight, not by number of atoms.)

Note that for a composition of, say, 50% Cu–50% Ni, the alloy begins to solidify at a temperature of 1313 °C (2395 °F), and solidification is complete at 1249 °C (2280 °F). Above 1313 °C, a homogeneous liquid of 50% Cu–50% Ni exists. When cooled slowly to 1249 °C, a homogeneous solid solution of 50% Cu–50% Ni results.

However, between the liquidus and solidus curves, and at a temperature of 1288 °C (2350 °F), there is a two-phase region: a **solid phase** composed of 42% Cu–58% Ni, and a **liquid phase** of 58% Cu–42% Ni. To determine the *solid composition*, we go left horizontally to the solidus curve and read down, obtaining 42% Cu. We obtain the *liquid composition* (58%) similarly, by going to the right to the liquidus curve. The procedure for determining the compositions of various phases in phase diagrams (called the **lever rule**) is described in detail in texts on materials science and metallurgy.

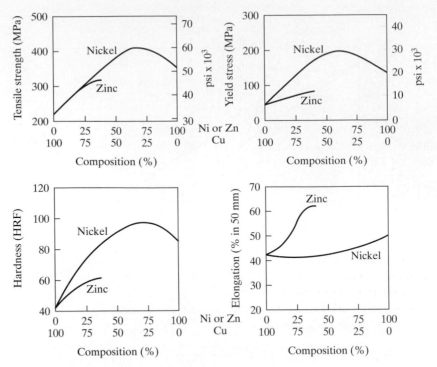

FIGURE 4.6   Mechanical properties of copper–nickel and copper–zinc alloys as a function of their composition. The curves for zinc are short, because zinc has a maximum solid solubility of 40% in copper. *Source*: L. H. Van Vlack; *Materials for Engineering*. Addison-Wesley Publishing Co., Inc., 1982.

The *completely solidified* alloy in the phase diagram shown in Fig. 4.5 is a **solid solution** because the alloying element (Cu, solute atom) is completely dissolved in the host metal (Ni, solvent atom), and each grain has the same composition. The atomic radius of copper is 0.128 nm and that of nickel is 0.125 nm, and both elements are of face-centered cubic structure; the Hume-Rothery rules are obeyed.

The mechanical properties of solid solutions of Cu–Ni depend on their composition (Fig. 4.6). Up to a point, the properties of pure copper are improved upon by increasing the nickel content. There is an optimal percentage of nickel that gives the highest strength and hardness to the Cu–Ni alloy. Figure 4.6 also shows how zinc, as an alloying element in copper, changes the mechanical properties of the alloy.

Note the maximum of 40% solid solubility for zinc (solute) in copper (solvent), whereas copper and nickel are completely soluble in each other. The improvements in properties are due to pinning (blocking) of dislocations at substitutional nickel or zinc atoms, which may also be regarded as impurity atoms. As a result, dislocations cannot move as freely, and the strength of the alloy increases.

Another example of a two-phase diagram is shown in Fig. 4.7, for the lead–tin system. The single phases alpha and beta are solid solutions. Note that the single-phase regions are separated from the liquid phase by two two-phase regions: *alpha + liquid* and *beta + liquid*.

Figure 4.7 shows the composition of the alloy (61.9% Sn–38.1% Pb) that has the *lowest* temperature at which the alloy is still completely liquid, namely, 183 °C (361 °F). This point is known as the **eutectic point**, and it is the point at which the liquid solution decomposes into the components alpha and beta. The word **eutectic** is from the Greek *eutektos*, meaning easily melted.

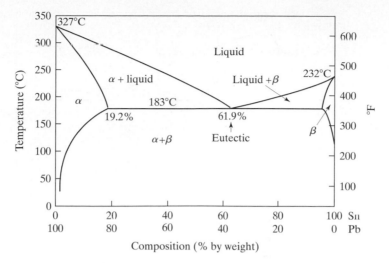

FIGURE 4.7   The lead–tin phase diagram. Note that the composition of the eutectic point for this alloy is 61.9% Sn–38.1% Pb. A composition either lower or higher than this ratio will have a higher liquidus temperature.

Eutectic points are important in applications such as soldering (Section 30.3), where low temperatures may be required to prevent thermal damage to parts during joining. Although there are various types of solders, tin–lead solders are commonly used for general applications; they have composition ranging from 5% Pb–95% Sn to 70% Pb–30% Sn. Each composition has its own melting point.

4.4   THE IRON–CARBON SYSTEM

As described in Chapter 5, steels, ferrous alloys, cast irons, and cast steels are used extensively because of their versatile properties and low cost. Steels and cast irons are represented by the iron–carbon binary system. Commercially pure iron contains up to 0.008% carbon, steels up to 2.11% carbon, and cast irons up to 6.67% carbon, although most cast irons contain less than 4.5% carbon. In this section the iron–carbon system is discussed, and we will explain how to evaluate and modify the properties of these important materials for specific applications.

The **iron–iron carbide phase diagram** is shown in Fig. 4.8. Although this diagram can be extended to the right—to 100% carbon (pure graphite)—the range that is significant to engineering applications is up to 6.67% carbon, because Fe_3C is a stable phase.

Pure iron melts at a temperature of 1538 °C (2798 °F), as shown at the left boundary in Fig. 4.8. As iron cools, it first forms delta ferrite, then austenite, and finally alpha ferrite.

4.4.1   Ferrite

Alpha ferrite, or simply **ferrite**, is a solid solution of body-centered cubic iron; it has a maximum solid solubility of 0.022% carbon at a temperature of 727 °C (1341 °F). Delta ferrite is stable only at very high temperatures and is of no practical significance in engineering. Just as there is a solubility limit for salt in water (with any extra amount precipitating as solid salt at the bottom of the container), so there is a solid solubility limit for carbon in iron.

Ferrite is relatively soft and ductile; it is magnetic from room temperature to 768 °C (1414 °F), the so-called *Curie temperature* (after M. Curie, 1867–1934). Although very lit-

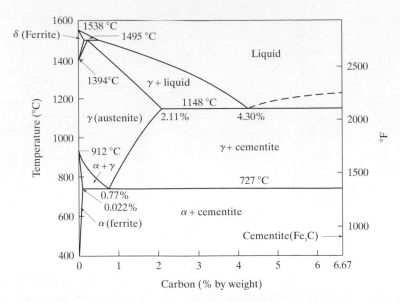

FIGURE 4.8   The iron–iron carbide phase diagram. Because of the importance of steel as an engineering material, this diagram is one of the most important of all phase diagrams.

tle carbon can dissolve interstitially in bcc iron, the amount of carbon can significantly affect the mechanical properties of ferrite. Furthermore, significant amounts of chromium, manganese, nickel, molybdenum, tungsten, and silicon can be contained in iron in solid solution, imparting desirable properties.

4.4.2 Austenite

Between 1394 °C (2541 °F) and 912 °C (1674 °F) iron undergoes a **polymorphic transformation** from the bcc to an fcc structure, becoming what is known as *gamma iron* or, more commonly, **austenite** (after W. R. Austen, 1843–1902). This structure has a solid sol-

FIGURE 4.9   The unit cells for (a) austenite, (b) ferrite, and (c) martensite. The effect of percentage of carbon (by weight) on the lattice dimensions for martensite is shown in (d). Note the interstitial position of the carbon atoms (see Fig. 1.9). Note, also, the increase in dimension *c* with increasing carbon content; this effect causes the unit cell of martensite to be in the shape of a rectangular prism.

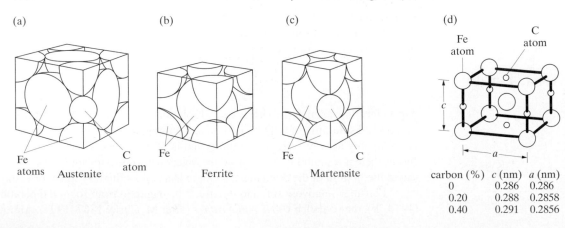

carbon (%)	c (nm)	a (nm)
0	0.286	0.286
0.20	0.288	0.2858
0.40	0.291	0.2856

ubility of up to 2.11% carbon at 1148 °C (2098 °F). Because the fcc structure has more interstitial positions, the solid solubility of austenite is about two orders of magnitude higher than that of ferrite, with the carbon occupying the interstitial positions (Fig. 4.9a).

Austenite is an important phase in the heat treatment of steels (Section 4.7). It is denser than ferrite, and its single-phase fcc structure is ductile at elevated temperatures; consequently it possesses good formability. Large amounts of nickel and manganese can also be dissolved in fcc iron to impart various properties. Steel is nonmagnetic in the austenitic form, either at high temperatures or, for austenitic stainless steels, at room temperature.

4.4.3 Cementite

The right boundary of Fig. 4.8 represents **cementite**, which is 100% iron carbide (Fe_3C), having a carbon content of 6.67%. Cementite, from the Latin *caementum* (meaning "stone chips"), is also called **carbide**. This carbide should not be confused with other carbides which are used as dies, cutting tools, and abrasives, such as tungsten carbide, titanium carbide, and silicon carbide (Chapters 8 and 21).

Cementite is a very hard and brittle intermetallic compound and has a significant influence on the properties of steels. It can include other alloying elements such as chromium, molybdenum, and manganese.

4.5 THE IRON–IRON CARBIDE PHASE DIAGRAM AND THE DEVELOPMENT OF MICROSTRUCTURES IN STEELS

The region of the iron–iron carbide phase diagram that is up to 2.11% carbon and that is significant for steels is shown in Fig. 4.10, which is an enlargement of the lower left-hand portion of Fig. 4.8. Various microstructures can be developed, depending on the carbon content, the amount of plastic deformation (working), and the method of heat treatment. For exam-

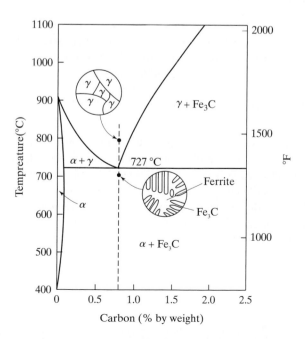

FIGURE 4.10 Schematic illustration of the microstructures for an iron–carbon alloy of eutectoid composition (0.77% carbon), above and below the eutectoid temperature of 727 °C (1341 °F).

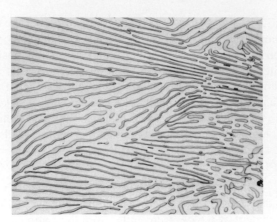

FIGURE 4.11
Microstructure of pearlite in 1080 steel, formed from austenite of eutectoid composition. In this lamellar structure, the lighter regions are ferrite, and the darker regions are carbide. Magnification: 2500×. *Source*: Courtesy of USX Corporation.

ple, let's consider the eutectic point of iron with a 0.77% carbon content, while it is being cooled very slowly from a temperature of, say, 1100 °C (2000 °F) in the austenite phase.

The reason for *slow* cooling is to maintain equilibrium; higher rates of cooling are employed in heat treating, as explained in Section 4.7. At 727 °C (1341 °F) a reaction takes place in which austenite is transformed into alpha ferrite (bcc) and cementite. Because the solid solubility of carbon in ferrite is only 0.022%, the extra carbon forms cementite.

This reaction is called a **eutectoid** (meaning *eutecticlike*) **reaction**; this term means that, at a certain temperature, a single solid phase (austenite) is transformed into two other solid phases (ferrite and cementite). The structure of eutectoid steel is called **pearlite**, because, at low magnifications, it resembles mother-of-pearl (Fig. 4.11). The microstructure of pearlite consists of alternating layers (**lamellae**) of ferrite and cementite. Consequently, the mechanical properties of pearlite are intermediate between those of ferrite (soft and ductile) and cementite (hard and brittle).

In iron with less than 0.77% carbon, the microstructure formed consists of a pearlite phase (ferrite and cementite) and a ferrite phase. The ferrite in the pearlite is called **eutectoid ferrite**. The ferrite phase is called **proeutectoid ferrite** (*pro* meaning before). It forms at a temperature higher than the eutectoid temperature of 727 °C (1341 °F) in the *alpha + gamma* region.

If the carbon content is higher than 0.77%, the austenite transforms into pearlite and cementite. The cementite in the pearlite is called **eutectoid cementite**, and the cementite phase is called **proeutectoid cementite** because it forms in the *alpha + Fe₃C* region, at a temperature higher than the eutectoid temperature.

4.5.1 Effects of Alloying Elements in Iron

Although carbon is the basic element that transforms iron into steel, other elements are also added to impart a variety of desirable properties. The main effect of these alloying elements on the iron–iron carbide phase diagram is to shift the eutectoid temperature and eutectoid composition (percentage of carbon in steel at the eutectoid point); they shift other phase boundaries as well.

The eutectoid temperature may be raised or lowered from 727 °C (1341 °F), depending on the particular alloying element. On the other hand, alloying elements always lower the eutectoid composition; that is, its carbon content is lower than 0.77%. Lowering the eutectoid temperature means increasing the austenite range. As result, an alloying element such as nickel is known as an **austenite former**. Because nickel has an fcc structure, it favors the fcc structure of austenite. Conversely, chromium and molybdenum have a bcc structure, thus favoring the bcc structure of ferrite. These elements are, therefore, known as **ferrite stabilizers**.

4.6 CAST IRONS

The term **cast iron** refers to a family of ferrous alloys composed of iron, carbon (ranging from 2.11% to about 4.5%), and silicon (up to about 3.5%). Cast irons are usually classified according to their solidification morphology from the eutectic temperature, as follows (see also Section 12.3):

a. Gray cast iron, or gray iron;

b. Ductile cast iron, nodular cast iron, or spheroidal graphite cast iron;

c. White cast iron;

d. Malleable iron;

e. Compacted graphite iron.

Cast irons are also classified by their structure: ferritic, pearlitic, quenched and tempered, or austempered.

The equilibrium phase diagram relevant to cast irons is shown in Fig. 4.12, in which the right boundary is 100% carbon, that is, pure graphite. The eutectic temperature is 1154 °C (2109 °F), and so cast irons are completely liquid at temperatures lower than those required for liquid steels. Consequently, iron with high carbon content can be cast (see Part II) at lower temperatures than can steels.

Although cementite exists in steels almost indefinitely, it is not completely stable—instead, it is **metastable**, with an extremely low rate of decomposition. Cementite can, however, be made to decompose into alpha ferrite and graphite. The formation of graphite (**graphitization**) can be controlled, promoted, and accelerated by modifying the composition and the rate of cooling, and by the addition of silicon.

FIGURE 4.12   Phase diagram for the iron–carbon system with graphite (instead of cementite) as the stable phase. Note that this figure is an extended version of Fig. 4.8.

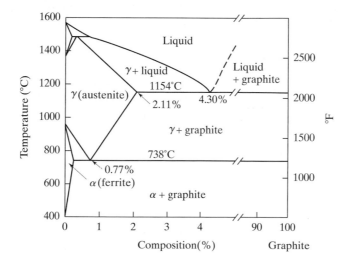

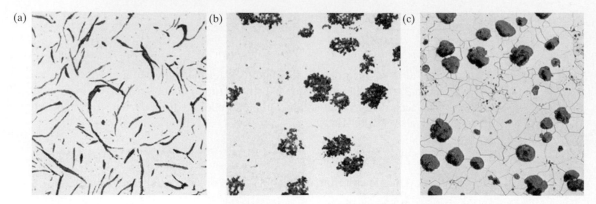

FIGURE 4.13   Microstructure for cast irons. Magnification: 100 $\times$. (a) Ferritic gray iron with graphite flakes. (b) Ferritic ductile iron (nodular iron), with graphite in nodular form. (c) Ferritic malleable iron; this cast iron solidified as white cast iron, with the carbon present as cementite, and was heat treated to graphitize the carbon. *Source*: ASM International.

4.6.1 Gray Cast Iron

In this structure, graphite exists largely in the form of *flakes* (Fig. 4.13a). It is called **gray cast iron**, or **gray iron**, because, when it is broken, the fracture path is along the graphite flakes and has, therefore a gray, sooty appearance. These flakes act as stress raisers. As a result, gray iron has negligible ductility, and it is weak in tension, although strong in compression, as are other brittle materials.

On the other hand, the presence of graphite flakes gives this material the capacity to dampen vibrations caused by internal friction and, consequently, the ability to dissipate energy. This capacity makes gray cast iron a suitable and commonly used material for constructing machine-tool bases and structures (Section 24.3).

The types of gray cast iron are called **ferritic**, **pearlitic**, and **martensitic**. Because of the different structures, each has different properties and applications. In ferritic gray iron, also known as *fully gray iron*, the structure consists of graphite flakes in an alpha-ferrite matrix.

Pearlitic gray iron has a structure of graphite in a matrix of pearlite. Although still brittle, it is stronger than fully gray iron. Martensitic gray iron is obtained by austenitizing a pearlitic gray iron and then rapidly quenching it, to produce a structure of graphite in a martensite matrix; as a result, this cast iron is very hard.

4.6.2 Ductile Iron (Nodular Iron)

In the ductile-iron structure, graphite is in a **nodular** or **spheroid** form (Fig. 4.13b). This shape permits the material to be somewhat ductile and shock-resistant. The shape of graphite flakes is changed into nodules (spheres) by small additions of magnesium and/or cerium to the molten metal prior to pouring. Ductile iron can be made ferritic or pearlitic by heat treatment. It can be heat treated to obtain, alternatively, a structure of tempered martensite (Section 4.7.6).

4.6.3 White Cast Iron

The white-cast-iron structure is very hard, wear-resistant, and brittle because of the presence of large amounts of iron carbide (instead of graphite). White cast iron is obtained either by cooling gray iron rapidly or by adjusting the composition by keeping the carbon and silicon content low. This type of cast iron is also called **white iron** because of the white crystalline appearance of the fracture surface.

4.6.4 Malleable Iron

Malleable iron is obtained by annealing white cast iron in an atmosphere of carbon monoxide and carbon dioxide, at between 800 °C and 900 °C (1470 °F and 1650 °F), for up to several hours, depending on the size of the part. During this process the cementite decomposes (*dissociates*) into iron and graphite. The graphite exists as *clusters* or *rosettes* (Fig. 4.13c) in a ferrite or pearlite matrix; consequently, malleable iron has a structure similar to that of nodular iron. This structure promotes ductility, strength, and shock resistance—hence, the term **malleable** (from the Latin *malleus* "can be hammered").

4.6.5 Compacted-Graphite Iron

The graphite in this structure is in the form of short, thick, and interconnected flakes having undulating surfaces and rounded extremities. The mechanical and physical properties of this cast iron are intermediate between those of flake-graphite and nodular-graphite cast irons.

4.7 HEAT TREATMENT OF FERROUS ALLOYS

The various microstructures described thus far can be modified by **heat-treatment** techniques, that is, by controlled heating and cooling of the alloys at various rates. These treatments induce **phase transformations** that greatly influence such mechanical properties as the strength, the hardness, the ductility, the toughness, and the wear resistance of the alloys.

The effects of thermal treatment depend on the alloy, on its composition and microstructure, on the degree of prior cold work, and on the rates of heating and cooling during heat treatment. The processes of recovery, recrystallization, and grain growth (Section 1.6) are examples of thermal treatment, involving changes in the grain structure of the alloy.

This section will focus on the microstructural changes in the iron–carbon system. Because of their technological significance, the structures considered are pearlite, spheroidite, bainite, martensite, and tempered martensite. The heat-treatment processes described are annealing, quenching, and tempering.

4.7.1 Pearlite

If the ferrite and cementite lamellae in the pearlite structure of the eutectoid steel shown in Fig. 4.11 are thin and closely packed, the microstructure is called **fine pearlite**. If they are thick and widely spaced, it is called **coarse pearlite**. The difference between the two depends on the rate of cooling through the eutectoid temperature, the site of a reaction in which austenite is transformed into pearlite. If the rate of cooling is relatively high, as it is in air, fine pearlite is produced; if cooling is slow, as it is in a furnace, coarse pearlite is produced.

The transformation from austenite to pearlite (among other structures) is best illustrated by Figs. 4.14b and c. These diagrams are called **isothermal transformation (IT) diagrams**, or *time-temperature-transformation (TTT) diagrams*. They are constructed from the data given in Fig. 4.14a, which shows the percentage of austenite transformed into pearlite as a function of temperature and time. The higher the temperature or the longer the time, the greater is the percentage of austenite transformed to pearlite.

Note that for each temperature there is a minimum time for the transformation to begin. This period defines the critical cooling rate; with longer times, austenite begins to transform into pearlite. This transformation can be traced in Figs. 4.14b and c.

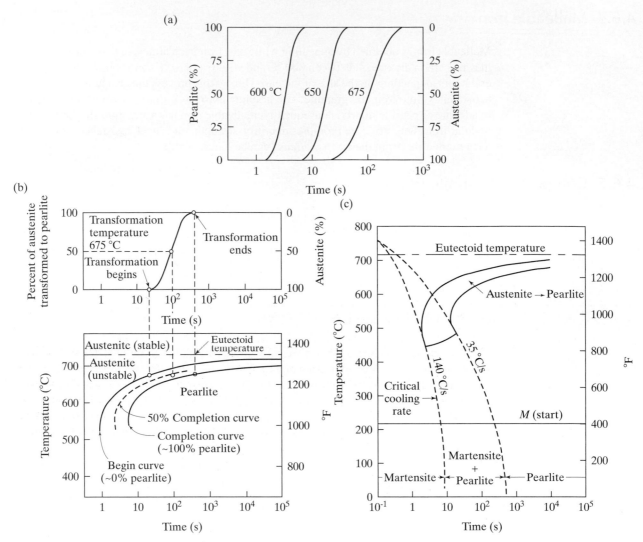

FIGURE 4.14 (a) Austenite-to-pearlite transformation of iron–carbon alloy as a function of time and temperature. (b) Isothermal transformation diagram obtained from (a) for a transformation temperature of 675 °C (1247 °F). (c) Microstructures obtained for a eutectoid iron–carbon alloy as a function of cooling rate. *Source*: ASM International.

The differences in the hardness and the toughness of the various structures obtained are shown in Fig. 4.15. Fine pearlite is harder and less ductile than coarse pearlite. The effects of various percentages of carbon, cementite, and pearlite on other mechanical properties of steels are shown in Fig. 4.16.

4.7.2 Spheroidite

When pearlite is heated to just below the eutectoid temperature and then held at that temperature for a period of time (**subcritical annealing**, Section 4.11.1), such as for a day at

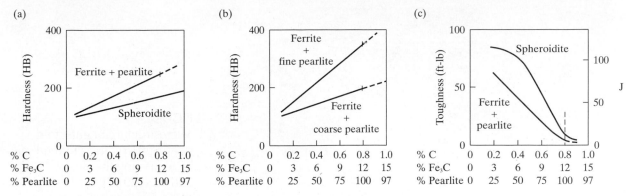

FIGURE 4.15   (a) and (b) Hardness and (c) toughness for annealed plain-carbon steels, as a function of carbide shape. Carbides in the pearlite are lamellar. Fine pearlite is obtained by increasing the cooling rate. The spheroidite structure has spherelike carbide particles. Note that the percentage of pearlite begins to decrease after 0.77% carbon. *Source*: L. H. Van Vlack; *Materials for Engineering*. Addison-Wesley Publishing Co., Inc., 1982.

700 °C (1300 °F), the cementite lamellae transform to roughly *spherical* shapes (Fig. 4.17). Unlike the lamellar shapes of cementite, which act as stress raisers, **spheroidites** (spherical particles) are less conducive to stress concentration because of their rounded shapes.

Consequently, this structure has higher toughness and lower hardness than the pearlite structure. In this form, it can be cold-worked, because the ductile ferrite has high toughness, and the spheroidal carbide particles prevent the initiation of cracks within the material.

FIGURE 4.16   Mechanical properties of annealed steels, as a function of composition and microstructure. Note (in (a)) the increase in hardness and strength and (in (b)) the decrease in ductility and toughness, with increasing amounts of pearlite and iron carbide. *Source*: L. H. Van Vlack; *Materials for Engineering*. Addison-Wesley Publishing Co., Inc., 1982.

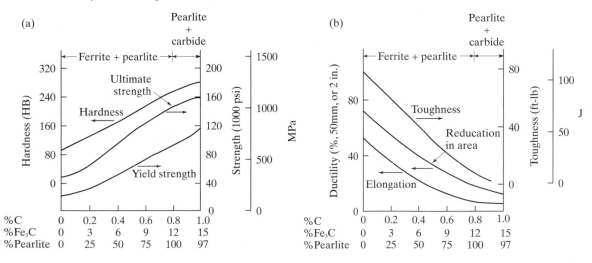

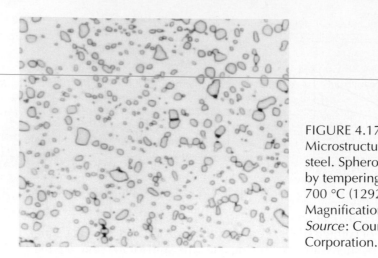

FIGURE 4.17
Microstructure of eutectoid steel. Spheroidite is formed by tempering the steel at 700 °C (1292 °F). Magnification: 1000 × . *Source*: Courtesy of USX Corporation.

4.7.3 Bainite

Visible only by using electron microscopy, **bainite** is a very fine microstructure consisting of ferrite and cementite, somewhat like a pearlitic but having a different morphology. It can be produced in steels with alloying elements and at cooling rates that are higher than those required for transformation to pearlite. This structure, called **bainitic steel** (after E. C. Bain, 1891–1971), is generally stronger and more ductile than pearlitic steels at the same hardness level.

4.7.4 Martensite

When austenite is cooled at a high rate, such as by quenching it in water, its fcc structure is transformed to a **body-centered tetragonal (bct)** structure. This structure can be described as a body-centered rectangular prism which is slightly elongated along one of its principal axes (Fig. 4.9d). This microstructure is called **martensite** (after A. Martens, 1850–1914).

Because martensite does not have as many slip systems as a bcc structure (and the carbon is in interstitial positions), it is extremely hard and brittle (Fig. 4.18); it lacks tough-

FIGURE 4.18   (a) Hardness of martensite, as a function of carbon content. (b) Micrograph of martensite containing 0.8% carbon. The gray platelike regions are martensite; they have the same composition as the original austenite (white regions). Magnification: 1000 × . *Source*: Courtesy of USX Corporation.

(a)

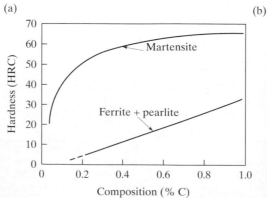

(b)

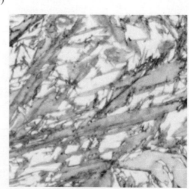

ness, and, therefore, has limited use. Martensite transformation takes place almost instantaneously (Fig. 4.14c) because it involves not the diffusion process but a slip mechanism (plastic deformation), a time-dependent phenomenon that is the mechanism in other transformations as well.

The material undergoes volume changes because of the differences in densities that result from phase transformations. For example, when austenite transforms to martensite, its volume increases (and its density decreases) by as much as 4%. A similar but smaller volume expansion also occurs when austenite transforms to pearlite. These expansions, and the thermal gradients present in a quenched part, cause internal stresses within the body. They may cause parts to undergo *distortion* or even to crack during heat treatment; **quench cracking** of steels is caused by rapid cooling during quenching.

Distortion is an irreversible dimensional change of the part. It is a general term and may consist of size distortion or shape distortion. *Size distortion* involves changes in the dimensions of the part without a change in shape, whereas *shape distortion* involves bending, twisting, and similar nonsymmetrical dimensional changes. Distortion can be reduced by proper control of heating and cooling cycles, by improved part design, and by more localized heat treatment of the part (see also Section 4.13).

4.7.5 Retained Austenite

If the temperature to which the alloy is quenched is not sufficiently low, only a portion of the structure is transformed to martensite. The rest is **retained austenite**, which is visible as white areas in the structure along with the dark, needlelike martensite. Retained austenite can cause dimensional instability and cracking, and it lowers the hardness and strength of the alloy.

4.7.6 Tempered Martensite

Martensite is tempered in order to improve its mechanical properties. **Tempering** is a heating process by which hardness is reduced and toughness is improved. The body-centered tetragonal martensite is heated to an intermediate temperature, typically 150 °C - 650 °C (300 °F - 1200 °F), where it decomposes to a two-phase microstructure consisting of body-centered cubic alpha ferrite and small particles of cementite.

With increasing tempering time and temperature, the hardness of tempered martensite decreases (Fig. 4.19). The reason is that the cementite particles coalesce and grow, and the distance between the particles in the soft ferrite matrix increases as the less stable and smaller carbide particles dissolve.

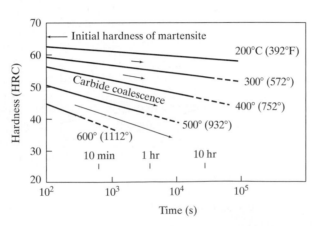

FIGURE 4.19   Hardness of tempered martensite, as a function of tempering time, for 1080 steel quenched to 65 HRC. Hardness decreases because the carbide particles coalesce and grow in size, thereby increasing the interparticle distance of the softer ferrite.

4.8 HARDENABILITY OF FERROUS ALLOYS

The capability of an alloy to be hardened by heat treatment is called its **hardenability**. It is a measure of the *depth* of hardness that can be obtained by heating and subsequent quenching. The term hardenability should not be confused with hardness, which is the resistance of a material to indentation or scratching (Section 2.6).

From the discussion thus far, it can be seen that hardenability of ferrous alloys depends on the carbon content, on the grain size of the austenite, on the alloying elements present in the material, and on the cooling rate. A test (the Jominy test) has been developed in order to determine the hardenability of an alloy.

4.8.1 The End-Quench Hardenability Test

In the commonly used **Jominy test** (after W. E. Jominy, 1893–1976), a round test bar 100 mm (4 in.) long, made from the particular alloy, is **austenitized**, that is, heated to the proper temperature to form 100% austenite. It is then quenched directly at one end (Fig. 4.20a) with a stream of water at 24 °C (75 °F).

The cooling rate thus varies throughout the length of the bar, the rate being highest at the lower end which is in direct contact with the water. The hardness along the length of the

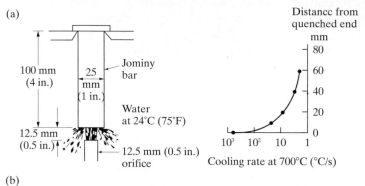

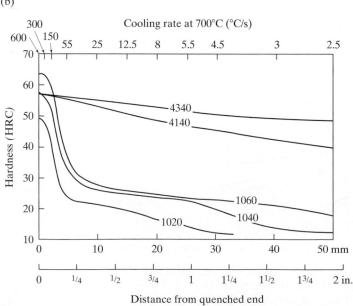

FIGURE 4.20 (a) End-quench test and cooling rate. (b) Hardenability curves for five different steels, as obtained from the end-quench test. Small variations in composition can change the shape of these curves. Each curve is actually a band, and its exact determination is important in the heat treatment of metals, for better control of properties. *Source*: L. H. Van Vlack; *Materials for Engineering*. Addison-Wesley Publishing Co., Inc., 1982.

bar is then measured at various distances from the quenched end and plotted as shown in Fig. 4.20b.

As expected from our discussion of the effects of cooling rates in Section 4.7, the hardness decreases away from the quenched end of the bar. The greater the depth to which the hardness penetrates, the greater is the hardenability of the alloy. Each composition of an alloy has its particular **hardenability band**. Note that the hardness at the quenched end increases with increasing carbon content; note also that 1040, 4140, and 4340 steels have the same carbon content (0.40%) and so they have the same hardness (57 HRC) at the quenched end.

Because small variations in composition and in grain size can affect the shape of hardenability curves, each lot of an alloy should be tested individually. The data may be plotted as a band, rather than as a single curve. Hardenability curves are necessary in predicting the hardness of heat-treated parts (such as gears, cams, and various other components) as a function of their composition.

4.8.2 Quenching Media

The fluid used for quenching the heated alloy also has an effect on hardenability. Quenching may be carried out in water, in brine (saltwater), in oils, in molten salts, or in air. Caustic solutions, polymer solutions, and gases are also used. Because of the differences in the thermal conductivities, the specific heats, and the heats of vaporization of these media, the rate of cooling of the alloy (**severity of quench**) is also different.

In relative terms and in decreasing order, the cooling capacities of several quenching media are as follows:

agitated brine, 5;

still water, 1;

still oil, 0.3;

cold gas, 0.1;

still air, 0.02.

Agitation is also a significant factor in the rate of cooling. The more vigorous the agitation, the higher is the rate of cooling. In tool steels the quenching medium is specified by a letter (see Table 5.7), such as W for water hardening, O for oil hardening, and A for air hardening.

The cooling rate also depends on the surface-area-to-thickness or surface-area-to-volume ratio of the part. The higher this ratio, the higher is the cooling rate. Thus, for example, a thick plate cools more slowly than a thin plate with the same surface area. These considerations are also significant in the cooling of metals and of plastics in casting and in molding processes.

Water is a common medium for rapid cooling. However, the heated metal may form a **vapor blanket** along its surfaces due to the water-vapor bubbles that form when water boils at the metal–water interface. This blanket creates a barrier to heat conduction, because of the lower thermal conductivity of the vapor.

Agitating the fluid or the part helps to reduce or eliminate the blanket. Also, water may be sprayed onto the part under high pressure. Brine is an effective quenching medium, because salt helps to nucleate bubbles at the interfaces; this effect improves agitation. Brine can, however, corrode the part.

Polymer quenchants have been used for almost thirty years for ferrous as well as for nonferrous alloy quenching, and new compositions are developed regularly. They have cooling characteristics that, generally, are between those of water and those of petroleum oils.

Typical polymer quenchants are polyvinyl alcohol, polyalkaline oxide, polyvinyl pyrrolidone, and polyethyl oxazoline. These quenchants have such advantages as better control of hardness results, elimination of fumes and fire (such as occur when oils are used as a quenchant), and reduction of corrosion (such as occurs when water is used). The quenching rate can be controlled by varying the concentration of the solutions.

4.9 HEAT TREATMENT OF NONFERROUS ALLOYS AND STAINLESS STEELS

Nonferrous alloys and some stainless steels generally cannot be heat treated by the techniques used on ferrous alloys. The reason is that nonferrous alloys do not undergo phase transformations like those in steels. The hardening and strengthening mechanisms for these alloys are fundamentally different.

Heat-treatable aluminum alloys, copper alloys, martensitic stainless steels, and some other stainless steels are hardened and strengthened by a process called **precipitation hardening**. This heat treatment is a technique in which small particles (of a different phase, and called **precipitates**) are uniformly dispersed in the matrix of the original phase (Fig. 4.3a). In this process, precipitate forms because the solid solubility of one element (one component of the alloy) in the other is exceeded.

Three stages are involved in precipitation hardening. They can best be described by reference to the phase diagram for the aluminum–copper system (Fig. 4.21a). For an alloy

FIGURE 4.21   (a) Phase diagram for the aluminum–copper alloy system. (b) Various microstructures obtained during the age-hardening process. *Source*: L. H. Van Vlack; *Materials for Engineering.* Addison-Wesley Publishing Co., Inc., 1982.

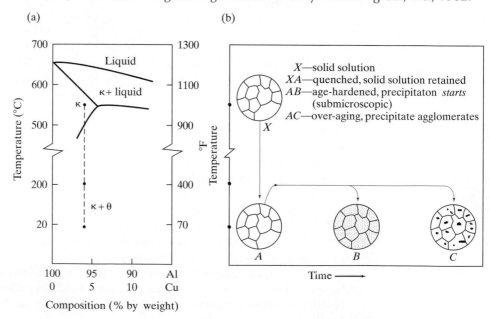

with the composition 95.5% Al–4.5% Cu, a single-phase (kappa) substitutional solid solution of copper (solute) in aluminum (solvent) exists between 500 °C and 570 °C (930 °F and 1060 °F).

This kappa phase is aluminum-rich, has a fcc structure, and is ductile. Below the lower temperature (that is, below the lower solubility curve) there are two phases: kappa and theta (a hard intermetallic compound of $CuAl_2$). This alloy can be heat treated, and its properties are modified by two different methods: *solution treatment* and *precipitation*.

4.9.1 Solution Treatment

In **solution treatment**, the alloy is heated to within the solid-solution kappa phase, say 540 °C (1000 °F), and then cooled rapidly—for instance, by quenching it in water. The structure obtained soon after quenching (*A* in Fig. 4.21b) consists only of the single phase kappa. This alloy has moderate strength and considerable ductility.

4.9.2 Precipitation Hardening

The structure obtained in *A* in Fig. 4.21b can be made stronger by **precipitation hardening**. The alloy is reheated to an intermediate temperature and then held there for a period of time, during which precipitation takes place. The copper atoms diffuse to nucleation sites and combine with aluminum atoms; this process produces the theta phase, which forms as submicroscopic precipitates (shown in *B* by the small dots within the grains of the kappa phase). This structure is stronger than that in *A*, although it is less ductile. The increase in strength is due to increased resistance to dislocation movement in the region of the precipitates.

Aging. Because the precipitation process is one of time and temperature, it is also called **aging**, and the property improvement is known as **age hardening**. If carried out above room temperature, the process is called **artificial aging**. However, several aluminum alloys harden and become stronger over a period of time at room temperature; this process is called **natural aging**.

Such alloys are first quenched; then, if it is so desired, they are shaped by plastic deformation at room temperature; finally, they are allowed to gain strength and hardness by aging naturally. Natural aging can be slowed down by refrigerating the quenched alloy (**cryogenic treatment**).

In the precipitation process, if the reheated alloy is held at the elevated temperature for an extended period of time, the precipitates begin to coalesce and grow. They become larger but fewer, as is shown by the larger dots in *C* in Fig. 4.21b. This process is called **overaging**, and the resulting alloy is softer and weaker.

There is an optimal time–temperature relationship in the aging process that must be observed in order to obtain desired properties (Fig. 4.22). Obviously, an aged alloy can be used only up to a certain maximum temperature in service; otherwise, it will overage and so lose its strength and hardness. Although weaker, an overaged part has better dimensional stability.

Maraging. This is a precipitation-hardening treatment for a special group of high-strength iron-base alloys. The word **maraging** is derived from *martensite age hardening*. In this process, one or more intermetallic compounds are precipitated in a matrix of low-carbon martensite. A typical maraging steel may contain 18% nickel in addition to other elements, and aging is done at 480 °C (900 °F).

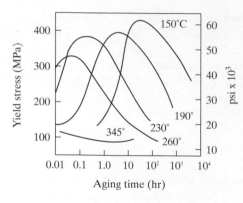

FIGURE 4.22   The effect of aging time and temperature on the yield stress of 2014-T4 aluminum alloy. Note that, for each temperature, there is an optimal aging time for maximum strength.

Hardening by maraging does not depend on the cooling rate; consequently, uniform full hardness can be obtained throughout large parts with minimal distortion. Typical uses of maraging steels are in dies and tooling for casting, molding, forging, and extrusion (Parts II and III).

4.10 CASE HARDENING

The heat treatment processes described thus far involve microstructural alterations and property changes in the *bulk* of the material or component, by means of *through hardening*. In many situations, however, alteration of only the *surface* properties of a part (hence, the term **case hardening**) is desirable. This method is particularly useful for improving resistance to surface indentation, fatigue, and wear.

Typical applications for case hardening are gear teeth, cams, shafts, bearings, fasteners, pins, automotive clutch plates, tools, and dies. Through hardening of these parts would not be desirable, because a hard part lacks the necessary toughness for these applications. A small surface crack could propagate rapidly through such a part and cause total failure.

Various surface-hardening processes are available (Table 4.1):

a. Carburizing (gas, liquid, and pack carburizing);
b. Carbonitriding;
c. Cyaniding;
d. Nitriding;
e. Boronizing;
f. Flame hardening;
g. Induction hardening; and
h. Laser hardening.

Basically, these are operations in which the component is heated in an atmosphere containing elements (such as carbon, nitrogen, or boron) that alter the composition, microstructure, and properties of surfaces. For steels with sufficiently high carbon content, surface hardening takes place without using any of these additional elements. Only the heat-treatment processes described in Section 4.7 are needed to alter the microstructures, usually by either flame hardening or induction hardening, as outlined in Table 4.1.

Laser beams and **electron beams** (Sections 26.7 and 26.8), also, are used effectively to harden both small and large surfaces, such as these of gears, valves, punches, and lo-

TABLE 4.1   Outline of Heat Treatment Processes for Surface Hardening

Process	Metals hardened	Element added to surface	Procedure	General characteristics	Typical applications
Carburizing	Low-carbon steel (0.2% C), alloy steels (0.08–0.2% C)	C	Heat steel at 870–950 °C (1600–1750 °F) in an atmosphere of carbona-ceous gases (gas carbu-rizing) or carbon-containing sol-ids (pack carburizing). Then quench.	A hard, high-carbon surface is produced. Hardness 55 to 65 HRC. Case depth <0.5–1.5 mm (<0.020 to 0.060 in.). Some dis-tortion of part during heat treatment.	Gears, cams, shafts, bear-ings, piston pins, sprockets, clutch plates
Carbonitriding	Low-carbon steel	C and N	Heat steel at 700–800 °C (1300–1600 °F) in an atmosphere of carbona-ceous gas and am-monia. Then quench in oil.	Surface hardness 55 to 62 HRC. Case depth 0.07 to 0.5 mm (0.003 to 0.020 in.). Less dis tortion than in carburizing.	Bolts, nuts, gears
Cyaniding	Low-carbon steel (0.2% C), alloy steels (0.08–0.2% C)	C and N	Heat steel at 760–845 °C (1400–1550 °F) in a molten bath of solu-tions of cyanide (e.g., 30% sodium cyanide) and other salts.	Surface hardness up to 65 HRC. Case depth 0.025 to 0.25 mm (0.001 to 0.010 in.). Some distortion.	Bolts, nuts, screws, small gears
Nitriding	Steels (1% Al, 1.5% Cr, 0.3% Mo), alloy steels (Cr, Mo), stainless steels, high-speed tool steels	N	Heat steel at 500–600 °C (925–1100 °F) in an atmosphere of ammo-nia gas or mixtures of molten cyanide salts. No further treatment.	Surface hardness up to 1100 HV. Case depth 0.1 to 0.6 mm (0.005 to 0.030 in.) and 0.02 to 0.07 mm (0.001 to 0.003 in.) for high speed steel.	Gears, shafts, sprockets, valves, cutters, boring bars, fuel-injection pump parts
Boronizing	Steels	B	Part is heated using boron-containing gas or solid in contact with part.	Extremely hard and wear resistant surface. Case depth 0.025–0.075 mm (0.001–0.003 in.).	Tool and die steels
Flame hardening	Medium-carbon steels, cast irons	None	Surface is heated with an oxyacetylene torch, then quenched with water spray or other quenching methods.	Surface hardness 50 to 60 HRC. Case depth 0.7 to 6 mm (0.030 to 0.25 in.). Little distortion.	Gear and sprocket teeth, axles, crankshafts, piston rods, lathe beds and centers
Induction hardening	Same as above	None	Metal part is placed in copper induction coils and is heated by high frequency current, then quenched.	Same as above	Same as above

comotive cylinders. These methods are also used for through hardening of relatively small parts. The main advantages of laser surface hardening are close control of power input, low distortion, and the ability to reach areas that would be inaccessible by other means. Capital costs can be high, however, and the depth of the case-hardened layer is usually less than 2.5 mm (0.1 in.).

Because case hardening is a localized heat treatment, case-hardened parts have a hardness gradient. Typically, the hardness is a maximum at the surface and decreases below the surface, with the rate of decrease depending on the composition of the metal and on the process variables.

Surface-hardening techniques can also be used for *tempering* (Section 4.11.3), to modify the properties of surfaces that have been subjected to heat treatment. Various other processes and techniques for surface hardening, such as shot peening and surface rolling, improve wear resistance and various other characteristics (Section 33.2).

Decarburization is the phenomenon in which alloys containing carbon lose carbon from their surfaces as a result of heat treatment or of hot-working in a medium, usually oxygen, that reacts with the carbon. Decarburization is undesirable, because it affects the hardenability of the surfaces of the part (by lowering its carbon content). It also adversely affects the hardness, the strength, and the fatigue life of steels, by significantly lowering their endurance limit. Decarburization is best avoided by processing in an inert atmosphere or a vacuum or by using neutral salt baths during heat treatment.

4.11 ANNEALING

Annealing is a general term used to describe the restoration of a cold-worked or heat-treated alloy to its original properties—for instance, so as to increase ductility (hence formability) and reduce hardness and strength, or so as to modify the microstructure. Annealing is also used to relieve residual stresses in a manufactured part, for the sake of improved machinability and of dimensional stability (Section 4.11.2). The term annealing also applies to the thermal treatment of glasses and similar products, of castings, and of weldments.

The annealing process consists of the following steps:

1. heating the workpiece to a specific range of temperature in a furnace;
2. holding it at that temperature for a period of time (soaking); and
3. air or furnace cooling.

The process may be carried out in an inert or a controlled atmosphere, or it may performed at lower temperatures to prevent or minimize surface oxidation.

An *annealing temperature* may be higher than the material's recrystallization temperature, depending on the degree of cold work. For example, the recrystallization temperature for copper ranges between 200 °C and 300 °C (400 °F and 600 °F), whereas the annealing temperature needed to recover the original properties fully ranges from 260 °C to 650 °C (500 °F to 1200 °F), depending on the degree of prior cold work (see also Section 1.6).

Full annealing is a term applied to the annealing of ferrous alloys, generally low- and medium-carbon steels. The steel is heated to above A_1 or A_3 (Fig. 4.23), and the cooling takes place slowly (typically at 10 °C (20 °F) per hour), in a furnace, after it is turned off. The structure obtained through full annealing is coarse pearlite, which is soft and ductile and has small, uniform grains.

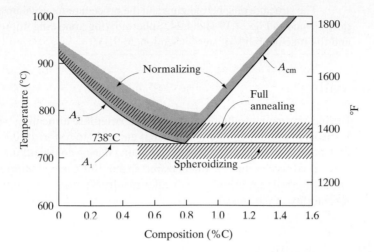

FIGURE 4.23   Heat-treating temperature ranges for plain-carbon steels, as indicated on the iron–iron carbide phase diagram. *Source*: ASM International.

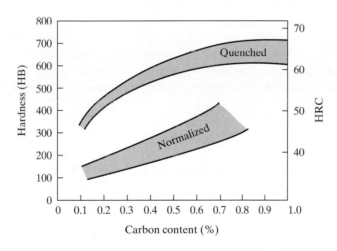

FIGURE 4.24   Hardness of steels in the quenched and normalized conditions, as a function of carbon content.

To avoid excessive softness from the annealing of steels, the cooling cycle may be done completely in still air. This process is called **normalizing**, to indicate that the part is heated to a temperature above A_3 or A_{cm} in order to transform the structure to austenite. Normalizing results in somewhat higher strength and hardness and in lower ductility than does full annealing (Fig. 4.24). The structure obtained is fine pearlite, with small, uniform grains. Normalizing is generally carried out to refine the grain structure, to obtain uniform structure (homogenization), to decrease residual stresses, and to improve machinability.

The structure of spheroidizing and the procedure for obtaining it were described in Section 4.7 and in Figs. 4.17 and 4.24. Spheroidizing annealing improves the cold workability and the machinability of steels (Section 20.9.1).

4.11.1 Process Annealing

During process annealing (also called **intermediate annealing**, **subcritical annealing**, or **in-process annealing**), the workpiece is annealed to restore its ductility, part or all of which may have been exhausted by work hardening during cold-working. Afterwards, the part can be worked further into the final desired shape. If the temperature is high and/or the time of annealing is long, grain growth may result (Section 1.6), with adverse effects on the formability of the annealed parts.

4.11.2 Stress-Relief Annealing

To reduce or eliminate residual stresses, a workpiece is generally subjected to **stress-relief annealing**, or simply **stress relieving**. The temperature and time required for this process depend on the material and on the magnitude of the residual stresses present. The residual stresses may have been induced during forming, machining, or other shaping processes or may have been caused by volume changes during phase transformations.

For steels, the part is not heated to as high as A_1, in order to avoid phase transformations. Slow cooling, such as occurs in still air, is generally employed. Stress relieving promotes dimensional stability in situations where subsequent relaxing of residual stresses may cause distortion of the part when it is in service over a period of time. It also reduces the tendency toward stress-corrosion cracking (Sections 2.10 and 3.8).

4.11.3 Tempering

If steels are hardened by heat treatment, then **tempering** or **drawing**—not to be confused with wire drawing or with the *deep drawing* described in Section 16.9 is used in order to reduce brittleness, to increase ductility and toughness, and to reduce residual stresses. The term tempering is used for glasses also (Section 17.11). In tempering, the steel is heated to a specific temperature, depending on composition, and then cooled at a prescribed rate.

The results of tempering for an oil-quenched AISI 4340 steel are shown in Fig. 4.25. Alloy steels may undergo **temper embrittlement**, which is caused by the segregation of impurities along the grain boundaries at temperatures between 480 °C and 590 °C (900 °F and 1100 °F).

4.11.4 Austempering

In **austempering**, the heated steel is quenched from the austenitizing temperature rapidly enough to avoid formation of ferrite or pearlite. It is held at a certain temperature until isothermal transformation from austenite to bainite is complete. It is then cooled to room temperature, usually in still air and at a moderate rate in order to avoid thermal gradients within the part. The quenching medium most commonly used is molten salt, at temperatures ranging from 160 °C to 750 °C (320 °F to 1380 °F).

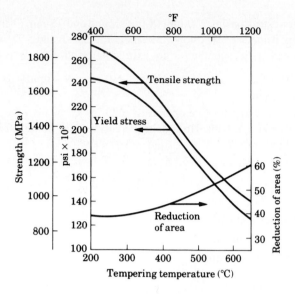

FIGURE 4.25   Mechanical properties of oil-quenched 4340 steel, as a function of tempering temperature. *Source*: Courtesy of LTV Steel Company.

Austempering is often substituted for conventional quenching and tempering, either to reduce the tendency toward cracking and distortion during quenching or to improve ductility and toughness while maintaining hardness. Because of the shorter cycle time involved, this process is economical for many applications.

In **modified austempering**, a mixed structure of pearlite and bainite is obtained. The best example of this practice is **patenting**, which provides high ductility and moderately high strength, such as in the patented wire used in the wire industry (Section 15.11).

4.11.5 Martempering (Marquenching)

In **martempering**, the steel or cast iron is first quenched from the austenitizing temperature in a hot-fluid medium, such as hot oil or molten salt. Next, it is held at that temperature until the temperature is uniform throughout the part; then it is cooled at a moderate rate, such as in air, in order to avoid temperature gradients within the part. Usually, the part is then tempered, because the structure obtained is otherwise primarily untempered martensite and is not suitable for most applications.

Martempered steels have less tendency to crack, distort, and develop residual stresses during heat treatment. In **modified martempering** the quenching temperature is lower, and thus the cooling rate is higher. The process is suitable for steels with lower hardenability.

4.11.6 Ausforming

In **ausforming**, also called **thermomechanical processing**, the steel is formed into desired shapes within controlled ranges of temperature and time to avoid formation of nonmartensitic transformation products. The part is then cooled at various rates to obtain the desired microstructures. Ausformed parts have superior mechanical properties.

Example: Heat Treatment of an Extrusion Die

As we have seen, heat treatment of parts to obtain a certain hardness involves several considerations regarding the material and its desired properties. The specific heat-treating process has to be planned carefully, and it often requires considerable experience, as is noted in this example.

A hot-extrusion die, 200-mm (8-in.) around and 75-mm (3-in.) long and having a hole of 75 mm, is made of H21 hot-work steel (Tables 5.6 and 5.7). A typical method for heat treating such a die, suitable for hot extrusion (Section 15.4), is outlined as follows:

1. Preheat the die at 815 to 845 °C, either in a slightly oxidizing atmosphere or in neutral salt.
2. Transfer it to a furnace operating at 1175 °C, in a 6% to 12% reducing atmosphere or neutral salt bath. Hold it in the furnace for about 20 minutes after the die has reached 1175 °C.
3. Cool it in still air to about 65 °C.
4. Temper it at 565 °C for four hours.
5. Cool it to near room temperature.
6. Retemper it at 650 °C for four hours.
7. Cool the die in air.

Source: ASM International.

4.12 HEAT-TREATING FURNACES AND EQUIPMENT

Two basic types of furnaces are used for heat treating: *batch* furnaces and *continuous* furnaces. Because they consume great amounts of energy, their insulation and efficiency are important design considerations, as are their initial cost, the personnel needed for their operation and maintenance, and their safe use.

Uniform temperature and accurate control of temperature–time cycles are important, so modern furnaces are equipped with various electronic controls. New developments in furnaces include computer-controlled systems, programmed to run through a complete heat-treating cycle repeatedly and with reproducible accuracy.

Heating-system fuels are usually gas, oil, or electricity (for resistance or induction heating). The type of fuel used affects the furnace's atmosphere: Unlike electric heating, gas or oil introduces the products of combustion into the furnace (a disadvantage). Electrical heating, however, has a slower startup time, and it is more difficult to adjust and control.

4.12.1 Batch Furnaces

In a batch furnace the parts to be heat treated are loaded into and unloaded from the furnace in individual batches. The furnace basically consists of an insulated chamber, a heating system, and an access door or doors. Batch furnaces are of the following basic types:

a. A **box furnace** is a horizontal rectangular chamber with one or two access doors through which parts are loaded. This type of furnace is commonly used and versatile, simple to construct and to use, and available in several sizes. A variation of this type is the **car-bottom furnace**. The parts to be heat treated, usually long or large, are loaded onto a flatcar which then moves on rails into the furnace.

b. A **pit furnace** is a vertical pit below ground level (having a lid) into which the parts are lowered. This type of furnace is particularly suitable for long parts, such as rods, shafts, and tubing, because they can be suspended by one end and, consequently, are less likely to warp during processing than if positioned horizontally within a box furnace.

c. A **bell furnace** is a round or rectangular box furnace without a bottom. It is lowered over stacked parts that are to be heat treated. This type of furnace is particularly suitable for coils of wire, for rods, and for sheet metal.

d. In the case of an **elevator furnace**, the parts to be heat treated are loaded onto a car platform, rolled into position, and then raised into the furnace. This type of furnace saves space in the plant. It can be especially suitable for alloys that have to be quenched rapidly, because a quenching tank can be placed directly under the furnace.

4.12.2 Continuous Furnaces

In this type, parts to be heat-treated move continuously through the furnace on conveyors of various designs that use trays, belts, chains, and other mechanisms. Continuous furnaces are suitable for high production runs and can be designed and programmed so that complete heat-treating cycles can be performed under tight control.

4.12.3 Salt-Bath Furnaces

Because of their high heating rates and better control of uniformity of temperature, salt baths are commonly used in various heat-treating operations, particularly for nonferrous strip and wire. Heating rates are high because of the higher thermal conductivity of liquid salts compared to that of air or gases.

Depending on the electrical conductivity of the salt, heating may be done externally (for nonconducting salts) or by immersed or submerged electrodes using low-voltage alternating current. Direct current cannot be used because it subjects the salt to electrolysis. Salt baths are available for a wide range of temperatures. Lead can be used as the heating medium instead.

4.12.4 Fluidized Beds

Dry, fine, and loose solid particles, usually aluminum oxide, are heated and suspended in a chamber by an upward flow of hot gas at various speeds. The parts to be heat treated are then placed within the floating particles—hence, the term **fluidized bed**. Because of its constant agitation, the system is efficient, the temperature distribution is uniform, and the heat-transfer rate is high. These furnaces are used for various batch-type applications.

4.12.5 Induction Heating

The part is heated rapidly by the electromagnetic field generated by an *induction coil* carrying alternating current, which induces eddy currents in the part. The coil, which can be shaped to fit the contour of the part to be heat treated (Fig. 4.26), is made of copper or of a copper-base alloy; usually, it is water-cooled. The coil may be designed to quench the part as well. Induction heating is desirable for localized heat treating, such as that required for gear teeth and cams.

4.12.6 Furnace Atmospheres

The atmospheres in furnaces can be controlled so to avoid (or cause) oxidation, tarnishing, and decarburization of ferrous alloys heated to elevated temperatures. Oxygen causes oxi-

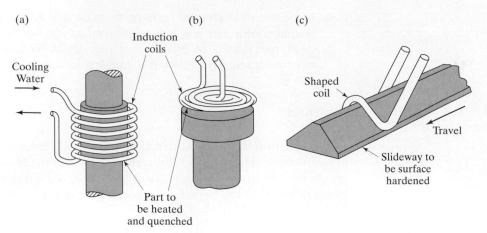

FIGURE 4.26   Types of coils used in induction heating of various surfaces of parts.

dation (corrosion, rusting, and scaling). Carbon dioxide has various effects; it may be neutral or decarburizing, depending on its concentration in the furnace atmosphere. Water vapor in the furnace causes oxidation of steels, resulting in a blue color.

Nitrogen is a common neutral atmosphere, and a vacuum provides a completely neutral atmosphere. The term **bluing** is used to describe formation of a thin blue film of oxide on finished parts to improve their appearance and their resistance to oxidation.

4.13 DESIGN CONSIDERATIONS FOR HEAT TREATING

In addition to the metallurgical factors, successful heat treating involves design considerations for avoiding problems such as cracking, distortion, and nonuniformity of the properties throughout the heat-treated part. The rate of cooling during quenching may not be uniform, particularly in complex shapes having varying cross-sections and thicknesses; this nonuniformity may produce severe temperature gradients. They can lead to variations in contraction, resulting in thermal stresses that may cause cracking of the part.

Furthermore, nonuniform cooling causes residual stresses in the part, which can lead to stress-corrosion cracking. The quenching method selected, the care taken in the quenching, and the proper choice of quenching medium and temperature are, consequently, important considerations.

As a general guideline for part design for heat treating, sharp internal or external corners should be avoided; otherwise, stress concentrations at these corners may raise the level of stresses high enough to cause cracking. A part should have its thicknesses as nearly uniform as possible; also, the transition between regions of different thicknesses should be made smooth.

Parts with holes, grooves, keyways, splines, and asymmetrical shapes may likewise be difficult to heat treat, because they may crack during quenching. Large surfaces with thin cross-sections are likely to warp. Hot forgings and hot steel-mill products may have a **decarburized skin** (loss of carbon, Section 4.10); as a result, they may not respond successfully to heat treatment.

SUMMARY

- Commercially pure metals generally do not have sufficient strength for many engineering applications; they must be alloyed with various elements which change their structures and properties. Important concepts in alloying are the solubility of alloying elements in a host metal and the phases present at various ranges of temperature and composition.

- Alloys come basically in two forms: solid solutions, and intermetallic compounds. Solid solutions may be substitutional or interstitial. There are certain conditions pertaining to the crystal structure and atomic radii that have to be met in order to develop these structures.

- Phase diagrams show the relationships among the temperature, the composition, and the phases present in a particular alloy system. As temperature is decreased at various rates, correspondingly various transformations take place in microstructures that have widely varying characteristics and properties. Among the binary systems, the most important is the iron–carbon system, which includes a wide range of steels and cast irons. Important components in this system are ferrite, austenite, and cementite. The basic types of cast irons are the following: gray iron, ductile (nodular) iron, white iron, malleable iron, compacted-graphite iron.

- The mechanisms for hardening and strengthening metal alloys involve thermal treatments: heating the alloy, and subsequently quenching it at varying rates. As a result, important phase transformations take place, producing structures such as pearlite (fine or coarse), spheroidite, bainite, and martensite. Heat treating of nonferrous alloys and of stainless steels involves solution treatment and precipitation hardening.

- The control of the furnace atmosphere, the quenchants used, the characteristics of the equipment, and the shape of the parts to be heat treated are important considerations. Hardenability is the capability of an alloy to be hardened by heat treatment. The end quench hardenability test (Jominy) is a method commonly used to determine hardenability bands for alloys.

- Case hardening is an important process for improving the wear and fatigue resistance of parts. Several methods are available, among then carburizing, nitriding, induction hardening, and laser hardening.

- Annealing includes several alternative processes (normalizing, process annealing, stress-relieving, tempering, austempering, and martempering), each having the purpose of enhancing the ductility and toughness of heat-treated parts.

TRENDS

- Studies on better methods of controlling the atmospheres in heat-treating furnaces are being conducted by computer modeling. Improvements in furnace insulation have resulted in significant energy savings.

- Studies are continuing on how to narrow the hardenability bands of alloys in order to obtain better control of the properties of heat-treated parts.

- Investigations are being conducted in which hot workpieces are quenched directly after they are hot-worked (for example, by forging). Hot-forged parts do not have to be re-heated for quenching; this shortcut improves efficiency and results in energy savings.

- Heat-treating facilities are being automated with the aid of computer programs that monitor and control all aspects of their operations.
- Electronic sensing systems are being developed for monitoring and detecting cracks, changes in part shape, and variations in the workpiece material during heat treating.

KEY TERMS

Age hardening	Equilibrium diagram	Phase diagram
Aging	Eutectic point	Phase transformations
Alloy	Eutectoid reaction	Precipitation hardening
Annealing	Ferrite	Pure metals
Austenite	Hardenability	Solute
Bainite	Heat treatment	Solution treatment
Case hardening	Intermetallic compounds	Solvent
Cast iron	Jominy test	Spheroidites
Cementite	Martensite	Stress relieving
Curie temperature	Normalizing	Tempering
Decarburization	Overaging	
Distortion	Pearlite	

BIBLIOGRAPHY

ASM Handbook, Vol. 3: *Alloy Phase Diagrams*. ASM International, 1992.

ASM Handbook, Vol. 4: *Heat Treating*. ASM International, 1991.

Brooks, C.R., *Principles of the Heat Treatment of Plain Carbon and Low Alloy Steel*, ASM International, 1996.

Bryson, B., *Heat Treatment, Selection, and Application of Tool Steels*. Hanser Gardner, 1997.

Heat Treater's Guide: Practices and Procedures for Irons and Steels. ASM International, 1995.

Heat Treater's Guide: Practices and Procedures for Nonferrous Alloys. ASM International, 1996.

Krauss, G., *Steels: Heat Treatment and Processing Principles*. ASM International, 1990.

Totten, G.E., and M.A.H. Howes (eds.), *Steel Heat Treatment Handbook*. Marcel Dekker, 1997.

REVIEW QUESTIONS

4.1 Describe the difference between a solute and a solvent.

4.2 What is a solid solution?

4.3 What are the conditions for obtaining (a) substitutional and (b) interstitial solid solutions?

4.4 What is the difference between a single-phase and a two-phase system?

4.5 Explain what is meant by "second-phase particle."

4.6 Describe the features of a phase diagram.

4.7 What do the terms "equilibrium" and "constitutional", as applied to phase diagrams, indicate?

4.8 What is the difference between "eutectic" and "eutectoid?"

4.9 What is tempering? Why is it done?

4.10 Explain what is meant by severity of quenching.

4.11 What are precipitates? Why are they significant in precipitation hardening?

4.12 What is the difference between natural and artificial aging?

4.13 Describe the characteristics of ferrite, austenite, and cementite.

4.14 What is the purpose of annealing?

QUALITATIVE PROBLEMS

4.15 You may have seen some technical literature on products stating that certain parts in those products are "heat treated." Describe briefly your understanding of this term and why the manufacturer mentions it.

4.16 Describe the engineering significance of the existence of a eutectic point in phase diagrams.

4.17 Explain the difference between hardness and hardenability.

4.18 Refer to Table 4.1, and explain why the items listed under "typical applications" are suitable for surface hardening.

4.19 Why is it generally not desirable to use steels in their as-quenched condition?

4.20 Describe the differences between case hardening and through hardening, insofar as engineering applications are concerned.

4.21 Describe the characteristics of (a) an alloy, (b) pearlite, (c) austenite, (d) martensite, and (e) cementite.

4.22 Explain why carbon, of all the elements, is so effective in imparting strength to iron in the form of steel.

4.23 How does the shape of graphite in cast iron affect its properties?

4.24 In Section 4.8, we listed several fluids in terms of their cooling capacity in quenching. Which physical properties of these fluids influence their cooling capacity?

4.25 Why is it important to know the characteristics of heat-treating furnaces?

4.26 Explain why, in the abscissa of Fig. 4.15, the percentage of pearlite begins to go down after 100% carbon content is reached.

4.27 What is the significance of decarburization? Give some examples.

4.28 Explain your understanding of size distortion and of shape distortion in heat-treated parts, and describe their causes.

4.29 Comment on your observations regarding Fig. 4.20.

QUANTITATIVE PROBLEMS

4.30 Using Fig. 4.5, estimate the following quantities for a 20% Cu–80% Ni alloy: (a) the liquidus temperature, (b) the solidus temperature, (c) the percentage of nickel in the liquid at 1400 °C (2550 °F), (d) the major phase at 1400 °C, and (e) the ratio of solid to liquid at 1400 °C.

4.31 Extrapolating the curves in Fig. 4.19, estimate the time that it would take for 1080 steel to soften to 53 HRC at (a) 200 °C and (b) 300 °C.

4.32 A typical steel for tubing is AISI 1040, one for music wire 1085. Considering their applications, explain the reason for the difference in their carbon contents.

SYNTHESIS AND DESIGN

4.33 We stated in this chapter that, in parts design, sharp corners should be avoided, in order to reduce the tendency toward cracking during heat treatment. If it is necessary for the part to have sharp corners in order to function properly, and it still requires heat treatment, what method would you recommend for manufacturing this part?

4.34 The heat-treatment processes for surface hardening are given in Table 4.1. Each of these processes involves different equipment, procedures, and cycle times; as a result, each incurs different costs. Examine available literature, and contact various facilities; then, make a similar table outlining the costs involved in each process.

4.35 We have seen that, as a result of heat treatment, parts can undergo size distortion and shape distortion to various degrees. By referring to the bibliography at the end of this chapter, make a survey of the technical literature, and report quantitative data regarding the distortions of parts having different shapes.

4.36 Figure 4.20 shows hardness distributions in end-quench tests, as measured *along the length* of the round bar. Make a simple qualitative sketch showing the hardness distribution *across the diameter* of the bar. Would the shape of the curve depend on the bar's carbon content? Explain.

4.37 Throughout this chapter you have seen the importance and the benefits of heat treating parts (or certain regions of parts), and you have seen some specific examples. Make a survey of the heat-treatment literature available, by referring to the bibliography at the end of this chapter; then, compile several examples and illustrations of parts that have been heat treated.

5

Ferrous Metals and Alloys: Production, General Properties, and Applications

5.1 INTRODUCTION

By virtue of their wide range of mechanical, physical, and chemical properties, **ferrous metals and alloys** are among the most useful of all metals. Ferrous metals and alloys contain iron as their base metal; the general categories are carbon and alloy steels, stainless steels, tool and die steels, cast irons, and cast steels.

Ferrous alloys are produced as (a) sheet steel for automobiles, appliances, and containers; (b) plates for boilers, ships, and bridges; (c) structural members such as I-beams, bar products, axles, crankshafts, and railroad rails; (d) gears, as stock for tools and dies; (e) music wire; and (f) fasteners such as bolts, rivets, and nuts.

A typical U.S. passenger car contains about 800 kg (1750 lb) of steel, accounting for about 55% to 60% of its weight. As an example of their widespread use, ferrous materials make up 70% to 85% by weight of structural members and mechanical components. Carbon steels are the least expensive of all structural metals.

The use of iron and steel as structural materials has been one of the most important technological developments. Primitive ferrous tools first appeared in about 4000–3000 B.C. They were made from meteoritic iron, obtained from meteorites that had struck the earth. True ironworking began in Asia Minor in about 1100 B.C. and signaled the advent of the iron age. Invention of the blast furnace, in about 1340 A.D., made possible the production of large quantities of iron and steel.

In this chapter, both traditional and modern methods of steelmaking are described. This chapter also describes the properties and characteristics of major categories of ferrous alloys, as produced by various methods.

5.2 PRODUCTION OF IRON AND STEEL

5.2.1 Raw Materials

The three basic materials used in iron- and steelmaking are **iron ore**, **limestone**, and **coke**. Although it does not occur in a free state in nature, iron is one of the most abundant elements in the world, making up about 5% of the earth's crust (in the form of various ores). The principal iron ores are *taconite* (a black flintlike rock), *hematite* (an iron oxide mineral), and *limonite* (an iron oxide containing water).

After it is mined, the ore is crushed into fine particles, the impurities are removed by various means such as magnetic separation, and the ore is formed into pellets, balls, or briquettes, using binders and water. Typically, pellets are about 65% pure iron and about 25 mm (1 in.) in diameter. The concentrated iron ore is referred to as *beneficiated* (as are other concentrated ores). Some iron-rich ores are used directly without pelletizing.

Coke is obtained from special grades of bituminous coal, which are heated in vertical ovens to temperatures of up to 1150 °C (2100 °F) and then cooled with water in quenching towers. Coke has several functions in steelmaking. One is to generate the high level of heat required for the chemical reactions in ironmaking to take place. A second is to produce carbon monoxide (a reducing gas, meaning that it removes oxygen), which is then used to reduce iron oxide to iron. The chemical by-products of coke are used in the making of plastics and of chemical compounds. Gases evolved during the conversion of coal to coke are used as fuel for plant operations.

The function of limestone (calcium carbonate) is to remove impurities from the molten iron. The limestone reacts chemically with impurities, acting like a **flux** (meaning to flow as a fluid) that causes the impurities to melt at a low temperature. The limestone combines with the impurities and forms a **slag**, which is light, floats over the molten metal, and is subsequently removed. *Dolomite* (an ore of calcium magnesium carbonate) is used as a flux. The slag is later used in making cement, fertilizers, glass, building materials, rock-wool insulation, and road ballast.

5.2.2 Ironmaking

The three raw materials are carried to the top of the **blast furnace** and dumped into it (Fig. 5.1); this process is called *charging the furnace*. The principle of this furnace was developed in Central Europe; the first blast furnace built in the United States began operating in 1621. The blast furnace is basically a large steel cylinder lined with refractory (heat-resistant) brick; it has the height of about a ten-story building.

The charge mixture is melted in a reaction at 1650 °C (3000 °F) with air preheated to about 1100 °C (2000 °F) and *blasted* into the furnace (hence the term "blast furnace") through nozzles (*tuyeres*). Although a number of reactions may take place, the basic reaction is that of oxygen with carbon to produce carbon monoxide, which in turn reacts with the iron oxide and reduces it to **iron**. Preheating the incoming air is necessary because the burning coke alone does not produce sufficiently high temperatures for the reactions to occur.

The molten metal accumulates at the bottom of the blast furnace, while the impurities float to the top of the metal. At intervals of four to five hours, the molten metal is drawn off (*tapped*) into ladle cars, each holding as much as 160 tons of molten iron.

The molten metal at this stage is called **pig iron**, or simply **hot metal**. It has a typical composition of 4% carbon, 1.5% silicon, 1% manganese, 0.04% sulfur, and 0.4% phosphorus, with the rest being pure iron. Use of the word **pig** comes from the early practice of pouring the molten iron into small sand molds, arranged like a litter of small pigs around a main channel. The solidified metal (pig) is then used in making iron and steels.

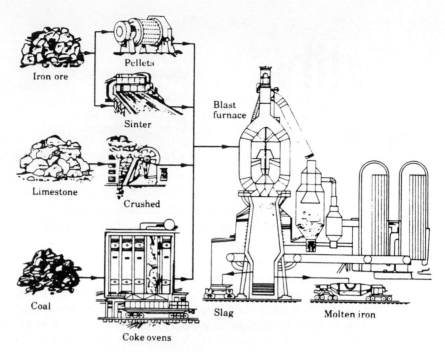

FIGURE 5.1   Schematic illustration of a blast furnace. *Source*: Courtesy of American Iron and Steel Institute.

5.2.3 Steelmaking

Steel was first produced in China and Japan in about 600–800 a.d. The steelmaking process is essentially one of refining the pig iron by the reduction of the percentage of manganese, silicon, carbon, and other elements, and of controlling the composition of the output by the addition of various elements. The molten metal from the blast furnace is transported into one of three types of furnaces: **open-hearth, electric, or basic oxygen**.

The label "open-hearth" derives from the shallow hearth shape that is directly open to the flames that melt the metal. Developed in the 1860s, the open-hearth furnace is still important industrially, but it is being replaced rapidly by electric furnaces and by the basic-oxygen process, because the latter two are more efficient and produce steels of better quality.

1. **Electric furnace**. The electric furnace was first introduced into the United States in 1906. The source of heat is a continuous electric arc that is formed between the electrodes and the charged metal (Fig. 5.2). Temperatures as high as 1925 °C (3500 °F) are generated in this type of furnace. There are usually three graphite electrodes, and they can be as large as 750 mm (30 in.) in diameter and 1.5 to 2.5 m (5 to 8 ft) in length. Their height in the furnace can be adjusted in response to the amount of metal present and the amount of wear of the electrodes.

   Steel scrap and a small amount of carbon and limestone are dropped into the electric furnace through the open roof. (Electric furnaces can also be charged with 100% scrap). The roof is then closed, and the electrodes are lowered. Power is turned on, and, within a period of about two hours, the metal melts. The current is then shut off, the electrodes are raised, the furnace is tilted, and the molten metal is poured into a **ladle**, which is a receptacle used for transferring and pouring molten metal.

   Electric-furnace capacities range from 60 to 90 tons of steel per day. The quality of steel produced is better than that from the open-hearth or the basic-oxygen process.

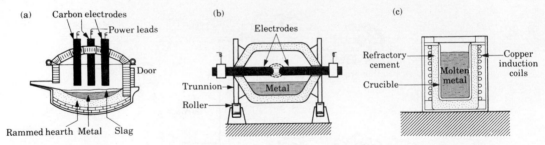

FIGURE 5.2   Schematic illustration of types of electric furnaces: (a) direct arc, (b) indirect arc, and (c) induction.

For smaller quantities, electric furnaces can be of the **induction** type. The metal is placed in a **crucible**, a large pot made of refractory material and surrounded with a copper coil through which alternating current is passed (Fig. 5.2c). The induced current in the charge melts the metal. These furnaces are also used for remelting metal for casting.

2. **Basic-oxygen furnace**. The basic-oxygen furnace (BOF) is the newest and fastest steel-making process. Typically, 200 tons of molten pig iron and 90 tons of scrap are charged (fed) into a vessel (Fig. 5.3a). Pure oxygen is then blown into the furnace for about 20 minutes through a water-cooled **lance** (which is a long tube), under a pressure of about 1250 kPa (180 psi) (Fig. 5.3b). Fluxing agents, such as lime, are added through a chute.

The vigorous agitation of the oxygen refines the molten metal by an oxidation process in which iron oxide is produced. The oxide then reacts with the carbon in the molten metal, producing carbon monoxide and carbon dioxide. The lance is retracted and the furnace is tapped by tilting it; note the opening in Fig. 5.3c for the molten metal. The slag is then removed by tilting the furnace in the opposite direction.

FIGURE 5.3   Schematic illustrations showing (a) charging, (b) melting, and (c) pouring of molten iron in a basic-oxygen process. *Source*: Inland Steel Company.

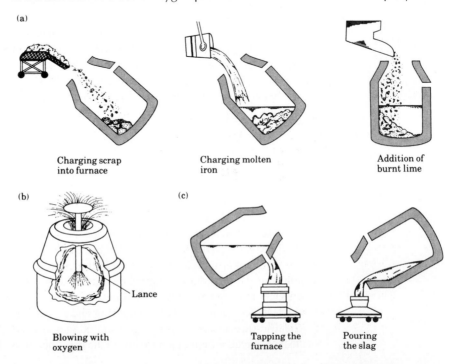

The BOF process is capable of refining 250 tons of steel in 35 to 50 minutes. Most BOF steels, which have low impurity levels and, hence, are of better quality than open-hearth furnace steels, are processed into plates, sheets, and various structural shapes, such as I-beams and channels (see Fig. 13.1).

3. **Vacuum furnace**. Steel may also be melted in induction furnaces from which the air has been removed, similar to the one shown in Fig. 5.2c. Because the process removes gaseous impurities from the molten metal, vacuum melting produces high-quality steels.

5.3 CASTING OF INGOTS

Traditionally, the next step in the steelmaking process is the shaping of the molten steel into a solid form (**ingot**) for such further processing as rolling it into shapes, casting it into semifinished forms, or forging it. (This shaping process is being rapidly replaced by **continuous casting** (Section 5.4), which improves efficiency by eliminating the need for ingots.) The molten metal is poured (teemed) from the ladle into ingot molds, in which the metal solidifies.

Molds are usually made of cupola iron or of blast-furnace iron, with 3.5% carbon; they are tapered, in order to facilitate the removal of the solidified metal. The bottoms of the molds may be closed or open; if they are open, the molds are placed on a flat surface.

The cooled ingots are removed (stripped) from the molds and lowered into **soaking pits**, where they are reheated to a uniform temperature of about 1200 °C (2200 °F) for subsequent processing by rolling. Ingots may be square, rectangular, or round in cross-section, and their weight ranges from a few hundred pounds to 40 tons.

Certain reactions take place during the solidification of an ingot; these reactions have an important influence on the quality of the steel produced. For example: Significant amounts of oxygen and other gases can dissolve in the molten metal during steelmaking. Most of these gases are rejected during the solidification of the metal, because the solubility limit of gases in the metal decreases sharply as its temperature decreases (see Fig. 10.14). Rejected oxygen combines with carbon, forming carbon monoxide, which causes porosity in the solidified ingot.

Depending on the amount of gas evolved during solidification, three types of steel ingots can be produced: killed, semi-killed, and rimmed.

1. **Killed steel**. Killed steel is a fully deoxidized steel; that is, oxygen is removed and porosity is thus eliminated. In the deoxidation process, the dissolved oxygen in the molten metal is made to react with elements such as aluminum, silicon, manganese, and vanadium that are added to the melt. These elements have an affinity for oxygen and form metallic oxides. If aluminum is used, the product is called aluminum-killed steel. The term *killed* comes from the fact that the steel lies quietly after being poured into the mold.

   The oxide inclusions in the molten bath, if sufficiently large, float out and adhere to (or are dissolved in) the slag. A fully killed steel is thus free of any porosity caused by gases. It is also free of any **blowholes** (large spherical holes near the surfaces of the ingot).

   Consequently, the chemical and mechanical properties of an ingot of a killed steel are relatively uniform throughout. Because of shrinkage during the solidification, however, an ingot of this type develops a **pipe** at the top (also called a **shrinkage cavity**); it has the appearance of a funnel-like shape. This pipe can take up a substantial volume of the ingot; it has to be cut off and scrapped.

2. **Semi-killed steel**. Semi-killed steel is a partially deoxidized steel. It contains some porosity (generally in the upper central section of the ingot), but it has little or no pipe; as a result, scrap is reduced. Although the piping in semi-killed steels is less, that advantage is offset by the presence of porosity in that region. Semi-killed steels are economical to produce.

3. **Rimmed steel**. In a rimmed steel, which generally has a low carbon content (less than 0.15 %), the evolved gases are "killed" (or controlled) only partially, by the addition

of elements such as aluminum. The gases produce blowholes along the outer rim of the ingot—hence the term *rimmed*. Blowholes are generally not objectionable, unless they break through the outer skin of the ingot.

Rimmed steels have little or no piping, and they have a ductile skin with good surface finish. However, blowholes may break through the skin if they are not controlled properly. Furthermore, impurities and inclusions tend to segregate toward the center of the ingot. Thus, products made from this steel may be defective and should be inspected.

Refining.   The properties and manufacturing characteristics of ferrous alloys are adversely affected by the amount of impurities, inclusions, and other elements present (see Section 2.10). The removal of impurities is known as *refining*; much of it is done in melting furnaces or in ladles, by means of the addition of various elements.

There is an increasing demand for cleaner steels, ones having improved and more uniform properties and greater consistency of composition. Refining is particularly important in producing high-grade steels and alloys for high-performance and critical applications, such as occur in aircraft manufacture. Moreover, warranty periods on shafts, camshafts, crankshafts for diesel trucks, and similar parts can be increased significantly by using higher-quality steels.

The trend in steelmaking is for **secondary refining** in ladles (**ladle metallurgy**) and vacuum chambers. New methods of ladle refining (**injection refining**) generally consist of melting and processing in a vacuum. Several processes using controlled atmospheres, such as electron-beam melting, vacuum-arc remelting, argon–oxygen decarburization, and vacuum-arc double-electrode remelting, have been developed.

5.4 CONTINUOUS CASTING

The traditional method of casting ingots is a batch process; that is, each ingot has to be stripped from its mold after solidification and processed individually. Furthermore, piping and microstructural and chemical variations are present throughout the ingot. These problems are alleviated by *continuous-casting* processes, which produce higher-quality steels at reduced cost (see also Section 13.7 on *minimills*).

Conceived in the 1860s, continuous or **strand casting** was first developed for casting non-ferrous metal strip. The process is now used for steel production, with major efficiency and productivity improvements and with significant cost reduction. One system for continuous casting is shown schematically in Fig. 5.4. The molten metal in the ladle is cleaned; then it is equalized in temperature by the blowing of nitrogen gas through it for five to ten minutes.

The metal is then poured into a refractory-lined intermediate pouring vessel (**tundish**), where impurities are skimmed off. The tundish holds as much as three tons of metal. The molten metal travels downward through water-cooled copper molds and begins to solidify into a path supported by rollers (*pinch rolls*).

Before starting the casting process, a solid *starter bar* (*dummy bar*) is inserted into the bottom of the mold. When the molten metal is first poured, it freezes onto the dummy bar. The bar is withdrawn at the same rate at which the metal is poured. The cooling rate is such that the metal develops a solidified skin (shell), so as to support itself during its travel downward—typically, at speeds of about 25 mm/s (1 in./s).

The shell thickness at the exit end of the mold is about 12 to 18 mm (0.5 to 0.75 in.). Additional cooling is provided by water sprays along the travel path of the solidifying metal. The molds are generally coated with graphite or similar solid lubricants, in order to reduce both friction and adhesion at the mold–metal interfaces. The molds are vibrated in order to reduce friction and sticking (Section 32.11).

The continuously cast metal may be cut into desired lengths by shearing or by computer-controlled torch cutting, or it may be fed directly into a rolling mill for further reduction in thickness and for shape-rolling of products such as channels and I-beams. In

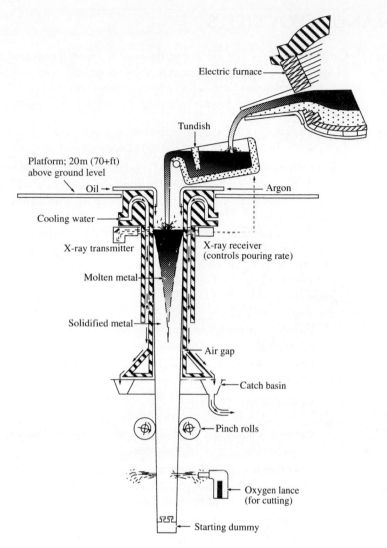

FIGURE 5.4   The continuous-casting process for steel. Typically, the solidified metal descends at a speed of 25 mm/s (1 in./s). Note that the platform is about 20 m (70 ft) above ground level. *Source*: *Metalcaster's Reference and Guide*, American Foundrymen's Society.

addition to costing less, continuously cast metals have more uniform compositions and properties than those obtained by ingot casting.

Although the thickness of steel strand is usually about 250 mm (10 in.), new developments have reduced this thickness to about 25 mm (1 in.). The thinner strand reduces the number of rolling operations required and improves the economy of the overall operation. Modern facilities use computer-controlled rolling operations on continuously cast strands, with final sheet thicknesses on the order of 2-6 mm (0.08-0.25 in.) for carbon, stainless, and electrical steels and with capabilities for rapid switchover from one type of steel to another.

After they are hot rolled, steel plates or shapes undergo one or more further processes, such as (a) cleaning and pickling by chemicals to remove surface oxides, (b) cold rolling to improve strength and surface finish, (c) annealing, and (d) coating (galvanizing or aluminizing) to improve resistance to corrosion.

5.5 CARBON AND ALLOY STEELS

Carbon and alloy steels are among the most commonly used metals and have a wide variety of applications (Table 5.1). The compositions and the processing of steels are controlled in a manner that makes them suitable for numerous applications. They are available in various basic product shapes: plate, sheet, strip, bar, wire, tube, castings, and forgings.

5.5.1 Effects of Various Elements in Steels

Various elements are added to steels, in order to impart the properties of hardenability, strength, hardness, toughness, wear resistance, workability, weldability, and machinability. These elements are listed below in alphabetic order, with summaries of their beneficial and detrimental effects.

Generally, the higher the percentages of these elements in steels, the greater are the particular properties that they impart; for example, the higher the carbon content, the greater the hardenability of the steel and the greater its strength, hardness, and wear resistance. On the other hand, ductility, weldability, and toughness are reduced with increasing carbon content.

Boron improves hardenability, without the loss of (or even with some improvement in) machinability and formability.

Calcium deoxidizes steels, improves toughness, and may improve formability and machinability.

Carbon improves hardenability, strength, hardness, and wear resistance; it reduces ductility, weldability, and toughness.

Cerium controls the shape of inclusions and improves toughness in high-strength, low-alloy steels; it deoxidizes steels.

Chromium improves toughness, hardenability, wear and corrosion resistance, and high-temperature strength; it increases the depth of hardness penetration resulting from heat treatment, by promoting carburization.

Cobalt improves strength and hardness at elevated temperatures.

Copper improves resistance to atmospheric corrosion and, to a lesser extent, increases strength, with little loss in ductility; it adversely affects hot-working characteristics and surface quality.

TABLE 5.1   Typical Selection of Carbon and Alloy Steels for Various Applications

Product	Steel	Product	Steel
Aircraft forgings, tubing, fittings	4140, 8740	Differential gears	4023
		Gears (car and truck)	4027, 4032
Automobile bodies	1010	Landing gear	4140, 4340, 8740
Axles	1040, 4140	Lock washers	1060
Ball bearings and races	52100	Nuts	3130
Bolts	1035, 4042, 4815	Railroad rails and wheels	1080
Camshafts	1020, 1040	Springs (coil)	1095, 4063, 6150
Chains (transmission)	3135, 3140	Springs (leaf)	1085, 4063, 9260, 6150
Coil springs	4063	Tubing	1040
Connecting rods	1040, 3141, 4340	Wire	1045, 1055
Crankshafts (forged)	1045, 1145, 3135, 3140	Wire (music)	1085

Lead improves machinability; it causes liquid-metal embrittlement.

Magnesium has the same effects as cerium.

Manganese improves hardenability, strength, abrasion resistance, and machinability; it deoxidizes the molten steel and reduces hot shortness; and it decreases weldability.

Molybdenum improves hardenability, wear resistance, toughness, elevated-temperature strength, creep resistance, and hardness; it minimizes temper embrittlement.

Nickel improves strength, toughness, and corrosion resistance; it improves hardenability.

Niobium (*columbium*) imparts fineness of grain size and improves strength and impact toughness; it lowers transition temperature; and it may decrease hardenability.

Phosphorus improves strength, hardenability, corrosion resistance, and machinability; it severely reduces ductility and toughness.

Selenium improves machinability.

Silicon improves strength, hardness, corrosion resistance, and electrical conductivity; it decreases magnetic hysteresis loss, machinability, and cold formability.

Sulfur improves machinability when combined with manganese; it lowers impact strength and ductility; it impairs surface quality and weldability.

Tantalum has effects similar to those of niobium.

Tellurium improves machinability, formability, and toughness.

Titanium improves hardenability; it deoxidizes steels.

Tungsten has the same effects as cobalt.

Vanadium improves strength, toughness, abrasion resistance, and hardness at elevated temperatures; it inhibits grain growth during heat treatment.

Zirconium has the same effects as cerium.

5.5.2 Residual Elements in Steels

During steel production, refining, and processing, some *residual elements* (**trace elements**) may still remain. Although we can also consider some of the elements in the preceding list as residuals, the following are generally considered unwanted residual elements; their effects are shown.

Antimony and **arsenic** cause temper embrittlement.

Hydrogen severely embrittles steels; however, heating during processing drives out most of the hydrogen.

Nitrogen improves strength, hardness, and machinability; in aluminum-deoxidized steels, it controls the size of inclusions and improves strength and toughness; it decreases ductility and toughness.

Oxygen slightly increases the strength of rimmed steels; it severely reduces toughness.

Tin causes hot shortness and temper embrittlement.

5.5.3 Designations for Steels

The American Iron and Steel Institute (AISI) and the Society of Automotive Engineers (SAE) designate carbon and alloy steels by using four digits. The first two digits indicate the alloying elements and their percentages, and the last two digits indicate the carbon content, by weight.

Another numbering system is the American Society for Testing and Materials (ASTM) designations, which incorporate the AISI–SAE designations and include standard specifications for steel products. For ferrous metals, the designation consists of the letter "A" followed by arbitrary numbers (generally three).

The latest numbering system for all metals has been developed cooperatively by several organizations; it is known as the *Unified Numbering System* (UNS). It consists of a letter indicating the general class of the alloy, followed by five digits designating its chemical composition.

5.5.4 Carbon Steels

Carbon steels are generally classified by their proportion (by weight) of carbon content.

  a. **Low-carbon steel**, also called **mild steel**, has less than 0.30% carbon. It is generally used for common industrial products, such as bolts, nuts, sheet, plate, and tubes, and for machine components that do not require high strength.

  b. **Medium-carbon steel** has 0.30% to 0.60% carbon. It is generally used in applications requiring higher strength than is available in low-carbon steels, such as in machinery, in automotive and agricultural equipment parts (gears, axles, connecting rods, crankshafts), in railroad equipment, and in parts for metalworking machinery.

  c. **High-carbon steel** has more than 0.60% carbon. It is generally used for parts requiring strength, hardness, and wear resistance, such as cutting tools, cable, music wire, springs, and cutlery. After being manufactured into shapes, the parts are usually heat treated and tempered (Chapter 4). The higher the carbon content of the steel, the higher is its hardness, strength, and wear resistance after heat treatment.

  d. Carbon steels containing sulfur and phosphorus are also available; they are known as **resulfurized** carbon steels (11xx series) and **rephosphorized and resulfurized** carbon steels (12xx series). For example, 1112 steel is a resulfurized steel with a carbon content of 0.12%. These steels have improved machinability, as described in Section 20.9.1.

The general mechanical properties of carbon and alloy steels are shown in Table 5.2. The machinability, formability, and weldability of such steels are described in various chapters.

TABLE 5.2   Typical Mechanical Properties of Selected Carbon and Alloy Steels in the Hot-Rolled, Normalized, and Annealed Condition

AISI	Condition	Ultimate tensile strength (MPa)	Yield strength (MPa)	Elongation in 50 mm (%)	Reduction of area (%)	Hardness (HB)
1020	As-rolled	448	346	36	59	143
	Normalized	441	330	35	67	131
	Annealed	393	294	36	66	111
1080	As-rolled	1010	586	12	17	293
	Normalized	965	524	11	20	293
	Annealed	615	375	24	45	174
3140	Normalized	891	599	19	57	262
	Annealed	689	422	24	50	197
4340	Normalized	1279	861	12	36	363
	Annealed	744	472	22	49	217
8620	Normalized	632	385	26	59	183
	Annealed	536	357	31	62	149

5.5.5 Alloy Steels

Steels containing significant amounts of alloying elements are called **alloy steels**; they are usually made with more care than are carbon steels. **Structural-grade** alloy steels, as identified by ASTM specifications, are used mainly in the construction and transportation industries, because of their high strength. Other alloy steels are used in applications where strength, hardness, creep and fatigue resistance, and toughness are required. These steels may also have been heat treated, in order to obtain the desired properties.

5.5.6 High-Strength Low-Alloy Steels

In order to improve the strength-to-weight ratio of steels, a number of **high-strength, low-alloy (HSLA)** steels have been developed. These steels have a low carbon content (usually less than 0.30%). They are characterized by a microstructure consisting of fine-grain ferrite as one phase and a hard second phase of martensite and austenite.

First developed in the 1930s, HSLA steels are usually produced in sheet form, by microalloying and controlled hot-rolling. Plates, bars, and structural shapes are made from these steels. The ductility, formability, and weldability of HSLA steels are, however, generally inferior to those of conventional low-alloy steels. To improve these properties, **dual-phase steels** have been developed (see below).

Sheet products of HSLA steels typically are used for parts of automobile bodies (in order to reduce weight and hence fuel consumption), in other transportation equipment, and in mining, agricultural, and various other industrial applications. HSLA plates are used in ships, in bridges, and in building construction, and shapes such as I-beams, channels, and angles are used in buildings and in various structures.

Designations.   Three categories compose the system of AISI designations for high-strength sheet steel (Table 5.3). *Structural quality* (S) includes the elements C, Mn, P, and N. *Low alloys* (X) contain Nb, Cr, Cu, Mo, Ni, Si, Ti, V, and Zr, either singly or in combination.

Weathering steels (W) have environmental corrosion resistance that is approximately four times greater than that of conventional low-carbon steels and contain Si, P, Cu, Ni,

TABLE 5.3   AISI Designation for High-Strength Sheet Steel

Yield Strength		Chemical composition	Deoxidation practice
psi $\times$ 10³	MPa		
35	240	S = structural quality	F = killed plus sulfide inclusion control
40	275		
45	310		
50	350	X = low alloy	
60	415		K = killed
70	485	W = weathering	
80	550		O = nonkilled
100	690	D = dual phase	
120	830		
140	970		

EXAMPLE

50 X 10³ psi min — 50 — yield strength   X — low alloy   F — killed plus sulfide inclusion control

and Cr in various combinations. In addition, the formability of these sheet steels is graded F (excellent), K (good), and O (fair).

5.5.7 Dual-Phase Steels

Dual-phase steels, designated with the letter "D" in Table 5.3, are processed specially to have a mixed ferrite and martensite structure. Developed in the late 1960s, these steels have a high work-hardening characteristic (high n value in Eq. 2.8), which improves their ductility and formability.

The SAE designations for these steels are similar to those given in Table 5.3, with the exception that another letter is added to indicate the carbon content. Thus, 050XF becomes 050XLF, where L indicates the proportion of carbon (in this case L meaning low carbon).

5.6 STAINLESS STEELS

Stainless steels are characterized primarily by their corrosion resistance, high strength and ductility, and high chromium content. They are called *stainless* because in the presence of oxygen (air) they develop a thin, hard adherent film of chromium oxide that protects the metal from corrosion (*passivation*). This protective film builds up again in the event that the surface is scratched. For passivation to occur, the minimum chromium content should be 10% to 12% by weight.

In addition to chromium, other alloying elements in stainless steels typically are nickel, molybdenum, copper, titanium, silicon, manganese, columbium, aluminum, nitrogen, and sulfur. The L is used to identify low-carbon stainless steels. The higher the carbon content is, the lower is the corrosion resistance of stainless steels. The reason is that the carbon combines with the chromium in the steel and forms chromium carbide; the reduced availability of chromium lowers the passivity of the steel. Still worse, the chromium carbide introduces a second phase and, thereby, promotes galvanic corrosion. (The soldiers in the Korean War Veterans Memorial in Washington, D.C. are cast in 316L stainless steel.)

Developed in the early 1900s, stainless steels are made by using electric furnaces or the basic-oxygen process and then techniques similar to those used in other types of steelmaking. The level of purity is controlled by various refining techniques. Stainless steels are available in a wide variety of shapes. Typical applications include cutlery, kitchen equipment, health care and surgical equipment, and the chemical, food-processing, and petroleum industries.

Stainless steels are generally divided into five types (Table 5.4).

a. **Austenitic (200 and 300 series)**. These steels are generally composed of chromium, nickel, and manganese in iron. They are nonmagnetic and have excellent corrosion resistance, but they are susceptible to stress-corrosion cracking. Austenitic stainless steels are hardened by cold-working. They are the most ductile of all stainless steels, and so they can easily be formed, although, with increasing cold work, their formability is reduced. These steels are used in a wide variety of applications, such as kitchenware, fittings, welded construction, lightweight transportation equipment, furnace and heat-exchanger parts, and components for severe chemical environments.

b. **Ferritic (400 series)**. These steels have a high chromium content—up to 27%. They are magnetic and have good corrosion resistance, but they have lower ductility than austenitic stainless steels. Ferritic stainless steels are hardened by cold-working and

TABLE 5.4   Room-Temperature Mechanical Properties and Typical Applications of Selected Annealed Stainless Steels

AISI (UNS)	Ultimate tensile strength (MPa)	Yield strength (MPa)	Elongation in 50 mm (%)	Characteristics and typical applications
303 (S30300)	550–620	240–260	53–50	Screw machine products, shafts, valves, bolts, bushings, and nuts; aircraft fittings; bolts; nuts; rivets; screws; studs.
304 (S30400)	565–620	240–290	60–55	Chemical and food processing equipment, brewing equipment, cryogenic vessels, gutters, downspouts, and flashings.
316 (S31600)	550–590	210–290	60–55	High corrosion resistance and high creep strength. Chemical and pulp handling equipment, photographic equipment, brandy vats, fertilizer parts, ketchup cooking kettles, and yeast tubs.
410 (S41000)	480–520	240–310	35–25	Machine parts, pump shafts, bolts, bushings, coal chutes, cutlery, tackle, hardware, jet engine parts, mining machinery, rifle barrels, screws, and valves.
416 (S41600)	480–520	275	30–20	Aircraft fittings, bolts, nuts, fire extinguisher inserts, rivets, and screws.

are not heat-treatable. They are generally used for nonstructural applications such as kitchen equipment and automotive trim.

  c. **Martensitic (400 and 500 series)**. Most martensitic stainless steels do not contain nickel and are hardenable by heat treatment. Their chromium content may be as much as 18%. These steels are magnetic, and they have high strength, hardness, and fatigue resistance, good ductility, and moderate corrosion resistance. Martensitic stainless steels are typically used for cutlery, surgical tools, instruments, valves, and springs.

  d. **Precipitation-hardening (PH)**. These steels contain chromium and nickel, along with copper, aluminum, titanium, or molybdenum. They have good corrosion resistance and ductility, and they have high strength at elevated temperatures. Their main application is in aircraft and aerospace structural components.

  e. **Duplex structure**. These steels have a mixture of austenite and ferrite. They have good strength, and they have higher resistance to both corrosion (in most environments) and stress-corrosion cracking than do the 300 series of austenitic steels. Typical applications are in water-treatment plants and in heat-exchanger components.

Example: Use of Stainless Steels in Automobiles

The types of stainless steel usually selected by materials engineers for use in automobile parts are 301, 409, 430, and 434. Because of its good corrosion resistance and mechanical properties, type 301 is used for wheel covers. Cold-working during the forming process increases its yield strength (by means of strain-hardening) and so gives the wheel cover a spring action.

Type 409 is used extensively for catalytic converters. Type 430 had been used for automotive trim, but it is not as resistant as type 434 is to the de-icing salts used in winter in colder climates; as a result, its use is now limited. In addition to being more corrosion-resistant, type 434 closely resembles the color of chromium plating, so it has become an attractive alternative to 430.

Stainless steels are well-suited for use in other automobile components as well: exhaust manifolds (replacing cast-iron manifolds to reduce weight, increase durability, and provide higher thermal conductivity and reduced emissions), mufflers and tailpipes (to offer better corrosion protection in harsh environments), and brake tubing.

5.7 TOOL AND DIE STEELS

Tool and die steels are specially alloyed steels (Tables 5.5 and 5.6). They are designed for high strength, impact toughness, and wear resistance at room and elevated temperatures. They are commonly used in forming and machining of metals (Parts III and IV).

TABLE 5.5   Basic Types of Tool and Die Steels

Type	AISI
High speed	M (molybdenum base)
	T (tungsten base)
Hot work	H1 to H19 (chromium base)
	H20 to H39 (tungsten base)
	H40 to H59 (molybdenum base)
Cold work	D (high carbon, high chromium)
	A (medium alloy, air hardening)
	O (oil hardening)
Shock resisting	S
Mold steels	P1 to P19 (low carbon)
	P20 to P39 (others)
Special purpose	L (low alloy)
	F (carbon-tungsten)
Water hardening	W

TABLE 5.6   Processing and Service Characteristics of Common Tool and Die Steels

AISI designation	Resistance to decarburization	Resistance to cracking	Approximate hardness (HRC)	Machinability	Toughness	Resistance to softening	Resistance to wear
M2	Medium	Medium	60–65	Medium	Low	Very high	Very high
T1	High	High	60–65	Medium	Low	Very high	Very high
T5	Low	Medium	60–65	Medium	Low	Highest	Very high
H11, 12, 13	Medium	Highest	38–55	Medium to high	Very high	High	Medium
A2	Medium	Highest	57–62	Medium	Medium	High	High
A9	Medium	Highest	35–56	Medium	High	High	Medium to high
D2	Medium	Highest	54–61	Low	Low	High	High to very high
D3	Medium	High	54–61	Low	Low	High	Very high
H21	Medium	High	36–54	Medium	High	High	Medium to high
H26	Medium	High	43–58	Medium	Medium	Very high	High
P20	High	High	28–37	Medium to high	High	Low	Low to medium
P21	High	Highest	30–40	Medium	Medium	Medium	Medium
W1, W2	Highest	Medium	50–64	Highest	High	Low	Low to medium

Source: Adapted from *Tool Steels*, American Iron and Steel Institute, 1978.

5.7.1 High-Speed Steels

High-speed steels (HSS) are the most highly alloyed tool and die steels. First developed in the early 1900s, they maintain their hardness and strength at elevated operating temperatures. There are two basic types of high-speed steels: the **molybdenum type** (M series) and the **tungsten type** (T series).

The **M-series** steels contain up to about 10% molybdenum, with chromium, vanadium, tungsten, and cobalt as other alloying elements. The **T-series** steels contain 12% to 18% tungsten, with chromium, vanadium, and cobalt as other alloying elements. The M-series steels generally have higher abrasion resistance than the T-series steels, undergo less distortion in heat treatment, and are less expensive. The M series constitutes about 95% of all the high-speed steels produced in the United States. High-speed steel tools can be coated with titanium nitride and titanium carbide for better wear resistance (Section 21.6).

5.7.2 Hot-Work, Cold-Work, and Shock-Resisting Die Steels

Hot-work steels (H series) are designed for use at elevated temperatures. They have high toughness as well as high resistance to wear and cracking. The alloying elements are generally tungsten, molybdenum, chromium, and vanadium.

Cold-work steels (A, D, and O series) are used for cold-working operations. They generally have high resistance to wear and cracking. These steels are available as oil-hardening or air-hardening types.

Shock-resisting steels (S series) are designed for impact toughness and are used in applications such as header dies, punches, and chisels. Other properties of these steels depend on the particular composition.

Various tool and die materials for a variety of manufacturing applications are presented in Table 5.7.

SUMMARY

- The major categories of ferrous metals and alloys are carbon steels, alloy steels, stainless steels, and tool and die steels. Their wide range of properties and generally low cost have made them among the most useful of all metallic materials.
- Steelmaking processes have been improved rapidly, notably the continuous-casting and secondary-refining techniques; these advances have resulted in higher quality steels and in higher efficiency and productivity in steelmaking operations.
- Alloying elements greatly influence mechanical, physical, chemical, and manufacturing properties (hardenability, castability, formability, machinability, and weldability) and performance in service.
- Carbon steels are generally classified as low-carbon (mild), medium-carbon, and high-carbon steels. Alloy steels contain a variety of alloying elements, particularly chromium, nickel, and molybdenum. Stainless steels are generally classified as austenitic, ferritic, martensitic, and precipitation-hardening.
- Tool and die steels are among the most important materials and are used widely in casting, machining, and forming operations for both metallic and nonmetallic materials. They generally consist of high-speed steels (molybdenum and tungsten types), hot- and cold-work steels, and shock-resisting steels.

TABLE 5.7   Typical Tool and Die Materials for Metalworking

Process	Material
Die casting	H13, P20
Powder metallurgy	
Punches	A2, S7, D2, D3, M2
Dies	WC, D2, M2
Molds for plastics and rubber	S1, O1, A2, D2, 6F5, 6F6, P6, P20, P21, H13
Hot forging	6F2, 6G, H11, H12
Hot extrusion	H11, H12, H13, H21
Cold heading	W1, W2, M1, M2, D2, WC
Cold extrusion	
Punches	A2, D2, M2, M4
Dies	O1, W1, A2, D2
Coining	52100, W1, O1, A2, D2, D3, D4, H11, H12, H13
Drawing	
Wire	WC, diamond
Shapes	WC, D2, M2
Bar and tubing	WC, W1, D2
Rolls	
Rolling	Cast iron, cast steel, forged steel, WC
Thread rolling	A2, D2, M2
Shear spinning	A2, D2, D3
Sheet metals	
Shearing	
Cold	D2, A2, A9, S2, S5, S7
Hot	H11, H12, H13
Pressworking	Zinc alloys, 4140 steel, cast iron, epoxy composites, A2, D2, O1
Deep drawing	W1, O1, cast iron, A2, D2
Machining	Carbides, high-speed steels, ceramics, diamond, cubic boron nitride

Notes: Tool and die materials are usually hardened to 55 to 65 HRC for cold working, and 30 to 55 for hot working. Tool and die steels contain one or more of the following major alloying elements: chromium, molybdenum, tungsten, and vanadium. For further details see the bibliography at the end of this chapter.

TRENDS

- The highly competitive international market for steel has led to cost control through improved productivity, elimination of obsolete and inefficient equipment and procedures, and reduced labor costs.

- New developments, such as specialty mills and minimills (which use mostly scrap metal, Section 13.7), allow economical production of specialty products or of one kind of product. Another trend is to use iron that is reduced directly (from iron oxide ores), rather than by melting it in blast furnaces.

- Computer controls and methods of process optimization are being implemented to improve efficiency and quality in all aspects of steelmaking.

- New compositions, treatments, and techniques for refining steels are being developed to improve various properties, such as formability, machinability, weldability, service life, and response to heat treatment.

- Continuous casting is increasingly applied in producing continuous steel shapes and smaller cross-sections.
- Zinc-coated, prepainted, and prelubricated sheet steels are reducing the number of processing steps in automotive applications, in appliances, and in a variety of other products.

KEY TERMS

Alloy steels	High-strength low-alloy steels	Refining
Basic-oxygen furnace	Ingot	Rimmed steel
Blast furnace	Integrated mills	Semi-killed steel
Carbon steels	Killed steel	Stainless steels
Continuous casting	Open-hearth furnace	Strand casting
Dual-phase steels	Pig	Tool and die steels
Electric furnace	Pig iron	Trace elements

BIBLIOGRAPHY

ASM Handbook, Vol. 1: *Properties and Selection: Iron, Steels, and High-Performance Alloys.* ASM International, 1990.

ASM Specialty Handbook: Carbon and Alloy Steels. ASM International, 1995.

ASM Specialty Handbook: Tool Materials. ASM International, 1995.

Bryson, B., *Heat Treatment, Selection and Application of Tool Steels.* Hanser Gardner, 1997.

Llewellyn, D.T., *Steels: Metallurgy and Applications* (2nd ed.). Butterworth-Heinemann, 1994.

Roberts, G.A., G. Krauss, and R. Kennedy, *Tool Steels* (5th ed.). ASM International, 1998.

REVIEW QUESTIONS

5.1 What are the major categories of ferrous alloys?

5.2 List the basic raw materials used in making iron and steel, and explain their functions.

5.3 List the types of furnaces commonly used in steelmaking and describe their characteristics.

5.4 List and explain the characteristics of the types of steel ingots.

5.5 What does refining mean? How is it done?

5.6 What advantages does continuous casting have over casting into ingots?

5.7 Name the four alloying elements that have the greatest effect on the properties of steels.

5.8 What are trace elements?

5.9 What are the percentage carbon contents of low-carbon, medium-carbon, and high-carbon steels?

5.10 How do stainless steels become stainless?

5.11 List the types of stainless steels.

5.12 What are the major alloying elements in tool and die steels and high-speed steels?

5.13 How does chromium affect the surface characteristics of stainless steels?

5.14 What kind of furnaces are used to refine steels?

5.15 How is iron extracted from ores?

5.16 What is high-speed steel?

5.17 What purpose does a tundish serve in continuous casting?

5.18 Why is limestone used in iron production?

5.19 Where does the term "pig iron" come from?

5.20 What are the advantages of a high carbon content in steel? What is the advantage of a low carbon content?

QUALITATIVE PROBLEMS

5.21 Identify several different products that are made of stainless steel, and explain why they are made of this material.

5.22 As you may know, professional cooks prefer carbon-steel to stainless-steel knives, even though the latter are more popular with consumers. Explain the reasons for those preferences.

5.23 Why is the control of ingot structure important?

5.24 Explain why continuous casting has been such an important technological advancement.

5.25 Certain alloying elements are commonly used in tool and die steels. Explain why these elements are essential in these steels.

5.26 Describe applications in which you would not want to use carbon steels.

5.27 Explain what would happen if the speed of the continuous-casting process (Fig. 5.4) is (a) higher or (b) lower than that indicated (typically 25 mm/s (1 in./sec)).

5.28 The cost of mill products of metals increases with decreasing thickness and section size. Explain why.

5.29 In Table 5.3, why is steel with sulfide inclusion control identified separately (as F) from killed steel?

5.30 Describe your observations regarding the information given in Table 5.7.

5.31 How do trace elements affect the ductility of steels?

5.32 Comment on your observations regarding Table 5.1.

5.33 In Table 5.7, D2 steel is listed as a tool and die material for most applications. Why is this so?

5.34 List the common impurities in steel. Which of these are the ones most likely to be minimized if the steel is melted in a vacuum furnace?

5.35 In Fig. 5.4, argon is used, but it is not listed as a common impurity of steel. Explain the purpose of argon in this application.

5.36 Explain the purpose of the oil in Fig. 5.4, given that the molten steel temperatures are far above the ignition temperatures of the oil.

5.37 Recent research has identified mold-surface textures that will either (a) inhibit a solidified steel from separating from the mold or (b) force it to stay in contact in continuous casting. What is the advantage of a mold which maintains intimate contact with the steel?

5.38 Add a column to the data given in Table 5.6 to give the common applications for the tool and die steels listed. Also, explain the significance of the machinability of the steel to the applications.

5.39 Identify products which cannot be made of steel and explain why this is so. For example, electrical contacts are commonly made of gold or copper, because their softness results in low contact resistance, while for steel the contact resistance would be very high.

QUANTITATIVE PROBLEMS

5.40 By referring to the available literature, estimate the cost of the raw materials for (a) an aluminum beverage can, (b) a stainless steel two-quart cooking pot, and (c) the steel hood of a car.

5.41 In Table 5.1, more than one type of steel is listed for some applications. By referring to data in the technical literature, determine the range of properties for these steels in various conditions such as cold-worked, hot-worked, and annealed.

5.42 Some soft drinks are now available in steel cans (with aluminum tops) that look similar to aluminum cans. Obtain one of each, weigh them when empty, and determine their respective wall thicknesses.

5.43 Using strength and density data, determine the minimum weight of a two-foot long tension member which must support 1000 lb., if it is manufactured from (a) annealed 303 stainless steel, (b) normalized 8620 steel, (c) as-rolled 1080 steel, (d) any two aluminum alloys, (e) any brass alloy, or (e) pure copper.

5.44 The endurance limit (fatigue life) of steel is approximately one-half the ultimate strength (see Fig. 2.16), but never higher than 100 ksi (700 MPa). For irons, the endurance limit is 40 % of the ultimate strength, but never higher than 24 ksi (170 MPa). Plot endurance limit vs. the ultimate strength for the steels described in this chapter and for the cast irons in Table 12.3. On the same plot, show the effect of surface finish by plotting the endurance limit assuming the material is in the as-cast state (see Fig. 2.28).

SYNTHESIS AND DESIGN

5.45 Based on the information given in Section 5.5.1, make a table with columns for each improved property, such as hardenability, strength, toughness, and machinability. In each column, list the elements that improve that property, and identify the element that has the most influence.

5.46 Assume that you are in charge of public relations for a steel-producing company. Outline all the attractive characteristics of steels that you would like your customers to know about.

5.47 Assume that you are in competition with the steel industry and are asked to list all the characteristics of steels that are not attractive. Make a list of these characteristics and explain their engineering relevance.

5.48 Assume that you are in charge of the research department of a large steel-producing company. Make a list of the research projects that you would like to initiate to improve products and expand their applications, explaining the reasons for your choices.

5.49 In Section 5.5.1, we noted the effects of various individual elements, such as either lead alone or sulfur alone, on the properties and characteristics of steels. We did not, however, discuss the role of combinations of elements, such as lead and sulfur together. Review the available technical literature, and prepare a table indicating the combined effects of several elements on steels.

5.50 In the past, waterfowl hunters used lead shot in their shotguns, but this practice resulted in lead poisoning of unshot birds that ingested lead pellets (along with gravel) to help them digest food. Recently, steel and tungsten have been used as replacement materials. If all pellets have the same velocity upon exiting the shotgun barrel, what concerns would you have regarding this material substitution? Consider environmental and performance effects.

5.51 Aluminum has been cited as a possible substitute material for steel in automobiles. What concerns would you have before purchasing an aluminum automobile?

5.52 In the 1940s, the Yamato was the largest battleship that had ever been built. Find out the weight of this this ship, and determine how many automobiles could be built from the steel in this one ship. How long would it take to cast this much steel by continuous casting?

6

Nonferrous Metals and Alloys: Production, General Properties, and Applications

6.1 INTRODUCTION

Nonferrous metals and alloys cover a wide range of materials, from the more common metals such as aluminum, copper, and magnesium to high-strength high-temperature alloys, such as those of tungsten, tantalum, and molybdenum. Although generally more expensive than ferrous metals (Table 6.1), nonferrous metals and alloys have important applications because of properties such as corrosion resistance, high thermal and electrical conductivity, low density, and ease of fabrication (Table 6.2).

Typical examples of the applications of nonferrous metals and alloys are aluminum for cooking utensils and aircraft bodies, copper wire for electricity, copper tubing for residential water supply, zinc for galvanized sheet metal for car bodies, titanium for jet-engine turbine blades and for orthopedic implants, and tantalum for rocket engines.

A turbofan jet engine for the Boeing 757 aircraft typically contains the following nonferrous metals and alloys: 38% titanium, 37% nickel, 12% chromium, 6% cobalt, 5% alu-

TABLE 6.1   Approximate Cost per Unit Volume for Wrought Metals and Plastics Relative to Cost of Carbon Steel

Gold	60,000	Magnesium alloys	2–4
Silver	600	Aluminum alloys	2–3
Molybdenum alloys	200–250	High-strength low-alloy steels	1.4
Nickel	35	Gray cast iron	1.2
Titanium alloys	20–40	Carbon steel	1
Copper alloys	5–6	Nylons, acetals, and silicon rubber*	1.1–2
Zinc alloys	1.5–3.5	Other plastics and elastomers*	0.2–1
Stainless steels	2–9		

*As molding compounds.
Note: Costs vary significantly with quantity of purchase, supply and demand, size and shape, and various other factors.

TABLE 6.2   General Characteristics of Nonferrous Metals and Alloys

Material	Characteristics
Nonferrous alloys	More expensive than steels and plastics; wide range of mechanical, physical, and electrical properties; good corrosion resistance; high-temperature applications.
Aluminum	High strength-to-weight ratio; high thermal and electrical conductivity; good corrosion resistance; good manufacturing properties.
Magnesium	Lightest metal; good strength-to-weight ratio.
Copper	High electrical and thermal conductivity; good corrosion resistance; good manufacturing properties.
Superalloys	Good strength and resistance to corrosion at elevated temperatures; can be iron-, cobalt-, and nickel-base.
Titanium	Highest strength-to-weight ratio of all metals; good strength and corrosion resistance at high temperatures.
Refractory metals	Molybdenum, niobium (columbium), tungsten, and tantalum; high strength at elevated temperatures.
Precious metals	Gold, silver, and platinum; generally good corrosion resistance.

minum, 1% niobium (columbium), and 0.02% tantalum. Without these materials, a jet engine (Fig. 6.1) could not be designed, manufactured, and operated at the power and efficiency levels required.

This chapter introduces the general properties, the production methods, and the important engineering applications for nonferrous metals and alloys. The manufacturing properties of these materials, such as formability, machinability, and weldability, are described in various chapters throughout this text.

6.2 ALUMINUM AND ALUMINUM ALLOYS

The important factors in selecting **aluminum** (Al) and its alloys are their high strength-to-weight ratio, their resistance to corrosion by many chemicals, their high thermal and electrical conductivity, their nontoxicity, reflectivity, and appearance, and their ease of formability and of machinability; they are also nonmagnetic.

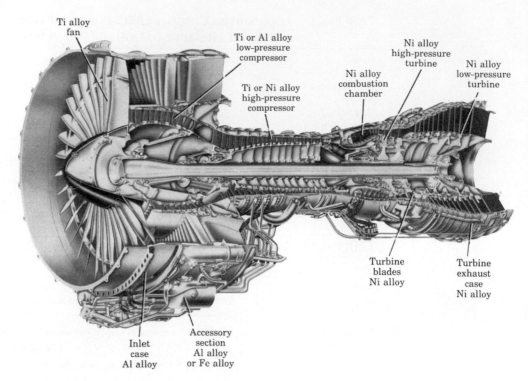

FIGURE 6.1   Cross-section of a jet engine (PW2037) showing various components and the alloys used in manufacturing them. *Source*: Courtesy of United Aircraft Pratt & Whitney.

The principal uses of aluminum and its alloys, in decreasing order of consumption, are in containers and packaging (aluminum cans and foil), in buildings and other types of construction, in transportation (aircraft and aerospace applications, buses, automobiles, railroad cars, and marine craft), in electrical applications (economical and nonmagnetic electrical conductor), in consumer durables (appliances, cooking utensils, and furniture), and in portable tools (Tables 6.3 and 6.4). Nearly all high-voltage transmission wiring is made of aluminum. In its structural (load-bearing) components, 82% of a Boeing 747 aircraft (and 79% of a Boeing 757 aircraft) is aluminum.

TABLE 6.3   Properties of Selected Aluminum Alloys at Room Temperature

Alloy (UNS)	Temper	Ultimate tensile strength (MPa)	Yield strength (MPa)	Elongation in 50 mm (%)
1100 (A91100)	O	90	35	35–45
1100	H14	125	120	9–20
2024 (A92024)	O	190	75	20–22
2024	T4	470	325	19–20
3003 (A93003)	O	110	40	30–40
3003	H14	150	145	8–16
5052 (A95052)	O	190	90	25–30
5052	H34	260	215	10–14
6061 (A96061)	O	125	55	25–30
6061	T6	310	275	12–17
7075 (A97075)	O	230	105	16–17
7075	T6	570	500	11

TABLE 6.4   Manufacturing Properties and Typical Applications of Selected Wrought Aluminum Alloys

Alloy	Characteristics*			Typical applications
	Corrosion resistance	Machinability	Weldability	
1100	A	C–D	A	Sheet metal work, spun hollow ware, tin stock
2024	C	B–C	B–C	Truck wheels, screw machine products, aircraft structures
3003	A	C–D	A	Cooking utensils, chemical equipment, pressure vessels, sheet metal work, builders' hardware, storage tanks
5052	A	C–D	A	Sheet metal work, hydraulic tubes, and appliances; bus, truck and marine uses
6061	B	C–D	A	Heavy-duty structures where corrosion resistance is needed, truck and marine structures, railroad cars, furniture, pipelines, bridge railings, hydraulic tubing
7075	C	B–D	D	Aircraft and other structures, keys, hydraulic fittings

* A, excellent; D, poor.

Aluminum alloys are available as mill products, that is, as wrought products made into various shapes by rolling, extrusion, drawing, and forging (Chapters 13-15). Aluminum ingots are available for casting, as is aluminum in powder form for powder-metallurgy applications (Chapter 17). Techniques have been developed whereby most aluminum alloys can be machined, formed, and welded with relative ease.

There are two types of wrought alloys of aluminum:

a. alloys that can be *hardened by cold-working* and are not heat-treatable, and

b. alloys that can be *hardened by heat treatment.*

Designation of Wrought-Aluminum Alloys.   Wrought-aluminum alloys are identified by four digits and by a **temper designation** that shows the condition of the material. The major alloying element is identified by the first digit. Here is the system:

1xxx—commercially pure aluminum—excellent corrosion resistance; high electrical and thermal conductivity; good workability; low strength; not heat treatable.

2xxx—copper—high strength-to-weight ratio; low resistance to corrosion; heat treatable.

3xxx—manganese—good workability; moderate strength; not generally heat-treatable.

4xxx—silicon—lower melting point; forms an oxide film of a dark-gray to charcoal color; not generally heat-treatable.

5xxx—magnesium—good corrosion resistance and weldability; moderate to high strength; not heat-treatable.

6xxx—magnesium and silicon—medium strength; good formability, machinability, weldability, and corrosion resistance; heat treatable.

7xxx—zinc—moderate to very high strength; heat treatable.

8xxx—other element.

The second digit in these designations indicates modifications of the alloy. For the 1xxx series, the third and fourth digits stand for the minimum amount of aluminum in the alloy—for example, "1050" indicates a minimum of 99.50% aluminum, "1090" indicates a minimum of 99.90% aluminum. In other series, the third and fourth digits identify the different alloys in the group and have no numerical significance.

Designation of Cast Aluminum Alloys.   Designations for cast aluminum alloys also consist of four digits. The first digit indicates the major alloy group, as follows:

1xx.x—aluminum (99.00% minimum);
2xx.x—aluminum–copper;
3xx.x—aluminum–silicon, with copper and/or magnesium;
4xx.x—aluminum–silicon;
5xx.x—aluminum–magnesium;
6xx.x—unused series;
7xx.x—aluminum–zinc;
8xx.x—aluminum–tin.

In the 1xx.x series, the second and third digits indicate the minimum aluminum content, as do the third and fourth in wrought aluminum. For the other series, the second and third digits have no numerical significance. The fourth digit (to the right of the decimal point) indicates product form.

Temper Designations.   The temper designations for both wrought and cast aluminum are as follows:

- F—as fabricated (by cold- or hot-working or by casting);
- O—annealed (from the cold-worked or the cast state);
- H—strain-hardened by cold-working (for wrought products only);
- T—heat-treated;
- W—solution-treated only (unstable temper).

Production.   Aluminum was first produced in 1825. It is the most abundant metallic element, making up about 8% of the earth's crust. It is produced in a quantity second only to that of iron. The principal ore for aluminum is *bauxite*, which is hydrous (water-containing) aluminum oxide and includes various other oxides. After the clay and dirt are washed off, the ore is crushed into powder and then treated with hot caustic soda (sodium hydroxide) to remove impurities. Alumina (aluminum oxide) is extracted from this solution and then dissolved in a molten sodium-fluoride and aluminum-fluoride bath at 940 °C–980 °C (1725 °F–1800 °F).

This mixture is then subjected to direct-current electrolysis. Aluminum metal forms at the cathode (negative pole), while oxygen is released at the anode (positive pole). *Commercially pure aluminum* is up to 99.99% aluminum, also referred to in industry as "four nines" aluminum. The production process consumes a great deal of electricity and so contributes significantly to the cost of aluminum.

Porous Aluminum.   Blocks of aluminum have recently been produced that are 37% lighter than solid aluminum and have uniform permeability (*microporosity*). This characteristic allows their use in applications where a vacuum or differential pressure has to be maintained. Examples are the vacuum holding of fixtures for assembly and automation and the vacuum forming or thermoforming of plastics (Section 18.6). These blocks are 70% to 90% aluminum powder; the rest is epoxy resin. They can be machined with relative ease and can be joined together using adhesives.

Example: An All-Aluminum Automobile

Aluminum usage in automobiles and in light trucks has been climbing steadily. As recently as 1990, there were no aluminum-structured passenger cars in production anywhere in the world, but in 1997 there were seven of them, including the Plymouth Prowler and the Audi A8. With weight savings of up to 47% over steel vehicles, such cars use less fuel, create less pollution, and are recyclable.

New alloys and new design and manufacturing methodologies had to be developed; as examples, welding and adhesive bonding procedures had to be refined, the structural frame design had to be optimized, and new tooling designs (to allow forming of aluminum) had to be created. Because of these new technologies, the desired environmental savings were able to be realized without an accompanying drop in performance or safety. In fact, the Audi A8 is the first luxury-class car to earn a dual five-star (highest safety) rating for both driver and front-seat passenger in the National Highway Transportation Safety Administration (NHSTA) New Car Assessment Program.

(a)

(b)

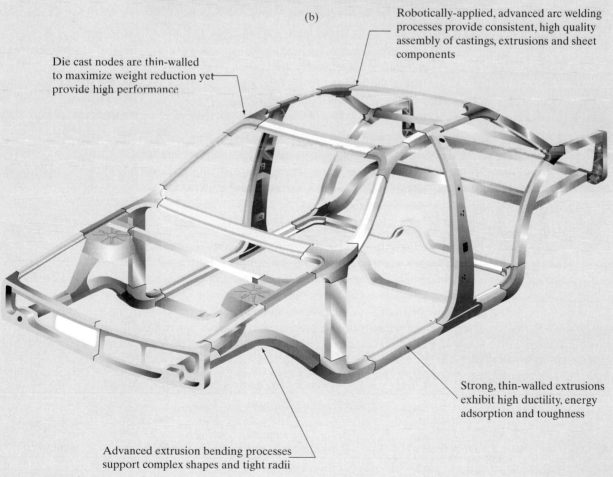

Robotically-applied, advanced arc welding processes provide consistent, high quality assembly of castings, extrusions and sheet components

Die cast nodes are thin-walled to maximize weight reduction yet provide high performance

Strong, thin-walled extrusions exhibit high ductility, energy adsorption and toughness

Advanced extrusion bending processes support complex shapes and tight radii

FIGURE 6.2 (a) The Audi A8 automobile which has an all-aluminum body structure. (b) The aluminum body structure, showing various components made by extrusion, sheet forming, and casting processes. *Source*: Courtesy of ALCOA, Inc.

6.3 MAGNESIUM AND MAGNESIUM ALLOYS

Magnesium (Mg) is the lightest engineering metal available, and it has good vibration-damping characteristics. Its alloys are used in structural and nonstructural applications wherever weight is of primary importance. Magnesium is also an alloying element in various nonferrous metals.

Typical uses of magnesium alloys are in aircraft and missile components, material-handling equipment, portable power tools (such as drills and sanders), ladders, luggage, bicycles, sporting goods, and general lightweight components. These alloys are available either as castings or as wrought products, such as extruded bars and shapes, forgings, and rolled plate and sheet. Magnesium alloys are also used in printing and textile machinery, to minimize inertial forces in high-speed components.

Because it is not sufficiently strong in its pure form, magnesium is alloyed with various elements (Table 6.5) in order to gain certain specific properties, particularly a high strength-to-weight ratio. A variety of magnesium alloys have good casting, forming, and machining characteristics. Because they oxidize rapidly (that is, they are *pyrophoric*), a fire hazard exists, and precautions must be taken when machining, grinding, or sand-casting magnesium alloys. Products made of magnesium and its alloys are, nonetheless, not a fire hazard in normal use.

Designation of Magnesium Alloys.   Magnesium alloys are designated as follows:

a. one or two prefix letters, indicating the principal alloying elements;
b. two or three numerals, indicating the percentage of the principal alloying elements, rounded off to the nearest decimal;
c. a letter of the alphabet (except the letters I and O) indicating the standardized alloy, with minor variations in composition;
d. a symbol for the temper of the material, following the system used for aluminum alloys.

For example, take the alloy AZ91C-T6:

- The principal alloying elements are aluminum (A, 9%, rounded off) and zinc (Z, 1%).
- The letter C, the third letter of the alphabet, indicates that this alloy was the third one standardized (later than A and B, which were the first and second alloys, respectively, that were standardized).
- T6 indicates that this alloy has been solution-treated and artificially aged.

Production.   Magnesium is the third most abundant metallic element (2%) in the earth's crust, coming after iron and aluminum. Most magnesium comes from sea water, which contains 0.13% magnesium in the form of magnesium chloride. First produced in 1808, magnesium metal can be obtained electrolytically or by thermal reduction.

In the electrolytic method, seawater is mixed with lime (calcium hydroxide) in settling tanks. Magnesium hydroxide precipitates to the bottom, and is filtered and mixed with hydrochloric acid. This solution is subjected to electrolysis (as is done with aluminum); that

TABLE 6.5   Properties and Typical Forms of Selected Wrought Magnesium Alloys

Alloy	Al	Zn	Mn	Zr	Condition	Ultimate tensile strength (MPa)	Yield strength (MPa)	Elongation in 50 mm (%)	Typical forms
AZ31 B	3.0	1.0	0.2		F	260	200	15	Extrusions
					H24	290	220	15	Sheet and plates
AZ80A	8.5	0.5	0.2		T5	380	275	7	Extrusions and forgings
HK31A			3Th	0.7	H24	255	200	8	Sheet and plates
ZK60A		5.7		0.55	T5	365	300	11	Extrusions and forgings

operation produces magnesium metal, which is then cast into ingots for further processing into various shapes.

In the thermal-reduction method, mineral rock containing magnesium (dolomite, magnesite, and other rocks) is broken down with reducing agents (such as powdered ferrosilicon—an alloy of iron and silicon), by heating the mixture in a vacuum chamber. As a result of this reaction, vapors of magnesium form, and they condense into magnesium crystals. These crystals are then melted, refined, and poured into ingots to be processed further into various shapes.

6.4 COPPER AND COPPER ALLOYS

First produced in about 4000 B.C., **copper** (Cu) and its alloys have properties somewhat similar to those of aluminum and its alloys. In addition, they are among the best conductors of electricity and heat (Tables 3.1 and 3.2), and they have good corrosion resistance. They can be processed easily by various forming, machining, casting, and joining techniques.

Copper alloys often are attractive for applications in which a combination of electrical, mechanical, nonmagnetic, corrosion-resistant, thermally conductive, and wear-resistant qualities are required. Applications include electrical and electronic components; springs; cartridges for small arms; plumbing; heat exchangers; marine hardware, and consumer goods, such as cooking utensils, jewelry, and other decorative objects. Pure copper can also be used as a solid lubricant in hot-metal forming operations (Section 32.11.3).

Copper alloys can acquire a wide variety of properties by the addition of alloying elements and by heat treatment, to improve their manufacturing characteristics. The most common copper alloys are brasses and bronzes. **Brass**, which is an alloy of copper and zinc, is one of the earliest alloys developed and has numerous applications, including decorative objects (Table 6.6).

Bronze is an alloy of copper and tin (Table 6.7). There are also other bronzes, such as aluminum bronze, which is an alloy of copper and aluminum, and tin bronzes. Beryllium copper, or **beryllium bronze**, and **phosphor bronze** have good strength and hardness for applications such as springs and bearings. Other major copper alloys are copper nickels and nickel silvers.

Designation of Copper Alloys. In addition to being identified by their composition, copper and copper alloys are known by various names (Tables 6.5 and 6.6). The temper designations, such as *1/2 hard*, *extra hard*, *extra spring*, and so on, are based on percentage reduction by cold-working (such as by rolling or drawing).

TABLE 6.6 Properties and Typical Applications of Selected Wrought Copper and Brasses

Type and UNS number	Nominal composition (%)	Ultimate tensile strength (MPa)	Yield strength (MPa)	Elongation in 50 mm (%)	Typical applications
Electrolytic tough pitch copper (C11000)	99.90 Cu, 0.04 O	220–450	70–365	55–4	Downspouts, gutters, roofing, gaskets, auto radiators, busbars, nails, printing rolls, rivets
Red brass, 85% (C23000)	85.0 Cu, 15.0 Zn	270–725	70–435	55–3	Weather-stripping, conduits, sockets, fasteners, fire extinguishers, condenser and heat exchanger tubing
Cartridge brass, 70% (C26000)	70.0 Cu, 30.0 Zn	300–900	75–450	66–3	Radiator cores and tanks, flashlight shells, lamp fixtures, fasteners, locks, hinges, ammunition components, plumbing accessories
Free-cutting brass (C36000)	61.5 Cu, 3.0 Pb, 35.5 Zn	340–470	125–310	53–18	Gears, pinions, automatic high-speed screw machine parts
Naval brass (C46400 to C46700)	60.0 Cu, 39.25 Zn, 0.75 Sn	380–610	170–455	50–17	Aircraft turnbuckle barrels, balls, bolts, marine hardware, propeller shafts, rivets, valve stems, condenser plates

TABLE 6.7   Properties and Typical Applications of Selected Wrought Bronzes

Type and UNS number	Nominal composition (%)	Ultimate tensile strength (MPa)	Yield strength (MPa)	Elongation in 50 mm (%)	Typical applications
Architectural bronze (C38500)	57.0 Cu, 3.0 Pb, 40.0 Zn	415 (As extruded)	140	30	Architectural extrusions, store fronts, thresholds, trim, butts, hinges
Phosphor bronze, 5% A (C51000)	95.0 Cu, 5.0 Sn, trace P	325–960	130–550	64–2	Bellows, clutch disks, cotter pins, diaphragms, fasteners, wire brushes, chemical hardware, textile machinery
Free-cutting phosphor bronze (C54400)	88.0 Cu, 4.0 Pb, 4.0 Zn, 4.0 Sn	300–520	130–435	50–15	Bearings, bushings, gears, pinions, shafts, thrust washers, valve parts
Low silicon bronze, B (C65100)	98.5 Cu, 1.5 Si	275–655	100–475	55–11	Hydraulic pressure lines, bolts, marine hardware, electrical conduits, heat exchanger tubing
Nickel silver, 65–10 (C74500)	65.0 Cu, 25.0 Zn, 10.0 Ni	340–900	125–525	50–1	Rivets, screws, slide fasteners, hollow ware, nameplates

Production.   Copper is found in several types of ores, the most common being sulfide ores. The ores are generally of low grade (although some contain up to 15% copper) and are usually obtained from open-pit mines. The ore is first crushed and then formed into a slurry (a watery mixture with insoluble solid particles). The slurry is ground into fine particles in ball mills (rotating cylinders with metal balls inside to crush the ore—Fig. 17.6). Chemicals and oil are then added, and the mixture is agitated. The mineral particles form a froth, which is scraped and dried.

The dry copper concentrate, as much as one-third of which is copper, is traditionally **smelted** (melted and fused) and refined. This process is known as **pyrometallurgy**, because heat is used to refine the metal. For applications such as electrical conductors, the copper is further refined electrolytically to a purity of at least 99.95% (oxygen-free electrolytic copper). A more recent technique for processing copper is **hydrometallurgy**, a process involving chemical and electrolytic reactions.

6.5 NICKEL AND NICKEL ALLOYS

Nickel (Ni), a silver-white metal discovered in 1751, is a major alloying element that imparts strength, toughness, and corrosion resistance. It is used extensively in stainless steels and in nickel-base alloys (also called **superalloys**). Nickel alloys are used in high-temperature applications, such as jet engine components, rockets, and nuclear power plants, in food-handling and chemical-processing equipment, in coins, and in marine applications.

Because nickel is magnetic, nickel alloys are also used in electromagnetic applications, such as solenoids. The principal use of nickel as a metal is in the electroplating of parts for the sake of appearance and of improving their corrosion and wear resistance.

Nickel alloys have high strength and corrosion resistance at elevated temperatures. Alloying elements in nickel are chromium, cobalt, and molybdenum. The behavior of nickel alloys in machining, forming, casting, and welding can be modified by various other alloying elements.

A variety of nickel alloys, having a range of strengths at different temperatures, have been developed (Table 6.8). *Monel* is a nickel-copper alloy. *Inconel* is a nickel-chromium alloy with a tensile strength of up to 1400 MPa (200 ksi). A nickel-molybdenum-chromium

TABLE 6.8   Properties and Typical Applications of Selected Nickel Alloys (All are Trade Names)

Type and UNS number	Nominal composition (%)	Ultimate tensile strength (MPa)	Yield strength (MPa)	Elongation in 50 mm (%)	Typical applications
Nickel 200 (annealed)	None	380–550	100–275	60–40	Chemical and food processing industry, aerospace equipment, electronic parts
Duranickel 301 (age hardened)	4.4 Al, 0.6 Ti	1300	900	28	Springs, plastics extrusion equipment, molds for glass, diaphragms
Monel R-405 (hot rolled)	30 Cu	525	230	35	Screw-machine products, water meter parts
Monel K-500 (age hardened)	29 Cu, 3 Al	1050	750	30	Pump shafts, valve stems, springs
Inconel 600 (annealed)	15 Cr, 8 Fe	640	210	48	Gas turbine parts, heat-treating equipment, electronic parts, nuclear reactors
Hastelloy C-4 (solution-treated and quenched)	16 Cr, 15 Mo	785	400	54	High temperature stability, resistance to stress-corrosion cracking

alloy (*Hastelloy*) has good corrosion resistance and high strength at elevated temperatures. *Nichrome*, an alloy of nickel, chromium, and iron, has high electrical resistance and a high resistance to oxidation and is used for electrical heating elements. *Invar*, an alloy of iron and nickel, has relatively low sensitivity to temperature (Section 3.6).

Production.   The main sources of nickel are sulfide and oxide ores, all of which have low concentrations of nickel. Nickel metal is produced by preliminary sedimentary and thermal processes, followed by electrolysis; this sequence yields 99.95% pure nickel. Although nickel is also present in the ocean bed in significant amounts, undersea mining of it is not yet economical.

6.6 SUPERALLOYS

Superalloys are important in high-temperature applications; hence, they are also known as **heat-resistant** or as **high-temperature alloys**. Major applications of superalloys are in jet engines and gas turbines; other applications are in reciprocating engines, in rocket engines, in tools and dies for hot-working of metals, and in the nuclear, chemical, and petrochemical industries. Superalloys generally have good resistance to corrosion, to mechanical and thermal fatigue, to mechanical and thermal shock, to creep, and to erosion at elevated temperatures.

These alloys are referred to as *iron-base*, *cobalt-base*, or *nickel-base superalloys*. They contain nickel, chromium, cobalt, and molybdenum as major alloying elements; other alloying elements are aluminum, tungsten, and titanium. Generally, superalloys are identified by trade names or by special numbering systems, and they are available in a variety of shapes. Most superalloys have a maximum service temperature of about 1000 °C (1800 °F) in structural applications. The temperatures can be as high as 1200 °C (2200 °F) for non-load-bearing components.

a. **Iron-base superalloys** generally contain from 32% to 67% iron, from 15% to 22% chromium, and from 9% to 38% nickel. Common alloys in this group are the *Incoloy* series.

TABLE 6.9   Properties and Typical Applications of Selected Nickel-Base Superalloys at 870 °C (1600 °F) (All are Trade Names)

Alloy	Condition	Ultimate tensile strength (MPa)	Yield strength (MPa)	Elongation in 50 mm (%)	Typical applications
Astroloy	Wrought	770	690	25	Forgings for high temperature
Hastelloy X	Wrought	255	180	50	Jet engine sheet parts
IN-100	Cast	885	695	6	Jet engine blades and wheels
IN-102	Wrought	215	200	110	Superheater and jet engine parts
Inconel 625	Wrought	285	275	125	Aircraft engines and structures, chemical processing equipment
Inconel 718	Wrought	340	330	88	Jet engine and rocket parts
MAR-M 200	Cast	840	760	4	Jet engine blades
MAR-M 432	Cast	730	605	8	Integrally cast turbine wheels
René 41	Wrought	620	550	19	Jet engine parts
Udimet 700	Wrought	690	635	27	Jet engine parts
Waspaloy	Wrought	525	515	35	Jet engine parts

b. **Cobalt-base superalloys** generally contain from 35% to 65% cobalt, from 19% to 30% chromium, and up to 35% nickel. Cobalt (Co) is a white-colored metal that resembles nickel. These superalloys are not as strong as nickel-base superalloys, but they retain their strength at higher temperatures.

c. **Nickel-base superalloys** are the most common of the superalloys, and they are available in a wide variety of compositions (Table 6.9). The proportion of nickel is from 38% to 76%; they also contain up to 27% chromium and 20% cobalt. Common alloys in this group are the *Hastelloy, Inconel, Nimonic, René, Udimet, Astroloy,* and *Waspaloy* series.

6.7 TITANIUM AND TITANIUM ALLOYS

Titanium (Ti), named after the giant Greek god Titan, was discovered in 1791, but it was not produced commercially until the 1950s. Although it is expensive, its high strength-to-weight ratio and its corrosion resistance at room and elevated temperatures make it attractive for many applications. They include aircraft, jet-engine (see Fig. 6.1), racing-car, chemical, petrochemical, and marine components, submarine hulls, and biomaterials, such as orthopedic implants (Table 6.10). Titanium alloys have been developed for service at 550 °C (1000 °F) for long periods of time and at up to 750 °C (1400 °F) for shorter periods.

Unalloyed titanium, known as commercially pure titanium, has excellent corrosion resistance for applications where strength considerations are secondary. Aluminum, vanadium, molybdenum, manganese, and other alloying elements are added to titanium alloys to impart properties such as improved workability, strength, and hardenability.

The properties and manufacturing characteristics of titanium alloys are extremely sensitive to small variations in both alloying and residual elements. Control of composition and processing are, therefore, important, especially the prevention of surface contamination by hydrogen, oxygen, or nitrogen during processing. These elements cause embrittlement of titanium and, consequently, reduce toughness and ductility.

TABLE 6.10 Properties and Typical Applications of Selected Wrought Titanium Alloys at Various Temperatures

Nominal composition (%)	UNS	Condition	Ultimate tensile strength (MPa)	Yield strength (MPa)	Elongation (%)	Reduction of area (%)	Temp. (°C)	Ultimate tensile strength (MPa)	Yield strength (MPa)	Elongation in 50 mm (%)	Reduction of area (%)	Typical applications
99.5 Ti	R50250	Annealed	330	240	30	55	300	150	95	32	80	Airframes; chemical, desalination, and marine parts; plate type heat exchangers
5 Al, 2.5 Sn	R54520	Annealed	860	810	16	40	300	565	450	18	45	Aircraft engine compressor blades and ducting; steam turbine blades
6 Al, 4V	R56400	Annealed	1000	925	14	30	300 425 550	725 670 530	650 570 430	14 18 35	35 40 50	Rocket motor cases; blades and disks for aircraft turbines and compressors; structural forgings and fasteners; orthopedic implants
		Solution + age	1175	1100	10	20	300	980	900	10 12 22	28 35 45	
13 V, 11 Cr, 3 Al	R58010	Solution + age	1275	1210	8	—	425	1100	830	12	—	High strength fasteners; aerospace components; honeycomb panels

The body-centered cubic structure of titanium (beta-titanium, above 880 °C (1600 °F) is ductile, whereas its hexagonal close-packed structure (alpha-titanium) is somewhat brittle and is very sensitive to stress corrosion. A variety of other structures (alpha, near-alpha, alpha-beta, and beta) can be obtained by alloying and heat treating, so that the properties can be optimized for specific applications.

Recent developments include the so-called **titanium aluminide intermetallics**, TiAl and Ti$_3$Al. They have higher stiffness and lower density than conventional titanium alloys, and they can withstand higher temperatures.

Production. Ores containing titanium are first reduced to titanium carbide in an arc furnace, then converted to titanium chloride in a chlorine atmosphere. This compound is reduced further by distillation and by leaching (dissolving); this sequence forms *sponge titanium*. The sponge is then pressed into billets, melted, and poured into ingots, to be processed later into various shapes. The complexity of these operations adds considerably to the cost of titanium.

6.8 REFRACTORY METALS AND ALLOYS

There are four **refractory metals**: molybdenum, niobium, tungsten, and tantalum; they are called *refractory* because of their high melting point. Although these refractory elements were discovered about 200 years ago (and have since been used as important alloying elements in steels and superalloys), their use as engineering metals and alloys did not begin until about the 1940s.

More than most other metals and alloys, these metals maintain their strength at elevated temperatures. They are, therefore, of great importance and use—in rocket engines, gas turbines, and various other aerospace applications; in the electronics, nuclear-power, and chemical industries; and as tool and die materials. The temperature range for some of these applications is on the order of 1100 °C –2200 °C (2000 °F – 4000 °F), where strength and oxidation are of major concern.

6.8.1 Molybdenum

Molybdenum (Mo), a silvery-white metal, was discovered in the 18th century. It has a high melting point, a high modulus of elasticity, good resistance to thermal shock, and good electrical and thermal conductivity. Molybdenum is used in greater amounts than is any other refractory metal. Typical applications of molybdenum are in solid-propellant rockets, jet engines, honeycomb structures, electronic components, heating elements, and dies for die casting.

The principal alloying elements for molybdenum are titanium and zirconium. It is itself also an important alloying element, in such casting and wrought alloys as steels and in heat-resistant alloys; it imparts strength, toughness, and corrosion resistance. A major disadvantage of molybdenum alloys is their low resistance to oxidation at temperatures above 500 °C (950 °F), which necessitates the use of protective coatings.

Production. The main source for molybdenum is the mineral molybdenite (molybdenum disulfide, mentioned also in Section 32.11 (on *solid lubricants*)). The ore is first processed and concentrated; later it is reduced by reaction with oxygen and then with hydrogen. Powder-metallurgy techniques are also used to produce ingots for further processing into various shapes.

6.8.2 Niobium (Columbium)

Niobium (Nb, for niobium, after Niobe, the daughter of mythical Greek king Tantalus; also referred to as **columbium**, after its source mineral, columbite) possesses good ductility and formability, and it has greater oxidation resistance than other refractory metals. With various alloying elements, niobium alloys can be produced with moderate strength and good fabrication characteristics. These alloys are used in rockets and missiles and in nuclear, chemical, and superconductor applications.

Niobium, first identified in 1801, is also an alloying element in various alloys and superalloys. It is processed from ores by reduction and refinement and from powder by melting and shaping into ingots.

6.8.3 Tungsten

Tungsten (W, for wolfram, its European name, from its source mineral, wolframite; in Swedish, *tung* means heavy and *sten* means stone.) was first identified in 1781; it is the most plentiful of all the refractory metals. Tungsten has the highest melting point of any metal (3410 °C, 6170 °F), and, as a result, it is characterized by high strength at elevated temperatures. On the other hand, it has high density, is brittle at low temperatures, and offers poor resistance to oxidation.

Tungsten and its alloys are used for applications involving temperatures above 1650 °C (3000 °F), such as nozzle throat liners in missiles and in the hottest parts of jet and rocket engines, circuit breakers, welding electrodes, and spark-plug electrodes. The filament wire in incandescent light bulbs is made of pure tungsten; the wire is produced by the use of powder-metallurgy and wire-drawing techniques.

Because of its high density, tungsten is also used as the material of balancing weights and counterbalances in mechanical systems, including self-winding watches. Tungsten is an important element in tool and die steels (Section 5.7), imparting strength and hardness at elevated temperatures. Tungsten carbide, with cobalt as a binder for the carbide particles, is one of the most important tool and die materials (Section 21.5).

Tungsten is processed from ore concentrates by chemical decomposition and is then reduced. It is further processed by powder metallurgy techniques in a hydrogen atmosphere.

6.8.4 Tantalum

Identified in 1802, **tantalum** (Ta, after the mythical Greek king Tantalus) is characterized by high melting point (3000 °C, 5425 °F), good ductility, and resistance to corrosion. It has, however, high density and poor resistance to chemicals at temperatures above 150 °C (300 °F). Tantalum is also used as an alloying element.

Tantalum is used extensively in electrolytic capacitors and in various components in the electrical, electronic, and chemical industries; it is also used for thermal applications, such as in furnaces and in acid-resistant heat exchangers. A variety of tantalum-base alloys is available; they come in many forms for use in missiles and aircraft. Tantalum is processed by techniques similar to those used for processing niobium.

6.9 BERYLLIUM

Steel gray in color, **beryllium** (Be) has a high strength-to-weight ratio. Unalloyed beryllium is used in rocket nozzles, space and missile structures, aircraft disc brakes, and precision instruments and mirrors. In nuclear and x-ray applications, it is used because of its low neutron absorption.

Beryllium is also an alloying element, and its alloys of copper and nickel are used in applications including springs (beryllium–copper), electrical contacts, and nonsparking tools for use in such explosive environments as mines and metal-powder production (Section 17.2). Beryllium and its oxide are toxic; their associated dust and fumes should not be inhaled.

6.10 ZIRCONIUM

Zirconium (Zr) is silvery in appearance; it has good strength and ductility at elevated temperatures, and it has good corrosion resistance because of an adherent oxide film. The element is used in electronic components; in nuclear-power reactor applications, it is used because of its low neutron absorption.

6.11 LOW-MELTING ALLOYS

Low-melting alloys are so named because of their relatively low melting points (see Table 3.1). The major metals in this category are lead, zinc, and tin and their alloys.

6.11.1 Lead

Lead (Pb, after plumbum, the root for the word plumber) has properties of high density, resistance to corrosion (by virtue of the stable lead-oxide layer that forms to protect the surface), softness, low strength, ductility, and good workability. Alloying it with various elements (such as antimony and tin) enhances lead's desirable properties, making it suitable for piping, collapsible tubing, bearing alloys, cable sheathing, roofing, and lead–acid storage batteries. Lead is also used for damping sound and vibrations, in radiation shielding against x-rays, in ammunition, as weights, and in the chemical industry.

The oldest known lead artifacts were made in about 3000 B.C. Lead pipes made by the Romans and installed in the Roman baths in Bath, England, two millennia ago are still in use. Lead is also an alloying element in *solders* (30.3.1), steels, and copper alloys; it promotes corrosion resistance and machinability (Section 20.9.1). An additional use of lead is as a solid lubricant for hot-metal forming operations (Section 32.11.3). Because of its toxicity, however, environmental contamination by lead (causing lead poisoning) is a major concern.

The important source mineral for lead is galena (PbS). It is mined, smelted, and refined by chemical treatments.

6.11.2 Zinc

Zinc (Zn), which is bluish-white in color, is the metal fourth most utilized industrially, coming after iron, aluminum, and copper. Although known for many centuries, zinc was not studied and developed until the 18th century. It has two major uses: for galvanizing iron, steel sheet, and wire; and as an alloy base for casting. In **galvanizing**, zinc serves as an anode and protects the steel (cathode) from corrosive attack, should the coating be scratched or punctured. Zinc is also used as an alloying element. Brass, for example, is an alloy of copper and zinc.

Another major use of zinc is structural, but pure zinc is rarely used for this purpose. Major alloying elements in zinc-based alloys are aluminum, copper, and magnesium; they impart strength, and they provide dimensional control during casting of the metal. Zinc-based alloys are used extensively in die casting (Section 11.12), for making such products as fuel pumps and grills for automobiles, components for household appliances such as vacuum cleaners, washing machines, and kitchen equipment, and various machinery parts and photoengraving equipment.

Another use for zinc is in superplastic alloys, which have good formability characteristics by virtue of their capacity to undergo large deformation without failure. Very fine-grained 78% Zn–22% Al sheet is a common example of a superplastic zinc alloy that can be formed by methods used for forming plastics or metals.

Production. A number of minerals containing zinc are found in nature; the principal source mineral is zinc sulfide, also called zincblende. The ore is first roasted in air and converted to zinc oxide. It is then reduced to zinc either electrolytically, using sulfuric acid, or by heating it in a furnace with coal, which causes molten zinc to separate.

6.11.3 Tin

Although used in small amounts, **tin** (Sn, from Latin "stannum") is an important metal. The most extensive use of tin, a silvery-white, lustrous metal, is as a protective coating on the steel sheet (tin plate) that is used in making containers (**tin cans**) for food and for various other products. The low shear strength of the tin coatings on steel sheet improves its performance in deep drawing and in general pressworking. Unlike the case of galvanized steels, however, if this coating is punctured, then it is the steel that corrodes, because tin is cathodic to it.

Unalloyed tin is used in such applications as lining material for water distillation plants and as a molten layer of metal over which plate glass is made. Tin-based alloys (also called **white metals**) generally contain copper, antimony, and lead. The alloying elements impart hardness, strength, and corrosion resistance.

Because of their low friction coefficients, which result from low shear strength and low adhesion, some tin alloys are used as journal-bearing materials. These alloys are known as **babbitts** (after I. Babbitt, 1799–1862) and contain tin, copper, and antimony. **Pewter** is an alloy of tin, copper, and antimony. It was developed in the 15th century and is used for tableware, hollowware, and decorative artifacts. Organ pipes are made of tin alloys.

Tin is an alloying element for dental alloys and for bronze (copper–tin alloy), titanium, and zirconium alloys. Tin–lead alloys are common soldering materials (Section 30.3.1), with a wide range of compositions and melting points.

Production. The most important tin mineral is cassiterite (tin oxide), which is of low grade. The ore is mined, concentrated by various techniques, smelted, refined, and cast into ingots for further processing.

6.12 PRECIOUS METALS

Gold, silver, and platinum are the most important **precious** (that is, costly) metals; they are also called **noble metals**.

a. **Gold** (Au, from Latin "aurum") is soft and ductile, and it has good corrosion resistance at any temperature. Typical applications include jewelry, coinage, reflectors, gold leaf for decorative purposes, dental work, electroplating, and electrical contacts and terminals.

b. **Silver** (Ag, from Latin "argentum") is a ductile metal, and it has the highest electrical and thermal conductivity of any metal (Table 3.2). It does, however, develop an oxide film that affects its surface characteristics and appearance. Typical applications for silver include tableware, jewelry, coinage, electroplating, photographic film, electrical contacts, solders, bearing linings, and food and chemical equipment. *Sterling silver* is an alloy of silver and 7.5% copper.

c. **Platinum** (Pt) is a soft, ductile, grayish-white metal that has good corrosion resistance even at elevated temperatures. Platinum alloys are used as electrical contacts, for spark-plug electrodes, as catalysts for automobile pollution-control devices, in filaments, in nozzles, in dies for extruding glass fibers (Section 17.10), in thermocouples, in the electrochemical industry, as jewelry, and in dental work.

6.13 SHAPE-MEMORY ALLOYS

Shape-memory alloys are unique in that, after being plastically deformed at room temperature into various shapes, they return to their original shapes upon heating. For example, a piece of straight wire made of this material can be wound into a helical spring. When heated with a match, the spring uncoils and returns to the original straight shape. A typical shape-memory alloy is 55% Ni–45% Ti; other such alloys are copper–aluminum–nickel, copper–zinc–aluminum, iron–manganese–silicon, and nickel–titanium.

Shape-memory alloys generally have such properties as good ductility, good corrosion resistance, and high electrical conductivity. They can be used to generate motion and/or force in temperature-sensitive actuators. Their behavior can also be *reversible*, that is, the shape can switch back and forth repeatedly upon application and removal of heat.

For example, a nickel–titanium antiscald valve has been made to protect people from being scalded in sinks, tubs, and showers. It is installed directly in the piping system and brings the water flow down to a trickle within 3 seconds after the water temperature reaches 47 °C (116 °F). Other applications are in eyeglass frames, connectors, clamps, and fasteners and in seals that are easy to install.

6.14 AMORPHOUS ALLOYS (METALLIC GLASSES)

A class of metal alloys which, unlike metals, do not have a long-range crystalline structure are called **amorphous alloys**. They have no grain boundaries, and the atoms are randomly and tightly packed. The amorphous structure was first obtained in the late 1960s by extremely **rapid solidification** of the molten alloy (Section 11.16). Because their structure resembles that of glasses, these alloys are also called **metallic glasses**.

Amorphous alloys typically contain iron, nickel, and chromium, alloyed with carbon, phosphorus, boron, aluminum, and silicon. They are available as wire, ribbon, strip, and powder. One application is for face-plate inserts on golf-club heads; that alloy has a composition of zirconium, beryllium, copper, titanium, and nickel and is made by die casting.

These alloys exhibit excellent corrosion resistance, good ductility, high strength, and very low loss from magnetic hysteresis. The latter property is utilized in the making of magnetic steel cores for transformers, generators, motors, lamp ballasts, magnetic amplifiers, and linear accelerators, and it provides greatly improved efficiency. However, fabrication costs have been significant. A major application for the superalloys of rapidly-solidified powders is consolidation into near-net shapes for parts used in aerospace engines.

6.15 NANOMATERIALS

Important recent developments involve the production of materials with grains, fibers, films, and composites having particles that are on the order of 1-100 nm in size. First investigated in the early 1980s and generally called **nanomaterials**, they have some properties that are frequently superior to traditional and commercially available materials. These characteristics can include strength, hardness, ductility, wear resistance and corrosion resistance suitable for structural (load-bearing) and nonstructural applications, in combination with unique electrical, magnetic, and optical properties.

The composition of a nanomaterial can be any combination of chemical elements; among the more important compositions are carbides, oxides, nitrides, metals and alloys, organic polymers, and various composites. Synthesis methods include inert gas condensation, plasma synthesis, electrodeposition, sol-gel synthesis, and mechanical alloying or ball milling.

Synthesized powders are consolidated into bulk materials by various techniques; compaction and sintering is one. They are available in a variety of shapes and are called by many names—for example, nanocrystalline materials, nanostructured materials, nanophase materials, nanopowders, nanowires, nanotubes, nanofilms. Because the synthesis of these products is done at atomic levels, their purity (on the order of 99.9999%), their homogeneity, and the uniformity of their microstructure are highly controlled; as a result, their mechanical, physical, and chemical properties can also be precisely controlled.

Among the current and potential applications for nanomaterials are the following:

a. cutting tools and inserts made of nanocrystalline carbides and other ceramics (Section 21.11);

b. nanophase ceramics that are ductile and machinable (Sections 8.2.5 and 20.9.3);

c. powders for powder-metallurgy processing (Section 17.2.1);

d. next-generation computer chips using nanocrystalline starting materials with very high purity, better thermal conductivity, and more durable interconnections;

e. flat-panel displays for laptop computers, made by synthesizing nanocrystalline phosphorus to improve screen resolution;

f. spark-plug electrodes, igniters for rockets, medical implants, high-sensitivity sensors, catalysts for elimination of pollutants, high-power magnets, and high-energy-density batteries.

SUMMARY

- Nonferrous metals and alloys cover a very broad range of materials. They can consist of aluminum, magnesium, and copper and of their alloys, which have a wide range of applications. For higher-temperature service, they consist of nickel, titanium, and refractory alloys (molybdenum, niobium, tungsten, tantalum) and of superalloys. Other nonferrous categories include low-melting alloys (lead, zinc, tin) and precious metals (gold, silver, platinum).

- Nonferrous alloys have a wide variety of desirable properties, such as: strength, toughness, hardness, and ductility; resistance to high temperature, creep, and oxidation; and a wide range of physical, thermal, and chemical properties. They can be heat-treated to impart certain desired properties. Among their attractive properties are high strength-to-weight and stiffness-to-weight ratios, particularly for aluminum and titanium.

- As in all materials, the selection of a nonferrous material for a particular application requires consideration of many factors, such as design and service requirements, long-term effects, chemical affinity to other materials, environmental attack, and cost.

- Among more recent developments are shape-memory alloys, amorphous alloys (metallic glasses), and nanomaterials all having some properties superior to those of conventional materials. Each has several unique applications in product design and in manufacturing.

TRENDS

- Aluminum is competing strongly to become an important structural metal, by reducing the weight and improving the corrosion resistance of automobiles. Aluminum-lithium alloys are being developed (particularly for aircraft components) that provide increased stiffness and reduced density.

- The purity and the corrosion resistance of magnesium alloys are being improved, particularly for automotive and computer applications.

- High-purity titanium is being developed for electronic and aerospace applications.

- Techniques for refining superalloys are being developed to improve their mechanical and physical properties and their corrosion resistance. The aim is to produce cleaner metals and alloys, using various melting techniques.

- Single-crystal nickel-base alloys are finding important high-temperature applications.

- Superalloys that are intermetallic compounds of nickel, chromium, molybdenum, and aluminum are being developed for high-temperature applications in critical gas-turbine components.

KEY TERMS

Amorphous alloys	Metallic glasses	Refractory metals
Babbitts	Nanomaterials	Shape-memory alloys
Brass	Pewter	Smelting
Bronze	Precious metals	Superalloys
Galvanizing	Pyrometallurgy	Temper designation
Low-melting alloys		

BIBLIOGRAPHY

ASM Handbook, Vol. 2: *Properties and Selection: Nonferrous Alloys and Special-Purpose Materials.* ASM International, 1990.

ASM Specialty Handbook: Heat-Resistant Materials. ASM International, 1997.

Edelstein, A.S., and R.C. Cammarata (eds.), *Nanomaterials: Systhesis, Properties, and Applications.* Institute of Physics, 1998.

Fremond, M., and S. Miyazaki, *Shape Memory Alloys.* Springer Verlag, 1996.

REVIEW QUESTIONS

6.1 Given the abundance of aluminum in the earth's crust, explain why it is more expensive than steel.

6.2 Why is magnesium often used as a structural material in power hand tools? Why are its alloys used instead of pure magnesium?

6.3 What are the major uses of copper? What are the alloying elements in brass and bronze, respectively?

6.4 What are superalloys? Why are they so named?

6.5 What properties of titanium make it attractive for use in race-car and jet-engine components? Why is titanium not widely used for engine components in passenger cars?

6.6 What are the individual properties of each of the major refractory metals that define its most useful applications?

6.7 What are metallic glasses? Why is the word "glass" used for these materials?

6.8 What is the composition (a) of babbitts, (b) of pewter, (c) of sterling silver?

6.9 Which of the materials described in this chapter has the highest (a) density, (b) electrical conductivity, (c) thermal conductivity, (d) strength, (e) cost?

6.10 What are the major uses of gold, other than in jewelry?

6.11 What are the advantages to using zinc as a coating for steel?

6.12 What are nanomaterials? Why are they being developed?

6.13 Why are aircraft skins made of aluminum alloys, even though magnesium is the lightest metal?

6.14 What are the major uses of lead?

QUALITATIVE PROBLEMS

6.15 Explain why cooking utensils are generally made of stainless steels, aluminum, or copper.

6.16 Would it be advantageous to plot the data in Table 6.1 in terms of cost per unit weight rather than of cost per unit volume? Explain, and give some examples.

6.17 Inspect Table 6.2, and comment on which of the two hardening processes (heat treating and work hardening) is more effective in improving the strength of aluminum alloys.

6.18 Other than mechanical strength, what other factors should be considered in selecting metals and alloys for high-temperature applications?

6.19 Explain why you would want to know the ductility of metals and alloys before selecting them.

6.20 Explain the techniques you would use to strengthen aluminum alloys.

6.21 Assume that, for geopolitical reasons, the price of copper increases rapidly. Name two metals with similar mechanical and physical properties that can be substituted for copper. Comment on your selection and observations.

6.22 If planes such as a Boeing 757 are made of 79% aluminum, why are automobiles predominantly made of steel?

6.23 Portable (notebook) computers have their housing made of magnesium. Why?

6.24 Table 6.3 lists the manufacturing properties of wrought aluminum alloys. Compare their relative characteristics with those of other metals.

6.25 Most household wiring is made of copper wire. By contrast, grounding wire leading to satellite dishes and the like is made of aluminum. Explain the reason for this.

QUANTITATIVE PROBLEMS

6.26 A simply-supported rectangular beam is 20 mm wide and 1 m long, and it is subjected to a vertical load of 25 kg at its center. Assume that this beam could be made of any of the materials listed in Table 6.1. Select three different materials and calculate for each the beam's height that causes each beam to have the same maximum deflection. Calculate the ratio of the cost for each of the three beams.

6.27 Obtain a few aluminum beverage cans, cut them, and measure their wall thicknesses. Using data in this chapter and simple formulas for thin-walled, closed-end pressure vessels, calculate the maximum internal pressure these cans can withstand before yielding.

6.28 Beverage cans are usually stacked on top of each other in stores. By using information from Problem 6.27 above, and by referring to textbooks on the mechanics of solids, make an estimate of the crushing load each of these cans can withstand.

6.29 Using strength and density data, determine the minimum weight of a two-foot long tension member which must support 1000 pounds, if it is manufactured from (a) 3003-O aluminum, (b) 5052-H34 aluminum, (c) AZ31B-F magnesium, (d) any brass alloy, and (e) any bronze alloy.

6.30 An automobile engine operates at up to 6000 rpm. If the stroke length for a piston is 6 in., and the piston is made of a 10-lb. steel casting, estimate the inertial stress on the 1-in. diameter connecting rod. If the piston is replaced by the same volume of aluminum alloy, what would be the speed for the same inertia-induced stress?

6.31 Plot the following for the materials described in this chapter: (a) yield strength vs. density, (b) modulus of elasticity vs. strength, and (c) modulus of elasticity vs. relative cost.

SYNTHESIS AND DESIGN

6.32 Because of the number of processes involved in making them, the cost of raw materials for metals depends on their condition (hot or cold rolled), shape (plate, sheet, bar, tubing), and size. Make a survey of the available literature and price lists, or get in touch with suppliers, and prepare a list indicating the cost per 100 kg of the nonferrous materials described in this chapter, as available in different conditions, shapes, and sizes.

6.33 The materials described in this chapter have numerous applications. Make a survey of the available literature, and prepare a list of several specific products and applications, indicating the types of materials used.

6.34 Name products that would not have been developed to their advanced stages (as we find them today) if alloys having high strength, high corrosion resistance, and high creep resistance, all at elevated temperatures, had not been developed.

6.35 Assume that you are the technical sales manager of a company that produces nonferrous metals. Choose any one of the metals and alloys described in this chapter, and prepare a brochure, including some illustrations, for use as sales literature by your staff in their contact with potential customers.

6.36 Inspect several metal products and components, and make an educated guess as to what materials each is made from. Give reasons for your guesses. If you list two or more possibilities, explain your reasoning.

6.37 Give applications for (a) amorphous metals, (b) precious metals, (c) low-melting alloys, (d) nanomaterials.

6.38 Describe the advantages of making products with multilayer materials; for example, aluminum bonded to the bottom of stainless-steel pots.

6.39 Describe applications and designs utilizing shape-memory alloys.

6.40 The Bronze Age is so known because the hardest metals known at the time were bronzes; tools, weapons, and armor were therefore made from bronze. Investigate the geographical sources of the metals needed for bronze, and identify the known sources in the Bronze Age. (*Note*: Does this explain the Greek interest in the British Islands?)

6.41 Aluminum beverage can tops are made from 5182 alloy, while the bottoms are made from 3004 alloy. Study the properties of these alloys and explain why they are used for these applications.

6.42 Obtain specimens of pure copper, pure aluminum, and alloys of copper and aluminum. Conduct tension tests on each, plot the stress-strain diagrams, and evaluate the results.

7

Polymers: Structure, General Properties, and Applications

7.1 INTRODUCTION

Although the word "plastics," first used as a noun around 1909, is commonly employed as a synonym for "polymers," **plastics** are one of numerous polymeric materials and have extremely large molecules (*macromolecules*). Consumer and industrial products made of polymers include food and beverage containers, packaging, signs, housewares, textiles, medical devices, foams, paints, safety shields, toys, appliances, lenses, gears, electronic and electrical products, and automobile bodies and components.

Because of their many unique and diverse properties, polymers have increasingly replaced metallic components in applications such as automobiles, civilian and military aircraft, sporting goods, toys, appliances, and office equipment. These substitutions reflect the advantages of polymers in terms of the following characteristics:

a. corrosion resistance and resistance to chemicals;

b. low electrical and thermal conductivity;

c. low density;

d. high strength-to-weight ratio, particularly when reinforced;

e. noise reduction;

f. wide choice of colors and transparencies;

g. ease of manufacturing and complexity of design possibilities;

h. relatively low cost (see Table 6.1);

i. others that may or may not be desirable, depending on the application, such as low strength and stiffness (Table 7.1), high coefficient of thermal expansion, low useful temperature range (up to about 350 °C (660 °F)), and less dimensional stability in service over a period of time.

The word *plastic* is from the Greek word *plastikos*, meaning "able to be molded and shaped." Plastics can be machined, cast, formed, and joined into many shapes with relative ease. Minimal additional surface-finishing operations, if any at all, are required; that characteristic provides an important advantage over metals. Plastics are commercially available as sheet, plate, film, rods, and tubing of various cross-sections.

The word **polymer** was first used in 1866. The earliest polymers were made of **natural organic materials** from animal and vegetable products; *cellulose* is the most common example. By means of various chemical reactions, cellulose is modified into cellulose acetate, which is used in making photographic films (celluloid), sheets for packaging, and textile fibers; into cellulose nitrate for plastics and explosives; into rayon (a cellulose textile fiber); and into varnishes. The earliest **synthetic** (manmade) polymer was a phenol-formaldehyde, a thermoset developed in 1906 and called *Bakelite* (a trade name, after L. H. Baekeland, 1863–1944).

The development of modern plastics technology began in the 1920s, when the raw materials necessary for making polymers were extracted from coal and petroleum products. Ethylene was the first example of such a raw material; it became the building block for polyethylene. Ethylene is the product of the reaction between acetylene and hydrogen, and acetylene is the product of the reaction between coke and methane. The commercial poly-

TABLE 7.1   Range of Mechanical Properties for Various Engineering Plastics at Room Temperature

Material	UTS (MPa)	E (GPa)	Elongation (%)	Poisson's ratio (ν)
ABS	28–55	1.4–2.8	75–5	—
ABS, reinforced	100	7.5	—	0.35
Acetal	55–70	1.4–3.5	75–25	—
Acetal, reinforced	135	10	—	0.35–0.40
Acrylic	40–75	1.4–3.5	50–5	—
Cellulosic	10–48	0.4–1.4	100–5	—
Epoxy	35–140	3.5–17	10–1	—
Epoxy, reinforced	70–1400	21–52	4–2	—
Fluorocarbon	7–48	0.7–2	300–100	0.46–0.48
Nylon	55–83	1.4–2.8	200–60	0.32–0.40
Nylon, reinforced	70–210	2–10	10–1	—
Phenolic	28–70	2.8–21	2–0	—
Polycarbonate	55–70	2.5–3	125–10	0.38
Polycarbonate, reinforced	110	6	6–4	—
Polyester	55	2	300–5	0.38
Polyester, reinforced	110–160	8.3–12	3–1	—
Polyethylene	7–40	0.1–1.4	1000–15	0.46
Polypropylene	20–35	0.7–1.2	500–10	—
Polypropylene, reinforced	40–100	3.5–6	4–2	—
Polystyrene	14–83	1.4–4	60–1	0.35
Polyvinyl chloride	7–55	0.014–4	450–40	—

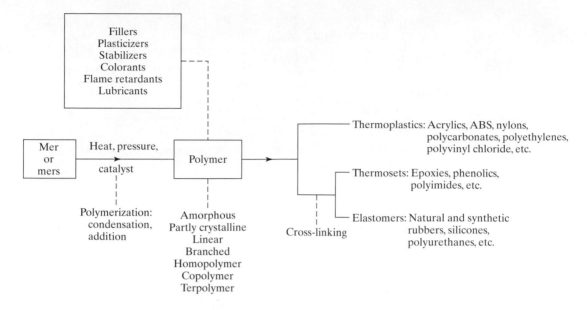

FIGURE 7.1   Outline of the topics described in Chapter 7.

mers, including polypropylene, polyvinyl chloride, polymethylmethacrylate, polycarbonate, and others, are all made in a similar manner; these materials are known as **synthetic organic polymers**.

An outline of the basic process of making various synthetic polymers is illustrated in Fig. 7.1. In polyethylene, only carbon and hydrogen atoms are involved, but other polymer compounds can be obtained by including chlorine, fluorine, sulfur, silicon, nitrogen, and oxygen. As a result, an extremely wide range of polymers, having among them an equally wide range of properties, has been developed.

This chapter describes the relationship of the structure of a polymer to its properties and behavior, both during manufacturing and during its service life under various physical and environmental conditions. An outline of the topics presented is given in Fig. 7.1. This chapter also describes the properties and engineering applications of plastics, rubbers, and elastomers. Reinforced plastics are described in Chapter 9 and processing methods for plastics and reinforced plastics in Chapter 18.

7.2 THE STRUCTURE OF POLYMERS

The properties of polymers depend largely on the structures of individual polymer molecules, on molecule shape and size, and on how they are arranged to form a polymer structure. Polymer molecules are characterized by their very large size, a feature that distinguishes them from most other organic chemical compositions.

Polymers are **long-chain molecules** (sometimes called **macromolecules** or **giant molecules**) that are formed by polymerization, that is, by the linking and cross-linking of different monomers. A **monomer** is the basic building block of a polymer. The word **mer**, from the Greek *meros*, meaning part, indicates the smallest repetitive unit; its use is similar to that of the term "unit cell" in connection with crystal structures of metals (Chapter 1).

The term **polymer** means "many mers" (or units), generally repeated hundreds or thousands of times in a chainlike structure. Most monomers are *organic* materials in which

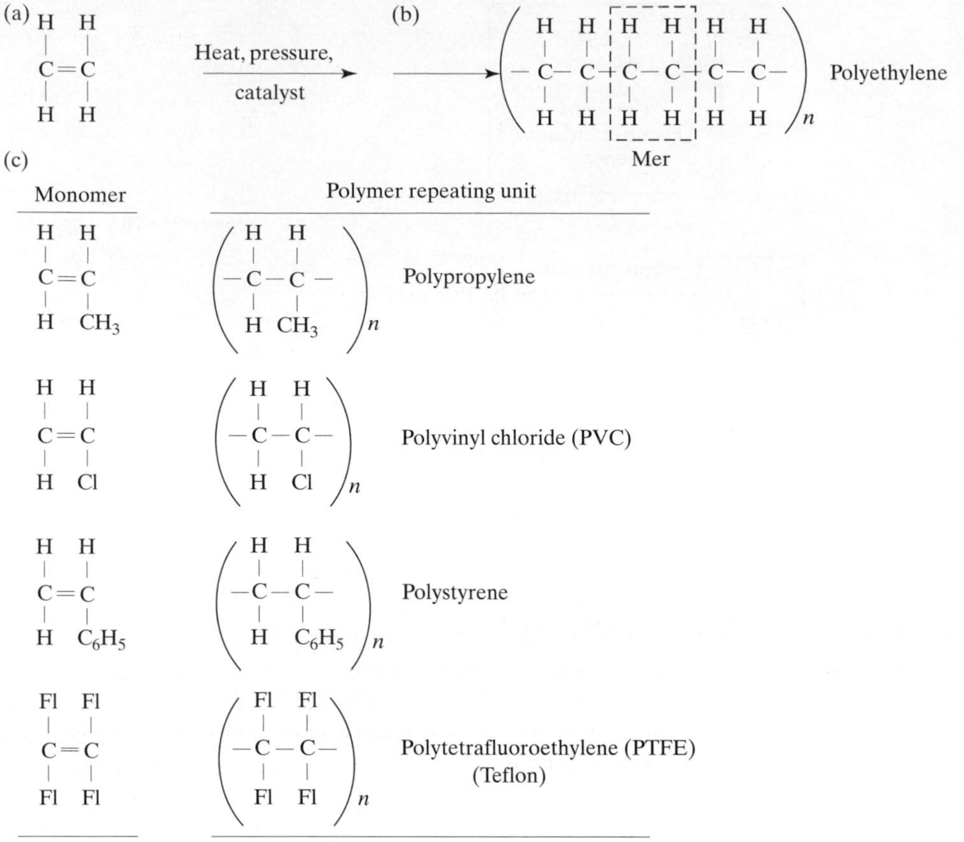

FIGURE 7.2   Basic structure of polymer molecules: (a) ethylene molecule; (b) polyethylene, a linear chain of many ethylene molecules; (c) molecular structure of various polymers. These are examples of the basic building blocks for plastics.

carbon atoms are joined in *covalent* (electron-sharing) bonds with other atoms such as hydrogen, oxygen, nitrogen, fluorine, chlorine, silicon, and sulfur. An ethylene molecule (Fig. 7.2a) is an example of a simple monomer consisting of carbon and hydrogen atoms.

7.2.1 Polymerization

Monomers can be linked into polymers in repeating units, to make longer and larger molecules, by a chemical process called a **polymerization reaction**. Polymerization processes are complex; they will be described only briefly here. Although there are many variations, two polymerization processes are basic: condensation and addition polymerization.

In **condensation polymerization**, polymers are produced by the formation of bonds between two types of reacting mers. A characteristic of this reaction is that reaction by-products such as water are condensed out (hence the name). This process is also known as **step-growth** or **step-reaction polymerization**, because the polymer molecule grows, step by step, until all of one reactant is consumed.

In **addition polymerization**, also called **chain-growth** or **chain-reaction polymerization**, bonding takes place without reaction by-products. It is called "chain-reaction" because of the high rate at which long molecules form simultaneously, usually within a few seconds. This rate is much higher than that for condensation polymerization. In this reaction, an initiator is added to open the double bond between two carbon atoms; it begins the linking process by adding many more monomers to a growing chain. For example, ethylene monomers (Fig. 7.2a) link to produce the polymer polyethylene (Fig. 7.2b); other examples of addition-formed polymers are shown in Fig. 7.2c.

Molecular Weight.   The sum of the molecular weights of the mers in a representative chain is known as the **molecular weight** of the polymer. The higher the molecular weight of a given polymer, the greater the average chain length. Most commercial polymers have a molecular weight between 10,000 and 10,000,000. Because polymerization is a random event, the polymer chains produced are not all of equal length, but the chain lengths produced fall into a traditional distribution curve. We determine and express the average molecular weight of a polymer on a statistical basis by averaging.

The spread of the chains' molecular weights is referred to as the **molecular weight distribution (MWD)**. A polymer's molecular weight and its MWD have a strong influence on its properties. For example, the tensile and the impact strength, the resistance to cracking, and the viscosity (in the molten state) of the polymer all increase with increasing molecular weight (Fig. 7.3).

Degree of Polymerization.   In some cases, it is more convenient to express the size of a polymer chain in terms of the **degree of polymerization (DP)**, defined as the ratio of the molecular weight of the polymer to the molecular weight of the repeating unit. For example, polyvinyl chloride (PVC) has a mer weight of 62.5, so the DP of PVC having a molecular weight of 50,000 is $50,000/62.5 = 800$. In terms of polymer processing (Chapter 18), the higher the DP is, the higher is the polymer's viscosity, or resistance to flow (Fig. 7.3); high viscosity adversely affects the ease of shaping and thus raises the overall cost of processing.

Bonding.   During polymerization, the monomers are linked together by **covalent bonds**, forming a polymer chain. Because of their strength, covalent bonds are also called **primary bonds**. The polymer chains are, in turn, held together by **secondary bonds**, such as van der Waals bonds, hydrogen bonds, and ionic bonds. Secondary bonds are weaker than primary bonds by one to two orders of magnitude. In a given polymer, the increase in

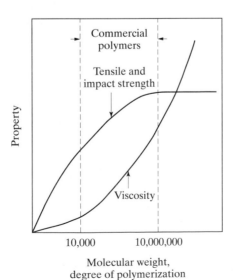

FIGURE 7.3   Effect of molecular weight and degree of polymerization on the strength and viscosity of polymers.

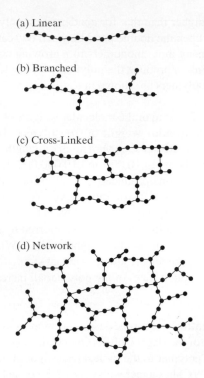

(a) Linear

(b) Branched

(c) Cross-Linked

(d) Network

FIGURE 7.4 Schematic illustration of polymer chains. (a) Linear structure—thermoplastics such as acrylics, nylons, polyethylene, and polyvinyl chloride have linear structures. (b) Branched structure, such as in polyethylene. (c) Cross-linked structure—many rubbers or elastomers have this structure, and the vulcanization of rubber produces this structure. (d) Network structure, which is basically highly cross-linked—examples are thermosetting plastics, such as epoxies and phenolics.

strength and viscosity with molecular weight comes in part from the fact that the longer the polymer chain is, the greater is the energy needed to overcome the combined strength of the secondary bonds. For example, ethylene polymers having DPs of 1, 6, 35, 140, and 1350 at room temperature are, respectively, in the form of gas, liquid, grease, wax, and hard plastic.

Linear Polymers.   The chainlike polymers shown in Fig. 7.2 are called **linear polymers** because of their sequential structure (Fig. 7.4a). A linear molecule is not necessarily straight in shape. In addition to those shown, other linear polymers are polyamides (nylon 6,6) and polyvinyl fluoride. Generally, a polymer consists of more than one type of structure; a linear polymer may contain some branched and cross-linked chains. As a result of branching and cross-linking, the polymer's properties can change.

Branched Polymers.   The properties of a polymer depend not only on the type of monomers, but also on their arrangement in the molecular structure. In **branched polymers** (Fig. 7.4b), side-branch chains are attached to the main chain during the synthesis of the polymer. Branching interferes with the relative movement of the molecular chains; as a result, deformation resistance and stress-crack resistance are increased. The density of branched polymers is lower than that of linear-chain polymers, because branches interfere with the packing efficiency of polymer chains.

The behavior of branched polymers can be compared to that of linear-chain polymers by making an analogy with a pile of tree branches (branched polymers) and a bundle of straight logs (linear). You will note that it is more difficult to move a branch within the pile of branches than to move a log within its bundle. The three-dimensional entanglements of branches make movements more difficult, a phenomenon akin to increased strength.

Cross-Linked Polymers.   Generally three-dimensional in structure, **cross-linked polymers** have adjacent chains linked by covalent bonds (Fig. 7.4c). Polymers with cross-

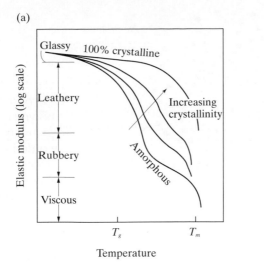
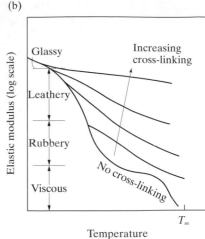

FIGURE 7.5   Behavior of polymers as a function of temperature and (a) degree of crystallinity and (b) cross-linking. The combined elastic and viscous behavior of polymers is known as viscoelasticity.

linked chain structure are called **thermosets**, or **thermosetting plastics**; examples are epoxies, phenolics, and silicones. Cross-linking has a major influence on the properties of polymers (generally imparting hardness, strength, stiffness, brittleness, and better dimensional stability; see Fig. 7.5), as well as in the **vulcanization** of rubber.

Network Polymers.   These consist of spatial (three dimensional) networks of three or more active covalent bonds (Fig. 7.4d). A highly cross-linked polymer is also considered a network polymer. Thermoplastic polymers that have already been formed or shaped can be cross-linked, to obtain greater strength, by subjecting them to high-energy radiation, such as ultraviolet light, x-rays, or electron beams, but excessive radiation can cause degradation of the polymer.

Copolymers and Terpolymers.   If the repeating units in a polymer chain are all of the same type, the molecule is called a **homopolymer**. However, as with solid-solution metal alloys (Section 4.2.1), two or three different types of monomers can be combined to impart certain special properties and characteristics to the polymer, such as improved strength, toughness, and formability of the polymer. **Copolymers** contain two types of polymers—for example, styrene–butadiene, which is used widely for automobile tires. **Terpolymers** contain three types—for example, ABS (acrylonitrile–butadiene–styrene), which is used for helmets, telephones, and refrigerator liners.

7.2.2 Crystallinity

Polymers such as polymethylmethacrylate, polycarbonate, and polystyrene are generally **amorphous**; that is, the polymer chains exist without long-range order (see also amorphous alloys, Section 6.14). The amorphous arrangement of polymer chains is often described as being like a bowl of spaghetti or like worms in a bucket, all intertwined with each other. In some polymers, however, it is possible to impart some crystallinity and thereby to modify their characteristics. This arrangement may be fostered either during the synthesis of the polymer or by deformation during its subsequent processing.

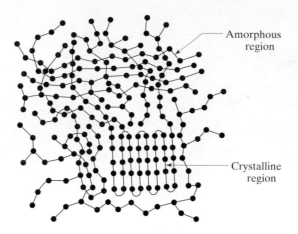

FIGURE 7.6   Amorphous and crystalline regions in a polymer. The crystalline region (crystallite) has an orderly arrangement of molecules. The higher the crystallinity, the harder, stiffer, and less ductile the polymer.

The crystalline regions in polymers are called **crystallites** (Fig. 7.6). These crystals are formed when the long molecules arrange themselves in an orderly manner, similar to the folding of a fire hose in a cabinet or of facial tissues in a box. We can regard a partially crystalline (**semi-crystalline**) polymer as a two-phase material, one phase being crystalline and the other amorphous.

By controlling the rate of solidification during cooling and chain structure, it is possible to impart different **degrees of crystallinity** to polymers, although never 100%. Crystallinity ranges from an almost complete crystal (up to about 95% by volume in the case of polyethylene) to slightly crystallized but mostly amorphous polymers.

The degree of crystallinity is also affected by branching. A linear polymer can become highly crystalline. A highly branched polymer cannot; it may develop some low level of crystallinity, but it will never achieve a high crystallite content, because the branches interfere with the alignment of the chains into a regular crystal array.

Effects of Crystallinity.   The *mechanical and physical properties* of polymers are greatly influenced by the degree of crystallinity. As it increases, polymers become stiffer, harder, less ductile, more dense, less rubbery, and more resistant to solvents and heat (Fig. 7.5). The increase in density with increasing crystallinity is called *crystallization shrinkage* and is caused by a more efficient packing of the molecules in the crystal lattice.

For example, the highly crystalline form of polyethylene, known as high-density polyethylene (HDPE), has a specific gravity in the range of from 0.941 to 0.970 (80% to 95% crystalline); it is stronger, stiffer, tougher, and less ductile than low-density polyethylene (LDPE), which is about 60% to 70% crystalline and has a specific gravity of about 0.910 to 0.925.

Optical properties are also affected by the degree of crystallinity. The reflection of light from the boundaries between the crystalline and the amorphous regions in the polymer causes opaqueness. Furthermore, because the index of refraction is proportional to density, the greater the density difference between the amorphous and crystalline phases, the greater is the opaqueness of the polymer. Polymers that are completely amorphous can be transparent, such as polycarbonate and acrylics.

7.2.3 Glass-Transition Temperature

Amorphous polymers do not have a specific melting point, but they do undergo a distinct change in their mechanical behavior across a narrow range of temperature. At low temperatures, they are hard, rigid, brittle, and glassy; at high temperatures, they are rubbery or leathery. The temperature at which a transition occurs is called the **glass-transition tem-**

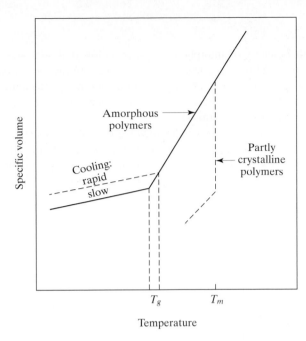

FIGURE 7.7   Specific volume of polymers as a function of temperature. Amorphous polymers, such as acrylic and polycarbonate, have a glass-transition temperature, T_g, but do not have a specific melting point, T_m. Partly crystalline polymers, such as polyethylene and nylons, contract sharply while passing through their melting temperatures during cooling.

perature (T_g); it is also called the **glass point** or **glass temperature**. The term "glass" is used in this description because glasses, which are amorphous solids, behave in the same manner; recall metallic glasses, in Section 6.14.

Although most amorphous polymers exhibit this behavior, there are some exceptions, such as polycarbonate which is neither rigid nor brittle below its glass-transition temperature. Polycarbonate is tough at ambient temperature and is thus used for safety helmets and shields.

To determine T_g, we measure the specific volume of the polymer and plot it against temperature, looking for a sharp change in the slope of the curve (Fig. 7.7). In the case of highly cross-linked polymers, the slope of the curve changes only gradually near T_g, and so it is difficult to determine T_g for these polymers.

The glass-transition temperature varies with different polymers (Table 7.2). For example, room temperature is above T_g for some polymers, below it for others. Unlike amorphous polymers, partly crystalline polymers have a distinct melting point, T_m (Fig. 7.7; see also Table 7.2). Because of the structural changes (first-order changes) occurring, the specific volume of the polymer drops suddenly as its temperature is reduced.

TABLE 7.2   Glass-Transition and Melting Temperatures of Some Polymers

Material	T_g (°C)	T_m (°C)
Nylon 6,6	57	265
Polycarbonate	150	265
Polyester	73	265
Polyethylene		
High density	−90	137
Low density	−110	115
Polymethylmethacrylate	105	—
Polypropylene	−14	176
Polystyrene	100	239
Polytetrafluoroethylene	−90	327
Polyvinyl chloride	87	212
Rubber	−73	—

7.2.4 Polymer Blends

The brittle behavior of amorphous polymers below their glass-transition temperature can be reduced by blending them, usually with small quantities of an **elastomer**. These tiny particles are dispersed throughout the amorphous polymer, enhancing its toughness and impact strength by improving its resistance to crack propagation. These polymer blends are known as **rubber modified polymers**.

More recent trends in blending involve several components, creating "**polyblends**" that utilize the favorable properties of different polymers. Some advances have been made in **miscible blends** (mixing without separation of two phases), created by a process similar to the alloying of metals that enables polymer blends to become more ductile. Polymer blends account for about 20% of all polymer production.

7.3 THERMOPLASTICS

We noted earlier that, within each molecule the bonds between adjacent long-chain molecules (secondary bonds) are much weaker than the covalent bonds between mers (primary bonds). It is the strength of the secondary bonds that determines the overall strength of the polymer; linear and branched polymers have weak secondary bonds.

For certain polymers, as the temperature is raised above the glass-transition temperature T_g or melting point T_m, we find that it becomes easier to form or mold them into desired shapes. The increased temperature weakens the secondary bonds (through thermal vibration of the long molecules), and the adjacent chains can thus move more easily under the shaping forces. If we then cool the polymer, it returns to its original hardness and strength; in other words, the process is reversible. Polymers that exhibit this behavior are known as **thermoplastics**, typical examples of which are acrylics, cellulosics, nylons, polyethylenes, and polyvinyl chloride.

The behavior of thermoplastics depends on other variables as well as their structure and their composition. Among the most important are temperature and rate of deformation. Below the glass-transition temperature, most polymers are *glassy* (brittle) and behave like an elastic solid; that is, the relationship between stress and strain is linear (see Fig. 2.2). For example, polymethylmethacrylate (PMMA) is glassy below its T_g; polycarbonate is one that is not glassy below its T_g.

The glassy behavior can be represented by a spring whose stiffness is equivalent to the modulus of elasticity of the polymer. When the applied stress is increased, the polymer eventually fractures, just as a piece of glass does at ambient temperature. Plastics, just as metals, undergo fatigue and creep phenomena. Typical stress–strain curves for some thermoplastics and thermosets at room temperature are shown in Fig. 7.8. Note that these plastics exhibit different behaviors, which we may describe as rigid, soft, brittle, flexible, and so on.

The mechanical properties of several polymers listed in Table 7.1 indicate that thermoplastics are about two orders of magnitude less stiff than metals. Their ultimate tensile strength is about one order of magnitude lower than that of metals (see Table 2.1).

Effects of Temperature.   If we raise the temperature of a thermoplastic polymer above its T_g, it first becomes *leathery*, and then, with increasing temperature, *rubbery* (Fig. 7.5). Finally, at higher temperatures (e.g., above T_m for crystalline thermoplastics), it becomes a *viscous fluid*; its viscosity decreases with increasing temperature. At still higher temperatures, the response of a thermoplastic can be likened to ice cream. It can be softened, molded into shapes, refrozen, resoftened, and remolded a number of times. In practice, however, repeated heating and cooling cause **degradation**, or **thermal aging**, of thermoplastics.

The typical effect of temperature on the strength and elastic modulus of thermoplastics is similar to that of metals; with increasing temperature, the strength and the modulus of elastici-

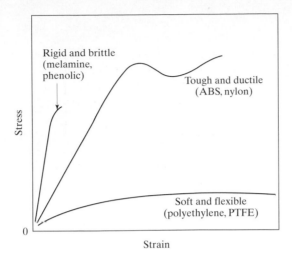

FIGURE 7.8   General terminology describing the behavior of three types of plastics. PTFE (polytetrafluoroethylene) has *Teflon* as its trade name. *Source*: R. L. E. Brown.

ty decrease and the toughness increases (Fig. 7.9). The effect of temperature on impact strength is shown in Fig. 7.10. Note the large difference in the impact behaviors of various polymers.

Effect of Rate of Deformation.   The behavior of thermoplastics is similar to the strain-rate sensitivity of metals, indicated by the strain-rate sensitivity exponent m in Eq. (2.9). Thermoplastics in general have high m values, indicating that they can undergo large uniform deformations in tension before fracture (Fig. 7.11). Note how (unlike in ordinary metals) the necked region elongates considerably.

We can easily demonstrate this phenomenon by stretching a piece of the plastic holder for 6-pack beverage cans. Observe the sequence of necking and stretching behavior shown in Fig. 7.11a. This characteristic, which is the same in the superplastic metals, enables the thermoforming of thermoplastics into such complex shapes as meat trays, lighted signs, and bottles for soft drinks.

Orientation.   When thermoplastics are deformed, say by stretching, the long-chain molecules tend to align in the general direction of the elongation. This process is called **orientation** and, just as in metals, the polymer becomes anisotropic (see also Section 1.5). The specimen becomes stronger and stiffer in the elongated (stretched) direction than in its transverse direction. Stretching is an important technique for enhancing the strength and the toughness of polymers. However, orientation weakens the polymer in the transverse direction.

Crazing.   Some thermoplastics (such as polystyrene and polymethylmethacrylate) when subjected to tensile stresses or to bending, develop localized, wedge-shaped, narrow

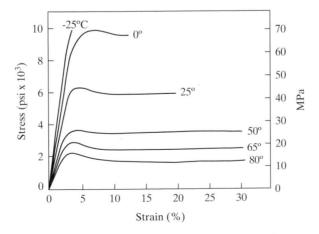

FIGURE 7.9   Effect of temperature on the stress-strain curve for cellulose acetate, a thermoplastic. Note the large drop in strength and the large increase in ductility with a relatively small increase in temperature. *Source*: After T. S. Carswell and H. K. Nason.

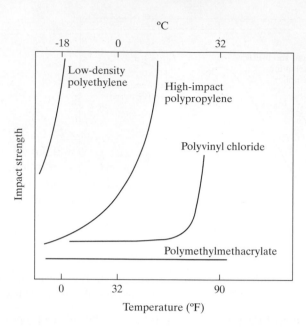

°C

FIGURE 7.10   Effect of temperature on the impact strength of various plastics. Small changes in temperature can have a significant effect on impact strength. *Source*: P. C. Powell.

FIGURE 7.11   (a) Load-elongation curve for polycarbonate, a thermoplastic. *Source*: R. P. Kambour and R. E. Robertson. (b) High-density polyethylene tensile-test specimen, showing uniform elongation (the long, narrow region in the specimen).

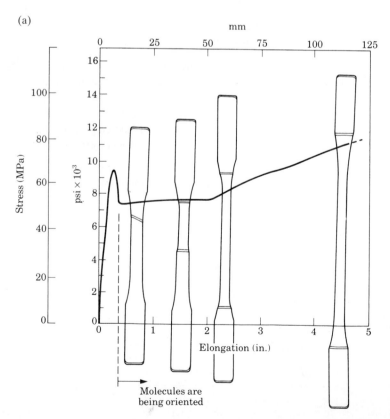

regions of highly deformed material, a phenomenon called **crazing**. Although they may appear to be like cracks, crazes are spongy material, typically containing about 50% voids. With increasing tensile load on the specimen, these voids coalesce to form a crack, which can eventually lead to fracture of the polymer. Crazing has been observed both in transparent glassy polymers and in other types.

The environment (particularly the presence of solvents, lubricants, or water vapor) can enhance the formation of crazes (*environmental stress cracking* and *solvent crazing*). Residual stresses in the material contribute to crazing and cracking of the polymer. Radiation, especially ultraviolet radiation, can increase the crazing behavior in certain polymers.

A related phenomenon is **stress whitening**. When subjected to tensile stresses, such as those caused by folding or bending, the plastic becomes lighter in color. This phenomenon is usually attributed to the formation of microvoids in the material. As a result, the material becomes less translucent (transmits less light) or more opaque. You can easily demonstrate this result by bending plastic components commonly found in colored binder strips for report covers, household products, and toys.

Water Absorption.   An important characteristic of some polymers, such as nylons, is their ability to absorb water. Water acts as a plasticizing agent (Section 7.5); that is, it makes the polymer more plastic. In a sense, it lubricates the chains in the amorphous region. With increasing moisture absorption, the glass-transition temperature, the yield stress, and the elastic modulus of the polymer typically are lowered severely. Dimensional changes also occur because of water absorption, especially in a humid environment.

Thermal and Electrical Properties.   Compared to metals, plastics are generally characterized by low thermal and electrical conductivity, low specific gravity (ranging from 0.90 to 2.2), and high coefficient of thermal expansion (about an order of magnitude higher). (See Tables 3.1 and 3.2.)

Because most polymers have low electrical conductivity, they can be used for insulators and as packaging material for electronic components. The electrical conductivity of some polymers can be increased by **doping** (introducing impurities into the polymer, such as metal powder, salts, and iodides). Discovered in the late 1970s, **electrically conducting polymers** include polyacetylene, polyaniline, polypyrrole, and polythiophene. The electrical conductivity of polymers increases with moisture absorption; their electronic properties can also be changed by irradiation.

Applications for conducting polymers include adhesives, microelectronic devices, rechargeable batteries, capacitors, catalysts, fuel cells, fuel-level sensors, deicer panels, radar dishes, antistatic coatings, and thermoactuating motors (for linear-motion applications such as power antennae, sun roofs, and power windows).

Creep and Stress Relaxation.   Because of their viscoelastic behavior, thermoplastics are particularly susceptible to creep and to stress relaxation, and to a larger extent than metals (Section 2.8). The extent of these phenomena depends on the polymer, the stress level, the temperature, and time. Thermoplastics exhibit creep and stress relaxation at room temperature; most metals do so only at elevated temperatures.

Example: Use of Electrically Conducting Polymers in Rechargeable Batteries

One of the earliest applications of conducting polymers was in rechargeable batteries. The cathode is made of a conducting polymer; the anode is lithium (a soft, silvery-white element that is the lightest metal known) or a lithium alloy. Developments are now taking place in making battery cells in which both electrodes are made of conducting polymers; one has been constructed with a capacity of 3.5 V.

7.4 THERMOSETTING PLASTICS

When the long-chain molecules in a polymer are cross-linked in a three-dimensional arrangement, the structure in effect becomes one *giant molecule* with strong covalent bonds. As previously stated, these polymers are called **thermosetting polymers**, or **thermosets**, because, during polymerization, the network is completed and the shape of the part is permanently set. This **curing (cross-linking)** reaction, unlike that of thermoplastics, is *irreversible*.

The response of a thermosetting plastic to sufficiently elevated temperature can be likened to what happens in the baking of a cake or in the boiling of an egg; once the cake is baked and cooled, or the egg boiled and cooled, reheating it will not change its shape. Some thermosets (such as epoxy, polyester, and urethane) cure at room temperature, because the heat produced by the exothermic reaction is sufficient to cure the plastic.

The polymerization process for thermosets generally takes place in two stages. The first occurs at the chemical plant, where the molecules are partially polymerized into linear chains. The second stage occurs at the parts-producing plant, where cross-linking is completed under heat and pressure during the molding and shaping of the part.

Thermosetting polymers do not have a sharply defined glass-transition temperature. Because of the nature of the bonds, the strength and hardness of a thermoset are, unlike those of thermoplastics, not affected by temperature or by rate of deformation. If the temperature is increased sufficiently, the thermosetting polymer instead begins to burn up, degrade, and char.

Thermosetting plastics generally possess better mechanical, thermal, and chemical properties, electrical resistance, and dimensional stability than do thermoplastics. A typical thermoset is *phenolic*, which is a product of the reaction between phenol and formaldehyde. Common products made from this polymer are the handles and knobs on cooking pots and pans and components of light switches and outlets.

7.5 ADDITIVES IN PLASTICS

In order to impart certain specific properties, polymers are usually compounded with **additives**. These additives modify and improve certain characteristics of the polymer, such as stiffness, strength, color, weatherability, flammability, arc resistance (for electrical applications), and ease of subsequent processing.

  a. **Plasticizers** are added to polymers to impart *flexibility* and *softness* by lowering their glass-transition temperature. Plasticizers are low-molecular-weight solvents with high boiling points (nonvolatile). They reduce the strength of the secondary bonds between the long-chain molecules and thus make the polymer soft and flexible. The most common use of plasticizers is in polyvinyl chloride (PVC), which remains flexible during its many uses. Other applications of plasticizers are in thin sheets, films, tubing, shower curtains, and clothing materials.

  b. Most polymers are adversely affected by *ultraviolet radiation* (such as from sunlight) and by *oxygen*; they weaken and break the primary bonds and so cause the *scission* (splitting) of the long-chain molecules. The polymer then degrades and becomes stiff and brittle. On the other hand, degradation may be beneficial, as in the disposal of plastic objects by subjecting them to environmental attack (see also Section 7.8).

  A typical example of protection against ultraviolet radiation is the compounding of certain plastics and rubber with **carbon black** (soot). The carbon black absorbs a high percentage of the ultraviolet radiation. Protection against degradation caused by oxidation, particularly at elevated temperatures, is achieved by adding *antioxidants* to the polymer. Various *coatings* are another means of protecting polymers.

c. **Fillers** used are generally wood flour (fine sawdust), silica flour (fine silica powder), clay, powdered mica, talc, calcium carbonate, and short fibers of cellulose, glass, or asbestos. Because of their low cost, fillers are important in reducing the overall cost of polymers. Depending on their type, fillers may also improve the strength, hardness, toughness, abrasion resistance, dimensional stability, or stiffness of plastics. These properties are greatest at specific percentages of different types of polymer–filler combinations. As with reinforced plastics, a filler's effectiveness depends on the nature of the bond between the filler material and the polymer chains.

d. The wide variety of colors available in plastics is obtained by adding **colorants**, either organic (*dyes*) or inorganic (*pigments*). The selection of a colorant depends on service temperature and on the expected amount of exposure to light. Pigments are dispersed particles; they generally have greater resistance than do dyes to temperature and to light.

e. If the temperature is sufficiently high, most polymers will ignite and burn. The **flammability** (ability to support combustion) of polymers varies considerably, depending on their composition (especially on their chlorine and fluorine content). Flame colors are usually yellow or blue. The flammability of polymers can be reduced either by making them from less flammable raw materials or by the addition of **flame retardants**, such as compounds of chlorine, bromine, and phosphorus. Cross-linking also reduces polymer flammability.

   The following list gives several common polymers with different burning characteristics:

   1. Plastics that do not burn:
      fluorocarbons (Teflon).
   2. Plastics that do burn but are self-extinguishing:
      carbonate, nylon, vinyl chloride.
   3. Plastics that burn and are *not* self-extinguishing:
      Acetal, acrylic, acrylonitrile–butadiene–styrene, cellulose, polyester, propylene, styrene.

f. **Lubricants** may be added to polymers to reduce friction during their subsequent processing into useful products and to prevent parts from sticking to the molds. Typical lubricants are linseed oil, mineral oil, and waxes (natural and synthetic); metallic soaps such as calcium stearate and zinc stearate are also used. Lubrication is also important in preventing thin polymer films from sticking to each other.

7.6 GENERAL PROPERTIES AND APPLICATIONS OF THERMOPLASTICS

The general characteristics and typical applications of major thermoplastics, particularly as they relate to the manufacturing and the service life of plastic products, are outlined in this section. General recommendations for various plastics applications are given in Table 7.3.

Acetals (from *acetic* and *alcohol*) have good strength, good stiffness, and good resistance to creep, abrasion, moisture, heat, and chemicals. Typical applications include: mechanical parts and components from which high performance is required over a long period: bearings, cams, gears, bushings, and rollers; and impellers, wear surfaces, pipes, valves, shower heads, and housings.

Acrylics (polymethylmethacrylate, PMMA) possess moderate strength, good optical properties, and weather resistance. They are transparent (but can be made opaque), are generally resistant to chemicals, and have good electrical resistance. Typical applications include: lenses, lighted signs, displays, window glazing, skylights, bubble tops, automotive lenses, windshields, lighting fixtures, and furniture.

TABLE 7.3   General Recommendations for Plastic Products

Design requirement	Applications	Plastics
Mechanical strength	Gears, cams, rollers, valves, fan blades, impellers, pistons	Acetal, nylon, phenolic, polycarbonate
Functional and decorative	Handles, knobs, camera and battery cases, trim moldings, pipe fittings	ABS, acrylic, cellulosic, phenolic, polyethylene, polypropylene, polystyrene, polyvinyl chloride
Housings and hollow shapes	Power tools, pumps, housings, sport helmets, telephone cases	ABS, cellulosic, phenolic, polycarbonate, polyethylene, polypropylene, polystyrene
Functional and transparent	Lenses, goggles, safety glazing, signs, food-processing equipment, laboratory hardware	Acrylic, polycarbonate, polystyrene, polysulfone
Wear resistance	Gears, wear strips and liners, bearings, bushings, roller-skate wheels	Acetal, nylon, phenolic, polyimide, polyurethane, ultrahigh molecular weight polyethylene

Acrylonitrile–butadiene–styrene (ABS) is dimensionally stable and rigid. It has good impact, abrasion, and chemical resistance; good strength and toughness; good low-temperature properties; and high electrical resistance. Typical applications include: pipes, fittings, chrome-plated plumbing supplies, helmets, tool handles, automotive components, boat hulls, telephones, luggage, housing, appliances, refrigerator liners, and decorative panels.

Cellulosics have a wide range of mechanical properties, depending on composition. They can be made rigid, strong, and tough. However, they weather poorly, and they are affected by heat and chemicals. Typical applications include: tool handles, pens, knobs, frames for eyeglasses, safety goggles, machine guards, helmets, tubing and pipes, lighting fixtures, rigid containers, steering wheels, packaging film, signs, billiard balls, toys, and decorative parts.

Fluorocarbons possess good resistance to high temperature (with a melting point of 327 °C, (621 °F) for Teflon), to chemicals, to weather, and to electricity. They also have unique nonadhesive properties and low friction. Typical applications include: linings for chemical-process equipment, nonstick coatings for cookware, electrical insulation for high-temperature wire and cable, gaskets, low-friction surfaces, bearings, and seals.

Polyamides (from the words *poly*, *amine*, and *carboxyl acid*) are available in two main types: *nylons* and *aramids*.

a. **Nylons** (a coined word) have good mechanical properties and abrasion resistance. They are self-lubricating, and they are resistant to most chemicals. All nylons are hygroscopic (absorb water); the moisture absorption reduces desirable mechanical properties and increases part dimensions. Typical applications include: gears, bearings, bushings, rollers, fasteners, zippers, electrical parts, combs, tubing, wear-resistant surfaces, guides, and surgical equipment.

b. **Aramids** (aromatic polyamides) have very high tensile strength and stiffness. Typical applications include: fibers for reinforced plastics (composite materials; Chapter 9), bulletproof vests, cables, and radial tires.

Polycarbonates are versatile. They have good mechanical and electrical properties, they have high impact resistance, and they can be made resistant to chemicals. Typical applications include: safety helmets, optical lenses, bullet-resistant window glazing, signs, bottles, food-processing equipment, windshields, load-bearing electrical components, electrical insulators, medical apparatus, business machine components, guards for machinery, and parts requiring dimensional stability.

Polyesters. (See also Section 7.7.) Thermoplastic polyesters have good mechanical, electrical, and chemical properties; good abrasion resistance; and low friction. Typical applications include: gears, cams, rollers, load-bearing members, pumps, and electromechanical components.

Polyethylenes possess good electrical and chemical properties. Their mechanical properties depend on composition and structure. Three major classes are (a) *low density* (LDPE), (b) *high density* (HDPE), and (c) *ultrahigh molecular weight* (UHMWPE). Typical applications for LDPE and HDPE are housewares, bottles, garbage cans, ducts, bumpers, luggage, toys, tubing, bottles, and packaging materials. UHMWPE is used in parts requiring high-impact toughness and resistance to abrasive wear; examples include artificial knee and hip joints.

Polyimides have the structure of a thermoplastic but the nonmelting characteristic of a thermoset. (See also Section 7.7.)

Polypropylenes have good mechanical, electrical, and chemical properties and good resistance to tearing. Typical applications include automotive trim and components, medical devices, appliance parts, wire insulation, TV cabinets, pipes, fittings, drinking cups, dairy-product and juice containers, luggage, ropes, and weather stripping.

Polystyrenes are inexpensive, have generally average properties, and are somewhat brittle. Typical applications include disposable containers, packaging, trays for meats, cookies and candy, foam insulation, appliances, automotive and radio/TV components, housewares, and toys and furniture parts (as a wood substitute).

Polysulfones have excellent resistance to heat, water, and steam; they have dielectric properties that are virtually unaffected by humidity, and they are highly resistant to some chemicals but are attacked by organic solvents. Typical applications include: steam irons, coffeemakers, hot water containers, medical equipment that requires sterilization, power-tool and appliance housings, aircraft cabin interiors, and electrical insulators.

Polyvinyl chloride (PVC) has a wide range of properties, is inexpensive and water-resistant, and can be made rigid or flexible. It is not suitable for applications requiring strength and heat resistance. *Rigid* PVC is tough and hard; it is used for signs and in the construction industry (for example, in pipes and conduits). *Flexible* PVC is used in wire and cable coatings, in low-pressure flexible tubing and hose, and in footwear, imitation leather, upholstery, records, gaskets, seals, trim, film, sheet, and coatings.

7.6.1 Common Trade Names for Thermoplastics

The following are some of the more common trade names for thermoplastics:

Trade name	**Type**
Alathon	Ethylene
Cycolac	Acrylonitrile–butadiene–styrene
Dacron	Polyester
Delrin	Acetal
Dylene	Styrene
Envex	Polyimide
Hyzod	Polycarbonate
Implex	Acrylic, rubber-modified
Kapton	Polyimide
Kevlar	Aramid
Kodel	Polyester
Kydex	Acrylic–polyvinyl chloride

Kynar	Polyvinylidene fluoride
Lexan	Polycarbonate
Lucite	Acrylic
Mylar	Polyester
Noryl	Polyphenylene oxide
Nylon	Polyamide
Orlon	Acrylic
Plexiglas	Acrylic
Royalite	Acrylonitrile–butadiene–styrene
Saran	Polyvinyl chloride
Sintra	Polyvinyl chloride
Styrofoam	Polystyrene
Teflon	Fluorocarbon
Torlon	Polyimide
Tygon	Polyvinyl chloride
Ultem	Polyetherimide
Vespel	Polyimide
Zerlon	Styrene–methylmethacrylate
Zytel	Polyamide

7.7 GENERAL PROPERTIES AND APPLICATIONS OF THERMOSETTING PLASTICS

This section outlines the general characteristics and typical applications of the major thermosetting plastics.

Alkyds (from *alkyl*, meaning alcohol, and *acid*) possess good electrical insulating properties, impact resistance, and dimensional stability, and they have low water absorption. Typical applications are in electrical and electronic components.

Aminos (**urea** and **melamine**) have properties that depend on composition. Generally, aminos are hard and rigid and are resistant to abrasion, creep, and electrical arcing. Typical applications include small appliance housings, countertops, toilet seats, handles, and distributor caps. Urea typically is used for electrical and electronic components, melamine for dinnerware.

Epoxies have excellent mechanical and electrical properties, and good dimensional stability, strong adhesive properties, and good resistance to heat and chemicals. Typical applications include electrical components requiring mechanical strength and high insulation, tools and dies, and adhesives. **Fiber-reinforced epoxies** have excellent mechanical properties and are used in pressure vessels, rocket-motor casings, tanks, and similar structural components.

Phenolics, although brittle, are rigid and dimensionally stable, and they have high resistance to heat, water, electricity, and chemicals. Typical applications include: knobs, handles, laminated panels, and telephones; bond material to hold abrasive grains together in grinding wheels; and electrical components, such as wiring devices, connectors, and insulators.

Polyesters. (See also Section 7.6.) Thermosetting polyesters have good mechanical, chemical, and electrical properties. Polyesters are generally reinforced with glass (or other) fibers. They also are available as casting resins. Typical applications include: boats, luggage, chairs, automotive bodies, swimming pools, and materials for impregnating cloth and paper.

Polyimides possess good mechanical, physical, and electrical properties at elevated temperatures. They also have good creep resistance and low friction and wear characteristics. Polyimides have the nonmelting characteristic of a thermoset but the structure of a thermoplastic. Typical applications include pump components (bearings, seals, valve seats, retainer rings, and piston rings), electrical connectors for high-temperature use, aerospace parts, high-strength impact-resistant structures, sports equipment, and safety vests.

Silicones have properties that depend on composition. Generally, they weather well, possess excellent electrical properties over a wide range of humidity and temperature, and resist chemicals and heat. (See also Section 7.9.) Typical applications include electrical components requiring strength at elevated temperatures, oven gaskets, heat seals, and waterproof materials.

Example: Materials for Refrigerator Door Liner

In the selection of candidate materials for a refrigerator door liner—where eggs, butter, salad dressings, and small bottles are stored—the following factors should be considered:

1. **Mechanical requirements:** strength, toughness (to withstand impact, door slamming, racking), stiffness, resilience, and resistance to scratching and wear at operating temperatures.
2. **Physical requirements:** dimensional stability and electrical insulation.
3. **Chemical requirements:** resistance to staining, to odor, to chemical reactions with food and beverages, and to cleaning fluids.
4. **Appearance:** color, stability of color, surface finish, texture, and feel.
5. **Manufacturing properties:** methods of manufacturing and assembly; effects of processing on material properties and behavior over a period of time; compatibility with other components in the door; and cost of materials and manufacturing.

An extensive study, considering all the factors involved, identified two candidate materials for door liners: ABS (acrylonitrile–butadiene–styrene) and HIPS (high-impact polystyrene). One aspect of the study involved the effect of vegetable oils, such as from salad dressing stored in the door shelf, on the strength of these plastics.

Experiments showed that the presence of vegetable oils significantly reduced the load-bearing capacity of HIPS. It was found that HIPS becomes brittle in the presence of oils (solvent stress cracking), whereas ABS is not affected to any significant extent.

7.8 BIODEGRADABLE PLASTICS

Plastic wastes contribute about 10% of municipal solid waste; on a volume basis, they contribute between two and three times their weight. One-third of plastic production goes into disposable products, such as bottles, packaging, and garbage bags. With the growing use of plastics, and with increasing concern over environmental issues regarding the disposal of plastic products and the shortage of landfills, major efforts are underway to develop completely biodegradable plastics. The first attempts were made in the 1980s as a possible solution to roadside litter.

Most plastic products have traditionally been made from synthetic polymers that are derived from nonrenewable natural resources, are not biodegradable, and are difficult to recycle. **Biodegradability** means that microbial species in the environment (e.g., microorganisms in soil and water) will degrade a portion of (or even the entire) polymeric material, under the right environmental conditions, and without producing toxic by-products.

The end products of the degradation of the biodegradable portion of the material are carbon dioxide and water. Because of the variety of constituents in biodegradable plastics, these plastics can be regarded as composite materials; consequently, only a portion of these plastics may be truly biodegradable.

Three different **biodegradable plastics** have thus far been developed. They have different degradability characteristics, and they degrade over different periods of time (anywhere from a few months to a few years).

a. The **starch-based** system is the farthest along in terms of production capacity. Starch may be extracted from potatoes, wheat, rice, and corn. In this system, starch granules are processed into a powder, which is heated and becomes a sticky liquid. The liquid is then cooled, formed into pellets, and processed in conventional plastic-processing equipment (which is described in Chapter 18). Various additives and binders are blended with the starch, to impart special characteristics to the bioplastic materials. For example, a composite of polyethylene and starch is now commercially produced as degradable garbage bags.

b. In the **lactic-based** system, fermenting feed stocks produce lactic acid, which is then polymerized to form a polyester resin. Typical uses include medical and pharmaceutical applications.

c. In the third system (**fermentation of sugar**), organic acids are added to a sugar feed stock. With the use of a specially developed process, the resulting reaction produces a highly crystalline and very stiff polymer which, after further processing, behaves in a manner similar to polymers developed from petroleum.

Numerous attempts are now being made to produce fully biodegradable plastics, by means of the use of various agricultural waste (*agrowastes*), plant carbohydrates, plant proteins, and vegetable oils.

Typical applications include the following:

- disposable tableware made from a cereal substitute, such as rice grains or wheat flour;
- plastics made almost entirely from starch extracted from potatoes, wheat, rice, and corn;
- plastic articles made from coffee beans and rice hulls, dehydrated and molded under high pressure and temperature;
- water-soluble and compostable polymers, for medical and surgical applications;
- food and beverage containers (made from potato starch, limestone, cellulose, and water) that can dissolve in storm sewers and oceans without affecting marine life or wildlife.

Because the development of biodegradable plastics is relatively new, their long-range performance, both during their useful life-cycle as products and in landfills, has not been fully assessed. There is also concern that emphasis on biodegradability will divert attention from the issue of *recyclability* of plastics and the efforts for *conservation* of materials and energy.

A major consideration is the fact that the cost of today's biodegradable polymers is substantially higher than that of synthetic polymers. Consequently, a mixture of agricultural waste—including hulls from corn, wheat, rice, and soy—(major component) and biodegradable polymers (minor component) is an attractive alternative.

Recycling.   For a number of years now, much effort has been expended by almost all municipalities on the collecting and recycling of used plastic products. Thermoplastics are recycled by remelting them and then reforming them into other products. These products carry *recycling symbols*, in the shape of a triangle outlined by three clockwise arrows and having a number in the middle. These numbers correspond to the following plastics:

1—PETE (polyethylene);

2—HDPE (high-density polyethylene);

3—V (vinyl);

4—LDPE (low-density polyethylene);

5—PP (polypropylene);

6—PS (polystyrene);

7—Other.

Recycled plastics are increasingly being used for a variety of products. For example, a recycled polyester, filled with glass fibers and minerals, has been selected for the engine cover for an F-series Ford pickup truck; it has the appropriate stiffness, chemical resistance, and shape retention up to 180 °C (350 °F).

A similar material was selected for the front-end panel assembly for the 1997 Chevrolet Malibu, for its impact strength and dimensional stability. Other automotive applications for such recycled plastics include heat/sound shields, duct-vent doors, fog-lamp brackets, and parking-brake wells.

7.9 ELASTOMERS (RUBBERS)

Elastomers compose a large family of amorphous polymers having a low glass-transition temperature. They have a characteristic ability to undergo large elastic deformations without rupture. They are soft, and they have a low elastic modulus. The term **elastomer** is derived from the words *elastic* and *mer*.

The structure of these polymers is highly kinked (tightly twisted or curled). They stretch, but then they return to their original shape after the load is removed (Fig. 7.12). They can also be cross-linked; the best example of that process is the elevated-temperature **vulcanization** of rubber with sulfur, discovered by C. Goodyear in 1839 and named for Vulcan, the Roman god of fire. Once the elastomer is cross-linked, it cannot be reshaped. For example, an automobile tire, which is one giant molecule, cannot be softened and reshaped.

The terms *rubber* and *elastomer* are often used interchangeably. Generally, an **elastomer** is defined as being capable of recovering substantially in shape and size after the load has been removed. A **rubber** is defined as being capable of recovering from large deformations quickly.

One property of elastomers is their hysteresis loss in stretching or compression (Fig. 7.12). The clockwise loop indicates energy loss, whereby mechanical energy is converted into heat. This property is desirable for absorbing vibrational energy (damping) and sound deadening.

The hardness of elastomers, which is measured with a durometer (Section 2.6.1), increases with cross-linking of the molecular chains. As with plastics, a variety of additives can be blended into elastomers to impart specific properties. Elastomers have a wide range of applications—for example, high-friction and nonskid surfaces, protection against corrosion and abrasion, electrical insulation, and shock and vibration insulation. Examples include tires, hoses, weatherstripping, footwear, linings, gaskets, seals, printing rolls, and flooring.

Natural Rubber.   The base for natural rubber is **latex**, a milklike sap obtained from the inner bark of a tropical tree. It has good resistance to abrasion and fatigue, and it has high frictional properties, but it has low resistance to oil, heat, ozone, and sunlight. Typical applications are tires, seals, shoe heels, couplings, and engine mounts.

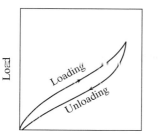

FIGURE 7.12   Typical load-elongation curve for rubbers. The clockwise loop, indicating the loading and the unloading paths, displays the hysteresis loss. Hysteresis gives rubbers the capacity to dissipate energy, damp vibration, and absorb shock loading, as is necessary in automobile tires and in vibration dampers placed under machinery.

Synthetic Rubbers.   Further developed than natural rubbers are the synthetic rubbers. Examples are synthetic natural rubber, butyl, styrene butadiene, polybutadiene, and ethylene propylene. Compared to natural rubbers, they have better resistance to heat, gasoline, and chemicals, and they have a higher range of useful temperatures.

Examples of synthetic rubbers that are resistant to oil are neoprene, nitrile, urethane, and silicone. Typical applications of synthetic rubbers are tires, shock absorbers, seals, and belts.

Silicones.   Silicones (see also Section 7.7) have the highest useful temperature range (up to 315 °C; 600 °F), but such other properties as strength and resistance to wear and oils are generally inferior to those in other elastomers. Typical applications of silicones are seals, gaskets, thermal insulation, high-temperature electrical switches, and electronic apparatus.

Polyurethane.   This elastomer has very good overall properties of high strength, stiffness, and hardness, and it has exceptional resistance to abrasion, cutting, and tearing. Typical applications are seals, gaskets, cushioning, diaphragms for the rubber forming of sheet metals (Section 16.10), and auto body parts.

SUMMARY

- Polymers are a major class of materials and possess a very wide range of mechanical, physical, chemical, and optical properties. Compared to metals, polymers are generally characterized by lower density, strength, elastic modulus, thermal and electrical conductivity, and cost, and by higher strength-to-weight ratio, higher resistance to corrosion, higher thermal expansion, wider choice of colors and transparencies, and greater ease of manufacturing into complex shapes.

- Plastics are composed of polymer molecules and various additives. The smallest repetitive unit in a polymer chain is called a mer. Monomers are linked by polymerization processes (condensation and addition) to form larger molecules. The glass-transition temperature separates the region of brittle behavior in polymers from that of ductile.

- The properties of polymers depend on the molecular weight, on the structure (linear, branched, cross-linked, or network), on the degrees of polymerization and crystallinity, and on additives. Additives have such functions as improving strength, flame retardation, and lubrication, imparting flexibility and color, and providing stability against ultraviolet radiation and oxygen. Polymer structures can be modified by several means to impart a wide range of desirable properties to plastics.

- Two major classes of polymers are the thermoplastics and the thermosets. Thermoplastics become soft and easy to form at elevated temperatures; they return to their original properties when cooled. Their mechanical behavior can be characterized by various spring and damping models; it includes such phenomena as creep and stress relaxation, crazing, and water absorption. Thermosets, which are obtained by cross-linking polymer chains, do not become soft to any significant extent with increasing temperature. They are much more rigid and harder than thermoplastics, and they offer many fewer choices of color.

- Elastomers have a characteristic ability to undergo large elastic deformations and then return to their original shapes when unloaded. Consequently, they have important applications in tires, seals, footwear, hoses, belts, and shock absorbers.

- Among important developments in polymers are recyclability and the biodegradable plastics, several formulations of which are being developed.

TRENDS

- Developments are taking place in the production of ultrahigh-purity polymers, high-temperature polymers, polymer blends, high-strength fibers, optical fibers, and multilayer films for optical applications, lenses, and recording media.

- The recyclability of plastics will continue to be an important topic in terms of environmental protection. Several biodegradable plastics are under development.

- Improvements are being made in water absorption, flammability, and degradation of plastics, as well as in their physical properties.

KEY TERMS

Additives
Biodegradability
Bonding
Branched polymers
Colorants
Crazing
Cross-linked polymers
Crystallites
Curing
Degradation
Degree of crystallinity
Degree of polymerization
Doping

Elastomer
Fillers
Flame retardants
Glass-transition temperature
Latex
Linear polymers
Lubricants
Mer
Molecular weight
Monomer
Network polymers
Orientation
Plasticizers

Plastics
Polyblends
Polymerization
Polymers
Primary bonds
Rubber
Secondary bonds
Stress whitening
Thermal aging
Thermoplastics
Thermosets
Vulcanization

BIBLIOGRAPHY

Berins, M.L., *Plastics Engineering Handbook* (5th ed.). Chapman & Hall, 1994.

Buckley, C.P., C.B. Bucknall, and N.G. McCrum, *Principles of Polymer Engineering* (2d ed.). Oxford University Press, 1997.

Colling, D.A., and T. Vasilos, *Industrial Materials: Polymers, Ceramics and Composites*. Prentice Hall, 1995.

Chanda, M., and S.K. Roy, *Plastics Technology Handbook* (3d ed.). Marcel Dekker, 1998.

Charrier, J.-M., *Polymeric Materials and Processing: Plastics, Elastomers, and Composites*. Hanser, 1991.

Domininghaus, H., *Plastic for Engineers: Materials, Properties, Applications*. Hanser Gardner, 1993.

Engineered Materials Handbook, Vol. 2: *Engineering Plastics*. ASM International, 1988.

Engineering Plastics and Composites (2d ed.). ASM International, 1993.

Fatigue and Tribological Properties of Plastics and Elastomers. William Andrew Inc., 1995.

Feldman, D., and A. Barbalata, *Synthetic Polymers: Technology, Properties, Applications*. Chapman & Hall, 1996.

Harper, C., *Handbook of Plastics, Elastomers, and Composites* (3d ed.). McGraw-Hill, 1996.

MacDermott, C.P., and A.V. Shenoy, *Selecting Thermoplastics for Engineering Applications* (2d ed.). Marcel Dekker, 1997.

Nielsen, L.E., and R.F. Landel, *Mechanical Properties of Polymers and Composites* (2d ed.). Marcel Dekker, 1994.

Rosen, S.L., *Fundamental Principles of Polymeric Materials* (2d ed.). Wiley, 1993.

Salamone, J.C. (ed.), *Concise Polymeric Materials Encyclopedia.* CRC Press, 1999.

Sperling, L.H., *Polymeric Multicomponent Materials: An Introduction.* Wiley, 1997.

Strong, A.B., *Plastics: Materials and Processing.* Prentice Hall, 1996.

REVIEW QUESTIONS

7.1 Summarize the important mechanical and physical properties of plastics.

7.2 What are the major differences between (a) the mechanical and (b) the physical properties of plastics and metals?

7.3 What are (a) polymerization and (b) degree of polymerization? What properties are influenced by the degree of polymerization?

7.4 What are the differences between linear, branched, and cross-linked polymers?

7.5 Why would we want to synthesize a polymer with a high degree of crystallinity?

7.6 What is a glass-transition temperature?

7.7 What additives are used in plastics? Why?

7.8 What is crazing?

7.9 What are polyblends?

7.10 What are the differences between thermoplastics and thermosets?

7.11 What is an elastomer?

7.12 What is a terpolymer?

7.13 What effects does a plasticizing agent have on a polymer?

7.14 Define the following acronyms: PMMA, PVC, ABS, HDPE, LDPE.

QUALITATIVE PROBLEMS

7.15 Inspect various plastic components in your automobile, and state whether you think that they are made of thermoplastic materials or of thermosetting plastics.

7.16 Give applications for which flammability of plastics would be of major importance.

7.17 What properties do elastomers have that thermoplastics in general do not have?

7.18 Do you think that the substitution of plastics for metals, in products traditionally made of metal, is viewed negatively by the public at large? If so, why?

7.19 Name three plastics that are suitable for use at elevated temperatures.

7.20 Is it possible for a material to have a hysteresis behavior that is the opposite of that shown in Fig. 7.12, so that the arrows run counterclockwise? Explain.

7.21 Observe the behavior of the specimen shown in Fig. 7.11, and state whether the material has a high or a low strain-rate sensitivity exponent m. (See Section 2.2.7.) Explain why it does.

7.22 Add more to the applications column in Table 7.3.

7.23 Discuss the significance of the glass-transition temperature, T_g, in engineering applications.

7.24 Why does cross-linking improve the strength of polymers?

7.25 Describe the methods by which optical properties of polymers can be altered.

7.26 Can polymers be made to conduct electricity? How?

7.27 Explain the reasons for which elastomers were developed. Are there any substitutes for elastomers? Explain.

7.28 Give several examples of plastic products or components in which creep and stress relaxation are important considerations.

7.29 Describe your opinions regarding the recycling of plastics vs. the development of plastics that are biodegradable.

7.30 Explain how you would go about determining the hardness of plastics.

7.31 Compare the values of the elastic modulus from Table 7.1 to the values for metals given in Chapters 2, 5, and 6.

7.32 Why is there so much variation in the stiffness of polymers?

7.33 Explain why thermoplastics are easier to recycle than thermosets.

7.34 Give an example of a process where crazing is desirable.

7.35 List and explain some environmental pros and cons of using plastic shopping bags instead of paper bags.

7.36 What characteristics are required of a polymer insert for a total hip replacement?

7.37 How can you tell whether a part is made of a thermoplastic?

7.38 As you know, there are plastic paper clips available in various colors. Why are there no plastic staples?

QUANTITATIVE PROBLEMS

7.39 Calculate the areas under the stress-strain curve (toughness) for the materials in Fig. 7.9, plot them as a function of temperature, and describe your observations.

7.40 Note in Fig. 7.9 that, as expected, the elastic modulus of the polymer decreases as temperature increases. Using the stress-strain curves in the figure, make a plot of the modulus of elasticity vs. the temperature. Comment on the shape of the curve.

7.41 A rectangular cantilever beam 120 mm high, 20 mm wide, and 1.5 m long is subjected to a concentrated load of 100 kg at its end. From Table 7.1, select three unreinforced and three reinforced materials, and calculate the maximum deflection of the beam in each case. Then select aluminum and steel for the same beam dimensions, calculate the maximum deflection, and compare the results.

7.42 Determine the dimensions of a tubular steel drive shaft for a typical automobile. If you now replace this shaft with an unreinforced and then with a reinforced plastic, what should be its new dimensions in each case, in order to transmit the same torque? Choose the materials from Table 7.1 and assume a Poisson's ratio of 0.4.

7.43 Estimate the number of molecules in a typical automobile tire. Estimate the number of atoms.

7.44 Using strength and density data, determine the minimum weight of a 2-ft long tension member which must support a load of 1000 lbs., if it is manufactured from (a) high-molecular-weight polyethylene, (b) polyester, (c) rigid polyvinyl chloride, (d) ABS, (e) polystyrene, (e) reinforced nylon. Where appropriate, calculate a range of weights for the same polymer.

7.45 Plot the following for any five polymers described in this chapter: (a) UTS vs. density, and (b) elastic modulus vs. UTS. Where appropriate, plot a range of values.

SYNTHESIS AND DESIGN

7.46 Describe the design considerations involved in replacing a metal beverage container with one made of plastic.

7.47 Assume that you are manufacturing a product in which all the gears are made of metal. A salesman visits you and asks you to consider replacing some of these metal gears with plastic ones. Make a list of the questions that you would raise before making a decision.

7.48 Sections 7.6 and 7.7 list several plastics and their applications. Rearrange this information by making a table of products (gears, helmets, luggage, electrical parts, etc.) which shows the types of plastic that can be used to make these products.

7.49 Make a list of products or parts that are not currently made of plastics, and offer some reasons why they are not. Support the reasons.

7.50 Review the three curves in Fig. 7.8, and give applications for each type of behavior. Explain your choices.

7.51 Repeat Problem 7.50 for the curves in Fig. 7.10.

7.52 In order to use a steel or aluminum container for an acidic substance, such as tomato sauce, a polymeric barrier must be placed between the container and its contents. Describe methods of producing such a barrier.

7.53 Perform a study of plastics used for some products; measure the hardness and stiffness of these plastics. (For example, dog chew toys use plastics with a range of properties.)

7.54 Add a column to Table 7.1 which describes the appearance of these plastics, especially available colors and opaqueness.

8

Ceramics, Graphite, and Diamond: Structure, General Properties, and Applications

8.1 INTRODUCTION

The metallic and nonmetallic materials described in the preceding chapters are not suitable for certain engineering applications—for example, (a) an electrical insulator to be used at high temperatures; (b) floor tiles to resist spills, scuffing, and abrasion; (c) a transparent baking dish; (d) a small ball bearing that is light, rigid, hard, and resists high temperatures; (e) the surfaces of the space shuttle orbiter, made of aluminum, when its skin temperature reaches 1450 °C (2650 °F) as it takes off and as it reenters the atmosphere.

We soon realize that we need materials that have properties such as high-temperature strength; hardness; inertness to chemicals, food, and environment; resistance to wear and corrosion; and low electrical and thermal conductivity. The materials described in this chapter generally have such desirable properties.

Ceramics are compounds of metallic and nonmetallic elements. The term *ceramics* (from the Greek words *keramos* meaning potter's clay and *keramikos* meaning clay products) refers both to the material and to the ceramic product itself. Because of the large number of possible combinations of elements, a great variety of ceramics is now available for a wide range of consumer and industrial applications.

The earliest use of ceramics was in pottery and bricks, dating back to before 4000 B.C. Ceramics have been used for many years in automotive spark plugs, as an electrical insulator and for high-temperature strength. They have become increasingly important in tool and die materials, in heat engines, and in automotive components such as exhaust-port liners, coated pistons, and cylinder liners.

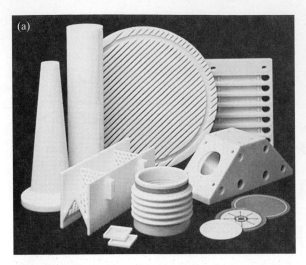
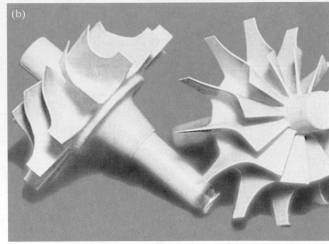

FIGURE 8.1   A variety of ceramic components. (a) Hight-strength alumina for high-temperature applications. (b) Gas-turbine rotors made of silicon nitride. *Source*: Wesgo Div., GTE.

Ceramics can be divided into two general categories:

a. traditional, such as whiteware, tiles, brick, sewer pipe, pottery, and abrasive wheels; and

b. industrial ceramics, also called **engineering**, **high-tech**, or **fine ceramics**, such as turbine, automotive, and aerospace components (Fig. 8.1); heat exchangers; semi-conductors; seals; prosthetics; and cutting tools.

This chapter describes the general characteristics and applications of those ceramics, glasses, and glass ceramics that are of importance in engineering applications and manufacturing. Because of their unique characteristics, the properties and uses of two forms of carbon, namely graphite and diamond, are also discussed here. The manufacturing of ceramic and of glass components and various shaping and finishing operations are detailed in Chapter 17. Composites, which are an important group of materials composed of ceramics, metals, and polymers, are described in Chapter 9.

8.2 THE STRUCTURE OF CERAMICS

The structure of ceramic crystals, containing various atoms of different sizes, is among the most complex of all material structures. The bonding between these atoms is generally **co-valent** (electron sharing, hence strong bonds) or **ionic** (primary bonding between oppositely charged ions, thus strong bonds). Such bonds are much stronger than metallic bonds. Consequently, properties such as hardness and thermal and electrical resistance are significantly higher in ceramics than in metals (Tables 3.1 and 3.2).

Ceramics are available as a *single crystal* or in *polycrystalline* form, consisting of many grains. Grain size has a major influence on the strength and properties of ceramics. The finer the grain size (hence the term *fine ceramics*), the higher are the strength and toughness.

8.2.1 Raw Materials

Among the oldest of the raw materials used for making ceramics is **clay**, which has a fine-grained sheetlike structure. The most commonly given example is *kaolin* (from Kao-ling, a hill in China). It is a white clay, consisting of silicate of aluminum with alternating, weakly bonded layers of silicon and aluminum ions. When added to kaolinite, water attaches itself to the layers (adsorption), making them slippery, and gives wet clay both its well-known softness and the plastic properties (*hydroplasticity*) that make it formable.

Other major raw materials for ceramics that are found in nature are *flint* (a rock composed of very fine-grained silica, SiO_2) and *feldspar* (a group of crystalline minerals consisting of aluminum silicates plus potassium, calcium, or sodium). In their natural state, these raw materials generally contain impurities of various kinds, which have to be removed prior to further processing of the materials into useful products with reliable performance. Highly refined raw materials produce ceramics with improved properties.

8.2.2 Oxide Ceramics

There are two major types of oxide ceramics: alumina and zirconia (Table 8.1).

Alumina.   Also called **corundum** or **emery**, *alumina* (aluminum oxide, Al_2O_3) is the most widely used *oxide ceramic*, either in pure form or as a raw material to be mixed

TABLE 8.1   Types and General Characteristics of Ceramics

Type	General Characteristics
Oxide ceramics	
Alumina	High hardness, moderate strength; most widely used ceramic; cutting tools, abrasives, electrical and thermal insulation.
Zirconia	High strength and toughness; thermal expansion close to cast iron; suitable for heat engine components.
Carbides	
Tungsten carbide	Hardness, strength, and wear resistance depend on cobalt binder content; commonly used for dies and cutting tools.
Titanium carbide	Not as tough as tungsten carbide; has nickel and molybdenum as the binder; used as cutting tools.
Silicon carbide	High-temperature strength and wear resistance; used for heat engines and as abrasives.
Nitrides	
Cubic boron nitride	Second-hardest substance known, after diamond; used as abrasives and cutting tools.
Titanium nitride	Gold in color; used as coatings because of low frictional characteristics.
Silicon nitride	High resistance to creep and thermal shock; used in heat engines.
Sialon	Consists of silicon nitrides and other oxides and carbides; used as cutting tools.
Cermets	Consist of oxides, carbides, and nitrides; used in high-temperature applications.
Silica	High temperature resistance; quartz exhibits piezoelectric effect; silicates containing various oxides are used in high-temperature nonstructural applications.
Glasses	Contain at least 50 percent silica; amorphous structures; several types available with a range of mechanical and physical properties.
Glass ceramics	Have a high crystalline component to their structure; good thermal-shock resistance and strong.
Graphite	Crystalline form of carbon; high electrical and thermal conductivity; good thermal shock resistance.
Diamond	Hardest substance known; available as single crystal or polycrystalline form; used as cutting tools and abrasives and as dies for fine wire drawing.

with other oxides. It has high hardness and moderate strength. Although alumina exists in nature, it contains unknown amounts of impurities and possesses nonuniform properties. As a result, its behavior is unreliable. Aluminum oxide, silicon carbide, and many other ceramics are now manufactured almost totally synthetically, so that their quality can be controlled.

First made in 1893, synthetic aluminum oxide is obtained by the fusion of molten bauxite (an aluminum oxide ore that is the principal source of aluminum), iron filings, and coke in electric furnaces. The cooled product is crushed, and then it is graded by size by passing the particles through standard screens. Parts made of aluminum oxide are cold-pressed and sintered (white ceramics). Their properties are improved by minor additions of other ceramics, such as titanium oxide and titanium carbide.

Structures containing alumina and various other oxides are known as mullite and spinel; they are used as refractory materials for high-temperature applications. The mechanical and physical properties of alumina are particularly suitable in applications such as electrical and thermal insulation and in cutting tools and abrasives (Sections 21.7 and 25.2).

Zirconia.   Zirconia (zirconium oxide, ZrO_2, white in color) has good toughness; good resistance to thermal shock, wear, and corrosion; low thermal conductivity; and a low friction coefficient. **Partially stabilized zirconia (PSZ)** has high strength and toughness and better reliability in performance than does zirconia. It is obtained by doping the zirconia with oxides of calcium, yttrium, or magnesium.

This process forms a material with fine particles of tetragonal zirconia in a cubic lattice. Typical applications include dies for hot extrusion of metals (Section 15.4.1) and zirconia beads used as grinding and dispersion media for aerospace coatings, for automotive primers and topcoats, and for fine glossy print on flexible food packaging.

Other important characteristics of PSZ are its coefficient of thermal expansion (only about 20% lower than that of cast iron) and its thermal conductivity (about one-third that of other ceramics). Because of these properties PSZ is very suitable for heat-engine components, such as cylinder liners and valve bushings, to keep the cast-iron engine assembly intact. New developments to further improve the properties of PSZ include **transformation-toughened zirconia (TTZ)**, which has higher toughness because of dispersed tough phases in the ceramic matrix.

8.2.3 Other Ceramics

Other major ceramics may be classified as follows.

Carbides.   Typical examples of **carbides** are those of tungsten (WC) and titanium (TiC), used as cutting tools and die materials, and that of silicon (SiC), used as an abrasive (especially in grinding wheels (Sections 21.5 and 25.2)).

a. **Tungsten carbide** consists of tungsten–carbide particles with cobalt as a binder. The amount of binder has a major influence on the material's properties. Toughness increases with cobalt content, whereas hardness, strength, and wear resistance decrease.

b. **Titanium carbide** has nickel and molybdenum as the binder and is not as tough as tungsten carbide.

c. Silicon carbide has good resistance to wear, thermal shock, and corrosion. It has a low friction coefficient, and it retains strength at elevated temperatures. It is suitable for high-temperature components in heat engines and is also used as an abrasive. First produced in 1891, synthetic silicon carbide is made from silica sand, coke, and small amounts of sodium chloride and sawdust. The process is similar to that for making synthetic aluminum oxide (Section 8.2.1).

Nitrides. Another important class of ceramics is the **nitrides**, particularly cubic boron nitride (CBN), titanium nitride (TiN), and silicon nitride (Si_3N_4).

a. Cubic boron nitride, the second hardest known substance (after diamond), has special applications, such as in cutting tools and for abrasives in grinding wheels. It does not exist in nature; it was first made synthetically in the 1970s, by means of techniques similar to those used in making synthetic diamond.

b. Titanium nitride is used widely as a coating on cutting tools. It improves tool life by virtue of its low frictional characteristics.

c. Silicon nitride has high resistance to creep at elevated temperatures, low thermal expansion, and high thermal conductivity; consequently, it resists thermal shock (Section 3.6). It is suitable for high-temperature structural applications, such as in automotive-engine and gas-turbine components, in cam-follower rollers, in bearings, in sand-blast nozzles, and in components for the paper industry.

Sialon. **Sialon** consists of silicon nitride with various additions of aluminum oxide, yttrium oxide, and titanium carbide. The word sialon is derived from silicon, aluminum, oxygen, and nitrogen. It has higher strength and thermal-shock resistance than silicon nitride; so far, it is used primarily as a cutting-tool material (Section 21.9).

Cermets. **Cermets** are combinations: a *ceramic* phase bonded with a *metallic* phase. Introduced in the 1960s and also called **black ceramics** or hot-pressed ceramics, they combine the high-temperature oxidation resistance of ceramics with the toughness, thermal-shock resistance, and ductility of metals. An application of cermets is in cutting tools, a typical composition being 70% aluminum oxide and 30% titanium carbide.

Other cermets contain various oxides, carbides, and nitrides. They have been developed for high-temperature applications, such as nozzles for jet engines and brakes for aircraft. Cermets can be regarded as composite materials; they can be used in various combinations of ceramics and metals bonded by powder-metallurgy techniques (Chapter 17).

8.2.4 Silica

Abundant in nature, **silica** is a polymorphic material—that is, it can have different crystal structures. The cubic structure is found in refractory bricks used for high-temperature furnace applications. Most glasses contain more than 50% silica. The most common form of silica is **quartz**, which is a hard, abrasive hexagonal crystal. It is used extensively in communications applications as an oscillating crystal of fixed frequency, because it exhibits the piezoelectric effect (Section 3.7).

Silicates are products of the reaction of silica with oxides of aluminum, magnesium, calcium, potassium, sodium, and iron. Examples are clay, asbestos, mica, and silicate glasses. **Lithium aluminum silicate** has very low thermal expansion and thermal conductivity and good thermal-shock resistance. However, it has very low strength and fatigue life. Thus it is suitable only for nonstructural applications, such as catalytic converters, regenerators, and heat-exchanger components.

8.2.5 Nanophase Ceramics and Composites

In order to improve the ductility and manufacturing properties of ceramics, particle size in ceramics has been reduced using various techniques such as gas condensation. Called **nanophase ceramics**, these materials consist of atomic clusters containing a few thousand atoms. Control of particle size, distribution, and contamination are important in these ceramics.

Nanophase ceramics exhibit ductility at significantly lower temperatures than do conventional ceramics. They are stronger and easier to fabricate and to machine, with fewer flaws. Applications are in the automotive industry (such as valves, rocker arms, turbocharger rotors, and cylinder liners) and in jet-engine components.

Nanocrystalline second-phase particles (on the order of 100 nm or less) and fibers are also being used as reinforcements in composites (Chapter 9). These composites have enhanced such properties as tensile strength and creep resistance. (See also Section 6.15 on *nanomaterials*.)

8.3 GENERAL PROPERTIES AND APPLICATIONS OF CERAMICS

Compared to metals, ceramics have the following relative characteristics: brittleness; high strength and hardness at elevated temperatures; high elastic modulus; and low toughness, density, thermal expansion, and thermal and electrical conductivity. However, because of the wide variety of ceramic-material compositions and grain sizes, the mechanical and physical properties of ceramics vary significantly. For example, the electrical conductivity of ceramics can be modified from poor to good (this change is the principle behind semiconductors (Chapter 34)).

Because of their sensitivity to flaws, to defects, and to surface or internal cracks, to the presence of different types and levels of impurities, and to different methods of manufacturing, ceramics can have a wide range of properties. Although the individual characteristics of ceramics were stated in Section 8.2, their general mechanical and physical properties are described next.

8.3.1 Mechanical Properties

The mechanical properties of several engineering ceramics are presented in Table 8.2. Note that their strength in tension (transverse rupture strength, Section 2.5) is approximately one order of magnitude lower than their compressive strength. The reason is their sensitivity to cracks, impurities, and porosity.

Such defects lead to the initiation and propagation of cracks under tensile stresses; such propagation reduces tensile strength severely. Thus, reproducibility and reliability (acceptable performance over a specified period of time) is an important aspect in the service life of ceramic components.

The tensile strength of polycrystalline ceramic parts increases with decreasing grain size and porosity. The latter relationship is approximately represented by the expression

$$UTS = UTS_o e^{-nP}, \tag{8.1}$$

TABLE 8.2   Properties of Various Ceramics at Room Temperature

Material	Symbol	Transverse rupture strength (MPa)	Compressive strength (MPa)	Elastic modulus (GPa)	Hardness (HK)	Poisson's ratio (ν)	Density (kg/m^3)
Aluminum oxide	Al_2O_3	140–240	1000–2900	310–410	2000–3000	0.26	4000–4500
Cubic boron nitride	CBN	725	7000	850	4000–5000	—	3480
Diamond	—	1400	7000	830–1000	7000–8000	—	3500
Silica, fused	SiO_2	—	1300	70	550	0.25	—
Silicon carbide	SiC	100–750	700–3500	240–480	2100–3000	0.14	3100
Silicon nitride	Si_3N_4	480–600	—	300–310	2000–2500	0.24	3300
Titanium carbide	TiC	1400–1900	3100–3850	310–410	1800–3200	—	5500–5800
Tungsten carbide	WC	1030–2600	4100–5900	520–700	1800–2400	—	10,000–15,000
Partially stabilized zirconia	PSZ	620	—	200	1100	0.30	5800

Note: These properties vary widely depending on the condition of the material.

where P is the volume fraction of pores in the solid, UTS_o is the tensile strength at zero porosity, and the exponent n ranges between 4 and 7.

The modulus of elasticity of ceramics is approximately related to porosity by the expression

$$E = E_o(1 - 1.9P + 0.9P^2),\qquad(8.2)$$

where E_o is the modulus at zero porosity.

Unlike most metals and thermoplastics, ceramics generally lack impact toughness and thermal-shock resistance, because of their inherent lack of ductility. Once initiated, a crack propagates rapidly. In addition to undergoing fatigue failure under cyclic loading, ceramics (and particularly glasses—Section 8.4) exhibit a phenomenon called **static fatigue**.

When subjected to a static tensile load over a period of time, these materials may suddenly fail. This phenomenon occurs in environments where water vapor is present. Static fatigue, which does not occur in a vacuum or in dry air, has been attributed to a mechanism similar to stress-corrosion cracking of metals (Section 2.10.2).

Ceramic components that are to be subjected to tensile stresses may be **prestressed**, in much the same way that concrete is prestressed. Prestressing the shaped ceramic components subjects them to compressive stresses. Methods used include the following:

a. heat treatment and chemical tempering (Section 17.11);
b. laser treatment of surfaces;
c. coating with ceramics having different thermal-expansion coefficients; and
d. surface-finishing operations, such as grinding, in which compressive residual stresses are induced on the surfaces.

Significant advances are being made in improving the toughness and other properties of ceramics, including the development of **machinable ceramics**. Among these advances are the proper selection and processing of raw materials, the control of purity and structure, and the use of reinforcements, with particular emphasis during design on advanced methods of stress analysis in ceramic components.

8.3.2 Physical Properties

Most ceramics have a relatively low specific gravity, ranging from about 3 to 5.8 for oxide ceramics, compared to 7.86 for iron (Table 3.1). They have very high melting or decomposition temperatures.

Thermal conductivity in ceramics varies by as much as three orders of magnitude, depending on their composition, whereas in metals it varies by only one order. Thermal conductivity of ceramics, like that of other materials, decreases with increasing temperature and porosity, because air is a poor thermal conductor.

The thermal conductivity k is related to porosity by

$$k = k_o(1 - P), \tag{8.3}$$

where k_o is the thermal conductivity at zero porosity and P is the porosity as a fraction of the total volume. Thus, if porosity is 15%, then $P = 0.15$.

Thermal expansion and thermal conductivity induce stresses that can lead to thermal shock or to thermal fatigue. The tendency toward **thermal cracking** (called **spalling** when a piece or a layer from the surface breaks off) is lower with low thermal expansion and high thermal conductivity. For example, fused silica has high thermal-shock resistance, because of its virtually zero thermal expansion.

A familiar example that illustrates the importance of low thermal expansion is heat-resistant ceramics for cookware and stove tops. (See also *glass ceramics*, Section 8.5.) They can sustain high thermal gradients, from hot to cold and vice versa. Moreover, the similar thermal expansion of ceramics and of metals is an important reason for the use of ceramic components in heat engines. The fact that the thermal conductivity of partially stabilized zirconia components is close to that of the cast iron in engine blocks is an additional advantage to the use of PSZ in heat engines.

An additional characteristic is the **anisotropy of thermal expansion** exhibited by oxide ceramics (like that exhibited by hexagonal close-packed metals); thermal expansion varies with differing direction through the ceramic (by as much as 50% for quartz). This behavior causes thermal stresses that can lead to cracking of the ceramic component.

The *optical* properties of ceramics can be controlled by using various formulations and by controlling the structure; these methods make possible the imparting of different degrees of transparency and of different colors. Single-crystal sapphire, for example, is completely transparent; zirconia is white; fine-grained polycrystalline aluminum oxide is a translucent gray. Porosity influences the optical properties of ceramics much in the same way as air trapped in ice cubes; it makes the material less transparent and gives it a white appearance.

Although, ceramics are basically resistors, they can be made electrically conducting by alloying them with certain elements, in order to make the ceramic act like a semiconductor or even like a superconductor.

8.3.3 Applications

Ceramics have numerous consumer and industrial applications. Several types of ceramics are used in the electrical and electronics industry, because they have high electrical resistivity, high dielectric strength (voltage required for electrical breakdown per unit thickness), and magnetic properties suitable for such applications as magnets for speakers. An example is **porcelain**, which is a white ceramic composed of kaolin, quartz, and feldspar; its largest use is in appliances and sanitaryware.

The capability of ceramics to maintain their strength and stiffness at elevated temperatures makes them very attractive for high-temperature applications. Their high resistance to wear makes them suitable for applications such as cylinder liners, bushings, seals, and bearings. The higher operating temperatures made possible by the use of ceramic components mean more efficient burning of fuel and reduction of emissions in automobiles. Currently, internal combustion engines are only about 30% efficient, but with the use of ceramic components the operating performance can be improved by at least 30%.

Much research has been conducted on developing materials and techniques for an all-ceramic heat engine capable of operating at temperatures up to 1000 °C (1830 °F). The development of such an engine has, however, been slower than expected because of such problems as unreliability, lack of sufficient toughness, difficulty with lubricating bearings and hot components, an unmet need for reliable nondestructive evaluation techniques, and a lack of the capability for structural ceramics (such as silicon nitride and silicon carbide) to be produced economically in near-net shape, as weighed against the need for the machining and finishing processes required for dimensional accuracy of the engine.

Consequently, all-ceramic engines are not expected until the next century. Ceramics that are being used successfully, especially in automotive gas-turbine engine components (as rotors), are silicon nitride, silicon carbide, and partially stabilized zirconia.

Coating metal with ceramics is another application; it may be done to reduce wear, to prevent corrosion, or to provide a thermal barrier. The tiles on the *space shuttle*, for example, are made of silica fibers having an open cellular structure that consists of 5% silica. The rest of the tile structure is air, so the tile is not only very light in weight but is also an excellent heat barrier. The tiles (34,000 on each shuttle) are bonded to the aluminum skin of the space shuttle with several layers of silicon-based adhesives. The skin temperature on the shuttle reaches 1400 °C (2550 °F), because of frictional heat from contact with the atmosphere.

Other attractive properties of ceramics are their low density and their high elastic modulus. They enable engine weight to be reduced and, in other applications, allow the inertial forces generated by moving parts to be lower. Ceramic turbochargers, for example, are about 40% lighter than conventional ones. High-speed components for machine tools are also candidates for ceramics (Chapter 24). Furthermore, the high elastic modulus of ceramics makes them attractive for improving the stiffness, while reducing the weight, of machines.

Bioceramics.   Because of their strength and inertness, ceramics are used as biomaterials (**bioceramics**) to replace joints in the human body, as prosthetic devices, and in dental work. Furthermore, ceramic implants can be made porous; bone can grow into the porous structure (likewise with porous titanium implants) and develop a strong bond, having high structural integrity, between them. Commonly used bioceramics are aluminum oxide, silicon nitride, and various compounds of silica.

Example: Ceramic Ball Bearings and Races

Silicon-nitride ceramic ball bearings are being used in machines, particularly in high-performance spindle bearings for machine tools. The ceramic spheres have a diameter tolerance of 0.13 μm (5 μin.) and a surface roughness of 0.02 μm (0.8 μin.). They have high wear resistance and high fracture toughness, and they perform well with little or no lubrication. The balls have a coefficient of thermal expansion one-fourth that of steel, and they can withstand temperatures of up to 1400 °C (2550 °F).

A more recent development is ball bearings and races made of a hybrid of metal and ceramic. Produced from titanium and carbon nitride by the use of powder-metallurgy techniques, the full-density titanium carbonitride (TiCN) material (mentioned in Section 21.6.3) is twice as hard as chromium steel and 40% lighter. Components up to 300 mm (12 in.) in diameter can be produced.

8.4 GLASSES

Glass is an amorphous solid with the structure of a liquid. In other words, it has been *supercooled*, that is, cooled at a rate too high to allow crystals to form. Technically, we define a glass as an inorganic product of fusion that has cooled to a rigid condition without crystallizing. Glass has no distinct melting or freezing point; its behavior is similar to that of amorphous alloys ("metallic glasses"—Section 6.14) and amorphous polymers (Section 7.2).

Glass beads were first produced in about 2000 B.C., glass-blowing followed in about 200 B.C. Silica was used for all glass products until the late 1600s. Rapid developments in glasses began in the early 1900s. Currently, there are some 750 different types of commercially available glasses.

The varieties of glass range from window glass to glass for containers, lighting, TV tubes and CRTs, and cookware to glasses with special mechanical, electrical, high-temperature, anti-chemical, corrosion, and optical characteristics. Special glasses are used in fiber optics (for communication by light with little loss in signal power) and in glass fibers with very high strength (for use in reinforced plastics—Section 9.2).

All glasses contain at least 50% silica, which is known as a **glass former**. The composition and properties of glasses, except their strength, can be modified greatly by the addition of oxides of aluminum, sodium, calcium, barium, boron, magnesium, titanium, lithium, lead, and potassium. Depending on their function, these oxides are known as **intermediates** (or **modifiers**). Glasses are generally resistant to chemical attack; they are ranked by their resistance to corrosion by acids, alkalis, or water.

8.4.1 Types of Glasses

Almost all *commercial glasses* are categorized by type (Table 8.3).

    a. soda-lime glass (the most common);

    b. lead-alkali glass;

    c. borosilicate glass;

    d. aluminosilicate glass;

    e. 96%-silica glass;

    f. fused silica glass.

TABLE 8.3   Properties of Various Glasses

	Soda-lime glass	Lead glass	Borosilicate glass	96 Percent silica	Fused silica
Density	High	Highest	Medium	Low	Lowest
Strength	Low	Low	Moderate	High	Highest
Resistance to thermal shock	Low	Low	Good	Better	Best
Electrical resistivity	Moderate	Best	Good	Good	Good
Hot workability	Good	Best	Fair	Poor	Poorest
Heat treatability	Good	Good	Poor	None	None
Chemical resistance	Poor	Fair	Good	Better	Best
Impact-abrasion resistance	Fair	Poor	Good	Good	Best
Ultraviolet-light transmission	Poor	Poor	Fair	Good	Good
Relative cost	Lowest	Low	Medium	High	Highest

Glasses are also classified as colored, opaque (white and translucent), multiform (variety of shapes), optical, photochromatic (darkens when exposed to light, as in sunglasses), photosensitive (changing from clear to opaque), fibrous (drawn into long fibers, as in fiberglass), and foam or cellular (containing bubbles, thus a good thermal insulator).

Glasses can be referred to as **hard** and **soft**, usually in the sense of a thermal property rather than a mechanical one. A soft glass softens at a lower temperature than does a hard glass. Soda–lime and lead–alkali glasses are considered soft, the rest hard.

8.4.2 Mechanical Properties

For all practical purposes, the behavior of glass, like that of most ceramics, is regarded as perfectly elastic and brittle (Section 2.10). The modulus of elasticity for commercial glasses ranges mostly from 55 GPa to 90 GPa (8 to 13 million psi), and their Poisson's ratios from 0.16 to 0.28. Hardness of glasses, as a measure of resistance to scratching, ranges from 5 to 7 on the Mohs scale; that is equivalent to a range approximately from 350 HK to 500 HK. (See Fig. 2.16.)

Glass in *bulk* form has a strength of less than 140 MPa (20 ksi). The relatively low strength of bulk glass is attributed to the presence of small flaws and microcracks on its surface, some or all of which may be introduced during normal handling of the glass by inadvertent abrading. These defects reduce the strength of glass by two to three orders of magnitude, compared to its ideal (defect-free) strength. Glasses can be strengthened by thermal or chemical treatments, to obtain high strength and toughness.

The strength of glass can theoretically reach as high as 35 GPa (5 million psi). When molten glass is freshly drawn into fibers (fiberglass), its tensile strength ranges from 0.2 GPa to 7 GPa (30 ksi to 1000 ksi), with an average value of about 2 GPa (300 ksi). Such glass fibers are stronger than steel; they are used to reinforce plastics in such applications as boats, automobile bodies, furniture, and sports equipment (Tables 2.1 and 9.1).

The strength of glass is usually measured by bending it. The surface of the glass is first thoroughly abraded (roughened) to ensure that the test gives a strength level that is reliable for actual service under adverse conditions. The phenomenon of static fatigue, observed in ceramics (Section 8.3), is also exhibited by glasses. If a glass item must withstand a load for 1000 hours or longer, the maximum stress that can be applied to it is approximately one-third the maximum stress that the same item can withstand during the first second of loading.

8.4.3 Physical Properties

Glasses have low thermal conductivity and high electrical resistivity and dielectric strength. Their thermal expansion coefficients are lower than those for metals and for plastics; they may even approach zero. For example, titanium silicate glass (a clear, synthetic high-silica glass) has a near-zero coefficient of expansion.

Fused silica, a clear, synthetic amorphous silicon dioxide of very high purity, also has a near-zero coefficient of expansion. The optical properties of glasses (such as reflection, absorption, transmission, and refraction) can be modified by varying their composition and treatment.

8.5 GLASS CERAMICS

Although glasses are amorphous, **glass ceramics** (such as *Pyroceram*, a trade name) have a high crystalline component to their microstructure. Glass ceramics contain large proportions of several oxides, and thus their properties are a combination of those for glass and those for ceramics. Most glass ceramics are stronger than glass. These products are first shaped and then heat treated, with **devitrification** (recrystallization) of the glass occurring. Unlike most glasses, which are clear, glass ceramics are generally white or gray in color.

The hardness of glass ceramics ranges approximately from 520 HK to 650 HK. They have a near-zero coefficient of thermal expansion; as a result, they have good thermal-shock resistance. They are strong, because of the absence of the porosity usually found in conventional ceramics. The properties of glass ceramics can be improved by modifying their composition and by heat-treatment techniques. First developed in 1957, glass ceramics are suitable for cookware, for the heat exchangers in gas turbine engines, for radomes (housings for radar antennas), and for electrical and electronics applications.

8.6 GRAPHITE

Graphite is a crystalline form of carbon having a *layered structure* with basal planes or sheets of close-packed carbon atoms. (See Fig. 1.4.) Consequently, graphite is weak when sheared along the layers. This characteristic, in turn, gives graphite its low frictional properties as a solid lubricant. However, its frictional properties are low only in an environment of air or moisture; in a vacuum, graphite is abrasive and is a poor lubricant. Unlike in other materials, strength and stiffness in graphite increase with temperature. Amorphous graphite is known as **lampblack** (black soot) and is used as a pigment.

Although brittle, graphite has high electrical and thermal conductivity and good resistance to thermal shock and to high temperature (although it begins to oxidize at 500 °C (930 °F). It is, therefore, an important material for applications such as electrodes, heating

FIGURE 8.2   Various engineering components made of graphite. *Source*: Poco Graphite, Inc., a Unocal Co.

elements, brushes for motors, high-temperature fixtures and furnace parts, mold materials (such as crucibles for the melting and casting of metals), and seals (Fig. 8.2).

A characteristic of graphite is its resistance to chemicals; for that reason, it is used in filters for corrosive fluids. Also, its low absorption cross-section and high scattering cross-section for thermal neutrons make graphite suitable for nuclear applications. Ordinary pencil "lead" is a mixture of graphite and clay.

Graphite is available commercially in square, rectangular, or round shapes of various sizes, and is generally graded in decreasing order of grain size: *industrial*, *fine-grain*, and *micrograin*. As in ceramics, the mechanical properties of graphite improve with decreasing grain size. Micrograin graphite can be impregnated with copper; in this form, it is used for electrodes in electrical-discharge machining and for furnace fixtures. Graphite is usually processed first by molding or forming, then by oven baking, and finally by machining to the final shape.

Graphite Fibers.   An important use of graphite is as fibers in reinforced plastics and composite materials (Section 9.2.1).

Carbon Foam.   A recent development is microcellular **carbon foam**, having isotropic strength characteristics and uniform porosity. Possible applications include its use for reinforcing components in aerospace structures (thus creating a composite material) that can be shaped directly.

Buckyballs.   A more recent development is the production of soccer-ball-shaped carbon molecules, called **buckyballs** (after Buckminster Fuller (1895–1983), inventor of the geodesic dome). Also called **fullerenes**, these chemically-inert spherical molecules are produced from soot and act much like solid lubricant particles (Section 32.11.1). Fullerenes become superconductors when mixed with metals.

8.7 DIAMOND

The second principal form of carbon is **diamond**, which has a covalently bonded structure. It is the hardest substance known (7000 HK–8000 HK). Diamond is brittle, and it begins to decompose in air at about 700 °C (1300 °F); in nonoxidizing environments, it resists higher temperatures.

Synthetic or **industrial diamond** was first made in 1955; it is used extensively in industrial applications. One method of manufacturing it is to subject graphite to a hydrostatic pressure of 14 GPa (2 million psi) and a temperature of 3000 °C (5400 °F). Synthetic diamond is identical to natural diamond, and it has superior properties because of its lack of impurities. It is available in various sizes and shapes; for abrasive machining, the most common grit size is 0.01 mm (0.004 in.) in diameter. Diamond particles can also be *coated* with nickel, copper, or titanium for improved performance in grinding operations.

A more recent development is **diamond-like carbon (DLC)**. It is used as a diamond film coating, as described in Section 33.13.

Gem-quality synthetic diamond is now made; its electrical conductivity is 50 times higher than that of natural diamond, and it is 10 times more resistant to laser damage. Possible applications are as heat sinks for computers, in telecommunications, in the integrated-circuit industries, and as windows for high-power lasers.

Because of its favorable characteristics, diamond has many important applications, such as the following:

a. cutting-tool material, as a single crystal or in polycrystalline form (Section 21.10);

b. abrasive in grinding wheels, for grinding hard materials (Section 25.2);

c. dressing of grinding wheels (i.e., sharpening of the abrasive grains);

d. dies for drawing wire less than 0.06 mm (0.0025 in.) in diameter; and

e. coatings for cutting tools and dies (Sections 21.10 and 33.13.).

SUMMARY

- Several nonmetallic materials are of great importance in engineering applications and in manufacturing processes. Ceramics, which are compounds of metallic and nonmetallic elements, are generally characterized by high hardness, high compressive strength, high elastic modulus, low thermal expansion, high temperature resistance, good chemical inertness, low density, and low thermal and electrical conductivity. On the other hand, they are brittle and they have low toughness. Nanophase ceramics are being developed, having better properties than common ceramics. Porosity in ceramics has important effects on their properties.

- Ceramics are generally categorized as either traditional or industrial (or high-tech) ceramics. The latter are particularly attractive for applications such as heat-engine components, cutting tools, and components requiring resistance against wear and corrosion. Ceramics of importance in design and manufacturing are the oxide ceramics (alumina and zirconia), the tungsten and silicon carbides, the nitrides, and the cermets.

- Glasses are supercooled liquids; that is, their rate of cooling is so high that they do not have time to solidify into a crystalline structure. Glasses are available in a wide variety of compositions and of mechanical, physical, and optical properties. Glass ceramics are predominantly crystalline in structure and have properties that are more desirable than those of glasses.

- Glass in bulk form has relatively low strength, but glasses can be strengthened by thermal and chemical treatments, in order to obtain high strength and toughness. Glass fibers are widely used as a reinforcing material in composite materials, such as in fiber-reinforced plastics.

- Graphite, fullerenes, and diamond are forms of carbon which display unusual combinations of properties. These materials have unique and emerging applications in engineering and manufacturing. Graphite has high-temperature and electrical applications; graphite fibers are used to reinforce plastics and other composite materials. Diamond (both the natural and the synthetic (or industrial)) is used as cutting tools for fine machining operations, as dies for thin-wire drawing, and as abrasives for grinding wheels. Diamond-like carbon has been developed for applications as a coating material giving improved wear resistance.

TRENDS

- Efforts are under way to improve the strength, the toughness, and the resistance to corrosion, fatigue, wear, and thermal shock of ceramics, as well as the reproducibility of their properties and their reliability in service.

- Standardized and nondestructive test methods and techniques are being developed for inspection of and for the detection of flaws in ceramic components and for the assessment of impact and of fatigue damage to components, particularly large components.

- Laser treatments and ion-implantation techniques are being developed for modifying ceramic surfaces and their properties.

- Diamond-like carbon (DLC) films are being increasingly applied to surfaces to enhance their friction and wear properties; coatings as thin as five nanometers have been used.

KEY TERMS

Alumina	Feldspar	Nitrides
Bioceramics	Flint	Oxide ceramics
Buckyballs	Fullerenes	Partially stabilized zirconia
Carbides	Glass	Porcelain
Carbon	Glass ceramics	Porosity
Carbon foam	Glass fibers	Sialon
Ceramics	Glass former	Silica
Cermets	Graphite	Static fatigue
Clay	Industrial ceramics	Transformation-toughened zirconia
Devitrification	Industrial diamond	White ceramics
Diamond	Ion implantation	Zirconia
Diamond-like carbon	Nanophase ceramics	

BIBLIOGRAPHY

Bioceramics: *Materials and Applications*. American Ceramic Society, Vol. I, 1995; Vol. II, 1996, Vol. III, 1999.

Concise Encyclopedia of Advanced Ceramics. The MIT Press, 1991.

Ellis, W.S., *Glass*, Avon Books, 1998.

Edinsinghe, M.J., *An Introduction to Structural Engineering Ceramics*. Ashgate Pub. Co., 1997.

Engineered Materials Handbook, Vol. 4: *Ceramics and Glasses*. ASM International, 1991.

Green, D.J., *An Introduction to the Mechanical Properties of Ceramics*. Cambridge Univ. Press, 1998.

Handbook of Ceramics and Composites, 3 vols. Marcel Dekker, 1991.

Hench, L.L. and J. Wilson (eds), *An Introduction to Bioceramics*. World Scientific Pub., 1993.

Mostaghaci, H. (ed.), *Advanced Ceramic Materials*. Trans Tech Pub., 1996.

Pfaender, H.G. (ed.), *Schott Guide to Glass*. Chapman & Hall, 1996.

Pierson, H.O., *Handbook of Carbon, Graphite, Diamond and Fullerenes: Properties, Processing and Applications*: Noyes Pub., 1993.

Prelas, M.A., G. Popovichi, and L.K. Bigelow (eds.), *Handbook of Industrial Diamonds and Diamond Films*. Marcel Dekker, 1998.

Rice, R.W., *Porosity of Ceramics*. Marcel Dekker, 1998.

Richerson, D. W., *Modern Ceramic Engineering* (2d ed.). Marcel Dekker, 1992.

Schwartz, M. M. (ed.), *Handbook of Structural Ceramics*. McGraw-Hill, 1992.

Shackelford, J.F. (ed.), *Bioceramics*, 1999.

Wachtman, Jr., J.B., *Mechanical Properties of Ceramics*. Wiley, 1996.

Weimer, A. (ed.), *Carbide, Nitride and Boride Materials Synthesis and Processing*. Chapman & Hall, 1997.

REVIEW QUESTIONS

8.1 Compare the major differences between the properties of ceramics and those of metals and plastics.

8.2 List the major types of ceramics that are useful in engineering applications.

8.3 What do the following materials consist of? (a) carbides; (b) cermets; (c) sialon.

8.4 List the major limitations of ceramics.

8.5 What is porcelain?

8.6 What is glass? Why is it called a supercooled material?

8.7 What is devitrification?

8.8 List the major types of glasses and their applications.

8.9 What is static fatigue?

8.10 Describe the major uses of graphite.

8.11 What is the significance of Al_2O_3 in this chapter?

8.12 How are alumina ceramics produced?

8.13 What is the difference between a carbide and a nitride?

8.14 What features of partially-stabilized zirconia differentiate it from other ceramics?

8.15 Is diamond a ceramic? Why or why not?

8.16 What is a buckyball?

8.17 What are the major uses of diamonds?

QUALITATIVE PROBLEMS

8.18 Explain why ceramics are weaker in tension than in compression.

8.19 What are the advantages of cermets? Suggest applications in addition to those given in the text.

8.20 Explain why the electrical and thermal conductivity of ceramics decreases with increasing porosity.

8.21 Explain why the mechanical property data in Table 8.1 have such a broad range. What is the significance in engineering practice?

8.22 What reasons can you think of that encouraged the development of synthetic diamond?

8.23 Explain why the mechanical properties of ceramics are generally better than those of metals.

8.24 How are ceramics made tougher?

8.25 Mention and describe applications in which static fatigue can be important.

8.26 How does porosity affect the mechanical properties of ceramics, and why does it do so?

8.27 What properties are important in making heat-resistant ceramics for use on oven tops? Why?

8.28 Describe the differences between the properties of glasses and those of ceramics.

8.29 A large variety of glasses is now available. Why is this so?

8.30 What is the difference between the structure of graphite and that of diamond? Is it important? Explain.

8.31 What materials are suitable for use as a coffee cup? Explain.

8.32 Aluminum oxide and partially stabilized zirconia are described as white in appearance. Can they be colored? If they can, how would you accomplish this?

8.33 Both ceramics and metal castings (Part II) are known to be stronger in compression than in tension. What similar causative reasons exist for these behaviors?

8.34 Why does the strength of a ceramic part depend on its size?

8.35 In old castles and churches in Europe, the glass windows display pronounced ripples and are thicker at the bottom than at the top. Explain why this has occurred.

8.36 Ceramics are hard and strong in compression and shear. Why, then, are they not used as nails or other fasteners?

8.37 It was stated in the text that ceramics have a wider range of strengths in tension than metals. List reasons why this is so, with respect to both the ceramic properties that cause variations and the difficulties in obtaining repeatable results.

QUANTITATIVE PROBLEMS

8.38 If a fully dense ceramic has the properties that $UTS_o = 180$ MPa and $E_o = 300$ GPa, what are these properties at 20% porosity for values of $n = 4, 5, 6,$ and 7, respectively?

8.39 Plot the UTS, E, and k values for ceramics as a function of porosity P, and describe and explain the trends that you observe in their behavior.

8.40 What would be the tensile strength and the modulus of elasticity of the ceramic in Problem 8.38, for porosities of 10% and 30%, for the four n values given?

8.41 Calculate the thermal conductivities for ceramics at porosities of 10%, 20%, and 30%, for $k_o = 0.7$ W/m $\cdot$ K.

8.42 A ceramic has $k_o = 0.65$ W/m $\cdot$ K. If this ceramic is shaped into a cylinder with a porosity distribution given by $P = 0.1(x/L)(1 - x/L)$, where x is the distance from one end of the cylinder and L is the total cylinder length, plot the porosity as a function of distance, evaluate the average porosity, and calculate the average thermal conductivity.

8.43 It can be shown that the minimum weight of a column which will support a given load depends on the ratio of the material's stiffness to the square root of its density. Plot this property for a ceramic as a function of porosity.

SYNTHESIS AND DESIGN

8.44 Make a list of the ceramic parts that you can find around your house and in your car. Explain why those parts are made of ceramics.

8.45 Assume that you are in technical sales and are fully familiar with all the advantages and limitations of ceramics. Which of the markets traditionally using nonceramic materials do you think ceramics can penetrate? What would you say to your potential customers during your sales visits? What kind of questions do you think they will ask?

8.46 Describe applications in which a ceramic material with a near-zero coefficient of thermal expansion would be desirable.

8.47 The modulus of elasticity of ceramics is largely maintained at elevated temperatures. What engineering applications could benefit from this characteristic?

8.48 List and discuss the factors that you would take into account when replacing a metal component with a ceramic component.

8.49 Obtain some data from the available technical literature, and quantitatively show the effect of temperature on the strength and the modulus of elasticity of several ceramics. Comment on how the shape of these curves differs from those for metals.

8.50 Assume that the cantilever beam in Quantitative Problem 3.16 in Chapter 3 is made of ceramic. How different would your answer be, compared to that of a beam made of metal? Explain clearly, giving numerical examples.

8.51 It was noted in Section 8.4.1 that there are several basic types of glasses available. Make a survey of the available technical literature, and prepare a table for these glasses, indicating various mechanical, physical, and optical properties.

8.52 Ceramic pistons are being considered for a high-speed combustion engine. List the benefits and concerns that you would have regarding this application.

8.53 Pyrex cookware displays a unique phenomenon: it functions well for a large number of cycles and then shatters into many pieces. Investigate this phenomenon, list the probable causes, and discuss the manufacturing considerations that may alleviate or contribute to such failures.

9

Composite Materials: Structure, General Properties, and Applications

9.1 INTRODUCTION

Among the major developments in materials in recent years are **composite materials**. In fact, composites are now one of the most important classes of **engineered materials**, because they offer several outstanding properties as compared to conventional materials. A composite material is a combination of two or more chemically distinct and insoluble phases; its properties and structural performance are superior to those of the constituents acting independently.

In Chapter 7 it was shown that plastics possess mechanical properties that are generally inferior to those of metals and alloys—in particular, low strength, stiffness, and creep resistance. These properties can be improved by embedding reinforcements of various types (such as glass or graphite fibers) to produce **reinforced plastics**. Metals and ceramics, as well, can be embedded with particles or fibers, to improve their properties; these combinations are known as **metal-matrix** and **ceramic-matrix** composites. As shown in Table 7.1, fiber reinforcements improve the strength, the stiffness, and the creep resistance of plastics, as well as their strength-to-weight and stiffness-to-weight ratios.

Composite materials have found increasingly wider applications in aircraft (Fig. 9.1), space vehicles, offshore structures, piping, electronics, automobiles, boats, and sporting goods. The oldest example of composites is the addition of straw to clay in the making of mud huts and of bricks for structural use; this combination dates back to 4000 B.C. In that application, the straws are the reinforcing fibers, and the clay is the matrix.

Another example of a composite material is the reinforcement of masonry and concrete with iron rods, which was begun in the 1800s. In fact, concrete itself is a composite material,

221

FIGURE 9.1 Application of advanced composite materials in Boeing 757-200 commercial aircraft. *Source*: Boeing Commercial Airplane Company.

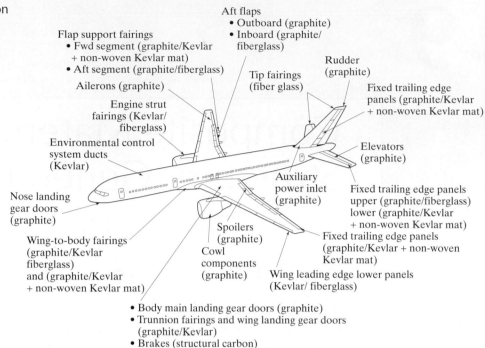

Flap support fairings
• Fwd segment (graphite/Kevlar + non-woven Kevlar mat)
• Aft segment (graphite/fiberglass)

Aft flaps
• Outboard (graphite)
• Inboard (graphite/ fiberglass)

Ailerons (graphite)

Engine strut fairings (Kevlar/ fiberglass)

Tip fairings (fiber glass)

Rudder (graphite)

Fixed trailing edge panels (graphite/Kevlar + non-woven Kevlar mat)

Environmental control system ducts (Kevlar)

Elevators (graphite)

Auxiliary power inlet (graphite)

Nose landing gear doors (graphite)

Fixed trailing edge panels upper (graphite/fiberglass) lower (graphite/Kevlar + non-woven Kevlar mat)

Spoilers (graphite)

Fixed trailing edge panels (graphite/Kevlar + non-woven Kevlar mat)

Wing-to-body fairings (graphite/Kevlar fiberglass) and (graphite/Kevlar + non-woven Kevlar mat)

Cowl components (graphite)

Wing leading edge lower panels (Kevlar/ fiberglass)

• Body main landing gear doors (graphite)
• Trunnion fairings and wing landing gear doors (graphite/Kevlar)
• Brakes (structural carbon)

consisting of cement, sand, and gravel. In reinforced concrete, steel rods impart the necessary tensile strength to the composite; concrete by itself is brittle, and it generally has little or no useful tensile strength.

This chapter describes the structure of composite materials, the types of reinforcing fibers used and their characteristics, and some of the major applications of these materials. The processing and the shaping of composite materials are described in Chapter 18.

9.2 THE STRUCTURE OF REINFORCED PLASTICS

Reinforced plastics, also known as **polymer-matrix composites (PMC)** and **fiber-reinfoced plastics (FRP)**, consist of **fibers** (the discontinuous or dispersed phase) in a plastic **matrix** (the continuous phase), as shown in Fig. 9.2. Commonly used fibers are glass, graphite, aramids, and boron.

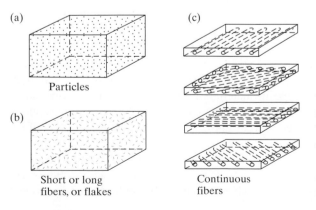

(a) Particles

(b) Short or long fibers, or flakes

(c) Continuous fibers

FIGURE 9.2 Schematic ilustration of methods of reinforcing plastics (matrix) with (a) particles, and (b) short or long fibers or flakes. The four layers of continuous fibers in illustration (c) are assembled into a laminate structure.

TABLE 9.1   Types and General Characteristics of Composite Materials

Material	Characteristics
Fibers	
Glass	High strength, low stiffness, high density; lowest cost; E (calcium aluminoborosilicate) and S (magnesia-aluminosilicate) types commonly used.
Graphite	Available as high-modulus or high-strength; low cost; less dense than glass.
Boron	High strength and stiffness; highest density; highest cost; has tungsten filament at its center.
Aramids (Kevlar)	Highest strength-to-weight ratio of all fibers; high cost.
Other fibers	Nylon, silicon carbide, silicon nitride, aluminum oxide, boron carbide, boron nitride, tantalum carbide, steel, tungsten, molybdenum.
Matrix materials	
Thermosets	Epoxy and polyester, with the former most commonly used; others are phenolics, fluorocarbons, polyethersulfone, silicon, and polyimides.
Thermoplastics	Polyetheretherketone; tougher than thermosets but lower resistance to temperature.
Metals	Aluminum, aluminum-lithium, magnesium, and titanium; fibers are graphite, aluminum oxide, silicon carbide, and boron.
Ceramics	Silicon carbide, silicon nitride, aluminum oxide, and mullite; fibers are various ceramics.

These fibers are strong and stiff (Table 9.1), and they have high specific strength (strength-to-weight ratio) and specific stiffness (stiffness-to-weight ratio), as shown in Fig. 9.3. Generally, however, they are brittle and abrasive, lack toughness, and can degrade chemically when exposed to the atmosphere. As also noted in the bottom of Table 9.2, the properties of fibers can vary significantly, depending on the quality of the material and on the method of processing.

The fibers by themselves have little structural value. The plastic matrix is less strong and less stiff, but it is tougher than the fibers. Reinforced plastics possess the advantages of each of the two constituents. The percentage of fibers (by volume) in reinforced plastics usually ranges between 10% and 60%.

Practically, the percentage of fiber in a matrix is limited by the average distance between adjacent fibers or particles. The highest practical fiber content is 65%; higher percentages generally result in lower structural properties. When more than one type of fiber

FIGURE 9.3   Specific tensile strength (tensile strength-to-density ratio) and specific tensile modulus (modulus of elasticity-to-density ratio) for various fibers used in reinforced plastics. Note the wide range of specific strengths and stiffnesses available.

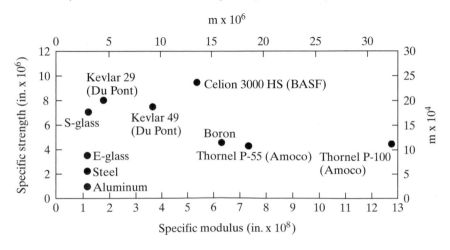

is used in a reinforced plastic, the composite is called a **hybrid**; hybrids generally have even better properties, but they are more costly.

In addition to high specific strength and specific stiffness, reinforced-plastic structures have improved fatigue resistance, greater toughness, and higher creep resistance than those made of unreinforced plastics. Such structures are relatively easy to design, fabricate, and repair.

9.2.1 Reinforcing Fibers

Reinforcing fibers for polymer-matrix composites are generally glass, graphite, aramids, or boron (Table 9.2).

Glass.   Glass fibers are the most widely used and the least expensive of all fibers. The composite material is called **glass-fiber reinforced plastic (GFRP)** and may contain between 30% and 60% glass fibers by volume. Glass fibers are made by drawing molten glass through small openings in a platinum die.

There are several principal types of glass fibers:

a. **E type**, a calcium aluminoborosilicate glass—the type most commonly used;
b. **S type**, a magnesia-aluminosilicate glass, offering higher strength and stiffness but at greater cost;
c. **E-CR** type, a more recently developed, high-performance glass fiber, offering higher resistance to elevated temperatures and acid corrosion than does the E glass.

Graphite.   Graphite fibers (Fig. 9.4a), although more expensive than glass fibers, have a combination of low density, high strength, and high stiffness. The product is called **carbon-fiber reinforced plastic (CFRP)**. All graphite fibers are made by **pyrolysis** of organic **precursors**, commonly *polyacrylonitrile* (PAN) because of its low cost. *Rayon* and *pitch* (the residue from catalytic crackers in petroleum refining) can also be used as precursors.

Pyrolysis is the process of inducing chemical changes by heat—for instance, by burning a length of yarn and causing the material to carbonize and become black in color. The temperatures for carbonizing range up to about 1500 °C (2730 °F); for graphitizing, to 3000 °C (5400 °F).

TABLE 9.2   Typical Properties of Reinforcing Fibers

Type	Tensile strength (MPa)	Elastic modulus (GPa)	Density $\left(kg/m^3\right)$	Relative cost
Boron	3500	380	2600	Highest
Carbon				
High strength	3000	275	1900	Low
High modulus	2000	415	1900	Low
Glass				
E type	3500	73	2480	Lowest
S type	4600	85	2540	Lowest
Kevlar				
29	2800	62	1440	High
49	2800	117	1440	High

Note: These properties vary significantly depending on the material and method of preparation.

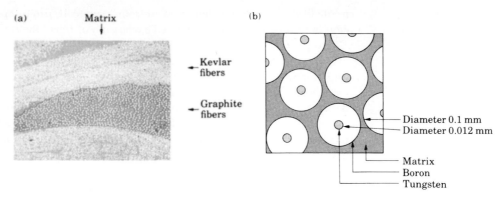

FIGURE 9.4   (a) Cross-section of a tennis racket, showing graphite and aramid (Kevlar) reinforcing fibers. *Source*: J. Dvorak, Mercury Marine Corporation, and F. Garrett, Wilson Sporting Goods Co. (b) Cross-section of boron fiber-reinforced composite material.

The difference between **carbon** and **graphite**, although the words are often used interchangeably, depends on the temperature of pyrolysis and the purity of the material. Carbon fibers are generally 80% to 95% carbon; graphite fibers are usually more than 99% carbon. A typical carbon fiber usually contains amorphous (noncrystalline) carbon and graphite (crystalline carbon). The fibers are classified by their elastic modulus, which ranges from 35 GPa to 800 GPa: *low*, *intermediate*, *high*, and *very high modulus*. Tensile strengths range from 250 MPa to 2600 MPa.

Conductive graphite fibers are now being produced, to make it possible to enhance the electrical and thermal conductivity of reinforced plastic components. The fibers are coated with a metal, usually nickel, using a continuous electroplating process. The coating is typically 0.5 μm thick, on a 7 μm-diameter graphite fiber core. Available in a chopped or a continuous form, the fibers are incorporated directly into the injection-molded plastic parts (Section 18.3). Applications include electromagnetic and radio-frequency shielding and lightning-strike protection.

Aramids.   Aramids (Section 7.6) are among the toughest fibers; they have very high specific strengths (Fig. 9.3). A common aramid is marketed under the trade name **Kevlar**. Aramids can undergo some plastic deformation before fracture, and so they have higher toughness than brittle fibers. However, aramids absorb moisture (hygroscopic); this propensity degrades their properties and complicates their application.

Boron.   Boron fibers consist of boron deposited (by chemical vapor-deposition techniques) onto tungsten fibers (Fig. 9.4b), although boron can also be deposited onto carbon fibers. These fibers have desirable properties, such as high strength and stiffness both in tension and in compression and resistance to high temperatures. Because of the high density of tungsten, they are, however, heavy, and are also expensive; their use increases the weight and the cost of the reinforced-plastic component.

Other Fibers.   Other fibers that are being used are nylon, silicon carbide, silicon nitride, aluminum oxide, sapphire, steel, tungsten, molybdenum, boron carbide, boron nitride, and tantalum carbide. **Whiskers** are also used as reinforcing fibers. They are tiny needlelike single crystals that grow to from 1 μm to 10 μm (40 μin. to 400 μin.) in diameter; they have aspect ratios (defined as the ratio of fiber length to diameter) ranging from 100 to 15,000.

Because of their small size, whiskers are either free of imperfections or the imperfections they contain do not significantly affect their strength, which approaches the theoretical strength of the material (size effect). The elastic moduli of whiskers range between 400 GPa and 700 GPa, and their tensile strength is on the order of 15 GPa to 20 GPa.

A high-performance polyethylene fiber is now available; called **Spectra** fiber (a trade name), it has ultra-high molecular weight and high molecular-chain orientation. The fiber has better abrasion resistance and flexural-fatigue resistance than the aramid fiber, yet a similar cost. In addition, because of its lower density (970 kg/m^3), it has higher specific strength and specific stiffness than the aramid fiber. A low melting point and poor adhesion to other polymers are its major limitations in various applications.

9.2.2 Fiber Size and Length

The mean diameter of fibers used in reinforced plastics is usually less than 0.01 mm (0.0004 in.). The fibers are very strong and stiff in tension. The reason is that the molecules in the fibers are oriented in the longitudinal direction, and their cross-sections are so small that the probability is low that any defects exist in the fiber. Glass fibers, for example, can have tensile strengths as high as 4600 MPa (650 ksi), whereas the strength of glass in bulk form is much lower.

Fibers are classified as **short** or **long** fibers, also called **discontinuous** or **continuous** fibers, respectively. Short fibers generally have aspect ratios between 20 and 60, long fibers have between 200 and 500. The designations "short" and "long" fiber are, in general, based on the following distinction: In a given type of fiber, if the mechanical properties improve as a result of increasing the average fiber length, then it is called a *short fiber*. If no such improvement in properties occurs, it is called a *long fiber*.

Reinforcing elements may also be in the form of chopped fibers, particles, or flakes, or even in the form of continuous *roving* (slightly twisted strand of fibers), *woven* fabric (similar to cloth), *yarn* (twisted strand), and *mats* of various combinations. Hybrid yarns are also available.

9.2.3 Matrix Materials

The matrix in reinforced plastics has three functions:

a. to support the fibers in place and transfer the stresses to them, while they carry most of the load;

b. to protect the fibers against physical damage and the environment.

c. to reduce the propagation of cracks in the composite, by virtue of the greater ductility and toughness of the plastic matrix.

Matrix materials are usually thermoplastics or thermosets; they commonly consist of epoxy, polyester, phenolic, fluorocarbon, polyethersulfone, or silicon (Sections 7.6 and 7.7). The most commonly used are the epoxies (80% of all reinforced plastics) and the polyesters, which are less expensive than the epoxies. Polyimides, which resist exposure to temperatures in excess of 300 °C (575 °F), are being developed for use with graphite fibers.

Some thermoplastics, such as polyetheretherketone (PEEK), are also used as matrix materials. They generally have higher toughness than thermosets, but their resistance to temperature is lower, being limited to 100 °C–200 °C (200 °F–400 °F).

9.3 PROPERTIES OF REINFORCED PLASTICS

The mechanical and physical properties of reinforced plastics depend on the kind, the shape, and the orientation of the reinforcing material, the length of the fibers, and the volume fraction (percentage) of the reinforcing material. Short fibers are less effective than long fibers (Fig. 9.5), and their properties are strongly influenced by time and temperature. Long fibers transmit the load through the matrix better, so they are commonly used in critical applications, particularly at elevated temperatures.

Fiber reinforcement also affects other properties of composites; physical properties and resistance to fatigue, creep, and wear depend on the type and amount of reinforcement. Reinforced plastics may also be made from various other materials and with other shapes for the polymer matrix, in order to impart specific properties (such as permeability and dimensional stability), to make processing easier, and to reduce production costs.

A critical factor in reinforced plastics is the strength of the bond between the fiber and the polymer matrix, because the load is transmitted through the fiber–matrix interface. Weak bonding causes **fiber pullout** and **delamination** of the structure, particularly under adverse environmental conditions.

FIGURE 9.5   The effect of type of fiber on various properties of fiber-reinforced nylon (6,6). *Source*: NASA.

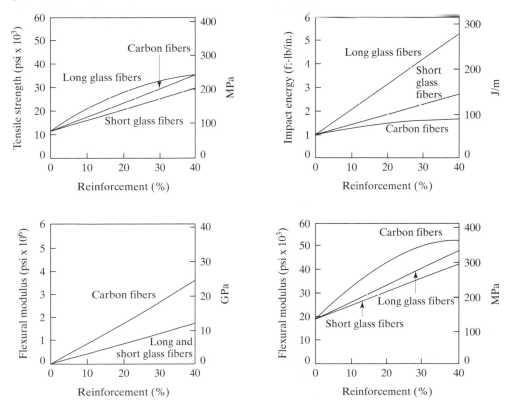

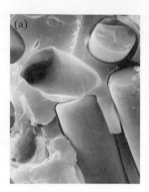

FIGURE 9.6   (a) Fracture surface of glass-fiber reinforced epoxy composite. The fibers are 10 μm (400 μin.) in diameter and have random orientation. (b) Fracture surface of a graphite-fiber reinforced epoxy composite. The fibers, 9 μm–11 μm in diameter, are in bundles and are all aligned in the same direction. *Source*: L. J. Broutman.

Adhesion at the interface can be improved by special surface treatments, such as coatings and coupling agents. Glass fibers, for example, are treated with a chemical called **silane** (a silicon hybride), for improved wetting and bonding between the fiber and the matrix. The importance of proper bonding can be appreciated by inspecting the fracture surfaces of reinforced plastics shown in Figs. 9.6a and b. Note, for example, the separation between the fibers and the matrix; obviously, better adhesion between them improves the overall strength of the composite.

Generally, the highest stiffness and strength in reinforced plastics is obtained when the fibers are aligned in the direction of the tension force. This composite is, of course, highly anisotropic (Fig. 9.7). As a result, other properties of the composite, such as stiffness, creep resistance, thermal and electrical conductivity, and thermal expansion, are also anisotropic. The transverse properties of such a unidirectionally reinforced structure are much lower than the longitudinal properties. Note, for example, how strong fiber-reinforced packaging tape is when pulled in tension, yet how easily it can split when pulling in the width direction.

For a specific service condition, we can give a reinforced plastic part an optimal configuration. For example, if the reinforced plastic part is to be subjected to forces in different directions (such as in thin-walled, pressurized vessels), (a) the fibers can be crisscrossed in the matrix, or (b) layers of fibers oriented in different directions can be built up into a laminate having improved properties in more than one direction. (See *filament winding*, Section 18.12.2.)

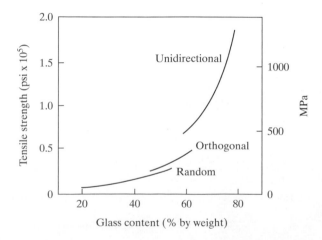

FIGURE 9.7   The tensile strength of glass-reinforced polyester as a function of fiber content and fiber direction in the matrix. *Source*: R. M. Ogorkiewicz, *The Engineering Properties of Plastics*. Oxford: Oxford University Press, 1977.

A composite flywheel rotor has been produced using a special weaving technique, in which the reinforcing fibers (E-glass) are aligned in the radial direction as well as in the hoop direction. Designed for mechanical-energy storage systems in low-emissions electric and hybrid vehicles, the flywheel can operate at speeds up to 50,000 rpm.

Example: Strength and Elastic Modulus of Reinforced Plastics

The strength and elastic modulus of a reinforced plastic with longitudinal fibers can be determined in terms of the strength and moduli both of the fibers and of the matrix and in terms of the volume fraction of fibers in the composite. In the following equations, c refers to the composite, f to the fiber, and m to the matrix. The total load P_c on the composite is shared by the fiber (P_f) and the matrix (P_m); thus,

$$P_c = P_f + P_m, \tag{9.1}$$

which we can write as

$$\sigma_c A_c = \sigma_f A_f + \sigma_m A_m, \tag{9.2}$$

where A_c, A_f, and A_m are the cross-sectional areas of the composite, the fiber, and the matrix, respectively; thus $A_c = A_f + A_m$.

Let's now denote x as the area fraction of the fibers in the composite. (Note that x also represents the volume fraction, because the fibers are uniformly longitudinal in the matrix.) We may now rewrite Eq. (9.2) as follows:

$$\sigma_c = x\sigma_f + (1 - x)\sigma_m. \tag{9.3}$$

We can now calculate the fraction of the total load carried by the fibers. First, we note that, in the composite under a tension load, the strains sustained by the fibers and the matrix are the same (that is, $e_c = e_f = e_m$). Next, we recall, from Section 2.2, that

$$e = \frac{\sigma}{E} = \frac{P}{AE}.$$

Consequently,

$$\frac{P_f}{P_m} = \frac{A_f E_f}{A_m E_m}. \tag{9.4}$$

We know the relevant quantities for a specific situation, so by using Eq. (9.1), we can determine the fraction P_f/P_c. Then, using the foregoing relationships, we can calculate the elastic modulus, E_c, of the composite, by replacing σ in Eq. (9.3) with E. Thus,

$$E_c = xE_f + (1 - x)E_m. \tag{9.5}$$

Let us now assume that a graphite–epoxy reinforced plastic with longitudinal fibers contains 20% graphite fibers. The elastic modulus of the fiber is 300 GPa, and that of the epoxy matrix is 100 GPa. Calculate the elastic modulus of the composite and the fraction of the load supported by the fibers.

Solution: The data given are $x = 0.2$, $E_f = 300$ GPa, and $E_m = 100$ GPa. Using Eq. (9.5), we find that

$$E_c = 0.2(300) + (1 - 0.2)100 = 60 + 80 = 140 \text{ GPa}.$$

We obtain the load fraction P_f/P_m from Eq. (9.4):

$$\frac{P_f}{P_m} = 0.2\frac{(300)}{0.8(100)} = 0.75.$$

Because

$$P_c = P_f + P_m \quad \text{and} \quad P_m = \frac{P_f}{0.75},$$

we find that

$$P_c = P_f + \frac{P_f}{0.75} = 2.33P_f, \quad \text{or} \quad P_f = 0.43P_c.$$

We have shown that the fibers support 43% of the load, even though they occupy only 20% of the cross-sectional area (and hence volume) of the composite.

9.4 APPLICATIONS OF REINFORCED PLASTICS

The first application of reinforced plastics (in 1907) was for an acid-resistant tank, made of a phenolic resin with asbestos fibers. *Formica*, commonly used for counter tops, was developed in the 1920s. Epoxies were first used as a matrix material in the 1930s. Beginning in the 1940s, boats were made with fiberglass, and reinforced plastics were used for aircraft, electrical equipment, and sporting goods. Major developments in composites began in the 1970s; those materials are now called **advanced composites**. Glass- or carbon-fiber reinforced hybrid plastics are now being developed for high-temperature applications, with continuous use ranging up to about 300 °C (550 °F).

Reinforced plastics are typically used in military and commercial aircraft and in rocket components, helicopter blades, automobile bodies, leaf springs, drive shafts, pipes, ladders, pressure vessels, sporting goods, sports and military helmets, boat hulls, and various other structures and components. In order to save weight in the transmissions of appliances, gears have been made consisting of glass-fiber reinforced acetal copolymer, by means of the injection-molding process (Section 18.3). These gears have the proper strength and the close tolerances necessary to offer a lengthy projected service life.

Applications of reinforced plastics include components in the DC-10, the L-1011, and the Boeing 727, 757, 767, and 777 commercial aircraft. The Boeing 777 is made of about 9% composites by total weight; that proportion is triple the composite content of previous Boeing transport aircraft. The floor beams and panels and most of the vertical and horizontal tail are made of composite materials. By virtue of the resulting weight savings, reinforced plastics have reduced fuel consumption by about 2%.

Substituting graphite–epoxy reinforced plastics for aluminum in large commercial aircraft could reduce both weight and production costs by 30%, while offering improved resistance to fatigue and corrosion. The structure of the Lear Fan 2100 passenger aircraft is almost totally made of graphite–epoxy reinforced plastic. Nearly 90% of the structure of the lightweight Voyager aircraft, which circled the earth without refueling, was made of carbon-reinforced plastic.

The contoured frame of the Stealth bomber is made of composites consisting of carbon and glass fibers, epoxy-resin matrices, high-temperature polyimides, and other advanced materials. Boron-fiber reinforced composites are used in military aircraft, in golf-club shafts, in tennis rackets, in fishing rods, and in sailboards (Fig. 9.8).

The processing of reinforced plastics presents significant challenges; several innovative techniques have been developed for manufacturing both large and small parts, particularly by molding, forming, cutting, and assembly. Careful inspection and testing of reinforced plastics is essential in critical applications, in order to ensure that good bonding between the reinforcing fiber and the matrix has been obtained throughout the structure. In some instances, the cost of inspection can be as high as one-quarter of the total cost of the composite product.

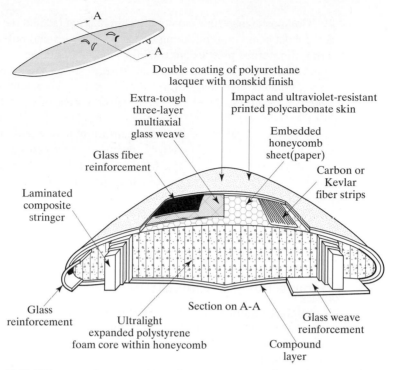

A

A

Double coating of polyurethane
lacquer with nonskid finish

Extra-tough
three-layer
multiaxial
glass weave

Impact and ultraviolet-resistant
printed polycarbonate skin

Glass fiber
reinforcement

Embedded
honeycomb
sheet(paper)

Laminated
composite
stringer

Carbon or
Kevlar
fiber strips

Glass
reinforcement

Section on A-A

Ultralight
expanded polystyrene
foam core within honeycomb

Glass weave
reinforcement

Compound
layer

FIGURE 9.8   Cross-section of a composite sailboard, an example of advanced materials construction. *Source*: K. Easterling, *Tomorrow's Materials* (2d ed.), p. 133. Institute of Metals, 1990.

Example: Composite Blades for Helicopters

Metal blades on helicopters are now being replaced by blades made of composite materials, principally S-glass fibers in an epoxy matrix (because S glass has a higher fatigue life than E glass). These blades have high stiffness, strength, resilience, and resistance to temperature and fatigue. They also have high impact strength; consequently, as compared to metal blades, composites can withstand a major ballistic impact without catastrophic failure and the helicopter can return safely to its base.

Furthermore, repairs of damaged blades can be made in the field, whereas metal blades require more extensive maintenance. It has also been shown that glass-reinforced composite blades have a better cost/performance ratio, and they are superior to aramid- or carbon-reinforced composites as well.

Example: Fiberglass Ladders

The traditional material for ladders is wood or aluminum. Partly because of its weight, a wood ladder gives the user a sense of security. However, wood can have internal and external defects that, if undetected, can significantly reduce the strength of the ladder. When dry, wood does not conduct electricity; when wet, however, it does so, and one should, therefore, not use a wet wood ladder near exposed electrical wiring.

Aluminum ladders are lightweight, and they can be designed for high strength and stiffness. They are longer-lasting than wood ladders, and they require little maintenance, but they conduct electricity.

Composite materials are now used in making ladders for various uses. Fiberglass is the most common reinforcing fiber, with epoxies and polyesters as the matrix material. Reinforced plastics are used for the rails of ladders, while the rungs are made of aluminum. These ladders have advantages similar to aluminum, and because they do not conduct electricity they are preferred by electricians. Fiberglass-reinforced ladders have a rugged feel and give the user a sense of security, and they can be made in various colors.

Fiberglass ladders can, however, absorb moisture and undergo surface weathering when exposed to outdoor environments, especially in warm and moist climates and in sunlight (Section 7.3). There is a loss of color and gloss, and the surface becomes rougher, on account of fiber prominence due to erosion of the matrix resin and to fiber blooming (exposure of fibers). These ladders can be coated with polyurethane for surface protection. Proper maintenance and periodic inspection of fiberglass ladders are important.

Example: Composite Military Helmets

A composite military helmet has been developed which, although weighing about the same as a conventional manganese–steel helmet, covers more of the head and offers twice the ballistic and fragmentation protection. To stop a bullet, a composite material must first deform or flatten it; this process occurs when the bullet's tip comes into contact with as many individual fibers of the composite as possible without the fibers' being pushed aside.

A composite helmet has a nonwoven fiber construction, made with ultrahigh-molecular-weight polyethylene fibers in a thermosetting polymer matrix, which effectively stops the bullet by flattening it as it strikes the first layer of material. *Source*: AlliedSignal Corp. and CGS Gallet SA.

9.5 METAL-MATRIX COMPOSITES (MMC)

The advantages of a **metal matrix** over a polymer matrix are its higher elastic modulus, its resistance to elevated temperatures, and its higher toughness and ductility. The limitations are higher density and greater difficulty in processing parts.

Matrix materials in these composites are usually aluminum, aluminum–lithium, magnesium, copper, titanium, and superalloys. Fiber materials can be graphite, aluminum oxide, silicon carbide, boron, molybdenum, and tungsten. The elastic modulus of nonmetallic fibers ranges between 200 GPa and 400 GPa, with tensile strengths being in the range from 2000 MPa to 3000 MPa.

Typical compositions and applications for metal-matrix composites are given in Table 9.3. Because of their high specific stiffness, light weight, and high thermal conductivity, boron fibers in an aluminum matrix have been used for structural tubular supports in the Space Shuttle orbiter.

Metal-matrix composites having silicon-carbide fibers and a titanium matrix are being used for the skin, beams, stiffeners, and frames of the hypersonic aircraft under development. Other applications are in bicycle frames and sporting goods. Studies are in progress on developing techniques for optimal bonding of fibers to the metal matrix.

TABLE 9.3   Metal-Matrix Composite Materials and Applications

Fiber	Matrix	Applications
Graphite	Aluminum	Satellite, missile, and helicopter structures
	Magnesium	Space and satellite structures
	Lead	Storage-battery plates
	Copper	Electrical contacts and bearings
Boron	Aluminum	Compressor blades and structural supports
	Magnesium	Antenna structures
	Titanium	Jet-engine fan blades
Alumina	Aluminum	Superconductor restraints in fission power reactors
	Lead	Storage-battery plates
	Magnesium	Helicopter transmission structures
Silicon carbide	Aluminum, titanium	High-temperature structures
	Superalloy (cobalt-base)	High-temperature engine components
Molybdenum, tungsten	Superalloy	High-temperature engine components

9.6 CERAMIC-MATRIX COMPOSITES (CMC)

Composites with a **ceramic matrix** are another important development in engineered materials because of their resistance to high temperatures and corrosive environments. As was described in Chapter 8, ceramics are strong and stiff, and they resist high temperatures, but they generally lack toughness. Matrix materials that retain their strength up to 1700 °C (3000 °F) are silicon carbide, silicon nitride, aluminum oxide, and mullite (a compound of aluminum, silicon, and oxygen).

Carbon–carbon matrix composites retain much of their strength up to 2500 °C (4500 °F), although they lack oxidation resistance at high temperatures. Fiber materials are usually carbon and aluminum oxide.

Various techniques for improving the mechanical properties of ceramic-matrix composites, particularly their toughness, are being investigated. Applications are in jet and automotive engines, deep-sea mining equipment, pressure vessels, structural components, cutting tools, and dies for the extrusion and the drawing of metals.

9.7 OTHER COMPOSITES

Composites may also consist of coatings of various kinds on base metals or substrates (Chapter 33). Examples are (a) plating of aluminum and other metals over plastics, generally for decorative purposes, (b) enamels, and (c) vitreous (glasslike) coatings on metal surfaces for various functional or ornamental purposes.

Composites are made into cutting tools and dies, such as cemented carbides and cermets (Chapter 21). Other composites are grinding wheels made of aluminum oxide, silicon carbide, diamond, or cubic boron nitride abrasive particles, held together with various organic, inorganic, or metallic binders (Chapter 25).

A composite developed more recently consists of granite particles in an epoxy matrix. It has high strength, good vibration-damping capacity (better than gray cast iron), and good frictional characteristics. It is used in machine-tool beds for some precision grinders (Section 24.3).

SUMMARY

- Composites are an important class of materials that have numerous attractive properties. Three major categories are fiber- reinforced plastics and metal-matrix and ceramic-matrix composites. They have a wide range of applications in the aircraft, aerospace, and transportation industries, in sporting goods, and in structural components.

- In fiber-reinforced plastics, the fibers are usually glass, graphite, aramids, or boron, while polyester and epoxies commonly serve as the matrix material. These composites have particularly high toughness and strength-to-weight and stiffness-to-weight ratios.

- In metal-matrix composites, the fibers are graphite, boron, aluminum oxide, silicon carbide, molybdenum, or tungsten; matrix materials generally consist of aluminum, aluminum–lithium, magnesium, copper, titanium, and superalloys.

- For ceramic-matrix composites, the fibers are usually carbon and aluminum oxide, and the matrix materials are silicon carbide, silicon nitride, aluminum oxide, carbon, or mullite (a compound of aluminum, silicon, and oxygen).

- In addition to the type and quality of the materials used, important factors in the structure of composite materials are the size and length of the fibers, their volume percentage compared with that of the matrix, the strength of the bond at the fiber-matrix interface, and the orientation of the fibers in the matrix.

TRENDS

- Improvements are being made in methods of fabrication, in quality assurance, in reproducibility, in reliability, and in the predictability of the behavior of composite materials during their service life.

- Developments are taking place in techniques for three-dimensional reinforcement of plastics and for improvement in their resistance to compression, buckling, and impact.

- An important area of study is reduction in the costs of raw materials and of fabrication for composite materials.

- Major developments in ceramic-matrix composites are expected in the area of improving the strength, toughness, and failure resistance under nonaxial or impact loading.

- Extensive developments in metal-matrix composites are found in aerospace applications requiring strength and stiffness at elevated temperatures, particularly continuous-fiber-reinforced titanium alloy composites.

- Particulate-reinforced metal-matrix composites have attracted great attention in automotive applications that are very cost-sensitive; developments are focused on the reproducibility of material properties.

- Ceramic-matrix cutting tools are being developed, made of silicon carbide-reinforced alumina, with greatly improved tool life. Carbon whisker-reinforced ceramic-matrix materials are being developed for valves and bushings, because of their high hardness and their favorable properties with respect to wear, friction, and lubrication.

- An important area of research is the use of fiber-reinforced polymers in high-cycle fatigue applications.

KEY TERMS

Advanced composites	Fiber pullout	Precursor
Ceramic matrix	Fibers	Pyrolysis
Composite materials	Hybrid	Reinforced plastics
Delamination	Matrix	Silane
Engineered materials	Metal matrix	Whiskers

BIBLIOGRAPHY

Agarwal, B.D., and L.J. Broutman, *Analysis and Performance of Fiber Composites* (2d ed.). Wiley, 1990.

Bittence, J.C. (ed.), *Engineering Plastics and Composites*. ASM International, 1990.

Bertholet, J.-M., *Composite Materials: Mechanical Behavior and Structural Analysis*. Springer, 1999.

Chawla, K.K., *Composite Materials: Science and Engineering* (2d ed.), Springer, 1998.

Cheremisinoff, N.P., and P.N. Cheremisinoff, *Fiberglass Reinforced Plastics*. Noyes Publications, 1995.

Engineered Materials Handbook, Vol. 1: *Composites*. ASM International, 1987.

Engineering Plastics and Composites (2d ed.). ASM International, 1993.

Fitzer, E., and L.M. Manocha, *Carbon Reinforcements and Carbon/Carbon Composites*. Springer, 1998.

Handbook of Ceramics and Composites, 3 vols. Marcel Dekker, 1991.

Harper, C., *Handbook of Plastics, Elastomers, and Composites* (3d ed.). McGraw-Hill, 1996.

Hull, D., and T.W. Clyne, *An Introduction to Composite Materials*. Cambridge Univ. Press, 1996.

Jang, B.Z., *Advanced Polymer Composites: Principles and Applications*. ASM International, 1994.

Kelley, A., R.W. Cahn, and M.B. Bever (eds.), *Concise Encyclopedia of Composite Materials* (Rev. ed.). Pergamon, 1994.

Mallick, P.K., *Composites Engineering Handbook*. Marcel Dekker, 1997.

Mileiko, S.T., *Metal and Ceramic Based Composites*. Elsevier, 1997.

Peters, S. (ed.), *Handbook of Composites*. Chapman & Hall, 1997.

Pilato, L.A., and M.J. Michno, *Advanced Composite Materials*. Springer, 1994.

Potter, K., *Introduction to Composite Products: Design, development and manufacture*. Chapman & Hall, 1997.

Schwartz, M., *Composite Materials*, Vol. 1: *Properties, Nondestructive Testing, and Repair*; Vol. 2: *Processing, Fabrication, and Applications*. Prentice Hall, 1997.

Starr, T., and K. Forsdyke, *Phenolic Composites*. Chapman & Hall, 1997.

REVIEW QUESTIONS

9.1 Distinguish between composites and metal alloys.

9.2 Describe the functions of the matrix and of the reinforcing fibers. What fundamental differences are there in the characteristics of the two materials?

9.3 What reinforcing fibers are generally used to make composites? Which type of fiber is the strongest? Which type is the weakest?

9.4 What is the range in length and diameter of reinforcing fibers?

9.5 List the important factors that determine the properties of reinforced plastics.

9.6 Compare the advantages and limitations of metal-matrix composites, reinforced plastics, and ceramic-matrix composites.

9.7 What are the most commonly used matrix materials?

9.8 What is a hybrid composite?

9.9 What material properties are improved by the addition of reinforcing fibers?

9.10 What is the purpose of the matrix material?

9.11 Is there a difference between a carbon fiber and a graphite fiber? Explain.

9.12 What is a whisker? What is the difference between a whisker and a fiber?

9.13 What do boron fibers consist of? Why are they heavy?

9.14 Why are metal-matrix composites of interest?

QUALITATIVE PROBLEMS

9.15 How do you think the use of straw in clay originally came about in making brick for dwellings?

9.16 What products have you personally seen that are made of reinforced plastics? How can you tell?

9.17 Identify metals and alloys that have strengths comparable to those of reinforced plastics.

9.18 The many advantages of composite materials were described in this chapter. What limitations or disadvantages do these materials have? What suggestions would you make to overcome these limitations?

9.19 What factors contribute to the cost of reinforcing fibers? (See also Table 9.2).

9.20 Give examples of composite materials other than those stated in this chapter.

9.21 A hybrid composite is defined as one containing two or more different types of reinforcing fibers. What advantages would such a composite have over others?

9.22 Explain why the behavior of the materials given in Fig. 9.5 is as shown.

9.23 Why are fibers capable of supporting a major portion of the load in composite materials?

9.24 Do metal-matrix composites have advantages over reinforced plastics? Explain.

9.25 Give reasons for the development of ceramic-matrix composites. Name some possible applications.

9.26 Explain how you would go about determining the hardness of reinforced plastics and of composite materials. Are hardness measurements on these types of materials meaningful? Does the size of the indentation make a difference? Explain.

9.27 How would you go about trying to determine the strength of a fiber?

9.28 It has been stated that glass fibers are much stronger than bulk glass. Why is this so?

9.29 Under what circumstances could a glass be used as a matrix?

9.30 When the American Plains states were settled, no trees existed for the construction of housing. Pioneers cut bricks from sod—basically, prairie soil as a matrix and grass and its root system as reinforcement. Explain why this would work. Also, if you were a pioneer, would you stack the bricks with the grass horizontally or vertically? Explain.

QUANTITATIVE PROBLEMS

9.31 Calculate the average increase in the properties of the plastics given in Table 7.1, as a result of their reinforcement, and describe your observations.

9.32 In the example in Section 9.3, what would be the percentage of the load supported by the fibers if their strength is 1100 MPa and the matrix strength is 200 MPa? What if the fiber stiffness is doubled and the matrix stiffness is halved?

9.33 Make a survey of the recent technical literature, and present data indicating the effects of fiber length on such mechanical properties as the strength, the elastic modulus, and impact energy of reinforced plastics.

9.34 Calculate the percent increase in the mechanical properties of reinforced nylon, from the data shown in Fig. 9.4.

9.35 Plot E/ρ and $E/\rho^{0.5}$ for the composite materials listed in Table 9.1, and make a comparison to the properties of the materials described in Chapters 4 through 8. (See also Table 9.2.)

9.36 Calculate the stress in the fibers and in the matrix for the Example in Section 9.3. Assume that the cross-sectional area is 0.1 in² and $P_c = 500$ lb

9.37 Repeat the calculations in the Example on page 229, (a) if a high-modulus carbon fiber is used and (b) if Kevlar 29 is used.

9.38 Refer to the properties listed in Table 7.1. If acetal is reinforced with E-type glass fibers, what is the range of fiber content in glass-reinforced acetal?

9.39 Plot the elastic modulus and strength of an aluminum metal-matrix composite with high-modulus carbon fibers, as a function of fiber content.

9.40 For the data in the example in Section 9.3, what should be the fiber content so that the fibers and the matrix fail simultaneously? Use an allowable fiber stress of 200 MPa and a matrix strength of 50 MPa.

SYNTHESIS AND DESIGN

9.41 What applications for composite materials can you think of other than those listed in Section 9.4? Why do you think your applications are suitable for these materials?

9.42 Using the information given in this chapter, develop special designs and shapes for new applications of composite materials.

9.43 Would a composite material with a strong and stiff matrix and soft and flexible reinforcement have any practical uses? Explain.

9.44 Make a list of products for which the use of composite materials could be advantageous because of their anisotropic properties.

9.45 Inspect Fig. 9.1, and explain what other components of an aircraft, including parts in the cabin, could be made of composites.

9.46 Name applications in which both specific strength and specific stiffness (Fig. 9.2) are important.

9.47 What applications for composite materials can you think of in which high thermal conductivity would be desirable?

9.48 As with other materials, the mechanical properties of composites are obtained by preparing appropriate specimens and then testing them. Explain what problems you might encounter in preparing specimens for and in testing tension. Suggest methods for making appropriate specimens, including their shape and how they are clamped into the jaws of testing machines.

9.49 Design and describe a test method to determine the mechanical properties of reinforced plastics in their thickness direction.

9.50 In the Trends section of this chapter, it was stated that developments are taking place in techniques for three-dimensional reinforcement of plastics. Describe (a) applications in which strength in the thickness direction of the composite is important, and (b) your ideas on how to achieve this strength. Include simple sketches of the structure utilizing such reinforced plastics.

9.51 As described in this chapter, reinforced plastics can be adversely affected by environment—in particular, by moisture, by chemicals, and by temperature variations. Design and describe test methods to determine the mechanical properties of composite materials subjected to these conditions.

9.52 Comment about your observations on the design of the sailboard shown in Fig. 9.8.

9.53 Describe the similarities and differences between ordinary corrugated cardboard and a honeycomb structure.

9.54 Suggest product designs in which corrugated cardboard can be used. Comment on the advantages and limitations.

9.55 Suggest consumer-product designs that could utilize honeycomb structures.

9.56 Make a survey of various sports equipment, and identify the components made of composite materials. Explain the reasons for and the advantages of using composites in these specific applications.

9.57 Several material combinations and structures were described in this chapter. In relative terms, identify those that would be suitable for applications involving one of the following: (a) very low temperatures, (b) very high temperatures, (c) vibrations, (d) high humidity.

9.58 Obtain a textbook on composite materials, and investigate the effective stiffness of a continuous fiber-reinforced polymer. Plot the stiffness of such a composite as a function of orientation with respect to the fiber direction.

9.59 Derive a general expression for the coefficient of thermal expansion for a continuous fiber-reinforced composite in the fiber direction.

Part II
Metal-Casting Processes and Equipment

Several different methods, such as casting, molding, forming, powder metallurgy, and machining, are available to shape metals into useful products. One of the oldest processes is **casting**, which basically involves pouring molten metal into a mold cavity where, upon solidification, it takes the shape of the cavity. Casting was first used around 4000 B.C. to make ornaments, copper arrowheads, and various other objects.

The casting process is capable of producing intricate shapes in one piece, including those with internal cavities, such as engine blocks. A wide variety of products can be cast. Figure II.1, for example, shows cast components in a typical automobile, a product that was used in the Introduction to Part I to illustrate the selection and use of a variety of materials.

Many casting processes have been developed over many years (Fig. II.2). As in all manufacturing, each process has its own characteristics, applications, advantages, limitations, and costs. Casting processes are most often selected over other manufacturing methods, for the following reasons:

- Casting can produce complex shapes with internal cavities or hollow sections;
- It can produce very large parts;
- It can utilize workpiece materials that are difficult or uneconomical to process by other means;
- Casting is competitive with other processes.

Almost all metals can be cast in, or nearly in, the final shape desired, often with only minor finishing operations required. This capability places casting among the most impor-

FIGURE II.1   Cast parts in a typical automobile.

239

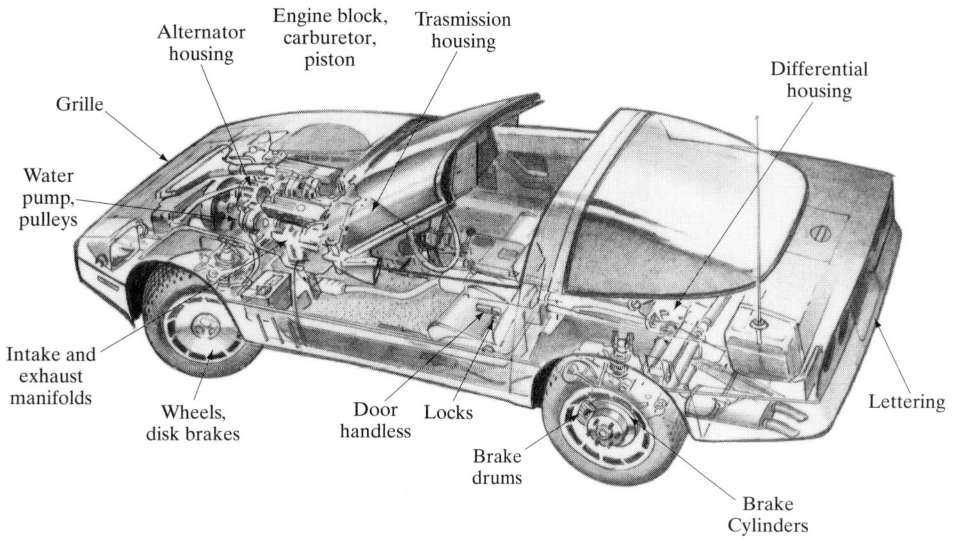

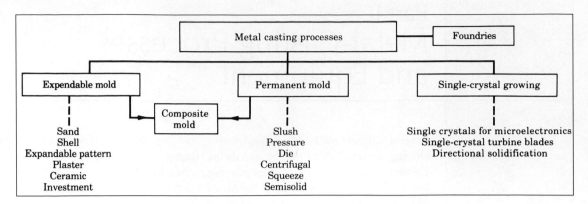

FIGURE II.2   Outline of metal-casting processes described in Part II.

tant **net-shape manufacturing** technologies, along with net-shape forging (Chapter 14), stamping of sheet metal (Chapter 16), and powder metallurgy and metal-injection molding (Chapter 17). With modern processing techniques and control of chemical composition, mechanical properties of castings can equal those made by other processes.

10

Fundamentals of Metal-Casting

10.1 INTRODUCTION

The **casting** process basically involves (a) pouring molten metal into a mold patterned after the part to be manufactured, (b) allowing it to cool, and (c) removing the metal from the mold. As with all other manufacturing processes, an understanding of the fundamentals is essential—both for the production of good quality and economical castings, and to establish proper techniques for mold design and casting practice.

Important considerations in casting operations are as follows:

- the flow of the molten metal into the mold cavity;
- the solidification and cooling of the metal in the mold;
- the influence of the type of mold material.

This chapter describes the relationship among the many factors involved in casting. The flow of molten metals into the mold cavity is discussed in terms of mold design and fluid flow characteristics. Solidification and cooling of metals in the mold are affected by several factors, including the metallurgical and thermal properties of the metal. The type of mold has an important influence because it affects the rate of cooling of the metal in the mold. Factors influencing defect formation are also described.

Industrial metal casting processes, design considerations, and casting materials are described in Chapters 11 and 12. The casting of ceramics and of plastics, which involves similar methods and procedures, are described in Chapters 17 and 18, respectively.

10.2 SOLIDIFICATION OF METALS

After molten metal is poured into a **mold**, a series of events takes place during the solidification of the casting and its cooling to ambient temperature. These events greatly influence the size, shape, uniformity, and chemical composition of the grains formed throughout the casting, which in turn influence its overall properties. The significant factors affecting these events are the type of metal; the thermal properties of both the metal and the mold; the geometric relationship between volume and surface area of the casting; and the shape of the mold.

10.2.1 Pure Metals

Because a pure metal has a clearly defined melting (or freezing) point, it solidifies at a constant temperature. Pure aluminum, for example, solidifies at 660 °C (1220 °F), iron at 1537 °C (2798 °F), and tungsten at 3410 °C (6170 °F). (See also Table 3.1 and Fig. 4.4.)

After the temperature of the molten metal drops to its freezing point, its temperature remains constant while the *latent heat of fusion* is given off. The solidification front (solid-liquid interface) moves through the molten metal, solidifying from the mold walls in toward the center. Once solidification has taken place at any point, cooling resumes. The solidified metal, called the *casting*, is taken out of the mold and is allowed to cool to ambient temperature.

The grain structure of a pure metal cast in a square mold is shown in Fig. 10.1a. At the mold walls, which are at ambient temperature, the metal cools rapidly. Rapid cooling produces a solidified **skin**, or *shell*, of fine equiaxed grains. The grains grow in a direction op-

FIGURE 10.1   Schematic illustration of three cast structures of metals solidified in a square mold: (a) pure metals; (b) solid-solution alloys; and (c) structure obtained by using nucleating agents. *Source*: G. W. Form, J. F. Wallace, J. L. Walker, and A. Cibula.

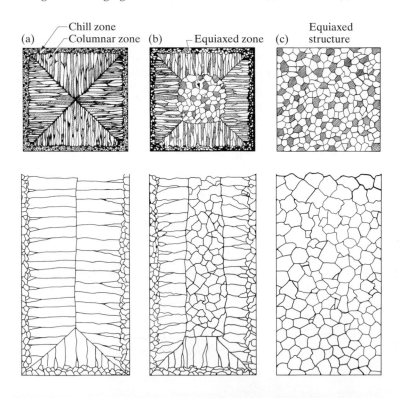

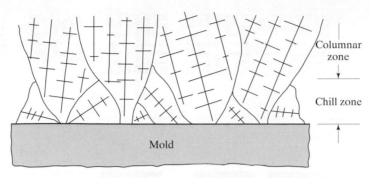

FIGURE 10.2   Development of a preferred texture at a cool mold wall. Note that only favorably oriented grains grow away from the surface of the mold.

posite to that of the heat transfer out through the mold. Those grains that have favorable orientation will grow preferentially and are called **columnar grains** (Fig. 10.2).

As the driving force of the heat transfer is reduced away from the mold walls, the grains become equiaxed and coarse. Those grains that have substantially different orientations are blocked from further growth. Such grain development is known as **homogenous nucleation**, meaning that the grains (crystals) grow upon themselves, starting at the mold wall.

10.2.2 Alloys

Solidification in alloys begins when the temperature drops below the liquidus, T_L, and is complete when it reaches the solidus, T_S (Fig. 10.3). Within this temperature range, the alloy is

FIGURE 10.3   Schematic illustration of alloy solidification and temperature distribution in the solidifying metal. Note the formation of dendrites in the mushy zone.

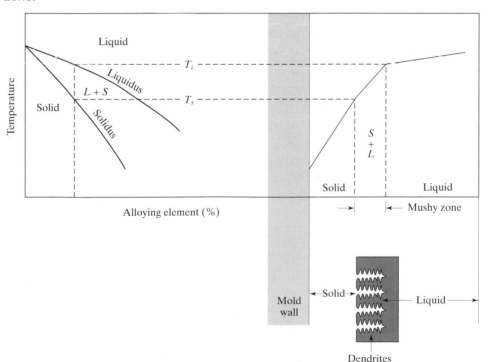

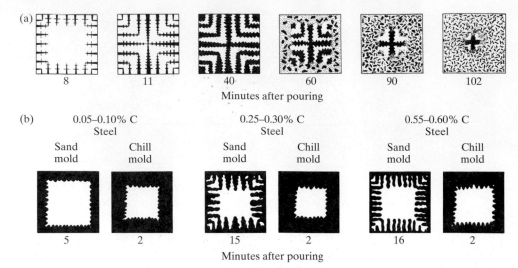

FIGURE 10.4   (a) Solidification patterns for gray cast iron in a 180-mm (7-in.) square casting. Note that after 11 min. of cooling, dendrites reach each other, but the casting is still mushy throughout. It takes about two hours for this casting to solidify completely. (b) Solidification of carbon steels in sand and chill (metal) molds. Note the difference in solidification patterns as the carbon content increases. *Source*: H. F. Bishop and W. S. Pellini.

in a mushy or pasty state with **columnar dendrites** (from the Greek *dendron*, meaning "akin to," and *drys*, meaning "tree").

Note the presence of liquid metal between the dendrite arms. Dendrites have three-dimensional arms and branches (secondary arms) which eventually interlock, as can be seen in Fig. 10.4. The study of dendritic structures, although complex, is important because such structures contribute to detrimental factors such as compositional variations, segregation, and microporosity.

The width of the **mushy zone**, where both liquid and solid phases are present, is an important factor during solidification. This zone is described in terms of a temperature difference, known as the **freezing range**, as follows:

$$\text{Freezing range} = T_L - T_S. \qquad (10.1)$$

It can be seen in Fig. 10.3 that pure metals have a freezing range that approaches zero, and that the solidification front moves as a plane front without forming a mushy zone. *Eutectics* (Section 4.3) solidify in a similar manner, with an approximately plane front.

The type of solidification structure developed depends on the composition of the eutectic. In alloys with a nearly symmetrical phase diagram, the structure is generally lamellar, with two or more solid phases present, depending on the alloy system. When the volume fraction of the minor phase of the alloy is less than about 25%, the structure generally becomes fibrous. These conditions are particularly important for cast irons.

For alloys, although it is not precise, a *short freezing range* generally involves a temperature difference of less than 50 °C (90 °F), and a *long freezing range* greater than 110 °C (200 °F). Ferrous castings generally have narrow mushy zones, whereas aluminum and magnesium alloys have wide mushy zones. Consequently, these alloys are in a mushy state throughout most of the solidification process.

Effects of Cooling Rates.   Slow cooling rates (on the order of 10^2 K/s) or long local solidification times result in *coarse* dendritic structures with large spacing between the den-

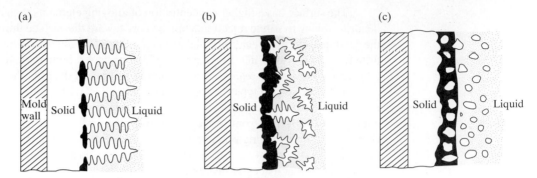

FIGURE 10.5   Schematic illustration of three basic types of cast structures:(a) columnar dendritic; (b) equiaxed dendritic; and (c) equiaxed nondendritic. *Source*: D. Apelian.

drite arms. For faster cooling rates (on the order of 10^4 K/s) or short local solidification times, the structure becomes *finer* with smaller dendrite arm spacing. For still higher cooling rates (on the order of from 10^6 to 10^8 K/s) the structures developed are amorphous, as described in Section 6.14.

The structures developed and the resulting grain size influence the properties of the casting. As grain size decreases, the strength and the ductility of the cast alloy increase, microporosity (interdendritic shrinkage voids) in the casting decreases, and the tendency for the casting to crack (*hot tearing*, see Fig. 10.11) during solidification decreases. Lack of uniformity in grain size and grain distribution results in castings with *anisotropic* properties.

A criterion describing the kinetics of the liquid-solid interface is the ratio G/R, where G is the *thermal gradient* and R is the *rate* at which the liquid-solid interface moves. Typical values for G range from 10^2 to 10^3 K/m and for R from 10^{-3} to 10^{-4} m/s. Dendritic type structures (Figs. 10.5a and b) typically have an R ratio in the range of 10^5 to 10^7, whereas ratios of 10^{10} to 10^{12} produce a plane-front, nondendritic liquid-solid interface (Fig. 10.6).

10.2.3 Structure-Property Relationships

Because all castings are expected to possess certain properties to meet design and service requirements, the relationships between properties and the structures developed during solidification are important aspects of casting. In this section, we describe these relationships in terms of dendrite morphology and the concentration of alloying elements in various regions.

The compositions of dendrites and the liquid metal are given by the *phase diagram* of the particular alloy (Section 4.3). When the alloy is cooled very slowly, each dendrite develops a uniform composition. Under the normal (faster) cooling rates encountered in practice, however, **cored dendrites** are formed. Cored dendrites have a surface composition different from that at their centers (this difference is referred to as a *concentration gradient*).

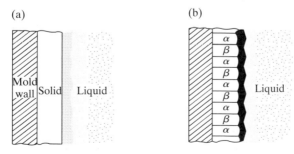

FIGURE 10.6   Schematic illustration of cast structures in (a) plane front, single phase, and (b) plane front, two phase. *Source*: D. Apelian.

The surface has a higher concentration of alloying elements than does the core of the dendrite, owing to solute rejection from the core toward the surface during solidification of the dendrite (**microsegregation**). The darker shading in the interdendritic liquid near the dendrite roots in Fig. 10.5 indicates that these regions have a higher solute concentration; microsegregation in these regions is much more pronounced than in others.

There are several types of **segregation**. In contrast with microsegregation, **macrosegregation** involves differences in composition throughout the casting itself. In situations where the solidifying front moves away from the surface of a casting as a plane front (Fig. 10.6), lower-melting point constituents in the solidifying alloy are driven toward the center (**normal segregation**). Consequently, such a casting has a higher concentration of alloying elements at its center than at its surfaces.

In dendritic structures such as those found in solid-solution alloys (Fig. 10.1b), the opposite occurs: the center of the casting has a lower concentration of alloying elements (**inverse segregation**). The reason is that liquid metal (having a higher concentration of alloying elements) enters the cavities developed from solidification shrinkage in the dendrite arms, which have solidified sooner.

Another form of segregation is due to gravity. **Gravity segregation** describes the process whereby higher-density inclusions or compounds sink, and lighter elements (such as antimony in an antimony–lead alloy) float to the surface.

A typical cast structure of a solid-solution alloy with an inner zone of equiaxed grains is shown in Fig. 10.1b. This inner zone can be extended throughout the casting, as shown in Fig. 10.1c, by adding an **inoculant** (*nucleating agent*) to the alloy. The inoculant induces nucleation of the grains throughout the liquid metal (**heterogeneous nucleation**).

Because of the presence of thermal gradients in a solidifying mass of liquid metal, and because of gravity and the resultant density differences, *convection* has a strong influence on the structures developed. Convection promotes the formation of an outer chill zone; refines grain size; and accelerates the transition from columnar to equiaxed grains. The structure shown in Fig. 10.5b can also be obtained by increasing convection within the liquid metal, whereby dendrite arms separate (**dendrite multiplication**). Conversely, reducing or eliminating convection results in coarser and longer columnar dendritic grains.

The dendrite arms are not particularly strong and can be broken up by agitation or mechanical vibration in the early stages of solidification (**semisolid metal forming** and **rheocasting**; see Section 11.14.2). This process results in finer grain size, with equiaxed nondendritic grains distributed more uniformly throughout the casting (Fig. 10.5c). Convection can be enhanced by the use of mechanical or electromagnetic methods.

Experiments are now being conducted during space flights concerning the effects of gravity on the microstructure of castings. Lack of gravity (or **microgravity**, as it is now called in regard to space travel) means that, unlike on Earth, there are no significant density differences or thermal gradients (and therefore no convection) during solidification. This lack of convection affects solidification structure and distribution of impurities. Recent experiments involve the growth of crystals for production of cadmium-zinc telluride, mercury-zinc telluride, and selenium-doped gallium arsenide semiconductor samples.

10.3 FLUID FLOW

To emphasize the importance of fluid flow, let's briefly describe the basic casting system as shown in Fig. 10.7. The molten metal is poured through a **pouring basin** or **cup**. It then flows through the **gating system** (sprue, runners and gates) into the mold cavity. As described in Section 11.2.2 and illustrated in Fig. 11.3, the **sprue** is a vertical channel through which the molten metal flows downward in the mold.

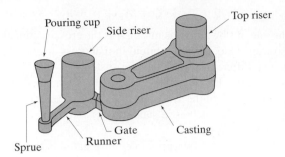

FIGURE 10.7   Schematic illustration of a typical riser-gated casting. Risers serve as reservoirs, supplying molten metal to the casting as it shrinks during solidification. See also Fig. 11.4. *Source*: American Foundrymen's Society.

Runners are the channels that carry the molten metal from the sprue to the mold cavity, or connect the sprue to the gate. The **gate** is that portion of the runner through which the molten metal enters the mold cavity. **Risers** serve as reservoirs to supply the molten metal necessary to prevent shrinkage during solidification.

Although such a gating system appears to be relatively simple, successful casting requires proper design and control of the solidification process to ensure adequate fluid flow in the system. For example, one of the most important functions of the gating system in sand casting is to trap contaminants (such as oxides and other inclusions) in the molten metal by having the contaminants adhere to the walls of the gating system, thereby preventing them from reaching the actual mold cavity.

Furthermore, a properly designed gating system avoids or minimizes problems such as premature cooling, turbulence, and gas entrapment. Even before it reaches the mold cavity, the molten metal must be handled carefully to avoid the formation of oxides on molten metal surfaces from exposure to the environment or introduction of impurities into the molten metal.

Two basic principles of fluid flow are relevant to gating design: Bernoulli's theorem and the law of mass continuity.

Bernoulli's Theorem.   This theorem is based on the principle of conservation of energy and relates pressure, velocity, the elevation of the fluid at any location in the system, and the frictional losses in a system that is full of liquid according to the equation

$$h + \frac{p}{\rho g} + \frac{v^2}{2g} = \text{constant}, \tag{10.2}$$

where h is the elevation above a certain reference plane, p is the pressure at that elevation, v is the velocity of the liquid at that elevation, r is the density of the fluid (assuming that it is incompressible), and g is the gravitational constant. Conservation of energy requires that, at a particular location in the system, the relationship

$$h_1 + \frac{p_1}{\rho g} + \frac{v_1^2}{2g} = h_2 + \frac{p_2}{\rho g} + \frac{v_2^2}{2g} + f \tag{10.3}$$

be satisfied, where the subscripts 1 and 2 represent two different elevations, respectively, and f represents the frictional loss in the liquid as it travels downward through the system. The frictional loss includes such factors as energy loss at the liquid-mold wall interfaces and turbulence in the liquid.

Continuity.   The law of mass continuity states that for incompressible liquids and in a system with impermeable walls, the rate of flow is constant. Thus,

$$Q = A_1 v_1 = A_2 v_2, \tag{10.4}$$

where Q is the rate of flow (such as m^3/s), A is the cross-sectional area of the liquid stream, and v is the average velocity of the liquid in that cross-sectional location. The subscripts 1 and 2 refer to two different locations in the system.

According to this law, the flow rate must be maintained anywhere in the system. The permeability of the walls of the system is important because otherwise some liquid will permeate through the walls (such as in sand molds) and the flow rate will decrease as the liquid moves through the system.

An application of the two principles just stated is the traditional tapered design of sprues (shown in Fig. 10.7); we can determine the shape of the sprue by using Eqs. (10.3) and (10.4). Assuming that the pressure at the top of the sprue is equal to the pressure at the bottom and that there are no frictional losses, the relationship between height and cross-sectional area at any point in the sprue is given by the parabolic relationship

$$\frac{A_1}{A_2} = \sqrt{\frac{h_2}{h_1}}, \tag{10.5}$$

where, for example, the subscript 1 denotes the top of the sprue and 2 denotes the bottom. Moving downward from the top, the cross-sectional area of the sprue must decrease. Depending on the assumptions made, expressions other than Eq. (10.5) can also be obtained. For example, we may assume a certain molten-metal velocity V_1 at the top of the sprue. Then, using Eqs. (10.3) and (10.4), we can obtain an expression for the ratio A_1/A_2 of the cross-sectional areas as a function of h_1, h_2, and V_1.

Recall that in a free-falling liquid (such as water from a faucet) the cross-sectional area of the stream decreases as it gains velocity downward. If we design a sprue with a constant cross-sectional area and pour the molten metal into it, regions may develop where the liquid loses contact with the sprue walls. As a result **aspiration**, a process whereby air is sucked in or entrapped in the liquid, may take place. On the other hand, tapered sprues are now replaced in many systems by straight-sided sprues with a **choke** to allow the metal to flow smoothly.

Flow Characteristics.   An important consideration in fluid flow in gating systems is the presence of **turbulence**, as opposed to the *laminar flow* of fluids. We use the *Reynolds number*, Re, to quantify this aspect of fluid flow; it represents the ratio of the *inertia* to the *viscous* forces in fluid flow, and is defined as

$$\text{Re} = \frac{vD\rho}{\eta}, \tag{10.6}$$

where v is the velocity of the liquid, D is the diameter of the channel, and ρ and η are the density and viscosity, respectively, of the liquid. The higher this number, the greater the tendency for turbulent flow. In ordinary gating systems, Re ranges from 2,000 to 20,000.

An Re value of up to 2,000 represents laminar flow; between 2,000 and 20,000, it represents a mixture of laminar and turbulent flow. Such a mixture is generally regarded as harmless in gating systems. Re values in excess of 20,000, however, represent severe turbulence, resulting in air entrainment and the formation of *dross* (the scum that forms on the surface of molten metal) from the reaction of the liquid metal with air and other gases. Techniques for minimizing turbulence generally involve avoidance of sudden changes in flow direction and in the geometry of channel cross-sections in gating system design.

Dross or slag can be almost completely eliminated only by vacuum casting (Section 11.8). Conventional atmospheric casting mitigates dross or slag by skimming, by using properly designed pouring basins and runner systems, or by using filters. Filters are usually made of ceramics, mica, or fiberglass, and their proper location and placement are important for effective filtering of dross and slag. Filters also can eliminate turbulent flow in the runner system.

10.4 FLUIDITY OF MOLTEN METAL

The capability of the molten metal to fill mold cavities is called *fluidity*; it consists of two basic factors: (1) characteristics of the molten metal, and (2) casting parameters. The following characteristics of molten metal influence fluidity:

a. **Viscosity.** As viscosity and its sensitivity to temperature (*viscosity index*) increase, fluidity decreases.

b. **Surface tension.** A high surface tension of the liquid metal reduces fluidity. Because of this, oxide films on the surface of the molten metal have a significant adverse effect on fluidity; for example, an oxide film on the surface of pure molten aluminum triples the surface tension.

c. **Inclusions.** As insoluble particles, inclusions can have a significant adverse effect on fluidity. This effect can be verified by observing the viscosity of a liquid such as oil with and without sand particles in it; the former has a higher viscosity.

d. **Solidification pattern of the alloy.** The manner in which solidification takes place, as described in Section 10.2, can influence fluidity. Moreover, fluidity is inversely proportional to the freezing range. The shorter the range (as in pure metals and eutectics), the higher the fluidity. Conversely, alloys with long freezing ranges (such as solid-solution alloys) have lower fluidity.

The following casting parameters influence fluidity and also influence the fluid flow and thermal characteristics of the system:

a. **Mold design.** The design and dimensions of the sprue, runners, and risers all influence fluidity.

b. **Mold material and its surface characteristics.** The higher the thermal conductivity of the mold and the rougher the surfaces, the lower the fluidity of the molten metal. Although heating the mold improves fluidity, it slows down solidification of the metal and the casting develops coarse grains and hence has lower strength.

c. **Degree of superheat.** Defined as the increment of temperature above the melting point of an alloy, superheat improves fluidity by delaying solidification.

d. **Rate of pouring.** The slower the rate of pouring molten metal into the mold, the lower the fluidity because of the higher rate of cooling.

e. **Heat transfer.** This factor directly affects the viscosity of the liquid metal (see below).

Although the interrelationships are complex, we use the general term **castability** to describe the ease with which a metal can be cast to obtain a part with good quality. This term includes not only fluidity but casting practices as well.

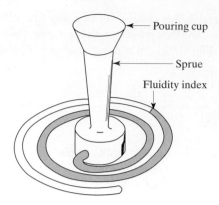

FIGURE 10.8   A test method for fluidity using a spiral mold. The *fluidity index* is the length of the solidified metal in the spiral passage. The greater the length of the solidified metal, the greater is its fluidity.

10.4.1 Tests for Fluidity

Several tests have been developed to quantify fluidity, although none is accepted universally. In one such test, shown in Fig. 10.8, the molten metal is made to flow along a channel that is at room temperature. The distance the metal flows before it solidifies and stops is a measure of its fluidity. Obviously this length is a function of the thermal properties of the metal and the mold, as well as of the design of the channel. Such tests are useful and simulate casting situations to a reasonable degree.

10.5 HEAT TRANSFER

An important consideration in casting is the heat transfer during the complete cycle from pouring to solidification and cooling to room temperature. Heat flow at different locations in the system is a complex phenomenon, and depends on many factors relating to the casting material and the mold and process parameters. For instance, in casting thin sections, the metal flow rates must be high enough to avoid premature chilling and solidification. However, the flow rate must not be so high as to cause excessive turbulence with its detrimental effects on the casting process.

A typical temperature distribution at the mold liquid-metal interface is shown in Fig. 10.9. Heat from the liquid metal is given off through the mold wall and the surrounding air. The temperature drop at the air-mold and mold-metal interfaces is caused by the presence of boundary layers and imperfect contact at these interfaces. The shape of the curve depends on the thermal properties of the molten metal and the mold.

10.5.1 Solidification Time

During the early stages of solidification, a thin, solidified skin begins to form at the cool mold walls and, as time passes, the skin thickens (Fig. 10.10). With flat mold walls, this thickness is proportional to the square root of time. Therefore, doubling the time will make the skin $\sqrt{2} = 1.41$ times, or 41%, thicker.

The **solidification time** is a function of the volume of a casting and its surface area (*Chvorinov's rule*); that is,

$$\text{Solidification time} = C\left(\frac{\text{volume}}{\text{surface area}}\right)^2, \tag{10.7}$$

where C is a constant that reflects mold material, metal properties (including latent heat), and temperature.

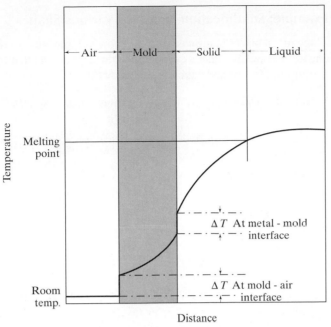

FIGURE 10.9   Temperature distribution at the interface of the mold wall and the liquid metal during solidification of metals in casting.

Thus, a large solid sphere solidifies and cools to ambient temperature at a much slower rate than does a smaller sphere; the reason is that the volume of a sphere is proportional to the cube of its diameter, and the surface area is proportional to the square of its diameter. Similarly, it can be shown that molten metal in a cube-shaped mold will solidify faster than in a spherical mold of the same volume (see example below).

The effects of mold geometry and elapsed time on skin thickness and shape are shown in Fig. 10.10. As illustrated, the unsolidified molten metal has been poured from the mold at different time intervals, ranging from five seconds to 6 minutes. Note that the skin thickness increases with elapsed time, but that the skin is thinner at internal angles (location *A* in the figure) than at external angles (location *B*). This latter condition is caused by slower cooling at internal angles than at external angles.

FIGURE 10.10   Solidified skin on a steel casting. The remaining molten metal is poured out at the times indicated in the figure. Hollow ornamental and decorative objects are made by a process called slush casting, which is based on this principle. *Source*: H. F. Taylor, J. Wulff, and M. C. Flemings.

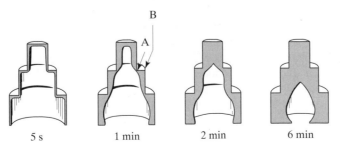

Example: Solidification Times for Various Shapes

Three metal pieces being cast have the same volume but different shapes; one is a sphere, one a cube, and the other a cylinder with its height equal to its diameter. Which piece will solidify the fastest and which one the slowest?

Solution: The volume is unity, so we have, from Eq. (10.7),

$$\text{Solidification time} \propto \frac{1}{(\text{surface area})^2}.$$

The respective surface areas are as follows:

Sphere: $V = \left(\frac{4}{3}\right)\pi r^3, \quad r = \left(\frac{3}{4\pi}\right)^{1/3},$

and $A = 4\pi r^2 = 4\pi\left(\frac{3}{4\pi}\right)^{2/3} = 4.84;$

Cube: $V = a^3, \quad a = 1, \quad \text{and} \quad A = 6a^2 = 6;$

Cylinder: $V = \pi r^2 h = 2\pi r^3, \quad r = \left(\frac{1}{2\pi}\right)^{1/3}, \quad \text{and}$

$$A = 2\pi r^2 + 2\pi rh = 6\pi r^2 = 6\pi\left(\frac{1}{2\pi}\right)^{2/3} = 5.54.$$

Thus, the respective solidification times are

$$t_{\text{sphere}} = 0.043C, \quad t_{\text{cube}} = 0.028C, \quad \text{and} \quad t_{\text{cylinder}} = 0.033C.$$

Hence the cube-shaped casting will solidify the fastest and the sphere-shaped casting will solidify the slowest.

10.5.2 Shrinkage

Because of their thermal expansion characteristics, metals shrink (contract) during solidification and cooling. *Shrinkage*, which causes dimensional changes and, sometimes, cracking, is the result of the following three events:

a. contraction of the molten metal as it cools prior to its solidification.

b. contraction of the metal during phase change from liquid to solid (latent heat of fusion).

c. contraction of the solidified metal (the casting) as its temperature drops to ambient temperature.

The largest amount of shrinkage occurs during cooling of the casting. The amount of contraction during solidification of various metals is shown in Table 10.1. Note that gray cast iron expands. The reason is that graphite has a relatively high specific volume, and when it precipitates as graphite flakes during solidification, it causes a net expansion of the metal. Shrinkage is further discussed in Section 12.2.1 in connection with design considerations in casting.

TABLE 10.1   Solidification Contraction for Various Cast Metals

Metal or alloy	Volumetric solidification contraction (%)	Metal or alloy	Volumetric solidification contraction (%)
Aluminum	6.6	70%Cu–30%Zn	4.5
Al–4.5%Cu	6.3	90%Cu–10%Al	4
Al–12%Si	3.8	Gray iron	Expansion to 2.5
Carbon steel	2.5–3	Magnesium	4.2
1% carbon steel	4	White iron	4–5.5
Copper	4.9	Zinc	6.5

Source: After R. A. Flinn.

10.6 DEFECTS

As will be seen in this section as well as other sections throughout Parts II-VI, various defects can develop in manufacturing processes, depending on factors such as materials, part design, and processing techniques. While some defects affect only the appearance of parts, others can have major adverse effects on the structural integrity of the parts made (see also Chapters 11 and 12).

Several defects can develop in castings (Figs. 10.11 and 10.12). Because different names have been used in the past to describe the same defect, the International Committee of Foundry Technical Associations has developed a standardized nomenclature consisting of seven basic categories of casting defects identified with boldface capital letters:

A. **Metallic projections**, consisting of fins, flash, or massive projections such as swells and rough surfaces.

B. **Cavities**, consisting of rounded or rough internal or exposed cavities, including blowholes, pinholes, and shrinkage cavities (see "porosity," below).

FIGURE 10.11   Examples of hot tears in castings. These defects occur because the casting cannot shrink freely during cooling, owing to constraints in various portions of the molds and cores. Exothermic (heat-producing) compounds may be used (as exothermic padding) to control cooling at critical sections to avoid hot tearing.

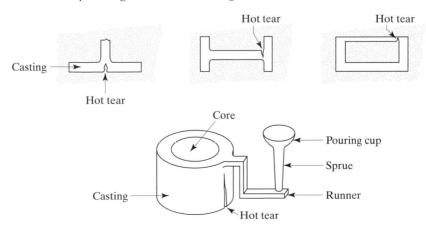

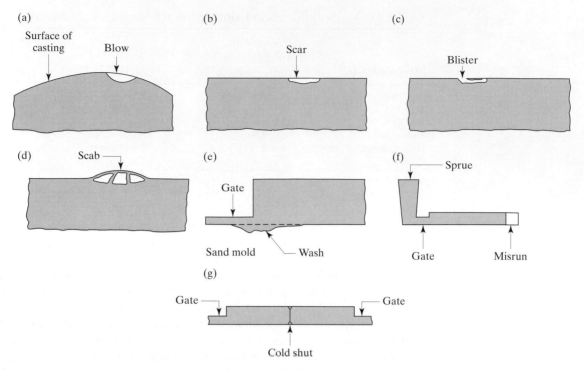

FIGURE 10.12   Examples of common defects in castings. These defects can be minimized or eliminated by proper design and preparation of molds and control of pouring procedures. *Source*: J. Datsko.

C. **Discontinuities**, such as cracks, cold or hot tearing, and cold shuts. If the solidifying metal is constrained from shrinking freely, cracking and tearing can occur. Although many factors are involved in tearing, coarse grain size and the presence of low melting point segregates along the grain boundaries (*intergranular*) increase the tendency for hot tearing. *Cold shut* is an interface in a casting that lacks complete fusion because of the meeting of two streams of liquid metal from different gates.

D. **Defective surface**, such as surface folds, laps, scars, adhering sand layers, and oxide scale.

E. **Incomplete casting**, such as misruns (due to premature solidification), insufficient volume of the metal poured, and runout (due to loss of metal from mold after pouring). Incomplete castings can result from the molten metal being at too low a temperature or from pouring the metal too slowly.

F. **Incorrect dimensions or shape**, owing to factors such as improper shrinkage allowance, pattern mounting error, irregular contraction, deformed pattern, or warped casting.

G. **Inclusions**, which form during melting, solidification and molding. Generally nonmetallic, they are regarded as harmful because they act as stress raisers and reduce the strength of the casting. Particles as small as 30 μm can be filtered out during processing of the molten metal. Inclusions may form during melting when molten metal reacts with the environment (usually oxygen) or with the crucible or mold material. Chemical reactions among components in the molten metal may produce inclusions; slags and other foreign material entrapped in the molten metal also become inclusions. Spalling of the mold and core surfaces also produces inclusions, indicating the importance of the quality of molds and of their maintenance.

10.6.1 Porosity

Porosity in a casting may be caused by *shrinkage* or *gases* or both. Porosity is detrimental to the ductility of a casting and its surface finish, making it permeable and thus affecting pressure tightness of a cast pressure vessel.

Porous regions can develop in castings because of **shrinkage** of the solidified metal. Thin sections in a casting solidify sooner than thicker regions; as a result, molten metal cannot be fed into the thicker regions that have not yet solidified. Porous regions may develop at their centers because of contraction as the surfaces of the thicker region begin to solidify first. *Microporosity* can also develop when the liquid metal solidifies and shrinks between dendrites and between dendrite branches (Section 10.2.3).

Porosity caused by shrinkage can be reduced or eliminated by various means. Adequate liquid metal should be provided to avoid cavities caused by shrinkage. Internal or external **chills**, used in sand casting (Fig. 10.13), also are an effective means of reducing shrinkage porosity. The function of chills is to increase the rate of solidification in critical regions. Internal chills are usually made of the same material as the casting and are left in the casting. However, there may be problems involved in proper fusion of the internal chills with the casting; foundries try to avoid use of internal chills for this reason. External chills may be made of the same material or may be iron, copper, or graphite.

With alloys, porosity can be reduced or eliminated by making the temperature gradient steep. For example, mold materials that have higher thermal conductivity may be used. Subjecting the casting to *hot isostatic pressing* is another method of reducing porosity (Section 17.3.2).

Liquid metals have much greater solubility for **gases** than do solid metals (Fig. 10.14). When a metal begins to solidify, the dissolved gases are expelled from the solution. Gases may also result from reactions of the molten metal with the mold materials. Gases either accumulate in regions of existing porosity (such as in interdendritic regions) or they cause microporosity in the casting, particularly in cast iron, aluminum, and copper.

FIGURE 10.13   Various types of (a) internal and (b) external chills (dark areas at corners), used in castings to eliminate porosity caused by shrinkage. Chills are placed in regions where there is a larger volume of metal, as shown in (c).

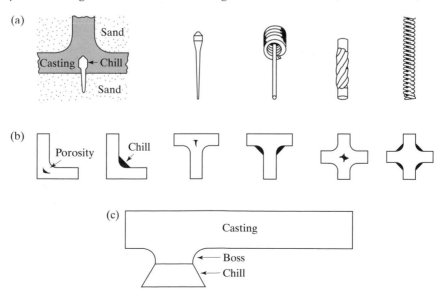

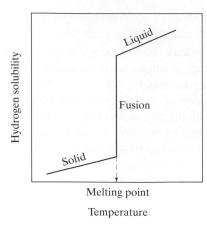

FIGURE 10.14   Solubility of hydrogen in aluminum. Note the sharp decrease in solubility as the molten metal begins to solidify.

Dissolved gases may be removed from the molten metal by flushing or purging with an inert gas, or by melting and pouring the metal in a vacuum. If the dissolved gas is oxygen, the molten metal can be *deoxidized*. Steel is usually deoxidized with aluminum, silicon, copper-based alloys with phosphorus copper, titanium, and zirconium-bearing materials (see also Section 5.2).

Whether microporosity is a result of shrinkage or is caused by gases may be difficult to determine. If the porosity is spherical and has smooth walls (much like the shiny holes in Swiss cheese), it is generally from gases. If the walls are rough and angular, porosity is likely from shrinkage between dendrites. Gross porosity is from shrinkage and is usually called a **shrinkage cavity**.

Example: Casting of U.S. Cannons in the 1860s

An innovative process for casting cannons was developed by Colonel Thomas J. Rodman while he was the commander of the Rock Island Arsenal, in Illinois, in the 1860s. In this process the cast iron gun was cooled from the interior while keeping the exterior in a liquid state. (Referring to Fig. 10.3, for example, assume that the mold wall on the left is the interior surface of the cannon.)

The inner walls of the gun solidified first and as the outer layers began to solidify, they underwent shrinkage, subjecting the already solidified inner wall to compressive residual stress. The result was a stronger and more reliable cannon, called the Rodman Gun, which reportedly lasted twenty times longer than existing guns.

This process revolutionized the art of cannon making world-wide. Some historians credit the invention with discouraging European naval forces from intervening in the U.S. Civil War (1861–1865). In making cylindrical high-pressure vessels, the shrinking of successive layers of concentric tubes over each other is now a well-known technique. With this method, the inner layers of the vessel are subjected to high levels of compressive residual stresses which, in turn, allow the vessel to sustain high internal pressures.

SUMMARY

- Casting is a solidification process in which molten metal is poured into a mold and allowed to cool. The metal may flow through a variety of passages (including pouring basins, sprues, runners, risers, and gating systems) before reaching the final mold cavity. Bernoulli's theorem, the continuity law, and the Reynolds number are the analytical tools used in designing, with the goals of an appropriate flow rate and the elimination of defects associated with fluid flow.

- Solidification of pure metals takes place at a constant temperature; solidification of alloys occurs over a range of temperatures, depending on composition. Phase diagrams are important tools for identifying the solidification point or points for technologically important materials.

- Composition and cooling rates of the melt affect the size and shape of grains and dendrites in the solidifying alloy. In turn, the size and structure of grains and dendrites influence properties of the solidified casting. Solidification time is a function of the volume of a casting and its surface area (Chvorinov's rule).

- The grain structure of castings can be controlled by various means to obtain the desired properties. Because metals contract during solidification and cooling, cavities can form in the casting. Porosity caused by gases evolved during solidification can be a significant problem, particularly because of its adverse effect on the mechanical properties of the castings. Various defects can develop in castings from lack of control of material and process variables.

- Although most metals shrink during solidification, gray cast iron and some aluminum alloys actually expand. Dimensional changes and cracking (hot tearing) are difficulties which can arise during solidification and cooling. Seven basic categories of casting defects have been identified.

- Melting practices have a direct effect on the quality of castings, as do foundry operations such as pattern and mold making, pouring of the melt, removal of cast parts from molds, cleaning, heat treatment, and inspection.

TRENDS

- Argon-oxygen decarburization and deoxidation, as well as electroslag remelting, ladle metallurgy, plasma refining, and calcium wire injection for the production of high-quality steels, are now being practiced by modern foundries.

- Investigation of the following is underway: electromagnetic stirring of the molten metal in the mold and vibration of the mold to obtain smaller and more uniform grain size during solidification; counter-gravity pouring; and shrouding the pouring stream.

- Computer-aided design and manufacturing techniques are being used to predict solidification patterns, prevent casting defects, and calculate weights, volumes, and dimensions for proper mold design and economical production.

- Improvements in the efficiency of furnaces, molten metal quality, and purifying and filtering techniques are being made.

KEY TERMS

Aspiration
Bernoulli's theorem
Casting
Chills
Columnar dendrites
Columnar grains

Cored dendrites
Dendrites
Fluidity
Freezing range
Gate
Gating system

Heterogeneous nucleation
Homogeneous nucleation
Inoculant
Macrosegregation
Microsegregation
Mold
Mushy zone

Porosity	Runners	Solidification
Pouring basin	Segregation	Sprue
Reynolds number	Shrinkage	Turbulence
Risers	Skin	

BIBLIOGRAPHY

ASM Handbook, Vol 15: *Casting*. ASM International, 1988.
Heine, R., *Principles of Metal Casting*. McGraw-Hill, 1999.
Liebermann, H.H., (ed.), *Rapidly Solidified Alloys*. Marcel Dekker, 1993.
Mikelonis, P.J. (ed.), *Foundry Technology: A Source Book*. ASM International, 1982.

Minkoff, I., *Solidification and Cast Structure*. Wiley, 1986.
Steel Castings Handbook (6th ed.). Steel Founders' Society of America, 1995.
Szekely, J., *Fluid Flow Phenomena in Metals Processing*. Academic Press, 1979.

REVIEW QUESTIONS

10.1 Why is casting an important manufacturing process?

10.2 What is the difference between the solidification of pure metals and metal alloys?

10.3 What are dendrites?

10.4 State the difference between short and long freezing ranges. How is range determined?

10.5 Describe the parameters on which solidification time depends.

10.6 Define shrinkage and porosity. How can you tell whether cavities in a casting are due to porosity or to shrinkage?

10.7 What is the function of chills?

10.8 How are dissolved gases removed from molten metal?

10.9 Describe the features of a gating system.

10.10 How is fluidity defined? Why is it important?

10.11 Explain the reasons for hot tearing in castings.

10.12 Name various defects in castings.

10.13 Why is it important to remove dross or slag during the pouring of molten metal into the mold? What methods are used to remove them?

10.14 What are the effects of mold materials on fluid flow and heat transfer?

10.15 Why is Bernoulli's equation important in casting?

10.16 What is a riser?

10.17 What is the purpose of an inoculant?

QUALITATIVE PROBLEMS

10.18 Describe the stages involved in the contraction of metals during casting.

10.19 Explain the reasons why heat transfer and fluid flow are important in metal casting.

10.20 We know that pouring metal at a high rate into a mold has certain disadvantages. Are there any disadvantages to pouring it very slowly?

10.21 Describe the events depicted in Fig. 10.4.

10.22 Would you be concerned about the fact that parts of internal chills are left within the casting? What materials do you think chills should be made of, and why?

10.23 What practical demonstrations can you offer to indicate the relationship of solidification time to volume and surface area?

10.24 Do you think early formation of dendrites in a mold can impede the free flow of molten metal into the mold? Give an illustration.

10.25 Explain why you may want to subject a casting to various heat treatments.

10.26 Why does porosity have detrimental effects on the mechanical properties of castings? Would physical properties such as thermal and electrical conductivity also be affected by porosity? Explain.

10.27 A spoked handwheel is to be cast in gray iron. In order to prevent hot tearing of the spokes, would you insulate the spokes or chill them? Explain.

10.28 Which of the following considerations is/are important for a riser to function properly? Must it: (a) have a surface area larger than the part being cast, (b) be kept open to atmospheric pressure, and/or (c) solidify first? Why?

10.29 Explain why the constant C in Eq. (10.7) depends on mold material, metal properties, and temperature.

10.30 Are external chills as effective as internal chills? Explain.

10.31 Explain why gray cast iron undergoes expansion rather than contraction during solidification, as shown in Table 10.1.

10.32 Referring to Fig. 10.10, explain why internal corners (such as A) develop a thinner skin than external corners (such as B) during solidification.

10.33 Note the shape of the two risers in Fig. 10.7, and discuss your observations with respect to Eq. (10.7).

10.34 Is there any difference in the tendency for shrinkage void formation for metals with short and long freezing ranges, respectively? Explain.

10.35 What is the influence of the cross-sectional area of the spiral channel in Fig. 10.8 on fluidity test results? What is the effect of sprue height? If this test is run with the test setup heated to elevated temperatures, would the test results be more useful? Explain.

10.36 Make a list of safety considerations and precautions that should be taken concerning all aspects of melting and casting of metals, including the equipment involved.

10.37 It has long been observed by foundrymen and ingot casters that low pouring temperatures, i.e., low superheat, promote formation of equiaxed grains over columnar grains. Also, equiaxed grains become finer as the pouring temperature decreases. Explain these phenomena.

10.38 What would you expect to occur if, in casting metal alloys, the mold was aggressively agitated (vibrated) after the molten metal had been in the mold for a sufficient amount of time to form a skin?

10.39 If you examine a typical ice cube, you will see pockets and cracks in the cube. However, some ice cubes are tubular in shape and do not have noticeable air pockets or cracks in their structure. Explain these phenomena.

QUANTITATIVE PROBLEMS

10.40 Sketch a graph of specific volume vs. temperature for a metal that shrinks as it cools from the liquid state to room temperature. On the graph, mark the area where shrinkage is compensated for by risers.

10.41 A round casting is 0.2 m (7.9 in.) in diameter and 0.5 m (19.7 in.) in length. Another casting of the same metal is elliptical in cross-section, with a major to minor axis ratio of 2, and has the same length and cross-sectional area as the round casting. Both pieces are cast under the same conditions. What is the difference in the solidification times of the two castings?

10.42 A 100-mm (4-in.) thick square plate and a right circular cylinder with a radius of 100 mm (4 in.) and a height of 50 mm each have the same volume. If each is to be cast using a cylindrical riser, will each part require the same size riser to ensure proper feeding? Explain.

10.43 Determine the dimensions of each of the parameters in the Reynolds number given in Eq. (10.6), and check for consistency.

10.44 Assume that the top of a round sprue has a diameter of 3 in. (75 mm) and is at a height of 8 in. (200 mm) from the runner. Based on Eq. (10.5), plot the profile of the sprue diameter as a function of its height. Assume that the sprue wall has a diameter of 0.25 in. (6 mm) at the bottom.

10.45 Pure aluminum is poured into a sand mold. The metal level in the pouring basin is 8 in. above the metal level in the mold, and the runner is circular with a 0.5-in. diameter. What is the velocity and rate of flow of the metal into the mold? Is the flow turbulent or laminar?

10.46 For the sprue described in Problem 10.45, what diameter runner is needed to ensure a Reynolds number of 2000? How long will a 25 in³ casting take to fill with such a runner?

10.47 A sprue is 10 in. long and has a diameter of 5 in. at the top, where the metal is poured. If a desired flow rate of 40 in³/sec is to be achieved, what should be the diameter of the bottom of the sprue? Will this sprue aspirate? Explain.

SYNTHESIS AND DESIGN

10.48 Can you devise fluidity tests other than that shown in Fig. 10.8? Explain the features of your test methods.

10.49 The figures below indicate various defects and discontinuities in cast products. Review each one and offer solutions to avoid them.

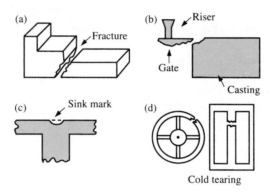

10.50 The fluidity test shown in Fig. 10.8 only illustrates the principle of this test. Design a setup for such a test, showing the type of materials and the equipment to be used. Explain the method by which you would determine the length of the solidified metal in the spiral passage.

10.51 Utilizing the equipment and materials available in a typical kitchen, design an experiment to reproduce results similar to those shown in Fig. 10.10. Comment on your observations.

10.52 One method of relieving stress concentrations in a part is to apply a small uniform plastic deformation to it. Make a list of your concerns and recommendations if such an approach is suggested for a casting.

10.53 If a casting of a given shape is to be doubled in volume, describe the effects on mold design, including the required change in the size of risers, runners, chokes, and sprues.

10.54 Conduct a literature search on the solidification of eutectic-type alloys and the casting defects which occur.

11

Metal-Casting Processes

11.1 INTRODUCTION

The first castings were made during the period 4000–3000 B.C., using stone and metal molds for casting copper. Various casting processes have been developed over a long period of time, each with its own characteristics and applications, to meet specific engineering and service requirements (Table 11.1). Many parts and components are made by casting, including cameras (Fig. 11.1), carburetors, engine blocks, crankshafts, automotive components (Fig. 11.2), agricultural and railroad equipment, pipes and plumbing fixtures, power tools, gun barrels, frying pans, and very large components for hydraulic turbines (Fig. 11.3).

TABLE 11.1   Summary of Casting Processes, Their Advantages and Limitations

Process	Advantages	Limitations
Sand	Almost any metal cast; no limit to size, shape or weight; low tooling cost.	Some finishing required; somewhat coarse finish; wide tolerances.
Shell mold	Good dimensional accuracy and surface finish; high production rate.	Part size limited; expensive patterns and equipment required.
Expendable pattern	Most metals cast with no limit to size; complex shapes.	Patterns have low strength and can be costly for low quantities.
Plaster mold	Intricate shapes; good dimensional accuracy and finish; low porosity.	Limited to nonferrous metals; limited size and volume of production; mold making time relatively long.
Ceramic mold	Intricate shapes; close tolerance parts; good surface finish.	Limited size.
Investment	Intricate shapes; excellent surface finish and accuracy; almost any metal cast.	Part size limited; expensive patterns, molds, and labor.
Permanent mold	Good surface finish and dimensional accuracy; low porosity; high production rate.	High mold cost; limited shape and intricacy; not suitable for high-melting-point metals.
Die	Excellent dimensional accuracy and surface finish; high production rate.	Die cost is high; part size limited; usually limited to nonferrous metals; long lead time.
Centrifugal	Large cylindrical parts with good quality; high production rate.	Equipment is expensive; part shape limited.

Two trends are currently having a major impact on the casting industry. The first is continuing mechanization and automation of the casting process, which has led to significant changes in the use of equipment and labor. Advanced machinery and automated process-control systems have replaced traditional methods of casting. The second major trend is the increasing demand for high-quality castings with close dimensional tolerances and no defects (Table 11.2).

FIGURE 11.1   (a) The Polaroid PDC-2000 digital camera with a AZ91D die-cast, high-purity magnesium case. (b) Two-piece Polaroid camera case made by the hot-chamber die casting process. *Source*: Courtesy of Polaroid Corporation and Chicago White Metal Casting, Inc.

FIGURE 11.2   Typical gray-iron castings used in automobiles, including transmission valve body (left) and hub rotor with disk-brake cylinder (front). *Source*: Courtesy of Central Foundry Division of General Motors Corporation.

FIGURE 11.3   A cast trasmission housing.

TABLE 11.2   General Characteristics of Casting Processes

Process	Typical materials cast	Weight (kg)		Typical surface finish (μm, R_a)	Porosity*	Shape complexity*	Dimensional accuracy*	Section thickness (mm)	
		Minimum	Maximum					Minimum	Maximum
Sand	All	0.05	No limit	5–25	4	1–2	3	3	No limit
Shell	All	0.05	100+	1–3	4	2–3	2	2	—
Expendable mold pattern	All	0.05	No limit	5–20	4	1	2	2	No limit
Plaster mold	Nonferrous (Al, Mg, Zn, Cu)	0.05	50+	1–2	3	1–2	2	1	—
Investment	All (High melting pt.)	0.005	100+	1–3	3	1	1	1	75
Permanent mold	All	0.5	300	2–3	2–3	3–4	1	2	50
Die	Nonferrous (Al, Mg, Zn, Cu)	< 0.05	50	1–2	1–2	3–4	1	0.5	12
Centrifugal	All	—	5000+	2–10	1–2	3–4	3	2	100

*Relative rating: 1 best, 5 worst.
Note: These ratings are only general; significant variations can occur, depending on the methods used.

This chapter is organized around the major classifications of casting practices (see Fig. II.2 in the Introduction to Part II). These classifications are related to mold materials, molding processes, and methods of feeding the mold with the molten metal. The major categories are as follows:

1. **Expendable molds**, which are made of sand, plaster, ceramics, and similar materials. These are generally mixed with various binders, or bonding agents. As described in Chapter 8, these materials are refractories, that is, they are capable of withstanding the high temperatures of molten metals. After the casting has solidified, the mold in these processes is broken up to remove the casting.

2. **Permanent molds**, which are made of metals that maintain their strength at high temperatures. As the name implies, they are used repeatedly and are designed in such a way that the casting can be easily removed and the mold used for the next casting. Because metal molds are better heat conductors than expendable nonmetallic molds, the solidifying casting is subjected to a higher rate of cooling, which in turn affects the microstructure and grain size within the casting (Chapter 10).

3. **Composite molds**, which are made of two or more different materials, such as sand, graphite, and metal, combining the advantages of each material. They are used in various casting processes to improve mold strength, control the cooling rates, and optimize the overall economics of the process.

The major expendable-mold processes are introduced in Sections 11.2–11.8, and the permanent-mold processes are introduced in Sections 11.9–11.14. Because of their unique characteristics and applications, particularly in manufacturing microelectronic devices, basic crystal-growing techniques are also described. The chapter concludes with an overview of modern foundries.

11.2 SAND CASTING

The traditional method of casting metals is in sand molds and has been used for millennia. Simply stated, *sand casting* consists of (a) placing a pattern having the shape of the desired casting in sand to make an imprint, (b) incorporating a gating system, (c) filling the resulting cavity with molten metal, (d) allowing the metal to cool until it solidifies, (e) breaking away the sand mold, and (f) removing the casting (Fig. 11.4). The production steps for a typical sand-casting operation are shown in Fig. 11.5.

Although the origins of sand casting date to ancient times, it is still the most prevalent form of casting. In the United States alone, about 15 million tons of metal are cast by this method each year.

11.2.1 Sands

Most sand casting operations use silica sand (SiO_2), which is the product of the disintegration of rocks over extremely long periods of time. Sand is inexpensive and is suitable as mold material because of its resistance to high temperatures. There are two general types of sand: **naturally bonded** (*bank* sand) and **synthetic** (*lake* sand). Because its composition can be controlled more accurately, synthetic sand is preferred by most foundries.

Several factors are important in the selection of sand for molds. Sand having fine, round grains can be closely packed and forms a smooth mold surface. Although fine-grained sand enhances mold strength, the fine grains also lower mold *permeability*. Good permeability of molds and cores allows gases and steam evolved during casting to escape easily.

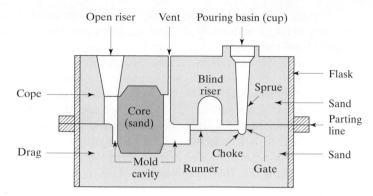

FIGURE 11.4   Schematic illustration of a sand mold, showing various features.

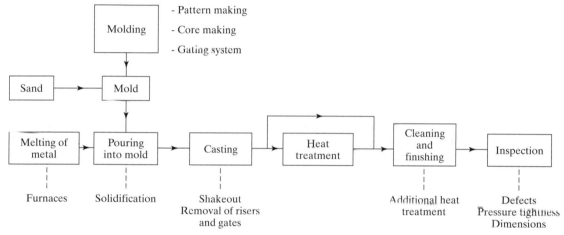

FIGURE 11.5   Outline of production steps in a typical sand-casting operation.

The mold should have good *collapsibility* (to allow for the casting to shrink while cooling) to avoid defects in the casting, such as hot tearing and cracking (Section 10.5). Thus the selection of sand involves certain tradeoffs with respect to properties. Sand is typically conditioned before use.

Mulling machines are used to uniformly and thoroughly mull (mix) sand with additives. Clay (bentonite) is used as a cohesive agent to bond sand particles, giving the sand strength. Zircon ($ZrSiO_4$), olivine (Mg_2SiO_4), and iron silicate (Fe_2SiO_4) sands are often used in steel foundries for their low thermal expansion. Chromite ($FeCr_2O_4$) is used for its high heat-transfer characteristics.

11.2.2 Types of Sand Molds

Sand molds are characterized by the types of sand that comprise them and by the methods used to produce them. There are three basic types of sand molds: green-sand, cold-box, and no-bake molds.

The most common mold material is **green molding sand**, which is a mixture of sand, clay, and water. The term "green" refers to the fact that the sand in the mold is moist or damp while the metal is being poured into it. Green-sand molding is the least expensive method of making molds.

In the **skin-dried** method, the mold surfaces are dried, either by storing the mold in air or by drying it with torches. These molds are generally used for large castings because of their higher strength.

Sand molds are also oven dried (*baked*) prior to pouring the molten metal; they are stronger than green-sand molds and impart better dimensional accuracy and surface finish to the casting. However, this method has drawbacks: distortion of the mold is greater; the castings are more susceptible to hot tearing because of the lower collapsibility of the mold; and the production rate is slower because of the drying time required.

In the **cold-box mold** process, various organic and inorganic *binders* are blended into the sand to bond the grains chemically for greater strength. These molds are dimensionally more accurate than green-sand molds but are more expensive.

In the **no-bake mold** process, a synthetic liquid resin is mixed with the sand; the mixture hardens at room temperature. Because bonding of the mold in this and in the cold-box process takes place without heat, they are called **cold-setting processes**.

The following are the major components of sand molds (Fig. 11.4):

1. The mold itself, which is supported by a **flask**. Two-piece molds consist of a **cope** on top and a **drag** on the bottom. The seam between them is the parting line. When more than two pieces are used, the additional parts are called *cheeks*.

2. A **pouring basin** or *pouring cup*, into which the molten metal is poured.

3. A **sprue**, through which the molten metal flows downward.

4. The **runner system**, which has channels that carry the molten metal from the sprue to the mold cavity. *Gates* are the inlets into the mold cavity.

5. **Risers**, which supply additional metal to the casting as it shrinks during solidification. Figure 11.4 shows two different types of risers: a *blind riser* and an *open riser*.

6. **Cores**, which are inserts made from sand. They are placed in the mold to form hollow regions or otherwise define the interior surface of the casting. Cores are also used on the outside of the casting to form features such as lettering on the surface of a casting or deep external pockets.

7. **Vents**, which are placed in molds to carry off gases produced when the molten metal comes into contact with the sand in the mold and core. They also exhaust air from the mold cavity as the molten metal flows into the mold.

11.2.3 Patterns

Patterns are used to mold the sand mixture into the shape of the casting. They may be made of wood, plastic, or metal. The selection of a pattern material depends on the size and shape of the casting, the dimensional accuracy, the quantity of castings required, and the molding process (Table 11.3).

Because patterns are used repeatedly to make molds, the strength and durability of the material selected for patterns must reflect the number of castings that the mold will produce. They may be made of a combination of materials to reduce wear in critical regions. Patterns are usually coated with a **parting agent** to facilitate their removal from the molds.

Patterns can be designed with a variety of features to fit application and economic requirements. **One-piece patterns**, also called *loose* or *solid patterns*, are generally used for simpler shapes and low-quantity production. They are generally made of wood and are inexpensive. **Split patterns** are two-piece patterns made such that each part forms a portion of the cavity for the casting; in this way, castings with complicated shapes can be produced.

TABLE 11.3   Characteristics of Pattern Materials

Characteristic	Rating[a]				
	Wood	*Aluminum*	*Steel*	*Plastic*	*Cast iron*
Machinability	E	G	F	G	G
Wear resistance	P	G	E	F	E
Strength	F	G	E	G	G
Weight[b]	E	G	P	G	P
Repairability	E	P	G	F	G
Resistance to:					
Corrosion[c]	E	E	P	E	P
Swelling[c]	P	E	E	E	E

[a]E, excellent; G, good; F, fair; P, poor.

[b]As a factor in operator fatigue.

[c]By water.

Source: D.C. Ekey and W.R Winter, *Introduction to Foundry Technology*. New York. McGraw-Hill, 1958.

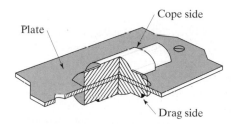

FIGURE 11.6   A typical metal match-plate pattern used in sand casting.

Match-plate patterns are a popular type of mounted pattern in which two-piece patterns are constructed by securing each half of one or more split patterns to the opposite sides of a single plate (Fig. 11.6). In such constructions, the gating system can be mounted on the drag side of the pattern. This type of pattern is used most often in conjunction with molding machines and large production runs to produce smaller castings.

An important recent development is the application of **rapid prototyping** (Chapter 19) to mold and pattern making. In sand casting, for example, a pattern can be fabricated in a rapid prototyping machine and fastened to a backing plate at a fraction of the time and cost of machining a pattern. There are several rapid prototyping techniques with which these tools can be produced quickly.

Pattern design is a crucial aspect of the total casting operation. The design should provide for **metal shrinkage**, ease of removal from the sand mold by means of a taper or draft (Fig. 11.7), and proper metal flow in the mold cavity. These topics are described in greater detail in Chapter 12.

FIGURE 11.7   Taper on patterns for ease of removal from the sand mold.

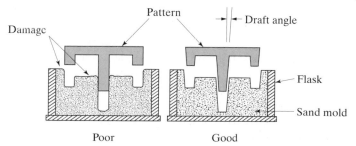

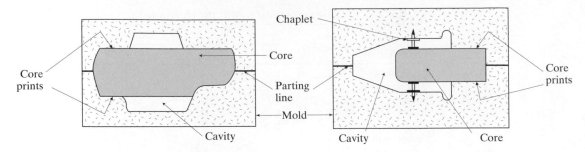

FIGURE 11.8   Examples of sand cores showing core prints and chaplets to support cores.

11.2.4 Cores

For castings with internal cavities or passages, such as those found in an automotive engine block or a valve body, *cores* are utilized. Cores are placed in the mold cavity before casting to form the interior surfaces of the casting and are removed from the finished part during shakeout and further processing. Like molds, cores must possess strength, permeability, ability to withstand heat, and collapsibility; therefore, cores are made of sand aggregates.

The core is anchored by **core prints**. These are recesses that are added to the pattern to support the core and to provide vents for the escape of gases (Fig. 11.8). A common problem with cores is that for some casting requirements, as in the case where a recess is required, they may lack sufficient structural support in the cavity. To keep the core from shifting, metal supports (**chaplets**) may be used to anchor the core in place (Fig. 11.8).

Cores are generally made in a manner similar to that used in making molds; the majority are made with shell, no-bake, or cold-box processes. Cores are formed in *core boxes*, which are used in much the same way that patterns are used to form sand molds. The sand can be packed into the boxes with sweeps, or blown into the box by compressed air from *core blowers*. The latter have the advantages of producing uniform cores and operating at very high production rates.

11.2.5 Sand-Molding Machines

The oldest known method of molding, which is still used for simple castings, is to compact the sand by hand hammering (tamping) or ramming it around the pattern. For most operations, however, the sand mixture is compacted around the pattern by *molding machines* (Fig. 11.9). These machines eliminate arduous labor, offer high-quality casting by improving the application and distribution of forces, manipulate the mold in a carefully controlled manner, and increase production rate.

Mechanization of the molding process can be further assisted by **jolting** the assembly. The flask, molding sand, and pattern are first placed on a pattern plate mounted on an anvil, and then jolted upward by air pressure at rapid intervals. The inertial forces compact the sand around the pattern. Jolting produces the highest compaction at the horizontal parting line, whereas in squeezing, compaction is highest at the squeezing head (Fig. 11.9). Thus, more uniform compaction can be obtained by combining squeezing and jolting.

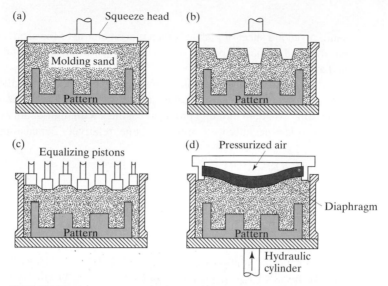

FIGURE 11.9   Various designs of squeeze heads for mold making: (a) conventional flat head; (b) profile head; (c) equalizing squeeze pistons; and (d) flexible diaphragm. *Source*: © Institute of British Foundrymen. Used with permission.

In **vertical flaskless molding**, the halves of the pattern form a vertical chamber wall against which sand is blown and compacted (Fig. 11.10). Then, the mold halves are packed horizontally, with the parting line oriented vertically and moved along a pouring conveyor. This operation is simple and eliminates the need to handle flasks, allowing for very high production rates, particularly when other aspects of the operation (such as coring and pouring) are automated.

Sandslingers fill the flask uniformly with sand under high-pressure stream. They are used to fill large flasks and are typically operated by machine. An impeller in the machine throws sand from its blades or cups at such high speeds that the machine not only places the sand but also rams it appropriately.

In **impact molding**, the sand is compacted by controlled explosion or instantaneous release of compressed gases. This method produces molds with uniform strength and good permeability.

In **vacuum molding**, also known as the "*V*" *process*, the pattern is covered tightly by a thin sheet of plastic. A flask is placed over the coated pattern and is filled with dry binderless

FIGURE 11.10   Vertical flaskless molding. (a) Sand is squeezed between two halves of the pattern. (b) Assembled molds pass along an assembly line for pouring.

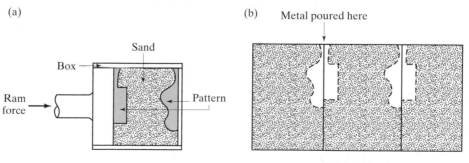

sand. A second sheet of plastic is then placed on top of the sand, and a vacuum action hardens the sand so that the pattern can be withdrawn. Both halves of the mold are made this way and assembled.

During pouring, the mold remains under a vacuum but the casting cavity does not. When the metal has solidified, the vacuum is turned off and the sand falls away, releasing the casting. Vacuum molding produces castings with high-quality detail and dimensional accuracy. It is especially well suited for large, relatively flat castings.

11.2.6 The Sand-Casting Operation

After the mold has been shaped and the cores have been placed in position, the two halves (cope and drag) are closed, clamped, and weighted down. They are weighted to prevent the separation of the mold sections under the pressure exerted when the molten metal is poured into the mold cavity.

The design of the gating system is important for proper delivery of the molten metal into the mold cavity. As described in Section 10.3, turbulence must be minimized, air and gases must be allowed to escape by such means as vents, and proper temperature gradients must be established and maintained to minimize shrinkage and porosity. The design of risers is also important in order to supply the necessary molten metal during solidification of the casting. The pouring basin may also serve as a riser. A complete sequence of operations in sand casting is shown in Fig. 11.11.

After solidification, the casting is shaken out of its mold, and the sand and oxide layers adhering to the casting are removed by vibration (using a shaker) or by sand blasting. Ferrous castings are also cleaned by blasting with steel shot (shot blasting) or grit. The risers and gates are cut off by oxyfuel–gas cutting, sawing, shearing, and abrasive wheels, or they are trimmed in dies. Gates and risers on steel castings are also removed with air carbon-arc (Section 27.9) or powder-injection torches. Castings may be cleaned by electrochemical means or by pickling with chemicals to remove surface oxides.

The characteristics of sand casting and other casting processes are given in Table 11.2 (see also Chapter 12). Almost all commercially-used metals can be sand cast. The surface finish obtained (Fig. 11.12) is largely a function of the materials used in making the mold. Dimensional accuracy is not as good as that of other casting processes. However, intricate shapes can be cast by this process, such as cast-iron engine blocks and very large propellers for ocean liners. Sand casting can be economical for relatively small production runs, and equipment costs are generally low.

The surface of castings is important in subsequent machining operations, because machinability can be adversely affected if the castings are not cleaned properly and sand particles remain on the surface. If regions of the casting have not formed properly or have formed incompletely, the defects may be repaired by filling them with weld metal. Sand-mold castings generally have rough, grainy surfaces, depending on the quality of the mold and the materials used.

The casting may subsequently be heat-treated (Chapter 4) to improve certain properties needed for its intended service use; these processes are particularly important for steel castings. Finishing operations may involve machining straightening, or forging with dies to obtain final dimensions.

Minor surface imperfections may also be filled with a metal-filled epoxy, especially for cast-iron castings because they are difficult to weld. Inspection (Section 36.9) is an important final step and is carried out to ensure that the casting meets all design and quality-control requirements.

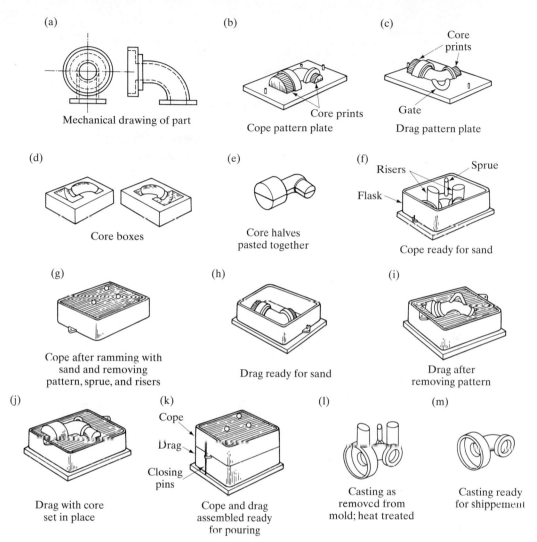

(a) Mechanical drawing of part

(b) Cope pattern plate — Core prints

(c) Core prints — Gate — Drag pattern plate

(d) Core boxes

(e) Core halves pasted together

(f) Risers — Sprue — Flask — Cope ready for sand

(g) Cope after ramming with sand and removing pattern, sprue, and risers

(h) Drag ready for sand

(i) Drag after removing pattern

(j) Drag with core set in place

(k) Cope — Drag — Closing pins — Cope and drag assembled ready for pouring

(l) Casting as removed from mold; heat treated

(m) Casting ready for shippement

FIGURE 11.11 Schematic illustration of the sequence of operations for sand casting. *Source*: Steel Founders' Society of America. (a) A mechanical drawing of the part is used to generate a design for the pattern. Considerations such as part shrinkage and draft must be built into the drawing. (b–c) Patterns have been mounted on plates equipped with pins for alignment. Note the presence of core prints designed to hold the core in place. (d–e) Core boxes produce core halves, which are pasted together. The cores will be used to produce the hollow area of the part shown in (a). (f) The cope half of the mold is assembled by securing the cope pattern plate to the flask with aligning pins, and attaching inserts to form the sprue and risers. (g) The flask is rammed with sand and the plate and inserts are removed. (h) The drag half is produced in a similar manner, with the pattern inserted. A bottom board is placed below the drag and aligned with pins. (i) The pattern, flask, and bottom board are inverted, and the pattern is withdrawn, leaving the appropriate imprint. (j) The core is set in place within the drag cavity. (k) The mold is closed by placing the cope on top of the drag and securing the assembly with pins. The flasks are then subjected to pressure to counteract buoyant forces in the liquid, which might lift the cope. (l) After the metal solidifies, the casting is removed from the mold. (m) The sprue and risers are cut off and recycled, and the casting is cleaned, inspected, and heat treated (when necessary).

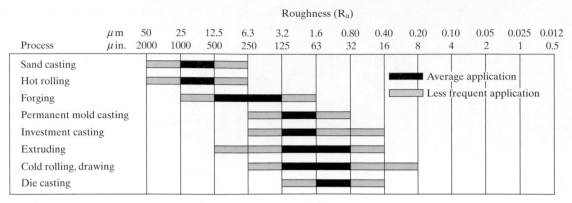

Process	μm μin.	50 2000	25 1000	12.5 500	6.3 250	3.2 125	1.6 63	0.80 32	0.40 16	0.20 8	0.10 4	0.05 2	0.025 1	0.012 0.5

Roughness (Rₐ)

Sand casting
Hot rolling
Forging
Permanent mold casting
Investment casting
Extruding
Cold rolling, drawing
Die casting

■ Average application
▨ Less frequent application

FIGURE 11.12   Surface roughness in casting and other metalworking processes. See also Figs. 22.14 and 26.4 for comparison with other manufacturing processes.

11.3 SHELL-MOLD CASTING

Shell-mold casting was first developed in the 1940s and has grown significantly because it can produce many types of castings with close dimensional tolerances and good surface finish at low cost. In this process, (a) a mounted pattern made of a ferrous metal or aluminum is heated to 175 °C–370 °C (350 °F–700 °F), (b) coated with a parting agent such as silicone, and (c) clamped to a box or chamber.

The box contains fine sand, mixed with 2.5% to 4% thermosetting resin *binder* (such as phenol-formaldehyde) that coats the sand particles. The box is either rotated upside down (Fig. 11.13) or the sand mixture is blown over the pattern, allowing it to coat the pattern.

The assembly is then placed in an oven for a short period of time to complete the curing of the resin. In most shell-molding machines the oven is a metal box with gas-fired burners that swing over the shell mold to cure it. The shell hardens around the pattern and is removed from the pattern using built-in ejector pins. Two half-shells are made in this manner and are bonded or clamped together in preparation for pouring.

The thickness of the shell can be accurately determined by controlling the time that the pattern is in contact with the mold. In this way, the shell can be formed with the re-

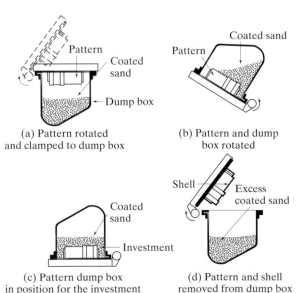

(a) Pattern rotated and clamped to dump box

(b) Pattern and dump box rotated

(c) Pattern dump box in position for the investment

(d) Pattern and shell removed from dump box

FIGURE 11.13   A common method of making shell molds. Called *dump-box* technique, the limitations are the formation of voids in the shell and peelback (when sections of the shell fall off as the pattern is raised). *Source*: ASM International.

quired strength and rigidity to hold the weight of the molten liquid. The shells are light and thin (usually 5 mm–10 mm, 0.2 in.–0.4 in.), and consequently their thermal characteristics are different from those for thicker molds.

Shell sand has a much lower permeability than sand used for green-sand molding, because a sand of much smaller grain size is used for shell molding. The decomposition of the shell-sand binder also produces a high volume of gas; unless the molds are properly vented, trapped air and gas can cause serious problems in shell molding of ferrous castings.

Shell molds are generally poured with the parting line horizontal and may also be supported by sand. The walls of the mold are relatively smooth, offering low resistance to flow of the molten metal and producing castings with sharper corners, thinner sections, and smaller projections than are possible in green-sand molds. With the use of multiple gating systems, several castings can be produced in a single mold.

Nearly any metal suited for sand casting may be cast by the shell-mold process and may be more economical than other casting processes, depending on various production factors. The cost of the resin binders is offset somewhat by the fact that only one-twentieth of the sand used in sand casting is necessary. The relatively high cost of metal patterns becomes a smaller factor as the size of production runs increases.

The high quality of the finished casting can significantly reduce cleaning, machining, and other finishing costs. Complex shapes can be produced with less labor, and the process can be automated fairly easily. Shell-molding applications include small mechanical parts requiring high precision, such as gear housings, cylinder heads, and connecting rods; the process is also widely used in producing high-precision molding cores.

11.3.1 Composite Molds

Composite molds are made of two or more different materials and are used in shell molding and other casting processes. They are generally employed in casting complex shapes such as impellers for turbines. Examples of composite molds are shown in Figs. 11.14a and

FIGURE 11.14   (a) Schematic illustration of a semipermanent composite mold. *Source: Steel Castings Handbook*, 5th ed. Steel Founders' Society of America, 1980. (b) A composite mold used in casting an aluminum-alloy torque converter. This part was previously cast in an all-plaster mold. *Source: Metals Handbook*, vol. 5, 8th ed.

(a)   (b)

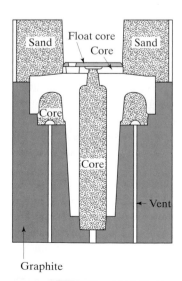

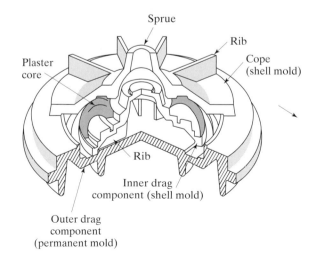

11.14b. Molding materials commonly used are shells (made as previously described), plaster, sand with binder, metal, and graphite.

Composite molds may also include cores and chills to control the rate of solidification in critical areas of castings. Composite molds increase the strength of the mold, improve the dimensional accuracy and surface finish of castings, and may help reduce overall costs and processing time.

11.3.2 Sodium Silicate Process

The mold material in the *sodium silicate process* is a mixture of sand and 1.5% to 6% sodium silicate (waterglass) as a binder. The mixture is packed around the pattern and hardened by blowing carbon dioxide (CO_2) gas through it. This process, also known as *silicate-bonded sand* or the *carbon-dioxide process*, was first used in the 1950s and has been developed further, for example, by using various other chemicals for binders. Cores made through this process reduce the tendency for parts to tear because of their compliance at elevated temperatures.

11.3.3 Rammed Graphite Molding

In this process, rammed graphite is used to make molds for casting reactive metals such as titanium and zirconium. Sand cannot be used because these metals react vigorously with silica. The molds are packed rather like sand molds (Section 11.2.5), air dried, baked at 175 °C (350 °F), fired at 870 °C (1600 °F), then stored under controlled humidity and temperature. The casting procedures are similar to those for sand molds.

11.4 EXPENDABLE-PATTERN CASTING (LOST FOAM)

The *expendable-pattern casting* process uses a polystyrene pattern, which evaporates upon contact with molten metal to form a cavity for the casting. The process is also known as *evaporative-pattern* or *lost-pattern casting*, and under the trade name *Full-Mold* process. It was formerly known as the "expanded polystyrene process," and has become one of the more important casting processes for ferrous and nonferrous metals, particularly for the automotive industry.

In this process, raw expendable polystyrene (EPS) beads, containing 5% to 8% pentane (a volatile hydrocarbon), are placed in a preheated die which is usually made of aluminum. The polystyrene expands and takes the shape of the die cavity; additional heat is applied to fuse and bond the beads together. The die is then cooled and opened, and the polystyrene pattern is removed. Complex patterns may also be made by bonding various individual pattern sections using hot-melt adhesive (Section 30.4).

The pattern is coated with a water-based refractory slurry, dried, and placed in a flask. The flask is then filled with loose fine sand, which surrounds and supports the pattern (Fig.11.15) and may be dried or mixed with bonding agents to give it additional strength. The sand is periodically compacted by various means (see Fig. 11.9). Then, without removing the polystyrene pattern, the molten metal is poured into the mold.

This action immediately vaporizes the pattern (an ablation process) and fills the mold cavity, completely replacing the space previously occupied by the polystyrene pattern. The heat degrades (depolymerizes) the polystyrene and the degradation products are vented into the surrounding sand.

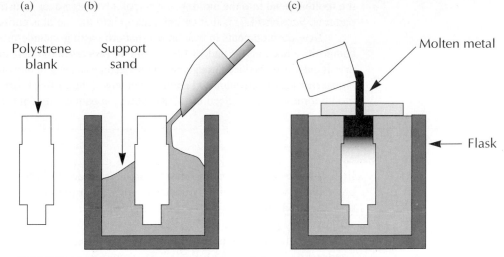

FIGURE 11.15   Schematic illustration of the expendable pattern casting process, also known as lost foam or evaporative casting.

The flow velocity in the mold depends on the rate of degradation of the polymer. Studies have shown that the flow of the molten metal is basically laminar, with Reynolds numbers in the range of 400 to 3000 (Section 10.3.1). The velocity of the molten metal at the metal–polymer pattern front is estimated to be in the range of 0.1 m/s–1.0 m/s. The velocity can be controlled by producing patterns with cavities or hollow sections; thus the velocity will increase as the molten metal crosses these hollow regions, similar to pouring it into an empty cavity as is done in sand casting.

Because the polymer requires considerable energy to degrade, large thermal gradients are present at the metal-polymer interface; in other words, the molten metal cools faster than it would if it were poured into a cavity. Consequently, fluidity (Section 10.3.2) is less than in sand casting. This has important effects on the microstructure throughout the casting and also leads to directional solidification of the metal.

The evaporative-pattern process has a number of advantages over other casting methods:

a. The process is relatively simple because there are no parting lines, cores, or riser systems; hence it has design flexibility.

b. Inexpensive flasks are sufficient for the process.

c. Polystyrene is inexpensive and can be easily processed into patterns having complex shapes, various sizes, and fine surface detail.

d. The casting requires minimum finishing and cleaning operations.

e. The process can be automated and is economical for long production runs. A major factor is the cost to produce the die used for expanding the polystyrene beads to make the pattern.

Typical applications for this process are cylinder heads, crankshafts, brake components and manifolds for automobiles, and machine bases. Aluminum engine blocks and other components of the General Motors Saturn automobiles are made by this process. Recent developments include the use of polymethylmethacrylate (PMMA) and polyalkylene carbonate as pattern materials for ferrous castings.

In a modification of the evaporative-pattern process, a polystyrene pattern is surrounded by a ceramic shell (*Replicast C-S process*). The pattern is burned out prior to pouring the molten metal into the mold. Its principal advantage over investment casting (using wax patterns, Section 11.7) is that carbon pickup into the metal is entirely avoided.

New developments in evaporative-pattern casting include production of metal-matrix composites (Sections 9.5 and 18.13). During the process of molding the polymer pattern, fibers or particles are embedded throughout. These become an integral part of the casting. Further techniques include modification and grain refinement of the casting by the use of grain refiners and modifier master alloys (Section 11.18) within the pattern while it is being molded.

11.5 PLASTER-MOLD CASTING

In the *plaster-mold casting* process, the mold is made of plaster of paris (gypsum, or calcium sulfate), with the addition of talc and silica flour to improve strength and to control the time required for the plaster to set. These components are mixed with water, and the resulting slurry is poured over the pattern.

After the plaster sets, usually within 15 minutes, the pattern is removed and the mold is dried at 120 °C–260 °C (250 °F–500 °F) to remove the moisture. Higher drying temperatures may be used depending on the type of plaster. The mold halves are assembled to form the mold cavity and are preheated to about 120 °C (250 °F). The molten metal is then poured into the mold.

Because plaster molds have very low permeability, gases evolved during solidification of the metal cannot escape. Consequently, the molten metal is poured either in a vacuum or under pressure. Mold permeability can be increased substantially by the *Antioch* process in which the molds are dehydrated in an autoclave (pressurized oven) for 6–12 hours, then rehydrated in air for 14 hours. Another method of increasing permeability is to use foamed plaster containing trapped air bubbles.

Patterns for plaster molding are generally made of aluminum alloys, thermosetting plastics, brass, or zinc alloys. Wood patterns are not suitable for making a large number of molds because they are repeatedly in contact with the water-based plaster slurry. Since there is a limit to the maximum temperature that the plaster mold can withstand (generally about 1200 °C; 2200 °F), plaster-mold casting is used only for aluminum, magnesium, zinc, and some copper-based alloys.

The castings have fine details with good surface finish. Because plaster molds have lower thermal conductivity than others, the castings cool slowly, and the more uniform grain structure is obtained with less warpage. Wall thickness of parts can be 1 mm–2.5 mm (0.04 in.–0.1 in.).

This process and the ceramic-mold and investment casting processes (described below) are known as **precision casting** because of the high dimensional accuracy and good surface finish obtained. Typical parts made are lock components, gears, valves, fittings, tooling, and ornaments. Castings usually weigh less than 10 kg (22 lb) and are typically in the range of 125–250 g (1/4–1/2 lb), although parts as light as 1 g (0.035 oz) have been made.

11.6 CERAMIC-MOLD CASTING

The *ceramic-mold casting* process, also called *cope-and-drag investment casting*, is similar to the plaster-mold process, with the exception that it uses refractory mold materials suitable for high-temperature applications. The slurry is a mixture of fine-grained zircon (ZrSiO$_4$), aluminum oxide, and fused silica, which are mixed with bonding agents and poured over the pattern (Fig. 11.16), which has been placed in a flask.

The pattern may be made of wood or metal. After setting, the molds (ceramic facings) are removed, dried, burned off to remove volatile matter, and baked. The molds are clamped firmly and used as all-ceramic molds. In the *Shaw process*, the ceramic facings

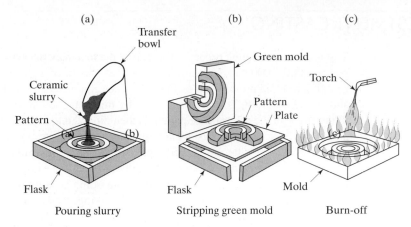

FIGURE 11.16   Sequence of operations in making a ceramic mold. *Source*: *Metals Handbook*, vol. 5, 8th ed.

are backed by fireclay (clay used in making firebricks that resist high temperatures) to give strength to the mold. The facings are then assembled into a complete mold, ready to be poured (Fig. 11.17).

The high-temperature resistance of the refractory molding materials allows these molds to be used in casting ferrous and other high-temperature alloys, stainless steels, and tool steels. The castings have good dimensional accuracy and surface finish over a wide range of sizes and intricate shapes, but the process is somewhat expensive. Typical parts made are impellers, cutters for machining operations, dies for metalworking, and molds for making plastic or rubber components. Parts weighing as much as 700 kg (1500 lb) have been cast by this process.

FIGURE 11.17   A typical ceramic mold (Shaw process) for casting steel dies used in hot forging. *Source*: *Metals Handbook*, vol. 5, 8th ed.

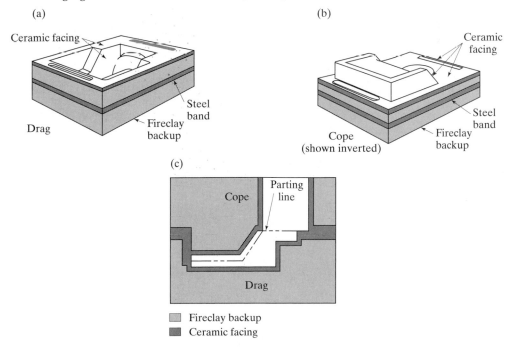

11.7 INVESTMENT CASTING

The *investment-casting* process, also called the **lost-wax process**, was first used during the period 4000–3000 B.C. The pattern is made of wax or of a plastic (such as polystyrene) by molding or rapid prototyping techniques. The sequences involved in investment casting are shown in Fig. 11.18. The pattern is made by injecting molten wax or plastic into a metal die in the shape of the pattern. The pattern is then dipped into a slurry of refractory material such as very fine silica and binders, including water, ethyl silicate, and acids. After this initial coating has dried, the pattern is coated repeatedly to increase its thickness.

The term *investment* derives from the fact that the pattern is invested with the refractory material. Wax patterns require careful handling because they are not strong enough to withstand the forces involved during mold making. However, unlike plastic patterns, wax can be recovered and reused.

FIGURE 11.18   Schematic illustration of investment casting (lost-wax process). Castings by this method can be made with very fine detail and from a variety of metals. *Source*: Steel Founders' Society of America.

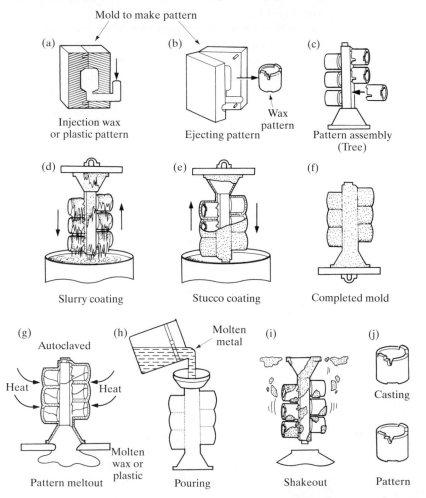

The one-piece mold is dried in air and heated to a temperature of 90 °C–175 °C (200 °F–375 °F). It is held in an inverted position for about 12 hours to melt out the wax. The mold is then fired to 650 °C–1050 °C (1200 °F–1900 °F) for about 4 hours, depending on the metal to be cast, to drive off the water of crystallization (chemically combined water) and burn off any residual wax. After the metal has been poured and has solidified, the mold is broken up and the casting is removed. A number of patterns can be joined to make one mold, called a **tree** (Fig. 11.18c), significantly increasing the production rate.

For small parts, the tree can be inserted into a permeable flask and filled with liquid slurry investment. The investment is then placed into a chamber and evacuated to remove air bubbles in it until the mold solidifies. The flask is then treated as the mold shown in Fig. 11.18, except that it is commonly placed in a vacuum-casting machine, so that molten metal is drawn into the permeable mold and onto the part, producing fine detail.

Although the labor and materials involved make the lost-wax process costly, it is suitable for casting high-melting-point alloys with good surface finish and close dimensional tolerances. Therefore, few or no finishing operations, which would otherwise add significantly to the total cost of the casting, are required.

This process is capable of producing intricate shapes, with parts weighing from 1 g to 35 kg (0.035 oz to 75 lb), from a wide variety of ferrous and nonferrous metals and alloys. Typical parts made are components for office equipment as well as mechanical components such as gears, cams, valves, and ratchets. Parts up to 1.5 m (60 in.) in diameter and weighing as much as 1140 kg (2500 lb) have been successfully manufactured through this process.

Example: Eliminating Porosity in Casting

In investment casting of an aluminum-alloy valve body, porosity developed at the core–casting interface. The mold was originally heated to 200 °C (400 °F), which was too high for the metal around the core to solidify at a sufficiently high rate.

The casting began to solidify from the outside wall toward the core, and the gas (hydrogen) expelled during freezing of the metal accumulated at the area near the core-metal interface, resulting in porosity. By lowering the mold temperature to around 90 °C (200 °F), the metal around the core solidified at a high enough rate to prevent expulsion of gases around the core area, thus eliminating porosity.

Ceramic-Shell Investment Casting.   A variation of the investment-casting process is *ceramic-shell casting*. It uses the same type of wax or plastic pattern, which is dipped first in ethyl silicate gel and subsequently into a fluidized bed of fine-grained fused silica or zircon flour. The pattern is then dipped into coarser-grained silica to build up additional coatings and proper thickness so that the pattern can withstand the thermal shock of pouring. The rest of the procedure is similar to investment casting. This process is economical and is used extensively for precision casting of steels and high-temperature alloys.

The sequence of operations involved in making a turbine disk by this method is shown in Fig. 11.19. If ceramic cores are used in the casting, they are removed by leaching with caustic solutions under high pressure and temperature. The molten metal may be poured in a vacuum to extract evolved gases and reduce oxidation, thus improving the quality of the casting. To further reduce microporosity, the castings made by this and other processes are subjected to hot isostatic pressing (see Section 17.3). Aluminum castings, for example, are subjected to a gas pressure up to 100 MPa (15 ksi) at 500 °C (900 °F).

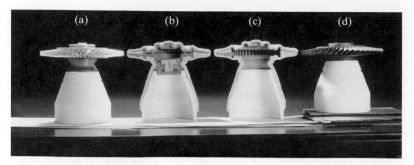

FIGURE 11.19   Investment casting of an integrally cast rotor for a gas turbine. (a) Wax pattern assembly. (b) Ceramic shell around wax pattern. (c) Wax is melted out and the mold is filled, under a vacuum, with molten superalloy. (d) The cast rotor, produced to net or near-net shape. *Source*: Howmet Corporation.

Example: Investment-Cast Superalloy Components for Gas Turbines

Since the 1960s, investment-cast superalloys have been replacing wrought counterparts in high-performance gas turbines. Much development has been taking place in producing cleaner superalloys (nickel-based and cobalt-based). Improvements have been made in melting and casting techniques, such as vacuum-induction melting and using microprocessor controls. Impurity and inclusion levels have continually been reduced, improving the strength and ductility of these components. Such control is essential because these parts operate at a temperature only about 50 °C (90 °F) below the solidus (Section 4.3).

The microstructure of an integrally investment-cast, gas-turbine rotor is shown in the upper portion of Fig. 11.20. Note the fine, uniform, equiaxed grains throughout the cross-section. Recent techniques to obtain this result include the use of a nucleant addition to the molten metal, as well as close control of its superheat, pouring techniques, and control of cooling rate of the casting.

In contrast, the lower portion of Fig. 11.20 shows the same type of rotor cast conventionally; note the coarse grain structure. This rotor will have inferior properties compared with the fine-grained rotor. Due to developments in these processes, the proportion of cast parts to other parts in aircraft engines has increased from 20% to about 45% by weight.

FIGURE 11.20   Cross-section and microstructure of two rotors: (top) investment-cast; (bottom) conventionally cast. *Source*: *Advanced Materials and Processes*, October 1990, p. 25. ASM International.

FIGURE 11.21   Schematic illustration of the vacuum-casting process. Note that the mold has a bottom gate. (a) Before and (b) after immersion of the mold into the molten metal. *Source*: From R. Blackburn, "Vacuum Casting Goes Commercial," *Advanced Materials and Processes*, February 1990, p. 18. ASM International.

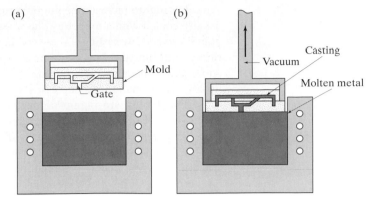

Induction furnace

11.8 VACUUM CASTING

A schematic illustration of the *vacuum-casting* process, or *counter-gravity low-pressure* (*CL*) *process* (not to be confused with the vacuum-molding process described in Section 11.2.5), is shown in Fig. 11.21. A mixture of fine sand and urethane is molded over metal dies and cured with amine vapor. The mold is then held with a robot arm and partially immersed into molten metal held in an induction furnace.

The metal may be melted in air (*CLA process*) or in a vacuum (*CLV process*). The vacuum reduces the air pressure inside the mold to about two-thirds of atmospheric pressure, thus drawing the molten metal into the mold cavities through a gate in the bottom of the mold. The molten metal in the furnace is at a temperature usually 55 °C (100 °F) above the liquidus temperature; consequently, it begins to solidify within a fraction of a second. After the mold is filled, it is withdrawn from the molten metal.

This process is an alternative to investment, shell-mold, and green-sand casting, and is particularly suitable for thin-walled (0.75 mm; 0.03 in.) complex shapes with uniform properties. Carbon, low- and high-alloy steel, and stainless steel parts weighing as much as 70 kg (155 lb) have been vacuum cast by this method.

CLA parts are easily made at high volume and relatively low cost. CLV parts usually involve reactive metals, such as aluminum, titanium, zirconium, and hafnium. These parts, which are often in the form of superalloys for gas turbines, may have walls as thin as 0.5 mm (0.02 in.). The process can be automated and production costs are similar to those for green-sand casting.

11.9 PERMANENT-MOLD CASTING

In the *permanent-mold casting process*, also called *hard-mold casting*, two halves of a mold are made from materials such as cast iron, steel, bronze, graphite, or refractory metal alloys. The mold cavity and gating system are machined into the mold and thus become an integral part. To produce castings with internal cavities, cores made of metal or sand aggregate are placed in the mold prior to casting.

Typical core materials are oil-bonded or resin-bonded sand, plaster, graphite, gray iron, low-carbon steel, and hot-work die steel. Gray iron is the most commonly used, particularly for large molds in aluminum and magnesium casting. Inserts are also used for various parts of the mold.

In order to increase the life of permanent molds, the surfaces of the mold cavity are usually coated with a refractory slurry (such as sodium silicate and clay) or sprayed with graphite every few castings. These coatings also serve as parting agents and as thermal barriers, controlling the rate of cooling of the casting. Mechanical ejectors (such as pins located in various parts of the mold) may be needed for removal of complex castings; ejectors usually leave small round impressions.

The molds are clamped together by mechanical means and heated to about 150 °C–200 °C (300 °F–400 °F) to facilitate metal flow and reduce thermal damage to the dies due to high temperature gradients. The molten metal is then poured through the gating system. After solidification, the molds are opened and the casting is removed. Special means that are employed to cool the mold include water or the use of fins similar to those found on motorcycle or lawnmower engines that cool the engine block.

Although the permanent-mold casting operation can be performed manually, the process can be automated for large production runs. This process is used mostly for aluminum, magnesium, copper alloys, and gray iron because of their generally lower melting points. Steels can also be cast using graphite or heat-resistant metal molds.

This process produces—at high production rates—castings with good surface finish, close dimensional tolerances, and uniform and good mechanical properties. Typical parts made are automobile pistons, cylinder heads, connecting rods, gear blanks for appliances, and kitchenware. Parts that can be made economically generally weigh less than 25 kg (55 lb), although special castings weighing a few hundred kilograms have been made using this process.

Although equipment costs can be high because of die costs, labor costs can be kept low by mechanizing the process. Permanent-mold casting is not economical for small production runs, and because of the difficulty in removing the casting from the mold, intricate shapes cannot be cast by this process. However, easily collapsed sand cores can be used and removed from castings to leave intricate internal cavities. The process is then called **semipermanent-mold casting**.

11.10 SLUSH CASTING

It was noted in Fig. 10.10 that a solidified skin develops first in a casting and that this skin then becomes thicker with time. Hollow castings with thin walls can be made by permanent-mold casting using this principle, a process called *slush casting*. The molten metal is poured into the metal mold; after the desired thickness of solidified skin is obtained, the mold is inverted or slung, and the remaining liquid metal is poured out. The mold halves are then opened and the casting is removed.

Slush casting is suitable for small production runs and is generally used for making ornamental and decorative objects (such as lamp bases and stems) and toys from low-melting-point metals such as zinc, tin, and lead alloys.

11.11 PRESSURE CASTING

In the two permanent-mold processes described above, the molten metal flows into the mold cavity by gravity. In the *pressure-casting process*, also called *pressure pouring* or *low-pressure casting* (Fig. 11.22a), the molten metal is forced upward by gas pressure into a graphite or metal mold. The pressure is maintained until the metal has completely solidified in the mold. The molten metal may also be forced upward by a vacuum, which also removes dissolved gases and produces a casting with lower porosity.

Pressure casting is generally used for high-quality castings—for example, steel railroad-car wheels. These wheels may also be cast in sand molds or semipermanent molds made of graphite and sand (Fig. 11.22b).

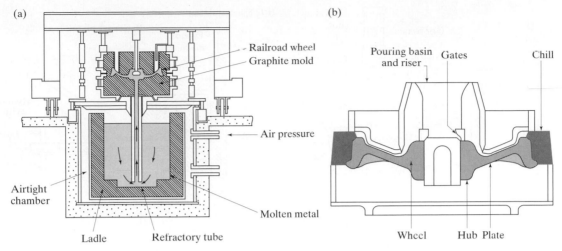

FIGURE 11.22   (a) The bottom-pressure casting process utilizes graphite molds for the production of steel railroad wheels. *Source*: The Griffin Wheel Division of Amsted Industries Incorporated. (b) Gravity-pouring method of casting a railroad wheel. Note that the pouring basin also serves as a riser. Railroad wheels can also be manufactured by forging.

11.12 DIE CASTING

The *die-casting* process, developed in the early 1900s, is a further example of permanent-mold casting. The molten metal is forced into the die cavity at pressures ranging from 0.7 MPa–700 MPa (0.1 ksi–100 ksi). The European term *pressure-die casting*, or simply die casting, which is described in this section, is not to be confused with the term *pressure casting* (described in Section 11.11).

Typical parts made through die casting are motors, business-machine and appliance components, hand tools, and toys. The weight of most castings ranges from less than 90 g (3 oz) to about 25 kg (55 lb). There are two basic types of die-casting machines: hot-chamber and cold-chamber.

11.12.1 Hot-Chamber Process

The *hot-chamber process* (Fig. 11.23a) involves the use of a piston, which traps a certain volume of molten metal and forces it into the die cavity through a gooseneck and nozzle. Pressures range up to 35 MPa (5000 psi), with an average of about 15 MPa (2000 psi). The metal is held under pressure until it solidifies in the die. To improve die life and to aid in rapid metal cooling (thereby reducing cycle time) dies are usually cooled by circulating water or oil through various passageways in the die block.

Cycle times usually range up to 200–300 *shots* (individual injections) per hour for zinc, although very small components such as zipper teeth can be cast at 18,000 shots per hour. Low-melting-point alloys such as zinc, magnesium, tin, and lead are commonly cast using this process.

11.12.2 Cold-Chamber Process

In the *cold-chamber process* (Fig. 11.23b), molten metal is poured into the injection cylinder (*shot chamber*). The shot chamber is not heated, hence the term *cold chamber*. The metal is forced into the die cavity at pressures usually ranging from 20 MPa to 70 MPa (3 ksi to 10 ksi), although they may be as high as 150 MPa (20 ksi). The machines may be horizontal (Figs. 11.24a and b) or vertical, in which case the shot chamber is vertical and the machine is similar to a vertical press.

(a)

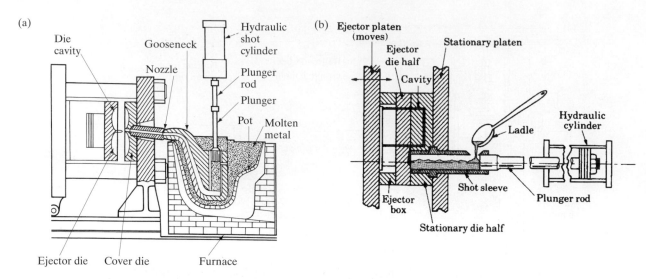

FIGURE 11.23   (a) Schematic illustration of the hot-chamber die-casting process. (b) Schematic illustration of the cold-chamber die-casting process. *Source*: Courtesy of *Foundry Management and Technology.*

FIGURE 11.24   (a) Schematic illustration of a cold-chamber die-casting machine. These machines are large compared to the size of the casting because large forces are required to keep the two halves of the dies closed. (b) 800-ton hot-chamber die-casting machine, DAM 8005 (made in Germany in 1998). This is the largest hot-chamber machine in the world and costs about $1.25 million.

(a)

(b)

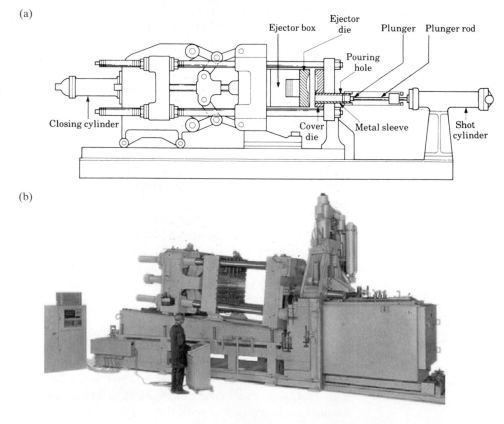

High-melting-point alloys of aluminum, magnesium, and copper are normally cast using this method, although other metals (including ferrous metals) can also be cast in this manner. Molten-metal temperatures start at about 600 °C (1150 °F) for aluminum and some magnesium alloys, and increase considerably for copper-based and iron-based alloys.

11.12.3 Process Capabilities and Machine Selection

Because of the high pressures involved, dies have a tendency to part unless clamped together tightly. Die-casting machines are rated according to the clamping force that can be exerted to keep the dies closed. The capacities of commercially available machines range from about 25 tons to 3000 tons. Other factors involved in the selection of die-casting machines are die size, piston stroke, shot pressure, and cost.

Die-casting dies (Fig. 11.25) may be single-cavity, multiple-cavity (with several identical cavities), combination-cavity (with several different cavities), or unit dies (simple small dies that can be combined in two or more units in a master holding die). Typically, the ratio of die weight to part weight is 1000 to 1, so the die for a casting weighing 2 kg would weigh about 2000 kg.

Dies are usually made of hot-work die steels or mold steels. Die wear increases with the temperature of the molten metal. **Heat checking** of dies (surface cracking from repeated heating and cooling of the die, discussed in Section 3.6) can be a problem. When die materials are selected and properly maintained, dies may last more than half a million shots before any significant die wear takes place.

Die design includes taper (draft) to allow the removal of the casting. The sprues and runners may be removed either manually or by using trim dies in a press. The entire die casting and finishing process can be highly automated. Lubricants (parting agents) are often applied as thin coatings on die surfaces. They are usually water-based lubricants with graphite or other compounds in suspension. Because of the high cooling capacity of water, these fluids are also effective in keeping die temperatures low.

Die casting has the capability for rapid production of strong, high-quality parts with complex shapes. It also produces good dimensional accuracy and surface details, so that parts require little or no subsequent machining or finishing operations (**net-shape forming**). Because of the high pressures involved, walls as thin as 0.38 mm (0.015 in.) are produced. They are thinner than those obtained by other casting methods. Ejector marks remain, as do small amounts of flash (thin material squeezed out between the dies) at the die parting line.

A typical part made by die casting is shown in Fig. 11.1b; note the intricate shape and fine surface detail. In the fabrication of certain parts, die casting can compete favorably with other manufacturing methods, such as sheet-metal stamping and forging, or other casting processes.

FIGURE 11.25   Various types of cavities in a die-casting die. *Source*: Courtesy of American Die Casting Institute.

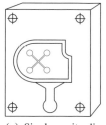 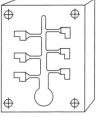  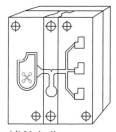

(a) Single-cavity die   (b) Multiple-cavity die   (c) Combination die   (d) Unit die

(a) 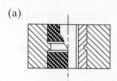   (b) 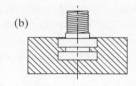   FIGURE 11.26   Examples of cast-in-place inserts in die casting. (a) Knurled bushing. (b) Grooved threaded rod.

TABLE 11.4   Properties and Typical Applications of Common Die-Casting Alloys

Alloy	Ultimate tensile strength (MPa)	Yield strength (MPa)	Elongation in 50 mm (%)	Applications
Aluminum 380 (3.5 Cu–8.5 Si)	320	160	2.5	Appliances, automotive components, electrical motor frames and housings
13 (12 Si)	300	150	2.5	Complex shapes with thin walls, parts requiring strength at elevated temperatures
Brass 858 (60 Cu)	380	200	15	Plumbing fixtures, lock hardware, bushings, ornamental castings
Magnesium AZ91 B (9 Al-0.7 Zn)	230	160	3	Power tools, automotive parts, sporting goods
Zinc No. 3 (4 Al)	280	—	10	Automotive parts, office equipment, household utensils, building hardware, toys
5 (4 Al–1 Cu)	320	—	7	Appliances, automotive parts, building hardware, business equipment

Source: Data from American Die Casting Institute.

In addition, because the molten metal chills rapidly at the die walls, the casting has a fine-grained, hard skin with higher strength. Consequently, the strength-to-weight ratio of die-cast parts increases with decreasing wall thickness. With good surface finish and dimensional accuracy, die casting can produce bearing surfaces that are normally machined.

Components such as pins, shafts, and threaded fasteners can be die cast integrally. Called **insert molding**, this process is similar to placing wooden sticks in popsicles prior to freezing (see also Section 18.3). For good interfacial strength, inserts may be knurled, grooved, or splined (Fig. 11.26). In selecting insert materials, the possibility of galvanic corrosion should be taken into account. Steel, brass, and bronze inserts, for example, are commonly used in die casting alloys. If galvanic corrosion is a potential problem, the insert can be insulated, plated, or surface-treated.

Equipment costs, particularly the cost of dies, are somewhat high, but labor costs are generally low because the process is semi- or fully automated. Die casting is economical for large production runs. The properties and typical applications of common die-casting alloys are given in Table 11.4.

11.13 CENTRIFUGAL CASTING

As its name implies, the *centrifugal-casting* process utilizes the inertial forces caused by rotation to distribute the molten metal into the mold cavities. This method was first suggested in the early 1800s. There are three types of centrifugal casting: true centrifugal casting, semicentrifugal casting, and centrifuging.

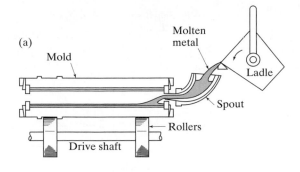

(a)

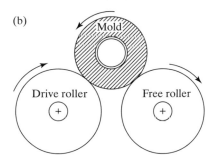

(b)

FIGURE 11.27   Schematic illustration of the centrifugal casting process. Pipes, cylinder liners, and similarly shaped parts can be cast with this process.

a. **True centrifugal casting**. In *true centrifugal casting*, hollow cylindrical parts, such as pipes, gun barrels, and streetlamp posts, are produced by the technique shown in Fig.11.27, in which molten metal is poured into a rotating mold. The axis of rotation is usually horizontal but can be vertical for short workpieces. Molds are made of steel, iron, or graphite, and may be coated with a refractory lining to increase mold life.

The mold surfaces can be shaped so that pipes with various outer shapes, including square or polygonal, can be cast. The inner surface of the casting remains cylindrical because the molten metal is uniformly distributed by centrifugal forces. However, –because of density differences, lighter elements such as dross, impurities, and pieces of the refractory lining tend to collect on the inner surface of the casting.

Cylindrical parts ranging from 13 mm (0.5 in.) to 3 m (10 ft) in diameter and 16 m (50 ft) long can be cast centrifugally, with wall thicknesses ranging from 6 mm to 125 mm (0.25 in. to 5 in.). The pressure generated by the centrifugal force is high, as much as 150 g's, and such high pressure is necessary for casting thick-walled parts. Castings of good quality, dimensional accuracy, and external surface detail are obtained by this process. In addition to pipes, typical parts made are bushings, engine-cylinder liners, and bearing rings with or without flanges.

b. **Semicentrifugal casting**. An example of *semicentrifugal casting* is shown in Fig. 11.28a. This method is used to cast parts with rotational symmetry such as a wheel with spokes.

c. **Centrifuging**. In *centrifuging*, also called *centrifuge casting*, mold cavities of any shape are placed at a certain distance from the axis of rotation. The molten metal is poured from the center and is forced into the mold by centrifugal forces (Fig. 11.28b). The properties of castings vary by distance from the axis of rotation.

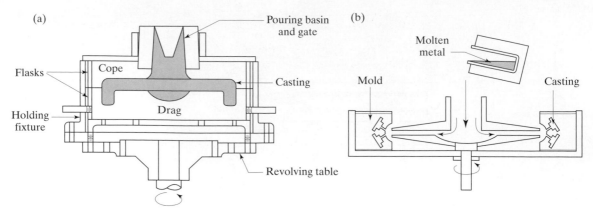

FIGURE 11.28   (a) Schematic illustration of the semicentrifugal casting process. Wheels with spokes can be cast by this process. (b) Schematic illustration of casting by centrifuging. The molds are placed at the periphery of the machine, and the molten metal is forced into the molds by centrifugal force.

11.14 SQUEEZE CASTING AND SEMISOLID METAL FORMING

There are two casting processes that are basically combinations of casting and forging (Chapter 14), namely, *squeeze casting* and *semisolid metal forming*.

11.14.1 Squeeze Casting

The *squeeze casting*, or *liquid-metal forging*, process was developed in the 1960s and involves solidification of the molten metal under high pressure (Fig. 11.29). The machinery includes a die, punch, and ejector pin. The pressure applied by the punch keeps the entrapped gases in solution, and the contact under high pressure at the die–metal interface promotes rapid heat transfer, resulting in a fine microstructure with good mechanical properties.

The application of pressure also overcomes feeding problems that can arise when casting metals with a long freezing range (Section 10.2.2). The pressures required in squeeze casting are lower than those for hot or cold forging.

Parts can be made to *near-net shape*, with complex shapes and fine surface detail, from both nonferrous and ferrous alloys. Typical products made are automotive components and mortar bodies (a short-barreled cannon).

FIGURE 11.29   Sequence of operations in the squeeze-casting process. This process combines the advantages of casting and forging.

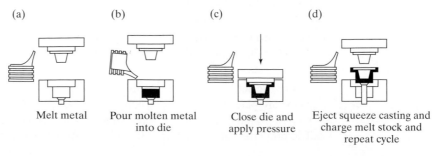

(a)	(b)	(c)	(d)
Melt metal	Pour molten metal into die	Close die and apply pressure	Eject squeeze casting and charge melt stock and repeat cycle

Example: Front Steering Knuckle Made by Squeeze Casting

The front steering knuckle for the 1997 Ford Taurus, Mercury Sable, and Lincoln Continental was redesigned to be made of squeeze-cast aluminum, replacing a ductile-iron knuckle made by green-sand casting. Although the cost of squeeze casting was higher than that of iron casting, its net-shape characteristic resulted in substantially reduced machining operations.

In addition to a 50% weight saving, the 3.85 kg (8.5 lb) aluminum knuckle had lower porosity, the same stiffness, and higher yield strength and toughness than the ductile-iron part. The part was subjected to finite-element analysis to optimize its strength and stiffness properties. *Source*: CMI International.

11.14.2 Semisolid Metal Forming

Also called *semisolid metalworking*, semisolid metal forming was developed in the 1970s. The metal or alloy has a nondendritic, roughly spherical, fine-grained structure when it enters the die or mold. The alloy exhibits **thixotropic** behavior (hence the process is also called **thixoforming**), that is, its viscosity decreases when agitated. For example, at rest and above its solidus temperature (Fig. 10.3), the alloy has the consistency of table butter, but when agitated vigorously its consistency is more like motor oils.

This behavior has been utilized in developing technologies combining casting and forging of parts, using cast billets that are forged when 30% to 40% liquid. Magnesium parts, for example, have been made in machines that combine the processes of die casting and injection molding of plastics with reciprocating screws (Section 18.3). Semisolid metal forming technology was in commercial production by 1981 and is also used in making cast metal-matrix composites (Section 18.13).

Another technique for forming in the semisolid state is **rheocasting**, in which a slurry is produced in a mixer and delivered to the mold or die. However, this process has not yet been commercially successful.

Example: Cast Automotive-Engine Components Replaced with Semisolid Forgings

The aluminum rocker-shaft pedestal for a Chrysler 3.5 L 24-valve V-6 engine was originally designed to be produced by permanent-mold casting; however, the resulting part did not have sufficient strength. The function of this part is to attach the valve-actuation mechanism to the cylinder head. Ductile (nodular) iron was considered for this part, but it weighed three times as much.

The process was replaced with semisolid forging in which specially cast aluminum slugs were forged when semisolid, about 50% solid and 50% liquid. It was found that the parts had higher strength, better dimensional accuracy and surface finish, and less porosity with better controlled microstructure, and that their cost was lower than that for cast parts.

The semisolid forging process was also used to make an aluminum timing-belt tensioner-puller pivot bracket for this engine, redesigned from a ductile iron design. The new bracket had good dimensional tolerances, did not require any significant additional machining processes, and cost $2.15 less per piece than the ductile iron bracket. *Source*: *Advanced Materials & Processes*, June 1993.

11.15 CASTING TECHNIQUES FOR SINGLE CRYSTAL COMPONENTS

The characteristics of single-crystal (*monocrystal*) and polycrystalline structures in metals were described in Chapter 1. This section describes the techniques used to cast single-crystal components such as gas turbine blades, which are generally made of nickel-based superalloys (Section 6.6) and used in the hot stages of the engine. The procedures involved can also be used for other alloys and components.

a. **Conventional casting of turbine blades**. The *conventional casting process* uses a ceramic mold. The molten metal is poured into the mold and begins to solidify at the ceramic walls. The grain structure developed is polycrystalline and is similar to that shown in Fig. 10.1c. The presence of grain boundaries makes this structure susceptible to creep and cracking along the boundaries under the centrifugal forces and elevated temperatures commonly encountered in an operating gas turbine.

b. **Directionally solidified blades**. In the *directional solidification process* (Fig. 11.30a), first developed in 1960, the ceramic mold is preheated by radiant heating. The mold is supported by a water-cooled chill plate. After the metal is poured into the mold, the assembly is slowly lowered. Crystals begin to grow at the chill-plate surface and upward, like the columnar grains shown in Fig. 10.2. The blade is thus directionally solidified, with longitudinal but no transverse grain boundaries. Consequently, the blade is stronger in the direction of centrifugal forces developed in the gas turbine.

c. **Single-crystal blades**. In *crystal growing*, developed in 1967, the mold has a constriction in the shape of a corkscrew or helix (Figs. 11.30b and c), the cross-section of which is so small that it allows only one crystal to fit through. The mechanism of crystal growth is such that only the most favorably oriented crystals are able to grow

FIGURE 11.30 Methods of casting turbine blades: (a) directional solidification; (b) method to produce a single-crystal blade; and (c) a single-crystal blade with the constriction portion still attached. *Source*: (a) and (b) B. H. Kear, *Scientific American*, October 1986; (c) *Advanced Materials and Processes*, October 1990, p. 29, ASM International.

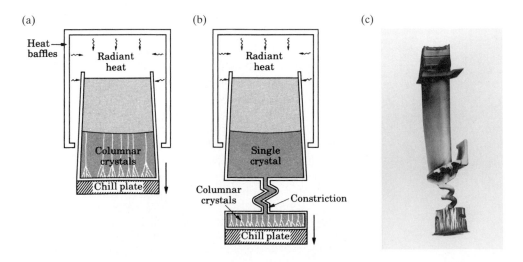

integrated facilities for all aspects of their operations. They produce a wide variety and sizes of castings at high production rates, at low cost, and with good quality control.

As outlined in Fig. 11.5, foundry operations initially involve two separate groups of activities. The first group is pattern and mold making. Computer-aided design and manufacturing and rapid prototyping techniques are now being used to minimize trial and error and improve efficiency in these areas. A variety of automated machinery is used to minimize labor costs, which can be significant in the production of castings. The second group of activities is melting the metals, controlling their composition and impurities, and pouring them into molds.

The rest of the operations (such as pouring into molds carried along conveyors, shakeout, cleaning, heat treatment, and inspection) are also automated. Automation minimizes labor, reduces the possibility of human error, increases the production rate, and attains higher quality levels. Industrial robots (Section 38.7) are being used extensively in foundry operations such as cleaning, riser cutting, mold venting, mold spraying, pouring, sorting, inspection, and automatic storage and retrieval systems for cores and patterns using automated guided vehicles (Section 38.6).

The level of automation in foundries is an important economic consideration, particularly in view of the fact that many foundries are small businesses. The degree of automation depends on the type of products made. A die-casting facility or a foundry making parts for the automotive industry may involve production runs in the hundreds of thousands; thus, a high level of automation is desirable. Such facilities can afford automation.

On the other hand, a jobbing foundry producing short production runs may not be as automated. Furthermore, foundries in general have been viewed as somewhat hot, dirty, and labor-intensive operations, and it can be difficult to find qualified personnel to work in such an environment. Consequently, automation has become increasingly necessary to compensate for the decline in worker competency.

Safety in Foundries. As in all other manufacturing operations, safety in foundries is an important consideration (See also Section 37.3.) Safety is particularly important in these operations because of the following factors:

a. Dust from sand and other compounds used in casting. Because of dust, proper ventilation and safety equipment for the personnel is necessary.

b. Fumes from molten metals, as well as splashing of the molten metal during transfer or pouring into molds.

c. The presence of fuels for furnaces, the control of their pressure, the proper operation of valves, etc.

d. The presence of water and moisture in crucibles, molds, and other locations, since it rapidly converts to steam, creating severe danger of explosion.

e. Improper handling of fluxes, which are hygroscopic and create a danger when they absorb moisture.

f. Inspection of crucibles, tools, and other equipment for wear, cracks, etc.

g. Inspection of equipment, such as pyrometers, for accuracy and proper calibration.

h. The need for proper personal safety equipment such as gloves, aprons, face shields, and shoes.

SUMMARY

- Casting processes are generally classified as expendable-mold or permanent-mold casting. The most common expendable-mold processes are sand, shell-mold, plaster-mold, ceramic-mold, and investment casting. Common permanent-mold processes include slush casting, pressure casting, die casting, and centrifugal casting. Expendable-mold casting usually involves lower mold and equipment costs, but produces less dimensional accuracy.

- The molds used in permanent-mold casting are made of metal or graphite, and are used repeatedly to produce a large number of parts. Because metals are good heat conductors but do not allow gases to escape, permanent molds have fundamentally different effects on casting than sand or other aggregate mold materials.

- In permanent-mold casting, die and equipment costs are relatively high, but the processes are economical for large production runs. Scrap loss is low and dimensional accuracy is relatively high, with good surface details.

- Other casting processes include squeeze casting (combination of casting and forging), semisolid metal forming, rapid solidification for the production of amorphous alloys (metallic glasses), and casting of single-crystal components such as turbine blades for the hot stages of jet engines.

- Melting processes are also important in casting operations. They include proper melting of the metals; preparation for alloying; removal of slag and dross; and pouring the molten metal into the molds. Inspection of castings for any internal or external defects is also important.

- Castings may subsequently be subjected to further processing, such as heat treatment and various machining operations, to produce final desired shapes and surface characteristics.

TRENDS

- Computer-aided design and manufacturing of castings, molds and dies, and gating and runner systems are being implemented at a rapid rate.

- Automation of molding and casting processes to reduce costs, using computer controls, sensors, and industrial robots, is an important area of continuing development and implementation.

- Research is in progress into the automated inspection of castings using, for instance, machine vision and fiber optics to inspect internal surfaces of castings that cannot be viewed directly.

- Improvements in melting and remelting techniques and the refinement of molten metal prior to pouring are in progress, including the use of exothermic materials to prevent choking in runners.

- Investment casting continues to be an efficient metal-shaping technology, with larger and more complex structural castings being made, particularly for high-temperature aerospace applications.

- Expendable-pattern and investment casting are being increasingly used in the automotive industry.
- Semisolid metal forming is an emerging technology with applications for aluminum-alloy parts for military, aerospace, and automotive uses. Other metals are also being developed using this technology.
- Environmental impact of foundry operations is an important aspect of casting metals.

KEY TERMS

Binders
Centrifugal casting
Ceramic-mold casting
Chaplets
Composite molds
Core prints
Cores
Crystal growing
Die casting
Expendable-pattern casting
Expendable molds
Fluxes
Foundry

Green molding sand
Insert molding
Investment casting
Levitation melting
Lost foam process
Lost-wax process
Master alloys
Parting agent
Patterns
Permanent mold casting
Permanent molds
Plaster-mold casting
Precision casting

Pressure casting
Rammed graphite molding
Rapid prototyping
Rapid solidification
Rheocasting
Sand casting
Semisolid metal forming
Shell-mold casting
Slush casting
Sodium silicate process
Squeeze casting
Thixotropy
Vacuum casting

BIBLIOGRAPHY

Allsop, D.F., and D. Kennedy, *Pressure Die Casting—Part II: The Technology of the Casting and the Die*. Pergamon, 1983.
An Introduction to Die Casting. American Die Casting Institute, 1981.
ASM Handbook, Vol. 15: *Casting*. ASM International, 1988.
Bradley, E.F., *High-Performance Castings: A Technical Guide*. Edison Welding Institute, 1989.
Clegg, A.J., *Precision Casting Processes*. Pergamon, 1991.
Kaye, A., and A.C. Street, *Die Casting Metallurgy*. Butterworths, 1982.

Product Design for Die Casting. Diecasting Development Council, 1988.
Steel Castings Handbook (5th ed.). Steel Founders' Society of America, 1995.
Street, A.C.; *The Diecasting Book* (2d ed.). Portcullis Press, 1986.
The Metallurgy of Die Castings. Society of Die Casting Engineers, 1986.
Young, K.P., *Semi-solid Processing*. Chapman & Hall, 1997.

REVIEW QUESTIONS

11.1 Describe the differences between expendable and permanent molds.

11.2 Name the important factors in selecting sand for molds.

11.3 What are the major types of sand molds? What are their characteristics?

11.4 List important considerations when selecting pattern materials.

11.5 What is the function of a core? What are core prints?

11.6 Name and describe the characteristics of the types of sand-molding machines.

11.7 What is the difference between sand- and shell-mold casting?

11.8 What are composite molds? Why are they used?

11.9 Describe the features of plaster-mold casting.

11.10 Why is the investment-casting process capable of producing fine surface detail on castings?

11.11 Name the type of materials used for permanent-mold casting processes.

11.12 What are the advantages of pressure casting?

11.13 List the advantages and limitations of die casting.

11.14 What are parting agents?

11.15 Describe the methods used for producing single-crystal parts.

11.16 What is the purpose of a riser? A vent?

11.17 What is the difference between true centrifugal and semicentrifugal casting?

11.18 Give examples of reasons to use die inserts.

11.19 What is the function of a core?

QUALITATIVE PROBLEMS

11.20 Explain why a casting may have a slightly different shape than the pattern used to make the mold.

11.21 What are the reasons for the large variety of casting processes that have been developed over the years? Explain with specific examples.

11.22 Describe the advantages and limitations of hot-chamber and cold-chamber die casting processes, respectively.

11.23 Explain why processes such as sand, shell-mold, plaster, and investment casting can produce parts with greater shape complexity than others such as permanent-mold, die, and centrifugal casting.

11.24 Why is it that die casting can produce the smallest parts?

11.25 What differences, if any, would you expect in the properties of castings made by permanent mold versus sand casting?

11.26 Would you recommend preheating the molds used in permanent-mold casting? Would you remove the casting soon after it has solidified? Explain your reasons.

11.27 Describe the advantages of composite molds. Where would you use them?

11.28 Referring to Fig. 11.4, do you think it is necessary to weigh down or clamp the two halves of the mold? Explain your reasons. Do you think that the kind of metal cast, such as gray cast iron vs. aluminum, should make a difference in the clamping force? Explain.

11.29 Give a step-by-step procedure for the following processes: (a) investment casting, (b) die casting, and (c) lost foam.

11.30 Explain why squeeze casting produces parts with better mechanical properties, dimensional accuracy, and surface finish than do expendable-mold processes.

11.31 In a sand-casting operation, what factors determine the time at which you would remove the casting from the mold?

11.32 What would you do to improve the surface finish in expendable-mold casting processes?

11.33 How would you attach the individual wax patterns on a "tree" in investment casting?

11.34 Describe the measures that you would take to reduce core shifting in sand casting.

11.35 You have seen that even though die casting produces thin parts, there is a limit to how thin they can be. Why can't even thinner parts be made by this process?

11.36 Describe the function of a blind riser. How important is it? Explain.

11.37 Describe the characteristics of chaplet materials. Should they melt while molten metal is being poured and solidified in the mold? Explain.

11.38 Explain the use of risers. Why can blind risers be smaller than open-top risers?

11.39 How are hollow parts with various cavities made by die casting? Are cores used? If so, how? Explain.

11.40 Explain why the strength-to-weight ratio of die-cast parts increases with decreasing wall thickness.

11.41 The volume of the mold in sand casting takes up a certain proportion of the total sand volume. Explain the factors involved in selecting the proportion of mold to total sand volume.

11.42 How are risers and sprues placed in sand molds? Explain with appropriate sketches.

11.43 Section 10.3.5 briefly outlined the three factors involved in shrinkage during casting. With numerical data obtained from the technical literature, show the relative shrinkage due to these factors.

11.44 In shell-mold casting, the curing process is critical to the quality of the finished mold. In this part of the process, the shell-mold assembly and cores are placed in an oven for a short period of time to complete the curing of the resin binder. List probable causes of unevenly cured cores or of uneven core thicknesses.

11.45 In addition to being an excellent way to produce hollow cylindrical parts, centrifugal casting provides a way of centrifuging lightweight, nonmetallic contaminants (slag) to the inside diameter of the part. Here the contaminants may be easily machined away after casting, rather than dispersed throughout the part. (a) Explain how this happens; (b) list several variables in the process that govern the effectiveness of this separation process; and (c) explain why, if the metal is poured at too low a temperature, the separation effect may not occur.

11.46 Why does the die-casting machine shown in Figure 11.24a have such a large clamp?

11.47 Chocolate is available in hollow shapes. What process is used to make these candies?

11.40 What are the benefits and drawbacks to heating the mold in investment casting before pouring in the molten metal?

11.49 In semi-centrifugal casting, metals such as aluminum are commonly spun in a horizontal plane, while platinum is usually spun in a vertical plane. Why?

11.50 Dendrites which derive their name from the Greek word for tree, can have secondary arms, called branches. Why don't trees in investment casting have branches extending from the central sprue with parts located off the branches?

11.51 The slushy state of alloys refers to that state between the solidus and liquidus temperatures, as described in Section 10.2. Pure metals do not have such a slushy state. Does this mean that pure metals cannot be slush cast? Explain.

QUANTITATIVE PROBLEMS

11.52 Estimate the clamping force for a die-casting machine in which the casting is rectangular with projected dimensions of 125 mm x 175 mm (5 in. x 7 in.). Would your answer depend on whether it is a hot-chamber or cold-chamber process? Explain.

11.53 The blank for the spool shown in the figure below is to be sand cast out of A-319, an aluminum casting alloy. Make a sketch of the wooden pattern for this part, and include all necessary allowances for shrinkage and machining.

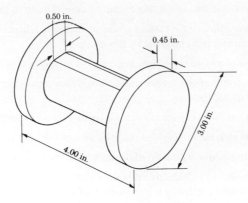

11.54 Repeat Problem 11.53, but assume that the aluminum spool is to be cast using expendable-pattern casting. Explain the important differences between the two patterns.

11.55 In sand casting, it is important that the cope mold half be held down with sufficient force to keep it from floating when the molten metal is poured in. For the casting shown in the figure below, calculate the minimum amount of weight necessary to keep the cope from floating up as the molten metal is poured in. (*Hint*: The buoyancy force exerted by the molten metal on the cope is dependent on the effective height of the metal head above the cope.)

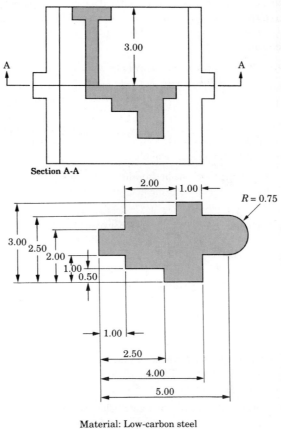

Section A-A

Material: Low-carbon steel
Density: $0.26 \, \text{lb/in}^3$
All dimensions in inches

11.56 Estimate the required clamping force for die casting toy soldiers from lead, recognizing that the fluid pressures are on the low end of the cold-chamber process scale. The soldiers are approximately 100 mm high and 50 mm wide. How many can be cast in each shot of a die-casting machine with a 1 MN capacity?

11.57 Calculate the production rate of single-crystal silicon from the two methods illustrated in Figure 11.31.

11.58 If an acceleration of 100 g's is necessary to produce a part in true centrifugal casting, and the part has an inner diameter of 10 in., a mean outer diameter of 14 in., and a length of 25 ft, what rotational speed is needed?

11.59 A jeweler wishes to produce twenty gold rings in one investment casting operation. The wax parts are fastened to a wax central sprue of 0.5 in. diameter. The rings are located in four rows, each 0.5 in. from the other on the sprue. The rings require a 0.125-in. diameter, 0.5-in. long runner to the sprue. Estimate the weight of gold needed to completely fill the rings, runners, and sprues. The specific gravity of gold is 19.3.

SYNTHESIS AND DESIGN

11.60 Make a list of the mold and die materials used in the casting processes described in this chapter. Under each type of material, list the casting processes that are employed, and explain why these processes are suitable for that particular mold or die material.

11.61 The optimum shape of a riser is spherical to ensure that it cools more slowly than the casting it feeds. Spherically-shaped risers, however, are difficult to cast. (a) Sketch the shape of a blind riser that is easy to mold, but also has the smallest possible surface area-to-volume ratio. (b) Compare the solidification time of the riser in part (a) to that of a riser shaped like a right circular cylinder. Assume that the volume of each riser is the same and that, for each, the height is equal to the diameter. (See the example in Section 10.3.4.)

11.62 This chapter described briefly the characteristics of melting furnaces for casting. Make a survey of the technical literature and prepare a table, outlining the applications, advantages, and limitations of these furnaces. Include your comments on trends in furnace design and developments.

11.63 Sketch an automated casting line (using conveyors, sensors, machinery, robots, etc.) that could automatically perform the expendable-pattern casting process.

11.64 Describe a test that could be performed to measure the permeability of sand for sand casting.

11.65 If you need only five units of a casting, which process(es) would you use? Why?

11.66 Which of the casting processes would be most suitable for making small toys? Why?

11.67 Describe the procedures that would be involved in making a bronze statue. Which casting process(es) would be suitable? Why?

11.68 Write a brief report on the permeability of molds and the techniques that are used to determine permeability.

11.69 A common method of producing shell molds is illustrated in Fig. 11.13. Make a survey of the casting literature and illustrate other methods of making these molds.

11.70 Light metals are commonly cast in vulcanized rubber molds. Perform a literature search on the mechanics of this process.

11.71 The sand casting shown in Figure 11.11 requires only a few finishing operations, namely the removal of risers and runners from the final part. Assume that the part has to be machined for special surface-finish requirements on the flanges. How would you change the design to allow the part to be placed in a fixture in the proper machine tool without changing the casting process in any other way?

11.72 Sometimes, it is desirable to cool metals more slowly than they would if the molds were maintained at room temperature. List and explain methods of slowing down the cooling process.

11.73 Make a scale drawing of a street lamp and the required mold to centrifugally cast this part. Compare it with Figure 11.27.

11.74 Prepare a detailed part drawing of an axe head. Suggest ways of casting this part, then prepare detailed drawings of necessary tools or patterns necessary for production.

12

Metal Casting: Design, Materials, and Economics

12.1 INTRODUCTION

In the preceding two chapters, it was noted that successful casting practice requires careful control of a large number of variables. These variables pertain to the particular characteristics of the metals and alloys cast, the method of casting, the mold and die materials, the mold design, and various process parameters. The flow of the molten metal in the mold cavities, the gating systems, the rate of cooling, and the gases evolved all influence the quality of a casting.

This chapter describes the general design considerations and guidelines for metal casting and presents suggestions for avoiding defects. It also describes the characteristics of the alloys that are commonly cast, together with their typical applications. The economics of casting operations are just as important as the technical considerations that have already been described, so this chapter also outlines the basic economic factors relevant to casting operations.

12.2 DESIGN CONSIDERATIONS

As in all manufacturing operations, certain guidelines and *design principles* pertaining to casting have been developed over many years. These principles were established primarily through practical experience, but new analytical methods, process modeling, and computer-aided design and manufacturing techniques are now coming into wider use, improving productivity and the quality of castings and resulting in significant cost savings.

12.2.1 Design for Expendable-Mold Casting

The guidelines that follow apply to all types of castings generally. The most significant design considerations are identified and addressed.

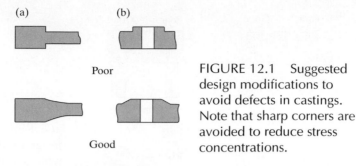

FIGURE 12.1   Suggested design modifications to avoid defects in castings. Note that sharp corners are avoided to reduce stress concentrations.

1. **Corners, angles, and section thickness.** Sharp corners, angles, and fillets should be avoided (Fig. 12.1), because they act as stress raisers and may cause cracking and tearing of the metal (as well as of the dies) during solidification. Fillet radii should be selected to reduce stress concentrations and to ensure proper liquid-metal flow during the pouring process. Fillet radii usually range from 3 mm to 25 mm (1/8 in. to 1 in.), although smaller radii may be permissible in small castings and in limited applications. On the other hand, if the fillet radii are too large, the volume of the material in those regions is also large and, consequently, the rate of cooling is lower.

   Section changes in castings should be smoothly blended into each other. The location of the largest circle that can be inscribed in a particular region is critical so far as shrinkage cavities are concerned (Figs. 12.2a and b). Because the cooling rate in regions with larger circles is lower, they are called **hot spots**. These regions could develop **shrinkage cavities** and **porosity** (Figs. 12.2c and d). Cavities at hot spots can be eliminated with small cores. Although they produce cored holes in the casting (Fig. 12.2e), these holes do not significantly affect its strength.

   Other examples of design principles that can be used to avoid shrinkage cavities are shown in Fig. 12.3. Although they increase the cost of production, metal paddings in the mold can eliminate or minimize hot spots. These paddings act as external chills, such as that shown for casting of a hollow cylindrical part with internal ribs in Fig. 12.4. It is important to maintain, as much as possible, uniform cross-sections and wall thicknesses throughout the casting to avoid shrinkage cavities.

2. **Flat areas.** Large flat areas (plain surfaces) should be avoided, because they may warp during cooling because of temperature gradients or develop poor surface finish (because of uneven flow of metal during pouring). Flat surfaces can be broken up with ribs and serrations.

FIGURE 12.2   Examples of designs showing the importance of maintaining uniform cross-sections in castings to avoid hot spots and shrinkage cavities.

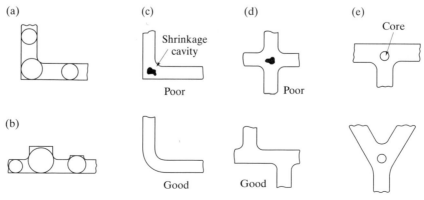

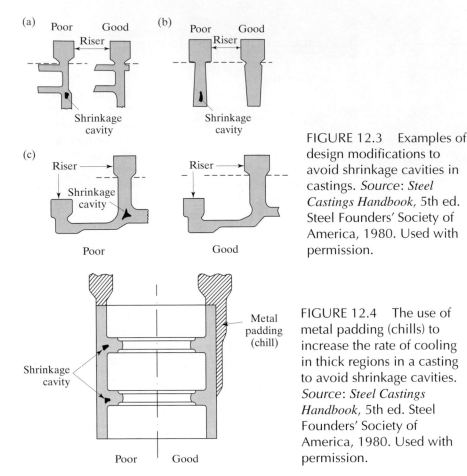

FIGURE 12.3 Examples of design modifications to avoid shrinkage cavities in castings. *Source*: *Steel Castings Handbook*, 5th ed. Steel Founders' Society of America, 1980. Used with permission.

FIGURE 12.4 The use of metal padding (chills) to increase the rate of cooling in thick regions in a casting to avoid shrinkage cavities. *Source*: *Steel Castings Handbook*, 5th ed. Steel Founders' Society of America, 1980. Used with permission.

3. **Shrinkage.** To avoid cracking of the casting, there should be allowances for shrinkage during solidification. In castings with intersecting ribs, the tensile stresses can be reduced by staggering the ribs or by changing the intersection geometry.

   Pattern dimensions should also provide for shrinkage of the metal during solidification and cooling. Allowances for shrinkage, also known as **patternmaker's shrinkage allowances**, usually range from about 10 mm/m to 20 mm/m (1/8 in./ft to 1/4 in./ft). Table 12.1 gives the normal shrinkage allowance for metals commonly sand cast.

TABLE 12.1 Normal Shrinkage Allowance for Some Metals Cast in Sand Molds

Metal	Percent
Gray cast iron	0.83–1.3
White cast iron	2.1
Malleable cast iron	0.78–1.0
Aluminum alloys	1.3
Magnesium alloys	1.3
Yellow brass	1.3–1.6
Phosphor bronze	1.0–1.6
Aluminum bronze	2.1
High-manganese steel	2.6

(a)

Irregular parting line

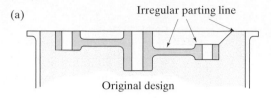

Original design

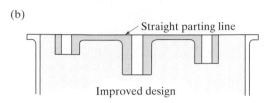

(b)

Straight parting line

Improved design

FIGURE 12.5   Redesign of a casting by making the parting line straight to avoid defects. *Source*: *Steel Casting Handbook*, 5th ed. Steel Founders' Society of America, 1980. Used with permission.

4. **Parting line.** The parting line is the line, or plane, separating the upper (cope) and lower (drag) halves of molds (Figs. 11.4 and 12.5). In general, it is desirable for the parting line to be along a flat plane, rather than contoured. Whenever possible, the parting line should be at the corners or edges of castings, rather than on flat surfaces in the middle of the casting, so that the **flash** at the parting line (material squeezing out between the two halves of the mold) will not be as visible.

   The location of the parting line is important because it influences mold design, ease of molding, number and shape of cores, method of support, and the gating system. Three examples of casting design modifications are shown in Fig. 12.6.

5. **Draft.** As seen in Fig. 11.7, a small *draft* (taper) is provided in sand-mold patterns to enable removal of the pattern without damaging the mold. Typical drafts range from

(a)

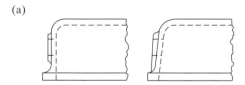

(b)

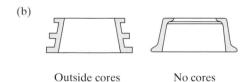

Outside cores   No cores

(c)

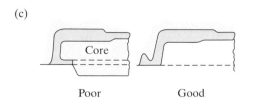

Core

Poor   Good

FIGURE 12.6   Examples of casting design modifications. *Source*: *Steel Casting Handbook*, 5th ed. Steel Founders' Society of America, 1980. Used with permission.

(a)

(b)

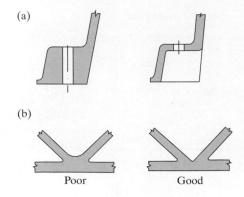

Poor   Good

FIGURE 12.7 Examples of undesirable and desirable design practices for die-cast parts. Note that section-thickness uniformity is maintained throughout the part. *Source*: American Die Casting Institute.

5 mm/m to 15 mm/m (1/16 in./ft to 3/16 in./ft). Depending on the quality of the pattern, draft angles usually range from 0.5° to 2°. The angles on inside surfaces are typically twice this range. They have to be higher than those for outer surfaces because the casting shrinks inward toward the core.

6. **Dimensional tolerances.** Dimensional tolerances depend on the particular casting process, size of the casting, and type of pattern used. Tolerances are smallest within one region of the mold, but because they are cumulative, increase between different regions of the mold. Tolerances should be as wide as possible, within the limits of good part performance; otherwise, the cost of the casting increases. In commercial practice, tolerances are usually in the range of ±0.8 mm (1/32 in.) for small castings and increase with the size of castings. Tolerances for large castings, for instance, may be ±6 mm ($\frac{1}{4}$ in.).

7. **Machining allowance.** Because most expendable-mold castings require some additional finishing operations, such as machining, allowances should be made in casting design for these operations. *Machining allowances*, which are included in pattern dimensions, depend on the type of casting and increase with the size and section thickness of castings. Allowances usually range from about 2 mm to 5 mm (0.1 in. to 0.2 in.) for small castings to more than 25 mm (1 in.) for large castings.

8. **Residual stresses.** The different cooling rates within the body of a casting cause residual stresses. Stress relieving (Section 4.11) may thus be necessary to avoid distortions in critical applications.

12.2.2 Design for Permanent-Mold Casting

The design principles for permanent-mold casting are generally similar to those for expendable-mold casting. Typical design guidelines and examples for permanent-mold casting are shown schematically for die casting in Fig. 12.7. Note that the cross-sections have been reduced in order to decrease the solidification time and save material.

Special considerations are involved in designing and tooling for die casting. Although designs may be modified to eliminate the draft for better dimensional accuracy, a draft angle of 1/2° or even 1/4° is usually required. Otherwise, galling may take place between the part and the dies and cause distortion.

12.3 CASTING ALLOYS

Chapters 5 and 6 described the general properties and applications of ferrous and nonferrous metals and alloys, respectively. This section describes the properties and applications of cast metals and alloys; their properties and casting and manufacturing characteristics are summarized in Fig.12.8 and Tables 12.2 to 12.5.

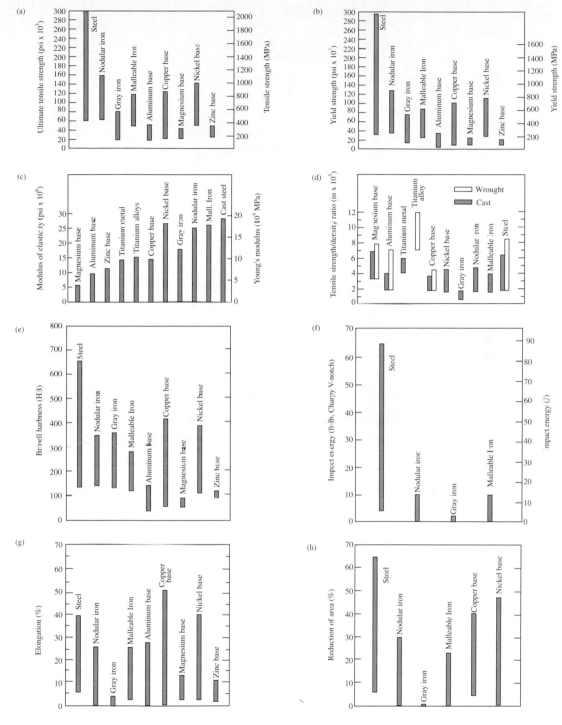

FIGURE 12.8   Mechanical properties for various groups of cast alloys. Note that gray iron has very little ductility and toughness, compared with most other cast alloys, some of which undergo considerable elongation and reduction of area in tension. Note also that even within the same group, the properties of cast alloys vary over a wide range, particularly for cast steels. *Source*: Steel Founders' Society of America.

TABLE 12.2 Typical Applications for Castings and Casting Characteristics

Type of alloy	Application	Castability*	Weldability*	Machinability*
Aluminum	Pistons, clutch housings, intake manifolds	E	F	G–E
Copper	Pumps, valves, gear blanks, marine propellers	F–G	F	F–G
Ductile iron	Crankshafts, heavy-duty gears	G	D	G
Gray iron	Engine blocks, gears, brake disks and drums, machine bases	E	D	G
Magnesium	Crankcase, transmission housings	G–E	G	E
Malleable iron	Farm and construction machinery, heavy-duty bearings, railroad rolling stock	G	D	G
Nickel	Gas turbine blades, pump and valve components for chemical plants	F	F	F
Steel (carbon and low alloy)	Die blocks, heavy-duty gear blanks, aircraft undercarriage members, railroad wheels	F	E	F
Steel (high alloy)	Gas turbine housings, pump and valve components, rock crusher jaws	F	E	F
White iron	Mill liners, shot blasting nozzles, railroad brake shoes, crushers and pulverizers	G	VP	VP
Zinc	Door handles, radiator grills,	E	D	E

*E, excellent; G, good; F, fair; VP, very poor; D, difficult.

TABLE 12.3 Properties and Typical Applications of Cast Irons

Cast iron	Type	Ultimate tensile strength (MPa)	Yield strength (MPa)	Elongation in 50 mm (%)	Typical applications
Gray	Ferritic	170	140	0.4	Pipe, sanitary ware
	Pearlitic	275	240	0.4	Engine blocks, machine tools
	Martensitic	550	550	0	Wearing surfaces
Ductile (Nodular)	Ferritic	415	275	18	Pipe, general service
	Pearlitic	550	380	6	Crankshafts, highly stressed parts
	Tempered martensite	825	620	2	High-strength machine parts, wear-resistant parts
Malleable	Ferritic	365	240	18	Hardware, pipe fittings, general engineering service
	Pearlitic	450	310	10	Railroad equipment, couplings
	Tempered martensite	700	550	2	Railroad equipment, gears, connecting rods
White	Pearlitic	275	275	0	Wear-resistant parts, mill rolls

TABLE 12.4   Mechanical Properties of Gray Cast Irons

ASTM class	Ultimate tensile strength (MPa)	Compressive strength (MPa)	Elastic modulus (GPa)	Hardness (HB)
20	152	572	66 to 97	156
25	179	669	79 to 102	174
30	214	752	90 to 113	210
35	252	855	100 to 119	212
40	293	965	110 to 138	235
50	362	1130	130 to 157	262
60	431	1293	141 to 162	302

TABLE 12.5   Properties and Typical Applications of Cast Nonferrous Alloys

Alloys (UNS)	Condition	Ultimate tensile strength (MPa)	Yield strength (MPa)	Elongation in 50 mm (%)	Typical applications
Aluminum alloys					
195 (AO1950)	Heat treated	220 280	110–220	8.5–2	Sand castings
319 (AO3190)	Heat treated	185–250	125–180	2–1.5	Sand castings
356 (AO3560)	Heat treated	260	185	5	Permanent mold castings
Copper alloys					
Red brass (C83600)	Annealed	235	115	25	Pipe fittings, gears
Yellow brass (C86400)	Annealed	275	95	25	Hardware, ornamental
Manganese bronze (C86100)	Annealed	480	195	30	Propeller hubs, blades
Leaded tin bronze (C92500)	Annealed	260	105	35	Gears, bearings, valves
Gun metal (C90500)	Annealed	275	105	30	Pump parts, fittings
Nickel silver (C97600)	Annealed	275	175	15	Marine parts, valves
Magnesium alloys					
AZ91A	F	230	150	3	Die castings
AZ63A	T4	275	95	12	Sand and permanent mold castings
AZ91C	T6	275	130	5	High strength
EZ33A	T5	160	110	3	Elevated temperature
HK31A	T6	210	105	8	Elevated temperature
QE22A	T6	275	205	4	Highest strength

12.3.1 Nonferrous Casting Alloys

Commonly cast nonferrous alloys are as follows:

1. **Aluminum-based alloys.** Alloys with an aluminum base have a wide range of mechanical properties, mainly because of various hardening mechanisms and heat treatments that can be used with them (Section 4.9). Their fluidity depends on alloying elements and oxides in the metal. These alloys have high electrical conductivity and

generally good atmospheric corrosion resistance. However, their resistance to some acids and all alkalis is poor, and care must be taken to prevent galvanic corrosion. They are nontoxic and lightweight and have good machinability. Except for alloys with silicon, however, they generally have low resistance to wear and abrasion.

Aluminum-based alloys have many applications, including architectural and decorative use. Engine blocks of some automobiles are made of aluminum-alloy castings. Parts made of aluminum-based and magnesium-based alloys are known as **light-metal** castings.

2. **Magnesium-based alloys.** The lowest density of all commercial casting alloys are those in the magnesium-based group. They have good corrosion resistance and moderate strength, depending on the particular heat treatment used.

3. **Copper-based alloys.** Although somewhat expensive, copper-based alloys have the advantages of good electrical and thermal conductivity, corrosion resistance, and nontoxicity, as well as wear properties suitable for bearing materials. Mechanical properties and fluidity are influenced by the alloying elements.

4. **Zinc-based alloys.** A low-melting-point alloy group, zinc-based alloys have good fluidity and sufficient strength for structural applications. These alloys are commonly used in die casting.

5. **High-temperature alloys.** High-temperature alloys have a wide range of properties and typically require temperatures of up to 1650 °C (3000 °F) for casting titanium and superalloys, and higher for refractory alloys. Special techniques such as single-crystal growing (Section 11.15) are used to cast these alloys into parts for jet- and rocket-engine components. Some of these alloys are more suitable and economical for casting than for shaping by other manufacturing methods, such as forging.

12.3.2 Ferrous Casting Alloys

Commonly cast ferrous alloys are as follows:

1. **Cast irons.** Cast irons represent the largest amount of all metals cast, and can easily be cast into intricate shapes. They generally possess several desirable properties, such as wear resistance, hardness, and good machinability.

   The term *cast iron* refers to a family of alloys. As described in Section 4.6, they are classified as gray cast iron (gray iron), ductile (nodular or spheroidal) iron, white cast iron, malleable iron, and compacted graphite iron. The characteristics of each of these cast irons are presented next. Their general properties and typical applications are given in Tables 12.3 and 12.4.

   a. **Gray cast iron.** Castings of gray cast iron have relatively few shrinkage cavities and little porosity. Various forms of gray cast iron are termed *ferritic*, *pearlitic*, and *martensitic*. Because of differences in their structures, each type has different properties. Typical uses of gray cast iron are in engine blocks, machine bases, electric-motor housings, pipes, and wear surfaces for machines. Gray cast irons are specified by a two-digit ASTM designation. Class 20, for example, specifies that the material must have a minimum tensile strength of 20 ksi (140 MPa). The mechanical properties for several classes of gray cast iron are given in Table 12.4.

   b. **Ductile (nodular) iron.** Typically used for machine parts, pipe, and crankshafts, ductile irons are specified by a set of two-digit numbers. For example, class or grade 80-55-06 indicates that the material has a minimum tensile strength of 80 ksi (550 MPa), a minimum yield strength of 55 ksi (380 MPa), and 6% elongation in 2 in. (50 mm).

   c. **White cast iron.** Because of its extreme hardness and wear resistance, white cast iron is used mainly in liners for machinery to process abrasive materials, rolls for rolling mills, and railroad-car brake shoes.

d. **Malleable iron.** The principal use of malleable iron is for railroad equipment and various types of hardware. Malleable irons are specified by a five-digit designation. "35018", for example, indicates that the yield strength of the material is 35 ksi (240 MPa), and its elongation is 18% in 2 in. (50 mm).

e. **Compacted graphite iron.** First produced commercially in 1976, compacted graphite iron (CGI) has properties that fall between those of gray and ductile irons. Gray iron has good damping and thermal conductivity but low ductility, whereas ductile iron has poor damping and thermal conductivity but high tensile strength and fatigue resistance.

Compacted graphite iron has damping and thermal properties similar to gray iron and strength and stiffness comparable to those of ductile iron. Because of its strength, parts made of CGI can be lighter. It is easy to cast, has consistent properties throughout the casting, and its machinability is better than that of ductile iron, an important consideration since it is used for automotive engine blocks and cylinder heads.

2. **Cast steels.** Because of the high temperatures required to melt cast steels (up to about 1650 °C, or 3000 °F), casting them requires considerable knowledge and experience. The high temperatures involved present difficulties in the selection of mold materials, particularly in view of the high reactivity of steels with oxygen, in melting and pouring the metal.

Steel castings possess properties that are more uniform (isotropic) than those made by mechanical working processes, which are described in Part III. Cast steels can be welded; however, welding alters the cast microstructure in the heat-affected zone (see Section 29.2.2), influencing the strength, ductility, and toughness of the base metal.

Subsequent heat treatment must be performed to restore the mechanical properties of the casting. Cast weldments have gained importance where complex configurations, or the size of the casting, may prevent casting the part economically in one location.

3. **Cast stainless steels.** Casting of stainless steels involves considerations similar to those for steels. Stainless steels generally have long freezing ranges and high melting temperatures. They develop several structures, depending on their composition and processing parameters. Cast stainless steels are available in various compositions and can be heat treated and welded. These products have high heat and corrosion resistance. Nickel-based casting alloys are used for severely corrosive environments and very high-temperature service.

12.4 THE ECONOMICS OF CASTING

When reviewing various casting processes, it was noted that some require more labor than others, some require expensive dies and machinery, and some take a great deal of time to produce (Table 12.6). Each of these individual factors affects to varying degrees the overall cost of a casting operation.

As described in greater detail in Chapter 40, the cost of a product includes the costs of materials, labor, tooling, and equipment. Preparations for casting a product include the production of molds and dies that require raw materials, time, and effort, which influence product cost. As can be seen in Table 12.6, relatively little cost is involved in molds for sand casting; on the other hand, die-casting dies require expensive materials and a great deal of machining and preparation. In addition to molds and dies, facilities are required for melting and pouring the molten metal into molds or dies. These facilities include furnaces and related machinery; their costs depend on the level of automation.

Finally, costs are involved in heat treating, cleaning, and inspecting castings. Heat treating is an important part of the production of many alloy groups, especially ferrous castings, and may be necessary to produce improved mechanical properties. However, heat

TABLE 12.6   General Cost Characteristics of Casting Processes

Process	Cost * Die	Equipment	Labor	Production rate (Pc/hr)
Sand	L	L	L–M	<20
Shell-mold	L–M	M-H	L–M	<50
Plaster	L–M	M	M–H	<10
Investment	M–H	L-M	H	<1000
Permanent mold	M	M	L–M	<60
Die	H	H	L–M	<200
Centrifugal	M	H	L–M	<50

* L, low; M, medium; H, high.

treating also introduces another set of production problems, such as scale formation and warpage, which can be a significant aspect of production costs.

The amount of labor and skills required for these operations can vary considerably, depending on the particular process and level of automation. Investment casting, for example, requires a great deal of labor because of the large number of steps involved in this operation. On the other hand, operations such as highly automated die casting can maintain high production rates with little labor required.

It should be noted that the cost of equipment per casting (**unit cost**) will decrease as the number of parts cast increases. Sustained high production rates, therefore, can justify the high cost of dies and machinery. However, if demand is relatively small, the cost per casting increases rapidly. It then becomes more economical to manufacture the parts by sand casting or with other manufacturing processes as described in Parts III and IV.

The two processes compared above (sand and die casting) produce castings with significantly different dimensional and surface-finish characteristics (Table 11.1). Not all manufacturing decisions are based purely on economic considerations. In fact, as can be seen throughout the rest of this text, parts can usually be made by more than one or two processes. The final decision depends on both economic and technical considerations (Chapter 40).

SUMMARY

- General principles have been established to aid designers in producing castings free from defects and meet dimensional tolerances, service requirements, and specifications and standards. These principles concern the shape of the casting and various techniques to minimize hot spots that could lead to shrinkage cavities. Because of the large number of variables involved, close control of all parameters is essential, particularly those related to the nature of liquid metal flow into the molds and dies and the rate of cooling in different regions of the mold or die.

- Several nonferrous and ferrous casting alloys are available, with a wide range of properties, casting characteristics, and applications. Because many castings are designed and produced to be assembled with other mechanical components and structures (subassemblies), various other considerations, such as weldability, machinability, and surface conditions, are also important.

- Within the limits of good performance, the economic aspects of casting are just as important as technical considerations. Factors affecting the overall cost are the cost of materials, molds, dies, equipment, and labor, each of which varies with the particular casting process. An important parameter is the cost per casting, which, for large production runs, can justify large expenditures for automated machinery and computer controls.

TRENDS

- Methods of casting high-strength gray iron, high-temperature ductile iron, and austempered ductile iron are being developed.
- Developments are being pursued in high-strength low-alloy compositions through microalloying, and carbon steels without heat treating.
- Cast stainless steels with improved corrosion resistance and higher strength have been introduced in the last few years and are being used in many applications.
- Computer-aided design and manufacturing and rapid prototyping of molds and dies are important areas being studied and implemented.
- Labor costs continue to become a smaller component of the total cost of casting due to increased use of automation and rapid prototyping.
- Modern casting plants are being built with state-of-the-art facilities, including computer control of all aspects of casting and inspection, in order to produce quality castings economically.

KEY TERMS

Cast iron	Flash	Patternmaker's shrinkage allowance
Compacted graphite iron	Hot spots	Porosity
Design principles	Machining allowance	Shrinkage cavities
Draft	Parting line	Unit cost

BIBLIOGRAPHY

ASM Handbook, Vol. 15: *Casting*. ASM International, 1988.

ASM Specialty Handbook: Cast Irons. ASM International, 1996.

Bradley, E.F., *High-Performance Castings: A Technical Guide*. Edison Welding Institute, 1989.

Casting Defects Handbook. American Foundrymen's Society, 1972.

Kaye, A., and A.C. Street, *Die Casting Metallurgy*. Butterworths, 1982.

Mikelonis, P.J. (ed.), *Foundry Technology: A Source Book*. ASM International, 1982.

Powell, G.W., S.-H. Cheng and C.E. Mobley, Jr., *A Fractography Atlas of Casting Alloys*. Battelle Press, 1992.

Rowley, M.T. (ed.), *International Atlas of Casting Defects*. American Foundrymen's Society, 1974.

Steel Castings Handbook (5th ed.). Steel Founders' Society of America, 1995.

Walton, C.F., and T.J. Opar (eds.), *Iron Castings Handbook* (3d ed.). Iron Castings Society, 1981.

REVIEW QUESTIONS

12.1 List the general design considerations in casting.

12.2 What are hot spots?

12.3 What is shrinkage allowance? Machining allowance?

12.4 Why are drafts necessary in some molds?

12.5 What are light-metal castings?

12.6 Name the types of cast irons available and list their major characteristics.

12.7 Why are steels more difficult to cast than cast irons?

12.8 Name the important factors involved in the economics of casting operations.

12.9 Describe your observations concerning Figs. 12.2 through 12.5.

QUALITATIVE PROBLEMS

12.10 Describe the procedure you would follow to determine whether a defect in a casting is a shrinkage cavity or porosity caused by gases.

12.11 Explain how you would go about avoiding hot tearing.

12.12 If you need only a few castings of the same design, which three processes would be the most expensive per piece?

12.13 Do you generally agree with the cost ratings in Table 12.6? If so, why?

12.14 Explain how ribs and serrations are helpful in casting flat surfaces that otherwise may warp. Give an illustration.

12.15 Describe the nature of the design changes made in Fig. 12.6. What general principles do you observe?

12.16 In Fig. 12.8 you will note that the ductility of some cast alloys is very little. Do you think this should be a significant concern in engineering applications of castings?

12.17 Do you think there will be fewer defects in a casting made by gravity pouring vs. one made by pouring under pressure?

12.18 Why are allowances provided for in the production of patterns? What do they depend on?

12.19 Explain the difference in importance of drafts in green-sand casting versus permanent-mold casting.

12.20 What type of cast iron would be suitable for a heavy machine base? Why?

12.21 Explain the advantages and limitations of sharp and rounded fillets, respectively, in casting design.

12.22 Referring to Tables 10.1 and 12.1, do you think that there is a contradiction regarding the behavior of gray cast iron? Explain.

12.23 Explain why the elastic modulus E of gray cast iron varies so widely, as shown in Table 12.4.

QUANTITATIVE PROBLEMS

12.24 When designing patterns for casting, patternmakers use special rulers that automatically incorporate solid shrinkage allowances into their designs. Therefore, a 12-in. patternmaker's ruler is longer than a foot. How long is a patternmaker's ruler designed for the making of patterns for (a) aluminum castings? (b) high-manganese steel?

12.25 Using the data given in Table 12.2, obtain rough plots of (a) castability vs. weldability, and (b) castability vs. machinability for at least five of the materials listed.

SYNTHESIS AND DESIGN

12.26 Porosity developed in the boss of the casting is illustrated in the figure below. Show that by simply repositioning the parting line of this casting, this problem can be eliminated.

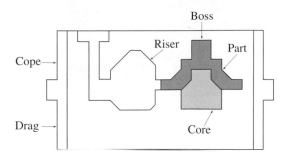

12.27 For the wheel illustrated in the figure below, show how (a) riser placement, (b) core placement, (c) padding, and (d) chills may be used to help feed molten metal and eliminate porosity in the isolated hub boss.

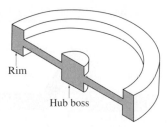

12.28 In view of the material covered in preceding chapters and based on the information given in Fig. 12.8, what general statements would you make about the mechanical properties of castings?

12.29 Assume that the introduction to this chapter is missing. Write a brief introduction to highlight the importance of the topics covered in it.

12.30 In the figure below, the original casting design shown in (a) was changed to the design shown in (b). The casting is round, with a vertical axis of symmetry. As a functional part, what advantages do you think the new design has over the old one?

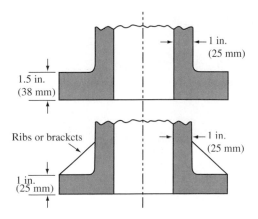

12.31 An incorrect and a correct design for casting are shown in the figure below. Review the changes made and comment on their advantages.

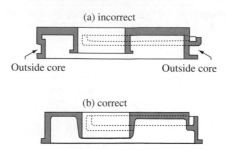

12.32 Three sets of designs for die casting are shown below. Note the changes made to die design 1 and comment on the reasons.

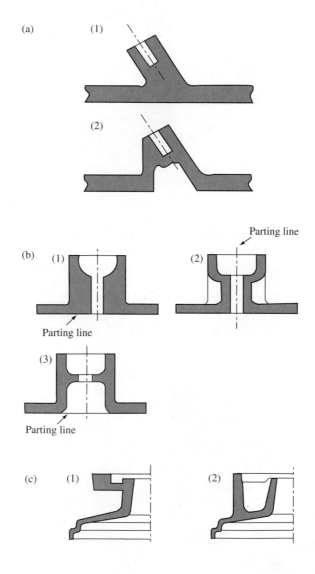

Part III
Forming and Shaping Processes and Equipment

We generally tend to take for granted many of the products that we use, or that we come across every day, and the materials and components from which they are made. When we inspect these products, we soon realize that a wide variety of materials and processes have been used to make them (Fig. III.1).

We also note that some products consist of a few parts (stapler, pipe wrench, light fixture), and others consist of thousands or even millions of parts (automobiles, computers, airplanes). Some products are thin (aluminum foil, plastic film, electrical-resistance wire for toasters), whereas others are thick (ship hulls, boiler plates, machine bases).

Some products have simple shapes with smooth curvatures (bicycle handles, ball bearings, cooking pots), but others have complex configurations and detailed surface features (coins, silverware, engine blocks). Some products are used in critical applications (turbine blades, connecting rods for engines, elevator cables), whereas others are used in routine applications (watering cans, spoons, paper clips).

The initial material used in forming and shaping metals is usually molten metal, which is cast into individual ingots or, more recently, continuously cast into slabs, rod, or pipe. Cast structures are converted to wrought ("worked") structures by the deformation processes described in Part III. In addition to cast and wrought structures, the raw material for making products may consist of metal powders. For plastics, the starting material is usually pellets, flakes, or powder, and for ceramics it is clays and oxides, obtained from ores or produced synthetically.

Note that the words *forming* and *shaping* are both used in the title for this section. Although the distinction between the two is not rigid, forming means changing the shape of an existing solid body. The body, which is called the workpiece, stock, or blank throughout the rest of this text, may be in the shape of a plate, a sheet, a bar, a rod, wire, or tubing of various cross-sections.

FIGURE III.1   Formed and shaped parts in a typical automobile.

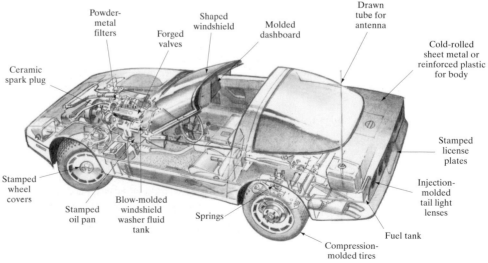

317

An ordinary wire coat hanger, for example, is made by forming a straight piece of wire by bending and twisting it into the shape of a hanger. A metal body for an automobile is made by forming sheet metal in dies, starting with flat sheet. The initial material for a typical translucent advertising sign is a flat piece of plastic; it is formed by heating it and then forcing it under a vacuum of air pressure into a mold. These are called **forming processes**.

Shaping processes usually involve molding and casting. The resulting product is usually at or near the final desired shape and may require little or no further finishing. A plastic coat hanger, for example, is made by forcing molten plastic into a mold in the shape of the hanger. Telephone receivers, keys for keyboards, and beverage bottles are made by shaping molten plastic in a mold. The white ceramic insulator for an automotive spark plug is made by shaping clay in a mold, then drying and firing it in a furnace.

Some of these manufacturing operations produce long *continuous* products, such as plates, sheets, tubing, and bars with various cross-sections. Rolling, extrusion, and drawing processes are capable of making such products out of metallic and nonmetallic materials, including reinforced plastics; they are then cut into the desired lengths. On the other hand, processes such as forging, powder metallurgy, and most forming and shaping processes for nonmetallic materials produce *discrete* products, such as turbine disks, gears, and bolts.

TABLE III.1 General Characteristics of Forming and Shaping Processes

Process	Characteristics
Rolling	
Flat	Production of flat plate, sheet, and foil in long lengths, at high speeds, and with good surface finish, especially in cold rolling; requires high capital investment; low to moderate labor cost.
Shape	Production of various structural shapes, such as I-beams, at high speeds; includes thread rolling; requires shaped rolls and expensive equipment; low to moderate labor cost; moderate operator skill.
Forging	Production of discrete parts with a set of dies; some finishing operations usually required; similar parts can be made by casting and powder-metallurgy techniques; usually performed at elevated temperatures; die and equipment costs are high; moderate to high labor cost; moderate to high operator skill.
Extrusion	Production of long lengths of solid or hollow products with constant cross-section; usually performed at elevated temperatures; product is then cut into desired lengths; can be competitive with roll forming; cold extrusion has similarities to forging and is used to make discrete products; moderate to high die and equipment cost; low to moderate labor cost; low to moderate operator skill.
Drawing	Production of long rod and wire, with round or various cross-sections; smaller cross-sections than extrusions; good surface finish; low to moderate die, equipment, and labor costs; low to moderate operator skill.
Sheet-metal forming	Production of a wide variety of shapes with thin walls and simple or complex geometries; generally low to moderate die, equipment, and labor costs; low to moderate operator skill.
Powder metallurgy	Production of simple or complex shapes by compacting and sintering metal powders; can be competitive with casting, forging, and machining processes; moderate die and equipment cost; low labor cost and skill.
Processing of plastics and composite materials	Production of a variety of continuous or discrete products by extrusion, molding, casting, and fabricating processes; can be competitive with sheet-metal parts; moderate die and equipment costs; high operator skill in processing of composite materials.
Forming and shaping of ceramics	Production of discrete ceramic products by a variety of shaping, drying, and firing processes; low to moderate die and equipment cost; moderate to high operator skill.

In Part III, the important factors involved in each forming and shaping process are described, along with how material and process variables influence the quality of a product (Table III.1). We explain both why some materials can be processed only by certain manufacturing methods and not by others and why parts with particular shapes can be processed only by certain techniques and not by others. The characteristics of the machinery and the equipment used in these processes also significantly affect the quality of the product, its rate of production, and the economics of the manufacturing operation.

An important consideration is the workability and formability of materials, meaning the maximum amount of deformation a material can withstand in a particular forming and shaping process without failure. The term **workability** is generally applied to bulk deformation processes (such as forging, rolling, and extrusion) in which the forces applied to the workpiece are predominantly compressive in nature. In contrast, the term **formability** is usually used for sheet-forming processes (such as bending, stamping, stretch forming, and deep drawing) in which the forces applied are primarily tensile.

The first half of Part III specifically describes the rolling of flat and shaped products, the forging of discrete parts, the extrusion of long pieces with various cross-sections, and the drawing of rod, wire, and tube. These processes are called *bulk-deformation processes*, because the workpieces and products have a relatively high ratio of volume to surface area or of volume to thickness. The second half describes sheet-forming processes, powder metallurgy techniques, the processing of polymers, of composites, of ceramics, and of glasses, and, finally, rapid prototyping operations.

13

Rolling of Metals

13.1 INTRODUCTION

Rolling is the process of reducing the thickness (or changing the cross-section) of a long workpiece by compressive forces applied through a set of **rolls** (Fig. 13.1); the process is similar to the rolling of dough with a rolling pin to reduce its thickness. Rolling, which accounts for about 90% of all metals produced by metalworking processes, was first developed in the late 1500s. The basic operation is flat rolling, or simply rolling, where the rolled products are flat plate and sheet.

Plates, which are generally regarded as having a thickness greater than 6 mm (1/4 in.), are used for structural applications, such as machine structures, ship hulls, boilers, bridges, and nuclear vessels. Plates can be as much as 0.3 m (12 in.) thick for the supports for large boilers, 150 mm (6 in.) thick for reactor vessels, and 100–125 mm (4–5 in.) thick for battleships and tanks.

Sheets are generally less than 6 mm thick; they are provided to manufacturing facilities as flat pieces or as strip in coils for further processing into various products. They are used for automobile and aircraft bodies, appliances, food and beverages containers, and kitchen and office equipment.

Commercial aircraft fuselages are usually made of a minimum of 1 mm (0.040 in.) thick aluminum-alloy sheet. For example, the skin thickness of a Boeing 747 is 1.8 mm (0.071 in.); that of a Lockheed L1011 is 1.9 mm (0.075 in.). Aluminum beverage cans are now made from sheets 0.28 mm (0.011 in.) thick, which are reduced to a final can wall thickness of 0.1 mm (0.004 in.). Aluminum **foil**, typically used to wrap candy and cigarettes, has a thickness of 0.008 mm (0.0003 in.).

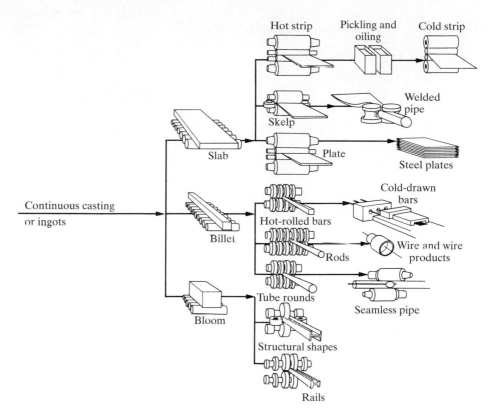

FIGURE 13.1   Schematic outline of various flat- and shape-rolling processes. *Source*: American Iron and Steel Institute.

This chapter describes the basic process of **flat rolling** and **shape rolling** operations, the production of seamless tubing and pipe, and the important factors involved in rolling practices. Traditionally, the initial material form for rolling is an ingot. As stated in Section 5.4, however, this practice is now being rapidly replaced by that of continuous casting and rolling, at much higher efficiency and a lower cost.

Rolling is first carried out at elevated temperatures (hot rolling); during this phase, the coarse-grained, brittle, and porous structure of the ingot or the continuously cast metal is broken down into a **wrought structure** having finer grain size and enhanced properties.

13.2 FLAT ROLLING

A schematic illustration of the **flat rolling** process is shown in Fig. 13.2a. A strip of thickness h_0 enters the **roll gap** and is reduced to thickness h_f by a pair of rotating rolls, each roll being powered through its own shaft by electric motors. The surface speed of the rolls is V_r. The velocity of the strip increases from its entry value, V_o, as it moves through the roll gap, in the same way fluid must flow faster as it moves through a converging channel.

The velocity of the strip is highest at the exit from the roll gap; we denote it as V_f there. Because the surface speed of the roll is constant, there is relative sliding between the roll and the strip along the arc of contact in the roll gap, L.

At one point along the contact length, called the **neutral point** or **no-slip point**, the velocity of the strip is the same as that of the roll. To the left of this point, the roll moves

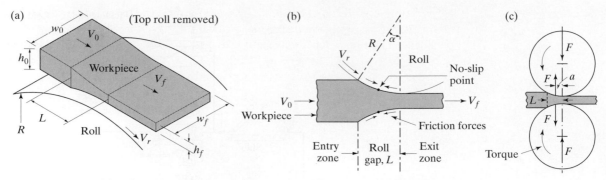

FIGURE 13.2   (a) Schematic illustration of the flat-rolling process. (b) Friction forces acting on strip surfaces. (c) The roll force, F, and the torque acting on the rolls. The width w of the strip usually increases during rolling, as is shown in Fig. 13.5.

faster than the strip; to the right of this point, the strip moves faster than the roll. Hence, the frictional forces, which oppose motion, act on the strip as shown in Fig. 13.2b.

13.2.1 Frictional Forces

The rolls pull the material into the roll gap through a *net frictional force* on the material. It can be seen that this net frictional force must be to the right in Fig. 13.2b; consequently, the frictional force to the left of the neutral point must be higher than the friction force to the right.

Although friction is necessary for rolling materials, energy is dissipated in overcoming friction; thus, increasing friction means increasing forces and power requirements. Furthermore, high friction could damage the surface of the rolled product. A compromise has to be made, one which induces low coefficients of friction by using effective lubricants.

The maximum possible **draft**, defined as the difference between the initial and final thicknesses, $(h_o - h_f)$, is a function of the coefficient of friction, μ, and the roll radius, R:

$$h_o - h_f = \mu^2 R. \tag{13.1}$$

Thus, the higher the friction and the larger the roll radius, the greater the maximum possible draft (and reduction in thickness) becomes. This situation is similar to the use of large tires (high R) and rough treads (high μ) on farm tractors and on off-road earth-moving equipment, which permit the vehicles to travel over rough terrain without skidding.

13.2.2 Roll Force and Power Requirement

Because the rolls apply pressure on the material in order to reduce its thickness, a force perpendicular to the arc of contact (Fig. 13.2c) is needed. Note, in Fig. 13.2c, that this **roll force**, F, is shown as perpendicular to the plane of the strip rather than as at an angle. This alignment is used because the arc of contact is generally very small compared to the roll radius, so we can assume the roll force to be perpendicular without causing significant error.

The roll force in flat rolling can be estimated from the formula

$$F = LwY_{\text{avg}}, \tag{13.2}$$

where L is the roll-strip contact length, w is the width of the strip, and Y_{avg} is the average true stress of the strip in the roll gap. Equation (13.2), ideally, is for a frictionless situation.

The higher the coefficient of friction is between the rolls and the strip, the greater becomes the divergence, and the formula predicts a lower roll force than the actual force.

The power required per roll can be estimated by assuming that the force F acts in the middle of the arc of contact: In Fig. 13.2c, $a = L/2$. **Torque per roll** is the product of F and a. Therefore, the *power per roll* in S.I. units is

$$\text{Power} = \frac{\pi F L N}{60,000\ kW},$$ (13.3)

where F is in newtons, L is in meters, and N is the rpm of the roll.

In traditional English units the power can be expressed as

$$\text{Power} = \frac{\pi F L N}{33,000\ hp},$$ (13.4)

where F is in lb. and L is in ft.; these formulas are applied in the example below.

Example: Calculation of Roll Force and Torque

An annealed copper strip, 9 in. (228 mm) wide and 1.00 in. (25 mm) thick, is rolled to a thickness of 0.80 in. (20 mm) in one pass. The roll radius is 12 in. (300 mm), and the rolls rotate at 100 rpm. Calculate the roll force and the power required in this operation.

Solution: The roll force is determined from Eq. (13.2), in which L is the roll-strip contact length. It can be shown from simple geometry that this length is approximately given by

$$L = \sqrt{R(h_o - h_f)} = \sqrt{12(1.00 - 0.80)} = 1.55 \text{ in.}$$

We now must determine Y_{avg} for annealed copper. The absolute value of the true strain that the strip undergoes in this operation is

$$\varepsilon = \ln\left(\frac{1.00}{0.80}\right) = 0.223.$$

Upon referring to Fig. 2.6, we note that annealed copper has a true stress of about 12,000 psi in the unstrained condition, while at a true strain of 0.223 the true stress is 40,000 psi. Thus the average stress, Y_{avg}, is about 26,000 psi. The roll force can now be determined as follows:

$$F = L w Y_{avg} = (1.55)(9)(26,000) = 363,000 \text{ lb} = 1.6 \text{ MN}.$$

The power per roll is calculated from Eq. (13.4), where $N = 100$. Thus,

$$\text{Power} = 2\pi F L N / 33,000 = 2\pi(363,000)(1.55/12)(100)/33,000$$

$$= 898 \text{ hp} = 670 \text{ kW}.$$

Because there are two rolls, the total power in rolling is 1796 hp = 1340 kW.

Exact calculation of the force (and of the power requirements) in rolling is difficult because of the difficulties involved in determining the exact contact geometry and in accurately estimating both the coefficient of friction and the strength of the material in the roll gap, particularly for hot rolling, and the sensitivity of the material to deformation at elevated temperatures.

Reducing Roll Force.   Roll forces can cause deflection and flattening of the rolls; such changes will, in turn, adversely affect the rolling operation. Also, the **roll stand**, including the housing, chocks, and bearings (Fig. 13.3), may stretch under the roll forces to such an extent

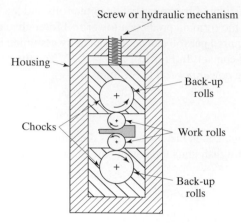

Screw or hydraulic mechanism

Housing

Back-up rolls

Chocks

Work rolls

Back-up rolls

FIGURE 13.3 Schematic illustration of a four-high rolling-mill stand, showing its various features. The stiffnesses of the housing, the rolls, and the roll bearings are all important in controlling and maintaining the thickness of the rolled strip.

that the roll gap can open up significantly. Consequently, the rolls have to be set closer than was calculated, to compensate for this deflection and to obtain the desired final thickness.

Roll forces can be reduced by any of the following means:

a. reducing friction;
b. using smaller-diameter rolls, to reduce the contact area;
c. taking smaller reductions per pass, to reduce the contact area; and
d. rolling at elevated temperatures, to lower the strength of the material.

Another effective method of reducing roll forces is to apply longitudinal **tensions** to the strip during rolling. As a result, the compressive stresses required to deform the material plastically become smaller. Because they require high roll forces, tensions are particularly important in rolling high-strength metals. Tensions can be applied to the strip either at the entry zone (**back tension**) or at the exit zone (**front tension**) or both.

Back tension is applied to the sheet by applying a braking action to the reel which supplies the sheet to the roll gap (the *pay-off* reel), by some suitable means. Front tension is applied by increasing the rotational speed of the *take-up* reel. Rolling can also be carried out by front tension only, with no power supplied to the rolls; this process is known as **Steckel rolling**.

13.2.3 Geometric Considerations

Because of the forces acting on them, rolls undergo certain geometric changes. Just as a straight beam deflects under a transverse load, roll forces tend to bend the rolls elastically during rolling (Fig. 13.4a); the higher the elastic modulus of the roll material, the smaller the roll deflection.

As a result of roll bending, the rolled strip tends to be thicker (have a **crown**) at its center than at its edges. The usual method of avoiding this problem is to grind the rolls so that their diameter at the center is slightly larger than at their edges (give them **camber**). Thus, when the roll bends, its contact along the width of the strip becomes straight and the strip being rolled has a constant thickness along its width.

For rolling sheet metals, the radius of the maximum camber point is generally 0.25 mm (0.01 in.) greater than that at the edges of the roll. When properly designed, cambered rolls produce flat strips (Fig. 13.4b). However, a particular camber is correct only for a certain load and a certain strip width. To reduce the effects of deflection, the rolls can be subjected to bending, by the application of moments at their bearings (a similar technique to bending a wooden stick at its ends); this manipulation simulates camber.

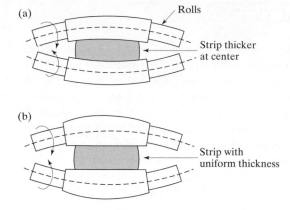

FIGURE 13.4   (a) Bending of straight cylindrical rolls, caused by the roll force. (b) Bending of rolls ground with camber, producing a strip with uniform thickness.

Because of the heat generated by plastic deformation during rolling, rolls can become slightly barrel-shaped (**thermal camber**). (Unless compensated for by some means, this condition can produce strips that are thinner at the center than at the edges.) Consequently, the total (or final) camber can be controlled by varying the location of the coolant on the rolls during hot rolling.

Roll forces also tend to **flatten** the rolls elastically, producing an effect much like the flattening of automobile tires. This flattening of the rolls is undesirable; it produces, in effect, a larger roll radius and, hence, a larger contact area for the same draft. The roll force, in turn, increases with increased flattening.

Spreading.   In the rolling of plates and sheet having high width-to-thickness ratios, the width of the material remains effectively constant during rolling. With smaller ratios, however, such as with a square cross-section, the width increases considerably in the roll gap, as a result of the same effect that occurs in the rolling of dough with a rolling pin. This increase in width is called *spreading* (Fig. 13.5). In the calculation of the roll force, the width w in Eq. (13.2a) is taken as an average width.

It can be shown that spreading increases with a decrease in the width-to-thickness ratio of the entering material (because of reduction in the width constraint), with an increase in the friction, and with a decrease in the ratio of the roll's radius to the strip's thickness (the latter two being due to increased longitudinal constraint of the material flow in the roll gap). Spreading can be prevented by the use of vertical rolls in contact with the edges of the rolled product (as in *edger mills*).

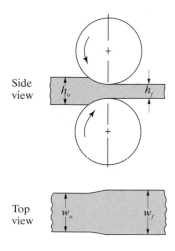

FIGURE 13.5   Increase in the width (spreading) of a strip in flat rolling (see also Fig. 13.2a). Similarly, spreading can be observed when dough is rolled with a rolling pin.

13.3 FLAT-ROLLING PRACTICE

The initial breaking down of an ingot or of a continuously cast slab is done by **hot rolling**. As was described in Section 10.2 and illustrated in Fig. 10.1, a **cast** structure is typically dendritic, and it includes coarse and nonuniform grains. This structure is usually brittle and may contain porosities. Hot rolling (above the recrystallization temperature of the metal, Section 1.6), converts the cast structure to a **wrought** structure (Fig. 13.6). This structure has finer grains and enhanced ductility, both resulting from the breaking up of brittle grain boundaries and the closing up of internal defects, especially porosity.

As described in Section 5.4, traditional methods of casting ingots are now being rapidly replaced by continuous casting (see also Section 13.7). Temperature ranges for hot rolling are typically about 450 °C (850 °F) for aluminum alloys, up to 1250 °C (2300 °F) for alloy steels, and up to 1650 °C (3000 °F) for refractory alloys (see also Table 14.1).

The product of the first hot-rolling operation is called a **bloom** or **slab** (Fig. 13.1). A bloom usually has a square cross-section, at least 150 mm (6 in.) on the side; a slab is usually rectangular in cross-section. Blooms are processed further, by *shape rolling*, into structural shapes, such as I-beams and railroad rails (Section 13.5). Slabs are rolled into plates and sheet.

Billets are usually square, with a cross-sectional area smaller than blooms; they are later rolled into various shapes, such as round rods and bars, by the use of shaped rolls. Hot-rolled round rods are used as the starting material for rod and wire drawing (Section 15.10); they are called **wire rods**.

In hot rolling blooms, billets, and slabs, the surface of the material is usually **conditioned** (prepared for a subsequent operation) prior to rolling. Conditioning is done by various means, such as the use of a torch (*scarfing*) to remove heavy scale or of rough grinding to smoothen surfaces. Prior to cold rolling, the scale developed during hot rolling may be removed by *pickling* with acids (acid etching) or by such mechanical means as blasting with water (or grinding, to remove other defects as well).

Cold rolling is carried out at room temperature (Section 1.7) and, compared to hot rolling, produces sheet and strip with much better surface finish (because of lack of scale), dimensional tolerances, and mechanical properties (because of strain hardening).

Pack rolling is a flat-rolling operation in which two or more layers of metal are rolled together; this process improves productivity. Aluminum foil, for example, is pack rolled in two layers. One side of aluminum foil is matte, the other side shiny: The foil-to-foil side has

FIGURE 13.6   Changes in the grain structure of cast or of large-grain wrought metals during hot rolling. Hot rolling is an effective way to reduce grain size in metals, for improved strength and ductility. Cast structures of ingots or continuous castings are converted to a wrought structure by hot working.

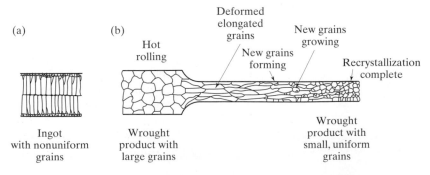

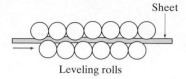

FIGURE 13.7   A method of roller leveling to flatten rolled sheets. See also Fig. 15.22.

a matte and satiny finish, but the foil-to-roll side is shiny and bright, because it has been in contact with the polished rolls.

Mild steel, when stretched during sheet-forming operations, undergoes *yield-point elongation*, a phenomenon that causes surface irregularities called *stretcher strains* or *Lueder's bands* (Section 16.3). To correct this situation, the sheet metal is subjected to a final light pass of 0.5% to 1.5% reduction, known as **temper rolling** or *skin pass*.

A rolled sheet may not be sufficiently flat as it leaves the roll gap, because of variations in the material or in the processing parameters during rolling. To improve flatness, the rolled strip is passed through a series of **leveling rolls**. Several different roller arrangements are used, one of which is shown in Fig. 13.7. Each roll is usually driven separately, by an individual electric motor. The strip is flexed in opposite directions as it passes through the sets of rollers.

13.3.1 Defects in Rolled Plates and Sheets

Defects may be present on the surfaces of rolled plates and sheets, or there may be internal structural defects. Defects are undesirable, not only because they degrade surface appearance but also because they may adversely affect the strength, the formability, and other manufacturing characteristics.

A number of surface defects, such as scale, rust, scratches, gouges, pits, and cracks, have been identified for sheet metals. These defects may be caused by inclusions and impurities in the original cast material or by various other conditions related to material preparation and to the rolling operation.

Wavy edges on sheets (Fig. 13.8a) are the result of roll bending. The strip is thinner along its edges than at its center (see Fig. 13.3a); because the edges elongate more than the center, they buckle, because they are restrained from expanding freely in the longitudinal (rolling) direction. The cracks shown in Figs. 13.8b and c are usually the result of poor material ductility at the rolling temperature.

Alligatoring (Fig. 13.8d) is a complex phenomenon and may be caused by nonuniform deformation during rolling or by the presence of defects in the original cast billet. Because the quality of the edges of the sheet is important in sheet-metal forming operations, edge defects in rolled sheets are often removed by shearing and slitting operations (Section 16.2.2).

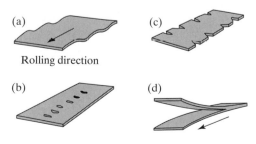

FIGURE 13.8   Schematic illustration of typical defects in flat rolling: (a) wavy edges; (b) zipper cracks in the center of the strip; (c) edge cracks; and (d) alligatoring.

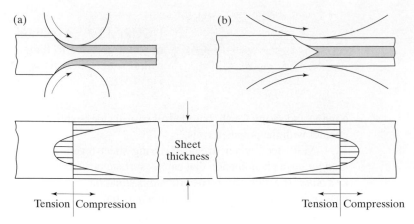

FIGURE 13.9   (a) Residual stresses developed in rolling with small rolls or at small reductions in thickness per pass. (b) Residual stresses developed in rolling with large rolls or at high reductions per pass. Note the reversal of the residual stress patterns.

13.3.2 Other Characteristics

Residual Stresses.   Because of nonuniform deformation of the material in the roll gap, residual stresses can develop in rolled plates and sheets, especially during cold rolling. Small-diameter rolls or small reductions per pass tend to deform the metal plastically at its surfaces (Fig. 13.9a). This situation produces compressive residual stresses on the surfaces (which can be beneficial for improved fatigue life) and tensile stresses in the middle.

On the other hand, large-diameter rolls and high reductions tend to deform the bulk more than the surfaces (Fig. 13.9b); this is due to the frictional constraint at the surfaces along the arc of contact between the roll and the strip. This situation produces residual stresses that are opposite of those in the case of small-diameter rolls.

Dimensional Tolerances.   Thickness tolerances for cold-rolled sheet usually range from ± 0.1 mm to 0.35 mm (0.004 in. to 0.014 in.). Tolerances are much greater for hot-rolled plates. Flatness tolerances are usually within ± 15 mm/m (3/16 in./ft) for cold rolling and ± 55 mm/m (5/8 in./ft) for hot rolling.

Surface Roughness.   The ranges of surface roughness in cold and hot rolling were given in Fig. 11.12; for comparison, it includes ranges for some of the other manufacturing processes. Note that cold rolling can produce a very fine surface finish, so products made of cold-rolled sheet may not require additional finishing operations. Note also that hot rolling and sand casting (Section 11.2) produce the same range of surface roughness.

Gage Numbers.   The thickness of a sheet is usually identified by a *gage number:* the smaller the number, the thicker the sheet. Several numbering systems are used, depending on the type of sheet metal being classified. Rolled sheets of copper and of brass are also identified by thickness changes during rolling, such as 1/4 hard, 1/2 hard, and so on.

13.4 ROLLING MILLS

Several types of rolling mills and equipment are built; they use diverse roll arrangements. Although the equipment for hot and cold rolling is essentially the same, there are differences in the roll materials, process parameters, lubricants, and cooling systems.

FIGURE 13.10   A general view of a rolling mill. *Source*: Inland Steel

The design, construction, and operation of **rolling mills** (Fig. 13.10) require major investments. Highly automated mills produce close-tolerance, high-quality plates and sheet at high production rates and low cost per unit weight, particularly when integrated with continuous casting (see Fig. 5.4).

The width of rolled products may range up to 5 m (200 in.) and be as thin as 0.0025 mm (0.0001 in.). Rolling speeds may range up to 25 m/s (about a mile a minute) for cold rolling, or even higher in highly automated and computer-controlled facilities.

Two-high or **three-high** rolling mills (Figs. 13.11a and b) are used for hot rolling in initial breakdown passes (primary roughing or **cogging mills**) on cast ingots or in continuous casting, with roll diameters ranging from 0.6 to 1.4 m (24 in. to 55 in.). In the three-high or **reversing mill**, the direction of material movement is reversed after each pass; the plate being rolled is repeatedly raised to the upper roll gap, rolled, and then lowered to the lower roll gap by elevators and various manipulators.

Four-high mills (Fig. 13.11c) and **cluster mills** (**Sendzimir** or **Z mill**; Fig. 13.11d) are based on the principle that small-diameter rolls lower roll forces and power requirements and reduce spreading. Moreover, when worn or broken, small rolls can be replaced at less cost than can large ones. However, small rolls deflect more under roll forces and have to be supported by other rolls, as is done in four-high and cluster mills. Although the cost of a Sendzimir mill facility can be millions of dollars, it is particularly suitable for cold rolling thin sheet of high-strength metals. Common rolled widths are 0.66 m (26 in.), with a maximum of 1.5 m (60 in.).

FIGURE 13.11   Schematic illustration of various roll arrangements: (a) two-high; (b) three-high; (c) four-high; (d) cluster (Sendzimir) mill.

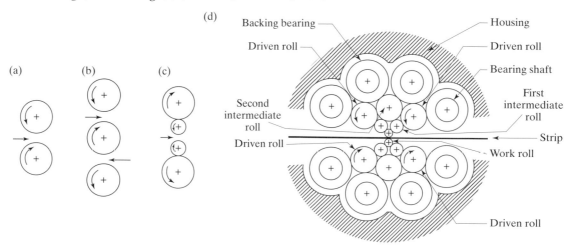

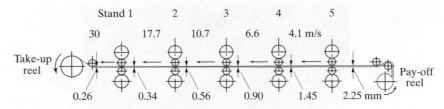

FIGURE 13.12   A tandem rolling operation.

In **tandem rolling** (Fig. 13.12) the strip is rolled continuously, through a number of **stands** (see Fig. 13.4), to smaller gages with each pass. Each stand consists of a set of rolls with its own housing and controls. A group of stands is called a *train*. The control of the gage and of the speed at which the sheet travels through each roll gap is critical. Electronic and computer controls, along with extensive hydraulic controls (particularly in precision rolling), are used in tandem rolling operations.

Rolls. The basic requirements for roll material are strength and resistance to wear. Common roll materials are cast iron, cast steel, and forged steel. Tungsten carbides are also used for small-diameter rolls, such as the working roll in a cluster mill. Forged-steel rolls, although more costly, have greater strength, stiffness, and toughness than cast-iron rolls (see also Sections 4.6 and 12.3.2). Rolls for cold rolling are ground to a fine finish; for special applications, they are polished.

Note that the bottom surface of an aluminum beverage can appears to have longitudinal scratches on it. This surface is a replica of the roll surface, which is produced by grinding (Chapter 25); in this way, we can easily determine the rolling direction of the original aluminum sheet.

Rolls made for cold rolling should not be used for hot rolling, because they may crack from thermal cycling (heat checking) and spalling (cracking or flaking of surface layers). Note from earlier discussions that the elastic modulus of the roll influences roll deflection and flattening.

Lubricants. Hot rolling of ferrous alloys is usually carried out without lubricants, although graphite may be used. Water-based solutions are used to cool the rolls and to break up the scale on the rolled material. Nonferrous alloys are hot rolled with a variety of compounded oils, emulsions, and fatty acids. Cold rolling is carried out with water-soluble oils or low-viscosity lubricants, such as mineral oils, emulsions, paraffin, and fatty oils (Section 32.10).

The heating medium used in heat treating billets and slabs may also act as a lubricant. For example, residual salts from molten-salt baths (Section 4.12.3) offer effective lubrication during rolling.

Example: A Tandem Rolling Operation

A typical tandem sheet-rolling operation is shown in Fig. 13.12, which indicates the thickness and the speed of the sheet after each reduction in the stands. The 2.25-mm (0.088-in.) sheet is supplied from a pay-off reel. The surface speed of the sheet after the first reduction (stand 5) is 4.1 m/s (820 ft/min). Four additional reductions are taken through the rest of the stands. The final thickness of the sheet is 0.26 mm (0.010 in.), and the sheet is taken up by the take-up reel at a speed of 30 m/s (6000 ft/min). The total reduction taken is $(2.25 - 0.26)/2.25 = 0.88$, or 88%.

13.5 SHAPE-ROLLING OPERATIONS

In addition to flat rolling, various shapes can be produced by **shape rolling**. Straight and long structural shapes, such as solid bars (with various cross-sections), channels, I-beams, and railroad rails, are rolled by passing the stock through a set of specially designed rolls (Fig. 13.13; also Fig. 13.1). Because the material's cross-section is to be reduced nonuniformly, the design of a series of rolls (**roll-pass design**) requires considerable experience in order to avoid external and internal defects, to hold dimensional tolerances, and to reduce roll wear.

13.5.1 Ring Rolling

In the **ring-rolling** process, a thick ring is expanded into a large diameter ring with a reduced cross section. The ring is placed between two rolls, one of which is driven (Fig. 13.14a), and its thickness is reduced by bringing the rolls closer together as they rotate. Since the volume of the ring remains constant during deformation, the reduction in thickness is compensated by an increase in the ring's diameter.

The ring-shaped blank may be produced by such means as by cutting from a plate, by piercing (see Section 14.4), or by cutting a thick-walled pipe. Various shapes can be ring rolled by the use of shaped rolls (Fig. 13.14b). Typical applications of ring rolling are large rings for rockets and turbines, gearwheel rims, ball-bearing and roller-bearing races, flanges, and reinforcing rings for pipes.

The ring-rolling process can be carried out at room or at elevated temperature, depending on the size, strength, and ductility of the workpiece material. Compared to other manufacturing processes capable of making the same part, the advantages of this process are short production times, material savings, close dimensional tolerances, and favorable grain flow in the product.

FIGURE 13.13   Stages in the shape rolling of an H-section part. Various other structural sections, such as channels and I-beams, are also rolled by this kind of process.

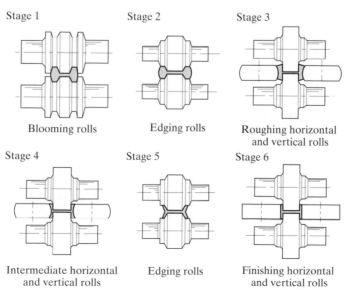

Stage 1	Stage 2	Stage 3
Blooming rolls	Edging rolls	Roughing horizontal and vertical rolls

Stage 4	Stage 5	Stage 6
Intermediate horizontal and vertical rolls	Edging rolls	Finishing horizontal and vertical rolls

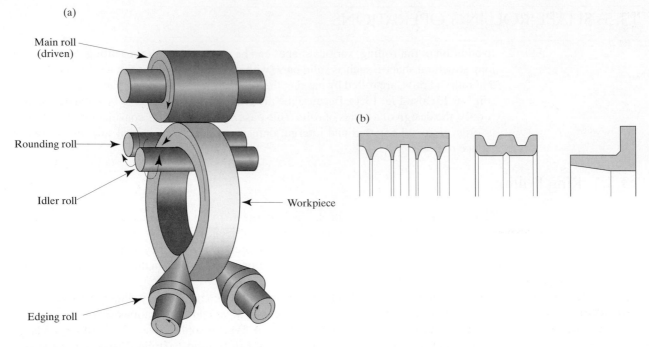

FIGURE 13.14   (a) Schematic illustration of a ring-rolling operation. Thickness reduction results in an increase in the part diameter. (b) Examples of cross-sections that can be formed by ring rolling.

13.5.2 Thread Rolling

The **thread-rolling** process is a cold-forming process by which straight or tapered threads are formed on round rods, by passing them between dies. Threads are formed on the rod or wire with each stroke of a pair of flat reciprocating dies (Fig. 13.15a). Typical products are screws, bolts, and similar threaded parts. Depending on die design, the major diameter of a rolled thread may or may not be larger than a machined thread (Fig. 13.16a)—that is, the same as the blank diameter. In either case, volume constancy is maintained, because no material is removed.

The process is capable of generating similar shapes, such as grooves and various gear forms, on other surfaces, and it can be used in the production of almost all threaded fasteners at high production rates. In another method, threads are formed with rotary dies (Fig. 13.15b) at production rates as high as 80 pieces per second.

The thread-rolling process has the advantages of generating threads without any loss of material (scrap) and with a good strength (due to cold working). The surface finish is very smooth, and the process induces compressive residual stresses on the workpiece surfaces, thus improving fatigue life.

Thread rolling is superior to the other methods of manufacturing threads, because machining the threads cuts through the grain-flow lines of the material, whereas rolling the threads leaves a grain-flow pattern that improves the strength of the thread (Fig. 13.16b).

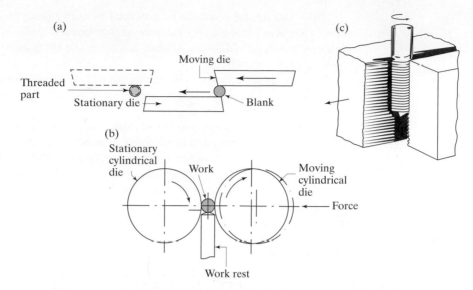

FIGURE 13.15   Thread-rolling processes: (a) and (c) reciprocating flat dies; (b) two-roller dies. Threaded fasteners, such as bolts, are made economically by these processes, at high rates of production.

Threads are rolled on metals in the soft condition, because of ductility requirements; however, they can subsequently be subjected to heat treatment and, if necessary, to final machining or to grinding. For metals in the hard condition, threads are machined and/or ground. Rolled threads are readily available in the most widely used standard thread forms; uncommon or special-purpose threads are usually machined.

FIGURE 13.16   (a) Features of a machined or rolled thread. (b) Grain flow in machined and rolled threads. Unlike machining, which cuts through the grains of the metal, the rolling of threads causes improved strength, because of cold working and favorable grain flow.

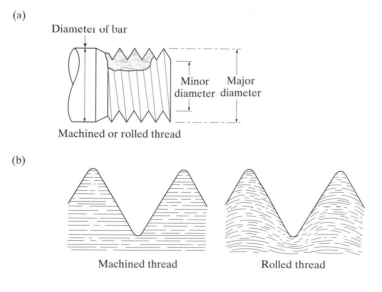

Spur and helical gears can be produced by cold-rolling processes similar to thread rolling. (See also Section 23.8.) The process may be carried out on solid cylindrical blanks or on precut gears. Cold rolling of gears has extensive applications in automatic transmissions and in power tools.

Internal thread rolling can be carried out with a fluteless **forming tap**. (See also Section 22.10.) This operation is similar to external thread rolling, and it produces accurate internal threads having good strength.

Lubrication is important in thread rolling operations in order to obtain good surface finish and surface integrity and to minimize defects. The manner in which the material deforms during plastic deformation is important, because internal defects can easily form. (See, for example, Fig. 14.20.) Usually made of hardened steel, dies are expensive to make because of their complex shape. They usually cannot be reground after they become worn. With proper die materials and preparation, however, die life may range up to millions of pieces.

13.6 PRODUCTION OF SEAMLESS PIPE AND TUBING

Rotary tube piercing is a hot-working process for making long, thick-walled *seamless* pipe and tubing (Fig. 13.17). It is based on the principle that when a round bar is subjected to radial compressive forces, tensile stresses develop at the center of the bar. (See Fig. 2.11.) When it is subsequently subjected to cyclic compressive stresses (Fig. 13.17b), a cavity begins to form at the center of the bar. This phenomenon can be demonstrated with a short piece of round eraser, by rolling it back and forth on a hard flat surface, as shown in Fig. 13.17b.

Rotary tube piercing (**Mannesmann process**) is carried out using an arrangement of rotating rolls (Fig. 13.17c). The axes of the rolls are skewed, in order to pull the round bar through the rolls by the axial component of the rotary motion. An internal mandrel assists the operation, by expanding the hole and sizing the inside diameter of the tube. The man-

FIGURE 13.17   Cavity formation in a solid round bar and its utilization in the rotary tube piercing process for making seamless pipe and tubing. (The Mannesmann mill was developed in the 1880s.)

(a)   (b)   (c)

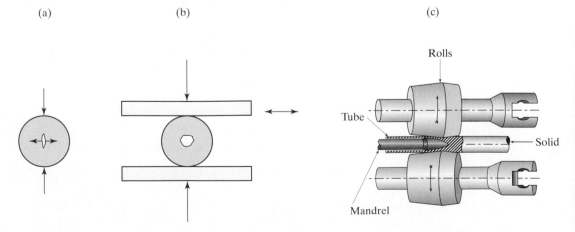

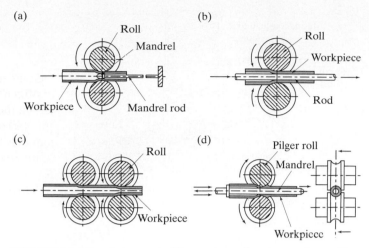

FIGURE 13.18   Schematic illustration of various tube-rolling processes: (a) with fixed mandrel; (b) with moving mandrel; (c) without mandrel; and (d) pilger rolling over a mandrel and a pair of shaped rolls. Tube diameters and thicknesses can also be changed by other processes, such as drawing, extrusion, and spinning.

drel may be held in place by a long rod, or it may be a floating mandrel without a support. Because of the severe deformation that the bar undergoes, the material must be high in quality and free from defects.

The diameter and thickness of tubes and pipes can be reduced by **tube rolling**, which uses shaped rolls (Fig. 13.18). Some of those operations can be carried out either with or without an internal mandrel. In the **pilger mill**, the tube and an internal mandrel undergo a reciprocating motion; the rolls are specially shaped and are rotated continuously. During the gap cycle on the roll, the tube is advanced and rotated, starting another cycle of tube reduction. Other processes for tube manufacturing are given in Chapter 15.

13.7 CONTINUOUS CASTING AND ROLLING; INTEGRATED MILLS AND MINIMILLS

The advantages of **continuous casting** were described in Section 5.4. This operation, also called **strand casting**, is highly automated and reduces the product's cost significantly. It is an important development and most companies are rapidly converting their facilities to this type of operation. Also, because the number of operations involved can make conventional production of tubes and pipes costly, a method of **spray casting** (*Osprey process*) can also be employed (Fig. 13.19).

Integrated Mills.   These are large facilities that involve complete activities from the production of hot metal in a blast furnace (Fig. 5.1) to the casting and the rolling of finished products (Section 5.4) that are ready to be shipped to the customer.

Minimills.   Competition in the steel industry has led to the development of *minimills*, a relatively new, yet important, operation. In a minimill, scrap metal is melted in electric-arc furnaces, cast continuously, and rolled directly into specific lines of products. Each minimill produces essentially one kind of rolled product (rod, bar, or structural sec-

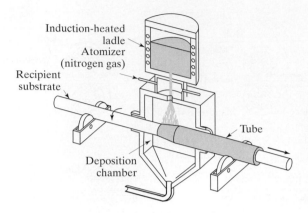

FIGURE 13.19   Spray casting (Osprey process), in which molten metal is sprayed over a rotating mandrel to produce seamless tubing and pipe. *Source*: J. Szekely, *Scientific American*, July 1987.

tions such as angle iron) from basically one type of metal or alloy. The scrap metal, which is obtained locally to reduce transportation costs, is usually old machinery, cars, and farm equipment.

Minimills have the economic advantages of low-investment optimal operations for each type of metal and product line and of low labor and energy costs. The products are usually oriented to markets in the mill's particular geographic area. One minimill in the northeast United States, for instance, supplies 95% of the domestic steel rod (for reinforced concrete) used in that region.

SUMMARY

- Rolling is the process of reducing the thickness or changing the cross-section of a long workpiece by compressive forces applied through a set of rolls. In addition to flat rolling, shape rolling is used to make products with various cross-sections. Products made by rolling include: plate, sheet, foil, rod, seamless pipe, and tubing; shape-rolled products, such as I-beams and structural shapes; and bars of various cross-section. Other rolling operations include ring rolling and thread rolling.

- Rolling may be carried out at room temperature (cold rolling) or at elevated temperatures (hot rolling). The process involves several material and process variables, including roll diameter (relative to material thickness), reduction per pass, speed, lubrication, and temperature. Spreading, bending, and flattening are important considerations for controlling the dimensional accuracy of the rolled stock.

- Rolling mills have a variety of roll configurations, such as two-high, three-high, four-high, cluster (Sendzimir), and tandem. Front and/or back tension may be applied to the material, to improve performance and to reduce roll forces.

- Continuous casting and rolling of ferrous and of nonferrous metals into semifinished products have become a common practice because of its economic benefits.

- Large facilities involving the complete sequence of activities, from the production of hot metal in a blast furnace to the casting and the rolling of finished products ready to be shipped to the customer, are known as integrated mills. On a much smaller scale, minimills utilize scrap metal which is melted in electric-arc furnaces, cast, and continuously rolled into specific lines of products.

TRENDS

- Continuous casting and rolling of both ferrous and nonferrous metals are being implemented at a rapid rate.
- Spray forming of near-net-shape flat products is beginning to compete with direct strip casting. Also, the Osprey process of spray casting of tubes, sheet, and billets is beginning to reach production status.
- Further developments are taking place in minimills, in order to roll specialized products efficiently and economically.
- Computer controls are being implemented in all aspects of the rolling and of the subsequent processing of plates, sheets, and shapes.
- Rolling operations are being conducted with better control of material properties and microstructure, and they are, increasingly, producing smoother surfaces.
- Ring rolling continues to displace machining operations in the production of bearing races.
- There is an increasing trend toward pursuing environmentally-friendly lubricants. Tighter control of residual lubricants (mill oil) is being investigated, in order to improve its reliability for further processing.

KEY TERMS

Alligatoring	Hot rolling	Sendzimir mill
Back tension	Mannesmann process	Shape rolling
Billet	Minimill	Sheet
Bloom	Neutral point	Slab
Camber	Osprey process	Spray casting
Cast structure	Pack rolling	Spreading
Cogging mill	Pilger mill	Stand
Cold rolling	Plate	Steckel rolling
Crown	Ring rolling	Tandem rolling
Draft	Roll	Temper rolling
Flat rolling	Roll stand	Thread rolling
Foil	Rolling	Wrought structure
Front tension	Rolling mill	
Gage number	Rotary tube piercing	

BIBLIOGRAPHY

Blazynski, T.Z., *Plasticity and Modern Metal-forming Technology*. Elsevier, 1989.

Ginzburg, V.B., *High-Quality Steel Rolling: Theory and Practice*. Marcel Dekker, 1993.

____, *Steel-Rolling Technology: Theory and Practice*. Marcel Dekker, 1989.

Hosford, W.F., and R.M. Caddell, *Metal Forming: Mechanics and Metallurgy* (2d ed.). Prentice Hall, 1993.

Lange, K. (ed.), *Handbook of Metal Forming*. McGraw-Hill, 1985.

Larke, E.C., *The Rolling of Strip, Sheet, and Plate* (2d ed.). Chapman & Hall, 1963.

Roberts, W.L., *Cold Rolling of Steel*. Marcel Dekker, 1978.

____, *Hot Rolling of Steel*. Marcel Dekker, 1983.

Starling, C.W., *The Theory and Practice of Flat Rolling*. The University of London Press, 1962.

Underwood, L.R., *The Rolling of Metals*, Vol. 1. Wiley, 1950.

Wusatowski, Z., *Fundamentals of Rolling*. Pergamon, 1969.

REVIEW QUESTIONS

13.1 What is the difference between a plate and a sheet?

13.2 Define (a) roll gap, (b) neutral point, (c) draft.

13.3 What factors contribute to spreading in flat rolling?

13.4 Explain the types of deflection that rolls undergo.

13.5 Describe the difference between a bloom, a slab, and a billet.

13.6 Why is roller leveling necessary?

13.7 List the defects commonly observed after flat rolling.

13.8 Explain the features of different types of rolling mills.

13.9 What is the advantage of tandem rolling?

13.10 Make a list of some parts that can be made by shape rolling.

13.11 How are seamless tubes produced?

13.12 Describe types of products that can be made by thread rolling.

13.13 Explain the features and advantages of continuous casting.

QUALITATIVE PROBLEMS

13.14 Rolling reduces the thickness of plates and sheets. It is possible, instead, to reduce the thickness by simply stretching the material. Would this be a feasible process? Explain.

13.15 It is said that necessity is the mother of invention. Explain why the rolling process was invented and developed.

13.16 Explain how the residual stress patterns shown in Fig. 13.9 become reversed when the roll radius or reduction per pass is changed.

13.17 Explain whether it would be practical to apply the roller-leveling technique shown in Fig. 13.7 to thick plates.

13.18 How does applying tensions affect flat-rolling practice?

13.19 Describe the factors that influence the roll force, F, in Fig. 13.2c.

13.20 Explain how you would go about applying front and back tensions to sheet metals during rolling.

13.21 In Section 13.2.2, we noted that rolls tend to flatten under roll forces. Describe the methods by which flattening can be reduced. Which property or properties of the roll material can be increased to reduce flattening?

13.22 Spreading in flat rolling increases with (a) decreasing width-to-thickness ratio of the entering material, (b) decreasing friction, and (c) decreasing ratio of the roll radius to the strip thickness. Explain why these increases occur.

13.23 Explain the technical and economic reasons for taking larger rather than smaller reductions per pass in flat rolling.

13.24 In Fig. 11.12, we note that surface roughness in hot rolling is much higher than in cold rolling. Explain why.

13.25 As stated in this chapter, flat rolling can be carried out by front tension only, using idling rolls (Steckel rolling). Thus the torque on the rolls is zero. Where, then, is the energy coming from to supply the work of deformation in rolling?

13.26 What is the consequence of applying too high a back tension in rolling?

13.27 In Fig. 13.11d, note that the driven rolls (powered rolls) are the third set from the work roll. Why isn't power supplied through the work roll itself? Is it even possible? Explain.

13.28 Describe the importance of controlling roll speeds, roll gaps, temperature, and other process variables in a tandem rolling operation, such as the one shown in the example in Section 13.4.

13.29 In Fig. 13.9a, if you remove the top compressive layer by, say, grinding, will the strip remain flat? If not, which way will it curve, and why?

13.30 Name several products made by each of the processes shown in Fig. 13.1.

13.31 Inspect some machine bolts, and comment on whether you think that they are made by thread rolling or machining.

QUANTITATIVE PROBLEMS

13.32 Using simple geometric relationships and the inclined-plane principle for friction, prove Eq. (13.1).

13.33 Show that the maximum angle α (known as the *angle of acceptance*—Fig. 13.2b) at which a plate can be pulled into the roll gap is equal to $\tan^{-1}\mu$, where μ is the coefficient of friction.

13.34 Calculate the roll force and the torque for AISI 1020 carbon steel strip, 400 mm wide and 10 mm thick, rolled to a thickness of 7 mm. The roll radius is 200 mm, and it rotates at 200 rpm.

13.35 In the example in Section 13.2.2, calculate the roll force, F, and the power, for the case in which the workpiece material is 1100-O aluminum and the roll radius R is 8 in.

13.36 Calculate the individual drafts in each of the stands in the tandem rolling example given in Section 13.4.

13.37 Assume that you are an instructor covering the topics in this chapter. Prepare three quantitative problems to test the knowledge of your students concerning the contents of this chapter. Give your own answers for each problem.

SYNTHESIS AND DESIGN

13.38 Figure 13.4 shows a simple sketch for a four-high mill stand. Make a survey of the available technical literature, and present a more detailed sketch for such a stand, one showing the major components.

13.39 Obtain a piece of soft round rubber eraser, such as that at the end of pencils, and duplicate the process shown in Fig. 13.17b. Note how the central portion of the eraser will begin to erode away, producing a hole.

13.40 If you repeat the experiment in Problem 13.39, but with the type of harder eraser used for erasing ink, you will note that the whole eraser will begin to crumble. Explain why.

13.41 Comment on the statements given in the Trends section at the end of this chapter.

14

Forging of Metals

14.1 INTRODUCTION

Forging is a process in which the workpiece is shaped by compressive forces applied through various dies and tools. It is one of the oldest metalworking operations, dating back at least to 4000 B.C.—perhaps as far back as 8000 B.C. Forging was first used to make jewelry, coins, and various implements by hammering metal with tools made of stone.

Simple forging operations can be performed with a heavy hand hammer and an anvil, as was traditionally done by blacksmiths. Most forgings, however, require a set of dies and such equipment as a press or a forging hammer. Unlike rolling operations, which generally produce continuous plates, sheets, strip, or various structural cross-sections, forging operations produce *discrete* parts.

Typical forged products are bolts and rivets, connecting rods, shafts for turbines, gears (Fig. 14.1a), hand tools, and structural components for machinery, aircraft (Figs. 14.1b and c), railroads, and a variety of other transportation equipment. The sequence of processes involved in forging operations is shown in Fig. 14.2.

Metal flow and grain structure can be controlled, so forged parts have good strength and toughness; they can be used reliably for highly stressed and critical applications

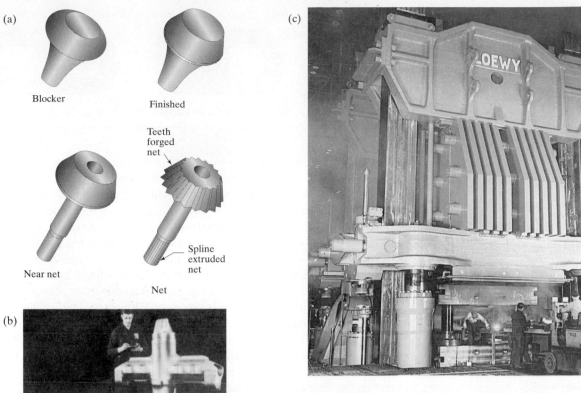

(a)

Blocker   Finished

Teeth
forged
net

Near net

Net

Spline
extruded
net

(b)

(c)

FIGURE 14.1   (a) Schematic illustration of the steps involved in forging a bevel gear with a shaft. *Source*: Forging Industry Association. (b) Landing-gear components for the C5A and C5B transport aircraft, made by forging. (c) General view of a 445 MN (50,000 ton) hydraulic press. *Source* for b and c: Wyman-Gordon Company.

FIGURE 14.2   Outline of forging and related operations.

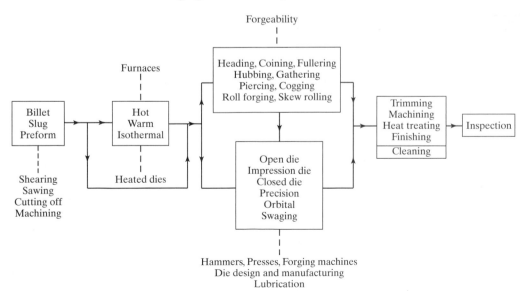

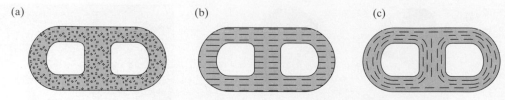

FIGURE 14.3   A part made by three different processes, showing grain flow.
(a) casting, (b) machining, (c) forging. *Source*: Forging industry Association.

(Fig. 14.3). Forging may be done at room temperature (*cold forging*) or at elevated temperatures (*warm* or *hot forging*, depending on the temperature, Section 1.7).

Because of the higher strength of the material, cold forging requires greater forces, and the workpiece materials must have sufficient ductility at room temperature. Cold-forged parts have good surface finish and dimensional accuracy. Hot forging requires smaller forces, but it produces dimensional accuracy and surface finish that are not as good.

Forgings generally require additional finishing operations, such as heat treating, to modify properties, and then machining to obtain accurate finished dimensions. These operations can be minimized by *precision forging*, which is an important example of the trend toward *net-shape* or *near-net shape* forming processes. This trend significantly reduces the number of operations required, and hence the manufacturing cost to make the final product.

A component that can be forged successfully may also be manufactured economically by other methods, such as by casting (Part II), by powder metallurgy (Chapter 17), or by machining (Part IV). However, as you might expect, each process will produce a part having different characteristics and limitations, particularly with regard to strength, toughness, dimensional accuracy, surface finish, and internal or external defects.

14.2 OPEN-DIE FORGING

Open-die forging is the simplest forging process (Table 14.1). Although most open-die forgings generally weigh 15 kg–500 kg (30 lb–1000 lb), forgings as heavy as 300 tons have

TABLE 14.1   Characteristics of Forging Processes

Process	Advantages	Limitations
Open die	Simple, inexpensive dies; useful for small quantities; wide range of sizes available; good strength characteristics	Limited to simple shapes; difficult to hold close tolerances; machining to final shape necessary; low production rate; relatively poor utilization of material; high degree of skill required
Closed die	Relatively good utilization of material; generally better properties than open-die forgings; good dimensional accuracy; high production rates; good reproducibility	High die cost for small quantities; machining often necessary
Blocker type	Low die costs; high production rates	Machining to final shape necessary; thick webs and large fillets necessary
Conventional type	Requires much less machining than blocker type; high production rates; good utilization of material	Somewhat higher die cost than blocker type
Precision type	Close tolerances; machining often unnecessary; very good material utilization; very thin webs and flanges possible	Requires high forces, intricate dies, and provision for removing forging from dies

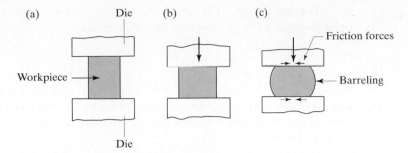

FIGURE 14.4   (a) Solid cylindrical billet upset between two flat dies. (b) Uniform deformation of the billet without friction. (c) Deformation with friction. Note barreling of the billet caused by friction forces at the billet–die interfaces.

been made. Sizes may range from very small parts up to shafts some 23 m (75 ft) long (in the case of ship propellers).

The open-die forging process can be depicted by a solid workpiece placed between two flat dies and reduced in height by compressing it (Fig. 14.4a). This process is also called **upsetting** or *flat-die forging*. The die surfaces in open-die forging may have simple cavities, to produce relatively simple forgings. The deformation of the workpiece under *ideal* conditions is shown in Fig. 14.4b. Because constancy of volume is maintained, any reduction in height increases the diameter of the forged part.

Note that, in Fig. 14.4b, the workpiece is deformed *uniformly*. In actual operations, the part develops a *barrel* shape (Fig. 14.4c); this deformation is also known as *pancaking*. **Barreling** is caused primarily by frictional forces at the die-workpiece interfaces that oppose the outward flow of the materials at these interfaces. Barreling can be minimized if an effective lubricant is used.

Barreling can also occur in upsetting hot workpieces between cold dies. The material at and near the interfaces cools rapidly, while the rest of the workpiece remains relatively hot. Thus, the material at the ends of the workpiece has higher resistance to deformation than the material at its center. Consequently, the central portion of the workpiece expands laterally to a greater extent than do its ends. Barreling from thermal effects can be reduced or eliminated by using heated dies; thermal barriers such as glass cloth at the die–workpiece interfaces are also used.

Cogging, also called *drawing out*, is basically an open-die forging operation in which the thickness of a bar is reduced by successive forging steps at specific intervals (Fig. 14.5). Because the contact area per stroke is small, a long section of a bar can be reduced in thickness without requiring large forces or machinery. Blacksmiths perform such operations with a hammer and an anvil using hot pieces of metal; iron fences of various design are often made by this process.

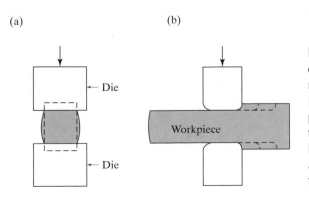

FIGURE 14.5   Two views of a cogging operation on a rectangular bar. Blacksmiths use this process to reduce the thickness of bars by hammering the part on an anvil. Note the barreling of the workpiece.

Forging Force. The forging force, F, in an open-die forging operation on a solid cylindrical piece can be estimated from the formula

$$F = Y_f \pi r^2 \left(1 + \frac{2\mu r}{3h} \right), \tag{14.1}$$

where Y_f is the *flow stress* of the material (see next example), μ is the coefficient of friction, and r and h are the radius and height of the workpiece, respectively. Derivation of this formula and of others for various forging processes are given in the bibliography listed at the end of this chapter.

Example: Calculation of Forging Force

A solid cylindrical slug made of 304 stainless steel is 150 mm (6 in.) in diameter and 100 mm (4 in.) high. It is reduced in height by 50% at room temperature, by open-die forging with flat dies. Assuming that the coefficient of friction is 0.2, calculate the forging force at the end of the stroke.

Solution: The forging force at the end of the stroke is calculated using Eq. (14.1), in which the dimensions pertain to the final dimensions of the forging. Thus, the final height $h = 100/2 = 50$ mm, and the final radius, r, is determined from volume constancy. Equating the volumes before and after deformation, we have

$$(\pi)(75)^2(100) = (\pi)(r)^2(50).$$

Therefore, $r = 106$ mm (4.17 in.).

The quantity Y_f in Eq. (14.1) is the flow stress of the material, which is the stress required to continue plastic deformation of the workpiece at a particular true strain. The absolute value of the true strain that the workpiece has undergone in this operation is

$$\varepsilon = \ln \left(\frac{100}{50} \right) = 0.69.$$

Referring to Fig. 2.6, we note that the flow stress for 304 stainless steel at a true strain of 0.69 is about 1000 MPa (140 ksi). We now now calculate the forging force, noting that for this problem the units in Eq. (14.1) must be in N and m. Thus,

$$F = (1000)(10^6)(\pi)(0.106)^2 1 + \frac{(2)(0.2)(0.106)}{(3)(0.050)}$$

$$= 4.5 \times 10^7 \text{ N} = 45 \text{ MN} = 10^7 \text{ lb} = 5000 \text{ tons}.$$

14.3 IMPRESSION-DIE AND CLOSED-DIE FORGING

In *impression-die forging*, the workpiece acquires the shape of the die cavities (impressions) while being forged between two shaped dies (Fig. 14.6). Note that some of the material flows outward and forms a **flash**. The flash has a significant role in the flow of material in impression-

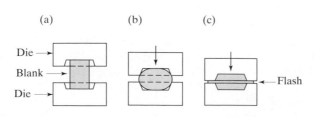

(a) (b) (c)

Die →
Blank →
Die →

← Flash

FIGURE 14.6 Stages in impression-die forging of a solid round billet. Note the formation of flash, which is excess metal that is subsequently trimmed off (see Fig. 14.8).

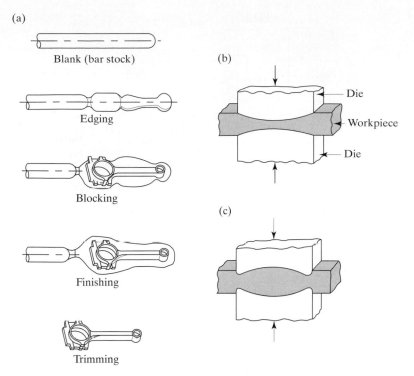

(a) Blank (bar stock)

Edging

Blocking

Finishing

Trimming

(b) Die / Workpiece / Die

(c)

FIGURE 14.7   (a) Stages in forging a connecting rod for an internal combustion engine. Note the amount of flash required to ensure proper filling of the die cavities. (b) Fullering, and (c) edging operations to distribute the material when preshaping the blank for forging.

die forging: The thin flash cools rapidly, and, because of its frictional resistance, it subjects the material in the die cavity to high pressures, thereby encouraging the filling of the die cavity.

The blank to be forged is prepared by such means as (a) cutting or *cropping* from an extruded or drawn bar stock, (b) a preform in operations such as powder metallurgy (Section 17.5), (c) casting, or (d) a preform blank in a prior forging operation. The blank is placed on the lower die and, as the upper die begins to descend, the blank's shape gradually changes, as is shown for the forging of a connecting rod in Fig. 14.7a.

Preforming processes, such as fullering and edging (Figs. 14.7b and c), are used to distribute the material into various regions of the blank, much as they are in shaping dough to make pastry. In **fullering**, material is distributed away from an area; in **edging**, it is gathered into a localized area. The part is then formed into the rough shape of a connecting rod by a process called **blocking**, using *blocker dies*. The final operation is the finishing of the forging in *impression dies* that give the forging its final shape. The flash is removed usually by a trimming operation (Fig. 14.8).

The examples shown in Figs. 14.6 and 14.7a are also referred to as **closed-die forgings**. However, in true closed-die or **flashless** forging, flash does not form and the workpiece completely fills the die cavity (right side of Fig. 14.9b). Accurate control of the volume of material and proper die design are essential in order to obtain a closed-die forging of the desired dimensions and tolerances. Undersize blanks prevent the complete filling of the die cavity; conversely, oversize blanks generate excessive pressures and may cause dies to fail prematurely or to jam.

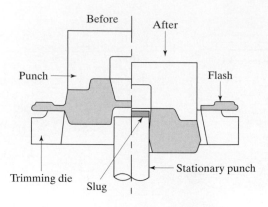

FIGURE 14.8 Trimming flash from a forged part. Note that the thin material at the center is removed by punching.

FIGURE 14.9 Comparison of closed-die forging to precision or flashless forging of a cylindrical billet. *Source*: H. Takemasu, V. Vazquez, B. Painter, and T. Altan.

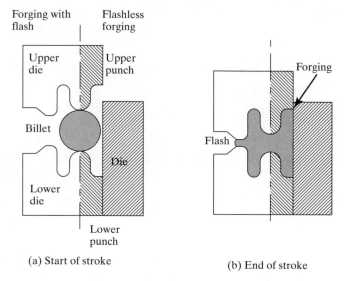

(a) Start of stroke

(b) End of stroke

14.3.1 Precision Forging

For economic reasons the trend in forging operations today is toward greater *precision*, which reduces the number of additional finishing operations. Operations in which the part formed is close to the final dimensions of the desired component are known as **near-net-shape** or **net-shape forging**. The advantages of net-shape forming were described in the General Introduction. In such a process, there is little excess material on the forged part, and it is subsequently removed (generally by trimming or grinding).

In **precision forging**, special dies produce parts having greater accuracies than those from impression-die forging and requiring much less machining. The process requires higher-capacity equipment, because of the greater forces required to obtain fine details on the part. Because of the relatively low forging loads and temperatures that they require, aluminum and magnesium alloys are particularly suitable for precision forging; also, little die wear takes place and the surface finish is good. Steels and titanium can also be precision-forged. Typical precision-forged products are gears, connecting rods, housings, and turbine blades.

Precision forging requires special and more complex dies, precise control of the billet's volume and shape, accurate positioning of the billet in the die cavity, and hence higher investment. However, less material is wasted, and much less subsequent machining is required, because the part is closer to the final desired shape. Thus, the choice between con-

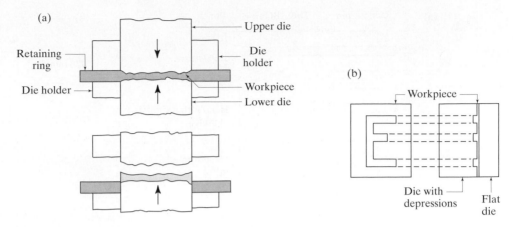

FIGURE 14.10   (a) Schematic illustration of the coining process. The earliest coins were made by open-die forging and lacked sharp details. (b) An example of a coining operation to produce an impression of the letter E on a block of metal.

ventional forging and precision forging requires an economic analysis, particularly in regard to the production volume.

14.3.2 Coining

Coining essentially is a closed-die forging process typically used in minting coins, medallions, and jewelry (Figs. 14.10a and b). The slug is coined in a completely closed die cavity. In order to produce fine details the pressures required can be as high as five or six times the strength of the material. Note, for example, the detail on newly minted coins. On some parts, several coining operations may be required. Lubricants cannot be applied in coining, because they can become entrapped in the die cavities and, being incompressible, prevent the full reproduction of die-surface details.

The coining process is also used with forgings and with other products, to improve surface finish and to impart the desired dimensional accuracy. This process, called **sizing**, involves high pressures, with little change in part shape during sizing. *Marking* of parts with letters and numbers can be done rapidly by a process similar to coining.

14.3.3 Forging Force

The forging force, F, required to carry out an impression-die forging operation can be estimated from the formula

$$F = kY_f A, \qquad (14.2)$$

where k is a multiplying factor (obtained from Table 14.2), Y_f is the flow stress of the material at the forging temperature, and A is the projected area of the forging, including the flash. In hot-forging operations, the actual forging pressure for most metals ranges from 550 MPa to 1000 MPa (80 ksi to 140 ksi).

TABLE 14.2   Range of k Values for Eq. (14.2)

Simple shapes, without flash	3–5
Simple shapes, with flash	5–8
Complex shapes, with flash	8–12

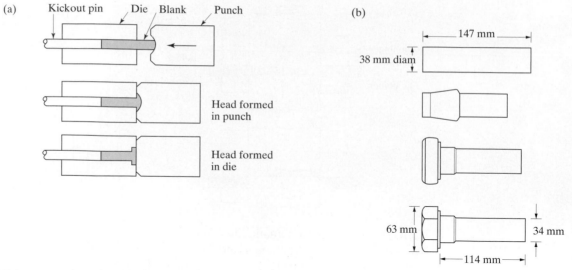

FIGURE 14.11   (a) Heading operation, to form heads on fasteners such as nails and rivets. (b) Sequence of operations to produce a bolt head by heading.

14.4   RELATED FORGING OPERATIONS

A number of other forging operations are carried out in order to impart the desired shape and features to forged products.

14.4.1   Heading

Heading is essentially an upsetting operation, usually performed at the end of a round rod or wire in order to produce a larger cross-section. Typical examples are the heads of bolts, screws, rivets, nails, and other fasteners (Fig. 14.11a). Heading processes can be carried out cold, warm, or hot; they are performed on machines called **headers**, which are usually highly automated. Production rates are hundreds of pieces per minute for small parts. These machines tend to be noisy; soundproof enclosure or the use of ear protectors is required. Heading operations can be combined with cold-extrusion processes (Section 15.5) to make various parts.

An important aspect of heading is the tendency for the bar to buckle if its unsupported length-to-diameter ratio is too high. This ratio is usually limited to less than 3 : 1, but it can be higher, depending on the die geometry. For example, higher ratios can be accommodated if the diameter of the die cavity is not more than 1.5 times the diameter of the bar.

Example: Manufacturing of a Bolt by Heading Operations

The starting material for the steel bolt shown in Fig. 14.11b is a round rod 147 mm (5.8 in.) long and 38 mm (1.5 in.) in diameter, sheared from a long drawn rod. The first operation consists of preforming: gathering material at one end of the rod to prepare it for heading. The second operation produces a round head, while reducing the diameter of the long section to 34 mm (1.34 in.).

The last operation produces a hexagonal head on the bolt. All the operations are performed at room temperature; they cold-work the material and so improve its mechanical properties and produce a good surface finish and dimensional accuracy.

FIGURE 14.12   A pierced round billet, showing grain flow pattern. *Source*: Courtesy of Ladish Co., Inc.

14.4.2 Piercing

Piercing is a process of indenting (but not breaking through) the surface of a workpiece with a punch in order to produce a cavity or an impression (Fig. 14.12). The workpiece may be confined in a die cavity, or it may be unconstrained. Piercing may be followed by punching, to produce a hole in the part. Piercing is also performed to produce hollow regions in forgings, using side-acting auxiliary equipment.

The *piercing force* depends on the cross-sectional area and the tip geometry of the punch, on the strength of the material, and on the magnitude of friction at the sliding interfaces. The pressure may range from three to five times the strength of the material—roughly the same level of stress required to make an indentation in hardness testing (Section 2.6.2).

14.4.3 Other Operations

Hubbing consists of pressing a hardened punch, having a particular tip geometry, into the surface of a block of metal. The cavity produced is then used as a die for forming operations, such as occur in the making of tableware. The die cavity is usually shallow, but, for deeper cavities, some material may be removed from the surface by machining prior to hubbing.

In **roll forging**, the cross-section of a bar is reduced or shaped by passing it through a pair of rolls with shaped grooves (Fig. 14.13). Roll forging is used to produce tapered shafts and leaf springs, table knives, and hand tools; it may also be used as a preliminary forming operation, to be followed by other forging processes.

A process similar to roll forging is **skew rolling**, typically used for making ball bearings (Fig. 14.14a). Round wire or rod is fed into the roll gap, and roughly spherical blanks are formed continually by the action of the rotating rolls. Another method of forming near-spherical blanks for ball bearings is to shear pieces from a round bar and then to upset them in ball headers, between two dies with hemispherical cavities (Fig. 14.14b). The balls are later ground and polished in special machinery (Sections 25.6 and 25.10).

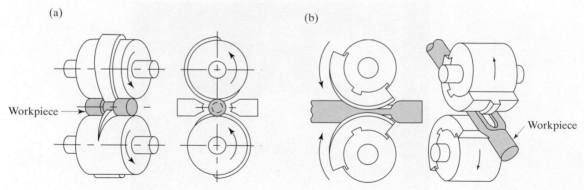

FIGURE 14.13   Two examples of the roll-forging operation, also known as *cross-rolling*. Tapered leaf springs and knives can be made by this process. *Source*: (a) J. Holub; (b) reprinted with permission of General Motors Corporation.

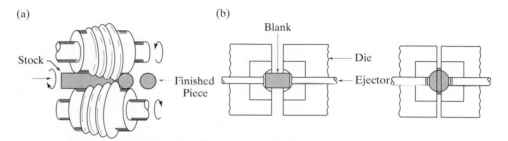

FIGURE 14.14   (a) Production of steel balls by the skew-rolling process. (b) Production of steel balls by upsetting a cylindrical blank. Note the formation of flash. The balls made by these processes are subsequently ground and polished for use in ball bearings (see Sections 25.6 and 25.10).

Orbital forging is a process in which the upper die moves along an orbital path (Fig. 14.15a) and forms the part *incrementally*. The operation is similar to the action of a mortar and pestle. Typical components forged by this process are disk-shaped and conical parts (Fig. 14.15b), such as bevel gears. The forging force is relatively small because, at any instant, the die contact is concentrated onto a small area of the workpiece. The operation is relatively quiet, and parts can be formed within 10–20 cycles of the orbiting die.

Incremental forging is a process in which a blank is forged into a shape with a tool that forms the blank in several small steps; this concept is somewhat similar to the cogging operation (Fig. 14.5), in which the die penetrates the blank to different depths across the surface. Consequently, this process requires much lower forces, as compared to conventional impression-die forging, and the tools are simpler and less costly. Two 7075 aluminum-alloy parts for the bulkhead of the Airbus aircraft have been made by incremental forging.

In **isothermal forging**, also known as **hot-die forging**, the dies are heated to the same temperature as that of the hot workpiece. Because the workpiece remains hot, its low strength and high ductility are maintained during forging; the forging load is low, and material flow within the die cavity is improved. Complex parts with good dimensional accuracy can be forged to near-net shape by one stroke in a hydraulic press. The dies for hot forging are usually made of nickel or molybdenum alloys.

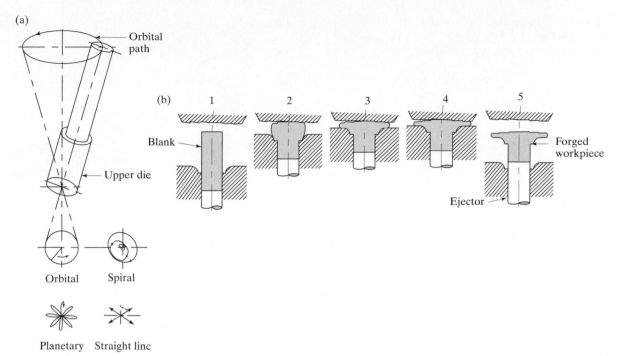

FIGURE 14.15   (a) Various movements of the upper die in orbital forging (also called rotary, swing, or rocking-die forging); the process is similar to the action of a mortar and pestle. (b) An example of orbital forging. Bevel gears, wheels, and rings for bearings can be made by this process.

Isothermal forging is expensive, and production is slow. However, it can be economical for intricate forgings made of materials such as titanium and superalloys, provided that the quantity required is sufficiently high to justify the die costs.

14.5 ROTARY SWAGING

In *rotary swaging*, also known simply as **swaging** or *radial forging*, a solid rod or tube is subjected to radial impact forces by a set of reciprocating dies (Figs. 14.16a and b). The die movements are obtained by means of a set of rollers in a cage, in an action similar to that of a roller bearing. The workpiece is stationary and the dies rotate, striking the workpiece at rates as high as 20 strokes per second.

In *die-closing swaging machines*, die movements are obtained through the reciprocating motion of wedges (Fig. 14.16c). The dies can be opened wider than those in rotary swagers, and thereby accommodate large-diameter or variable-diameter parts. In another type of machine, the dies do not rotate but move radially in and out. Typical products are screwdriver blades and soldering-iron tips (Fig. 14.16d).

In **tube swaging**, the internal diameter and/or the thickness of the tube can be controlled with or without the use of internal mandrels (Figs. 14.17a and b). For small-diameter tubing, high-strength wire is used as a mandrel. Mandrels can also be made with longitudinal grooves, to allow swaging of internally shaped tubes (Fig. 14.17c). The rifling in gun barrels, for example, is made by swaging a tube over a mandrel having spiral grooves. Special machinery has been built to swage gun barrels and other parts with starting diameters as large as 350 mm (14 in.).

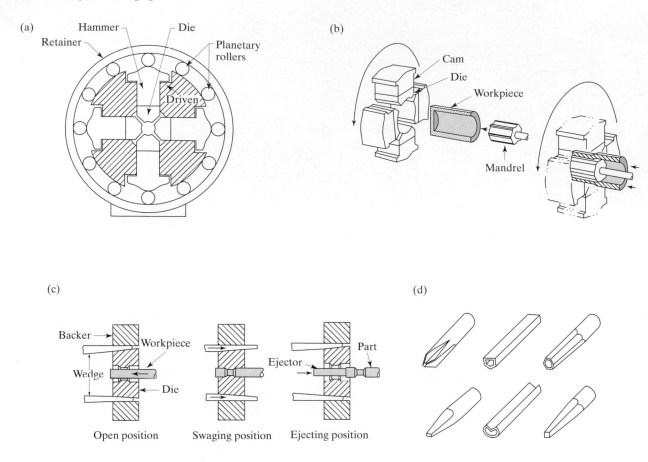

FIGURE 14.16   (a) Schematic illustration of the rotary-swaging process.
(b) Forming internal profiles on a tubular workpiece by swaging. (c) A die-closing
type swaging machine, showing forming of a stepped shaft. (d) Typical parts made
by swaging.

The swaging process can be used to assemble fittings over cables and wire; in such cases the tubular fitting is swaged directly onto the cable. This process is also used for operations such as *pointing* (tapering the tip of a cylindrical part) and *sizing* (finalizing the dimensions of a part).

Swaging is usually limited to a maximum workpiece diameter of about 150 mm (6 in.); parts as small as 0.5 mm (0.02 in.) have been swaged. Tolerances range from ±0.05 mm to ±0.5 mm (0.002 in. to 0.02 in.). Swaging is suitable for medium to high rates of production (rates as high as 50 parts per minute are possible, depending on the complexity of the part). It is a versatile process, and it is limited in length only by the length of the bar supporting the mandrel, if one is needed.

As with other cold-working processes, parts produced by swaging have improved mechanical properties. Lubricants are used for improved surface finish and die life. For workpieces having low ductility at room temperature, swaging can be performed at elevated temperatures.

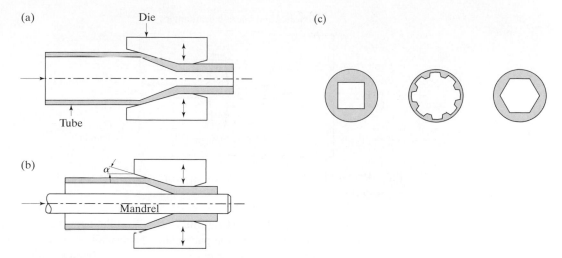

FIGURE 14.17   (a) Swaging of tubes without a mandrel; note the increase in wall thickness in the die gap. (b) Swaging with a mandrel; note that the final wall thickness of the tube depends on the mandrel diameter. (c) Examples of cross-sections of tubes produced by swaging on shaped mandrels. Rifling (spiral grooves) in small gun barrels can be made by this process.

14.6 FORGING-DIE DESIGN

The design of forging dies requires a knowledge of the strength and ductility of the workpiece material, its sensitivity to deformation rate and temperature, its frictional characteristics, and the shape and complexity of the workpiece. Die distortion under high forging loads is an important consideration, particularly if close tolerances are required.

The most important rule in die design is the fact that the part will flow in the direction of least resistance. Thus the workpiece (*intermediate shape*) should be shaped so that it properly fills the die cavities. An example of the intermediate shapes for a connecting rod were shown in Fig. 14.7a. The importance of preforming can be appreciated by noting how a piece of dough is preshaped to make a pie crust or how ground meat is preshaped to make a hamburger.

Preshaping.   In a properly preshaped workpiece, the material should not flow easily into the flash, the grain flow pattern should be favorable, and excessive sliding at the workpiece–die interfaces should be minimized in order to reduce wear. Selection of shapes requires considerable experience and involves calculations of cross-sectional areas at each location in the forging.

Computer-aided design techniques have been developed to expedite these calculations, as well as to predict the material-flow pattern in the die cavity and to predict the formation of defects. Because the material undergoes different degrees of deformation (and at different rates) in various regions in the die cavity, the mechanical properties depend on the particular location in the forging.

Die Design Features.   The terminology for forging dies is shown in Fig. 14.18, and the significance of various features is described below. Some of these considerations are similar to those for casting (Section 12.2).

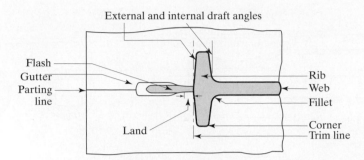

FIGURE 14.18   Standard terminology for various features of a typical impression-forging die.

For most forgings, the **parting line** is usually at the largest cross-section of the part. For simple symmetrical shapes, the parting line is normally a straight line at the center of the forging, but for more complex shapes the line may not lie in a single plane. The dies are then designed in such a way that they lock during engagement, in order to avoid side thrust, balance forces, and maintain die alignment during forging.

After sufficiently constraining lateral flow to ensure proper die filling, the flash material is allowed to flow into a *gutter*, so that the extra flash does not increase the forging load unnecessarily. A general guideline for flash clearance between dies is 3% of the maximum thickness of the forging. The length of the *land* is usually two to five times the flash thickness. Several gutter designs have been developed throughout the years.

Draft angles are necessary in almost all forging dies, in order to facilitate the removal of the part from the die. Upon cooling, the forging shrinks both radially and longitudinally, so internal draft angles are made larger than external ones. Internal angles are about 7° to 10°, external angles about 3° to 5°.

Selection of the proper radii for corners and fillets is important, in order to ensure smooth flow of the metal into the die cavity and to improve die life. Small radii are generally undesirable, because of their adverse effect on metal flow and their tendency to wear rapidly (as a result of stress concentration and thermal cycling). Small fillet radii also can cause fatigue cracking of the dies. As a general rule, these radii should be as large as can be permitted by the design of the forging.

Instead of being made as one piece, dies may be assembled with *die inserts* (Fig. 14.19), particularly for complex shapes; this alternative reduces the cost of making several similar dies. The inserts can be made of stronger and harder materials, and they can be changed easily in the case of wear or failure in a particular section of the die.

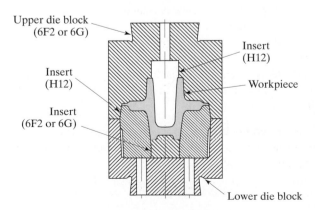

FIGURE 14.19   Die inserts used in dies for forging an automotive axle housing. (See Tables 5.5 to 5.7 for die materials.) *Source: Metals Handbook, Desk Edition.* ASM International, Metals Park, Ohio, 1985. Used with permission.

As with the patterns used in casting, *allowances* are provided in forging-die design because machining the forging may be necessary to obtain final desired dimensions and surface finish. Machining allowance should be provided at flanges, at holes, and at mating surfaces.

14.7 DIE MATERIALS AND LUBRICATION

Among important aspects of forging (as well as of other manufacturing processes discussed in Part III) are die materials and lubrication.

Die Materials.   Most forging operations, particularly for large parts, are carried out at elevated temperatures. General requirements for die materials therefore are (a) strength and toughness at elevated temperatures, (b) hardenability and ability to harden uniformly, (c) resistance to mechanical and thermal shock, and (d) wear resistance, particularly resistance to abrasive wear, because of the presence of scale in hot forging.

Selection of proper die materials depends on such factors as the die size, the composition and the properties of the workpiece, the complexity of the shape, the forging temperature, the type of forging operation, the cost of the die materials, and the number of forgings required. Heat transfer from the hot workpiece to the dies (and subsequent distortion of the dies) is also an important factor.

Common die materials are tool and die steels containing chromium, nickel, molybdenum, and vanadium (see Tables 5.5 and 5.6). Dies are made from die blocks, which themselves are forged from castings and then machined and finished to the desired shape and surface finish.

Die failures usually result from a variety of the reasons described in Section 14.10. Die manufacturing methods are also described in that section.

Lubrication.   Lubricants greatly influence friction and wear; consequently, they affect the forces required (Eq. 14.1) and the flow of the metal in die cavities. They can also act as a thermal barrier between the hot workpiece and the relatively cool dies, slowing the rate of cooling of the workpiece and improving metal flow. Another important role of the lubricant is to serve as a *parting agent*, that is, one which inhibits the forging from sticking to the dies and helps in its release from the die.

A wide variety of lubricants can be used in forging. (See also Chapter 32.) For hot forging, graphite, molybdenum disulfide, and sometimes glass are used. For cold forging, mineral oils and soaps are common lubricants, applied after *conversion coating* of the blanks (Section 32.12). In hot forging, the lubricant is usually applied directly to the dies; in cold forging, it is applied to the workpiece. The method of application and the uniformity of the lubricant's thickness on the blank are important to product quality.

14.8 FORGEABILITY

Forgeability is generally defined as the capability of a material to undergo deformation without cracking. A number of tests have been developed to quantify forgeability, although none is accepted universally. A commonly used test is to **upset** a solid cylindrical specimen and observe any cracking on the barreled surfaces (see Fig. 2.19d); the greater the deformation prior to cracking, the greater the forgeability of the metal.

Upsetting tests can be performed at various temperatures and deformation rates. If notch sensitivity of the material is high, surface defects will affect the results by causing premature cracking. A typical surface defect is a **seam**, which may be a string of inclusions, a longitudinal scratch, or folds introduced during prior working of the material.

TABLE 14.3   Classification of Metals in
Decreasing Order of Forgeability

Metal or alloy	Approximate range of hot forging temperature (°C)
Aluminum alloys	400–550
Magnesium alloys	250–350
Copper alloys	600–900
Carbon and low–alloy steels	850–1150
Martensitic stainless steels	1100–1250
Austenitic stainless steels	1100–1250
Titanium alloys	700–950
Iron-base superalloys	1050–1180
Cobalt-base superalloys	1180–1250
Tantalum alloys	1050–1350
Molybdenum alloys	1150–1350
Nickel-base superalloys	1050–1200
Tungsten alloys	1200–1300

In the **hot-twist test**, a round specimen is twisted continuously in the same direction until it fails. The test is performed on a number of specimens at different temperatures, and the number of turns that each specimen undergoes before failure is observed. The optimum forging temperature is then chosen. The hot-twist test is particularly useful for steels.

The forgeabilities of several metals and alloys are given in Table 14.3, in decreasing order of forgeability. These ratings should be regarded only as general guidelines. They arc based on considerations of ductility and strength, of forging temperature required, of frictional behavior, and of the quality of the forgings produced. Because of differences in ductility at different temperatures, two-phase alloys (such as titanium) are more difficult to forge than single-phase alloys, and they require careful selection and control of forging temperature.

Typical *hot* forging temperature ranges for various metals and alloys are included in Table 14.3. Note that higher forging temperature does not necessarily indicate greater difficulty in forging that material. For *warm* forging, temperatures range from 200 °C to 300 °C (400 °F to 600 °F) for aluminum alloys and from 550 °C to 750 °C (1000 °F to 1400 °F) for steels.

Forging Defects.   In addition to surface cracking during forging, other defects can develop as a result of the material flow pattern in the die. If there is an insufficient volume of material to fill the die cavity, the web may buckle during forging and develop laps (Fig. 14.20a). On the other hand, if the web is thick, the excess material flows past the already formed portions of the forging and develops internal cracks (Fig. 14.20b).

The various radii in the forging die cavity can significantly influence the formation of such defects. Internal defects may also develop from nonuniform deformation of the material in the die cavity, from temperature gradients throughout the workpiece during forging, and from microstructural changes caused by phase transformations.

Although it may not be considered a flaw, another important aspect of quality in a forging is the *grain flow pattern* (see Fig. 14.12). There are situations in which the flow lines reach a surface perpendicularly, exposing the grain boundaries directly to the environment; this condition is known as **end grains**. In service, they can be attacked by the environment, develop a rough surface, and act as stress raisers.

Forging defects can cause fatigue failures, and they may lead to such other problems as corrosion and wear during the service life of the component. The importance of inspecting forgings prior to their placement in service, particularly in critical applications, is obvious; inspection techniques are described in Sections 36.2 and 36.3.

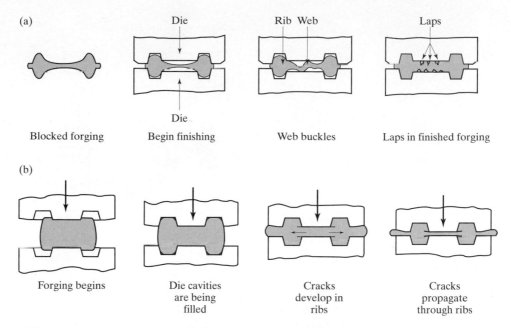

FIGURE 14.20   Examples of defects in forged parts. (a) Laps formed by web buckling during forging; web thickness should be increased to avoid this problem. (b) Internal defects caused by oversized billet; die cavities are filled prematurely, and the material at the center flows past the filled regions as the dies close.

14.9 FORGING MACHINES

A variety of forging machines are in use, with a range of capacities, speeds, and speed-stroke characteristics (Table 14.4). These machines are generally classified as **presses** or **hammers**.

14.9.1 Presses

Hydraulic Presses.   These presses operate at constant speeds and are *load limited*, or load restricted. In other words, a press stops if the load required exceeds its capacity. Large amounts of energy can be transmitted to a workpiece by a constant load throughout a stroke, the speed of which can be controlled. Because forging in a hydraulic press takes longer than in other types of forging machines, the workpiece may cool rapidly unless the dies are heated (see *isothermal forging*, Section 14.4). Compared to mechanical presses, hydraulic presses are slower and involve higher initial cost, but they require less maintenance.

TABLE 14.4   Speed Range of Forging Equipment

Equipment	m/s
Hydraulic press	0.06–0.30
Mechanical press	0.06–1.5
Screw press	0.6–1.2
Gravity drop hammer	3.6–4.8
Power drop hammer	3.0–9.0
Counterblow hammer	4.5–9.0

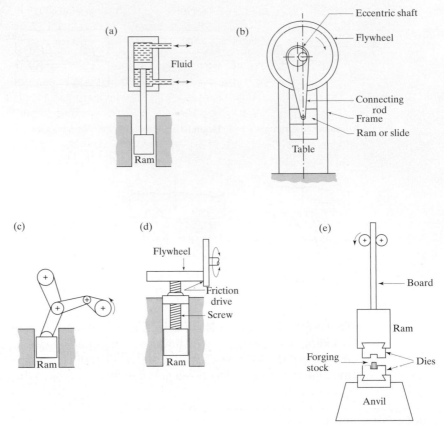

FIGURE 14.21   Schematic illustration of the principles of various forging machines. (a) Hydraulic press. (b) Mechanical press with an eccentric drive; the eccentric shaft can be replaced by a crankshaft to give the up-and-down motion to the ram. (c) Knuckle-joint press. (d) Screw press. (e) Gravity drop hammer.

A hydraulic press typically consists of a frame with two or four columns, pistons, cylinders (Fig. 14.21a), rams, and hydraulic pumps driven by electric motors. The ram speed can be varied during the stroke. Press capacities range up to 125 MN (14,000 tons) for open-die forging, and up to 450 MN (50,000 tons) in North America, 640 MN (72,000 tons) in France, and 730 MN (82,000 tons) in Russia for closed-die forging. The main landing-gear support beam for the Boeing 747 aircraft is forged in a 450-MN (50,000-ton) hydraulic press, shown in Fig. 14.1c (with the part in the forefront). This part is made of a titanium alloy and weighs approximately 1350 kg (1.5 tons).

Mechanical Presses.   These presses are basically of either the crank or the eccentric type (Fig. 14.21b). The speed varies from a maximum at the center of the stroke to zero at the bottom of the stroke, so they are *stroke limited*. The energy in a mechanical press is generated by a large flywheel powered by an electric motor. A clutch engages the flywheel to an eccentric shaft. A connecting rod translates the rotary motion into a reciprocating linear motion. A *knuckle-joint* mechanical press is shown in Fig. 14.21c. Because of the linkage design, very high forces can be applied in this type of press (see also Fig. 11.24a).

The force available in a mechanical press depends on the stroke position; it becomes extremely high at the bottom dead center. Thus proper setup is essential to avoid breaking the dies or equipment components. Mechanical presses have high production rates; they are easier to automate and require less operator skill than do other types of forging machines. Press capacities generally range from 2.7 MN (300 tons) to 107 MN (12,000 tons).

Screw Presses.   These presses (Fig. 14.21d) derive their energy from a flywheel; hence they are *energy limited*. The forging load is transmitted through a vertical screw, and the ram comes to a stop when the flywheel energy is dissipated. If the dies do not close at the end of the cycle, the operation is repeated until the forging is completed.

Screw presses are used for various open-die and closed-die forging operations; they are particularly suitable for small production quantities and precision parts, such as turbine blades. Capacities range from 1.4 MN to 280 MN (160 tons to 31,500 tons).

14.9.2 Hammers

Hammers derive their energy from the potential energy of the ram, which is converted into kinetic energy (Fig. 14.21e); thus they are *energy limited*. Unlike hydraulic presses, they operate at high speeds, and the resulting low forming time minimizes the cooling of a hot forging. Low cooling rates allow the forging of complex shapes, particularly those with thin and deep recesses. To complete the forging, several successive blows are usually made in the same die. Hammers are available in a variety of designs; they are the most versatile and the least expensive type of forging equipment.

Gravity Drop Hammers.   In the operation of this hammer, a process called **drop forging**, the energy is derived from the free-falling ram (the hammer shown in Fig. 14.21e is known as a *board hammer*). The available energy of the hammer is the product of the ram's weight and the height of its drop. Ram weights range from 180 kg to 4500 kg (400 lb to 10,000 lb), with energy capacities ranging up to 120 kJ (90,000 ft-lb).

Power Drop Hammers.   In this hammer, the ram's downstroke is accelerated by steam, air, or hydraulic pressure at about 750 kPa (100 psi). Ram weights range from 225 kg to as much as 22,500 kg (500 lb to 50,000 lb), with energy capacities ranging up to 1150 kJ (850,000 ft-lb).

Counterblow Hammers.   This hammer has two rams that simultaneously approach each other horizontally or vertically to forge the part. As in open-die forging operations, the part may be rotated between blows for proper shaping of the workpiece during forging. Counterblow hammers operate at high speeds and transmit less vibration to their bases. Capacities range up to 1200 kJ (900,000 ft-lb).

High-Energy-Rate Machines.   In a high-energy-rate machine, the ram is accelerated by inert gas at high pressure, and the part is forged in one blow at a very high speed. Although there are several types of these machines, various problems associated with their operation and maintenance, with die breakage, and with safety considerations have greatly limited their actual use in forging plants.

14.9.3 Selection of Forging Machines

Several considerations are important in the selection of forging machines: force or energy requirements; the size, shape and complexity of the forging; the strength of the workpiece material; and the sensitivity of the material to the rate of deformation. Additional factors include production rate, dimensional accuracy, maintenance, operating skills required, noise level, and cost.

In general, presses are preferred for use with aluminum, magnesium, beryllium, bronze, and brass. Hammers are usually preferred for use with steels, titanium, copper, and refractory-metal alloys. A forging may also be made on two or more types of equipment, that is, first on a hammer, then on a hydraulic or mechanical press.

14.10 FORGING PRACTICE AND PROCESS CAPABILITIES

A typical forging operation involves the following sequence of steps (see also Fig. 14.2):

1. Prepare a slug, billet, or preform by shearing (cropping), sawing, or cutting off, either cold or hot. If necessary, clean surfaces by such means as shot blasting.

2. For hot forging, heat the workpiece in a suitable furnace and, if necessary, descale it after heating with a wire brush, a water jet, or steam or by scraping. Descaling may also occur during the initial stages of forging, when the scale, which is usually brittle, falls off during plastic deformation of the part.

3. For hot forging, preheat and lubricate the dies; for cold forging, lubricate the blank.

4. Forge in appropriate dies and in the proper sequence. If necessary, remove any excess material, such as flash, by trimming, machining, or grinding.

5. Clean the forging, check its dimensions, and, if necessary, machine it to final dimensions and tolerances.

6. Perform additional operations, such as straightening and heat treating, for improved mechanical properties. Perform any finishing operations that may be required.

7. Inspect the forging for external and internal defects.

The quality, dimensional tolerances, and surface finish of a forging depend on how well these operations are performed and controlled. Generally, tolerances range between $\pm 0.5\%$ and $\pm 1\%$ of the dimensions of the forging. In good practice, tolerances for hot forging of steel are usually less than ± 6 mm (1/4 in.), and in precision forging they can be as low as ± 0.25 mm (0.01 in.).

Other factors that contribute to dimensional inaccuracy are draft angles, radii, die wear, die closure, and mismatching of the dies. Surface finish of the forging depends on the effectiveness of the lubricant, preparation of the blank, die surface finish, and die wear.

Automation in Forging. Many forging machines and facilities have been automated, and operations are now computer controlled. Blanks and forgings are handled by robots and by other automatic handling equipment (Sections 38.6 and 38.7); this handling may include loading into and unloading from furnaces. Mechanical manipulators are used to move and position billets in the dies. Lubrication and other operations, such as the trimming, heat treating, and transporting of billets, have been automated.

Production rates have been increased through better control of all aspects of forging operations. Automation has been particularly effective in producing high-quantity parts, such as gears, axles, nuts, bolts, and bearing races.

Plant layout for forging depends on factors such as the size of the forging and the equipment involved. New developments in forging include elimination of intermediate steps by direct melting and forging into net or near-net shapes. Such improvements can significantly reduce the cost of forgings by saving labor, equipment, and material. (See also Section 11.14 on *Squeeze Casting* and *Semisolid Metal Forming*).

14.11 DIE MANUFACTURING METHODS

Various manufacturing methods, either singly or in combination, are used in making dies. These processes include casting, forging, machining, grinding, and electrical and electrochemical methods of die sinking. The process of hubbing, either cold or hot, may also be used to make small dies with shallow cavities. Dies are usually heat treated for greater hardness and wear resistance. If necessary, their surface profile and finish are improved by finish grinding and polishing, either by hand or by programmable industrial robots.

The choice of a die manufacturing method depends on the particular operation in which the die is to be used and on its size and shape. Cost often dictates the process selected, because tool and die costs can be significant in manufacturing operations. For example, a set of dies for automotive body panels can cost $2 million. Even small and relatively simple dies can cost hundreds of dollars. On the other hand, because a large number of parts are usually made from the same die, die cost per piece is generally only a small portion of a part's manufacturing cost.

Dies may be classified as male and female; they may also be classified by their size. Small dies generally are those that have a surface area of $10^3 \, \text{mm}^2 - 10^4 \, \text{mm}^2 (2 \, \text{in}^2 - 15 \, \text{in}^2)$, whereas large dies have surface areas of $1 \, \text{m}^2 \, (9 \, \text{ft}^2)$ and larger, such as those used for pressworking automotive body panels.

Dies of various sizes and shapes can be **cast** from steels, cast irons, and nonferrous alloys. The processes used range from sand casting (for large dies weighing many tons) to shell molding (for small dies). Several die materials, such as tool and die steels, high-speed steels, and carbides, are described in Section 5.7, Chapter 21, and Tables 5.5-5.7. Cast steels are generally preferred for dies for large workpieces, because of their strength and toughness and because of the ease with which their composition, grain size, and properties can be controlled and modified.

Depending on how they solidify, cast dies, unlike those made of wrought metal by forging or rolling, may not have directional properties; they may exhibit the same properties on all working surfaces. However, because of shrinkage, control of dimensional tolerances in cast dies can be difficult as compared to that in machined dies.

Most commonly, dies are **machined** from **forged** die blocks by processes such as milling, turning, grinding, and electrical and electrochemical machining. Typically, a die for hot working operations is machined by milling on computer-controlled machine tools that use various software. Machining can be difficult for high-strength and wear-resistant die materials that are hard or are heat treated.

These operations can be time consuming. As a result, nontraditional machining processes are used extensively, particularly for small- or medium-sized dies. These processes are generally faster and more economical, and the dies usually do not require additional finishing. Diamond dies for drawing fine wire are manufactured by producing holes with a thin rotating needle coated with diamond dust, using oil as a lubricant.

For improved hardness, wear resistance, and strength, die steels are usually *heat treated*. Improper heat treatment is one of the most common causes of die failure. Heat treatment may distort dies through the action of microstructural changes and of uneven thermal cycling. Particularly important are the condition and composition of the die surfaces. The proper selection of temperatures and atmospheres for heat treatment, of quenching media, of quenching practice, of tempering procedures, and of handling are important. Dies may be subjected to various surface treatments for improved frictional and wear characteristics.

After heat treatment, dies are subjected to **finishing operations**, such as grinding, polishing, and chemical and electrical processes, to obtain the desired surface finish and dimensional accuracy. The grinding process, if not controlled properly, can cause surface damage from excessive heat and can induce harmful tensile residual stresses on the surface of the die, which will reduce its fatigue life. Scratches on a die's surface can act as stress raisers. Likewise, commonly used die-making processes, such as electrical-discharge machining, can cause surface damage and cracks, unless the process parameters are carefully controlled.

14.12 DIE FAILURES

Failure of dies in manufacturing operations generally results from one or more of the following causes: (a) improper design, (b) defective material, (c) improper heat treatment and finishing operations, (d) overheating and heat checking (cracking caused by temperature cycling), (e) excessive wear, (f) overloading, (g) misuse, and (h) improper handling. Some of the major factors leading to die failure are described below. Although these factors apply to dies made of tool and die steels, many are also applicable to other die materials.

The proper design of dies is as important as the proper selection of die materials. In order to withstand the forces in manufacturing processes, a die must have proper cross-sections and clearances. Sharp corners, radii, and fillets, as well as abrupt changes in cross-section, act as stress raisers and can have detrimental effects on die life. Dies may be made in segments and prestressed during assembly for improved strength.

The proper handling, installation, assembly, and aligning of dies are essential. Overloading of tools and dies can cause premature failure. For example, a common cause of failure of cold extrusion dies is the failure of the operator or of a programmable robot to remove a formed part from the die before loading it with another blank.

In spite of their hardness and resistance to abrasion, die materials such as carbides and diamond are susceptible to cracking and chipping from impact forces or from thermal stresses caused by temperature gradients within the die. Surface preparation and finishing are important. Even metalworking fluids (Chapter 32) can adversely affect tool and die materials. Sulfur and chlorine additives in lubricants and coolants, for example, can leach away the cobalt binder in tungsten carbide and lower its strength and toughness.

Even if they are manufactured properly, dies are subjected to high stresses and high temperatures during their use, factors which cause wear and (hence) shape changes. Die wear is important because when the die shape changes, the parts, in turn, have improper dimensions. In both these ways, the economics of the manufacturing operation is adversely affected.

During use, dies may also undergo heat checking from thermal cycling, particularly in die casting. To reduce heat checking (which has the appearance of parched land) and eventual die breakage in hot working operations, dies are usually preheated to temperatures of about 1500 °C to 2500 °C (3000 °F to 5000 °F). Cracked or worn dies may be repaired by welding and metal-deposition techniques, including lasers.

Dies may be designed and constructed with inserts that can be replaced when worn or cracked. The proper design and placement of these inserts is important, because, if it is ignored, the inserts themselves can crack. Die failure and fracture in manufacturing plants can be hazardous to employees.

It is not unusual for a set of dies resting on the floor or on a shelf to disintegrate suddenly, because of the highly stressed internal condition (residual stresses) of its components. The broken pieces are propelled at high speed and can cause serious injury or fatality. Highly stressed dies and tooling should always be surrounded by metal shielding. These shields should be properly designed and sufficiently strong to contain the fractured pieces in the event of die failure.

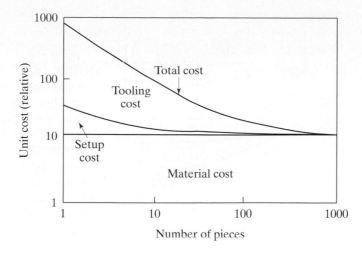

FIGURE 14.22   Typical unit cost (cost per piece) in forging; note how the setup and the tooling costs per piece decrease as the number of pieces forged increases, if all pieces use the same die.

14.13 THE ECONOMICS OF FORGING

Several factors are involved in the cost of forgings. Tool and die costs range from moderate to high, depending on the complexity of the forging. However, as in other manufacturing operations, this cost is spread over the number of parts forged with that particular die set. Thus, even though the cost of material per piece is constant, setup and tooling costs per piece decrease as the number of pieces forged increases (Fig. 14.22).

The ratio of the cost of the material to the total cost of forging the part increases with the weight of forgings; the more expensive the material, the higher the cost of the material relative to the total cost. Because dies must be made and forging operations must be performed regardless of the size of forging, the cost of dies and of the forging operation relative to material cost is high for small parts, and, conversely, material costs are relatively low.

As part size increases, the share of material cost in the total cost also increases, but at a lower rate. This occurs because (a) the incremental increase in die cost is relatively small, (b) the machinery and operations involved are essentially the same regardless of part size, and (c) the amount of labor involved per piece is not that much higher. The total cost involved in a forging operation is not influenced to any major extent by the type of materials forged.

Labor costs in forging are generally moderate; they have been reduced significantly by automated and computer-controlled operations. Die design and manufacturing are now being performed by computer-aided design and manufacturing techniques, which yield significant savings in time and effort.

The cost of forging a part compared to that of making it by various casting techniques, by powder metallurgy, by machining, or by other methods is an important consideration in a competitive marketplace. For example, all other factors being the same, and depending on the number of pieces required, manufacturing a certain part by, say, expendable-mold casting may well be more economical than doing so by forging (Fig. 14.23). This casting method does not require expensive molds and tooling, whereas forging requires expensive dies. Competitive aspects of manufacturing are discussed in greater detail in Chapter 40.

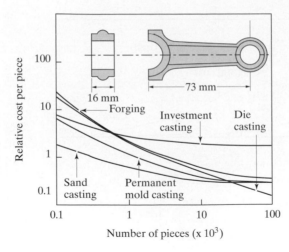

FIGURE 14.23   Relative unit costs of a small connecting rod made by various forging and casting processes. Note that, for large quantities, forging is more economical. Sand casting is the more economical process for fewer than about 20,000 pieces.

SUMMARY

- Forging denotes a family of metalworking processes in which deformation of the workpiece is carried out by compressive forces applied through a set of dies. Forging is capable of producing a wide variety of structural parts with favorable characteristics such as strength, toughness, dimensional accuracy, and reliability in service.

- The forging process can be carried out at room, warm, or high temperatures (above the recrystallization temperature). Workpiece material behavior during deformation, friction, heat transfer, and material-flow characteristics in the die cavity are important considerations, as are the proper selection of die materials, lubricants, workpiece and die temperatures, speeds, and equipment.

- Various defects can develop if the process is not controlled properly, especially in workpiece quality, billet or preform shape, and die geometry. Computer-aided design and manufacturing techniques are now being used extensively in die design and manufacturing, in preform design, in predicting material flow, and in preparing for the possibility of internal and external defects during forging.

- A variety of forging machines are available, each with its own characteristics and capabilities. Forging operations have been highly automated, using industrial robots and computer controls.

- In swaging, a solid rod or a tube is reduced in diameter by the reciprocating radial movement of a set of two or four dies. Swaging is suitable for producing short or long lengths of bar or tubing with various internal or external profiles.

- Because die failure has a major economic impact, die design, die material selection, and die manufacturing methods are of major importance. A variety of die materials and manufacturing methods are available, including advanced material-removal processes (especially electrical-discharge machining) and subsequent treatment and surface finishing operations.

TRENDS

- Computer-aided design and manufacturing are being implemented increasingly in all aspects of forging design and manufacturing. Techniques being used include: modeling of the deformation of the workpiece during forging by *finite-element analysis*; die design; preform design; calculation of forces and energy requirements; and prediction of forging defects, die wear, and die failure.

- Near-net-shape or net-shape forging applications continue to increase.

- Further developments in automation, in robust sensors, in computer control, in real-time hot-dimensional measuring capabilities, in internal inspection of ingots, and in the use of industrial robots for material handling and for processing are taking place.

- Improvements in heating-furnace design, reduction in heating cycles, warm forging, flashless hot forging, controlled cooling after forging to obtain better mechanical properties, heating systems to eliminate scale, improved die materials for significantly better die life, and overall efficiency and energy savings in hot-forging operations are taking place.

- Dies are being designed for rapid exchange to promote flexibility in forging operations.

- Economical methods to convert scale to usable products are being investigated.

KEY TERMS

Barreling	Hammers	Piercing
Closed-die forging	Heading	Precision forging
Cogging	Hot-twist test	Presses
Coining	Hubbing	Roll forging
Edging	Impression-die forging	Sizing
End grain	Incremental forging	Skew rolling
Flash	Isothermal forging	Swaging
Forgeability	Net-shape forging	Upsetting
Forging	Open-die forging	
Fullering	Orbital forging	

BIBLIOGRAPHY

Altan, T., S.I. Oh, and H.C. Gegel, *Metal Forming—Fundamentals and Applications*. ASM International, 1983.

____, *Forging: Equipment, Materials and Practices*. Battelle Memorial Institute, 1973.

ASM Handbook, Vol. 14: *Forming and Forging*. ASM International, 1988.

Blazynski, T.Z., *Plasticity and Modern Metal-forming Technology*. Elsevier, 1989.

Byrer, T.G. (ed.), *Forging Handbook*. ASM International, 1985.

Hosford, W.F., and R.M. Caddell, *Metal Forming: Mechanics and Metallurgy* (2d ed.). Prentice Hall, 1993.

Lange, K. (ed.), *Handbook of Metal Forming*. McGraw-Hill, 1985.

Open Die Forging Manual (3d ed.). Forging Industry Association, 1982.

Prasad, Y.V.R.K., and S. Sasidhara (eds.), *Hot Working Guide: A Compendium of Processing Maps*. ASM International, 1997.

Product Design Guide for Forging. Forging Industry Association, 1997.

Thomas, A., *DFRA Forging Handbook: Die Design*. Drop Forging Research Association, 1980.

REVIEW QUESTIONS

14.1 What is the difference between cold, warm, and hot forging?

14.2 Explain the difference between open-die and impression-die forging.

14.3 What does breaking down a cast ingot mean?

14.4 Explain the difference between fullering, edging, and blocking.

14.5 What factors are involved in precision forging?

14.6 Describe orbital forging and explain how it differs from conventional forging operations.

14.7 What type of parts is rotary swaging capable of producing?

14.8 Explain the features of a typical forging die.

14.9 Why is intermediate shape important in forging operations?

14.10 How is forgeability defined?

14.11 Explain what is meant by "load limited," "energy limited," and "stroke limited," as these terms pertain to forging machines.

14.12 What is flash?

14.13 Why is hubbing an attractive alternative to producing simple dies?

14.14 Explain the principles of different forging machines.

14.15 Explain the concerns in the layout of upsetting dies.

14.16 Describe the capabilities and limitations of common forging equipment.

14.17 What is the difference between piercing and punching?

QUALITATIVE PROBLEMS

14.18 Explain the function of flash in impression-die forging.

14.19 How can you tell whether a certain part is forged or cast? Explain the features that you would investigate.

14.20 Why is control of the volume of the blank important in closed-die forging?

14.21 What are the advantages and limitations of a cogging operation?

14.22 Describe your observations concerning Fig. 14.19.

14.23 What are the advantages and limitations of using die inserts?

14.24 Explain why inner draft angles are larger than outer angles. Is this also true for permanent-mold casting?

14.25 Explain why there are so many different types of forging machines.

14.26 In Part II it was noted that very large parts can be made by casting. Is this also true for forging? Explain the technical and economic aspects of such operations.

14.27 Comment on your observations regarding the grain flow pattern in Fig. 14.12.

14.28 What are the advantages of isothermal forging?

14.29 Perform simple cogging operations on pieces of clay, using a flat piece of wood, and make observations regarding the spread of the pieces as a function of the original cross-sections of the clay specimens—for example, square, or rectangular with different thickness-to-width ratios.

14.30 Would you design a forging die whose flash has no gutter (see Fig. 14.18)? Explain your reasons.

14.31 How would the temperature of a hot workpiece change as it is forged, using room-temperature dies, in (a) a slow-acting hydraulic press, and (b) a drop hammer. Explain.

14.32 Why should grain flow patterns in forging be studied? Explain.

14.33 If you section, polish, and etch metal balls made by the processes shown in Fig. 14.14, what would the grain flow lines be like? Explain your answer.

14.34 By inspecting some forged products, such as a pipe wrench, you can see that the lettering on them is raised rather than sunk. Offer an explanation about why they are made that way.

14.35 Discuss the environmental concerns regarding the operations described in this chapter.

14.36 What are the advantages and disadvantages of using a lubricant in forging?

14.37 If you were selecting machinery for a mass-produced part to be made by forging, which machinery would you immediately eliminate from consideration?

14.38 Explain why glass is used as a lubricant in hot forging.

14.39 In isothermal forging, dies typically may last for only a few parts. Explain the significance of this fact for the unit costs shown in Figure 14.22.

14.40 Describe the difficulties in defining forgeability.

14.41 Explain why one cannot go from stock to finished forging in one press stroke.

QUANTITATIVE PROBLEMS

14.42 Calculate the forging force for a solid cylindrical workpiece, made of 1020 steel, that is 3.5 in. high and 5 in. diameter and is to be reduced in height by 30%. Let the coefficient of friction be 0.2.

14.43 Using Eq. (14.2), estimate the forging force for the workpiece in Problem 14.42, assuming that it is a complex forging and that the projected area of the flash is 40% greater than the projected area of the forged workpiece.

14.44 Determine the temperature rise in the specimen in Problem 14.30, assuming that the process is adiabatic and the temperature is uniform throughout the specimen.

14.45 Take two solid cylindrical specimens of equal diameter but different heights and compress them (frictionless) to the same percent reduction in height. Show that the final diameters will be the same.

14.46 In the example in Section 14.2, calculate the forging force, assuming that the material is 1100-O aluminum and that the coefficient of friction is 0.2.

14.47 Using Eq. (14.1), make a plot of the forging force, F, as a function of the radius, r, of the workpiece. Assume that the flow stress, Y_f, of the material is constant, and remember that the volume of the material remains constant during forging; thus, as h decreases, r increases.

14.48 How would you go about calculating the punch force required in a hubbing operation, assuming that the material is mild steel and the projected area of the impression is 0.5 in^2? Explain clearly. (*Hint*: See Section 2.6 on hardness.)

14.49 A mechanical press is powered by a 30-hp motor and operates at forty strokes per minute. It uses a flywheel, so that the crankshaft speed does not vary appreciably during the stroke. If the stroke is 6 in., what is the maximum constant force that can be exerted over the entire stroke length?

14.50 For the same mechanical press as in Problem 14.49, to what thickness can a cylinder 3 in. in diameter and 2 in. high of 5052-O aluminum be forged before the press stalls? (See Problem 14.42.)

14.51 If a hydraulic cylinder has an 8-in. internal bore and has a pump which can generate 1000 psi, what is the largest-diameter mild steel cylinder that can be upset in this press?

SYNTHESIS AND DESIGN

14.52 Devise an experimental method whereby you can measure only the force required for forging the flash in impression-die forging.

14.53 Assume that you represent the forging industry and that you are facing a representative of the casting industry. What would you tell that person about the merits of forging processes? How would you prepare yourself to face questions about any limitations of forging relative to casting?

14.54 The accompanying illustration shows a round impression-die forging, made from a cylindrical blank as shown on the left. As described in this chapter, such parts are made in a sequence of forging operations. Suggest a sequence of intermediate forging steps to make this part and sketch the shape of the dies needed.

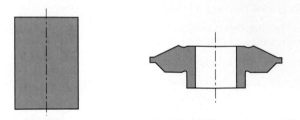

14.55 Gears can be made by forging, especially bevel gears. Make a survey of the technical literature and describe the sequence of manufacturing steps involved. Comment on the quality of such a gear as compared to one made by the casting processes described in Chapter 11.

14.56 Forging is one method of producing turbine blades for jet engines. Study the design of such blades and the relevant technical literature, then prepare a step-by-step procedure to produce such blades by forging operations. Comment on the possible problems that could be encountered and offer solutions. How would the properties differ, if at all, from those for cast blades? Explain.

14.57 In comparing forged parts with those that are cast, we have noted that the same part may be made by either process. Comment on the pros and cons of each process, considering factors such as part size and shape complexity, design flexibility, mechanical properties developed, performance in service, and whatever else you think relevant.

14.58 From the data given in Table 14.3, obtain the approximate value of the yield strength of these materials at hot-forging temperatures. Plot a bar chart showing the maximum diameter of a hot-forged part produced on a press with a 60 ton capacity, as a function of the material.

14.59 In hot-forging operations, flames are seen to surge from the dies when they are opened. Explain why this occurs.

14.60 Obtain a number of bolts, nails and screws of different sizes. Measure the volume of the heads and calculate the original unsupported length-to-diameter ratio for these parts. Discuss these numbers with respect to the discussion in the text.

15

Extrusion and Drawing of Metals

15.1 INTRODUCTION

In the **extrusion** process, a billet (generally round) is forced through a die (Fig. 15.1), in a manner similar to squeezing toothpaste from a tube. Almost any solid or hollow cross-section may be produced by extrusion, which can create essentially semifinished parts (Fig. 15.2). Because the die geometry remains the same throughout the operation, extruded products have a constant cross-section.

Depending on the ductility of the material, extrusion may be carried out at room or at an elevated temperature. Because a chamber is involved, each billet is extruded individually, and thus extrusion is a batch or semicontinuous process.

Extrusion is often combined with forging operations, in which case it is generally known as **cold extrusion**. It has numerous important applications, including fasteners and components for automobiles, bicycles, motorcycles, heavy machinery, and transportation equipment.

Typical products made by extrusion are railings for sliding doors, tubing having various cross-sections, structural and architectural shapes, and door and window frames. Extruded products can be cut into desired lengths, which then become discrete parts such as

369

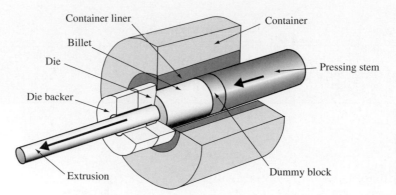

FIGURE 15.1   Schematic illustration of the direct extrusion process.

brackets, gears, and coat hangers (Fig. 15.2). Commonly extruded materials are aluminum, copper, steel, magnesium, and lead (lead pipes were made by extrusion in the eighteenth century). Other metals and alloys can also be extruded, with various levels of difficulty. Extrusion of plastics is described in Section 18.2.

Drawing is an operation, developed between A.D. 1000 and 1500, in which the cross-section of solid rod, wire, or tubing is reduced or changed in shape by *pulling* it through a die. Drawn rods are used for shafts, spindles, and small pistons and as the raw material for fasteners such as rivets, bolts, and screws. In addition to round rods, various profiles can also drawn. The term *drawing* is also used to refer to making cup-shaped parts by sheet forming operations (Section 16.9).

The distinction between the terms **rod** and **wire** is somewhat arbitrary, rod merely being larger in cross-section than wire. In industry, wire is generally defined as a rod that has been drawn through a die at least once. Wire drawing involves smaller diameters than rod drawing, with sizes down to 0.01 mm (0.0005 in.) for magnet wire, and even smaller for use in very low-current fuses.

Wire and wire products cover a wide range of applications, such as electrical and electronic wiring, cables, tension-loaded structural members, welding electrodes, springs, paper clips, spokes for bicycle wheels, and stringed musical instruments.

(a)

(b)

(c)

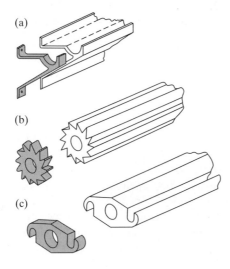

FIGURE 15.2   Extrusions, and examples of products made by sectioning off extrusions. *Source*: Kaiser Aluminum.

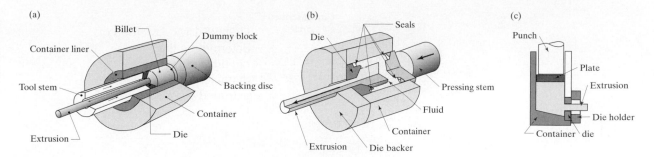

(a)

Billet

Container liner

Tool stem

Extrusion

Dummy block

Backing disc

Container

Die

(b)

Die

Seals

Pressing stem

Fluid

Container

Extrusion   Die backer

(c)

Punch

Plate

Extrusion

Die holder

Container   die

FIGURE 15.3   Types of extrusion: (a) indirect; (b) hydrostatic; (c) lateral.

15.2 THE EXTRUSION PROCESS

In the basic extrusion process, called **direct**, or **forward**, **extrusion**, a round billet is placed in a *chamber* (container) and forced through a die opening by a hydraulically-driven ram or pressing stem (Fig. 15.1). The die opening may be round, or it may have various shapes. Other types of extrusion are indirect, hydrostatic, and impact extrusion. In **indirect** extrusion (reverse, inverted, or backward extrusion), the die moves toward the billet (Fig. 15.3a).

In **hydrostatic** extrusion (Fig. 15.3b), the billet is smaller in diameter than the chamber, which is filled with a fluid, and the pressure is transmitted to the billet by a ram. Unlike in direct extrusion, there is no friction to overcome along the container walls. Another type of extrusion is **lateral**, or **side**, **extrusion** (Fig. 15.3c).

As can be seen in Fig. 15.4, the geometric variables in extrusion are the die angle, α, and the ratio of the cross-sectional area of the billet to that of the extruded product, A_o/A_f, called the **extrusion ratio**, R. Other variables in extrusion are the temperature of the billet, the speed at which the ram travels, and the type of lubricant used.

A parameter describing the shape of the extruded product is the **circumscribing-circle diameter (CCD)**, which is the diameter of the smallest circle into which the extruded cross-section will fit (Fig. 15.5). Thus the CCD for a square cross-section is its diagonal dimension. The complexity of an extrusion is a function of the ratio of the perimeter of the extruded product to its cross-sectional area, known as the **shape factor**. Obviously, a solid round extrusion has the smallest shape factor, whereas the parts shown in Fig. 15.2 have high shape factors.

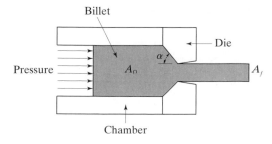

Billet

Pressure

A_o

α

Die

A_f

Chamber

FIGURE 15.4   Process variables in direct extrusion. The die angle, reduction in cross-section, extrusion speed, billet temperature, and lubrication all affect the extrusion pressure.

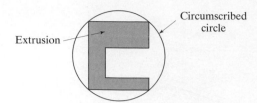

FIGURE 15.5   Method of determining the circumscribing-circle diameter (CCD) of an extruded cross-section.

15.2.1 Extrusion Force

The force required for extrusion depends on the strength of the billet material, the extrusion ratio, friction between the billet and the chamber and die surfaces, and process variables such as the temperature of the billet and the speed of extrusion. We can estimate the *extrusion force, F,* from the formula

$$F = A_o k \ln \left(\frac{A_o}{A_f} \right) \tag{15.1}$$

where k is the **extrusion constant**, and A_o and A_f are the billet and extruded product areas, respectively. The k values for several metals are given in Fig. 15.6, for a range of temperatures.

Example: Calculation of Force in Hot Extrusion

A round billet made of 70-30 brass is extruded at a temperature of 675 °C (1250 °F). The billet diameter is 5 in. (125 mm) and the diameter of the extrusion is 2 in. (50 mm). Calculate the extrusion force required.

Solution: The extrusion force is calculated using Eq. (15.1), in which the extrusion constant, k, is obtained from Fig. 15.6. For this material, we find that $k = 35,000$ psi (250 MPa) at the extrusion temperature. Thus,

$$F = \pi(2.5)^2(35,000) \ln \left[\frac{\pi(2.5)^2}{\pi(1.0)^2} \right] = 1.26 \times 10^6 \text{ lb}$$

$$= 630 \text{ tons} = 5.5 \text{ MN}.$$

See Section 15.9 for capacities of extrusion presses.

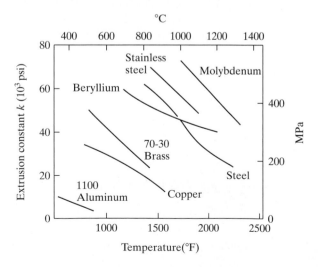

FIGURE 15.6   Extrusion constant k for various metals at different temperatures. *Source:* P. Loewenstein.

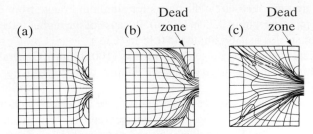

FIGURE 15.7   Types of metal flow in extruding with square dies. (a) Flow pattern obtained at low friction, or in indirect extrusion. (b) Pattern obtained with high friction at the billet–chamber interfaces. (c) Pattern obtained at high friction, or with cooling of the outer regions of the billet in the chamber. This type of pattern, observed in metals whose strength increases rapidly with decreasing temperature, leads to a defect known as pipe, or extrusion defect.

15.2.2 Metal Flow in Extrusion

The metal flow pattern in extrusion, as in other forming processes, is important because of its influence on the quality and the mechanical properties of the final product. The material flows longitudinally, much like incompressible fluid flow in a channel; thus extruded products have an elongated grain structure (preferred orientation). We will describe in Section 15.8 how improper metal flow during extrusion can produce various defects in the extruded product.

A common technique for investigating the flow pattern is to section the round billet in half lengthwise and then mark one face with a square grid pattern. The two halves are placed in the chamber together and extruded. The products are then taken apart and studied. Figure 15.7 shows typical flow patterns obtained by this technique in direct extrusion with **square dies** (90° die angle).

The conditions under which these different flow patterns occur are described in the figure caption. Note the **dead-metal zones** in Figs. 15.7b and c, where the metal at the corners is essentially stationary. This situation is similar to stagnation of fluid flow in channels that have sharp turns.

15.3 EXTRUSION PRACTICE

Because they have sufficient ductility, aluminum, copper, magnesium, and their alloys and steels and stainless steels are extruded with relative ease into numerous shapes. Other metals such as titanium and refractory metals can be extruded, but only with some difficulty and considerable die wear.

Extrusion ratios, R, usually range from about 10 to 100. They may be higher for special applications (400) or lower for less ductile materials, although they usually need to be at least 4 to work the material plastically through the bulk of the workpiece. Extruded products are usually less than 7.5 m (25 ft) long, because of the difficulty in handling greater lengths, but they can be as long as 30 m (100 ft).

Circumscribed-circle diameters for aluminum range from 6 mm to 1 m (0.25 in. to 40 in.); most are within 0.25 m (10 in.). Because of the higher forces required, the maximum CCD for steel is usually limited to 0.15 m (6 in.).

Ram speeds may range up to 0.5 m/s (100 ft/min). Generally, lower speeds are preferred for aluminum, magnesium, and copper, higher speeds for steels, titanium, and refractory alloys.

Most extruded products, particularly those with small cross-sections, require straightening and twisting. These operations are accomplished by stretching the extruded product, usually in a hydraulic stretcher equipped with jaws. Dimensional tolerances in extrusion are usually in the range of ±0.25 mm–2.5 mm (±0.01 in.–0.1 in.), and they increase with increasing cross-section.

The presence of a die angle causes a small portion of the end of the billet to remain in the chamber after the operation has been completed. This portion, called scrap or the *butt end*, is subsequently removed by cutting off the extrusion at the die exit. Alternatively, another billet or a graphite block may be placed in the chamber to extrude the piece remaining from the previous extrusion.

In **coaxial extrusion** or **cladding**, coaxial billets are extruded together, provided that the strength and ductility of the two metals are compatible. An example is copper clad with silver. *Stepped extrusions* are produced by extruding the billet partially in one die, then in one or more larger dies. (See also *cold extrusion*, Section 15.5.) Lateral extrusion (Fig. 15.3c) is used for the sheathing of wire and the coating of electric wire with plastic.

Although it is a batch or semicontinuous process, extrusion can be economical for large production runs as well as for short ones. Tool costs are generally low, particularly for producing simple solid cross-sections.

15.4 HOT EXTRUSION

Extrusion is carried out at elevated temperatures—for metals and alloys that do not have sufficient ductility at room temperature, or in order to reduce the forces required (Table 15.1). As in all other hot working operations, hot extrusion has special requirements because of the high operating temperatures.

For example, die wear can be excessive, and cooling of the hot billet in the chamber can be a problem which results in highly nonuniform deformation (Fig. 15.7c). To reduce cooling of the billet and to prolong die life, extrusion dies may be preheated, as is done in hot forging operations.

Because the billet is hot, it develops an oxide film unless heated in an inert-atmosphere furnace. This film can be abrasive, and it can affect the flow pattern of the material. It also results in an extruded product that may be unacceptable in cases in which good surface finish is important.

TABLE 15.1 Extrusion Temperature Ranges for Various Metals

	°C
Lead	200–250
Aluminum and its alloys	375–475
Copper and its alloys	650–975
Steels	875–1300
Refractory alloys	975–2200

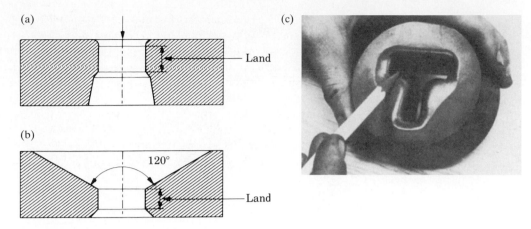

FIGURE 15.8 Typical extrusion-die configurations: (a) die for nonferrous metals; (b) die for ferrous metals; (c) die for T-shaped extrusion, made of hot-work die steel and used with molten glass as a lubricant. *Source* for (c): Courtesy of LTV Steel Company.

In order to avoid the formation of oxide films on the hot extruded product, the dummy block placed ahead of the ram (Fig. 15.1) is made a little smaller in diameter than the container. As a result, a thin cylindrical shell (*skull*), consisting mainly of the oxidized layer, is left in the container. The extruded product is thus free of oxides; the skull is later removed from the chamber.

15.4.1 Die Design and Die Materials

Die design (Fig. 15.8) requires considerable experience. *Square dies* (**shear dies**) are used in extruding nonferrous metals, especially aluminum. Square dies develop dead-metal zones, which in turn form a die angle (see Fig. 15.7b and c) along which the material flows in the deformation zone. The dead-metal zones produce extrusions with bright finishes.

Tubing is extruded from a solid or hollow billet to wall thicknesses as small as 1 mm (0.040 in.). For solid billets, the ram is fitted with a mandrel that pierces a hole in the billet. Billets with a previously pierced hole may also be extruded in this way. Because of friction and the severity of deformation, thin-walled extrusions are more difficult to produce than thick-walled extrusions. Wall thickness is usually limited to 1 mm (0.040 in.) for aluminum, 3 mm (0.125 in.) for carbon steels, and 5 mm (0.20 in.) for stainless steels.

Hollow cross-sections (Fig. 15.9a) can be extruded by welding-chamber methods and the use of various dies known as **spider dies**, **porthole dies**, and **bridge dies** (Fig. 15.9b). During extrusion, the metal divides and flows around the supports for the internal mandrel into strands; these strands are then rewelded under the high pressures existing in the welding chamber, before they exit through the die. This condition is much like that of air flowing around a moving car and rejoining downstream.

The welding-chamber process is suitable only for aluminum and some of its alloys, because of their capacity for developing a strong weld under pressure. Lubricants cannot be used because they prevent rewelding of the metal in the die.

Guidelines for proper die design in extrusion are illustrated in Fig. 15.10. Note the importance of symmetry of cross-section; note also the avoidance of sharp corners and of extreme changes in die dimensions within the cross-section.

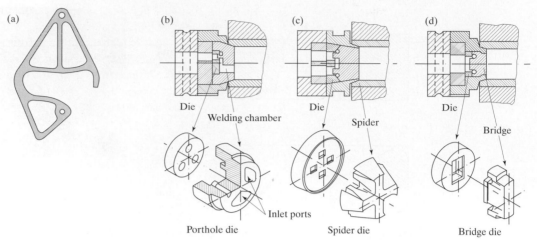

FIGURE 15.9   (a) An extruded 6063-T6 aluminum ladder lock for aluminum extension ladders. This part is 8 mm (5/16 in.) thick and is sawed from the extrusion (see Fig. 15.2). (b)-(d) Components of various dies for extruding intricate hollow shapes. *Source* for (b)-(d): K. Laue and H. Stenger, *Extrusion—Processes, Machinery, Tooling.* American Society for Metals, Metals Park, Ohio, 1981. Used with permission.

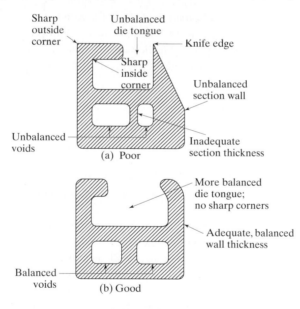

FIGURE 15.10   Poor and good examples of cross-sections to be extruded. Note the importance of eliminating sharp corners and of keeping section thicknesses uniform. *Source*: J. G. Bralla (ed.); *Handbook of Product Design for Manufacturing.* New York: McGraw-Hill Publishing Company, 1986. Used with permission.

15.4.2 Die Materials and Lubrication

Die materials for hot extrusion are usually hot-work die steels (Section 5.7). Coatings such as zirconia may be applied to the dies to extend their life. Partially-stabilized zirconia dies (Section 8.2.2) are also being used for hot extrusion of tubes and rods; however, they are not suitable for making dies for extruding complicated shapes, because of the severe stress gradients developed in the die.

   Lubrication is important in hot extrusion. *Glass* is an excellent lubricant for steels, stainless steels, and high-temperature metals and alloys. In a process developed in the 1940s and known as the **Séjournet process** (after J. Séjournet), a circular glass pad is placed at the die entrance in the chamber. The hot billet conducts heat to the glass pad, which acts as a reservoir of molten glass, lubricating the die interface as extrusion progresses. Before the billet is placed in the chamber, its cylindrical surface is coated with a layer of powdered glass, to provide lubrication at the billet–chamber interface.

For metals that have a tendency to stick to the container and the die, the billet can be enclosed in a thin-walled container made of a softer, lower-strength metal such as copper or mild steel. This procedure is called **jacketing** or **canning**. In addition to acting as a low-friction interface, this jacket prevents contamination of the billet by the environment (or, if the billet material is toxic or radioactive, the jacket prevents it from contaminating the environment). This technique can also be used for extruding reactive metal powders (Section 17.3).

15.5 COLD EXTRUSION

Developed in the 1940s, *cold extrusion* is a general term often denoting a combination of operations, such as direct and indirect extrusion and forging (Fig. 15.11). Cold extrusion has gained wide acceptance in industry, particularly for tools and for components in automobiles, motorcycles, bicycles, appliances, and transportation and farm equipment.

This process uses slugs cut from cold-finished or hot-rolled bar, wire, or plate. Slugs that are less than about 40 mm (1.5 in.) in diameter are sheared, and their ends are squared by grinding or upsetting. Larger-diameter slugs are machined from bars into specific lengths. Parts weighing as much as 45 kg (100 lb) and having lengths of up to 2 m (80 in.) have been made, although most cold-extruded parts weigh much less. Powder-metal slugs (preforms) are also cold extruded.

Cold extrusion has the following advantages over hot extrusion:

- improved mechanical properties resulting from work-hardening, provided that the heat generated by plastic deformation and friction does not recrystallize the extruded metal;
- good control of dimensional tolerances, reducing the need for subsequent machining or finishing operations;
- improved surface finish, due partly to lack of an oxide film, provided that lubrication is effective;
- elimination of the need for billet heating;
- production rates and costs that are competitive with those of other methods of producing the same part; some machines are capable of producing more than 2000 parts per hour.

The magnitude of the stresses on the tooling in cold extrusion, however, is very high, especially with steel workpieces, being on the order of the hardness of the workpiece material. The punch hardness usually ranges between 60 HRC and 65 HRC, the die hardness between 58 HRC and 62 HRC. Punches are a critical component, as they must have not only sufficient strength but also sufficient toughness and resistance to wear and fatigue.

The design of tooling and the selection of appropriate tool and die materials is crucial to the success of cold extrusion. (See Table 5.7.) Also important is the control of workpiece material with regard to its quality, the accuracy of the slug dimensions, and its surface condition.

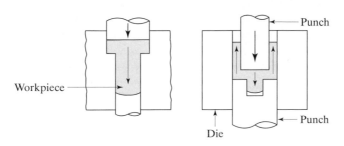

FIGURE 15.11   Two examples of cold extrusion. Thin arrows indicate the direction of metal flow during extrusion.

Lubrication is critical, especially with steels, because of the possibility of sticking (*seizure*) between the workpiece and the tooling if the lubricant breaks down. The most effective means of lubrication is application of a phosphate **conversion coating** on the workpiece, followed by a coating of soap or wax (Section 32.12).

Example: Cold-Extruded Part

A typical cold-extruded product, similar to the metal component of an automotive spark plug, is shown in Fig. 15.12. First a slug is sheared off the end of a round rod (Fig. 15.12, left); it is then cold extruded (Fig. 15.12, middle), in an operation similar to those shown in Fig. 15.11, but with a blind hole. The material at the bottom of the blind hole is then punched out, producing the small slug shown. Note the diameters of the slug and of the hole at the bottom of the sectioned part, respectively.

Studying material flow during deformation helps avoid defects and leads to improvements in punch and die design. The part is usually sectioned in the midplane, then polished and etched to show the grain flow, as shown in Fig. 15.13. (See also Fig. 14.12).

FIGURE 15.12   Production steps for a cold extruded spark plug. *Source*: National Machinery Company.

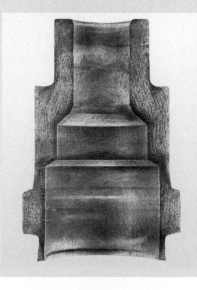

FIGURE 15.13   A cross-section of the metal part in Fig. 15.12, showing the grain flow pattern. *Source*: National Machinery Company.

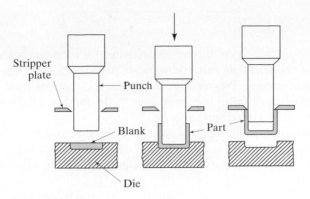

FIGURE 15.14   Schematic illustration of the impact-extrusion process. The extruded parts are stripped by the use of a stripper plate, because they tend to stick to the punch.

15.6 IMPACT EXTRUSION

Impact extrusion is similar to indirect extrusion; it is often included in the cold-extrusion category. The punch descends rapidly on the blank (slug), which is extruded backward (Fig. 15.14). Because of volume constancy, the thickness of the tubular extruded section is a function of the clearance between the punch and the die cavity.

Typical products made by this process are shown in Fig. 15.15a and b. Another example of cold extrusion is the production of collapsible tubes, such as for toothpaste (Fig. 15.15b). Most nonferrous metals can be impact-extruded in vertical presses and at production rates as high as two parts per second.

The diameter of the parts made can approach 150 mm (6 in.). The impact-extrusion process can produce thin-walled tubular sections, ones having thickness-to-diameter ratios as small as 0.005. Consequently, the symmetry of the part and the concentricity of the punch and the blank are important.

FIGURE 15.15   (a) Two examples of products made by impact extrusion. These parts may also be made by casting, by forging, or by machining; the choice of process depends on the dimensions and the materials involved and on the properties desired. Economic considerations are also important in final process selection. (b) and (c) Impact extrusion of a collapsible tube by the *Hooker process*.

(a)   (b)   (c)

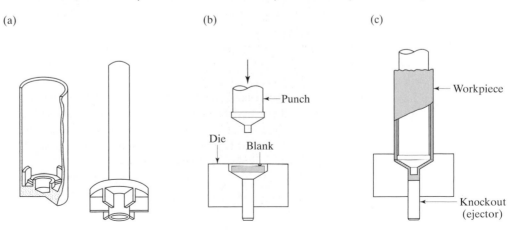

15.7 HYDROSTATIC EXTRUSION

In *hydrostatic extrusion*, the pressure required for extrusion is supplied through an incompressible fluid medium surrounding the billet (Fig. 15.3b). Consequently, there is no container-wall friction. Pressures are usually on the order of 1400 MPa (200 ksi). The high pressure in the chamber transmits some of the fluid to the die surfaces, where it significantly reduces friction and forces.

Hydrostatic extrusion, which was developed in the early 1950s, has been improved by extruding the part into a second pressurized chamber, which is under lower pressure (**fluid-to-fluid extrusion**). Because of the compressive environment, this operation reduces the defects in the extruded product.

Hydrostatic extrusion is usually carried out at room temperature, typically using vegetable oils as the fluid (particularly castor oil, because it is a good lubricant and because its viscosity is not influenced significantly by pressure). For elevated-temperature extrusion, waxes, polymers, and glass are used as the fluid. These materials also serve as thermal insulators and help maintain the billet temperature during extrusion.

Brittle materials can be extruded successfully by this method, because the hydrostatic pressure increases the ductility of the material. However, the main reasons for this success appear to be low friction and the use of small die angles and high extrusion ratios. Most commercial hydrostatic-extrusion operations involve ductile materials. However, a variety of metals and polymers, solid shapes, tubes and other hollow shapes, and even some honeycomb and clad profiles have been extruded successfully.

In spite of the success obtained, hydrostatic extrusion has had limited industrial applications, largely because of the somewhat complex nature of the tooling, the experience needed with high pressures and the design of specialized equipment, and the long cycle times required.

15.8 EXTRUSION DEFECTS

Depending on material condition and on process variables, extruded products can develop several types of defects that can significantly affect their strength and product quality. Some defects are visible to the naked eye; others can be detected only by the techniques described in Section 36.9. There are three principal *extrusion defects:* surface cracking, pipe, and internal cracking.

1. **Surface cracking.** If extrusion temperature, friction, or speed is too high, surface temperatures rise significantly, and this condition may cause surface cracking and tearing (**fir-tree cracking** or **speed cracking**). These cracks are intergranular (along the grain boundaries; see Fig. 2.26) and are usually caused by **hot shortness** (Section 1.4.3). These defects occur especially in aluminum, magnesium, and zinc alloys, although they may also occur in high-temperature alloys. This situation can be avoided by lowering the billet temperature and the extrusion speed.

   Surface cracking may also occur at lower temperatures, where it has been attributed to periodic sticking of the extruded product along the die land. When the product being extruded sticks to the die land, the extrusion pressure increases rapidly. Shortly thereafter, the product moves forward again and the pressure is released. The cycle is then repeated continually, producing periodic circumferential cracks on the surface. Because of the similarity in appearance to the surface of a bamboo stem which it causes, it is known as **bamboo defect**.

2. **Pipe.** The type of metal-flow pattern shown in Fig. 15.7c tends to draw surface oxides and impurities toward the center of the billet, much like a funnel. This defect is known as **pipe defect**, also *tailpipe* or *fishtailing*. As much as one-third of the length of the extruded product may contain this type of defect and have to be cut off as scrap.

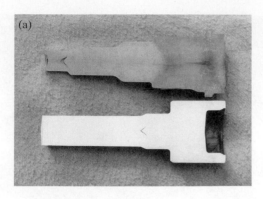
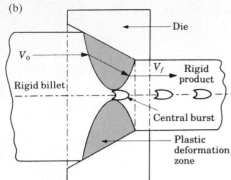

FIGURE 15.16   (a) Chevron cracking (central burst) in extruded round steel bars. Unless the products are inspected, such internal defects may remain undetected, and later cause failure of the part in service. This defect can also develop in the drawing of rod, of wire, and of tubes. (b) Schematic illustration of rigid and plastic zones in extrusion. The tendency toward chevron cracking increases if the two plastic zones do not meet. Note that the plastic zone can be made larger either by decreasing the die angle or by increasing the reduction in cross-section (or both). *Source*: B. Avitzur.

Piping can be minimized by modifying the flow pattern to a more uniform one; for example, by controlling friction and minimizing temperature gradients. Another method is to machine the billet's surface prior to extrusion, so that scale and surface impurities are removed. These impurities can also be removed by chemical etching of the surface oxides prior to extrusion.

3. **Internal cracking.** The center of the extruded product can develop cracks variously called **center cracking**, **center-burst**, **arrowhead fracture**, or **chevron cracking** (Fig. 15.16a). These cracks are attributed to a state of hydrostatic tensile stress at the centerline in the deformation zone in the die (Fig. 15.16b), a situation similar to the necked region in a tensile-test specimen (see Fig. 2.22).

    The tendency for center cracking:
    a. increases with increasing die angle;
    b. increases with increasing amount of impurities; and
    c. decreases with increasing extrusion ratio and friction.

    These cracks have also been observed in tube extrusion and in tube spinning (Section 16.11.3); they appear on the inside surfaces of tubes and for the same reasons.

15.9 EXTRUSION EQUIPMENT

The basic equipment for extrusion is a horizontal hydraulic press (Fig. 15.17). (See also Section 14.9.) These presses are suitable for extrusion, because the stroke and speed of the operation can be controlled. They are capable of applying a constant force over a long stroke; thus, long billets can be used, and the production rate increased. Hydraulic presses with a ram-force capacity as high as 120 MN (14,000 tons) have been built; they are used for hot extrusion of large billets.

Vertical hydraulic presses are generally used for cold extrusion. They generally have less capacity than those used for hot extrusion, but they take up less floor space. In addition

FIGURE 15.17 General view of a 9-MN (1000-ton) hydraulic-extrusion press. *Source*: Courtesy of Jones & Laughlin Steel Corporation.

to such presses, crankjoint and knucklejoint mechanical presses are also used for cold extrusion and for impact extrusion, to mass produce small components. Multistage operations, where the cross-sectional area is reduced in a number of operations, are also carried out on specially designed presses.

15.10 THE DRAWING PROCESS

In **drawing**, the cross-section of a round rod or wire is typically reduced or changed by pulling it through a die (Fig. 15.18). The major variables in drawing are similar to those in extrusion: reduction in cross-sectional area, die angle, friction along the die–workpiece interfaces, and drawing speed. The die angle influences the drawing force and the quality of the drawn product.

It can be shown that, for a certain reduction in diameter and a certain frictional condition, there is an optimum die angle at which the drawing force is a minimum. This calculation does not, however, mean that the process should be carried out at this "optimum" angle because, as described below, there are other product-quality considerations.

Drawing Force. The expression for the *drawing force* under frictionless conditions is similar to that for extrusion; it is given by the expression

$$F = Y_{avg} A_f \ln\left(\frac{A_o}{A_f}\right). \tag{15.2}$$

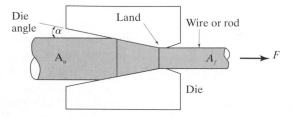

FIGURE 15.18 Process variables in wire drawing. The die angle, the reduction in cross-sectional area per pass, the speed of drawing, the temperature, and the lubrication all affect the drawing force, F.

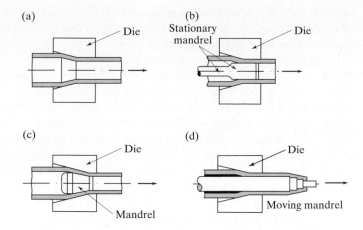

FIGURE 15.19   Examples of tube-drawing operations, with and without an internal mandrel. Note that a variety of diameters and wall thicknesses can be produced from the same initial tube stock (which has been made by other processes).

where Y_{avg} is the average true stress of the material in the die gap. (See Example in Section 13.2.2.) Because more work has to be done to overcome friction, the force increases with increasing friction.

As reduction increases, the drawing force increases. However, there has to be a limit to the magnitude of the force, because when the tensile stress due to the drawing force reaches the yield stress of the metal being drawn, the workpiece will simply yield and, eventually, break. It can be shown that, ideally, the maximum reduction in cross-sectional area per pass is 63%. Thus, for example, a 10-mm diameter rod can at most be reduced to a diameter of 6.1 mm in one pass without failure.

Drawing of Other Shapes.   Various solid cross-sections can be produced by drawing through dies with different profiles. The initial cross-section is usually round or square. Proper die design and the proper selection of reduction sequence per pass require considerable experience to ensure proper material flow in the die, reduce internal or external defects, and improve surface quality.

The wall thickness, diameter, or shape of tubes that have been produced by extrusion or by other processes can be further reduced by tube drawing processes (Fig. 15.19). Tubes as large as 0.3 m (12 in.) in diameter can be drawn by these techniques. Mandrels of various profiles are available for these operations.

Wedge-shaped dies are used in drawing flat strips. This process, although not of major industrial significance, is the fundamental deformation process in **ironing**, used extensively in making aluminum beverage cans (Section 16.9.3).

15.11 DRAWING PRACTICE

As in all metalworking processes, successful drawing operations require careful selection of process parameters and consideration of many factors. Drawing speeds depend on the material and on the reduction in cross-sectional area; they may range from 1 m/s, to 2.5 m/s (200 ft/min to 500 ft/min) for heavy sections, to as much as 50 m/s (10,000 ft/min) for very fine wire, such as that used for electromagnets. Because the product does not have sufficient time to dissipate the heat generated, temperatures can rise substantially at high drawing speeds and can have detrimental effects on product quality.

Reductions in cross-sectional area per pass range from near zero to about 45%; usually, the smaller the initial cross-section, the smaller the reduction per pass. Fine wires are usually drawn at 15% to 25% reduction per pass, larger sizes at 20% to 45%. Reductions of more than 45% may result in lubricant breakdown and resultant surface-finish deterioration. Drawing large solid or hollow sections can be done at elevated temperatures.

A light reduction, called a **sizing pass**, may also be taken on rods to improve surface finish and dimensional accuracy. Because they basically deform only the surface layers, however, light reductions usually produce highly nonuniform deformation of the material and its microstructure. Consequently, the properties of the material vary with location within the cross-section.

Because of work hardening, intermediate annealing (Section 4.11) between passes may be necessary to maintain sufficient ductility during cold drawing. Drawn copper and brass wires are designated by their temper, such as 1/4 hard, 1/2 hard, etc.

High-carbon steel wires for springs and for musical instruments are made by heat treating (**patenting**) the drawn wire; the microstructure so obtained is fine pearlite. These wires have ultimate tensile strengths as high as 5 GPa (700 ksi) and tensile reduction of area of about 20%.

Bundle Drawing.   Although very fine wire can be produced by drawing, the cost can be high. One method employed to increase productivity is to draw many wires (as many as several thousand) simultaneously as a *bundle*. The wires are separated from one another by a suitable metallic material with similar properties but lower chemical resistance (so that it can subsequently be leached out from the drawn wire surfaces).

Bundling produces wires that are somewhat polygonal in cross-section rather than round. In addition to continuous lengths, techniques have been developed to produce fine wire that is broken into various sizes and shapes. The wires produced can be as small as 4 μm (0.00016 in.) in diameter; they can be made from such materials as stainless steels, titanium, and high-temperature alloys. Applications include electrically conductive plastics, heat-resistant and electrically conductive textiles, filter media, radar camouflage, and medical implants.

15.11.1 Die Design

The characteristic features of a typical die design for drawing are shown in Fig. 15.20. Die angles usually range from 6° to 15°. Note, however, that there are two angles (entering and approach) in a typical die. The basic design for this type of die was developed through years

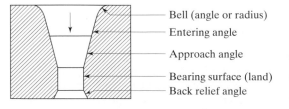

Bell (angle or radius)
Entering angle
Approach angle
Bearing surface (land)
Back relief angle

FIGURE 15.20
Terminology of a typical die used for drawing round rod or wire.

of trial and error. The purpose of the bearing surface (*land*) is to set the final diameter of the product (called **sizing**). Also, when a worn die is reground, the land maintains the exit dimension of the die opening.

A set of dies is required for **profile drawing** for various stages of deformation. The dies may be made in one piece or, depending on the complexity of the cross-sectional profile, with several segments held together in a ring. Computer-aided design techniques are being implemented to design dies for smooth material flow through the dies and to minimize defects.

A set of idling cylindrical or shaped rolls is also used in drawing rods or bars of various shapes. This arrangement (*Turk's head*) is more versatile than that in ordinary drawing dies because the rolls can be adjusted to different positions and angles.

15.11.2 Die Materials

Die materials for drawing are usually tool steels and carbides; diamond dies are used for fine wire (Table 5.7). For improved wear resistance, steel dies may be chromium plated, and carbide dies may be coated with titanium nitride. Mandrels for tube drawing are usually made of hardened tool steels or of carbides.

Diamond dies are used for drawing fine wire with diameters ranging from 2 μm to 1.5 mm (0.0001 in. to 0.06 in.). They may be made from a single-crystal diamond or else in polycrystalline form, with diamond particles in a metal matrix (compacts). Because of their cost and their lack of tensile strength and toughness, carbide and diamond dies are used as inserts or nibs, which are supported in a steel casing (Fig. 15.21). For hot drawing, cast-steel dies are used, because of their high resistance to wear at elevated temperatures.

15.11.3 Lubrication

Proper lubrication is essential in drawing, in order to improve die life, reduce drawing forces and temperature, and improve surface finish. In tube drawing, lubrication is particularly critical, because of the difficulty of maintaining a sufficiently thick lubricant film at the mandrel–tube interface. The following are the basic types of lubrication (see also Chapter 32):

a. **Wet drawing.** The dies and the rod are completely immersed in the lubricant, which typically consists of oils and emulsions containing fatty or chlorinated additives and various chemical compounds.

b. **Dry drawing.** The surface of the rod to be drawn is coated with a lubricant, such as soap, by passing it through a box filled with the lubricant (*stuffing box*).

c. **Coating.** The rod or wire is coated with a soft metal that acts as a solid lubricant. Copper or tin, for example, can be chemically deposited on the surface of the metal to serve this purpose.

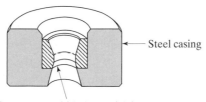

Steel casing

Tungsten - carbide insert (nib)

FIGURE 15.21   Tungsten-carbide die insert in a steel casing. Diamond dies, used in drawing thin wire, are encased in a similar manner.

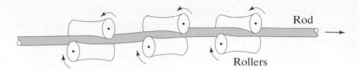

FIGURE 15.22   Schematic illustration of roll straightening of a drawn round rod (see also Fig. 13.7).

  d. Ultrasonic vibration of the dies and mandrels. This technique has been utilized successfully to reduce the friction in drawing solid or hollow sections, as well as in other metalworking processes. When it is done properly, the vibrations reduce forces, improve surface finish and die life, and allow larger reductions per pass without failure.

15.12 DEFECTS AND RESIDUAL STRESSES

Typical defects in drawn rod and wire are similar to those observed in extrusion—especially, center cracking. (See Fig. 15.16.) An additional type of defect in drawing is **seams**, which are longitudinal scratches or folds in the material. Seams may open up during subsequent forming operations, such as upsetting, heading, thread rolling, or bending of the rod or wire, and they can cause serious quality-control problems in production. Various other surface defects, such as scratches and die marks, can also result from improper selection of the drawing-process parameters, poor lubrication, or unsatisfactory die condition.

  Because they undergo nonuniform deformation during drawing, cold-drawn products usually have residual stresses. From light reductions of a few percent, the longitudinal surface residual stresses are compressive, while the middle is in tension, and so fatigue life is improved. Conversely, heavier reductions induce tensile surface stresses, while the middle is in compression. Residual stresses can be significant in causing stress-corrosion cracking of the part over a period of time. Moreover, they cause the component to warp if a layer of material is subsequently removed, such as by slitting, machining, or grinding (see Fig. 2.30).

  Rods and tubes that are not sufficiently straight (or are supplied as coil) can be straightened by passing them through an arrangement of rolls placed at different axes (Fig. 15.22). The rolls subject the product to a series of bending and unbending operations, a process similar to roller leveling (see Fig. 13.7).

15.13 DRAWING EQUIPMENT

Although it comes in several designs, the equipment for drawing is basically of two types: draw bench, and bull block.

  A **draw bench** contains a single die, and its design is similar to that of a long horizontal tension-testing machine (Fig. 15.23). The pulling force is supplied by a chain drive or is activated hydraulically. Draw benches are used for single-length drawing of straight rods and tubes with diameters larger than 20 mm (0.75 in.). Lengths may be up to 30 m (100 ft.). Machine capacities reach 1.3 MN (300 klb) of pulling force, with a speed range of 6 m/min to 60 m/min (20 ft/min to 200 ft/min).

  Very long rod and wire (many kilometers) and wire of smaller cross-sections, usually less than 13 mm (0.5 in.), are drawn by a rotating **drum** (**bull block**, **capstan**, Fig. 15.24). The tension in this setup provides the force required for drawing the wire, usually through multiple dies.

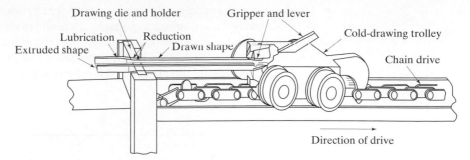

FIGURE 15.23   Cold drawing of an extruded channel on a draw bench, to reduce its cross-section. Individual lengths of straight rod or of cross-sections are drawn by this method. *Source*: Courtesy of The Babcock and Wilcox Company, Tubular Products Division.

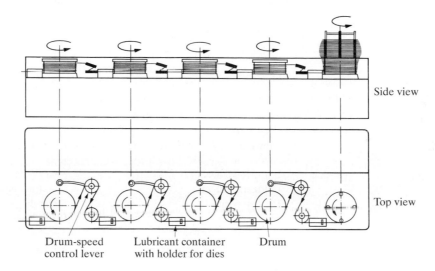

FIGURE 15.24   Two views of a multistage wire-drawing machine that is typically used in the making of copper wire for electrical wiring. *Source*: H. Auerswald.

SUMMARY

- Extrusion is the process of forcing a billet through a die, to reduce its cross-section or to produce a wide range of solid or hollow cross-sections. The process is generally carried out at elevated temperatures, to reduce forces and to improve the ductility of the material.

- Important factors in extrusion are die design, extrusion ratio, billet temperature, lubrication, and extrusion speed. Although the term cold extrusion applies to extrusion at room temperature, it is also the name for a process which is a combination of extrusion and forging operations. Cold extrusion is capable of economically producing discrete parts in various shapes, with good mechanical properties and dimensional tolerances.

- Rod, wire, and tube drawing basically involve the process of pulling the material through a die (or a set of dies in tandem). Although the cross-sections of most drawn products are round, other shapes can also be drawn. Drawing tubular products, to reduce either their diameter or their thickness, usually requires internal mandrels.

- The die design, the reduction in cross-sectional area per pass, and the selection of die materials and lubricants are all important parameters in obtaining drawn products of high quality and of good surface finish. Both external defects and internal defects (chevron cracking) can develop both in extrusion and in drawing; their minimization depends principally on the die angle, the reduction per pass, and the quality of the workpiece material.

TRENDS

- Computer-aided die design and manufacturing are being implemented, to improve material flow in extrusion and in drawing and to reduce defects.
- Ceramic dies are being used in high-temperature extrusion of small cross-sections.
- Improvements are taking place in die materials and in coatings to extend die life.

KEY TERMS

Bamboo defect	Draw bench	Pipe defect
Bridge die	Drawing	Porthole die
Bull block	Extrusion	Rod
Bundle drawing	Extrusion constant	Seam
Canning	Extrusion defects	Séjournet process
Capstan	Extrusion ratio	Shear die
Center cracking	Fir-tree cracking	Sizing pass
Chevron cracking	Hydrostatic extrusion	Speed cracking
Circumscribing-circle diameter	Impact extrusion	Spider die
Cold extrusion	Ironing	Turk's head
Conversion coating	Jacketing	Wire
Dead-metal zone	Patenting	

BIBLIOGRAPHY

Extrusion

Alexander, J.M., and B. Lengyel, *Hydrostatic Extrusion*. Mills and Boon, 1971.

ASM Handbook, Vol. 14: *Forming and Forging*. ASM International, 1988.

Blazynski, T.Z., *Plasticity and Modern Metal-forming Technology*. Elsevier, 1989.

Hosford, W.F., and R.M. Caddell, *Metal Forming: Mechanics and Metallurgy* (2d ed.). Prentice Hall, 1993.

Inoue, N., and M. Nishihara (eds.), *Hydrostatic Extrusion: Theory and Applications*. Elsevier, 1985.

Lange, K. (ed.), *Handbook of Metal Forming*. McGraw-Hill, 1985.

Laue, K., and H. Stenger, *Extrusion—Processes, Machinery, Tooling*. ASM International, 1981.

Michaeli, W., *Extrusion Dies*, (2d ed.) Hanser, 1992.

Sheppard, T., *Extrusion of Aluminum Alloys*. Chapman & Hall, 1997.

Drawing

Hosford, W.F., and R.M. Caddell, *Metal Forming: Mechanics and Metallurgy* (2d ed.). Prentice Hall, 1993.

Lange, K. (ed.), *Handbook of Metal Forming*. McGraw-Hill, 1985.

Nonferrous Wire Handbook, 2 vols. The Wire Association International, Inc., 1977 and 1981.

Steel Wire Handbook, vol. 1, 1968; vol. 2, 1969; vol. 3, 1972; vol. 4, 1980. Wire Association International.

REVIEW QUESTIONS

15.1 How does extrusion differ from rolling and forging?

15.2 What is the difference between extrusion and drawing?

15.3 Define circumscribing-circle diameter (CCD).

15.4 What is shape factor? Why is it important?

15.5 Describe the types of metal flow that occur in extrusion. Why are they important?

15.6 What is a dead-metal zone?

15.7 Define (a) cladding, (b) dummy block, (c) shear dies, (d) skull, (e) canning.

15.8 Why is glass a good lubricant in hot extrusion?

15.9 Explain why cold extrusion has become an important manufacturing process.

15.10 What types of defects may occur in extrusion and in drawing?

15.11 Name the important process variables in the drawing of rod and wire.

15.12 What is the difference between direct and reverse extrusion?

15.13 What is a land?

15.14 What is a bull block?

15.15 How are tubes extruded? How are they drawn?

15.16 How are gears extruded? What further processing is necessary?

QUALITATIVE PROBLEMS

15.17 Explain why extrusion is a batch or semicontinuous process. Do you think it can be made into a continuous process? Explain.

15.18 Explain the different ways by which changing the die angle affects the extrusion process.

15.19 Glass is a good lubricant in hot extrusion. Would you use glass for impression-die forging also? Explain.

15.20 Extrusion ratio, speed, and temperature all affect the extrusion force. Explain why they do.

15.21 How would you go about avoiding center cracking defects in extrusion? Explain why your methods would be effective.

15.22 Assume that you are reducing the diameter of two rods, one by simple tension and the other by frictionless indirect extrusion. Which method will require more force? Why?

15.23 What is the purpose of a stripper plate in impact extrusion?

15.24 If the impact extrusion process did not exist, how else would you make the parts shown in Fig. 15.15a?

15.25 Table 15.1 gives temperature ranges for extruding various metals. Describe the consequences of extruding at a temperature (a) below and (b) above these ranges.

15.26 Will the force in direct extrusion vary as the billet gets shorter and shorter? If so, why?

15.27 What changes would you expect in the strength, hardness, and ductility of a metal after it has been drawn through dies at room temperature?

15.28 Comment on the significance of grain-flow patterns, such as those shown in Fig. 15.7.

15.29 In which applications could you use the type of impact-extruded parts shown in Fig. 15.15?

15.30 Can spur gears be made (a) by drawing, (b) by extrusion? Helical gears? Explain.

15.31 Is there any particular advantage in extruding with square dies? Explain.

15.32 Why do you think the two dies shown in Fig. 15.8a and b are suitable for extruding nonferrous and ferrous metals, respectively?

15.33 We have seen in Chapter 13 that applying back tension in rolling reduces the roll force. What advantages, if any, would applying back tension in rod or wire drawing have? Explain.

15.34 Determine a technique for starting a drawing operation; that is, how would you prepare the end of a wire so as to be able to feed it through a die, so that a drawing operation can commence?

15.35 Are capstans and bull blocks useful for rods?

15.36 What is the purpose of a dummy block?

15.37 In hydrostatic extrusion, complex seals are used between the ram and the container, but not between the extrusion and the die. Why?

15.38 Describe your observations concerning Fig. 15.9.

15.39 Occasionally, steel wire drawing will take place within a sheath of a soft metal such as copper or lead. Why would this sheath be useful?

QUANTITATIVE PROBLEMS

15.40 Calculate the force required in extruding copper at 700 °C, if the billet diameter is 125 mm and the extrusion ratio is 20.

15.41 Assuming an ideal drawing process, what is the smallest final diameter to which a 50-mm diameter rod can be drawn?

15.42 If you include friction in Problem 15.41, would the final diameter be different? Explain.

15.43 Calculate the extrusion force for a round billet, 200 mm in diameter, made of beryllium, and extruded at 1000 °C to a diameter of 50 mm.

15.44 Show that, for a perfectly plastic material with a yield stress Y, and under frictionless conditions, the pressure p in direct extrusion is

$$p = Y \ln \left(\frac{A_o}{A_f} \right).$$

15.45 Show that, for the conditions stated in Problem 15.44, the drawing stress σ_d in wire drawing is

$$\sigma_d = Y \ln \left(\frac{A_o}{A_f} \right).$$

15.46 Plot the equations given in Problems 15.44 and 15.45, as a function of the percent reduction of area. Describe your observations.

15.47 Refer to Fig. 15.10, and determine the diameters of the circumscribing circles for the two examples. (You may need to enlarge the figures to obtain accurate measurements.)

15.48 Assume that you are an instructor covering the topics in this chapter. Prepare three quantitative problems, to test the knowledge of your students concerning the contents of this chapter. Give your own answers for each problem.

15.49 Calculate the final temperature of the billet in Problem 15.40. Assume that all of the work of deformation is dissipated into heat in the workpiece and that no heat is conducted through the tooling.

15.50 A planned extrusion operation involves steel at 800 °C, with an initial diameter of 100 mm and a final diameter 20 mm. Two presses, one with capacity of 20 MN and the other with a capacity of 10 MN, are available for the operation. Obviously, the larger press requires greater care and more expensive tooling. Is the smaller press sufficient for this operation? If not, what recommendations would you make to allow the use of the smaller press?

SYNTHESIS AND DESIGN

15.51 Assume that you are the technical director of trade association of manufacturers of extruders and extruding machines. Prepare a technical leaflet for potential customers, stating all the advantages of extrusion.

15.52 Assume that the summary to this chapter is missing. Write a one-page summary of the highlights to the wire-drawing process.

15.53 Review the technical literature, and make a detailed list of the manufacturing steps involved in the manufacture of long, metallic hypodermic needles.

15.54 Figure 15.2 shows three examples of products that are obtained by slicing long extruded sections into small pieces. Name several other products that can be made similarly.

15.55 Describe the similarities and differences between extrusion and drawing, and name several specific products that can be made either by one of these processes or by the forging processes described in Chapter 14.

15.56 Make an extensive list of products that are either made of, or have one or more components made of, (a) wire and (b) rods of various cross-sections.

15.57 Survey the technical literature, and explain how external vibrations can be applied to wire drawing to reduce friction. Comment also on the possible directions of vibration, such as longitudinal or torsional.

15.58 Describe products that can be made using the lateral extrusion process shown in Fig. 15.3c.

15.59 Survey the technical literature, and write a brief essay on the technology of glass lubrication in hot extrusion.

15.60 A popular child's toy is a miniature extrusion press, used with a soft dough or a putty to make various shapes. Obtain such a toy, and demonstrate the surface defects that may develop.

15.61 Although extruded products are typically straight, it is possible to design dies in such a way that the product develops a constant curvature as it comes out of the die. (a) Describe your ideas on how this can be achieved. (b) What applications would curved extrusions have?

15.62 Assume that the plastic-deformation zone in extrusion can be approximated by an isosceles right triangle, with the die/workpiece contact length being the hypotenuse. If chevron cracking occurs when the deformation zones fail to overlap, obtain an expression for when chevron cracking will occur, as a function of die angle and reduction.

16

Sheet-Metal Forming Processes

16.1 INTRODUCTION

Products made by **sheet-metal forming** processes are all around us; they include metal desks, file cabinets, appliances, car bodies, aircraft fuselages, and beverage cans. Sheet forming dates back to 5000 B.C., when household utensils and jewelry were made by hammering and stamping gold, silver, and copper.

Compared to those made by casting and by forging, sheet-metal parts offer the advantages of light weight and versatile shape. Because of its low cost and generally good strength and formability characteristics, low-carbon steel is the most commonly used sheet metal. For aircraft and aerospace applications, the common sheet materials are aluminum and titanium.

This chapter first describes the methods by which blanks are cut from large rolled sheets, then further processed into desired shapes by a wide variety of traditional methods as well as by such techniques as superplastic forming and diffusion bonding. The chapter

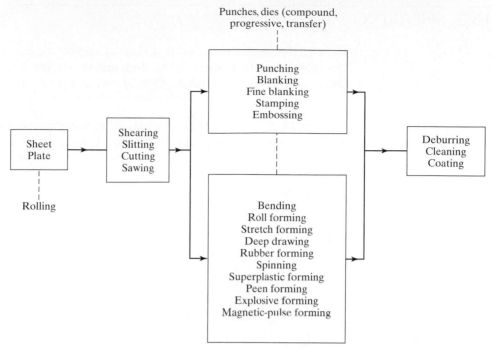

FIGURE 16.1   Outline of sheet-metal forming processes.

also includes discussions on the characteristic features of sheet metals, the techniques used to determine their formability, and the construction of forming-limit diagrams. All the major processes of sheet forming and all the equipment used to make sheet-metal products, as outlined in Fig. 16.1 and Table 16.1, are also described.

TABLE 16.1   Characteristics of Sheet-Metal Forming Processes

Process	Characteristics
Roll forming	Long parts with constant complex cross-sections; good surface finish; high production rates; high tooling costs.
Stretch forming	Large parts with shallow contours; suitable for low-quantity production; high labor costs; tooling and equipment costs depend on part size.
Drawing	Shallow or deep parts with relatively simple shapes; high production rates; high tooling and equipment costs.
Stamping	Includes a variety of operations, such as punching, blanking, embossing, bending, flanging, and coining; simple or complex shapes formed at high production rates; tooling and equipment costs can be high, but labor cost is low.
Rubber forming	Drawing and embossing of simple or complex shapes; sheet surface protected by rubber membranes; flexibility of operation; low tooling costs.
Spinning	Small or large axisymmetric parts; good surface finish; low tooling costs, but labor costs can be high unless operations are automated.
Superplastic forming	Complex shapes, fine detail and close tolerances; forming times are long, hence production rates are low; parts not suitable for high-temperature use.
Peen forming	Shallow contours on large sheets; flexibility of operation; equipment costs can be high; process is also used for straightening parts.
Explosive forming	Very large sheets with relatively complex shapes, although usually axisymmetric; low tooling costs, but high labor cost; suitable for low-quantity production; long cycle times.
Magnetic-pulse forming	Shallow forming, bulging, and embossing operations on relatively low-strength sheets; most suitable for tubular shapes; high production rates; requires special tooling.

16.2 SHEARING

Before a sheet-metal part is made, a *blank* of suitable dimensions is first removed from a large sheet (usually from a coil) by **shearing**; that is, the sheet is cut by subjecting it to shear stresses, typically ones developed between a punch and a die (Fig. 16.2a). Typical

FIGURE 16.2 (a) Schematic illustration of shearing with a punch and die, indicating some of the process variables. Characteristic features of (b) a punched hole and (c) the slug. Note that the scales of the two figures are different.

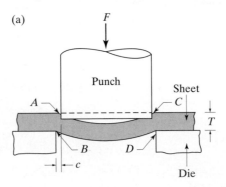

(a)

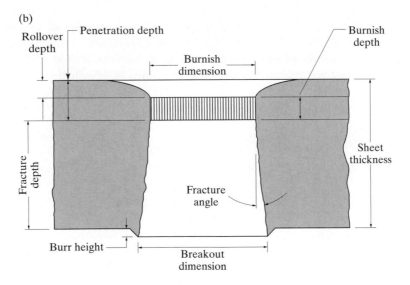

(b)

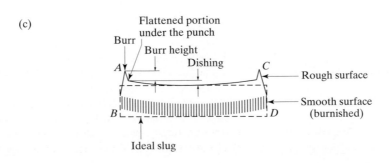

(c)

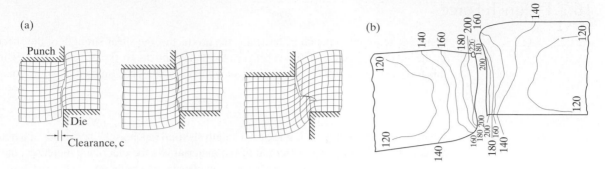

FIGURE 16.3   (a) Effect of the clearance, c, between punch and die on the deformation zone in shearing. As the clearance increases, the material tends to be pulled into the die rather than be sheared. In practice, clearances usually range between 2% and 10% of the thickness of the sheet. (b) Microhardness (HV) contours for a 6.4-mm (0.25-in.) thick AISI 1020 hot-rolled steel in the sheared region. *Source*: H. P. Weaver and K. J. Weinmann.

features of the sheared edges of the sheet and of the slug are shown in Figs. 16.2b and c, respectively. Note that the edges are not smooth, nor are they perpendicular to the plane of the sheet.

Shearing usually starts with the formation of cracks on both the top and bottom edges of the workpiece (A and B, and C and D in Fig. 16.2a). These cracks eventually meet each other and separation occurs. The rough *fracture surfaces* are due to these cracks; the smooth and shiny *burnished surfaces* on the hole and the slug are from the contact and rubbing of the sheared edge against the walls of the punch and die.

The major processing parameters in shearing are the shape of and the materials for the punch and die, the speed of the punching, the lubrication, and the **clearance**, c, between the punch and the die. The clearance is a major factor in determining the shape and the quality of the sheared edge. As the clearance increases, the sheared edge becomes rougher, and the zone of deformation (Fig. 16.3a) becomes larger. The sheet tends to be pulled into the clearance zone, and the edges of the sheared zone become rougher. Unless such edges are acceptable as produced, secondary operations (which will add to the production cost) may be required, to make them smoother.

The ratio of the burnished to the rough areas on the sheared edge increases with increasing ductility of the sheet metal, and decreases with increasing sheet thickness and clearance. The width of the deformation zone in Fig. 16.3 depends on *punch speed*. With increasing speed, the heat generated by plastic deformation is confined to a smaller and smaller zone; consequently, the sheared zone is narrower, and the surface is smoother and exhibits less burr formation.

A **burr** is a thin edge or ridge, as shown in Figs. 16.2b and c. Burr height increases with increases in the clearance and in the ductility of the sheet metal. Dull tool edges contribute greatly to burr formation. The height, shape, and size of the burr can significantly affect subsequent forming operations. Several **deburring** processes are described in Section 25.11.

Edge quality has been found to improve with increasing punch speed; speeds may be as high as 10-12 m/s (33-39 ft/s). As shown in Fig. 16.3b, sheared edges can undergo severe cold working, which is due to the high shear strains involved. The resultant work hardening can adversely affect the formability of the sheet during subsequent operations.

16.2.1 Punch Force

The force required to punch is, basically, the product of the shear strength of the sheet metal by the area being sheared. Friction between the punch and the workpiece can, however, increase this force substantially. The *maximum punch force*, *F*, can be estimated from the equation

$$F = 0.7TL(\text{UTS}), \qquad\qquad (16.1)$$

where T is sheet thickness, L is the total length sheared (such as the perimeter of a hole), and UTS is the ultimate tensile strength of the material. As the clearance increases, the punch force decreases, and the wear on dies and punches is also reduced.

In addition to the punch force, a force is also required to strip the punch from the sheet during its return stroke. This second force is difficult to estimate, because of the many factors involved. The effects of punch shape and die shape on punch forces are described in Section 16.2.3.

Example: Calculation of Punch Force

Estimate the force required for punching a 1-in. (25-mm) diameter hole through a $\frac{1}{8}$-in. (3.2-mm) thick annealed titanium-alloy Ti-6Al-4V sheet at room temperature.

Solution: The force is estimated from Eq. (16.1). The UTS for this alloy is found from Table 6.10 to be 1000 MPa, or 140,000 psi. Thus,

$$F = 0.7\left(\frac{1}{8}\right)(\pi)(1)(140{,}000) = 38{,}500 \text{ lb} = 19.25 \text{ tons} = 0.17 \text{ MN}.$$

16.2.2 Shearing Operations

Several operations based on the shearing process are performed. We first define two terms. In **punching**, the sheared slug is discarded (Fig. 16.4a). In **blanking**, the slug is the part and the rest is scrap. Many of the operations described below, as well as those described throughout the rest of this chapter, can now be carried out on computer-numerical-controlled machines (see Chapter 39) with quick-change toolholders. Such

FIGURE 16.4   (a) Punching (piercing) and blanking. (b) Examples of various shearing operations on sheet metal.

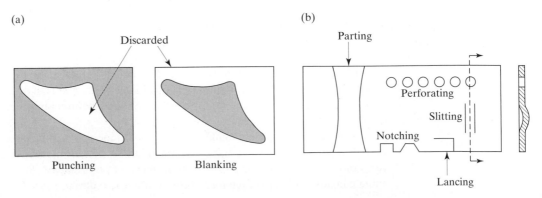

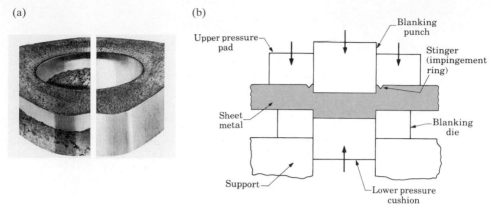

FIGURE 16.5   (a) Comparison of sheared edges produced by conventional (left) and by fine-blanking (right) techniques. (b) Schematic illustration of one setup for fine blanking. *Source*: Feintool U.S. Operations.

machines are particularly useful in making those prototypes of sheet-metal parts that require several operations.

Die Cutting. Die cutting is a shearing process that consists of the following operations (Fig. 16.4b):

a. **perforating**—punching a number of holes in a sheet;
b. **parting**—shearing the sheet into two or more pieces;
c. **notching**—removing pieces (or various shapes) from the edges; and
d. **lancing**—leaving a tab without removing any material.

Parts produced by these processes have various uses, particularly in assembly with other components. Perforated sheet metals, with hole diameters ranging from around 1 mm (0.040 in.) to 75 mm (3 in.), have uses as filters, as screens, in ventilation, as guards for machinery, in noise abatement, and in weight reduction. They are punched in crank presses (see Fig. 14.21b) at rates as high as 300,000 holes per minute, using special dies and equipment.

Fine Blanking.   Very smooth and square edges can be produced by *fine blanking* (Fig. 16.5a). One basic die design is shown in Fig. 16.5b. A V-shaped stinger, or impingement, locks the sheet tightly in place and prevents the type of distortion of the material shown in Figs. 16.2b and 16.3. The fine-blanking process, which was developed in the 1960s, involves clearances on the order of 1% of the sheet thickness, which may range from 0.5 mm to 13 mm (0.02 in. to 0.5 in.). Dimensional tolerances are on the order of ±0.05 mm (0.002 in.) in most cases, and less than 0.025 mm (0.001 in.) in the case of edge perpendicularity.

The fine-blanking operation is usually carried out on triple-action hydraulic presses, where the movements of the punch, of the pressure pad, and of the die are separately controlled. The process usually involves a part having holes that are punched simultaneously with its blanking. Suitable sheet hardness is typically between 50 and 90 HRB.

Slitting.   Shearing operations can be carried out by means of a pair of circular blades similar to those in a can opener (Fig. 16.6); this process is called *slitting*. The blades follow either a straight line or a circular or curved path. A slit edge normally has a burr, which may

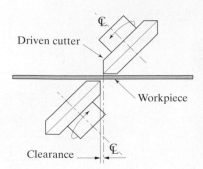

FIGURE 16.6   Slitting with rotary knives. This process is similar to opening cans.

be plastically folded over the sheet surface by rolling the sheet between two rolls. There are two types of slitting equipment. In the *driven* type, the blades are powered. In the *pull-through* type, the strip is pulled through idling blades. Slitting operations, if not performed properly, may cause various distortions of the sheared edges.

Steel Rules.   Soft metals (as well as paper, leather, and rubber) can be blanked with *steel-rule dies*. Such a die consists of a thin strip of hardened steel, bent into the shape to be produced (a concept similar to that of a cookie cutter) and held on its edge on a flat wooden base. The die is pressed against the sheet, which rests on a flat surface, and it shears the sheet along the shape of the steel rule.

Nibbling.   In *nibbling*, a machine called a *nibbler* moves a small straight punch up and down rapidly into a die. A sheet is fed through the gap, and many overlapping holes are made. This operation is similar to the making of a large elongated slot in a sheet of paper by the successive punching of holes with a paper punch. By the use of manual control, sheets can be cut along any desired path. An advantage of nibbling, in addition to its flexibility, is that intricate slots and notches, such as those shown in Fig. 16.4b, can be produced with standard punches. The process is economical for small production runs, because no special dies are required.

Scrap in Shearing.   The amount of scrap (the *trim loss*) produced in shearing operations can be significant; it can be as high as 30% on large stampings. A significant factor in manufacturing cost, scrap can be reduced substantially by proper arrangement of the shapes on the sheet to be cut (**nesting**). Computer-aided design techniques have been developed to minimize the scrap from shearing operations.

Tailor-Welded Blanks.   Consisting of two or more pieces of flat sheet metal butt-welded together (as in the example below), these are becoming increasingly important, particularly to the automotive industry. Because each subpiece can have a different thickness, grade, coating, or other property, tailor-welded blanks possess the needed properties in the desired locations in the blank. The result is improved productivity, reduction in the weight of scrap, elimination of the need for subsequent spot welding in the making of the car body, and better control of dimensions.

The most commonly used welding technique is laser-beam welding (Section 27.8). Because of the small thicknesses involved, the proper alignment of the sheets prior to welding is important.

Example: Laser-Welded Sheet Metal for Forming

In the forming processes to be described throughout this chapter, the sheet blank is usually one piece and of one thickness, blanked from a large sheet. An important trend involves *laser butt welding* of pieces of sheet metal of different shapes and thicknesses; the welded assembly is subsequently formed into a final shape. One such example is the production of an automobile outer side panel (shown in Fig. 16.7).

Note that five different pieces are first blanked; four of them are 1 mm thick, one is 0.8 mm thick. These pieces are laser butt welded and then stamped into the final shape. In this way, the blanks can be tailored for a particular application, not only as to shape and thickness, but also by the use of different quality sheets (with or without coatings).

Laser welding techniques (Section 27.8) are now highly developed; as a consequence, weld joints are very strong. The growing trend toward welding and forming sheet-metal pieces makes possible significant flexibility in product design, structural stiffness, crash behavior, and formability; it also makes possible the use of different materials in one component, weight savings, and cost reduction in materials, scrap, equipment, assembly, and labor.

There are a growing number of applications for this type of production in U.S. and Japanese automotive companies. The various components shown in Fig. 16.8 utilize the advantages outlined above. For example, note, in part (b), that the strength and stiffness required for the support of the shock absorber are achieved by the welding of a round piece onto the surface of the large sheet. The sheet thickness in these components varies, depending on its location and on its contribution to such characteristics as stiffness and strength, and thereby makes possible significant weight savings.

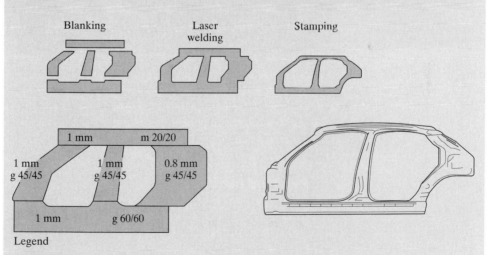

Legend

g 60/60 (45/45)   Hot galvanized alloy steel sheet. Zinc amount: 60/60 (45/45) g/m².
m20/20   Double-layered iron-zinc alloy electroplated steel sheet. Zinc amount 20/20 g/m².

FIGURE 16.7   Production of an outer side panel of a car body, by laser butt-welding and stamping. *Source*: After M. Geiger and T. Nakagawa.

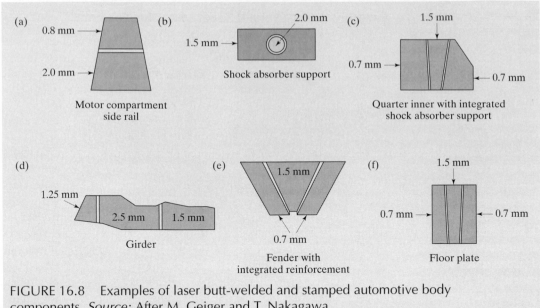

FIGURE 16.8   Examples of laser butt-welded and stamped automotive body components. *Source*: After M. Geiger and T. Nakagawa.

16.2.3 Shearing Dies

The features and types of various shearing dies are described in this section.

Clearances.   Because the formability of the sheared part can be influenced by the quality of its sheared edges, clearance control is important. The appropriate clearance is a function of the type of material, its temper, and its thickness and of the size of the blank and its proximity to the edges of the original sheet. As a general guideline, clearances for soft materials are less than those for harder grades. Also, the thicker the sheet is, the larger the clearance must be. Holes which are small (as compared to sheet thickness) require greater clearances than ones which are larger.

Clearances generally range between 2% and 8% of the sheet thickness, but they may be as small as 1% or as large as 30%. In the use of larger clearances, attention must be paid to the rigidity and the alignment of the presses and to the dies and their setups. The smaller the clearance, the better the quality of the edge. In a process called **shaving** (Fig. 16.9), the extra material from a rough sheared edge is trimmed by cutting.

Punch and Die Shapes.   Note in Fig. 16.2a that the surfaces of the punch and of the die are both flat. The punch force, therefore, builds up rapidly during shearing, because the entire thickness is sheared at the same time. The location of the regions being sheared at any moment can be controlled by beveling the punch and die surfaces (Fig. 16.10). The geometry is similar to that of a paper punch; you can see that by looking closely at the tip of the

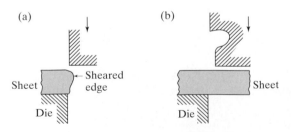

FIGURE 16.9   Schematic illustrations of the shaving of a sheared edge. (a) Shaving a sheared edge. (b) Shearing and shaving, combined in one stroke.

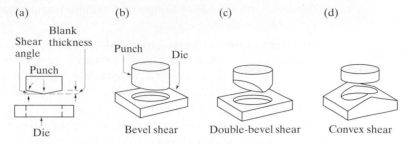

FIGURE 16.10   Examples of the use of shear angles on punches and dies.

punch. Beveling is particularly suitable for the shearing of thick blanks, because it reduces the force at the beginning of the stroke; it also reduces the operation's noise level.

Note, in Figs. 16.10c and d, that, because of the symmetry of the punch tip, there are no lateral forces acting on the punch. By contrast, the punch in Fig. 16.10b has a single taper, and so a lateral force does act on the punch. Consequently, the punch and press setups in this latter case must have sufficient lateral rigidity so that they neither produce a hole that is located improperly nor allow the punch to hit the edge of the lower die (as it might at points *B* or *D* in Fig. 16.2a), causing damage.

Compound Dies.   Several operations on the same strip may be performed in one stroke at one station with a *compound die* (Figs. 16.11a and b). Such combined operations are usually limited to relatively simple shapes, because they are somewhat slow and be-

FIGURE 16.11   Schematic illustrations: (a) before and (b) after blanking a common washer in a compound die. Note the separate movements of the die (for blanking) and the punch (for punching the hole in the washer). (c) Schematic illustration of making a washer in a progressive die. (d) Forming of the top piece of an aerosol spray can in a progressive die. Note that the part is attached to the strip until the last operation is completed.

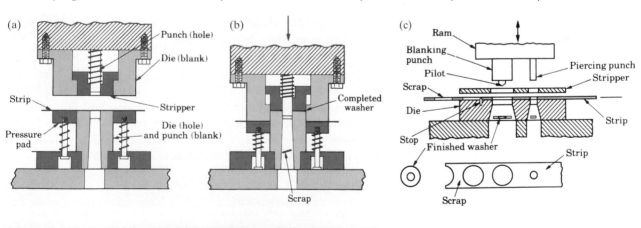

cause the dies (with increasing complexity) rapidly become much more expensive than those for individual shearing operations.

Progressive Dies.   Parts requiring multiple operations, such as punching, blanking, and notching, can be made at high production rates in *progressive dies*. The sheet metal is fed through as a coil strip, and a different operation is performed at the same station with each stroke of a series of punches (Fig. 16.11c). An example of a part made in progressive dies is shown in Fig. 16.11d.

Transfer Dies.   In a *transfer die* setup, the sheet metal undergoes different operations at different stations, which are arranged along a straight line or a circular path. After each step, the part is transferred to the next station for further operations.

Tool and Die Materials.   Tool and die materials for shearing are generally tool steels and, for high production rates, carbides (see Table 5.7). Lubrication is important for reducing tool and die wear and improving edge quality.

16.2.4 Other Methods of Cutting Sheet Metal

There are several other methods of cutting sheets and, particularly, plates:

a. The sheet or plate may be cut with a **band saw**; this method is a chip removal process (like those described in Section 23.6).

b. **Flame cutting** (Section 27.9) is another common method, particularly for thick steel plates; it is widely used in shipbuilding and on heavy structural components.

c. **Laser-beam cutting** (Section 26.7) has become an important process. It is used, with computer-controlled equipment, to cut a variety of shapes consistently and in various thicknesses. This process can be combined with punching and shearing; the two processes cover different and complementary ranges. Parts with certain features can be produced best by one process; some with other features can be produced best by the other process. Combination machines incorporating both capabilities have been designed and built. (See also the Example at the end of Section 26.7.)

d. **Friction sawing** involves a disk or blade which rubs against the sheet or plate at high surface speeds (Section 23.6.2).

e. **Water-jet cutting** (Section 26.9) is an important cutting process that is effective on many metallic materials as well as nonmetallic ones.

16.3 SHEET-METAL CHARACTERISTICS

After a blank is cut from a larger sheet, it is formed into various shapes. Basically, all sheet-forming processes employ various dies and tooling to stretch and bend the sheet. Before we consider these processes, however, certain characteristics of sheet metals must be reviewed, because of their important effects on the overall operation (Table 16.2).

16.3.1 Elongation

Although sheet-forming operations rarely involve simple uniaxial stretching like that in a tension test, observations concerning tensile testing can be useful for understanding the behavior of sheet metals. Recall, from Section 2.2, that a specimen subjected to tension first undergoes **uniform elongation**; only when the load exceeds the ultimate tensile strength does the specimen begin to neck.

Because the material is usually being stretched in sheet forming, high uniform elongation is desirable for good formability. The true strain at which necking begins is numerically equal to the *strain-hardening exponent* (n) shown in Eq. (2.8); thus, a high n value indicates large uniform elongation (see Table 2.3).

TABLE 16.2   Characteristics of Metals Important in Sheet Forming

Characteristic	Importance
Elongation	Determines the capability of the sheet metal to stretch without necking and failure; high strain-hardening exponent (n) and strain-rate sensitivity exponent (m) desirable.
Yield-point elongation	Observed with mild-steel sheets; also called Lueder's bands and stretcher strains; causes flamelike depressions on the sheet surfaces; can be eliminated by temper rolling, but sheet must be formed within a certain time after rolling.
Anisotropy (planar)	Exhibits different behavior in different planar directions; present in cold-rolled sheets because of preferred orientation or mechanical fibering; causes earing in drawing; can be reduced or eliminated by annealing but at lowered strength.
Anisotropy (normal)	Determines thinning behavior of sheet metals during stretching; important in deep-drawing operations.
Grain size	Determines surface roughness on stretched sheet metal; the coarser the grain, the rougher the appearance (orange peel); also affects material strength.
Residual stresses	Caused by nonuniform deformation during forming; causes part distortion when sectioned and can lead to stress-corrosion cracking; reduced or eliminated by stress relieving.
Springback	Caused by elastic recovery of the plastically deformed sheet after unloading; causes distortion of part and loss of dimensional accuracy; can be controlled by techniques such as overbending and bottoming of the punch.
Wrinkling	Caused by compressive stresses in the plane of the sheet; can be objectionable or can be useful in imparting stiffness to parts; can be controlled by proper tool and die design.
Quality of sheared edges	Depends on process used; edges can be rough, not square, and contain cracks, residual stresses, and a work-hardened layer, which are all detrimental to the formability of the sheet; quality can be improved by control of clearance, tool and die design, fine blanking, shaving, and lubrication.
Surface condition of sheet	Depends on rolling practice; important in sheet forming as it can cause tearing and poor surface quality; see also Section 13.3.

Necking may be *localized* or it may be *diffuse*, depending on the *strain-rate sensitivity* (m) of the material; this relationship is given in Eq. (2.9). The higher the value of m, the more diffuse the neck becomes; diffuseness is desirable in sheet-forming operations.

In addition to uniform elongation and necking, the **total elongation** of the specimen (in terms of that for a 50 mm (2 in.) gage length) is also a significant factor in the formability of sheet metals. Obviously, the total elongation of the material increases with increasing values of both n and m.

16.3.2 Yield-Point Elongation

Low-carbon steels exhibit a behavior called *yield-point elongation*, one having upper and lower yield points (Fig. 16.12a). This behavior indicates that, after the material yields, the sheet stretches farther in certain regions without any increase in the lower yield point, while other regions in the sheet have not yet yielded. Aluminum–magnesium alloys also exhibit this behavior.

This behavior produces **Lueder's bands (stretcher strain marks** or *worms*) on the sheet (Fig. 16.12b); they are elongated depressions on the surface of the sheet, such as can be found on the bottom of cans used for common household products (Fig. 16.12c). They may be objectionable in the final product, because coarseness in the surface degrades appearance and causes difficulties in subsequent coating and painting operations.

The usual method of avoiding these marks is to eliminate or to reduce yield-point elongation, by reducing the thickness of the sheet 0.5% to 1.5% by cold rolling (**temper** or **skin rolling**). Because of strain aging (Section 2.10.1), however, the yield-point elongation

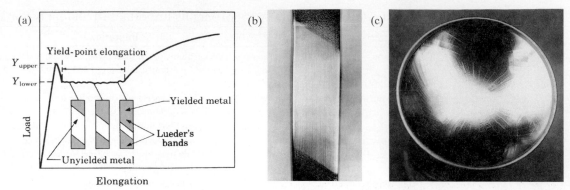

FIGURE 16.12   (a) Yield-point elongation in a sheet-metal specimen. (b) Lueder's bands in a low-carbon steel sheet. *Source*: Courtesy of Caterpillar Inc. (c) Stretcher strains at the bottom of a steel can for household products.

reappears after a few days at room temperature—or after a few hours at higher temperatures. To prevent this undesirable occurrence, one should form the material within a certain time limit (which depends on the type of the steel).

16.3.3 Anisotropy

An important factor that influences sheet-metal forming is *anisotropy* (directionality) of the sheet. Recall that anisotropy is acquired during the thermo-mechanical processing of the sheet, and that there are two types of anisotropy (Section 1.5): *crystallographic anisotropy* (preferred orientation of the grains) and *mechanical fibering* (alignment of impurities, inclusions, and voids throughout the thickness of the sheet). This subject is discussed further in Section 16.9.

16.3.4 Grain Size

The grain size of the sheet metal is important for two reasons. As described in Section 1.4, grain size affects mechanical properties, and it influences the surface appearance of the formed part (**orange peel**). The coarser the grain, the rougher is the surface appearance. An ASTM grain size of 7 or finer (Table 1.1) is preferred for general sheet-metal forming operations.

16.4 TEST METHODS FOR FORMABILITY OF SHEET METALS

Sheet-metal **formability** is of great technological and economic interest. It is normally defined as the ability of the sheet metal to undergo the desired shape change without such failure as necking or tearing. As we shall see throughout the rest of this chapter, sheet metals may (depending on part geometry) undergo two basic modes of deformation: (a) *stretching* and (b) *drawing* (described in Section 16.9).

There are important distinctions between these two modes, and different parameters are involved in determining formability under these different conditions. This section describes the methods that are generally used in manufacturing industries to predict formability.

16.4.1 Cupping Tests

Because sheet-forming is basically a process of stretching the material, the earliest tests developed to predict formability were cupping tests (Fig. 16.13a). The sheet-metal specimen

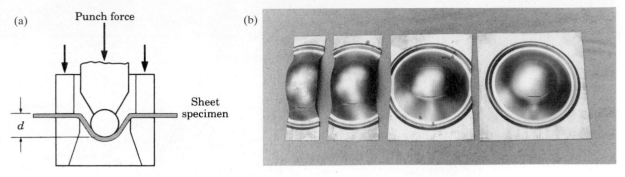

(a)   Punch force

Sheet specimen

d

(b)

FIGURE 16.13   (a) A cupping test (the Erichsen test) to determine the formability of sheet metals. (b) Bulge-test results on steel sheets of various widths. The specimen farthest left is subjected to, basically, simple tension. The specimen farthest right is subjected to equal biaxial stretching. *Source*: Inland Steel Company.

is clamped between two circular flat dies, and a steel ball or round punch is pushed hydraulically into the sheet metal until a crack begins to appear on the stretched specimen.

The greater the value is of the punch depth d, the greater is the formability of the sheet. Although such tests are easy to perform (and *are* approximate indicators of formability), they do not simulate the exact conditions of actual sheet-forming operations.

16.4.2 Forming-Limit Diagrams

An important development in testing the formability of sheet metals is the **forming-limit diagram (FLD)**. The sheet is marked with a grid pattern of circles, typically 2.5 to 5 mm (0.1 to 0.2 in.) in diameter, using electrochemical or photoprinting techniques. The blank is then stretched over a punch, and the deformation of the circles is observed and measured in regions where failure (*necking* and *tearing*) has occurred. For improved accuracy of measurement, the circles are made as small as practicable.

In order to develop unequal stretching, as in actual sheet-forming operations, the specimens are cut to varying widths (Fig. 16.13b). Note that a square specimen (farthest right in the figure) produces **equal biaxial stretching** (such as that achieved in blowing up a spherical balloon), whereas a narrow specimen (farthest left in the figure) approaches a state of **uniaxial stretching** (simple tension). After a series of such tests is performed on a particular sheet metal at different widths, a forming-limit diagram showing the boundaries between *failure* and *safe* regions is constructed (Fig. 16.14).

In order to develop the forming-limit diagram, the major and minor engineering strains, as measured from the deformation of the original circles, are obtained as follows. Note in Fig. 16.14a that the original circle has deformed into an ellipse. The *major axis* of the ellipse represents the major direction and magnitude of stretching. The major strain is the *engineering strain* in this direction, and is always *positive*, because of sheet-metal stretching. The *minor axis* of the ellipse represents the magnitude of the stretching or shrinking in the *transverse* direction of the sheet metal.

Note that the minor strain can be either *negative* or *positive*. If, for example, a circle is placed in the center of a tensile-test specimen and then stretched, the specimen becomes narrower as it is stretched (Poisson effect), and the minor strain is negative. (This behavior can easily be demonstrated by stretching a rubber band.) On the other hand, if we place a circle on a spherical rubber balloon and inflate it, the minor and major strains are both positive and equal in magnitude.

(a)   (b)

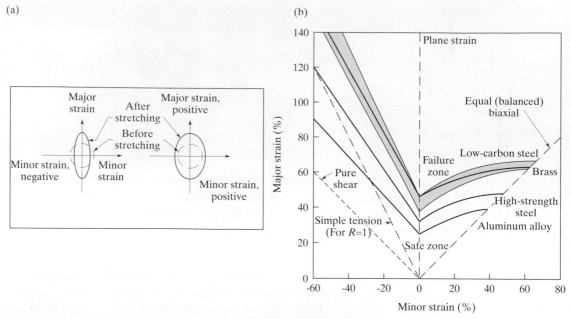

FIGURE 16.14   (a) Strains in deformed circular grid patterns. (b) Forming-limit diagrams (FLD) for various sheet metals. Although the major strain is always positive (stretching), the minor strain may be either positive or negative. In the lower left of the diagram, *R* is the normal anisotropy of the sheet, as described in Section 16.9.2. *Source*: S. S. Hecker and A. K. Ghosh.

By comparing the *surface areas* of the original circle and the deformed circle on the formed sheet, we can also determine whether the thickness of the sheet has changed. Because the volume remains constant in plastic deformation, we know that if the area of the deformed circle is larger than the original circle, the sheet has become thinner. This phenomenon can be observed by blowing up a balloon and noting that it becomes more translucent (because of getting thinner) as it is stretched.

The data obtained from different locations in each of the samples shown in Fig. 16.13b are plotted in the form shown in Fig. 16.14b. The curves represent the boundaries between failure and safe zones. Thus, if a circle underwent major and minor strains of plus and minus 40%, respectively, there would be no tear in that region of the specimen. On the other hand, if the major and minor strains in an aluminum-alloy specimen were plus 80% and minus 40%, respectively, there would be a tear in that region of the specimen.

An example of a formed sheet-metal part with a grid pattern is shown in Fig. 16.15. Note the tear, and note the deformation of the circular patterns in the vicinity of the tear re-

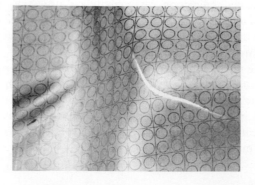

FIGURE 16.15   The deformation of the grid pattern and the tearing of sheet metal during forming. The major and minor axes of the circles are used to determine the coordinates on the forming-limit diagram in Fig. 16.14b. *Source*: S. P. Keeler.

gion. Figure 16.14b shows that different materials have different forming-limit diagrams and that the higher the curve, the better the formability of the material.

It is important to note that a compressive minor strain of, say, 20% is associated with a higher major strain than is a tensile (positive) minor strain of the same magnitude. In other words, it is desirable for the minor strain to be negative (shrinking in the minor direction). In the forming of complex sheet-metal parts, special tooling can be designed to take advantage of the beneficial effect of negative minor strains on formability.

The effect of sheet-metal thickness on forming-limit diagrams is to raise the curves in Fig. 16.14b. The thicker the sheet, the higher its formability curve, and the more formable it is. On the other hand, in actual forming operations, a thick blank may not bend as easily around small radii without cracking (Section 16.5).

The friction and the lubrication at the interface between the punch and the sheet metal are important factors in the test results. With well-lubricated interfaces, the strains are more uniformly distributed over the punch. Furthermore, surface scratches, deep gouges, and blemishes can reduce formability and can thereby cause premature tearing and failure.

16.5 BENDING SHEET AND PLATE

Bending is one of the most common forming operations. We merely have to look at the components in an automobile or an appliance—or at a paper clip or a file cabinet—to appreciate how many parts are shaped by bending. Bending is used not only to form flanges, seams, and corrugations but also to impart stiffness to the part (by increasing its moment of inertia).

The terminology used in bending is shown in Fig. 16.16. Note that, in bending, the outer fibers of the material are in tension, while the inner fibers are in compression. Because of the Poisson's ratio, the width of the part (bend length, L) in the outer region is smaller, and in the inner region it is larger, than the original width (see Fig. 16.17c). This phenomenon may easily be observed by bending a rectangular rubber eraser.

As shown in Fig. 16.16, the **bend allowance** is the length of the *neutral axis* in the bend and is used to determine the blank length for a bent part. However, the position of the neutral axis depends on the radius and angle of bend (as described in texts on mechanics of materials). An approximate formula for the bend allowance, L_b, is given by

$$L_b = \alpha(R + kT),\qquad(16.2)$$

where α is the bend angle (in radians), T is the sheet thickness, R is the bend radius, and k is a constant. Note that, for the ideal case, the neutral axis is at the center of the sheet thickness, $k = 0.5$, and, hence,

$$L_b = \alpha\left[R + \left(\frac{T}{2}\right)\right].\qquad(16.3)$$

In practice, k values usually range from 0.33 (for $R < 2T$) to 0.5 (for $R > 2T$).

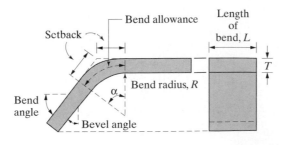

FIGURE 16.16   Bending terminology. Note that the bend radius is measured to the inner surface of the bent part.

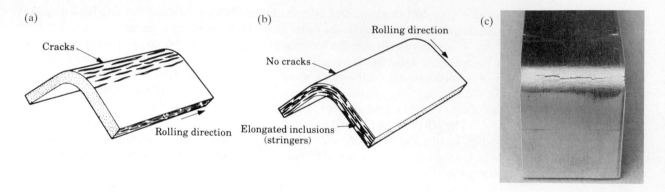

FIGURE 16.17   (a) and (b) The effect of elongated inclusions (stringers) on cracking, as a function of the direction of bending with respect to the original rolling direction of the sheet. (c) Cracks on the outer surface of an aluminum strip bent to an angle of 90°. Note the narrowing of the top surface due to Poisson effect.

16.5.1 Minimum Bend Radius

The engineering strain on a sheet during bending is

$$e = \frac{1}{(2R/T) + 1}.$$

(16.4)

As R/T decreases (the ratio of the bend radius to the thickness becomes smaller), the tensile strain at the outer fiber increases, and the material eventually cracks (Fig. 16.17).

The ratio at which a crack appears on the outer surface of the bend is referred to as the **minimum bend radius** for the material. It is usually expressed (reciprocally) in terms of the thickness, such as $2T$, $3T$, $4T$, and so on. Thus, a $3T$ minimum bend radius indicates that the *smallest radius* to which the sheet can be bent, without cracking, is three times its thickness. The minimum bend radius for various materials is given in Table 16.3.

There is an inverse relationship between **bendability** and the tensile reduction of area of the material (Fig. 16.18). The minimum bend radius is, approximately,

$$R = T\left(\frac{50}{r - 1}\right),$$

(16.5)

TABLE 16.3   Minimum Bend Radius for Various Materials at Room Temperature

Material	Condition	
	Soft	Hard
Aluminum alloys	0	$6T$
Beryllium copper	0	$4T$
Brass, low-leaded	0	$2T$
Magnesium	$5T$	$13T$
Steels		
Austenitic stainless	$0.5T$	$6T$
Low-carbon, low-alloy, and HSLA	$0.5T$	$4T$
Titanium	$0.7T$	$3T$
Titanium alloys	$2.6T$	$4T$

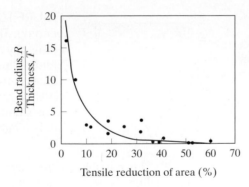

FIGURE 16.18   Relationship between R/T ratio and tensile reduction of area for sheet metals. Note that sheet metal with a 50% tensile reduction of area can be bent over itself, in a process like the folding of a piece of paper, without cracking. *Source*: After J. Datsko ans C.T. Yang.

where r is the tensile reduction of area of the sheet metal. Note that for $r = 50$, the minimum bend radius is zero; that is, the sheet can be folded over itself, in much the same way as a piece of paper. To increase the bendability of metals, we may increase their tensile reduction of area, either by heating or by bending in a high-pressure environment.

Bendability depends on the *edge condition* of the sheet. Since rough edges are points of stress concentration, bendability decreases as edge roughness increases. Another significant factor in edge cracking is the amount and shape of inclusions in the sheet metal and the amount of cold working that the edges undergo during shearing. Because of their pointed shape, inclusions in the form of stringers are more detrimental than globular-shaped inclusions. The removal of the cold-worked regions by, for example, machining the part, or by annealing it to improve its ductility, greatly improves the resistance to edge cracking.

Anisotropy of the sheet is an important factor in bendability. As shown in Fig. 1.13, cold rolling produces anisotropy by *preferred orientation* and by *mechanical fibering* due to the alignment of whatever impurities, inclusions, and voids may be present. Prior to the bending of such a sheet, caution should be exercised in cutting it in the proper direction from a rolled sheet (although this choice may not always be possible).

Whether or not a sheet is anisotropic can be determined by observing the direction of cracking in the cupping test (Fig. 16.13). If the crack is as shown in Fig. 1.13, the sheet is anisotropic; if it is circular, the sheet is isotropic.

16.5.2 Springback

Because all materials have a finite modulus of elasticity, plastic deformation is followed, when the load is removed, by some elastic recovery (see Fig. 2.3). In bending, this recovery is called *springback*; you can easily observe it by bending then releasing a piece of sheet metal or wire. As noted in Fig. 16.18, the final bend angle after springback is smaller, and the final bend radius is larger, than before bending. Springback occurs not only in flat sheets and plate, but also in rod, wire, and bar with any cross-section.

Springback can be calculated approximately in terms of the radii R_i and R_f (Fig. 16.19), as

$$\frac{R_i}{R_f} = 4\left(\frac{R_i Y}{ET}\right)^3 - 3\left(\frac{R_i Y}{ET}\right) + 1. \qquad \textbf{(16.6)}$$

Note from this formula that springback increases (a) as the R/T ratio and the yield stress Y of the material increase and (b) as the elastic modulus E decreases.

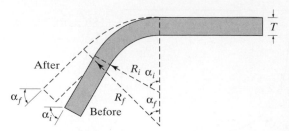

FIGURE 16.19   Springback in bending. The part tends to recover elastically after bending, and its bend radius becomes larger. Under certain conditions, it is possible for the final bend angle to be smaller than the original angle (negative springback).

In V-die bending (Fig. 16.20), it is possible for the material to exhibit *negative*, as well as positive, springback. This condition is caused by the nature of the deformation which is occurring just as the punch completes the bending operation at the end of the stroke. Negative springback does not occur in air bending (*free bending*) because of the lack of the constraints that a V-die imposes.

Compensation for Springback.   In forming operations, springback is usually compensated for by *overbending* the part (Figs. 16.20a and b); several trials may be necessary to obtain the desired results. Another method is to *coin* the bend area by subjecting it to high localized compressive stresses between the technique tip of the punch and the die surface (Figs. 16.20c and d); this technique is known as *bottoming* the punch. Another method is *stretch bending*, in which the part is subjected to tension while being bent. In order to reduce springback bending may also be carried out at elevated temperatures.

16.5.3 Bending Force

Bending forces can be estimated by assuming that the process is one of simple bending of a rectangular beam. The bending force in that case is a function of the strength of the material, the length L of the bend, the thickness T of the sheet, and the size, W, of the die opening (Fig. 16.21). Excluding friction, the *maximum bending force*, P, is

$$P = \frac{kYLT^2}{W},$$ (16.7)

where the factor k ranges from about 0.3 for a wiping die, to about 0.7 for a U-die, to about 1.3 for a V-die, and Y is the yield stress of the material. (See Section 2.2.)

For a V-die, this equation can often be approximated as

$$P = \frac{(\text{UTS})LT^2}{W},$$ (16.8)

FIGURE 16.20   Methods of reducing or eliminating springback in bending operations. *Source*: V. Cupka, T. Nakagawa, and H. Tyamoto.

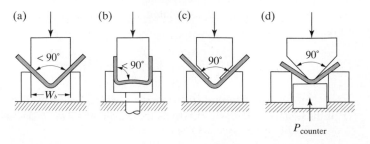

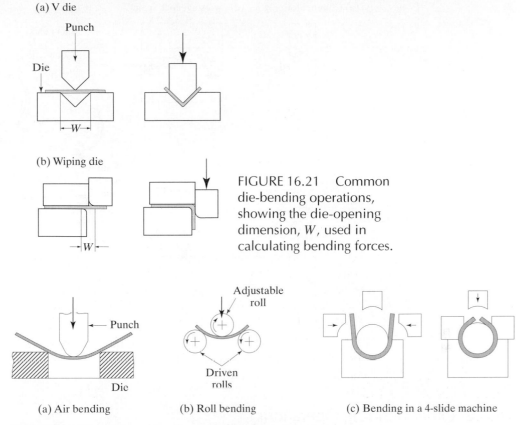

FIGURE 16.21   Common die-bending operations, showing the die-opening dimension, *W*, used in calculating bending forces.

FIGURE 16.22   Examples of various bending operations.

where UTS is the ultimate tensile strength of the material. This equation applies well to situations in which the punch radius and the sheet thickness are small compared to the die opening, *W*.

The bending force is also a function of the progress of the punch through the bending cycle. It increases from zero to a maximum, and it may even decrease as the bend is completed; it then increases sharply as the punch reaches the bottom of its stroke during die bending. In air bending (Fig. 16.22a), or free bending, the force does not increase again after it begins to decrease.

16.6 COMMON BENDING OPERATIONS

Several bending operations commonly used in industry are described in this section.

16.6.1 Press Brake Forming

Sheet metal or plate can be bent easily with simple fixtures using a press. Sheets 7 m (20 ft) or longer, and other relatively narrow pieces, are usually bent in a *press brake* (Fig. 16.23). This machine utilizes long dies in a mechanical or hydraulic press and is suitable for small production runs. The tooling is simple, and it is adaptable to a wide variety of shapes; furthermore, the process can be easily automated.

Die materials for press brakes may range from hardwood (for low-strength materials and small production runs) to carbides. For most applications, carbon-steel or gray-iron dies are generally used. (See also Section 5.7.)

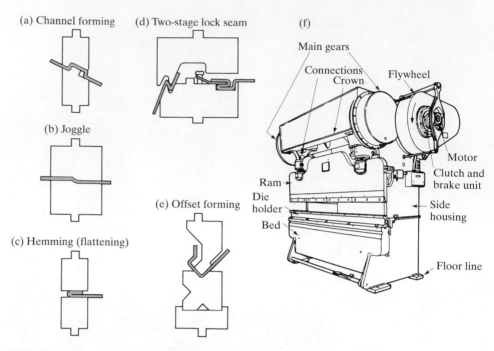

FIGURE 16.23 (a) through (e) Schematic illustrations of various bending operations in a press brake. (f) Schematic illustration of a press brake. *Source*: Verson Allsteel Company.

16.6.2 Other Bending Operations

Sheet metal may also be bent by a variety of processes, as described below.

Roll-Bending. In this process (Fig. 16.22b), plates are bent using a set of rolls. By adjusting the distance between the three rolls, various curvatures can be obtained.

Bending in a 4-Slide Machine. Bending of relatively short pieces can also be done on machines such as that shown in Fig. 16.22c. These machines are available in a variety of designs, and the lateral movements of the dies are controlled and synchronized with the vertical die movement to form the part to desired shapes.

Beading. In *beading*, the periphery of the sheet metal is bent into the cavity of a die (Figs. 16.24a and b). The bead imparts stiffness to the part by increasing the moment of in-

FIGURE 16.24 (a) Bead forming with a single die. (b) Bead forming with two dies, in a press brake.

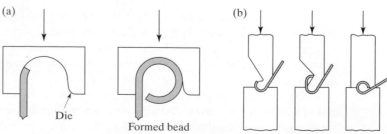

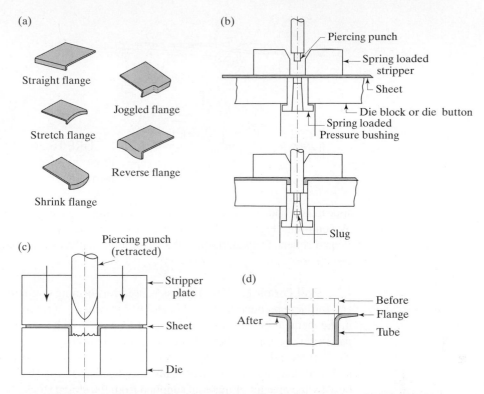

FIGURE 16.25   Various flanging operations. (a) Flanges on flat sheet. (b) Dimpling. (c) The piercing of sheet metal to form a flange. In this operation, a hole does not have to be prepunched before the punch descends. Note, however, the rough edges along the circumference of the flange. (d) The flanging of a tube; note the thinning of the edges of the flange.

ertia of that section. Also, it improves the appearance of the part and eliminates exposed sharp edges.

Flanging.   *Flanging* is a process of bending the edges of sheet metals, usually to 90°. In **shrink flanging** (Fig. 16.25a), the flange is subjected to compressive hoop stresses which, if excessive, can cause the flange edges to wrinkle. The wrinkling tendency increases with a decrease in the radius of curvature of the flange. In **stretch flanging**, the flange edges are subjected to tensile stresses that, if excessive, can lead to cracking along the periphery.

Dimpling.   In this operation (Fig. 16.25b), first a hole is punched, and then it is expanded into a flange. Flanges may be produced by **piercing** with a shaped punch (Fig. 16.25c). The ends of tubes also can be flanged by a similar process (Fig. 16.25d). When the bend angle is less than 90°, as in fittings with conical ends, the process is called **flaring**.

The condition of the edges (see Fig. 16.3) is important in these operations. Stretching the material causes high tensile stresses at the edges, which could lead to cracking and tearing of the flange. As the ratio of flange diameter to hole diameter increases, the strains increase proportionately. The rougher the edge, the greater will be the tendency for cracking. Sheared or punched edges may be shaven off with a sharp tool (see Fig. 16.9), to improve the surface finish of the edge and thus reduce the possibility of cracking.

Hemming.   In the *hemming* process (also called *flattening*), the edge of the sheet is folded over itself (Fig. 16.23c). Hemming increases the stiffness of the part, improves its

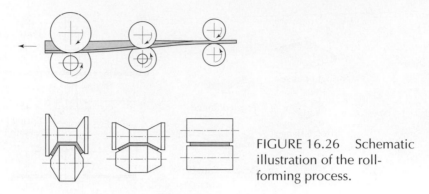

FIGURE 16.26 Schematic illustration of the roll-forming process.

appearance, and eliminates sharp edges. **Seaming** involves joining two edges of sheet metal by hemming (Fig. 16.23d). Double seams are made by a similar process, using specially shaped rollers, for watertight and airtight joints, such as are needed in food and beverage containers.

Roll Forming. This process is used for forming continuous lengths of sheet metal and for large production runs; it is also called *contour roll forming* or *cold roll forming*. In it, the metal strip is bent in stages by passing it through a series of rolls (Fig. 16.26). The parts are then usually sheared and stacked continuously.

Typical products made are channels, gutters, siding, panels, door and picture frames, and pipes and tubing with lock seams (see Section 30.5). The length of the part is limited only by the amount of material supplied from the coiled stock. The sheet thickness usually ranges from about 0.125 mm to 20 mm (0.005 in. to 0.75 in.). Forming speeds are generally below 1.5 m/s (300 ft/min), although they can be much higher for special applications.

The design and sequencing of the rolls, which usually are mechanically driven, requires considerable experience. Tolerances, springback, and tearing and buckling of the strip have to be considered. The rolls are generally made of carbon steel or of gray iron, and they may be chromium plated for better surface finish of the formed product and for better wear resistance of the rolls. Lubricants may be used to improve roll life and surface finish and to cool the rolls and the workpiece.

16.7 TUBE BENDING AND FORMING

The bending and forming of tubes and of other hollow sections requires special tooling in order to avoid buckling and folding. The oldest and simplest method of bending a tube or pipe is first, to pack the inside with loose particles, commonly sand, and then to bend it in a suitable fixture. The filling prevents the tube from buckling. After the tube has been bent, the sand is shaken out. Tubes can also be plugged with various flexible internal mandrels (Fig. 16.27). A relatively thick tube having a large bend radius can be bent without filling it with particulates and without using plugs.

Bulging. This process involves placing a tubular, conical, or curvilinear part into a split-female die and then expanding it, usually with a polyurethane plug (Fig. 16.28a). The punch is then retracted, the plug returns to its original shape, and the formed part is removed by opening the dies. Typical products made are coffee or water pitchers, barrels, and beads on drums. For parts with complex shapes, the plug, instead of being cylindrical, may be shaped in order to apply higher pressure at critical regions. The major advantage of using

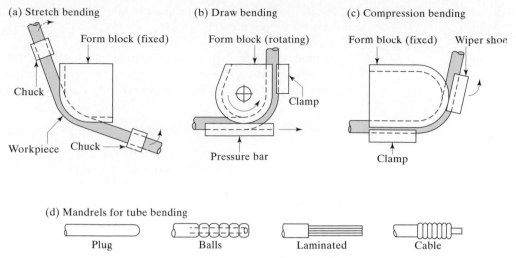

FIGURE 16.27   Methods of bending tubes. Internal mandrels, or the filling of tubes with particulate materials such as sand, are often necessary to prevent collapse of the tubes during bending. Solid rods and structural shapes can also be bent by these techniques.

polyurethane plugs is that they are very resistant to abrasion, wear, and lubricants; furthermore, they do not damage the surface finish of the part being formed.

Forming of tubes and of tubular shapes such as exhaust pipes, fuel filler tubes, and exhaust manifolds can also be done using internal fluid pressure (replacing the polyurethane plug), with the ends of the tubes sealed by mechanical means. The part expands in a

FIGURE 16.28   (a) The bulging of a tubular part with a flexible plug. Water pitchers can be made by this method. (b) Production of fittings for plumbing, by expanding tubular blanks under internal pressure. The bottom of the piece is then punched out to produce a "T." *Source*: J. A. Schey, *Introduction to Manufacturing Processes* (2d ed.). New York: McGraw-Hill Publishing Company, 1987.

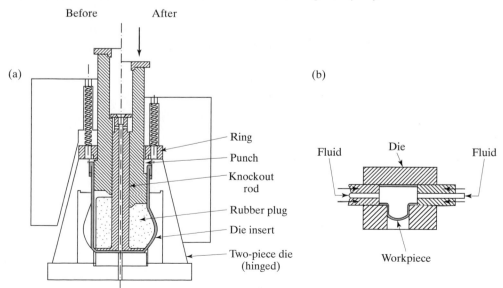

split-female die at pressures on the order of 600 MPa (90,000 psi); the die is then opened to remove the formed part (Fig. 16.28b).

Segmented Dies.   These dies consist of individual segments that are placed inside the part, then mechanically expanded in a generally radial direction, and finally retracted. Segmented dies are relatively inexpensive, and they can be used for large production runs.

Example: Manufacturing of Bellows

Bellows are manufactured by a bulging process, as shown in Fig. 16.29. After the tube is bulged at several equidistant locations, it is compressed axially to collapse the bulged regions, thus forming bellows. The tube material must be able to undergo the large strains involved during the collapsing process.

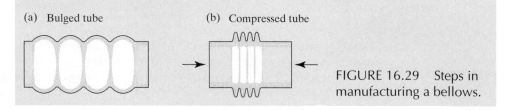

(a) Bulged tube

(b) Compressed tube

FIGURE 16.29   Steps in manufacturing a bellows.

16.8 STRETCH FORMING

In *stretch forming*, the sheet metal is clamped along its edges and then stretched over a die or *form block*, which moves upward, downward, or sideways, depending on the particular machine (Fig. 16.30). Stretch forming is used primarily to make aircraft wing-skin panels, automobile door panels, and window frames. Aluminum skins for the Boeing 767 and 757 aircraft are made by stretch forming, with a tensile force of 9 MN (2 million lb). The rectangular sheets are 12 m $\times$ 2.5 m $\times$ 6.4 mm (40 ft $\times$ 8.3 ft $\times$ 0.25 in.).

In most operations, the blank is a rectangular sheet, clamped along its narrower edges and stretched lengthwise, thus allowing the material to shrink in width. Controlling the amount of stretching is important to avoid tearing. Stretch forming cannot produce parts with sharp contours or with re-entrant corners (depressions on the surface of the die).

FIGURE 16.30   Schematic illustration of a stretch-forming process. Aluminum skins for aircraft can be made by this method. *Source*: Cyril Bath Co.

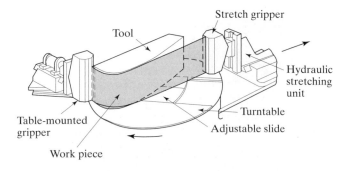

Dies for stretch forming are generally made of zinc alloys, steel, plastics, or wood. Most applications require little or no lubrication. Various accessory equipment can be used in conjunction with stretch forming, including additional forming with both male and female dies while the part is in tension. Although this process is generally used for low-volume production, it is versatile and economical.

16.9 DEEP DRAWING

Many parts made of sheet metal are cylindrical or box-shaped: for example, pots and pans, containers for food and beverages (Fig. 16.31), kitchen sinks, and automotive fuel tanks. Such parts are usually made by a process in which a punch forces a flat sheet-metal blank into a die cavity

FIGURE 16.31   The metal-forming processes involved in manufacturing a two-piece aluminum beverage can.

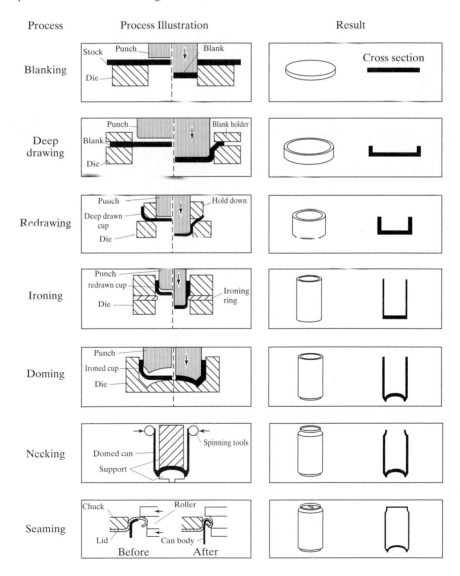

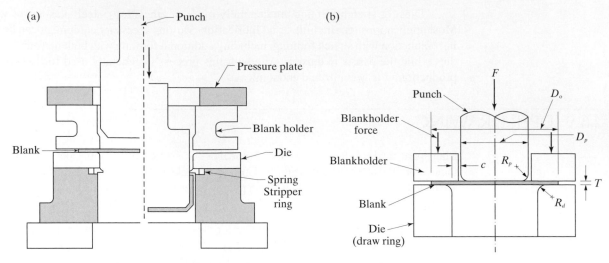

FIGURE 16.32 (a) Schematic illustration of the deep-drawing process on a circular sheet-metal blank. The stripper ring facilitates the removal of the formed cup from the punch. (b) Process variables in deep drawing. Except for the punch force, F, all the parameters indicated in the figure are independent variables.

(Fig. 16.32a). Although the process is generally called *deep drawing*, on account of its capability of producing deep parts, it is also used to make parts that are shallow or have moderate depth.

16.9.1 The Deep-Drawing Process

In the basic method, a round sheet-metal blank is placed over a circular die opening and is held in place with a **blankholder**, or *hold-down ring* (Fig. 16.32b). The punch travels downward and forces the blank into the die cavity, forming a cup. The important variables in deep drawing are the properties of the sheet metal, the ratio of blank diameter (D_o) to punch diameter (D_p), the clearance (c) between punch and die, the punch radius (R_p), the die-corner radius (R_d), the blankholder force, and friction and lubrication.

During the **drawing** operation, the movement of the blank into the die cavity induces compressive circumferential (hoop) stresses in the flange, which tend to cause the flange to **wrinkle** during drawing. This phenomenon can be demonstrated by trying to force a circular piece of paper into a round cavity such as a drinking glass. Wrinkling can be reduced or eliminated if a blankholder is kept under the effect of a certain force. In order to improve performance the magnitude of this force can be controlled as a function of punch travel.

The cup wall, which is already formed, is subjected principally to a longitudinal tensile stress. Elongation causes the cup wall to thin; if excessive, it causes tearing. Because of the many variables involved, the punch force F is difficult to calculate; it increases with increase in the strength, the diameter, and the thickness of the sheet-metal blank.

16.9.2 Deep Drawability

In a deep-drawing operation, failure generally results from a *thinning* of the cup wall under high longitudinal tensile stresses. If we follow the movement of the material into the die cavity, it can be seen that the sheet metal must be capable of undergoing a reduction in width due to reduction in diameter; the sheet should also resist thinning under the longitudinal

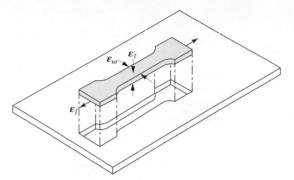

FIGURE 16.33   Strains on a tensile-test specimen removed from a piece of sheet metal. These strains are used in determining the normal and planar anisotropy of the sheet metal.

tensile stresses in the cup wall. *Deep drawability* is generally expressed by the **limiting drawing ratio (LDR)**:

$$LDR = \frac{\text{Maximum blank diameter}}{\text{Punch diameter}} = \frac{D_o}{D_p}. \tag{16.9}$$

Whether a sheet metal can successfully be deep drawn into a round cup-shaped part has been found to be a function of the *normal anisotropy*, R, of the sheet metal, also called its **plastic anisotropy**. Normal anisotropy is defined in terms of the true strains that the specimen undergoes in tension (Fig. 16.33):

$$R = \frac{\text{Width strain}}{\text{Thickness strain}} = \frac{\varepsilon_w}{\varepsilon_t}. \tag{16.10}$$

In order to obtain the value of R, a tensile-test specimen is first prepared and then subjected to an elongation of from 15% to 20%, and the true strains are calculated in the manner discussed in Section 2.2. Because cold-rolled sheets generally have anisotropy in their *planar* direction, the R value of a specimen cut from a rolled sheet will depend on its orientation with respect to the rolling direction of the sheet. In this case, an average value $\left(R_{avg}\right)$ is calculated from the equation

$$R_{avg} = \frac{R_0 + 2R_{45} + R_{90}}{4}, \tag{16.11}$$

where the angles are relative to the rolling direction of the sheet. Some typical R_{avg} values are given in Table 16.4.

The experimentally determined relationship between R_{avg} and the limiting drawing ratio is shown in Fig. 16.34. No other mechanical property of sheet metal shows as consistent a relationship to LDR as does R_{avg}. Thus, by using a tensile-test result and by obtaining the normal anisotropy of the sheet metal, the limiting drawing ratio of a material can be determined.

TABLE 16.4   Typical Range of Average Normal Anisotropy, R, for Various Sheet Metals

Zinc alloys	0.4–0.6
Hot-rolled steel	0.8–1.0
Cold-rolled rimmed steel	1.0–1.4
Cold-rolled aluminum-killed steel	1.4–1.8
Aluminum alloys	0.6–0.8
Copper and brass	0.6–0.9
Titanium alloys (α)	3.0–5.0
Stainless steels	0.9–1.2
High-strength low-alloy steels	0.9–1.2

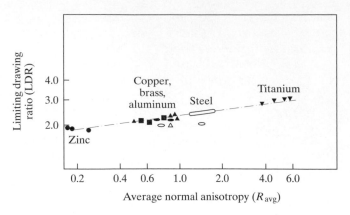

FIGURE 16.34   The relationship between average normal anisotropy and the limiting drawing ratio for various sheet metals. *Source*: M. Atkinson.

Earing and Planar Anisotropy.   In drawing, the edges of cups may become wavy; this phenomenon is called *earing* (Fig. 16.35). This condition is caused by the *planar anisotropy* of the sheet, indicated by ΔR. It is defined in terms of directional R values from the equation

$$\Delta R = \frac{R_0 - 2R_{45} + R_{90}}{2}. \qquad (16.12)$$

When $\Delta R = 0$, no ears form. The height of the ears increases as ΔR increases. The number of ears produced may be two, four, or eight. Ears are objectionable on drawn cups, because they have to be trimmed off, resulting in scrap.

It can be seen that deep drawability is enhanced by a high R_{avg} value and a low ΔR. Generally, however, sheet metals with high R_{avg} also have high ΔR values. Sheet-metal textures are being developed to improve drawability, by controlling the type of alloying elements in the material as well as various processing parameters, during rolling of the sheet.

16.9.3 Deep Drawing Practice

Certain guidelines have been established for successful deep drawing practice. The blankholder pressure is generally chosen as 0.7% to 1.0% of the sum of the yield strength

FIGURE 16.35   Earing in a drawn steel cup, caused by the planar anisotropy of the sheet metal.

and the ultimate tensile strength of the sheet metal. Too high a blankholder force increases the punch force and causes the cup wall to tear; on the other hand, wrinkling will occur if the blankholder force is too low.

Clearances are usually 7% to 14% greater than sheet thickness. If the clearance is too small, the blank may be simply pierced or sheared by the punch. The corner radii of the punch and of the die are also important. If they are too small, they can cause fracture at the corners; if they are too large, the cup wall may wrinkle (in a phenomenon called *puckering*).

Drawbeads (Fig. 16.36a) are often necessary to control the flow of the blank into the die cavity. Beads restrict the flow of the sheet metal by bending and unbending it during drawing; they thereby increase the force required to pull the sheet into the die cavity. Drawbeads also help to reduce the required blankholder forces, because the beaded sheet has a higher stiffness and hence a lower tendency to wrinkle. Drawbead diameters may range from 13 mm to 20 mm (0.50 in. to 0.75 in.), the latter being for large stampings such as automotive panels.

Deep drawing of *box-shaped* and of *nonsymmetric* parts can present significant difficulties in practice (Figs. 16.36b and c). Note in sketch (c), for example, that various regions of the part undergo different types of deformation during drawing.

In order to avoid tearing of the sheet metal during forming, it is important to incorporate such factors as (1) large die radii, (2) effective lubrication, (3) the design and location of draw beads, (4) the development of proper blank size and shape, (5) the cutting off of corners of square or rectangular blanks at 45° to reduce tensile stresses during drawing, and (6) the use of blanks free of internal and external defects.

Ironing.   Note in Fig. 16.32 that if the clearance is large, the drawn cup will have thicker walls at its rim than at its base. The reason is that the rim consists of material from the outer diameter of the blank, which was reduced in diameter more than that constituting the rest of the cup wall. As a result, the cup will have a nonuniform wall thickness. *Ironing* is a process in which the wall thickness of a drawn cup is made constant by the pushing of

FIGURE 16.36   (a) Schematic illustration of a draw bead. (b) Metal flow during the drawing of a box-shaped part, while using beads to control the movement of the material. (c) Deformation of circular grids in the flange in deep drawing.

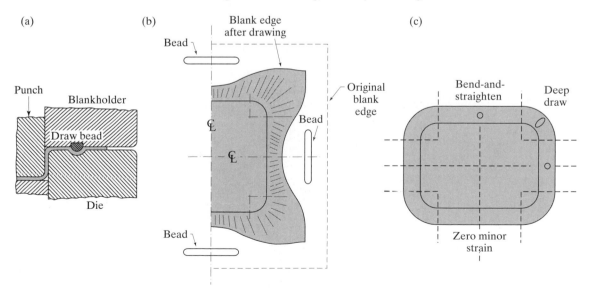

the cup through ironing rings (see Fig. 16.31). Aluminum beverage cans, for example, undergo two or three ironing operations in one stroke in which the drawn cup is pushed through a set of ironing rings.

Redrawing.   Containers or shells that are too difficult to draw in one operation generally undergo *redrawing*. (See Fig. 16.31.) Because of volume constancy, the cup becomes longer as it is redrawn to smaller diameters. In *reverse* redrawing, the cup is placed upside down in the die and thus subjected to bending in the direction opposite to its original configuration.

Drawing without Blankholder.   Deep drawing may also be carried out successfully without a blankholder, provided that the sheet metal is sufficiently thick to prevent wrinkling. A typical range is

$$D_o - D_p < 5T, \tag{16.13}$$

where T is the sheet thickness. The dies are specially contoured for this operation.

Embossing.   This is an operation consisting of shallow or moderate draws, made with male and female matching dies (Fig. 16.37). Embossing is used principally for the stiffening of flat panels and for purposes of decoration.

Lubrication.   In deep drawing, lubrication lowers forces, increases drawability, and reduces defects in the parts and wear on the tooling. In general, lubrication of the punch should be held to a minimum, because friction between the punch and the cup improves drawability by reducing tensile stresses in the cup. For general applications, commonly used lubricants are mineral oils, soap solutions, and heavy-duty emulsions. For more difficult applications, coatings, wax, and solid lubricants are used.

Tooling and Equipment for Drawing.   The most common tool and die materials for deep drawing are tool steels and cast irons, although other materials, such as carbides and plastics, may also be used. The equipment for deep drawing is usually a *double-action* hydraulic press or a mechanical press, the latter being generally favored because of its higher punch speed. The double-action hydraulic press controls the punch and the blankholder independently. Punch speeds generally range between 0.1 m/s and 0.3 m/s (20 ft/min and 60 ft/min).

Modern production facilities are highly automated. For example, a single plant can produce up to 100,000 automotive oil-filter cans per day. The blanks are fed and transferred automatically with robot-controlled mechanical fingers (Section 38.7). Lubricant spraying is

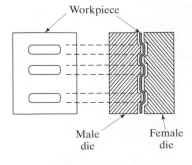

FIGURE 16.37   An embossing operation with two dies. Letters, numbers, and designs on sheet-metal parts and thin ash trays can be produced by this process.

Workpiece

Male die   Female die

synchronized with press stroke and the parts are transferred with magnetic or vacuum devices. Inspection systems monitor the entire drawing operation (see Section 36.11).

16.10 RUBBER FORMING

In the processes described in the preceding sections, it has been noted that the dies are generally made of solid materials. However, in *rubber forming*, one of the dies in a set can be made of a flexible material, such as a polyurethane membrane. Polyurethanes are used widely, because of their resistance to abrasion, their resistance to cutting by burrs or by sharp edges on the sheet metal, and their long fatigue life.

In the bending and embossing of sheet metal, the female die is replaced with a rubber pad (Fig. 16.38). Note that the outer surface of the sheet is protected from damage or scratches because it is not in contact with a hard metal surface during forming. Pressures in rubber forming are usually on the order of 10 MPa (1500 psi).

In the **hydroform** or *fluid-forming* process (Fig. 16.39), the pressure over the rubber membrane is controlled throughout the forming cycle, with maximum pressures of up to 100 MPa (15,000 psi). This procedure allows close control of the part during forming, to prevent wrinkling or tearing. Deeper draws are obtained than in conventional deep drawing, because the pressure around the rubber membrane forces the cup against the punch. As a result, the friction at the punch–cup interface increases; this increase reduces the longitudinal tensile stresses in the cup and delays fracture.

FIGURE 16.38   Examples of the bending and the embossing of sheet metal with a metal punch and with a flexible pad serving as the female die. *Source*: Polyurethane Products Corporation.

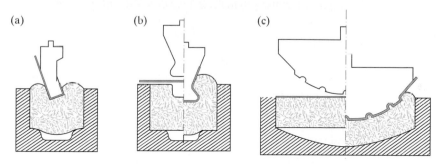

FIGURE 16.39   The hydroform (or fluid forming) process. Note that, in contrast to the ordinary deep-drawing process, the pressure in the dome forces the cup walls against the punch. The cup travels with the punch; in this way, deep drawability is improved.

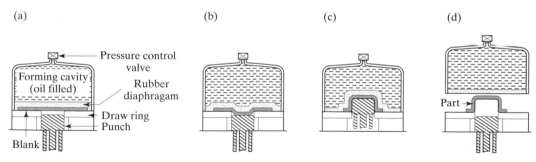

The control of frictional conditions in rubber forming and in other sheet-forming operations can be a critical factor in making parts successfully. The use of proper lubricants and application methods is also important.

When selected properly, rubber-forming processes have the advantages of (a) low tooling cost, (b) flexibility and ease of operation, (c) low die wear, (d) avoidance of damage to the surface of the sheet, and (e) capability to form complex shapes. Parts can also be formed with laminated sheets of various nonmetallic materials or coatings.

16.11 SPINNING

Spinning is an old process which involves the forming of axisymmetric parts over a mandrel, by the use of various tools and rollers. This process is somewhat similar to that of forming clay on a potter's wheel. As this section describes, there are three basic types of spinning techniques: conventional (or manual), shear, and tube spinning. The equipment used in these processes is similar to a lathe, but it has special features.

16.11.1 Conventional Spinning

In *conventional spinning*, a circular blank of flat or preformed sheet metal is held against a mandrel and rotated, while a rigid tool deforms and shapes the material over the mandrel (Fig. 16.40a). The tool may be activated either manually or by a computer-controlled hydraulic mechanism. The process involves a sequence of passes, and it requires considerable skill.

Conventional spinning is particularly suitable for conical and curvilinear shapes, which otherwise would be difficult or uneconomical to produce (Fig. 16.40b). Part diameters may range up to 6 m (20 ft). Although most spinning is performed at room temperature, thick parts, or metals with high strength or low ductility, require spinning at elevated temperatures.

16.11.2 Shear Spinning

Also known as *power spinning*, *flow turning*, *hydrospinning*, and *spin forging*, *shear spinning* produces an axisymmetric conical or curvilinear shape, while maintaining the part's maximum diameter and reducing its thickness (Fig. 16.41a). Although a single roller can be used, two rollers are preferable in order to balance the forces acting on the mandrel. Typical parts made are rocket-motor casings and missile nose cones.

FIGURE 16.40   (a) Schematic illustration of the conventional spinning process. (b) Types of parts conventionally spun. All parts are axisymmetric.

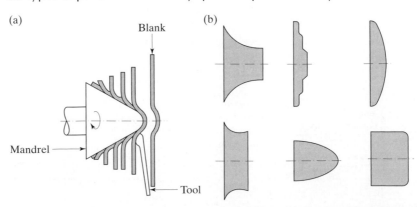

(a)

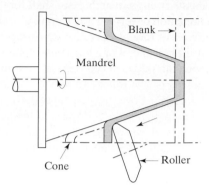

(b)

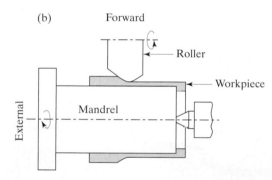

FIGURE 16.41   (a) Schematic illustration of the shear spinning process for making conical parts. The mandrel can be shaped so that curvilinear parts can be spun. (b) Schematic illustration of the tube spinning process.

Parts up to 3 m (10 ft) in diameter can be formed by shear spinning. The operation wastes little material, and it can be completed in a relatively short time— as little as a few seconds. Various shapes can be spun with fairly simple tooling, which is generally made of tool steel. Because of the large deformations involved, this process generates considerable heat and so necessitates the use of water-based fluids during spinning.

The **spinnability** of a metal is defined as the maximum reduction in thickness to which a part can be subjected by spinning, without fracture. Spinnability is related to the tensile reduction of area of the material, just as bendability is. (See Fig. 16.18.) If a metal has a tensile reduction of area of some 50% (or higher), its thickness can be reduced by as much as 80% in just one spinning pass. Materials with low ductility are spun at elevated temperatures.

16.11.3 Tube Spinning

In *tube spinning*, the thickness of cylindrical parts is reduced by spinning them on a cylindrical mandrel using rollers (Fig. 16.41b). Note that the operation may be carried out externally or internally. The part may be spun *forward* or *backward* (this nomenclature is similar to that of a drawing or a backward extrusion process (Chapter 15)). In either case, the reduction in wall thickness results in a longer tube.

The maximum reduction per pass in tube spinning is related to the tensile reduction of area of the material, as it is in shear spinning. Tube spinning can be used to make pressure vessels, automotive components such as car and truck wheels, and rocket, missile, and jet-engine parts.

Example: Manufacturing a Jet-Engine Compressor Shaft

The Rolls-Royce Olympus jet-engine compressor shaft for the supersonic Concorde aircraft is made by a combination of forging and spinning operations (Fig. 16.42). First, a preform is made by a series of forging operations on a superalloy blank. The preform is then machined to fit over the mandrel of a horizontal spinning machine.

The first forming operation (pass 1) consists of tube spinning, applied to the small end of the forged blank by a pair of rollers. In pass 2, the annular section is formed into a conical shape by shear spinning over the conical section of the mandrel. The last three passes consist of gradually reducing the thickness of the larger end of the part, by tube spinning. (Note the profile produced on the outer diameter of the shaft.) The formed part is then machined, in order to obtain certain desired dimensional tolerances and geometric features.

A number of alternative methods have been considered for the manufacturing of this part and of similar axisymmetric parts for this jet engine. In the end, the most economical method was found to be the one shown in Fig. 16.42. Forging the part closer to the final shape (to reduce the number of spinning passes) was not economical: The cost of forging such parts increases significantly as their length-to-diameter ratio increases, particularly for thin-walled components.

Several other parts of this jet engine also are made by spinning them on a two-roller, 100-hp (75-kW) spinning machine. The operations are performed at room temperature, using a water-based lubricant that acts mainly as a coolant to carry away the substantial heat generated during the spinning process.

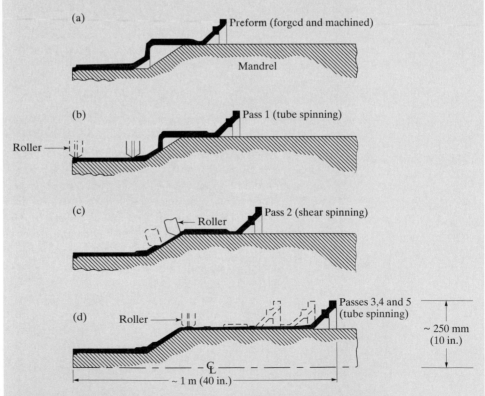

FIGURE 16.42   Steps in tube and shear spinning of a compressor shaft for the Olympus jet engine of the supersonic Concorde aircraft.

16.12 SUPERPLASTIC FORMING

Section 2.2.7 described the superplastic behavior of certain metals and alloys (such as Zn–Al and titanium) having very fine grains (less than 10 to 15 μm—for instance, ASTM No. 10 in Table 1.1), where very large tensile elongations (up to 2000%) are obtained within certain temperature ranges and at low strain rates. These alloys can be formed into complex shapes by *superplastic forming*, a process that employs common metalworking or polymer-processing techniques. (See Chapter 18).

The very high ductility and the relatively low strength of superplastic alloys offer the following advantages:

a. Lower strength is required of the tooling, because of the low strength of the material at forming temperatures; hence, tooling costs are lower.

b. Complex shapes can be formed out of one piece, with fine detail and close tolerances and with elimination of secondary operations.

c. Weight and material savings can be realized, because of the formability of the materials.

d. Little or no residual stress occurs in the formed parts.

Superplastic forming has the following limitations.

a. The material must not be superplastic at service temperatures.

b. Because of the extreme strain-rate sensitivity of the superplastic material, it must be formed at sufficiently low rates (typically at strain rates of 10^{-4} to 10^{-2}/s). Forming times range anywhere from a few seconds to several hours. Thus, cycle times are much longer than those of conventional forming processes; superplastic forming is therefore a batch-forming process.

Superplastic alloys (particularly Zn-22Al and Ti-6Al-4V) can be formed by such bulk deformation processes as compression molding, closed-die forging, coining, hubbing, and extrusion. Sheet forming of these materials can also be carried out using such operations as thermoforming, vacuum forming, and blow molding (Chapter 18).

An important development is the ability to fabricate sheet-metal structures by combining **diffusion bonding** with superplastic forming (**SPF/DB**). Typical structures in which flat sheets are diffusion bonded (as described in Section 28.7) and formed are shown in Fig. 16.43. After diffusion bonding the selected locations of the sheets, the unbonded regions (*stop-off*) are expanded into a mold by pressurized argon gas. These structures are thin, and they have high stiffness-to-weight ratios. As a result, they are particularly important in aircraft and aerospace applications.

This process improves productivity by eliminating mechanical fasteners, and it produces parts with good dimensional accuracy and low residual stresses. The technology is now well advanced for titanium structures for aerospace applications. Structures made of 7475-T6 aluminum alloy are also being developed using this technique; other metals for superplastic forming are the Inconel 100 and Incoloy 718 nickel alloys and some iron-based, high-carbon alloys.

Commonly used die materials in superplastic forming are low-alloy steels, cast tool steels, ceramics, graphite, and plaster of paris. Selection depends on the forming temperature and the strength of the superplastic alloy.

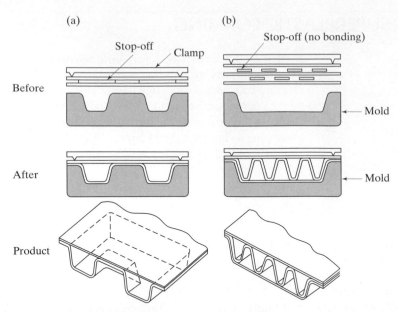

FIGURE 16.43   Types of structures made by diffusion bonding and superplastic forming of sheet metal. Such structures have a high stiffness-to-weight ratio. *Source*: Rockwell International Corp.

Example: Applications of Superplastic Forming/Diffusion Bonding

The majority of applications for SPF/DB produce titanium parts for military aircraft, such as the Toronado and the Mirage 2000—for example, fuselage bulkheads, leading-edge slats, heat-exchanger ducts, and cooler outlet ducts. The nozzle fairing of the F-15 fighter aircraft also is made by this process. Parts are also being made for the European Fighter Aircraft from Ti-6Al-4V titanium alloy and 7475 aluminum alloys. In civilian applications, the Airbus A340 has its water-closet, drain, and fresh-water maintenance panels made of Ti-6Al-4V.

The superplastic forming process is usually carried out at about 900 °C (1650 °F) for titanium alloys and at about 500 °C (930 °F) for aluminum alloys; temperatures for diffusion bonding are similar. However, the presence of an oxide layer on aluminum sheets is a significant problem that degrades the bond strength in diffusion bonding. To illustrate cycle times, 718 nickel-alloy sheets 2 mm (0.080 in.) in thickness were, in one application, superplastically formed in ceramic dies at 950 °C (1740 °F), by argon gas at a pressure of 2 MPa (300 psi) and with a cycle time of 4 hours.

16.13 EXPLOSIVE, MAGNETIC-PULSE, PEEN, AND OTHER FORMING PROCESSES

Although not as commonly used as the other processes reviewed thus far, several more sheet-forming processes are described in this section.

16.13.1 Explosive Forming

Explosives are used for many destructive purposes, in demolition work and in warfare. By controlling their quantity and shape, however, one can use explosives as a source of energy

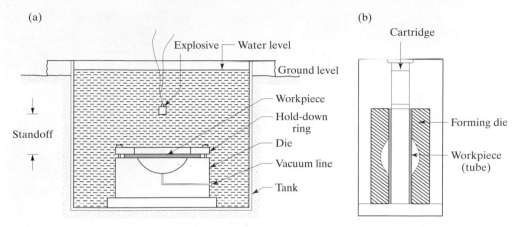

FIGURE 16.44   (a) Schematic illustration of the explosive forming process. (b) Illustration of the confined method of explosive bulging of tubes.

for metal forming. This energy was first utilized to form metals in the early 1900s. Typically, in *explosive forming*, the sheet-metal blank is clamped over a die, and the entire assembly is lowered into a tank filled with water (Fig. 16.44a). The air in the die cavity is evacuated, an explosive charge is placed at a certain height, and the charge is detonated.

The rapid conversion of the explosive charge into gas generates a shock wave. The pressure of this wave is sufficient to form sheet metals. The peak pressure, p, due to the explosion, generated in water, is given by the expression

$$p = K\left(\frac{\sqrt[3]{W}}{R}\right)^a, \tag{16.14}$$

where p is in psi, K is a constant which depends on the type of explosive (e.g., 21,600 for TNT (trinitrotoluene)), W is the weight of the explosive in pounds, R is the distance of the explosive from the workpiece surface (*standoff*) in feet, and a is a constant, generally taken to be 1.15.

A variety of shapes can be formed by the use of this process, provided that the material is ductile at the high rates of deformation characteristic of the explosive nature of the process. Explosive forming is versatile—there is virtually no limit to the size of the workpiece—and it is particularly suitable for low-quantity production runs of large parts, such as occur in aerospace applications.

Steel plates 25 mm (1 in.) thick and 3.6 m (12 ft) in diameter have been formed by this method. Tubes having walls as thick as 25 mm (1 in.) have been bulged by explosive-forming techniques.

The mechanical properties of parts made by this process are basically the same as those of parts made by conventional forming methods. Depending on the number of parts to be produced, dies may be made of aluminum alloys, steel, ductile iron, zinc alloys, reinforced concrete, wood, plastics, or composite materials.

Another explosive forming method is shown in Fig. 16.44b: Only a *cartridge* (canned explosive) is used as the source of energy. This second process can also be used for bulging and expanding thin-walled tubes.

16.13.2 Magnetic-Pulse Forming

In *magnetic-pulse forming*, or *electromagnetic forming*, the energy stored in a capacitor bank is discharged rapidly through a magnetic coil. In a typical example, a ring-shaped coil

(a)

(b)

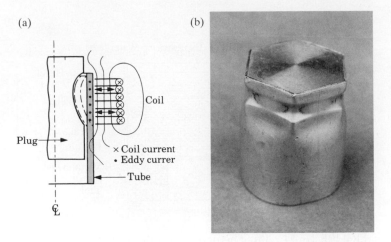

FIGURE 16.45 (a) Schematic illustration of the magnetic pulse forming process used to form a tube over a plug. (b) Aluminum tube collapsed over a hexagonal plug by the magnetic-pulse forming process.

is placed over a tubular workpiece. The tube is then collapsed over another solid piece by magnetic forces, making the assembly an integral part (Fig. 16.45).

The magnetic field produced by the coil crosses the metal tube (a conductor) and so generates *eddy currents* in the tube. These currents, in turn, produce their own *magnetic field* (Fig. 16.45a). The forces produced by the two magnetic fields oppose each other; consequently, there is a repelling force between the coil and the tube. The forces generated collapse the tube over the inner piece.

The higher the electrical conductivity of the workpiece, the higher are the magnetic forces. It is not necessary for the workpiece material to have magnetic properties. Flat magnetic coils are also available, for the operations of embossing and of shallow drawing on sheet metals.

Magnetic-pulse forming is used for collapsing thin-walled tubes over rods, cables, and plugs, for compression-crimp sealing of automotive oil filter canisters, for bulging and flaring operations, and for swaging end fittings onto torque tubes for the Boeing 777 aircraft.

16.13.3 Peen Forming

Peen forming is used to produce curvatures on thin sheet metals by **shot peening** (see Section 33.2) one surface of the sheet. In peen forming, the surface of the sheet is subjected to compressive stresses, which tend to expand the surface layer. Because the material below the peened surface remains rigid, the surface expansion causes the sheet to develop a curvature. The process also induces compressive surface residual stresses, which improve the fatigue strength of the sheet.

Peening is done with cast-iron or steel shot, discharged either from a rotating wheel or, by an air blast, from a nozzle. Peen forming is used by the aircraft industry to generate smooth and complex curvatures on aircraft wing skins. Cast-steel shot about 2.5 mm (0.1 in.) in diameter, traveling at speeds of 60 m/s (200 ft/s), have been used to form wing panels 25 m (80 ft) long. For heavy sections, shot diameters as large as 6 mm $\left(\frac{1}{4}\text{ in.}\right)$ may be used. The peen-forming process is also used for straightening twisted or bent parts; out-of-round rings, for example, can be straightened by this method.

16.13.4 Other Sheet-Forming Processes

Several other types of sheet-forming processes are also used, although somewhat rarely.

a. **Laser forming** of sheet metal involves the application of laser beams in specific regions of a part, in order to induce steep thermal gradients through the thickness of the sheet. The thermal stresses developed are sufficiently high to cause localized plastic deformation of the sheet and result in, for example, in a bent sheet.

b. In **laser-assisted forming**, certain operations can be carried out using lasers as a localized heat source, to reduce the flow stress of the sheet metal at specific locations and to improve formability and increase process flexibility. Examples are the straightening, bending, embossing, and forming of complex tubular or flat components. The possible adverse effects of such localized heating on product integrity should be investigated.

c. In **electrohydraulic forming** (*underwater spark* or *electric-discharge forming*), the source of energy is a spark between electrodes connected by a thin wire. The rapid discharge of the energy from a capacitor bank through the electrodes generates a shock wave (similar to those created by explosives) and forms the part. This process has been used in making relatively small parts, at energy levels lower than those in explosive forming—typically a few kJ.

d. **Gas mixtures** in a closed container have been utilized as an energy source. When one is ignited, the pressures generated are sufficient to form parts. The principle is similar to that used for the generation of pressure in an internal combustion engine.

e. **Liquefied gases**, such as liquid nitrogen, may also be used to develop pressures high enough to form sheet metals. When allowed to reach room temperature in a closed container, liquefied nitrogen becomes gaseous and expands, developing the necessary pressure to form the part.

16.14 THE MANUFACTURING OF HONEYCOMB STRUCTURES

The **honeycomb structure** consists basically of a core of honeycomb (or of other corrugated shapes) bonded to two thin outer skins (Fig. 16.46). The most common example of such a structure is corrugated cardboard, which has a high stiffness-to-weight ratio and is used extensively in packaging for consumer and industrial goods.

There are two principal methods of manufacturing honeycomb materials. In the **expansion** process (Fig. 16.46a), the more common method, sheets are cut from a coil, and an adhesive is applied at intervals (node lines). The sheets are stacked and cured in an oven, so that strong bonds develop at the adhesive joints. The block is then cut into slices of the desired dimension and stretched to produce a honeycomb structure. This procedure is similar to that used in expanding folded paper structures into the shapes of decorative objects.

In the **corrugation** process (Fig. 16.46b), which is similar to the process used in making corrugated cardboard, the sheet passes through a pair of specially designed rolls, becoming a corrugated sheet, which is then cut into desired lengths. Again, adhesive is applied to the node lines, and the block is cured. Note that no expansion process is involved. The honeycomb material is then made into a sandwich structure (Fig. 16.46c): Face sheets are joined by adhesives to the top and bottom surfaces.

Honeycomb structures are most commonly made of 3000-series aluminum, but they are also made of titanium, stainless steels, and nickel alloys. Recent developments include

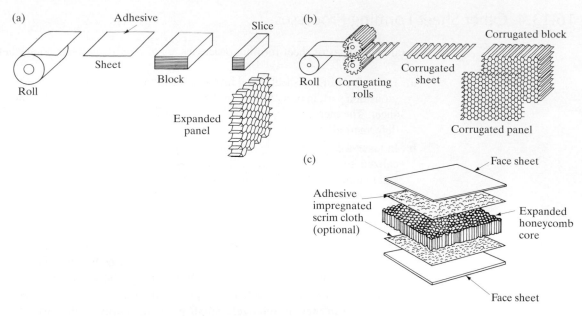

FIGURE 16.46   Methods of manufacturing honeycomb structures: (a) Expansion process; (b) Corrugation process; (c) Assembling a honeycomb structure into a laminate.

the use of reinforced plastics, such as aramid–epoxy. Bonding between the core and the skins is accomplished either by adhesives or by brazing. Because of their light weight and their high resistance to bending forces, honeycomb structures are used for aircraft and aerospace components in buildings, and in transportation equipment.

16.15 THE DENT RESISTANCE OF SHEET-METAL PARTS

Dents are commonly found on cars, appliances, office furniture, and kitchen utensils. Dents are usually caused by dynamic forces from moving objects that hit the sheet metal. In typical automotive panels, for example, velocities at impact range up to 45 m/s (150 ft/s). Thus, it is the *dynamic yield stress* (yield stress under high rates of deformation) rather than the static yield stress that is the significant strength parameter (Section 2.2).

Dynamic forces tend to cause *localized* dents; static forces tend to spread the dented area. Try to dent a piece of flat sheet metal, first by pushing a ball-peen hammer against it, and then by striking it with the hammer; note how localized the dent is in the latter case.

Dent resistance of sheet-metal parts has been found to (a) increase as the sheet's yield stress and its thickness increase and (b) decrease as its elastic modulus and its overall panel stiffness increase. Panels rigidly held at their edges, therefore, have lower dent resistance.

16.16 EQUIPMENT FOR SHEET-METAL FORMING

For most pressworking operations, the basic equipment consists of mechanical, hydraulic, pneumatic, or pneumatic-hydraulic presses. Section 14.9 described basic features and characteristics of such presses. Typical designs for press frames are shown in Fig. 16.47. (See also Fig. 14.21.) The proper design, construction, and stiffness of such equipment is essential to efficient operation, high production rate, good dimensional control, and high product quality.

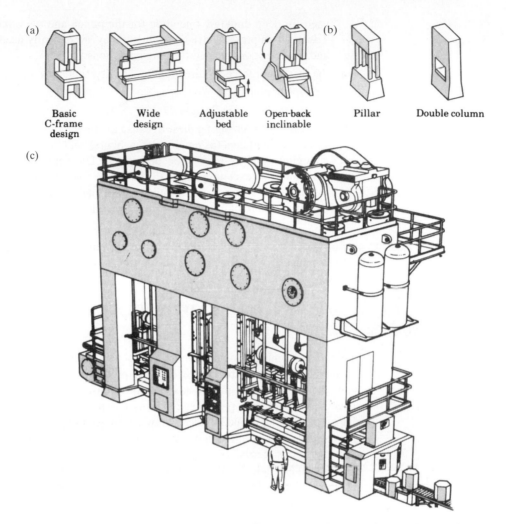

(a)

Basic
C-frame
design

Wide
design

Adjustable
bed

Open-back
inclinable

(b)

Pillar

Double column

(c)

FIGURE 16.47   (a) and (b) Schematic illustrations of types of press frames for sheet-forming operations. Each type has its own characteristics of stiffness, capacity, and accessibility. *Source*: *Engineer's Handbook*, VEB Fachbuchverlag, 1965. (c) A large stamping press. *Source*: Verson Allsteel Company.

The traditional **C-frame** structure (Fig. 16.47a) has been widely used for ease of tool and workpiece accessibility. It is, however, not as stiff as the **box-type** (O-type) pillar and double-column frame structures (Fig. 16.47b). Furthermore, advances in automation and in the use of industrial robots and computer controls (Chapters 38 and 39) have made accessibility less important.

Press selection for sheet-metal forming operations depends on several factors:

a. the type of forming operation and the size and shape of the dies and tooling required;

b. the size and shape of workpiece;

c. the length of stroke of the slide or slides, the number of strokes per minute, the speed, and the *shut height* (distance from the top of the bed to the bottom of the slide, with the stroke down);

d. the number of slides. Single-action presses have one reciprocating slide. Double-action presses have two slides, reciprocating in the same direction; they are typically used for deep drawing, one slide for the punch and the other for the blankholder. Triple-action presses have three slides; they are typically used for reverse redrawing and for other complicated forming operations.

e. the maximum force required (press capacity, tonnage rating);

f. the type of controls;

g. safety features—see Section 37.3;

h. the features for changing dies. Because the time required for changing dies in presses can be significant (as much as a few hours), and thus affect productivity, rapid die-changing systems have been developed. Die setups following a system called **single-minute exchange of die (SMED)** can now be changed in less than ten minutes, by the use of automated hydraulic or pneumatic systems. These techniques are particularly important in automated and computer-integrated manufacturing systems.

Because a press is a major capital investment, its use for a variety of parts and applications should be investigated. Versatility and multiple use are important factors in its selection, particularly for product modifications and for the making of new products to respond to changes in market demand.

16.17 THE ECONOMICS OF SHEET-METAL FORMING PROCESSES

Sheet-metal forming involves economic considerations similar to those for the other processes that have been described. Sheet-forming processes compete with each other (as well as with other processes) more than do other operations. Sheet-forming operations are versatile, so a number of different processes can be used to produce the same part. For example, a cup-shaped part can be formed by deep drawing, by spinning, by rubber forming, or by explosive forming; moreover it can be formed by impact extrusion, by casting, or by fabricating it from different pieces.

As an example, the part shown in Fig. 16.48 can be made either by deep drawing or by conventional spinning—but the die costs for the two processes are significantly different. Deep-drawing dies have many components, and they cost much more than the relatively simple mandrels and tools employed in spinning.

Consequently, the die cost per part in drawing will be high if few parts are needed. On the other hand, this part can be formed by deep drawing in a much shorter time than by spinning, even if the latter operation is automated. Furthermore, spinning requires more skilled labor.

Considering these factors, the breakeven point is at about 700 parts, and deep drawing is more economical for quantities greater than that. Chapter 40 describes further details of the economics of manufacturing.

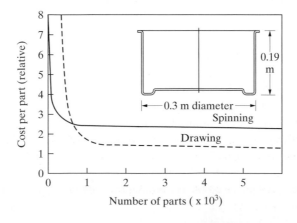

FIGURE 16.48   Cost comparison for manufacturing a round sheet-metal container either by conventional spinning or by deep drawing. Note that for small quantities, spinning is more economical.

SUMMARY

- Sheet-metal forming processes are among the most versatile of all operations. They are generally used on workpieces having high ratios of surface area to thickness. Unlike in bulk deformation processes such as forging and extrusion, the thickness of the material in sheet forming is generally prevented from being reduced, to avoid necking and tearing.

- Important material parameters are the quality of the sheared edge of the sheet metal prior to forming, the capability of the sheet to stretch uniformly, and the material's resistance to thinning, its normal and planar anisotropy, its grain size, and its yield-point elongation (for low-carbon steels).

- The forces and energy required in sheet-metal forming processes are transmitted to the workpiece through solid tools and dies, through flexible rubber or polyurethane members, or by electrical, chemical, magnetic, and gaseous means.

- Because of the relatively thin materials used, springback, buckling, and wrinkling are significant problems in sheet forming. Springback is a function of the yield stress, the elastic modulus, and the ratio of bend radius to thickness. These problems can be reduced or eliminated by proper tool and die design, by minimizing the unsupported length of the sheet during processing, and by controlling the thickness of the incoming sheet and its mechanical properties.

- Among important developments is the superplastic forming of diffusion-bonded sheets. The process is capable of producing complex sheet-metal structures, particularly for aerospace applications, (which require particularly high stiffness-to-weight ratios).

- Several test methods have been developed for predicting the formability of sheet metals. In bending operations, the tensile reduction of the area of the sheet gives an indication of its bendability (minimum bend radius); this also applies to the parameter spinnability of metals (maximum reduction in thickness per pass).

- For general stamping operations, forming-limit diagrams are very useful, because they establish quantitative relationships among the major and minor principal strains that limit safe forming. For deep-drawing operations, the important parameter is the normal or plastic anisotropy of the sheet (the ratio of width strain to thickness strain, in tensile testing).

TRENDS

- Studies are continuing on techniques to determine the formability of sheet metals under various conditions. For example, computer-controlled blankholder forces are being investigated to optimize drawability.

- Various sheet-metal textures are being developed and controlled to improve formability.

- Tool surface textures are being designed and applied to control friction and to improve sheet formability.

- Computer-aided die design and manufacturing and finite-element analysis are being implemented to improve productivity and reduce costs.

- Automated systems for changing press dies quickly are being implemented.

- Hydroforming is finding increased applications in the automotive and aerospace industries.

- Diffusion bonding, combined with superplastic forming technology, continues to increase in applications requiring weight and cost savings, particularly for the aerospace industry.

- Tailor-welded sheet blanks are finding increased applications, particularly in the automotive industry.

KEY TERMS

Beading	Embossing	Planar anisotropy
Bendability	Explosive forming	Plastic anisotropy
Bend allowance	Fine blanking	Press brake
Bending	Flanging	Progressive dies
Blankholder	Formability	Punching
Blanking	Forming-limit diagram	Redrawing
Bulging	Hemming	Roll forming
Burnished surface	Honeycomb structures	Rubber forming
Burr	Hydroform process	Shaving
Clearance	Ironing	Shearing
Compound dies	Laser forming	Slitting
Deburring	Limiting drawing ratio	Spinning
Deep drawing	Lueder's bands	Springback
Dent resistance	Magnetic-pulse forming	Steel rule
Dimpling	Minimum bend radius	Stretch forming
Drawbead	Nesting	Superplastic forming
Drawing	Nibbling	Tailor-welded blanks
Earing	Normal anisotropy	Transfer dies
Electrohydraulic forming	Peen forming	Wrinkling

BIBLIOGRAPHY

ASM Handbook, Vol. 14: *Forming and Forging*. ASM International, 1988.

Benson, S., *Press Brake Technology*. Society of Manufacturing Engineers, 1997.

Bitzer, T., *Honeycomb Technology: Materials, Design, Manufacturing, Applications and Testing*. Chapman & Hall, 1997.

Blazynski, T.Z., *Plasticity and Modern Metal-forming Technology*. Elsevier, 1989.

Fundamentals of Tool Design (4th ed.). Society of Manufacturing Engineers, 1998.

Gillanders, J., *Pipe and Tube Bending Manual*. FMA International, 1994.

Hosford, W.F., and R.M. Caddell, *Metal Forming: Mechanics and Metallurgy* (2d ed.). Prentice Hall, 1993.

Morgan, E., *Tinplate and Modern Canmaking Technology*. Pergamon, 1985.

Pearce, R., *Sheet Metal Forming*. Chapman & Hall, 1997.

Smith, D., *Die Design Handbook* (3d ed.). Society of Manufacturing Engineers, 1990.

____, *Fundamentals of Pressworking*. Society of Manufacturing Engineers, 1994.

Suchy, I., *Handbook of Die Design*. McGraw-Hill, 1997.

Tool and Manufacturing Engineers Handbook (4th ed.), Vol. 2: *Forming*. Society of Manufacturing Engineers, 1984.

REVIEW QUESTIONS

16.1 How does sheet-metal forming differ from rolling, forging, and extrusion?

16.2 What causes burrs? How can they be reduced or eliminated?

16.3 Explain the difference between punching and blanking.

16.4 List the various operations performed by die cutting. What types of applications do these processes have in manufacturing?

16.5 Describe the difference between compound, progressive, and transfer dies.

16.6 Name the various methods by which sheet-metal blanks can be cut from a large sheet.

16.7 List the characteristics of sheet metals that are important in sheet-forming operations. Explain why they are important.

16.8 What is the significance of anisotropy?

16.9   Describe the features of forming-limit diagrams (FLD).

16.10   List the properties of materials that influence springback. Explain why they do.

16.11   Make a list of common bending operations, giving one application for each.

16.12   Why do tubes buckle when bent?

16.13   Explain why normal anisotropy is important in determining the deep drawability of a material.

16.14   Describe earing and why it occurs.

16.15   What are the advantages of rubber forming?

16.16   Explain the features of unconventional forming methods for sheet metal.

16.17   What is the difference between deep drawing and redrawing?

16.18   Why is ironing an important process?

16.19   What are the differences and similarities between conventional spinning and shear spinning?

16.20   How is hydroforming similar to rubber forming?

16.21   How is roll forming fundamentally different from rolling?

16.22   What is the purpose of a draw bead?

QUALITATIVE PROBLEMS

16.23   Outline the differences that you have observed between products made of sheet metals and those made by casting and forging.

16.24   Describe the cutting process that takes place when a pair of scissors cuts through aluminum foil.

16.25   Identify the material and process variables that influence the punch force in shearing, and explain how each of these affects this force.

16.26   Explain why springback in bending depends on yield stress, elastic modulus, sheet thickness, and bend radius.

16.27   What is the significance of the size of the circles in the grid patterns shown in Fig. 16.15? What is the significance of the thickness of the lines?

16.28   Explain why cupping tests may not predict the formability of sheet metals in actual forming processes.

16.29   The text stated that the thicker the sheet metal, the higher the curves in Fig. 16.14b become. Why do you think this effect occurs?

16.30   Identify the factors that influence the deep-drawing force, F, in Fig. 16.32b, and explain why they do.

16.31   Inspect the earing shown in Fig. 16.35, and identify the direction in which the blank was cut from a cold-rolled sheet.

16.32   Why are the beads in Fig. 16.36b placed in those particular locations?

16.33   Describe the factors that influence the size and length of beads in drawing operations.

16.34   Duplicate the peen-forming process by hammering aluminum sheets of various thicknesses with a ball-peen hammer. Describe your observations about the curvatures produced.

16.35   Describe the features of the different types of presses shown in Fig. 16.47. What are typical applications for each one?

16.36   A general rule for dimensional relationships for successful drawing without a blankholder is given by Eq. (16.13). Explain what would happen if this limit were exceeded.

16.37   Describe (a) the similarities and (b) the dissimilarities between the bulk deformation processes described in Chapters 13 through 15 and the sheet-forming processes described in this chapter.

16.38   Inspect a common paper punch, comment on the shape of the punch tip, and compare it with those shown in Fig. 16.10. Comment on your observations.

16.39   Section 16.2 described the secondary operations that may be necessary to make sheared edges smoother. Make a list of processes that you think could be suitable for this additional secondary operation, and explain their characteristics.

16.40 Section 16.2.1 stated that the punch stripping force is difficult to estimate, because of the many factors involved. Make a list of these factors, with brief explanations about why they would affect the stripping force.

16.41 Is it possible for the forming-limit diagram shown in Fig. 16.14b to have a negative major strain? Explain.

16.42 Inspect Fig. 16.14b and explain clearly whether in a sheet-forming operation you would like to develop a state of strain that is to the left or to the right of the forming-limit diagram.

16.43 Is it possible to have ironing take place in an ordinary deep-drawing operation? What is the most important factor?

16.44 Note the roughness of the periphery of the flanged hole in Fig. 16.25c, and comment on its possible effects when the part is used in a product.

16.45 What recommendations would you make in order to eliminate cracking of the bent piece shown in Fig. 16.17c? Explain your reasons.

16.46 As you can see, the forming-limit diagram axes pertain to engineering strains, given as a percentage. Describe your thoughts about whether the use of true strains, as in Eq. (2.7), would have any significant advantage.

16.47 It has been stated that the drawability of a material is higher in the hydroform process than in the deep-drawing process. Explain why.

16.48 Give several specific examples from this chapter in which friction is desirable and several in which it is not desirable.

16.49 As you can see, the operations described in this chapter produce considerable scrap. Describe your thoughts regarding the reuse, recycling, or disposal of this scrap. Consider its size, its shape, and its contamination by metalworking fluids.

16.50 In the manufacture of automotive body panels from carbon-steel sheet, stretcher strains (or Lueder's bands) are observed, and they detrimentally affect surface finish. How can these be eliminated?

16.51 A coil of sheet metal is taken to a furnace and annealed, in order to improve its ductility. It is found, however, that the sheet has a lower limiting drawing ratio than it had before annealing. Explain why this effect has occurred.

16.52 What effect does friction have on a forming-limit diagram? Why are lubricants generally used in sheet-metal forming?

16.53 Through changes in clamping, a sheet-metal forming operation can allow the material to undergo a negative minor strain. Explain how this effect can be advantageous.

16.54 Do you think the term SMED a misnomer? Explain.

QUANTITATIVE PROBLEMS

16.55 Calculate R_{avg} for a metal where the R values for the 0°, 45°, and 90° directions are 0.9, 1.6, and 1.75, respectively. What is the limiting drawing ratio for this material?

16.56 Calculate the value of ΔR for the case in Question 16.55. Will any ears form when this material is deep drawn? Explain.

16.57 Estimate the limiting drawing ratio (LDR) for the materials listed in Table 16.4.

16.58 Prove Eq. (16.4).

16.59 Regarding Eq. (16.4), it has been stated that, in bending, actual values of the strain e on the outer fibers (in tension) are higher than those on the inner fibers (in compression), the reason being that the neutral axis shifts during bending. With an appropriate sketch, explain this phenomenon.

16.60 Using Eq. (16.14) and the K value for TNT, plot the pressure as a function of weight (W) and R, respectively. Describe your observations.

16.61 Section 16.5 states that the k values in bend allowance depend on the relative magnitudes of R and T. Explain why this relationship exists.

16.62 In explosive forming, calculate the peak pressure in water for 0.3 lb of TNT at a standoff distance of 3 ft. Comment on whether or not the magnitude of this pressure is sufficiently high to form sheet metals.

16.63 Why is the bending force P proportional to the square of the sheet thickness, as seen in Section 16.5.4?

16.64 In Fig. 16.14a, measure the respective areas of the solid outlines, compare them with the areas of the original circles, and calculate the final thicknesses of the sheets, assuming that the original sheet is 1 mm thick.

16.65 With the aid of a free-body diagram, prove the existence of compressive hoop stresses in the flange in a deep-drawing operation.

16.66 Plot Eq. (16.6) in terms of the elastic modulus, E, and the yield stress, Y, and describe your observations.

16.67 What is the minimum bend radius for a 2-mm thick sheet metal with a tensile reduction of area of 30%? Does the bend angle affect your answer? Explain.

16.68 When a round sheet-metal blank is deep drawn, it is found that it does not exhibit any earing. Its R values in the 0° and 90° directions to rolling are 1.4 and 1.8, respectively. What is the R value in the 45° direction?

16.69 Survey the technical literature, and explain the mechanism by which negative springback takes place in bending. Explain why negative springback does not occur in air bending.

16.70 Using the data in Table 16.3, and referring to Eq. (16.5), calculate the tensile reduction of area for the materials and conditions listed in the table.

16.71 Obtain an aluminum beverage container, and cut it in half lengthwise with a pair of tin snips. Using a micrometer, measure the thickness of the bottom and of the wall. Estimate the thickness reductions in ironing and the diameter of the original blank.

16.72 What is the force required to punch a square hole, 100 mm on each side, from a 1-mm thick 5052-O aluminum sheet, by the use of flat dies? What would be your answer if beveled dies are used?

SYNTHESIS AND DESIGN

16.73 Examine some of the products in your home that are made of sheet metal, and discuss the process (or combination of processes) by which you think they were made.

16.74 Consider several shapes to be blanked from a large sheet (such as oval, triangular, L-shaped, and so forth) by laser-beam cutting, and sketch a nesting layout to minimize scrap generation. (See Section 16.2.2.)

16.75 Give several product applications for hemming and for seaming.

16.76 Many missile components are made by spinning. What other methods could you use if spinning processes were not available?

16.77 Give several structural applications in which diffusion bonding and superplastic forming are used jointly.

16.78 Inspect sheet-metal parts in an automobile, and describe your thoughts as to which of the processes (or combinations of processes) were used in making them. Comment on the reasons why more than one process had to be used.

16.79 Name several parts that can be made in compound dies and several that can be made in transfer dies.

16.80 On the basis of experiments, it has been suggested that concrete, either plain or reinforced, can be a suitable material for dies in metal forming operations. Describe your thoughts regarding this suggestion, considering die geometry and any other factors that may be relevant.

16.81 Metal cans are either two-piece (in which the bottom and sides are integral) or three-piece (in which the sides, the bottom, and the top are each separate pieces). For a three-piece can, should the seam (a) be in the rolling direction, (b) be normal to the rolling direction, or (c) be oblique to the rolling direction? Prove your answer, using equations from solid mechanics.

16.82 Locate a drum cymbal, and describe the manufacturing processes used in its production.

16.83 Investigate methods for determining optimum blank shapes for deep-drawing operations. Sketch the optimally shaped blanks for rectangular cups, and optimize their layout on a large sheet of metal.

17

Processing of Powder Metals, Ceramics, Glass, and Superconductors

17.1 INTRODUCTION

In the manufacturing processes described in the preceding chapters, the raw materials used are metals and alloys, either in a molten state or in solid form. This chapter describes the processes used for making parts from metal powders, ceramics, glass, and superconductors.

We will first see how metal parts are made by compacting fine metal powders in suitable dies and *sintering*, that is, heating without melting. This process, called **powder metallurgy (P/M)**, was first used by the Egyptians, in 3000 B.C., to make iron tools. One of its first modern uses was in the early 1900s, to make the tungsten filaments for incandescent light bulbs. (See Section 2.2 in the General Introduction.) The availability of a wide range of powder compositions, the ability to produce parts to net dimensions (**net-shape forming**), and the economics of the overall operation make this process attractive for many applications (Table 17.1).

Typical products made by powder-metallurgy techniques (Figs. 17.1a, b, and c) range from tiny balls for ball-point pens, to gears, cams, and bushings, to cutting tools, to porous products, such as filters and oil-impregnated bearings, to a variety of automotive components

TABLE 17.1   Typical Applications for Metal Powders

Application	Metals	Uses
Abrasives	Fe, Sn, Zn	Cleaning, abrasive wheels
Aerospace	Al, Be, Nb	Jet engines, heat shields
Automotive	Cu, Fe, W	Valve inserts, bushings, gears
Electrical/electronic	Ag, Au, Mo	Contacts, diode heat sinks
Heat treating	Mo, Pt, W	Furnace elements, thermocouples
Joining	Cu, Fe, Sn	Solders, electrodes
Lubrication	Cu, Fe, Zn	Greases, abradable seals
Magnetic	Co, Fe, Ni	Relays, magnets
Manufacturing	Cu, Mn, W	Dies, tools, bearings
Medical/dental	Ag, Au, W	Implants, amalgams
Metallurgical	Al, Ce, Si	Metal recovery, alloying
Nuclear	Be, Ni, W	Shielding, filters, reflectors
Office equipment	Al, Fe, Ti	Electrostatic copiers, cams

Source: R. M. German.

(which now constitute about 70% of the PM market), such as piston rings, valve guides, connecting rods, and hydraulic pistons. A typical family car now contains, on the average, 11 kg (25 lb) of precision metal parts made by powder metallurgy, and it is estimated that the amount will soon rise to 22 kg (50 lb).

The most commonly used metals in P/M are iron, copper, aluminum, tin, nickel, titanium, and the refractory metals. For parts made of brass, bronze, steels, and stainless steels, *prealloyed powders* are used, where each powder particle itself is an alloy.

Powder metallurgy has become competitive with processes such as casting, forging, and machining, particularly for relatively complex parts made of high-strength and hard alloys. Although most parts weigh less than 2.5 kg (5 lb), they can weigh as much as 50 kg (100 b). Advances in technology now permit structural parts of aircraft, such as landing gear, engine-mount supports, engine disks, impellers, and engine nacelle frames, to be made by P/M.

(a)

(c)

(b)

FIGURE 17.1   (a) Examples of typical parts made by powder-metallurgy processes. (b) Upper trip lever for a commercial irrigation sprinkler, made by P/M. This part is made of unleaded brass alloy; it replaces a die-cast part, with a 60% savings. *Source*: Reproduced with permission from *Success Stories on P/M Parts*, 1998. Metal Powder Industries Federation, Princeton, New Jersey, 1998. (c) Main-bearing powder metal caps for 3.8 and 3.1 liter General Motors automotive engines. *Source*: Courtesy of Zenith Sintered Products, Inc., Milwaukee, Wisconsin.

The properties, and various important applications, of ceramics and glasses were described in Chapter 8. In this chapter we describe the techniques used in processing them into useful products. Generally, ceramics are processed through the following steps: crushing or grinding the raw materials into very fine particles, mixing them with various additives to impart certain characteristics, and then shaping, drying, and firing the material. They may be subjected to additional processing for better control of dimensions and surface finish.

Glass products are processed by melting the glass and forming it in molds, machines, and various devices—or by blowing. Shapes produced include flat sheet and plate, rods, glass fibers, tubing, and discrete products such as bottles. The strength of glass can be improved by thermal and chemical treatments.

17.2 PRODUCTION OF METAL POWDERS

The powder-metallurgy process basically consists of the following operations in sequence (Fig. 17.2):

1. **Powder production**;
2. **Blending**;
3. **Compaction**;
4. **Sintering**;
5. **Finishing operations**.

To improve quality and dimensional accuracy, or in special applications, additional processing such as coining, sizing, forging, machining, infiltration, and resintering may be carried out.

17.2.1 Methods of Powder Production

There are several methods of producing metal powders, and most of them can be produced by more than one method; the choice depends on the requirements of the end product. Particle sizes range from 0.1 μm to 1000 μm (4 μin. to 0.04 in.). Metal sources are generally bulk metals and alloys, ores, salts, and other compounds.

The shape, the size distribution, the porosity, the chemical purity, and the bulk and surface characteristics of the particles depend on the particular process used (Figs. 17.3 and 17.4).

FIGURE 17.2   Outline of processes and operations involved in making powder-metallurgy parts.

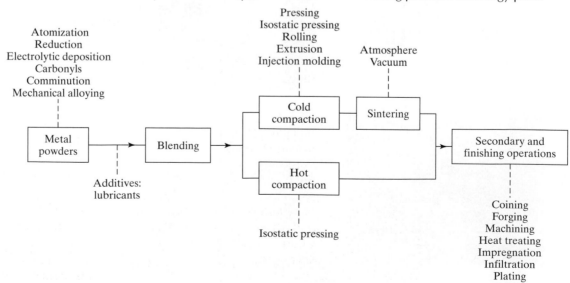

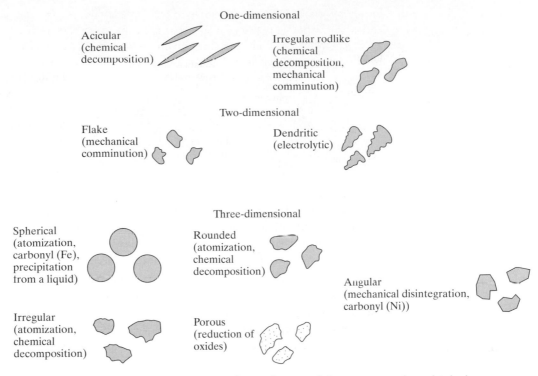

One-dimensional

Acicular
(chemical
decomposition)

Irregular rodlike
(chemical
decomposition,
mechanical
comminution)

Two-dimensional

Flake
(mechanical
comminution)

Dendritic
(electrolytic)

Three-dimensional

Spherical
(atomization,
carbonyl (Fe),
precipitation
from a liquid)

Rounded
(atomization,
chemical
decomposition)

Angular
(mechanical disintegration,
carbonyl (Ni))

Irregular
(atomization,
chemical
decomposition)

Porous
(reduction of
oxides)

FIGURE 17.3   Particle shapes in metal powders, and the processes by which they are produced. Iron powders are produced by many of these processes.

These characteristics are important, because they significantly affect the flow and permeability during compaction and in subsequent sintering operations.

1. **Atomization.** *Atomization* produces a liquid-metal stream by injecting molten metal through a small orifice (Fig. 17.5a). The stream is broken up by jets of inert gas, air, or water. The size of the particles formed depends on the temperature of the metal, the rate of flow, the nozzle size, and jet characteristics. In one variation of this method, a consumable electrode is rotated rapidly in a helium-filled chamber (Fig. 17.5b). The centrifugal force breaks up the molten tip of the electrode into metal particles.

FIGURE 17.4   (a) Scanning-electron-microscopy photograph of iron-powder particles made by atomization. (b) Nickel-based superalloy (Udimet 700) powder particles made by the rotating electrode process; see Fig. 17.5b. *Source*: Courtesy of P.G. Nash, Illinois Institute of Technology, Chicago.

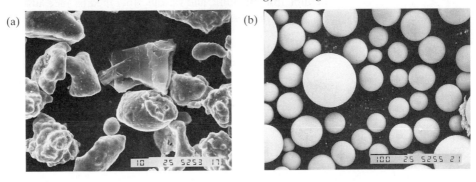

(a)

(b)

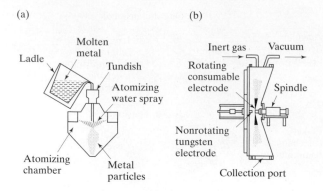

(a)   (b)

FIGURE 17.5   Methods of metal-powder production by atomization; (a) melt atomization; (b) atomization with a rotating consumable electrode.

2. **Reduction.** The *reduction* of metal oxides (removal of oxygen) uses gases, such as hydrogen and carbon monoxide, as reducing agents; by this means, very fine metallic oxides are reduced to the metallic state. The powders produced by this method are spongy and porous, and they have uniformly sized spherical or angular shapes.

3. **Electrolytic deposition.** *Electrolytic deposition* utilizes either aqueous solutions or fused salts. The powders produced are among the purest available.

4. **Carbonyls.** Metal *carbonyls*, such as iron carbonyl ($Fe(CO)_5$) and nickel carbonyl ($Ni(CO)_4$), are formed by letting iron or nickel react with carbon monoxide. The reaction products are then decomposed to iron and nickel, and they turn into small, dense, uniformly spherical particles of high purity.

5. **Comminution.** Mechanical *comminution* (*pulverization*) involves crushing (Fig. 17.6), milling in a ball mill, or grinding brittle or less ductile metals into small particles. A *ball mill* is a machine (Fig. 17.6b) with a rotating hollow cylinder partly filled with steel or white-cast-iron balls. With brittle materials, the powder particles produced have angular shapes; with ductile metals, they are flaky, and they are not particularly suitable for powder metallurgy applications.

6. **Mechanical alloying.** In *mechanical alloying*, developed in the 1960s, powders of two or more pure metals are mixed in a ball mill. Under the impact of the hard balls, the powders fracture and join together by diffusion, forming alloy powders.

7. **Other methods.** Other less commonly used methods are (a) **precipitation** from a chemical solution, (b) production of fine metal chips by **machining**, and (c) **vapor condensation**. New developments include techniques based on high-temperature *extractive metallurgical processes*. Metal powders are being produced using high-temperature processing techniques based on (a) the reaction of volatile halides (a compound of halogen and an electropositive element) with liquid metals, and (b) the controlled reduction and reduction/carburization of solid oxides.

8. **Nanopowders.** New developments include production of *nanopowders* of copper, aluminum, iron, titanium, and various other metals. (See, also, *nanomaterials* in Section 6.15 and *nanoceramics* in Sections 8.2.5.) Because these powders are pyrophoric

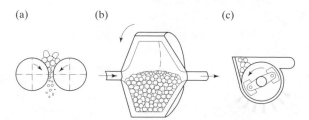

(a)   (b)   (c)

FIGURE 17.6   Methods of mechanical comminution, to obtain fine particles: (a) roll crushing, (b) ball mill, and (c) hammer milling.

(ignite spontaneously) or are readily contaminated when exposed to air, they are shipped as thick slurries under hexane gas (which itself is highly volatile and combustible).

When the material is subjected to large plastic deformation by compression and shear, at stress levels of 5500 MPa (800 ksi), during processing of the powders, the particle size is reduced, and the material becomes pore-free and possesses enhanced properties.

9. **Microencapsulated powders.** These metal powders are completely coated with a binder. For electrical applications, such as magnetic components of ignition coils and other pulsed AC and DC applications, the binder acts like an insulator, preventing electricity from flowing between particles and so reducing eddy-current losses. The powders are compacted by warm pressing; they are used with the binder still in place. (See also *metal injection molding* in Section 17.3.3.)

17.2.2 Particle Size, Distribution, and Shape

Particle size is usually measured by *screening*, that is, by passing the metal powder through screens (sieves) of various mesh sizes. Screen analysis is achieved by using a vertical stack of screens, with the mesh size becoming finer as the powder flows downward through the screens. The larger the mesh size, the smaller is the opening in the screen. For example, a mesh size of 30 has an opening of 600 μm, size 100 has 150 μm, and size 400 has 38 μm. (This method is similar to the numbering of abrasive grains: The larger the number, the smaller the size of the abrasive particle—see Section 25.2).

In addition to screen analysis, several other methods are also available for particle size analysis:

a. **sedimentation**, which involves measuring the rate at which particles settle in a fluid;

b. **microscopic analysis**, which may include the use of transmission and scanning electron microscopy;

c. **light scattering** from a laser that illuminates a sample consisting of particles suspended in a liquid medium. (The particles cause the light to be scattered; a detector then digitizes the signals and computes the particle size distribution.)

d. **optical** means, such as particles blocking a beam of light that is then sensed by a photocell;

e. **suspending particles** in a liquid and then detecting particle size and distribution by electrical sensors.

The *size distribution* of particles is an important consideration, because it affects the processing characteristics of the powder. The distribution of particle size is given in terms of a *frequency distribution* plot (See Section 36.5 for details.) The maximum is called the *mode size*.

Particle shape has a major influence on processing characteristics. The shape is usually described in terms of aspect ratio or shape factor. *Aspect ratio* is the ratio of the largest dimension to the smallest dimension of the particle. This ratio ranges from unity (for a spherical particle) to about 10 for flakelike or needlelike particles.

Shape factor (SF), or shape index, is a measure of the ratio of the surface area of the particle to its volume, normalized by reference to a spherical particle of equivalent volume. Thus, for example, the shape factor for a flake is higher than that for a sphere.

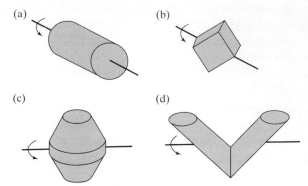

FIGURE 17.7 Some common equipment geometries for mixing or blending powders: (a) cylindrical, (b) rotating cube, (c) double cone, and (d) twin shell. *Source:* Reprinted with permission from R.M. German, *Powder Metallurgy Science.* Princeton, NJ; Metal Powder Industries Federation, 1984.

17.2.3 Blending Metal Powders

Blending (mixing) powders is the second step in powder metallurgy processing. It is carried out for the following purposes:

a. Because the powders made by various processes have different sizes and shapes, they must be mixed to obtain uniformity. The ideal mix is one in which all the particles of each material are distributed uniformly.

b. Powders of different metals and other materials can be mixed in order to impart special physical and mechanical properties and characteristics to the P/M product.

c. Lubricants can be mixed with the powders to improve their flow characteristics. The results are reduced friction between the metal particles, improved flow of the powder metals into the dies, and longer die life. Lubricants typically are stearic acid or zinc stearate, in a proportion of from 0.25% to 5% by weight.

Powder mixing must be carried out under controlled conditions, to avoid contamination or deterioration. Deterioration is caused by excessive mixing, which may alter the shape of the particles and work-harden them and thus make the subsequent compacting operation more difficult. Powders can be mixed in air, in inert atmospheres (to avoid oxidation), or in liquids, which act as lubricants and make the mix more uniform. Several types of blending equipment are available (Fig. 17.7). To improve and maintain quality, these operations increasingly are being controlled by microprocessors.

Hazards. Because of their high surface area-to-volume ratio, metal powders are explosive, particularly aluminum, magnesium, titanium, zirconium, and thorium. Great care must be exercised both during blending and in storage and handling. Precautions include (a) grounding equipment, (b) preventing sparks (by using nonsparking tools and avoiding friction as a source of heat), and (c) avoiding dust clouds, open flames, and chemical reactions.

17.3 COMPACTION OF METAL POWDERS

Compaction is the step in which the blended powders are pressed into shapes in dies (Figs. 17.8a and b). The presses used are actuated either hydraulically or mechanically. The purposes of compaction are to obtain the required shape, density, and particle-to-particle contact and to make the part sufficiently strong to be further processed.

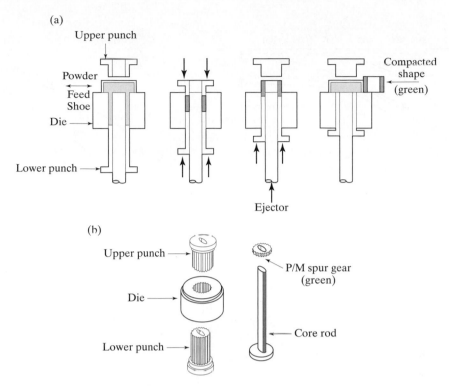

FIGURE 17.8 (a) Compaction of metal powder to form a bushing. The pressed powder part is called green compact. (b) Typical tool and die set for compacting a spur gear. *Source*: Metal Powder Industries Federation.

The pressed powder is known as a **green compact**. The powder must flow easily to feed properly into the die cavity. Pressing is generally carried out at room temperature, although it can be done at elevated temperatures.

The *density* of the green compact depends on the pressure applied (Fig. 17.9a). As the compacting pressure is increased, its density approaches the density of the metal in its bulk form. Another important factor is the size distribution of the particles. If all the particles are of the same size, there will always be some porosity when they are packed together (theoretically, at least 24% by volume). Imagine, for example, a box filled with tennis balls; there are always open spaces between the balls. However, introducing smaller particles will fill the spaces between the larger particles and, thus, result in a higher density of the compact. (See also *porous aluminum*, Section 6.2.)

The higher the density, the higher the strength and the elastic modulus of the part (Fig. 17.9b). The reason is that the higher the density, the higher the amount of solid metal in the same volume, and hence the greater its resistance to external forces. Because of friction between the metal particles in the powder and friction between the punches and the die walls, the density within the part can vary considerably.

This variation can be minimized by proper punch and die design and by control of friction. It may be necessary, for example, to use multiple punches, with separate movements, in order to ensure that the density is more nearly uniform throughout the part (Fig. 17.10). Recall a similar discussion regarding compaction of sand in mold making. (See Fig. 11.7.)

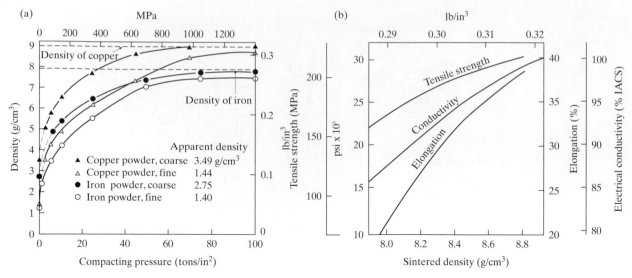

FIGURE 17.9   (a) Density of copper- and iron-powder compacts as a function of compacting pressure. Density greatly influences the mechanical and physical properties of P/M parts. *Source*: F. V. Lenel, *Powder Metallurgy: Principles and Applications.* Princeton, NJ; Metal Powder Industries Federation, 1980. (b) Effect of density on tensile strength, elongation, and electrical conductivity of copper powder. IACS means International Annealed Copper Standard for electrical conductivity.

FIGURE 17.10   Density variation in compacting metal powders in various dies: (a) and (c) single-action press; (b) and (d) double-action press. Note in (d) the greater uniformity of density, from pressing with two punches with separate movements, compared with (c). (e) Pressure contours in compacted copper powder in a single-action press. *Source*: P. Duwez and L. Zwell.

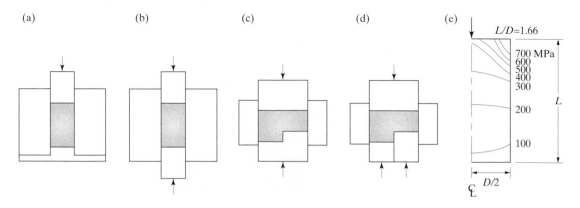

TABLE 17.2   Compacting Pressures for Various Metal Powders

Metal	Pressure (MPa)
Aluminum	70–275
Brass	400–700
Bronze	200–275
Iron	350–800
Tantalum	70–140
Tungsten	70–140
Other materials	
Aluminum oxide	110–140
Carbon	140–165
Cemented carbides	140–400
Ferrites	110–165

FIGURE 17.11
A 7.3 MN (825 ton) mechanical press for compacting metal powder. *Source*: Courtesy of Cincinnati Incorporated.

17.3.1 Equipment

The pressure required for pressing metal powders ranges from 70 MPa (10 ksi), for aluminum, to 800 MPa (120 ksi), for high-density iron parts (Table 17.2). The compacting pressure required depends on the characteristics and shape of the particles, on the method of blending, and on the lubricant.

Press capacities are on the order of 1.8 MN–2.7 MN (200 tons–300 tons), although presses with much higher capacities are used for special applications. Most applications require less than 100 tons. For small tonnage, crank- or eccentric-type mechanical presses are used; for higher capacities, toggle or knucklejoint presses are employed (see Fig. 14.21). Hydraulic presses (Fig. 17.11) with capacities as high as 45 MN (5000 tons) can be used for large parts.

The selection of the press depends on part size and configuration, on density requirements, and on production rate. However, the higher the pressing speed, the greater the tendency for the press to trap air in the die cavity and prevent proper compaction.

17.3.2 Isostatic Pressing

Compaction can also be carried out or improved by additional processing, such as isostatic pressing, rolling, and forging. Because the density of compacted powders can vary significantly, green compacts may be subjected to *hydrostatic pressure* in order to achieve more uniform compaction.

In **cold isostatic pressing (CIP)**, the metal powder is placed in a flexible rubber mold made of neoprene rubber, urethane, polyvinyl chloride, or another elastomer (Fig. 17.12). The assembly is then pressurized hydrostatically in a chamber, usually by water. The most common pressure is 400 MPa (60 ksi), although pressures of up to 1000 MPa (150 ksi) may be used. The applications of CIP and other compacting methods, in terms of the size and complexity of a part, are shown in Fig. 17.13; a typical application is automotive cylinder liners.

In **hot isostatic pressing (HIP)**, the container is usually made of a high-melting-point sheet metal, and the pressurizing medium is inert gas or a vitreous (glasslike) fluid (Fig. 17.14). Common conditions for HIP are 100 MPa (15 ksi) at 1100 °C (2000 °F), although the trend is toward higher pressures and temperatures. The main advantage of HIP

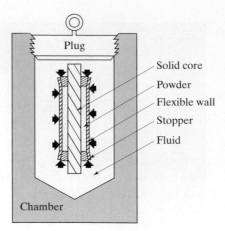

FIGURE 17.12 Schematic diagram of cold isostatic pressing, as applied to forming a tube. The powder is enclosed in a flexible container around a solid core rod. Pressure is applied isostatically to the assembly inside a high-pressure chamber. *Source*: Reprinted with permission from R.M. German, *Powder Metallurgy Science.* Princeton, NJ; Metal Powder Industries Federation, 1984.

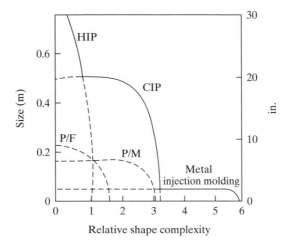

FIGURE 17.13 Capabilities, with respect to part size and shape complexity, available from various P/M operations. P/F means powder forging. *Source*: Metal Powder Industries Federation.

FIGURE 17.14 Schematic illustration of hot isostatic pressing. The pressure and temperature variation vs. time are shown in the diagram. *Source*: Reprinted with permission from R.M. German, *Powder Metallurgy Science.* Princeton, NJ; Metal Powder Industries Federation, 1984.

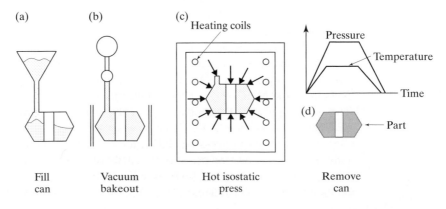

is its ability to produce compacts having almost 100% density, good metallurgical bonding of the particles, and good mechanical properties.

The HIP process is used mainly in making superalloy components for the aircraft and aerospace industries and in military, medical, and chemical applications. The process is also used to close internal porosity and to improve properties in superalloy and titanium-alloy castings for the aerospace industry. It is routinely used, also, as a final densification step for tungsten–carbide cutting tools and P/M tool steels.

The main advantages of isostatic pressing are the following:

a. Because of the uniformity of pressure from all directions and the absence of die-wall friction, it produces fully-dense compacts of practically uniform grain structure and density (hence, isotropic properties), irrespective of shape. Parts with high length-to-diameter ratios have been produced with very uniform density, strength, and toughness and good surface detail.

b. It is capable of handling much larger parts than are other compacting processes.

The limitations are as follows:

a. wider dimensional tolerances than are caused by other compacting processes.

b. greater cost and time than are required by other processes.

c. applicability only to relatively small production quantities (e.g., less than 10,000 parts per year).

17.3.3 Other Compacting and Shaping Processes

Metal Injection Molding (MIM).   In *metal injection molding*, also called *injection molding*, very fine metal powders ($<10\ \mu$m) are blended with either a polymer or a wax-based binder. The mixture then undergoes a process similar to die casting. (See Section 11.12; see also *injection molding of plastics* in Section 18.3). The molded greens are placed in a low-temperature oven, to burn off the plastic—or else the binder is removed by solvent extraction; then they are sintered in a furnace.

Metals suitable for metal-injection molding are carbon and stainless steels, tool steels, copper, bronze, and titanium. Typical parts made are components for watches, small-caliber gun barrels, heat sinks, automobiles, and surgical knives.

The following are the major advantages of metal injection molding over conventional compaction:

a. Complex shapes, having wall thicknesses as small as 5 mm (0.2 in.), can be molded and then easily removed from the dies.

b. Mechanical properties are nearly equal to those of wrought products.

c. Dimensional tolerances are good.

d. High production rates can be achieved by the use of multicavity dies.

Parts produced by the MIM process compete well against investment-cast parts (Section 11.7), small forgings (Chapter 14), and complex machined parts (Chapters 22 and 23). MIM does not, however, compete well with zinc and aluminum die casting (Section 11.12) and with screw machining (Section 22.5). The major limitation of this process, which is due to the high cost of the fine metal powders required, is that parts must be relatively small and are usually limited to about 250 g (0.55 lb.).

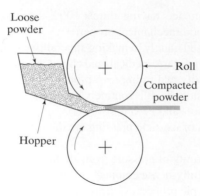

FIGURE 17.15   An example of powder rolling. *Source*: *Metals Handbook* (9th ed.), Vol. 7. American Society for Metals.

Rolling.   In *powder rolling*, also called **roll compaction**, the powder is fed to the roll gap in a two-high rolling mill (Fig. 17.15; also Fig. 13.11), and is compacted into a continuous strip at speeds of up to 0.5 m/s (100 ft/min). The rolling process can be carried out at room or at elevated temperature. Sheet metal for electrical and electronic components and for coins can be made by this process.

Extrusion.   Powders can be compacted by *extrusion* (Chapter 15); the powder is encased in a metal container and extruded. After sintering, preformed P/M parts may be reheated and then forged in a closed die to their final shape. Superalloy powders, for example, are hot extruded for improved properties.

Pressureless Compaction.   In *pressureless compaction*, the die is filled with metal powder by gravity, and the powder is sintered directly in the die. Because of the resulting low density, pressureless compaction is used principally for porous parts such as filters.

Ceramic Molds.   Ceramic molds for shaping metal powders are made by the technique used in investment casting. After the mold is made, it is filled with metal powder and placed in a steel container. The space between the mold and the container is filled with particulate material. The container is then evacuated, sealed, and subjected to hot isostatic pressing. Titanium-alloy compressor rotors for missile engines, for example, have been made by this process.

Spray Deposition.   Spray deposition is a shape-generation process, an example of which is shown is shown in Fig. 13.19. The basic components of the spray-deposition process for metal powders are (a) an atomizer, (b) a spray chamber with inert atmosphere, and (c) a mold for producing preforms. The mold may be made in various shapes, such as billets, tubes, disks, and cylinders.

Although there are several variations, the best known is the *Osprey* process. After the metal is atomized, it is deposited onto a cooled preform mold, usually made of copper or ceramic, where it solidifies. The metal particles bond together, developing a density that is normally above 99% of the solid-metal density.

Spray-deposited preforms may be subjected to additional shaping and consolidation processes, such as forging, rolling, and extrusion. The grain size is fine and the mechanical properties are comparable to those for wrought products made of the same alloy.

17.3.4 Punch and Die Materials

The selection of punch and die materials for P/M depends on the abrasiveness of the powder metal and on the number of parts to be produced. Most common die materials are air- or oil-hardening tool steels, such as D2 or D3, with a hardness range of 60–64 HRC (Table 5.7). Because of their higher hardness and wear resistance, tungsten-carbide dies are used for more severe applications. Punches are generally made of similar materials.

Close control of die and punch dimensions is essential for proper compaction and die life. Too large a clearance between the punch and the die will allow the metal powder to enter the gap, where it will interfere with the operation and cause eccentric parts. Diametral clearances are generally less than 25 μm (0.001 in.). Die and punch surfaces must be lapped or polished—and in the direction of tool movements—for improved die life and overall performance.

17.4 SINTERING

Sintering is the process whereby green compacts are heated in a controlled-atmosphere furnace to a temperature below the melting point, but sufficiently high to allow bonding (fusion) of the individual particles. Prior to sintering, the compact is brittle, and its strength, known as **green strength**, is low. The nature and strength of the bond between the particles, and, hence, that of the sintered compact, depend on the mechanisms of diffusion, plastic flow, evaporation of volatile materials in the compact, recrystallization, grain growth, and pore shrinkage.

The principal variables in sintering are temperature, time, and the furnace atmosphere. Sintering temperatures (Table 17.3) are generally within 70% to 90% of the melting point of the metal or alloy. Sintering times (Table 17.3) range from a minimum of about 10 minutes for iron and copper alloys to as much as 8 hours for tungsten and tantalum. Continuous sintering-furnaces, which are used for most production today, have three chambers:

1. a burn-off chamber for volatilizing the lubricants in the green compact, in order to improve bond strength and prevent cracking;
2. a high-temperature chamber for sintering; and
3. a cooling chamber.

TABLE 17.3   Sintering Temperature and Time for Various Metals

Material	Temperature (° C)	Time (Min)
Copper, brass, and bronze	760–900	10–45
Iron and iron-graphite	1000–1150	8–45
Nickel	1000–1150	30–45
Stainless steels	1100–1290	30–60
Alnico alloys (for permanent magnets)	1200–1300	120–150
Ferrites	1200–1500	10–600
Tungsten carbide	1430–1500	20–30
Molybdenum	2050	120
Tungsten	2350	480
Tantalum	2400	480

To obtain optimum properties, proper control of the furnace atmosphere is important for successful sintering. An oxygen-free atmosphere is essential, to control the carburization and decarburization of iron and iron-based compacts and to prevent oxidation of powders. A vacuum is generally used for sintering refractory-metal alloys and stainless steels. The gases most commonly used for sintering a variety of other metals are hydrogen, dissociated or burned ammonia, partially combusted hydrocarbon gases, and nitrogen.

Sintering mechanisms are complex; they depend on the composition of the metal particles as well as on processing parameters (Fig. 17.16). As temperature increases, two adjacent particles begin to form a bond by a **diffusion** mechanism (*solid-state bonding*). As a result, the strength, the density, the ductility, and the thermal and electrical conductivities of the compact increase. At the same time, however, the compact shrinks; hence, allowances should be made for shrinkage, as is done in casting.

A second sintering mechanism is **vapor-phase transport**. Because the material is heated to very close to its melting temperature, metal atoms will release to the vapor phase from the particles. At convergent geometries (the interface of two particles), the melting temperature is locally higher, and the vapor phase resolidifies. Thus, the interface grows and strengthens, while each particle shrinks as a whole.

If two adjacent particles are of different metals, *alloying* can take place at the interface of the two particles. One of the particles may have a lower melting point than the other; in that case, one particle may melt and, because of surface tension, surround the particle that has not melted (**liquid-phase sintering**). An example is cobalt in tungsten-carbide tools and dies (Section 21.5). Stronger and denser parts can be obtained in this way.

In liquid-phase sintering, the concentration of heavier components may be higher at the bottom than at the top of the part because of the effects of gravity. In order to obtain a more uniform distribution, experiments are being conducted in space shuttles under conditions of **microgravity**, just as is being tried in metal casting. (See Section 10.2.3.)

FIGURE 17.16   Schematic illustration of two mechanisms for sintering metal powders: (a) solid-state material transport; (b) liquid-phase material transport. R = particle radius, r = neck radius, and ρ = neck profile radius.

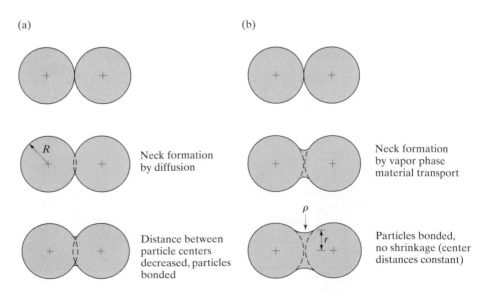

(a)

(b)

R

Neck formation by diffusion

Distance between particle centers decreased, particles bonded

Neck formation by vapor phase material transport

ρ

r

Particles bonded, no shrinkage (center distances constant)

Another method, which is still at an experimental stage, is **spark sintering**. In this process, loose metal powders are placed in a graphite mold, heated by an electric current, subjected to a high-energy discharge, and compacted, all in one step. The rapid discharge strips contaminants (or any oxide coating, such as on aluminum) from the surfaces of the particles and thus encourages good bonding during compaction at elevated temperatures.

Mechanical Properties.   Depending on temperature, time, and processing history, different structures and porosities can be obtained in a sintered compact, to affect its properties. Porosity cannot be completely eliminated, because voids remain after compaction and because gases evolve during sintering. Porosities may consist either of a network of interconnected pores or of closed holes. Generally, if the density of the material is less than 80% of its theoretical density, the pores are interconnected. Porosity is an important characteristic for making P/M filters and bearings.

Typical mechanical properties for several sintered P/M alloys are given in Table 17.4. Note the effect of heat treating on the properties of metals. To evaluate the differences between the properties of P/M, wrought, and cast metals and alloys, compare this table to the ones in Parts I and II.

The effects of various processes on the mechanical properties of a titanium alloy are shown in Table 17.5. Note that hot isostatically pressed (HIP) titanium has properties that are similar to those for cast and forged titanium. It should be remembered, however, that forged components are likely (unless they have been precision-forged to net shape) to require additional machining processes that a P/M component may not require. Powder metallurgy is becoming a competitive alternative to most small forgings.

TABLE 17.4   Mechanical Properties of Selected P/M Materials

Designation	MPIF type	Condition	Ultimate tensile strength (MPa)	Yield strength (MPa)	Hardness	Elongation in 25 mm (%)	Elastic modulus (GPa)
Ferrous							
FC-0208	N	AS	225	205	45 HRB	<0.5	70
		HT	295	—	95 HRB	<0.5	70
	R	AS	415	330	70 HRB	1	110
		HT	550	—	35 HRC	<0.5	110
	S	AS	550	395	80 HRB	1.5	130
		HT	690	655	40 HRC	<0.5	130
FN-0405	S	AS	425	240	72 HRB	4.5	145
		HT	1060	880	39 HRC	1	145
	T	AS	510	295	80 HRB	6	160
		HT	1240	1060	44 HRC	1.5	160
Aluminum							
601 AB, pressed bar		AS	110	48	60 HRH	6	—
		HT	252	241	75 HRH	2	—
Brass							
CZP-0220	T	—	165	76	55 HRH	13	—
	U	—	193	89	68 HRH	19	—
	W	—	221	103	75 HRH	23	—
Titanium							
Ti-6Al-4V		HIP	917	827	—	13	—
Superalloys							
Stellite 19		—	1035	—	49 HRC	<1	—

MPIF: Metal Powder Industries Federation. AS: as sintered, HT: heat treated, HIP: hot isostatically pressed.

TABLE 17.5   Mechanical Property Comparison for Ti-6AI-4V

Process(*)	Density (%)	Yield strength (MPa)	Ultimate strength (MPa)	Elongation (%)	Reduction of area (%)
Cast	100	840	930	7	15
Cast and forged	100	875	965	14	40
Blended elemental (P+S)	98	786	875	8	14
Blended elemental (HIP)	>99	805	875	9	17
Prealloyed (HIP)	100	880	975	14	26

(*) P+S = pressed and sintered, HIP = hot isostatically pressed.
Source: R.M. German.

Example: Shrinkage in Sintering

In solid-state bonding during sintering of a powder-metal green compact, the linear shrinkage is 4%. If the desired sintered density is 95% of the theoretical density of the metal, what should be the density of the green compact?

Solution: Linear shrinkage is defined as $\Delta L/L_o$, where L_o is the original length; the volume shrinkage during sintering is, then,

$$V_{sint} = V_{green}\left(1 - \frac{\Delta L}{L_o}\right)^3. \tag{17.1}$$

The volume of the green compact must be higher than that of the sintered part, but the mass does not change during sintering. We can, therefore, rewrite this expression in terms of the density ρ:

$$\rho_{green} = \rho_{sint}\left(1 - \frac{\Delta L}{L_o}\right)^3. \tag{17.2}$$

Thus,

$$\rho_{green} = 0.95(1 - 0.04)^3 = 0.84, \text{ or } 84\%.$$

17.5 SECONDARY AND FINISHING OPERATIONS

In order to improve the properties of sintered P/M products further or to impart special characteristics, several additional operations may be carried out after sintering.

1. **Coining** and **sizing** are compaction operations, performed under high pressure in presses. The purposes of these operations are to impart dimensional accuracy to the sintered part and to improve its strength and surface finish by further densification.

2. An important development is the use of *preformed* and *sintered* alloy powder compacts, which are subsequently cold or hot **forged** to the desired final shapes, sometimes by **impact forging**. (See Section 14.9.2.) These products have a good surface finish, good dimensional tolerances, and a uniform and fine grain size. The superior properties obtained make this technology particularly suitable for such applications as highly stressed automotive and jet-engine components.

3. The inherent porosity of P/M components can be utilized by **impregnating** them with a fluid. A typical application is to impregnate the sintered part with oil, usually by immersing the part in heated oil. Bearings and bushings that are internally lubricated, with up to 30% oil by volume, are made by this method. Such components have a continuous supply of lubricant, by capillary action, during their service lives. Universal joints are now made by means of grease-impregnated P/M techniques, and no longer require grease fittings.

4. **Infiltration** is a process whereby a slug of a lower-melting-point metal is placed against the sintered part and then the assembly is heated to a temperature sufficient to melt the slug. The molten metal infiltrates the pores, by capillary action, to produce a relatively pore-free part having good density and strength. The most common application is the infiltration of iron-base compacts by copper.

   The advantages of infiltration are that hardness and tensile strength are improved and that the pores are filled (the latter prevents moisture penetration, which could cause corrosion). Infiltration may also be used with lead: Because of the low shear strength of lead, the infiltrated part develops lower frictional characteristics than the one not infiltrated. Some bearing materials are formed in this way.

5. Powder-metal parts may be subjected to other finishing operations, including the following:

   - **heat treating**, for improved hardness and strength;
   - **machining**, for producing various geometric features by milling, by drilling, and by tapping (to produce threaded holes);
   - **grinding**, for improved dimensional accuracy and surface finish;
   - **plating**, for improved appearance and resistance to wear and corrosion.

Example: Powder-Metallurgy Gears for a Garden Tractor

Such components as the gears, the bushings, and some structural parts of garden tractors can now be made by P/M techniques instead of by the traditional casting or forging methods. Gears have been manufactured competitively by the use of high-quality powders having high compressibility (and thus requiring low compacting pressures). These parts have from medium to high density and are suitable for severe applications with high loads and for high-wear surfaces.

In one application, a reduction gear for a garden tractor was made from iron powder and infiltrated with copper. Although its strength was acceptable, the wear rate under high loads was too high. This wear resulted in loss of tooth profile, in side loading on the bearings, and in a high noise level. To improve wear resistance and strength, a new powder was selected, one containing 2.0% nickel, 0.5% graphite, 0.5% molybdenum—the balance was atomized iron powder. Because of the size of the part, the pressing loads were very high. The part was redesigned, and the tooling was made with three punches, to compact the part to three different densities. The entire part required a compacting load of 4 MN (450 tons).

By this method, high density was obtained in those sections of the part that required high strength and wear resistance. The high density also permitted carburization for hardness improvement. The presintered part was pressed again, to a new density of 7.3–7.5 g/cm^3 in the tooth area, for improved strength, while the hub of the gear remained at its pressed density of 6.4–6.6 g/cm^3. The weight of the gear was 1 kg (2.25 lb).

Example: Production of Tungsten Carbide for Tools and Dies

Tungsten carbide is an important tool and die material, mostly because of its hardness, strength, and wear resistance over a wide range of temperatures. (See Section 21.5). Powder-metallurgy techniques are used in making such carbides. First, powders of tungsten and carbon are blended together in a ball mill or a rotating mixer. The mixture (basically 94% tungsten and 6% carbon, by weight) is heated to approximately 1500 °C (2800 °F) in a vacuum-induction furnace.

As a result, the tungsten is carburized and forms tungsten carbide in fine powder form. A binding agent (usually cobalt) is then added to the tungsten carbide (together with an organic fluid such as hexane), and the mixture is ball milled to produce a uniform and homogenous mix. This process can take several hours, or even days.

The mixture is then dried and consolidated, usually by cold compaction under pressures of about 200 MPa (30,000 psi). The part is then sintered in a hydrogen atmosphere or vacuum furnace, at a temperature of from 1350 °C to 1600 °C (from 2500 °F to 2900 °F), depending on its composition. At this temperature, the cobalt is in a liquid phase and acts as a binder for the carbide particles. (Powders may also be hot pressed at the sintering temperature, using graphite dies.)

During sintering, the tungsten carbide undergoes a linear shrinkage of about 16%; the reduction corresponds to a volume shrinkage of about 40%. Thus, control of size and shape is important for producing tools with accurate dimensions. A combination of other carbides, such as titanium carbide and tantalum carbide, can also be produced, using mixtures made by the method described.

The trend now is to use finer and finer particles, in order to enhance the mechanical properties of such composite structures (*nanostructures*, described in Sections 8.2.5 and 17.2.1).

17.6 DESIGN CONSIDERATIONS FOR POWDER METALLURGY

Because of the unique properties of metal powders, their flow characteristics in the die, and the brittleness of green compacts, the following design principles have been established (Fig. 17.17):

a. The shape of the compact must be as simple and uniform as possible. Sharp changes in contour, thin sections, variations in thickness, and high length-to-diameter ratios should be avoided.

b. Provision must be made for ejecting the green compact from the die without damaging the compact; for example, holes or recesses should be parallel to the axis of punch travel. Chamfers should also be provided, to avoid chipping along the edges and corners of the compact.

c. As with most other processes, P/M parts should be made with the widest dimensional tolerances that are consistent with their intended applications, in order to increase tool and die life and to reduce production costs.

d. Dimensional tolerances of sintered P/M parts are usually on the order of ±0.05–0.1 mm (±0.002–0.004 in.); tolerances improve significantly with additional operations such as sizing, machining, and grinding.

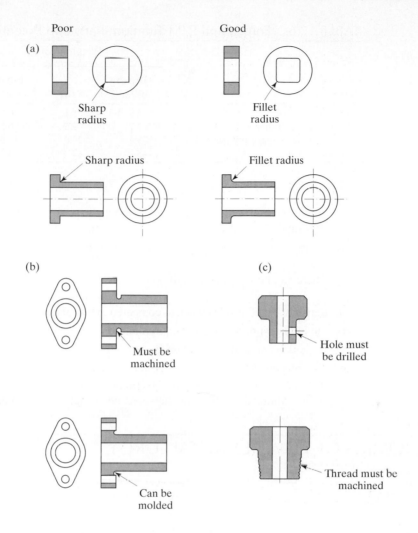

FIGURE 17.17   Examples of P/M parts, showing poor designs and good ones. Note that sharp radii and reentry corners should be avoided, and that threads and transverse holes have to be produced separately by additional machining operations.

17.7 PROCESS CAPABILITIES

The process capabilities of powder metallurgy may be summarized as follows:

a. It is a technique for making parts from high-melting-point refractory metals, parts which may be difficult or uneconomical to produce by other methods.

b. It offers high production rates on relatively complex parts, by the use of automated equipment requiring little labor.

c. It offers good dimensional control and, in many instances, resultant elimination of machining and finishing operations; in this way, it reduces scrap and waste and saves energy.

d. The availability of a wide range of compositions makes it possible to obtain special mechanical and physical properties, such as stiffness, damping, hardness, density,

TABLE 17.6   Forged and P/M Titanium Parts and Potential Cost Savings

	Weight (kg)			Potential cost saving (%)
Part	Forged billet	P/M	Final part	
F-14 Fuselage brace	2.8	1.1	0.8	50
F-18 Engine mount support	7.7	2.5	0.5	20
F-18 Arrestor hook support fitting	79.4	25.0	12.9	25
F-14 Nacelle frame	143	82	24.2	50

toughness, and specific electrical and magnetic properties. Some of the highly alloyed new superalloys can be manufactured into parts only by P/M processing.

e. It offers capability for impregnation and infiltration for special applications.

There are, however, certain limitation to P/M:

a. the high cost of metal powder, as compared to that of raw materials to be cast or wrought;

b. the high cost of tooling and equipment for small production runs;

c. limitations on part size and on shape complexity;

d. resulting mechanical properties, such as strength and ductility, that are generally lower than those obtained by forging. The properties of full-density P/M parts made by HIP, or by additional forging, can, however, be as high as those made by other processes.

17.8 ECONOMICS OF POWDER METALLURGY

Because P/M can produce parts at or near net shape and thus eliminate many secondary manufacturing and assembly operations, it has become increasingly competitive with casting, forging, and machining. On the other hand, the high initial cost of punches, dies, and equipment for P/M processing means that production volume must be sufficiently high to warrant this expenditure. Although there are exceptions, the process is generally economical for quantities over 10,000 pieces.

The near-net-shape capability of P/M reduces or eliminates scrap. For example, weight comparisons of aircraft components produced by forging and by P/M processes are shown in Table 17.6. Note that these P/M parts are subjected to further machining processes; thus the final parts weigh less than those made by either of the two processes alone.

17.9 SHAPING CERAMICS

Several techniques are available for processing ceramics into useful products (Table 17.7). Generally, the procedure involves the following steps: (a) crushing or grinding the raw materials into very fine particles; (b) mixing them with additives to impart certain desirable characteristics, and (c) shaping, drying, and firing the material (Fig. 17.18).

The first step in processing ceramics is the *crushing* (also called *comminution* or *milling*) of the raw materials (see Section 17.2.1). Crushing is generally done in a ball mill, either dry or wet. (See Fig. 17.6.) Wet crushing is more effective, because it keeps the particles together and prevents the suspension of fine particles in the air. The particles may then be sized (sieved), filtered, and washed.

TABLE 17.7   Characteristics of Ceramics Processing

Process	Advantages	Limitations
Slip casting	Large parts, complex shapes; low equipment cost.	Low production rate; limited dimensional accuracy.
Extrusion	Hollow shapes and small diameters; high production rate.	Parts have constant cross section; limited thickness.
Dry pressing	Close tolerances; high production rate with automation.	Density variation in parts with high length-to-diameter ratios; dies require high abrasive-wear resistance; equipment can be costly.
Wet pressing	Complex shapes; high production rate.	Part size limited; limited dimensional accuracy; tooling costs can be high.
Hot pressing	Strong, high-density parts.	Protective atmospheres required; die life can be short.
Isostatic pressing	Uniform density distribution.	Equipment can be costly.
Jiggering	High production rate with automation; low tooling cost.	Limited to axisymmetric parts; limited dimensional accuracy.
Injection molding	Complex shapes; high production rate.	Tooling can be costly.

The ground particles are then mixed with *additives*, the functions of which are one or more of the following:

a. **binder** for the ceramic particles;
b. **lubricant**, to aid mold release and to reduce internal friction between particles during molding;
c. **wetting agent**, to improve mixing.
d. **plasticizer**, to make the mix more plastic and formable.
e. Various **agents** to control foaming and sintering;
f. **Deflocculent**, to make the ceramic–water suspension more uniform. Deflocculation changes the electrical charges on the particles of clay, so that they repel rather than attract each other. Water is added to make the mixture more pourable and less viscous. Typical deflocculents are Na_2CO_3 and Na_2SiO_3, in amounts of less than 1%.

The three basic shaping processes for ceramics are casting, plastic forming, and pressing. They are described in the subsections that follow.

FIGURE 17.18   Processing steps involved in making ceramic parts.

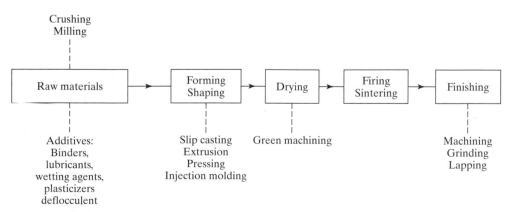

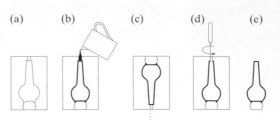

(a)   (b)   (c)   (d)   (e)

FIGURE 17.19   Sequence of operations in slip-casting a ceramic part. After the slip has been poured, the part is dried and fired in an oven to give it strength and hardness. *Source*: F.H. Norton, *Elements of Ceramics*. Addison-Wesley Publishing Company, Inc. 1974.

17.9.1 Casting

The most common casting process is **slip casting**, also called **drain casting** (Fig. 17.19). A **slip** is a suspension of *colloidal* (small particles that do not settle) ceramic particles in an immiscible (insoluble in each other) liquid, which is generally water. In this process, the slip is poured into a porous mold made of plaster of paris. The slip must have sufficient fluidity and low enough viscosity to flow easily into the mold—much like the fluidity of molten metals described in Section 10.3. Air entrapment can be a significant problem during slip casting.

After the mold has absorbed some of the water from the outer layers of the suspension, it is inverted, and the remaining suspension is poured out (for the making of hollow objects, as in the slush casting of metals described in Section 11.10). The top of the part is then trimmed, the mold is opened, and the part is removed.

Large and complex parts, such as plumbing ware, art objects, and dinnerware, can be made by slip casting. Dimensional control is poor and the production rate is low, but mold and equipment costs are also low. In some applications, components of the product (such as handles for cups and pitchers) are made separately and then joined, using the slip as an adhesive. Molds may also consist of multicomponents. Iron and other magnetic materials are removed using in-line magnetic separators.

For solid ceramic parts, the slip is supplied continuously into the mold to replenish the absorbed water; the suspension is not drained from the mold. At this stage, the part is a soft solid or is semirigid. The higher the concentration of solids is in the slip, the less water has to be removed. The part, called *green* (as in powder metallurgy), is then fired.

While the ceramic parts are green, they may be carefully machined. Because of the delicate nature of the green compacts, machining is usually done manually or with simple tools. For example, the flashing in a slip casting may be removed gently, with a fine wire brush, or holes can be drilled. Detailed work, such as the tapping of threads, is generally not done on green compacts, because warpage due to firing makes such machining not viable. (See Section 17.9.4.)

Doctor-Blade Process.   Thin sheets of ceramics, less than 1.5–mm (0.06–in.) thick, can be made by a casting technique called the *doctor-blade process*. The slip is cast over a moving plastic belt and its thickness is controlled by a blade.

Among other processes are these two: **rolling** the slip between pairs of rolls; **casting** the slip over a paper tape, which then burns off during firing.

17.9.2 Plastic Forming

Plastic forming, also called *soft*, *wet*, or *hydroplastic forming*, can be carried out by various methods, such as extrusion, injection molding, or molding and jiggering (Fig. 17.20). Plastic

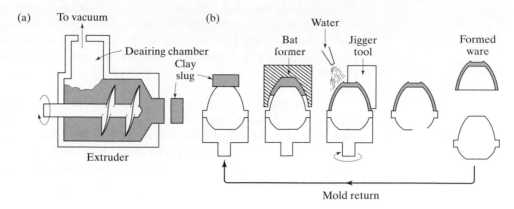

FIGURE 17.20   (a) Extruding and (b) jiggering operations. *Source*: R.F. Stoops.

forming tends to orient the layered structure of clay along the direction of material flow and so tends to cause anisotropic behavior of the material, both in subsequent processing and in the final properties of the ceramic product.

In **extrusion**, the clay mixture, containing 20% to 30% water, is forced through a die opening by screw-type equipment. The cross-section of the extruded product is constant (Chapter 15), and there are limitations to wall thickness for hollow extrusions. Tooling costs are low, and production rates are high. The extruded products may be subjected to additional shaping operations.

17.9.3 Pressing

Dry Pressing.   A technique similar to powder-metal compaction, *dry pressing*, is used for relatively simple shapes. Typical parts are whiteware, refractories, and abrasive products. The process has the same high production rates and close control of dimensional tolerances as in P/M. The moisture content of the mixture is generally below 4%, but it may be as high as 12%. Organic and inorganic binders, such as stearic acid, wax, starch, and polyvinyl alcohol, are usually added to the mixture, and they also act as lubricants.

The pressing pressure is from 35 MPa to 200 MPa (5 ksi to 30 ksi). Modern presses used for dry pressing are highly automated. Dies, usually made of carbides or of hardened steel, must have high wear resistance, to withstand the abrasive ceramic particles, so they can be expensive.

As in P/M compaction, density can vary significantly in dry-pressed ceramics, because of friction among the particles and at the mold walls. Density variations cause warping during the firing. Warping is particularly severe for parts having high length-to-diameter ratios; the recommended maximum ratio is 2:1. Several methods may be used to minimize density variations; design of tooling is important. Vibratory pressing and impact forming are used, particularly for nuclear-reactor fuel elements. Isostatic pressing also reduces density variations.

Wet Pressing.   In *wet pressing*, the part is formed in a mold while under high pressure in a hydraulic or mechanical press. This process generally is used to make intricate shapes. Moisture content usually ranges from 10% to 15%. Production rates are high; however, part size is limited, dimensional control is difficult to achieve because of shrinkage during drying, and tooling costs can be high.

Isostatic Pressing.   Used extensively in powder metallurgy, *isostatic pressing* is also used for ceramics, in order to obtain uniform density distribution throughout the part. Automotive spark-plug insulators, for example, are made by this method; silicon-nitride vanes for high-temperature applications (see Fig. 8.1) are made by *hot* isostatic pressing.

Jiggering.   A combination of processes is used to make ceramic plates. Clay slugs are first extruded, then formed into a *bat* over a plaster mold, and finally jiggered on a rotating mold (Fig. 17.20). *Jiggering* is a motion in which the clay bat is formed by means of templates or rollers. The part is then dried and fired. The process is limited to axisymmetric parts and has limited dimensional accuracy, but the operation can be automated.

Injection Molding.   We have previously described the advantages of *injection molding* of powder metals (Section 17.3.3. See also Section 18.3, on injection molding of plastics). This process is now used extensively for the precision forming of ceramics for high-technology applications, such as in rocket-engine components. The raw material is mixed with a binder, such as a thermoplastic polymer (e.g., polypropylene, low-density polyethylene, or ethylene vinyl acetate) or a wax. The binder usually is removed by pyrolysis; the part is then sintered by firing.

This process can produce thin sections, typically less than 10 mm–15 mm (0.4 in.–0.6 in.) thick, from most engineering ceramics—for example, alumina, zirconia, silicon nitride, silicon carbide, and sialon. Thicker sections require careful control of the materials used and of processing parameters, in order to avoid internal voids and cracks, especially those due to shrinkage.

Hot Pressing.   In *hot pressing*, also called *pressure sintering*, pressure and temperature are applied simultaneously. This method makes the part denser and stronger, by reducing porosity. Protective atmospheres are usually employed, and graphite is a commonly used punch and die material.

Hot isostatic pressing (HIP—Section 17.3.2) may also be used, particularly to improve shape accuracy and the quality of such high-technology ceramics as silicon carbide and silicon nitride. Glass-encapsulated HIP processing has been shown to be effective for this purpose.

17.9.4 Drying and Firing

The next step in ceramic processing is to dry and fire the part to give it the proper strength and hardness. *Drying* is a critical stage, because of the tendency for the part to warp, or crack, from variations in the moisture content and the thickness within the part. Control of atmospheric humidity and of temperature is important in order to reduce warping and cracking.

Loss of moisture results in shrinkage of the part by as much as 15% to 20% from the original moist size (Fig. 17.21). In a humid environment, the evaporation rate is low, and consequently the moisture gradient across the thickness of the part is lower than that in a dry environment. This low moisture gradient, in turn, prevents a large, uneven gradient in shrinkage from the surface to the interior during drying.

A ceramic part that has been shaped by any of the methods described above is in the *green* state (as in powder metallurgy). This part can be *machined* (Chapters 22 and 23)

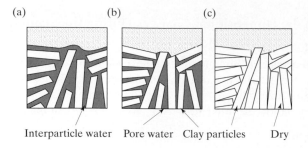

FIGURE 17.21   Shrinkage of wet clay caused by removal of water during drying. Shrinkage may be as much as 20% by volume. *Source*: F.H. Norton, *Elements of Ceramics*. Addison-Wesley Publishing Company, Inc. 1974.

relatively easily, to bring it closer to a near-net shape. Although it should be handled carefully, machining it is not particularly difficult, because of its relative softness.

Firing, also called **sintering**, involves heating the part to an elevated temperature in a controlled environment, a process similar to the sintering employed in powder metallurgy. Some shrinkage occurs during firing. Firing gives the ceramic part its strength and hardness. This improvement in properties results from (a) development of a strong bond between the complex oxide particles in the ceramic and (b) reduced porosity. A new technology, although not yet commercialized, involves the **microwave sintering** of ceramics in furnaces operating at more than 2 GHz. Its cost effectiveness will depend on the availability of inexpensive furnace insulation.

Nanophase ceramics (described in Section 8.2.5) can be sintered at lower temperatures than those used for conventional ceramics. They are easier to fabricate, because they can be compacted at room temperature to high densities, hot pressed to theoretical density, and formed into net-shape parts without binders or sintering aids.

17.9.5 Finishing Operations

Because firing causes dimensional changes, additional operations may be performed to give the ceramic part its final shape, improve its surface finish and tolerances, and remove any surface flaws. The finishing processes used can be one or more of the following, described in various sections in Part IV:

1. *grinding* with a diamond wheel;
2. *lapping* and *honing*;
3. *ultrasonic machining*;
4. *drilling*, by the use of a diamond-coated drill;
5. *electrical-discharge machining*;
6. *laser-beam machining*;
7. *abrasive water-jet cutting*;
8. *tumbling*, to remove sharp edges and grinding marks.

The choice of the process is important, because of the brittle nature of most ceramics and because of the additional costs involved in these processes. The effect of the finishing operation on the properties of the product must also be considered; for instance, because of notch sensitivity, the finer the finish, the higher the part's strength. To improve their appearance and strength, and to make them impermeable, ceramic products are often coated with a **glaze** material, which forms a glassy coating after firing. (See Section 33.12).

Example: Dimensional Changes During the Shaping of Ceramic Components

A solid cylindrical ceramic part is to be made with a final length, L, of 20 mm. It has been established that, for this material, linear shrinkages during drying and firing are 7% and 6%, respectively, based on the dried dimension L_d. Calculate (a) the initial length L_o of the part and (b) the dried porosity, P_d if the porosity of the fired part, P_f, is 3%.

Solution:

a. On the basis of the information given (and noting that firing is preceded by drying), we can write

$$\frac{(L_d - L)}{L_d} = 0.06,$$

or

$$L = (1 - 0.06)L_d;$$

hence,

$$L_d = \frac{20}{094} = 21.28 \text{ mm},$$

$$L_o(1 + 0.07)L_d = (1.07)(21.28) = 22.77 \text{ mm}.$$

b. Because the final porosity is 3%, the actual volume, V_a, of the solid material in the part is

$$V_a = (1 - 0.03)V_f = 0.97V_f,$$

where V_f is the fired volume of the part. Because the linear shrinkage during firing is 6%, we can determine the dried volume V_d of the part as follows:

$$V_d = \frac{V_f}{(1 - 0.06)^3} = 1.2V_f.$$

Hence,

$$\frac{V_a}{V_d} = \frac{0.97}{1.2} = 0.81, \text{ or } 81\%.$$

Therefore, the porosity, P_d, of the dried part is 19%.

17.10 FORMING AND SHAPING OF GLASS

Glass is processed by melting it and then shaping it, either in molds and various devices or by blowing. Shapes produced include flat sheet and plate, rods, tubing, glass fibers, and discrete products such as bottles and headlights. The strength of glass can be improved by thermal and chemical treatments (Section 17.11), which induce compressive surface residual stresses, or by laminating it with a thin sheet of tough plastic.

Glass products can generally be categorized as follows:

1. flat sheet or plate, ranging in thickness from about 0.8 mm to 10 mm (0.03 in. to 0.4 in.), such as window glass, glass doors, and table tops;
2. rods and tubing, used for chemicals, neon lights, and decorative artifacts;
3. discrete products, such as bottles, vases, headlights, and television tubes;
4. glass fibers, to reinforce composite materials (Section 9.2.1) and for fiber optics.

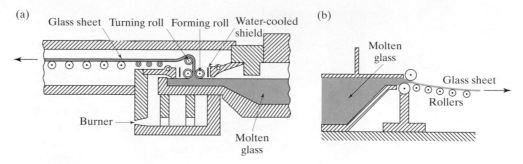

FIGURE 17.22   (a) Continuous process for drawing sheet glass from a molten bath. *Source*: W.D. Kingery, *Introduction to Ceramics*. Wiley, 1976. (b) Rolling glass to produce flat sheet.

All glass forming and shaping processes begin with molten glass (typically 1000 to 1200 °C [1830 to 2200 °F] for soda-lime-silica), which has the appearance of red-hot viscous syrup, supplied from a melting furnace or tank.

17.10.1 Flat Sheet and Plate

Flat sheet glass can be made by drawing or rolling from the molten state or by a floating method; all three methods are continuous processes.

The **drawing** process for making flat sheet or plate involves a machine in which the molten glass passes through a pair of rolls (Fig. 17.22a) which appear similar to an old-fashioned clothes wringer. The solidifying glass is squeezed between these rolls, formed into a sheet, and then moved forward over a set of smaller rolls.

In the **rolling** process (Fig. 17.22b), the molten glass is squeezed between rollers, forming a sheet. The surfaces of the glass may be embossed with a pattern by a texture on the roller surfaces; in this way, the glass surface becomes a replica of the roll surface. Glass sheet produced by drawing or rolling has a rough surface appearance. In the making of *plate glass*, both surfaces have to be subsequently ground parallel and then polished.

In the **float method** (Fig. 17.23), molten glass from the furnace is fed into a bath in which the glass, under a controlled atmosphere, floats on a bath of molten tin. The glass then moves over rollers into another chamber (*lehr*) where it solidifies. *Float glass* has a smooth (*fire-polished*) surface and needs no further grinding or polishing.

17.10.2 Tubing and Rods

Glass tubing is manufactured by the process shown in Fig. 17.24. Molten glass is wrapped around a rotating hollow cylindrical or cone-shaped mandrel, and is drawn out by a set of rolls. Air is blown through the mandrel to prevent the glass tube from collapsing. These machines may be horizontal, vertical, or slanted downward. Glass rods are made in a similar manner, but air is not blown through the mandrel; the drawn product becomes a solid rod.

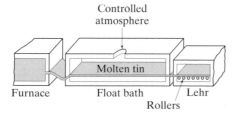

FIGURE 17.23   The float method of forming sheet glass. *Source*: Corning Glass Works.

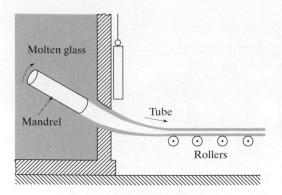

FIGURE 17.24
Manufacturing process for glass tubing. Air is blown through the mandrel to keep the tube from collapsing. *Source*: Corning Glass Works.

17.10.3 Glass Fibers

Continuous glass fibers are drawn through multiple orifices (200 to 400 holes) in heated platinum plates, at speeds as high as 500 m/s (1700 ft/s). Fibers as small as 2 μm (80 μin.) in diameter can be produced by this method. In order to protect their surfaces, fibers are subsequently coated with chemicals. Short glass fibers, used as a thermal insulating material (**glass wool**) or for acoustic insulation, are made by a **centrifugal spraying** process in which molten glass is fed into a rotating head.

17.10.4 Discrete Glass Products

Several processes are used in making discrete glass objects, as described below.

The **blowing** process is used to make hollow thin-walled glass items, such as bottles and flasks; it is similar to blow molding of thermoplastics (Section 18.4). The steps involved in the production of an ordinary glass bottle by the blowing process are shown in Fig. 17.25. Blown air expands a hollow gob of heated glass against the walls of the mold. The molds are usually coated with a parting agent, such as oil or emulsion, to prevent the glass from sticking to the mold.

The surface finish of products made by the blowing process is acceptable for most applications. It is difficult to control the wall thickness of the product, but the process is used for its high production rate. Incandescent light bulbs are made in automatic blowing machines, at a rate of over 1000 bulbs per minute. (See Fig. 3 in the General Introduction.)

In **pressing**, a gob of molten glass is placed into a mold and pressed into shape with the use of a plunger. The mold may be made in one piece (Fig. 17.26) or it may be split (Fig. 17.27). After being pressed, the solidifying glass acquires the shape of the mold-plunger cavity. Because of the confined environment, the product has higher dimensional accuracy than can be obtained with blowing. Pressing cannot, however, be used on thin-walled items, nor can it be used for products (such as bottles) from which the plunger cannot be retracted.

The **centrifugal casting** process, also known in the glass industry as **spinning** (Fig. 17.28), is similar to that used for metals (see Section 11.13). The centrifugal force pushes the molten glass against the mold wall, where it solidifies. Typical products made are TV picture tubes and missile nose cones.

Shallow dish-shaped or lightly embossed glass parts can be made by the **sagging** process. A sheet of glass is placed over the mold and heated; the glass sags by its own weight and takes the shape of the mold. The process is similar to the thermoforming of thermoplastics (Section 18.6), but it works without pressure or a vacuum. Typical applications are dishes, sunglass lenses, mirrors for telescopes, and lighting panels.

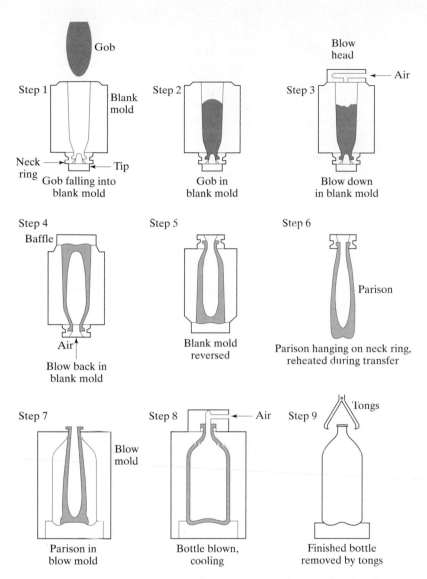

FIGURE 17.25   Stages in manufacturing an ordinary glass bottle. *Source*: F.H. Norton, *Elements of Ceramics*. Addison-Wesley Publishing Company, Inc. 1974.

FIGURE 17.26   Manufacturing a glass item by pressing glass in a mold. *Source*: Corning Glass Works.

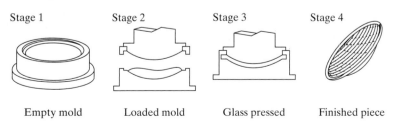

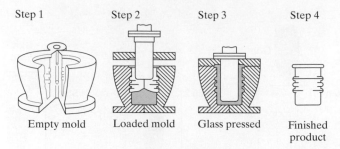

Step 1   Step 2   Step 3   Step 4

Empty mold   Loaded mold   Glass pressed   Finished product

FIGURE 17.27   Pressing glass in a split mold. *Source*: E.B. Shand, *Glass Engineering Handbook*. McGraw-Hill, 1958.

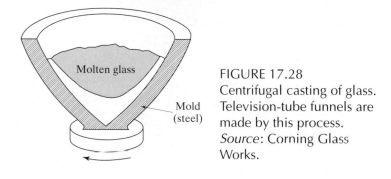

Molten glass

Mold (steel)

FIGURE 17.28 Centrifugal casting of glass. Television-tube funnels are made by this process. *Source*: Corning Glass Works.

17.11 TECHNIQUES FOR STRENGTHENING AND TREATING GLASS

Glass can be strengthened by the processes described in this section. Glass products may also be subjected to heat treatment (annealing) and to other finishing operations.

a. Thermal tempering. Also called *physical tempering* or *chill tempering*, this process cools the surfaces of the hot glass rapidly (Fig. 17.29). As a result, the surfaces shrink, and, at first, tensile stresses develop on the surfaces. As the bulk of the glass begins

FIGURE 17.29   Residual stresses in tempered glass plate, and stages involved in inducing compressive surface residual stresses for improved strength.

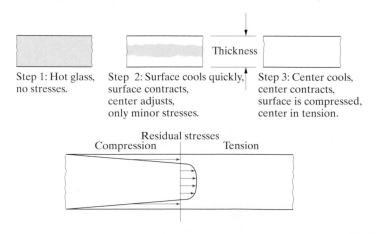

Thickness

Step 1: Hot glass, no stresses.

Step 2: Surface cools quickly, surface contracts, center adjusts, only minor stresses.

Step 3: Center cools, center contracts, surface is compressed, center in tension.

Residual stresses

Compression   Tension

to cool, it contracts. The already solidified surfaces are forced to contract, and so they develop residual compressive surface stresses, while the interior develops tensile stresses. (See also Section 2.11.) Compressive surface stresses improve the strength of the glass, in the same way that they do in other materials.

The higher the coefficient of thermal expansion of the glass and the lower its thermal conductivity, the higher will be the level of residual stresses developed, and, hence, the stronger the glass becomes. Thermal tempering takes a relatively short time (minutes) and can be applied to most glasses. Because of the large amount of energy stored in residual stresses, **tempered glass** shatters into a large number of pieces when broken.

b. Chemical tempering. In this process the glass is heated in a bath of molten KNO_3, K_2SO_4, or $NaNO_3$, depending on the type of glass. Ion exchange takes place, with larger atoms replacing the smaller atoms in the surface of the glass. As a result, residual compressive stresses are developed on the surface. This condition is similar to that created by forcing a wedge between two bricks in a wall.

The time required for chemical tempering is about one hour longer than that for thermal tempering. It may be performed at various temperatures. At low temperatures, part distortion is minimal, and complex shapes can therefore be treated; at elevated temperatures, there may be some distortion of the part, but the product can then be used at higher temperatures without loss of strength.

c. Laminated glass. This product results from another strengthening method, called *laminate strengthening*; it consists of two pieces of flat glass with a thin sheet of tough plastic between them. When laminated glass is broken, its pieces are held together by the plastic sheet. This phenomenon can be observed in a shattered automobile windshield.

Finishing Operations.   As in metal products, residual stresses can develop in glass products if they are not cooled at a sufficiently slow rate. In order to ensure that the product is free from these stresses, it is **annealed** by a process similar to the stress-relief annealing of metals. (See Section 4.11.2.) The glass is heated to a certain temperature and then cooled gradually. Depending on the size, the thickness, and the type of the glass, annealing times may range from a few minutes to as long as the 10 months as in the case of a 600–mm (24–in.) mirror for a telescope.

In addition to annealing, glass products may be subjected to further operations such as cutting, drilling, grinding, and polishing (Part IV). Sharp edges and corners can be smoothed by grinding, an effect seen in glass tops for desks and shelves, or by holding a torch against the edges (**fire polishing**); this method rounds them by localized softening and by surface tension.

17.12 DESIGN CONSIDERATIONS FOR CERAMICS AND GLASSES

Ceramic and glass products require careful selection of composition, processing methods, finishing operations, and methods of assembly. Limitations such as general lack of tensile strength, sensitivity to internal and external defects, and low impact toughness are important. These limitations have to be balanced against such desirable characteristics as hardness, scratch resistance, compressive strength at room and elevated temperatures, and diverse physical properties.

Control of processing parameters and of the quality and level of impurities in the raw materials is important. As in all design decisions, there are priorities and limitations, and several factors should be considered, including the number of parts needed and the costs of tooling, equipment, and labor.

Dimensional changes and warping and cracking possibilities during processing are significant factors in selecting methods for shaping these materials. When a ceramic or glass component is part of a larger assembly, compatibility with other components is another important consideration. Particularly important are thermal expansion (as in seals) and the type of loading. The potential consequences of part failure are always a significant factor in designing ceramic products.

17.13 PROCESSING OF SUPERCONDUCTORS

Although superconductors (Section 3.7) have major energy-saving potential in the generation, storage, and distribution of electrical energy, their processing into useful shapes and sizes for practical applications has presented significant difficulties. Two basic types of superconductors are metals (**low-temperature superconductors, LTSC**, including combinations of niobium, tin, and titanium) and ceramics (**high-temperature superconductors, HTSC**, including various copper oxides). Here "high" temperature means closer to ambient temperature. The HTSC are of greater pratical use.

Ceramic superconducting materials are available in powder form. The fundamental difficulty in manufacturing them is their inherent brittleness and anisotropy, which make it difficult to align the grains in the proper direction for high efficiency. The smaller the grain size, the more difficult it is to align the grains.

The basic manufacturing process consists of the following steps:

a. preparing the powder, mixing it, and grinding it in a ball mill to a grain size of 0.5 μm to 10 μm;

b. forming it into shape; and

c. heat treating it.

The most common forming process is **oxide powder in tube (OPIT)**. In this process, the powder is packed into silver tubes (because silver has the highest electrical conductivity) and sealed at both ends. The tubes are then mechanically worked, by such deformation processes as swaging, drawing, extrusion, isostatic pressing, and rolling, into final shapes, which may be wire, tape, coil, or bulk.

Other principal superconductor-shaping processes are (a) the coating of silver wire with superconducting material, (b) the deposition of superconductor films by laser ablation, (c) the doctor-blade process (see Section 17.9.1), (d) explosive cladding, and (e) chemical spraying. The purpose of heat treatment of the formed part is to improve grain alignment.

SUMMARY

Powder Metallurgy

- Powder metallurgy is a net-shape forming process, consisting of producing metal powders, blending them, compacting them in dies, and sintering them to impart strength, hardness, and toughness. Compaction may also be carried out by cold or hot isostatic pressing, for improved properties. Although the size and the weight of its products are limited, the P/M process is capable of producing relatively complex parts economically, in net-shape form, to close dimensional tolerances, from a wide variety of metal and alloy powders.

- Secondary and finishing operations may be performed on P/M parts to improve their dimensional accuracy, surface finish, mechanical and physical properties, and appearance. These further operations include forging, heat treating, machining, grinding, plating, infiltration (such as with oil), and impregnation (such as with low-melting-point metals).

- Control of powder shape and quality, of process variables, and of sintering atmospheres are important considerations in product quality. Density and mechanical and physical properties can be controlled by tooling design and by compacting pressure.

- An important P/M process is metal injection molding, which involves mixing the very fine metal powders with polymers, to make them flow more easily into molds of complex shape during compaction. The polymers subsequently evaporate during sintering.

- Design considerations for powder metallurgy include the shape of the part, the ability to eject the green compact from the die, and dimensional tolerances acceptable for the particular application. The P/M process is suitable for medium- to high-volume production runs and for relatively small parts, and it has some competitive advantages over other methods of production, such as casting, forging, and machining.

Ceramics, Glasses, and Superconductors

- Ceramic products are shaped by various casting, plastic-forming, or pressing techniques; the parts are then dried and fired, to impart strength and hardness. Finishing operations (such as machining and grinding) may be performed to give the part its final shape, or to subject it to surface treatments. Because of their inherent brittleness, ceramics are processed with due consideration of distortion and cracking. Control of raw-material quality and of processing parameters are also important factors.

- Glass products are made by several shaping processes that are similar to those used for plastics and ceramics. Glasses are available in a wide variety of forms, of compositions, and of mechanical, physical, and optical properties. Their strength can be improved by thermal and chemical treatments.

- Continuous methods of glass processing are drawing, rolling, and floating. Discrete glass products can be manufactured by blowing, pressing, centrifugal casting, or sagging. The parts may subsequently be annealed to relieve residual stresses.

- Design considerations for ceramics and glasses are guided by such factors as their general lack of tensile strength and toughness and their sensitivity to external and internal defects. Warping and cracking during production are important considerations.

- Manufacturing superconductors into useful products is a challenging area, because of the anisotropy and the inherent brittleness of the materials involved (both metals and ceramics). Although other processes are also being developed, the basic and common process consists of packing the powder into a silver tube and deforming it plastically into desired shapes.

TRENDS

Powder Metallurgy

- The trend in P/M applications is toward the production of larger parts and the increased use of hot isostatic pressing.

- New alloys are being developed for P/M parts; these alloys cannot easily be processed into shapes by other processes.

- Powders are being made by mechanical alloying and by rapid-solidification techniques, to impart desirable properties. Machinable prealloyed powders are being developed.
- Although P/M products are traditionally aimed mostly at the automotive industry, major efforts are being expended on producing parts for the aerospace and other industries.
- Metal injection molding and P/M hot forging are becoming viable production processes.
- Small, high-strength steel P/M parts are being made in impact-forging hammers at rates higher than in hydraulic presses.
- Larger-capacity hot isostatic presses are being built, and HIP quenching is being developed, to reduce cycle times.
- In accordance with the general trend towards near-net-shape manufacturing, P/M is increasingly being applied to a variety of products.
- Computer programs are being developed to simulate, and thereby help optimize, various aspects of P/M processing.

Ceramics, Glasses, and Superconductors

- Shaping processes for ceramics are being controlled more precisely, to minimize defects, to improve dimensional accuracy, and to impart higher strength and reliability to the product.
- Machining, grinding, and finishing operations for ceramics are being improved, for better precision and of enhanced surface properties.
- Surfaces of ceramic parts are being subjected to laser treatments, for improved properties and friction and wear characteristics.
- Two-phase ceramics are being developed, ones having superplastic behavior characteristics that allow them to be shaped into products like those made from superplastic metals.
- Microwave sintering of ceramics is a technology being developed.
- Several processes are being developed to make superconductors into useful shapes; among them are coating, deposition, cladding, and chemical spraying.

KEY TERMS

Powder Metallurgy

Atomization
Blending
Carbonyls
Cold isostatic pressing
Comminution
Compaction
Diffusion
Electrolytic deposition
Green compact
Green strength
Hot isostatic pressing
Impregnation
Infiltration
Injection molding

Mechanical alloying
Metal injection molding
Oxide powder in tube process
Powder metallurgy
Pressureless compaction
Reduction
Shape factor
Sintering
Spark sintering

Ceramics, Glasses, and Superconductors

Binder
Blowing

Centrifugal casting
Chemical tempering
Deflocculent
Doctor-blade process
Drawing
Fire polishing
Firing
Float method
High-temperature superconductors
Hot pressing
Injection molding
Jiggering
Laminated glass
Low-temperature superconductors
Microwave sintering
Oxide-powder-in-tube process

Plastic forming	Sagging	Tempered glass
Plasticizer	Slip	Thermal tempering
Pressing	Slip casting	Wetting agent

BIBLIOGRAPHY

Powder Metallurgy

ASM Handbook, Vol. 7: *Powder Metal Technologies and Applications*. ASM International, 1998.

Fayed, M., and L. Otten (eds.), *Handbook of Powder Science and Technology* (2d ed.). Chapman & Hall, 1997.

German, R.M., *Powder Injection Molding*. Metal Powder Industries Federation, 1990.

_____, *Powder Metallurgy Science*. Metal Powder Industries Federation, 1984.

_____, *Sintering Theory and Practice*. Wiley, 1996.

_____, and A. Bose, *Injection Molding of Metals and Ceramics*. Metal Powder Industries Federation, 1997.

Hausner, H.H., and M.K. Mall, *Handbook of Powder Metallurgy*. Chemical Publishing Company, 1982.

Kahn, H.A., and B.L. Ferguson, *Powder Forging*. Metal Powder Industries Federation, 1990.

Lawley, A., *Atomization: The Production of Metal Powders*. Metal Powder Industries Federation, 1992.

Lenel, F.V., *Powder Metallurgy: Principles and Applications*. American Powder Metallurgy Institute, 1980.

Powder Metallurgy Design Guidebook. American Powder Metallurgy Institute, revised periodically.

Ceramics, Glasses, and Superconductors

Bourdillon, A., *High Temperature Superconductors: Processing and Science*. Academic Press, 1994.

Concise Encyclopedia of Advanced Ceramics. The MIT Press, 1991.

Engineered Materials Handbook, Vol. 4: *Ceramics and Glasses*. ASM International, 1991.

German, R.M., and A. Bose, *Injection Molding of Metals and Ceramics*. Metal Powder Industries Federation, 1997.

Ghosh, A., B. Hiremath and J. Halloran (eds.), *Design for Manufacturability of Ceramic Components*. American Ceramic Society, 1995.

Green, D.J., *An Introduction to the Mechanical Properties of Ceramics*. Cambridge Univ. Press, 1998.

Handbook of Ceramics and Composites (3 vols.). Marcel Dekker, 1991.

Hiremath, B., T. Gupta and K.M. Nair (eds.), *Ceramic Manufacturing Practices and Technologies*. American Ceramic Society, 1997.

Hiremath, B., A. Bruce and A. Ghosh (eds.), *Manufacture of Ceramic Components*. American Ceramic Society, 1995.

Hlavac, J., *The Technology of Glass and Ceramics*. Elsevier, 1983.

Kingery, W.D., H.K. Bowen, and D.R. Uhlmann, *Introduction to Ceramics* (2d ed.). Wiley, 1976.

McHale, A.E. (ed.), *Phase Diagrams and Ceramic Processes*. Chapman & Hall, 1997.

McLellen, G.W., and E.B. Shand, *Glass Engineering Handbook*. McGraw-Hill, 1984.

Mistler, R.E., and E.R. Twiname, *Tape Casting: Theory and Practice*. American Ceramic Society, 1999.

Musikant, S., *What Every Engineer Should Know About Ceramics*. Marcel Dekker, 1991.

Mutsuddy, B.C., *Ceramic Injection Molding*. Chapman & Hall, 1995.

Norton, F.H., *Elements of Ceramics* (2d ed.). Addison-Wesley, 1974.

Rahaman, M.N., *Ceramics Processing and Sintering*. Marcel Dekker, 1998.

Reed, J.S., *Principles of Ceramics Processing* (2d ed.). Wiley, 1995.

Reimanis, I., C. Henager and A. Tomsia (eds.), *Ceramic Joining*. American Ceramic Society, 1997.

Richerson, D. W., *Modern Ceramic Engineering*. (2d ed.). Marcel Dekker, 1992.

Sabia, R., V. Greenhurt and C. Pantano (eds.), *Finishing of Advanced Ceramics and Glasses*. American Ceramic Society, 1999.

Schwartz, M. M. (ed.), *Handbook of Structural Ceramics*. McGraw-Hill, 1992.

Wachtman, J.B (ed), *Ceramic Innovations in the 20th Century*. American Ceramic Society, 1999.

Weimer, A. (ed.), *Carbide, Nitride and Boride Materials Synthesis and Processing*. Chapman & Hall, 1997.

Powder Metallurgy

REVIEW QUESTIONS

17.1 Describe briefly the production steps involved in making powder-metallurgy parts.

17.2 Name the various methods of powder production, and explain the types of powders produced.

17.3 Explain why metal powders are blended.

17.4 What is meant by *green*? Is green strength important? Explain.

17.5 Name the methods used in metal powder compaction. Why is there density variation in the compacting of powders?

17.6 What is the magnitude of the stresses and of the forces involved in compaction?

17.7 Are there hazards involved in P/M processing? List them, and explain their causes.

17.8 Give the reasons that injection molding of metal powders is becoming an important process.

17.9 What requirements should punches and dies meet in P/M processing?

17.10 Describe what happens during sintering.

17.11 Why might secondary and finishing operations be performed on P/M parts?

17.12 Explain the difference between impregnation and infiltration. Give some examples for each.

17.13 What is mechanical alloying? What are its advantages over the conventional alloying of metals?

17.14 Why are protective atmospheres necessary in sintering? What would be the effects on the properties of P/M parts if such atmospheres were not used?

17.15 How arc spherical powders produced? How are aggressive, sharp-edged powders produced?

17.16 Explain why powder-metal parts are commonly used for machine elements requiring good frictional and wear characteristics and for mass produced parts.

17.17 What is screening?

17.18 What type of equipment is used in powder compaction?

17.19 Describe the features of sintering furnaces.

QUALITATIVE PROBLEMS

17.20 Why do mechanical and physical properties depend on the density of P/M parts?

17.21 What are the effects of the different shapes and sizes of metal particles in P/M processing?

17.22 Describe the relative advantages and limitations of cold and hot isostatic pressing.

17.23 What are the advantages and limitations of metal injection molding compared to those of other shaping processes?

17.24 Are the requirements for punch and die materials in powder metallurgy different from those for forging and extrusion? Explain.

17.25 Explain why powder metallurgy has become highly competitive with casting, forging, and machining processes.

17.26 Explain the reasons for the shapes of the curves shown in Fig. 17.9 and for their relative positions.

17.27 Should green compacts be brought up to the sintering temperature slowly or rapidly? Explain your reasoning.

17.28 Because they undergo special processing, metal powders are more expensive than the same metals in bulk form. How is the additional cost justified in powder-metallurgy parts?

17.29 Explain the effects of using fine powders and those of using coarse powders in the making of P/M parts.

17.30 What type of press is required to compact parts with the set of punches shown in Fig. 17.10d?

17.31 In Fig. 17.10e, we note that the pressure is not uniform across the diameter of the compact at a particular distance from the punch. What is the reason for this variation?

17.32 Why do the compacting pressure and the sintering temperature depend on the type of powder metal?

17.33 Comment on the shapes and the ranges of the curves of process capabilities in Fig. 17.13.

17.34 It is possible to infiltrate P/M parts with various resins as well as with metals. What possible applications can benefit from resin infiltration? Explain.

17.35 Assume that you are to give a quiz on the topics covered in this chapter. Prepare several qualitative problems and supply the answers.

QUANTITATIVE PROBLEMS

17.36 Estimate the maximum tonnage required to compact a brass slug 2.0 in. in diameter. Would the height of the slug make any difference in your answer? Explain your reasoning.

17.37 Refer to Fig. 17.9; what should be the volume of loose, fine iron powder in order to make a solid cylindrical compact 20 mm in diameter and 10 mm high?

17.38 Determine the shape factors for (a) a cylinder with dimensional ratios of 1:1:1 and (b) a flake with ratios of 1:10:10.

17.39 Estimate the number of particles in a 300-g sample of iron powder, if the particle size is 75 μm.

17.40 Assume that the surface of a copper particle is covered by an oxide layer 0.1 mm in thickness. What is the volume (and the percentage of volume) occupied by this layer, if the copper particle itself is 50 μm in diameter?

17.41 Survey the technical literature to obtain data on shrinkage during the sintering of P/M parts. Comment on your observations.

17.42 Plot the total surface area of a 100-gram sample of aluminum, as a function of the natural log of particle size.

17.43 A coarse copper powder is compacted in a mechanical press at a pressure of 20 tons/in^2. During sintering, the green part shrinks an additional 8%. What is the final density?

17.44 A gear is to be manufactured from iron powder. It is desired that it have a final density 90% that of cast iron, and it is known that the shrinkage in sintering will be approximately 5%. For a gear that is 3 in. in diameter and has a 0.75 in. hub, what is the required press force?

SYNTHESIS AND DESIGN

17.45 Describe several P/M products in which density variations would be desirable.

17.46 Compare the design considerations for P/M products to those for (a) casting and (b) forging. Describe your observations.

17.47 Describe the design considerations in the making of powder-metallurgy parts. How different are those in the casting and forging of metals?

17.48 Are there applications in which you would not use a P/M product? Explain.

17.49 Describe in detail other methods of manufacturing the parts shown in Fig. 17.1a.

17.50 How large is the grain size of metal powders that can be produced in atomization chambers? Conduct a literature search to determine the answer.

17.51 Plot the opening size versus the mesh size for screens used in powder-size sorting.

17.52 Use the Internet to locate suppliers of metal powders, and compare the cost of the powder to the cost of ingots for five different materials.

17.53 It is known that in the design of P/M gears, the hub outside diameter should be as far as possible from the root of the gear. Explain why this is the case.

Ceramics, Glasses, and Superconductors

REVIEW QUESTIONS

17.54 What are the steps involved in processing ceramics?

17.55 List and describe the functions of additives.

17.56 Describe the slip-casting process.

17.57 What is the doctor-blade process?

17.58 Explain the relative advantages of dry, of wet, and of isostatic pressing.

17.59 What is jiggering? What shapes does it produce?

17.60 Name the factors that are important in drying ceramic products.

17.61 What types of finishing operations are used on ceramics?

17.62 List the categories into which glass products are generally classified.

17.63 Describe briefly the methods by which flat sheet glass is made.

17.64 How are glass tubing and glass rods produced?

17.65 Explain the glass-blowing process.

17.66 What is the difference between the physical and the chemical tempering of glass?

17.67 What are the advantages of laminated glass?

17.68 How are glass fibers made?

17.69 Describe the tempering processes.

17.70 What are the similarities and the differences between the processing of ceramics and that of powder metals?

17.71 How are ceramic particles produced?

17.72 What is greenware?

17.73 What are the important characteristics of slip-casting molds?

17.74 What types of materials are used for superconductors?

QUALITATIVE PROBLEMS

17.75 What should be the requirements for the metal balls in a ball mill?

17.76 What is the reason for the shrinkage during drying of ceramic products?

17.77 Which property of glasses allows them to be expanded and shaped into bottles by blowing?

17.78 Explain why ceramic parts may distort or warp during drying. What precautions would you take to avoid this situation?

17.79 What properties should plastic sheet have when used in laminated glass? Why?

17.80 It is stated that the higher the coefficient of thermal expansion of a glass and the lower its thermal conductivity, the higher the level of the residual stresses developed. Explain why.

17.81 Other than the methods shown in Fig. 17.6, can you think of additional methods for crushing ceramics? Describe your ideas with appropriate sketches.

17.82 What do you think is the purpose of the operation shown in Fig. 17.19d?

17.83 Are any of the processes used for making discrete glass products similar to ones described in preceding chapters? Describe them, if any.

17.84 Injection molding is a process that is used for powder metals, for ceramics, and for plastics. Why is this so?

17.85 Are there any similarities between the strengthening mechanisms used on glass and those used on other metallic and nonmetallic materials? Explain.

17.86 Describe and explain the differences in the manner in which each of the following flat surfaces would fracture when struck with a large piece of rock: (a) ordinary window glass, (b) tempered glass, (c) laminated glass.

17.87 Is there any flash which results from slip casting? How would you propose to remove such flash?

17.88 What are the similarities between slip casting and shell-mold casting?

QUANTITATIVE PROBLEMS

17.89 In the example at the end of Section 17.9, calculate (a) the porosity of the dried part, if the porosity of the fired part is to be 9%; and (b) the initial length L_o of the part, if the linear shrinkages during drying and firing are 8% and 7%, respectively.

17.90 What would be the answers to Problem 17.89 if the quantities given were halved?

SYNTHESIS AND DESIGN

17.91 Describe similarities and differences between the processes described in this chapter and (a) those in Part II on metal casting, (b) those in Part III.

17.92 Consider some ceramic products with which you are familiar, and outline a sequence of processes to manufacture them.

17.93 Make a survey of the technical literature, and describe the differences, if any, between the quality of glass fibers made for reinforced plastics and that of those made for fiber-optic communications. Comment on your observations.

17.94 How different are the design considerations for ceramics from those for other materials?

17.95 Locate a local ceramics/pottery shop, and investigate the different techniques for coloring and decorating a ceramic part. What are the different methods of applying a metallic finish on the part?

17.96 Perform an Internet search, and construct a list of automotive parts made of ceramics.

17.97 One method of producing superconducting wire and strip is by compacting powders of these materials, placing them into a tube, and drawing them through dies (or rolling them). Describe your thoughts concerning the steps and problems involved in such production.

18

Forming and Shaping Plastics and Composite Materials

18.1 INTRODUCTION

The processing of plastics involves operations similar to those used to form and shape metals; those operations were described in the preceding chapters. Plastics can be molded, cast, formed, machined and joined; they can be processed into many shapes with relative ease and in few operations (Table 18.1). As was shown in Chapter 7, plastics melt or cure at relatively low temperatures; hence, unlike metals, they are easy to handle and require less energy to process. The properties of plastic parts and components are, however, influenced greatly by the method of manufacture and by the processing parameters, so the proper control of these conditions is important for part quality.

Plastics are usually shipped to manufacturing plants as pellets or powders, and they are melted (for thermoplastics) just before the shaping process. Plastics are also available as sheet, plate, rod, and tubing, which may be formed into a variety of products. Liquid plastics are used especially in the making of reinforced-plastic parts.

TABLE 18.1   Characteristics of Forming and Shaping Processes for Plastics
and Composite Materials

Process	Characteristics
Extrusion	Long, uniform, solid or hollow complex cross-sections; high production rates; low tooling costs; wide tolerances.
Injection molding	Complex shapes of various sizes, eliminating assembly; high production rates; costly tooling; good dimensional accuracy.
Structural foam molding	Large parts with high stiffness-to-weight ratio; less expensive tooling than in injection molding; low production rates.
Blow molding	Hollow thin-walled parts of various sizes; high production rates and low cost for making containers.
Rotational molding	Large hollow shapes of relatively simple shape; low tooling cost; low production rates.
Thermoforming	Shallow or relatively deep cavities; low tooling costs; medium production rates.
Compression molding	Parts similar to impression-die forging; relatively inexpensive tooling; medium production rates.
Transfer molding	More complex parts than compression molding and higher production rates; some scrap loss; medium tooling cost.
Casting	Simple or intricate shapes made with flexible molds; low production rates.
Processing of composite materials	Long cycle times; tolerances and tooling cost depend on process.

This chapter follows the outline shown in Fig. 18.1, and it describes the basic processes and economics of forming and shaping plastics and reinforced plastics. We also describe processing techniques for metal-matrix and ceramic-matrix composites; these engineered materials have become increasingly important in applications with critical requirements.

18.2 EXTRUSION

In *extrusion*, raw materials in the form of thermoplastic pellets, granules, or powder are placed into a hopper and fed into the extruder barrel (Fig. 18.2). The barrel is equipped with a *screw* that blends the pellets and conveys them down the barrel. The internal friction from the mechanical action of the screw, along with heaters around the extruder's barrel, heats the pellets and liquefies them. The screw action also builds up pressure in the barrel.

Screws have three distinct sections:

1. A *feed* section that conveys the material from the hopper area into the central region of the barrel;
2. A *melt*, or *transition*, section where the heat generated by the shearing of the plastic and by the heaters causes melting to begin; and
3. A *pumping* section where additional shearing and melting occurs, with pressure buildup at the die.

The lengths of these sections can be changed to accommodate the melting characteristics of different plastics. The molten plastic or elastomer is forced through a die, in a process similar to that of extruding metals. The extruded product is then cooled, either by

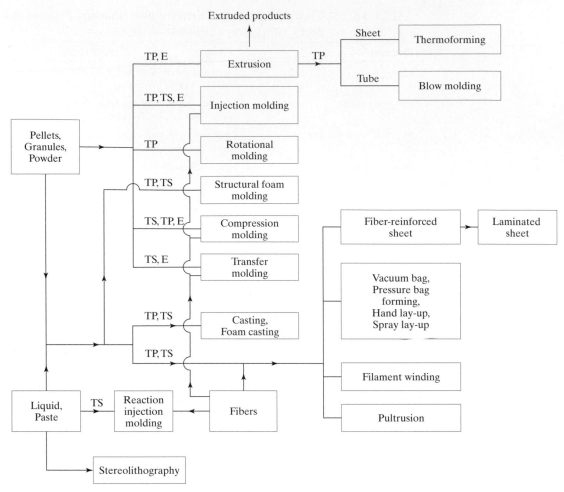

FIGURE 18.1   Outline of forming and shaping processes for plastics, elastomers, and composite materials. (TP, Thermoplastic; TS, Thermoset; E, Elastomer.)

FIGURE 18.2   Schematic illustration of a typical extruder. *Source: Encyclopedia of Polymer Science and Engineering* (2d ed.). Copyright © 1985. Reprinted by permission of John Wiley & Sons, Inc.

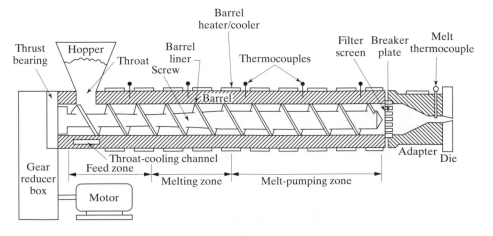

exposing it to air or by passing it through a water-filled channel. Controlling the rate and uniformity of cooling is important to minimize product shrinkage and distortion.

Complex shapes with constant cross-section can be extruded with relatively inexpensive tooling. The extruded product can also be *drawn* (*sized*) by a puller after it has cooled; the extruded product is then coiled or cut into desired lengths.

Because there is a continuous supply of raw material on the hopper, long products, such as solid rods, channels, tubing, pipe, window frames, architectural components, and sheet can be extruded. A more recent development is the extrusion of rigid plastic tubing by a process in which the die is *rotated*; consequently, the polymer is sheared and biaxially oriented during extrusion. The tube has higher crushing strength and higher strength-to-weight ratio than conventionally extruded tubes.

Plastic-coated electrical wire, cable, and strips are also extruded and coated by this process. The wire is fed into the die opening at a controlled rate with the extruded plastic in order to produce a uniform coating.

Pellets, which are used for other plastics-processing methods described in this chapter, are made by extrusion. Here, the extruded product is a small-diameter rod, which is *chopped* into short lengths (pellets) as it is extruded. With some modifications, extruders can also be used as simple melters for other shaping processes such as injection molding and blow molding (Sections 18.3 and 18.4).

Process parameters such as extruder-screw speed, barrel-wall temperatures, die design, and cooling and drawing speeds should be controlled in order to extrude products having uniform dimensional accuracy. To filter out unmelted or congealed resin, a metal screen is usually placed just before the die; it is replaced periodically.

Extruders are generally rated by the diameter D of the barrel and by the length-to-diameter (L/D) ratio of the barrel. Typical commercial units are from 25 to 200 mm (from 1 to 8 in.) in diameter, with L/D ratios ranging from 5 to 30. Extrusion equipment costs can be on the order of $300,000, including the cost for the equipment for downstream cooling and winding of the extruded product. Large production runs are generally required to justify such an expenditure.

Sheet and Film Extrusion.   Polymer *sheet* and *film* can be produced by the use of a flat extrusion die, such as that shown in Fig. 18.3. The polymer is extruded by forcing it through a specially designed die, after which the extruded sheet is taken up first on water-cooled rolls and then by a pair of rubber-covered pull-off rolls.

Thin polymer films and common plastic bags are made from a tube produced by an extruder (Fig. 18.4). In this process (*blown film*), a thin-walled tube is extruded vertically

FIGURE 18.3   Die geometry (coat-hanger die) for extruding sheet. *Source: Encyclopedia of Polymer Science and Engineering* (2d ed.). Copyright © 1985. Reprinted by permission of John Wiley & Sons, Inc.

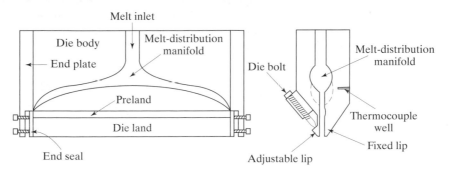

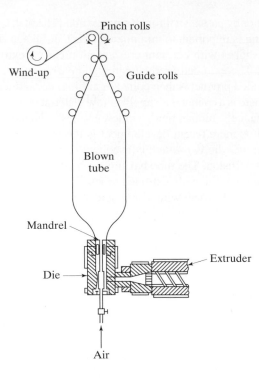

FIGURE 18.4   Schematic illustration of the production of thin film and plastic bags from tube first produced by an extruder and then blown by air. *Source*: D.C. Miles and J.H. Briston, *Polymer Technology*, 1979. Reproduced by permission of Chemical Publishing Co., Inc.

upward and then expanded into a balloon shape by blowing air through the center of the extrusion die until the desired film thickness is reached. The balloon is usually cooled by air from a cooling ring around it, which can also act as a barrier to further expansion of the balloon to control its dimensions.

Blown film is marketed as wrapping film (after slitting the cooled bubble) and as bags (where the bubble is pinched and cut off). Film is also produced by shaving solid round billets of plastics, especially polytetrafluoroethylene (PTFE); the process is called **skiving**, that is, *shaving* with specially designed knives. (See also Section 23.8.4.)

Example: Blown Film

Assume that a typical plastic shopping bag, made by blown film, has a lateral (width) dimension of 400 mm. (a) What should be the extrusion die diameter? (b) These bags are relatively strong in use—how is this strength achieved?

Solution:

a. The perimeter of the bag, when it is flat, is $(2)(400) = 800$ mm. As the original cross-section of the film is round, the blown diameter should be $\pi D = 800$, so $D = 255$ mm. Recall that, in this process, a tube is expanded to from 1.5 to 2.5 times the extrusion-die diameter. Taking the maximum value of 2.5, we calculate the die diameter as $255/2.5 = 100$ mm.

b. Note, in Fig. 18.4, that, after being extruded, the balloon is being pulled upward by the pinch rolls. Thus, in addition to diametral stretching and the attendant molecular orientation, the film is *stretched* and *oriented* in the longitudinal direction. The resulting biaxial orientation of the polymer molecules significantly improves the strength and toughness of the blown film.

18.3 INJECTION MOLDING

Injection molding is essentially the same process as hot-chamber die casting (Fig. 18.5; also Section 11.12). Just as in extrusion, the barrel (cylinder) is heated to promote melting. However, with-injection molding machines, a far greater portion of the heat transferred to the polymer is due to frictional heating. The pellets or granules are fed into the heated cylinder, and the melt is forced into a split-die chamber, either by a hydraulic *plunger* or by the *rotating screw* system of an extruder.

Newer equipment is of the *reciprocating screw* type (Fig. 18.5b). As the pressure builds up at the mold entrance, the rotating screw begins to move backward under pressure to a predetermined distance; this movement controls the volume of material to be injected. The screw then stops rotating and is pushed forward hydraulically, forcing the molten plastic into the mold cavity. Injection-molding pressures usually range from 70 MPa to 200 MPa (10,000 psi to 30,000 psi).

Typical injection-molded products are cups, containers, housings, tool handles, knobs, electrical and communication components (such as telephone receivers), toys (Fig. 18.5c), and plumbing fittings. For thermoplastics, the molds are relatively cool, but thermosets are molded in heated molds, where *polymerization* and *cross-linking* take place.

In either case, after the part is sufficiently cooled (for thermoplastics) or cured (for thermosets), the molds are opened and the part is ejected. The molds are then closed, and the process is repeated automatically. Elastomers also are injection-molded by these processes.

Because the material is molten when injected into the mold, complex shapes and good dimensional accuracy can be achieved. Molds with moving and unscrewing mandrels are also used; they allow the molding of parts having multiple cavities or internal or external threads.

To accommodate part design, molds may have several components: runners (such as are used in metal-casting dies—see Fig. 11.25), cores, cavities, cooling channels, inserts, knockout pins, and ejectors. There are three basic types of molds:

FIGURE 18.5   Injection molding with (a) plunger, (b) reciprocating rotating screw, (c) a typical part made from an injection molding machine cavity, showing a number of parts made from one shot; note also mold features such as sprues, runners. and gates.

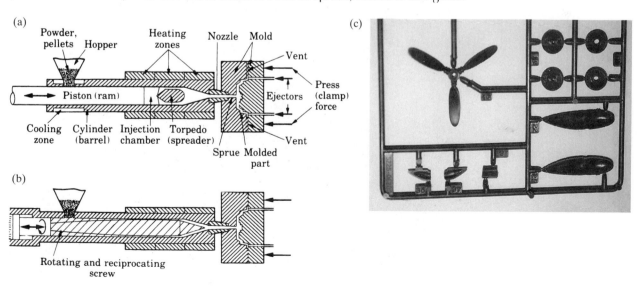

a. **the cold-runner two-plate** mold (this design is the simplest);
b. **the cold-runner three-plate** mold, in which the runner system is separated from the part when the mold opens;
c. **the hot-runner** mold (also called the **runnerless** mold), in which the molten plastic is kept hot in a heated runner plate.

In cold-runner molds, the solidified plastic in the channels that connect the mold cavity to the end of the barrel must be removed, usually by trimming. This scrap can be chopped and recycled. In hot-runner molds, which are more expensive, there are no gates, runners, or sprues attached to the molded part. Cycle times are shorter, because only the injection-molded part must be cooled and ejected.

Metallic components, such as screws, pins, and strips, can also be placed in the mold cavity and become an integral part of the injection-molded product (**insert molding**, Fig. 18.6). The most common examples of such combinations are electrical components.

Multicomponent injection molding (also called *coinjection* or *sandwich* molding) allows the forming of parts with a combination of colors and shapes. An example is the multicolor molding of rear-light covers for automobiles made of different materials. Also, printed film can be placed in the mold cavity, so that parts need not be decorated or labeled after molding.

Overmolding.   This is a term used for producing hinge joints and ball-and-socket joints in one operation and without any post-molding assembly. Two different plastics have thus far been used, to ensure that no bond will form between the molded halves of the joint, because otherwise motion would be impeded.

A new process, called **ice-cold molding**, uses the same type of plastic to form both components of the joint; its use can be seen in a typical door hinge. The process is carried out in one cycle in a standard injection-molding machine. It involves a two-cavity mold and uses cooling inserts positioned in the area of contact between the first and the second molded component of the joint. In this way, no bond forms between the two pieces.

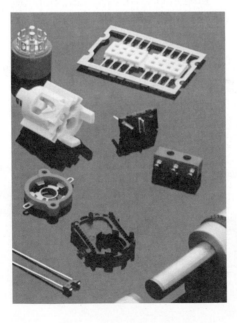

FIGURE 18.6   Typical products made by injection molding, including examples of insert molding. *Source*: Plainfield Molding Inc.

Process Capabilities. Injection molding is a high-rate production process and permits good dimensional control. Typical cycle times range from 5 to 60 seconds, but they can be several minutes for thermosetting materials. The molds are generally made of tool steels, beryllium–copper, or aluminum, and they may have multiple cavities, so that more than one part can be made in one cycle. (See also Fig. 11.25.) Mold costs can be as high as $100,000; mold life may be on the order of 2 million cycles for steel molds, but it is only about 10,000 cycles for aluminum molds.

Mold design and the control of material flow in the die cavities are important factors in the quality of the product. Much progress has been made in the analysis and design of molds and of material flow in injection molding. (See also Section 18.15.) *Modeling techniques* have been developed for studying optimum gating systems, mold filling, mold cooling, and part distortion; they take into account such factors as injection pressure, temperature, and the condition of the resin. Software programs are now available to expedite the design process for molding parts with good dimensions and characteristics.

Machines. Injection-molding machines are usually horizontal (Fig. 18.7). Vertical machines are used for making small close-tolerance parts and for insert molding. The clamping force on the dies is generally supplied by hydraulic means, although electrical means are now available. Electrically driven models weigh less and are quieter than hydraulic machines.

Injection-molding machines are rated according to the capacity of the mold and the clamping force. In most machines, this force ranges from 0.9 to 2.2 MN (100 to 250 tons). The largest machine in operation has a capacity of 45 MN (5000 tons), and it can produce parts weighing 25 kg (55 lb) (most parts weigh from 100 to 600 g (from 3 to 20 oz)). The

FIGURE 18.7 A 2.2-MN (250-ton) injection-molding machine. The tonnage is the force applied to keep the dies closed during injection of molten plastic into the mold cavities. *Source*: Courtesy of Cincinnati Milacron, Plastics Machinery Division.

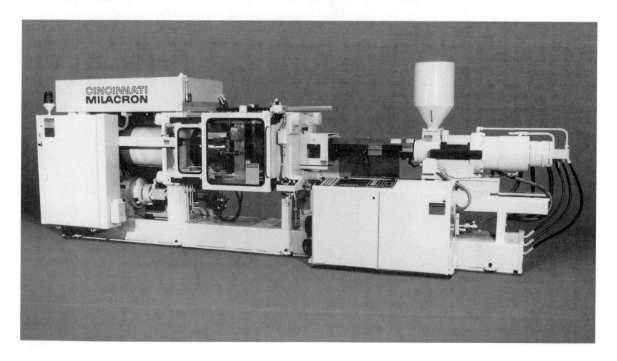

cost of a 100-ton machine ranges from about $60,000 to about $90,000, that of a 300-ton machine from about $85,000 to about $140,000.

The high cost of dies—typically from $20,000 to $200,000—means that high-volume production is necessary to justify such an expenditure. Modern machines are equipped with microprocessors and microcomputers in a control panel and monitor all aspects of the operation.

Example: Injection Molding of Parts

A 250-ton injection-molding machine is to be used to make spur gears 4.5 - in. in diameter and 0.5 in. thick. The gears have a fine tooth profile. How many gears can be injection-molded in one set of molds? Does the thickness of the gears influence your answer?

Solution: Because of the fine detail involved (fine gear teeth), let's assume that the pressures required in the mold cavity will be on the order of 100 MPa (15 ksi). The cross-sectional (projected) area of the gear is $\pi(4.5)^2/4 = 15.9$ in^2. If we assume that the parting plane of the two halves of the mold is in the middle of the gear, the force required is $(15.9)(15,000) = 238,500$ lb.

The capacity of the machine is 250 tons, so we have $(250)(2000) = 500,000$ lb of clamping force available. Therefore, the mold can accommodate two cavities and produce two gears per cycle. Because it does not influence the cross-sectional area of the gear, the thickness of the gear does not directly influence the pressures involved, and so it does not change the answer.

18.3.1 Reaction-Injection Molding

In the *reaction-injection molding* (RIM) process, developed in 1969, a mixture of resin with two or more reactive fluids is forced into the mold cavity at high speed (Fig. 18.8). Chemical reactions take place rapidly in the mold, and the polymer solidifies into a thermoset part.

Major applications of this process produce automotive bumpers and fenders, thermal insulation for refrigerators and freezers, water skis, and stiffeners for structural components.

FIGURE 18.8   Schematic illustration of the reaction-injection molding process. *Source*: *Modern Plastics Encyclopedia.*

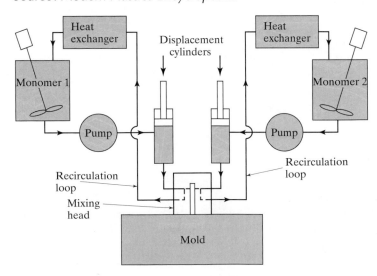

Various reinforcing fibers, such as glass or graphite, may also be used to improve the product's strength and stiffness. Depending on the number of parts to be made and on the part quality required, molds can be made of steel, aluminum, or similar materials.

18.3.2 Structural-Foam Molding

The *structural-foam molding* process is used to make plastic products with a solid outer skin and a cellular inner structure. Typical products made are furniture components, TV cabinets, business-machine housings, and storage-battery cases. Although there are several foam-molding processes, they are all basically similar to injection molding and to extrusion. Both thermoplastics and thermosets can be used for foam molding, but thermosets are in a liquid processing form similar to the condition of polymers in reaction-injection molding.

In **injection foam molding**, thermoplastics are mixed with a blowing agent (usually an inert gas such as nitrogen), which expands the material. The core of the part is cellular, and the skin is rigid. The thickness of the skin can be as much as 2 mm (0.08 in.), and part densities are as low as 40% of the density of the solid plastic. Thus parts have a desirably high stiffness-to-weight ratio, even when weighing as much as 55 kg (120 lb).

18.4 BLOW MOLDING

Blow molding is a modified extrusion- and injection-molding process. In **extrusion blow molding**, a tube (usually turned so that it is vertical) is first extruded, then clamped into a mold with a cavity much larger than the tube diameter, and finally blown outward to fill the mold cavity (Fig. 18.9a). Blowing is usually done with an air blast at a pressure of from 350 kPa to 700 kPa (50 psi – 100 psi). In some operations the extrusion is continuous and the molds move with the tubing.

The molds close around the tubing, close off both ends (thereby breaking the tube into sections), and then move away as air is injected into the tubular piece. The part is then cooled and ejected. Corrugated pipe and tubing are made by continuous blow molding in which the pipe or tubing is extruded horizontally and blown into moving molds.

In **injection blow molding**, a short tubular piece (**parison**) is first injection-molded (Fig. 18.9b). The dies then open and the parison is transferred to a blow-molding die. Hot air is injected into the parison, which expands to the walls of the mold cavity. Typical products made are plastic beverage bottles and hollow containers.

Multilayer blow molding involves the use of coextruded tubes or parisons and so permits the production of multilayer structures. A typical example of multilayer structures is plastic packaging for food and beverage having such characteristics as odor and permeation barrier, taste and aroma protection, scuff resistance, the capability of being printed, and the ability to be filled with hot fluids. Other applications are in the cosmetics and the pharmaceutical industries.

18.5 ROTATIONAL MOLDING

Most thermoplastics and some thermosets can be formed into large hollow parts by *rotational molding*. The thin-walled metal mold is made of two pieces (split female mold) and is designed to be rotated about two perpendicular axes (Fig. 18.10). A premeasured quantity of powdered plastic material is placed inside the warm mold. The powder is obtained from a polymerization process that precipitates a powder from a liquid. The mold is then heated, usually in a large oven, while it is rotated about the two axes.

(a)

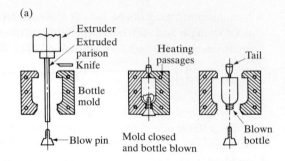

(b)

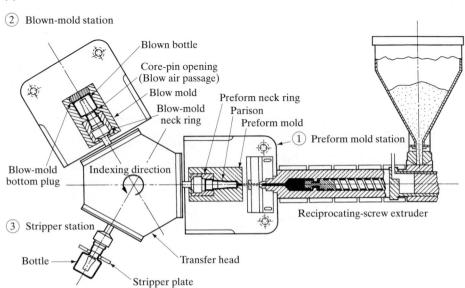

FIGURE 18.9   Schematic illustrations of (a) the blow-molding process for making plastic beverage bottles, and (b) a three-station injection blow-molding machine. *Source*: *Encyclopedia of Polymer Science and Engineering* (2d ed.). Copyright © 1985. Reprinted by permission of John Wiley & Sons, Inc.

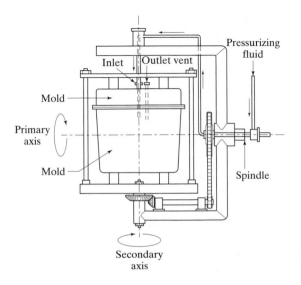

FIGURE 18.10   The rotational molding (rotomolding or rotocasting) process. Trash cans, buckets, and plastic footballs can be made by this process.

This action tumbles the powder against the mold, where heating fuses the powder without melting it. In some parts, a chemical cross-linking agent is added to the powder, and cross-linking occurs after the part is formed in the mold from continued heating. Typical parts made by rotational molding are tanks of various sizes, trash cans, boat hulls, buckets, housings, toys, carrying cases, and footballs. Various metallic or plastic inserts may also be integrally molded into the parts made by this process.

Liquid polymers called **plastisols** (vinyl plastisols being the most common) also can be used in **slush molding**. This is a process in which the mold is simultaneously heated and rotated. The particles of plastic material are forced against the inside walls of the heated mold by the tumbling action. Upon contact with the wall, the material melts and coats the walls of the mold. The part is cooled while it is still rotating and then removed by opening the mold.

Rotational molding can produce parts with complex hollow shapes and with wall thicknesses as small as 0.4 mm (0.016 in.). Parts as large as 1.8 m $\times$ 1.8 m $\times$ 3.6 m (6 ft $\times$ 6 ft $\times$ 12 ft) have been formed. The outer surface finish of the part is a replica of the surface finish of the mold walls. Cycle times are longer than in other molding processes, but equipment costs are low. Quality control considerations usually involve accurate weight of the powder placed in the mold, proper rotation of the mold, and temperature-time relationship during the oven cycle.

18.6 THERMOFORMING

Thermoforming is a series of processes for forming thermoplastic sheet or film over a mold, by means of the application of heat and pressure (Fig. 18.11). In this process, a sheet is heated in an oven to the *sag* point (softening but not to the melting point). The sheet is then removed from the oven, placed over a mold, and forced against the mold through the application of a vacuum. The mold is usually at room temperature, hence the shape of the plastic becomes set upon contact with the mold. Because of the low strength of the materials formed, the pressure differential caused by the vacuum is usually sufficient for forming, although air pressure or mechanical means are also applied for some parts.

Typical parts made by thermoforming are advertising signs, refrigerator liners, packaging, appliance housings, and panels for shower stalls. Because thermoforming is a drawing and stretching operation, much like sheet-metal forming, the material should exhibit

FIGURE 18.11   Various thermoforming processes for thermoplastic sheet. These processes are commonly used in making advertising signs, cookie and candy trays, panels for shower stalls, and packaging.

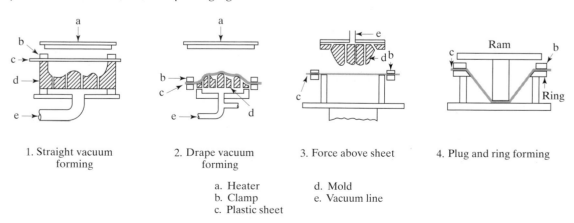

| 1. Straight vacuum forming | 2. Drape vacuum forming | 3. Force above sheet | 4. Plug and ring forming |

a. Heater   d. Mold
b. Clamp   e. Vacuum line
c. Plastic sheet

high uniform elongation; otherwise it will neck and fail. Thermoplastics have high capacities for uniform elongation, by virtue of their high strain-rate sensitivity exponents, *m*. (See Section 2.2.7.) The sheets used in thermoforming are made by sheet extrusion. Parts with openings or holes cannot be formed by this process, because the pressure differential cannot be maintained during forming.

Molds for thermoforming are usually made of aluminum, because high strength is not a requirement. The holes in the molds (to pull a vacuum) are usually less than 0.5 mm (0.02 in.), in order not to leave any marks on the formed parts. Tooling is inexpensive. Quality considerations include tears, nonuniform wall thickness, improperly filled molds, and poor part definition (surface details).

18.7 COMPRESSION MOLDING

In *compression molding*, a preshaped charge of material, a premeasured volume of powder, or a viscous mixture of liquid resin and filler material is placed directly into a heated mold cavity. Forming is done under pressure from a plug or from the upper half of the die (Fig. 18.12). Compression molding results in the formation of flash, which is subsequently removed by trimming or by other means.

FIGURE 18.12   Types of compression molding, a process similar to forging: (a) positive, (b) semipositive, and (c) flash. The flash in part (c) has to be trimmed off. (d) Die design for making a compression-molded part with undercuts.

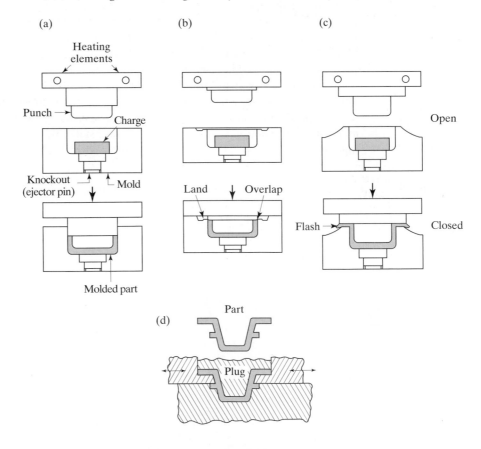

Typical parts made are dishes, handles, container caps, fittings, electrical and electronic components, washing-machine agitators, and housings. Fiber-reinforced parts with long chopped fibers are formed by this process exclusively.

Compression molding is used mainly with thermosetting plastics, with the original material being in a partially polymerized state. Cross-linking is completed in the heated die; curing times range from 0.5 to 5 minutes, depending on the material and on part thickness and geometry. The thicker the material is, the longer it will take to cure. Elastomers are also shaped by compression molding.

Three types of compression molds are available:

a. **flash-type**, for shallow or flat parts;
b. **positive**, for high density parts;
c. **semipositive**, for quality production.

Undercuts in parts are not recommended; however, dies can be designed to open sideways (Fig. 18.12d) to allow removal of the molded part. In general, the available complexity of parts is less than that from injection molding, but dimensional control is better. Because of their relative simplicity, dies for compression molding are generally less costly than those used in injection molding.

18.8 TRANSFER MOLDING

Transfer molding represents a further development of compression molding. The uncured thermosetting material is placed in a heated transfer pot or chamber (Fig. 18.13). After the material is heated, it is injected into heated closed molds. A ram, a plunger, or a rotating-screw feeder (depending on the type of machine used) forces the material to flow through the narrow channels into the mold cavity.

FIGURE 18.13   Sequence of operations in transfer molding for thermosetting plastics. This process is particularly suitable for intricate parts with varying wall thickness.

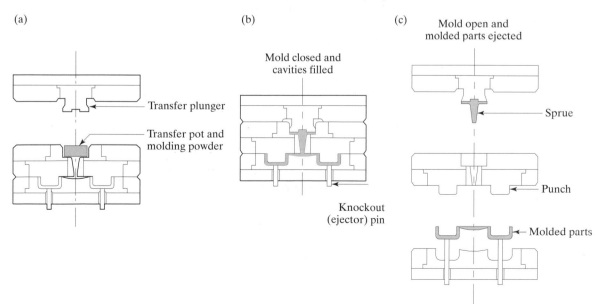

This flow generates considerable heat, which raises the temperature of the material and homogenizes it. Curing takes place by cross-linking. Because the resin is molten as it enters the molds, the complexity of the parts and the dimensional control approach those of injection molding.

Typical parts made by transfer molding are electrical and electronic components and rubber and silicone parts. The process is particularly suitable for intricate shapes with varying wall thicknesses. The molds tend to be more expensive than those for compression molding, and some material is left in the channels of the mold during filling. (See also Resin Transfer Molding, Section 18.12.1.)

18.9 CASTING

Some thermoplastics (e.g., nylons and acrylics) and thermosetting plastics (e.g., epoxies, phenolics, polyurethanes, polyester) can be *cast*, in either rigid or flexible molds, into a variety of shapes (Fig. 18.14a). Typical parts cast are gears, bearings, wheels, thick sheets, and components requiring resistance to abrasive wear.

a. In the conventional casting of thermoplastics, a mixture of monomer, catalyst, and various additives is heated and poured into the mold. The part forms after polymerization takes place at ambient pressure. Intricate shapes can be produced with flexible molds, which are then peeled off. Degassing may be necessary for product integrity.

b. **Centrifugal casting.** This process is also used with plastics, including reinforced plastics with short fibers. (See Section 11.13.) Thermosets are cast in a similar manner; typical parts produced are similar to those made by thermoplastic castings.

c. **Potting and encapsulation.** A variation of casting that is important to the electrical and electronics industry is potting and encapsulation. This process involves casting the plastic around an electrical component to embed it in the plastic.

   Potting (Fig. 18.14b) is done in a housing or case, which is an integral part of the product. In *encapsulation* (Fig. 18.14c), the component is coated with a layer of the solidified plastic. In both applications, the plastic serves as a dielectric (nonconductor). Structural members, such as hooks and studs, may be partly encapsulated.

FIGURE 18.14   Schematic illustration of (a) casting, (b) potting, (c) encapsulation of plastics.

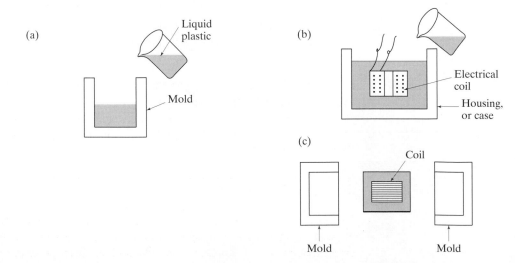

d. Foam molding and casting. Products such as styrofoam cups and food containers, insulating blocks, and shaped packaging materials (such as for cameras, appliances, and electronics), are made by *foam molding*. The material is expandable polystyrene. Polystyrene **beads** (obtained by polymerization of styrene monomer) are placed in a mold with a blowing agent and exposed to heat, usually by steam. As a result, the beads expand to as much as 50 times their original size and take the shape of the mold. The amount of expansion can be controlled by varying temperature and time.

A common method of molding is to use *pre-expanded beads*, in which beads are partially expanded by steam (although hot air, hot water, or an oven can also be used) in an open-top chamber. The beads are then placed in a storage bin and allowed to stabilize for a period of from 3 to 12 hours. They can then be molded into shapes in the manner described above.

Polystyrene beads are available in three sizes: small, for cups; medium, for molded shapes; and large, for the molding of insulating blocks (which can then be cut to size). The bead size selected depends on the minimum wall thickness of the product. Beads can also be colored prior to expansion, and they are available integrally colored.

Polyurethane **foam** processing, for products such as cushions and insulating blocks, involves several processes. Basically, it starts with the mixing of two or more chemical components; the reaction forms a cellular structure which solidifies in the mold. Various low-pressure and high-pressure machines, having computer controls for proper mixing, are available.

18.10 COLD FORMING AND SOLID-PHASE FORMING

Processes that have been used in the cold working of metals, such as rolling, deep drawing, extrusion, closed-die forging, coining, and rubber forming, can also be used to form many thermoplastics at room temperature (*cold forming*). Typical materials formed are polypropylene, polycarbonate, ABS, and rigid PVC. The important considerations are the following:

1. The material must be sufficiently ductile at room temperature (consequently polystyrenes, acrylics, and thermosets cannot be formed).
2. The material's deformation must be nonrecoverable (to minimize springback and creep).

The advantages of cold forming of plastics over other methods of shaping are threefold:

a. Strength, toughness, and uniform elongation are increased.
b. Plastics with high molecular weights can be used, to make parts with superior properties.
c. Forming speeds are not affected by part thickness, because there is no heating or cooling involved; cycle times are generally shorter than molding processes.

Solid-phase forming is carried out at a temperature from 10 °C to 20 °C (20 °F—40 °F) below the melting temperature of the plastic (if it is a crystalline polymer), while it is still in a solid state. The advantages over cold forming are that forming forces and springback are lower. These processes are not as widely used as hot-processing methods; they are generally restricted to special applications.

18.11 PROCESSING ELASTOMERS

Elastomers (Section 7.9) can be shaped by a variety of processes also used for shaping thermoplastics. Thermoplastic elastomers are commonly shaped by extrusion or injection molding, extrusion being the more economical and the faster process. In terms of its processing

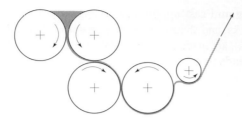

FIGURE 18.15   Schematic illustration of calendering. Sheets produced by this process are subsequently used in thermoforming.

characteristics, a thermoplastic elastomer is a polymer; in terms of its function and performance, it is a rubber.

These polymers can also be formed by blow molding or by thermoforming. Thermoplastic polyurethane can be shaped by all conventional methods; it can also be blended with thermoplastic rubbers, polyvinyl chloride compounds, ABS, and nylon. Dryness of the materials is important. For extrusion, the temperatures are in the range of from 170 °C to 230 °C (from 340 °F to 440 °F), for molding, they are up to 60 °C (140 °F). Typical extruded-elastomer products are tubing, hoses, molding, and inner tubes. Injection-molded products cover a broad range of applications, such as components for automobiles and appliances.

Rubber and some thermoplastic sheets are formed by the **calendering** process (Fig. 18.15), wherein a warm mass of the compound is fed into a series of rolls and is **masticated**; it is stripped off in the form of a sheet. The rubber may also be formed over both surfaces of a fabric liner.

Discrete rubber products, such as gloves, are made by dipping a metal form (in the shape of a hand) repeatedly into a liquid compound that adheres to the form. It is then vulcanized, usually in steam, and stripped from the form.

18.12 PROCESSING REINFORCED PLASTICS

As described in Chapter 9, reinforced plastic, a type of **composite**, is among the most important materials. It can be engineered to meet specific design requirements, such as high strength-to-weight and stiffness-to-weight ratios and creep resistance. Because of their unique structure, reinforced plastics require special methods to shape them into useful products (Fig. 18.16).

FIGURE 18.16   Reinforced-plastic components for a Honda motorcycle. The parts shown are front and rear forks, a rear swingarm, a wheel, and brake disks.

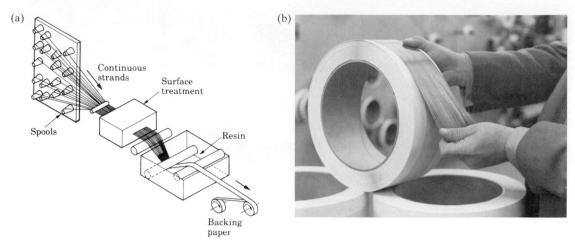

FIGURE 18.17   (a) Manufacturing process for polymer-matrix composite. *Source*:
T.-W. Chou, R.L. McCullough, and R.B. Pipes. (b) Boron-epoxy prepreg tape.
Source: Avco Specialty Materials/Textron.

The care required and the several steps involved in manufacturing reinforced plastics make processing costs substantial, and, generally, they are not competitive with traditional materials and shapes. This situation has necessitated the careful assessment and integration of the design and manufacturing processes (concurrent engineering) in order to minimize costs while maintaining product integrity and production rate. An important safety and environmental concern in reinforced plastics is the dust generated during processing—for example, airborne carbon fibers are known to remain in the work area long after fabrication of parts has been completed.

Reinforced plastics can usually be fabricated by the methods described in this chapter, plus some provision for the presence of more than one type of material in the composite. The reinforcement may be chopped fibers, woven fabric or mat, roving or yarn (slightly twisted fiber), or continuous lengths of fiber (Section 9.2.1).

In order to obtain good bonding between the reinforcing fibers and the polymer matrix, as well as to protect them during subsequent processing, fibers are surface treated by impregnation (*sizing*). Short fibers are commonly added to thermoplastics for injection molding; milled fibers can be used for reaction-injection molding; longer chopped fibers are used primarily in the compression molding of reinforced plastics.

When the impregnation is carried out as a separate step, the resulting partially cured sheets are called by various terms:

a. Prepregs. In a typical procedure for making reinforced- plastic *prepregs* (Fig. 18.17a), the continuous fibers are first aligned and then subjected to surface treatment to enhance adhesion to the polymer matrix. They are then coated by dipping them in a resin bath and finally made into a sheet or tape (Fig. 18.17b). Individual pieces of the sheet are then assembled into laminated structures (Fig. 18.18a), such as the horizontal stabilizer for the F-14 fighter aircraft.

Special computer-controlled tape-laying machines have been developed for this purpose (Fig. 18.18b). Typical products made from prepregs are flat or corrugated architectural paneling, panels for construction and for electrical insulation, and structural components of aircraft requiring good property retention and fatigue strength under hot or wet conditions.

b. Sheet-molding compound (SMC). Continuous strands of reinforcing fiber are first chopped into short fibers (Fig. 18.19) and then deposited in random directions over a layer of resin paste (usually a polyester mixture which may contain fillers such as

(a)

(b)

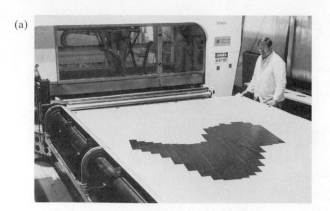

FIGURE 18.18   (a) Single-ply layup of boron-epoxy tape for the horizontal stabilizer for F-14 fighter aircraft. *Source*: Grumman Aircraft Corporation. (b) A 10 axis computer-numerical-controlled tape-laying system. This machine is capable of laying up 75 mm and 150 mm (3 in. and 6 in.) wide tapes, on contours of up to ±30° and at speeds of up to 0.5 m/s (1.7 ft/s). *Source*: Courtesy of The Ingersoll Milling Machine Company.

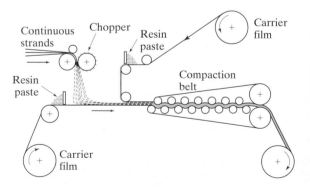

FIGURE 18.19   The manufacturing process for producing reinforced-plastic sheets. The sheet is still viscous at this stage; it can later be shaped into various products. *Source*: T.-W. Chou, R. L. McCullough, and R. B. Pipes.

various mineral powders) carried on a polymer film such as polyethylene. A second layer of resin paste is deposited on top, and the sheet is pressed between rollers.

The product is gathered into rolls, or placed into containers in layers, and stored until it has undergone a maturation period and reached the desired molding viscosity. The maturing process takes place under controlled temperature and humidity, and usually takes one day.

The molding compounds should be stored at a temperature sufficiently low to delay curing. They have a limited shelf life (usually around 30 days) and must be processed within this period. Alternatively, the resin and the fibers can be mixed together only at the time they are placed into the mold.

c. **Bulk-molding compound (BMC).** These compounds are in the shape of billets (hence the term bulk) generally up to 50 mm (2 in.) in diameter, and they are made in the same manner as SMCs, by the use of the extrusion process (Chapter 15) to obtain a bulk form. When processed into products, BMCs have flow characteristics similar to those of dough, so they are also called *dough-molding compounds* (DMC).

d. **Thick-molding compound (TMC).** Thick-molding compound combines a characteristic of BMC (lower cost) with one of SMC (higher strength). It is usually injection-molded, using chopped fibers of various lengths. One application is in electrical components, because of the high dielectric strength of TMC.

Example: Tennis Rackets Made of Composite Materials

In order to have certain desirable characteristics, such as light weight and stiffness, composite-material tennis rackets are being manufactured with graphite, fiberglass, boron, ceramic (silicon carbide), and Kevlar as the reinforcing fibers. These rackets have a foam core; some have unidirectional, others braided reinforcement.

Rackets with boron fibers have the highest stiffness, followed by those with graphite (carbon), then glass, then Kevlar fibers. The racket with the lowest stiffness has 80% fiberglass, the stiffest has 95% graphite and 5% boron, and so it has the highest percentage of inexpensive reinforcing fiber and the smallest percentage of the most expensive fiber.

18.12.1 Molding

There are several molding processes for reinforced plastics described in this section.

a. In **compression molding**, the material is placed between two molds and pressure is applied. Depending on the material, the molds may be either at room temperature or heated to accelerate hardening. The material may be in bulk form (bulk-molding compound, which is a viscous, sticky mixture of polymers, fibers, and additives). It is generally shaped into a log that subsequently is cut into the desired shape. Fiber lengths generally range from 3 to 50 mm (0.125 to 2 in.), although longer fibers (say, 75 mm or 3 in.) may also be used.

Sheet-molding compounds also can be used in molding. These compounds are similar to BMC, except that the resin–fiber mixture is laid between plastic sheets, to make a sandwich that can be easily handled. The sheets are removed when the SMC is placed in the mold.

b. In **vacuum-bag molding** (Fig. 18.20), prepregs are laid in a mold to form the desired shape. In this case, the pressure required to shape the product and develop good bonding is obtained by covering the lay-up with a plastic bag and creating a vacuum. If additional heat and pressure are desired, the entire assembly is put into an autoclave. Care

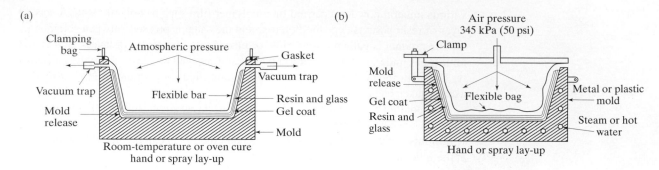

FIGURE 18.20   (a) Vacuum-bag forming. (b) Pressure-bag forming. *Source*: T. H. Meister.

should be exercised to maintain fiber orientation, if specific fiber orientations are desired. In chopped-fiber materials, no specific orientation is intended.

In order to prevent the resin from sticking to the vacuum bag and to facilitate removal of excess resin, several sheets of various materials (*release cloth, bleeder cloth*) are placed on top of the prepreg sheets. The molds can be made of metal, usually aluminum, but they are more often made from the same resin (with reinforcement) as the material to be cured. This practice eliminates any problem with difference in thermal expansion between the mold and the part.

c. **Contact molding** processes use a single male or female mold (Fig. 18.21) made of materials such as reinforced plastics, wood, or plaster. Contact molding is used in making products with high surface-area-to-thickness ratios, such as swimming pools, boats, tub and shower units, and housings. This is a "wet" method, in which the reinforcement is impregnated with the resin at the time of molding.

The simplest method is called **hand lay-up.** The materials are placed and shaped in the mold by hand (Fig. 18.21a), and the squeezing action expels any trapped air and compacts the part. Molding may also be done by spraying (**spray-up;** Fig. 18.21b).

Although spraying can be automated, these processes are relatively slow, and labor costs are high. However, they are simple, and the tooling is inexpensive. Only the mold-side surface of the part needs to be smooth, and the choice of materials is limited. Many types of boats are made by this process.

d. **Resin transfer molding** is based on transfer molding (Section 18.8): A resin is mixed with a catalyst and is forced by a piston-type positive displacement pump into the mold

FIGURE 18.21   Manual methods of processing reinforced plastics: (a) hand lay-up and (b) spray-up. These methods are also called *open-mold* processing.

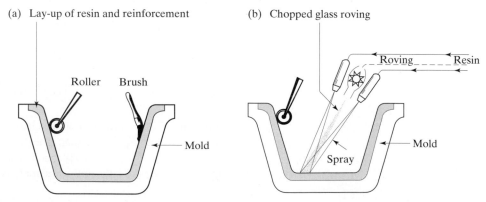

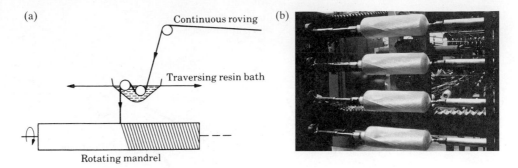

FIGURE 18.22   (a) Schematic illustration of the filament-winding process. (b) Fiberglass being wound over aluminum liners, for slide-raft inflation vessels for the Boeing 767 aircraft. *Source*: Brunswick Corporation, Defense Division.

cavity that is filled with fiber reinforcement. The process is a viable alternative to hand lay-up, spray-up, and compression molding for low- or intermediate-volume production.

e. Transfer/injection molding. This is an automated operation for manufacturing that combines compression molding, injection molding, and transfer molding. The potential of this process is being investigated, in view of the good surface finish, dimensional stability, and mechanical properties of compression molding combined with the high automation capability and low cost of injection molding and transfer molding that it affords.

18.12.2 Filament Winding, Pultrusion, and Pulforming

a. Filament winding. This is a process in which the resin and fibers are combined at the time of curing (Fig. 18.22a). Axisymmetric parts, such as pipes and storage tanks, and even asymmetric parts are produced on a rotating mandrel. The reinforcing filament, tape, or roving is wrapped continuously around the form. The reinforcements are impregnated by passing them through a polymer bath. The process can be modified by wrapping the mandrel with prepreg material.

The products made by filament winding are very strong, because of their highly reinforced structure. This process has also been used for strengthening cylindrical or spherical pressure vessels (Fig. 18.22b) made of materials such as aluminum and titanium. The presence of a metal inner lining makes the part impermeable.

Filament winding can be used directly over solid-rocket propellant forms. Seven-axis computer-controlled machines have been developed for making asymmetric parts that automatically dispense several unidirectional prepregs. Typical asymmetric parts made are aircraft engine ducts, fuselages, propellers, blades, and struts.

b. Pultrusion. Long shapes with various uniform cross-sections, such as rods, profiles, and tubing—types similar to drawn metal products—are made by the *pultrusion* process. Developed in the early 1950s, the continuous reinforcement (roving or fabric) is pulled first through a thermosetting polymer bath and then through a long heated steel die (Fig. 18.23). The product is cured during its travel through the die. It is then cut into desired lengths. To improve fiber impregnation with the resin, ambient pressures as high as 2800 kPa (400 psi) are used.

The most common material used in pultrusion is polyester with glass reinforcements. Typical products made are golf clubs, drive shafts, and such structural members as ladders, walkways, and handrails.

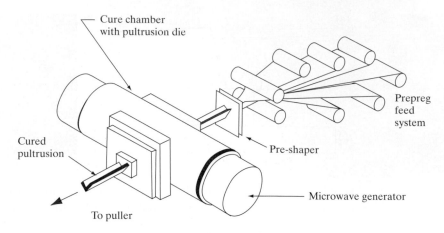

FIGURE 18.23   Schematic illustration of the pultrusion process.

c. **Pulforming.** Continuously reinforced products other than constant cross-sectional profiles are made by *pulforming*. After being pulled through the polymer bath, the composite is clamped between the two halves of a die and cured into a finished product. The dies recirculate and shape the products successively. Commonly made products are hammer handles reinforced by glass fiber and curved automotive leaf springs.

Example: Polymer Automotive-Body Panels Shaped by Various Processes

The trend toward the use of polymeric materials for automobile panels has been increasing at an accelerating rate. Among U.S.-manufactured automobiles using various polymeric body panels are the Pontiac Trans Sport, the Chevrolet Lumina, the Oldsmobile Silhouette, all Saturn models, the Chevrolet Camaro, and the Pontiac Firebird. Typical parts are vertical panels, such as fenders and quarter panels and front and rear fascias, and flat horizontal components such as hoods.

The following are the three commonly used and competing processing methods:

1. injection-molded thermoplastics and elastomers;
2. reaction-injection molded polyurea/polyurethanes;
3. compression-molded sheet-molding compound (SMC); also, some resin-transfer-molded polyester and vinylester.

The Saturn utilizes *injection-molded* body panels and other large exterior components. Its front fenders and rear quarter panels are made of polyphenylene-ether/nylon, its door outer panels are made of polycarbonate/ABS, and its fascias are made of thermoplastic polyolefin. These materials are selected for design flexibility, impact strength and toughness, corrosion resistance, high durability, and low mass. Vertical panels and fascias are made in multicavity molds on 5000-ton injection-molding machines, then assembled mechanically to a steel frame. New developments include injection-molded thermoplastic polyester fenders.

Large exterior body parts are also made of *reaction-injection molded* (RIM) polyurethane, although polyureas are becoming important for body panels and bumpers. Most thermoset fascias are made of reinforced RIM polyurethane, such as those for the General Motors All-Purpose Vehicle (APV); however, preference is now being given to new polyureas, because of their higher thermal stability, their low-temperature toughness, and the lower cycle times possible.

Large horizontal exterior body panels, such as hoods, roofs, and rear decks, are made of reinforced polyester or vinylester in the form of *compression-molded* sheet-molding compounds. Lower-volume parts, however, are now being made by *resin transfer molding* (RTM), largely because of the relatively low tooling costs.

Environmental and recycling considerations in material and process selection for automobiles have become increasingly important. Polyphenylene oxide, used for the Jeep Cherokee and the Plymouth Acclaim/Dodge Spirit overhead consoles, is being replaced with polycarbonate made out of 100% recycled or reclaimed materials.

18.12.3 Quality Considerations in the Processing of Reinforced Plastics

The major quality considerations in the processes described in this section involve internal voids and gaps between successive layers of material. Volatile gases that develop during processing must be allowed to escape from the lay-up through the vacuum bag, in order to avoid porosity due to trapped gases. Microcracks may develop during improper curing or during transportation and handling. These defects can be detected using ultrasonic scanning and other techniques (see Section 36.9).

18.13 PROCESSING METAL-MATRIX COMPOSITES

The three basic methods of manufacturing metal-matrix composites (MMC) into near-net-shape parts are described in this section.

a. **Liquid-phase processing** basically consists of casting the liquid matrix and the solid reinforcement, using either conventional casting processes (Chapter 11) or pressure infiltration casting. In the latter process, pressurized gas is used to force the liquid matrix metal into a preform (usually shaped out of sheet or wire) made of the reinforcing fibers.

b. **Solid-phase processes** consist basically of powder-metallurgy techniques, including cold and hot isostatic pressing (Section 17.3.2). Proper mixing, to obtain homogeneous distribution of the fibers, is important. An example of this technique, employed in tungsten-carbide tool and die manufacturing, with cobalt as the matrix material, is given in the last Example in Section 17.5.

In the making of complex MMC parts with whisker or fiber reinforcement, die geometry and the control of process variables are very important for ensuring proper distribution and orientation of the fibers within the part. MMC parts made by powder-metallurgy processes are generally heat treated for optimum properties.

c. The techniques used in **two-phase (liquid/solid) processing** consist of rheocasting, described in Section 11.14.2, and spray atomization and deposition. In the latter processes, the reinforcing fibers are mixed with a matrix that contains both liquid and solid phases.

> **Example: Metal-Matrix Composite Brake Rotors and Cylinder Liners**
>
> Some brake rotors are currently being made of composites consisting of an aluminum-based matrix reinforced with 20% silicon carbide (SiC) particles. The particles are stirred into molten aluminum alloys, and the mixture is cast into ingots. The ingots are then remelted and cast into shapes, such as brake rotors and drums, by the use of casting processes, such as green-sand, bonded-sand, investment, permanent-mold, and squeeze casting. (See Chapter 11.) These rotors are about one-half the weight of those made of gray-cast-iron; they conduct heat three times faster; and they add the stiffness and wear-resistance characteristic of ceramics and reduce noise and vibration.
>
> To improve the wear- and heat-resistance of cast-iron cylinder liners in aluminum engine blocks, aluminum-matrix liners are being developed. The MMC layer consists of 12% aluminum oxide (Al_2O_3) fiber and 9% graphite fiber and has a thickness that ranges from 1.5 to 2.5 mm (0.06 to 0.1 in.).

18.14 PROCESSING CERAMIC-MATRIX COMPOSITES

Several processes used in making ceramic-matrix composites (CMC) are described in this section. In addition to these processes, new techniques such as melt infiltration, controlled oxidation, and hot-press sintering, which are still largely in the experimental stage, are being developed for improving the properties and performance of these composites.

Slurry infiltration is the most common process. It involves the preparation of a fiber preform that is hot pressed and then impregnated with a slurry (which contains the matrix powder), a carrier liquid, and an organic binder. A further improvement of this process is **reaction bonding** or **reaction sintering** of the slurry. High strength, toughness, and uniform structure are obtained by slurry infiltration, but the product has limited high-temperature properties, because of the low melting temperature of the matrix materials used.

Chemical synthesis processes involve the sol-gel and the polymer-precursor techniques. In the **sol-gel process**, a *sol* (a colloidal fluid having the liquid as its continuous phase) containing fibers is converted to a *gel*, which is then subjected to heat treatment to produce a ceramic-matrix composite. The **polymer-precursor** method is analogous to the process used in making ceramic fibers.

In **chemical vapor infiltration**, a porous fiber preform is infiltrated with the matrix phase by the use of the chemical vapor deposition technique (Section 33.5). The product has very good high-temperature properties, but the process is costly and time-consuming.

18.15 DESIGN CONSIDERATIONS AND ECONOMICS OF FORMING AND SHAPING PLASTICS

Design considerations in forming and shaping plastics are somewhat similar to those used in processing of metals. The selection of an appropriate material from an extensive list requires consideration of service requirements and of possible long-range effects on properties and behavior (such as dimensional stability and wear) as well as of ultimate disposal after completion of the life cycle. Some of these issues are described in the General Introduction under *Environmentally Conscious Manufacturing* and in Sections 7.8 and 37.4.

Compared to metals, plastics have lower strength and stiffness, although the strength-to-weight and stiffness-to-weight ratio for reinforced plastics is higher than for many metals. Section sizes should, therefore, be selected accordingly, with a view to maintaining a sufficiently high section modulus, for improved stiffness. Reinforcement with fibers or particles can also be highly effective in achieving this objective, as can designing cross-sections with a high moment of inertia to area ratio.

One of the major design advantages of reinforced plastics is the directional nature of the strength of the composite. (See, for example, Fig. 9.7.) Forces applied to the material are transferred by the resin matrix to the fibers which are much stronger and stiffer than the matrix. (See Chapter 9.) When the fibers are all oriented in one direction, the resulting composite material is exceptionally strong in the fiber direction. This property is often utilized in designing reinforced-plastic structures.

For strength in two principal directions, individually unidirectional layers are often laid at the corresponding angles to each other. If strength in the third (thickness) direction is desired, a different type of composite is used to form a sandwich structure.

Physical properties, especially a high coefficient of thermal expansion (hence contraction), are important. Improper part design or assembly can lead to warping and shrinking (Fig. 18.24a). Plastics can easily be molded around metallic parts and inserts. However, their compatibility with metals when so assembled is an important consideration.

The overall part geometry often determines the particular shaping or molding process. Even after a particular process is selected, the designs of the part and the die should be such that they will not cause problems concerning shape generation (Fig. 18.24b), dimensional control, and surface finish. As in the casting of metals and alloys, material flow in the mold cavities should be properly controlled. The effects of molecular orientation during processing should also be considered, especially in extrusion, thermoforming, and blow molding.

Large variations in cross-sectional sizes (Fig. 18.24c) and abrupt changes in geometry should be avoided, for better product quality and increased mold life. Furthermore, contraction in large cross-sections tends to cause porosity in plastic parts. Conversely, a lack of stiffness may make it more difficult to remove thin sections from molds after shaping them.

The low elastic modulus of plastics further requires that shapes be selected properly for improved stiffness of the component (Fig. 18.24d), particularly when saving materials is important. These considerations are similar to those in designing metal castings and forgings.

The properties of the final product depend on the original material and on its processing history. Cold working of polymers improves their strength and toughness. On the other hand, because of the nonuniformity of deformation (even in simple rolling), residual

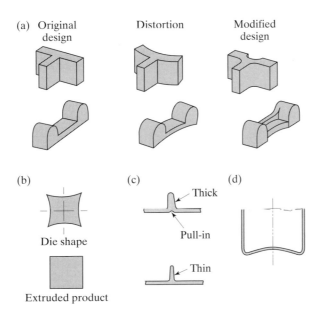

(a) Original design   Distortion   Modified design

(b)   Die shape   Extruded product

(c)   Thick   Pull-in   Thin

(d)

FIGURE 18.24   Examples of design modifications to eliminate or minimize distortion of plastic parts. (a) Suggested design changes to minimize distortion. *Source*: F. Strasser. (b) Die design (exaggerated) for extrusion of square sections. Without this design, product cross-sections swell because of the recovery of the material; this effect is known as die swell. (c) Design change in a rib, to minimize pull-in caused by shrinkage during cooling. (d) Stiffening the bottoms of thin plastic containers by doming—this technique is similar to the process used to make the bottoms of aluminum beverage cans.

stresses develop in polymers, just as they do in metals. These stresses can also be generated by thermal cycling of the part. The magnitude and direction of residual stresses, however produced, are important factors. These stresses can relax over a period of time and cause distortion of the part during its service life.

Economics. As in all processes, design and manufacturing decisions are ultimately based on performance and cost, including the costs of equipment, tooling, and production. The final selection of a process depends greatly on production volume. High equipment and tooling costs can be acceptable if the production run is large, as is the case in casting and forging. Various types of equipment are used in processes for forming and shaping plastics. The most expensive are injection-molding machines, with costs being directly proportional to clamping force.

The optimum number of cavities in the die for making the product in one cycle is an important consideration, as it is in all die casting. For small parts, several cavities can be accommodated in a die, with runners to each cavity. If a part is large, then it may be that only one cavity can be accommodated. As the number of cavities increases, so does the cost of the die.

Larger dies may be considered for the sake of a larger number of cavities, at the expense of increasing die cost even further; on the other hand, more parts will be produced per machine cycle, and so the production rate will increase. A detailed analysis has to be made, to determine the optimum number of cavities, die size, and machine capacity. Similar considerations apply to other plastics-processing methods.

General guidelines to economical processing of plastics and of composite materials are given in Tables 18.2 and 18.3. Note the high capital costs for molding plastics and the wide range of production rates. For composite materials, equipment and tooling costs for most molding operations are generally high, and production rates and economical production quantities vary widely.

TABLE 18.2   Comparative Costs and Production Volumes for Processing of Plastics

	Equipment capital cost	Production rate	Tooling cost	Typical production volume, number of parts
Machining	Medium	Medium	Low	10 – $\sim 2\times10^2$
Compression molding	High	Medium	High	10^3 – 10^6
Transfer molding	High	Medium	High	10^3 – 10^6
Injection molding	High	High	High	10^4 – 10^7
Extrusion	Medium	High	Low	10 *
Rotational molding	Low	Low	Low	10^2 – 10^3
Blow molding	Medium	Medium	Medium	10^3 – 10^6
Thermoforming	Low	Low	Low	10^2 – 10^3
Casting	Low	Very low	Low	10 – 10^2
Forging	High	Low	Medium	10 – 10^2
Foam molding	High	Medium	Medium	10^4 – 10^7

Source: After R.L.E. Brown, *Design and Manufacture of Plastic Parts*. Copyright (c) 1980 by John Wiley & Sons, Inc. Reprinted by permission of John Wiley & Sons, Inc.
*Continuous process.

TABLE 18.3 Economic Production Quantities for Various
Molding Methods

Molding method	Relative investment required		Relative production rate	Economic production quantity
	Equipment	Tooling		
Hand lay-up	VL	L	L	VL
Spray-up	L	L	L	L
Casting	M	L	L	L
Vacuum-bag molding	M	L	VL	VL
Compression-molded BMC	H	VH	H	H
SIVIC and preform	H	VH	H	H
Pressure-bag molding	H	H	L	L
Centrifugal casting	H	H	M	M
Filament winding	H	H	L	L
Pultrusion	H	H	H	H
Rotational molding	H	H	L	M
Injection molding	VH	VH	VH	VH

Source: J.G. Bralla (ed.), *Handbook of Product Design for Manfacturing*. McGraw-Hill, 1986.
VL, very low; L, low; M, medium; H, high; VH, very high.

SUMMARY

- Thermoplastics can be formed and shaped by a variety of processes, such as extrusion, molding, casting, and thermoforming, as well as by some of the processes used in metalworking. The raw material is usually in the form of pellets and powders. The high strain-rate sensitivity of thermoplastics allows extensive stretching in forming operations; thus complex and deep shapes can be produced. Thermosetting plastics are generally molded or cast.

- Fiber-reinforced plastics are processed into structural components using liquid plastics, prepregs, and bulk- and sheet-molding compounds. Fabricating techniques include various molding methods, filament winding, and pultrusion. The type and orientation of the fibers and the strength of the bond between fibers and matrix and between layers of materials are important considerations.

- The design of plastic parts must take into account their low strength and stiffness and their physical properties, such as high thermal expansion and generally low resistance to temperature. Inspection techniques are available to determine the integrity of these products.

- Because of their expanding use in critical applications, the processing of metal-matrix and ceramic-matrix composites has undergone important developments to ensure product integrity and to reduce costs. Metal-matrix composites are processed by liquid-phase, solid-phase, and two-phase processes. Ceramic-matrix composites can be processed by slurry infiltration, by chemical synthesis, or by chemical-vapor infiltration.

- Because of the variety of low-cost materials and manufacturing techniques available, the economics of processing plastics and reinforced plastics is an important consideration (particularly when compared to that of metal components). It includes die costs, cycle times, and production volume as important parameters.

TRENDS

- Reinforced-plastic parts and components are being developed at a rapid pace, for applications requiring high stiffness and strength-to-weight ratio.
- Computer-aided mold design is being implemented, particularly for injection molding of complex shapes. Various analytical and computer techniques are being developed to study material flow in molds, to optimize and make consistent part quality.
- Computer-controlled machinery and concurrent-engineering approaches are being developed to improve the quality and the production rate of reinforced-plastic structures, as well as to reduce costs.
- Composite-manufacturing automation techniques are being developed, to compete economically with conventional materials and fabrication methods.
- Computer-generated filament-winding designs and computer-driven winding machines are becoming prevalent.
- Tougher composites are being developed: double-layer structures consisting of soft, ductile, high-modulus, high-toughness layers alternated with hard, brittle, high-modulus, and low-toughness layers. The brittle layers are infiltrated with a ductile constituent.

KEY TERMS

Blow molding
Bulk-molding compound
Calendering
Casting
Chemical synthesis
Chemical-vapor infiltration
Cold forming
Compression molding
Contact molding
Encapsulation
Extrusion
Extrusion blow molding
Filament winding

Foam molding
Ice-cold forming
Injection molding
Insert molding
Liquid-phase processing
Overmolding
Parison
Pellets
Plastisols
Potting
Prepregs
Pulforming
Pultrusion

Reaction-injection molding
Resin transfer molding
Rotational molding
Sheet-molding compound
Slurry infiltration
Slush molding
Solid-phase forming
Structural foam molding
Thermoforming
Thick-molding compound
Transfer molding
Two-phase processing
Vacuum-bag molding

BIBLIOGRAPHY

Berins, M.L. (ed.), *Plastics Engineering Handbook* (5th ed.). Chapman & Hall, 1995.

Bhowmick, A.K., *Rubber Products Manufacturing Technology.* Marcel Dekker, 1994.

Bitzer, T., *Honeycomb Technology: Materials, Design, Manufacturing, Applications and Testing.* Chapman & Hall, 1997.

Campbell, P.D.O., *Plastic Component Design.* Industrial Press, 1996.

Chabot, J.F., Jr., *The Development of Plastics Processing Machinery and Methods.* Wiley, 1992.

Chanda, J.M., and S.K. Roy, *Plastics Technology Handbook* (3d ed.). Marcel Dekker, 1998.

Cracknell, P.S., and R.W. Dyson, *Handbook of Thermoplastics Injection Mould Design.* Chapman & Hall, 1994.

Engineering Materials Handbook, Vol. 1: *Composites.* ASM International, 1987.

Feldman, D., and A. Barbalata, *Synthetic Polymers: Technology, properties, applications*. Chapman & Hall, 1996.

Griskey, R.G., *Polymer Process Engineering*. Chapman & Hall, 1995.

Gutowski, T.G., *Advanced Composites Manufacturing*. Wiley, 1997.

Karszes, W.M., *Extrusion Coating: Equipment and Materials*. Tappi Press, *1997*.

Macosko, C.W., *Fundamentals of Reaction-Injection Molding*. Oxford University Publishers, 1989.

Mallick, P.K. (ed.), *Composites Engineering Handbook*. Marcel Dekker, 1997.

Malloy, R.A., *Plastic Part Design for Injection Molding—An Introduction*. Hanser–Gardner, 1994.

Mayer, R.M., and N. Hancox, *Design Data for Reinforced Plastics: A guide for engineers and designers*. Chapman & Hall, 1994.

Meyer, R.W., *Handbook of Pultrusion Technology*. Methuen, 1985.

Mills, N., *Mechanical Design of Polymer Foam Products*. Chapman & Hall, 1997.

Modern Plastics Encyclopedia. McGraw-Hill, annual.

Muccio, E.A., *Plastic Part Technology*. ASM International, 1991.

_____, *Plastics Processing Technology*. ASM International, 1994.

Potter, K., *Resin Transfer Moulding*. Chapman & Hall, 1997.

Pye, R.G.W., *Injection Mold Design* (4th ed.). Wiley, 1989.

Quinn, J.A., *Composites Design Manual*. Technomic, 1999.

Rauwendaal, C., *Polymer Extrusion* (3d ed.). Hanser, 1994.

Rosato, D.V., *Plastics Processing Data Handbook*, (2d ed.). Chapman & Hall, 1997.

Rosato, D.V., D.P. DiMattia, and D.V. Rosato, *Designing with Plastics and Composites: A Handbook*. Van Nostrand Reinhold, 1991.

Ryan, A., *Polymer Processing and Structure Development*. Chapman & Hall, 1997.

Schwartz, M.M., *Composite Materials,* Vol. 2: *Processing, Fabrication, and Applications*. Prentice Hall, 1996.

_____, *Joining of Composite-Matrix Materials*. ASM International, 1995.

Shastri, R., *Plastics Product Design*. Marcel Dekker, 1996.

Stevens, M.J., and J.A. Covas, *Extruder Principles and Operation*. Chapman & Hall, 1996.

Strong, A.B., *Plastics: Materials and Processing*. Prentice Hall, 1996.

Sweeney, F.M., *Reaction Injection Molding Machinery and Processes*. Marcel Dekker, 1987.

Tool and Manufacturing Engineers Handbook (4th ed.), Vol. 8: *Plastic Part Manufacturing*. Society of Manufacturing Engineers, 1996.

Winchaeli, W., *Extrusion Dies for Plastics and Rubber* (2d ed.). Hanser, 1992.

REVIEW QUESTIONS

18.1 What are the forms of raw materials for processing plastics into products?

18.2 Describe the features of an extruder.

18.3 Why is injection molding capable of producing parts with complex shapes and fine detail?

18.4 How are injection-molding machines rated?

18.5 Describe the blow molding process.

18.6 What is (a) a parison, (b) a plastisol, (c) a prepreg?

18.7 How is thin plastic film produced?

18.8 List several products that can be made by thermoforming.

18.9 What similarities are there between compression molding and closed-die forging?

18.10 Explain the difference between potting and encapsulation.

18.11 Describe the advantages of cold forming of plastics over other processing methods.

18.12 Name the major methods used in processing reinforced plastics.

18.13 What are the characteristics of filament-wound products?

18.14 Describe the methods used to make tubular plastic products.

18.15 List the major design considerations in forming and shaping reinforced plastics.

18.16 What is pultrusion? Pulforming?

18.17 Describe the principal manufacturing processes used to make metal-matrix composites.

18.18 How are plastic sheet and thick plastic film produced?

18.19 How are foam drinking cups produced?

18.20 If a polymer is in the form of a thin sheet, is it a thermoplastic or thermoset? Why?

QUALITATIVE PROBLEMS

18.21 Describe the advantages of applying traditional metal forming techniques (Chapters 13 through 16) to forming plastics.

18.22 Explain the reasons that some forming processes are more suitable for certain plastics than for others.

18.23 Describe the problems involved in recycling products made from reinforced plastics.

18.24 List several possible applications for filament-wound plastics.

18.25 Explain the difference between extrusion and pultrusion.

18.26 Would you use thermosetting plastics for injection molding? Explain.

18.27 By inspecting plastic containers, such as ones for baby powder, you can see that the integral lettering on them is raised rather than depressed. Can you offer an explanation about why they are molded in that way?

18.28 Describe the differences among the three major types of compression molding.

18.29 Outline the precautions that you would take in shaping reinforced plastics.

18.30 What are the factors that contribute to the cost of each forming and shaping process described in this chapter?

18.31 An injection-molded nylon gear is found to contain small pores. It is recommended that the material be dried before molding it. Explain why drying will solve this problem.

18.32 Explain why operations such as blow molding and film-bag making are performed vertically. Why is the movement upward?

18.33 Describe the operation shown in Fig. 18.5b.

18.34 Comment on the principle of operation of the tape laying machine shown in Fig. 18.18b.

18.35 Typical production volumes are given in Table 18.2. Comment on your observations, and explain why there is such a wide range.

18.36 Give several examples of injection-molded parts.

18.37 What determines the cycle time (a) for injection molding (b) for thermoforming?

18.38 Think of plastic parts that are made using two or more of the processes described in this chapter.

18.39 Does the pull-in defect shown in Fig. 18.24c also occur in metal forming and casting processes? Explain.

18.40 Describe the differences between compression-molded and injection-molded parts.

18.41 What are the differences between the barrel section of an extruder and that of an injection molding machine?

18.42 What is the function of the torpedo in the injection chamber in Fig. 18.5a?

18.43 List processes that use plastic powder as raw material and those that use plastic pellets.

18.44 Which processes are reasonable for making small production runs (for example, 100 parts) of plastic parts?

18.45 Examine common plastic poker chips. How are they manufactured?

QUANTITATIVE PROBLEMS

18.46 Estimate the die-clamping force required for injection molding five identical 6-in. diameter disks in one die. Include the runners of appropriate length and diameter.

18.47 A two-liter plastic beverage bottle is made from a parison that has a diameter which is the same as that of the threaded neck of the bottle and has a length of 5 in. Assuming uniform deformation during blow molding, estimate the wall thickness of the tubular portion of the parison.

18.48 Consider a foam drinking cup. Measure the volume of the cup and the weight. From this, estimate the percent increase in volume of the polystyrene beads.

18.49 In the sterilization process for producing intravenous (IV) bags for medical applications, the bags are subjected to an internal pressure of 30 psi. If the bag diameter is 4 in., and it can be approximated as a thin-walled cylindrical pressure vessel, what wall thickness is required to ensure that the bag does not burst during sterilization? Assume that the allowable tensile stress is 10 ksi.

SYNTHESIS AND DESIGN

18.50 Give examples of several parts suitable for insert molding. How would you manufacture these parts if insert molding were not available?

18.51 Give other examples of design modifications in addition to those shown in Fig. 18.24.

18.52 With specific examples, discuss the design issues involved in making products out of plastics as against reinforced plastics.

18.53 Inspect various plastic components in your car, and identify the processes that could have been used in making them.

18.54 Explain the design considerations involved in replacing a metal beverage can with one made of plastic.

18.55 Inspect several electrical components, such as light switches, outlets, and circuit breakers, and describe the process(es) used in making them.

18.56 Inspect several similar products that are made either from metals or from plastics, such as a metal bucket and a plastic bucket of similar shape and size. Comment on their respective thicknesses and explain the reasons for their differences, if any.

18.57 Write a brief technical paper on how plastic coatings are applied to (a) electrical wiring, (b) sheet-metal panels, (c) wire baskets, racks, and similar structures, and (d) handles for tools, such as wire cutters and pliers needing electrical insulation.

18.58 Based on experiments, it has been suggested that polymers (plain or reinforced) can be a suitable material for dies in sheet-forming operations. Describe your thoughts regarding this suggestion, considering die geometry and any other factors that can be relevant.

18.59 As we know, plastic forks, spoons, and knives are not particularly strong or rigid. What suggestions would you have to make them better? Describe processes that could be used for this purpose, and comment on the production costs involved.

18.60 For ease of sorting for recycling, a rapidly increasing number of plastic products are now identified with a triangular symbol and a single-digit number at its center. What do these numbers indicate?

18.61 What are the similarities and differences between the product design principles for the processes described in this chapter and those for the chapters in Part III? Describe your observations.

18.62 Obtain a kit for producing a model car or plane. Examine the injection-molded parts provided, and describe your thoughts on the layout of the molds.

18.63 Using the Internet, obtain the following information:

    a. costs of raw polystyrene beads;

    b. cost of raw polyethylene pellets;

    c. the range of sizes of injection molding machines;

    d. the melt properties (glass transition temperatures, melting temperatures, etc.) of plastics;

    e. the availability of polymer additives, such as coloring agents and flow property additives.

18.64 In injection-molding operations, it is common practice to remove the part from its runner and then to place the runner in a shredder and recycle the resultant pellets. List the concerns you would have in using such recycled pellets as against so-called virgin pellets.

18.65 An increasing environmental concern is the long time required for degradation of polymers in landfills. Perform a literature search on the trends and developments in the production of biodegradable plastics.

19

Rapid-Prototyping Operations

19.1 INTRODUCTION

In the development of a new product, there is invariably a need to produce a single example, or **prototype**, of a designed part or system, before the allocation of large amounts of capital to new production facilities or assembly lines. The main reason for this need is that the capital cost is so high, and production tooling takes so much time to prepare; consequently, a working prototype is needed for troubleshooting and for design evaluation, before a complicated system is ready to be produced and marketed.

In Fig. 6 in the General Introduction, a typical product development process is outlined. When errors are discovered in, or when more efficient or better design solutions are gleaned from the study of, an earlier-generation prototype, the iterative procedure naturally occurs. The main problem with this usual approach, however, is that the production of a prototype can be extremely time-consuming: Tooling can take many months to prepare, and the production of a single complicated part by conventional manufacturing operations is very difficult. While waiting for a prototype, facilities and staff still generate costs.

An even more important concern is the speed with which a product flows from concept to marketable product. In a competitive marketplace, it is well known that products which are introduced before their competitors are generally more profitable and enjoy a larger share of the market. At the same time, there are important concerns regarding production of high-quality products (Chapter 36). For these reasons, there is a concerted effort to bring high-quality products to market quickly.

A new technology which considerably speeds the iterative product development process is the concept and practice of **rapid prototyping** (Fig.19.1). The advantages of rapid prototyping include the following:

(a) 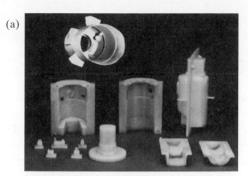   (b)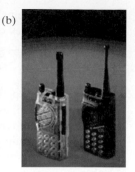

FIGURE 19.1   (a) Examples of parts made by rapid prototyping processes. (b) Stereolithography model of cellular phone. *Source*: 3D Systems.

- Physical models of parts produced from CAD data files can be manufactured in a matter of hours, to allow rapid evaluation of manufacturability and design effectiveness. In this way, rapid prototyping serves as an important tool for visualization and for concept verification.

- With suitable materials, the prototype can be used in subsequent manufacturing operations to obtain the final parts. In this way, rapid prototyping serves as an important manufacturing technology.

- Rapid prototyping operations can be used in some applications to produce tooling for manufacturing operations. In this way, one can obtain tooling in a matter of a few days.

Rapid-prototyping processes can be classified into three major groups: **subtractive**, **additive**, and **virtual**. As the names imply, subtractive processes involve material removal from a workpiece larger than the final part; additive processes build up a part by adding material incrementally; and virtual processes use advanced computer-based visualization technologies.

Almost all materials can be manufactured through a rapid-prototyping operation, but polymers are the workpiece material most commonly used today (Table 19.1). New processes

TABLE 19.1   Characteristics of Rapid Prototyping Technologies

Supply phase	Process	Layer creation technique	Phase change type	Materials
Liquid	Stereolithography	Liquid layer curing	Photopolymerization	Photopolymers (acrylates, epoxies, colorable resins, filled resins)
	Solid-based curing	Liquid layer curing and milling	Photopolymerization	Photopolymers
	Fused-deposition modeling	Extrusion of melted polymer	Solidification by cooling	Polymers (ABS, polyacrylate, etc.), wax, metals and ceramics with binder.
	Ballistic-particle manufacturing	Droplet deposition	Solidification by cooling	Polymers, wax
Powder	Three-dimensional printing	Layer of powder and binder droplet deposition	No phase change	Ceramic, polymer and metal powders with binder.
	Selective laser sintering	Layer of powder	Laser driven sintering melting and solidification	Polymers, metals with binder, metals, ceramics and sand with binder.
Solid	Laminated-object manufactuning	Deposition of sheet material	No phase change	Paper, polymers.

are continually being introduced and existing processes improved. This chapter is intended to serve as a survey of the most common rapid prototyping operations.

19.2 SUBTRACTIVE PROCESSES

Making a prototype has traditionally involved manufacturing processes using a variety of tooling and machines; usually it takes anywhere from weeks to months, depending on part complexity. Until recently, this approach has required highly-skilled operators, using conventional metal cutting and finishing machinery (see Part IV), to execute operations, one by one, until the prototype was finished. Today, subtractive processes use computer-based technologies to speed the process.

Essential to this approach are the following technologies:

- **Computer-based drafting packages**, which can produce three-dimensional representations of parts;
- **Interpretation software**, which can translate the CAD file into a format usable by manufacturing software;
- **Manufacturing software**, which is capable of planning the machining operations required to produce the desired shape; and
- **Computer-numerical-control machinery**, with the capabilities required to manufacture the parts.

When a prototype is needed only for shape verification, a soft material (usually a polymer or a wax) is used as the workpiece, in order to reduce machining problems. The material intended for the actual application can be the one machined instead, but this approach may be more time-consuming. Subtractive systems can take many forms; they are similar in approach to manufacturing cells (Section 39.9).

Operators may or may not be involved, although handling of the part is usually a human task. Depending on part complexity and on machining capabilities, prototypes can be produced in a matter of from a few days to a few weeks. These operations are covered in detail in Chapters 22 and 23.

19.3 ADDITIVE PROCESSES

Additive rapid-prototyping operations all build parts in *layers*. They are summarized in Table 19.1. In order to visualize the approach used, it is beneficial to think of constructing a loaf of bread by stacking individual slices on top of each other. All of the processes described in this section *build* parts slice by slice. The main difference between the various processes lies in the approach taken to produce the individual slices.

All additive rapid-prototyping operations require elaborate software. As an example, note the solid part shown in Fig. 19.2a. The first step is to obtain a CAD file description of the part. The computer then constructs slices of the three-dimensional part (Fig. 19.2b). Each slice is analyzed separately, and a set of instructions is compiled, in order to provide the rapid-prototyping machine with detailed information regarding the manufacture of the part. Figure 19.2d shows the paths of the extruder in the fused-deposition modeling operation. (See Section 19.3.1.)

Rapid prototyping, in this approach, requires operator input in the setup of the proper computer files and in the initiation of the production process. Following this stage, the machines generally operate unattended and provide a rough part after a few hours. The part

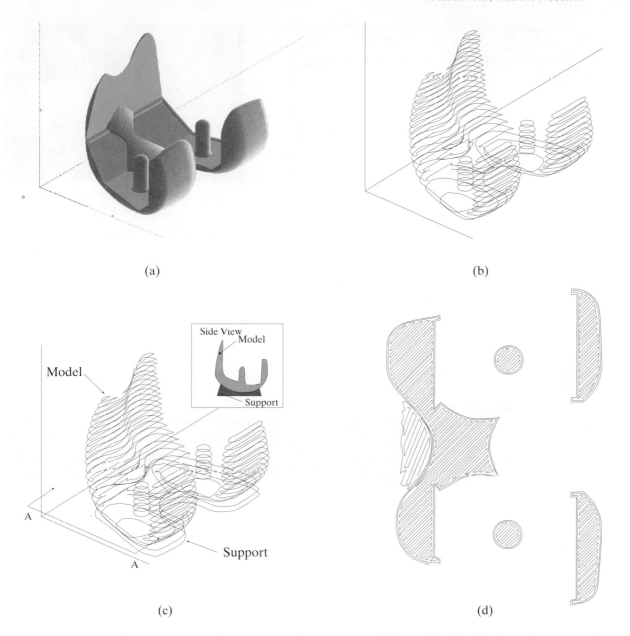

FIGURE 19.2   The computational steps in producing a stereolithography file. (a) Three-dimensional description of part. (b) The part is divided into slices (only one in 10 is shown). (c) Support material is planned. (d) A set of tool directions is determined to manufacture each slice. Shown is the extruder path at section A-A from (c), for a fused-deposition-modeling operation.

is then put through a series of finishing manual operations (such as sanding and painting), in order to complete the rapid-prototyping process.

It should be recognized that the setup and finishing operations are very labor-intensive and that the production time is only a part of the time required to obtain a prototype. In general, however, additive processes are much faster than subtractive processes; they can take as little as from a few minutes to a few hours to produce a part.

(a)

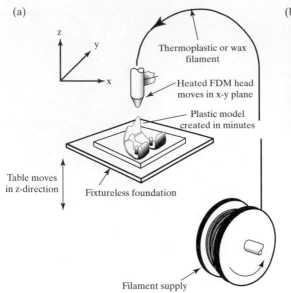

Thermoplastic or wax filament

Heated FDM head moves in x-y plane

Plastic model created in minutes

Table moves in z-direction

Fixtureless foundation

Filament supply

(b)

FIGURE 19.3 (a) Schematic illustration of the fused-deposition-modeling process. (b) The FDM 5000, a fused-deposition-modeling-machine. *Source*: Courtesy of Stratysis, Inc.

19.3.1 Fused-Deposition Modeling

In the *fused-deposition-modeling (FDM)* process (Fig.19.3), a gantry-robot-controlled extruder head moves in two principal directions over a table. The table can be raised and lowered as needed. A thermoplastic or wax filament is extruded through the small orifice of a heated die. The initial layer is placed on a foam foundation by extruding the filament at a constant rate while the extruder head follows a predetermined path (Fig. 19.2d). When the first layer is completed, the table is lowered so that subsequent layers can be superposed. More machines for FDM are currently being sold in the United States than for any other system of rapid prototyping.

Occasionally, complicated parts are required, such as the one shown in Fig. 19.4. This part is difficult to manufacture directly, because once the part has been constructed up to

FIGURE 19.4 (a) A part with a protruding section which requires support material. (b) Common support structures used in rapid-prototyping machines. *Source*: P.F. Jacobs, *Rapid Prototyping & Manufacturing: Fundamentals of Stereolithography*. Society of Manufacturing Engineers, 1992.

(a)

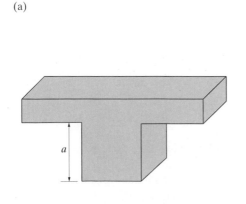

(b)

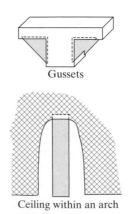

Gussets

Ceiling within an arch

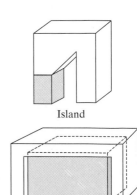

Island

Ceiling

height *a*, the next slice would require the filament to be placed in a location where no material exists to support it. The solution is to extrude a support material separately from the modeling material, so that a filament can be placed safely in the center of the part. The support material is extruded with a less dense spacing of filament on a layer, so that it is weaker than the model material and can be broken off after the part is completed.

The layers in an FDM machine are determined by the extruder-die diameter; they are typically from 0.50 mm to 0.25 mm (from 0.02 in. to 0.01 in.). This thickness represents the best achievable tolerance in the vertical direction. In the *x-y* plane, dimensional accuracy can be as fine as 0.025 mm (0.001 in.), as long as a filament can be extruded into the feature.

Close examination of an FDM-produced part will indicate that a stepped surface exists on oblique exterior planes. If this surface roughness is objectionable, a heated tool can be used to smoothen the surface, or a coating can be applied, often in the form of a polishing wax. However, the overall tolerances are then compromised, unless care is taken in these finishing operations.

Some FDM machines can be obtained for around $30,000, but others can cost as much as $150,000. The main difference among the machines is the maximum size of the parts that can be produced. A wide variety of polymers and waxes are available for different applications.

19.3.2 Stereolithography

Another very common rapid-prototyping process, one actually developed prior to fused-deposition modeling, is stereolithography (Fig. 19.5). The *stereolithography* process is based on the principle of *curing* (hardening) a liquid photopolymer into a specific shape. A vat, containing a mechanism whereby a platform can be lowered and raised, is filled with a photocurable liquid acrylate polymer. The liquid is a mixture of acrylic monomers, oligomers (polymer intermediates), and a photoinitiator.

When the platform is at its highest position, depth *a*, the layer of liquid above it is shallow. A *laser*, generating an ultraviolet beam, is now focused upon a selected surface area of the photopolymer and then moved in the *x-y* direction. The beam cures that portion of the photopolymer (say, a ring-shaped portion) and thereby produces a solid body. The platform is then lowered sufficiently to cover the cured polymer with another layer of liquid polymer, and the sequence is repeated. In Fig. 19.5, the process is repeated until level *b* is reached. Thus far we have generated a cylindrical part with a constant wall thickness. Note that the platform is now lowered by a vertical distance *ab*.

FIGURE 19.5   Schematic illustration of the stereolithography process. *Source*: Ultra Violet Products, Inc.

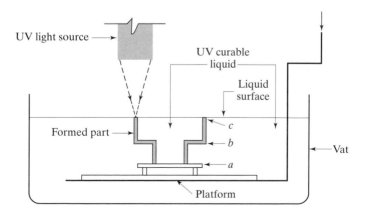

At level *b*, the *x*-*y* movements of the beam are wider, so that we now have a flange-shaped portion that is being produced over the previously formed part. After the proper thickness of the liquid has been cured, the process is repeated, producing another cylindrical section between levels *b* and *c*. Note that the surrounding liquid polymer is still fluid, because it has not been exposed to the ultraviolet beam, and that the part has been produced from the bottom up in individual "slices". The unused portion of the liquid polymer can be used again to make another part or another prototype.

Note that the term stereolithography, as used to describe this process, comes from the facts that the movements are three-dimensional and that the process is similar to lithography, in which the image to be printed on a flat surface is ink-receptive and the blank areas are ink-repellent. Also note that stereolithography can, like FDM, need a weaker support material; in stereolithography, this support takes the form of perforated structures. After its completion, the part is removed from the platform, blotted, and cleaned ultrasonically and with an alcohol bath; then the support structure is removed, and the part is subjected to a final curing cycle.

The smallest tolerance which can be achieved in stereolithography depends on the focus sharpness of the laser; typically, it is around 0.0125 mm (0.0005 in). Oblique surfaces can also can be of very high quality. An interesting technique can be used to construct two layers and then produce a transition from one layer to the next. The platform is lowered below the fluid level, then raised above the fluid, so that the photocurable polymer forms a meniscus between these layers. The meniscus is then cured with the laser, to form a smoother surface.

Solid parts can be produced by applying special laser-scanning patterns to speed production. For example, by spacing scan lines in stereolithography, volumes or pockets of uncured polymer can be formed around cured shells. When the part is later placed in a post processing oven, the pockets cure, and a solid part forms. Similarly, parts to be investment-cast (see Section 19.5) will have a drainable honeycomb structure which permits a significant fraction of the part to remain uncured.

Total cycle times in stereolithography range from a few hours to a day, without postprocessing (sanding, painting, etc.). Depending on their capacity, the cost of the necessary machines is in the range of $100,000 to $400,000; the cost of the liquid polymer is on the order of $300 per gallon. Maximum part size is 0.5 m $\times$ 0.5 m $\times$ 0.6 m (19 in. $\times$ 19 in. $\times$ 24 in.).

Example: Computer Mouse Design

When contacted by a major computer manufacturer (and potential first-time customer), Logitech Company quoted a bid for building a two-button computer mouse of unique design within two weeks (Fig.19.6). Stereolithography was efficiently employed within a concurrent-engineering approach. (See Section 3 in the General Introduction.) The customer gave Logitech control drawings on the new mouse, and concurrent-engineering development took place with two design teams: an electrical-engineering team emphasizing control circuitry, and a mechanical-engineering team emphasizing casing layout and button geometry.

On the first day, both engineering teams began their design work. Overnight on the first day, the stereolithography machine produced the first prototype of the mouse bottom. Design work on the mouse top and the complicated button mechanism was completed during the second day, and the parts were sent to the stereolithography machine and produced before the end of the third day. By this time, completed prototype circuitry boards had been constructed and were ready to be assembled into the prototype. The total elapsed time between launch and the completed functional prototype was seven days.

The company was able to demonstrate the design with working prototypes within the two week deadline. The company now ships over one million units each year to the computer manufacturer.
Source: Courtesy Logitech and 3D Systems, Inc.

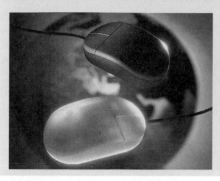

FIGURE 19.6   A two-button computer mouse.

19.3.3 Selective Laser Sintering

Selective laser sintering (SLS) is a process based on the sintering of nonmetallic (or, less commonly, metallic) powders selectively into an individual object (see also Chapter 17). The basic elements in this process are shown in Fig. 19.7. The bottom of the processing chamber is equipped with two cylinders:

   a. a powder feed cylinder, which is raised incrementally to supply powder to the part-build cylinder through a roller mechanism; and
   b. a part-build cylinder, which is lowered incrementally to where the sintered part is formed.

   Λ thin layer of powder is first deposited in the part build cylinder. Λ laser beam, guided by a process-control computer using instructions generated by the 3-D CAD

FIGURE 19.7   Schematic illustration of the selective laser sintering process.
Source: After C. Deckard and P.F. McClure.

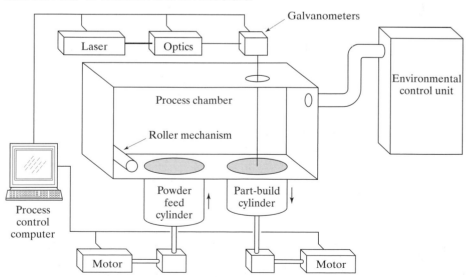

program of the desired part, is then focused on that layer, tracing and sintering a particular cross-section into a solid mass. The powder in other areas remains loose, yet it supports the sintered portion. Another layer of powder is now deposited; this cycle is repeated again and again until the entire three-dimensional part has been produced. The loose particles are then shaken off, and the part is recovered. The part does not require further curing, unless it is a ceramic.

A variety of materials can be used in this process, including polymers (ABS, PVC, nylon, polyester, polystyrene, epoxy—see also Chapter 7), wax, metals, and ceramics with appropriate binders. It is most common to use polymers, because of the smaller, less expensive, less complicated lasers required for sintering. With ceramics and metals, it is common to sinter only a polymer binder which has been blended with the ceramic or metal powders and then to complete the sintering in a furnace.

19.3.4 Solid-Base Curing

The *solid-base curing* process, also called *solid ground curing*, is unique in that entire slices of a part are manufactured at one time; as a result, a large throughput is achieved compared to that from other rapid-prototyping processes. This process is, however, among the most expensive, so its adoption has been less common than that of other types of rapid prototyping.

The basic approach is illustrated in Fig. 19.8. It consists of the following steps:

1. Once a slice is created by the computer software, a mask of the slice is printed on a glass sheet, by the use of an electrostatic printing process similar to that used in laser printers. A mask is required, because the area of the slice where solid material is desired remains transparent (steps A through C in Fig. 19.8).

FIGURE 19.8   Schematic illustration of the solid-base-curing process. *Source:* After M. Burns, *Automated Fabrication*, Prentice Hall, 1993.

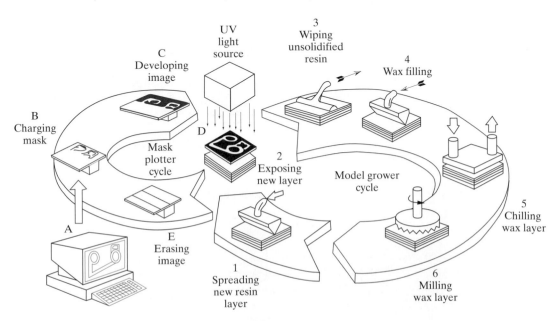

2. While the mask is being prepared, a thin layer of photoreactive polymer is laid down on the work surface and spread evenly (step 1).

3. The photomask is placed over the work surface, and an ultraviolet floodlight is projected through the mask. Wherever the mask is clear, the light shines through to cure the polymer and causes the desired slice to be hardened (step D).

4. The unaffected resin, still liquid, is vacuumed off the surface (step 3).

5. Water-soluble liquid wax is spread across the work area, filling the cavities previously occupied by the unexposed liquid polymer. Since the workpiece is on a chilling plate and the workspace remains cool, the wax hardens quickly (steps 4 and 5).

6. The layer is then milled (see Section 23.2) to achieve the correct thickness and good flatness (step 6).

7. The process is repeated, layer by layer, until the part is completed.

Solid base curing has the advantage of high production rate, both because entire slices are produced at once and because two glass screens are used concurrently. That is, while one mask is being used to expose the polymer, the next mask is already being prepared, and it is ready as soon as the milling operation is completed.

The wax support is water soluble; it may be removed immediately, or it may remain in place as protection during shipping of the part. Use of the wax support means that any shape can be manufactured, including "ship-in-the-bottle" types of parts where removal of a solid support would be difficult. Usually, no finishing operation is required, but occasionally the polymer will be cleaned in a slightly acidic solution to bleach the surface and to obtain a smoother finish.

19.3.5 Ballistic Particle Manufacturing

In the *ballistic particle manufacturing* process, a stream of a material, such as a plastic, a ceramic, a metal, or wax, is ejected through a small orifice at a surface (target), by the use of an ink-jet-style mechanism. The mechanism uses a piezoelectric pump, which operates when an electric charge is applied, generating a shock wave that propels 50-μm droplets at a rate of 10,000 per second. The operation is repeated, in a manner similar to other processes, to form the part, with layers of wax deposited on top of each other. The ink-jet head is guided by a three-axis robot.

Three-dimensional printing (3DP) is related to ballistic particle manufacturing, except that, instead of depositing the part material, the print head deposits an inorganic binder material (such as colloidal silica). The binder is directed onto a layer of ceramic or metal powders, as shown in Fig. 19.9. A piston supporting the powder bed is lowered incrementally, and with each step a layer is deposited and then unified by the binder. Commonly used powder materials are aluminum oxide, silicon carbide, silica, and zirconia. (See Chapter 8.)

A common part produced by 3DP is a ceramic casting shell (see Section 11.6), in which an aluminum-oxide or aluminum-silica powder is fused with a silica binder. The molds need to be post processed in two steps: curing at around 150 °C (300 °F), and then firing at 1000 °C–1500 °C (1840 °F–2740 °F).

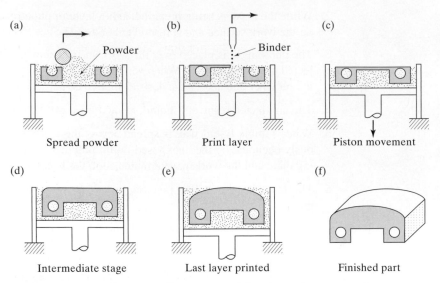

FIGURE 19.9 Schematic illustration of the three-dimensional-printing process. *Source*: After E. Sachs and M. Cima.

19.3.6 Laminated-Object Manufacturing

Lamination implies a laying down of layers which are adhesively bonded to one another. *Laminated-object manufacturing (LOM)* uses layers of paper or plastic sheets with a heat-activated glue on one side to produce parts. The desired shapes are burned into the sheet with a laser, and the parts are built layer by layer (Fig.19.10).

Once the part is completed, the excess material must be removed manually. This process is simplified by programming the laser to burn perforations in criss-crossed patterns; the resulting grid lines make the part appear as if it had been constructed from gridded paper. LOM uses sheets as thin as 0.05 mm (0.002 in.) although 0.02 in. thickness is more commonly used, so that it can achieve tolerances similar to those available from stereolithography and from fused-deposition modeling. The compressed paper has the appearance and strength of soft wood, and it is often mistaken for elaborate wood carvings. The paper parts are easy to finish or coat.

FIGURE 19.10 (a) Schematic illustration of the laminated-object-manufacturing process. *Source*: Helysis, Inc. (b) Crankshaft-part example made by LOM. *Source*: After L. Wood.

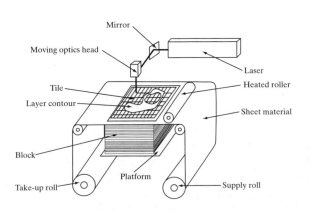

These systems, compared to other rapid prototyping operations, use very inexpensive media, and the lower-end systems are the least expensive of such machines. Referred to as **desktop rapid prototyping machines**, they use standard labels as media, but they have limited workspace. Another limitation of the process is that the workpieces, being produced from paper, do not lend themselves well to further manufacturing operations.

19.4 VIRTUAL PROTOTYPING

Virtual prototyping, a totally software form of prototyping, uses advanced graphics and virtual-reality environments to allow designers to examine a part. In a way, this technology is used by CAD packages to render a part, so that the designer can observe and evaluate the part as it is drawn. However, virtual prototyping systems should be recognized as extreme cases of rendering detail.

The simplest forms of such systems use complex software and three-dimensional graphics routines to allow viewers to change the view of parts on a computer screen. More complicated versions will use virtual-reality headgear and gloves with appropriate sensors, to let the user observe a computer-generated prototype of the desired part in a completely virtual environment.

Virtual prototyping has the advantage of instantaneous rendering of parts for evaluation, but the more advanced systems are costly. Because familiarity with software interfaces is a necessary prerequisite to their application, these systems have very steep learning curves. Furthermore, many manufacturing and design practitioners prefer a physical prototype to evaluate, rather than a video-screen rendering. They often perceive virtual-reality prototypes to be inferior to mechanical prototypes, even when designers debug as many or more errors in the virtual environment.

There have been some important examples of complicated products which have been produced without any physical prototype whatsoever. Perhaps the best-known example is the Boeing 777 aircraft, where mechanical fits and interferences were evaluated on a CAD system, and difficulties were corrected before manufacture of the first production model (Chapter 39).

19.5 APPLICATIONS OF RAPID-PROTOTYPING TECHNOLOGY TO THE MANUFACTURE OF ACTUAL PARTS

While extremely beneficial as a demonstration and visualization tool, rapid-prototyping processes have also been used as a manufacturing step in production. There are two basic methodologies used: (a) direct production of the desired parts in rapid prototyping, and (b) production of tooling by rapid prototyping, for use in further manufacturing operations.

19.5.1 Production of Individual Parts

The polymer parts which can be obtained from various rapid-prototyping operations are useful not only for design evaluation and troubleshooting; occasionally these processes can even be used to manufacture marketable products directly. Unfortunately, it is often desirable, for functional reasons, to use metallic parts, while the best-developed and most-available rapid-prototyping operations involve polymeric workpieces.

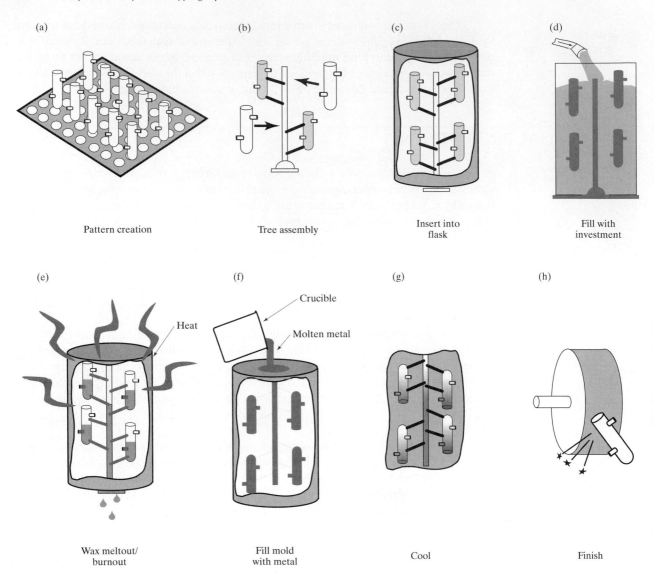

FIGURE 19.11   Manufacturing steps for investment casting that uses rapid-prototyped wax parts as blanks. This approach uses a flask for the investment, but a shell method can also be used. *Source*: 3D Systems, Inc.

The solution is to use the components manufactured through rapid prototyping as aids in further processing. As an example, an approach for investment casting is shown in Fig. 19.11. (See also Section 11.7.) Here the individual patterns are made in a rapid-prototyping operation (in this case stereolithography) and then used as the blanks in assembling a tree for investment casting.

It should be noted that this approach requires a polymer which will melt and burn from the ceramic mold completely; such polymers are available for all forms of polymer rapid-prototyping operations. Furthermore, the parts as drawn in CAD programs are usually software-modified to account for shrinkage; it is the modified part which is produced in the rapid-prototyping machinery.

Rapid prototyping processes are now being used to produce engineering components (**direct manufacturing**), but not economically for large quantityes. The advantage of rapid prototyping is that it makes traditionally costly processes economical for very short production runs—often for merely one part.

19.5.2 Rapid Tooling

The main difficulty which must be overcome in applying rapid-prototyping operations beyond prototyping is the long time required. Recall that the advantage of rapid-prototyping is short production time for *individual* parts compared to other approaches. A part which can be contained in a 150-mm (6-in.) cube and can be manufactured through stereolithography in eight or so hours is produced much faster that way than through other processes. However, if a batch of a few thousand of these parts is to be manufactured, the time needed to produce all of the components directly through rapid prototyping is excessive.

A number of approaches have been devised for the rapid production of tooling by means of rapid-prototyping operations. For example, in Fig. 19.12, a sand-casting operation is shown, one in which the pattern plates have been manufactured via rapid-prototyping approaches, while the remainder of the process is identical to conventional sand casting (see Section 11.2). The advantage to this approach is the short time needed to produce the pattern plate compared to that in conventional manufacturing. The main shortcoming is the reduced pattern life, as compared to that obtained from machined high-strength metals.

Another common application is injection molding (see Section 18.3). Here, the mold (or, more typically, a mold insert) is manufactured via rapid prototyping and is used in injection-molding machines. Two approaches are used for the production of the tooling. Either a high-melting-point thermoplastic or a stable thermoset is used for low-temperature injection molding, or an investment cast insert is produced using the approach described in Section 19.4.1.

Molds for slip casting of ceramics can also be produced in this manner. (See Section 17.9.1.) To produce individual molds, rapid-prototyping processes are used directly, but the molds will be shaped with the desired permeability. For example, in fused-deposition modeling, this requirement mandates that the filaments be placed onto the individual slices with a small gap between adjacent filaments. These filaments will later be positioned at right angles in adjacent layers.

The result is a mold (or mold insert) which can be used for the manufacture of plastic components without the time lag (several months) traditionally required for the procurement of tooling. Furthermore, the design is simplified, because the designer need only analyze a CAD file of the desired part. Software then produces the tool geometry and automatically compensates for shrinkage.

Consider, again, the investment-casting approach shown in Fig. 19.11. Obviously, for large production runs, the time required to produce the blanks individually in a rapid-prototyping machine will be excessive. Injection-molded patterns produced from rapid-prototyped tooling, however, can be used to speed production while still dramatically reducing lead time. The main concerns are (a) that the resulting parts offer only limited dimensional accuracy and surface finish, compared to those available from traditionally produced molds, and (b) that the life of the tooling is short, especially when polymer inserts are being used.

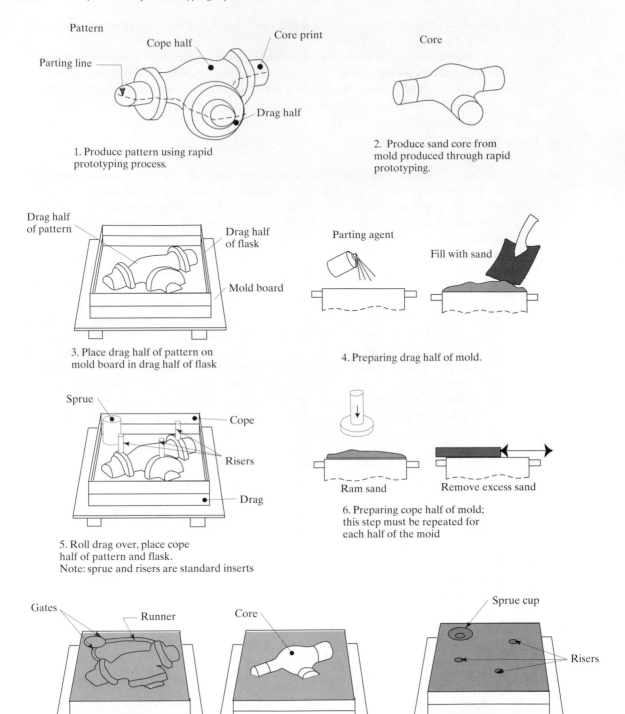

1. Produce pattern using rapid prototyping process.

2. Produce sand core from mold produced through rapid prototyping.

3. Place drag half of pattern on mold board in drag half of flask

4. Preparing drag half of mold.

5. Roll drag over, place cope half of pattern and flask. Note: sprue and risers are standard inserts

6. Preparing cope half of mold; this step must be repeated for each half of the moid

7. Seperate flask — remove all patterns. Place core in place, close flask.

8. Flask closed and clamped, ready for pouring of molten metal.

FIGURE 19.12   Manufacturing steps in sand casting that uses rapid-prototyped patterns. *Source*: 3D Systems, Inc.

Example: Automotive Rear-Wiper Motor Cover

Manufacturing engineers at Ford Motor Company were faced with a dilemma when it was realized that, to meet production goals, a prototype rear-wiper motor cover was needed for the 1994 Explorer within a six-week time frame (Fig.19.13). Ford's tooling supplier could not meet this deadline; to machine, then to grind, and finally to verify dimensions usually took many times longer.

From a CAD file, a prototype was created and, as an example of classical rapid-prototyping utility, was produced by stereolithography and was fitted over the wiper motor. As often occurs with new designs and assemblies, an interference problem was discovered, one requiring a redesign. The wax prototype was machined by hand, the new fit was verified, and the modified part served as the template for adjusting the CAD drawing. From the revised CAD drawing, a new prototype was produced and the fit was assured.

Using mold-design software, "negative" patterns of the parts were produced that incorporated shrink factors to compensate for the prototype resin, the A2 steel (Section 5.7) to be used as the tooling, and the polypropylene end material. These mold patterns were produced using an investment-casting-compatible wax on a stereolithography system and then cast using A2 steel. The first molds were then evaluated, and improvements were made in the cooling channels and the injector-pin components of the tool. A second set of tools were investment-cast, to yield 30,000 pieces per month. Total turnaround time was four weeks.

Source: Courtesy of Ford Motor Company and 3D Systems.

FIGURE 19.13   Rapid tooling for a rear-wiper-motor cover.

SUMMARY

- Rapid prototyping has grown into its own unique manufacturing discipline within the past two decades. As a physical-model-producing technology, it is a useful technique for identifying and correcting design errors. Several techniques exist for producing parts through rapid prototyping.

- Fused-deposition modeling consists of a computer-controlled extruder through which a polymer filament is deposited to produce a part slice by slice.

- Stereolithography involves a computer-controlled laser-focusing system that cures a liquid thermosetting polymer containing a photosensitive curing agent.

- Solid-base curing involves curing an entire layer at one time with an ultraviolet lamp, and then wiping it with a water-soluble wax to fill in uncured locations. It results in higher throughput than other processes.
- Laminated-object manufacturing first uses a laser beam to cut the slices on paper or plastic sheets (laminations), then applies an adhesive layer, and finally stacks the sheets to produce the part.
- Ballistic-particle manufacturing (and the related process of three-dimensional printing) uses an inkjet mechanism to deposit liquid droplets of the prototyping material (or to deposit a liquid binder onto powders, respectively).
- Selective laser sintering uses a high-powered laser beam to sinter powders in a desired pattern.
- Rapid prototyping techniques have made possible much faster product-development times and, in addition, are having a major effect on other manufacturing processes. When appropriate materials are used, rapid-prototyping machinery can produce blanks for investment casting or for similar processes, so that metallic parts can be obtained quickly and inexpensively, even for lot sizes as small as one part. Such approaches can also be applied to producing molds for operations such as injection molding and thereby can significantly reduce lead time between design and manufacture.

TRENDS

- Rapid-prototyping systems continue to become more economical and at the same time more accurate and faster.
- With increases in computational speeds, virtual prototyping is gaining greater acceptance. Indeed, simple virtual-prototyping capabilities exist in almost all commercially available CAD programs.
- Rapid-prototyping technologies are increasingly applied as manufacturing machinery, in order to produce blanks for tooling that is to be completed via such processes as investment casting, or in order to make tooling and tooling inserts directly.
- New polymers are becoming available that are environmentally more friendly and that have higher strength, especially with respect to impact resistance.

KEY TERMS

Additive processes	Photopolymer	Stereolithography
Ballistic-particle manufacturing	Prototype	Subtractive processes
Desktop machines	Rapid tooling	Three-dimensional printing
Fused-deposition modeling	Selective laser sintering	Virtual prototyping
Laminated-object manufacturing	Solid-base curing	

BIBLIOGRAPHY

Beaman, J.J., J.W. Barlow, D.L. Bourell, and R. Crawford, *Solid Freeform Fabrication*. Kluwer Academic Pub., 1997.

Bennett, G. (ed.), *Developments in Rapid Prototyping and Tooling*. Institution of Mechanical Engineers, 1997.

Burns, M., *Automated Fabrication*. Prentice Hall, 1993.

Chua, C.K., and L.K. Fua, *Rapid Prototyping: Principles and Applications in Manufacturing*. Wiley, 1997.

Jacobs, P.F., *Rapid Prototyping and Manufacturing: Fundamentals of StereoLithography*. McGraw-Hill, 1993.

———, *StereoLithography and Other RP&M Technologies: From Rapid Prototyping to Rapid Tooling*. Society of Manufacturing Engineers, 1995.

Wood, L., *Rapid Automated Prototyping: An Introduction*. Industrial Press, 1993.

REVIEW QUESTIONS

19.1 What is stereolithography?

19.2 Can rapid-prototyped parts be made of paper?

19.3 What is virtual prototyping, and how does it differ from additive methods?

19.4 What is FDM?

19.5 What are the steps in producing a part through solid-base curing?

19.6 What is meant by rapid tooling?

19.7 Outline methods of producing metal parts using the processes described in this chapter.

QUALITATIVE PROBLEMS

19.8 Examine a coffee cup, and decide in which orientation you would choose to produce the part, if using (a) fused-deposition manufacturing, (b) laminated-object manufacturing.

19.9 How would you quickly manufacture tooling for injection molding?

19.10 Summarize the rapid-prototyping processes and the materials which can be used for them.

19.11 Which processes described in this chapter are best suited for production of ceramic parts? Why?

19.12 Why are so few parts in commercial products directly manufactured through rapid-prototyping operations?

19.13 What is the main advantage to physical rapid prototyping?

19.14 Why are cleaning and finishing operations necessary for rapid-prototyping processes?

19.15 Careful analysis of a rapid-prototyped part indicates that it is made up of layers, with a clear filament outline visible on a layer. Is the material a thermoset or a thermoplastic?

19.16 Why is solid-base curing not as popular, in terms of machines sold, as other rapid-prototyping techniques?

QUANTITATIVE PROBLEMS

19.17 Using an approximate cost of $500 per gallon, estimate the material cost of a rapid-prototyped rendering of a computer mouse.

19.18 The extruder head in a fused-deposition modeling setup has a diameter of 1.25 mm (0.05 in.) and produces layers 0.25-mm (0.01-in.) thick. If the extruder head and polymer extrudate velocities are 50 mm per second, estimate the production time for the generation of a 50-mm (2-in.) solid cube. Assume that there is a 15-second delay between layers as the extruder head is moved over a wire brush for cleaning.

19.19 Using the data for Problem 19.18, and also noting that the porosity for the support material is 50%, calculate the production rate for making a cup 100-mm (4-in.) high and having an outside diameter of 88 mm (3.5 in.) and wall thickness of 6-mm (0.25 in.). Consider both the case with the closed end up and that with it down.

19.20 If parts are to be investment-cast, they can be produced more quickly if they have a solid shell and a porous interior. Estimate the material and production-time reduction for producing a hollow cylinder 125-mm (5 in.) high and 62.5-mm (2.5 in.) in diameter. Assume that either stereolithography or FDM can be analyzed, with a 0.625-mm (0.025 in.) focus width or filament diameter, respectively. To ensure part integrity, two contours will be traced around the periphery of the part on each surface. Use a laser traverse or extruder-head speed of 50 mm per second.

SYNTHESIS AND DESIGN

19.21 A current topic of research is to produce parts from rapid-prototyping operations and then to use them in experimental stress analysis, in order to infer the strength of final parts produced by means of conventional manufacturing operations. List your concerns with this approach, and outline means of addressing these concerns.

19.22 Because of relief of residual stresses during curing, long unsupported overhangs in parts from stereolithography will tend to curl. Suggest methods of controlling or eliminating this curl.

19.23 Because rapid prototyping machines represent a large capital investment, few companies can justify the purchase of their own system. Service companies which produce parts based on their customers' drawings have become common. Perform an informal survey of such service companies, and determine the classes of rapid-prototyping machines used and their percentages.

19.24 One of the major advantages of stereolithography is that it can use semi-transparent polymers, so that internal details of parts can be readily discerned. List parts in which this feature is valuable.

PART IV
Material-Removal Processes and Machines

Parts manufactured by casting, forming, and shaping processes, described in Parts II and III and including many of those made with near-net or net-shape methods, often require further operations before the product is ready for use. Moreover, in many engineering applications, parts must be *interchangeable* to function properly and reliably during their expected service lives. Such is the case with automobile parts (Fig. IV.1). Note, for example, the dimensional tolerances specified on the part shown in Fig. IV.2, and the presence of a threaded end.

A brief review will show that none of the processes described thus far can produce a part with such accuracy. Critical choices have to be made about the extent of shaping and forming versus the extent of machining to be done on a workpiece to economically produce an acceptable part.

Machining, the broad term used to describe **removal of material** from a workpiece, covers several processes. These are usually divided into the following categories:

- **Cutting**, which generally involves single-point or multipoint cutting tools, each with a clearly defined tool shape;
- **Abrasive processes** such as grinding;
- **Advanced machining processes** that utilize electrical, chemical, thermal, and hydrodynamic methods, as well as lasers.

FIGURE IV.1   Typical machined parts on an automobile.

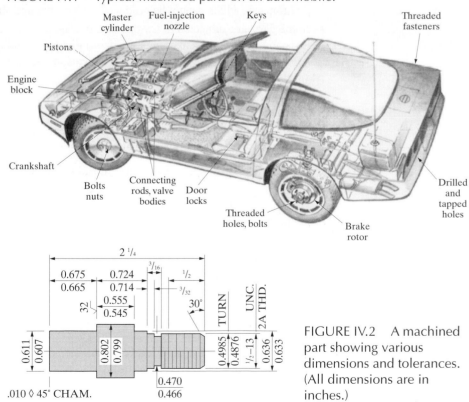

FIGURE IV.2   A machined part showing various dimensions and tolerances. (All dimensions are in inches.)

531

FIGURE IV.3   A forged crankshaft before and after machining of bearing surfaces. *Source*: Courtesy of Wyman-Gordon Company.

Material-removal processes are desirable or even necessary in manufacturing operations for the following reasons:

- Closer **dimensional accuracy** may be required than is available from casting, forming, or shaping processes alone. For example, in the forged crankshaft shown in Fig. IV.3, the bearing surfaces and the holes cannot be produced with good dimensional accuracy and surface finish solely by forming and shaping processes.
- Parts may have external and internal **geometric features**, as well as sharp corners and flatness, which cannot be produced by forming and shaping processes.
- Some parts are subjected to various heat treatments for improved hardness and wear resistance. Since these parts may undergo distortion and surface discoloration, they generally require additional **finishing operations**, such as grinding, to obtain the desired final dimensions and surface finish.
- Parts may require special **surface characteristics** or surface texture that cannot be produced by other means.
- Machining the part may be more **economical** than manufacturing it by other processes, particularly if the number of parts desired is relatively small.

Against these advantages, material-removal processes have certain limitations:

- Removal processes inevitably **waste material** and generally require more energy, capital, and labor than forming and shaping operations. Therefore, they should be avoided whenever possible.
- Unless carried out properly, material-removal processes can have **adverse effects** on the surface quality and properties of the product.
- Removing a volume of material from a workpiece generally takes **longer** than it does to shape it by other processes.

Material-removal processes and machines are indispensable to manufacturing technology. Ever since lathes were introduced in the 1700s, many processes have been continuously developed. We now have available a variety of computer-controlled machines, as well as new techniques using lasers and electrical, chemical, thermal, and hydrodynamic energy sources.

Following the outline shown in Fig. IV.4, Part IV will first describe the basic mechanics of chip formation in cutting processes. Among the most important aspects of cutting operations is the type of tools used. Improper tool selection can have a major economic

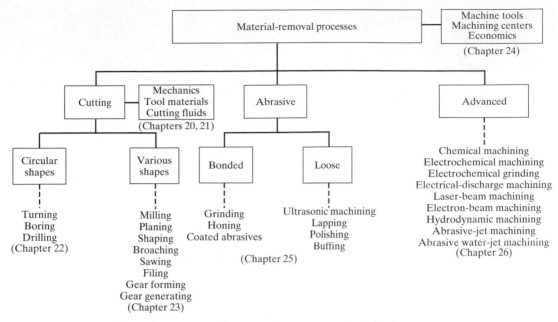

FIGURE IV.4   Outline of the material-removal processes described in Part IV.

impact on the operation. Tool materials have been developed to meet the challenges of machining new materials, including composite materials, with high strength and toughness.

A variety of shapes can be produced by machining. We will describe all major cutting processes and their capabilities, typical applications, and limitations. The machines on which material-removal operations are performed are generally called **machine tools**. Their construction and characteristics greatly influence these operations, as well as product quality, surface finish, and dimensional accuracy.

It is important to view machining and manufacturing operations as a *system* consisting of the **workpiece**, the **cutting tool**, and the **machine**. Machining operations cannot be carried out efficiently and economically without a knowledge of the interactions among these elements.

Part IV will also identify important machine-tool characteristics, including their structure and stiffness, and new developments in machine-tool design and the materials used in their construction. Among new developments are **machining centers**, which are versatile machine tools controlled by computers and capable of performing a variety of machining operations efficiently.

We then describe processes in which removal of material to a high dimensional accuracy is carried out by **abrasive processes**. The most common example is a grinding wheel, in which the abrasive particles are held together with a bond. Other examples of abrasive operations are sanding with coated abrasives (sandpaper, emery paper), and honing, lapping, buffing, polishing, shot-blasting, and ultrasonic machining.

For technical and economic reasons, certain parts cannot be manufactured satisfactorily either by cutting or by abrasive processes. Since the 1940s, important developments have taken place in advanced machining processes such as electrical, chemical, thermal, and hydrodynamic means of material removal. As a result, chemical, electrochemical, electrical-discharge, laser- and electron-beam, abrasive-jet, and hydrodynamic machining have now become major manufacturing processes.

The knowledge gained in Part IV will enable us to assess the capabilities and limitations of material-removal processes and equipment, their proper selection for maximum productivity and low product cost, and how these processes fit into the broader scheme of manufacturing operations.

20

Fundamentals of Cutting

20.1 INTRODUCTION

Cutting processes remove material from the surface of a workpiece by producing **chips**. Although these processes will be described in Chapters 22 and 23 in greater detail, some of the more common cutting processes are illustrated in Fig. 20.1.

In the **turning** operation (Fig. 20.1a) the workpiece is rotated and a cutting tool removes a layer of material as it moves to the left; (b) shows a **cutting-off** operation, where the cutting tool moves radially inward and separates the right piece from the bulk of the blank; (c) shows a **slab-milling** operation, in which a rotating cutting tool removes a layer of material from the surface of the workpiece; and (d) shows an **end-milling** operation, in which a rotating cutter travels along a certain depth in the workpiece and produces a cavity.

One of the most common processes is turning, illustrated in Fig. 20.2. The cutting tool is set at a certain *depth of cut* (measured in mm or in.) and travels to the left with a certain velocity as the workpiece rotates. The *feed* or *feed rate* is the distance the tool travels per unit revolution of the workpiece (mm/rev or in./rev). As a result of this action, a chip is produced which moves up the face of the tool.

In order to analyze this process in detail, a two-dimensional model of it is presented in Fig. 20.3. In this idealized model, a cutting tool moves to the left along the workpiece at a constant velocity, V, and depth of cut, t_o. A chip is produced ahead of the tool by deforming and shearing the material continuously along the shear plane.

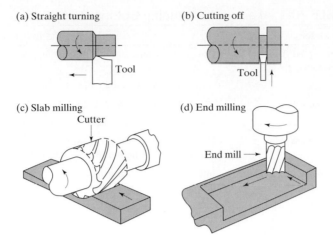

(a) Straight turning

Tool

(b) Cutting off

Tool

(c) Slab milling

Cutter

(d) End milling

End mill →

FIGURE 20.1   Examples of cutting processes.

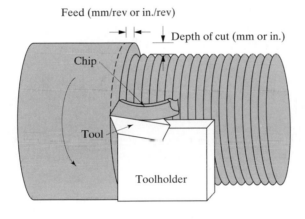

Feed (mm/rev or in./rev)

Depth of cut (mm or in.)

Chip

Tool

Toolholder

FIGURE 20.2   Basic principle of the turning operation.

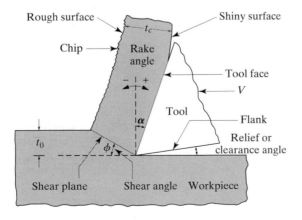

Rough surface

Shiny surface

Chip

t_c

Rake angle

Tool face

V

− + +

α

Tool

Flank

Relief or clearance angle

t_0

ϕ

Shear plane

Shear angle   Workpiece

FIGURE 20.3   Schematic illustration of a two-dimensional cutting process, also called orthogonal cutting. Note that the tool shape and its angles, depth of cut, t_o, and the cutting speed, V, are all independent variables.

TABLE 20.1   Factors Influencing Cutting Processes

Parameter	Influence and interrelationship
Cutting speed, depth of cut, feed, cutting fluids	Forces, power, temperature rise, tool life, type of chip, surface finish.
Tool angles	As above; influence on chip flow direction; resistance to tool chipping.
Continuous chip	Good surface finish; steady cutting forces; undesirable in automated machinery.
Built-up edge chip	Poor surface finish; thin stable edge can protect tool surfaces.
Discontinuous chip	Desirable for ease of chip disposal; fluctuating cutting forces; can affect surface finish and cause vibration and chatter.
Temperature rise	Influences tool life, particularly crater wear, and dimensional accuracy of workpiece; may cause thermal damage to workpiece surface.
Tool wear	Influences surface finish, dimensional accuracy, temperature rise, forces and power.
Machinability	Related to tool life, surface finish, forces and power.

In comparing Figs. 20.2 and 20.3, note that the feed in turning is now equivalent to t_o, and the depth of cut in turning is equivalent to the width of cut (dimension perpendicular to the page) in the idealized model. These relationships can be visualized by rotating Fig. 20.3 clockwise by 90°.

Table 20.1 outlines the factors that influence a cutting process. The major *independent variables* in the cutting process are as follows:

- Tool material, coatings, and tool condition.
- Tool shape, surface finish, and sharpness.
- Workpiece material, condition, and temperature.
- Cutting parameters, such as speed, feed, and depth of cut.
- Cutting fluids.
- The characteristics of the machine tool, such as its stiffness and damping.
- Workholding and fixturing.

Dependent variables—those that are influenced by changes in the independent variables—are the following:

- Type of chip produced.
- Force and energy dissipated in the cutting process.
- Temperature rise in the workpiece, the chip, and the tool.
- Wear and failure of the tool.
- Surface finish produced on the workpiece after machining.

When unacceptable conditions result from machining operations, the manufacturing engineer must ask questions to determine the cause of the problem.

a. If, for example, the surface finish of the workpiece being cut is poor and unacceptable, which of the independent variables should be changed first? The angle of the tool? If so, should it be increased or decreased?

b. If the cutting tool wears and rapidly becomes dull, should the cutting speed, the depth of cut, or the tool material be changed?

c. If the tool and the machine begin to vibrate, what should be done to eliminate or reduce vibrations?

This chapter describes the mechanics of chip formation; chip types; force and power requirements; temperature rise caused by the cutting action; tool life; surface finish; and machinability. With this knowledge, we can plan efficient and economical machining operations and can select the proper equipment and tooling.

20.2 THE MECHANICS OF CHIP FORMATION

In order to understand the basic metal-cutting process, let's first study the mechanism of chip formation. This is a subject that has been studied extensively since the early 1940s; several models of the cutting mechanism, with varying degrees of complexity, have been proposed. This text will discuss only one theory (by M. E. Merchant), which is sufficient for our purposes.

Although almost all cutting processes are three-dimensional in nature (Chapters 22 and 23), the model shown in Fig. 20.3 is useful in studying the basic mechanics of cutting. In this model, known as **orthogonal cutting**, the tool has a **rake angle** of α (positive, as shown in the figure) and a **relief (clearance) angle**.

Microscopic examinations have revealed that chips are produced by the *shearing* process shown in Fig. 20.4a, and that shearing takes place along a **shear zone** (usually referred to as the **shear plane**). This plane is at an angle ϕ, called the **shear angle**, with the surface of the workpiece. Section 20.3 will describe this zone in greater detail, since it has a major influence on the quality of the machined surface.

Below the shear plane the workpiece is undeformed, and above it is the chip, already formed and moving up the face of the tool as cutting progresses. Note from Fig. 20.4a that the shearing process in chip formation is similar to the motion of cards in a deck sliding against each other. The dimension d in the figure is highly exaggerated to show the mechanism involved; in reality, this dimension is only on the order of 10^{-2} to 10^{-3} mm (10^{-3} to 10^{-4} in.).

It can be seen that the thickness of the chip, t_c, can be determined by knowing the depth of cut t_o, α, and ϕ. The ratio of t_o/t_c is known as the **cutting ratio**, r, which can be expressed as

$$r = \frac{t_o}{t_c} = \frac{\sin\phi}{\cos(\phi - \alpha)}. \qquad \textbf{(20.1)}$$

The chip thickness is always greater than the depth of cut; therefore, the value of r is always less than unity. The reciprocal of r is known as the *chip compression ratio* and is a measure of how thick the chip has become compared to the depth of cut. Thus the chip compression ratio is always greater than unity.

FIGURE 20.4   (a) Schematic illustration of the basic mechanism of chip formation in metal cutting. (b) Velocity diagram in the cutting zone. See also Section 20.5.3. *Source*: M. E. Merchant.

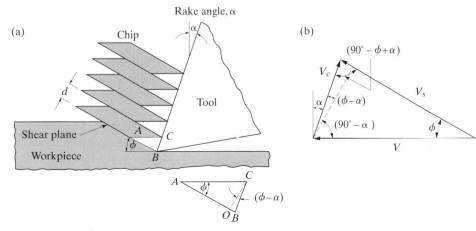

It should also be noted that although t_o has been referred to here as the depth of cut, in the machining processes described in Chapters 22 and 23, this quantity is known as the *feed*. Assume, for instance, that the workpiece in Fig. 20.2 was a thin-walled tube or pipe and the width of the cut was the same as the thickness of the tube. We would then visualize the situation by rotating Fig. 20.3 clockwise by 90° and noting that it is now similar to the view in Fig. 20.2. Consequently, the depth of cut is the same as the feed.

The cutting ratio is an important and useful parameter for evaluating cutting conditions. Since the undeformed chip thickness, t_o, is a machine setting and is therefore known (an independent variable), the cutting ratio can be easily calculated by measuring the chip thickness with a micrometer or dial caliper. With the rake angle also known for a particular cutting operation, Eq. (20.1) allows calculation of the shear angle in orthogonal cutting.

On the basis of Fig. 20.4a, we can express the **shear strain**, γ, that the material undergoes (see also Fig. 2.12) as

$$\gamma = \frac{AB}{OC} = \frac{AO}{OC} + \frac{OB}{OC},$$

or

$$\gamma = \cot \phi + \tan (\phi - \alpha). \tag{20.2}$$

Note that large shear strains are associated with low shear angles or low or negative rake angles. Shear strains of 5 or higher have been observed in actual cutting operations. Compared to forming and shaping processes, the material undergoes greater deformation during cutting.

Also, deformation in cutting generally takes place within a very narrow deformation zone; that is, the dimension $d = OC$ in Fig. 20.4a is very small. Therefore, the rate at which shearing takes place is high. The nature and size of the deformation zone is further discussed in Section 20.3.

The shear angle has great significance in the mechanics of cutting operations. It influences force and power requirements, chip thickness, and temperature (because of the work of deformation). Consequently, much attention has been focused on determining the relationships between the shear angle and workpiece material properties and cutting process variables.

One of the earliest analyses was based on the assumption that the shear angle adjusts itself to minimize the cutting force, or that the shear plane is a plane of maximum shear stress. The analysis yielded the expression

$$\phi = 45° + \frac{\alpha}{2} - \frac{\beta}{2}, \tag{20.3}$$

where β is the **friction angle** and is related to the *coefficient of friction*, μ, at the tool–chip interface (rake face) by the expression (see also Fig. 20.11)

$$\mu = \tan\beta. \tag{20.4}$$

Equation (20.3) indicates that, as the rake angle decreases and/or the friction at the tool-chip interface increases, the shear angle decreases and the chip becomes thicker. Thicker chips mean more energy dissipation because the shear strain is higher (Eq. (20.2)). Because work done during cutting is converted into heat, temperature rise is also higher. The effects of these phenomena are described throughout the rest of this chapter.

From Fig. 20.3, note that since chip thickness is greater than the depth of cut, the velocity of the chip, V_c, has to be lower than the cutting speed, V. Since mass continuity has to be maintained, we have

$$V t_o = V_c t_c \quad \text{or} \quad V_c = Vr.$$

Hence,

$$V_c = \frac{V \sin \phi}{\cos (\phi - \alpha)}. \tag{20.5}$$

We can also construct a velocity diagram (Fig. 20.4b) and, from trigonometric relationships, obtain the equation

$$\frac{V}{\cos (\phi - \alpha)} = \frac{V_s}{\cos \alpha} = \frac{V_c}{\sin \phi}, \tag{20.6a}$$

where V_s is the velocity at which shearing takes place in the shear plane. Note also that

$$r = \frac{t_o}{t_c} = \frac{V_c}{V}. \tag{20.6b}$$

These velocity relationships will be utilized further in Section 20.5.3 regarding power requirements in cutting operations.

20.3 THE TYPES OF CHIPS PRODUCED IN METAL-CUTTING

When we observe actual chip formation under different metal-cutting conditions, we find significant deviations from the ideal model shown in Figs. 20.3 and 20.4a. The types of metal chips commonly observed in practice and their photomicrographs are shown in Fig. 20.5. Because the types of chips produced significantly influence the surface finish of the workpiece and the overall cutting operation (for instance tool life, vibration, and chatter), the *types of chips* are described in the following order:

- **Continuous**
- **Built-up edge**
- **Serrated** or **segmented**
- **Discontinuous**

Let's first note that a chip has two surfaces: one that is in contact with the tool face (rake face), and the other from the original surface of the workpiece. The tool side of the chip surface is shiny, or *burnished*, which is caused by the rubbing of the chip as it moves up the tool face. The other surface of the chip does not come into contact with any solid body. This surface has a jagged, rough appearance (as in Fig. 20.3), which is caused by the shearing mechanism shown in Fig. 20.4a.

20.3.1 Continuous Chips

Continuous chips are usually formed with ductile materials at high cutting speeds and/or high rake angles (Fig. 20.5a). The deformation of the material takes place along a narrow shear zone, the **primary shear zone**. Continuous chips may, because of friction, develop a **secondary shear zone** at the tool–chip interface (Fig. 20.5b). The secondary zone becomes thicker as tool–chip friction increases.

In continuous chips, deformation may also take place along a wide primary shear zone with curved boundaries (Fig. 20.5c). Note that the lower boundary is below the machined surface, subjecting the machined surface to distortion, as depicted by the distorted vertical lines. This situation occurs particularly in machining soft metals at low speeds and low rake angles. It can produce poor surface finish and induce residual surface stresses, which may be detrimental to the properties of the machined part.

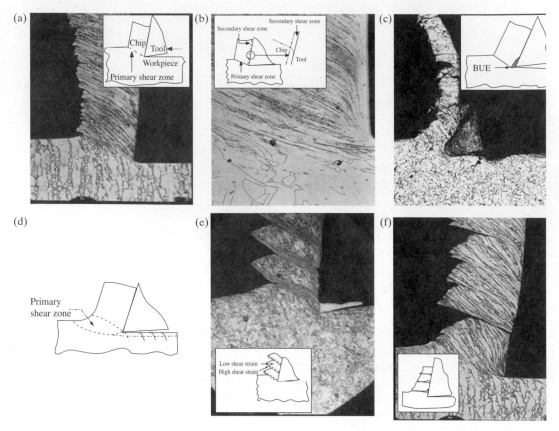

FIGURE 20.5   Basic types of chips and their photomicrographs produced in metal cutting: (a) continuous chip with narrow, straight primary shear zone; (b) secondary shear zone at the chip–tool interface; (c) continuous chip with large primary shear zone; (d) continuous chip with built-up edge; (e) segmented or nonhomogeneous chip; and (f) discontinuous chip. *Source*: After M. C. Shaw, P.K. Wright, and S. Kalpakjian.

Although they generally produce good surface finish, continuous chips are not always desirable, particularly in the computer-controlled machine tools widely used today (Chapter 24). They tend to become tangled around the tool holder, the fixturing, and the workpiece, as well as chip-disposal systems, and the operation has to be stopped to clear away the chips. This problem can be alleviated with **chip breakers** (Section 20.3.7) and by changing machining parameters, such as cutting speed, feed, and cutting fluids.

20.3.2 Built-up Edge Chips

A *built-up edge (BUE)*, consisting of layers of material from the workpiece that are gradually deposited on the tool (hence the term *built-up*), may form at the tip of the tool during cutting (Fig. 20.5d). As it becomes larger, the BUE becomes unstable and eventually breaks up. Part of the BUE material is carried away by the tool side of the chip; the rest is deposited randomly on the workpiece surface. The process of BUE formation and destruction is repeated continuously during the cutting operation, unless measures are taken to eliminate it.

The built-up edge is commonly observed in practice. It is one of the factors that most adversely affects surface finish in cutting, as can be seen in Figs. 20.5c and 20.6. A built-up edge, in effect, changes the geometry of the cutting edge. Note, for example, the large tip radius of the BUE and the rough surface finish produced.

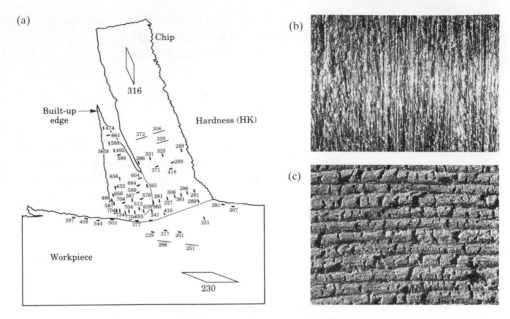

FIGURE 20.6   (a) Hardness distribution in the cutting zone for 3115 steel. Note that some regions in the built-up edge are as much as three times harder than the bulk metal. (b) Surface finish in turning 5130 steel with a built-up edge. (c) Surface finish on 1018 steel in face milling. Magnifications: 15X. *Source*: Courtesy of Metcut Research Associates, Inc.

Because of work hardening and deposition of successive layers of material, BUE hardness increases significantly (Fig. 20.6a). Although BUE is generally undesirable, a thin, stable BUE is usually regarded as desirable because it reduces wear by protecting the rake face of the tool.

As the cutting speed increases, the size of the BUE decreases; in fact it may not form at all. The tendency for a BUE to form is also reduced by any of the following practices:

a. Decreasing the depth of cut,

b. Increasing the rake angle,

c. Using a sharp tool, and

d. Using an effective cutting fluid.

In general, the higher the affinity (tendency to form a bond) of the tool and workpiece materials, the greater the tendency for BUE formation. In addition, a cold-worked metal generally has less tendency to form BUE than one that has been annealed.

20.3.3 Serrated Chips

Serrated chips (also called *segmented* or *nonhomogeneous* chips) are semicontinuous chips with zones of low and high shear strain (Fig. 20.5e). Metals with low thermal conductivity and strength that decreases sharply with temperature, such as titanium, exhibit this behavior. The chips have a sawtoothlike appearance. (This type of chip should not be confused with the illustration in Fig. 20.4a, in which the dimension *d* is highly exaggerated.)

20.3.4 Discontinuous Chips

Discontinuous chips consist of segments that may be firmly or loosely attached to each other (Fig. 20.5f). Discontinuous chips usually form under the following conditions:

1. Brittle workpiece materials, because they do not have the capacity to undergo the high shear strains involved in cutting.

2. Workpiece materials that contain hard inclusions and impurities, or have structures such as the graphite flakes in gray cast iron.
3. Very low or very high cutting speeds.
4. Large depths of cut.
5. Low rake angles.
6. Lack of an effective cutting fluid.
7. Low stiffness of the machine tool.

Because of the discontinuous nature of chip formation, forces continually vary during cutting. Consequently, the stiffness or rigidity of the cutting-tool holder, the workholding devices, and the machine tool are important in cutting with both discontinuous-chip and serrated-chip formation. If it is not stiff enough, the machine tool may begin to vibrate and chatter (as discussed in Section 24.4). This, in turn, adversely affects the surface finish and dimensional accuracy of the machined component, and may damage the cutting tool or cause excessive wear.

20.3.5 Chip Curl

In all cutting operations on metals, as well as nonmetallic materials such as plastics and wood, chips develop a curvature (*chip curl*) as they leave the workpiece surface (Figs. 20.3, 20.5d, and 20.8). The reasons for chip curl are still not clearly understood. Among the possible factors contributing to the phenomenon are the distribution of stresses in the primary and secondary shear zones, thermal effects, the work-hardening characteristics of the workpiece material, and the geometry of the rake face of the cutting tool.

Process variables, as well as material properties, also affect chip curl. Generally, the radius of curvature decreases—the chip becomes curlier—as depth of cut decreases; this increases the rake angle, and decreases friction at the tool–chip interface. The use of cutting fluids and various additives in the workpiece material also influence chip curl.

20.3.6 Chip Breakers

As stated in Section 20.3.1, long, continuous chips are undesirable because they are a potential safety hazard; they tend to become entangled and interfere with cutting operations. This situation is especially troublesome in high-speed automated machinery and in untended machining cells using computer numerically controlled machines (Chapters 24 and 39). If all the independent machining variables are under control, the usual procedure employed to avoid such a situation is to break the chip intermittently with a *chip breaker*.

Although the chip breaker has traditionally been a piece of metal clamped to the rake face of the tool (Figs. 20.7a and b) which bends the chip and breaks it, most cutting tools and inserts (Section 21.5.3) are now equipped with built-in chip breaker features of various designs (Figs. 20.7c and 21.2) for individual inserts. Chip breakers increase the effective rake angle of the tool and, consequently, increase the shear angle.

Chips can also be broken by changing the tool geometry, thereby controlling chip flow, as in the turning operations shown in Fig. 20.8. Experience has indicated that the ideal chip is in the shape of the letter C or the number 9 and fits within a 25 mm (1 in.) square block.

With soft workpiece materials such as pure aluminum or copper, chip breaking by such means is generally not effective. Common techniques used with such materials, include machining at small increments and then pausing (so that a chip is not generated) or reversing the feed by small increments. In interrupted cutting operations, such as milling (Chapter 23), chip breakers are generally not necessary, since the chips already have finite lengths because of the intermittent nature of the operation.

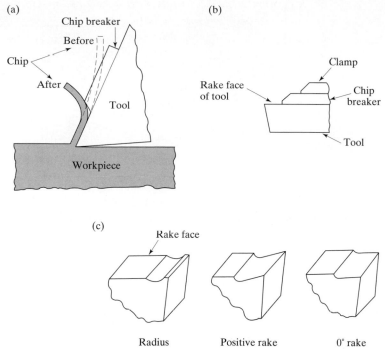

(a)

(b)

(c)

FIGURE 20.7   (a) Schematic illustration of the action of a chip breaker. Note that the chip breaker decreases the radius of curvature of the chip. (b) Chip breaker clamped on the rake face of a cutting tool. (c) Grooves in cutting tools acting as chip breakers; see also Fig. 21.2.

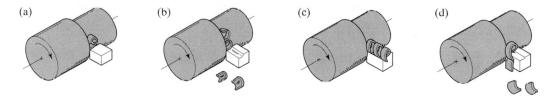

FIGURE 20.8   Various chips produced in turning: (a) tightly curled chip; (b) chip hits workpiece and breaks; (c) continuous chip moving away from workpiece; and (d) chip hits tool shank and breaks off. *Source*: G. Boothroyd, *Fundamentals of Metal Machining and Machine Tools*. Copyright © 1975; McGraw-Hill Publishing Company. Used with permission.

20.3.7 Chip Formation in Nonmetallic Materials

Many of the discussions for metals are also generally applicable to nonmetallic materials. A variety of chips are obtained in cutting thermoplastics, depending on the type of polymer as well as process parameters such as depth of cut, tool geometry, and cutting speed. Because they are brittle, thermosetting plastics and ceramics generally produce discontinuous chips. (See also Section 20.9.3.)

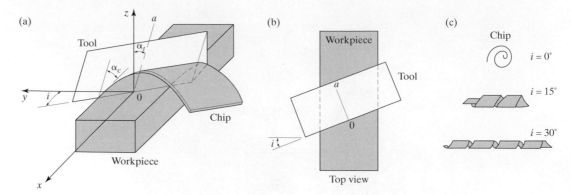

FIGURE 20.9   (a) Schematic illustration of cutting with an oblique tool. (b) Top view showing the inclination angle, i. (c) Types of chips produced with different inclination

20.4 THE MECHANICS OF OBLIQUE CUTTING

The majority of cutting operations involve tool shapes that are three-dimensional (*oblique*). The basic difference between two-dimensional and oblique cutting is shown in Fig. 20.9a. As we have seen, in orthogonal cutting the tool edge is perpendicular to the movement of the tool and the chip slides directly up the face of the tool.

In oblique cutting, the cutting edge is at an angle i, called the **inclination angle** (Fig. 20.9b). Note the lateral direction of chip movement in oblique cutting. This situation is similar to an angled snow-plow blade, which throws the snow sideways.

Note that the chip in Fig. 20.9a flows up the rake face of the tool at angle α_c (**chip flow angle**), which is measured in the plane of the tool face. Angle α_n, the **normal rake angle**, is a basic geometric property of the tool. This is the angle between the normal oz to the workpiece surface and the line oa on the tool face.

The workpiece material approaches the tool at a velocity V and leaves the surface (as a chip) with a velocity V_c. The effective rake angle α_e is calculated in the plane of these two velocities. Assuming that the chip flow angle α_c is equal to the inclination angle i—and this assumption has been found, through experiments, to be approximately correct—the effective rake angle α_e is

$$\alpha_e = \sin^{-1}\left(\sin^2 i + \cos^2 i \sin\alpha_n\right). \tag{20.7}$$

Since both i and α_n can be measured directly, the effective rake angle can be calculated. As i increases, the effective rake angle increases and the chip becomes thinner and longer. The influence of the inclination angle on chip shape is shown in Fig. 20.9c.

A typical single-point turning tool used on a lathe is shown in Fig. 20.10a. Note the various angles involved, each of which has to be properly selected for efficient cutting. Although these angles on cutting tools can usually be produced by grinding (Chapter 25), it is a time-consuming process.

Cutting tools are now widely available as **inserts** (Fig. 20.10b), which are mounted on tool holders with various angles for positioning the inserts for different applications. Various three-dimensional cutting tools are described in greater detail in Chapters 22 and 23. These include tools for drilling, tapping, milling, planing, shaping, broaching, sawing, and filing.

Shaving and Skiving.   Thin layers of material can be removed from straight or curved surfaces by a process similar to the use of a plane to shave wood. *Shaving* is particularly useful in improving the surface finish and dimensional accuracy of sheared parts and punched slugs (Fig. 16.9). Another application of shaving is in finishing gears with a cutter that has the shape of the gear tooth (see Section 23.8.4).

(a)

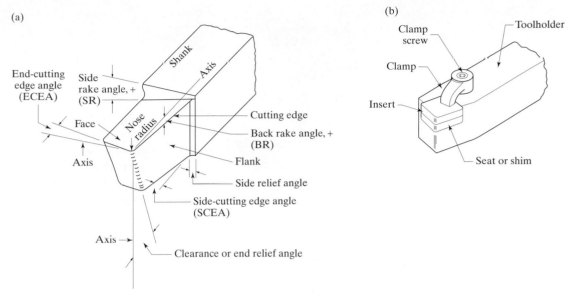

(b)

FIGURE 20.10   (a) Schematic illustration of a right-hand cutting tool. Although these tools have traditionally been produced from solid tool-steel bars, they have been largely replaced by carbide or other inserts of various shapes and sizes, as shown in (b). The various angles on these tools and their effects on machining are described in Section 22.3.1.

Parts that are long or have a combination of shapes are shaved by skiving with a specially-shaped cutting tool. The tool moves tangentially across the length of the workpiece.

20.5 CUTTING FORCES AND POWER

Knowledge of the *forces* and *power* involved in cutting operations is important for the following reasons:

1. Power requirements must be known to enable the selection of a machine tool with adequate power.
2. Data on cutting forces is required so that:
   a. Machine tools can be properly designed to avoid excessive distortion of the machine elements and maintain the desired dimensional tolerances for the finished part, tooling and toolholders, and workholding devices, and
   b. It can be determined, in advance of actual production, whether the workpiece is capable of withstanding the cutting forces without excessive distortion.

The forces acting on the tool in orthogonal cutting are shown in Fig. 20.11. The **cutting force**, F_c, acts in the direction of the cutting speed, V, and supplies the energy required for cutting. The **thrust force**, F_t, acts in a direction normal to the cutting velocity, that is, perpendicular to the workpiece. These two forces produce the **resultant force**, R.

Note that the resultant force can be resolved into two components on the tool face: a **friction force**, F, along the tool-chip interface, and a **normal force**, N, perpendicular to it. Using Fig. 20.11, it can be shown that

$$F = R \sin\beta, \tag{20.8}$$

and

$$N = R \cos\beta. \tag{20.9}$$

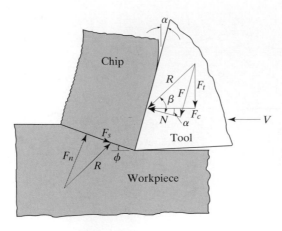

FIGURE 20.11   Forces acting on a cutting tool in two-dimensional cutting. Note that the resultant force, R, must be colinear to balance the forces.

Note also that the resultant force is balanced by an equal and opposite force along the shear plane and is resolved into a **shear force**, F_s, and a **normal force**, F_n. It can be shown that these forces can be expressed as follows:

$$F_s = F_c \cos\phi - F_t \sin\phi \qquad \textbf{(20.10)}$$

and

$$F_n = F_c \sin\phi + F_t \cos\phi. \qquad \textbf{(20.11)}$$

Because we can calculate the area of the shear plane by knowing the shear angle and the depth of cut, we can determine the shear and normal stresses in the shear plane.

The ratio of F to N is the **coefficient of friction**, μ, at the tool–chip interface, and the angle β is the **friction angle** (as in Eq. 20.4). We can express μ as

$$\mu = \frac{F}{N} = \frac{F_t + F_c \tan\alpha}{F_c - F_t \tan\alpha}. \qquad \textbf{(20.12)}$$

The coefficient of friction in metal cutting generally ranges from about 0.5 to 2, indicating that the chip encounters considerable frictional resistance while moving up the rake face of the tool.

Although the magnitude of forces in actual cutting operations is generally on the order of a few hundred newtons, the local *stresses* in the cutting zone and the pressures on the tool are very high because the contact areas are very small. The chip–tool contact length (see Fig. 20.3), for example, is typically on the order of 1 mm (0.04 in.). Thus, the tool is subjected to very high stresses, which lead to wear and sometimes chipping and fracture of the tool.

20.5.1 Thrust Force

A knowledge of the thrust force in cutting is important because the tool holder, the work-holding devices, and the machine tool must be sufficiently stiff to minimize deflections caused by this force. For example, if the thrust force is too high or if the machine tool is not sufficiently stiff, the tool will be pushed away from the surface being machined. This movement will, in turn, reduce the depth of cut, resulting in lack of dimensional accuracy in the machined part.

Refer again to Fig. 20.11 and note that the thrust force acts downward. As the rake angle increases and/or friction at the rake face decreases, this force can act upward. This situation can be visualized by noting that when $\mu = 0$ (that is, $\beta = 0$), the resultant force, R, coincides with the normal force, N. In this case, R will have a thrust-force component that is upward. Also note that when $\mu = 0$ and $\beta = 0$, the thrust force is zero.

Example: Direction of Thrust Force

We note from Fig. 20.11 that

$$F_t = R \sin(\beta - \alpha)$$

or

$$F_t = F_c \tan(\beta - \alpha).$$

The magnitude of F_c is always positive (as shown in Fig. 20.11); the sign of F_t can be either positive or negative, depending on the relative magnitudes of β and α. When $\beta > \alpha$, the sign of F_t is positive (downward) and when $\beta < \alpha$, it is negative (upward). It is therefore possible to have an upward thrust force at high rake angles and/or with low friction at the tool–chip interface.

20.5.2 Measuring Cutting Forces

Cutting forces can be measured by using suitable **dynamometers** (with resistance-wire strain gages) or **force transducers** (such as piezoelectric crystals) mounted on the machine tool. Forces can also be calculated from the amount of **power consumption** that occurs during cutting, often measured by a power monitor, provided that the mechanical efficiency of the machine tool can be determined.

20.5.3 Power

Power is the product of force and velocity. Referring to Fig. 20.11, we see that the power input in cutting is

$$\text{Power} = F_c V \tag{20.13}$$

This power is dissipated mainly in the shear zone (due to the energy required to shear the material) and on the rake face of the tool (due to tool–chip interface friction).

From Figs. 20.4b and 20.11, it can be seen that the power dissipated in the shear plane is

$$\text{Power for shearing} = F_s V_s. \tag{20.14}$$

If we let w be the width of cut, then the **specific energy for shearing**, u_s, is given by

$$u_s = \frac{F_s V_s}{w t_o V}. \tag{20.15}$$

Similarly, the power dissipated in friction is

$$\text{Power for friction} = F V_c, \tag{20.16}$$

and the **specific energy for friction**, u_f, is

$$u_f = \frac{F V_c}{w t_o V} = \frac{F r}{w t_o}. \tag{20.17}$$

The **total specific energy**, u_t, is thus

$$u_t = u_s + u_f. \tag{20.18}$$

Because of the many factors involved, the reliable prediction of cutting forces and power is still based largely on experimental data, such as those given in Table 20.2. The wide

TABLE 20.2 Approximate Energy Requirements in Cutting Operations (at drive motor, corrected for 80% efficiency; multiply by 1.25 for dull tools).

Material	Specific energy	
	$W \cdot s/mm^3$	$hp \cdot min/in.^3$
Aluminum alloys	0.4–1.1	0.15–0.4
Cast irons	1.6–5.5	0.6–2.0
Copper alloys	1.4–3.3	0.5–1.2
High-temperature alloys	3.3–8.5	1.2–3.1
Magnesium alloys	0.4–0.6	0.15–0.2
Nickel alloys	4.9–6.8	1.8–2.5
Refractory alloys	3.8–9.6	1.1–3.5
Stainless steels	3.0–5.2	1.1–1.9
Steels	2.7–9.3	1.0–3.4
Titanium alloys	3.0–4.1	1.1–1.5

range of values shown can be attributed to differences in strength within each material group and to various other factors, such as friction, use of cutting fluids, and processing variables.

The sharpness of the tool tip also influences forces and power. Because it rubs against the machined surface and makes the deformation zone ahead of the tool larger, duller tools require higher forces and power.

Example: Relative Energies in Cutting

In an orthogonal cutting operation, depth of cut $t_o = 0.005$ in., cutting speed $V = 400$ ft/min, rake angle $\alpha = 10°$, and the width of cut = 0.25 in. It is observed that chip thickness $t_c = 0.009$ in., $F_c = 125$ lb, and $F_t = 50$ lb. Calculate what percentage of the total energy goes into overcoming friction at the tool–chip interface.

Solution: We can express the percentage as

$$\frac{\text{Friction energy}}{\text{Total energy}} = \frac{FV_c}{F_cV} = \frac{Fr}{F_c},$$

where

$$r = \frac{t_o}{t_c} = \frac{5}{9} = 0.555,$$

$$F = R\sin\beta,$$

$$F_c = R\cos(\beta - \alpha),$$

and

$$R = \sqrt{F_t^2 + F_c^2} = \sqrt{50^2 + 125^2} = 135 \text{ lb}.$$

Thus,

$$125 = 135\cos(\beta - 10),$$

so

$$\beta = 32°$$

and

$$F = 135 \sin 32° = 71.5 \text{ lb.}$$

Hence,

$$\text{Percentage} = \frac{(71.5)(0.555)}{125} = 0.32, \quad \text{or} \quad 32\%.$$

20.6 TEMPERATURE IN CUTTING

As in all metalworking operations, the energy dissipated in cutting operations is converted into heat, which, in turn, raises the temperature in the cutting zone. Knowledge of the *temperature rise* is important because of the following phenomena:

- Excessive temperature adversely affects the strength, hardness, and wear resistance of the cutting tool.
- Increased heat causes dimensional changes in the part being machined, making it difficult to control dimensional accuracy.
- Heat can induce thermal damage to the machined surface, adversely affecting its properties.
- The machine tool itself may be subjected to elevated and uneven temperatures, causing distortion of the machine and, therefore, poor dimensional control of the workpiece.

Because of the work done in shearing and in overcoming friction on the rake face of the tool, the main sources of heat generation are the primary shear zone and the tool–chip interface. Additionally, if the tool is dull or worn (as in, for example, Fig. 20.22), heat is also generated when the tool tip rubs against the machined surface.

Cutting temperatures increase with the strength of the workpiece material, with the cutting speed, and with the depth of cut; they decrease with increasing specific heat and with thermal conductivity of the workpiece material. The **mean temperature** in turning on a lathe is found to be proportional to the cutting speed and feed, or

$$\text{Mean temperature} \propto V^a f^b, \tag{20.19}$$

where a and b are constants that depend on the tool and workpiece materials, V is the cutting speed, and f is the feed of the tool—that is, how far the tool travels per revolution of the workpiece. Approximate values for the exponents a and b are as follows for two sample materials:

Tool material	a	b
Carbide	0.2	0.125
High-speed steel	0.5	0.375

A typical temperature distribution in the cutting zone is shown in Fig. 20.12. Note the presence of severe temperature gradients and note that the maximum temperature is about halfway up the face of the tool. The particular temperature pattern depends on factors such as the specific heat and thermal conductivity of the tool and workpiece materials, cutting speed, depth of cut, and the type of cutting fluid used (if any).

The temperatures developed in a turning operation on 52100 steel are shown in Fig. 20.13. The temperature distribution along the tool flank surface is shown in Fig. 20.13a

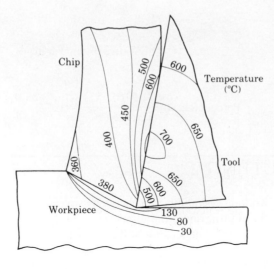

FIGURE 20.12 Typical temperature distribution in the cutting zone. Note the steep temperature gradients within the tool and the chip. *Source*: G. Vieregge.

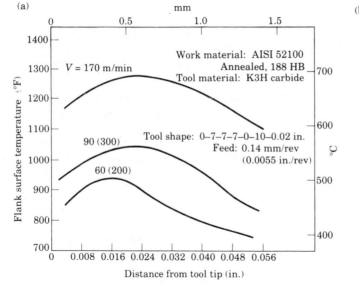

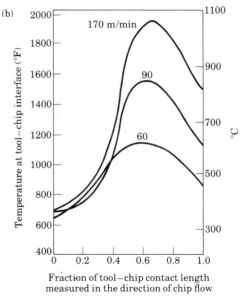

FIGURE 20.13 Temperatures developed in turning 52100 steel: (a) flank temperature distribution; and (b) tool–chip interface temperature distribution. *Source*: B. T. Chao and K. J. Trigger.

for cutting speeds *V* of 60, 90, and 170 m/min (200, 300, and 550 ft/min), respectively, as a function of distance from the tip of the cutting tool. Figure 20.13b shows the temperature distribution at the tool–chip interface for the same three cutting speeds and as a function of the fraction of the contact length. (Zero on the abscissa represents the tool tip, and 1.0 represents the end of the tool–chip contact length.)

Note that temperature increases with cutting speed and that the highest temperature is almost 1100 °C (2000 °F). The presence of such high temperatures can be verified by observing the dark-bluish color of chips (caused by oxidation) produced at high cutting speeds. Chips can become red hot, creating a safety hazard for the operator.

From Eq. (20.19) and the values for the exponent *a*, we can see that cutting speed greatly influences temperature. As speed increases, the time for heat dissipation decreases

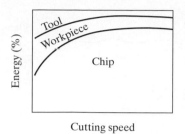

FIGURE 20.14
Percentage of the heat generated in cutting going into the workpiece, tool, and chip, as a function of cutting speed. Note that the chip carries away most of the heat.

and temperature rises. This effect can easily be demonstrated by rubbing your hands together faster and faster.

The chip carries away much of the heat generated (Fig. 20.14). As cutting speed increases, a larger proportion of the heat generated is carried away by the chip, and little heat goes into the workpiece. This is one reason why machining speeds used in practice have been increasing over the years (see *high-speed machining*, Section 22.4.1); another is the economic benefits of reducing machining costs (Section 24.5).

Techniques for measuring temperature. Temperatures and their distribution in the cutting zone may be determined from **thermocouples** embedded in the tool and/or the workpiece. This technique has been used successfully, although it involves considerable effort. It is easier to determine the average temperature with the **thermal emf** (electromotive force) at the tool–chip interface, which acts as a hot junction between two different materials (that is, tool and chip).

The **infrared radiation** from the cutting zone may also be monitored with a radiation pyrometer. However, this technique indicates only surface temperatures; the accuracy of the results depends on the emissivity of the surfaces, which is difficult to determine accurately.

20.7 TOOL LIFE: WEAR AND FAILURE

The preceding sections have shown that cutting tools are subjected to (a) high localized stresses, (b) high temperatures, (c) sliding of the chip along the rake face, and (d) sliding of the tool along the freshly cut surface (see also Chapter 32). These conditions induce **tool wear**, which, in turn, adversely affects tool life, the quality of the machined surface, and its dimensional accuracy, and consequently, the economics of cutting operations.

Tool wear is generally a gradual process, much like the wear of the tip of an ordinary pencil. The rate of tool wear depends on tool and workpiece materials, tool shape, cutting fluids, process parameters (such as cutting speed, feed, and depth of cut), and machine-tool characteristics. There are two basic types of wear, corresponding to two regions in a cutting tool: *flank wear* and *crater wear.*

20.7.1 Flank Wear

Flank wear occurs on the relief face of the tool (Figs. 20.15a and e; see also Fig. 20.3 and the side relief angle in Fig. 20.10a) and is generally attributed to (a) rubbing of the tool along the machined surface, causing adhesive and/or abrasive wear (Section 32.6), and (b) high temperatures, which affect tool-material properties as well as the workpiece surface.

In a classic study by F. W. Taylor on machining steels, published in 1907, the approximate relationship

$$VT^n = C,$$

(20.20)

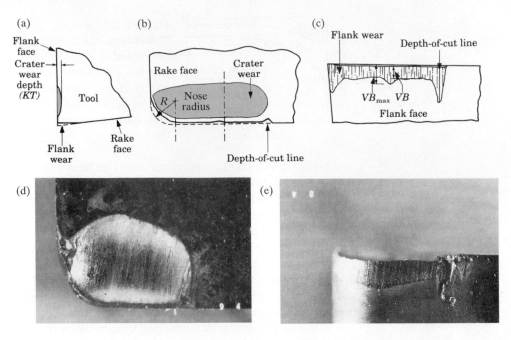

FIGURE 20.15 (a) Flank and crater wear in a cutting tool. Tool moves to the left. (b) View of the rake face of a turning tool, showing nose radius *R* and crater wear pattern on the rake face of the tool. (c) View of the flank face of a turning tool, showing the average flank wear land VB and the depth-of-cut line (wear notch). See also Fig. 20.18. (d) Crater and (e) flank wear on a carbide tool.
Source: Manufacturing Technology Laboratory, Lehigh University, J.C. Keefe.

was established, where *V* is the cutting speed, *T* is the time (in minutes) that it takes to develop a certain flank **wear land** (*VB* in Fig. 20.15c), *n* is an exponent that depends on tool and workpiece materials and cutting conditions, and *C* is a constant.

Note that *C* is the cutting speed at $T = 1$. Therefore, each combination of workpiece and tool materials and each cutting condition has its own *n* and *C* values, both of which are determined experimentally. The range of *n* values observed in practice is given in Table 20.3.

Cutting speed is the most significant process variable in tool life, although depth of cut and feed rate are also important. Thus, Eq. (20.20) can be replaced by

$$VT^n d^x f^y = C, \tag{20.21}$$

where *d* is the depth of cut and *f* is the feed rate (in mm/rev or in./rev) in turning.

The exponents *x* and *y* must be determined experimentally for each cutting condition. Taking $n = 0.15$, $x = 0.15$, and $y = 0.6$ as typical values encountered in practice, it can be seen that cutting speed, feed rate, and depth of cut are of decreasing importance.

Equation (20.21) can be rewritten as

$$T = C^{1/n} V^{-1/n} d^{-x/n} f^{-y/n}, \tag{20.22}$$

or

$$T \simeq C^7 V^{-7} d^{-1} f^{-4}. \tag{20.23}$$

The following observations can be made from Eq. (20.23) for a constant tool life:

1. If the feed rate or the depth of cut is increased, the cutting speed must be decreased, and vice versa.

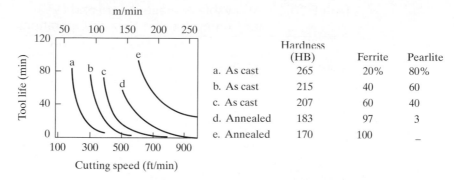

FIGURE 20.16   Effect of workpiece microstructure and hardness on tool life in turning ductile cast iron. Note the rapid decrease in tool life as the cutting speed increases. Tool materials have been developed that resist high temperatures, such as carbides, ceramics, and cubic boron nitride, as described in Chapter 21.

2. Depending on the exponents, a reduction in speed can result in an increase in the volume of the material removed because of the increased feed rate and/or depth of cut.

Tool-Life Curves.   *Tool-life curves* are plots of experimental data obtained by performing cutting tests on various materials under different conditions and with varying process parameters, such as cutting speed, feed, depth of cut, tool material and geometry, and cutting fluids. Note in Fig. 20.16, for example, (a) the rapid decrease in tool life as the cutting speed increases, and (b) the strong influence of the condition of the workpiece material on tool life. Also note the large difference in tool life for different workpiece material microstructures.

Heat treatment of the workpiece is important largely due to increasing workpiece hardness. For example, ferrite has a hardness of about 100 HB, pearlite 200 HB, and martensite 300–500 HB (see Chapter 4). Impurities and hard constituents in the material or on the surface of the workpiece, such as rust, scale, slag, etc., are also important considerations because their abrasive action reduces tool life.

Tool-life curves, from which the exponent n can be determined (Fig. 20.17), are generally plotted on log–log paper. These curves are usually linear over a limited range of cutting speeds but are rarely so over a wide range. Moreover, the exponent n can indeed become negative at low cutting speeds. Thus, tool-life curves may actually reach a maximum and then

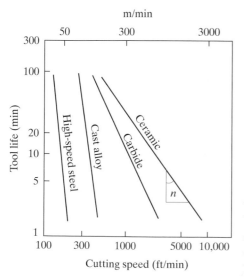

FIGURE 20.17   Tool-life curves for a variety of cutting-tool materials. The negative inverse of the slope of these curves is the exponent n in the Taylor tool-life equations and C is the cutting speed at $T = 1$ min.

TABLE 20.3   Range of n Values for Eq. (20.20) for Various Tool Materials

High-speed steels	0.08–0.2
Cast alloys	0.1–0.15
Carbides	0.2–0.5
Ceramics	0.5–0.7

TABLE 20.4   Allowable Average Wear Land (*VB*) for Cutting Tools in Various Operations

	Allowable wear land (mm)	
Operation	High-speed Steels	Carbides
Turning	1.5	0.4
Face milling	1.5	0.4
End milling	0.3	0.3
Drilling	0.4	0.4
Reaming	0.15	0.15

Note: 1 mm = 0.040 in.

curve downward. Because of this, caution should be exercised when using tool-life equations beyond the range of cutting speeds to which they are applicable.

Because temperature affects the physical and mechanical properties of materials, we can expect that it strongly influences wear. Investigations have confirmed that as temperature increases, flank wear rapidly increases.

Allowable Wear Land.   Just as we decide to sharpen a knife or a pair of scissors when the quality of the cut begins to deteriorate and the cutting forces required increase too much, we similarly resharpen or replace cutting tools when (a) the surface finish of the machined workpiece begins to deteriorate, (b) cutting forces increase significantly, and (c) temperature rises significantly. The *allowable wear land* (*VB* in Fig. 20.15c) for various machining conditions is given in Table 20.4. For improved dimensional accuracy and surface finish, the allowable wear land may be made smaller than the values given in the table.

The recommended cutting speed for a high-speed steel tool is generally the one that yields a tool life of 60 to 120 min (for carbide tools, 30 to 60 min). However, selected cutting speeds can vary significantly from these values, depending on the particular workpiece, the operation, and high productivity considerations due to the use of modern, computer-controlled machine tools.

Optimum Cutting Speed.   We have seen that, as cutting speed increases, tool life is rapidly reduced. On the other hand, if cutting speeds are low, tool life is long but the rate at which material is removed is also low. Thus, there is an *optimum cutting speed*, as described in Section 24.5.

Example: Effect of Cutting Speed on Material Removal

We can appreciate the effect of cutting speed on the volume of metal removed between tool resharpenings or replacements by analyzing Fig. 20.16. Assume that a material is being machined in the "a" condition, that is, as cast with a hardness of 265 HB.

If the cutting speed is 60 m/min, tool life is about 40 min. Therefore, the tool travels a distance of 60 m/min × 40 min = 2400 m before it is resharpened or replaced. If the cutting speed is increased to 120 m/min, tool life is about 5 min. Therefore, the tool travels 120 m/min × 5 min = 600 m.

Since the volume of material removed is directly proportional to the distance the tool has traveled, it should be clear that by decreasing the cutting speed, we can remove more material between tool changes. Note, however, that the lower the cutting speed, the longer the time required to machine a part. These variables have an important economic impact, and are discussed further in Section 24.5.

Example: Increasing Tool Life by Reducing the Cutting Speed

Using the Taylor Eq. (20.20) for tool life and letting $n = 0.5$ and $C = 400$, calculate the percentage increase in tool life when the cutting speed is reduced by 50%.

Solution: Since $n = 0.5$, we can rewrite the Taylor equation as $VT = 400$. Letting V_1 be the initial speed and V_2 the reduced speed, we note that for this problem $V_2 = 0.5 \, V_1$. Because C is a constant, we have the relationship

$$0.5 \, V_1 T_2 = V_1 T_1.$$

Simplifying this expression, we find that $T_2/T_1 = 1/0.25 = 4.0$.

This indicates that the tool life change is $(T_2 - T_1)/T_1 - (T_2/T_1) - 1 = 4 - 1 = 3$, or that it is increased by 300%. The reduction in cutting speed has resulted in a major increase in tool life. Note that, in this problem, the magnitude of C is not relevant.

20.7.2 Crater Wear

Crater wear occurs on the rake face of the tool (Figs. 20.15a, b, and d, and Fig. 20.18) and, by changing the chip–tool interface geometry, it affects the cutting process. The most significant factors influencing crater wear are (a) temperature at the tool–chip interface and

FIGURE 20.18   (a) Schematic illustrations of types of wear observed on various types of cutting tools. (b) Schematic illustrations of catastrophic tool failures. A study of the types and mechanisms of tool wear and failure is essential to the development of better tool materials. *Source*: V. C. Venkatesh.

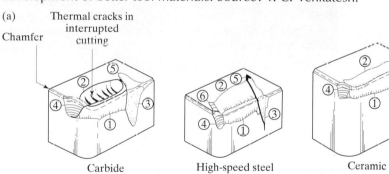

(a)

Carbide   High-speed steel   Ceramic

1. Flank wear (wear land)
2. Crater wear
3. Primary groove or depth-of-cut line

4. Secondary groove (oxidation wear)
5. Outer metal chip notch
6. Inner chip notch

(b)

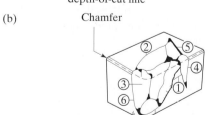 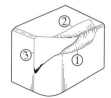

High-speed steel tool, thermal softening and plastic flow

Ceramic tool, chipping and fracture

1. Flank wear
2. Crater wear
3. Failure face

4. Primary groove or depth-of-cut line
5. Outer metal chip notch
6. Plastic flow around failure face

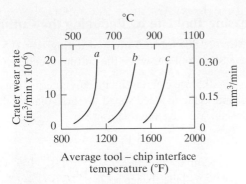

°C

FIGURE 20.19   Relationship between crater-wear rate and average tool–chip interface temperature: (a) High-speed steel; (b) C-1 carbide; and (c) C-5 carbide. Note how rapidly crater-wear rate increases as the temperature increases. *Source*: B. T. Chao and K. J. Trigger.

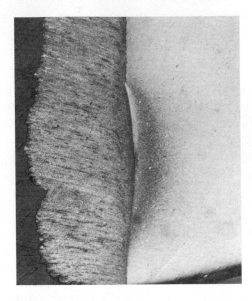

FIGURE 20.20   Cutting tool (right) and chip (left) interface in cutting plain-carbon steel. The discoloration of the tool indicates the presence of high temperatures. Compare this figure with Fig. 20.12. *Source*: P. K. Wright.

(b) the chemical affinity between the tool and workpiece materials. Additionally, the factors influencing flank wear also influence crater wear.

Crater wear has been described in terms of a **diffusion** mechanism, that is, the movement of atoms across the tool–chip interface. Since diffusion rate increases with increasing temperature, crater wear increases as temperature increases. Note in Fig. 20.19 how sharply crater wear increases within a narrow temperature range.

When we compare Figs. 20.12 and 20.15a, we see that the location of the maximum depth of crater wear (KT) coincides with the location of the maximum temperature at the tool–chip interface. An actual cross-section of this interface when steel is cut at high speeds is shown in Fig. 20.20. Note the location of the crater-wear pattern and the discoloration pattern of the tool by high temperatures.

20.7.3 Chipping

Chipping is the term used to describe the breaking away of a small piece from the cutting edge of the tool, a phenomenon similar to breaking the tip of a sharp pencil. The chipped pieces from the cutting tool may be very small (**microchipping** or **macrochipping**), or they may be relatively large (**gross chipping** or **fracture**). Unlike wear, which is a gradual process, chipping results in a sudden loss of tool material and a corresponding change in shape, and has a major detrimental effect on surface finish, surface integrity, and dimensional accuracy of the workpiece.

Two main causes of chipping are **mechanical shock** (impact due to interrupted cutting, as in milling or turning a splined shaft), and **thermal fatigue** (cyclic variations in temperature of the tool in interrupted cutting). Thermal cracks are usually perpendicular to the cutting edge of the tool (Fig. 20.18a). Major inconsistencies in the workpiece material composition or its structure also may cause chipping. Chipping may occur in a region in the tool where a small crack or defect already exists.

High positive rake angles can contribute to chipping because of the small included angle of the tool tip (as in Fig. 20.3). Also, it is possible for the crater-wear region to progress toward the tool tip, weakening the tip and causing chipping. Chipping or fracture can be reduced by selecting tool materials with high impact and thermal-shock resistance, as described in Chapter 21.

20.7.4 General Observations on Tool Wear

Because of the many factors involved, including the characteristics of the machine tool and the quality of a tool manufactured by a particular supplier, the wear behavior of cutting tools varies significantly. In addition to the wear processes already described, other phenomena also contribute to patterns of tool wear (Fig. 20.18).

For example, due to the decrease in yield strength resulting from the high temperatures generated during cutting, tools may soften and undergo plastic deformation. This type of deformation generally occurs when machining high-strength metals and alloys. Therefore, tools must be able to maintain their strength and hardness at the elevated temperatures encountered in cutting.

The wear **groove** or **notch** on cutting tools (Fig. 20.18) has been attributed to the fact that this region is the boundary where the chip is no longer in contact with the tool. This boundary, also known as the **depth-of-cut (DOC) line**, oscillates because of inherent variations in the cutting operation and accelerates the wear process. Furthermore, this region is in contact with the machined surface from the previous cut. Since a machined surface may develop a thin work-hardened layer, this contact could contribute to the formation of the wear groove.

Because they are hard and abrasive, scale and oxide layers on a workpiece surface increase wear. In such cases, the depth of cut should be greater than the thickness of the oxide film or the work-hardened layer. Therefore, the depth of cut in Fig. 20.2 should be greater than the thickness of the scale on the workpiece. In other words, light cuts should not be taken on rusted workpieces.

20.7.5 Tool-Condition Monitoring

With the rapidly increasing use of computer-controlled machine tools and the implementation of automated manufacturing (as discussed in Part VIII), the reliable and repeatable performance of cutting tools has become an important consideration. As described in Chapters 22–24, most modern machine tools, once programmed properly, now operate with little direct supervision by a machine operator. Consequently, the failure of a cutting tool can have serious effects on the quality of the machined part as well as on the efficiency and economics of the overall machining operation.

It is thus essential to continuously and indirectly monitor the condition of the cutting tool so as to note, for example, wear, chipping, or gross failure. In most state-of-the-art machine tools, tool-condition monitoring systems are integrated into computer numerical control and programmable logic controllers (as in Section 38.2.5). Techniques for tool-condition monitoring typically fall into two general categories: direct and indirect.

The **direct** method for observing the condition of a cutting tool involves optical measurement of wear, such as the periodic observation of changes in the tool profile. This is the most common and reliable technique and is done using a microscope (**toolmakers' microscope**). This procedure requires, however, that the cutting operation be stopped.

Indirect methods of measuring wear involve the correlation of the tool condition with process variables such as forces, power, temperature rise, surface finish, and vibrations. One important development is the **acoustic emission (AE) technique**, which utilizes a piezoelectric transducer attached to a tool holder. The transducer picks up acoustic emissions (typically above 100 kHz) that result from the stress waves generated during cutting. By analyzing the signals, tool wear and chipping can be monitored.

The acoustic-emission technique is particularly effective in precision machining operations where, because of the small amounts of material removed, cutting forces are low. One effective use of AE is in detecting the fracture of small carbide tools at high cutting speeds.

A similar indirect tool-condition monitoring system consists of **transducers** that are installed in original machine tools or are retrofitted on existing machines. They continually monitor torque and forces during cutting. The signals are preamplified and a microprocessor analyzes and interprets their content. The system is capable of differentiating the signals that come from tool breakage, tool wear, a missing tool, overloading of the machine, or colliding machine components. The system can also automatically compensate for tool wear and thus improve dimensional accuracy.

The design of the transducers must be such that they are (a) nonintrusive to the machining operation, (b) accurate and repeatable in signal detection, (c) resistant to abuse and shop-floor environment, and (d) cost effective. Continued progress is being made in the development of such sensors, including the use of infrared and fiber-optic techniques for temperature measurement during machining.

In lower cost computer-numerical control machine tools (as in Sections 22.3.9, 24.2, and 38.3), monitoring is done by *tool-cycle time*. In a production environment, once the life expectancy of a cutting tool or insert has been determined, it can be entered in the control so that the operator is prompted to make a tool or cutter change when this time is reached. This process is fairly reliable (although not totally so because of the inherent statistical variation in tool lives) and is inexpensive.

20.8 SURFACE FINISH AND SURFACE INTEGRITY

Surface finish influences not only the dimensional accuracy of machined parts, but also their properties. Whereas *surface finish* describes the *geometric* features of surfaces (Chapter 31), *surface integrity* pertains to *properties*, such as fatigue life and corrosion resistance, which are influenced strongly by the type of surface produced. Factors influencing surface integrity are (a) temperatures generated during processing, (b) residual stresses, (c) metallurgical (phase) transformations, and (d) surface plastic deformation, tearing, and cracking.

The built-up edge, with its significant effect on the tool-tip profile, has the greatest influence on surface finish. Figure 20.21 shows the surfaces obtained in two different cutting operations. The BUE damage is manifested in the scuffing marks, which deviate from the straight grooves that would result from normal machining (as in Fig. 20.2). Note the considerable damage to the surfaces from BUE. Ceramic and diamond tools generally produce better surface finish than other tools, largely because of their much lower tendency to form a BUE.

(a)  (b)

FIGURE 20.21   Surfaces produced on steel by cutting, as observed with a scanning electron microscope: (a) turned surface and (b) surface produced by shaping. *Source*: J. T. Black and S. Ramalingam.

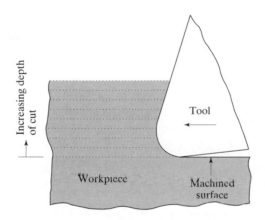

FIGURE 20.22   Schematic illustration of a dull tool in orthogonal cutting (exaggerated). Note that at small depths of cut, the positive rake angle can effectively become negative, and the tool may simply ride over and burnish the workpiece surface.

A tool that is not sharp has a large radius along its edges, just as a dull pencil or knife does. Figure 20.22 illustrates the relationship between the radius of the cutting edge and the depth of the cut in orthogonal cutting. Note that at small depths of cut, the rake angle can effectively become negative; the tool may simply ride over the workpiece surface and not remove chips.

This behavior can be simulated by trying to scrape the surface along the length of a stick of butter with a dull knife. You will note that it is not possible to remove a layer of butter at very small depths unless the knife is sharp. If this radius (not to be confused with the radius R in Fig. 20.15b) is large in relation to the depth of cut, the tool will rub over the machined surface. Rubbing generates heat and induces residual surface stresses, which, in turn, may cause surface damage such as tearing and cracking. Therefore, the depth of cut should generally be greater than the radius on the cutting edge.

In turning, as in other cutting operations, the tool leaves a spiral profile (**feed marks**) on the machined surface as it moves across the workpiece (Figs. 20.2 and 20.23). It can be seen that the higher the feed, f, and the smaller the tool-nose radius, R, the more prominent these marks. Although not significant in rough machining operations, these marks are important in finish machining. Feed marks and other surface-finish considerations for individual machining processes are discussed in Chapters 22–23.

Vibration and chatter are described in detail in Section 24.4. For now, it should be recognized that if the tool vibrates or chatters during cutting, it will adversely affect surface

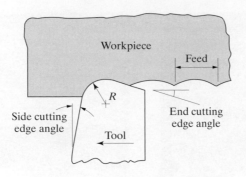

FIGURE 20.23   Schematic illustration of feed marks in turning (highly exaggerated). See also Fig. 20.2.

finish. The reason is that a vibrating tool periodically changes the dimensions of the cut. Excessive chatter can also cause chipping and premature failure of the more brittle cutting tools, such as ceramics and diamond.

20.9 MACHINABILITY

The *machinability* of a material is usually defined in terms of four factors:

1. Surface finish and integrity of the machined part;
2. Tool life obtained;
3. Force and power requirements;
4. Chip control.

Thus, good machinability indicates good surface finish and integrity, long tool life, and low force and power requirements. As for chip control, long and thin (stringy) curled chips, if not broken up, can severely interfere with the cutting operation by becoming entangled in the cutting zone.

Because of the complex nature of cutting operations, it is difficult to establish relationships that quantitatively define the machinability of a material. In manufacturing plants, tool life and surface roughness are generally considered to be the most important factors in machinability. Although not used much any more, approximate **machinability ratings** are available in the example below.

Example: Machinability Ratings

Machinability ratings are based on a tool life of $T = 60$ min. The standard material is AISI 1112 steel (resulfurized), which is given a rating of 100. For a tool life of 60 min, this steel should be machined at a cutting speed of 100 ft/min (30 m/min). Higher speeds will reduce tool life, and lower speeds will increase it.

For example, 3140 steel has a machinability rating of 55. This means that when it is machined at a cutting speed of 55 ft/min (17 m/min), tool life will be 60 min. Nickel has a rating of 200, indicating that it should be machined at 200 ft/min (60 m/min) to obtain a tool life of 60 min. Machinability ratings for various materials are as follows: free-cutting brass, 300 ft/min; 2011 wrought aluminum, 200; pearlitic gray iron, 70; Inconel, 30; and precipitation-hardening 17-7 steel, 20.

As the hardness of the material increases, its machinability rating decreases proportionately. Such ratings are only approximate, however, and should be used with caution.

20.9.1 Machinability of Steels

Because steels are among the most important engineering materials (as noted in Chapter 5), their machinability has been studied extensively. The machinability of steels has been mainly improved by adding lead and sulfur to obtain so-called **free-machining steels**.

Resulfurized and Rephosphorized Steels.   *Sulfur* in steels forms manganese sulfide inclusions (second-phase particles), which act as stress raisers in the primary shear zone. As a result, the chips produced break up easily and are small; this improves machinability. The size, shape, distribution, and concentration of these inclusions significantly influence machinability. Elements such as *tellurium* and *selenium*, which are both chemically similar to sulfur, act as inclusion modifiers in resulfurized steels.

Phosphorus in steels has two major effects. It strengthens the ferrite, causing increased hardness. Harder steels result in better chip formation and surface finish. Note that soft steels can be difficult to machine, with built-up edge formation and poor surface finish. The second effect is that increased hardness causes the formation of short chips instead of continuous stringy ones, thereby improving machinability.

Leaded Steels.   A high percentage of lead in steels solidifies at the tip of manganese sulfide inclusions. In non-resulfurized grades of steel, lead takes the form of dispersed fine particles. Lead is insoluble in iron, copper, and aluminum and their alloys. Because of its low shear strength, therefore, lead acts as a solid lubricant (Section 32.11) and is smeared over the tool–chip interface during cutting. This behavior has been verified by the presence of high concentrations of lead on the tool-side face of chips when machining leaded steels.

When the temperature is sufficiently high—for instance, at high cutting speeds and feeds (Section 20.6)—the lead melts directly in front of the tool, acting as a liquid lubricant. In addition to this effect, lead lowers the shear stress in the primary shear zone, reducing cutting forces and power consumption. Lead can be used in every grade of steel, such as 10xx, 11xx, 12xx, 41xx, etc. Leaded steels are identified by the letter *L* between the second and third numerals (for example, 10L45). (Note that in stainless steels, similar use of the letter *L* means "low carbon," a condition that improves their corrosion resistance.)

However, because lead is a well-known toxin and a pollutant, there are serious environmental concerns about its use in steels (estimated at 4500 tons of lead consumption every year in the production of steels). Consequently, there is a continuing trend toward eliminating the use of lead in steels (*lead-free steels*). **Bismuth** and **tin** are now being investigated as possible substitutes for lead in steels.

Calcium-Deoxidized Steels.   An important development is calcium-deoxidized steels, in which oxide flakes of calcium silicates (CaSO) are formed. These flakes, in turn, reduce the strength of the secondary shear zone, decreasing tool–chip interface friction and wear. Temperature is correspondingly reduced. Consequently, these steels produce less crater wear, especially at high cutting speeds.

Stainless Steels.   Austenitic (300 series) steels are generally difficult to machine. Chatter can be a problem, necessitating machine tools with high stiffness. However, ferritic stainless steels (also 300 series) have good machinability. Martensitic (400 series) steels are abrasive, tend to form a built-up edge, and require tool materials with high hot hardness and crater-wear resistance. Precipitation-hardening stainless steels are strong and abrasive, requiring hard and abrasion-resistant tool materials.

The Effects of Other Elements in Steels on Machinability.   The presence of *aluminum* and *silicon* in steels is always harmful because these elements combine with oxygen to form aluminum oxide and silicates, which are hard and abrasive. These compounds increase tool wear and reduce machinability. It is essential to produce and use clean steels.

Carbon and *manganese* have various effects on the machinability of steels, depending on their composition. Plain low-carbon steels (less than 0.15% C) can produce poor surface finish by forming a built-up edge. Cast steels are more abrasive, although their machinability is similar to that of wrought steels. Tool and die steels are very difficult to machine and usually require annealing prior to machining. Machinability of most steels is improved by cold working, which hardens the material and reduces the tendency for built-up edge formation.

Other alloying elements, such as *nickel*, *chromium*, *molybdenum*, and *vanadium*, which improve the properties of steels, generally reduce machinability. The effect of *boron* is negligible. Gaseous elements such as *hydrogen* and *nitrogen* can have particularly detrimental effects on the properties of steel. *Oxygen* has been shown to have a strong effect on the aspect ratio of the manganese sulfide inclusions; the higher the oxygen content, the lower the aspect ratio and the higher the machinability.

In selecting various elements to improve machinability, we should consider the possible *detrimental effects* of these elements on the properties and strength of the machined part in service. At elevated temperatures, for example, lead causes embrittlement of steels (liquid-metal embrittlement, hot shortness; see Section 1.4.3), although at room temperature it has no effect on mechanical properties.

Sulfur can severely reduce the hot workability of steels, because of the formation of iron sulfide, unless sufficient manganese is present to prevent such formation. At room temperature, the mechanical properties of resulfurized steels depend on the orientation of the deformed manganese sulfide inclusions (anisotropy). Rephosphorized steels are significantly less ductile, and are produced solely to improve machinability.

20.9.2 Machinability of Various Other Metals

Aluminum is generally very easy to machine, although the softer grades tend to form a built-up edge, resulting in poor surface finish. High cutting speeds, high rake angles, and high relief angles are recommended. Wrought aluminum alloys with high silicon content and cast aluminum alloys may be abrasive; they require harder tool materials. Dimensional tolerance control may be a problem in machining aluminum, since it has a high thermal coefficient of expansion and a relatively low elastic modulus .

Beryllium is similar to cast irons. Because it is more abrasive and toxic, though, it requires machining in a controlled environment.

Cast gray irons are generally machinable but are abrasive. Free carbides in castings reduce their machinability and cause tool chipping or fracture, necessitating tools with high toughness. Nodular and malleable irons are machinable with hard tool materials.

Cobalt-based alloys are abrasive and highly work-hardening. They require sharp, abrasion-resistant tool materials and low feeds and speeds.

Wrought **copper** can be difficult to machine because of built-up edge formation, although cast copper alloys are easy to machine. Brasses are easy to machine, especially with the addition of lead (*leaded free-machining brass*). Bronzes are more difficult to machine than brass.

Magnesium is very easy to machine, with good surface finish and prolonged tool life. However, care should be exercised because of its high rate of oxidation and the danger of fire (the element is pyrophoric).

Molybdenum is ductile and work-hardening, so it can produce poor surface finish. Sharp tools are necessary.

Nickel-based alloys are work-hardening, abrasive, and strong at high temperatures. Their machinability is similar to that of stainless steels.

Tantalum is very work-hardening, ductile, and soft. It produces a poor surface finish; tool wear is high.

Titanium and its alloys have poor thermal conductivity (indeed, the lowest of all metals), causing significant temperature rise and built-up edge; they can be difficult to machine.

Tungsten is brittle, strong, and very abrasive, so its machinability is low, although it greatly improves at elevated temperatures.

Zirconium has good machinability. It requires a coolant-type cutting fluid, however, because of the danger of explosion and fire.

20.9.3 Machinability of Various Materials

Graphite is abrasive; it requires hard, abrasion-resistant, sharp tools.

Thermoplastics generally have low thermal conductivity, low elastic modulus, and low softening temperature. Consequently, machining them requires tools with positive rake angles (to reduce cutting forces), large relief angles, small depths of cut and feed, relatively high speeds, and proper support of the workpiece. Tools should be sharp.

External cooling of the cutting zone may be necessary to keep the chips from becoming "gummy" and sticking to the tools. Cooling can usually be achieved with a jet of air, vapor mist, or water-soluble oils. Residual stresses may develop during machining. To relieve these stresses, machined parts can be annealed for a period of time at temperatures ranging from 80 °C to 160 °C (175 °F to 315 °F), and then cooled slowly and uniformly to room temperature.

Thermosetting plastics are brittle and sensitive to thermal gradients during cutting. Their machinability is generally similar to that of thermoplastics.

Because of the fibers present, **reinforced plastics** are very abrasive and are difficult to machine. Fiber tearing, pulling, and edge delamination are significant problems; they can lead to severe reduction in the load-carrying capacity of the component. Furthermore, machining of these materials requires careful removal of machining debris to avoid contact with and inhaling of the fibers.

The machinability of **ceramics** has improved steadily with the development of **nanoceramics** (Section 8.2.5) and with the selection of appropriate processing parameters, such as *ductile-regime cutting* (Section 22.4.2).

Metal–matrix and ceramic–matrix composites can be difficult to machine, depending on the properties of the individual components, i.e., reinforcing fibers or whiskers, as well as the matrix material.

20.9.4 Thermally Assisted Machining

Metals and alloys that are difficult to machine at room temperature can be machined more easily at elevated temperatures. In *thermally assisted machining* (**hot machining**), the source of heat—a torch, induction coil, high-energy beam (such as laser or electron beam), or plasma arc—is focused to an area just ahead of the cutting tool. The advantages are: (a) lower cutting forces, (b) increased tool life, (c) use of inexpensive cutting-tool materials, (d) higher material-removal rates, and (e) reduced tendency for vibration and chatter.

It may be difficult to heat and maintain a uniform temperature distribution within the workpiece. Also, the original microstructure of the workpiece may be adversely affected by elevated temperatures. Most applications of hot machining are in the turning of high-strength metals and alloys, although experiments are in progress to machine ceramics such as silicon nitride.

SUMMARY

- Material-removal processes are often necessary in order to impart the desired dimensional accuracy, geometric features, and surface finish characteristics to components, particularly those with complex shapes that cannot be produced economically or with other shaping techniques. On the other hand, these processes generally take longer, waste some material in the form of chips, and may have adverse effects on surfaces produced.

- Commonly observed chip types are continuous; built-up edge; discontinuous; and serrated. Important process variables in machining are tool shape and material; cutting conditions such as speed, feed, and depth of cut; use of cutting fluids; and the characteristics of the workpiece material and the machine tool. Parameters influenced by these variables are forces and power consumption; tool wear; surface finish and integrity; temperature; and dimensional accuracy of the workpiece.

- Temperature rise is an important consideration, since it can have adverse effects on tool life as well as on the dimensional accuracy and surface integrity of the machined part.

- Two major types of tool wear are flank wear and crater wear. Tool wear depends on workpiece and tool material characteristics; on cutting speed, feed, depth of cut, and cutting fluids; and on machine-tool characteristics.

- Surface finish of machined components can adversely affect product integrity. Important variables are the geometry and condition of the cutting tool, the type of chip produced, and process variables.

- Machinability is usually defined in terms of surface finish, tool life, force and power requirements, and chip control. Machinability of materials depends not only on their intrinsic properties and microstructure, but also on proper selection and control of process variables.

TRENDS

- Studies of cutting processes are continuing, particularly for new metallic and nonmetallic materials (as well as engineered materials), to find better ways of machining.

- Because of their importance in computer-controlled manufacturing and in planning tool changes, reliable tool-life-testing techniques and accurate prediction of tool life continue to be investigated.

- On-line tool-wear monitoring techniques and devices for computer-controlled machine tools are being developed and are currently in use.

- Control of chip flow and disposal, particularly in high-production machining, is being investigated.

KEY TERMS

Acoustic emission
Allowable wear land
Built-up edge
Chip
Chip breaker
Chip curl
Chipping of tool
Clearance angle
Continuous chip
Crater wear
Cutting force
Cutting ratio
Depth-of-cut line
Diffusion
Discontinuous chip
Feed marks

Flank wear
Friction angle
Hot machining
Inclination angle
Machinability
Machinability ratings
Machine tool
Machining
Notch wear
Oblique cutting
Orthogonal cutting
Primary shear zone
Rake angle
Relief angle
Rephosphorized steel
Resulfurized steel

Secondary shear zone
Serrated chip
Shaving
Shear angle
Shear plane
Skiving
Specific energy
Surface finish
Surface integrity
Taylor equation
Thermally-assisted machining
Thrust force
Tool-condition monitoring
Tool life
Turning
Wear land

BIBLIOGRAPHY

Armarego, E.J.A., and R.H. Brown, *The Machining of Metals.* Prentice Hall, 1969.

Astakhov, V.P., *Metal Cutting Mechanics.* CRC Press, 1998.

ASM Handbook, Vol. 16: *Machining*, ASM International, 1989.

Boothroyd, G., and W.A. Knight, *Fundamentals of Machining and Machine Tools*, (2d ed.) Marcel Dekker, 1989.

Kalpakjian, S. (ed.), *Tool and Die Failures: Source Book.* ASM International, 1982.

Oxley, P.L.B., *Mechanics of Machining—An Analytical Approach to Assessing Machinability.* Wiley, 1989.

Shaw, M.C., *Metal Cutting Principles.* Oxford, 1984.

Stephenson, D.A., and J.S. Agapiou, *Metal Cutting Theory and Practice.* Marcel Dekker, 1996.

Tool and Manufacturing Engineers Handbook (4th ed.). *Vol. 1: Machining.* Society of Manufacturing Engineers, 1983.

Trent, E.M., and P.K. Wright, *Metal Cutting* (4th ed.). Butterworth Heinemann, 1999.

Venkatesh, V.C., and H. Chandrasekaran, *Experimental Techniques in Metal Cutting* (Rev. ed.). Prentice Hall, 1987.

REVIEW QUESTIONS

20.1 List the (a) independent variables and (b) dependent variables in cutting.

20.2 Explain the difference between positive and negative rake angles.

20.3 Explain the difference between discontinuous chips and segmented chips.

20.4 Why are continuous chips not always desirable?

20.5 Is there any advantage to having a built-up edge? Explain.

20.6 Name the factors that contribute to the formation of discontinuous chips.

20.7 What is the function of chip breakers? How do they work?

20.8 Identify the forces involved in a cutting operation. Which force contributes to the power required?

20.9 Explain the features of different types of tool wear.

20.10 Name the techniques used for measuring tool wear. Describe their advantages and limitations.

20.11 Are the locations of maximum temperature and crater wear related? If so, why?

20.12 List the factors that contribute to poor surface finish in cutting.

20.13 Explain the term "machinability" and what it involves. Why does titanium have poor machinability?

20.14 What is the Taylor tool life equation?

20.15 When do serrated chips occur?

20.16 Is there a drawback to machining very slowly?

20.17 What are the common forms of chip breakers?

20.18 What is the difference between oblique and orthogonal cutting?

20.19 Is material ductility important for machinability? Explain.

20.20 Why is the rake angle of a tool important? Is the relief angle important?

20.21 What is turning? Describe its capabilities.

QUALITATIVE PROBLEMS

20.22 Explain why studying the types of chips produced is important in understanding cutting operations.

20.23 Why do you think the maximum temperature in orthogonal cutting is located at about the middle of the tool–chip interface? (*Hint*: Remember that the two sources of heat are a) shearing in the primary shear plane, and b) friction at the tool–chip interface.)

20.24 What are the effects of lowering the friction at the tool–chip interface (say, with a lubricant) on the mechanics of cutting operations?

20.25 Tool life can be almost infinite at low cutting speeds. Would you recommend that all machining be done at low speeds? Explain.

20.26 Explain the consequences of allowing temperatures to rise to high levels in cutting.

20.27 The cutting force increases with depth of cut and decreasing rake angle. Why?

20.28 Why is it not always advisable to increase cutting speed in order to increase production rate?

20.29 What are the consequences if tools chip?

20.30 Wood is a highly anisotropic (orthotropic) material. Explain the effects on chip formation in cutting wood at different angles to the grain direction.

20.31 What are the effects of performing a cutting operation with a dull tool?

20.32 To what factors do you attribute the difference in the specific energies when machining the materials shown in Table 20.2? Why is there a range of energies for each group of material?

20.33 Explain why it is possible to remove more material between tool resharpenings by lowering the cutting speed.

20.34 Noting that the dimension d in Fig. 20.4a is very small (on the order of less than 0.01 mm), explain why the shear strain rate in metal cutting is so high. (See also Table 2.3).

20.35 Explain the significance of Eq. (20.7).

20.36 We note in Eq. (20.19) that the cutting speed, V, has a greater influence on mean temperature than the feed, f. Why?

20.37 Comment on your observations regarding Fig. 20.9.

20.38 Would you have anticipated the general temperature distribution in metal cutting to be the one shown in Fig. 20.12? Explain.

20.39 Describe the consequences of exceeding the allowable wear land (Table 20.3) for various cutting-tool materials.

20.40 Comment on your observations regarding Fig. 20.6.

20.41 Why does the temperature in cutting depend on the cutting speed, feed, and depth of cut? Explain in terms of the relevant process variables.

20.42 You will note that the values of a and b in Eq. (20.19) are higher for high-speed steels than for carbides. Why is this so?

20.43 As shown in Fig. 20.14, the percentage of the total cutting energy carried away by the chip increases with cutting speed. Why?

20.44 In Table 20.4, we note that the allowable wear land for carbides is generally lower than that for high-speed steels. Why?

20.45 Describe in detail the effects that a dull tool can have on cutting operations.

20.46 Explain whether it is desirable to have a high or low n value in the Taylor tool-life equation. How about the value of C?

20.47 The tool-life curve for ceramic tools in Fig. 20.17 is to the right of those for other tool materials. Why?

20.48 What type of chips would be produced when machining gray cast iron? Explain.

20.49 It was noted in this chapter that the power in cutting is dissipated mainly in the primary shear zone and at the chip–tool interface. If the rake angle is $0°$, then the frictional forces are perpendicular to the cutting direction and do not consume machine power. Why, then, does this result in an increase in the power dissipated over a rake angle of, for example, $20°$?

20.50 Why are tool temperatures low at low cutting speeds and high at high cutting speeds?

20.51 What is the drawback to a large wear land?

20.52 The Taylor tool-life equation pertains to flank wear. Would you expect that a wear equation for crater wear would be substantially different? Explain.

20.53 Given your understanding of the basic metal-cutting process, what are the important physical and chemical properties of a cutting tool?

20.54 An aerospace aluminum alloy has a very high thermal conductivity and strength, but cutting it results in serrated chips. What would you say about the strength of the aluminum at high temperatures?

20.55 What is the importance of the cutting ratio?

QUANTITATIVE PROBLEMS

20.56 Let $n = 0.4$ and $C = 400$ in the Taylor equation for tool wear. What is the percent increase in tool life if the cutting speed is reduced by (a) 20%, and (b) 40%?

20.57 Assume that in orthogonal cutting the rake angle is $10°$ and the coefficient of friction is 0.5. Using Eq. (20.3), determine the percentage increase in chip thickness when the friction is doubled.

20.58 Derive Eq. (20.12).

20.59 Taking carbide as an example and using Eq. (20.19), determine how much the feed should be reduced in order to keep the mean temperature constant when the cutting speed is doubled.

20.60 Using trigonometric relationships, derive an expression for the ratio of shear energy to frictional energy in orthogonal cutting, in terms of angles α, β, and ϕ only.

20.61 An orthogonal cutting operation is being carried out under the following conditions: $t_o = 0.1$ mm, $t_c = 0.2$ mm, width of cut $= 5$ mm, $V = 2$ m/s, rake angle $= 10°$, $F_c = 500$ N, and $F_t = 200$ N. Calculate the percentage of the total energy that is dissipated in the shear plane.

20.62 Determine the C and n values for the four tool materials shown in Fig. 20.17.

20.63 The data in the following table are obtained in orthogonal cutting of AISI 4130 steel using a high-speed steel tool, and at a cutting speed $V = 90$ ft/min, depth of cut $t_o = 0.0025$ in., and width of cut $= 0.475$ in. Calculate the missing quantities in the table. Describe your observations concerning variations of forces and energies with increasing rake angle.

α	ϕ	γ	μ	β	F_c(lb)	F_t(lb)	$u_t\left(\dfrac{\text{in.-lb}}{\text{in.}^3}\right)$	u_s	u_f	$\dfrac{u_f}{u_t}(\%)$
25°	20.9°		1.46		380	224				
35	31.6		1.53		254	102				
40	35.7		1.54		232	71				
45	41.9		1.83		232	68				

20.64 Derive Eq. (20.1).

20.65 Assume that in orthogonal cutting, the rake angle, α, is 15° and the friction angle, β, is 30° at the chip–tool interface. Determine the percentage change in chip thickness when the friction angle is 50°. Do not use Eq. (20.3).

20.66 Determine the shear angle for the example given in Section 20.5.3. Is this an exact calculation or an estimate? Explain.

20.67 Using Eq. (20.19) and referring to Fig. 20.13a, estimate the magnitude of the constant a.

20.68 Show that for the same shear angle, there are two rake angles that give the same cutting ratio.

20.69 Do you agree with the following statement?: If the cutting speed, the shear angle, and the rake angle are known, the chip velocity up the face of the tool can be calculated. Explain.

20.70 With appropriate diagrams, show how the use of a cutting fluid can change the magnitude of the thrust force, F_t.

20.71 For a turning operation using a ceramic cutting tool, if the speed is to be doubled, by what factor must the feed rate be modified to obtain a constant tool life?

20.72 In the example given in Section 20.5.3, if the cutting speed, V, is doubled to 800 ft/min., will the answer be different? Explain.

20.73 The ideal surface roughness in turning (without built-up edge or vibrations, as shown in Fig. 20.23) is approximately

$$R_a = \frac{f^2}{8R},$$

where R_a is the arithmetic mean value (Section 31.5), f is the feed, and R is the tool nose radius. Select an appropriate feed for $R = 1$ mm and a desired roughness of 1 μm. How would you adjust this feed to allow for nose wear of the tool during extended cuts?

20.74 Assuming that the coefficient of friction in cutting is 0.3, calculate the maximum depth of cut for turning a hard aluminum alloy on a 20 hp lathe (mechanical efficiency = 80%) with a width of cut of 0.25 in, a rake angle of 10°, and a cutting speed of 300 ft/min. What is your estimate of the material's shear strength? Use the specific energy requirements given in Table 20.2.

20.75 Using a carbide cutting tool, the temperature in a cutting operation with a speed of 250 ft/min and feed of 0.0025 in./rev is measured as 1200 °F. What is the approximate temperature if the speed is doubled? What speed is required to lower the maximum cutting temperature to 800 °F?

SYNTHESIS AND DESIGN

20.76 As we have seen, chips carry away the majority of the heat generated in cutting. If chips did not have this capacity, what suggestions would you make in order to be able to carry out machining processes? Explain.

20.77 Tool life could be greatly increased if an effective means of cooling and lubrication were found. Design methods of delivering this fluid to the tool–workpiece interface and discuss the advantages and shortcomings of your design.

20.78 Design an experimental setup whereby orthogonal cutting can be simulated in a turning operation on a lathe.

20.79 Assume that you are an instructor covering the topics described in this chapter, and you are giving a quiz on the numerical aspects to test students' understanding. Prepare several quantitative problems and supply the answers.

20.80 Cutting tools are sometimes designed so that the chip–tool contact length is controlled by recessing it at the rake face some distance away from the tool tip. Explain the possible advantages of such a tool.

21

Cutting-Tool Materials and Cutting Fluids

21.1 INTRODUCTION

The selection of cutting-tool materials for a particular application is among the most important factors in machining operations, as is the selection of mold and die materials for forming and shaping processes (Part III). As noted in Chapter 20, the cutting tool is subjected to (a) high temperatures, (b) contact stresses, and (c) sliding along the tool–chip interface and along the machined surface. Consequently, a cutting tool must possess the following characteristics:

- **Hardness**, particularly at elevated temperatures (**hot hardness**), so that the hardness, strength, and wear resistance of the tool are maintained at the temperatures encountered in cutting operations (Fig. 21.1).
- **Toughness**, so that impact forces on the tool in interrupted cutting operations (such as milling or turning a splined shaft) or due to vibration and chatter during machining do not chip or fracture the tool.
- **Wear resistance**, so that an acceptable tool life is obtained before the tool is indexed or replaced.

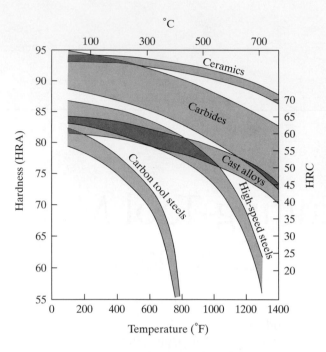

FIGURE 21.1 The hardness of various cutting-tool materials as a function of temperature (hot hardness). The wide range in each group of materials is due to the variety of tool compositions and treatments available for that group. See also Table 21.1 for melting or decomposition temperatures of these materials.

- **Chemical stability** or **inertness** with respect to the workpiece material, so that any adverse reactions contributing to tool wear are avoided.

Various cutting-tool materials with a wide range of mechanical, physical, and chemical properties are available (Tables 21.1 through 21.3). Tool materials are usually divided into the following general categories, listed in the order in which they were developed and implemented:

1. Carbon and medium-alloy steels
2. High-speed steels
3. Cast-cobalt alloys
4. Carbides
5. Coated tools
6. Alumina-based ceramics
7. Cubic boron nitride
8. Silicon-nitride-base ceramics
9. Diamond
10. Whisker-reinforced materials

Note that, as described in Parts II and III, many of these tool materials are also used for dies and molds. This chapter describes the characteristics, applications, and limitations of these tool materials in machining operations, including characteristics such as hot hardness, toughness, impact strength, wear resistance, thermal shock resistance, and costs, as well as the range of cutting speeds and depth of cut for optimal performance.

TABLE 21.1   Typical Properties of Tool Materials

Property	High-speed steels	Cast alloys	Carbides		Ceramics	Cubic boron nitride	Single-crystal diamond*
			WC	TiC			
Hardness	83–86 HRA	82–84 HRA 46–62 HRC	90–95 HRA 1800–2400 HK	91–93 HRA 1800–3200 HK	91–95 HRA 2000–3000 HK	4000–5000 HK	7000–8000 HK
Compressive strength							
MPa	4100–4500	1500–2300	4100–5850	3100–3850	2750–4500	6900	6900
psi $\times 10^3$	600–650	220–335	600–850	450–560	400–650	1000	1000
Transverse rupture strength							
MPa	2400–4800	1380–2050	1050–2600	1380–1900	345–950	700	1350
psi $\times 10^3$	350–700	200–300	150–375	200–275	50–135	105	200
Impact strength							
J	1.35–8	0.34–1.25	0.34–1.35	0.79–1.24	< 0.1	< 0.5	< 0.2
in.-lb	12–70	3–11	3–12	7–11	< 1	< 5	< 2
Modulus of elasticity							
GPa	200	–	520–690	310–450	310–410	850	820–1050
psi $\times 10^6$	30	–	75–100	45–65	45–60	125	120–150
Density							
kg/m^3	8600	8000–8700	10,000–15,000	5500–5800	4000–4500	3500	3500
lb/in.^{3}	0.31	0.29–0.31	0.36–0.54	0.2–0.22	0.14–0.16	0.13	0.13
Volume of hard phase, %	7–15	10–20	70–90	–	100	95	95
Melting or decomposition temperature							
°C	1300		1400	1400	2000	1300	700
°F	2370		2550	2550	3600	2400	1300
Thermal conductivity, W/m K	30–50	–	42–125	17	29	13	500–2000
Coefficient of thermal expansion, $\times 10^{-6}/°C$	12	–	4–6.5	7.5–9	6–8.5	4.8	1.5–4.8

*The values for polycrystalline diamond are generally lower, except impact strength, which is higher.

571

TABLE 21.2 General Characteristics of Cutting-Tool Materials. These Tool Materials Have a Wide Range of Compositions and Properties; Thus Overlapping Characteristics Exist in Many Categories of Tool Materials.

	Carbon and low- to medium-alloy steels	High-speed steels	Cast-cobalt alloys	Uncoated carbides	Coated carbides	Ceramics	Polycrystalline cubic boron nitride	Diamond
Hot hardness			Increasing					↑
Toughness	↓		Increasing					
Impact strength	↓		Increasing					
Wear resistance			Increasing					↑
Chipping resistance	↓		Increasing					
Cutting speed			Increasing					↑
Thermal-shock resistance	↓		Increasing					
Tool material cost			Increasing					↑
Depth of cut	Light to medium	Light to heavy	Light to heavy	Light to heavy	Light to heavy	Light to heavy	Light to heavy	Very light for single-crystal diamond
Finish obtainable	Rough	Rough	Rough	Good	Good	Very good	Very good	Excellent
Method of processing	Wrought	Wrought, cast, HIP* sintering	Cast and HIP sintering	Cold pressing and sintering	CVD or PVD†	Cold pressing and sintering or HIP sintering	High-pressure, high-temperature sintering	High-pressure, high-temperature sintering
Fabrication	Machining and grinding	Machining and grinding	Grinding	Grinding		Grinding	Grinding and polishing	Grinding and polishing

Source: R. Komanduri, Kirk-Othmer Encyclopedia of Chemical Technology, (3d ed.). New York: Wiley, 1978.

* Hot-isostatic pressing.

† Chemical-vapor deposition, physical-vapor deposition.

TABLE 21.3   Operating Characteristics of Cutting-Tool Materials

Tool materials	General characteristics	Modes of tool wear or failure	Limitations
High-speed steels	High toughness, resistance to fracture, wide range of roughing and finishing cuts, good for interrupted cuts	Flank wear, crater wear	Low hot hardness, limited hardenability, and limited wear resistance
Uncoated carbides	High hardness over a wide range of temperatures, toughness, wear resistance, versatile and wide range of applications	Flank wear, crater wear	Cannot use at low speed because of cold welding of chips and microchipping
Coated carbides	Improved wear resistance over uncoated carbides, better frictional and thermal properties	Flank wear, crater wear	Cannot use at low speed because of cold welding of chips and microchipping
Ceramics	High hardness at elevated temperatures, high abrasive wear resistance	Depth-of-cut line notching, microchipping, gross fracture	Low strength, low thermomechanical fatigue strength
Polycrystalline cubic boron nitride (cBN)	High hot hardness, toughness, cutting-edge strength	Depth-of-cut line notching, chipping, oxidation, graphitization	Low strength, low chemical stability at higher temperature
Polycrystalline diamond	Hardness and toughness, abrasive wear resistance	Chipping, oxidation, graphitization	Low strength, low chemical stability at higher temperature

Source: After R. Komanduri and other sources.

21.2 CARBON AND MEDIUM-ALLOY STEELS

Carbon steels are the oldest of tool materials and have been used widely for drills, taps, broaches, and reamers since the 1880s. Low-alloy and medium-alloy steels were developed later for similar applications but with longer tool life.

Although inexpensive and easily shaped and sharpened, these steels do not have sufficient hot hardness and wear resistance for cutting at high speeds (where, as we have seen, the temperature rises significantly). Note in Fig. 21.1, for example, how rapidly the hardness of carbon steels decreases as the temperature increases. Consequently, the use of these steels is limited to very low-speed cutting operations.

21.3 HIGH-SPEED STEELS

High-speed steel (HSS) tools are so named because they were developed to cut at higher speeds. First produced in the early 1900s, *high-speed steels* are the most highly alloyed of the tool steels (Section 5.7). They can be hardened to various depths, have good wear resistance, and are relatively inexpensive. Because of their toughness and high resistance to fracture, high-speed steels are especially suitable for high positive rake-angle tools (those with small included angles), for interrupted cuts, and for machine tools with low stiffness that are subject to vibration and chatter.

There are two basic types of high-speed steels: **molybdenum** (M series) and **tungsten** (T series). The M series contains up to about 10% molybdenum, with chromium, vanadium, tungsten, and cobalt as alloying elements. The T series contains 12% to 18% tungsten, with chromium, vanadium, and cobalt as alloying elements. The M series generally has higher abrasion resistance than the T series, undergoes less distortion during heat treating, and is less expensive. Consequently, 95% of all high-speed steel tools are made of M-series steels.

High-speed-steel tools are available in wrought, cast, and sintered (powder-metallurgy) forms. They can be **coated** for improved performance (Section 21.6). High-speed-steel tools may also be subjected to surface treatments, such as case hardening for improved hardness and wear resistance (see Section 4.10) or steam treatment at elevated temperatures to develop a black oxide layer for improved performance—for instance, to reduce built-up edge formation.

High-speed steels account for the largest tonnage of tool materials used today, followed by various die steels and carbides. They are used in a wide variety of cutting operations requiring complex tool shapes, such as drills, reamers, taps, and gear cutters (Chapters 22 and 23). Their most important limitation is the cutting speeds that can be employed, which are low relative to those of carbide tools.

21.4 CAST-COBALT ALLOYS

Introduced in 1915, *cast-cobalt alloys* have the following ranges of composition: 38% to 53% cobalt, 30% to 33% chromium, and 10% to 20% tungsten. Because of their high hardness (typically 58 to 64 HRC), they have good wear resistance and can maintain their hardness at elevated temperatures. They are not as tough as high-speed steels and are sensitive to impact forces. Consequently, they are less suitable than high-speed steels for interrupted cutting operations.

Commonly known as *Stellite* tools, these alloys are cast and ground into relatively simple tool shapes. Such tools are now used only for special applications that involve deep, continuous **roughing cuts** at relatively high feeds and speeds, as much as twice the rates possible with high-speed steels. (As described in Section 22.2, roughing cuts usually involve high feed rates and large-depth cuts; conversely, **finishing cuts** are at a lower feed and depth of cut.)

21.5 CARBIDES

The three groups of tool materials just described (alloy steels, high-speed steels, and cast alloys) possess the necessary toughness, impact strength, and thermal shock resistance, but also have important limitations, particularly with regard to strength and hardness, especially hot hardness. Consequently, they cannot be used as effectively where high cutting speeds, and therefore high temperatures, are involved.

To meet the challenge of higher speeds for higher production rates, *carbides* (also known as *cemented* or *sintered carbides*) were introduced in the 1930s. Because of their high hardness over a wide range of temperatures (Fig. 21.1), high elastic modulus and thermal conductivity, and low thermal expansion, carbides are among the most important, versatile, and cost-effective tool and die materials for a wide range of applications.

The two basic groups of carbides used for machining operations are *tungsten carbide* and *titanium carbide*. In order to differentiate them from coated tools (Section 21.6), plain carbide tools are usually referred to as **uncoated** carbides. (See Section 21.11 for a discussion of **micrograin** carbides.)

21.5.1 Tungsten Carbide

Tungsten carbide (WC) is a composite material consisting of tungsten-carbide particles bonded together in a cobalt matrix; an alternate name for WC is *cemented* carbides. These tools are manufactured with powder-metallurgy techniques (as shown in the example in Section 17.5), in which WC particles are combined with cobalt in a mixer, resulting in a cobalt matrix surrounding the WC particles.

These particles, which are 1–5 μm (40–200 μin.) in size, are then pressed and sintered into the desired insert shapes. (Because of this process, WC is also called *sintered carbides*.) Tungsten carbides are frequently compounded with carbides of titanium and niobium to impart special properties to the carbide.

The amount of cobalt present significantly affects the properties of carbide tools. As the cobalt content increases, the strength, hardness, and wear resistance of WC decrease, while its toughness increases because of the higher toughness of cobalt. Tungsten carbide tools are generally used for cutting steels, cast irons, and abrasive nonferrous materials, and have largely replaced HSS tools because of their better performance.

21.5.2 Titanium Carbide

Titanium carbide (TiC) has higher wear resistance than tungsten carbide but is not as tough. With a nickel–molybdenum alloy as the matrix, TiC is suitable for machining hard materials, mainly steels and cast irons, and for cutting at speeds higher than those appropriate for tungsten carbide.

21.5.3 Inserts

We have seen that carbon-steel and high-speed-steel tools are shaped in one piece and ground to various geometric features (Fig. 20.10a); other such tools include drill bits and milling cutters. After the cutting edge wears, the tool has to be removed from its holder and reground.

Although a supply of sharp or resharpened tools is usually available from tool rooms, tool-changing operations are time-consuming and inefficient. The need for a more effective method has led to the development of *inserts,* which are individual cutting tools with several cutting points (Fig. 21.2). A square insert, for example, has eight cutting points, and a triangular insert has six.

Inserts are usually clamped on the tool *shank* with various locking mechanisms (Figs. 21.3a-c). Although not as commonly used, inserts may also be *brazed* to the tool

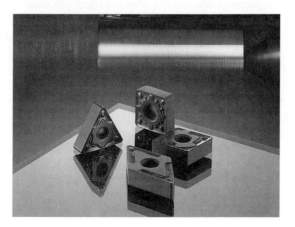

FIGURE 21.2   Typical carbide inserts with various shapes and chip-breaker features; round inserts are also available (Fig. 21.4). The holes in the inserts are standardized for interchangeability. *Source*: Courtesy of Kyocera Engineered Ceramics, Inc., and *Manufacturing Engineering Magazine*, Society of Manufacturing Engineers.

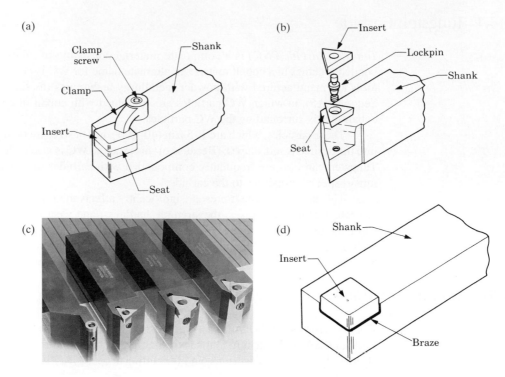

FIGURE 21.3   Methods of attaching inserts to toolholders: (a) Clamping, and (b) Wing lockpins. (c) Examples of inserts attached to toolholders with threadless lockpins, which are secured with side screws. *Source*: Courtesy of Valenite. (d) Insert brazed on a tool shank (see Section 30.2).

shank (Fig. 21.3d). Because of the difference in thermal expansion between the insert and the tool shank, however, brazing must be done carefully to avoid cracking or warping.

Clamping is the preferred method of securing an insert because each insert has a number of cutting points, and after one edge is worn, it is **indexed** (rotated in its holder) to make available another cutting point. In addition to the examples in this figure, a wide variety of other toolholders is available for specific applications, including those with quick insertion and removal features.

Carbide inserts are available in a wide variety of shapes, such as square, triangle, diamond, and round. The strength of the cutting edge of an insert depends on its shape. The smaller the included angle (Fig. 21.4), the lower the strength of the edge. In order to further improve edge strength and prevent chipping, all insert edges are usually honed, chamfered, or produced with a negative land (Fig. 21.5). Most inserts are honed to a radius of about 0.025 mm (0.001 in.).

Chip breaker features on cutting tools, described in Section 20.3.7, are for the purposes of (a) controlling chip flow during machining, (b) eliminating long chips, and (c) reducing vibration and heat generated. Most carbide inserts are now available with a wide variety of complex chip-breaker features, typical examples of which are shown in Fig. 21.2.

The selection of a particular chip-breaker feature depends on the feed and depth of cut of the operation, the workpiece material, the type of chip produced during cutting, and whether it is a roughing or finishing cut. Optimum chip breaker geometries are now being developed using computer-aided design and finite-element analysis techniques.

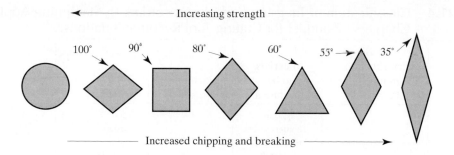

FIGURE 21.4   Relative edge strength and tendency for chipping and breaking of inserts with various shapes. Strength refers to the cutting edge shown by the included angles. *Source*: Kennametal, Inc.

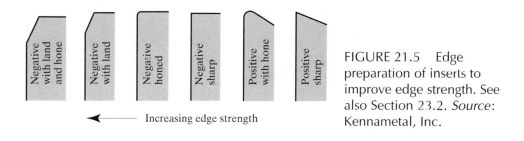

FIGURE 21.5   Edge preparation of inserts to improve edge strength. See also Section 23.2. *Source*: Kennametal, Inc.

Stiffness of the machine tool is of major importance when using carbide tools (See tion 24.4). Light feeds, low speeds, and chatter are detrimental because they tend to damage the tool's cutting edge. Light feeds, for example, concentrate the forces and temperature closer to the edges of the tool, increasing the tendency for the edges to chip off.

Low cutting speeds tend to encourage cold welding of the chip to the tool. Cutting fluids, if used to minimize the heating and cooling of the tool in interrupted cutting operations, should be applied continuously and in large quantities.

21.5.4 Classification of Carbide Tools

For a number of years, the American National Standards Institute (ANSI) has classified carbide tools as ranging from grades C-1 to C-8 (Table 21.4). With rapidly increasing trends in global manufacturing and with increasingly wider use of the ISO (International Organization for Standardization) standards, there has been, for some time, a major effort to standardize carbide classification.

Carbide grades are now being classified using the symbols P, M, and K for a range of applications (Table 21.5). The approximate equivalent ISO standards for the carbides listed are included in Table 21.4. Because of the wide variety of carbide compositions available and the broad range of machining applications and workpiece materials involved, however, efforts for ISO classification continue to be a difficult task. This is especially true when comparing ISO grades with the traditional C grades.

TABLE 21.4   Classification of Tungsten Carbides According to Machining Applications. See also Chapters 22 and 23 for Cutting Tool Recommendations.

ISO Standard	ANSI Classification number (Grade)	Materials to be machined	Machining operation	Type of carbide	Characteristics of	
					Cut	Carbide
K30–K40	C–1	Cast iron, nonferrous metals, and nonmetallic materials requiring abrasion resistance	Roughing	Wear-resistant grades; generally straight WC-Co with varying grain sizes	Increasing cutting speed	Increasing hardness and wear resistance
K20	C–2		General purpose			
K10	C–3		Light finishing			
K01	C–4		Precision finishing		Increasing feed rate	Increasing strength and binder content
P30–P50	C–5	Steels and steel alloys requiring crater and deformation resistance	Roughing	Crater-resistant grades; various WC-Co compositions with TiC and/or TaC alloys	Increasing cutting speed	Increasing hardness and wear resistance
P20	C–6		General purpose			
P10	C–7		Light finishing			
P01	C–8		Precision finishing		Increasing feed rate	Increasing strength and binder content

Note: The ISO and ANSI comparisons are approximate.

TABLE 21.5   ISO Classification of Carbide Cutting Tools According to Use

Symbol	Workpiece material	Color code	Designation in increasing order of wear resistance and decreasing order of toughness in each category, in increments of 5
P	Ferrous metals with long chips	Blue	P01, P05 through P50
M	Ferrous metals with long or short chips; nonferrous metals	Yellow	M10 through M40
K	Ferrous metals with short chips; nonferrous metals; nonmetallic materials	Red	K01, K10 through K40

21.6 COATED TOOLS

As described in Part I, new alloys and engineered materials are being developed continuously, particularly since the 1960s. These materials have high strength and toughness but are generally abrasive and chemically reactive with tool materials. The difficulty of machining these materials efficiently, and the need for improving the performance in machining the more common engineering materials, has led to important developments in *coated tools*.

Because of their unique properties, such as lower friction and higher resistance to cracks and wear, coated tools can be used at high cutting speeds, reducing both the time required for machining operations and costs. Cutting time has been reduced by a factor of more than 100 since 1900 (Fig. 21.6). Coated tools can have tool lives 10 times longer than those of uncoated tools.

21.6.1 Coating Materials

Commonly-used coating materials are titanium nitride (TiN), titanium carbide (TiC), titanium carbonitride (TiCN), and aluminum oxide (Al_2O_3). These coatings, generally in the

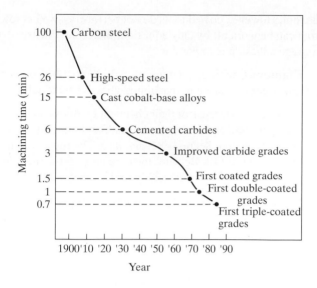

FIGURE 21.6   Relative time required to machine with various cutting-tool materials, indicating the year the tool materials were introduced. *Source*: Sandvik Coromant.

thickness range of 2–15 μm (80–600 μin.), are applied on cutting tools and inserts by the following techniques (Section 33.5):

a. Chemical-vapor deposition (CVD), including **plasma-assisted CVD**, and
b. Physical-vapor deposition (PVD).

The CVD process is the most commonly used method for carbide tools with multiphase and ceramic coatings, both of which are described later in this section. The PVD-coated carbides with TiN coatings, on the other hand, have higher cutting-edge strength, lower friction, lower tendency to form a built-up edge, and are smoother and more uniform in thickness (which is generally in the range of 2 to 4 μm (80 to 160 μin.)).

An emerging coating technology, used particularly for multiphase coatings, is **medium-temperature chemical-vapor deposition (MTCVD).** It is being developed to machine ductile (nodular) iron and stainless steels and to provide higher resistance to crack propagation than CVD coatings provide.

Coatings for cutting tools, as well as for dies, should have the following general characteristics:

- **High hardness** at elevated temperatures.
- **Chemical stability** with and **inertness** to the workpiece material.
- **Low thermal conductivity**.
- **Good bonding** to the substrate to prevent flaking or spalling.
- **Little or no porosity**.

The effectiveness of coatings, in turn, is enhanced by the hardness, toughness, and high thermal conductivity of the substrate (which may be carbide or high-speed steel). Honing of the cutting edges (see Section 25.10) is an important procedure for the maintainance of coating strength; otherwise, the coating may peel or chip off at sharp edges and corners.

Titanium Nitride.   Titanium-nitride coatings have low friction coefficients, high hardness, resistance to high temperature, and good adhesion to the substrate. Consequently, they greatly improve the life of high-speed-steel tools, as well as the lives of carbide tools, drill bits, and cutters. Titanium–nitride coated tools (gold in color) perform well at higher cutting speeds and feeds.

Flank wear is significantly lower than that of uncoated tools, and flank surfaces can be reground after use since regrinding the tool does not remove the coating on the rake face of the tool. However, coated tools do not perform as well at low cutting speeds because the coating can be worn off by chip adhesion; therefore, the use of appropriate cutting fluids to discourage adhesion is important.

Titanium Carbide.   Titanium-carbide coatings on tungsten–carbide inserts have high flank-wear resistance in machining abrasive materials.

Ceramics.   Because of their chemical inertness, low thermal conductivity, resistance to high temperature, and resistance to flank and crater wear, ceramics are suitable coating materials for tools (see Sections 8.2 and 8.3). The most commonly used ceramic coating is aluminum oxide (Al_2O_3). Because they are very stable (not chemically reactive), however, oxide coatings generally bond weakly to the substrate.

Multiphase Coatings.   The desirable properties of the coatings just described can be combined and optimized with the use of *multiphase coatings*. Carbide tools are now available with two or three layers of such coatings and are particularly effective in machining cast irons and steels.

For example, one could first layer TiC over the substrate, followed by Al_2O_3, and then TiN. The first layer should bond well with the substrate; the outer layer should resist wear and have low thermal conductivity. The intermediate layer should bond well and be compatible with both layers.

Typical applications of multiple-coated tools are as follows:

1. High-speed, continuous cutting: TiC/Al_2O_3.
2. Heavy-duty, continuous cutting: $TiC/Al_2O_3/TiN$.
3. Light, interrupted cutting: $TiC/TiC + TiN/TiN$.

FIGURE 21.7   Multiphase coatings on a tungsten-carbide substrate. Three alternating layers of aluminum oxide are separated by very thin layers of titanium nitride. Inserts with as many as thirteen layers of coatings have been made. Coating thicknesses are typically in the range of 2 to 10 μm. *Source*: Courtesy of Kennametal, Inc., and *Manufacturing Engineering Magazine*, Society of Manufacturing Engineers.

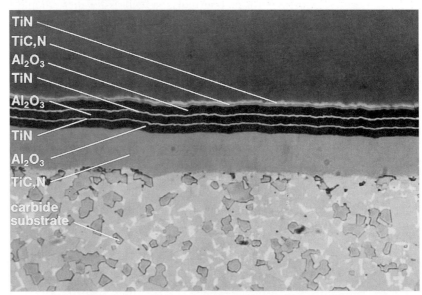

Coatings are also available in **alternating multiphase layers**. The thickness of these layers is on the order of 2 to 10 μm, thinner than regular multiphase coatings (Fig. 21.7). The reason for using thinner coatings is that coating hardness increases with decreasing grain size, a phenomenon that is similar to the increase in strength of metals with decreasing grain size (Section 1.4). Therefore, thinner layers are harder than thicker layers.

Example: Multiphase Coating on a Carbide Tool

An example of a recently developed coated carbide tool consists of the following, starting from the top layer:

TiN	Low friction
Al_2O_3	High thermal stability
TiCN	Fiber reinforced; good balance of resistance to flank wear and crater wear, particularly for interrupted cutting
A special carbide substrate (thin)	High fracture toughness
Carbide substrate (bulk)	Hard and resistant to plastic deformation

21.6.2 Diamond-Coated Tools

The properties and applications of diamond and diamond coatings are described in Sections 8.7 and 33.13, respectively, and their use as cutting tools is given in Section 21.10. A recent development concerns the use of polycrystalline diamond as a coating for cutting tools, particularly on tungsten–carbide and silicon–nitride inserts. Difficulties exist regarding adherence of the diamond film to the substrate and the difference in thermal expansion between the diamond and substrate materials. (See Table 21.1.)

Thin-film *diamond coated* inserts are now commercially available, as are thick-film diamond brazed-tip cutting tools. Thin films are deposited on substrates with PVD and CVD techniques. Thick films are obtained by growing a large sheet of pure diamond, which is then laser cut to shape and brazed to a carbide shank.

Diamond-coated tools are particularly effective in machining nonferrous and abrasive materials, such as aluminum alloys containing silicon, fiber-reinforced and metal-matrix composite materials, and graphite. As much as tenfold improvements in tool life have been obtained over other coated tools.

21.6.3 New Coating Materials

While titanium-nitride coatings made by chemical-vapor deposition are still common, advances are being made in the development and testing of new coating materials. **Titanium carbonitride (TiCN)** and **titanium aluminum nitride (TiAlN)** have been found to be effective in cutting stainless steels. TiCN, which is deposited with physical-vapor deposition techniques, is harder and tougher than TiN and can be used on carbides and high-speed steel tools. TiAlN is effective in machining aerospace alloys.

Chromium-based coatings, such as **chromium carbide (CrC)**, have been found to be effective in machining softer metals that tend to adhere to the cutting tool, such as aluminum, copper, and titanium. Other new materials include **zirconium nitride (ZrN)** and

hafnium nitride (HfN). Considerable experimental data is required before these coatings and their behavior can be fully assessed for proper applications in machining.

Recent developments include (a) **nanocoatings** (see also Section 6.15), including carbide, boride, nitride, oxide, or some combination, and (b) **composite coatings**, using a variety of materials. The hardness of some of these coatings approaches that of cubic boron nitride. Although they are still in experimental stages, it is expected that these coatings will have the combined benefits of various types of coatings as well as wider applications in machining operations.

21.6.4 Ion Implantation

In this process, ions are introduced into the surface of the cutting tool, improving its surface properties (Section 33.6). The process does not change the dimensions of tools. **Nitrogen-ion** implanted carbide tools have been used successfully on alloy steels and stainless steels. **Xenon-ion** implantation of tools is also under development.

21.7 ALUMINA-BASED CERAMICS

Ceramic tool materials, introduced in the early 1950s, consist primarily of fine-grained, high-purity **aluminum oxide**. (See also Chapter 8.) They are cold-pressed into insert shapes under high pressure and sintered at high temperature; the end product is referred to as **white**, or **cold-pressed**, ceramics. Additions of titanium carbide and zirconium oxide help improve properties such as toughness and thermal-shock resistance.

Alumina-based ceramic tools have very high abrasion resistance and hot hardness (Fig. 21.8). Chemically, they are more stable than high-speed steels and carbides, so they have less tendency to adhere to metals during cutting and a correspondingly lower tendency to form a built-up edge. Consequently, in cutting cast irons and steels, good surface finish is obtained with ceramic tools. However, ceramics lack toughness, and their use may result in premature tool failure by chipping or catastrophic failure. (See Fig. 20.18.)

Ceramic inserts are available in shapes similar to the shapes of carbide inserts. They are effective in high-speed, uninterrupted cutting operations, such as finishing or semifinishing by turning. To reduce thermal shock, cutting should be performed either dry or with a copious amount of cutting fluid, applied in a steady stream. Improper or intermittent applications of the fluid can cause thermal shock and fracture of the ceramic tool.

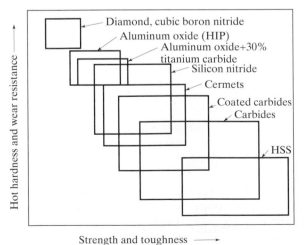

FIGURE 21.8   Ranges of properties for various groups of tool materials. See also Tables 21.1 through 21.5.

Ceramic tool shape and setup are important. Negative rake angles (large included angles) are generally preferred in order to avoid chipping due to the poor tensile strength of ceramics. Tool failure can be reduced by increasing the stiffness and damping capacity of machine tools, mountings, and workholding devices, thus reducing vibration and chatter (Section 24.4).

Cermets.   Black, or **hot-pressed**, ceramics (*carboxides*) were introduced in the 1960s. They typically contain 70% aluminum oxide and 30% titanium carbide, and are also called *cermets* (from ceramic and metal). Other cermets contain molybdenum carbide, niobium carbide, and tantalum carbide. (See Section 8.2.3.) Although they have chemical stability and resistance to built-up edge formation, their brittleness and high cost have been a problem.

Further refinements of these tools have resulted in improved strength, toughness, and reliability. Their performance is somewhere between that of ceramics and carbides and has been particularly suitable for light roughing cuts and high-speed finishing cuts. Chip-breaker features are important for cermet inserts. Although cermets can be coated, the benefits of coatings are somewhat controversial; the improvement in wear resistance appears to be marginal.

21.8 CUBIC BORON NITRIDE

Next to diamond, *cubic boron nitride* (cBN) is the hardest material presently available. Introduced in 1962, it is also used as an abrasive (Chapter 25). Cubic boron nitride is made by bonding a 0.5–1-mm (0.02–0.04-in.) layer of **polycrystalline cubic boron nitride** to a carbide substrate by sintering under pressure (Fig. 21.9). While the carbide provides shock resistance, the cBN layer provides very high wear resistance and cutting-edge strength (Fig. 21.10). Cubic boron nitride tools are also made in small sizes without a substrate.

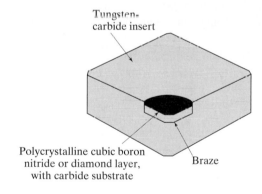

Tungsten-carbide insert

Polycrystalline cubic boron nitride or diamond layer, with carbide substrate

Braze

FIGURE 21.9
Construction of a polycrystalline cubic boron nitride or a diamond layer on a tungsten-carbide insert.

FIGURE 21.10   Inserts with polycrystalline cubic boron nitride tips (top row) and solid polycrystalline cBN inserts (bottom row). *Source*: Courtesy of Valenite.

At elevated temperatures, cBN is chemically inert to iron and nickel, and its resistance to oxidation is high. It is, therefore, particularly suitable for cutting hardened ferrous and high-temperature alloys. (See *hard turning*, Section 22.4.3.)

Because cBN tools are brittle, stiffness of the machine tool and fixturing is important in order to avoid vibration and chatter. Furthermore, in order to avoid cracking due to thermal shock, machining should generally be performed dry—i.e., cutting fluids should be avoided, particularly in interrupted cutting operations such as milling.

21.9 SILICON-NITRIDE BASED CERAMICS

Developed in the 1970s, *silicon-nitride* (SiN) *based ceramic* tool materials consist of silicon nitride with various additions of aluminum oxide, yttrium oxide, and titanium carbide. These tools have toughness, hot hardness, and good thermal-shock resistance.

An example of a SiN-base material is **sialon**, named after the elements of which it is composed: silicon, aluminum, oxygen, and nitrogen. It has higher thermal-shock resistance than silicon nitride, and is recommended for machining cast irons and nickel-based superalloys at intermediate cutting speeds. Because of chemical affinity to iron, SiN-based tools are not suitable for machining steels.

21.10 DIAMOND

Of all known materials, the hardest substance is diamond (Section 8.7). It has low friction, high wear resistance, and the ability to maintain a sharp cutting edge. Diamond is used when good surface finish and dimensional accuracy are required, particularly with soft nonferrous alloys and abrasive nonmetallic materials. **Single-crystal diamond** of various carats is used for special applications, such as machining copper-front precision optical mirrors for the Strategic Defense Initiative (SDI) program.

Because diamond is brittle, tool shape and sharpness are important. Low rake angles (large included angles) are generally used to provide a strong cutting edge. Special attention should be given to proper mounting and crystal orientation in order to obtain optimum tool life. Wear may occur through microchipping (caused by thermal stresses and oxidation) and through transformation to carbon (caused by the heat generated during cutting).

Single-crystal diamond tools have been largely replaced by **polycrystalline-diamond (PCD)** tools (*compacts*), which are also used as wire-drawing dies for fine wire (Section 15.11). These materials consist of very small synthetic crystals, fused by a high-pressure, high-temperature process to a thickness of about 0.5 to 1 mm (0.02 to 0.04 in.) and bonded to a carbide substrate; the result is similar to cBN tools (Figs. 21.9 and 21.10). The random orientation of the diamond crystals prevents the propagation of cracks through the structure, significantly improving its toughness.

Diamond tools can be used satisfactorily at almost any speed, but are most suitable for light, uninterrupted finishing cuts. In order to minimize tool fracture, the single-crystal diamond must be resharpened as soon as it becomes dull. Because of its strong chemical affinity, diamond is not recommended for machining plain-carbon steels or titanium, nickel, and cobalt-based alloys. Diamond is also used as an abrasive in grinding and polishing operations (Chapter 25) and as coatings (Sections 21.6 and 33.13).

21.11 WHISKER-REINFORCED AND NANOCRYSTALLINE TOOL MATERIALS

In order to further improve the performance and wear resistance of cutting tools, particularly in machining new materials and composites that are under continued investigation, progress is being made in developing new tool materials with enhanced properties such as the following:

a. High fracture toughness.

b. Resistance to thermal shock.

c. Cutting-edge strength.

d. Hot hardness.

Recent developments include the use of **whiskers** as reinforcing fibers (Section 9.2.1) in composite cutting-tool materials. Examples of *whisker-reinforced* materials include silicon-nitride base tools reinforced with silicon-carbide (SiC) whiskers, and aluminum-oxide-based tools reinforced with silicon-carbide whiskers, sometimes with the addition of *zirconium oxide* (ZrO_2). However, the high reactivity of silicon carbide with ferrous metals makes SiC-reinforced tools unsuitable for machining irons and steels.

Progress in **nanomaterials** (Section 6.15) has lead to the development of cutting tools made of very-fine-grained (**micrograin**) carbides (tungsten carbide, titanium carbide and tantalum carbide). Compared to traditional carbides, these tool materials are stronger, harder, and more wear resistant, improving productivity. In one application, microdrills with diameters on the order of 100 μm (0.004 in.) are being made from these materials and used in microelectronic circuits fabrication (Chapter 34).

21.12 CUTTING-TOOL RECONDITIONING

When tools, particularly high-speed steels, become worn, they are **reconditioned** (resharpened) for further use. They are usually ground on tool and cutter grinders in toolrooms having special fixtures (Section 25.6.5). The reconditioning may be carried out either by hand, which requires considerable operator skill, or on computer-controlled tool and cutter grinders. Other methods (as described in Chapter 26) may also be used to recondition tools and cutters. Reconditioning may also involve recoating used tools with titanium nitride.

Consistency and precision are important in reconditioning. Resharpened tools should be inspected for their shape and surface finish. Decisions about whether tools should be reconditioned or recycled depend on the relative costs involved. Skilled labor is costly, as are computer-controlled grinders, so an additional consideration is the recycling of tool materials and the costs involved in doing so (Table 21.6), since many contain expensive materials of strategic importance, such as tungsten and cobalt.

21.13 CUTTING FLUIDS

Also called *lubricants* and *coolants*, *cutting fluids* are used extensively in machining as well as abrasive machining processes (Chapter 25) to achieve the following results:

• Reduce friction and wear, thus improving tool life and surface finish.

• Reduce forces and energy consumption.

TABLE 21.6   Approximate Cost of Selected Cutting Tools

Tool	Size (in.)	Cost ($)
High-speed steel tool bits	$\frac{1}{4}$ sq. $\times$ $2\frac{1}{2}$ long	1–2
	$\frac{1}{2}$ sq. $\times$ 4	3–7
Carbide-tipped (brazed) tools for turning	$\frac{1}{4}$ sq.	2
	$\frac{3}{4}$ sq.	4
Carbide inserts, square $\frac{3}{16}''$ thick		
Plain	$\frac{1}{2}$ inscribed circle	5–9
Coated		6–10
Ceramic inserts, square	$\frac{1}{2}$ inscribed circle	8–12
Cubic boron nitride inserts, square	$\frac{1}{2}$ inscribed circle	60–90
Diamond-coated inserts	$\frac{1}{2}$ inscribed circle	50–60
Diamond-tipped inserts (polycrystalline)	$\frac{1}{2}$ inscribed circle	90–100

- Cool the cutting zone, thus reducing workpiece temperature and thermal distortion.
- Wash away the chips.
- Protect the machined surfaces from environmental corrosion.

A cutting fluid basically may be a **coolant** or a **lubricant**. Its effectiveness in cutting operations depends on a number of factors, such as the method of application, temperature, cutting speed, and type of machining operation. As shown in Section 20.6, temperature increases as cutting speed increases. Therefore, cooling of the cutting zone is of major importance at high cutting speeds.

Water is an excellent coolant; however, it causes rusting of workpieces and machine components and is a poor lubricant. On the other hand, if the speed is low, such as in broaching or tapping, lubrication (not cooling) is the important factor. By reducing the tendency for built-up edge formation, lubrication improves the workpiece surface finish.

The relative severity of various machining operations is defined as the magnitude of temperatures and forces encountered, the tendency for built-up edge formation, and the ease with which chips are disposed of from the cutting zone. As severity increases (such as in broaching, tapping, and threading), so does the need for cutting-fluid effectiveness.

There are situations, however, in which the use of cutting fluids can be detrimental. In interrupted cutting operations, such as milling, the cooling action of the cutting fluid increases the extent of cycles of alternate heating and cooling (*thermal cycling*) to which the cutter teeth are subjected. This condition can lead to thermal cracks (thermal fatigue or thermal shock). Cutting fluids may also cause the chip to become curlier, concentrating the stresses closer to the tool tip. These stresses, in turn, concentrate the heat closer to the tool tip, which reduces tool life.

21.13.1 Cutting-Fluid Action

Although the basic mechanisms of lubrication in metalworking operations are described in greater detail in Section 32.9, we briefly describe here the mechanisms by which cutting fluids influence machining operations. In view of the high contact pressures and high rate of relative sliding at the tool–chip interface, how does a cutting fluid penetrate this interface to influence the cutting process?

It appears that the fluid is drawn into the tool–chip interface by the **capillary action** of the interlocking network of surface asperities. (See also Section 32.2.) Studies have shown that the cutting fluid gains access to the interface by seeping from the sides of the chip.

Because of the small size of this capillary network, the cutting fluid should therefore have a small molecular size and possess proper wetting (surface tension) characteristics.

Example: Effect of Cutting Fluids on Machining

A machining operation is being carried out with a cutting fluid that is an effective lubricant. Explain the changes in the mechanics of the cutting operation and total energy consumption if the fluid is shut off.

Solution: Since the cutting fluid is a good lubricant, the friction at the tool–chip interface will increase when the fluid is shut off. The following chain of events takes place:

a. Fluid is shut off.
b. Friction at the tool–chip interface increases.
c. The shear angle decreases (Eq. 20.3).
d. The shear strain increases (Eq. 20.2).
e. The chip becomes thicker.
f. A built-up edge is likely to form.

The following events occur as a consequence of the preceding phenomena:

a. The shear energy in the primary zone increases (Section 20.5.3).
b. The friction energy in the secondary zone increases.
c. The total energy increases.
d. The temperature in the cutting zone increases, causing greater tool wear.
e. Surface finish is likely to deteriorate.
f. Dimensional tolerances may be difficult to maintain because of the increased temperature and expansion of the workpiece during machining.

21.13.2 Types of Cutting Fluids

Four general types of cutting fluids are commonly used in machining operations:

a. **Oils**.
b. **Emulsions**.
c. **Semisynthetics**.
d. **Synthetics**.

The characteristics of these fluids are described in Section 32.10, and cutting fluid recommendations for specific machining operations are given in Chapters 22, 23, and 25.

21.13.3 Methods of Application

There are three basic methods of cutting fluid application:

a. **Flood cooling** (Fig. 21.11). This is the most common method. Flow rates range from 10 L/min (3 gal/min) for single-point tools to 225 L/min (60 gal/min) per cutter for multiple-tooth cutters (for example, in milling). In operations such as gun drilling (Section 22.7.1) and end milling (Section 23.2.3), fluid pressures of 700 kPa–14,000 kPa (100 psi–2000 psi) are used to wash away the chips.

b. **Mist cooling.** Mist cooling supplies fluid to inaccessible areas and provides better visibility of the workpiece being machined. It is particularly effective with water-

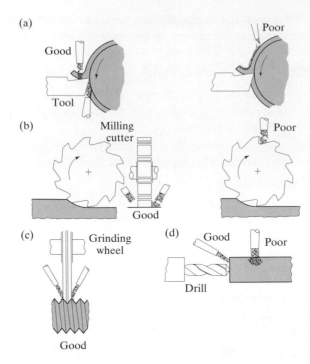

FIGURE 21.11   Schematic illustration of proper methods of applying cutting fluids in various machining operations: (a) turning, (b) milling, (c) thread grinding, and (d) drilling.

based fluids and in grinding operations, at air pressures of 70 kPa–600 kPa (10 psi–80 psi). Mist cooling requires venting (to prevent the inhalation of fluid particles by the machine operator and others nearby) and has limited cooling capacity,

c. **High-pressure systems.** With the increasing speed and power of modern, computer-controlled machine tools, heat generation in machining operations has become a significant factor. Recent developments include the use of high-pressure refrigerated coolant systems to improve the rate of heat removal from the cutting zone. High pressures are also used in delivering the cutting fluid to the cutting zone by specially designed nozzles that aim a powerful jet of fluid to the zone.

   The pressures employed, which are usually in the range of 5.5 MPa–35 MPa (800 psi–5000 psi), act as a chip breaker in situations where the chips produced would otherwise be long and continuous, interfering with the cutting operation. In order to avoid damage to the workpiece surface by impact from particles in the high-pressure jet, contaminant size in the coolant should not exceed 20 μm (800 μin.); proper and continuous filtering of the fluid is essential.

21.13.4 Effects of Cutting Fluids

The selection of a cutting fluid should also include considerations such as its potential effects on workpiece material and machine tools, biological factors, and environmental factors.

Effects on Workpiece Material.   When selecting a cutting fluid, one should consider whether the machined component will be subjected to environmental attack and high service stresses, possibly leading to stress-corrosion cracking. This consideration is particularly important for cutting fluids with sulfur and chlorine additives. For example, fluids containing chlorine should not be used when machining titanium. Another consideration is the possible staining of the workpiece by cutting fluids, especially copper and aluminum.

Machined parts should be cleaned and washed in order to remove any cutting-fluid residue (Section 33.16). This operation can be significant in time and cost; consequently, the trend is to use low-viscosity, water-based fluids for ease of cleaning and filtering.

Effects on Machine Tools.   Just as a cutting fluid may adversely affect the workpiece material, it can similarly affect the machine tool and its components, such as slideways and bearings. The choice of fluid must, therefore, include consideration of its compatibility with the various metallic and nonmetallic materials involved, including oils and grease that may be used as lubricants.

Biological and Environmental Effects.   Because the machine-tool operator is usually in close proximity to cutting fluids, the effects of operator contact with fluids should be of primary concern. Fumes, smoke, and odors from cutting fluids can cause severe skin reactions and respiratory problems. Considerable progress has been made in ensuring the safe use of cutting fluids in manufacturing plants.

Additionally, the effect on the environment, particularly with regard to air and water contamination, is very important. This has led to a trend toward **dry machining**, which may have its own advantages and limitations.

Cutting fluids, as well as other metalworking fluids used in manufacturing operations, may undergo chemical changes as they are used over time. These changes may be due to environmental effects or to contamination from various sources, including chips and metal fines produced during machining and tramp oil (from hydraulic leaks, way oils on machines, and lubricating systems for machine tools).

These changes involve the growth of microbes (bacteria, molds, and yeast), particularly in the presence of water, adversely affecting the properties and characteristics of the fluids.

Clarification, Recycling, and Disposal.   Several techniques, such as settling, skimming, centrifuging, and filtering, are available for clarifying used cutting fluids. Recycling involves treatment of the fluids with various additives, agents, biocides, and deodorizers, as well as water treatment (for water-based fluids). Disposal practices must comply with federal, state, and local laws and regulations, as described in Section 37.4.

SUMMARY

- A wide variety of cutting-tool materials have been developed over the past century, the most commonly used ones being high-speed steels, carbides, ceramics, and cubic boron nitride. Tool materials have a broad range of mechanical and physical properties, such as hot hardness, toughness, chemical stability and inertness, and resistance to chipping and wear.
- Various tool coatings have been developed, with major improvements in tool life, surface finish, and the economics of machining operations. Common coating materials are titanium nitride, titanium carbide, titanium carbonitride, and aluminum oxide; diamond coatings are also gaining acceptance. The trend is toward multiphase coatings for even better performance.

- The selection of appropriate tool materials depends not only on the material to be machined, but also on process parameters and the characteristics of the machine tool.
- Cutting fluids are important in machining operations and usually reduce friction, forces, and power requirements, thus improving tool life. Generally, slower cutting operations and those with high tool pressures require a fluid with good lubricating characteristics, whereas in high-speed operations, where temperature rise can be significant, fluids with cooling capacity are preferred.
- The selection of cutting fluids should include considerations of their possible adverse effects on the machined parts, machine tools, personnel, and the environment.

TRENDS

- Continual progress is being made in the development of new cutting-tool materials with improved properties, particularly for machining high-strength, high-temperature materials and composites containing abrasive fibers and particles.
- New tool materials include whisker-reinforced composite ceramics. Laser treatment of tools is being studied as a way to improve their hardness and wear resistance.
- The purity and porosity of tool materials, particularly in ceramics, is an important area of study aimed at improving toughness and reliability of performance.
- Efforts are continuing to standardize cutting-tool materials, testing for properties, and their applications.
- Many coatings, applied either in single or multiple layers, are becoming widely available to improve tool performance under various conditions, particularly at high cutting speeds. Both the level of adherence of coatings to the substrate and cutting-edge strength are being improved.
- Cutting fluids are continually being developed for improved performance and with improved biological and ecological characteristics.
- Dry machining is a new trend because of increased concern about environmental issues and strict government regulations regarding the use of cutting fluids.

KEY TERMS

Alumina-based ceramics
Carbides
Cast-cobalt alloys
Ceramics
Cermets
Chemical stability
Chip breaker
Coated tools
Coolants
Cubic boron nitride
Cutting fluids
Diamond coatings
Dry machining

Finishing cuts
Flood cooling
High-speed steels
Inserts
Lubricants
Micrograin carbides
Mist cooling
Multiphase coatings
Nanocrystalline
Polycrystalline cubic boron nitride
Polycrystalline diamond
Reconditioning of tools
Roughing cuts

Sialon
Silicon–nitride-based ceramics
Stellite
Titanium carbide
Titanium nitride
Tungsten carbide
Tool reconditioning
Toughness
Tungsten carbide
Uncoated carbides
Wear resistance
Whisker-reinforced tools

BIBLIOGRAPHY

ASM Handbook, Vol. 16: *Machining*. ASM International, 1989.

ASM Handbook, Vol. 3: *Properties and Selection: Stainless Steels, Tool Materials and Special Purpose Metals.* ASM International, 1980.

ASM Specialty Handbook: Tool Materials. ASM International, 1995.

Boothroyd, G., and W.A. Knight, *Fundamentals of Machining and Machine Tools*, (2d ed.). Marcel Dekker, 1989.

Kalpakjian, S. (ed.), *Tool and Die Failures: Source Book.* ASM International, 1982.

Komanduri, R., *Tool Materials*, in *Kirk-Othmer Encyclopedia of Chemical Technology*, (4th ed.). Vol. 24, 1997.

Machinery's Handbook. Industrial Press, revised periodically.

Machining Data Handbook, (3d ed.). 2 vols. Machinability Data Center, 1980.

Nachtman, E.S., and S. Kalpakjian, *Lubricants and Lubrication in Metalworking Operations.* Marcel Dekker, 1985.

Roberts, G.A., G. Krauss, and R. Kennedy, *Tool Steels*, (5th ed.). ASM International, 1997.

Schey, J.A., *Tribology in Metalworking–Friction: Wear and Lubrication.* ASM International, 1983.

Sluhan, C. (ed.), *Cutting and Grinding Fluids: Selection and Application.* Society of Manufacturing Engineers, 1992.

Stephenson, D.A., and J.S. Agapiou, *Metal Cutting Theory and Practice.* Marcel Dekker, 1996.

Trent, E.M., and P.K. Wright, *Metal Cutting*, (4th ed.). Butterworth Heinemann, 1999.

Tool and Manufacturing Engineers Handbook, (4th ed.). Vol. 1: *Machining*. Society of Manufacturing Engineers, 1983.

REVIEW QUESTIONS

21.1 What are the major properties required of cutting-tool materials?

21.2 What differences in composition and properties are there between carbon-steel and high-speed steel tools?

21.3 List the major elements in cast-cobalt tools.

21.4 What is the composition of a typical carbide tool?

21.5 Why were cutting-tool inserts developed?

21.6 Why are tools coated? What are the common coating materials?

21.7 Explain the applications and limitations of ceramic tools.

21.8 What is the composition of sialon?

21.9 How are cutting tools reconditioned?

21.10 List the various functions of cutting fluids.

21.11 Explain how cutting fluids penetrate the cutting zone.

21.12 List the methods by which cutting fluids are applied in machining operations.

21.13 What is a multiphase coating? What are its advantages?

21.14 Why are carbides also referred to as cemented carbides?

21.15 Describe the advantages and limitations of diamond tools.

21.16 What is the hardest known material, next to diamond?

21.17 What is a cermet? What are its advantages?

21.18 Explain the difference between M-series and T-series high- speed steels.

QUALITATIVE PROBLEMS

21.19 Explain why so many different types of cutting-tool materials have been developed.

21.20 Which tool materials would be suitable for interrupted cutting operations? Why?

21.21 Describe the reasons for coating cutting tools with multiple layers of different materials.

21.22 Make a list of the alloying elements used in high-speed steels. Explain why they are so effective in cutting tools. (See Chapter 5.)

21.23 What are the purposes of chamfers on inserts?

21.24 What is the economic impact of the trend shown in Fig. 21.6?

21.25 Why does temperature have such an important effect on the life of cutting tools?

21.26 Ceramic and cermet cutting tools have certain advantages over carbide tools. Why, then, are they not completely replacing carbide tools?

21.27 Can cutting fluids have any adverse effects? If so, what are they?

21.28 Describe the trends you observe in Table 21.2.

21.29 Why are chemical stability and inertness (non-reactivity) important in cutting tools?

21.30 How would you go about measuring the effectiveness of cutting fluids?

21.31 Titanium–nitride coatings on tools reduce the coefficient of friction at the tool–chip interface. What is the significance of this?

21.32 Describe the necessary conditions for optimal utilization of the capabilities of diamond and cubic boron nitride cutting tools.

21.33 List the advantages of coating high-speed steel tools.

21.34 Describe the limits of application when comparing tungsten-carbide and titanium-carbide cutting tools.

21.35 Negative rake angles are generally preferred for ceramic, diamond, and cubic boron nitride tools. Why?

21.36 Do you think that there is a relationship between the cost of a cutting tool and its hot hardness? Explain.

21.37 In Section 21.2, it is stated that carbon and medium-alloy steel tools are used for low-speed cutting operations. Make a survey of the technical literature and give some typical values for maximum cutting speeds for these tool materials.

21.38 Survey the technical literature and give some typical values of cutting speeds for high-speed-steel tools and for a variety of workpiece materials.

21.39 In Table 21.1, the last two properties listed can be important to the life of the cutting tool. Why?

21.40 It has been stated that titanium nitride coatings allow cutting speeds and feeds to be higher than those for uncoated tools. Survey the technical literature and prepare a table showing the percentage increase of speeds and feeds that would be made possible by coating the tools.

21.41 You will note, in Fig. 21.1, that all tool materials have a wide range of hardness for a particular temperature, especially carbides. Why is this so?

21.42 List and explain the considerations involved in the decision to recondition, recycle, or discard a cutting tool.

21.43 Referring to Table 21.1, state which tool materials would be suitable for interrupted cutting operations. Explain.

21.44 Diamond films are typically deposited on a substrate. What kind of substrates are suitable for this type of coating?

21.45 Which of the properties listed in Table 21.1 is, in your opinion, the least important in machining? Explain.

21.46 If a drill bit is intended for woodworking applications, what material is it most likely to be made from? (*Hint*: the temperatures rarely rise to 400 °C in woodworking.) Is there any reason why such a drill bit cannot be used to drill a few holes in a metal?

21.47 Emulsion cutting fluids are typically made up of 95% water and 5% soluble oil and chemical additives. Why is the ratio so unbalanced? Is the oil needed at all?

21.48 What are the consequences of a coating having a different coefficient of thermal expansion than a substrate, if the application is a cutting tool?

21.49 Discuss the relative advantages and limitations of dry machining, a new trend in response to environmental concerns. Consider all relevant technical and economic aspects.

QUANTITATIVE PROBLEMS

21.50 Make a recommendation for the ANSI grade of a carbide tool for a finishing pass in turning a steel shaft at a 0.050-in. depth of cut.

21.51 Repeat Problem 21.40, but for a turning operation on high-strength aluminum in which the same tool is to be used for both roughing and finishing passes.

SYNTHESIS AND DESIGN

21.52 Survey the technical literature and describe the trends in new cutting-tool materials development. Which of these is becoming available to industry?

21.53 Describe in detail your thoughts regarding the technical and economic factors involved in tool material selection.

21.54 One of the principal concerns with coolants is degradation due to biological attack by bacteria. To prolong life, chemical biocides are often added, but these biocides greatly complicate the disposal of coolants. Conduct a literature search regarding the latest developments in the use of environmentally benign biocides in cutting fluids.

21.55 Contact several different suppliers of cutting tools in your area, construct a table similar to Table 21.6, and make comparisons to the approximate costs given.

21.56 As you can see, there are several types of cutting-tool materials available today for machining operations. Yet, there is much research and development that is being carried out on these materials. Make a list of the reasons why you think such studies are being conducted; comment on each with a specific application or example.

21.57 Assume that you are in charge of a laboratory for developing new or improved cutting fluids. On the basis of the discussions presented in this and the previous chapter, suggest a list of topics for your staff to investigate. Explain why you chose those topics.

22

Machining Processes Used to Produce Round Shapes

22.1   INTRODUCTION

This chapter describes machining processes with the capability of producing parts that are basically round in shape. Typical products made include parts as small as miniature screws for eyeglass-frame hinges and as large as rolls for rolling mills, cylinders, gun barrels, and turbine shafts for hydroelectric power plants. These processes are usually performed by turning the workpiece on a lathe.

Turning means that the part is rotating while it is being machined. The starting material is usually a workpiece that has been made by other processes, such as casting, forging, extrusion, or drawing, as described in Parts II and III. Turning processes, which are outlined in Fig. 22.1 and Table 22.1, are very versatile. The following processes are capable of producing a wide variety of shapes:

- **Turning**, to produce straight, conical, curved, or grooved workpieces (Figs. 22.1a–d), such as shafts, spindles, and pins.
- **Facing**, to produce a flat surface at the end of the part (Fig. 22.1e), which is useful for parts that are attached to other components, or face grooving to produce grooves for O-ring seats (Fig. 22.1f).

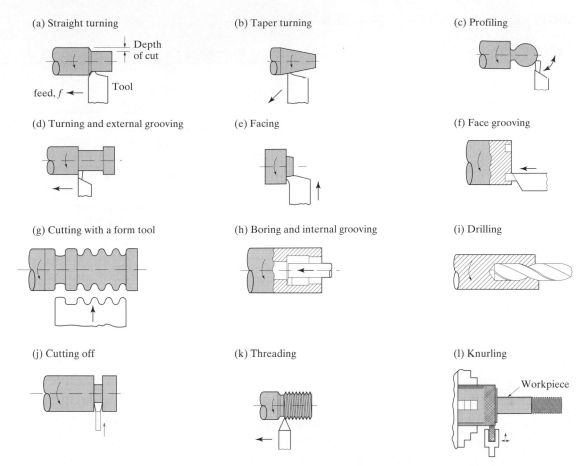

(a) Straight turning

Depth of cut

feed, f — Tool

(b) Taper turning

(c) Profiling

(d) Turning and external grooving

(e) Facing

(f) Face grooving

(g) Cutting with a form tool

(h) Boring and internal grooving

(i) Drilling

(j) Cutting off

(k) Threading

(l) Knurling

Workpiece

FIGURE 22.1 Various cutting operations that can be performed on a lathe. Note that all parts have circular symmetry.

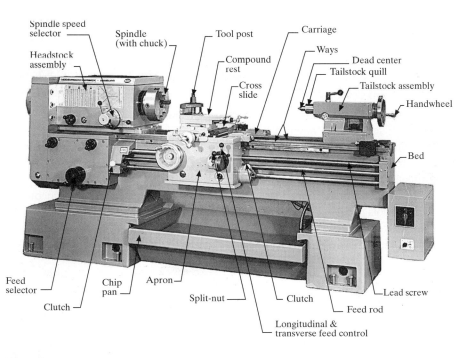

Spindle speed selector

Headstock assembly

Spindle (with chuck)

Tool post

Compound rest

Cross slide

Carriage

Ways

Dead center

Tailstock quill

Tailstock assembly

Handwheel

Bed

Feed selector

Clutch

Chip pan

Apron

Split-nut

Clutch

Feed rod

Lead screw

Longitudinal & transverse feed control

FIGURE 22.2
Components of a lathe.
Source: Courtesy of Heidenreich & Harbeck

TABLE 22.1   General Characteristics of Machining Processes Described in Chapters 22 and 23

Process	Characteristics	Commercial tolerances (±mm)
Turning	Turning and facing operations on all types of materials; uses single-point or form tools; requires skilled labor; low production rate, but medium to high with turret lathes and automatic machines, requiring less-skilled labor.	Fine: 0.05–0.13 Rough: 0.13 Skiving: 0.025–0.05
Boring	Internal surfaces or profiles, with characteristics similar to turning; stiffness of boring bar important to avoid chatter.	0.025
Drilling	Round holes of various sizes and depths; requires boring and reaming for improved accuracy; high production rate; labor skill required depends on hole location and accuracy specified.	0.075
Milling	Variety of shapes involving contours, flat surfaces, and slots; wide variety of tooling; versatile; low to medium production rate; requires skilled labor.	0.13–0.25
Planing	Flat surfaces and straight contour profiles on large surfaces; suitable for low-quantity production; labor skill required depends on part shape.	0.08–0.13
Shaping	Flat surfaces and straight contour profiles on relatively small workpieces; suitable for low-quantity production; labor skill required depends on part shape.	0.05–0.13
Broaching	External and internal flat surfaces, slots, and contours with good surface finish; costly tooling; high production rate; labor skill required depends on part shape.	0.025–0.15
Sawing	Straight and contour cuts on flat or structural shapes; not suitable for hard materials unless saw has carbide teeth or is coated with diamond; low production rate; requires only low labor skill.	0.8

- The use of **form tools** (Fig. 22.1g) to produce various shapes for functional purposes or for appearance.
- **Boring**, to enlarge a hole or cylindrical cavity made by a previous process or to produce circular internal grooves (Fig. 22.1h).
- **Drilling**, to produce a hole (Fig. 22.1i), which may be followed by boring to improve its accuracy and surface finish.
- **Parting**, also called **cutting off**, to cut a piece from the end of a part, as is done in the production of slugs or blanks for additional processing into discrete products (Fig. 22.1j).
- **Threading**, to produce external or internal threads (Fig. 22.1k).
- **Knurling**, to produce a regularly shaped roughness on cylindrical surfaces, as in making knobs (Fig. 22.1(l)).

These cutting operations are typically performed on a **lathe** (Fig. 22.2), which is now available in a variety of designs and computer-controlled features (as discussed in Section 22.3 and Chapter 24). Turning may be performed at various rotational speeds of the workpiece, depths of cut, d, and feeds, f (Fig. 22.3), depending on the workpiece and tool materials, the surface finish and dimensional accuracy required, and the characteristics of the machine tool.

This chapter describes turning process parameters, cutting tools, process capabilities, and the machine tools used to produce a variety of parts with round shapes. Because of their economic impact, high-speed machining and ultraprecision machining processes are also described. Finally, design considerations to improve productivity for each group of processes are also given.

22.2 TURNING PARAMETERS

The majority of turning operations involve the use of simple single-point cutting tools. The geometry of a typical right-hand cutting tool for turning is shown in Figs. 20.10 and 22.4. Such tools are described by a standardized nomenclature. Each group of tool and work-

FIGURE 22.3   (a) Schematic illustration of a turning operation showing depth of cut, d, and feed, f. Cutting speed is the surface speed of the workpiece at the tool tip. (b) Forces acting on a cutting tool in turning. F_c is the cutting force, F_t is the thrust or feed force (in the direction of feed), and F_r is the radial force that tends to push the tool away from the workpiece being machined. Compare this figure with Fig. 20.11 for a two-dimensional cutting operation.

(a)   (b)

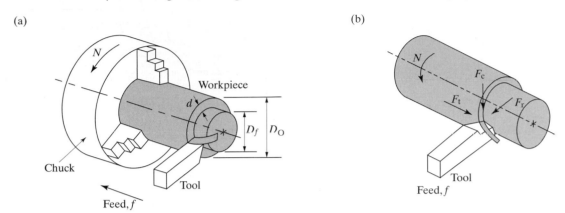

piece materials has an optimum set of tool angles, which have been developed largely through experience (Table 22.2).

In Chapter 20, we described the important process parameters that have a direct influence on machining processes and the importance of controlling these parameters for optimized productivity. This section outlines turning process parameters such as tool geometry and material removal rate, and gives data for recommended cutting practices, including cutting-tool materials, depth of cut, feed, cutting speed, and use of cutting fluids.

Tool Geometry.   The various angles in a single-point cutting tool have important functions in machining operations. **Rake angles** are important in controlling both the direction of chip flow and the strength of the tool tip. As described in Chapter 20, positive rake angles improve the cutting operation by reducing forces and temperatures. However, positive angles result in a small included angle of the tool tip (as in Fig. 20.3). Depending on the toughness of the tool material, this may cause premature tool chipping and failure.

The **side rake angle** is more important than the **back rake angle**, although the latter usually controls the direction of chip flow. **Relief angles** control interference and rubbing at the tool–workpiece interface. If the relief angle is too large, the tool tip may chip off; if it is too small, flank wear may be excessive. **Cutting-edge angles** affect chip formation, tool strength, and cutting forces to various degrees.

The **nose radius** affects surface finish and tool-tip strength. The smaller the nose radius (sharp tool), the rougher the surface finish of the workpiece and the lower the strength of the tool. However, large nose radii can lead to tool chatter. (See Section 24.4.)

Material Removal Rate.   The *material removal rate* (MRR) is the volume of material removed per unit time (such as mm^3/min or $in.^3/min$). Referring to Figs. 20.2 and 22.3a, note that for each revolution of the workpiece, we remove a ring-shaped layer of material with a cross-sectional area that equals the product of the distance the tool travels in one revolution (feed, f) and the depth of cut, d. The volume of this ring is the product of the cross-sectional area $(f)(d)$ and the average circumference of the ring, πD_{avg}, where

$$D_{avg} = \frac{(D_o + D_f)}{2}.$$

(a)

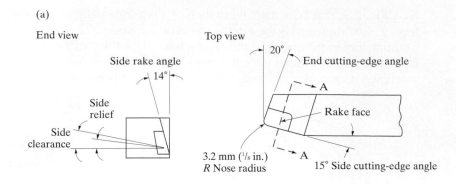

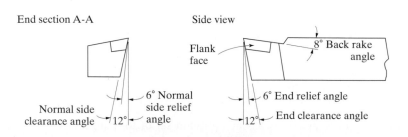

Tool Signature	Dimensions	Abbreviation
8	Back rake angle	BR
14	Side rake angle	SR
6	End relief angle	ER
12	End clearance angle	. . .
6	Side relief angle	SRF
12	Side clearance angle	. . .
20	End cutting-edge angle	ECEA
15	Side cutting-edge angle	SCEA
$^{1}/_{8}$	Nose radius	NR

(b)

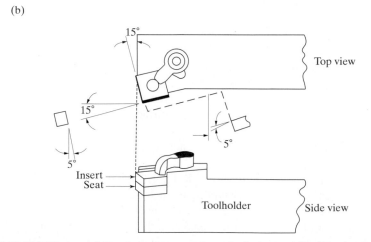

FIGURE 22.4   (a) Designations and symbols for a right-hand cutting tool; solid high-speed-steel tools have a similar designation. Right-hand means that the tool travels from right to left as shown in Fig. 22.1a. (b) Square insert in a right-hand toolholder for a turning operation. A wide variety of toolholders are available for holding inserts at various angles. *Source*: Kennametal Inc.

TABLE 22.2   General Recommendations for Turning Tool Angles

Material	High-speed steel					Carbide (inserts)				
	Back rake	Side rake	End relief	Side relief	Side and end cutting edge	Back rake	Side rake	End relief	Side relief	Side and end cutting edge
Aluminum and magnesium alloys	20	15	12	10	5	0	5	5	5	15
Copper alloys	5	10	8	8	5	0	5	5	5	15
Steels	10	12	5	5	15	−5	−5	5	5	15
Stainless steels	5	8–10	5	5	15	−5–0	−5–5	5	5	15
High-temperature alloys	0	10	5	5	15	5	0	5	5	45
Refractory alloys	0	20	5	5	5	0	0	5	5	15
Titanium alloys	0	5	5	5	15	−5	−5	5	5	5
Cast irons	5	10	5	5	15	−5	−5	5	5	15
Thermoplastics	0	0	20–30	15–20	10	0	0	20–30	15–20	10
Thermosets	0	0	20–30	15–20	10	0	15	5	5	15

For light cuts on large-diameter workpieces, the average diameter may be replaced by D_o.

The rotational speed of the workpiece is N, and the material removal rate per revolution is $(\pi)(D_{avg})(d)(f)$. Since we have N revolutions per minute, the removal rate is

$$\text{MRR} = (\pi)(D_{avg})(d)(f)(N). \tag{22.1}$$

The dimensional accuracy of this equation can be checked by substituting dimensions into the right-hand side. For instance, $(\text{mm})(\text{mm})(\text{mm/rev})(\text{rev/min}) = \text{mm}^3/\text{min}$, which indicates volume rate of removal. Similarly, the cutting time, t, for a workpiece of length l can be calculated by noting that the tool travels at a feed rate of $fN = (\text{mm/rev})(\text{rev/min}) = \text{mm/min}$. Since the distance traveled is l mm, the cutting time is

$$t = \frac{l}{fN}. \tag{22.2}$$

The cutting time does not include the time required for *tool approach* and *retraction*. Because the time spent in noncutting cycles of a machining operation is unproductive and adversely affects the overall economics, the time involved in approaching and retracting tools to and from the workpiece is an important consideration. Machine tools are now being designed and built to minimize this time. One method of accomplishing this is to rapidly traverse the tools during noncutting cycles followed by a slower movement as the tool engages the workpiece.

The foregoing equations and the terminology used are summarized in Table 22.3.

Forces in Turning.   The three forces acting on a cutting tool are shown in Fig. 22.3b. These forces are important in the design of machine tools, as well as in the deflection of tools and workpieces for precision machining operations.

The **cutting force**, F_c, acts downward on the tool tip (and therefore tends to deflect the tool downward). This is the force that supplies the energy required for the cutting operation. It can be calculated, using Table 20.1, from the energy per unit volume described in Section 20.5.

The **thrust force**, F_t, acts in the longitudinal direction. This force is also called the **feed force** because it is in the feed direction. The **radial force**, F_r, acts in the radial direction and tends to push the tool away from the workpiece.

TABLE 22.3   Summary of Turning Parameters and Formulas

N = Rotational speed of the workpiece, rpm

f = Feed, mm/rev or in./rev

v = Feed rate, or linear speed of the tool along workpiece length, mm/min or in./min

   = fN

V = Surface speed of workpiece, m/min or ft/min

   = $\pi D_o N$ (for maximum speed)

   = $\pi D_{\text{avg}} N$ (for average speed)

l = Length of cut, mm or in.

D_o = Original diameter of workpiece, mm or in.

D_f = Final diameter of workpiece, mm or in.

D_{avg} = Average diameter of workpiece, mm or in.

   = $(D_o + D_f)/2$

d = Depth of cut, mm or in.

   = $(D_o + D_f)/2$

t = Cutting time, s or min

   = l/fN

MRR = mm^3/min or $\text{in.}^3/\text{min}$

   = $\pi D_{\text{avg}} d\, fN$

Torque = $\text{N} \cdot \text{m}$ or $\text{lb} \cdot \text{ft}$

   = $(F_c)(D_{\text{avg}}/2)$

Power = kW or hp

   = (Torque) (ω), where $\omega = 2\pi N$ radians/min

Note: The units given are those that are commonly used; however, appropriate units must be used and checked in the formulas.

Forces F_t and F_r are difficult to calculate because of the many factors involved in the cutting process, so they are usually determined experimentally.

Roughing and Finishing Cuts.   In machining, the usual procedure is to (a) perform one or more *roughing cuts* at high feed rates and large depths of cut (and, therefore, high metal removal rates but little consideration of dimensional tolerance and surface roughness), and (b) follow it with a *finishing cut* at a lower feed and depth of cut for a good surface finish.

Tool Materials, Feeds, and Cutting Speeds.   The general characteristics of cutting-tool materials have been described in Chapter 21. A broad range of applicable cutting speeds and feeds for these tool materials is given in Fig. 22.5 as a general guideline in turning operations. Specific recommendations with regard to turning process parameters for various workpiece materials and cutting tools are given in Table 22.4.

Cutting Fluids.   Although many metallic and nonmetallic materials can be machined without a cutting fluid (*dry machining*), in many cases the application of a cutting fluid can improve the operation significantly. (See also Section 21.13.) General recommendations for cutting fluids appropriate to various workpiece materials are given in Table 22.5.

Example: Material Removal Rate and Cutting Force in Turning

A 6-in.-long, $\frac{1}{2}$-in.-diameter 304 stainless steel rod is being reduced in diameter to 0.480 in. by turning on a lathe. The spindle rotates at $N = 400$ rpm, and the tool is traveling at an axial speed of 8 in./min. Calculate the cutting speed, material removal rate, cutting time, power dissipated, and cutting force.

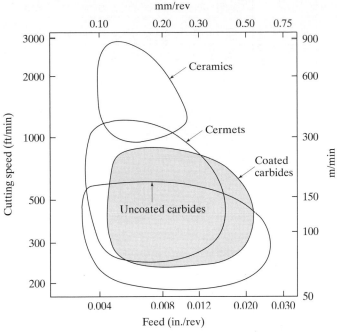

FIGURE 22.5   The range of applicable cutting speeds and feeds for a variety of tool materials. *Source*: Valenite.

Solution: The cutting speed is the tangential speed of the workpiece. The maximum cutting speed is at the outer diameter, D_o, and is obtained from the expression

$$V = \pi D_o N.$$

Thus,

$$V = (\pi)(0.500)(400) = 628 \text{ in./min} = 52 \text{ ft/min}.$$

The cutting speed at the machined diameter is

$$V = (\pi)(0.480)(400) = 603 \text{ in./min} = 50 \text{ ft/min}.$$

From the information given, we note that the depth of cut is

$$d = \frac{(0.500 - 0.480)}{2} = 0.010 \text{ in.}$$

and the feed is

$$f = \frac{8}{400} = 0.02 \text{ in./rev.}$$

According to Eq. (22.1), the material removal rate is then

$$\text{MRR} = (\pi)(0.490)(0.010)(0.02)(400) = 0.123 \text{ in.}^3/\text{min.}$$

The actual time to cut, according to Eq. (22.2), is

$$t = \frac{6}{(0.02)(400)} = 0.75 \text{ min.}$$ *(continued)*

TABLE 22.4   General Recommendations for Turning Operations

Workpiece material	Cutting tool	General-purpose starting conditions			Range for roughing and finishing		
		Depth of cut mm (in.)	Feed mm/rev (in./rev)	Cutting speed m/min (ft/min)	Depth of cut mm (in.)	Feed mm/rev (in./rev)	Cutting speed m/min (ft/min)
Low-C and free-machining steels	Uncoated carbide	1.5–6.3 (0.06–0.25)	0.35 (0.014)	90 (300)	0.5–7.6 (0.02–0.30)	0.15–1.1 (0.006–0.045)	60–135 (200–450)
	Ceramic-coated carbide	"	"	245–275 (800–900)	"	"	120–425 (400–1400)
	Triple-coated carbide	"	"	185–200 (600–650)	"	"	90–245 (300–800)
	TiN-coated carbide	"	"	105–150 (350–500)	"	"	60–230 (200–750)
	Al_2O_3 ceramic	"	0.25 (0.010)	395–440 (1300–1450)	"	"	365–550 (1200–1800)
	Cermet	"	0.30 (0.012)	215–290 (700–950)	"	"	105–455 (350–1500)
Medium and high-C steels	Uncoated carbide	1.2–4.0 (0.05–0.20)	0.30 (0.012)	75 (250)	2.5–7.6 (0.10–0.30)	0.15–0.75 (0.006–0.03)	45–120 (150–400)
	Ceramic-coated carbide	"	"	185–230 (600–750)	"	"	120–410 (400–1350)
	Triple-coated carbide	"	"	120–150 (400–500)	"	"	75–215 (250–700)
	TiN-coated carbide	"	"	90–200 (300–650)	"	"	45–215 (150–700)
	Al_2O_3 ceramic	"	0.25 (0.010)	335 (1100)	"	"	245–455 (800–1500)
	Cermet	"	0.25 (0.010)	170–245 (550–800)	"	"	105–305 (350–1000)

Work material	Tool material	Depth of cut mm (in.)	Feed mm/rev (in./rev)	Speed m/min (ft/min)	Depth of cut mm (in.)	Feed mm/rev (in./rev)	Speed m/min (ft/min)
Cast iron, gray	Uncoated carbide	1.25–6.3 (0.05–0.25)	0.32 (0.013)	90 (300)	0.4–12.7 (0.015–0.5)	0.1–0.75 (0.004–0.03)	75–185 (250–600)
	Ceramic-coated carbide	"	"	200 (650)	"	"	120–365 (400–1200)
	TiN-coated carbide	"	"	90–135 (300–450)	"	"	60–215 (200–700)
	Al_2O_3 ceramic	"	0.25 (0.010)	455–490 (1500–1600)	"	"	365–855 (1200–2800)
	SiN ceramic	"	0.32 (0.013)	730 (2400)	"	"	200–990 (650–3250)
Stainless steel, austenitic	Triple-coated carbide	1.5–4.4 (0.06–0.175)	0.35 (0.014)	150 (500)	0.5–12.7 (0.02–0.5)	0.08–0.75 (0.003–0.03)	75–230 (250–750)
	TiN-coated carbide	"	"	85–160 (275–525)	"	"	55–200 (175–650)
	Cermet	"	0.30 (0.012)	185–215 (600–700)	"	"	105–290 (350–950)
High-temperature alloys, nickel base	Uncoated carbide	2.5 (0.10)	0.15 (0.006)	25–45 (75–150)	0.25–6.3 (0.01–0.25)	0.1–0.3 (0.004–0.012)	15–30 (50–100)
	Ceramic-coated carbide	"	"	45 (150)	"	"	20–60 (65–200)
	TiN-coated carbide	"	"	30–55 (95–175)	"	"	20–85 (60–275)
	Al_2O_3 ceramic	"	"	260 (850)	"	"	185–395 (600–1300)
	SiN ceramic	"	"	215 (700)	"	"	90–215 (300–700)
	Polycrystalline cBN	"	"	150 (500)	"	"	120–185 (400–600)
Titanium alloys	Uncoated carbide	1.0–3.8 (0.04–0.15)	0.15 (0.006)	35–60 (120–200)	0.25–6.3 (0.01–0.25)	0.1–0.4 (0.004–0.015)	10–75 (30–250)
	TiN-coated carbide	"	"	30–50 (100–200)	"	"	10–100 (30–325)

(continued)

603

TABLE 22.4 (*continued*) General Recommendations for Turning Operations

Workpiece material	Cutting tool	General-purpose starting conditions			Range for roughing and finishing		
		Depth of cut mm (in.)	Feed mm/rev (in./rev)	Cutting speed m/min (ft/min)	Depth of cut mm (in.)	Feed mm/rev (in./rev)	Cutting speed m/min (ft/min)
Aluminum alloys, free machining	Uncoated carbide	1.5–5.0 (0.06–0.20)	0.45 (0.018)	490 (1600)	0.25–8.8 (0.01–0.35)	0.08–0.62 (0.003–0.025)	200–670 (650–2000)
	TiN-coated carbide	"	"	550 (1800)	"	"	60–915 (200–3000)
	Cermet	"	"	490 (1600)	"	"	215–795 (700–2600)
	Polycrystalline diamond	"	"	760 (2500)	"	"	305–3050 (1000–10,000)
high silicon	Polycrystalline diamond	"	"	530 (1700)	"	"	365–915 (1200–3000)
Copper alloys	Uncoated carbide	1.5–5.0 (0.06–0.20)	0.25 (0.010)	260 (850)	0.4–7.51 (0.015–0.3)	0.15–0.75 (0.006–0.03)	105–535 (350–1750)
	Ceramic-coated carbide	"	"	365 (1200)	"	"	215–670 (700–2200)
	Triple-coated carbide	"	"	215 (700)	"	"	90–305 (300–1000)
	TiN-coated carbide	"	"	90–275 (300–900)	"	"	45–455 (150–1500)
	Cermet	"	"	245–425 (800–1400)	"	"	200–610 (650–2000)
	Polycrystalline diamond	"	"	520 (1700)	"	"	275–915 (900–3000)
Tungsten alloys	Uncoated carbide	2.5 (0.10)	0.2 (0.008)	75 (250)	0.25–5.0 (0.01–0.2)	0.12–0.45 (0.005–0.018)	55–120 (175–400)
	TiN-coated carbide	"	"	85 (275)	"	"	60–150 (200–500)
Thermoplastics and thermosets	TiN-coated carbide	1.2 (0.05)	0.12 (0.005)	170 (550)	0.12–5.0 (0.005–0.20)	0.08–0.35 (0.003–0.015)	90–230 (300–750)
	Polycrystalline diamond	"	"	395 (1300)	"	"	150–730 (500–2400)
Composites, graphite reinforced	TiN-coated carbide	1.9 (0.075)	0.2 (0.008)	200 (650)	0.12–6.3 (0.005–0.25)	0.12–1.5 (0.005–0.06)	105–290 (350–950)
	Polycrystalline diamond	"	"	760 (2500)	"	"	550–1310 (1800–4300)

Source: Based on data from Kennametal Inc.

Note: Cutting speeds for high-speed-steel tools are about one-half those for uncoated carbides.

TABLE 22.5   General Recommendations
for Cutting Fluids for Machining

Material	Type of fluid
Aluminum	D, MO, E, MO + FO, CSN
Beryllium	MC, E, CSN
Copper	D, E, CSN, MO + FO
Magnesium	D, MO, MO + FO
Nickel	MC, E, CSN
Refractory	MC, E, EP
Steels (carbon and low alloy)	D, MO, E, CSN, EP
Steels (stainless)	D, MO, E, CSN
Titanium	CSN, EP, MO
Zinc	C, MC, E, CSN
Zirconium	D, E, CSN

Note: CSN, chemicals and synthetics; D, dry; E, emulsion;
EP, extreme pressure; FO, fatty oil; and MO, mineral oil.

We can calculate the power required by referring to Table 20.1 and taking an average value for stainless steel as $4 \text{ w} \cdot \text{s/mm}^3 = 4/2.73 = 1.47 \text{ hp} \cdot \text{min/in.}^3$. Therefore, the power dissipated is

$$\text{Power} = (1.47)(0.123) = 0.181 \text{ hp},$$

and since 1 hp = 396,000 in.-lb/min, the power dissipated is 71,700 in.-lb/min.

The cutting force, F_c, is the tangential force exerted by the tool. Power is the product of torque, T, and rotational speed in radians per unit time; hence,

$$T = \frac{(71,700)}{(400)(2\pi)} = 29 \text{ lb} - \text{in.}$$

Since $T = (F_c)(D_{avg}/2)$, we have

$$F_c = \frac{29}{(0.490/2)} = 118 \text{ lb}.$$

22.3 LATHES AND LATHE OPERATIONS

Lathes are generally considered to be the oldest machine tools. Although woodworking lathes were originally developed during the period 1000–1 B.C., metalworking lathes with lead screws were not built until the late 1700s. The most common lathe (Fig. 22.2) was originally called an **engine lathe** because it was powered with overhead pulleys and belts from nearby engines. Today these lathes are equipped with individual electric motors.

Although simple and versatile, an engine lathe requires a skilled machinist because all controls are manipulated by hand. Consequently, it is inefficient for repetitive operations and for large production runs. The rest of this section will describe the various types of automation that are usually added to improve efficiency.

22.3.1 Lathe Components

Lathes are equipped with a variety of components and accessories. The basic components of a common lathe are described below.

Bed.   The bed supports all major components of the lathe. Beds have a large mass and are rigidly built, usually from gray or nodular cast iron. (See also Section 24.3 on new materials for machine-tool structures.) The top portion of the bed has two **ways**, with various cross-sections, that are hardened and machined for wear resistance and dimensional accuracy during use. (See also Fig. 24.13.)

Carriage.   The carriage, or carriage assembly, slides along the ways and consists of an assembly of the *cross-slide*, *tool post*, and *apron*. The cutting tool is mounted on the *tool post*, usually with a *compound rest* that swivels for tool positioning and adjustment. The *cross-slide* moves radially in and out, controlling the radial position of the cutting tool in operations such as facing (Fig. 22.1e). The *apron* is equipped with mechanisms for both manual and mechanized movement of the carriage and the cross-slide by means of the *lead screw.*

Headstock.   The headstock is fixed to the bed and is equipped with motors, pulleys, and V-belts that supply power to the *spindle* at various rotational speeds. The speeds can be set through manually-controlled selectors. Most headstocks are equipped with a set of gears, and some have various drives to provide a continuously variable speed range to the spindle. Headstocks have a hollow spindle to which workholding devices, such as *chucks* and *collets* (Section 22.3.3), are attached, and long bars or tubing can be fed through for various turning operations.

Tailstock.   The tailstock, which can slide along the ways and be clamped at any position, supports the other end of the workpiece. It is equipped with a center that may be fixed (*dead center*) or may be free to rotate with the workpiece (*live center*). Drills and reamers can be mounted on the tailstock *quill* (a hollow cylindrical part with a tapered hole) to drill axial holes in the workpiece.

Feed Rod and Lead Screw.   The feed rod is powered by a set of gears from the headstock. It rotates during the operation of the lathe and provides movement to the carriage and the cross-slide by means of gears, a friction clutch, and a keyway along the length of the rod. Closing a split nut around the lead screw engages it with the carriage; it is also used for cutting threads accurately (as described in Section 22.5).

22.3.2 Lathe Specifications

A lathe is usually specified by (a) its *swing*, that is, the maximum diameter of the workpiece that can be machined (Table 22.6), (b) the maximum distance between the headstock and tailstock centers, and (c) the length of the bed. For example, a lathe may have the following size: 360 mm (14 in.) swing by 760 mm (30 in.) between centers by 1830 mm (6 ft) length of bed. Lathes are available in a variety of styles and types of construction and power.

Bench lathes are placed on a workbench; they have low power, are usually operated by hand feed, and are used to precision-machine small workpieces. *Toolroom lathes* have high precision, enabling the machining of parts to close tolerances. *Engine lathes* are available in a wide range of sizes and are used for a variety of turning operations. In *gap bed lathes*, a section of the bed in front of the headstock can be removed to accommodate larger-diameter workpieces.

Special-purpose lathes are used for applications such as railroad wheels, gun barrels, and rolling-mill rolls, with workpiece sizes as large as 1.7 m in diameter by 8 m in length (66 in. × 25 ft) and capacities of 450 kW (600 hp). The cost of engine lathes ranges from about $2000 for bench types to over $100,000 for larger units.

TABLE 22.6   Typical Capacities and Maximum Workpiece Dimensions for Machine Tools

Machine tool	Maximum dimension (m)	Power (kW)	Maximum rpm
Lathes (swing/length)			
Bench	0.3/1	<1	3000
Engine	3/5	70	4000
Turret	0.5/1.5	60	3000
Automatic screw	0.1/0.3	20	10,000
Boring machines (work diameter/length)			
Vertical spindle	4/3	200	300
Horizontal spindle	1.5/2	70	1000
Drilling machines			
Bench and column (drill diameter)	0.1	10	12,000
Radial (column to spindle distance)	3	—	—
Numerical control (table travel)	4	—	—

Note: Larger capacities are available for special applications.

Maximum spindle speeds are usually 2000 rpm, but may be only about 200 rpm for large lathes. For special applications, speeds may range from 4000 rpm to 10,000 rpm, or even up to 40,000 rpm for high-speed machining (Section 22.4.1).

22.3.3 Workholding Devices and Accessories

Workholding devices are particularly important in machine tools and machining operations. In a lathe, one end of the workpiece is clamped to the spindle by a chuck, collet, face plate, or mandrel.

A **chuck** is usually equipped with three or four *jaws*. *Three-jaw* chucks generally have a geared-scroll design that makes the jaws self-centering; they are used for round workpieces, such as bar stock, pipes, and tubing, which can be centered to within 0.025 mm (0.001 in.). *Four-jaw* (independent) chucks have jaws that can be moved and adjusted independently of each other; they can be used for square, rectangular, or odd-shaped workpieces. Because they are more ruggedly constructed than three-jaw chucks, they are used for heavy workpieces or for work requiring multiple chuckings where concentricity is important.

The jaws in some types of chucks can be reversed to permit clamping of the workpieces either on outside surfaces or on the inside surfaces of hollow workpieces such as pipes and tubing. Also available are jaws that are made of low-carbon steel (*soft jaws*) which can be machined into desired shapes; because of their low strength and hardness, they conform to small irregularities on workpieces and therefore result in better clamping.

Chucks can be *power actuated* or actuated *manually*, using a chuck wrench. Because they take longer to operate, manually actuated chucks are generally used only for toolroom and limited production runs. Chucks are available in various designs and sizes. Their selection depends on the type and speed of operation, workpiece size, production and accuracy requirements, and the jaw forces required.

By controlling the magnitude of jaw forces, an operator can ensure that the part does not slip in the chuck during machining. High spindle speeds can reduce jaw (clamping) forces significantly due to the effect of centrifugal forces; this effect is particularly important in precision tube turning. Modern jaw-actuating mechanisms permit higher clamping force for roughing and lower force for finishing operations.

To meet the increasing demands for stiffness, precision, versatility, power, and high cutting speeds in modern machine tools, major advances have been made in the design of workholding devices. **Power chucks**, actuated pneumatically or hydraulically, are used in automated equipment for high production rates, including the loading of parts using industrial robots. Also available are several types of power chucks with lever- or wedge-type mechanisms to actuate the jaws; these chucks have jaw movements (stroke) that are usually limited to about 13 mm (0.5 in.).

A **collet** is basically a longitudinally-split tapered bushing. The workpiece, which generally has a maximum diameter of 1 in., is placed inside the collet, and the collet is pulled (*draw-in* collet; Fig. 22.6a) or pushed (*push-out* collet; Fig. 22.6b) into the spindle mechanically. The tapered surfaces shrink the segments of the collet radially, tightening the workpiece. Collets are used for round workpieces as well as for other shapes (e.g., square or hexagonal workpieces) and are available in a wide range of incremental sizes.

One advantage to using a collet rather than a three- or four-jaw chuck is that the collet grips nearly all of the circumference of the part, making it particularly suited for parts with small cross-sections. Because the radial movement of the collet segments is small, workpieces should generally be within 0.125 mm (0.005 in.) of the nominal size of the collet.

Face plates are used for clamping irregularly shaped workpieces. The plates are round and have several slots and holes through which the workpiece is bolted or clamped.

Mandrels (Fig. 22.7) are placed inside hollow or tubular workpieces and are used to hold workpieces that require machining on both ends or on their cylindrical surfaces. Some mandrels are mounted between centers on the lathe.

Accessories.   Several devices are available as accessories and attachments for lathes. Among these devices are the following:

1. Carriage and cross-slide stops with various designs to stop the carriage at a predetermined distance along the bed,

FIGURE 22.6   (a) and (b) Schematic illustrations of a draw-in type collet. The workpiece is placed in the collet hole, and the conical surfaces of the collet are forced inward by pulling it with a draw bar into the sleeve. (c) A push-out type collet. (d) Workholding of a part on a face plate. *Source (photos b and d)*: M.P. Groover. *Fundamentals of Modern Manufacturing: Materials, Processes and Systems.* ©1996. Reprinted by permission of John Wiley and Sons.

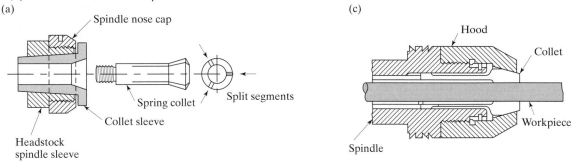

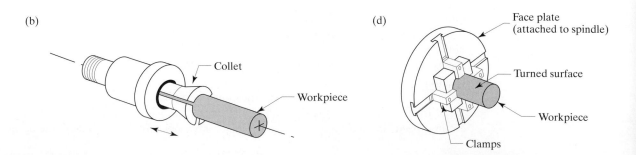

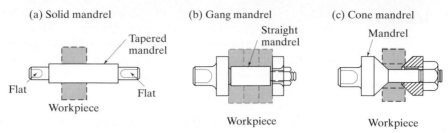

FIGURE 22.7   Various types of mandrels to hold workpieces for turning. These mandrels are usually mounted between centers on a lathe. Note that in (a), both the cylindrical and the end faces of the workpiece can be machined, whereas in (b) and (c), only the cylindrical surfaces can be machined.

2. Devices for turning parts with various tapers or radii,
3. Milling, sawing, gear-cutting, and grinding attachments, and
4. Various attachments for boring, drilling, and thread cutting.

22.3.4 Lathe Operations

In a typical turning operation, the workpiece is clamped by any one of the workholding devices described. Long and slender parts should be supported by a *steady rest* and *follow rest* placed on the bed; otherwise, the part will deflect under the cutting forces. These rests are usually equipped with three adjustable fingers or rollers, which support the workpiece while allowing it to rotate freely. Steady rests are clamped directly on the *ways* of the lathe (as in Fig. 22.2), whereas *follow rests* are clamped on the carriage and travel with it.

The cutting tool, attached to the tool post, which is driven by the lead screw, removes material by traveling along the bed. A *right-hand* tool travels toward the headstock, and a *left-hand* tool toward the tailstock. Facing operations are done by moving the tool radially with the cross-slide, and clamping the carriage for better dimensional accuracy.

Form tools are used to produce various shapes on round workpieces by turning (Fig. 22.1g). The tool moves radially inward to machine the part. Machining by form cutting is not suitable for deep and narrow grooves or sharp corners because they may cause vibration and result in poor surface finish. As a rule, (a) the formed length should not be greater than about 2.5 times the minimum diameter of the part, (b) the cutting speed should be reduced from turning settings, and (c) cutting fluids should be used.

Several other operations are also performed on a lathe, as described in greater detail throughout the rest of this chapter.

The **boring** operation on a lathe is similar to turning. Boring is performed inside hollow workpieces or in a hole made previously by drilling or other means. Out-of-shape holes can be straightened by boring. The workpiece is held in a chuck or in some other suitable workholding device. Boring of large workpieces is described in Section 22.6.

Drilling can be performed on a lathe by mounting the drill bit in a drill chuck into the tailstock quill (a tubular shaft). The workpiece is placed in a workholder on the headstock, and the quill is advanced by rotating the hand wheel. Holes drilled in this manner may not be concentric because of the tendency for the drill to drift radially. The concentricity of the hole is improved by subsequently boring the drilled hole. Drilled holes may be **reamed** on lathes in a manner similar to drilling, thus improving hole tolerances.

The tools for *parting*, *grooving*, *thread cutting*, and various other operations are specially shaped for their particular purpose or are available as inserts. *Knurling* is performed on a lathe with hardened rolls (see Fig. 22.1l) in which the surface of the rolls is a replica of the profile to be generated. The rolls are pressed radially against the rotating workpiece, while the tool moves axially along the part.

22.3.5 Tracer Lathes

Tracer lathes are machine tools with attachments that are capable of turning parts with various contours. Also called *duplicating lathes* or *contouring lathes*, the cutting tool follows a path that duplicates the contour of the template, similar to a pencil following the shape of a plastic template used in engineering drawing. A tracer finger follows the template and, through a hydraulic or electrical system, guides the cutting tool along the workpiece without operator intervention. Operations performed on a tracer lathe have been largely replaced by numerical-control lathes and turning centers (Section 24.2).

22.3.6 Automatic Lathes

Lathes have been increasingly automated over the years. Manual machine controls have been replaced by various mechanisms that enable cutting operations to follow a certain prescribed sequence. In a fully automatic machine, parts are fed and removed automatically, whereas in semiautomatic machines, these functions are performed by the operator.

Automatic lathes, which may have a horizontal or vertical spindle and do not have tailstocks, are also called *chucking machines*, or *chuckers*. They are used for machining individual pieces of regular or irregular shapes, and are available in either single- or multiple-spindle types. In another type of automatic lathe, the bar stock is fed periodically into the lathe and a part is machined and cut off at the end of the bar. Automatic lathes are suitable for medium- to high-volume production.

22.3.7 Automatic Bar Machines

Formerly called *automatic screw machines*, these machines are designed for high-production-rate machining of screws and similar threaded parts. Because they are capable of producing various other components, they are now called *automatic bar machines*.

All operations on these machines are performed automatically, with tools attached to a special turret. After each screw or part is machined to finished dimensions, the bar stock is fed forward automatically and then cut off. These machines may be equipped with single or multiple spindles. Capacities range from 3-mm to 150-mm (1/8-in. to 6-in.) diameter bar stock.

Single-spindle automatic bar machines are similar to turret lathes and are equipped with various cam-operated mechanisms. There are two types of single-spindle machines. In **Swiss-type automatics** (Fig. 22.8), the cylindrical surface of the rod is machined by a series of tools that move in radially, and in the same plane, toward the workpiece. The bar stock is clamped close to the headstock spindle, which minimizes deflections. These machines are capable of high-precision machining of small-diameter parts.

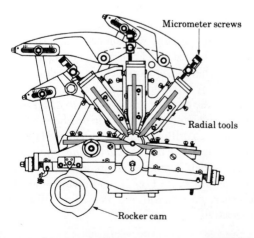

FIGURE 22.8   Schematic illustration of a Swiss-type automatic screw machine. *Source*: George Gorton Machine Company.

The other single-spindle machine (also called the *American type*) is similar to a small automatic turret lathe. The turret is on a vertical plane, and all motions of the machine components are controlled by cams. Automatic bar machines are now equipped with computer numerical controls, which eliminate the use of cams, and the operation is programmed for a particular product. (See Chapter 38.)

Multiple-spindle automatic bar machines have from four to eight spindles, arranged in a circle on a large drum, each carrying an individual workpiece. The cutting tools are arranged in various positions in the machine and move in both axial and radial directions. Each part is machined in stages as it moves from one station to the next. Because all operations are carried out simultaneously, cycle time per part is reduced.

22.3.8 Turret Lathes

Turret lathes are capable of performing multiple cutting operations, such as turning, boring, drilling, thread cutting, and facing (Fig. 22.9), on the same workpiece. Several cutting tools (usually as many as six) are mounted on the hexagonal *main turret*, which is rotated for each specific cutting operation.

The lathe usually has a *square turret* on the cross-slide, with as many as four cutting tools mounted on it. The workpiece, generally a long round rod, is advanced a preset distance through the chuck. After the part is machined, it is cut off by a tool mounted on the square turret which moves radially into the workpiece. The rod is then advanced the same preset distance into the work area, and the next part is machined.

Turret lathes (bar type or chucking type) are versatile, and operations may be carried out either by hand, using the turnstile (capstan wheel), or automatically. Once set up properly by a setup person, these machines do not require highly skilled operators. The turret lathe shown in Fig. 22.9 is known as a *ram-type* turret lathe, one in which the ram slides in a separate base on the saddle. The short stroke of the turret slide limits this machine to relatively short workpieces and light cuts, in both small- and medium-quantity production.

In another style, called the *saddle type*, the main turret is installed directly on the saddle, which slides directly on the bed. The length of the stroke is limited only by the length of the bed. This type of lathe is more heavily constructed and is used to machine large workpieces. Because of the heavy weight of the components, saddle-type lathe operations are slower than ram-type lathe operations. Vertical turret lathes are also available; they are more suitable for short, heavy workpieces with diameters as large as 1.2 m (48 in.).

FIGURE 22.9   Schematic illustration of the components of a turret lathe. Note the two turrets: square and hexagonal (main). *Source: American Machinist and Automated Manufacturing.*

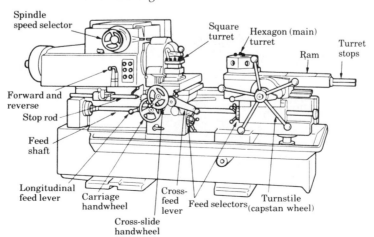

22.3.9 Computer-Controlled Lathes

In the most advanced lathes, movement and control of the machine and its components are actuated by *computer numerical controls* (CNC) as described in Section 24.2 and Chapters 38 and 39. The features of such a lathe are shown in Fig. 22.10. These lathes are usually equipped with one or more turrets (Figs. 22.11a and b). Each turret is equipped with a variety of tools and performs several operations on different surfaces of the workpiece.

FIGURE 22.10   A computer numerical control lathe. Note the two turrets on this machine. *Source*: Jones & Lamson, Textron, Inc.

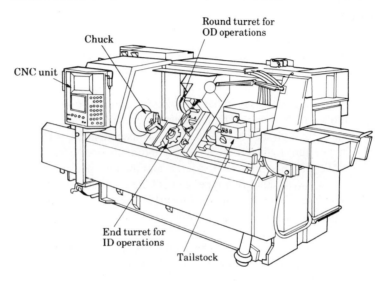

FIGURE 22.11   (a) A turret with six different tools for inside-diameter and outside-diameter cutting and threading operations. (b) A turret with eight different cutting tools. *Source*: Monarch Machine Tool Company.

(a)

(b)

These machines are highly automated, the operations are repetitive and maintain the desired dimensional accuracy, and less-skilled labor is required (after the machine is set up). They are suitable for low- to medium-volume production.

Example: Typical Parts Made on CNC Turning Machine Tools

The capabilities of CNC turning machine tools are illustrated in Fig. 22.12. Material and number of cutting tools used and machining times are indicated for each part. These parts can also be made on manual or turret lathes, although not as effectively or consistently. *Source:* Monarch Machine Tool Company.

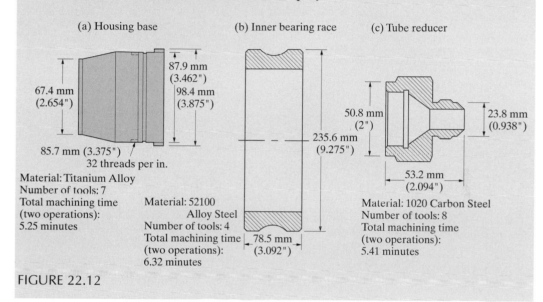

(a) Housing base

67.4 mm (2.654")
87.9 mm (3.462")
98.4 mm (3.875")
85.7 mm (3.375") / 32 threads per in.

Material: Titanium Alloy
Number of tools: 7
Total machining time (two operations): 5.25 minutes

(b) Inner bearing race

235.6 mm (9.275")
78.5 mm (3.092")

Material: 52100 Alloy Steel
Number of tools: 4
Total machining time (two operations): 6.32 minutes

(c) Tube reducer

50.8 mm (2")
23.8 mm (0.938")
53.2 mm (2.094")

Material: 1020 Carbon Steel
Number of tools: 8
Total machining time (two operations): 5.41 minutes

FIGURE 22.12

Example: Machining of Various Complex Shapes

Note that, in the preceding example, the parts are axisymmetric. The capabilities of CNC turning can be further illustrated by referring to Figs. 22.13, which shows three additional, more complex parts: a pump shaft, a crankshaft, and a tubular part with internal rope thread. As in most operations, the machining of these parts consists of both roughing and finishing cuts.

1. *Pump shaft* (Fig. 22.13a). This part, as well as a wide variety of similar parts with external and internal features (including camshafts), was produced on a CNC lathe with two turrets, similar in construction to the machine shown in Fig. 22.10. Each turret can hold as many as eight tools. Note that to produce this particular shape, the upper turret is programmed in such a manner that its radial movement is synchronized with shaft rotation.

   The spindle turning angle is monitored directly; a processor performs a high-speed calculation and the CNC issues a command to the cam turret in terms of that angle. It has absolute position feedback, using a high-accuracy scale system. The CNC compares the actual value with the commanded one and performs an automatic compensation, using a built-in learning function. The turret has a lightweight design for smooth operation (by reducing inertial forces).

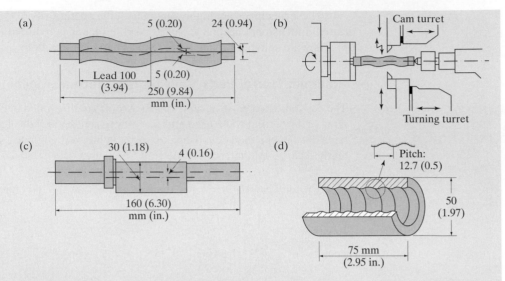

FIGURE 22.13

This shaft may be made of aluminum or stainless steel. The machining parameters for aluminum are given in Table 22.7; see item (a) in the first column of the table. These may be compared with the data in Table 22.4, which gives only a broad approximate range as a guideline. The inserts were K10 (C3) uncoated carbide and compacted (polycrystalline) diamond (Chapter 21). The OD machining in the table refers to the two straight cylindrical ends of the part.

The total machining time for an aluminum shaft was 24 min.; for stainless steel, it was 55 min. Note from Table 22.4 that the cutting speed for stainless steel is considerably lower than that for aluminum, lengthening the machining time.

TABLE 22.7

Operation	Cutting speed		Depth of cut	Feed	Tool
(a)					
OD roughing	1150 rpm	160 m/min (525 fpm)	3 mm (0.12 in.)	0.3 mm/rev (0.012 ipr)	K10 (C3)
OD finishing	1750	250 (820)	0.2 (0.008)	0.15 (0.0059)	K10 (C3)
Lead roughing	300	45 (148)	3 (0.12)	0.15 (0.0059)	K10 (C3)
Lead finishing	300	45 (148)	0.1 (0.004)	0.15 (0.0059)	Diamond compact
(b)					
Eccentric roughing	200 rpm	5-11 m/min (16-136 fpm)	1.5 mm (0.059 in)	0.2 mm/rev (0.008 ipr)	K10 (C3)
Eccentric finishing	200	5-11 (16-36)	0.1 (0.004)	0.05 (0.0020)	K10 (C3)
(c)					
Thread roughing	800 rpm	70 m/min (230 fpm)	1.6 mm (0.063 in.)	0.15 mm/rev (0.0059 ipr)	Coated carbide
Thread finishing	800	70 (230)	0.1 (0.004)	0.15 (0.0059)	Cermet

2. *Crankshaft* (Fig. 22.13b). This part is made of ductile (nodular) cast iron (Section 12.3.2). The machining parameters are shown in item (b) of Table 22.7. The insert was K10 carbide. The machining time was 25 min.; note that this time is on the same order of magnitude as that for the first part.

3. *Tubular part with internal rope thread* (Fig. 22.13c). Made of 304 stainless steel, this part was machined under the conditions given in item (c) in Table 22.7. The starting blank was a straight tubular piece, similar to a bushing. The cutting tools were coated carbide and cermet. The boring bar was made of tungsten carbide for increased stiffness (and, therefore, improved dimensional accuracy and surface finish). For the threaded portion, the dimensional accuracy was ±0.05 mm (0.002 in.), with a surface finish of $R_a = 2.5\ \mu$m (100 μin.).

    The machining time for this part was 1.5 min. Note that this time is much shorter than that for the other two examples. The reason is that this part is shorter, less material is removed, it does not have the eccentric features of the first two parts (so the radial movement of the cutting tool is not a function of the angular position of the part), and the cutting speed is higher. *Source*: Based on technical literature supplied by Okuma Corp.

22.3.10 Turning Process Capabilities

Relative *production rates* in turning, as well as in other cutting operations described in the rest of this chapter and in Chapter 23, are shown in Table 22.8. These rates have an important bearing on productivity in machining operations. Note that there are major differences in the production rate among these processes. These differences are not only due to the inherent characteristics of the processes and machine tools, but are also due to various other factors, such as setup times and the types and sizes of the workpieces involved. (See Section 24.5 and Chapter 40.)

TABLE 22.8 Typical Production Rates for Various Cutting Operations

Operation	Rate
Turning	
Engine lathe	Very low to low
Tracer lathe	Low to medium
Turret lathe	Low to medium
Computer-control lathe	Low to medium
Single-spindle chuckers	Medium to high
Multiple-spindle chuckers	High to very high
Boring	Very low
Drilling	Low to medium
Milling	Low to medium
Planing	Very low
Gear cutting	Low to medium
Broaching	Medium to high
Sawing	Very low to low

Note: Production rates indicated are relative: *Very low* is about one or more parts per hour; *medium* is approximately 100 parts per hour; *very high* is 1000 or more parts per hour.

The ratings in Table 22.8 are relative and there can be significant variations in special applications. For example, heat-treated high-carbon cast steel rolls (for rolling mills, Section 13.4) can be machined on special lathes at material removal rates as high as 6000 cm^3/min (370 in.^{3}/min) using multiple cermet tools. The important factor in this operation (also called *high removal rate machining*) is the very high rigidity of the machine tool (to avoid tool breakage due to chatter; see Section 24.4) and its high power—up to 450 kW (600 hp).

The surface finish (Figs. 22.14) and dimensional accuracy (Fig. 22.15) obtained in turning and related operations depend on factors such as the characteristics and condition of the machine tool; stiffness; vibration and chatter; process parameters; tool geometry and wear; the use of cutting fluids; the machinability of the workpiece material; and operator skill. As a result, a wide range of surface finishes can be obtained, as shown in Fig. 22.14. (See also Fig. 26.4.)

FIGURE 22.14 The range of surface roughnesses obtained in various machining processes. Note the wide range within each group, especially in turning and boring. See also Fig. 26.4.

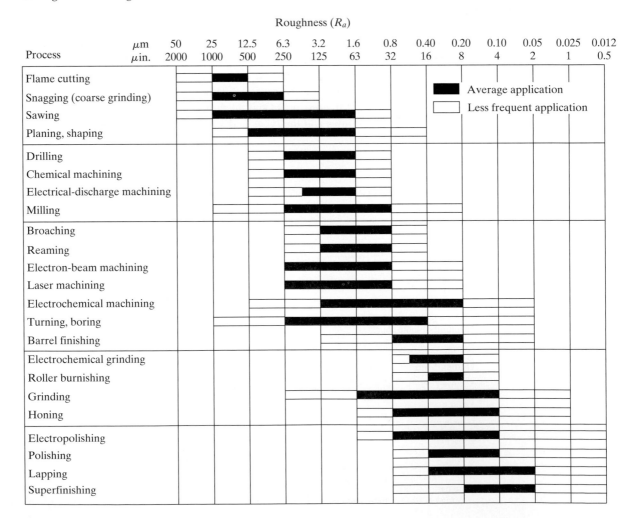

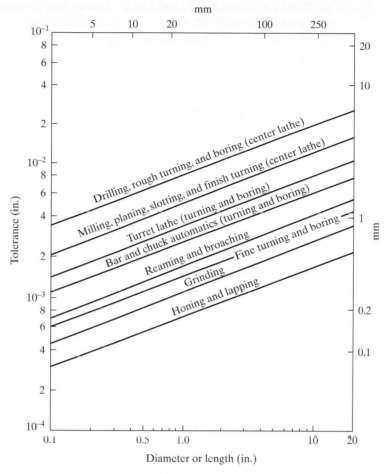

FIGURE 22.15   The range of dimensional tolerances obtained in various machining processes as a function of workpiece size. Note that there is an order of magnitude difference between small and large workpieces. *Source*: Adapted from *Manufacturing Planning and Estimating Handbook*, McGraw-Hill, 1963.

22.3.11 Design Considerations for Turning Operations

Several considerations are important in designing parts to be manufactured economically by turning operations. Because machining, in general, can take considerable time (increasing the production cost), wastes material, and is not as economical as forming or shaping parts, it should be avoided as much as possible. When turning operations are necessary, the following general design guidelines should be used:

a. Parts should be designed so that they can be fixtured and clamped in workholding devices with relative ease. Thin, slender workpieces are difficult to support properly to withstand clamping and cutting forces. (See also *flexible fixturing*, Section 38.9.)

b. The dimensional accuracy and surface finish specified should be as wide as permissible for the part to function properly.

c. Sharp corners, tapers, and major dimensional variations in the part should be avoided.

d. Blanks to be machined should be as close to final dimensions as possible (near-net-shape forming), so as to reduce production cycle time.

e. Parts should be designed so that cutting tools can travel across the workpiece without obstruction.

f. Design features should be such that commercially available standard cutting tools, inserts, and toolholders can be used.

g. Materials should, as much as possible, be selected for their machinability (Section 20.9).

22.3.12 Guidelines for Turning Operations

A general guide to the probable causes of problems in turning operations is given in Table 22.9. Recall that Chapters 20 and 21 described the factors influencing the parameters listed.

In addition to the various recommendations concerning tools and process parameters that have been described thus far, an important factor is the presence of *vibration* and *chatter* (Chapter 24). Vibration during cutting can cause poor surface finish, poor dimensional accuracy, and premature tool wear and failure. The following are some generally accepted guidelines for turning operations (because of the complexity of the problem, however, some of the guidelines have to be implemented on a trial-and-error basis):

a. Minimize tool overhang.

b. Support workpiece rigidly.

c. Use machine tools with high stiffness and high damping capacity.

d. When tools begin to vibrate and chatter, modify one or more of the process parameters, such as tool geometry, cutting speed, feed rate, depth of cut, or use of cutting fluid. (See also *adaptive control*, Section 38.5.)

22.3.13 Chip Collection Systems

The chips produced during machining must be collected and disposed of properly. The volume of chips produced can be very high, particularly in high-speed and high-removal-rate operations. For example, in a drilling operation on steel during which only 1 in^3 of metal is removed, the loose bulk volume of the chips can be in the range of 40 in^3-800 in^3, depending on chip type (Section 20.3). Likewise, the milling of 1 in^3 steel produces 30 in^3-45 in^3 of chips, and cast iron produces 7 in^3-15 in^3 of chips.

Sometimes called **chip management**, the process involves collecting chips from their source in the machine tool in an efficient manner and removing them from the work area.

TABLE 22.9   General Troubleshooting Guide for Turning Operations

Problem	Probable causes
Tool breakage	Tool material lacks toughness; improper tool angles; machine tool lacks stiffness; worn bearings and machine components; cutting parameters too high.
Excessive tool wear	Cutting parameters too high; improper tool material; ineffective cutting fluid; improper tool angles.
Rough surface finish	Built-up edge on tool; feed too high; tool too sharp, chipped or worn; vibration and chatter.
Dimensional variability	Lack of stiffness; excessive temperature rise; tool wear.
Tool chatter	Lack of stiffness; workpiece not supported rigidly; excessive tool overhang.

Long and stringy chips are more difficult to collect than short chips (using chipbreaker features on cutting tools; see Figs. 20.7 and 21.2). Therefore, the type of chip produced (*chip control*) is an integral aspect of the chip collecting system.

Chips can be collected by any of the following methods:

1. Allowing gravity to drop them on a steel conveyor belt,
2. Dragging the chips from a settling tank,
3. Using augers, with feed screws similar to those in meat grinders,
4. Using magnetic conveyors (for ferrous chips), and
5. Employing vacuum methods of removal.

Modern machine tools are designed with automated chip-handling features. It should be noted that there may be a considerable amount of cutting fluid mixed in with and adhering to the chips produced, so proper filtration or draining is important. The fluid and sludge can be removed using *chip wringers* (centrifuges). Chip processing systems usually require considerable floor space and can cost from $60,000 for small shops to over $1 million for large plants.

The collected chips may be recycled or dumped (provided they are free of harmful chemical components or fluids). Prior to their removal from a manufacturing plant, the large volume of chips can be reduced to as little as one-fifth of the loose volume by *compaction* (crushing) into briquettes or by *shredding*.

Dry chips are more valuable for recycling because of the reduced environmental contamination. The final method of chip disposal depends on economics as well as on compliance with local, state, and federal regulations. The trend is to recycle all chips as well as the used cutting fluids and the sludge.

22.4 HIGH-SPEED MACHINING, ULTRAPRECISION MACHINING, AND HARD TURNING

Important developments in cutting processes involve the implementation of high-speed machining, ultraprecision machining, and hard turning, as described in this section.

22.4.1 High-Speed Machining

With increasing demands for higher productivity and lower production costs, investigations have been carried out since the late 1950s to increase the material removal rate in machining, particularly for applications in the aerospace and automotive industries. One obvious possibility is to increase the cutting speed.

The term *high speed* is relative. As a general guide, an approximate range of cutting speeds may be defined as follows:

1. **High speed:** 600–1800 m/min (2000–6000 ft/min),
2. **Very high speed:** 1800–18,000 m/min (6000–60,000 ft/min),
3. **Ultrahigh speed:** >18,000 m/min.

Spindle rotational speeds today may range up to 40,000 rpm, although the automotive industry, for example, generally limits them to 15,000 rpm for better reliability and less downtime should a failure occur. The spindle power required in high-speed machining is generally on the order of 0.004 W/rpm (0.005 hp/rpm), whereas in traditional machining, it is in the range of 0.2 to 0.4 W/rpm (0.25 to 0.5 hp/rpm).

Spindle designs for high speeds generally involve an integral electric motor. The armature is built onto the shaft and the stator is placed in the wall of the spindle housing. The bearings may be rolling element or hydrostatic; the latter requires less space than the former.

Much research and development work has been carried out in the area of *high-speed machining* (turning, milling, boring, and drilling) of aluminum alloys, titanium alloys, steels, and superalloys. Much data have been collected regarding the effect of high cutting speeds on (a) the type of chips produced, (b) cutting forces and power, (c) temperatures generated, (d) tool wear, (e) surface finish, and (f) the economics of the process.

These studies have indicated that high-speed machining can be economical for certain applications. Consequently, it is now implemented for the machining of aircraft-turbine components and automotive engines with five to ten times the productivity of traditional machining. High-speed machining of complex 3- and 5-axis contours has been made possible only recently by advances in CNC control technology. (See also Chapters 24 and 38.)

A major factor in the adoption of high-speed machining has been the desire to improve tolerances in cutting operations. With high-speed machining, most of the heat generated in cutting is removed by the chip (Fig. 20.14), so the tool and (more importantly) the workpiece remain close to ambient temperature. This is beneficial because there is no thermal expansion or warping of the workpiece during machining.

The following are important machine factors in high-speed operations:

1. Power and stiffness of the machine tools,
2. Stiffness of toolholders and workholding devices,
3. Spindle design for high power and high rotational speeds,
4. Inertia of the machine-tool components,
5. Fast feed drives,
6. Level of automation, and
7. Selection of an appropriate cutting tool,

It is important to note, however, that high-speed machining should be considered almost exclusively for situations in which **cutting time** is a significant portion of the floor-to-floor time of the operation. As described in Section 38.6 and Chapter 40, other factors—such as **noncutting time** and *labor costs*—are also important considerations in the overall assessment of the benefits of high-speed machining for a particular application.

22.4.2 Ultraprecision Machining

Beginning in the 1960s, increasing demands have been made for the precision manufacturing of components for computer, electronic, nuclear energy, and defense applications. Some examples include optical mirrors, computer memory disks, and drums for photocopying machines. Surface finish requirements are in the tens of nanometer (10^{-9} m or 0.001 μm; 0.04 μin.) range and form accuracies in the μm and sub-μm range. (See also Chapter 31.)

Because the cutting tool for *ultraprecision machining* applications is almost exclusively a single-crystal diamond, the process is also called **diamond turning**. The diamond tool has a polished cutting-edge with a radius as small as a few nanometers. Wear of the diamond can be a significant problem, and recent advances include *cryogenic diamond turning*, in which the tooling system is cooled by liquid nitrogen to a temperature of about –120 °C (–184 °F).

The workpiece materials for ultraprecision machining to date include copper alloys, aluminum alloys, silver, gold, electroless nickel, infrared materials, and plastics (acrylics). The depth of cut involved is in the nanometer range. In this range, hard and brittle materials produce continuous chips (the process is known as **ductile-regime cutting**; see also *ductile-regime grinding* in Section 25.5.6); deeper cuts produce discontinuous chips.

The machine tools for these applications are built with very high precision and high machine, spindle, and workholding-device stiffnesses. These ultraprecision machines, parts of which are made of structural materials with low thermal expansion and good dimensional stability (Section 24.3), are located in a dust-free environment (i.e., clean rooms) where the temperature is controlled to within a fraction of one degree.

Vibrations from internal machine sources as well as from external sources, such as nearby machines on the same floor, are also avoided as much as possible. Laser metrology is used for feed and position control, and the machines are equipped with highly advanced computer control systems and with thermal and geometric error-compensating features.

General Considerations for Precision Machining.   There are several important factors involved in precision and ultraprecision machining and machine tools:

1. Machine-tool design, construction, and assembly; stiffness, damping, and geometric accuracy.
2. Motion control of various components, both linear and rotational.
3. Spindle technology.
4. Thermal growth of the machine tool, compensation for thermal growth, and control of the machine-tool environment.
5. Cutting-tool selection and application (Chapter 21).
6. Machining parameters (Chapters 20, 22, and 23).
7. Real-time performance of the machine tool, tool-condition monitoring, and control of both (Chapter 20).

Because of their often-complex interactions, these factors must be taken as a whole and treated as a *system*. Various details regarding these factors are described in Chapter 24.

22.4.3 Hard Turning

We have seen that, as the hardness of the workpiece increases, its machinability decreases and tool wear and fracture, as well as surface finish and surface integrity, can become significant problems. As described in Chapters 25 and 26, there are several other mechanical processes (particularly grinding) and nonmechanical methods of removing material economically from hard or hardened metals and alloys. However, it is still possible to apply traditional cutting processes to hard metals and alloys by selecting an appropriate tool material and by using machine tools with high stiffness.

One common example is the finish machining of heat-treated steel (in the range of 45 to 65 HRC) shafts, gears, pinions, and various automotive components using polycrystalline cubic boron nitride (PcBN), cermet, or ceramic cutting tools. Called *hard turning*, this process produces machined parts with good dimensional accuracy, surface finish (as low as 0.25 μm or 10 μin.), and surface integrity. The available power and stiffness of the machine tool and fixturing are important factors, as is edge preparation of the cutting tool to avoid premature failure (see Section 21.5.3).

From both technical and economic viewpoints, hard turning can compete successfully with the grinding process. For instance, hard turning is three times faster than grinding, requires fewer operations, and utilizes five times less energy. A comparative example of hard turning vs. grinding is presented in Section 25.6.9.

22.5 CUTTING SCREW THREADS

Screw threads are among the most important machine elements. A *screw thread* may be defined as a ridge of uniform cross-section that follows a helical or spiral path on the outside or inside of a cylindrical (*straight thread*) or tapered (conical) surface (*tapered thread*). Machine screws, bolts, and nuts have straight threads, as do threaded rods for applications such as the lead screw in lathes (Fig. 22.2). Threads may be *right-handed* or *left-handed*. Tapered threads are commonly used for water or gas pipes and plumbing supplies, which require a watertight or airtight connection.

Threads may be produced basically by (a) forming (*thread rolling;* see Section 13.5.2), which constitutes the largest quantity of threaded parts produced, or (b) cutting. It is also possible to cast threaded parts, but there are limitations to dimensional accuracy, surface finish, and minimum dimensions, and production rates are not as high as those obtained in other processes.

As shown in Fig. 22.1k, turning operations are capable of producing threads on round bar stock. When threads are produced externally or internally by cutting with a lathe-type tool, the process is called *thread cutting* or *threading*. When cut internally with a special threaded tool (*tap*), the process is called *tapping* (Section 22.10). External threads may also be cut with a *die* or by milling. Although it adds considerably to the cost, threads may subsequently be ground for improved dimensional accuracy and surface finish.

22.5.1 Screw-Thread Nomenclature

Standardization of screw threads began in the middle 1880s, and several thread forms have since been standardized. The nomenclature for screw threads is given in Fig. 22.16a. *Unified screw-thread* forms (Fig. 22.16b), based on the American National thread system, were adopted in the United States, Canada, and the United Kingdom in 1948 to obtain interchangeable screw threads. This standard has been revised periodically, particularly with regard to dimensional tolerances.

In 1969, the *ISO general-purpose screw-thread* form was developed with a wide range of metric sizes; it has since been adopted by many countries (Fig. 22.16c). Other types of threads are shown in Fig. 22.17.

In the Unified system, thread dimensional tolerances are specified as Class 1, 2, or 3, in decreasing order of looseness. In the ISO system, tolerance classes are a combination of tolerance grades and positions and are based on crest and pitch diameters.

The *tolerance grade* is expressed by numerals ranging from 3 to 9, in order of increasing coarseness (loose tolerance). Comparatively, grade 6 in the ISO system is roughly equivalent to grade 2 in the Unified system. The letters represent *tolerance positions* for the two diameters and indicate allowances (specified differences in size) according to the following system:

Allowance	External thread (bolt)	Internal thread (nut)
Large	e	—
Small	g	G
None	h	H

(a)

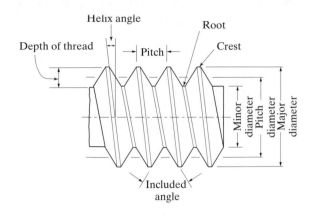

(b)   (c)

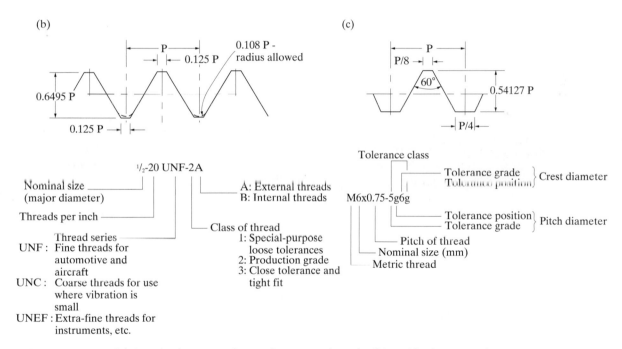

FIGURE 22.16   (a) Standard nomenclature for screw threads. (b) Unified National thread and identification of threads. (c) ISO metric thread and identification of threads.

22.5.2 Screw-Thread Cutting on a Lathe

Threads may be visualized as deep, coarse feed marks (Fig. 20.2). A typical thread-cutting operation on a lathe is shown in Fig. 22.18a. The cutting tool, whose shape depends on the type of thread to be cut, is mounted on a holder that is moved along the length of the workpiece by the *lead screw* on the lathe (Fig. 22.2). The movement is achieved by the engagement of a *split nut* (also called a *half nut*) inside the apron of the lathe (not shown in the figure).

The axial movement of the tool in relation to the rotation of the workpiece determines the *lead* of the screw thread, that is, the axial distance moved in one complete revolution of the screw. For a fixed spindle rpm, the slower the tool movement, the finer the thread will

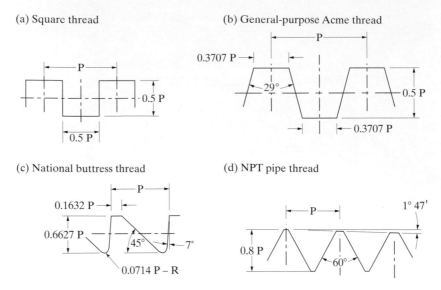

(a) Square thread

(b) General-purpose Acme thread

(c) National buttress thread

(d) NPT pipe thread

FIGURE 22.17   Various types of screw threads.

FIGURE 22.18   (a) Cutting screw threads on a lathe with a single-point cutting tool. (b) Cutting screw threads with a single-point tool in several passes, normally utilized for large threads. The small arrows in the figures show the direction of feed, and the broken lines show the position of the cutting tool as time progresses. Note that in radial cutting, the tool is fed directly into the workpiece. In flank cutting, the tool is fed into the piece along the right face of the thread. In incremental cutting, the tool is first fed directly into the piece at the center of the thread, then at its sides, and finally into the root. (c) A typical carbide insert and toolholder for cutting screw threads. (d) Cutting internal screw threads with a carbide insert. (See also Figs. 21.2 and 21.3.)

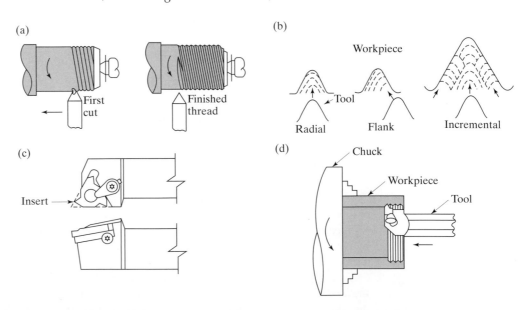

be. In thread cutting, the cutting tool may be fed radially into the workpiece, cutting both sides of the thread at the same time as in form cutting. However, this method usually produces a poor surface finish.

A number of passes in the sequence shown in Fig. 22.18b are generally required to produce good dimensional accuracy and surface finish. Figure 22.18c shows a carbide insert for screw thread cutting (*threading insert*), and Fig. 22.18d shows an internal screw-thread cutting process. Although cutting threads on lathes is an old and versatile method, it requires considerable operator skill and is a slow (i.e., uneconomical) process. Consequently, except for small production runs, it has been largely replaced by other methods, such as thread rolling, automatic screw machining, and use of CNC lathes.

The production rate in cutting screw threads can be increased with tools called *die-head chasers* (Figs. 22.19a and b). These tools typically have four cutters with multiple teeth and can be adjusted radially. After the threads are cut, the cutters open automatically (giving rise to the alternative name *self-opening die heads*) by rotating around their axes to allow the part to be removed.

Solid threading dies (Fig. 22.19c) are also available for cutting straight or tapered screw threads. These dies are used mostly to thread the ends of pipes and tubing and are not suitable for production work.

22.5.3 Design Considerations for Screw-Thread Cutting

The design considerations that must be taken into account in order to produce high-quality economical screw threads are as follows:

a. Designs should allow for the termination of threads before they reach a shoulder. Internal threads in blind holes should have an unthreaded length at the bottom.

b. Attempts should be made to eliminate shallow, blind tapped holes.

c. Chamfers should be specified at the ends of threaded sections to minimize finlike threads with burrs.

d. Threaded sections should not be interrupted with slots, holes, or other discontinuities.

e. Standard threading tooling and inserts should be used as much as possible.

f. Thin-walled parts should have sufficient thickness and strength to resist clamping and cutting forces. A good rule of thumb is that the minimum engagement length of a fastener should be 1.5 times the diameter.

g. Parts should be designed so that all cutting operations can be completed in one setup.

FIGURE 22.19   (a) Straight chasers for cutting threads on a lathe. (b) Circular chasers. (c) A solid threading die.

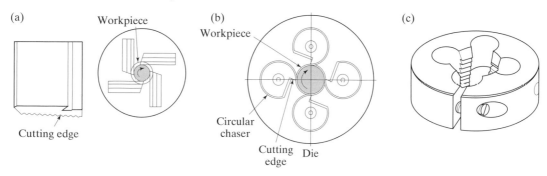

22.6 BORING AND BORING MACHINES

As carried out on a lathe, boring produces circular internal profiles in hollow workpieces (Fig. 22.1e) or on a hole made by drilling or another process. Boring is done with cutting tools that are similar to those used in turning. Because the *boring bar* (Fig. 22.20a) has to reach the full length of the bore, tool deflection and, therefore, maintainance of dimensional accuracy can be a significant problem.

The boring bar must be sufficiently stiff—that is, made of a material with high elastic modulus, such as tungsten carbide—to minimize deflection and avoid vibration and chatter. Boring bars have been designed with capabilities for damping vibration (Fig. 22.20b).

Although boring operations on relatively small workpieces can be carried out on a lathe, **boring mills** are used for large workpieces. These machines are either vertical or horizontal, and are capable of performing operations such as turning, facing, grooving, and chamfering. A *vertical boring machine* (Fig. 22.20c) is similar to a lathe but has a vertical axis of workpiece rotation.

The cutting tool (usually a single point made of M-2 and M-3 high-speed steel and C-7 and C-8 carbide) is mounted on the tool head, which is capable of vertical movement (for boring and turning) and radial movement (for facing), guided by the cross-rail. The head can be swiveled to produce conical (tapered) surfaces.

In **horizontal boring machines** (Fig. 22.21), the workpiece is mounted on a table that can move horizontally in both the axial and radial directions. The cutting tool is mounted on a spindle that rotates in the headstock, which is capable of both vertical and longitudinal movements. Drills, reamers, taps, and milling cutters can also be mounted on the machine spindle.

Boring machines are available with a variety of features. Although workpiece diameters are generally 1 m–4 m (3 ft–12 ft), workpieces as large as 20 m (60 ft) can be machined in some vertical boring machines. Machine capacities range up to 150 kW (200 hp). These machines are also available with computer numerical controls, which allow all movements to be programmed. With such controls, little operator involvement is required and consis-

FIGURE 22.20   (a) Schematic illustration of a steel boring bar with a carbide insert. Note the passageway in the bar for cutting fluid application. (b) Schematic illustration of a boring bar with tungsten-alloy "inertia disks" sealed in the bar to counteract vibration and chatter during boring. This system is effective for boring bar length-to-diameter ratios of up to 6. (c) Schematic illustration of the components of a vertical boring mill. *Source*: Kennametal Inc.

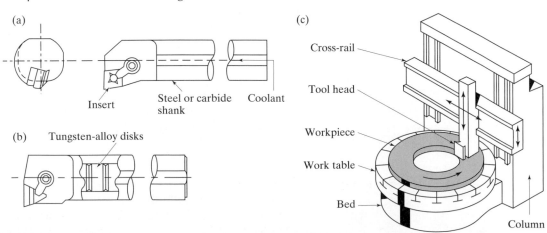

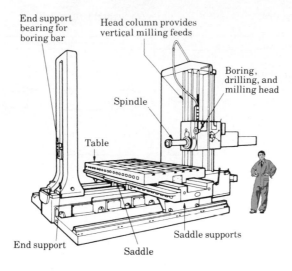

FIGURE 22.21   Horizontal boring mill. *Source*: Giddings and Lewis, Inc.

tency and productivity are improved. Cutting speeds and feeds for boring are similar to those for turning. (For capabilities of boring operations, see Table 22.8.)

Jig borers are vertical boring machines with high-precision bearings. Although they are available in various sizes and are used in tool rooms for making jigs and fixtures, they are now being replaced by more versatile numerical control machines.

Design Considerations for Boring.   Guidelines for efficient and economical boring operations are similar to those for turning. Additionally, the following factors should be considered:

a. Whenever possible, through holes rather than blind holes should be specified. (The term *blind hole* refers to a hole that does not go through the thickness of the workpiece; see, for example, Fig. 22.1i.)

b. The greater the length-to-bore-diameter ratio, the more difficult it is to hold dimensions because of the deflections of the boring bar due to cutting forces.

c. Interrupted internal surfaces should be avoided.

22.7 DRILLING AND DRILLS

When inspecting various products around us, we realize that the vast majority have several holes in them. Holes are generally used either for assembly with fasteners, such as bolts, screws, and rivets (each requiring a hole), or to provide access to the inside of a part. Note, for example, the number of rivets on an airplane's fuselage, or the bolts in engine blocks and various components under the hood of an automobile.

Holemaking is among the most important operations in manufacturing. In automotive engine production, the cost of holemaking is one of the largest machining costs. **Drilling** is a major and common holemaking proces; other processes for producing holes are punching (Section 16.2) and various advanced machining processes (Chapter 26).

22.7.1 Drills

Because *drills* usually have a high length-to-diameter ratio (Fig. 22.22), they are capable of producing relatively deep holes. They are somewhat flexible, however, depending on their diameter, and should be used with care in order to drill holes accurately and to prevent the drill from breaking. Furthermore, the chips that are produced within the workpiece have to

(a) Twist drill

(c) Straight-flute drill

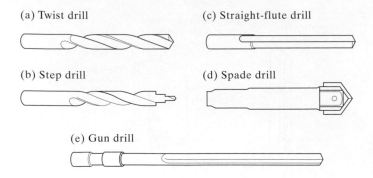

(b) Step drill

(d) Spade drill

(e) Gun drill

(f) Drill with brazed carbide tip

Carbide insert

Braze

Drill body (low-alloy steel)

(g) Drill with indexable carbide inserts

Carbide inserts

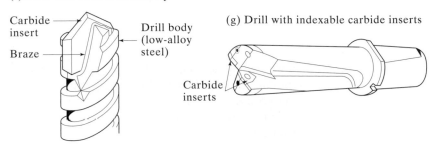

FIGURE 22.22   Various types of drills.

move in the direction opposite to the axial movement of the drill. Consequently, chip disposal and the effectiveness of cutting fluids can present significant difficulties in drilling.

Generally, the hole diameters produced by drilling are slightly larger than the drill diameter (*oversize*), as one can note by observing that a drill can be easily removed from the hole it has just produced. The amount of oversize depends on the quality of the drill and of the equipment used, as well as on the practices employed.

Depending on their thermal properties, some metals and nonmetallic materials expand significantly due to the heat produced by drilling, so the final hole could be smaller than the drill diameter. Also, drilled holes may be subjected to subsequent operations for better surface finish and dimensional accuracy, such as reaming and honing. Drills generally leave a *burr* on the bottom surface upon breakthrough, necessitating deburring operations (Section 25.10).

Twist Drill.   The most common drill is the conventional *standard-point twist drill* (Fig. 22.23a), the main features of which are the *point angle*, *lip-relief angle*, *chisel-edge angle*, and *helix angle*. The geometry of the drill tip is such that the normal rake angle and velocity of the cutting edge vary with the distance from the center of the drill.

Generally, two spiral grooves (*flutes*) run the length of the drill, and the chips produced are guided upward through these grooves. The grooves also serve as passageways to enable the cutting fluid to reach the cutting edges. Some drills have internal longitudinal holes through which cutting fluids are forced, improving lubrication and cooling as well as washing away the chips.

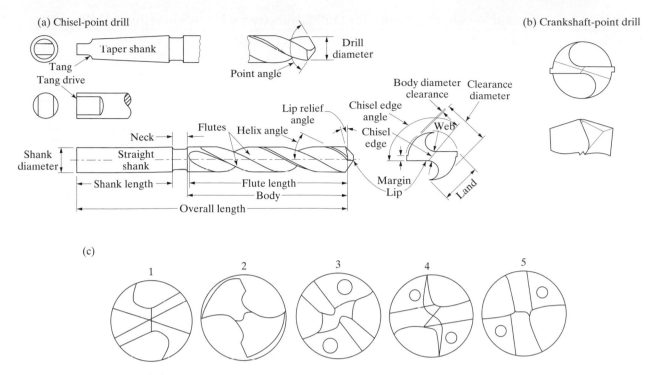

FIGURE 22.23   (a) Standard chisel-point drill indicating various features. The function of the pair of margins is to provide a bearing surface for the drill against walls of the hole as it penetrates into the workpiece; drills with four margins *(double-margin)* are available for improved drill guidance and accuracy. Drills with chip-breaker features are also available. (b) Crankshaft-point drill. (c) Various drill points and their manufacturers: 1. Four-facet split point, by Komet of America. 2. SE point, by Hertel. 3. New point, by Mitsubishi Materials. 4. Hosoi point, by OSG Tap and Die. 5. Helical point.

Drills are available with a **chip-breaker** feature ground along the cutting edges. This feature is important in drilling with automated machinery where disposal of long chips without operator assistance is necessary.

General drill geometry recommendations for various workpiece materials are given in Table 22.10. These angles are based on experience in drilling operations and are designed to produce accurate holes, minimize drilling forces and torque, and optimize drill life.

Drill Point Geometries.   Small changes in drill geometry can have a significant effect on the drill's performance, particularly in the chisel-edge region, which accounts for about 50% of the thrust force in drilling. For example, too small a lip relief angle (Fig. 22.23a) increases the thrust force, generates excessive heat, and increases wear. Conversely, too large an angle can cause chipping or breaking of the cutting edge. Consequently, in addition to conventional point drills, several other drill-point geometries have been developed to improve drill performance and increase the penetration rate (Fig. 22.23c). Special grinding techniques and equipment are used to produce these geometries.

Other Types of Drills.   Several types of drills are shown in Figs. 22.24. A *step drill* produces holes of two or more different diameters. A *core drill* is used to make an existing hole larger. *Counterboring* and *countersinking drills* produce depressions on the surface to

TABLE 22.10   General Recommendations for Drill Geometry for High-Speed Twist Drills

Workpiece material	Point angle	Lip-relief angle	Chisel-edge angle	Helix angle	Point
Aluminum alloys	90–118	12–15	125–135	24–48	Standard
Magnesium alloys	70–118	12–15	120–135	30–45	Standard
Copper alloys	118	12–15	125–135	10–30	Standard
Steels	118	10–15	125–135	24–32	Standard
High-strength steels	118–135	7–10	125–135	24–32	Crankshaft
Stainless steels, low strength	118	10–12	125–135	24–32	Standard
Stainless steels, high strength	118–135	7–10	120–130	24–32	Crankshaft
High-temp. alloys	118–135	9–12	125–135	15–30	Crankshaft
Refractory alloys	118	7–10	125–135	24–32	Standard
Titanium alloys	118–135	7–10	125–135	15–32	Crankshaft
Cast irons	118	8–12	125–135	24–32	Standard
Plastics	60–90	7	120–135	29	Standard

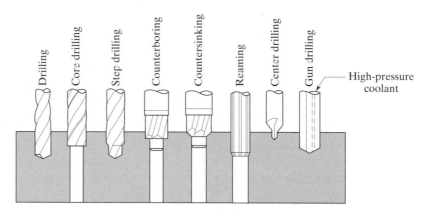

FIGURE 22.24   Various types of drilling and reaming operations.

accommodate the heads of screws and bolts. A *center drill* is short and is used to produce the hole at the end of a piece of stock so that it may be mounted between centers in a lathe (between the headstock and the tailstock, Fig. 22.2). A *spot drill* is used to spot (to start) a hole at the desired location on a surface.

Spade drills have removable tips or bits and are used to produce large and deep holes. They have the advantages of higher stiffness (because of the absence of flutes in the body of the drill), ease of grinding the cutting edges, and lower cost. *Crankshaft drills* (Fig. 22.23b) have good centering ability, and because chips tend to break up easily, these drills are suitable for producing deep holes.

Gun Drilling.   Developed originally for drilling gun barrels, *gun drilling* is used for drilling deep holes and requires a special drill (Figs. 22.22e and 22.25a). The depth-to-diameter ratios of holes produced can be 300:1 or even higher. The thrust force (the radial force that tends to push the drill sideways) is balanced by bearing pads on the drill that slide along the inside surface of the hole (Fig. 22.25a). Therefore, a gun drill is self-centering, an important feature when drilling straight, deep holes.

Cutting speeds in gun drilling are usually high and feeds are low. The cutting fluid is forced under high pressure through a longitudinal hole in the body of the drill (Fig. 22.25b).

(a)

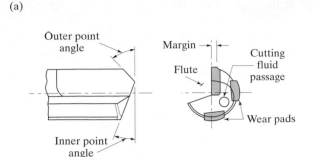

(b)

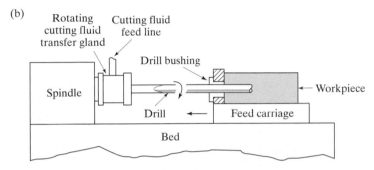

FIGURE 22.25 (a) A gun drill showing various features. (b) Method of gun drilling. *Source*: Eldorado Tool and Manufacturing Corporation.

In addition to lubricating and cooling, the fluid also flushes out chips that would otherwise be trapped in the deep hole being drilled, thus interfering with the drilling operation. The tool does not have to be retracted to clear the chips.

Trepanning. In *trepanning*, the cutting tool (Fig. 22.26a) produces a hole by removing a disk-shaped piece (*core*), usually from flat plates. A hole is produced without reducing all the material removed to chips, as is the case in drilling. The trepanning process can be used to make disks up to 150 mm (6 in.) in diameter from flat sheet or plate; it can also be used to make circular grooves in which O-rings are to be placed (see Fig. 22.1f).

Trepanning can be done on lathes, drill presses (Fig. 22.26b), or other machines, using single-point or multipoint tools. A variation of trepanning is **gun trepanning**, which uses a cutting tool similar to a gun drill except that the tool has a central hole.

FIGURE 22.26 (a) Trepanning tool. (b) Trepanning with a drill-mounted single cutter.

(a)   (b)

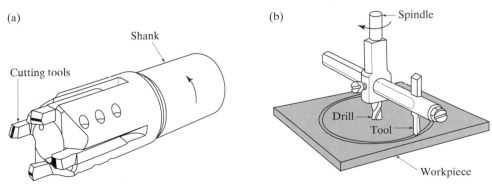

22.7.2 Material Removal Rate

The *material removal rate* (MRR) in drilling is the volume of material removed by the drill per unit time. For a drill with a diameter D, the cross-sectional area of the drilled hole is $\pi D^2/4$. The velocity of the drill perpendicular to the workpiece is the product of the feed f (the distance the drill penetrates per revolution) and the rotational speed N where $N = V/\pi D$. Thus,

$$\text{MRR} = \left(\frac{\pi D^2}{4}\right)(f)(N). \tag{22.3}$$

We can check the dimensional accuracy of this equation, as we did for Eq. (22.1), by noting that $\text{MRR} = (\text{mm}^2)(\text{mm/rev})(\text{rev/min}) = \text{mm}^3/\text{min}$, which is the correct unit for volume removed per unit time.

22.7.3 Thrust Force and Torque

The *thrust force* in drilling acts perpendicular to the hole axis; if this force is excessive, it can cause the drill to bend or break. An excessive thrust force can also distort the workpiece, particularly if it does not have sufficient stiffness (for example, thin sheet-metal structures), or it can cause the workpiece to slip into the workholding fixture.

Thrust forces range from a few newtons for small drills to as high as 100 kN (22.5 klb) for drilling high-strength materials with large drills. Similarly, drilling torque can range as high as 4000 N · m (3000 lb-ft). The thrust force depends on factors such as (a) the strength of the workpiece material, (b) feed, (c) rotational speed, (d) drill diameter, (e) drill geometry, and (f) cutting fluids. Accurate calculation of the thrust force on the drill is difficult. However, experimental data are available as an aid in designing and using drills and drilling equipment.

A knowledge of the magnitude of the *torque* in drilling is essential for estimating the power requirement. Excessive torque can distort the workpiece or cause it to slip in the workholding fixture. The torque during drilling is difficult to calculate. It can be obtained from the data given in Table 20.1 by noting that the power dissipated during drilling is the product of torque and rotational speed. Therefore, the torque on the drill can be calculated by first calculating the material-removal rate.

Example: Material Removal Rate and Torque in Drilling

A hole is being drilled in a block of magnesium alloy with a 10-mm drill bit at a feed of 0.2 mm/rev, with the spindle running at $N = 800$ rpm. Calculate the material removal rate and the torque on the drill.

Solution: The material removal rate is first calculated from Eq. (22.3):

$$\text{MRR} = \left[\frac{(\pi)(10)^2}{4}\right](0.2)(800) = 12{,}570 \text{ mm}^3/\text{min} = 210 \text{ mm}^3/\text{s}.$$

Referring to Table 20.1, let's take an average unit power of 0.5 W · s/mm³ for magnesium alloys. Therefore, the power required is

$$\text{Power} = (210)(0.5) = 105 \text{ W}.$$

Power is the product of the torque on the drill and the rotational speed, which in this case is $(800)(2\pi)/60 = 83.8$ radians per second. Noting that W = J/s and J = N · m, we have

$$T = \frac{105}{83.8} = 1.25 \text{ N·m}.$$

22.7.4 Drill Materials and Sizes

Drills are usually made of high-speed steels (M1, M7, and M10), and many are now coated with titanium nitride for increased wear resistance (Section 21.6). Carbide-tipped (Figs. 22.22f and g) or solid-carbide (C-2) drills are available for cast irons, steels, hard high-temperature metals, and abrasive materials, such as concrete and brick (*masonry drills*), and composite materials with abrasive fiber reinforcements, such as glass and graphite.

Polycrystalline-diamond coated drills are now commonly used for producing fastener holes in reinforced plastics, such as graphite-epoxy. Because of their high wear resistance, several thousand holes can be drilled with little damage to the material.

Standard twist-drill sizes consist of the following series:

a. **Numerical:** No. 97 (0.0059 in.) to No. 1 (0.228 in.).

b. **Letter:** A (0.234 in.) to Z (0.413 in.).

c. **Fractional:** Straight shank from $\frac{1}{64}$ in. to $1\frac{1}{4}$ in. (in $\frac{1}{64}$ in. increments) to $1\frac{1}{2}$ in. (in $\frac{1}{32}$ in. increments), and larger drills in larger increments. Taper shank from $\frac{1}{8}$ in. to $1\frac{3}{4}$ in. (in $\frac{1}{64}$ in. increments) to $3\frac{1}{2}$ in. (in $\frac{1}{16}$ in. increments).

d. **Millimeter:** From 0.05 mm (0.002 in.), in increments of 0.01 mm.

The capabilities of drilling and boring operations are shown in Table 22.11.

22.7.5 Drilling Practice

Drills and similar holemaking tools are usually held in *drill chucks* which may be tightened with or without keys. Special chucks and collets, with various quick-change features that do not require stopping the spindle, are available for use on production machinery.

Because a drill doesn't have a centering action, it tends to "walk" on the workpiece surface at the beginning of the operation. This problem is particularly severe with small-diameter drills. To start a hole properly, the drill should be guided, using fixtures (such as a bushing) to keep it from deflecting sideways.

A small starting hole can be made with a center drill (usually with a point angle of 60°), or the drill point may be ground to an *S* shape (*helical* or *spiral point*). This shape's self-centering characteristic eliminates the need for center drilling, produces accurate holes, and improves drill life. These factors are particularly important in automated production with CNC machines in which the usual practice is to use a spot drill with a point angle of 118°. The drill will "walk" less when the point angles of the spot drill and of the drill to be used are matched.

Because of its rotary motion, drilling produces holes with walls that have circumferential marks; in contrast, punched holes have longitudinal marks (see Fig. 16.5a). This difference is significant in terms of the hole's fatigue properties (Section 30.5).

TABLE 22.11   Capabilities of Drilling and Boring Operations

Tool type	Diameter range (mm)	Hole depth/diameter Typical	Hole depth/diameter Maximum
Twist	0.5–150	8	50
Spade	25–150	30	100
Gun	2–50	100	300
Trepanning	40–250	10	100
Boring	3–1200	5	8

TABLE 22.12   General Recommendations for Speeds and Feeds in Drilling

Workpiece material	Surface Speed		Feed, mm/rev (in./rev) Drill diameter		Rpm	
	m/min	ft/min	1.5 mm (0.060 in.)	12.5 mm (0.5 in.)	1.5 mm	12.5 mm
Aluminum alloys	30–120	100–400	0.025 (0.001)	0.30 (0.012)	6400–25,000	800–3000
Magnesium alloys	45–120	150–400	0.025 (0.001)	0.30 (0.012)	9600–25,000	1100–3000
Copper alloys	15–60	50–200	0.025 (0.001)	0.25 (0.010)	3200–12,000	400–1500
Steels	20–30	60–100	0.025 (0.001)	0.30 (0.012)	4300–6400	500–800
Stainless steels	10–20	40–60	0.025 (0.001)	0.18 (0.007)	2100–4300	250–500
Titanium alloys	6–20	20–60	0.010 (0.0004)	0.15 (0.006)	1300–4300	150–500
Cast irons	20–60	60–200	0.025 (0.001)	0.30 (0.012)	4300–12,000	500–1500
Thermoplastics	30–60	100–200	0.025 (0.001)	0.13 (0.005)	6400–12,000	800–1500
Thermosets	20–60	60–200	0.025 (0.001)	0.10 (0.004)	4300–12,000	500–1500

Note: As hole depth increases, speeds and feeds should be reduced. Selection of speeds and feeds also depends on the specific surface finish required.

Drilling Recommendations.   Recommended ranges for drilling speeds and feeds are given in Table 22.12. The speed is the *surface speed* of the drill at its periphery. Thus, a 0.5-in. (12.7 mm) drill rotating at 300 rpm has a surface speed of $\left(\frac{0.5}{2} \text{ in.}\right)$ $(300 \text{ rev/min})(2\pi \text{ rad/rev})\left(\frac{1}{12} \text{ ft/in.}\right) = 39 \text{ ft/min} = 12 \text{ m/min}$. When drilling holes smaller than 1 mm (0.040 in.) in diameter, rotational speeds can range up to 30,000 rpm, depending on the workpiece material.

The *feed* in drilling is the distance the drill travels into the workpiece per revolution. For example, Table 22.12 recommends that for most workpiece materials, a drill 1.5 mm (0.060 in.) in diameter should have a feed of 0.025 mm/rev. If the speed column in the table indicates that the drill should rotate at, say, 2000 rpm, then the drill should travel into the workpiece at a linear speed of $(0.025 \text{ mm/rev})(2000 \text{ rev/min}) = 50 \text{ mm/min} = 2 \text{ in./min}$.

Chip removal during drilling can be difficult, especially for deep holes in soft and ductile materials. The drill should be retracted periodically (*pecking*) to remove chips that may have accumulated along the flutes; otherwise, the drill may break because of excessive torque, or it may "walk" off location and produce a misshapen hole. A general guide to the probable causes of problems in drilling operations is given in Table 22.13.

Drill Reconditioning.   Drills are reconditioned by grinding them either manually or using special fixtures. Proper reconditioning of drills is important, particularly with automated manufacturing on computer numerical control machines. Hand grinding is difficult and requires considerable skill in order to produce symmetric cutting edges. Grinding on fixtures is accurate and is done on special computer-controlled grinders. Drills coated with titanium nitride can be recoated.

TABLE 22.13   General Troubleshooting Guide for Drilling Operations

Problem	Probable causes
Drill breakage	Dull drill; drill seizing in hole because of chips clogging flutes; feed too high; lip relief angle too small.
Excessive drill wear	Cutting speed too high; ineffective cutting fluid; rake angle too high; drill burned and strength lost when sharpened.
Tapered hole	Drill misaligned or bent; lips not equal; web not central.
Oversize hole	Same as above; machine spindle loose; chisel edge not central; side pressure on workpiece.
Poor hole surface finish	Dull drill; ineffective cutting fluid; welding of workpiece material on drill margin; improperly ground drill; improper alignment.

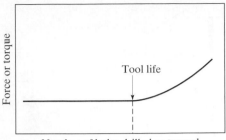

FIGURE 22.27   The determination of drill life by monitoring the rise in force or torque as a function of the number of holes drilled. This test is also used for determining tap life.

22.7.6 Measuring Drill Life

The resharpening or replacement of dull drills is important, particularly in automated production. The use of dull drills increases forces and power, causes surface damage, and produces inaccurate holes. The life of drills, as well as taps (Section 22.10), is usually measured by the number of holes drilled before they become dull.

The test procedure consists of clamping a block of material on a suitable dynamometer or force transducer and drilling a number of holes while recording the torque or force during each successive operation. After a number of holes have been drilled, the torque and force begin to increase because the tool is becoming dull (Fig. 22.27).

Drill life is defined as the number of holes drilled until this transition begins. Other techniques, such as monitoring vibration and acoustic emissions (Section 20.7.5), may also be used to determine drill life. These techniques are particularly important in computer-controlled operations.

22.8 DRILLING MACHINES

Drilling machines are used for drilling holes, tapping, reaming, and for small-diameter boring operations. The most common vertical type is the **drill press**, the major components of which are shown in Fig. 22.28a. The workpiece is placed on an adjustable table, either by clamping it directly into the slots and holes on the table or by using a vise, which in turn can be clamped to the table. The drill is lowered manually by hand wheel or by power feed at preset rates. Manual feeding requires some skill in judging the appropriate feed rate.

Drill presses are usually designated by the largest workpiece diameter that can be accommodated on the table. Sizes typically range from 150 mm to 1250 mm (6 in. to 50 in.).

In order to maintain proper cutting speeds at the cutting edges of drills, the spindle speed on drilling machines has to be adjustable to accommodate different drill sizes. Adjustments are made by means of pulleys, gear boxes, or variable-speed motors.

The types of drilling machines range from simple *bench-type* units, used to drill small-diameter holes, to large *radial drills* (Fig. 22.28b), which can accommodate large workpieces. The distance between the column and the spindle center can be as much as 3 m (10 ft). The drill head of *universal drilling machines* can be swiveled to drill holes at an angle.

Developments in drilling machines include numerically controlled three-axis machines; various drilling operations are performed automatically and in the desired sequence with the use of a turret (Fig. 22.29). Note that the turret holds several different tools. (See also Section 24.2.)

Drilling machines with multiple spindles (*gang drilling*) are used for high-production-rate operations. These machines are capable of drilling in one step as many as 50 holes of varying sizes, depths, and locations. These machines are also used for reaming and counterboring operations. Special drilling machines, such as those used to produce holes in continuous

(a)

(b)

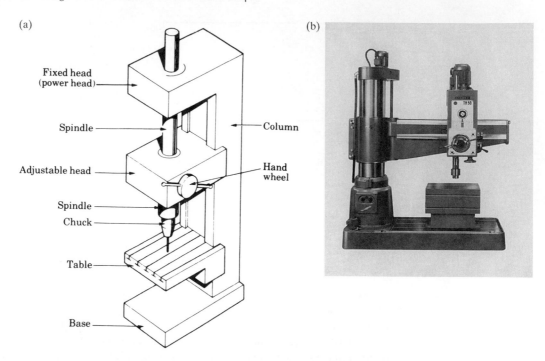

Fixed head
(power head)

Spindle

Column

Adjustable head

Hand
wheel

Spindle

Chuck

Table

Base

FIGURE 22.28   Schematic illustration of the components of (a) a vertical drill
press and (b) a radial drilling machine. *Source*: Willis Machinery and Tools.

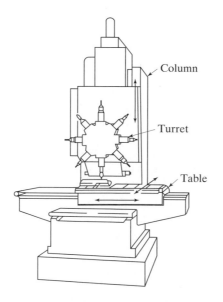

Column

Turret

Table

FIGURE 22.29   A three-
axis computer numerical
control drilling machine.
The turret holds as much as
eight different tools, such
as drills, taps, and reamers.

hinges (e.g., piano hinges), use twist drills 1 mm (0.040 in.) in diameter. These machines are
usually horizontal and produce holes in up to 3-m (10-ft) long segments on one cycle.

Workholding devices for drilling are important to ensure that the workpiece can be located properly. They also keep the workpiece from slipping or rotating during drilling. Workholding devices are available in various designs; the important features are three-point locating for
accuracy and three-dimensional workholding for secure fixturing. (See also Section 38.9.)

22.9 REAMING AND REAMERS

Reaming is an operation used to (a) make an existing hole dimensionally more accurate than can be obtained by drilling alone and (b) improve its surface finish. The most accurate holes are produced by the following sequence of operations:

1. Centering,
2. Drilling,
3. Boring, and
4. Reaming.

For even better accuracy and surface finish, holes may be *burnished* or internally ground and honed (Sections 25.6 and 25.10).

A *reamer* (Fig. 22.30a) is a multiple-cutting-edge tool with straight or helically fluted edges; that removes very little material. For soft metals, a reamer typically removes a minimum of 0.2 mm (0.008 in.) on the diameter of a drilled hole, and for harder metals about 0.13 mm (0.005 in.). Attempts to remove smaller layers can be detrimental, as the reamer may be damaged or the hole surface may become burnished. In this case, honing would be preferred. In general, reamer speeds should be one-half those of the same-sized drill, and three times the feed rate.

The basic types of reamers are hand and machine. *Hand reamers* are straight or have a tapered end in the first third of their length. Various *machine reamers*, also called chucking reamers because they are mounted in a chuck and operated by a machine, are available.

There are two types of chucking reamers. *Rose* reamers have cutting edges with wide margins and no relief (Fig. 22.30a); they remove considerable material and true up a hole for flute reaming. *Fluted* reamers have small margins and relief, with a rake angle of about 5°. They are usually used for light cuts of about 0.1 mm (0.004 in.) on the hole diameter.

Shell reamers, which are hollow and mounted on an arbor, are generally used for holes larger than 20 mm (0.75 in.). *Expansion* reamers are adjustable for small variations in hole size and also to compensate for wear of the reamer's cutting edges. *Adjustable* reamers (Fig. 22.30b) can be set for specific hole diameters and are, therefore, versatile.

Reamers are usually made of high-speed steels (M1, M2, and M7) or solid carbides (C-2) or have carbide cutting edges. Proper reamer maintenance and reconditioning are im-

FIGURE 22.30   (a) Terminology for a helical reamer. (b) Inserted-blade adjustable reamer.

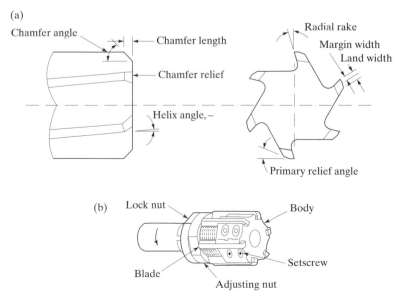

(a)

Chamfer angle
Chamfer length
Chamfer relief
Helix angle, –
Radial rake
Margin width
Land width
Primary relief angle

(b) Lock nut   Body
Blade
Adjusting nut
Setscrew

portant for hole accuracy and surface finish. Reamers may be held rigidly, as in a chuck, or they may *float* in their holding fixtures to ensure alignment or be *piloted* in guide bushings placed above and below the workpiece.

A further development in reaming consists of the *dreamer,* a tool which combines drilling and reaming; the tip of the tool produces a hole by drilling and the rest of the same tool performs a reaming operation. A similar development involves drilling and tapping in one stroke using a single tool.

22.10 TAPPING AND TAPS

Internal threads in workpieces can be produced by *tapping.* A *tap* is a chip-producing threading tool with multiple cutting teeth (Fig. 22.31a). Taps are generally available with two, three, or four flutes; the most common production tap is the two-flute spiral-point tap. The two-flute tap forces the chips into the hole so that the tap needs to be retracted only at the end of the cut. Three-fluted taps are stronger because more material is available in the flute. Tap sizes range up to 100 mm (4 in.).

Tapered taps are designed to reduce the torque required for tapping through holes. *Bottoming taps* are for tapping blind holes to their full depth. *Collapsible taps* are used in large-diameter holes; after tapping has been completed, the tap is mechanically collapsed and, without rotation, is removed from the hole.

Chip removal can be a significant problem during tapping because of the small clearances involved. If chips aren't removed properly, the excessive torque that results can break the tap. The use of a cutting fluid and periodic reversal and removal of the tap from the hole are effective means of chip removal and of improving the quality of the tapped hole.

A development for higher tapping productivity is the combination of drilling and tapping in a single tool (*drapping*). The tool has a drilling section at its tip, followed by a tapping section.

Tapping may be done by *hand* or with machines such as the following ones:

1. Drilling machines,
2. Lathes,
3. Automatic screw machines,
4. Vertical CNC milling machines combining the correct relative rotation and the longitudinal feed.

Special tapping machines are available with features for multiple tapping operations. Multiple-spindle tapping heads are used extensively, particularly in the automotive industry, where 30% to 40% of machining operations involve the tapping of holes. One system for automatic tapping of nuts is shown in Fig. 22.31b.

With proper lubrication, tap life may be as high as 10,000 holes. Tap life can be determined with the same technique used to measure drill life. (See Fig. 22.27.) Taps are usu-

FIGURE 22.31   (a) Terminology for a tap. (b) Tapping of steel nuts in production.

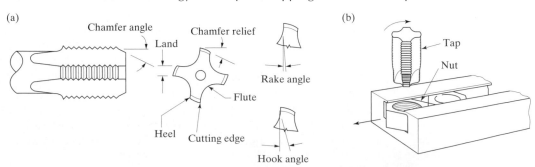

ally made of carbon steels for light-duty applications or of high-speed steels (M1, M2, M7, and M10) for production work.

Productivity in tapping operations can be improved by *high-speed tapping*, with surface speeds as high as 100 m/min (350 ft/min). *Self-reversing* tapping systems have also been improved significantly, and are now in use with modern computer-controlled machine tools. Several designs are available, with operating speeds as high as 5000 rpm, although actual cutting speeds in most applications are considerably lower.

Cycle times are typically on the order of 1-2 seconds. Also, some tapping systems now have capabilities for directing the cutting fluid to the cutting zone through the spindle and a hole in the tap, which also helps flush the chips out of the hole being tapped.

Chipless tapping is a process of internal thread rolling using a forming tap (Section 13.5.2).

22.11 DESIGN CONSIDERATIONS FOR DRILLING, REAMING, AND TAPPING

The basic design guidelines for drilling, reaming, and tapping operations are as follows:

a. Designs should allow holes to be drilled on flat surfaces and perpendicular to the drill motion; otherwise, the drill tends to deflect and the hole will not be located accurately. Exit surfaces for the drill should also be flat.

b. Interrupted hole surfaces should be avoided or minimized for improved dimensional accuracy.

c. Hole bottoms should, if possible, match standard drill-point angles (Table 22.10). Flat bottoms or odd shapes should be avoided.

d. Through holes are preferred over blind holes, as they are in boring operations. If holes with large diameters are required, the workpiece should have a preexisting hole, preferably made during fabrication of the part (e.g., by forming or casting).

e. Parts should be designed so that all drilling can be done with a minimum of fixturing and without repositioning the workpiece.

f. It may be difficult to ream blind or intersecting holes because of the possibility of tool breakage. Extra hole depth should be provided.

g. Blind holes must be drilled deeper than subsequent reaming or tapping operations that may be performed.

Example: Bone Screw Retainer

A cervical spine implant is shown in Fig. 22.32a. In the event that a patient requires cervical bony fusion at one or more vertebral levels, this implant can act as an internal stabilizer, decreasing the amount of motion in this region to help promote a successful fusion. The plate affixes to the anterior aspect of the spine with bone screws that go through the plate and into the bone. The undersurface of the plate has a very rough surface that helps hold the plate in place while the bone screws are being inserted.

One concern with this type of implant is the possibility of the bone screws loosening with time due to normal, repetitive loading from the patient. In extreme cases, this can result in a screw backing out, with the head of the screw no longer flush with the plate, a condition that is obviously undesirable. This implant uses a retainer to prevent the bone screw from backing out away from the plate. The part drawing for the retainer is shown in Figure 22.32b.

The retainer has a number of design features that are essential for it to function correctly and without complicating the surgical procedure. To ease its use in surgery, the plate is provided with the retainers already in place, with the circular notches aligned with the bone screw holes. This allows the surgeon to insert the bone screws without interference from the retainer. Once the screws are inserted, the surgeon turns the retainer a few degrees so that each screw head is then captured. In order to ensure the retainer's proper orientation in the plate, the thread of its shank must start in the same axial location as point S in Fig. 22.32b.

The manufacturing steps to produce this part are shown in Fig. 22.32c. First, a 0.5-in. diameter Ti-6Al-4V rod is placed in a CNC lathe and faced, then the threaded area is turned to the diameter necessary to machine the threads. The thread is turned on the shank, but over a longer length than ultimately required because of difficulties in obtaining high quality threads at the start of machining. The cap is then turned to the required diameter and the 0.10 in. radius is machined on the underside of the head.

The part is then removed, inspected, and placed in another CNC lathe and is faced to length. The spherical radius in the cap is machined and the center hole is drilled and the hex head broached. The cap is removed and inspected. If the desired length has not been achieved, it is lapped (Section 25.10.4) to the final dimension.

At this point, the retainer is placed in a CNC milling machine, using a specially designed fixture which consists basically of a threaded, tapered hole. By carefully applying a pre-determined torque on the retainer when placing it into the fixture, the starting location of the threads can be accurately controlled. Once the cap is located in the fixture, the three circular notches are machined per the drawing.

The retainer is then deburred and tumbled (Section 25.11) to remove all sharp corners, and the bottom is heavy grit blasted to match that of the underside of the plate. Finally, the parts are anodized (Section 33.9) and passivated to obtain the desired biocompatability.

Source: J. Mankowski and B. Pyszka, Master Metal Engineering Inc., and C. Lyle and M. Handwerker, Wright Medical Technology, Inc.

FIGURE 22.32

screw and retainer
inserted in plate

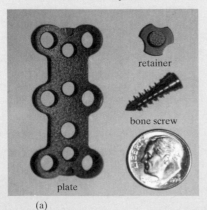

retainer

bone screw

plate

(a)

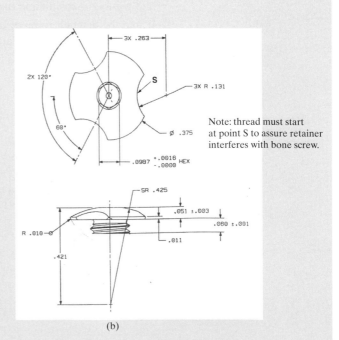

Note: thread must start
at point S to assure retainer
interferes with bone screw.

(b)

SUMMARY

- Cutting processes that produce external and internal circular profiles are turning, boring, drilling, and tapping. Because of the three-dimensional nature of these operations, chip movement and its control are important considerations. Chip removal can be a significant problem, especially in drilling and tapping, and can lead to tool breakage.
- Optimization of each cutting process requires an understanding of the interrelationships among design parameters (part shape, dimensional accuracy, surface finish) and process parameters (cutting speed, feed, depth of cut), tool material, tool shape, use of cutting fluids, and sequence of operations to be performed.
- High-speed machining, ultraprecision machining, and hard turning are developments that have helped reduce machining costs and produce parts with exceptional surface finish and dimensional accuracy for critical applications.
- The parts to be machined may have been produced by casting, forging, extrusion, or powder metallurgy. The closer the blank to be machined to the final shape desired, the fewer the number and extent of the subsequent machining processes required.

TRENDS

- The major trend in cutting processes is to optimize operations and minimize costs by automation, reducing the amount of labor needed.
- High-speed machining (with spindle speeds on the order of 20,000 rpm) and hard turning are in wider use and are becoming competitive with other removal processes in specialized applications.
- Much progress is being made in the ultraprecision machining of specialized components using very sharp single-crystal diamond tools.
- Sensors for measuring and monitoring forces, power, deflections, temperature, tool wear and fracture, and surface finish are in use as a means of on-line compensation to maintain quality and reduce defective parts.
- Machine tools are being designed and built such that setup time and idle time (e.g., time spent in non-cutting tool movements, retraction, acceleration and deceleration of tools, and turret indexing) are reduced.
- Machine tools are now capable of performing various simultaneous cutting operations on a workpiece, using multiple-spindle, -axis, and -turret systems, as well as of performing roughing and finishing operations in one setup.
- In-process gaging systems now monitor the cutting operation and provide real-time control feedback. These include automatic tool wear and breakage monitoring and detection as well as the implementation of inspection techniques for statistical process control.
- Computer-controlled turning machines are replacing screw machines in specialty fastener products.

KEY TERMS

Automatic bar machine	Diamond turning	Finishing cuts
Back rake angle	Drill life	Form tools
Bed	Drilling	Gun drilling
Boring	Drill press	Hard turning
Boring mill	Ductile-regime cutting	Headstock
Carriage	Engine lathe	High-speed machining
Chip management	Face plate	Holemaking
Chuck	Facing	Jig borer
Collet	Feed force	Knurling
Cutting-edge angle	Feed rod	Lathes

Lead screw
Mandrel
Material removal rate
Nose radius
Parting
Power chuck
Rake angle
Reamer

Reaming
Reconditioning
Relief angle
Roughing cuts
Screw threads
Side rake angle
Tailstock
Tapping

Threading
Trepanning
Turning
Turret lathe
Twist drill
Ultraprecision machining

BIBLIOGRAPHY

ASM Handbook, Vol. 16: *Machining*. ASM International, 1989.
Boothroyd, G., and W.A. Knight, *Fundamentals of Machining and Machine Tools*, (2d ed.) Marcel Dekker, 1989.
Brown, J., *Advanced Machining Technology Handbook*. McGraw-Hill, 1998.
Machinery's Handbook. Industrial Press, revised periodically.
Machining Data Handbook, (3d ed.), 2 vols. Machinability Data Center, 1980.

Metal Cutting Tool Handbook, (7th ed.) Industrial Press, 1989.
Stephenson, D.A., and J.S. Agapiou, *Metal Cutting Theory and Practice*. Marcel Dekker, 1996.
Tool and Manufacturing Engineering Handbook, (4th ed.), Vol. 1: *Machining*. Society of Manufacturing Engineers, 1983.
Walsh, R.A., *McGraw-Hill Machining and Metalworking Handbook*. McGraw-Hill, 1994.
Weck, M., *Handbook of Machine Tools*, 4 vols. Wiley, 1984.

REVIEW QUESTIONS

22.1 Describe the types of machining operations that can be performed on a lathe.
22.2 Explain the functions of different angles on a single-point lathe cutting tool.
22.3 What is the difference between feed rod and lead screw?
22.4 Why were power chucks developed?
22.5 Why can boring on a lathe be a difficult operation?
22.6 Why is there more than one turret in turret lathes?
22.7 Explain the reasoning behind the various design guidelines for turning.
22.8 List the features of automatic screw machines.
22.9 Describe the differences between boring a workpiece on a lathe and boring it on a boring mill.
22.10 Explain the consequences of drilling with a drill bit that has not been properly sharpened.
22.11 How is drill life determined?
22.12 Why are reaming operations performed?
22.13 Why can tapping be a difficult operation?
22.14 Describe the difference between a steady rest and a follow rest. Give an application of each.
22.15 Ram-type turret lathes are used more commonly than saddle-type turret lathes. Why?
22.16 Explain the functions of the saddle on a lathe.
22.17 Explain the functions of the margin in a twist drill (Fig. 22.23).
22.18 Explain why pipe threads are tapered.
22.19 Describe the relative advantages of (a) self-opening and (b) solid die heads for threading.
22.20 What are the ways in a lathe?
22.21 How is a boring mill different from a lathe?
22.22 On what kind of machine is knurling performed?
22.23 What is a tracer lathe?
22.24 What does "forming" mean with respect to machine shapes?
22.25 Explain how external threads are cut on a lathe.
22.26 What is the difference between a blind hole and a through hole?
22.27 Describe the kinds of operations that can be performed on a drill press.
22.28 Why does a roughing cut never follow a finishing cut?

22.76 Could the part shown on the left in Problem 22.75 be made with processes other than casting? Explain. How does the number of parts required influence your answer? Would you still need machining operations to complete the part, as shown on the right?

22.77 Suggest remedies for the problems encountered in turning operations as listed in Table 22.9. Explain why you are making these suggestions.

22.78 Explain why the drilling problems listed in Table 22.13 have those particular causes. Suggest remedies, and explain why you are making these suggestions.

22.79 With appropriate sketches, describe the principles of various fixturing methods and devices that can be used for the processes described in this chapter. Include three-point locating and three-dimensional workholding for drilling and similar operations.

22.80 Make a comprehensive table of the process capabilities of the machining processes described in this chapter. Use several columns to describe the machines involved, the type of tools and tool materials used, the shapes of blanks and parts produced, the typical maximum and minimum sizes, the surface finish, the dimensional tolerances, and the production rates.

22.81 Based on the data developed in the foregoing problem, describe your thoughts regarding the procedure to be followed in determining what type of machine tool to select for a particular part to be machined.

22.82 A large bolt is to be produced from extruded hexagonal stock by placing the hex stock into a chuck and machining the cylindrical shank of the bolt by turning. List the difficulties which may be presented by this operation.

22.83 The following part is a power transmitting shaft; it is to be produced on a lathe. List the operations that are needed to make this part and estimate the machining time.

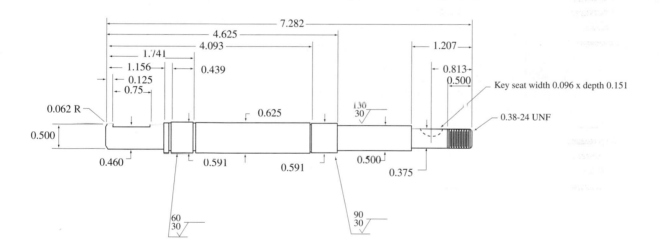

23

Machining Processes Used to Produce Various Shapes

23.1 INTRODUCTION

In addition to producing various external or internal round profiles, cutting operations can produce many other parts with more complex shapes (Fig. 23.1). As described in this chapter, several cutting processes and machine tools are capable of producing these shapes using multitooth and single-point cutting tools. (See also Table 22.1.)

This chapter begins with one of the most versatile processes: *milling*, in which a rotating, multitooth cutter removes material while traveling along various axes with respect to the workpiece. Other processes are then described, such as *planing*, *shaping*, and *broaching*, in which the tool or workpiece travels along a straight path, producing flat and shaped surfaces.

Next, we cover *sawing* processes, which are generally used to prepare blanks from rods and flat plate for subsequent forming, machining, and welding operations. Also briefly discussed is *filing*, which is used to remove small amounts of material, usually from edges and corners.

Recall that Part III included *gear manufacturing* by metal-forming processes, in which gear teeth are produced by plastic deformation. It was also stated that gears can be manufactured with casting and powder-metallurgy techniques. This chapter describes gear production by several machining processes that use special cutters, and describes the quality and properties of gears made by these processes.

646

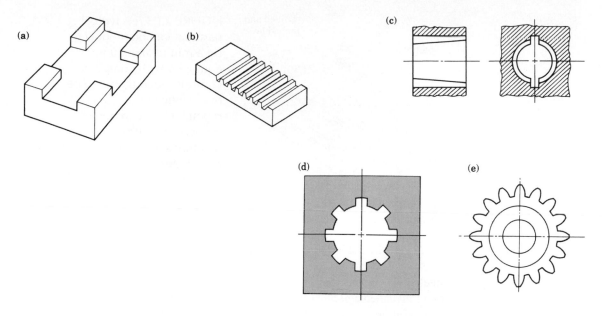

FIGURE 23.1   Typical parts and shapes produced with the machining processes described in this chapter.

23.2 MILLING OPERATIONS

Milling includes a number of highly versatile machining operations capable of producing a variety of configurations (Fig. 23.2) with the use of a **milling cutter**, a multitooth tool that produces a number of chips in one revolution. Parts such as the one shown in Fig. 23.3 can be machined efficiently with various types of milling cutters.

FIGURE 23.2   Some of the basic types of milling cutters and milling operations.

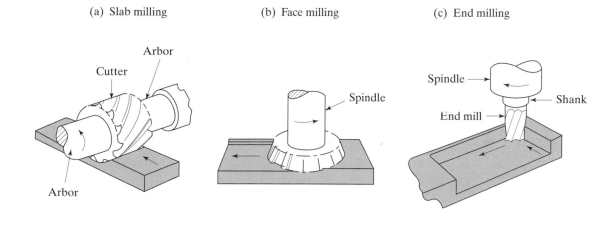

(a) Slab milling   (b) Face milling   (c) End milling

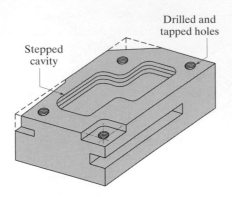

FIGURE 23.3   A typical part that can be produced on a milling machine equipped with computer controls. Such parts can be made efficiently and repetitively on computer numerical control (CNC) machines, without the need for refixturing or reclamping the part.

23.2.1 Slab Milling

In *slab milling*, also called *peripheral* milling, the axis of cutter rotation is parallel to the workpiece surface to be machined (Fig. 23.2a). The cutter, generally made of high-speed steel, has a number of teeth along its circumference, each tooth acting like a single-point cutting tool called a *plain mill*.

Cutters for slab milling may have *straight* or *helical teeth* resulting in, respectively, orthogonal or oblique cutting action. The helical teeth on the cutter shown in Fig. 23.2a are preferred over straight teeth because the load on the tooth is lower, resulting in a smoother operation and reducing tool forces and chatter. (See also Fig. 20.9.)

Conventional Milling and Climb Milling.   In *conventional milling*, also called *up milling*, the maximum chip thickness is at the end of the cut (Figs. 23.4a and b). The advantages are that tooth engagement is not a function of workpiece surface characteristics, and contamination or scale on the surface does not affect tool life. This is the common method of milling; the cutting process is smooth, provided that the cutter teeth are sharp. However, there may be a tendency for the tool to chatter and the workpiece has a tendency to be pulled upward, necessitating proper clamping.

In *climb milling*, also called *down milling*, cutting starts at the surface of the workpiece, where the chip is at its thickest. The advantage is that the downward component of the cutting forces holds the workpiece in place, particularly for slender parts. Because of the re-

FIGURE 23.4   (a) Schematic illustration of conventional milling and climb milling. (b) Slab milling operation, showing depth of cut, d, feed per tooth, f, chip depth of cut, t_c, and workpiece speed, v. (c) Schematic illustration of cutter travel distance l_c to reach full depth of cut.

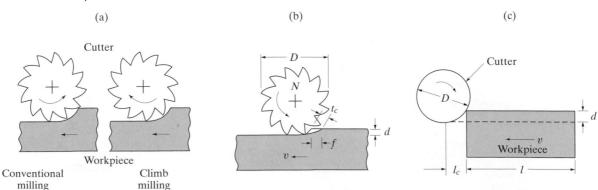

sulting high-impact forces when the teeth engage the workpiece, however, this operation must have a rigid setup, and backlash must be eliminated in the table feed mechanism.

Climb milling is not suitable for the machining of workpieces having surface scale, such as hot-worked metals, forgings, and castings. The scale is hard and abrasive and causes excessive wear and damage to the cutter teeth, shortening tool life. Climb milling is recommended, in general, for maximum cutter life in using computer numerical controlled (CNC) machine tools (Chapter 38).

Milling Parameters. The cutting speed, V, in milling is the peripheral speed of the cutter, or

$$V = \pi D N, \tag{23.1}$$

where D is the cutter diameter and N is the rotational speed of the cutter (Fig. 23.4b).

Note that the thickness of the chip in slab milling varies along its length because of the relative longitudinal motion between cutter and workpiece. For a straight-tooth cutter, we can determine the approximate *undeformed chip thickness* (*chip depth of cut*), t_c, from the equation

$$t_c = \frac{2fd}{D}, \tag{23.2}$$

where f is the feed per tooth of the cutter, measured along the workpiece surface (that is, the distance the workpiece travels per tooth of the cutter, in mm/tooth or in./tooth), and d is the depth of cut. As t_c becomes greater, the force on the cutter tooth increases.

Feed per tooth is determined from the equation

$$f = \frac{v}{Nn}, \tag{23.3}$$

where v is the linear speed (feed rate) of the workpiece and n is the number of teeth on the cutter periphery. We can check the dimensional accuracy of this equation by using appropriate units for the individual terms—for instance, $(\text{mm/tooth}) = (\text{m/min}) \left(10^3 \text{ mm/m}\right)/(\text{rev/min})(\text{number of teeth/rev})$.

The cutting time, t, is given by the expression

$$t = \frac{\left(l + l_c\right)}{v}, \tag{23.4}$$

where l is the length of the workpiece (Fig. 23.4c) and l_c is the extent of the cutter's first contact with the workpiece. Based on the assumption that $l_c \ll l$ (although this is not generally the case), the *material removal rate* is

$$\text{MRR} = \frac{lwd}{t} = wdv, \tag{23.5}$$

where w is the width of the cut (which, for a workpiece narrower than the length of the cutter, is the same as the width of the workpiece). As stated in Section 22.2, the distance that the cutter travels in the noncutting cycle of the milling operation is an important economic consideration and should be minimized.

Although the *power requirement* in slab milling can be calculated, the *forces* acting on the cutter (tangential, radial, and axial; see also Fig. 22.3b) are difficult to calculate because of the many variables involved (particularly cutting tool geometry). These forces can be measured experimentally for a variety of conditions.

TABLE 23.1   Summary of Milling Parameters and Formulas

N = Rotational speed of the milling cutter, rpm
f = Feed, mm/tooth or in./tooth
D = Cutter diameter, mm or in.
n = Number of teeth on cutter
v = Linear speed of the workpiece or feed rate, mm/min or in./min
V = Surface speed of cutter, m/min or ft/min
    $= D N$
f = Feed per tooth, mm/tooth or in./tooth
    $= v/N n$
l = Length of cut, mm or in.
t = Cutting time, s or min
    $= (l + l_c)/v$, where l_c = extent of the cutter's first contact with workpiece
MRR = mm^3/min or $in.^3/min$
    $= w\, d\, v$, where w is the width of cut
Torque = $N \cdot m$ or $lb \cdot ft$
    $= (F_c)(D/2)$
Power = kW or hp
    $= $ (Torque)(ω), where $\omega = 2\pi N$ radians/min

Note: The units given are those that are commonly used; however, appropriate units must be used in the formulas.

From the power, however, we can calculate the *torque* on the cutter spindle. (See the following example.) Although the torque is the product of the tangential force on the cutter and the cutter's radius, the tangential force per tooth will depend on how many teeth are engaged during the cut.

The foregoing equations and the terminology used are summarized in Table 23.1.

Example: Material Removal Rate, Power Required, Torque, and Cutting Time in Slab Milling

A slab-milling operation is being carried out on a 12-in. long, 4-in. wide annealed mild-steel block at a feed $f = 0.01$ in./tooth and a depth of cut $d = \frac{1}{8}$ in. The cutter is $D = 2$ in. in diameter, has 20 straight teeth, rotates at $N = 100$ rpm, and is wider than the block to be machined. Calculate the material removal rate, estimate the power and torque required for this operation, and calculate the cutting time.

Solution: From the information given, we can calculate the linear speed v of the workpiece from Eq. (23.3):

$$v = fNn = (0.01)(100)(20) = 20 \text{ in./min.}$$

From Eq. (23.5), the material removal rate is

$$\text{MRR} = (4)(\tfrac{1}{8})(20) = 10 \text{ in.}^3/\text{min.}$$

Since the workpiece is annealed mild steel, let's estimate unit power from Table 20.1 as 1.1 hp $\cdot$ min/in.^{3}. Hence, the power required can be estimated as

$$\text{Power} = (1.1)(10) = 11 \text{ hp.}$$

We can also calculate the torque acting on the cutter spindle by noting that power is the product of torque and the spindle rotational speed (in radians per unit time). Therefore,

$$\text{Torque} = \frac{\text{Power}}{\text{Rotational speed}}$$

$$= \frac{(11 \text{ hp})(33{,}000 \text{ lb-ft/min.hp})}{(100 \text{ rpm})(2\pi)} = 578 \text{ lb-ft.}$$

The cutting time is given by Eq. (23.4), in which the quantity l_c can be shown, from simple geometric relationships and for $D \gg d$, to approximate

$$l_c = \sqrt{Dd} = \sqrt{(2)(\tfrac{1}{8})} = 0.5 \text{ in.}$$

Thus, the cutting time is

$$t = \frac{(12 + 0.5)}{20} = 0.625 \text{ min} = 37.5 \text{ s.}$$

23.2.2 Face Milling

In *face milling*, the cutter is mounted on a spindle having an axis of rotation perpendicular to the workpiece surface (Fig. 23.2b). It removes material in the manner shown in Fig. 23.5a. The cutter rotates at a rotational speed N and the workpiece moves along a straight path at a linear speed v. When the cutter rotates as shown in Fig. 23.5b, the operation is *climb* milling; when it rotates in the opposite direction (Fig. 23.5c), the operation is *conventional* milling. The cutting tools are mounted on the cutter body as shown in Fig. 23.6.

Because of the relative motion between the cutting teeth and the workpiece, a face-milling cutter leaves *feed marks* on the machined surface (Figs. 23.5e and 23.7) similar to those left by turning operations (Fig. 20.2). Note that surface roughness of the workpiece depends on insert corner geometry and feed per tooth.

The terminology for a face-milling cutter, as well as the various angles, are shown in Fig. 23.8. The side view is shown in Fig. 23.9, where we note that, as in turning operations, the *lead angle* of the insert in face milling has a direct influence on the *undeformed chip thickness*. As the lead angle (positive as shown) increases, the undeformed chip thickness decreases (as does chip thickness), and the length of contact increases.

The range of lead angles for most face-milling cutters is from 0° to 45°. Note that the cross-sectional area of the undeformed chip remains constant. The lead angle also influences the forces in milling. It can be seen that as the lead angle decreases, there is a smaller and smaller vertical force component (axial force on the cutter spindle).

A wide variety of milling cutters is available. The cutter diameter should be chosen such that it will not interfere with fixtures and other components in the setup. In a typical face milling operation, the ratio of the cutter diameter, D, to the width of cut, w, should be no less than 3:2.

The relationship of cutter diameter and insert angles and their position relative to the surface to be milled is important in that it will determine the angle at which an insert *enters* and *exits* the workpiece. Note in Fig. 23.5b for climb milling that if the insert has zero axial and radial rake angles (see Fig. 23.8), the rake face of the insert engages the workpiece directly.

As seen in Figs. 23.10a and b, however, the same insert engages the workpiece at different angles, depending on the relative positions of the cutter and the workpiece. In illustration (a), the tip of the insert makes the first contact, so there is a possibility for the cutting edge to chip off.

In illustration (b), on the other hand, the first contacts (at entry, reentry, and the two exits) are at an angle and away from the tip of the insert. There is, therefore, less tendency for the insert to fail, because the forces on the insert vary more slowly. Note from Fig. 23.8 that the radial and axial rake angles will also have an effect.

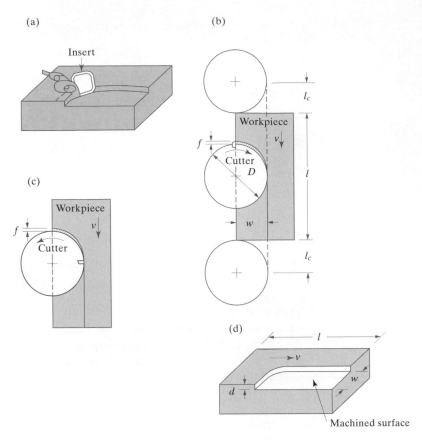

(a)

Insert

(b)

l_c

Workpiece

f v

Cutter D

w

l

l_c

(c)

Workpiece

f v

Cutter

(d)

l

v

d

w

Machined surface

FIGURE 23.5   Face-milling operation showing (a) action of an insert in face milling; (b) climb milling; (c) conventional milling; (d) dimensions in face milling. The width of cut, w, is not necessarily the same as the cutter radius. *Source*: Ingersoll Cutting Tool Company.

FIGURE 23.6   A face-milling cutter with indexable inserts. *Source*: Courtesy of Ingersoll Cutting Tool Company.

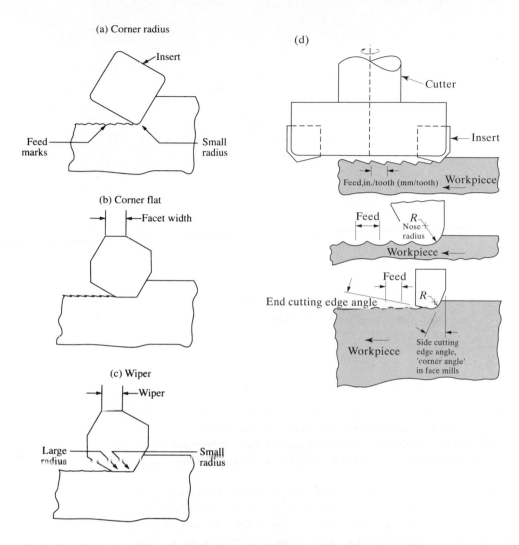

FIGURE 23.7   Schematic illustration of the effect of insert shape on feed marks on a face-milled surface: (a) small corner radius, (b) corner flat on insert, and (c) wiper, consisting of a small radius followed by a large radius which leaves smoother feed marks. *Source*: Kennametal Inc. (d) Feed marks due to various insert shapes.

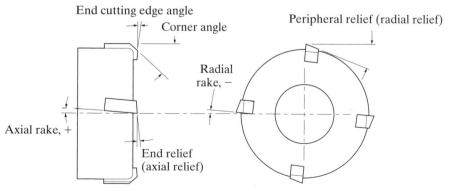

FIGURE 23.8   Terminology for a face-milling cutter.

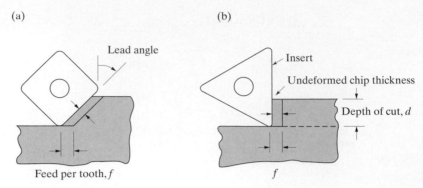

FIGURE 23.9   The effect of lead angle on the undeformed chip thickness in face milling. Note that as the lead angle increases, the chip thickness decreases, but the length of contact (i.e., chip width) increases. The insert in (a) must be sufficiently large to accommodate the contact length increase.

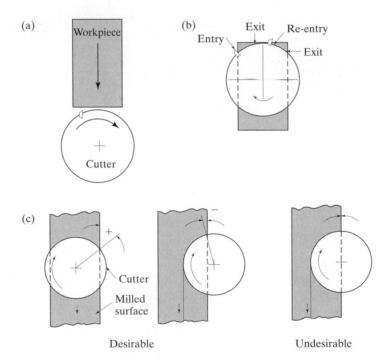

FIGURE 23.10   (a) Relative position of the cutter and insert as it first engages the workpiece in face milling, (b) insert positions towards the end of cut, and (c) examples of exit angles of insert, showing desirable (positive or negative angle) and undesirable (zero angle) positions. In all figures, the cutter spindle is perpendicular to the page.

Figure 23.10c shows the exit angles for various cutter positions. Note that in the first two examples, the insert exits the workpiece at an angle, causing the force on the insert to reduce to zero at a slower rate (desirable) than in the third example, where the insert exits the workpiece suddenly (undesirable).

Example: Material Removal Rate, Power Required, and Cutting Time in Face Milling

Refer to Fig. 23.5 and assume that $D = 150$ mm, $w = 60$ mm, $l = 500$ mm, $d = 3$ mm, $v = 0.6$ m/min, and $N = 100$ rpm. The cutter has 10 inserts, and the workpiece material is a high-strength aluminum alloy. Calculate the material removal rate, cutting time, and feed per tooth, and estimate the power required.

Solution: The cross-section of the cut is $(w)(d) = (60)(3) = 180$ m^2. Noting that the workpiece speed, v, is 0.6 m/min $= 600$ mm/min, we calculate the material removal rate as

$$\text{MRR} = (180)(600) = 108{,}000 \text{ mm}^3/\text{min}.$$

The cutting time is given by

$$t = \frac{(l + 2l_c)}{v}.$$

We note from Fig. 23.5 that for this problem, $l_c = \frac{D}{2} = 75$ mm. The cutting time, therefore, is

$$t = \frac{(500 + 150)}{10} = 65 \text{ s} = 1.08 \text{ min}.$$

We obtain the feed per tooth from Eq. (23.3). Noting that $N = 100$ rpm $= 1.67$ rev/s, we have

$$f = \frac{10}{(1.67)(10)} = 0.6 \text{ mm/tooth}.$$

For this material, let's estimate the unit power from Table 20.1 to be $1.1 \text{ W} \cdot \text{s/mm}^3$. Then the power is

$$\text{Power} = (1.1)(1800) = 1980 \text{ W} = 1.98 \text{ kW}.$$

23.2.3 End Milling

Flat surfaces as well as various profiles can be produced by *end milling*. The cutter in end milling (**end mill**) is shown in Fig. 23.2c; it has either straight or tapered shanks for smaller and larger cutter sizes, respectively. The cutter usually rotates on an axis perpendicular to the workpiece, although it can be tilted to machine-tapered surfaces.

End mills are also available with hemispherical ends (*ball nose*) for the production of curved surfaces, such as dies and molds. *Hollow end mills* have internal cutting teeth and are used to machine the cylindrical surface of solid round workpieces. End mills are made of high-speed steels or have carbide inserts.

High-Speed Milling.   High-speed machining and its applications were described in Section 22.4.1. One of the more common applications is *high-speed milling* using an end mill, which observes the same general provisions regarding the stiffness of machines, workholding devices, etc. A typical application is the milling of aluminum-alloy aerospace components and honeycomb structures (Section 16.14), with spindle speeds on the order of 20,000 rpm. Chip collection and disposal can be a significant problem in these operations (Section 22.3.13).

The production of cavities in small forging dies (**die sinking**) for parts like connecting rods is now being done using high-speed end milling with a TiAlN-coated 2-mm (0.040-in.) diameter ballnose end mill. The spindle is equipped with air bearings and can rotate at speeds as high as 50,000 rpm, and with a rotational accuracy of 10 μm.

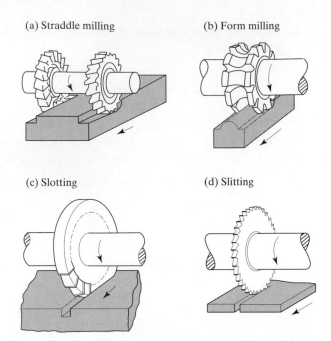

(a) Straddle milling

(b) Form milling

(c) Slotting

(d) Slitting

FIGURE 23.11   Cutters for (a) straddle milling, (b) form milling, (c) slotting, and (d) slitting with a milling cutter.

23.2.4 Other Milling Operations and Milling Cutters

Several other milling operations and cutters are used to machine various surfaces. In **straddle milling**, two or more cutters are mounted on an arbor and are used to machine two parallel surfaces on the workpiece (Fig. 23.11a). **Form milling**, which produces curved profiles, uses cutters that have specially shaped teeth (Fig. 23.11b); such cutters are also used for cutting gear teeth (Section 23.8.1).

Circular cutters for slotting and slitting are shown in Figs. 23.11c and d, respectively. The teeth may be staggered slightly, like those in a saw blade (Section 23.6), to provide clearance for the cutter when making deep slots. *Slitting saws* are relatively thin, usually less than 5 mm $\left(\frac{3}{16} \text{ in.}\right)$. *T-slot cutters* are used to mill T-slots (Fig. 23.12a), such as those found in machine-tool work tables for clamping workpieces. A slot is first milled with an end mill. The cutter then cuts the complete profile of the slot in one pass.

FIGURE 23.12   (a) T-slot cutting with a milling cutter. (b) A shell mill.

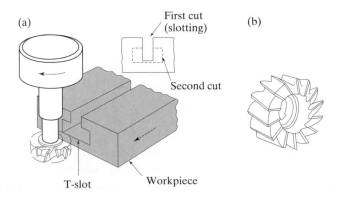

(a)

First cut (slotting)

(b)

Second cut

T-slot

Workpiece

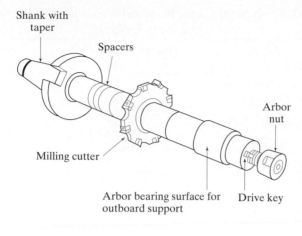

FIGURE 23.13   Mounting a milling cutter on an arbor for use on a horizontal milling machine.

Key seat cutters are used to make the semicylindrical key seats (Woodruff) for shafts. *Angle milling cutters* (single-angle or double-angle) are used to produce tapered surfaces with various angles.

Shell mills (Fig. 23.12b) are hollow inside and are mounted on a shank; this allows the same shank to be used for different-sized cutters. The use of shell mills is similar to that of end mills. Milling with a single cutting tooth mounted on a high-speed spindle is known as *fly cutting*; it is generally used in simple face-milling and boring operations. The tool can be shaped as a single-point cutting tool and can be placed in various radial positions on the spindle.

23.2.5 Tool Holders

Milling cutters are classified as either arbor cutters or shank cutters. *Arbor cutters* are mounted on an **arbor** (Fig. 23.13), for operations such as slab, face, straddle, and form milling. In *shank-type cutters*, the cutter and the shank are one piece. The most common examples of shank cutters are end mills. Though small end mills have straight shanks, larger end mills have tapered shanks for better clamping to resist the higher forces and torque involved.

Cutters with straight shanks are mounted in collet chucks or special end mill holders; those with tapered shanks are mounted in tapered tool holders. In addition to mechanical ones, hydraulic tool holders and arbors are also available. The stiffness of cutters and tool holders is important for surface quality and to reduce vibration and chatter during milling operations. Conventional tapered tool holders have a tendency to wear and bellmouth due to the radial forces involved in milling.

23.2.6 Milling Process Capabilities

In addition to the various characteristics of milling processes that have been described, milling process capabilities include parameters such as surface finish, dimensional tolerances, production rate, and cost considerations. Data on these capabilities are presented in Tables 22.1 and 22.7 and in Fig. 40.8 (production rate and times); Fig. 22.13 (surface finish); Figs. 22.14, 40.6, and 40.7 (tolerances); Table 23.2 (capabilities); and Table 23.3 (tooling costs).

The conventional ranges of feeds and cutting speeds for milling are given in Table 23.4. *Feeds* typically range from about 0.1 mm (0.004 in.) to 0.5 mm (0.02 in.) per tooth. Depths of cut are usually 1 mm–8 mm (0.04 in.–0.30 in.). *Cutting speeds* vary over a wide range, depending on workpiece material, cutting tool material, and process parameters; they

TABLE 23.2   Typical Capacities and Maximum Workpiece Dimensions
for Some Machine Tools

Machine tool	Maximum dimension m (ft)	Power (kW)	Maximum speed
Milling machines (table travel)			
Knee-and-column	1.4 (4.6)	20	4000 rpm
Bed	4.3 (14)		
Numerical control	5 (16.5)		
Planers (table travel)	10 (33)	100	1.7 m/s
Broaching machines (length)	2 (6.5)	0.9 MN	
Gear cutting (gear diameter)	5 (16.5)		

Note: Larger capacities are available for special applications.

TABLE 23.3   Approximate Cost of Selected Tools for Machining*

Tools	Size (in.)	Cost ($)
Drills, HSS, straight shank	$\frac{1}{4}$	1.00–2.00
	$\frac{1}{2}$	3.00–6.00
Coated (TiN)	$\frac{1}{4}$	2.60–3.00
	$\frac{1}{2}$	10–15
Tapered shank	$\frac{1}{4}$	2.50–7.00
	1	15–45
	2	80–85
	3	250
	4	950
Reamers, HSS, hand	$\frac{1}{4}$	10–15
	$\frac{1}{2}$	10–15
Chucking	$\frac{1}{2}$	5–10
	1	20–25
	$1\frac{1}{2}$	40–55
End mills, HSS	$\frac{1}{2}$	10–15
	1	15–30
Carbide-tipped	$\frac{1}{2}$	30–35
	1	45–60
Solid carbide	$\frac{1}{2}$	30–70
	1	180
Burs, carbide	$\frac{1}{2}$	10–20
	1	50–60
Milling cutters, HSS, staggered tooth, $\frac{3}{8}''$ wide	4	35–75
	8	130–260
Collets (5 core)	1	10–20

*Cost depends on the particular type of material and shape of tool, its quality, and the amount purchased.

usually range from 30 m/min (90 ft/min) to 3000 m/min (10,000 ft/min). For *cutting fluid* recommendations, see Table 22.5.

A general **troubleshooting guide** for milling operations is given in Table 23.5; the last four items in this table are illustrated in Fig. 23.14. *Back striking* involves double feed marks made by the trailing edge of the cutter (the lower half of the cutter in Fig. 23.10b). Note from this table that some recommendations (such as changing milling parameters or cutting tools) are easier to accomplish than others (such as changing tool angles, cutter geometry, and the stiffness of spindles and workholding devices).

TABLE 23.4   General Recommendations for Milling Operations

Workpiece material	Cutting tool	General-purpose starting conditions		Range of conditions	
		Feed mm/tooth (in./tooth)	Speed m/min (ft/min)	Feed mm/tooth (in./tooth)	Speed m/min (ft/min)
Low-C and free-machining steels	Uncoated carbide, coated carbide, cermets	0.13–0.20 (0.005–0.008)	120–180 (400–600)	0.085–0.38 (0.003–0.015)	90–425 (300–1400)
Alloy steels					
Soft	Uncoated, coated, cermets	0.10–0.18 (0.004–0.007)	90–170 (300–550)	0.08–0.30 (0.003–0.012)	60–370 (200–1200)
Hard	Cermets, PcBN	0.10–0.15 (0.004–0.006)	180–210 (600–700)	0.08–0.25 (0.003–0.010)	75–460 (250–1500)
Cast iron, gray					
Soft	Uncoated, coated, cermets, SiN	0.10–10.20 (0.004–0.008)	120–760 (400–2500)	0.08–0.38 (0.003–0.015)	90–1370 (300–4500)
Hard	Cermets, SiN, PcBN	0.10–0.20 (0.004–0.008)	120–210 (400–700)	0.08–0.38 (0.003–0.015)	90–460 (300–1500)
Stainless steel, austenitic	Uncoated, coated, cermets	0.13–0.18 (0.005–0.007)	120–370 (400–1200)	0.08–0.38 (0.003–0.015)	90–500 (300–1800)
High-temperature alloys, nickel base	Uncoated, coated, cermets, SiN, PcBN	0.10–0.18 (0.004–0.007)	30–370 (100–1200)	0.08–0.38 (0.003–0.015)	30–550 (90–1800)
Titanium alloys	Uncoated, coated, cermets	0.13–0.15 (0.005–0.006)	50–60 (175–200)	0.08–0.38 (0.003–0.015)	40–140 (125–450)
Aluminum alloys					
Free machining	Uncoated, coated, PCD	0.13–0.23 (0.005–0.009)	610–900 (2000–3000)	0.08–0.46 (0.003–0.018)	300–3000 (1000–10,000)
High silicon	PCD	0.13 (0.005)	610 (2000)	0.08–0.38 (0.003–0–015)	370–910 (1200–3000)
Copper alloys	Uncoated, coated, PCD	0.13–0.23 (0.005–0.009)	300–760 (1000–2500)	0.08–0.46 (0.003–0.018)	90–1070 (300–3500)
Thermoplastics and thermosets	Uncoated, coated, PCD	0.13–0.23 (0.005–0.009)	270–460 (900–1500)	0.08–0.46 (0.003–0.018)	90–1370 (300–4500)

Source: Based on data from Kennametal Inc.
Note: Depths of cut, *d*, usually are in the range of 1–8 mm (0.04–0.3 in.). PcBN: polycrystalline cubic boron nitride; PCD: polycrystalline diamond.
Note: See also Table 22.2 for range of cutting speeds within tool material groups.

23.2.7 Design and Operating Guidelines for Milling

Many of the guidelines for turning and boring (Chapter 22) are applicable to milling operations. Additional factors relevant to milling include the following:

a. Standard milling cutters should be used and costly special cutters should be avoided. Design features include shape, size, depth, width, and corner radii.

b. Chamfers should be used instead of radii because of the difficulty of smoothly matching various intersecting surfaces.

c. Internal cavities and pockets with sharp corners should be avoided due to the difficulty of milling them because cutters have a finite edge radius.

d. Workpieces should be sufficiently rigid to minimize any deflections resulting from clamping and cutting forces.

TABLE 23.5   General Troubleshooting Guide for Milling Operations

Problem	Probable causes
Tool breakage	Tool material lacks toughness; improper tool angles; cutting parameters too high.
Tool wear excessive	Cutting parameters too high; improper tool material; improper tool angles; improper cutting fluid.
Rough surface finish	Feed too high; spindle speed too low; too few teeth on cutter; tool chipped or worn; built-up edge; vibration and chatter.
Tolerances too broad	Lack of spindle stiffness; excessive temperature rise; dull tool; chips clogging cutter.
Workpiece surface burnished	Dull tool; depth of cut too low; radial relief angle too small.
Back striking	Dull cutting tools; cutter spindle tilt; negative tool angles.
Chatter marks	Insufficient stiffness of system; external vibrations; feed, depth, and width of cut too large.
Burr formation	Dull cutting edges or too much honing; incorrect angle of entry or exit; feed and depth of cut too high; incorrect insert geometry.
Breakout	Lead angle too low; incorrect cutting edge geometry; incorrect angle of entry or exit; feed and depth of cut too high.

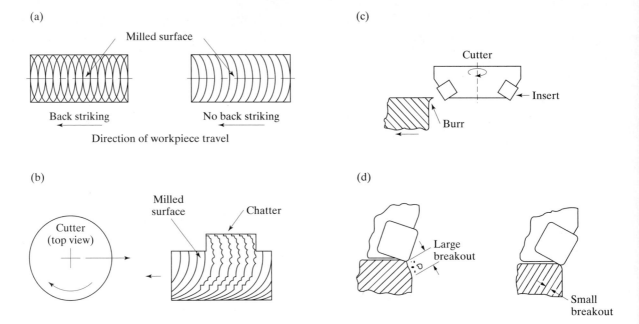

FIGURE 23.14   Surface features and corner defects in face milling operations; see also Fig. 23.7. For troubleshooting, see Table 23.5. *Source*: Kennametal Inc.

Guidelines for the avoidance of vibration and chatter in milling are similar to those for turning (Section 22.3.12). In addition, the following practices should be considered:

a. Cutters should be mounted as close to the spindle base as possible to reduce tool deflections.

b. Tool holders and fixturing should be as rigid as possible.

c. In case of vibration and chatter, tool shape and process condition should be modified, and cutters with fewer cutting teeth or with random tooth spacing should be used.

23.3 MILLING MACHINES

Because they are capable of performing a variety of cutting operations, milling machines are among the most versatile and useful machine tools. The oldest milling machine was built by Eli Whitney (1765–1825) in 1820. A wide selection of milling machines with numerous features is now available (Table 23.2).

23.3.1 Column-and-Knee Type Machines

Used for general-purpose milling operations, *column-and-knee type machines* are the most common milling machines. The spindle on which the milling cutter is mounted may be horizontal (Fig. 23.15) for slab milling, or vertical for face and end milling, boring, and drilling operations (Fig. 23.16). The basic components of these machines are as follows:

- A *work table*, on which the workpiece is clamped using T-slots. The table moves longitudinally relative to the saddle.
- A *saddle*, which supports the table and can move in the transverse direction.
- A *knee*, which supports the saddle and gives the table vertical movement so that the depth of cut can be adjusted.
- An *overarm* in horizontal machines, which is adjustable to accommodate different arbor lengths.
- A *head*, which contains the spindle and cutter holders. In vertical machines, the head may be fixed or it can be vertically adjustable, and it can be swiveled in a vertical planc on the column for cutting tapered surfaces.

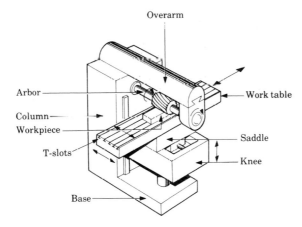

FIGURE 23.15   Schematic illustration of a horizontal-spindle column-and-knee type milling machine. *Source*: G. Boothroyd.

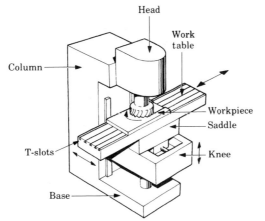

FIGURE 23.16   Schematic illustration of a vertical-spindle column-and-knee type milling machine (also called a *knee miller*). *Source*: G. Boothroyd.

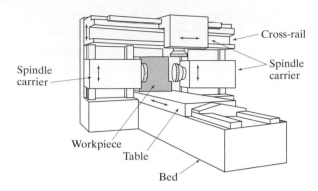

FIGURE 23.17   Schematic illustration of a bed-type milling machine. Note the single vertical-spindle cutter and two horizontal-spindle cutters. *Source*: ASM International.

Plain milling machines have three axes of movement, which are usually imparted manually or by power. In *universal column-and-knee milling machines*, the table can be swiveled on a horizontal plane. In this way, complex shapes (e.g., helical grooves at various angles) can be machined to produce such as parts as gears, drills, taps, and cutters.

23.3.2 Bed-Type Machines

In *bed-type machines*, the work table is mounted directly on the bed, which replaces the knee and can move only longitudinally (Fig. 23.17). These milling machines are not as versatile as other types, but they have great stiffness and are used for high-production work. The spindles may be horizontal or vertical, and of duplex or triplex types—that is, with two or three spindles, respectively, for the simultaneous machining of two or three workpiece surfaces.

23.3.3 Other Types of Milling Machines

Several other types of milling machines are available (see also *machining centers*, Section 24.2). *Planer-type milling machines*, which are similar to bed-type machines, are equipped with several heads and cutters to mill various surfaces. They are used for heavy workpieces and are more efficient than planers (Section 23.4) when used for similar purposes. *Rotary-table machines* are similar to vertical milling machines and are equipped with one or more heads for face-milling operations.

Various milling-machine components are being rapidly replaced by *computer numerical control machines*. These machine tools are versatile and capable of milling, drilling, boring, and tapping with repetitive accuracy (Fig. 23.18). Other developments include *profile milling machines*, which have five axes of movement (Fig. 23.19); note the three linear and two angular movements of the machine components.

23.3.4 Workholding Devices and Accessories

The workpiece to be milled must be clamped securely to the work table to resist cutting forces and prevent slippage during milling. Various fixtures and vises are generally used for this purpose. (See also Section 38.9 on *flexible fixturing*.) They are mounted and clamped to the work table using the T-slots seen in Figs. 23.16a and b.

Vises are used for small production work and small parts. Fixtures are used for higher production work and can be automated by various mechanical and hydraulic means.

Accessories for milling machines include various fixtures and attachments for the machine head as well as the work table designed to adapt them to different milling operations. The accessory that has been used most commonly in the past is the *universal dividing (index)*

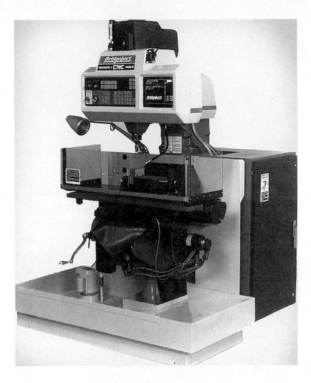

FIGURE 23.18   A computer numerical control, vertical-spindle milling machine. This machine is one of the most versatile machine tools. *Source*: Courtesy of Bridgeport Machines Division, Textron Inc.

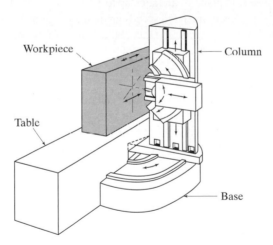

FIGURE 23.19   Schematic illustration of a five-axis profile milling machine. Note that there are three principal linear and two angular movements of machine components.

head. Manually operated, this fixture rotates (indexes) the workpiece to specified angles between individual machining steps. It has typically been used to mill parts with polygonal surfaces and to machine gear teeth. Dividing heads are now used only for low-volume, job-shop quantities; they have been replaced by CNC controls and machining centers.

23.4 PLANING AND SHAPING

Planing is a relatively simple cutting operation by which flat surfaces, as well as various cross-sections with grooves and notches, are produced along the length of the workpiece (Fig. 23.20). Planing is usually done on large workpieces—as large as 25 m $\times$ 15 m (75 ft $\times$ 40 ft).

(a)   (b)

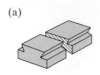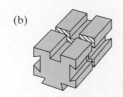

FIGURE 23.20   Typical parts that can be made on a planer.

In a *planer*, the workpiece is mounted on a table that travels along a straight path. A horizontal cross-rail, which can be moved vertically along the ways in the column, is equipped with one or more tool heads. The cutting tools are attached to the heads, and machining is done along a straight path. Because of the reciprocating motion of the workpiece, elapsed noncutting time during the return stroke is significant.

Consequently, these operations are neither efficient nor economical, except for low-quantity production. The efficiency of the operation can be improved by equipping planers with tool holders and tools that cut in both directions of table travel.

In order to prevent tool cutting edges from chipping when they rub along a workpiece during the return stroke, tools are either tilted away or lifted mechanically or hydraulically. Because of the length of the workpiece, it is essential to equip cutting tools with chip breakers. Otherwise, the chips produced can be very long, interfering with the operation as well as becoming a safety hazard.

Cutting speeds in planers can range up to 120 m/min (400 ft/min) with capacities of up to 110 kW (150 hp). Recommended speeds are in the range of 3 to 6 m/min (10 to 20 ft/min) for cast irons and stainless steels, and up to 90 m/min (300 ft/min) for aluminum and magnesium alloys. Feeds are usually in the range of 0.5 to 3 mm/stroke (0.02 to 0.125 in./stroke). The most common tool materials are M2 and M3 high-speed steels and C-2 and C-6 carbides.

Shaping is used to machine parts; it is much like planing, except that the parts are smaller. Cutting by shaping is basically the same as by planing. In a *horizontal shaper*, the tool travels along a straight path, and the workpiece is stationary. The cutting tool is attached to the tool head, which is mounted on the ram.

The ram has a reciprocating motion, and in most machines, cutting is done during the forward movement of the ram (*push cut*); in others, it is done during the return stroke of the ram (*draw cut*). Vertical shapers (*slotters*) are used to machine notches, keyways, and dies. Because of low production rates, only special-purpose shapers, such as gear shapers (Section 23.8.2), are in common use today.

23.5 BROACHING AND BROACHING MACHINES

The *broaching* operation is similar to shaping with multiple teeth and is used to machine internal and external surfaces, such as holes of circular, square, or irregular section, keyways, the teeth of internal gears, multiple spline holes, and flat surfaces (Fig. 23.21).

A **broach** is, in effect, a long multitooth cutting tool (Fig. 23.22a); the total depth of material removed in one stroke is the sum of the depths of cut of each tooth of the broach. A large broach can remove material as deep as 38 mm (1.5 in.) in one stroke.

Broaching is an important production process and can produce parts with very good surface finish and dimensional accuracy. It competes favorably with other processes, such as boring, milling, shaping, and reaming, to produce similar shapes. Although broaches can be expensive, the cost is justified with high-quantity production runs.

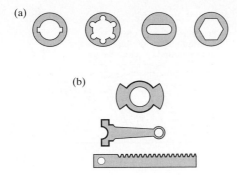

FIGURE 23.21   (a) Typical parts made by internal broaching. (b) Parts made by surface broaching. Heavy lines indicate broached surfaces. *Source*: General Broach and Engineering Company.

Broaches.   The terminology for a broach is given in Fig. 23.22b. The *rake* (hook) angle depends on the material cut (as it does in turning and other cutting operations), and usually ranges between 0° and 20°. The *clearance* angle is usually 1°–4°; finishing teeth have smaller angles. Too small a clearance angle causes rubbing of the teeth against the broached surface. The *pitch* of the teeth depends on factors such as the length of the workpiece (length of cut), tooth strength, and size and shape of chips.

The tooth depth and pitch must be sufficiently large to accommodate the chips produced during broaching, particularly for long workpieces; at least two teeth should be in contact with the workpiece at all times. The following formula may be used to obtain the pitch for a broach to cut a surface of length l:

$$\text{Pitch} = k\sqrt{l} \tag{23.6}$$

Here, k is a constant equal to 1.76 when l is in mm and 0.35 when l is in inches. An average pitch for small broaches is in the range of 3.2 to 6.4 mm (0.125 to 0.25 in.) and for large ones is in the range of 12.7 to 25 mm (0.5 to 1 in.). The cut per tooth depends on the workpiece material and on the surface finish desired; it is usually in the range of 0.025 to 0.075 mm (0.001 to 0.003 in.) for medium-size broaches but can be larger than 0.25 mm (0.01 in.) for larger broaches.

Broaches are available with various tooth profiles, including some with *chip breakers* (Fig. 23.23). Broaches are made for the production of various external and internal shapes. The variety of *surface* broaches include *slab* (for cutting flat surfaces), *slot, contour, dovetail, pot* (for precision external shapes), and *straddle*.

Internal broach types include *hole* (for close tolerance holes, round shapes, and other shapes; Fig. 23.24), *keyway, internal gear*, and *rifling* (for gun barrels). Irregular internal shapes are usually broached by starting with a round hole drilled or bored in the workpiece.

FIGURE 23.22   (a) Cutting action of a broach, showing various features. (b) Terminology for a broach.

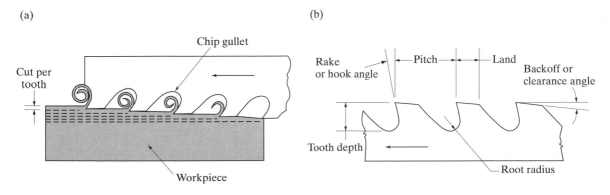

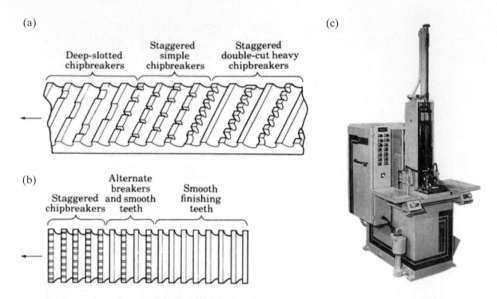

FIGURE 23.23   Chipbreaker features on (a) a flat broach and (b) a round broach. (c) Vertical broaching machine. *Source*: Ty Miles, Inc.

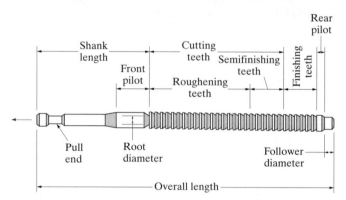

FIGURE 23.24   Terminology for a pull-type internal broach used for enlarging long holes.

Turn Broaching.   An advance in broaching technology is *turn broaching* of the bearing surfaces (Fig. IV.3) of crankshafts and similar applications. The crankshaft is rotated between centers, and the broach, which is equipped with multiple carbide inserts, passes tangentially across the bearing surfaces and removes material (Fig. 23.25).

This process is a combination of *shaving* and *skiving* (removing a thin layer of material with a specially-shaped cutting tool). Straight as well as circular broaches have been used successfully in turn broaching. Machines that broach a number of crankshafts simultaneously have also been built.

23.5.1 Broaching Machines

Broaching machines either pull or push the broaches and are made either horizontal or vertical. **Push broaches** are usually shorter, generally in the range of 150–350 mm (6–14 in.). **Pull broaches** tend to straighten the hole, whereas pushing permits the broach to follow any irregularity of the leader hole. Horizontal machines are capable of longer strokes.

FIGURE 23.25   Turn broaching of a crankshaft. The crankshaft rotates while the broaches pass tangentially across the crankshaft's bearing surfaces. *Source*: Courtesy of Ingersoll Cutting Tool Company.

The *force* required to pull or push the broach depends on the strength of the workpiece material, the total depth and width of cut, and the cutting speed. Tooth profile and cutting fluids also affect this force. The pulling force capacities of broaching machines are as high as 0.9 MN (100 tons).

Broaching machines are relatively simple in construction, have only linear motions, and are usually actuated hydraulically (although some are moved by crank, screw, or rack). Many styles of broaching machines are available, some with multiple heads, allowing a variety of shapes and parts to be produced, including helical splines and rifled gun barrels. Sizes range from machines for making needlelike parts to those used for broaching gun barrels.

23.5.2 Broaching Process Parameters

Cutting speeds for broaching may range from 1.5 m/min (5 ft/min) for high-strength alloys to as much as 15 m/min (50 ft/min) for aluminum and magnesium alloys. The most common broach materials are M2 and M7 high-speed steels and carbide inserts. The majority of broaches are now coated with titanium nitride for improved tool life and surface finish. Ceramic inserts are also used for finishing operations in some applications.

Smaller high-speed-steel blanks for broaches can be made with powder-metallurgy techniques (Chapter 17) for better control of quality. Although carbide or ceramic inserts can be indexed after they are worn, high-speed-steel broach teeth have to be resharpened by grinding (which, of course, alters the size of the broach). Cutting fluids are generally recommended for broaching.

23.5.3 Design Considerations for Broaching

Broaching, like other machining processes, requires that certain guidelines be followed in order to obtain economical and high-quality production. The major requirements are as follows:

a. Parts should be designed so that they can be clamped securely in broaching machines. Parts should have sufficient structural strength and stiffness to withstand cutting forces during broaching.

b. Blind holes, sharp corners, dovetail splines, and large flat surfaces should be avoided.

c. Chamfers are preferable to round corners.

Example: Broaching Internal Splines

The part shown in Fig. 23.26 was made of nodular iron (65-45-15; Section 12.3.2) with internal splines, each 50 mm (2 in.) long. The splines had 19 involute teeth with a pitch diameter of 63.52 mm (2.5009 in.). An M-2 high-speed-steel broach with 63 teeth, a length of 1.448 m (57 in.), and a diameter the same as the pitch diameter was used to produce the splines. The cut per tooth was 0.116 mm (0.00458 in.). The production rate was 63 pieces per hour. The number of parts per grind was 400, with a total broach life of about 6000 parts. *Source*: ASM International.

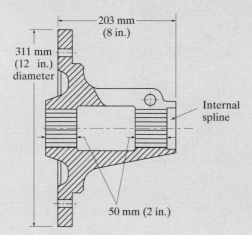

FIGURE 23.26

23.6 SAWING

Sawing is a cutting operation in which the cutting tool is a blade having a series of small teeth (**saw**), each tooth removing a small amount of material. This process is used for all metallic and nonmetallic materials that are machinable by other cutting processes and is capable of producing various shapes (Fig. 23.27). Sawing is an effective bulk-removal process and can produce near-net shapes from raw materials. The width of cut (**kerf**) in sawing is usually narrow, so the process wastes little material.

Typical saw-tooth and saw-blade configurations are shown in Fig. 23.28. Tooth spacing is usually in the range of 0.08 to 1.25 teeth per mm (2 to 32 per in.). A wide variety of tooth forms and spacing and blade thicknesses, widths, and sizes are available. Saw blades are made from carbon and high-speed steels (M-2 and M-7). Carbide or high-speed-steel-tipped steel blades are used to saw harder materials (Fig. 23.29).

Tooth set is important in that it provides a sufficiently wide kerf for the blade to move freely in the workpiece without binding and frictional resistance. This also reduces the heat generated; heat can have an adverse effect on the cut, especially when cutting thermoplastics. The tooth set also allows the blade to track accurately, following the pattern to be cut without wandering.

At least two or three teeth should always be engaged with the workpiece in order to prevent *snagging* (catching of the saw tooth on the workpiece). This is why sawing thin materials can be difficult. The thinner the stock, the finer the saw teeth should be, and the greater the number of teeth per unit length. Cutting speeds in sawing usually range up to 90 m/min (300 ft/min), with lower speeds for high-strength metals. Cutting fluids are generally used to improve the quality of cut and the life of the saw.

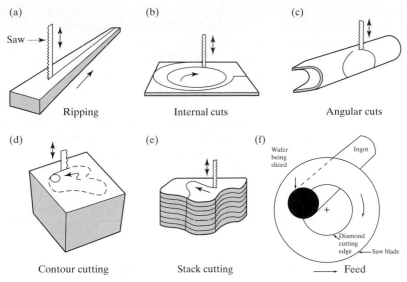

FIGURE 23.27   Examples of various sawing operations. *Source*: DoALL Company.

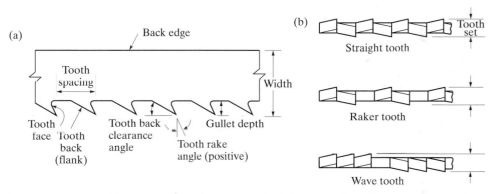

FIGURE 23.28   (a) Terminology for saw teeth. (b) Types of tooth set on saw teeth, staggered to provide clearance for the saw blade to prevent binding during sawing.

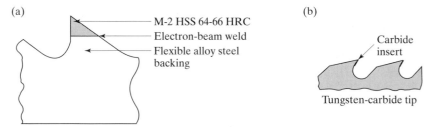

FIGURE 23.29   (a) High-speed-steel teeth welded on steel blade. (b) Carbide inserts brazed to blade teeth.

23.6.1 Types of Saws

Hacksaws have straight blades and reciprocating motions. Developed in the 1650s, they are generally used to cut off bars, rods, and structural shapes. They may be manually or power operated. Because cutting takes place during only one of the two reciprocating strokes, hacksaws are not as efficient as band saws (described later).

Power hacksaw blades are usually 1.2 to 2.5 mm (0.05 to 0.10 in.) thick and up to 610 mm (24 in.) long. Strokes per minute range from 30 for high-strength alloys to 180 for carbon steels. The hacksaw frame in power hacksaws is weighted by various mechanisms, applying as much as 1.3 kN (300 lb) of force to the workpiece to improve the cutting rate. Hand hacksaw blades are thinner and shorter than power hacksaw blades, with as many as 1.2 teeth per mm (32 per in.) for sawing sheet metal and thin tubing.

Circular saws, also called *cold saws* in cutting metal, are generally used for high-production-rate sawing (*cutting off*). Cutting-off operations can also be carried out with thin, abrasive disks (Section 25.6). Cold sawing is very commonly used, particularly for large cross-sections (such as products from rolling mills with various cross-sections; Fig. 13.1). These saws are available with a variety of tooth profiles and sizes, and can be fed at any angle into the workpiece. Cutting off with circular saws produces relatively smooth surfaces (Fig. 22.13) with good dimensional accuracy, due to the stiffness of the machines as well as that of the saws.

Band saws have continuous, long, flexible blades and have a continuous cutting action. Vertical band saws (i.e., the direction of blade travel is vertical) are used for straight as well as contour cutting of flat sheets and other parts supported on a horizontal table. Also available are computer-controlled band saws with the capability of guiding the contour path automatically. Horizontal band saws have higher productivity than power hacksaws.

With high-speed-steel blades, cutting speeds for sawing are about 9 m/min (30 ft/min) for high-strength alloys and 120 m/min (400 ft/min) for carbon steels. With high-carbon-steel blades, cutting speeds range up to 400 m/min (1300 ft/min) for aluminum and magnesium alloys.

Blades and high-strength wire can be *coated* with diamond powder (**diamond-edged blades** and **diamond wire saws**) so that the diamond particles act as cutting teeth (abrasive cutting); carbide particles are also used for this purpose. These blades and wires are suitable for sawing hard metallic, nonmetallic, and composite materials. (See also Section 34.3.) Wire diameters range from 13 mm (0.5 in.) for use in rock cutting to 0.08 mm (0.003 in.) for precision cutting. Hard materials can also be sawed with thin, abrasive disks (Section 25.6) and with the advanced machining processes (Chapter 26).

23.6.2 Friction Sawing

Friction sawing is a process in which a mild-steel blade, or disk, rubs against the workpiece at speeds of up to 7600 m/min (25,000 ft/min). The frictional energy is converted into heat, which rapidly softens a narrow zone in the workpiece. The action of the blade or disk, which is sometimes provided with teeth or notches, pulls and ejects the softened metal from the cutting zone.

The heat generated in the workpiece produces a heat-affected zone on the cut surfaces; therefore, workpiece properties can be adversely affected by the sawing process. Because only a small portion of the blade is engaged with the workpiece at any time, the blade cools rapidly as it passes through the air.

The friction-sawing process is suitable for hard ferrous metals and reinforced plastics, but not for nonferrous metals, because they have a tendency to stick to the blade. Friction sawing disks as large as 1.8 m (6 ft) in diameter are used to cut off large steel sections. Friction sawing is also commonly used to remove flash from castings (Chapter 11).

23.7 FILING AND FINISHING

Filing involves the small-scale removal of material from a surface, corner, or hole, including the removal of burrs. First developed around 1000 B.C., files are usually made of hardened steel and are available in a variety of cross-sections, including flat, round, half round, square, and triangular. Files have many tooth forms and grades of coarseness.

(a) High-speed-steel bur   (b) Carbide bur   (c) Rotary File

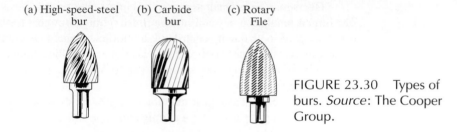

FIGURE 23.30   Types of burs. *Source*: The Cooper Group.

Although filing is usually done by hand, various machines with automatic features are available for high production rates, with files reciprocating at up to 500 strokes/min. *Band files* consist of file segments, each about 75 mm (3 in.) long, which are riveted to a flexible steel band and used in a manner similar to band saws. Disk-type files are also available.

Rotary files and **burs** (Fig. 23.30) are available for special applications such as removing material in die making, deburring, scale removal from surfaces, and producing chamfers on parts. These cutters are usually conical, cylindrical, or spherical in shape and have various tooth profiles. Their cutting action, which is similar to that of reamers, removes small amounts of material. The rotational speeds range from 1500 rpm for cutting steel with large burs to as high as 45,000 rpm for magnesium using small burs.

23.8 GEAR MANUFACTURING BY MACHINING

Several processes for making gears or producing gear teeth on various components were described in Parts II and III. Gears can be manufactured by casting, forging, extrusion, drawing, thread rolling, powder metallurgy, and blanking sheet metal (for making thin gears, such as those used in watches and small clocks). Nonmetallic gears can be made by injection molding and casting (Chapter 18). The standard nomenclature for an involute spur gear is shown in Fig. 23.31.

FIGURE 23.31   Nomenclature for an involute spur gear.

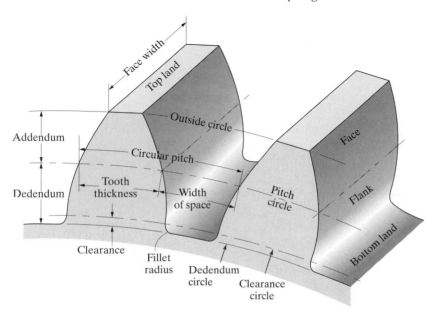

Gears may be as small as those used in watches or as large as 9 m (30 ft) in diameter. The dimensional accuracy and surface finish required for gear teeth depend on its intended use. Poor gear-tooth quality contributes to inefficient energy transmission and noise and adversely affects the gear's frictional and wear characteristics. Submarine gears, for example, have to be of extremely high quality so as to reduce noise levels, helping the submarine avoid detection.

There are two basic gear manufacturing methods which involve the machining of a wrought or cast gear blank: *form cutting* and *generating*.

23.8.1 Form Cutting

In *form cutting*, the cutting tool is similar to a form-milling cutter made in the shape of the space between the gear teeth (Fig. 23.32a). The gear-tooth shape is reproduced by cutting the gear blank around its periphery. The cutter travels axially along the length of the gear tooth at the appropriate depth to produce the gear tooth profile. After each tooth is cut, the cutter is withdrawn, the gear blank is rotated (*indexed*), and the cutter proceeds to cut another tooth. The process continues until all teeth are cut.

Each cutter is designed to cut a range of number of teeth. The precision of the form-cut tooth profile depends on the accuracy of the cutter and on the machine and its stiffness. Although inefficient, form cutting can be done on milling machines, with the cutter mounted on an arbor and the gear blank mounted in a dividing head.

FIGURE 23.32   (a) Producing gear teeth on a blank by form cutting. (b) Schematic illustration of gear generating with a pinion-shaped gear cutter. (c) Schematic illustration of gear generating in a gear shaper using a pinion-shaped cutter. Note that the cutter reciprocates vertically. (d) Gear generating with rack-shaped cutter.

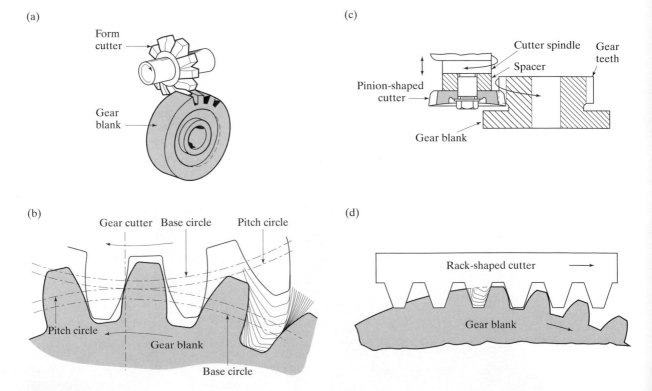

Because the cutter has a fixed geometry, form cutting can be used only to produce gear teeth that have constant width, that is, on spur or helical gears but not on bevel gears. Internal gears and gear teeth on straight surfaces, such as in rack and pinion, are form cut with a shaped cutter, using a machine similar to a shaper.

Broaching can also be used to produce gear teeth and is particularly applicable to internal teeth. The process is rapid and produces fine surface finish with high dimensional accuracy. However, because broaches are expensive and a separate broach is required for each gear size, this method is suitable almost exclusively for high-quantity production.

Gear teeth may be cut on special machines with a single-point cutting tool that is guided by a *template* in the shape of the gear-tooth profile. Because the template can be made much larger than the gear tooth, dimensional accuracy is improved.

Form cutting is a relatively simple process and can be used for cutting gear teeth with various profiles; however, it is a slow operation, and some types of machines require skilled labor. Consequently, it is suitable only for low-quantity production. Machines with semi-automatic features can be used economically for form cutting on a limited production basis.

23.8.2 Gear Generating

The cutting tool used in *gear generating* may be one of the following:

- A pinion-shaped cutter.
- A rack-shaped straight cutter.
- A hob.

a. The **pinion-shaped cutter** can be considered as one of the gears in a conjugate pair and the other as the gear blank (Fig. 23.32b); it is used on machines called *gear shapers* (Fig. 23.32c). The cutter has an axis parallel to that of the gear blank and rotates slowly with the blank at the same pitch-circle velocity in an axial reciprocating motion. A train of gears provides the required relative motion between the cutter shaft and the gear-blank shaft.

Cutting may take place at either the downstroke or the upstroke of the machine. Because the clearance required for cutter travel is small, gear shaping is suitable for gears that are located close to obstructing surfaces, such as flanges (as in the gear blank in Fig. 23.32c). The process can be used for low-quantity as well as high-quantity production.

b. On a **rack shaper**, the generating tool is a segment of a rack (Fig. 23.32d) which reciprocates parallel to the axis of the gear blank. Because it is not practical to have more than 6 to 12 teeth on a rack cutter, the cutter must be disengaged at suitable intervals and returned to the starting point; the gear blank remains fixed.

c. A gear-cutting **hob** (Fig. 23.33) is basically a worm, or screw, made into a gear-generating tool by machining a series of longitudinal slots or gashes into it to form the cutting teeth. When hobbing a spur gear, the angle between the hob and gear blank axes is 90° minus the lead angle at the hob threads. All motions in hobbing are rotary, and the hob and gear blank rotate continuously, much as two gears meshing until all teeth are cut.

Hobs are available with one, two, or three threads. If the hob has a single thread and the gear is to have 40 teeth, for example, the hob and gear spindle must be geared together so that the hob makes 40 revolutions while the gear blank makes one revolution. Similarly, if a double-threaded hob is used, the hob would make 20 revolutions to the gear blank's one revolution.

In addition, the hob must be fed parallel to the gear axis for a distance greater than the face width of the gear tooth (Fig. 23.31) in order to produce straight teeth on

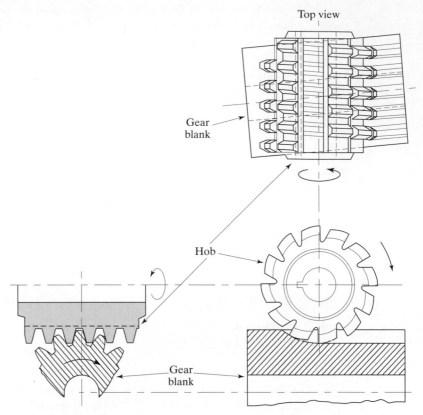

FIGURE 23.33   Schematic illustration of three views of gear cutting with a hob. *Source*: After E. P. DeGarmo and Society of Manufacturing Engineers.

spur gears. The same hobs and machines can be used to cut helical gears by tilting the axis of the hob spindle.

Because it produces a variety of gears rapidly and with good dimensional accuracy, gear hobbing is used extensively in industry. Although the process is suitable for low-quantity production, it is most economical for medium- to high-quantity production.

Gear-generating machines can also produce spiral-bevel and hypoid gears. Like most other machine tools, modern gear-generating machines are computer controlled. **Multiaxis computer-controlled machines** are capable of generating many types and sizes of gears using indexable milling cutters.

23.8.3 Cutting Bevel Gears

Straight bevel gears are generally roughed out in one cut with a form cutter on machines that index automatically. The gear is then finished to the proper shape on a gear generator. The generating method is analogous to the rack-generating method already described. The cutters reciprocate across the face of the bevel gear as does the tool on a shaper (Fig. 23.34a).

The machines for spiral bevel gears operate on essentially the same principle. The spiral cutter is basically a face-milling cutter that has a number of straight-sided cutting blades protruding from its periphery (Fig. 23.34b).

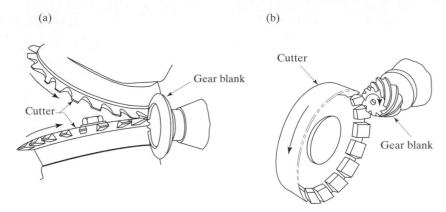

FIGURE 23.34   (a) Cutting a straight bevel-gear blank with two cutters. (b) Cutting a spiral bevel gear with a single cutter. *Source*: ASM International.

23.8.4 Gear-Finishing Processes

As produced by any of the processes described, the surface finish and dimensional accuracy of gear teeth may not be sufficiently accurate for certain applications. Moreover, the gears may be noisy or their mechanical properties, such as fatigue life, may not be sufficiently high.

Several *finishing processes* are available to improve the surface quality of gears. The choice of process is dictated by the method of gear manufacture and whether the gears have been hardened by heat treatment. As described in Chapter 4, heat treating can cause distortion of parts. Consequently, for precise gear-tooth profile, heat-treated gears should be subjected to appropriate finishing operations.

Shaving.   The gear shaving process involves a cutter, made in the exact shape of the finished tooth profile, which removes small amounts of metal from the gear teeth. The cutter teeth are slotted or gashed at several points along its width, making the process similar to fine broaching. The motion of the cutter is reciprocating. Shaving and burnishing (described later) can only be performed on gears with a hardness of 40 HRC or lower.

Although the tools are expensive and special machines are necessary, shaving is rapid and is the most commonly used process for gear finishing. It produces gear teeth with improved surface finish and improved accuracy of tooth profile. Shaved gears may subsequently be heat treated and then ground for improved hardness, wear resistance, and accurate tooth profile.

Burnishing.   The surface finish of gear teeth can also be improved by burnishing. Introduced in the 1960s, burnishing is basically a surface plastic-deformation process (Section 33.2) using a special hardened gear-shaped burnishing die that subjects the tooth surfaces to a surface-rolling action (**gear rolling**). Cold working of tooth surfaces improves the surface finish and induces surface compressive residual stresses on the gear teeth, thus their fatigue life. However, burnishing does not significantly improve gear-tooth accuracy.

Grinding, Honing, and Lapping.   For the highest dimensional accuracy, tooth spacing and form, and surface finish, gear teeth may subsequently be ground, honed, and lapped (Chapter 25). Specially-dressed grinding wheels are used for either forming or generating gear-tooth surfaces. There are several types of grinders for gears, with the single index form grinder being the most commonly available. In **form grinding**, the shape of the grinding

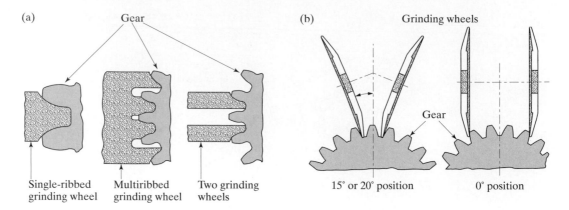

(a)   Gear   (b)   Grinding wheels

Single-ribbed grinding wheel   Multiribbed grinding wheel   Two grinding wheels

15° or 20° position   Gear   0° position

FIGURE 23.35   Finishing gears by grinding: (a) form grinding with shaped grinding wheels; (b) grinding by generating with two wheels.

wheel is identical to that of the tooth spacing (Fig. 23.35a). In **generating**, the grinding wheel acts in a manner similar to the gear generating cutter previously described (Fig. 23.35b).

The **honing** tool is a plastic gear impregnated with fine abrasive particles. The process is faster than grinding and is used to improve surface finish. To further improve the surface finish, ground gear teeth are **lapped** using abrasive compounds with either a gear-shaped lapping tool (made of cast iron or bronze) or a pair of mating gears that are run together. Although production rates are lower and costs are higher, these finishing operations are particularly suitable for producing hardened gears of very high quality, long life, and quiet operation.

23.8.5 Design Considerations for Gear Machining

Design considerations for gear-cutting operations may be summarized as follows:

a. The design of gear blanks is important, especially for complex gear teeth; provision should be made for clamping blanks securely to the machine.

b. The specified dimensional accuracy and surface finish on gear teeth should be as broad as possible for economical production.

c. Wide gears (face width) are more difficult to machine than narrow ones.

d. Gears should be machined prior to their assembly on shafts.

e. Sufficient clearance should be provided between the gear teeth and the flanges, shoulders, and other features, so that the cutting tool can function without interference.

f. Provision should be made for the use of standard cutters wherever possible.

23.8.6 The Economics of Gear Production

As in all cutting operations, the cost of gears increases rapidly with improved surface finish and quality. (See also Fig. 25.33 and Chapter 40.) Figure 23.36 shows the relative manufacturing cost of gears as a function of quality, as specified by AGMA (American Gear Manufacturers Association) and DIN (Deutsches Institut für Normung) numbers. The higher the number, the smaller the dimensional tolerance of gear teeth. Note how the cost can vary by an order of magnitude.

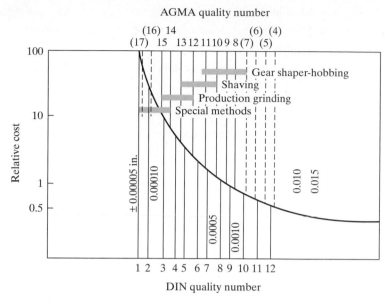

FIGURE 23.36   Gear manufacturing cost as a function of gear quality. The numbers along the vertical lines indicate tolerances. *Source*: Society of Manufacturing Engineers.

SUMMARY

- Various complex shapes can be machined by slab, face, and end milling, broaching, and sawing operations. Milling is one of the most common processes because it is capable of producing a variety of shapes on workpieces.

- Although these three processes are similar to processes such as turning, drilling, and boring, most of the latter processes utilize multitooth tools and cutters at various axes with respect to the workpiece.

- The machine tools for these operations are now mostly computer-controlled and have various features and flexibility in operation.

- In addition to the various forming and shaping processes described in previous chapters, gears are also produced by machining (form cutting or generating); the latter produces gears with better surface finish and higher dimensional accuracy. The surface finish and accuracy of tooth profile are further improved by finishing processes such as shaving, burnishing, grinding, honing, and lapping.

TRENDS

- Machine tools for milling, broaching, sawing, and gear cutting are being designed and constructed with more computer controlled features, improving productivity and product consistency and reducing the need for highly skilled labor.

- High-speed milling, especially end milling, is gaining wider acceptance because it increases productivity, product quality, and dimensional control. Associated with this trend is the design and development of lightweight spindles with high stiffness.

- Milling machines are being designed and built such that vertical and horizontal spindles are combined in one machine (machining center, Chapter 24).

- Machine tools are being made with higher power, cutting speed, and stiffness.
- Planers are being replaced with planer-type computer-controlled milling and similar machines.
- Cutting fluids are being developed with greater concern for environmental and biological considerations.

KEY TERMS

Arbor	Form cutting	Pull broach
Broaching	Friction sawing	Push broach
Bur	Gear generating	Rack shaper
Burnishing	High-speed milling	Sawing
Climb milling	Hob	Shaping
Die sinking	Honing	Shaving
End milling	Kerf	Slab milling
Face milling	Lapping	Tooth set
Filing	Milling	Turn broaching
Fly cutting	Planing	Workholding

BIBLIOGRAPHY

Arnone, M., *High Performance Machining*. Hanser, 1998.
ASM Handbook, Vol. 16: *Machining*. ASM International, 1989.
Boothroyd, G., and W.A. Knight, *Fundamentals of Machining and Machine Tools*, (2d ed.). Marcel Dekker, 1989.
Brown, J., *Advanced Machining Technology Handbook*. McGraw-Hill, 1998.
Ewert, R.H., *Gears and Gear Manufacture: The Fundamentals*. Chapman & Hall, 1997.
Machinery's Handbook. Industrial Press, revised periodically.
Machining Data Handbook, (3d ed.), 2 vols. Machinability Data Center, 1980.

Stephenson, D.A., and J.S. Agapiou, *Metal Cutting Theory and Practice*. Marcel Dekker, 1996.
Tool and Manufacturing Engineers Handbook (4th ed.), Vol. 1: *Machining*. Society of Manufacturing Engineers, 1983.
Townsend, D.P., *Dudley's Gear Handbook: The Design, Manufacturing, and Application of Gears*, (2d ed.). McGraw-Hill, 1991.
Walsh, R.A., *McGraw-Hill Machining and Metalworking Handbook*. McGraw-Hill, 1994.

REVIEW QUESTIONS

23.1 Why is milling a versatile machining process?
23.2 Describe the different types of cutters used in milling operations, and give an application of each.
23.3 What are the advantages of helical teeth over straight teeth on cutters for slab milling?
23.4 Describe the relative characteristics of climb milling and up milling.
23.5 What are the differences among planing and shaping operations and their applications?
23.6 Explain why broaching is a commonly used process. Give some typical applications.
23.7 Describe the features of a broach and explain their functions.
23.8 Why is sawing a commonly used process? Does it have any limitations? Explain.
23.9 Explain why hacksaws are not as productive as band saws.

23.10 Why do some saw blades have staggered teeth?

23.11 Why are some saw blades equipped with carbide or high-speed-steel cutting teeth?

23.12 Give reasons for the development of files as tools.

23.13 Explain the difference between shaving and burnishing.

23.14 What advantages do bed-type milling machines have over column-and-knee type machines for production operations?

23.15 Why is the axis of the hob tilted with respect to the axis of the gear blank?

23.16 Describe the difference between finishing by form grinding and by generating.

23.17 How are T-slots machined?

23.18 What is the difference between straddle milling and form milling?

23.19 What is a shell mill? Why are they commonly used?

23.20 Why is it difficult to saw very thin sections?

23.21 What is friction sawing?

23.22 Describe the motion of a hob.

23.23 What finishing processes are used for gears?

QUALITATIVE PROBLEMS

23.24 Explain why broaching crankshaft bearings is an attractive alternative to other machining processes.

23.25 Several guidelines were presented in this chapter for various cutting operations. Discuss the reasoning behind these guidelines.

23.26 In milling operations with horizontal- and vertical-spindle machines, which one is likely to hold dimensional accuracy better? Why?

23.27 What similarities and differences are there in slitting with a milling cutter and sawing?

23.28 Why do machined gears have to be subjected to finishing operations? Which of the finishing processes are not suitable for hardened gear teeth? Why?

23.29 How would you reduce the surface roughness shown in Fig. 23.7a?

23.30 Why are machines such as the one shown in Fig. 23.18 so useful?

23.31 Describe a type of product that could be produced efficiently on the type of machine shown in Fig. 23.19.

23.32 Comment on your observations concerning the designs shown in Fig. 23.21 and on the usefulness of broaching operations.

23.33 Explain how contour cutting could be started in a band saw as shown in Fig. 23.27d.

23.34 In Fig. 23.29a, high-speed-steel cutting teeth are welded to a steel blade. Would you recommend that the whole blade be made of high-speed steel? Explain your reasons.

23.35 Report your observations on the recommendations given in Table 23.4, and explain why those recommendations have been made.

23.36 Describe the factors that contribute to broaching force and explain why they do so.

23.37 Describe the conditions under which broaching would be the preferred method of machining.

23.38 List and explain the factors involved in the cost of producing gears by machining operations. Consider also the number of gears to be produced.

23.39 Explain whether the feed marks left on the workpiece by the face-milling cutter in Fig. 23.15a are segments of true circles. Describe the parameters you consider in answering this question.

23.40 With appropriate sketches, explain the differences between and similarities among shaving, broaching, and turn broaching operations.

23.41 Would you consider the machining processes described in this chapter to be net-shape processing? Explain, with appropriate examples.

23.42 Why is end milling such a versatile process? Explain with examples.

23.43 In milling and sawing, nonuniform spacing between the cutting teeth can be beneficial to the cutting operation. Why?

23.44 What determines the selection of the number of teeth on a milling cutter? Explain.

23.45 List and explain factors that contribute to poor surface finish in the processes described in this chapter.

23.46 Explain the possible reasons why a knife cuts better when it is moved back and forth. Consider factors such as the material cut, friction, and the dimensions of the cut.

23.47 Comment on the effect of positive and negative rake angles of the insert, respectively, on power consumption in face milling operations.

23.48 Emulsions used for milling operations have a slightly larger concentration of oil than those used for turning operations. Why is this the case?

23.49 Are there size limitations to parts to be sawed? Explain.

23.50 Why is it difficult to use friction sawing on non-ferrous metals?

23.51 What are the advantages and disadvantages of pull and push broaches?

23.52 Explain why the cutting tool may easily chip or break during climb milling.

23.53 Would you recommend broaching a keyway on a gear blank before or after machining the teeth? Why?

23.54 What operations can be performed on a drill press that cannot be performed on a milling machine?

23.55 How would you recommend machining dovetails onto air compressor blades?

QUANTITATIVE PROBLEMS

23.56 If you use a cylindrical bur to make a chamfer along the edge of a straight piece of metal, what type of surface finish will be produced? With appropriate sketches, describe the effects of the bur diameter, its rpm, the number of cutting teeth, the workpiece speed, and any other parameter that influences the surface finish.

23.57 Suggest methods whereby milling cutters of various designs, including end mills, can incorporate carbide inserts.

23.58 In describing the broaching operations and the design of broaches, we have not given equations regarding feeds, speeds, material removal rates, etc., as we have done in turning and milling operations. Study Figs. 23.21 through 23.24 and develop such equations.

23.59 In milling operations, the total cutting time can be significantly influenced by (a) the magnitude of the noncutting distance, l_c, shown in Figs. 23.4 and 23.5, and (b) the ratio of width of cut, w, to the cutter diameter, D. Sketch several combinations of these parameters, give dimensions, select feeds and cutting speeds, etc., and determine the total cutting time. Comment on your observations.

23.60 You are performing a slab-milling operation at a certain cutting speed (surface speed of the cutter) and feed per tooth. Explain the procedure for determining the table speed required.

23.61 Show that the distance l_c in slab milling is approximately equal to $\sqrt{Dd}$ for situations where $D \gg d$. See Fig. 23.4c.

23.62 In the example in Section 23.2.1, which of the quantities will be affected when the feed is increased to $f = 0.02$ in./tooth?

23.63 Calculate the chip depth of cut, t_c, and the torque for the example in Section 23.2.1.

23.64 Estimate the time required to face mill a 10-in.-long, 2-in.-wide brass block with a 6-in. diameter cutter with 10 high-speed-steel inserts.

23.65 A 10-in.-long, 1-in.-thick plate is being cut on a band saw at 150 ft/min. The saw has 12 teeth per in. If the feed per tooth is 0.003 in., how long will it take to saw the plate along its length?

23.66 A single-thread hob is used to cut 40 teeth on a spur gear. The cutting speed is 120 ft/min and the hob is 3 in. in diameter. Calculate the rotational speed of the spur gear.

23.67 Assume that in the face-milling operation shown in Fig. 23.5, the workpiece dimensions are 5 in. by 10 in. The cutter is 6 in. in diameter, has 8 teeth, and rotates at 300 rpm. The depth of cut is 0.125 in. and the feed is 0.005 in./tooth. Assume that the specific energy requirement for this material is

2 hp·min/in.^{3} and that only 75% of the cutter diameter is engaged during cutting. Calculate (a) the power required and (b) the material removal rate.

23.68 Allowing an approach distance of 0.1 in. for both entry and exit of the cutter into the workpiece, calculate the cutting time needed to mill the whole surface in Problem 23.67.

23.69 A slab milling operation will take place on a part 250 mm long and 50 mm wide. A helical cutter 75 mm in diameter with ten teeth will be used. If the feed per tooth is 0.2 mm/tooth and the cutting speed is 0.75 m/s, find the machining time and metal removal rate for removing 6 mm from the surface of the part.

23.70 A 10 in. by 1.5 in. workpiece will be face milled on a 3 in. diameter cutter with five cemented carbide inserts. The operations will take place at a spindle speed of 100 rpm, a feed of 0.01 in./tooth and depth of cut of 0.1 in. Find the machining time and the metal removal rate.

23.71 For the data in Problem 23.70, determine the feed per tooth and the metal removal rate if the desired machining time is one minute.

23.72 Calculate the ranges of typical machining times for face milling a 10-in.-long, 2-in.-wide cutter with a depth of cut of 0.1 in. for the following workpiece materials: (a) low-carbon steel, (b) titanium alloys, (c) aluminum alloys, and (d) thermoplastics.

SYNTHESIS AND DESIGN

23.73 The part shown in Fig. 23.3 is to be machined from a rectangular blank. Suggest the machine tool(s) required, the fixturing needed, and the types and sequence of operations to be performed. Discuss your answer in terms of the workpiece material, such as aluminum vs. stainless steel.

23.74 Referring to the illustration in Problem 23.73, would you prefer to machine this part from a preformed blank (near-net shape) rather than a rectangular blank? If so, how would you prepare such a blank? How would the number of parts required influence your answer?

23.75 Could the part shown in Fig. 23.3 be machined by any of the processes described in Chapter 22? Explain.

23.76 Assume that you are an instructor covering the topics described in this chapter, and you are giving a quiz on the numerical aspects to test the understanding of the students. Prepare several quantitative problems and supply the answers.

23.77 Some handbooks include tables of do and don'ts regarding machining operations and the equipment used. Survey the available literature and prepare such a table for milling operations.

23.78 With appropriate sketches, describe the principles of various fixturing methods and devices that can be used in the processes described in this chapter.

23.79 Make a comprehensive table of the process capabilities of the machining processes described in this chapter. Using several columns, list the machines involved, type of tools and tool materials used, shapes of blanks and parts produced, typical maximum and minimum sizes, surface finish, dimensional tolerances, and production rates.

23.80 Based on the data developed in Problem 23.79, describe your thoughts regarding the procedure to be followed in determining what type of machine tool to select when machining a particular part.

23.81 A trend in machining is the increased use of flexible fixturing. Conduct a literature search on the Internet regarding flexible fixturing and summarize your findings.

23.82 Using the Internet, obtain specifications on the smallest and largest milling machines available and compare your results to the results obtained by your classmates.

23.83 Scalping is an operation sometimes performed on cast billets before rolling (Chapter 13). Investigate and describe the capabilities and sizes of scalping machines.

23.84 If expanded honeycomb panels (Section 16.14) were to be machined in a form milling operation, what would you do to keep the sheet metal from buckling? Think up as many solutions as you can.

24

Machining and Turning Centers, Machine-Tool Structures, and Machining Economics

24.1 INTRODUCTION

This chapter describes major developments in the design and capabilities of computer-controlled machine tools. Known as **machining** and **turning centers**, these machines have flexibility and versatility that other machine tools do not have, and they have, consequently, become the first choice in machine-tool selection. Also described in this chapter are the material and design aspects of machine tools as structures and a review of new developments in the use of various materials and composites in their construction.

Included in these developments is an improved understanding of machine-tool performance, particularly with regard to stiffness and vibration, chatter, and damping characteristics. These are important considerations—not only for dimensional accuracy and the quality of surfaces produced, but also because of their influence on tool life and overall machining economics. The final section in this chapter describes the economics of machining operations, identifying the factors that contribute to machining costs and describing a simple analysis of cost minimalization.

24.2 MACHINING AND TURNING CENTERS

In descriptions of individual machining processes and machine tools in the preceding chapters, it was noted that each machine, regardless of how highly it is automated, is designed to perform basically one type of operation. Previous chapters have also shown that, in manufacturing, most parts require a number of different machining operations on their various surfaces.

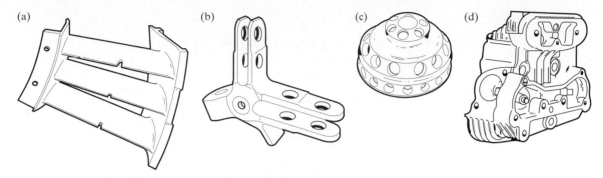

FIGURE 24.1   Examples of parts that can be machined on machining centers, using various processes such as turning, facing, milling, drilling, boring, reaming, and threading. Such parts would ordinarily require a variety of machine tools. *Source*: Toyoda Machinery.

Note, for example, that the parts shown in Fig. 24.1 have a variety of features and that all surfaces on these parts require different types of machining operations, such as milling, facing, boring, drilling, reaming, and threading, to obtain certain specified dimensional tolerances and surface finish. None of the machine tools described in Chapters 22 and 23 could, individually, produce these parts completely.

Traditionally, machining operations are performed by moving the workpiece from one machine tool to another until all machining is completed. This is a viable manufacturing method that can be highly automated; it is the principle behind **transfer lines**. Commonly used in high-volume or mass production, transfer lines consist of several machine tools arranged in a sequence (described in Section 38.2). The workpiece, such as an automotive engine block, moves from station to station, with a specific machining operation performed at each station. The workpiece is then transferred to the next machine for another operation, and so on.

There are products and situations, however, where transfer lines are not feasible or economical, particularly when the types of products to be machined are changed rapidly. An important concept, developed in the late 1950s, is that of machining centers. A **machining center** is a computer-controlled machine tool capable of performing a variety of cutting operations on different surfaces and different directions on a workpiece (Fig. 24.2). In general, the workpiece is stationary and the cutting tools rotate, as they do in milling and drilling operations.

FIGURE 24.2   A horizontal-spindle machining center, equipped with an automatic tool changer. Tool magazines can store 200 cutting tools. *Source*: Courtesy of Cincinnati Milacron, Inc.

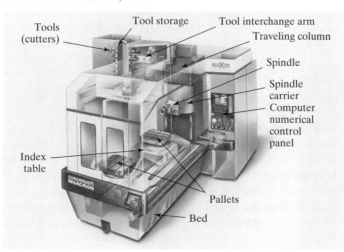

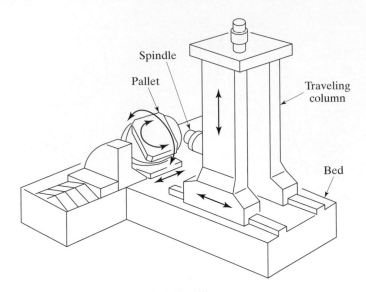

FIGURE 24.3   Schematic illustration of a five-axis machining center. Note that in addition to the three linear movements, the pallet can be swiveled (rotated) along two axes, allowing the machining of complex shapes such as those shown in Fig. 24.1. *Source*: Toyoda Machinery.

The development of machining centers is intimately related to advances in computer control of machine tools, the details of which are described in Chapter 38. Recall that as an example of the advances in modern lathes, Fig. 22.10 illustrated a numerically controlled lathe (*turning center*) with two turrets carrying several cutting tools for turning, facing, boring, and threading.

The workpiece in a machining center is placed on a **pallet** or *module* that can be moved and swiveled (oriented) in various directions (Fig. 24.3). After a particular cutting operation has been completed, the workpiece does not have to be moved to another machine (as has been done traditionally) for additional operations, such as drilling, reaming, or tapping. In other words, the tools and the machine are brought to the workpiece.

After all the cutting operations have been completed, the pallet automatically moves away with the finished workpiece, and another pallet containing another workpiece to be machined is brought into position by **automatic pallet changers** (Fig. 24.4). All movements are computer-controlled, and pallet-changing cycle times are on the order of 10 to 30 seconds. Pallet stations are available with multiple pallets serving the machining center. The machines can also be equipped with various automatic parts, such as loading and unloading devices.

The machining center is equipped with a programmable **automatic tool changer**. Depending on the design, up to 200 cutting tools can be stored in a magazine, drum, or chain (tool storage). Auxiliary tool storage is available on some special machining centers for many more cutting tools. The cutting tools are automatically selected with random access for the shortest route to the machine spindle. The **tool-exchange arm** shown in Fig. 24.5 is a common design. (See also Fig. 24.2.) It swings around to pick up a particular tool (each tool has its own toolholder) and places it in the spindle.

Tools are identified by coded tags, bar codes, or memory chips attached directly to the toolholders. *Tool-changing times* are typically between 5 and 10 seconds; they may be less

(a)

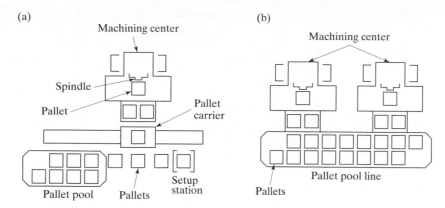

FIGURE 24.4   (a) Schematic illustration of the top view of a horizontal-spindle machining center showing the pallet pool, set-up station for a pallet, pallet carrier, and an active pallet in operation (shown directly below the spindle of the machine). (b) Schematic illustration of two machining centers with a common pallet pool. Various other arrangements are possible in such systems. *Source*: Hitachi Seiki Co., Ltd.

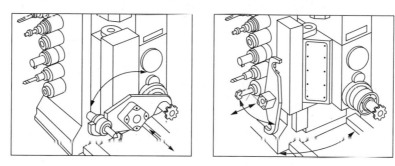

FIGURE 24.5   Swing-around tool changer on a horizontal-spindle machining center. *Source*: Cincinnati Milacron, Inc.

than one second for small tools, or up to 30 seconds for tools weighing 110 kg (250 lb). The trend in tool changers is to use simpler mechanisms, resulting in faster tool-changing times.

Machining centers may be equipped with a **tool-** and/or **part-checking station** that feeds information to the computer-numerical control to compensate for any variations in tool settings or tool wear. **Touch probes** (Fig. 24.6) can be automatically installed into a tool holder (as discussed in Sections 36.11, 38.3, and 38.4) to determine reference surfaces of the workpiece, for the selection of tool settings, and for the on-line inspection of parts being machined.

Note in Fig. 24.6 that several surfaces can be contacted (see also *sensor technology*, Section 38.8), and that their relative positions are determined and stored in the database of the computer software. The data are then used to program tool paths and to compensate for tool length and diameter, as well as for tool wear in more advanced machine tools.

24.2.1 Types of Machining and Turning Centers

Although there are various designs for machining centers, the two basic types are vertical spindle and horizontal spindle; many machines are capable of using both axes. The maximum dimensions that the cutting tools can reach around a workpiece in a machining center is known as the **work envelope**; this term was first used in connection with industrial robots (Section 38.7).

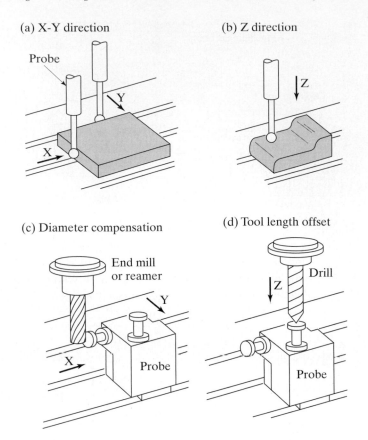

FIGURE 24.6   Touch probes used in machining centers for determining workpiece and tool positions and surfaces relative to the machine table or column. (a) Touch probe determining the X-Y (horizontal) position of a workpiece, (b) determining the height of a horizontal surface, (c) determining the planar position of the surface of a cutter (for instance, for cutter-diameter compensation), and (d) determining the length of a tool for tool-length offset. *Source*: Hitachi Seiki Co., Ltd.

Vertical-spindle machining centers, or *vertical machining centers*, are suitable for performing various machining operations on flat surfaces with deep cavities—for instance, mold and die making. A vertical-spindle machining center, which is similar to a vertical-spindle milling machine, is shown in Fig. 24.7. The tool magazine is on the left of the figure and all operations and movements are directed and modified through the computer-control panel on the right.

Because the thrust forces in vertical machining are directed downward, such machines have high stiffness and produce parts with good dimensional accuracy. These machines are generally less expensive than horizontal-spindle machines.

Horizontal-spindle machining centers, or *horizontal machining centers*, are suitable for large as well as tall workpieces that require machining on a number of their surfaces. The pallet can be swiveled on different axes (Fig. 24.3) to various angular positions.

Another category of horizontal-spindle machines is **turning centers**, which are computer-controlled lathes with several features. A three-turret computer numerical-controlled turning center is shown in Fig. 24.8. This machine is designed with two horizontal spindles and three turrets equipped with a variety of cutting tools used to perform several operations on a rotating workpiece.

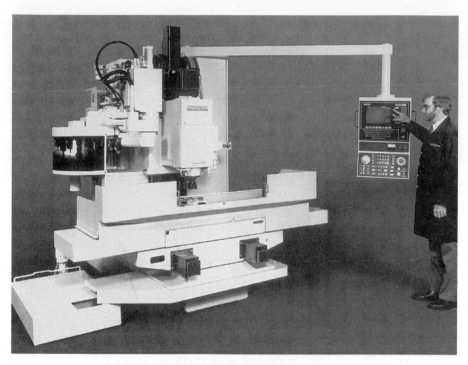

FIGURE 24.7   A vertical-spindle machining center. The tool magazine is on the left of the machine. The control panel on the right can be swiveled by the operator. *Source*: Courtesy of Cincinnati Milacron, Inc.

FIGURE 24.8   Schematic illustration of a three-turret, two-spindle computer numerical controlled turning center. *Source*: Hitachi Seiki Co., Ltd.

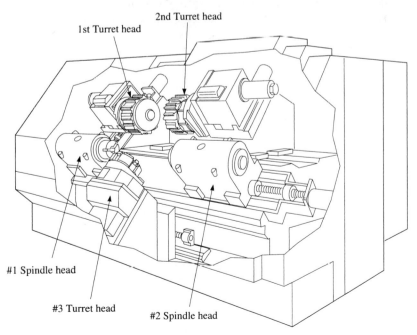

Universal machining centers are equipped with both vertical and horizontal spindles. They have a variety of features and are capable of machining all surfaces of a workpiece (vertical, horizontal, and diagonal).

24.2.2 Characteristics and Capabilities of Machining Centers

The following are the major characteristics of machining centers:

- They are capable of handling a variety of part sizes and shapes efficiently, economically, and with repetitively high dimensional accuracy; dimensional tolerances are on the order of ± 0.0025 mm (0.0001 in.).
- The machines are versatile, having as many as six axes of linear and angular movements, and are capable of quick changeover from one type of product to another, so the need for a variety of machine tools and floor space is significantly reduced.
- The time required for loading and unloading workpieces, changing tools, gaging, and troubleshooting is reduced, so productivity is improved, reducing labor requirements (particularly for skilled labor) and minimizing production costs.
- They are highly automated and relatively compact, so that one operator can attend two or more machines at the same time.
- The machines are equipped with tool-condition monitoring devices (Section 20.7.5) for the detection of tool breakage and wear, as well as probes for tool-wear compensation and for tool positioning.
- In-process and post-process gaging and inspection of machined workpieces are now features of machining centers. (See Section 36.11.)

Machining centers are available in a wide variety of sizes and features, and their costs range from about $50,000 to $1 million and higher. Typical capacities range up to 75 kW (100 hp) and maximum spindle speeds are usually in the range of 4000–8000 rpm; some are as high as 75,000 rpm for special applications using small-diameter cutters. Some pallets are capable of supporting workpieces weighing as much as 7,000 kg (15,000 lb), although higher capacities are available for special applications.

Many machines are now being constructed on a **modular** basis, so that various peripheral equipment and accessories can be installed and modified as the demand for different types of products changes. (Product changes are a major consideration in computer-integrated manufacturing, as described in Part VIII.)

Because of the high productivity of machining centers, large amounts of chips are produced and must be collected and disposed of properly (Section 22.3.13). Several designs are available for **chip collection**, one example of which is shown in Fig. 24.9. Note the two chip conveyors at the bottom of the cross-sectional view of a portion of a horizontal-spindle machining center. These particular conveyors are of the spiral (screw) type; they collect chips along the two troughs and deliver them to a collecting point. Other systems may use chain-type conveyors.

24.2.3 Machine-Tool Selection

Machining centers can require significant capital expenditures, so to be cost effective, they generally have to be used for at least two shifts per day. Consequently, there must be sufficient and continued demand for products made in machining centers to justify this purchase. Because of their inherent versatility, however, machining centers can be

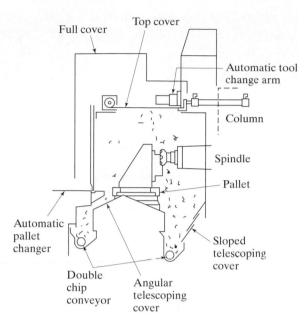

Full cover

Top cover

Automatic tool
change arm

Column

Spindle

Pallet

Automatic
pallet
changer

Double
chip
conveyor

Angular
telescoping
cover

Sloped
telescoping
cover

FIGURE 24.9   Schematic illustration of a chip-collecting system in a horizontal-spindle machining center. The chips that fall by gravity are collected by the two horizontal conveyors at the bottom of troughs. *Source*: Okuma Machinery Works Ltd.

used to produce a wide range of products, particularly with *just-in-time manufacturing* (Section 39.11).

The selection of the type and size of machining centers depends on several factors, among which are the following:

- The type of products, their size, and their shape complexity.
- The type of machining operations to be performed and the type and number of cutting tools required.
- The dimensional accuracy required.
- The production rate required.

Although versatility is the key factor in the selection of machining centers, these considerations must be weighed against the high capital investment required and compared to the costs of manufacturing the same products using a number of the more traditional machine tools.

Example: Machining Outer Bearing Races on a Turning Center

Outer bearing races (Fig. 24.10) are machined on a turning center. The starting material is hot-rolled 52100 steel tube 91 mm (3.592 in.) OD and 75.5 mm (2.976 in.) ID. The cutting speed is 95 m/min (313 ft/min) for all operations. All tools are carbide, including the cutoff tool (last operation), which is 3.18 mm $\left(\frac{1}{8}\text{ in.}\right)$ instead of 4.76 mm $\left(\frac{3}{16}\text{ in.}\right)$ for the high-speed steel cutoff tool that was formerly used.

The material saved by this change is significant because the width of the race is small. The turning center was able to machine these races at high speeds and with repeatable tolerances of ± 0.025 mm (0.001 in.). (See also the example in Section 22.3.9.) *Source*: McGill Manufacturing Company

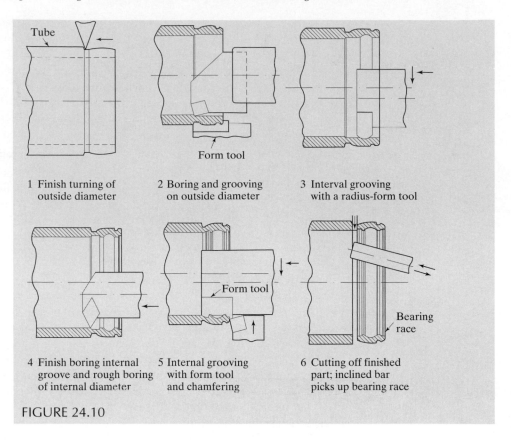

1 Finish turning of outside diameter

2 Boring and grooving on outside diameter

3 Interval grooving with a radius-form tool

4 Finish boring internal groove and rough boring of internal diameter

5 Internal grooving with form tool and chamfering

6 Cutting off finished part; inclined bar picks up bearing race

FIGURE 24.10

24.3 MACHINE-TOOL STRUCTURES

Today's markets have stringent requirements for quality and precision in manufactured products, which are often made with difficult-to-machine materials and with precise specifications concerning dimensional accuracy, surface finish, and product integrity. Consequently, the design and construction of machine tools are important aspects of manufacturing engineering. This section covers the material and design aspects of machine tools as structures that have certain desired characteristics.

24.3.1 Materials

The design of the frame of machine tools requires a thorough knowledge of (a) the materials available for construction, (b) their forms and properties, (c) the dynamics of the particular machining process, (d) the magnitude and nature of forces involved, and (e) thermal expansion of the machine tool.

The most common frame materials are (a) gray or ductile (nodular) cast iron, (b) wrought steel, and (c) polymer concrete. More recent developments include the use of ceramics and granite-epoxy composites.

Gray iron has the advantages of low cost and good damping capacity, but is heavy (Section 12.3). Most machine-tool structures are made of class 40 cast iron; some are made of class 50. Each casting requires a pattern (Chapter 11), the cost of which increases significantly with size.

Welded steels are the choice for lightweight structures because of the low cost of steel, its availability in various section sizes and shapes (such as channels, angles, and tubes), its desirable mechanical properties, and its other favorable characteristics (such as formability, machinability, and weldability). Tubes, for example, have high stiffness-to-weight ratios. On the other hand, the higher damping capacity of castings and composites isn't available with steels. However, a properly designed and assembled wrought-steel structure, with all its joints, can have as high a damping capacity as castings.

Polymer concretes are a mixture of crushed concrete and plastic (polymethylmethacrylate; see Chapter 7). They can easily be cast into desired shapes for machine bases and various components. They were first introduced in the 1980s, and several new compositions are being developed. Although they have good damping capacity, polymer concretes have low stiffness (about one-third that of class 40 cast iron) and poor thermal conductivity. These materials can also be used for sandwich construction with cast irons, however, combining the advantages of each type of material.

Concrete has been used for machine-tool bases since the early 1970s for specialized applications. Compared with cast iron, concrete is less expensive; its curing time is about three weeks (much shorter than that necessary for castings); and it has good damping capacity. However, concrete has low tensile strength and is brittle, so it is not suitable for applications involving impact loads. Concrete can also be poured into cast-iron base structures to increase their mass and improve machine-tool damping capacity. Filling the cavities of bases with loose sand is also an effective means of improving damping capacity.

Ceramic components are being used in advanced machine tools for their strength, stiffness, corrosion resistance, surface finish, and good thermal stability (Chapter 8). Ceramic machine-tool components were first introduced in the 1980s. Spindles and bearings can now be made of silicon nitride, which has better friction and wear characteristics than traditional metallic materials. Furthermore, the low density of ceramics makes them suitable for the components of high-speed machinery that undergo rapid reciprocal movements, in which low inertial forces are desirable to maintain the system's stability.

Composites may consist of polymer-, metal-, or ceramic-matrix with various reinforcing materials (Chapter 9). The compositions can be tailored to provide appropriate mechanical properties in selected axes of the machine tool. Although they are expensive and presently limited in use, composites are likely to become significant materials for high-accuracy, high-speed machining applications.

Granite-epoxy composite has been developed with a typical composition of 93% crushed granite and 7% epoxy binder. First used in precision centerless and internal grinders (Section 25.6) in the early 1980s, this composite material has several favorable properties: (a) good castability, which allows design versatility in machine tools; (b) a high stiffness-to-weight ratio; (c) thermal stability; (d) resistance to environmental degradation; and (e) good damping capacity (Section 24.4.3). Its compatibility with the metal sections to which it is joined is important.

24.3.2 Machine-Tool Design

Important considerations in machine tools generally involve the following factors: machine design and construction, materials used, spindle construction, thermal expansion, environmental control, and motion control. Various other parameters include the selection of cutting tools as well as processing parameters (such as speeds and feeds), tool-condition monitoring, and error compensation.

Stiffness and Damping. Among the most important factors in machine-tool structures are stiffness and damping. *Stiffness* is a function of the dimensions and geometry of

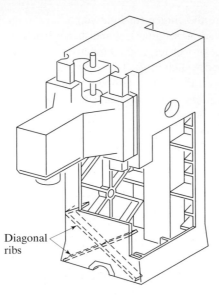

Diagonal
ribs

FIGURE 24.11   An example of a machine-tool structure. The box-type, one-piece design with internal diagonal ribs significantly improves the stiffness of the machine. *Source*: Okuma Machinery Works Ltd.

the structural components (including the spindle, bearings, drive train, and slideways) and the elastic modulus of the materials used (Table 2.2).

The stiffness of a machine tool can be enhanced by design improvements, such as the box-like, one-piece solid column structure shown in Fig. 24.11. The diagonally arranged inside ribs contribute significantly to the stiffness of this structure in all directions, improving machining accuracy. *Damping* involves the types of materials used, as well as the number and nature of the joints (for example, welded vs. bolted) in the structure (Section 24.4.)

Thermal Expansion.   An important factor that contributes to lack of precision of a machine tool is the *thermal expansion* of its components, which causes distortion of the machine. Furthermore, machines expand to different extents in different axes because of the different materials used and the differing dimensions of the components in the machine tool. It has been estimated that about 50% of machine-tool errors is due to temperature.

There are two sources of heat in machine tools:

1. *Internal*, from bearings, ballscrews, machine ways, spindle motors, pumps, servomotors, and heat generated from the cutting zone (Section 20.6). Directing the heat generated from these sources away from the machine-tool base is important, as is the quick removal of the chips produced during machining.

2. *External*, from nearby furnaces or heaters, sunlight, and fluctuations in ambient temperatures (including unexpected sources, such as air-conditioning units or vents or even just someone opening a door). The use of cutting fluids is also a significant factor, and control of coolant temperature is important in order to maintain dimensional accuracy.

These considerations are particularly important in **precision** and **ultraprecision machining**, including **diamond turning** (described in Section 22.4), where dimensional tolerances and surface finish are now in the nanometer range $(10^{-9}\,\text{m})$. The machines used for these high-precision operations are equipped with the following:

1. Various thermal and geometric real-time error-compensating features, including the modeling of heating and cooling and electronic compensation for accurate ballscrew positions,

2. Gas or fluid hydrostatic spindle bearings,

3. New designs for traction or friction drives for linear motion,

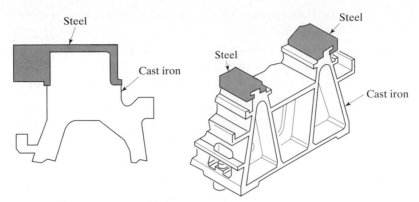

FIGURE 24.12   Steel guideways integrally-cast on top of the cast-iron bed of a machining center. Because of its higher elastic modulus, the steel provides higher stiffness than cast iron. *Source*: Hitachi Seiki Co., Ltd.

4. Extremely fine feed and position controls using microactuators,
5. Fluid-circulation channels in the machine-tool base for the maintainance of thermal stability.

The structural components of the machine tool can be made of materials with high dimensional stability and low thermal expansion, such as Super-Invar, granite, ceramics, and composites (Section 24.3.2). *Retrofitting* of older machine tools is also a viable option for enhanced performance.

Assembly Techniques.   Among recent developments in assembly techniques (Part V) are integral casting and resin bonding.

An example of **integral casting** is shown in Fig. 24.12. A hybrid casting technology is utilized whereby a steel guideway is cast integrally over a cast-iron bed. The steel provides higher stiffness (because its elastic modulus is higher than that of cast iron) and durability.

Resin bonding is also being used to assemble machine tools, which normally utilize mechanical fastening and welding. These adhesives have favorable characteristics for machine-tool construction, do not require special preparation, and are suitable for assembling both the nonmetallic and the metallic components of the machine tool. (See also Section 30.4.)

Guideways.   The preparation of guideways in machine tools requires significant effort. The plain cast-iron sliding way, which is the most common, requires much hand scraping to make it geometrically correct and long lasting. A variety of other materials are also being investigated, including molded epoxies, Teflon, and various polymer-base materials (Chapter 7).

The movements of various components in a machine tool along various axes have usually utilized conventional *ballscrew*, *rotating-screw drives*, and *rotary motors*. However, this system of mechanical and electrical components has several disadvantages, such as speed limitations, length restrictions, inertia effects, backlash (and other errors), wear of the components, and low efficiency.

The strong trend is now for **linear motor drives**. A linear motor is like a typical rotary electric motor that has been rolled out flat. The sliding surfaces in these drives are separated by an air gap and the load is supported by magnetic forces; this is the same principle used in some high-speed ground transportation systems in which the cars are supported by magnetic levitation.

Linear motor drives in machine tools have the following advantages:

a. Simplicity and minimal maintenance (there is one moving part and no mechanical linkages).

b. Better positioning accuracy and repeatability, in as much as submicron range; smooth operation.

c. A wide range of linear speeds, ranging from 1 μm/s to 5 m/s.

d. Acceleration as high as 4 g to 10 g.

e. Because there is no metal-to-metal contact between sliding surfaces, there is no wear.

Machine Foundations.   Equally important in machine-tool precision are foundations, their mass, and the manner in which they are installed in a plant. For example, in one special grinder for grinding 2.75-m (9-ft) diameter marine-propulsion gears with high precision, the concrete foundation is 6.7 m (22 ft) deep. The large mass of concrete and the machine base reduce the amplitude of vibrations and their adverse effects and isolates the base from external vibrations. Better results are obtained when the machine is installed on an *independent* concrete slab which, in turn, is isolated from the rest of the floor plant with shock-isolation devices.

24.3.3 Recent Developments in Machine-Tool Design

Significant developments concerning the design and the materials used for machine-tool bases and components have been taking place.

Lightweight designs are desirable because of ease of transportation, higher natural frequencies, and the lower inertial forces of the moving members. Lightweight designs and design flexibility require fabrication processes such as (a) the mechanical fastening (bolts and nuts) of individual components, and (b) welding. However, this approach to fabrication increases labor as well as material costs because of the preparations required.

With the goal of improving the stiffness of machine tools and therefore attaining extremely fine dimensional tolerances on machined components, the first truly innovative machine-tool structure is being developed, using a self-contained octahedral (eight-sided) machine frame. The machines are called variously **hexapods**, **parallel kinematic linked**, or **prism-shaped machines**, and are based on a mechanism called the Stewart platform (an invention used to position aircraft cockpit simulators).

The workpiece is fixtured on a fixed table. Pairs of telescoping tubes (struts or legs), equipped with ballscrews, are used to maneuver a rotating cutting tool. During machining, the machine controller shortens some tubes, while others are extended so that the cutter can follow a specified contour around the workpiece.

Six sets of coordinates are involved in these machines: three linear sets and three rotational sets. Every motion of the cutter, even a simple linear motion, is translated into six coordinated leg lengths moving in real time. The motions of the legs (each with its own motor) are rapid and, consequently, high accelerations and decelerations are involved and inertia forces are high.

These machines are still in their developmental stages, and their performance is continuously being evaluated in the areas of stiffness, dimensional accuracy, speed, and thermal expansion. The machines are basically portable, have high stiffness, and have high flexibility in the production of parts with various geometries and sizes without the necessity of refixturing parts.

24.4 VIBRATION AND CHATTER IN MACHINING OPERATIONS

In describing cutting processes and machine tools, it was pointed out that *machine stiffness* is as important as any other parameter in machining. Low stiffness affects the magnitude of *vibration and chatter* in tools and machines, and can have adverse effects on product quality. Uncontrolled vibration and chatter can result in the following:

FIGURE 24.13   Chatter marks (right of center of photograph) on the surface of a turned part. *Source*: General Electric Company.

- Poor surface finish (as shown in the right central region of Fig. 24.13).
- Loss of dimensional accuracy of the workpiece.
- Premature wear, chipping, and failure of the cutting tool, a crucial consideration with brittle tool materials, such as ceramics, some carbides, and diamond (Chapter 21).
- Possible damage to the machine-tool components from excessive vibration.
- Objectionable noise, particularly if it is of high frequency, such as the squeal heard when turning brass on a lathe.

Vibration and chatter in machining are complex phenomena. In cutting operations there are two basic types of vibration: forced vibration and self-excited vibration.

24.4.1 Forced Vibration

Forced vibration is generally caused by some *periodic* applied force present in the machine tool, such as that from gear drives, imbalance of the machine-tool components, misalignment, and motors and pumps. In processes such as milling or turning a splined shaft or a shaft with a keyway, forced vibrations are caused by the periodic engagement of the cutting tool with entry to and exit from the workpiece surface. (See, for example, Figs. 23.10 and 23.14.)

The basic solution to forced vibration is to isolate or remove the forcing element. If the forcing frequency is at or near the natural frequency of a component of the machine-tool system, one of the frequencies may be raised or lowered. The amplitude of vibration can be reduced by increasing the stiffness or by damping the system. Although changing the cutting parameters generally does not appear to greatly influence the magnitude of forced vibrations, changing the cutting speed and the tool geometry can be helpful.

24.4.2 Self-Excited Vibration

Generally called **chatter**, *self-excited vibration* is caused by the interaction of the chip-removal process and the structure of the machine tool. Self-excited vibrations usually have a very high amplitude. Chatter typically begins with a disturbance in the cutting zone. Such disturbances include (a) a lack of homogeneity in the workpiece material or its surface condition, (b) changes in the type of chips produced, or (c) changes in the frictional conditions at the tool–chip interface as influenced by cutting fluids and their effectiveness.

Regenerative Chatter.   The most important type of self-excited vibration is *regenerative chatter*. It is caused when a tool is cutting a surface that has a roughness or disturbances left from the previous cut. (See, for example, Fig. 20.23.) The depth of cut varies, and the resulting variations in the cutting force subject the tool to vibrations; the process continues repeatedly, making it "regenerative." This type of vibration can be observed while driving over a rough road (the so-called *washboard effect*).

Self-excited vibrations can generally be controlled by (a) increasing the dynamic stiffness of the system, and (b) damping. **Dynamic stiffness** is defined as the ratio of the amplitude of the force applied to the amplitude of the vibration. Because a machine tool has different stiffnesses at different frequencies, changes in cutting parameters can affect chatter.

24.4.3 Factors Influencing Chatter

The tendency for a particular workpiece to chatter during cutting is proportional to the cutting forces and to the depth and width of cut. Consequently, because cutting forces increase with strength (and hence hardness), the tendency to chatter generally increases as the hardness of the workpiece material increases. Therefore, aluminum and magnesium alloys have less tendency to chatter than do martensitic and precipitation-hardening stainless steels, nickel alloys, and high-temperature and refractory alloys. (See Chapters 5 and 6.)

An important factor in chatter is the *type of chip* produced during cutting operations. Continuous chips involve steady cutting forces; consequently, they generally do not cause chatter. Discontinuous chips and serrated chips (Fig. 20.5), on the other hand, may do so; these chips are produced periodically, and the resulting variations in force during cutting can cause chatter.

There are other factors that also contribute to chatter. Among these are the use of dull cutters, a lack of cutting fluids, and worn machine-tool ways.

24.4.4 Damping

Damping is defined as the rate at which vibrations decay. This effect is like testing your automobile's shock absorbers by pushing down on the car's front (or rear) end and observing how soon the motion stops. Damping is an important factor in controlling machine-tool vibration and chatter.

Internal Damping of Structural Materials. Internal damping results from the energy loss in materials during vibration. For example, steel has less damping capacity than gray cast iron, and composite materials (see Chapter 9 and Section 24.3) have more damping capacity than gray iron (Fig. 24.14). The difference in the damping capacity of materi-

FIGURE 24.14 The relative damping capacity of (a) gray cast iron and (b) epoxy-granite composite material. The vertical scale is the amplitude of vibration and the horizontal scale is time. *Source*: Cincinnati Milacron, Inc.

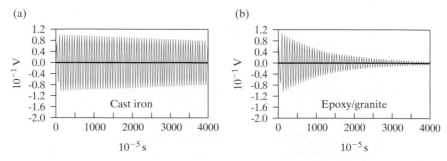

als can be observed by striking them with a gavel and listening to the sound. Try, for example, striking pieces of steel, concrete, and wood, and listen to the sound.

Joints in Machine-Tool Structures.   Although they are less significant than internal damping, bolted joints in the structure of a machine tool are also a source of damping; their effectiveness depends on size, position, and the number of joints. Because friction dissipates energy, small relative movements along dry (unlubricated) joints dissipate energy and help to improve damping. In joints where oil or adhesive polymers are present, the internal friction at the joint dissipates energy, which also contributes to damping.

All machine tools consist of a number of large and small components, assembled into a structure by various means. Consequently, this type of damping is cumulative due to the presence of a number of joints in the machine tool. Note in Fig. 24.15 that damping increases as the number of components on a lathe and their contact area increase.

The more joints, therefore, the greater the amount of energy dissipated and the higher the damping. However, overall system stiffness is usually reduced as the number of joints increases. Another method of damping (to reduce or eliminate vibration and chatter) is implemented in boring bars, as described and illustrated in Fig. 22.20b. Such damping is accomplished by various mechanical means, which dissipate energy by frictional resistance of the components within the structure of the boring bar.

External Damping.   External damping is accomplished with external dampers, which are similar to shock absorbers on automobiles. Special vibration absorbers have been developed and installed on machine tools for this purpose. Machine tools are also installed on specially prepared floors to isolate forced vibrations (such as those from nearby machines on the same floor) as an aid in improving damping.

It is evident from the foregoing discussion that a balance must be achieved between increased stiffness of a machine tool and the desirability of increased damping, particularly in the construction of high-precision machine tools. It has recently been suggested that stiffness and damping functions in a machine tool should be decoupled. Although difficult to achieve, innovative designs have been developed and implemented for advanced machine tools, such as high-precision grinders (Section 25.6).

FIGURE 24.15   The damping of vibrations as a function of the number of components on a lathe. Joints dissipate energy; the greater the number of joints, the higher the damping capacity of the machine. *Source*: J. Peters.

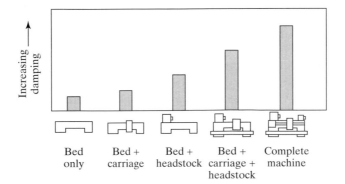

24.4.5 Guidelines for Reducing Vibration and Chatter in Machine Tools

Various sections in Chapters 22 and 23 have outlined general guidelines for reducing vibration and chatter in machining operations. The basic guidelines may be summarized as follows:

a. Minimize tool overhang.
b. Support workpiece rigidly.
c. Modify tool and cutter geometry.
d. Change process parameters, such as cutting speed, feed, depth of cut, and cutting fluids.
e. Increase the stiffness of the machine tool and its components by improving design, using larger cross-sections, and using materials with higher elastic modulus.
f. Improve the damping capacity of the machine tool.

24.5 MACHINING ECONOMICS

In the Introduction to Part IV, it was stated that the limitations of machining processes include the time required to machine a part and the amount of material wasted. Despite these drawbacks, machining is indispensable in many situations, particularly for producing complex workpiece shapes and obtaining good dimensional accuracy and surface finish.

We have also seen that machining involves a number of material variables and process parameters; the proper choice of these parameters is important in the productivity of machining operations. The preceding chapters in this part of the text have outlined the material and process parameters that are relevant to efficient machining operations. When analyzing the *economics* of machining, however, we have to consider several other factors.

As described in greater detail in Chapter 40, these considerations include the costs involved in (a) machine tools, fixtures, and cutting tools, (b) labor and overhead, (c) the time consumed in setting up the machine for a particular operation, (d) material handling and movement, such as loading the blank and unloading the machined part, (e) gaging, and (f) cutting times and noncutting times.

Actual machining time is an important consideration. Recall also the discussion in Section 22.4 on the importance of *noncutting time* in assessing the economic relevance of high-speed machining. Unless noncutting time is a significant portion of the floor-to-floor time, high-speed machining should not be considered. We describe the role of various aspects of computer-integrated manufacturing in these operations in Part VIII.

Minimizing Machining Cost. As in all manufacturing processes and operations, all relevant parameters in machining can be chosen and specified in such a manner that the **machining cost per piece**, as well as **machining time per piece**, is minimized.

Various methods and approaches have been developed to accomplish this goal, and with the increasing use of software and user-friendly computers, this task has now become easier. However, in order for the results to be reliable, it is essential that input data be accurate and up to date. Described below is one of the simpler and more common methods of analyzing machining costs in a turning operation.

In machining a part by turning, the total machining cost per piece, C, consists of

$$C = C_1 + C_2 + C_3 + C_4, \tag{24.1}$$

where

$C_1 =$ **Nonproductive cost:** labor, overhead, and machine-tool costs involved in setting up for machining, mounting the cutting tool, preparing the fixtures and the machine, and advancing and retracting the cutting tool.

$C_2 =$ **Machining cost:** labor, overhead, and machine-tool costs while the cutting operation is taking place.

$C_3 =$ **Tool-change cost:** labor, overhead, and machine-tool costs during tool change.

$C_4 =$ **Cutting tool cost.** It has been observed that the cost of cutting tools is often only about 5% of the total cutting operation. Consequently, using the least expensive tool is not always an effective way of reducing machining costs.

The result of such an analysis is shown qualitatively in Fig. 24.16. In a machining operation, it is important to identify all relevant parameters, to determine various cost factors, to obtain relevant tool-life curves for the particular operation, and to properly measure the various time intervals involved in the overall machining operation. Note in the figure that, depending on the shape of the curves obtained, small changes in cutting speed can have a significant effect on the minimum cost or minimum time per piece.

Three of the four cost variables listed above depend on cutting speed. As cutting speed increases, the machining time for a particular workpiece and the cost per piece decrease.

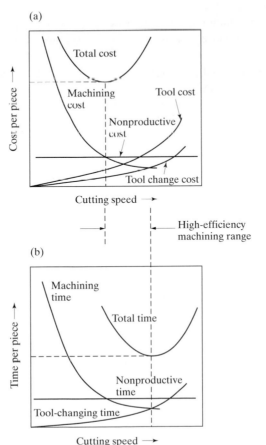

FIGURE 24.16   Graphs showing (a) cost per piece and (b) time per piece in machining. Note the optimum speeds for both cost and time. The range between the two is known as the *high-efficiency machining range.*

However, as shown in Section 20.7, tool life generally decreases with cutting speed; as a consequence, the tool cost increases, as does the tool-changing cost because tools have to be indexed or changed more frequently. Note, however, that the nonproductive cost C_1 does not depend on the cutting speed.

Each of these costs can be described by a mathematical equation in terms of its own relevant parameters, and all four can be added together as in Eq. (24.1). This equation is then differentiated with respect to the cutting speed, V, to determine the **optimum cutting speed** for minimum cost per piece (Fig. 24.16a).

Likewise, the *total time* required to machine the part is obtained by a similar mathematical equation, adding together the times involved in various phases of the total operation (such as loading and unloading the part, actual machining, and changing the tool). This equation is then differentiated with respect to the cutting speed to obtain minimum time per piece (Fig. 24.16b). Note from this figure that there is a difference between the two optimum cutting speeds. The range between these two speeds is sometimes called the **high-efficiency machining range**.

SUMMARY

- Because they are versatile and capable of performing a variety of cutting operations on small and large workpieces, machining centers and turning centers are among the most important developments in machine tools. Their selection depends on factors such as part complexity, the number and type of cutting operations to be performed, the number of cutting tools required, and the necessary dimensional accuracy and production rate.

- Vibration and chatter in machining are important considerations for workpiece dimensional accuracy, surface finish, and tool life. Stiffness and damping capacity of machine tools are important factors in controlling vibration and chatter. New materials are continually being developed and used for constructing machine-tool structures.

- The economics of machining processes depend on nonproductive costs, machining costs, tool-change costs, and tool costs. Optimum cutting speeds can be determined for both minimum machining time per piece and minimum cost per piece.

TRENDS

- Machining centers and turning centers, as well as computer controls on all types of machine tools, have progressed rapidly and continue to do so. Improvements are constantly being made in the power, speed, and stiffness of these machines.

- Machining centers and turning centers are being constructed with multitool heads and rapid-traverse features in all axes to reduce idle time. Because of their unique features, linear motor drives are being implemented at a rapid rate.

- The design of machining centers, including modular ones, is being reviewed and modified to make them fit and integrate better when placed in line with other machines in computer-integrated manufacturing systems (also known as flexible manufacturing cells or systems). These include modular machining centers.

- The characteristics of machine-tool structures and their construction are constantly being investigated in order to minimize distortions and deviations during cutting operations and to improve surface finish and dimensional accuracy.
- Sensors and controllers are being developed to automatically recognize chatter conditions and to modify machining parameters accordingly.
- New materials are being developed for machine-tool bases and components. Among these materials are epoxy-granite composites, ceramics, and various combinations of these materials.

KEY TERMS

Automatic pallet changer	High-efficiency machining range	Tool-exchange arm
Automatic tool changer	Linear-motor drive	Tool- and part-checking station
Chatter	Machining center	Touch probes
Chip collection	Modular construction	Turning center
Damping	Pallet	Universal machining center
Dynamic stiffness	Regenerative chatter	Work envelope
Forced vibration	Self-excited vibration	
Hexapods	Stiffness	

BIBLIOGRAPHY

ASM Handbook, Vol. 16: *Machining*. ASM International, 1989.

Boothroyd, G., and W.A. Knight, *Fundamentals of Machining and Machine Tools*, (2d ed.). Marcel Dekker, 1989.

Krar, S.F., and A.F. Check, *Technology of Machine Tools* (5th ed.). Glencoe/MacMillan McGraw-Hill, 1996.

Reshetov, D.N., and V.T. Portman, *Accuracy of Machine Tools*. American Society of Mechanical Engineers, 1989.

Rivin, E.I., *Stiffness and Damping in Mechanical Design*. Marcel Dekker, 1999.

Tool and Manufacturing Engineers Handbook, (4th ed.), Vol. 1: *Machining*. Society of Manufacturing Engineers, 1983.

Weck, M., *Handbook of Machine Tools*, 4 vols. Wiley, 1984.

REVIEW QUESTIONS

24.1 Describe the distinctive features of machining and turning centers. Why are these machines so versatile?

24.2 Why are pallet changers and tool changers integral parts of machining centers?

24.3 Explain the tooling system in a machining center and how it operates.

24.4 Describe the economic considerations involved in selecting machining centers.

24.5 Describe the adverse effects of vibration and chatter in machining.

24.6 Why is damping of machine tools important? How is it accomplished?

24.7 Explain the trends in materials used for machine-tool structures.

24.8 Why is thermal expansion of machine-tool components important?

24.9 What factors contribute to costs in machining operations?

24.10 What is the high-efficiency machining range?

24.11 What is chatter?

24.12 Explain the importance of foundations for installing machine tools.

24.13 What are the typical tool-changing times in a machining center?

24.14 What is the difference between a turret and a spindle?

24.15 What types of materials are machine-tool bases made from?

QUALITATIVE PROBLEMS

24.16 Explain the technical requirements that led to the development of machining centers.

24.17 Why do spindle speeds in machining centers vary over a wide range?

24.18 Why is the stiffness of machine tools important in machining operations?

24.19 Are there cutting operations that cannot be performed in machining centers? Why or why not?

24.20 Is the control of cutting-fluid temperature important? If so, in what way?

24.21 Explain how you would go about reducing each of the cost factors in machining operations. What difficulties would you encounter?

24.22 We know that we may be able to decrease machining costs by increasing the cutting speed. Explain which costs are likely to change, and how, as the cutting speed increases.

24.23 In addition to the number of joints in a machine tool, what other factors influence the rate at which damping increases, as shown in Fig. 24.15?

24.24 Would the parts shown in Problems 22.52 and 23.54 be suitable for machining on a machining center? Explain.

24.25 Other than the fact that they each have a minimum, are the overall shapes of the total-cost and total-time curves in Fig. 24.16 important? Explain.

24.26 Section 20.5.1 stated that the thrust force in cutting can be negative at high rake angles and/or low friction at the chip-tool interface. This can have an adverse effect on the stability of the cutting process. Explain why.

24.27 What are the advantages and disadvantages of cast machine-tool frames?

24.28 What are the advantages and disadvantages of welded-steel frames? Bolted steel frames?

24.29 What role does concrete play in controlling vibration in steel-framed machine tools?

24.30 Give examples of forced vibration or self-excited vibration.

24.31 What workpiece requirements would make a machining center preferable to conventional milling machines, lathes, and drill presses?

QUANTITATIVE PROBLEMS

24.32 A machining-center spindle and tool extend 12 in. from its machine tool frame. What temperature change can be tolerated to maintain a tolerance of 0.0001 in. in machining? A tolerance of 0.001 in.? Assume that the spindle is made of steel.

24.33 Using the Taylor tool-life equation, obtain the cost per part as a function of cutting speed for a turning operation. Assume that the nonproductive cost is a constant, the machining cost is the product of machining time and a prescribed rate of $25.00 per hour, and the tool change cost is the same rate times a constant time of 5 min per tool change. Assume a roughing cut on a brass piece, 0.5 in. wide, using a carbide tool with $C = 400$, and at 0.02 in./rev feed rate and spindle speed of 300 rpm. How would you expect the curve to change if the cutting tool is high-speed steel?

24.34 Perform the same analysis as in Problem 24.33, but obtain the production time as a function of the cutting speed.

SYNTHESIS AND DESIGN

24.35 If you were the chief engineer in charge of the design of machining and turning centers, what changes and improvements would you recommend on existing models?

24.36 Study the technical literature and outline the trends in the design of modern machine tools.

24.37 Make a list of components of machine tools that could be made of ceramics and explain why ceramics would be suitable.

24.38 Survey the available literature from various machine-tool manufacturers and prepare a comprehensive table, indicating the capabilities, sizes, costs, etc. of machining and turning centers. Comment on your observations.

24.39 As you can appreciate, the cost of machining and turning centers is considerably higher than more traditional machine tools. In view of the fact that many operations performed by these centers can also be done on conventional machines, how would you go about justifying the high cost of these centers? Explain with appropriate examples.

24.40 Perform an information search on the Internet and survey the capabilities and costs of machining centers.

24.41 Would it be possible to design and build machining and turning centers without the use of computer controls? Explain.

25

Abrasive Machining and Finishing Operations

25.1 INTRODUCTION

In many cases in manufacturing, the surface finish and dimensional accuracy requirements for a part are too *fine*, the workpiece material is too *hard*, or the workpiece material is too *brittle* to produce the part solely by any of the processes described in the preceding chapters. For example, ball and roller bearings, pistons, valves, cylinders, cams, gears, cutting tools and dies, and precision components for instrumentation generally require high dimensional accuracy and fine surface finish. One of the best methods for producing such parts is **abrasive machining**.

An **abrasive** is a small, nonmetallic hard particle having sharp edges and an irregular shape (unlike the cutting tools described earlier). Abrasives are capable of removing small amounts of material from a surface through a cutting process that produces tiny chips. Most of us are familiar with using bonded abrasives (**grinding wheels**, Fig. 25.1) to sharpen knives and tools, as well as using sandpaper to smoothen surfaces and sharp corners.

Abrasives are also used to hone, lap, buff, and polish workpieces. With the use of computer-controlled machines, abrasive processes are now capable of producing a wide va-

FIGURE 25.1   A variety of bonded abrasives used in abrasive machining processes. *Source*: Courtesy of Norton Company.

riety of workpiece geometries (Table 25.1 and Fig. 25.2) with very fine surface finish and close dimensional tolerances. (See Figs. 22.13, 22.14, and 26.4.)

Because they are hard, abrasives are also used in *finishing processes* for very hard or heat-treated parts—for instance, shaping hard nonmetallic materials, such as ceramics and glasses; removing unwanted weld beads and spatter; cutting off lengths of bars, structural shapes, masonry, and concrete; and cleaning surfaces with jets of air or water containing abrasive particles.

TABLE 25.1   General Characteristics of Abrasive Machining Processes and Machines

Process	Characteristics	Maximum dimension (m)*
Surface	Flat surfaces on most materials; production rate depends on table size and automation; labor skill depends on part; production rate is high on vertical-spindle rotary-table type.	Reciprocating table L: 6 Rotary table D: 3
Cylindrical	Round workpieces with stepped diameters; low production rate unless automated; labor skill depends on part shape.	Workpiece D: 0.8 Roll grinders D: 1.8 Universal grinders D: 2.5
Centerless	Round workpieces; high production rate; low to medium labor skill.	Workpiece D: 0.8
Internal	Bores in workpiece; low production rate; low to medium labor skill.	Hole D: 2
Honing	Bores and holes in workpiece; low production rate; low labor skill.	Spindle D: 1.2
Lapping	Flat surfaces; high production rate; low labor skill.	Table D: 3.7
Ultrasonic machining	Holes and cavities of various shapes, particularly in hard and brittle nonconducting materials.	—

*Larger capacities are available for special applications. L = length; D = diameter.

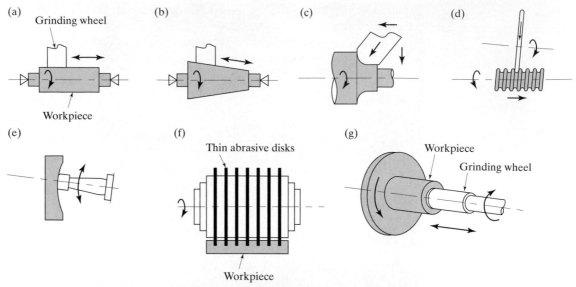

FIGURE 25.2   The types of workpieces and operations typical of grinding:
(a) cylindrical surfaces, (b) conical surfaces, (c) fillets on a shaft, (d) helical profiles,
(e) concave shape, (f) cutting off or slotting with thin wheels, and (g) internal
grinding. See also the illustrations in Section 25.6.

This chapter presents the characteristics of abrasives and how they are used in various material-removal processes. As with cutting operations, we will first describe the mechanics of these operations, because this knowledge will then allow us to establish the interrelationships of material and process variables and the quality and dimensional accuracy of the surfaces produced.

25.2 ABRASIVES

The following are abrasives commonly used in manufacturing processes:

Conventional abrasives
   a. Aluminum oxide (Al_2O_3)
   b. Silicon carbide (SiC)

Superabrasives
   c. Cubic boron nitride (cBN)
   d. Diamond

These abrasives (also discussed in Chapter 8) are much harder than conventional cutting-tool materials, as can be seen by comparing Tables 25.2 and 21.1. Because the last

TABLE 25.2   Knoop Hardness for Various Materials and Abrasives

Common glass	350–500	Titanium nitride	2000
Flint, quartz	800–1100	Titanium carbide	1800–3200
Zirconium oxide	1000	Silicon carbide	2100–3000
Hardened steels	700–1300	Boron carbide	2800
Tungsten carbide	1800–2400	Cubic boron nitride	4000–5000
Aluminum oxide	2000–3000	Diamond	7000–8000

two of the four listed above are the two hardest materials known, they are referred to as "**superabrasives**."

In addition to hardness, an important characteristic is **friability**—that is, the ability of abrasive grains to fracture (break down) into smaller pieces. This property gives abrasives their *self-sharpening* characteristics, which are crucial in maintaining the sharpness of the abrasives during use.

High friability indicates low strength or low fracture resistance of the abrasive, so a highly friable abrasive grain fragments more rapidly under grinding forces than one with low friability. For example, aluminum oxide has lower friability than silicon carbide, and correspondingly, less tendency to fragment.

The *shape* and *size* of the abrasive grain also affect its friability. Blocky grains, for example, which are analogous to negative-rake-angle cutting tools (shown in Fig. 20.3), are less friable than platelike grains. Also, because the probability of defects is lower in small grains (due to the *size effect*), they are stronger and less friable. The importance of friability to abrasive processes will be further described in Section 25.5.

Types of Abrasives.   The abrasives found in nature are *emery*, *corundum* (alumina), *quartz*, *garnet*, and *diamond*. These natural abrasives generally contain unknown amounts of impurities and possess nonuniform properties; consequently, their performance is inconsistent and unreliable. As a result, abrasives are now made synthetically.

a. Synthetic **aluminum oxide**, first made in 1893, is obtained by fusing bauxite, iron filings, and coke. Aluminum oxides are divided into two groups: fused and unfused.

   Fused aluminum oxides are categorized as dark (less friable), white (very friable), and monocrystalline. **Unfused alumina** (also known as *ceramic aluminum oxides*) can be harder than fused alumina, the purest (free of flaws) form of which is **seeded gel**.

   First introduced in 1987, seeded gel has a particle size on the order of 0.2 μm, which is much smaller than commonly used abrasive grains. These particles are sintered to form larger sizes. Because of their hardness and relatively high friability, seeded gels maintain their sharpness and are used for difficult-to-grind materials.

b. **Silicon carbide** (first discovered in 1891) is made with silica sand, petroleum coke, and small amounts of sodium chloride (table salt). Silicon carbides are divided into **black** (less friable) and **green** (more friable), and generally have higher friability than aluminum oxides; therefore, they have a greater tendency to fracture and remain sharp.

c. **Cubic boron nitride** was first developed in the 1970s; its properties and characteristics are described in Chapters 8 and 21.

d. **Diamond**, also known as synthetic or industrial diamond, was first used as an abrasive in 1955; its properties and characteristics are described in Chapters 8 and 21.

Grain Size.   As used in manufacturing processes, abrasives are generally very small compared to the size of cutting tools and inserts (described in Chapters 20 and 21). Also, abrasives have sharp edges, allowing the removal of very small quantities of material from the workpiece surface. Consequently, very fine surface finish and dimensional accuracy can be obtained.

The size of an abrasive *grain* is identified by **grit number**, which is a function of sieve size; the smaller the grain size, the larger the grit number. For example, number 10 is regarded as very coarse, 100 as fine, and 500 as very fine. Sandpaper and emery cloth are also identified in this manner, with grit number printed on the back of the abrasive paper or cloth.

25.3 BONDED ABRASIVES (GRINDING WHEELS)

Because each abrasive grain usually removes only a very small amount of material at a time, high rates of material removal can be achieved only if a large number of these grains act together. This is done by using **bonded abrasives**, typically in the form of a **grinding wheel.**

A simple grinding wheel is shown schematically in Fig. 25.3. The abrasive grains are held together by a **bonding** material (described below) which acts as supporting posts or braces between the grains. In bonded abrasives, porosity is essential to provide clearance for the chips being produced and to provide cooling; otherwise, the chips would interfere with the grinding process. It is impossible to utilize a grinding wheel with no porosity, one that is fully dense and solid. Porosity can be observed by looking at the surface of any grinding wheel. (Other features of Fig. 25.3 are described in Sections 25.4 and 25.5.)

Some of the more commonly used types of grinding wheels are shown in Fig. 25.4 for conventional abrasives, and in Fig. 25.5 for superabrasives. Note that, due to the high cost of the latter, only a small volume of these wheels consists of superabrasives. An estimated 250,000 different types and sizes of abrasive wheels are made today.

Bonded abrasives are marked with a standardized system of letters and numbers, indicating the type of abrasive, grain size, grade, structure, and bond type. Figure 25.6 shows the marking system for aluminum-oxide and silicon-carbide bonded abrasives and Fig. 25.7 shows the marking system for diamond and cubic boron nitride bonded abrasives.

The *cost* of grinding wheels depends on the type and size of wheel. Small wheels up to about 25 mm (1 in.) in diameter cost approximately $2–$10 for conventional abrasives, $30–$100 for diamond, and $50–$200 for cBN. For a large wheel, about 500 mm in diameter and 250 mm in width (20 in. by 10 in.), the costs are $500, $5000–$8000, and almost $20,000, respectively.

25.3.1 Bond Types

The common bond types for bonded abrasives are *vitrified, resinoid, rubber,* and *metal.* Most of these bonds are used for conventional abrasives as well as for superabrasives.

Vitrified.   Essentially a glass, a *vitrified bond* is also called a *ceramic bond,* particularly outside the United States. It is the most common and widely used bond. The raw materials consist of feldspar (a crystalline mineral) and clays. They are mixed with the abrasives, moistened, and molded under pressure into the shape of grinding wheels.

FIGURE 25.3   Schematic illustration of a physical model of a grinding wheel, showing its structure and wear and fracture patterns.

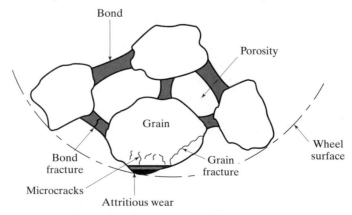

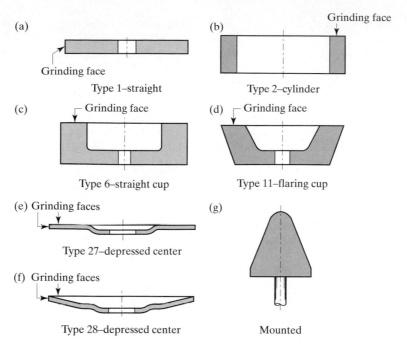

FIGURE 25.4   Common types of grinding wheels made with conventional abrasives. Note that each wheel has a specific grinding face; grinding on other surfaces is improper and unsafe.

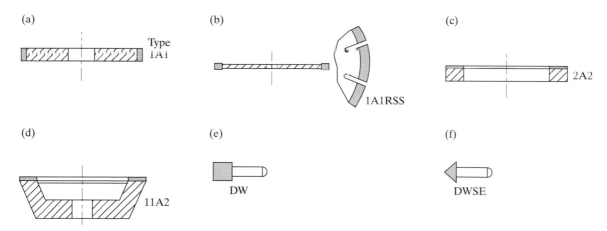

FIGURE 25.5   Examples of superabrasive wheel configurations. The annular regions (rim) are superabrasive grinding surfaces, and the wheel itself (core) is generally made of metal or composites. The bonding materials for the superabrasives are: (a), (d), and (e) resinoid, metal, or vitrified, (b) metal, (c) vitrified, and (f) resinoid.

These "green" products (which are similar to powder-metallurgy parts, Chapter 17) are fired slowly, up to a temperature of about 1250 °C (2300 °F), to fuse the glass and de-velop structural strength. The wheels are then cooled slowly to avoid thermal cracking, fin-ished to size, inspected for quality and dimensional accuracy, and tested for defects.

Wheels with vitrified bonds are strong, stiff, porous, and resistant to oils, acids, and water. They are brittle and lack resistance to mechanical and thermal shock, but vitrified

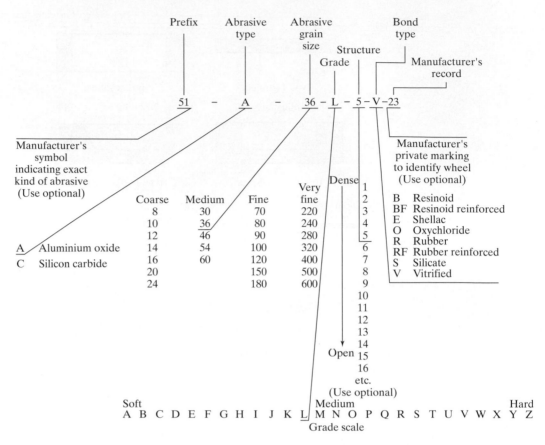

FIGURE 25.6   Standard marking system for aluminum-oxide and silicon-carbide bonded abrasives.

wheels are also available with steel backing plates or cups for better structural support during their use. The color of the wheel can be modified with various elements during its manufacture; in this way, wheels can be coded for use with specific workpiece materials, e.g., ferrous, nonferrous, ceramic, and so on.

Resinoid.   Resinoid bonding materials are *thermosetting resins*, and are available in a wide range of compositions and properties (Chapter 7). Because the bond is an organic compound, wheels with *resinoid bonds* are also called **organic wheels**. The basic manufacturing technique consists of mixing the abrasive with liquid or powdered phenolic resins and additives, pressing the mixture into the shape of a grinding wheel, and curing it at temperatures of about 175 °C (350 °F).

Because the elastic modulus of thermosetting resins is lower than that of glasses, resinoid wheels are more flexible than vitrified wheels. **Reinforced wheels** are widely used, in which one or more layers of *fiberglass mats* of various mesh sizes provide the reinforcement. Their purpose is to retard the disintegration of the wheel should it break for some reason, rather than to improve its strength. Large-diameter resinoid wheels can be additionally supported with one or more internal rings made of round steel bar, which are inserted during the molding of the wheel.

Rubber.   The most flexible bond used in abrasive wheels is rubber. The manufacturing process consists of mixing crude rubber, sulfur, and the abrasive grains together,

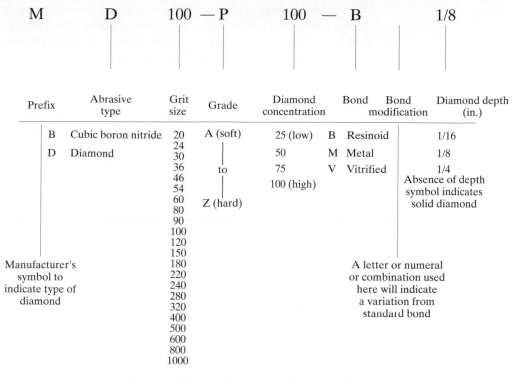

| M | D | 100 — P | 100 — B | 1/8 |

Prefix	Abrasive type	Grit size	Grade	Diamond concentration	Bond	Bond modification	Diamond depth (in.)
B Cubic boron nitride		20	A (soft)	25 (low)	B Resinoid		1/16
D Diamond		24		50	M Metal		1/8
		30		75	V Vitrified		1/4
		36	to	100 (high)			Absence of depth
		46					symbol indicates
		54					solid diamond
		60					
		80	Z (hard)				
		90					
		100					
		120					
		150					
Manufacturer's		180				A letter or numeral	
symbol to		220				or combination used	
indicate type of		240				here will indicate	
diamond		280				a variation from	
		320				standard bond	
		400					
		500					
		600					
		800					
		1000					

FIGURE 25.7   Standard marking system for cubic boron nitride and diamond bonded abrasives.

rolling the mixture into sheets, cutting out circles, and heating them under pressure to vulcanize the rubber. Thin wheels can be made in this manner and are used like saws for cutting-off operations (*cut-off blades*).

Metal Bonds.   Using powder-metallurgy techniques, the abrasive grains (usually diamond or cubic boron nitride) are bonded to the periphery of a metal wheel to depths of 6 mm (0.25 in.) or less (as in Fig. 25.5). Metal bonding is carried out under high pressure and temperature. The wheel itself (the core) may be made of aluminum, bronze, steel, ceramics, or composite materials, depending on the wheel requirements, such as strength, stiffness, and dimensional stability.

Other Bonds.   In addition to those described above, other bonds include silicate, shellac, and oxychloride bonds. However, they have limited uses, and will not be discussed further here. A new development is the use of *polyimide* (Section 7.7) as a substitute for the phenolic in resinoid wheels. It is tough and also resistant to high temperatures. Superabrasive wheels may also be *layered* so that a single abrasive layer is plated or brazed to a metal wheel with a particular desired shape. These wheels are lower in cost and are used for small-production quantities.

25.3.2 Wheel Grade and Structure

The **grade** of a bonded abrasive is a measure of the bond's strength; it includes both the *type* and the *amount* of bond in the wheel. Because strength and hardness are directly related (Section 2.6.2), the grade is also referred to as the *hardness* of a bonded abrasive. A hard wheel has a stronger bond and/or a larger amount of bonding material between the grains than a soft wheel. (See also the example in Section 25.5.5.)

The **structure** of a bonded abrasive is a measure of the *porosity* (spacing between the grains in Fig. 25.3). Some porosity is essential to provide clearance for the grinding chips; otherwise, they would interfere with the grinding process. The structure of bonded abrasives ranges from dense to open. (See Fig. 25.6.)

25.4 THE GRINDING PROCESS

Grinding is a chip-removal process that uses an individual abrasive grain as the cutting tool (Fig. 25.8a). The major differences between grain and single-point cutting tool actions are as follows:

a. The individual abrasive grains have *irregular shapes* and are spaced *randomly* along the periphery of the wheel (Fig. 25.9).

b. The average rake angle of the grains is highly negative, such as −60° or even lower. Consequently, grinding chips undergo much larger deformation than they do in other cutting processes. (See Section 20.2.)

c. The radial positions of the grains vary.

d. Cutting speeds are very high, typically 30 m/s (600 ft/min).

FIGURE 25.8   (a) Grinding chip being produced by a single abrasive grain. (A) chip, (B) workpiece, (C) abrasive grain. Note the large negative rake angle of the grain. The inscribed circle is 0.065 mm (0.0025 in.) in diameter. *Source*: M. F. Merchant. (b) Schematic illustration of chip formation by an abrasive grain with a wear flat. Note the negative rake angle of the grain and the small shear angle.

(a)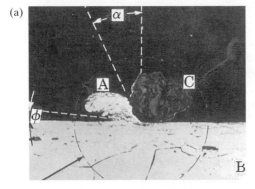

(b)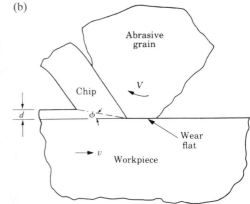

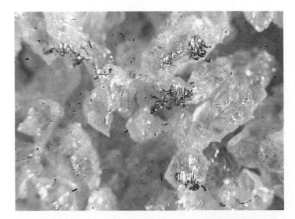

FIGURE 25.9   The surface of a grinding wheel (A46-J8V) showing abrasive grains, wheel porosity, wear flats on grains, and metal chips from the workpiece adhering to the grains. Note the random distribution and shape of abrasive grains. Magnification: 50X. *Source*: S. Kalpakjian.

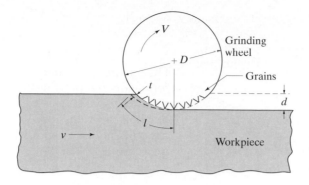

FIGURE 25.10   Schematic illustration of the surface grinding process, showing various process variables. The figure depicts conventional (up) grinding.

The grinding process and its parameters can best be observed in the *surface grinding* operation, shown schematically in Fig. 25.10. A straight grinding wheel (Fig. 25.4a) of diameter D removes a layer of metal at a depth d (**wheel depth of cut**). An individual grain on the periphery of the wheel moves at a tangential velocity V, while the workpiece moves at a velocity v. Each abrasive grain removes a small chip with an *undeformed thickness* (**grain depth of cut**) t and an *undeformed length l.*

Example: Chip Dimensions in Surface Grinding

By geometric relationships, it can be shown that the undeformed chip length, l, in surface grinding (Fig. 25.10) is given approximately by the expression

$$l = \sqrt{Dd} \qquad \textbf{(25.1)}$$

and the undeformed chip thickness t by the expression

$$t = \sqrt{(4v/VCr)}\,\sqrt{d/D}, \qquad \textbf{(25.2)}$$

where C is the number of cutting points per unit area of the periphery of the wheel and is estimated to be in the range of 0.1 to 10 per mm^2 (10^2 to 10^3 per $in.^2$). The quantity r is the ratio of chip width to average undeformed chip thickness and has an approximate value of between 10 and 20. Let's calculate l and t for the following process parameters: $D = 200$ mm, $d = 0.05$ mm, $v = 30$ m/min, and $V = 1800$ m/min.

Using the preceding formulas, we find that

$$l = \sqrt{(200)(0.05)} = 3.2 \text{ mm} = 0.13 \text{ in.}$$

Assuming that $C = 2$ per mm^2 and that $r = 15$, we obtain

$$t = \sqrt{\frac{(4)(30)}{(1800)(2)(15)}}\sqrt{\frac{0.05}{200}} = 0.006 \text{ mm} = 0.00023 \text{ in.}$$

Note that these chips are much smaller than those obtained in metal cutting operations in general. Furthermore, because of plastic deformation, the actual chip will be shorter and thicker than the calculated values. (See Fig. 25.8.)

25.4.1 Grinding Forces

A knowledge of grinding forces is necessary not only for estimating power requirements and designing grinding machines, but also for determining the deflections that the workpiece and the grinding machine may undergo; it is also helpful in the design and use of workholding

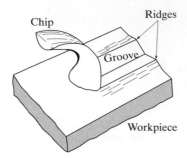

FIGURE 25.11   Chip formation and plowing of the workpiece surface by an abrasive grain. This action is similar to abrasive wear. (See Fig. 32.6.)

devices. Deflections, in turn, adversely influence dimensional accuracy and are critical in precision grinding.

If we assume that the cutting force on the grain is proportional to the cross-sectional area of the undeformed chip, it can be shown that the **grain force** (tangential force on the wheel) is proportional to process variables as follows:

$$\text{Grain force} \propto \left(\frac{v}{V} \sqrt{\frac{d}{D}} \right) \text{(strength of the material).} \qquad \textbf{(25.3)}$$

Because of the small dimensions involved, forces in grinding are usually much smaller than those in cutting operations (discussed in Chapters 22 and 23). Grinding forces should be kept low in order to avoid distortion and to maintain the dimensional accuracy of the workpiece.

The **energy** dissipated in producing a grinding chip consists of the energy required for the following phenomena:

1. Chip formation.
2. Plowing, as shown by the ridges in Fig. 25.11.
3. Friction caused by rubbing of the grain along the surface.

The grains develop a **wear flat** (Fig. 25.8b), which is similar to *flank wear* in cutting tools (Fig. 20.15), as a result of the grinding operation. The wear flat rubs along the ground surface and, because of friction, dissipates energy.

Typical **specific energy** requirements (energy per unit volume of material removed) in grinding are shown in Table 25.3. Note that these energy levels are much higher than those in machining operations (see Table 20.2). This difference can be attributed to factors such as the presence of a wear flat and chips produced with a high negative rake angle. From the specific energy data, we can calculate the grinding force (tangential to the

TABLE 25.3   Approximate Specific Energy Requirements for Surface Grinding

Workpiece material	Hardness	Specific energy	
		$\text{W} \cdot \text{s/mm}^3$	$\text{hp} \cdot \text{min/in.}^3$
Aluminum	150 HB	7–27	2.5–10
Cast iron (class 40)	215 HB	12–60	4.5–22
Low-carbon steel (1020)	110 HB	14–68	5–25
Titanium alloy	300 HB	16–55	6–20
Tool steel (T15)	67 HRC	18–82	6.5–30

wheel), F_t, and the thrust force (normal to the workpiece surface), F_n, as shown in the example below.

Example: Forces in Surface Grinding

Assume that you are performing a surface grinding operation on low-carbon steel, with a wheel of diameter $D = 10$ in. that is rotating at $N = 4000$ rpm, and a width of cut $w = 1$ in. The depth of cut is $d = 0.002$ in. and the feed rate of the workpiece, v, is 60 in./min. Calculate the cutting force (force tangential to the wheel), F_c, and the thrust force (normal to the workpiece surface), F_n.

Solution: We first determine the material removal rate (MRR), as follows:

$$\text{MRR} = dwv = (0.002)(1)(60) = 0.12 \text{ in.}^3/\text{min.}$$

The power consumed is given by

$$\text{Power} = (u)(\text{MRR})$$

where u is the specific energy, as obtained from Table 25.3. (See also Section 20.5.3.) For low-carbon steel, let us estimate it to be 15 hp·min/in.^{3}. Therefore,

$$\text{Power} = (15)(0.12) = 1.8 \text{ hp.}$$

By noting that 1 hp = 33,000 ft·lb/min = 396,000 in.·lb/min, we obtain

$$\text{Power} = (1.8)(396,000) = 712,800 \text{ in.·lb/min.}$$

Since power is defined as

$$\text{Power} = (T)(\omega),$$

where T is the torque and is equal to $T = (F_c)(D/2)$, and ω is the rotational speed of the wheel in radians per minute ($\omega = 2\pi N$), it follows that

$$712,800 = (F_c)\left(\tfrac{10}{2}\right)(2)(\pi)(4000),$$

and therefore, $F_c = 5.7$ lb.

The thrust force, F_n, can be estimated by noting (from experimental data in the technical literature) that it is about 30% higher than the cutting force, F_c. Consequently,

$$F_n = (1.3)(5.7) = 7.4 \text{ lb.}$$

25.4.2 Temperature

Temperature rise in grinding is an important consideration because it can adversely affect the surface properties and cause residual stresses on the workpiece. Furthermore, temperature gradients in the workpiece cause distortions by differential thermal expansion and contraction. When a portion of the heat generated is conducted into the workpiece, it expands the part being ground, making it difficult to control dimensional accuracy.

The **surface temperature rise** in grinding is related to process variables by the following expression:

$$\text{Temperature rise} \propto D^{1/4} d^{3/4} \left(\frac{V}{v}\right)^{1/2}. \tag{25.4}$$

Therefore, temperature increases with increasing depth of cut, wheel diameter, and wheel speed, and decreases with increasing workpiece speed. Note that the depth of cut, d, has the greatest influence on temperature.

Peak temperatures during grinding may reach 1600 °C (3000 °F). However, the time involved in producing a chip is extremely short (microseconds), so the chip may or may not melt. Because the chips carry away much of the heat generated, as do chips formed in machining processes using cutting tools (Fig. 20.14), only a fraction of the heat produced in grinding is conducted to the workpiece.

Sparks.   The sparks produced when grinding metals are actually chips that glow, resulting from the *exothermic* (heat-producing) reaction of the hot chips with oxygen in the atmosphere. Sparks do not occur when any metal is ground in an oxygen-free environment.

The color, intensity, and shape of the sparks depend on the composition of the metal being ground. Charts are available that help identify the type of metal being ground from the appearance of its sparks. If the heat generated due to exothermic reaction is sufficiently high, chips can melt and, owing to surface tension, acquire a spherical shape and solidify as metal particles.

Tempering.   Excessive temperature rise in grinding can cause *tempering* and *softening* of the workpiece surface. Process variables must therefore be selected carefully in order to avoid excessive temperature rise. The use of grinding fluids is an effective means of controlling temperature.

Burning.   Excessive temperature during grinding may burn the surface being ground. A *burn* is characterized by a bluish color on ground steel surfaces, an indication that high temperature caused oxidation. It can be detected by etching and metallurgical techniques. A burn may not be objectionable in itself. However, the surface layers may undergo *phase transformations* (Chapter 4), with martensite forming in higher-carbon steels from rapid cooling (**metallurgical burn**). This condition will influence the surface properties of ground parts, reducing surface ductility and toughness.

Heat Checking.   High temperatures in grinding may cause the workpiece surface to crack; this is known as *heat checking*. These cracks are usually perpendicular to the grinding direction. Under severe grinding conditions, however, parallel cracks may also appear. Such a surface lacks toughness and has low fatigue and corrosion resistance.

25.4.3 Residual Stresses

Temperature gradients within the workpiece during grinding are primarily responsible for *residual stresses*. Grinding fluids and the method of application, as well as process parameters such as depth of cut and speeds, significantly influence the magnitude and type of residual stresses developed (tension or compression).

Because of the adverse effect of tensile residual stresses on fatigue strength, process variables should be carefully selected. Residual stresses can usually be reduced by lowering wheel speed and increasing workpiece speed (**low-stress grinding**, or *gentle grinding*). Softer grade wheels, known as **free-cutting wheels**, may also be used.

25.5 GRINDING WHEEL WEAR

Grinding wheel wear is an important consideration because it adversely affects the shape and dimensional accuracy of ground surfaces, as does wear on cutting tools. Grinding wheel wear is caused by three different mechanisms: attritious grain wear, grain fracture, and bond fracture.

25.5.1 Attritious Grain Wear

In *attritious wear*, the cutting edges of an originally sharp grain become dull by attrition, developing a **wear flat** (Fig. 25.8b) that is similar to flank wear in cutting tools. Wear is caused by the interaction of the grain with the workpiece material, involving both physical and chemical reactions. These reactions are complex and involve diffusion, chemical degradation or decomposition of the grain, fracture at a microscopic scale, plastic deformation, and melting.

Attritious wear is low when the two materials (grain and workpiece) are *chemically inert* with respect to each other, much like what we saw with cutting tools. The more inert the materials, the lower the tendency for reaction and adhesion to occur between the grain and the workpiece.

For example, because aluminum oxide is relatively inert with respect to iron, its rate of attritious wear when used to grind steels is much lower than that of silicon carbide and diamond. On the other hand, silicon carbide can dissolve in iron, so it is not suitable for grinding steels. Cubic boron nitride has a higher inertness with respect to steels, so it is suitable for use as an abrasive.

The selection of the type of abrasive for low attritious wear is, therefore, based on the *reactivity* of the grain with the workpiece and on their relative mechanical properties, such as hardness and toughness. The environment and the type of grinding fluid used also have an influence on grain–workpiece interactions.

25.5.2 Grain Fracture

Because abrasive grains are brittle, their fracture characteristics in grinding are important. If the wear flat caused by attritious wear is excessive, the grain becomes dull and grinding becomes inefficient and produces undesirably high temperatures.

Optimally, the grain should fracture or fragment at a moderate rate, so that new sharp cutting edges are produced continuously during grinding. This is equivalent to breaking a dull piece of chalk or a stone into two or more pieces in order to expose new sharp edges. Section 25.2 described the *friability* of abrasives (the extent to which they are self-sharpening), an important factor in effective grinding.

The selection of grain type and size for a particular application also depends on the attritious wear rate. A grain–workpiece material combination with high attritious wear and low grain friability dulls grains and develops a large wear flat. Grinding then becomes inefficient, and surface damage (such as burning) is likely to occur.

25.5.3 Bond Fracture

The strength of the bond (grade) is a significant parameter in grinding. If the bond is too strong, dull grains cannot be dislodged. This prevents other sharp grains along the circumference of the grinding wheel from contacting the workpiece to remove chips, and the grinding process becomes inefficient. On the other hand, if the bond is too weak, the grains are easily dislodged and the wear rate of the wheel increases. In this case, maintaining dimensional accuracy becomes difficult.

In general, softer bonds are recommended for harder materials, and for reducing residual stresses and thermal damage to the workpiece. Hard-grade wheels are used for softer materials and for removing large amounts of material at high rates.

25.5.4 Dressing, Truing, and Shaping of Grinding Wheels

Dressing is the process of producing sharp new edges on grains, conditioning worn grains on the surface of a grinding wheel (conditioning), and truing (producing a true circle) an out-of-round wheel. Dressing is necessary when excessive attritious wear dulls the wheel, called **glazing** because of the shiny appearance of the wheel surface, or when the wheel becomes loaded.

Loading is when the porosities on the grinding surfaces of the wheel (Fig. 25.9) become filled or clogged with chips. Loading can occur in the grinding of soft materials or by improper selection of grinding wheels or process parameters. A loaded wheel cuts inefficiently, generating much frictional heat; this results in surface damage and loss of dimensional accuracy.

Three techniques are used to dress grinding wheels. In the first method, a specially shaped *diamond-point tool* or *diamond cluster* is moved across the width of the grinding face of a rotating wheel and removes a small layer from the wheel surface with each pass. This method can be either dry or wet, depending on whether the wheel is to be used dry or wet, respectively. In practice, however, the wear of the diamond can be significant with harder wheels, in which case a diamond disk or cup wheel can be used.

In the second dressing method, a set of *star-shaped steel disks* is manually pressed against the wheel. Material is removed from the wheel surface by crushing the grains. As a result, this method produces a coarse surface on the wheel and is used only for rough grinding operations on bench or pedestal grinders.

In the third method, abrasive sticks may be used to dress grinding wheels, particularly softer wheels. However, this technique is not appropriate for precision grinding operations.

Dressing techniques for metal-bonded diamond wheels involve the use of *electrical-discharge* and *electrochemical* material-removal techniques (Chapter 26). These processes erode away very thin layers of the metal bond, exposing new diamond cutting edges.

Dressing for form grinding involves *crush dressing*, or *crush forming*; it consists of pressing a metal roll on the surface of the grinding wheel, which is usually a vitrified wheel. The roll (made of high-speed steel, tungsten carbide, or boron carbide) has a machined or ground profile on its periphery, and reproduces a replica of this profile on the surface of the grinding wheel being dressed.

Dressing techniques and how frequently the wheel surface is dressed are important because they affect grinding forces and surface finish. Modern computer-controlled grinders are equipped with automatic dressing features which dress the wheel continually as grinding progresses. The first contact between the dressing tool and the grinding wheel is very important; it is usually monitored precisely by piezoelectric or acoustic-emission sensors (Section 38.8).

These features are particularly important for grinders with high stiffness and when using harder and more expensive abrasive wheels, because of the very small amounts of grinding-wheel material involved in dressing passes. For a typical aluminum oxide wheel, the depth removed during dressing is on the order of 5 to 15 μm (200 to 600 μin.), but for a cBN wheel it would be 2 to 10 μm (80 to 400 μin.). Consequently, modern dressing systems have a resolution as low as 0.25 to 1 μm (10 to 40 μin.). In the maintenance of grinding wheels, other devices (such as vibration sensors, power monitors, and strain gauges) are also used in combination.

Truing is a dressing operation by which a wheel is restored to its original shape; thus, a round wheel is dressed to make its circumference a true circle (hence the name). For softer wheels, truing and dressing are done separately, but for harder wheels (such as cBN), both are done in one operation.

Grinding wheels can be **shaped** to the form to be ground on the workpiece (Section 25.6.2). The grinding face on the Type 1 straight wheel shown in Fig. 25.4a is cylindrical and, therefore, produces a flat surface. However, this surface can be shaped by dressing it to various forms.

Although templates have been used for this purpose, modern grinders are equipped with computer-controlled shaping features, whereby the diamond dressing tool traverses the wheel

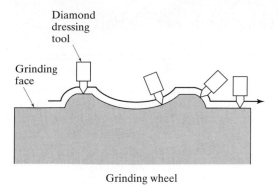

FIGURE 25.12   Shaping the grinding face of a wheel by dressing it with computer control. Note that the diamond dressing tool is normal to the surface at point of contact with the wheel. *Source*: Okuma Machinery Works Ltd.

face automatically along a certain prescribed path (Fig. 25.12). Note in this figure that the axis of the diamond dressing tool remains normal to the wheel face at the point of contact.

25.5.5 Grinding Ratio

Grinding wheel wear is generally correlated with the amount of workpiece material ground by a parameter called the **grinding ratio**, G, which is defined as

$$G = \frac{\text{Volume of material removed}}{\text{Volume of wheel wear}} \qquad \textbf{(25.5)}$$

Grinding ratios in practice vary widely, ranging from 2 to 200 and even higher, depending on the type of wheel, workpiece material, the grinding fluid, and process parameters such as depth of cut and speeds of wheel and workpiece.

During a grinding operation, a particular wheel may **act soft** (wear is high) or **act hard** (wear is low), regardless of the wheel grade. Note, for example, that an ordinary pencil acts soft when writing on rough paper, and acts hard when on soft paper. Acting hard or soft is a function of the force on the grain. The higher the force, the greater the tendency for the grains to fracture or be dislodged from the wheel surface, and the higher the wheel wear and the lower the grinding ratio.

From Eq. (25.1) we note that the grain force increases with the strength of the workpiece material, work speed, and depth of cut, and decreases with increasing wheel speed and wheel diameter. Thus a wheel acts soft when v and d increase or when V and D decrease.

Attempting to obtain a high grinding ratio in practice isn't always desirable because high ratios may indicate grain dulling and possible surface damage. A lower ratio may be acceptable when an overall economic analysis justifies it.

Example: Action of a Grinding Wheel

A surface-grinding operation is being carried out with the wheel running at a constant spindle speed. Will the wheel act soft or hard as the wheel wears down over a period of time? Assume that the depth of cut, d, remains constant and the wheel is dressed periodically.

Solution: Referring to Eq. (25.3), we note that the parameters that change by time in this operation are the wheel diameter, D, and V. As D becomes smaller, the relative grain force increases, and the wheel acts softer. Some grinding machines are equipped with variable-speed spindle motors to accommodate these changes, and also to make provision for accommodating wheels of different diameters.

25.5.6 Wheel Selection and Grindability of Materials

The type of grinding wheel used for a certain application can greatly influence the quality of surfaces produced, as well as the economics of the operation. Wheel selection involves not only the shape of the wheel with respect to the shape of the part to be produced, but the characteristics of the workpiece material as well. On the basis of the discussion thus far, it can be seen that the physical and mechanical properties of the workpiece material are important in the selection of a type of abrasive and a bond.

The **grindability** of materials, like machinability (Section 20.9), is difficult to precisely define. Grindability is a general indicator of how easy it is to grind a material. It includes considerations such as the quality of the surface produced, surface finish, surface integrity, wheel wear, cycle time, and overall economics. As in machinability, grindability of a material can be enhanced greatly by the proper selection of process parameters (Table 25.4), wheels, and grinding fluids, as well as of machine characteristics and fixturing methods.

Grinding practices are now well established for a wide variety of metallic and non-metallic materials, including newly developed materials for aerospace applications. Specific recommendations for selecting wheels (Table 25.5) and appropriate process parameters for metals can be found in various handbooks.

Ceramics are now ground with relative ease using diamond wheels, as well as carefully selected process parameters. It has been shown, for example, that with light passes and machines with high stiffness and damping capacity, it is possible to produce continuous chips and good surface integrity in grinding (Fig. 25.11), known as **ductile regime grinding**. Because ceramic chips are typically 1 μm-10 μm (40 μin.–400 μin.) in size, they are more difficult to remove from grinding fluids than metal chips, requiring fine filters and special methods.

TABLE 25.4   Typical Range of Speeds and Feeds for Abrasive Processes

Process variable	Conventional grinding	Creep-feed grinding	Buffing	Polishing
Wheel speed (m/min)	1500–3000	1500–3000	1800–3600	1500–2400
Work speed (m/min)	10–60	0.1–1	—	—
Feed (mm/pass)	0.01–0.05	1–6	—	—

TABLE 25.5   Typical Recommendations for Grinding Wheels for Use with Various Materials

Material	Type of grinding wheel
Aluminum	C46–K6V
Brass	C46–K6V
Bronze	A54–K6V
Cast iron	C60–L6V, A60–M6V
Carbides	C60–I9V, D150–R75B
Ceramics	D150–N50M
Copper	C60–J8V
Nickel alloys	B150H100V
Nylon	A36–L8V
Steels	A60–M6V
Titanium	A60–K8V
Tool steels (>50 HRC)	B120WB

Note: These recommendations vary significantly, depending on material composition, the particular grinding operation, and grinding fluids used.

25.6 GRINDING OPERATIONS AND MACHINES

Grinding operations are carried out with a variety of wheel–workpiece configurations. The selection of a grinding process for a particular application depends on part shape and size, ease of fixturing, and the production rate required.

The basic types of grinding operations—surface, cylindrical, internal, and centerless grinding—are described in this section. The relative movement of the wheel may be along the surface of the workpiece (*traverse* grinding, *through feed* grinding, *cross-feeding*), or it may be radially into the workpiece (*plunge* grinding). Surface grinders comprise the largest percentage of grinders used in industry, followed by bench grinders (usually with two wheels at each end of the spindle), cylindrical grinders, and tool and cutter grinders; the least common are internal grinders.

Grinding machines are available for various workpiece geometries and sizes. Modern grinding machines are computer controlled, with features such as automatic workpiece loading and unloading, clamping, cycling, gaging, dressing, and wheel shaping. Grinders can also be equipped with probes and gages for determining the relative position of the wheel and workpiece surfaces (see also Fig. 24.6) as well as with tactile sensing features whereby diamond dressing-tool breakage, if any, can readily be detected during the dressing cycle.

25.6.1 Surface Grinding

Surface grinding involves grinding flat surfaces and is one of the most common grinding operations (Fig. 25.13). Typically, the workpiece is secured on a *magnetic chuck* attached to the work table of the *grinder* (Fig. 25.14). Nonmagnetic materials generally are held by vises, special fixtures, vacuum chucks, or double-sided adhesive tapes.

A straight wheel is mounted on the *horizontal spindle* of the grinder. Traverse grinding occurs as the table reciprocates longitudinally and feeds laterally after each stroke. In *plunge grinding*, the wheel is moved radially into the workpiece, as it is when grinding a groove (Fig. 25.13b).

The size of a surface grinder is determined by the surface dimensions that can be ground on the machine. In addition to the surface grinder shown in Fig. 25.14, there are other types, with *vertical spindles* and *rotary tables* (referred to as *Blanchard* type, Fig. 25.13c). These configurations allow a number of pieces to be ground in one setup. Steel balls for ball bearings are ground in special setups at high production rates (Fig. 25.15).

FIGURE 25.13   Schematic illustrations of various surface grinding operations.
(a) Traverse grinding with a horizontal-spindle surface grinder. (b) Plunge grinding with a horizontal-spindle surface grinder, producing a groove in the workpiece.
(c) A vertical-spindle rotary-table grinder (also known as the *Blanchard* type).

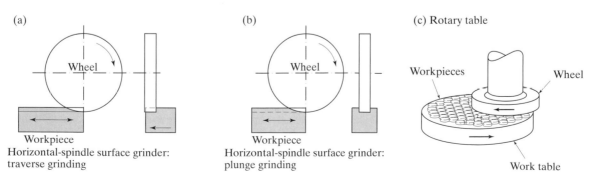

(a)

Wheel

Workpiece
Horizontal-spindle surface grinder:
traverse grinding

(b)

Wheel

Workpiece
Horizontal-spindle surface grinder:
plunge grinding

(c) Rotary table

Workpieces   Wheel

Work table

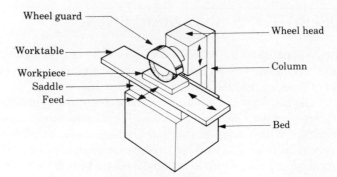

FIGURE 25.14   Schematic illustration of a horizontal-spindle surface grinder.

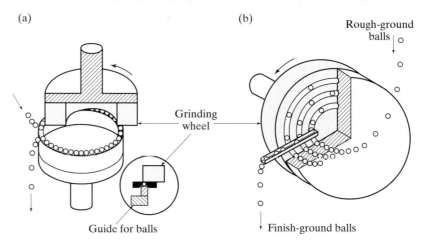

FIGURE 25.15   (a) Rough grinding of steel balls on a vertical-spindle grinder; the balls are guided by a special rotary fixture. (b) Finish grinding of balls in a multiple-groove fixture. The balls are ground to within 0.013 mm (0.0005 in.) of their final size. *Source: American Machinist.*

25.6.2 Cylindrical Grinding

In *cylindrical grinding*, also called *center-type* grinding (Fig. 25.16; see also Fig. 25.2), the external cylindrical surfaces and shoulders of the workpiece are ground. Typical applications include crankshaft bearings, spindles, pins, bearing rings, and rolls for rolling mills.

The rotating cylindrical workpiece reciprocates laterally along its axis. In grinders used for large and long workpieces, the grinding wheel reciprocates; called a *roll grinder*, it is capable of grinding rolls as large as 1.8 m (72 in.) in diameter for rolling mills (see Fig. 13.1).

The workpiece in cylindrical grinding is held between centers or in a chuck, or it is mounted on a faceplate in the headstock of the grinder. For straight cylindrical surfaces, the axes of rotation of the wheel and workpiece are parallel. Separate motors drive the wheel and workpiece at different speeds. Long workpieces with two or more diameters are also ground on cylindrical grinders. Cylindrical grinding can produce shapes (*form grinding* and *plunge grinding*) in which the wheel is dressed to the form to be ground (Fig. 25.17).

Cylindrical grinders are identified by the maximum diameter and length of the workpiece that can be ground, similar to engine lathes. In *Universal grinders*, both the workpiece and the wheel axes can be moved and swiveled around a horizontal plane, permitting the grinding of

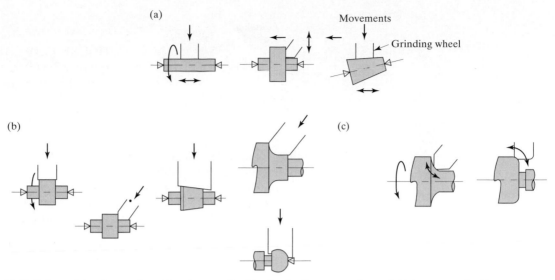

FIGURE 25.16   Examples of various cylindrical grinding operations. (a) Traverse grinding, (b) plunge grinding, and (c) profile grinding. *Source*: Okuma Machinery Works Ltd.

tapers and other shapes. These machines are equipped with computer controls, reducing labor and producing parts accurately and repetitively.

With computer-control features, *noncylindrical* parts (such as cams) can be ground on rotating workpieces. As Fig. 25.18 illustrates, the workpiece spindle rpm is synchronized such that the radial distance between the workpiece and wheel axes is varied continuously to produce a particular shape, such as the one shown in the figure.

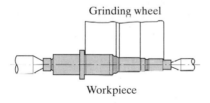

FIGURE 25.17   Plunge grinding of a workpiece on a cylindrical grinder with the wheel dressed to a stepped shape. See also Fig. 25.12.

FIGURE 25.18   Schematic illustration of grinding a noncylindrical part on a cylindrical grinder with computer controls to produce the shape. The part rotation and the distance x between centers is varied and synchronized to grind the particular workpiece shape.

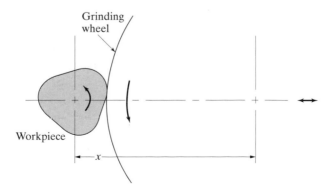

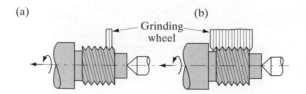

FIGURE 25.19   Thread grinding by (a) traverse, and (b) plunge grinding.

Thread grinding is done on cylindrical grinders with specially dressed wheels matching the shape of the threads (Fig. 25.19), as well as using centerless grinders (Section 25.6.4). Although costly, threads produced by grinding are the most accurate of any manufacturing process and have a very fine surface finish. The workpiece and wheel movements are synchronized to produce the pitch of the thread, usually in about six passes. (See also Section 25.6.4.)

Example: Cycle Patterns in Cylindrical Grinding

As in most grinding operations, the grinding wheel in cylindrical grinding usually makes several passes along a path in order to produce the final geometry on the workpiece. Figure 25.20 illustrates various cycle patterns for producing several shapes on a multifunctional computer-controlled precision grinder. The downward arrowheads with numbers indicate the start of the grinding cycle.

The determination of the optimum pattern for minimum cycle time with the least expense depends on the amount of material to be removed, part shape, and the process parameters chosen. These patterns are automatically generated by the software in the computer controls of the grinder. *Source*: Toyoda Machinery.

FIGURE 25.20

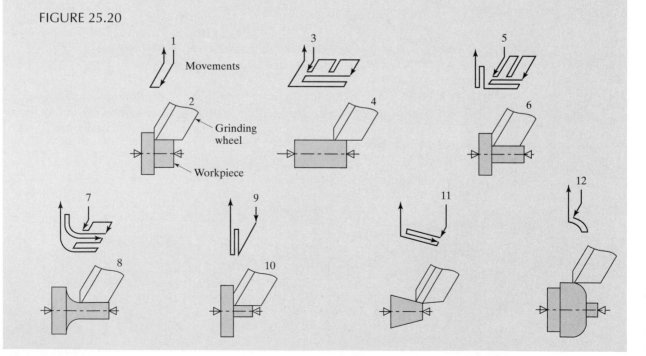

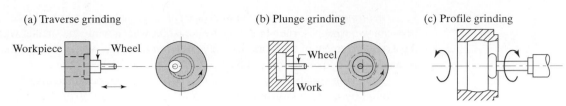

FIGURE 25.21   Schematic illustrations of internal grinding operations.

25.6.3 Internal Grinding

In *internal grinding* (Fig. 25.21), a small wheel is used to grind the inside diameter of the part, such as to bushings and bearing races. The workpiece is held in a rotating chuck and the wheel rotates at 30,000 rpm or higher. Internal profiles can also be ground with profile-dressed wheels that move radially into the workpiece. The headstock of internal grinders can be swiveled on a horizontal plane to grind tapered holes.

25.6.4 Centerless Grinding

Centerless grinding is a high-production process for continuously grinding cylindrical surfaces in which the workpiece is supported not by centers (hence the term "centerless") or chucks, but by a blade (Figs. 25.22a and b). Typical parts made by centerless grinding are roller bearings, piston pins, engine valves, camshafts, and similar components. This continuous production process requires little operator skill.

Parts with diameters as small as 0.1 mm (0.004 in.) can be ground. Centerless grinders (Fig. 25.22c) are now capable of wheel surface speeds on the order of 10,000 m/min (35,000 ft/min), using cubic boron nitride abrasive wheels.

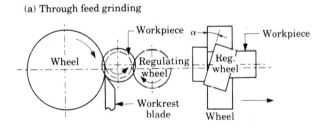

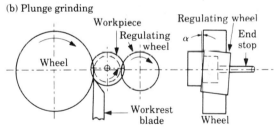

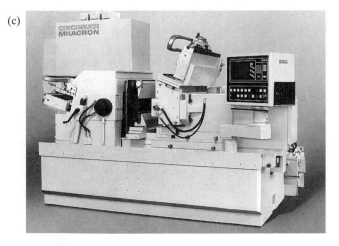

FIGURE 25.22   Schematic illustrations of centerless grinding operations: (a) through feed grinding. (b) Plunge grinding. (c) A computer numerical control cylindrical grinding machine. *Source*: Courtesy of Cincinnati Milacron, Inc.

In *through-feed grinding*, the workpiece is supported on a workrest blade and is ground between two wheels. Grinding is done by the larger wheel, while the smaller wheel regulates the axial movement of the workpiece. The *regulating wheel*, which is rubber bonded, is tilted and runs at a speed of only about $\frac{1}{20}$th of the grinding wheel speed.

Parts with variable diameters, such as bolts, valve tappets, and distributor shafts, can be ground by centerless grinding. Called *infeed*, or *plunge, grinding* (Fig. 25.22b), the process is similar to plunge or form grinding with cylindrical grinders. Tapered pieces are centerless ground by *end-feed grinding*. High-production-rate thread grinding can be done with centerless grinders using specially dressed wheels.

In *internal centerless grinding*, the workpiece is supported between three rolls and is internally ground. Typical applications are sleeve-shaped parts and rings.

25.6.5 Other Grinders

A variety of special-purpose grinders is available.

Universal tool and cutter grinders are used for grinding single-point or multipoint tools and cutters, including drills. They are equipped with special workholding devices for accurate positioning of the tools to be ground. A variety of CNC tool grinders is now available, making the operation simpler and faster, with consistent results. However, the cost of these grinders ranges from about $150,000 to $400,000.

Tool-post grinders are self-contained units and are usually attached to the tool post of a lathe (as in Fig. 22.2). The workpiece is mounted on the headstock and is ground by moving the tool post. These grinders are versatile, but the lathe components should be protected from abrasive debris.

Swing-frame grinders are used in foundries for grinding large castings. Rough grinding of castings is called **snagging**, and is usually done on floorstand grinders using wheels as large as 0.9 m (36 in.) in diameter. *Portable grinders* are driven either pneumatically or electrically, or with a flexible shaft connected to an electric motor or gasoline engine. They are used for operations such as grinding off weld beads and *cutting-off* operations using thin abrasive disks.

Bench grinders are used for routine offhand grinding of tools and small parts. They are usually equipped with two wheels mounted on the two ends of the shaft of an electric motor. One wheel is usually coarse for rough grinding, and the other is fine for finish grinding. *Pedestal* or *stand grinders* are placed on the floor and used much like bench grinders.

25.6.6 Creep-Feed Grinding

Grinding has traditionally been associated with small rates of material removal (Table 25.4) and fine finishing operations. However, grinding can also be used for large-scale metal removal operations similar to milling, broaching, and planing.

In *creep-feed grinding*, developed in the late 1950s, the wheel depth of cut, *d*, is as much as 6 mm (0.25 in.), and the workpiece speed is low (Fig. 25.23a). The wheels are mostly softer-grade resin bonded, and with open structure, to keep temperatures low and improve surface finish.

The machines used for creep-feed grinding have special features, such as power up to 225 kW (300 hp), high stiffness (because of the high forces due to the large depth of material removed), high damping capacity, variable spindle and work-table speeds, and ample capacity for grinding fluids. Grinders with capabilities for continuously dressing the grinding wheel with a diamond roll are now available.

(a)   (b)   (c)

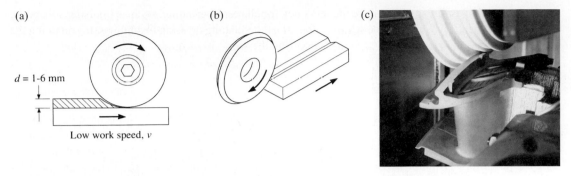

FIGURE 25.23   (a) Schematic illustration of the creep-feed grinding process. Note the large wheel depth of cut, d. (b) A shaped groove produced on a flat surface by creep-feed grinding in one pass. Groove depth is typically on the order of a few mm. (c) An example of creep-feed grinding with a shaped wheel. This operation can also be performed by some of the processes described in Chapter 26. *Source:* Courtesy of Blohm, Inc., and *Manufacturing Engineering Magazine*, Society of Manufacturing Engineers.

Its overall economics and competitive position with other material-removal processes indicate that creep-feed grinding can be competitive with other machining processes and economical for specific applications, such as the grinding of shaped punches, key seats, twist-drill flutes, the roots of turbine blades (Fig. 25.23c), and various complex, superalloy parts.

Because the wheel is dressed to the shape of the workpiece to be produced, the workpiece does not have to be previously milled, shaped, or broached. Therefore, near-net-shape castings and forgings are suitable parts for creep-feed grinding. Although generally one pass is sufficient, a second pass may be necessary for improved surface finish.

25.6.7 Heavy Stock Removal by Grinding

Grinding can be used for heavy stock removal by increasing process parameters. The process can be economical in specific applications and compete favorably with machining processes—particularly milling, but also turning and broaching. In this operation, surface finish is of secondary importance and the grinding wheel (or belt) is utilized to its fullest for minimum cost per piece. The dimensional tolerances in this process are on the same order as those obtained by other machining processes.

25.6.8 Grinding Chatter

Chatter is particularly important in grinding because it adversely affects surface finish and wheel performance. Vibrations during grinding may be caused by bearings, spindles, and the use of unbalanced wheels, as well as by external sources, such as nearby machinery. Also, the grinding process can itself cause regenerative chatter.

The analysis of chatter in grinding is similar to that of machining operations (Section 24.4). Thus, the important variables are stiffness of the machine tool, stiffness of work-holding devices, and damping. Additional factors that are unique to grinding chatter are nonuniformities in the grinding wheel, uneven wheel wear, and the dressing techniques used.

Because these variables produce characteristic **chatter marks** on ground surfaces, a study of these marks can often lead to the source of the problem. General guidelines have been established to reduce the tendency for chatter in grinding, such as (a) using soft-grade wheels, (b) dressing the wheel frequently, (c) changing dressing techniques, (d) reducing the material-removal rate, and (e) supporting the workpiece rigidly.

25.6.9 Safety in Grinding Operations

Because grinding wheels are brittle and rotate at high speeds, certain procedures must be carefully followed in their handling, storage, and use. Failure to follow these procedures and the instructions and warnings printed on individual wheel labels may result in serious injury or fatality. Grinding wheels should be stored properly and protected from environmental extremes (e.g., high temperature or humidity). They should be visually inspected for cracks and damage prior to installing them on grinders.

Damage to a grinding wheel can severely reduce its **bursting speed**, defined as the surface speed at which a freely rotating wheel bursts (explodes). The surface speed is, of course, related to the wheel diameter and its rotational speed, so bursting speed can be defined in terms of bursting rpm for a particular wheel.

The bursting speed depends on the type of wheel and on its bond, grade, and structure. In diamond and cBN wheels (Fig. 25.5), which are operated at high surface speeds, the type of core material used in the wheel affects the bursting speed; metal cores, as expected, have the highest bursting speed, on the order of about 250 m/s (800 ft/s).

Wheels should be mounted on spindles of proper size, so that they are neither forced (which may fracture the wheel at its center) nor loose (which can cause unbalance). Flanges should be of appropriate design and dimensions. Wheels should be *balanced*, because otherwise the surface produced will be wavy and the wheel will cause vibrations, possibly leading to wheel fracture. Some machine spindles and flanges provide for balancing the wheels.

Grinding wheels should be used according to their specifications and maximum operating speeds, and should not be dropped or abused. Wheel guarding, operator protection, and bystander safety also are very important.

Example: Grinding vs. Hard Turning

In Section 22.5 we described hard turning, an example of which is the machining of heat-treated steels (usually above 45 HRC) using a single-point polycrystalline cubic-boron-nitride cutting tool. In view of the discussions presented thus far, it is evident that grinding and hard turning will be competitive in specific applications. Consequently, there has been considerable debate regarding the respective merits of the two processes.

Hard turning continues to be increasingly competitive with grinding, and dimensional tolerances and surface finish are beginning to approach those obtained with grinding. As seen in Tables 20.2 and 25.3, turning requires much less energy than grinding. Also, thermal and other damage to the workpiece surface is less likely to occur; cutting fluids may not be necessary; and the machine tools are less expensive. In addition, finishing the part while still chucked in the lathe eliminates the need for material handling and setting the part in the grinder.

However, workholding devices for large and slender workpieces during hard turning can present significant problems because the cutting forces used are higher than grinding forces. Furthermore, tool wear and its control can be a significant problem as compared to the automatic dressing of grinding wheels. It is evident that the competitive position of hard turning vs. grinding must be evaluated individually for each application and in terms of product surface finish and integrity, quality, and overall economics.

25.7 GRINDING FLUIDS

The functions of grinding fluids are similar to those of cutting fluids (Section 21.13). Although grinding and other abrasive-removal processes can be performed dry, the use of a fluid is important. It prevents temperature rise in the workpiece and improves the part's surface finish and dimensional accuracy. Fluids also improve the efficiency of the operation by reducing wheel wear and loading and by lowering power consumption.

Grinding fluids are typically water-based emulsions for general grinding, and oils for thread grinding (Table 25.6). They may be applied as a stream (flood) or as mist, which is a mixture of fluid and air. Because of the high surface speeds involved, an airstream (*air blanket*) around the periphery of the wheel usually prevents the fluid from reaching the wheel–workpiece interface. Special *nozzles* that conform to the shape of the cutting surface of the grinding wheel have been designed in which the grinding fluid is applied effectively under high pressure.

The temperature of water-based grinding fluids can rise significantly as they remove heat from the grinding zone. Consequently, the workpiece can expand, making it difficult to control dimensional tolerances. The common method employed to maintain uniform workpiece temperature is to use refrigerating systems (chillers) through which the grinding fluid is circulated.

As described in Section 21.13 on cutting fluids, the biological and ecological aspects, disposal, treatment, and recycling of grinding fluids are among the most important considerations in their selection and use. The practices employed must comply with federal, state, and local laws and regulations (Section 37.4).

25.8 DESIGN CONSIDERATIONS FOR GRINDING

Design considerations for grinding operations are similar to those for machining. In addition, specific attention should be given to the following points:

a. Parts to be ground should be designed so that they can be held securely, either in chucks, magnetic tables, or suitable fixtures and workholding devices. Otherwise, thin straight or tubular workpieces may distort during grinding.

b. If high dimensional accuracy is required, interrupted surfaces, such as holes and keyways, should be avoided because they can cause vibrations.

c. In cylindrical grinding, parts should be balanced and long, slender designs should be avoided to minimize deflections. Fillets and corner radii should be as large as possible, or relief should be provided for by prior machining.

TABLE 25.6   General Recommendations for Grinding Fluids

Material	Grinding fluid
Aluminum	E, EP
Copper	CSN, E, MO + FO
Magnesium	D, MO
Nickel	CSN, EP
Refractory metals	EP
Steels	CSN, E
Titanium	CSN, E

D: dry; E: emulsion; EP: Extreme pressure; CSN: chemicals and synthetics; MO: mineral oil; FO: fatty oil.

d. In centerless grinding, short pieces may be difficult to grind accurately because of their lack of support on the blade. In through-feed grinding, only the largest diameter can be ground.

e. Designs requiring accurate form grinding should be kept simple to avoid frequent wheel dressing.

f. Deep and small holes, and blind holes requiring internal grinding, should be avoided or they should include a relief.

In general, design should require that a minimum amount of material be removed by grinding, except in creep-feed grinding. Moreover, in order to maintain good dimensional accuracy, designs should preferably allow for all grinding to be done without having to reposition the workpiece. (This guideline is also applicable to all manufacturing processes and operations.)

25.9 ULTRASONIC MACHINING

In *ultrasonic machining* (UM), material is removed from a surface by microchipping and erosion with fine abrasive grains in a slurry (Fig. 25.24a). The tip of the tool (*sonotrode*) vibrates at a frequency of 20 kHz and low amplitude (0.0125 mm–0.075 mm; 0.0005 in.–0.003 in.). This vibration, in turn, imparts a high velocity to abrasive grains between the tool and the workpiece.

The stress produced by the impact of abrasive particles on the workpiece surface is high because (a) the time of contact between the particle and the surface is very short (10 to 100 μs), and (b) the area of contact is very small. In brittle materials, these impact stresses are sufficiently high to cause microchipping and erosion of the workpiece surface.

The tip of the tool, which is attached to a transducer through the tool holder, is usually made of mild steel and undergoes wear. Special tooling is required for each shape to be produced. The grains are usually boron carbide, although aluminum oxide or silicon carbide are also used (Chapter 8). Grain sizes range from grit number 100 for roughing to grit number 1000 for finishing operations. The grains are carried in a water slurry, with concentrations of 20% to 60% by volume. The slurry also carries the debris away from the cutting zone.

Ultrasonic machining is best suited for materials that are hard and brittle, such as ceramics, carbides, precious stones, and hardened steels. Two applications of ultrasonic machining are shown in Figs. 25.24b and c.

Rotary Ultrasonic Machining (RUM). In this process, the abrasive slurry is replaced by a tool with metal-bonded diamond abrasives either impregnated or electroplated on the tool surface. The tool is rotated and ultrasonically vibrated, and the workpiece is

FIGURE 25.24 (a) Schematic illustration of the ultrasonic machining process. (b) and (c) Types of parts made by this process. Note the small size of holes produced.

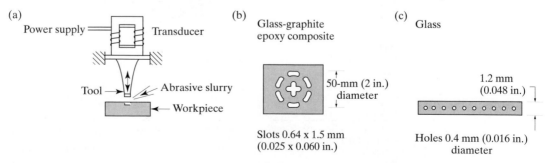

pressed against it at a constant pressure; the process is similar to a face milling operation (Fig. 23.6) with the inserts being replaced by abrasives. The chips produced are washed away by a coolant pumped through the core of the rotating tool. The rotary ultrasonic machining process is particularly effective in producing deep holes and at high material-removal rates in ceramic parts.

Design Considerations.   Design guidelines for ultrasonic machining include the following:

a. Avoid sharp profiles, corners, and radii because the abrasive slurry erodes away sharp corners.

b. Expect some taper for holes made with this process.

c. In order to avoid chipping of brittle materials at the exit end in producing through holes, support the bottom of the parts with a backup plate.

25.10 FINISHING OPERATIONS

In addition to those described thus far, several processes are also used on workpieces as the final finishing operation. These processes mainly utilize fine abrasive grains. Finishing operations can contribute significantly to production time and product cost. Thus, they should be specified with due consideration to their costs and benefits.

25.10.1 Coated Abrasives

Typical examples of *coated abrasives* are sandpaper and emery cloth, with grains that are more pointed than those used for grinding wheels. The majority of coated abrasives are made of aluminum oxide, with silicon carbide and zirconia alumina being the rest. They usually have a much more open structure than the abrasives on grinding wheels.

The grains are electrostatically deposited on flexible backing materials, such as paper, cotton, rayon polyester, polynylon, and various blends of these materials (Fig. 25.25), with their long axes perpendicular to the plane of the backing. The matrix (coating) is made of resins. Recent developments include the use of multiple layers of abrasives, particularly for belts (as described in the next example).

Coated abrasives are available as sheets, belts, and disks. They are used extensively to finish flat or curved surfaces of metallic and nonmetallic parts and metallographic specimens, and in woodworking. The precision of surface finish obtained depends primarily on grain size.

Belt Grinding.   Coated abrasives are also used as *belts* for high-rate material removal with good surface finish. *Belt grinding* has become an important production process, in some cases replacing conventional grinding operations. Grit numbers ranging from 16 to 1500 are available. Belt speeds are usually in the range of 700 to 1800 m/min (2500 to

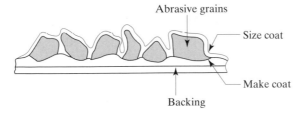

Abrasive grains
Size coat
Make coat
Backing

FIGURE 25.25   Schematic illustration of the structure of a coated abrasive. Sandpaper, developed in the 16th century, and emery cloth are common examples of coated abrasives.

6000 ft/min). Machines for abrasive-belt operations require proper belt support, and have rigid construction to minimize vibrations.

Conventional coated abrasives have randomly placed abrasives on their surface. A recent development is **microreplication** in which the abrasives, in the shape of tiny aluminum-oxide pyramids, are placed in a predetermined orderly arrangement on the belt surface. Used on stainless steels and superalloys, their performance is more consistent and the temperatures involved are lower. Typical applications include the belt grinding of surgical implants, golf clubs, firearms, turbine blades, and medical and dental instruments.

Example: Belt Grinding of Turbine Nozzle Vanes

The turbine nozzle vane shown in Fig. 25.26 was investment cast (Section 11.8) from a cobalt-base superalloy. To remove a thin diffusion layer from the root skirt and tip skirt sections of the vane, it was ground on a cloth-backed abrasive belt (aluminum oxide, grit number 60). The vanes were mounted on a fixture and ground at a belt speed of 1800 m/min (6000 ft/min) without a grinding fluid. Production rate was 93 seconds per piece. Each vane weighed 21.65 g before and 20.25 g after belt grinding. *Source*: ASM International.

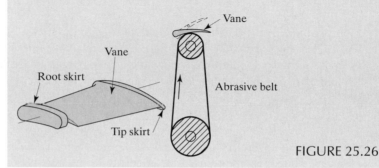

FIGURE 25.26

25.10.2 Wire Brushing

In the *wire brushing* process, the workpiece is held against a circular wire brush that rotates at high speed. The speed ranges from 1750 rpm for large wheels to 3500 rpm for small wheels.

The tips of the wire produce longitudinal scratches on the workpiece surface. This process is used to produce a fine surface texture. Some efforts are taking place to develop wire brushing as a light material-removal process.

25.10.3 Honing

Honing is an operation used primarily to give holes a fine surface finish (as in Fig. 22.13). The honing tool consists of a set of aluminum-oxide or silicon-carbide bonded abrasives, called *stones* (Fig. 25.27). They are mounted on a mandrel that rotates in the hole, applying a radial force with a reciprocating axial motion; this action produces a cross-hatched pattern. The stones can be adjusted radially for different hole sizes. Honing is also done on

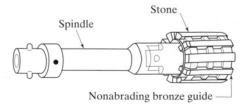

FIGURE 25.27   Schematic illustration of a honing tool used to improve the surface finish of bored or ground holes.

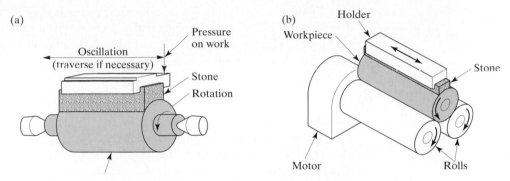

FIGURE 25.28   Schematic illustrations of the superfinishing process for a cylindrical part. (a) Cylindrical microhoning, (b) Centerless microhoning.

external cylindrical or flat surfaces and to remove sharp edges on cutting tools and inserts. (See Fig. 21.5.)

The fineness of surface finish can be controlled by the type and size of abrasive used, the pressure applied, and speed. Surface speeds range from about 45 m/min to 90 m/min (150 to 300 ft/min). A fluid is used to remove chips and to keep temperatures low. If not done properly, honing can produce holes that are neither straight nor cylindrical, but with shapes that are bellmouthed, wavy, barrel-shaped, or tapered.

In another honing process, called **superfinishing**, the pressure applied is very light and the motion of the stone has a short stroke. The process is controlled so that the grains do not travel along the same path on the surface of the workpiece being honed. Examples of external superfinishing of a round part are shown in Fig. 25.28.

25.10.4 Lapping

Lapping is a finishing operation used on flat or cylindrical surfaces. The lap (Fig. 25.29a) is usually made of cast iron, copper, leather, or cloth. The abrasive particles are embedded in the lap, or they may be carried through a slurry. Depending on the hardness of the workpiece, lapping pressures range from 7 kPa to 140 kPa (1 to 20 psi).

Dimensional tolerances on the order of ± 0.0004 mm (0.000015 in.) can be obtained with the use of fine abrasives up to grit size 900. Surface finish can be as smooth as 0.025 to 0.1 μm (1 to 4 μin.).

FIGURE 25.29   (a) Schematic illustration of the lapping process. (b) Production lapping on flat surfaces. (c) Production lapping on cylindrical surfaces.

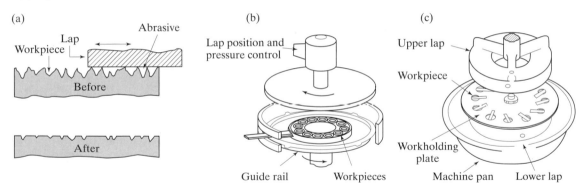

Production lapping on flat or cylindrical pieces is done on machines such as those shown in Figs. 25.29b and c. Lapping is also done on curved surfaces, such as spherical objects and glass lenses, using specially shaped laps. *Running-in* of mating gears can be done by lapping. (See also Section 32.6.)

25.10.5 Polishing

Polishing is a process that produces a smooth, lustrous surface finish. Two basic mechanisms are involved in the polishing process: (a) fine-scale abrasive removal, and (b) softening and smearing of surface layers by frictional heating during polishing. The shiny appearance of polished surfaces results from the smearing action.

Polishing is done with disks or belts made of fabric, leather, or felt that are coated with fine powders of aluminum oxide or diamond. In *double-sided polishing*, pads are fixed on the faces of platens that rotate horizontally and in opposite directions. Parts with irregular shapes, sharp corners, deep recesses, and sharp projections are difficult to polish.

25.10.6 Chemical Mechanical Polishing

Chemical mechanical polishing is a process in which a chemically reactive surface is polished with a ceramic slurry in a sodium hydroxide solution. A major application of this process is the polishing of silicon wafers (Section 34.3).

25.10.7 Electropolishing

Mirror-like finishes can be obtained on metal surfaces by *electropolishing*, a process that is the reverse of electroplating (Section 33.8). Because there is no mechanical contact with the workpiece, this process is particularly suitable for polishing irregular shapes.

The electrolyte attacks projections and peaks on the workpiece surface at a higher rate than the rest of the surface, producing a smooth surface. Electropolishing is also used for deburring operations (Section 25.11).

25.10.8 Polishing Processes Using Magnetic Fields

A more recent development in polishing involves the use of magnetic fields to support abrasive slurries in the polishing of ceramic balls and bearing rollers.

Magnetic float polishing of ceramic balls is illustrated schematically in Fig. 25.30a. A magnetic fluid (containing abrasive grains and extremely fine ferromagnetic particles in a carrier fluid, such as water or kerosene) is filled in the chamber within a guide ring. The ceramic balls are located between a drive shaft and a float. The abrasive grains, ceramic balls, and the float (which is made of a nonmagnetic material) are all suspended by magnetic forces. The balls are pressed against the rotating drive shaft and are polished by the abrasive action.

The forces applied by the abrasive particles on the balls are extremely small and controllable, so the polishing action is very fine. Because polishing times are much lower than those involved in other polishing methods, the process is very economical and the surfaces produced have few (if any) significant defects.

Magnetic-field-assisted polishing of ceramic rollers is illustrated in Fig. 25.30b. A ceramic or steel roller (the workpiece) is clamped and rotated on a spindle. The magnetic poles are oscillated, introducing a vibratory motion to the magnetic-abrasive conglomerate. This action polishes the cylindrical roller surface. Bearing steels of 63 HRC have been mirror-finished in 30 seconds with this process.

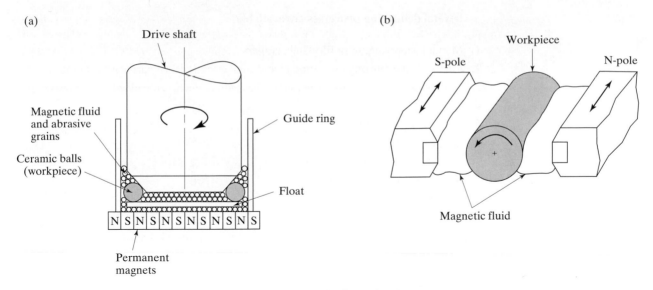

FIGURE 25.30   Schematic illustration of polishing of balls and rollers using magnetic fields. (a) Magnetic float polishing of ceramic balls. (b) Magnetic-field-assisted polishing of rollers. *Source*: R. Komanduri, M. Doc, and M. Fox.

25.10.9 Buffing

Buffing is similar to polishing, with the exception that very fine abrasives are used on soft disks made of cloth or hide. The abrasive is supplied externally from a stick of abrasive compound. Polished parts may subsequently be buffed to obtain an even finer surface finish.

25.11 DEBURRING

Burrs are thin ridges, usually triangular in shape, that develop along the edges of a workpiece from machining, from shearing sheet materials (as in Figs. 16.2 and 16.3), and from trimming forgings and castings. Burrs may interfere with the assembly of parts and can cause jamming of parts, misalignment, and short circuits in electrical components. Furthermore, burrs may reduce the fatigue life of components. Because they are usually sharp, they can be a safety hazard to personnel. On the other hand, burrs on thin drilled or tapped components, such as the tiny parts in watches, can provide extra thickness and, therefore, improve the holding torque of screws.

There are, as yet, no widely accepted standards for the definition of burrs. Burrs can be detected by simple means such as with a finger, toothpick, or pipe cleaner. Visual inspection may include magnifiers and microscopes.

Traditionally, burrs have been removed manually, a process which may account for up to 10% of the manufacturing cost of the part. The need for deburring may be reduced by adding chamfers to sharp edges on parts and by controlling processing parameters.

The cost-effectiveness of deburring operations depends on factors such as the extent of deburring required, part complexity and burr location, the number of parts, floor space available, and safety and environmental considerations.

Several **deburring processes** are available:

1. Manual deburring, with files and scrapers.
2. Mechanical deburring by cutting pieces such as cylindrical parts on a rotating spindle.
3. Wire brushing or using rotary nylon brushes with filaments embedded with abrasive grits.
4. Abrasive belts.
5. Ultrasonic machining.
6. Electropolishing.
7. Electrochemical machining.
8. Magnetic abrasive finishing.
9. Vibratory finishing.
10. Shot blasting or abrasive blasting.
11. Abrasive-flow machining, such as extruding a semi-solid abrasive media over the edges of the part.
12. Thermal energy, such as lasers or plasma.

The last four processes are described next; other processes are covered elsewhere in the text.

a. **Vibratory** and **barrel finishing** processes are used to improve the surface finish of and remove burrs from large numbers of relatively small workpieces. In this batch-type operation, specially shaped *abrasive pellets* or media are placed in a container along with the parts to be deburred. The container is either vibrated or tumbled.

   The impact of individual abrasives and metal particles removes the sharp edges and burrs from the parts. Depending on the application, this is a dry or wet process, and liquid compounds may be added for requirements such as degreasing and corrosion resistance of the part being deburred.

b. In **shot blasting**, also called **grit blasting**, abrasive particles (usually sand) are propelled by a high-velocity jet of air, or by a rotating wheel, onto the surface of the workpiece. Shot blasting is particularly useful in deburring metallic and nonmetallic materials and in stripping, cleaning, and removing surface oxides. The surface produced has a matte finish. Small-scale polishing and etching can also be done using this process on bench-type units (**microabrasive blasting**).

c. In **abrasive-flow machining**, abrasive grains, such as silicon carbide or diamond, are mixed in a putty-like matrix, which is then forced back and forth through the openings and passageways in the workpiece. The movement of the abrasive matrix under pressure erodes away both burrs and sharp corners and polishes the part.

   This process is particularly suitable for workpieces with internal cavities that are inaccessible by other means. Pressures applied range from 0.7 MPa to 22 MPa (100 psi to 3200 psi). External surfaces can also be deburred with this method by containing the workpiece within a fixture that directs the abrasive media to the edges and the areas to be deburred. The deburring of a turbine impeller by abrasive-flow machining is illustrated in Fig. 25.31.

d. The **thermal energy** method of deburring consists of placing the part in a chamber which is then injected with a mixture of natural gas and oxygen. When this mixture is ignited, a heat wave is produced with a temperature of 3300 °C (6000 °F). The burrs heat up instantly and are melted away, while the temperature of the part reaches only about 150 °C (300 °F).

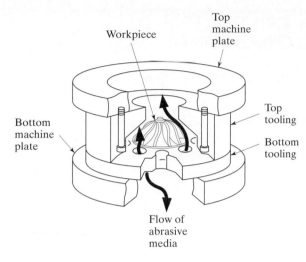

Workpiece

Top machine plate

Top tooling

Bottom tooling

Bottom machine plate

Flow of abrasive media

FIGURE 25.31 Schematic illustration of abrasive flow machining to deburr a turbine impeller. The arrows indicate movement of the abrasive media. Note the special fixture, which is usually different for each part design. *Source*: Extrude Hone Corp.

This process is effective in various applications on noncombustible parts. There are drawbacks, however: larger burrs or flashes tend to form beads after melting; the process can distort thin and slender parts; and it does not polish or buff the workpiece surfaces as do several other deburring processes.

Robotic Deburring.   Deburring and flash removal from finished products are now being performed increasingly by *programmable robots* (Section 38.7) using a force-feedback system for control. This method eliminates tedious manual labor and results in more consistent deburring.

One example of the robotic deburring of a die-cast part for an outboard motor housing is shown in Fig. 25.32. In another example, the manual deburring of a double-helical gear for a helicopter gearbox required 150 minutes, whereas with robotic deburring, the time required was reduced to 15 minutes.

FIGURE 25.32 A deburring operation on a robot-held die-cast part for an outboard motor housing, using a grinding wheel. Abrasive belts (Fig. 25.26) or flexible abrasive radial-wheel brushes can also be used for such operations. *Source*: Courtesy of Acme Manufacturing Company and *Manufacturing Engineering Magazine*, Society of Manufacturing Engineers.

25.12 ECONOMICS OF GRINDING AND FINISHING OPERATIONS

We have seen that grinding may be used both as a *finishing* operation and as a *large-scale removal* operation (as in creep-feed grinding). The use of grinding as a finishing operation is often necessary because forming and machining processes alone usually do not produce parts with the desired dimensional accuracy and surface finish.

Because it is an additional operation, grinding contributes significantly to product cost. On the other hand, creep-feed grinding has proved to be an economical alternative to machining operations such as milling, even though wheel wear is high. Also, grinding and hard turning have now become competitive for certain specific applications.

All finishing operations contribute to product cost. On the basis of the discussion thus far, it can be seen that as the surface-finish requirement increases, more operations are necessary, so the cost increases. Note in Fig. 25.33 how rapidly the cost increases as surface finish is improved by additional processes, such as grinding and honing.

Much progress has been made in automating the equipment involved in finishing operations, including computer controls. Consequently, labor costs and production times have been reduced, even though such machinery may require significant capital investment. If finishing is likely to be an important factor in manufacturing a particular product, the conceptual and design stages should involve an analysis of the level of surface finish and dimensional accuracy required.

Furthermore, all processes that precede finishing operations should be analyzed for their capability to produce a more acceptable surface finish and dimensional accuracy. This can be accomplished through proper selection of tools and process parameters and the characteristics of the machine tools involved.

FIGURE 25.33   Increase in the cost of machining and finishing a part as a function of the surface finish required. This is the main reason that the surface finish specified on parts should not be any finer than necessary for the part to function properly.

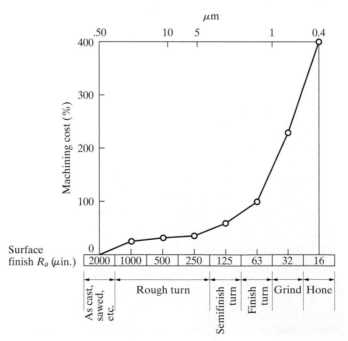

SUMMARY

- Abrasive machining is often necessary and economical when workpiece hardness is high, the materials are brittle, and surface finish and dimensional tolerance requirements are high.

- Conventional abrasives consist of aluminum oxide and silicon carbide, and superabrasives consist of cubic boron nitride and diamond. The friability of abrasive grains is an important factor in their performance, as are the shape and size of the grains.

- Grinding wheels consist of a combination of abrasive grains and bonding agents. Important characteristics of wheels are abrasive grain and bond types, grade, and hardness. Wheels may also be reinforced to maintain their integrity when a crack develops.

- Grinding wheel wear is an important consideration in product surface quality and integrity. The dressing and truing of wheels are important processes and are done by various techniques.

- A variety of abrasive machining processes and machinery are available for surface, external, and internal grinding. Abrasive machining is also used for large-scale material-removal processes, such as creep-feed grinding, making it competitive with processes such as milling and turning.

- The selection of abrasives and process variables, including grinding fluids, is important in order to obtain the desired surface finish and dimensional accuracy. Otherwise, damage to surfaces—such as burning, heat checking, detrimental residual stresses, and chatter—may develop.

- Several finishing operations are available for improved surface finish. Because they can contribute significantly to product cost, the appropriate selection and implementation of these operations are important.

- Deburring may be necessary for certain finished components. Commonly used methods are vibratory and barrel finishing and shot blasting, although thermal energy and other methods are also available.

TRENDS

- As with other machine tools, the trend for abrasive operations is for greater automation and computer control.

- Advanced controls on grinders are now capable of calculating when and how long a grinding wheel should be dressed; they can also automatically and continuously compensate for wheel-diameter reduction, feeds, and wheel surface speeds.

- The trend in the design of grinding machines is for higher machine and spindle stiffnesses, vibration-free structures, higher and more stable wheel speeds, continuous dressing, higher material removal rates, and lower cycle times.

- Cooling the workpiece in some grinding operations, such as creep feed grinding, is now requiring mist collection (from grinding fluids) and automatic fire-extinguishing systems.

- Grinding is capable of competing with some machining operations and performing roughing and finishing operations in one setup of the workpiece. Creep-feed grinding is now competing with milling and broaching processes.

- Developments in grinding wheels include better control of manufacturing parameters and greater uniformity of properties. Operating speeds of wheels are being increased for higher productivity. The design, guarding, and safe operation of grinding wheels is an important consideration.

KEY TERMS

Abrasive-flow machining	Glazing	Resinoid bond
Abrasives	Grade	Robotic deburring
Aluminum oxide	Grain depth of cut	Rotary ultrasonic machining
Attritious wear	Grain size	Seeded gel
Barrel finishing	Grindability	Shot blasting
Belt grinding	Grinding	Silicon nitride
Bonded abrasives	Grinding ratio	Snagging
Bonding	Grinding wheel	Sonotrode
Buffing	Grit number	Sparks
Burning	Hardness of wheel	Specific energy
Burr	Heat checking	Structure of wheel
Chatter marks	Honing	Superabrasives
Coated abrasives	Lapping	Superfinishing
Creep-feed grinding	Loading	Tempering
Cubic boron nitride	Low-stress grinding	Truing
Deburring	Magnetic float polishing	Ultrasonic machining
Diamond	Magnetic-field-assisted polishing	Vibratory finishing
Dressing	Metal bonding	Vitrified
Electropolishing	Metallurgical burn	Wear flat
Finishing	Microreplication	Wheel depth of cut
Free-cutting wheels	Polishing	Wire brushing
Friability	Reinforced wheels	

BIBLIOGRAPHY

Andrew, C., T.D. Howes, and T.R.A. Pearce, *Creep Feed Grinding.* Industrial Press, 1985.

ASM Handbook, Vol. 16: *Machining.* ASM International, 1989.

Borkowski, J., and A. Szymanski, *Uses of Abrasives and Abrasive Tools.* Ellis Horwood, 1992.

Farago, F.T., *Abrasive Methods Engineering*, Vol. 1, 1976; Vol. 2, 1980. Industrial Press.

Gillespie, L.K., *Deburring and Edge Finishing Handbook.* Society of Manufacturing Engineers, 1999.

King, R.I., and R.S. Hahn, *Handbook of Modern Grinding Technology.* Chapman & Hall/Methuen, 1987.

Krar, S., and E. Ratterman, *Superabrasives: Grinding and Machining with CBN and Diamond.* McGraw-Hill, 1990.

Machinery's Handbook, revised periodically. Industrial Press.

Machining Data Handbook, (3d ed.), 2 vols. Machinability Data Center, 1980.

Malkin, S., *Grinding Technology: Theory and Applications of Machining with Abrasives.* Wiley, 1989.

Maroney, M. L., *A Guide to Metal and Plastic Finishing.* Industrial Press, 1991.

Metzger, J.L., *Superabrasive Grinding.* Butterworths, 1986.

Shaw, M.C., *Principles of Abrasive Processing.* Oxford, 1996.

Tool and Manufacturing Engineers Handbook, (4th ed.), Vol. 1: *Machining.* Society of Manufacturing Engineers, 1983.

Webster, J.A., I.D. Marinescu and T.D. Trevor, *Abrasive Processes.* Marcel Dekker, 1999.

REVIEW QUESTIONS

25.1 What is an abrasive? What are superabrasives?

25.2 How is the size of an abrasive grain related to its number?

25.3 Why are most abrasives now made synthetically?

25.4 Describe the structure of a grinding wheel.

25.5 Explain the characteristics of each type of bond used in bonded abrasives.

25.6 Describe (a) the grade, and (b) the structure of bonded abrasives.

25.7 What causes grinding sparks?

25.8 Define metallurgical burn.

25.9 Explain the mechanisms by which grinding wheels wear.

25.10 Define (a) friability, (b) wear flat, (c) grinding ratio, (d) truing, and (e) dressing.

25.11 Explain what is meant by a grinding wheel acting soft or acting hard.

25.12 What is creep-feed grinding and what are its advantages?

25.13 What is the principle of ultrasonic machining? Why is it not suitable for ductile materials?

25.14 List the finishing operations commonly used in manufacturing operations. Why are they necessary? Explain why they should be minimized.

25.15 What are the differences between lapping, polishing, and buffing?

25.16 Name the major deburring operations and briefly describe their principles.

25.17 What are the functions of grinding fluids?

25.18 How is centerless grinding different from cylindrical grinding?

25.19 Why should you only grind on recommended faces of grinding wheels?

25.20 What is honing? What are its similarities to grinding?

25.21 What are the differences between coated and bonded abrasives?

25.22 Describe the methods used for thread grinding.

25.23 What is heat checking? What is its significance?

QUALITATIVE PROBLEMS

25.24 Why are grinding operations necessary for components that have previously been machined by the processes described in Chapters 22 and 23?

25.25 Explain why there are so many different types and sizes of grinding wheels.

25.26 Explain the reasons for the large difference between the specific energies involved in machining (Table 20.2) and grinding (Table 25.3).

25.27 Comment on the selection of grinding wheels for the applications shown in Table 25.5.

25.28 What precautions should you take when grinding with high precision? Make comments about the machine, process parameters, the grinding wheel, and grinding fluids.

25.29 What factors could contribute to chatter in grinding?

25.30 The grinding ratio, G, depends on the following: the type of grinding wheel, workpiece hardness, wheel depth of cut, wheel and workpiece speeds, and the type of grinding fluid. Explain why.

25.31 It is generally recommended that, when grinding hardened steels, the grinding wheel should be of a relatively soft grade. Explain the reason.

25.32 In Fig. 25.4, the proper grinding surfaces are shown with an arrow for each type of wheel. Explain why the other surfaces of the wheels should not be used for grinding.

25.33 Explain the factors involved in selecting the appropriate type of abrasive for a particular grinding operation.

25.34 What are the effects of a wear flat on the grinding process?

25.35 Would you encounter any difficulties in grinding thermoplastics? Thermosets? If so, what precautions would you take?

25.36 Is the grinding ratio important in evaluating the economics of a grinding operation? Explain.

25.37 We know that grinding can produce a very fine surface finish on a workpiece. Is this necessarily an indication of the quality of a part? Explain.

25.38 What are the consequences of allowing the temperature to rise during grinding?

25.39 What costs would be associated with dressing a grinding wheel? Explain.

25.40 If not done properly, honing can produce holes that are bellmouthed, wavy, barrel-shaped, or tapered. Explain how this is possible.

25.41 List and explain factors that contribute to poor surface finish in the processes described in this chapter.

25.42 What are the implications of using a smaller abrasive grain size (higher grit number) in a bonded grinding wheel?

25.43 Jewelry applications require the grinding of diamonds into desired shapes. How is this done, since diamond is the hardest material known?

25.44 Which of the processes described in this chapter are particularly suitable for workpieces made of (a) ceramics, (b) thermoplastics, and (c) thermosets? Why?

25.45 A new development in metal cutting is laser-assisted cutting, where a laser beam heats a localized area where cutting will take place. Is laser-assisted grinding viable? Explain.

25.46 Typical types of grinding wheels for use with various materials are listed Table 25.5. Other than cost, is there any reason that a grinding wheel intended for a hard workpiece cannot be used for a softer workpiece?

25.47 Why are speeds so much higher in grinding than in cutting?

25.48 Why does grinding temperature decrease with increasing work speed (Eq. 25.2)? Does this mean that for a work speed of zero, the temperature is infinite? Why isn't the work feed rate infinite? Explain.

QUANTITATIVE PROBLEMS

25.49 Calculate the chip dimensions for the example problem in Section 25.4 for the following process variables: $D = 8$ in., $d = 0.001$ in., $v = 100$ ft/min, $V = 6000$ ft/min, $C = 500$ per in.^{2}, and $r = 20$.

25.50 If the strength of the workpiece material is doubled, what should be the percentage decrease in the wheel depth of cut, d, in order to maintain the same grain force, all other variables being the same?

25.51 Assume that a surface grinding operation is being carried out under the following conditions: $D = 200$ mm, $d = 0.1$ mm, $v = 40$ m/min, and $V = 3000$ m/min. These conditions are then changed to the following: $D = 150$ mm, $d = 0.1$ mm, $v = 30$ m/min, and $V = 2500$ m/min. How different is the temperature rise from the rise that occurs with the initial conditions?

25.52 Estimate the percent increase in the cost of the grinding operation if the specification for the surface finish of a part is changed from 63 μin. to 16 μin.

25.53 Assume that the energy cost for grinding an aluminum part, with a specific energy requirement of 8 W·s/mm^3, is $0.90 per piece. What would be the energy cost of carrying out the same operation if the workpiece material is T15 tool steel?

25.54 On the basis of the information given in Chapters 22 and 25, comment on the feasibility of producing a 10-mm hole 100 mm deep in a copper alloy (a) by conventional drilling, and (b) by internal grinding.

25.55 In describing grinding processes, we have not given the type of equations regarding feeds, speeds, material removal rates, total grinding time, etc., as we have done in turning and milling operations in Chapters 22 and 23. Study the quantitative relationships involved and develop such equations for grinding operations.

25.56 What would be the answers to the example in Section 25.4.1 on grinding forces if the workpiece were high-strength titanium and the width of cut, w, 0.75 in.? Give your answers in newtons.

25.57 It is known that, in grinding, heat checking occurs when grinding with a spindle speed of 4000 rpm, a wheel diameter of 10 in., and a depth of cut of 0.0015 in. for a feed rate of 50 ft/min. For this reason, the standard operating procedure is to keep the spindle speed at 3500 rpm. If a new, 8-in. diameter wheel is used, what spindle speed can be used before heat checking occurs? What spindle speed should be used to keep the same grinding temperatures as those encountered with the existing operating conditions?

25.58 It is desired to grind a hard aerospace aluminum alloy. A depth of 0.003 in. is to be removed from a cylindrical section 10 in. long and 4 in. in diameter. If each part is to be ground in not more than one minute, what is the approximate power requirement for the grinder? What if the material is changed to a hard titanium alloy?

25.59 A grinding operation takes place with a ten-inch grinding wheel with a spindle speed of 3000 rpm. The workpiece feed rate is 60 ft/min and the depth of cut is 0.002 in. Contact thermometers record an approximate maximum temperature of 1800 °F. If the workpiece is steel, what is the temperature if the speed is increased to 4000 rpm? What if the speed is 10,000 rpm?

SYNTHESIS AND DESIGN

25.60 Assume that you are an instructor covering the topics described in this chapter, and you are giving a quiz on the numerical aspects to test the understanding of the students. Prepare several quantitative problems and supply the answers.

25.61 With appropriate sketches, describe the principles of various fixturing methods and devices that can be used for the processes described in this chapter.

25.62 Explain the major design guidelines for grinding.

25.63 Make a comprehensive table of the process capabilities of abrasive machining processes. Using several columns, describe the machines involved, the type of abrasive tools used, the shapes of blanks and parts produced, typical maximum and minimum sizes, surface finish, tolerances, and production rates.

25.64 Based on the data developed in the foregoing problem, describe your thoughts regarding the procedure to be followed in determining what type of machine tool to select for a particular part to be machined by abrasive means.

25.65 Vitrified grinding wheels (also called ceramic wheels) use a glasslike bond to hold the abrasive grains together. Given your understanding of ceramic part manufacture (Chapter 17), list ways of producing vitrified wheels.

25.66 A somewhat controversial subject in grinding is size effect; that is, there is an apparent increase in the strength of a workpiece when the depth of penetration by grinding abrasives is reduced. Design an experimental setup whereby this size effect could be examined.

25.67 Describe as many parameters as you can that could affect the final surface finish in grinding. Include process parameters as well as setup and equipment effects.

26

Advanced Machining Processes and Nanofabrication

26.1 INTRODUCTION

The machining processes described in the preceding chapters remove material by chip formation, abrasion, or microchipping. There are situations, however, where these processes are not satisfactory, economical, or even possible, for the following reasons:

- The **hardness** and **strength** of the material is very high (typically above 400 HB) or the material is too brittle.
- The workpiece is too **flexible**, slender, or delicate to withstand the cutting or grinding forces, or the parts are difficult to **fixture**—that is, to clamp in workholding devices.
- The **shape** of the part is complex (Figs. 26.1a and b), including such features as internal and external profiles or small-diameter holes in fuel-injection nozzles.
- **Surface finish** and **dimensional tolerance** requirements are more rigorous than those obtained by other processes.
- **Temperature rise** and **residual stresses** in the workpiece are not desirable or acceptable.

FIGURE 26.1 Examples of parts made by advanced machining processes. These parts are made by advanced machining processes and would be difficult or uneconomical to manufacture by conventional processes. (a) Cutting sheet metal with a laser beam. *Courtesy of Rofin-Sinar, Inc., and Manufacturing Engineering Magazine, Society of Manufacturing Engineers.* (b) Microscopic gear with a diameter on the order of 100 μm, made by a special etching process. *Courtesy of Wisconsin Center for Applied Microelectronics, University of Wisconsin-Madison.*

These requirements led to the development of chemical, electrical, laser, and other means of material removal. Beginning in the 1940s, these advanced methods, which in the past have been called *nontraditional* or *unconventional* machining, are outlined in Table 26.1 in the order they are described in this chapter.

Because they fall beyond traditional means of machining, some of the processes described in Chapter 25 could also be included in this chapter, as is done in some texts; examples include ultrasonic machining and some of the deburring operations, such as abrasive-flow machining and thermal energy (thermochemical) methods. The distinctions are, however, not particularly significant.

When selected and applied properly, advanced machining processes offer major technical and economic advantages over traditional machining methods. This chapter describes these processes, including their typical applications, limitations, and considerations of quality, dimensional accuracy, characteristics of surfaces produced, and economics.

26.2 CHEMICAL MACHINING

Chemical machining (CM) was developed based on the observation that chemicals attack metals and etch them, thereby removing small amounts of material from the surface. This process is carried out by chemical dissolution, using **reagents** or **etchants**, such as acids and alkaline solutions.

Chemical machining is the oldest of the nontraditional machining processes, and has been used to engrave metals and hard stones, in deburring, and more recently in the production of printed-circuit boards and microprocessor chips.

26.2.1 Chemical Milling

In *chemical milling*, shallow cavities are produced on plates, sheets, forgings, and extrusions, generally for overall reduction of weight (Fig. 26.2). This process has been used on a wide variety of metals, with depths of metal removal as large as 12 mm (0.5 in.). Selective attack by the chemical reagent on different areas of the workpiece surfaces is controlled by removable layers of material, called **masking** (Fig. 26.3a), or by partial immersion in the reagent.

TABLE 26.1   General Characteristics of Advanced Machining Processes

Process	Characteristics	Process parameters and typical material removal rate or cutting speed
Chemical machining (CM)	Shallow removal (up to 12 mm) on large flat or curved surfaces; blanking of thin sheets; low tooling and equipment cost; suitable for low production runs.	0.0025–0.1 mm/min.
Electrochemical machining (ECM)	Complex shapes with deep cavities; highest rate of material removal among nontraditional processes; expensive tooling and equipment; high power consumption; medium to high production quantity.	V: 5–25 dc; A: 1.5–8 A/mm^2; 2.5–12 mm/min, depending on current density.
Electrochemical grinding (ECG)	Cutting off and sharpening hard materials, such as tungsten-carbide tools; also used as a honing process; higher removal rate than grinding.	A: 1–3 A/mm^2; Typically 25 mm^3/s per 1000 A.
Electrical-discharge machining (EDM)	Shaping and cutting complex parts made of hard materials; some surface damage may result; also used as a grinding and cutting process; expensive tooling and equipment.	V: 50–380; A: 0.1–500; Typically 300 mm^3/min.
Wire EDM	Contour cutting of flat or curved surfaces; expensive equipment.	Varies with material and thickness.
Laser-beam machining (LBM)	Cutting and holemaking on thin materials; heat-affected zone; does not require a vacuum; expensive equipment; consumes much energy.	0.50–7.5 m/min.
Electron-beam machining (EBM)	Cutting and holemaking on thin materials; very small holes and slots; heat-affected zone; requires a vacuum; expensive equipment.	1–2 mm^3/min.
Water-jet machining (WJM)	Cutting all types of nonmetallic materials to 25 mm and greater in thickness; suitable for contour cutting of flexible materials; no thermal damage; noisy.	Varies considerably with material.
Abrasive water-jet machining (AWJM)	Single or multilayer cutting of metallic and nonmetallic materials.	Up to 7.5 m/min.
Abrasive-jet machining (AJM)	Cutting, slotting, deburring, deflashing, etching, and cleaning of metallic and nonmetallic materials; manually controlled; tends to round off sharp edges; hazardous.	Varies considerably with material.

The procedure for chemical milling consists of the following steps:

1. If the part to be machined has residual stresses from prior processing, the stresses should first be relieved (see Sections 2.11 and 4.11) in order to prevent warping after chemical milling.

2. The surfaces are thoroughly degreased and cleaned (see Section 33.16) to ensure good adhesion of the masking material and uniform material removal. Scale from heat treatment should also be removed.

3. The masking material is applied. Masking with tapes or paints (**maskants**) is a common practice, although elastomers (rubber and neoprene) and plastics (polyvinyl chloride, polyethylene, and polystyrene) are also used. The maskant material should not react with the chemical reagent.

4. The masking that covers various regions that require etching is peeled off by the scribe-and-peel technique.

5. The exposed surfaces are etched with etchants such as sodium hydroxide (for aluminum), solutions of hydrochloric and nitric acids (for steels), or iron chloride (for

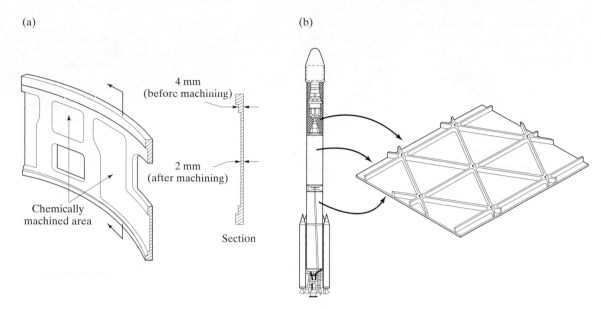

FIGURE 26.2   (a) Missile skin-panel section contoured by chemical milling to improve the stiffness-to-weight ratio of the part. (b) Weight reduction of space launch vehicles by chemical milling aluminum-alloy plates. These panels are chemically milled after the plates have first been formed into shape by processes such as roll forming or stretch forming. The design of the chemically machined rib patterns can be modified readily at minimal cost. *Source*: *Advanced Materials and Processes*, December 1990. ASM International.

stainless steels). Temperature control and stirring during chemical milling is important in order to obtain a uniform depth of material removed.

6. After machining, the parts should be washed thoroughly to prevent further reactions with any etchant residues.

7. The rest of the masking material is removed and the part is cleaned and inspected.

8. Additional finishing operations may be performed on chemically milled parts.

9. This sequence of operations can be repeated to produce stepped cavities and various contours (Fig. 26.3b).

Process Capabilities.   Chemical milling is used in the aerospace industry to remove shallow layers of material from large aircraft components, missile skin panels, and extruded parts for airframes. Tank capacities for reagents are as large as 3.7 m × 15 m

FIGURE 26.3   (a) Schematic illustration of the chemical machining process. Note that no forces or machine tools are involved in this process. (b) Stages in producing a profiled cavity by chemical machining; note the undercut.

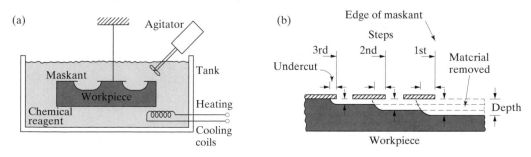

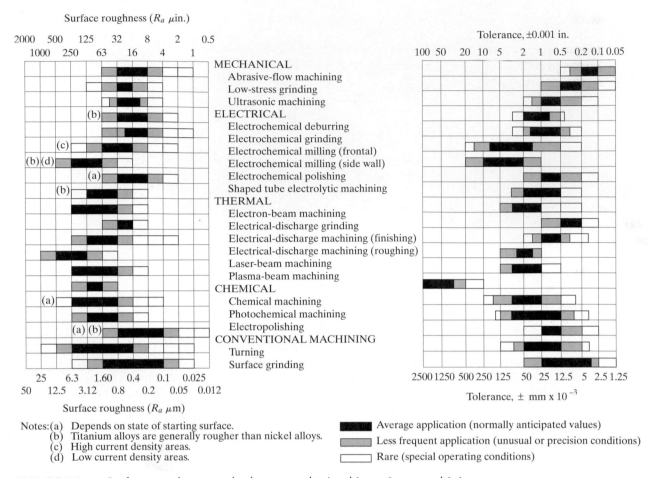

FIGURE 26.4 Surface roughness and tolerances obtained in various machining processes. Note the wide range within each process (see also Fig. 22.13). *Source: Machining Data Handbook*, 3rd ed. Copyright © 1980. Used by permission of Metcut Research Associates, Inc.

(12 ft × 50 ft). The process is also used to fabricate microelectronic devices (Chapter 34). The ranges of surface finish and tolerance obtained by chemical machining and other machining processes are shown in Fig. 26.4.

Some surface damage may result from chemical milling because of *preferential etching* and *intergranular attack*, which adversely affect surface properties. The chemical milling of welded and brazed structures (Part V) may result in uneven material removal. Chemical milling of castings may result in uneven surfaces caused by porosity in and nonuniformity of the material.

26.2.2 Chemical Blanking

Chemical blanking is similar to the blanking of sheet metal in that it is used to produce features which penetrate through the thickness of the material (as in Fig. 16.4), with the exception that material is removed by chemical dissolution rather than by shearing. Typical applications for chemical blanking are the burr-free etching of printed-circuit boards, decorative panels, and thin sheet-metal stampings, as well as the production of complex or small shapes.

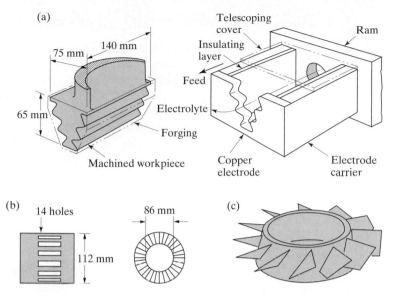

FIGURE 26.7   Typical parts made by electrochemical machining. (a) Turbine blade made of a nickel alloy, 360 HB; note the shape of the electrode on the right. *Source*: ASM International. (b) Thin slots on a 4340-steel roller-bearing cage. (c) Integral airfoils on a compressor disk.

Machines having current capacities as high as 40,000 A and as low as 5 A are available. The penetration rate of the tool is proportional to the current density. Because the metal removal rate is only a function of ion exchange rate, it is not affected by the strength, hardness, or toughness of the workpiece.

Process Capabilities.   Electrochemical machining is generally used to machine complex cavities in high-strength materials, particularly in the aerospace industry for the mass production of turbine blades, jet-engine parts, and nozzles (Fig. 26.7). It is also used to machine forging-die cavities (*die sinking*) and to produce small holes.

The ECM process leaves a burr-free surface; in fact, it can also be used as a deburring process. It does not cause any thermal damage to the part, and the lack of tool forces prevents distortion of the part. Furthermore, there is no tool wear, and the process is capable of producing complex shapes as well as machining hard materials.

However, the mechanical properties of components made by ECM should be compared carefully to those of other material-removal methods. Electrochemical machining systems are now available as *numerically-controlled machining centers*, with the capability of high production rates, high flexibility, and the maintenance of close dimensional tolerances.

Design Considerations for Electrochemical Machining

a. Because of the tendency for the electrolyte to erode away sharp profiles, electrochemical machining is not suited for producing sharp square corners or flat bottoms.

b. Controlling the electrolyte flow may be difficult, so irregular cavities may not be produced to the desired shape with acceptable dimensional accuracy.

c. Designs should make provision for a small taper for holes and cavities to be machined.

Example: Electrochemical Machining of a Biomedical Implant

A total knee replacement system consists of a femoral and tibial implant combined with an ultrahigh molecular weight polyethylene (UHMWPE) insert, as shown in Fig. 26.8a. The polyethylene (Chapter 7) has superior wear resistance and low friction against the cobalt-chrome alloy femoral implant. The UHMWPE insert is compression molded (Section 18.7) and the metal implant is cast and ground on its external mating surfaces.

Designers of implants, manufacturing engineers, and clinicians have been particularly concerned with the contact surface in the cavity of the metal implant that mates with a protrusion on the polyethylene insert. As the knee articulates during normal motion, the polyethylene slides against the metal part, becoming a potentially serious wear site. This geometry is necessary to ensure lateral stability of the knee (that is, to prevent the knee from buckling sideways).

In order to produce a smooth surface, the grinding of the bearing surfaces of the metal implant, using both hand-held and cam-mounted grinders, was a procedure that had been followed for many years. However, grinding produced marginal repeatability and quality. The interior surfaces of this part are extremely difficult to access for grinding, and the cobalt-chrome alloy is difficult to grind. Consequently, advanced machining processes, particularly electrochemical machining, were ideal candidates for this operation.

As shown in Fig. 26.8b, the current procedure consists of placing the metal implant in a fixture and bringing a tungsten electrode of the desired final contour in close proximity to the implant. The electrolyte is a sodium nitrate and water mixture and is pumped through the tool, filling the gap between the tool and implant. A power source (typically 10 V and 225 A) is applied, causing local electrochemical machining of the high spots on the implant surface and producing a polished surface.

The electrolyte flow volume can be controlled to maximize surface quality. When the flow rate is too low, defects appear on the machined surface as localized dimples; if the rate is too high, machining times become longer. Typical machining times for this part are four to six minutes.

Source: T. Hershberger and R. Redman, Biomet, Inc., Warsaw, Indiana.

(a)

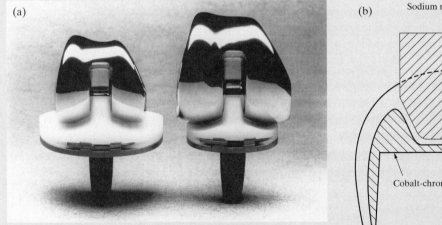

(b)

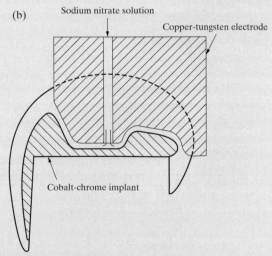

FIGURE 26.8   (a) Two total knee replacement systems showing metal implants (top pieces) with an ultrahigh molecular weight polyethylene insert (bottom pieces). (b) Cross-section of the ECM process as applied to the metal implant. *Source*: Biomet, Inc.

26.3.1 Pulsed Electrochemical Machining (PECM)

This process is a refinement of ECM; it uses very high current densities (on the order of 100 A/cm^2), but the current is *pulsed* rather than direct current. The purpose of pulsing is to eliminate the need for high electrolyte flow rates, which limit the usefulness of ECM in die and mold making (die sinking). Investigations have shown that PECM improves fatigue life, and the process has been proposed as a possible method for eliminating the recast layer left on die and mold surfaces by electrical discharge machining (see Section 26.5).

However, the usefulness of PECM in die sinking appears to be limited because (a) the process leaves metal residues floating in water (highly undesirable to the environment), and (b) it is difficult to maintain precise alignment of the tool and workpiece when moving from the EDM to the PECM machines. If misaligned by even a few microns, all polishing will occur where the gap is smallest, and passivation will occur where the gap is largest. A machine has been developed that performs both EDM and PECM; in this way, the need to move the tool and workpiece between the two processes is eliminated.

It appears that PECM might be very useful for micromachining, for the following reasons: (a) The metal removal requirements in micromachining (see Section 26.12) are very small, which suits the process well, and (b) the total lack of tool wear (since only hydrogen is generated at the cathode) implies that the process can be used for very high precision work, although the erosion problem due to stray current has to be overcome.

26.4 ELECTROCHEMICAL GRINDING

Electrochemical grinding (ECG) combines electrochemical machining with conventional grinding. The equipment used is similar to a conventional grinder, except that the wheel is a rotating cathode embedded with abrasive particles (Fig. 26.9a). The wheel is metal-bonded with diamond or aluminum-oxide abrasives, and rotates at a surface speed of from 1200 m/min to 2000 m/min (4000 to 7000 ft/min).

The abrasives have two functions: (a) to serve as insulators between the wheel and the workpiece, and (b) to mechanically remove electrolytic products from the working area. A flow of electrolyte solution (usually sodium nitrate) is provided for the electrochemical machining phase of the operation. Current densities range from 1 A/mm^2 to 3 A/mm^2 $(500 \text{ to } 2000 \text{ A/in.}^2)$.

The majority of metal removal in ECG is by electrolytic action, and typically less than 5% of metal is removed by the abrasive action of the wheel; therefore, wheel wear is very low. Finishing cuts are usually made by the grinding action but only to produce a surface with good finish and dimensional accuracy.

The ECG process is suitable for applications similar to those for milling, grinding, and sawing (Fig. 26.9b). It is not adaptable to cavity-sinking operations. This process has been successfully applied to carbides and high-strength alloys. It offers a distinct advantage over

FIGURE 26.9   (a) Schematic illustration of the electrochemical-grinding process. (b) Thin slot produced on a round nickel-alloy tube by this process.

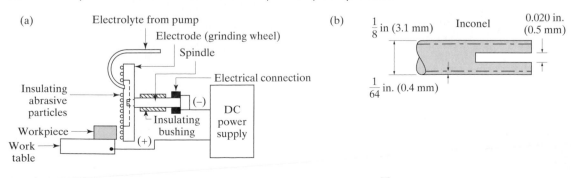

traditional diamond-wheel grinding when processing very hard materials, where wheel wear can be high. ECG machines are now available with numerical controls, improving dimensional accuracy, repeatability, and increased productivity.

Electrochemical honing combines the fine abrasive action of honing with electrochemical action. Although the equipment is costly, the process is as much as five times faster than conventional honing, and the tool lasts as much as ten times longer. It is used primarily for finishing internal cylindrical surfaces.

Design Considerations for Electrochemical Grinding.   In addition to those already listed for electrochemical machining, ECG requires two additional design considerations:

a. Designs should avoid sharp inside radii.

b. If flat surfaces are to be produced, the electrochemically ground surface should be narrower than the width of the grinding wheel.

26.5 ELECTRICAL-DISCHARGE MACHINING

The principle of *electrical-discharge machining* (EDM), also called *electrodischarge* or *spark-erosion machining*, is based on the erosion of metals by spark discharges. We know that when two current-conducting wires are allowed to touch each other, an arc is produced. If we look closely at the point of contact between the two wires, we note that a small portion of the metal has been eroded away, leaving a small crater.

Although this phenomenon has been known since the discovery of electricity, it was not until the 1940s that a machining process based on this principle was developed. The EDM process has become one of the most important and widely accepted production technologies in manufacturing industries.

Principle of Operation.   The basic EDM system consists of a shaped tool (*electrode*) and the workpiece, connected to a dc power supply and placed in a **dielectric** (electrically nonconducting) fluid (Fig. 26.10a). When the potential difference between the tool and the workpiece is sufficiently high, a transient spark discharges through the fluid, removing a very small amount of metal from the workpiece surface. The capacitor discharge is repeated at rates of between 50 kHz and 500 kHz, with voltages usually ranging between 50 V and 380 V and currents from 0.1 A to 500 A.

FIGURE 26.10   (a) Schematic illustration of the electrical-discharge machining process. This is one of the most widely used machining processes, particularly for die-sinking operations. (b) Examples of cavities produced by the electrical-discharge machining process, using shaped electrodes. Two round parts (rear) are the set of dies for extruding the aluminum piece shown in front (see also Fig. 15.9b). *Source:* Courtesy of AGIE USA Ltd. (c) A spiral cavity produced by EDM using a slowly rotating electrode, similar to a screw thread. *Source: American Machinist.*

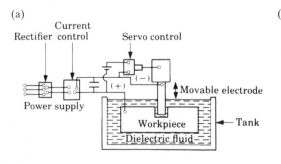

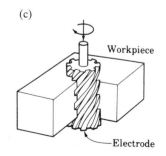

The functions of the dielectric fluid are to

1. Act as an insulator until the potential is sufficiently high,
2. Act as a flushing medium and carry away the debris in the gap, and
3. Provide a cooling medium.

The workpiece is fixtured within the tank containing the dielectric fluid, and its movements are controlled by numerically controlled systems. The gap between the tool and the workpiece (*overcut*) is critical; thus, the downward feed of the tool is controlled by a servomechanism, which automatically maintains a constant gap.

The most common dielectric fluids are mineral oils, although kerosene and distilled and deionized water are also used in specialized applications. Recent trends involve the use of clear, low-viscosity fluids; although more expensive, these fluids make cleaning easier. The machines are equipped with a pump and filtering system for the dielectric fluid.

The EDM process can be used on any material that is an electrical conductor. The melting point and the latent heat of melting are important physical properties that determine the volume of metal removed per discharge. As these quantities increase, the rate of material removal decreases. The volume of material removed per discharge is typically in the range of 10^{-6} to 10^{-4} mm^3 $\left(10^{-10} \text{ to } 10^{-8} \text{ in.}^3\right)$.

Because the process doesn't involve mechanical energy, the hardness, strength, and toughness of the workpiece material do not necessarily influence the removal rate. The frequency of discharge or the energy per discharge is usually varied to control the removal rate, as are the voltage and current. The removal rate and surface roughness increase with increasing current density and decreasing frequency of sparks.

Electrodes.   *Electrodes* for EDM are usually made of graphite, although brass, copper, or copper–tungsten alloy are also used. The tools are shaped by forming, casting, powder metallurgy, or machining techniques. Electrodes as small as 0.1 mm (0.005 in.) in diameter have been used, and the depth-to-hole diameter ratios can range up to 400:1.

Tool wear is an important factor because it affects dimensional accuracy and the shape produced. Tool wear is related to the melting points of the materials involved: the lower the melting point, the higher the wear rate. Consequently, graphite electrodes have the highest wear resistance. Tool wear can be minimized by reversing the polarity and using copper tools, a process called **no-wear EDM**.

Process Capabilities.   Electrical-discharge machining has numerous applications, such as the production of die cavities for large automotive-body components (**die-sinking machining centers**), deep small-diameter holes with tungsten wire as the electrode, narrow slots in parts, turbine blades, and various intricate shapes (Figs. 26.10b and c).

Stepped cavities can be produced by controlling the relative movements of the workpiece in relation to the electrode (Fig. 26.11). *Internal cavities* can be produced by using a rotating electrode with a movable tip. The electrode is rotated mechanically during machining (Fig. 26.12).

Metal-removal rates usually range from 2 to 400 mm^3/min. Because of the molten and resolidified (recast) surface structure, high rates produce a very rough surface finish with poor surface integrity and low fatigue properties. Therefore, finishing cuts are made at low removal rates, or the recast layer is removed subsequently by finishing operations. Recent techniques include the use of an oscillating electrode which provides very fine surface finish, requiring significantly less benchwork to produce lustrous cavities.

FIGURE 26.11 Stepped cavities produced with a square electrode by the EDM process. The workpiece moves in the two principal horizontal directions (x–y), and its motion is synchronized with the downward movement of the electrode to produce these cavities. Also shown is a round electrode capable of producing round or elliptical cavities. *Source*: Courtesy of AGIE USA Ltd.

(a)   (b)

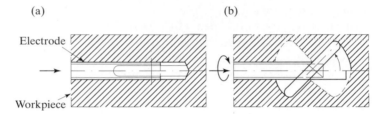

Electrode

Workpiece

FIGURE 26.12 Schematic illustration of producing an inner cavity by EDM, using a specially designed electrode with a hinged tip, which is slowly opened and rotated to produce the large cavity. *Source*: Luziesa France.

Design Considerations for EDM

a. Parts should be designed so that the required electrodes can be shaped properly and economically.

b. Deep slots and narrow openings should be avoided.

c. For economic production, the surface finish specified should not be too fine.

d. In order to achieve a high production rate, the bulk of material removal should be done by conventional processes (roughing out).

26.5.1 Electrical-Discharge Grinding

The grinding wheel in *electrical-discharge grinding* (EDG) is made of graphite or brass and contains no abrasives. Material is removed from the workpiece surface by repetitive spark discharges between the rotating wheel and the workpiece. The EDG process can be combined with electrochemical grinding. The process is then called **electrochemical-discharge grinding** (ECDG).

Material is removed by chemical action, with the electrical discharges from the graphite wheel breaking up the oxide film, and is washed away by the electrolyte flow. The process is used primarily for grinding carbide tools and dies but can also be used with fragile parts, such as surgical needles, thin-walled tubes, and honeycomb structures. The ECDG process is faster than EDG, but power consumption is higher.

In **sawing** with EDM, a setup similar to a band or circular saw (but without any teeth) is used with the same electrical circuit for EDM. Narrow cuts can be made at high rates of metal removal. Because cutting forces are negligible, the process can be used on thin and slender components as well.

26.6 WIRE EDM

A variation of EDM is *wire EDM* (Figs. 26.13a and b), or *electrical-discharge wire cutting*. In this process, which is similar to contour cutting with a band saw (Fig. 23.27), a slowly moving wire travels along a prescribed path, cutting the workpiece, with the discharge sparks acting like cutting teeth. This process is used to cut plates as thick as 300 mm (12 in.), and for making punches, tools, and dies from hard metals. It can also cut intricate components for the electronics industry.

The wire is usually made of brass, copper, or tungsten; zinc- or brass-coated and multi-coated wires are also used. The wire diameter is typically about 0.30 mm (0.012 in.) for roughing cuts and 0.20 mm (0.008 in.) for finishing cuts. The wire should have sufficient tensile strength and fracture toughness, as well as high electrical conductivity and capacity to flush away the debris produced during cutting.

The wire is generally used only once, as it is relatively inexpensive. It travels at a constant velocity in the range of 0.15 to 9 m/min (6 to 360 in./min), and a constant gap (kerf) is maintained during the cut. The trend in the use of dielectric fluids is toward clear, low-viscosity fluids.

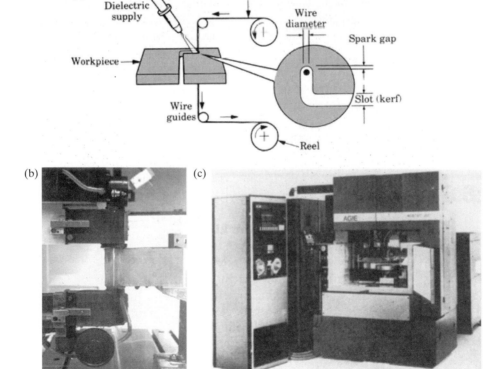

FIGURE 26.13   (a) Schematic illustration of the wire EDM process. As much as 50 hours of machining can be performed with one reel of wire, which is then discarded. (b) Cutting a thick plate with wire EDM. (c) A computer-controlled wire EDM machine. *Source*: Courtesy of AGIE USA Ltd.

The cutting speed is generally given in terms of the cross-sectional area cut per unit time. Typical examples are: 18,000 mm^2/hr $(28\ in.^2/hr)$ for 50-mm (2-in.) thick D2 tool steel, and 45,000 mm^2/hr $(70\ in.^2/hr)$ for 150-mm (6-in.) thick aluminum. These removal rates indicate a linear cutting speed of $18,000/50 = 360$ mm/hr $= 6$ mm/min, and $45,000/150 = 300$ mm/hr $= 5$ mm/min, respectively.

Modern wire EDM machines (**multiaxis EDM wire cutting machining centers**) are equipped with the following features:

1. Computer controls for controlling the cutting path of the wire (Fig. 26.13c),
2. Multiheads for cutting two parts at the same time,
3. Features such as controls for preventing wire breakage,
4. Automatic self-threading features in case of wire breakage, and
5. Programmed machining strategies to optimize the operation.

Two-axis computer-controlled machines can produce cylindrical shapes in a manner similar to a turning operation or cylindrical grinding. Many modern wire EDM machines allow the control of the feed and take-up ends of the wire to traverse independently in two principal directions, so tapered parts can be made. Depending on size, capability, and quality, the cost of wire EDM machines is in the range of $150,000 to $300,000.

26.7 LASER-BEAM MACHINING

In *laser-beam machining* (LBM), the source of energy is a **laser** (an acronym for *L*ight *Am*plification by *S*timulated *E*mission of *R*adiation), which focuses optical energy on the surface of the workpiece (Fig. 26.14a). The highly focused, high-density energy melts and evaporates portions of the workpiece in a controlled manner. This process, which does not require a vacuum, is used to machine a variety of metallic and nonmetallic materials.

There are several types of lasers used in manufacturing operations (Table 26.2):

a. CO_2 (*pulsed* or *continuous wave*).
b. Nd : YAG (neodymium:yttrium-aluminum-garnet).
c. Nd : glass, ruby.
d. Excimer lasers (from the words *Exci*ted and di*mer*, meaning two mers or two molecules of the same chemical composition).

FIGURE 26.14   (a) Schematic illustration of the laser-beam machining process. (b) and (c) Examples of holes produced in nonmetallic parts by LBM.

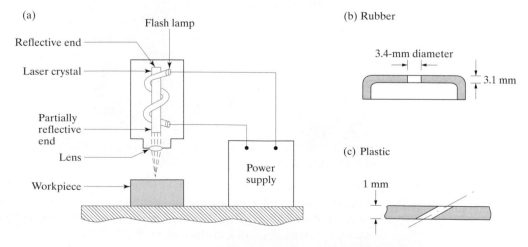

TABLE 26.2   General Applications of Lasers in Manufacturing

Application	Laser type
Cutting	
Metals	PCO_2, $CWCO_2$, $Nd:YAG$, ruby
Plastics	$CWCO_2$
Ceramics	PCO_2
Drilling	
Metals	PCO_2, $Nd:YAG$, $Nd:glass$, ruby
Plastics	Excimer
Marking	
Metals	PCO_2, $Nd:YAG$
Plastics	Excimer
Ceramics	Excimer
Surface treatment, metals	$CWCO_2$
Welding, metals	PCO_2, $CWCO_2$, $Nd:YAG$, $Nd:glass$, ruby

Note: P = pulsed, CW = continuous wave.

Important physical parameters in LBM are the *reflectivity* and *thermal conductivity* of the workpiece surface, and its specific heat and latent heats of melting and evaporation. The lower these quantities, the more efficient the process. The surface produced by LBM is usually rough and has a *heat-affected zone* (as discussed in Section 29.2) which, in critical applications, may have to be removed or heat treated. Kerf width is an important consideration, as it is in other cutting processes, such as sawing, wire EDM, and electron-beam machining.

Laser beams may be used in combination with a gas stream, such as oxygen, nitrogen, or argon (**laser-beam torch**), for cutting thin sheet materials. High-pressure, inert gas assisted laser cutting is used for stainless steel and aluminum; it leaves an oxide-free edge that can improve weldability. Gas streams also have the important function of blowing away molten and vaporized material from the workpiece surface.

Process Capabilities.   Laser-beam machining is widely used for drilling and cutting metals, nonmetallic materials, ceramics, and composite materials (Figs. 26.14b and c). The abrasive nature of composite materials and the cleanliness of the operation have made laser-beam machining an attractive alternative to traditional machining methods.

Holes as small as 0.005 mm (0.0002 in.), with hole depth-to-diameter ratios of 50 : 1, have been produced in various materials, although a more practical minimum is 0.025 mm (0.001 in.). Steel plates as thick as 32 mm (1.25 in.) can be cut with laser beams.

Laser-beam machining is being used increasingly in the electronics and automotive industries. Bleeder holes for fuel-pump covers and lubrication holes in transmission hubs are, for example, being drilled with lasers. The cooling holes in the first stage vanes of the Boeing 747 jet engines are also produced by lasers. Significant cost savings have been achieved by laser-beam machining, a process that is competing with electrical-discharge machining.

Laser beams are also used for the following:

1. **Welding** (Section 27.8),
2. Small-scale and localized **heat treating** (Chapter 4) of metals and ceramics to modify their surface mechanical and tribological properties, and
3. The **marking** of parts, such as letters, numbers, codes, etc. Marking can also be done by processes such as (a) with ink; (b) with mechanical devices such as punches, pins, stylus, scroll rolls, or stamping; and (c) by etching. Although the equipment is more

expensive than that used in other methods, marking and engraving with lasers has become increasingly common due to its accuracy, reproducibility, flexibility, ease of automation, and on-line application in manufacturing.

The inherent *flexibility* of the laser-cutting process, with its fiber-optic beam delivery, simple fixturing, and low setup times, and the availability of multi-kW machines and 2-D and 3-D computer-controlled laser-cutting systems are attractive features. Therefore, laser cutting can compete successfully with cutting sheet metal with the traditional punching processes described in Chapter 16. There are now efforts to combine the two processes for improved overall efficiency. (See the following example.)

Extreme caution should be exercised with lasers. Even low-power lasers can cause damage to the retina of the eye if proper precautions are not observed.

Design Considerations for Laser-Beam Machining

a. Reflectivity of the workpiece surface is an important consideration in laser-beam machining; because they reflect less, dull and unpolished surfaces are preferable.

b. Designs with sharp corners should be avoided since they can be difficult to produce. Deep cuts produce tapers.

c. Any adverse effects on the properties of the machined materials caused by the high local temperatures and heat-affected zone should be investigated.

Example: Combining Laser Cutting and Punching of Sheet Metal

As we have seen, laser cutting processes and punching processes have their respective advantages and limitations regarding both technical and economic aspects. Laser cutting advantages are generally (a) smaller batches, (b) the flexibility of the operation, (c) a wide range of thicknesses, (d) prototyping capability, (e) materials and composites that may otherwise be cut with difficulty, and (f) complex geometries that can be programmed.

Punching advantages and drawbacks include (a) large lot sizes, (b) relatively simple parts, (c) a small range of part thicknesses, (d) fixed and limited punch geometries even when using turrets, (e) rapid production, and (f) integration with subsequent processing after punching.

It is evident that the two processes cover different but complementary ranges. It is not difficult to visualize parts with some features that can be produced best by one process, and other features that are best produced by the other process.

Machines have been designed and built in such a manner that the processes and fixturing can be utilized jointly to their full extent but without interfering with each others' operational boundaries. The purpose of combining is to increase the overall efficiency and productivity of the manufacturing process for parts that are within the capabilities of each of the two processes, similar to the concept of the machining centers described in Section 24.2. For example, turret punch presses have been equipped with an integrated laser head; the machine can punch or laser cut, but it cannot do both simultaneously.

Several factors have to be taken into account in such a combination with respect to the characteristics of each operation: (a) the ranges of sizes, thicknesses, and shapes to be produced and how they are to be nested; (b) processing and setup times, including the loading, fixturing, and unloading of parts; (c) programming for cutting; and (d) the process capabilities of each method, including dynamic characteristics, vibrations, and shock from punching (and isolation) that may disturb adjustments and alignments of the laser components.

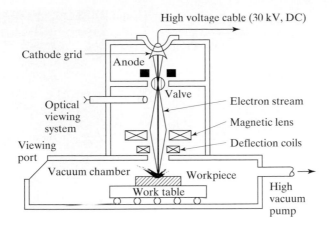

FIGURE 26.15 Schematic illustration of the electron-beam machining process. Unlike LBM, this process requires a vacuum, so workpiece size is limited to the size of the vacuum chamber.

26.8 ELECTRON-BEAM MACHINING AND PLASMA-ARC CUTTING

The source of energy in *electron-beam machining* (EBM) is high-velocity electrons, which strike the surface of the workpiece and generate heat (Fig. 26.15). The machines utilize voltages in the range of 50 kV–200 kV to accelerate the electrons to speeds of 50% to 80% of the speed of light. Its applications are similar to those of laser-beam machining, except that EBM requires a *vacuum*. Consequently, it is used much less than laser beam machining.

Electron-beam machining can be used for very accurate cutting of a wide variety of metals. Surface finish is better and kerf width is narrower than that for other thermal cutting processes. (See also Section 27.7 on *electron-beam welding*.) The interaction of the electron beam with the workpiece surface produces hazardous x-rays; the equipment should, therefore, be used only by highly trained personnel.

In **plasma-arc cutting (PAC)**, *plasma beams* (ionized gas) are used to rapidly cut ferrous and nonferrous sheets and plates (Section 27.5.3). The temperatures generated are very high (9400 °C; 17,000 °F, in the torch for oxygen as a plasma gas). Consequently, the process is fast, the kerf width is small, and the surface finish is good. Parts as thick as 150 mm (6 in.) can be cut. Material-removal rates are much higher than those associated with the EDM and LBM processes, and parts can be machined with good reproducibility. Plasma-arc cutting is highly automated today, using programmable controllers.

Design Considerations

a. The guidelines for LBM generally apply to EBM as well.

b. Because vacuum chambers have limited capacity, part sizes should closely match the size of the vacuum chamber for a high-production rate per cycle.

c. If a part requires electron-beam machining on only a small portion of the workpiece, consideration should be given to manufacturing it as a number of smaller components and assembling them after electron-beam machining.

26.9 WATER-JET MACHINING

When we put our hand across a jet of water or air, we feel a considerable concentrated force acting on it. This force results from the momentum change of the stream, and, in fact, is the principle on which the operation of water or gas turbines is based. In *water-jet machining*

(a)

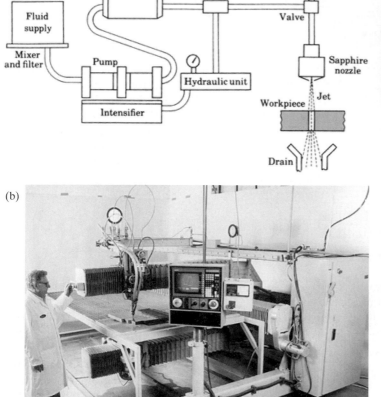

(c)

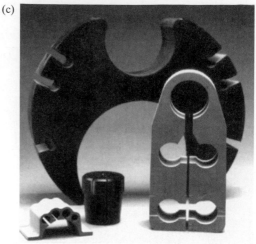

FIGURE 26.16   (a) Schematic illustration of water-jet machining. (b) A computer-controlled, water-jet cutting machine cutting a granite plate. (c) Example of various nonmetallic parts produced by the water-jet cutting process. *Source*: Courtesy of Possis Corporation.

(WJM), also called **hydrodynamic machining**, this force is utilized in cutting and deburring operations (Fig. 26.16). See also *water-jet peening*, Section 33.2.2.

The water jet acts like a saw and cuts a narrow groove in the material. A pressure level of about 400 MPa (60 ksi) is generally used for efficient operation, although pressures as high as 1400 MPa (200 ksi) can be generated. Jet-nozzle diameters range between 0.05 mm and 1 mm (0.002 in. and 0.040 in.).

A water-jet cutting machine and its operation are shown in Fig. 26.16b. A variety of materials can be cut, including plastics, fabrics, rubber, wood products, paper, leather, insulating materials, brick, and composite materials (Fig. 26.16c).

Depending on the materials, thicknesses can range up to 25 mm (1 in.) and higher. Vinyl and foam coverings for automobile dashboards, as well as some body panels, are being cut using multiple-axis, robot-guided water-jet machining equipment. Because it is an efficient and clean operation compared to other cutting processes, it is also used in the food processing industry for cutting and slicing food products.

The advantages of this process are that (a) cuts can be started at any location without the need for predrilled holes, (b) no heat is produced, (c) no deflection of the rest of the workpiece takes place (so the process is suitable for flexible materials), (d) little wetting of the workpiece takes place, and (e) the burr produced is minimal. It is also an environmentally safe manufacturing process.

26.9.1 Abrasive Water-Jet Machining

In *abrasive water-jet machining* (AWJM), the water jet contains abrasive particles (such as silicon carbide or aluminum oxide), which increase the material-removal rate above that of water-jet machining. Metallic, nonmetallic, and advanced composite materials of various thicknesses can be cut in single or multilayers.

This process is suitable particularly for heat-sensitive materials that cannot be machined by processes in which heat is produced. Cutting speeds can be as high as 7.5 m/min (25 ft/min) for reinforced plastics, but much lower for metals; consequently, this process may not be acceptable for situations requiring high production rates.

The minimum hole size that can be produced satisfactorily to date is about 3 mm (0.12 in.); maximum hole depth is on the order of 25 mm (1 in.). With multiple-axis and robotic-control machines, complex three-dimensional parts can be machined to finish dimensions. The optimum level of abrasives in the jet stream is controlled automatically in modern AWJM systems. Nozzle life has been improved by making nozzles from rubies, sapphires, and carbide-based composite materials.

26.10 ABRASIVE-JET MACHINING

In *abrasive-jet machining* (AJM), a high-velocity jet of dry air, nitrogen, or carbon dioxide, containing abrasive particles, is aimed at the workpiece surface under controlled conditions (Fig. 26.17). The impact of the particles develops a sufficiently concentrated force (see also Section 25.9) to perform operations such as (a) cutting small holes, slots, or intricate patterns in very hard or brittle metallic and nonmetallic materials, (b) deburring or removing small flash from parts, (c) trimming and beveling, (d) removing oxides and other surface films, and (e) general cleaning of components with irregular surfaces.

The gas supply pressure is on the order of 850 kPa (125 psi) and the abrasive-jet velocity can be as high as 300 m/s (100 ft/s) and is controlled by a valve. The hand-held nozzles are usually made of tungsten carbide or sapphire. The abrasive size is in the range of from 10 to 50 μm (400 to 2000 μin.). Because the flow of the free abrasives tends to round off corners, designs for abrasive-jet machining should avoid sharp corners; also, holes made in metal parts tend to be tapered.

There is some hazard involved in using this process because of airborne particulates. This problem can be avoided by using the abrasive water-jet machining process.

FIGURE 26.17   Schematic illustration of the abrasive-jet machining process.

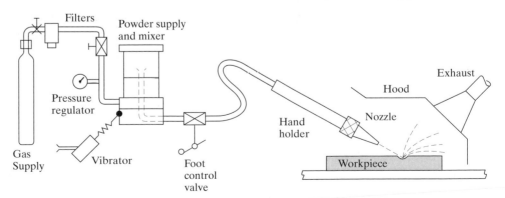

26.11 NANOFABRICATION

Nanofabrication involves the generation and manipulation of structures with characteristic lengths less than 1 μm (40 μin.), nano meaning 10^{-9}. While devices with scales on the order of micrometers have been produced for decades, nanoscale processes promise to provide major improvements and revolutionize small-scale devices. Potential applications of these materials and devices include electronics applications, drug delivery, revolutionary mechanical devices, sensors, and medical diagnostic systems.

A distinction should be made between (a) the *production* of nanoscale materials or particles (nanosynthesis; see Section 6.15) and (b) those processes which *manipulate* particles or geometries on a nanoscale (nanofabrication). Each of these has very different approaches and limitations.

Many of the nanofabrication processes are more accurate and precise versions of the processes used in integrated-circuit manufacture (Chapter 34), such as photolithography, lithography, and related processes. Some limited lithography can be performed on an **atomic force microscope** (AFM; see Section 31.5.3) which can even allow the manipulation of individual atoms.

With the extremely small length scales and associated close dimensional tolerances that must be maintained in the fabrication of nanoscale structures, **chemical etching** or **wet etching** (see Section 34.7) cannot be applied because of the tendency to undercut below a protective mask (see Figure 34.7). For this reason, extremely fine structures are produced with **reactive ion etching** (RIE) or **dry etching**. In this process, an ionized gas plasma is driven by radio frequency power applied to the workpiece electrode and strikes the (usually) metallic workpiece. This causes the metal to sputter, and can generate very high-quality etches with very high depth-to-width ratios.

Reactive ion etching shows great promise as a nanofabrication approach, but it will undercut a vertical wall. Recent developments include coating side walls with a one or two molecular layer thick polymer to eliminate undercut. Special care must be taken to eliminate residual stresses in the workpiece, since as material is removed, warpage is likely if such stresses are present.

Atomic force microscopes have been used in nanoscale lithography and have great potential for small-scale surface etching. These microscopes are mainly used as surface visualization tools (Chapter 31). However, when used with the proper cantilever, AFMs can perform lithography with atomic resolution, and have even been used to manipulate single molecules and atoms on surfaces.

Figure 26.18a shows an SEM image of a diamond-tipped, stainless-steel cantilever typically used for nanolithography, while Figure 26.18b shows the resulting scratch made with the cantilever shown in (a). Note that the depth of cut is less than 100 nm, and the resolution is extremely fine.

Nanofabrication has the potential to revolutionize many industries, including information storage, integrated circuit manufacture, and medical drug delivery systems. For example, it has been estimated that if a bit of information could be stored in 100 atoms, then all of the books ever written could be stored in a 0.5-mm cube. Scientists have envisioned the days when microscopic robots will be injected into the body and deliver drugs exactly where needed.

The greatest hindrance to nanofabrication thus far has been the limited capability of nanofabrication processes. For example, an atomic force microscope can only process a section of a surface approximately 0.01 mm^2 at a time, and typical lithography speeds are on the order of 10 μm per second. These are orders of magnitude too low for industrial uses other than for fundamental research, although new methods of increasing capacity are constantly being investigated.

(a)

(b)

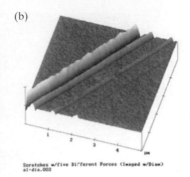

FIGURE 26.18   (a) A scanning electron microscope view of a diamond-tipped (triangular piece at the right) cantilever used with the atomic force microscope. The diamond tip is attached to the end of the cantilever with an adhesive. (b) Scratches produced on a surface by the diamond tip under different forces. Note the extremely small size of the scratches.

26.12   MICROMACHINING

An important area of continued investigation is the development of **microelectromechanical systems (MEMS)**, in which the typical dimensions of the components are on the order of micrometers. Examples of such systems are electromagnetic microactuators for rigid disk drives, microgimbals, microbellows, and various probes, sensors, and measuring devices. Micromachining operations for manufacturing these components usually involve *chemical etching* processes on a very fine scale, as described in this chapter and Chapter 34.

As an example, Fig. 26.19a shows a gear assembly used for actuation and orientation at microscales. The tiny rotor is 55 μm in diameter and has been driven at speeds up to 300,000 rpm, and can be rotated counterclockwise or clockwise. A detail of the rotor assembly is shown in Fig. 26.19b, where, for reference, a grain of sand and clusters of human red blood cells have been placed next to the rotor.

FIGURE 26.19   An example of micromachined microelectromechanical system; note the dimensional scale. Gear assembly driven by resonant combdrives (an electrostatic motor, also called comb drive). (a) View of entire assembly. (b) Detail of rotor driver portion of the gear assembly. *Source*: R. Muller, University of California, Berkeley.

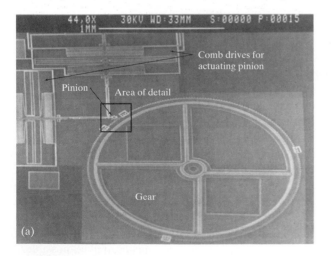

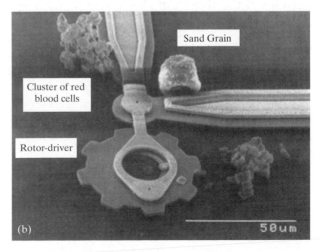

FIGURE 26.20   A micromirror made from polysilicon folded into an upright position. The mirror surface is gold plated. Note the dimensional scale.
Source: R. Muller, University of California, Berkeley.

To produce this rotor, the components are chemically etched in a recessed area of a wafer, then the surface is chemically-mechanically polished (see Section 25.10.6). Finally, the associated electronic circuit is fabricated in a continuous-batch complementary metal-oxide semiconductor (CMOS) manufacturing process (see Chapter 34 for details).

One area of interest for microelectromechanical systems is their use as probes and measuring devices, including aerospace and fluid-flow applications. Especially of interest is their incorporation into fiber-optic systems. One problem which can occur is that light can be directed onto a sensor which has been micromachined onto a surface, but if the light is parallel to the surface, it is more difficult to measure.

Figure 26.20 shows a micromirror which has been machined into a silicon wafer, plated with a gold reflecting surface and then folded upright so that it can be used in a micro interferometer. The elecrostatic drive allows the mirror to be manipulated at micrometer scales.

26.13 ECONOMICS OF ADVANCED MACHINING PROCESSES

Advanced machining processes have unique applications, particularly for difficult-to-machine materials and for parts with complex internal and external profiles. The economic production run for a particular process depends on the cost of tooling and equipment, operating costs, the material-removal rate required, and the level of operator skill required, as well as on secondary and finishing operations that may subsequently be necessary.

In chemical machining, an important factor is the cost of reagents, maskants, and disposal, together with the cost of cleaning the parts. In electrical-discharge machining, the cost of electrodes and the need to periodically replace them can be significant.

The rate of material removal, and with it production rate, can vary significantly in these processes. (See Table 26.1.) The cost of tooling and equipment also varies considerably, as does the operator skill required. The high capital investment for machines such as electrical and high-energy beam machining should be justified in terms of the production runs and the feasibility of manufacturing the same part by other means, if at all possible.

SUMMARY

- Advanced machining processes have unique capabilities, and involve chemical, electrochemical, electrical, laser, and high-energy-beam sources of energy. The mechanical properties of the workpiece material are not significant because these processes rely on mechanisms that do not involve the strength, hardness, ductility, or toughness of the material; rather, they involve physical, chemical, and electrical properties.

- Chemical and electrical methods of machining are particularly suitable for hard materials and complex shapes. They do not produce forces (and can therefore be used for thin, slender, and flexible workpieces), significant temperatures, or residual stresses. However, the effects of these processes on surface integrity must be investigated, as they can damage surfaces considerably, reducing the fatigue life of the product.

- High-energy-beam machining processes basically utilize laser beams, electron beams, and plasma arc. They have important industrial applications, possess high flexibility of operation, and are economically competitive with various other processes.

- Water-jet, abrasive water-jet, and abrasive-jet machining processes can be used for cutting as well as deburring operations. Because they do not utilize hard tooling, they have inherent flexibility of operation.

TRENDS

- The need for economical methods of material removal will increase further because of the development of new materials, ceramics, and composites as well as complex shapes that are difficult to machine with traditional processes.

- Electrochemical machining is becoming increasingly important because of the demanding requirements of computer-chip and microelectromechanical systems (MEMS) manufacture.

- In spite of their advantages, the effects of advanced machining processes on the properties and service life of workpieces are important considerations, particularly for critical applications.

- The trend in the machinery for advanced machining processes is for computer controls, using multiple-axis robots, as well as exploring possibilities of combining different processes for flexibility and improved productivity.

- Laser-beam and electrical-discharge machining of automotive and various other components is being implemented at an increasing rate.

KEY TERMS

Abrasive-jet machining	Electrochemical machining	No-wear EDM
Abrasive water-jet machining	Electrode	Photochemical blanking
Chemical blanking	Electrolyte	Photochemical machining
Chemical machining	Electron-beam machining	Photoetching
Chemical milling	Etchant	Photoresist
Die sinking	Hydrodynamic machining	Plasma beams
Dielectric	Laser	Plasma-arc cutting
Electrical-discharge grinding	Laser-beam machining	Pulsed electrochemical machining
Electrical-discharge machining	Masking	Reagent
Electrochemical grinding	Micromachining	Wire EDM
Electrochemical-discharge grinding	Micromechanical systems	Water-jet machining
Electrochemical honing	Nanofabrication	

BIBLIOGRAPHY

ASM Handbook, Vol. 16: *Machining*. ASM International, 1989.

Brown, J., *Advanced Machining Technology Handbook*. McGraw-Hill, 1998.

Crafer, R.C., and P.J. Oakley, *Laser Processing in Manufacturing*. Chapman & Hall, 1993.

Edelstein, A.S. and Cammarata, R.C., *Nanomaterials: Synthesis, Properties and Applications*. Institute of Physics Publishing, Bristol, 1996.

Gillespie, L., *Deburring and Edge Finishing Handbook*. Society of Manufacturing Engineers, 1999.

Guitrau, E.B., *The EDM Handbook*. Soho Press, 1997.

Jain, V.K., and P.C. Pandey, *Theory and Practice of Electrochemical Machining*. Wiley, 1993.

Kalpakjian, S. (ed.), *Tool and Die Failures: Source Book*. ASM International, 1982.

Lange, K. (ed.), *Handbook of Metal Forming* (Chapter 32, Die Manufacture). McGraw-Hill, 1985.

Machinery's Handbook, revised periodically. Industrial Press.

Machining Data Handbook (3d ed.), 2 vols. Machinability Data Center, 1980.

Madou, M.J., *Fundamentals of Microfabrication*. CRC Press, 1997.

McGeough, J.A., *Advanced Methods of Machining*. Chapman & Hall, 1988.

Migliore, L., *Laser Materials Processing*. Marcel Dekker, 1996.

Momber, A.W., and R. Kovacevic, *Principles of Abrasive Water Jet Machining*. Springer, 1998.

Powell, J., *CO_2 Laser Cutting* (2d ed.). Springer, 1998.

Raichoudhury, P. (ed.), *Handbook of Microlithography, Micromachining, and Microfabrication*. Society of Photo-optical Instrumentation Engineers, 1997.

Sommer, C., and S. Sommer, *Wire EDM Handbook*. Technical Advanced Publishing Co., 1992.

Tool and Manufacturing Engineers Handbook (4th ed.), Vol. 1: *Machining*. Society of Manufacturing Engineers, 1983.

REVIEW QUESTIONS

26.1 List the reasons for the development of advanced machining processes.

26.2 Name the processes involved in chemical machining. Describe briefly their principles.

26.3 What should be the properties of maskants?

26.4 Describe chemical blanking and compare it with conventional blanking using dies.

26.5 Explain the difference between chemical machining and electrochemical machining.

26.6 What is the underlying principle of electrochemical grinding?

26.7 Why has electrical-discharge machining become so widely used?

26.8 Explain how the EDM process is capable of producing complex shapes.

26.9 What are the capabilities of wire EDM? Could this process be used to make tapered pieces? Explain.

26.10 Describe the advantages of water-jet machining.

26.11 Why is the preshaping or premachining of parts sometimes desirable in the processes described in this chapter?

26.12 Why is electron-beam machining hazardous?

26.13 What is the difference between photochemical blanking and chemical blanking?

26.14 Can contoured cavities be machined chemically?

26.15 What type of workpiece is not suitable for laser beam machining?

26.16 What is an undercut and why must it be considered in chemical machining?

26.17 Describe your understanding of the capabilities and potential of nanofabrication.

QUALITATIVE PROBLEMS

26.18 Give possible technical and economic reasons why the processes described in this chapter might be preferred over those described in the preceding chapters, or even necessary.

26.19 Explain why the mechanical properties of workpiece materials are not significant in most of the processes described in this chapter.

26.20 In which of the manufacturing activities in industry is the wire EDM process most applicable?

26.21 Why do different material-removal processes affect the fatigue strength of materials to different degrees?

26.22 Explain why it is difficult to produce sharp profiles and corners with some of the processes described in this chapter.

26.23 Which of the advanced machining processes causes thermal damage? What is the consequence of such damage to workpieces?

26.24 In abrasive water-jet machining, at what stage is the abrasive introduced in the water jet? Survey the available literature, then draw a schematic outline of the equipment involved.

26.25 Describe your thoughts regarding the laser-beam machining of nonmetallic materials. Give several possible applications, including their advantages as compared to other processes.

26.26 Comment on the depth of material removed from a metal surface by abrasive-jet machining.

26.27 Are deburring operations are necessary for parts made by advanced machining processes? Explain and give several examples.

26.28 Do you think it should be possible to produce spur gears by advanced machining processes, starting with a round blank? Explain.

26.29 List and explain factors that contribute to poor surface finish in the processes described in this chapter.

26.30 Make a survey of the available technical literature and describe the types of surfaces produced by electron-beam, plasma-arc, and laser cutting.

26.31 It was stated that graphite is the preferred material for EDM tooling. Would graphite be suitable for wire EDM?

26.32 Does EDM affect the fatigue strength of cold worked metals? Explain.

26.33 What is the purpose of the abrasives in electrochemical grinding?

26.34 Why are lasers increasingly used to mark parts?

26.35 Which of the processes described are suitable for producing very small and deep holes? Why?

26.36 Is kerf important in wire EDM? Explain.

26.37 Are there similarities between photochemical machining and solid base curing? (See Section 19.3.)

26.38 If an electroless nickel plating (Section 33.8) was placed on a polymer part, could it then be cut with a wire EDM process?

QUANTITATIVE PROBLEMS

26.39 A 100-mm deep hole that is 20 mm in diameter is being produced by electrochemical machining. A high production rate is more important than machined surface quality. Estimate the maximum current and the time required to perform this operation.

26.40 If the operation in Problem 26.39 were performed on an electrical-discharge machine, what would be the estimated machining time?

26.41 A cutting off operation is being performed with a laser beam. The workpiece being cut is $\frac{3}{4}$ in. thick and 8 in. long. If the kerf is $\frac{3}{32}$ in. wide, estimate the time required to perform this operation.

26.42 Studies have indicated that it is possible to develop quantitative relationships between material properties and laser processing parameters, leading to recommendations as to optimum cutting speeds. Make a survey of the available technical literature regarding this aspect and describe your findings.

26.43 A 1.0-in.-thick copper plate is being machined through wire EDM. The wire moves at a speed of 5 ft/min and the kerf width is $\frac{1}{16}$ in. What is the required power? Note that it takes 1550 J (2100 ft-lb) to melt one gram of copper.

26.44 Conventional laser printers typically operate at 300 dots/in. If such a mechanism is used to prepare the mask in photochemical blanking, what is the best tolerance that can be achieved?

SYNTHESIS AND DESIGN

26.45 Would you consider designing a machine tool that combines, in one machine, two or more of the processes described in this chapter? Explain. For what types of parts would such a machine be useful? Give a preliminary sketch for such a machine.

26.46 Repeat Problem 26.45, combining processes described in (a) Chapters 13–16, (b) Chapters 22 and 23, and (c) Chapters 25 and 26. Give a preliminary sketch of a machine for each of the three groups. How would you convince a prospective customer of the merits of such machines?

26.47 Make a list of machining processes that may be suitable for each of the following materials: (a) ceramics, (b) cast iron, (c) thermoplastics, (d) thermosets, (e) diamond, and (f) annealed copper.

26.48 How would you manufacture a thin, large-diameter, conical round disk with a thickness that decreases from the center outward?

26.49 Describe the similarities and differences among the various design guidelines presented in this chapter.

26.50 We have seen that there are several holemaking methods. Based on the topics covered in Parts III and IV, make a comprehensive table of holemaking processes. Describe the advantages and limitations of each method, comment on the quality and surface integrity of the holes produced, and give examples of specific applications.

26.51 An example of combining laser cutting and the punching of sheet metal is given in Section 26.7. Considering the relevant parameters involved, design a system whereby both processes can be used in combination to produce parts from sheet metal.

26.52 Marking surfaces with numbers and letters for part identification purposes can be done not only with labels but by various mechanical and nonmechanical methods. Based on the processes described throughout this text thus far, make a list of these methods, explaining their advantages, limitations, and typical applications.

26.53 Precision engineering is a term that is used to describe manufacturing high-quality parts with close dimensional tolerances and good surface finish. Based on their process capabilities, make a comprehensive list of machining processes, with decreasing order of quality of parts produced. Include a brief commentary on each method.

26.54 With appropriate sketches, describe the principles of various fixturing methods and devices that can be used for the processes described in this chapter.

26.55 Make a comprehensive table of the process capabilities of the advanced machining processes described in this chapter. Use several columns describing the machines involved, the type of tools and tool materials used, the shapes of blanks and parts produced, the typical maximum and minimum sizes, surface finish, tolerances, and production rates.

26.56 One of the general concerns regarding advanced machining processes is that, in spite of their many advantages, they are generally slower than conventional machining processes. Make a survey of the speeds, machining times, and production rates involved and prepare a table comparing their respective process capabilities.

26.57 We have seen that several of the processes described in Part IV of this text can be employed, either singly or in combination, to make or finish dies for metalworking operations. Write a brief technical paper on these methods, describing their advantages and limitations, and typical applications.

26.58 Would the processes described in this chapter be difficult to perform on various nonmetallic or rubberlike materials? Explain your thoughts, commenting on the influence of various physical and mechanical properties of workpiece materials, part geometries, etc.

26.59 Using the Internet, obtain a list of suppliers of electrical-discharge machining equipment, and survey the capacities of these machines. Also, compare the wire electrode materials for wire EDM that are available in terms of sizes and costs.

26.60 Abrasion resistance is very important for wires used in wire EDM. Perform a technical literature search and write a summary regarding approaches used to improve the abrasion resistance of wires.

26.61 Survey the latest technical literature and make a list of components that can be made by nanofabrication techniques, including their size and shape complexity. What practical applications would such components have?

Part V
Joining Processes and Equipment

Some products are made of only one component: bolts, nails, steel balls for bearings, staples, screws, and paper clips. Almost all products, however, are assembled from components that were manufactured as individual parts. Even relatively simple products consist of at least two different parts joined by various means. Some kitchen knives, for example, have wooden handles that are attached to the knife blade with metal fasteners. Cooking pots and pans have plastic or wooden handles and knobs that are attached by various methods. The eraser of an ordinary pencil is attached with a brass sleeve.

Observe, for example, motorcycles, computers, washing machines, power tools, and airplanes, and how their numerous components are assembled and joined so that they can function reliably. A typical automobile has 15,000 components, a few of which are shown in Fig. V.1; all of them must be assembled, using several joining methods. A Boeing 747-400 aircraft has more than 6 million parts.

Joining is an all-inclusive term, covering processes such as welding, brazing, soldering, adhesive bonding, and mechanical fastening. These processes are an important and necessary aspect of manufacturing operations for the following reasons:

- The product is impossible to manufacture as a single piece. Consider, for example, the tubular part shown in Fig. V.2. Assume that each of the arms of this product is 5 m (15 ft) long, the tubes are 100 mm (4 in.) in diameter, and their wall thickness is 1 mm (0.04 in.). After reviewing all the manufacturing processes described in the preceding chapters, we would soon conclude that manufacturing this part in one piece would be impossible or uneconomical.

FIGURE V.1 Various parts in a typical automobile assembled using the processes described in Part V.

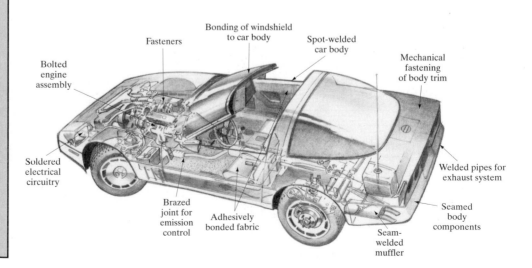

771

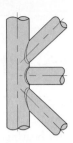

FIGURE V.2   A tubular part fabricated by joining individual components. This product cannot be manufactured in one piece by any of the methods described in previous chapters, if it consists of thin-walled, large-diameter, tubular-shaped long arms.

- The product, such as a cooking pot with a metal handle, is more economical to manufacture as individual components, which are then assembled.

- Products such as automobile engines, hair dryers, and printers need to be designed so as to be able to be taken apart for maintenance or repair.

- Different properties may be desirable for functional purposes of the product. For instance, surfaces subjected to friction, wear, corrosion, or environmental attack generally require characteristics different from those of the component's bulk. Examples are carbide cutting tips brazed to the shank of a drill (see Fig. 22.22f) and automotive brake shoes or grinding wheels bonded to a metal backing (see Fig. 25.1).

- Transporting the product in individual components and assembling them at home or at the customer's plant may be easier and less costly than transporting the completed item. Some bicycles, large toys, metal or wood shelving, and most machine tools and presses are assembled after the components or subassemblies have been transported to the appropriate site.

Although there can be different ways of categorizing the wide variety of available joining processes, this book follows the latest classification by the American Welding Society (AWS). Accordingly, joining processes fall into three major categories (Fig. V.3): (a) welding, (b) adhesive bonding, and (c) mechanical fastening.

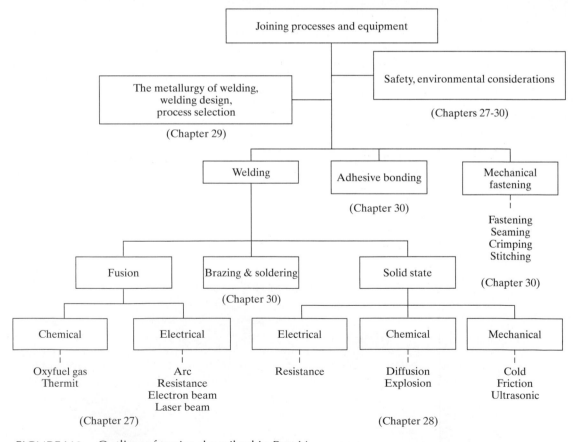

FIGURE V.3   Outline of topics described in Part V.

TABLE V.1   Comparison of Various Joining Methods

Method	Strength	Design variability	Small parts	Large parts	Tolerances	Reliability	Ease of maintenance	Visual inspection	Cost
	Characteristics								
Arc welding	1	2	3	1	3	1	2	2	2
Resistance welding	1	2	1	1	3	3	3	3	1
Brazing	1	1	1	1	3	1	3	2	3
Bolts and nuts	1	2	3	1	2	1	1	1	3
Riveting	1	2	3	1	1	1	3	1	2
Fasteners	2	3	3	1	2	2	2	1	3
Seaming, crimping	2	2	1	3	3	1	3	1	1
Adhesive bonding	3	1	1	2	3	2	3	3	2

Note: 1, very good; 2, good; 3, poor.

Welding processes are, in turn, divided into three basic categories: (a) fusion welding, (b) solid-state welding, and (c) brazing and soldering. Some types of welding processes can be classified into both the fusion and the solid-state categories.

The individual groups of joining processes described briefly below have various characteristics, outlined in Table V.1 as a guide to process selection.

Fusion welding is defined as the melting together and coalescing of materials by means of heat (usually supplied by chemical or electrical means); filler metals may or may not be used. This process constitutes a major category of welding; it comprises consumable or nonconsumable electrode arc welding and high-energy-beam welding processes. The welded joint undergoes important metallurgical and physical changes which, in turn, have a major effect on the properties and performance of the welded component or structure.

In **solid-state welding**, joining takes place without fusion; consequently, there is no liquid (molten) phase in the joint. The basic categories are diffusion bonding and cold, ultrasonic, friction, resistance, and explosion welding. Diffusion bonding, combined with superplastic forming, has become an important manufacturing process for complex shapes. **Brazing** and **soldering** use filler metals and involve lower temperatures than welding; the heat required is supplied externally.

Adhesive bonding has been developed into an important technology because of its several advantages; it has unique applications requiring strength, sealing, insulating, vibration damping, and resistance to corrosion between dissimilar metals. Included in this category are electrically-conducting adhesives for surface-mount technologies. **Mechanical fastening** involves traditional methods of using various fasteners, bolts, nuts, and rivets. **Joining plastics** can be accomplished by adhesive bonding, fusion by various external or internal heat sources, and mechanical fastening.

The choice of a joining process depends on several factors: (a) the application, (b) the joint design, (c) the materials involved; and (d) the shapes of the components to be joined, their thicknesses, and their sizes (Fig. V.4). Other considerations are the location of the joint within the product, the number of individual components involved, the operator skill required, and equipment and labor costs.

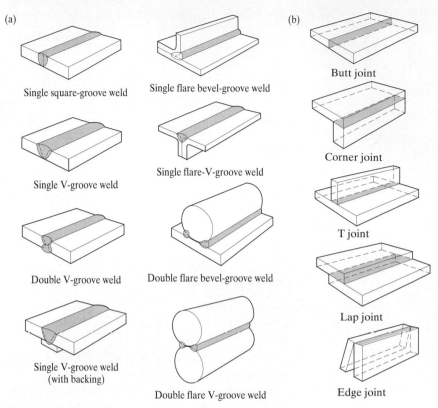

(a)

Single square-groove weld

Single flare bevel-groove weld

Single V-groove weld

Single flare-V-groove weld

Double V-groove weld

Double flare bevel-groove weld

Single V-groove weld
(with backing)

Double flare V-groove weld

(b)

Butt joint

Corner joint

T joint

Lap joint

Edge joint

FIGURE V.4   Examples of joints that can be made by various joining processes described in Part V.

27

Fusion-Welding Processes

27.1 INTRODUCTION

The welding processes described in this chapter involve the partial melting and fusion of the joint between two members. Here, **fusion welding** is defined as melting together and coalescing materials by means of heat. The thermal energy required for these welding operations is usually supplied by *chemical* or *electrical* means. **Filler metals**, which are metals added to the weld area during welding, may or may not be used. Fusion welds made without the addition of filler metals are known as *autogenous* welds.

This chapter describes the major classes of fusion-welding processes; it covers the basic principles of each process and the equipment used in it, its relative advantages and limitations, its capabilities, and the economic considerations affecting its selection (Table 27.1). These processes include the oxyfuel, arc, and high-energy-beam (electron-beam and laser-beam) welding processes that have important and unique applications in modern manufacturing.

27.2 OXYFUEL GAS WELDING

Oxyfuel gas welding (OFW) is a general term used to describe any welding process that uses a **fuel gas** combined with *oxygen* to produce a flame. This flame is the source of the

TABLE 27.1   General Characteristics of Fusion Welding Processes

Joining process	Operation	Advantage	Skill level required	Welding position	Current type	Distor- tion*	Cost of equip- ment
Shielded metal-arc	Manual	Portable and flexible	High	All	ac, dc	1 to 2	Low
Submerged arc	Automatic	High deposition	Low to medium	Flat and horizontal	ac, dc	1 to 2	Medium
Gas metal-arc	Semiautomatic or automatic	Most metals	Low to high	All	dc	2 to 3	Medium to high
Gas tungsten-arc	Manual or automatic	Most metals	Low to high	All	ac, dc	2 to 3	Medium
Flux-cored arc	Semiautomatic or automatic	High deposition	Low to high	All	dc	1 to 3	Medium
Oxyfuel	Manual	Portable and flexible	High	All	—	2 to 4	Low
Electron-beam, Laser-beam	Semiautomatic or automatic	Most metals	Medium to high	All	—	3 to 5	High

*1, highest; 5, lowest.

heat that is used to melt the metals at the joint. The most common gas-welding process uses *acetylene fuel*; it is known as *oxyacetylene welding* and is used typically for structural sheet-metal fabrication, automotive bodies, and various other repair work. Developed in the early 1900s, this process utilizes the heat generated by the combustion of acetylene gas (C_2H_2) in a mixture with oxygen.

The heat is generated in accordance with a pair of chemical reactions. The primary combustion process, which occurs in the inner core of the flame (Fig. 27.1), runs as follows:

$$C_2H_2 + O_2 \rightarrow 2CO + H_2 + \text{heat.} \tag{27.1}$$

This reaction dissociates the acetylene into carbon monoxide and hydrogen; it produces about one-third of the total heat generated in the flame. The secondary combustion process is

FIGURE 27.1   Three basic types of oxyacetylene flames used in oxyfuel-gas welding and cutting operations: (a) neutral flame; (b) oxidizing flame; (c) carburizing, or reducing, flame. The gas mixture in (a) is basically equal volumes of oxygen and acetylene.

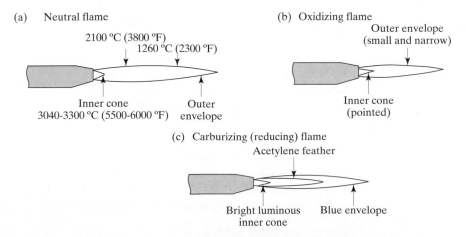

$$2CO + H_2 + 1.5O_2 \rightarrow 2CO_2 + H_2O + \text{heat}. \qquad \textbf{(27.2)}$$

This reaction consists of the further burning of the hydrogen and the carbon monoxide. This second reaction produces about two-thirds of the total heat. The temperatures developed in the flame as a result of these reactions can reach 3300 °C (6000 °F). Note that the reaction of hydrogen with oxygen produces water vapor.

27.2.1 Types of Flames

The proportions of acetylene and oxygen in the gas mixture are an important factor in oxyfuel gas welding. At a ratio of 1 : 1, that is, when there is no excess oxygen, it is considered to be a **neutral flame**.

With a greater oxygen supply, it becomes an **oxidizing flame**. This flame is harmful, especially for steels, because it oxidizes the steel. Only in the welding of copper and copper-based alloys is an oxidizing flame desirable, because in those cases a thin protective layer of *slag* forms over the molten metal. If the ratio of oxygen is deficient, the flame becomes a **reducing** or **carburizing flame**. The temperature of a reducing flame (one having excess acetylene) is lower, so it is suitable for applications requiring low heat, such as brazing, soldering, and flame-hardening.

Other fuel gases, such as hydrogen and methylacetylene propadiene, can be used in oxyfuel gas welding. The temperatures developed by these gases are low; they are therefore used for welding (a) metals with low melting points, such as lead, and (b) parts that are thin and small. The flame with pure hydrogen gas is colorless, so it is difficult to adjust the flame by eyesight. Most other gases, such as natural gas, propane, and butane, are not suitable for oxyfuel welding, because their heat output is low or because the flame is oxidizing.

27.2.2 Filler Metals

Filler metals are used to supply additional material to the weld zone during welding. They are available as rod or wire made of metals compatible with those to be welded. These consumable **filler rods** may be bare, or they may be coated with **flux**.

The purpose of the flux is to retard oxidation of the surfaces of the parts being welded, by generating a *gaseous shield* around the weld zone. The flux also helps to dissolve and remove oxides and other substances from the workpiece and so contributes to the formation of a stronger joint. The slag developed protects the molten puddle of metal against oxidation as it cools.

27.2.3 Welding Practice and Equipment

Oxyfuel gas welding can be used with most ferrous and nonferrous metals for almost any thickness of workpiece, but the relatively low heat input limits the process in practice to thicknesses of less than 6 mm (0.25 in.). A variety of joints can be produced by this method. The basic steps can be summarized as follows:

1. Prepare the edges to be joined, and establish and maintain their proper position by the use of clamps and fixtures.
2. Open the acetylene valve, and ignite the gas at the tip of the torch. Open the oxygen valve, and adjust the flame for the particular operation (Fig. 27.2).
3. Hold the torch at about 45° from the plane of the workpiece, with the inner flame near the workpiece and the filler rod at about 30°–40°.

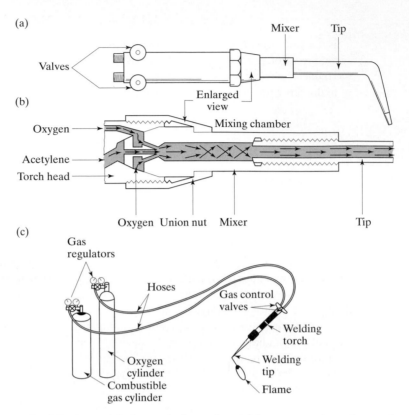

FIGURE 27.2   (a) General view of and (b) cross-section of a torch used in oxyacetylene welding. The acetylene valve is opened first; the gas is lit with a spark lighter or a pilot light; then the oxygen valve is opened and the flame adjusted. (c) Basic equipment used in oxyfuel-gas welding. To ensure correct connections, all threads on acetylene fittings are left-handed, whereas those for oxygen are right-handed. Oxygen regulators are usually painted green, acetylene regulators red.

4. Touch the filler rod to the joint and control its movement along the joint length by observing the rate of melting and filling of the joint.

Small joints may consist of a single weld bead, as shown in Fig. V.4; deep V-groove joints are made in multiple passes. Cleaning the surface of each weld bead prior to depositing a second layer is important for joint strength and for avoiding defects (see Chapter 29); wire brushes, hand or power, may be used for this purpose.

The equipment for oxyfuel gas welding basically consists of a **welding torch** (available in various sizes and shapes) connected by hoses to high-pressure gas cylinders and equipped with pressure gages and regulators (Fig. 27.2c). The use of safety equipment, such as goggles with shaded lenses, face shields, gloves, and protective clothing, is essential.

Proper connection of hoses to the cylinders is also an important factor in safety. Oxygen and acetylene cylinders have different threads, so that the hoses cannot be connected to the wrong cylinders. Gas cylinders should be anchored securely and should not be dropped or mishandled.

Process Capabilities.   The low cost of the equipment—usually less than $500 for smaller units—is an attractive feature of oxyfuel gas welding. Although it can be mechanized, this operation is essentially manual (and hence slow); it is used typically for fabrication and

(a)

(b)

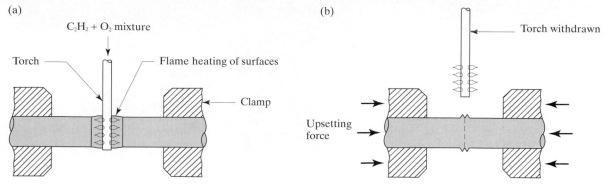

FIGURE 27.3   Schematic illustration of the pressure-gas welding process.

repair work. It has the advantages of being portable, versatile, and economical for simple and low-quantity work. Proper operator training and skill are essential.

27.2.4 Pressure Gas Welding

This method of welding two components starts with the heating of the interface by means of a torch using, typically, oxyacetylene gas (Fig. 27.3a). After the interface begins to melt, the torch is withdrawn, and a force is applied to press the two components together (Fig. 27.3b). The force is maintained until the interface solidifies. Note the formation of a flash due to the upsetting of the joined ends of the two components. (See also Fig. 28.3.)

27.3 ARC-WELDING PROCESSES: CONSUMABLE-ELECTRODE

In *arc welding,* developed in the mid-1800s, the heat required is obtained from electrical energy. The process involves either a *consumable* or a *nonconsumable electrode* (rod or wire). An arc is produced between the tip of the electrode and the workpiece to be welded, by the use of an AC or a DC power supply. This arc produces temperatures of about 30,000 °C (54,000 °F), much higher than those developed in oxyfuel gas welding. The "arc welding" category includes several welding processes, as described below.

27.3.1 Shielded Metal-Arc Welding

Shielded metal-arc welding (SMAW) is one of the oldest, simplest, and most versatile joining processes. About 50% of all industrial and maintenance welding is currently performed by this process. The electric arc is generated by touching the tip of a coated electrode against the workpiece and then withdrawing it quickly to a distance sufficient to maintain the arc (Fig. 27.4). The electrodes are in the shape of a thin, long stick, so this process is also known as **stick welding**. (See Section 27.4.)

The heat generated melts a portion of the tip of the electrode, of its coating, and of the base metal in the immediate area of the arc. A weld forms after the molten metal, a mixture of the base metal (workpiece), the electrode metal, and substances from the coating on the electrode, solidifies in the weld area. The electrode coating deoxidizes the weld area and provides a shielding gas to protect it from oxygen in the environment.

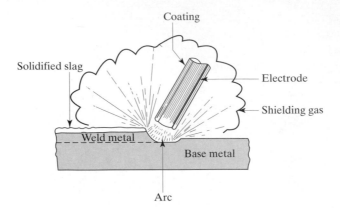

FIGURE 27.4   Schematic illustration of the shielded metal-arc welding process. About 50% of all large-scale industrial welding operations use this process.

A bare section at the end of the electrode is clamped to one terminal of the power source, while the other terminal is connected to the workpiece being welded (Fig. 27.5). The current usually ranges between 50 A and 300 A; power requirements are generally less than 10 kW. The current may be DC or AC. For sheet-metal welding, DC is preferred because of the steady arc it produces.

The *polarity* of the DC current, that is, the direction of current flow, can be important; its selection depends on such factors as type of electrode, the metals to be welded, and the depth of the heated zone. In **straight polarity**, the workpiece is positive and the electrode negative; it is preferred for sheet metals, because it produces shallow penetration, and for joints with very wide gaps. In **reverse polarity**, the electrode is positive, and deeper weld penetration is possible. In the AC method, the arc pulsates rapidly; this method is suitable for welding thick sections and for using large-diameter electrodes at maximum currents.

Process Capabilities.   The SMAW process has the advantages of being relatively simple and versatile and of requiring a smaller variety of electrodes. The equipment consists of a power supply, power cables, and an electrode holder, and the total cost of the equipment is typically below $1500. The use of safety equipment, similar to that used with oxyfuel gas welding, is essential.

The SMAW process is commonly used in general construction, in shipbuilding, on pipelines, and for maintenance work, because the equipment is portable and can be easily maintained. It is especially useful for work in remote areas, where a portable fuel-powered

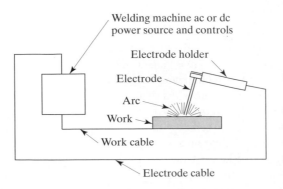

FIGURE 27.5   Schematic illustration of the shielded metal-arc welding operation (also known as stick welding, because the electrode is in the shape of a stick).

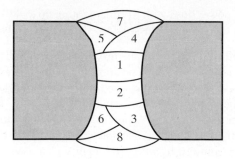

FIGURE 27.6   A deep weld showing the buildup sequence of individual weld beads.

generator can be used as the power supply. The process is best suited for workpiece thicknesses of 3 mm-19 mm (0.12 in.-0.75 in.), although this range can be easily extended by skilled operators using multiple-pass techniques (Fig. 27.6).

The multiple-pass process requires that the slag be cleaned after each weld bead. Unless removed completely, the solidified slag can cause severe corrosion of the weld area and lead to failure of the weld. Slag should be completely removed, such as by wire brushing, before another weld is applied for multiple-pass welding. As a result, both labor costs and material costs are high.

27.3.2 Submerged Arc Welding

In *submerged arc welding* (SAW), the weld arc is shielded by a *granular flux*, consisting of lime, silica, manganese oxide, calcium fluoride, and other compounds. The flux is fed into the weld zone by gravity flow through a nozzle (Fig. 27.7). The thick layer of flux completely covers the molten metal; it prevents spatter and sparks and suppresses the intense ultraviolet radiation and fumes characteristic of the SMAW process. The flux also acts as a thermal insulator, promoting deep penetration of heat into the workpiece.

The consumable electrode is a coil of bare round wire 1.5 mm–10 mm $\left(\frac{1}{16} \text{ in.-}\frac{3}{8} \text{ in.}\right)$ in diameter; it is fed automatically through a tube (**welding gun**). Electric currents typically range between 300 A and 2000 A. The power supplies are usually connected to standard

FIGURE 27.7   Schematic illustration of the submerged-arc welding process and equipment. The unfused flux is recovered and reused. *Source*: American Welding Society.

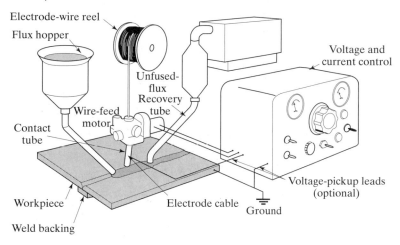

single- or three-phase power lines with a primary rating up to 440 V. The welder must wear gloves, but other than tinted safety glasses, face shields generally are not necessary.

Process Capabilities.   Because the flux is fed by gravity, the SAW process is largely limited to welds in a flat or horizontal position and having a backup piece. Circular welds can be made on pipes, provided that they are rotated during welding. As Fig. 27.7 shows, the unfused flux can be recovered, treated, and reused.

Developed in the 1940s, the SAW process can be automated for greater economy. It is used to weld a variety of carbon and alloy steel and stainless steel sheet or plate, often at speeds as high as 5 m/min (16 ft/min). The quality of the weld is very high, with good toughness, ductility, and uniformity of properties.

The SAW process provides very high welding productivity, depositing 4–10 times the amount of weld metal per hour as the SMAW process. Typical applications include thick plate welding for shipbuilding and for pressure vessels. Total cost for a welding system usually ranges from $2000 to $10,000, but it can be considerably higher for larger systems with multiple electrodes.

27.3.3 Gas Metal-Arc Welding

In *gas metal-arc welding* (GMAW), developed in the 1950s and formerly called *metal inert-gas* (MIG) *welding*, the weld area is shielded by an effectively inert atmosphere of argon, helium, carbon dioxide, or various other gas mixtures (Fig. 27.8). The consumable bare wire is fed automatically through a nozzle into the weld arc (Fig. 27.9).

As an addition to the use of inert shielding gases, deoxidizers are usually present in the electrode metal itself, in order to prevent oxidation of the molten weld puddle. Multiple weld layers can be deposited at the joint. Metal can be transferred by three methods in the GMAW process: the spray, the globular, and the short-circuiting.

In **spray transfer**, small droplets of molten metal from the electrode are transferred to the weld area at a rate of several hundred droplets per second. The transfer is spatter-free

FIGURE 27.8   Schematic illustration of the gas metal-arc welding process, formerly known as MIG (for metal inert gas) welding.

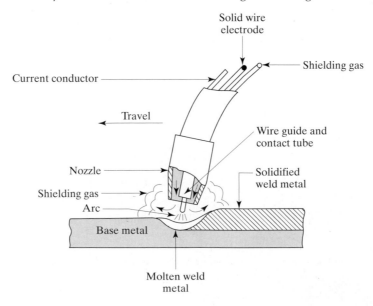

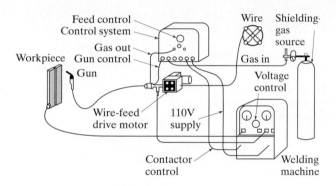

FIGURE 27.9   Basic equipment used in gas metal-arc welding operations. *Source*: American Welding Society.

and very stable. High DC current and voltages and large-diameter electrodes are used, with argon or an argon-rich gas mixture used as the shielding gas. The average current required in this process can be reduced by the use of a **pulsed arc**, which superimposes high-amplitude pulses onto a low, steady current, and the process can be used in all welding positions.

In **globular transfer**, carbon-dioxide-rich gases are utilized, and globules propelled by the forces of the electric arc transfer the metal, with considerable spatter. High welding currents are used; they make possible greater weld penetration and welding speed than are achieved in spray transfer. Heavier sections are commonly joined by this method.

In **short-circuiting**, the metal is transferred in individual droplets, more than 50 per second, as the electrode tip touches the molten weld metal and short-circuits. Low currents and voltages are utilized, with carbon-dioxide-rich gases and with electrodes made of small-diameter wire. The power required is about 2 kW.

The temperatures generated are relatively low; consequently, this method is suitable only for thin sheets and sections (less than 6 mm; 0.25 in.), otherwise incomplete fusion may occur. This process is easy to use, and it is very popular for welding ferrous metals in thin sections. Pulsed-arc systems, however, are gaining in usage for thin ferrous and nonferrous metals.

Process Capabilities.   The GMAW process is suitable for welding a variety of ferrous and nonferrous metals and is used extensively in the metal-fabrication industry. Because of the relatively simple nature of the process, the training of operators is easy. The process is versatile, rapid, and economical, and welding productivity is double that of the SMAW process. The GMAW process can easily be automated and lends itself readily to robotics and to flexible manufacturing systems (Chapters 38 and 39). The cost of the equipment usually ranges from $1000 to $3000.

27.3.4 Flux-Cored Arc Welding

The *flux-cored arc welding* (FCAW) process (Fig. 27.10) is similar to gas metal-arc welding, with the exception that the electrode is tubular in shape and is filled with flux (hence the term "flux-cored"). Cored electrodes produce a more stable arc, improve weld contour, and produce better mechanical properties of the weld metal.

The flux in these electrodes is much more flexible than the brittle coating used on SMAW electrodes, so the tubular electrode can be provided in long coiled lengths. The electrodes are usually 0.5 mm-4 mm (0.020 in.-0.15 in.) in diameter, and the power required is about 20 kW.

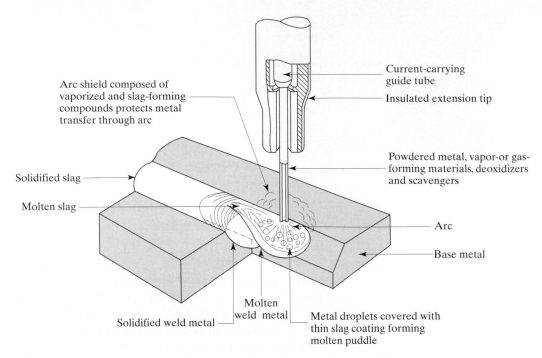

FIGURE 27.10   Schematic illustration of the flux-cored arc-welding process. This operation is similar to gas metal-arc welding, shown in Fig. 27.8.

Self-shielded cored electrodes are also available. These electrodes do not require external gas shielding, because they contain emissive fluxes that shield the weld area against the surrounding atmosphere. Advances in the manufacture of electrodes for FCAW and in the chemistry of the flux have made this process the fastest growing in welding.

Small-diameter electrodes have made the welding of thinner materials not only possible but often preferable. Also, small-diameter electrodes make it relatively easy to weld parts in different positions, and the flux chemistry permits the welding of many metals.

Process Capabilities.   The flux-cored arc-welding process combines the versatility of SMAW with the continuous and automatic electrode-feeding feature of GMAW. It is economical and versatile, so it is used for welding a variety of joints, mainly on steels, stainless steels, and nickel alloys. The higher weld-metal-deposition rate of the FCAW process compared with that of GMAW has led to its use in the joining of sections of all thicknesses. Recent development of *tubular electrodes* with very small diameters has extended the use of this process to workpieces of smaller section size.

A major advantage of FCAW is the ease with which specific weld-metal chemistries can be developed. By adding alloying elements to the flux core, virtually any alloy composition can be developed. This process is easy to automate and is readily adaptable to flexible manufacturing systems and robotics. The cost of equipment is generally in the range of $1000 to $3000.

27.3.5 Electrogas Welding

Electrogas welding (EGW) is used primarily for welding the edges of sections vertically in one pass, with the pieces placed edge to edge (butt joint). It is classified as a *machine-welding process*, because it requires special equipment (Fig. 27.11). The weld metal is

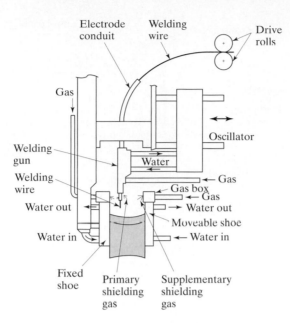

FIGURE 27.11　Schematic illustration of the electrogas welding process. *Source*: American Welding Society.

deposited into a weld cavity between the two pieces to be joined. The space is enclosed by two water-cooled copper dams (*shoes*) to prevent the molten slag from running off. Mechanical drives move the shoes upward. Circumferential welds, such as on pipes, are also possible, with the workpiece rotating.

Single or multiple electrodes are fed through a conduit, and a continuous arc is maintained, using flux-cored electrodes at up to 750 A, or solid electrodes at 400 A. Power requirements are about 20 kW. Shielding is done by means of an inert gas, such as carbon dioxide, argon, or helium, depending on the type of material being welded. The gas may be provided from an external source, or it may be produced from a flux-cored electrode, or from both.

Process Capabilities.　The equipment for electrogas welding is reliable, and training operators is relatively simple. Weld thickness ranges from 12 mm to 75 mm (0.5 in. to 3 in.) on steels, titanium, and aluminum alloys. Typical applications are in the construction of bridges, pressure vessels, thick-walled and large-diameter pipes, storage tanks, and ships. The cost of machines typically ranges from $15,000 to $25,000, although portable machines with less power cost as little as $5000.

27.3.6　Electroslag Welding

Developed in the 1950s, *electroslag welding* (ESW) and its applications are similar to electrogas welding (Fig. 27.12). The main difference is that the arc is started between the electrode tip and the bottom of the part to be welded. Flux is added and then is melted by the heat of the arc. After the molten slag reaches the tip of the electrode, the arc is extinguished. Heat is then produced continuously by the electrical resistance of the molten slag.

Because the arc is extinguished, ESW is not strictly an arc-welding process. Single or multiple solid as well as flux-cored electrodes may be used. The guide may be nonconsumable (conventional method) or consumable.

Process Capabilities.　Electroslag welding is capable of welding plates with thicknesses ranging from 50 mm to more than 900 mm (2 in.-36 in.). Welding is done in one

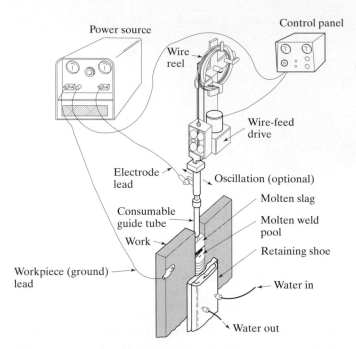

FIGURE 27.12   Equipment used for electroslag welding operations. *Source*: American Welding Society.

pass. The current required is about 600 A at 40 V-50 V, although higher currents are used for thick plates. Travel speed of the weld is in the range of 12 to 36 mm/min (0.5 to 1.5 in./min). Weld quality is good, and the process is used for heavy structural steel sections, such as heavy machinery and nuclear-reactor vessels. The cost of a typical ESW system ranges from $15,000 to $25,000—higher for multiple-electrode units.

27.4 ELECTRODES

Electrodes for the consumable arc-welding processes described are classified according to the strength of the deposited weld metal, the current (AC or ±DC), and the type of coating. Electrodes are identified by numbers and letters (Table 27.2), or by color code, particularly if they are too small to imprint with identification. Typical coated electrode dimensions are 150 to 460 mm (6 to 18 in.) in length and 1.5 to 8 mm $\left(\frac{1}{16} \text{ to } \frac{5}{16} \text{ in.}\right)$ in diameter. As the thickness of the sections to be welded decreases, the required current and electrode diameter also decrease.

Specifications for electrodes and for filler metals, including dimensional tolerances, quality control procedures, and processes, are stated by the American Welding Society (AWS) and the American National Standards Institute (ANSI); some appear in the Aerospace Materials Specifications (AMS) by the Society of Automotive Engineers (SAE).

Among other requirements, the specifications state that (a) the wire diameter must not vary more than 0.05 mm (0.002 in.) from nominal size, and (b) the coatings must be concentric with the wire. Electrodes are sold by weight and are available in a wide variety of sizes and specifications. Selection and recommendations for electrodes for a particular metal and its application can be found in supplier literature and in the various handbooks and references listed at the end of this chapter.

TABLE 27.2   Designations for Mild Steel Coated Electrodes

The prefix "E" designates arc welding electrode.
The first two digits of four-digit numbers and the first three digits of five-digit numbers
indicate minimum tensile strength:

E60XX	60,000 psi minimum tensile strength
E70XX	70,000 psi minimum tensile strength
E110XX	110,000 psi minimum tensile strength

The next-to-last digit indicates position:

EXX1X	All positions
EXX2X	Flat position and horizontal fillets

The last two digits together indicate the type of covering and the current to be used.
The suffix (Example: EXXXX-A1) indicates the approximate alloy in the weld deposit:

—A1	0.5% Mo
—B1	0.5% Cr, 0.5% Mo
—B2	1.25% Cr, 0.5% Mo
—B3	2.25% Cr, 1% Mo
—B4	2% Cr, 0.5% Mo
—B5	0.5% Cr, 1% Mo
—C1	2.5% Ni
—C2	3.25% Ni
—C3	1% Ni, 0.35% Mo, 0.15% Cr
—D1 and D2	0.25–0.45% Mo, 1.75% Mn
—G	0.5% min. Ni, 0.3% min. Cr, 0.2% min. Mo, 0.1% min. V, 1% min. Mn (only one element required)

Electrode Coatings.   Electrodes are *coated* with claylike materials that include silicate binders and powdered materials such as oxides, carbonates, fluorides, metal alloys, and cellulose (cotton cellulose and wood flour). The coating, which is brittle and participates in complex interactions during welding, has the following basic functions:

a. to stabilize the arc;

b. to generate gases to act as a shield against the surrounding atmosphere—the gases produced are carbon dioxide and water vapor (and carbon monoxide and hydrogen in small amounts);

c. to control the rate at which the electrode melts;

d. to act as a flux to (1) protect the weld against formation of oxides, nitrides, and other inclusions, and (2) with the resulting slag, protect the molten weld pool;

e. to add alloying elements to the weld zone to enhance the properties of the joint—among them, deoxidizers, to prevent the weld from becoming brittle.

The deposited electrode coating or slag must be removed after each pass in order to ensure a good weld. A wire brush (manual or power) can be used for this purpose. Bare electrodes and wire, made of stainless steels and aluminum alloys, are also available. They are used as filler metals in various welding operations.

27.5 ARC-WELDING PROCESSES: NONCONSUMABLE-ELECTRODE

Unlike the arc-welding processes that use consumable electrodes, which were described in Section 27.3, nonconsumable-electrode processes typically use a **tungsten electrode**. As one pole of the arc, it generates the heat required for welding. A shielding gas is supplied from an external source. Described below are the advantages, the limitations, and some typical applications of these processes.

27.5.1 Gas Tungsten-Arc Welding

In *gas tungsten-arc welding* (GTAW), formerly known as *TIG welding* (for "tungsten inert gas"), the filler metal is supplied from a **filler wire** (Fig. 27.13). Because the tungsten electrode is not consumed in this operation, a constant and stable *arc gap* is maintained at a constant current level. The filler metals are similar to the metals to be welded, and flux is not used. The shielding gas is usually argon or helium (or a mixture of the two). Welding with GTAW may be done without filler metals—for example, in the welding of close-fit joints.

Depending on the metals to be welded, the power supply is either DC at 200 A, or AC at 500 A (Fig. 27.14). In general, AC is preferred for aluminum and magnesium, because the cleaning action of AC removes oxides and improves weld quality. Thorium or zirconium may be used in the tungsten electrodes, to improve their electron emission characteristics. Power requirements range from 8 kW to 20 kW.

Contamination of the tungsten electrode by the molten metal can be a significant problem, particularly in critical applications, because it can cause discontinuities in the weld. Contact of the electrode with the molten metal pool should, therefore, be avoided.

Process Capabilities.   The GTAW process is used for a wide variety of metals and applications, particularly aluminum, magnesium, titanium, and the refractory metals. It is

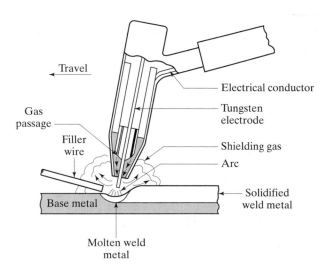

FIGURE 27.13   The gas tungsten-arc welding process, formerly known as TIG (for tungsten inert gas) welding.

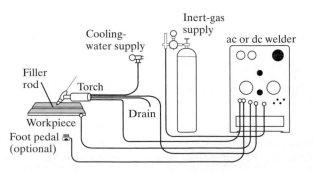

FIGURE 27.14   Equipment for gas tungsten-arc welding operations. *Source*: American Welding Society.

especially suitable for thin metals. The cost of the inert gas makes this process more expensive than SMAW but provides welds with very high quality and surface finish. It is used in a variety of critical applications, with a wide range of workpiece thicknesses and shapes. The equipment is portable, and typically costs from $1000 to $5000.

27.5.2 Atomic Hydrogen Welding

Atomic hydrogen welding (AHW) uses an arc in a shielding atmosphere of hydrogen. The arc is between two tungsten or carbon electrodes. Thus the workpiece is not part of the electrical circuit, as it is in GTAW. The hydrogen gas also cools the electrodes.

27.5.3 Plasma-Arc Welding

In *plasma-arc welding* (PAW), developed in the 1960s, a concentrated plasma arc is produced and is aimed at the weld area. The arc is stable and reaches temperatures as high as 33,000 °C (60,000 °F). A **plasma** is ionized hot gas, composed of nearly equal numbers of electrons and ions. The plasma is initiated between the tungsten electrode and the orifice by a low-current pilot arc.

Unlike other processes, the plasma arc is concentrated, because it is forced through a relatively small orifice. Operating currents are usually below 100 A, but they can be higher for special applications. When a filler metal is used, it is fed into the arc, as is done in GTAW. Arc and weld-zone shielding is supplied by means of an outer shielding ring and the use of gases, such as argon, helium, or mixtures.

There are two methods of plasma-arc welding. In the **transferred-arc** method (Fig. 27.15a), the workpiece being welded is part of the electrical circuit. The arc transfers from the electrode to the workpiece (hence, the term "transferred"). In the **nontransferred** method (Fig. 27.15b), the arc occurs between the electrode and the nozzle, and the heat is carried to the workpiece by the plasma gas. This thermal transfer mechanism is similar to that for oxyfuel flame (see Section 27.2).

Process Capabilities. Compared to other arc-welding processes, plasma-arc welding has higher energy concentration (and so permits deeper and narrower welds), better arc stability, less thermal distortion, and higher welding speeds, from 120 to 1000 mm/min (5 to 40 in./min). A variety of metals can be welded, with part thicknesses generally less than 6 mm (0.25 in.).

FIGURE 27.15   Two types of plasma-arc welding processes: (a) transferred, (b) nontransferred. Deep and narrow welds can be made by this process at high welding speeds.

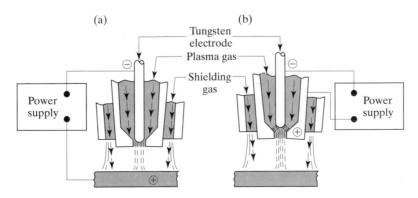

The high heat concentration can penetrate completely through the joint (**keyhole** technique), with thicknesses as much as 20 mm (0.75 in.) for some titanium and aluminum alloys. In the keyhole technique, the force of the plasma arc displaces the molten metal and produces a hole at the leading edge of the weld pool.

Plasma-arc welding, rather than the GTAW process, is often used for butt and lap joints, because of its higher energy concentration, better arc stability, and higher welding speeds. Proper training and skill are essential for operators who use this equipment. Safety considerations include protection against glare, spatter, and noise from the plasma arc. Equipment costs are typically in the range of $3000–$6000.

27.6 THERMIT WELDING

Thermit welding (TW) gets its name from the compounds named *thermite*, a name based on the word *therm*, meaning heat; the word *Thermit* is a registered trademark. The process involves exothermic (heat producing) reactions between metal oxides and metallic reducing agents. The heat of the reaction is then utilized in welding. This process dates back to the early 1900s.

The most common mixture of materials used in welding steel and cast iron is finely divided particles of iron oxide (Fe_3O_4), aluminum oxide (Al_2O_3), iron, and aluminum. This nonexplosive mixture produces a maximum theoretical temperature of from 3200 °C (5800 °F) in less than a minute; in practice, however, it reaches only about from 2200 to 2400 °C (4000 to 4350 °F).

The mixture may also contain other materials, to impart special properties to the weld. The reaction is started by applying a magnesium fuse to special compounds of peroxides, chlorates, or chromates, known as oxidizing agents, at an ignition temperature of about 1200 °C (2200 °F).

Thermit welding involves aligning the parts to be joined, but with a gap between them (usually filled with wax), around which a sand or ceramic mold is built. If the parts are thick, the mold cavity may be preheated to improve welding and to dry the mold. Drying the mold is very important; otherwise, superheated steam trapped in the mold can cause explosions. The superheated products of the reaction are allowed to flow into the gap, melting the edges of the parts being joined. Thermit welding is suitable for welding and repairing large forgings and castings, and can also be used to weld thick steel structural sections, railroad rails, and pipe.

27.7 ELECTRON-BEAM WELDING

In *electron-beam welding* (EBW), developed in the 1960s, heat is generated by high-velocity narrow-beam electrons. The kinetic energy of the electrons is converted into heat as they strike the workpiece. This process requires special equipment to focus the beam on the workpiece *in a vacuum*; the higher the vacuum , the more the beam penetrates and the greater the depth-to-width ratio.

Almost any metal can be welded by EBW, and workpiece thicknesses can range from foil to plate. The intense energy is also capable of producing holes in the workpiece (**keyhole**; Section 27.5.3). Generally, no shielding gas, flux, or filler metal is required. Capacities of electron beam guns range up to 100 kW.

Process Capabilities.   The EBW process has the capability of making high-quality welds that are almost parallel-sided, are deep and narrow, and have small heat-affected zones (see Section 29.2). Depth-to-width ratios range between 10 and 30. The sizes of welds made by EBW are much smaller than those of welds made by conventional processes. Using servo controls, parameters can be accurately controlled, and at welding speeds as high as 12 m/min (40 ft/min).

Almost any metal can be butt- or lap-welded with this process, at thicknesses up to 150 mm (6 in.). Distortion and shrinkage in the weld area is minimal. Weld quality is good and of very high purity. Typical applications include the welding of aircraft, missile, nuclear, and electronic components and of gears and shafts for the automotive industry.

Electron-beam welding equipment generates x-rays; hence, proper monitoring and periodic maintenance are essential. Depending on capacity, the cost of equipment ranges from about $75,000 to over $1 million.

27.8 LASER-BEAM WELDING

Laser-beam welding (LBW) utilizes a high-power laser beam as the source of heat, to produce a fusion weld. (See Fig. 26.14, Table 26.1, and Section 26.7.) Because the beam can be focused onto a very small area, it has high energy density and, therefore, deep-penetrating capability.

The beam can be directed, shaped, and focused precisely on the workpiece. Consequently, this process is particularly suitable for welding deep and narrow joints (Fig. 27.16), with depth-to-width ratios typically ranging from 4 to 10.

In the automotive industry, welding of transmission components is the most widespread application. Among numerous other applications is the welding of thin parts for electronic components.

The laser beam may be **pulsed** (in milliseconds) for applications such as spot welding of thin materials, with power levels up to 100 kW. **Continuous** multi-kW laser systems are used for deep welds on thick sections.

Process Capabilities.   Laser-beam welding produces welds of good quality, with minimum shrinkage and distortion. Laser welds have good strength and are generally ductile and free of porosity. The process can be automated so as to be used on a variety of materials with thicknesses of up to 25 mm (1 in.); it is particularly effective on thin workpieces.

FIGURE 27.16   Comparison of the size of weld beads in (a) electron-beam or laser-beam welding to that in (b) conventional (tungsten-arc) welding. *Source*: American Welding Society, *Welding Handbook* (8th ed.), 1991.

(a) 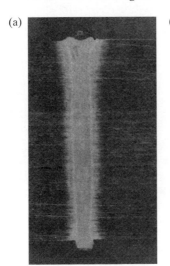 (b)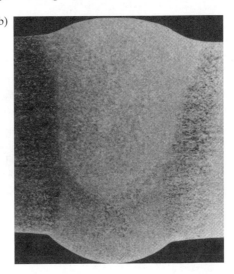

Typical metals and alloys welded include aluminum, titanium, ferrous metals, copper, superalloys, and the refractory metals. Welding speeds range from 2.5 m/min (8 ft/min) to as high as 80 m/min (250 ft/min) for thin metals.

Because of the nature of the process, the welding can be done in otherwise inaccessible locations. Safety is particularly important in laser-beam welding, because of the extreme hazards to the eye as well as the skin; solid-state (YAG) lasers are particularly dangerous.

The major advantages of LBW over EBW are the following:

a. A vacuum is not required, and so the beam can be transmitted through air.

b. Laser beams can be shaped, manipulated, and focused optically (using fiber optics), so the process can easily be automated.

c. The beams do not generate x-rays (as opposed to EBW).

d. The quality of the weld is better, with less tendency for incomplete fusion, spatter, and porosity and with less distortion.

As in other, similar automated welding systems, the operator skill required is minimal. The cost of equipment for LBW usually ranges from $40,000 to about $1 million.

Example: Laser Welding of Razor Blades

A closeup of the Gillette Sensor razor cartridge is shown in Fig. 27.17. Each of the two narrow, high-strength blades has 13 pinpoint welds, 11 of which can be seen (as darker spots, about 0.5 mm in diameter) on each blade in the photograph. You can inspect the welds on actual blades with a magnifying glass or a microscope.

The welds are made with a Nd:YAG laser equipped with fiber-optic delivery. This equipment provides very flexible beam manipulation and can target exact locations along the length of the blade. With a set of these machines, production is at a rate of 3 million welds per hour, with accurate and consistent weld quality. *Source*: Courtesy of Lumonics Corporation, Industrial Products Division.

FIGURE 27.17

27.9 CUTTING

In addition to mechanical means, a piece of material can be separated into two or more pieces or into various contours by the use of a heat source that melts and removes a narrow zone in the workpiece. The sources of heat can be torches, electric arcs, or lasers.

27.9.1 Oxyfuel Gas Cutting

Oxyfuel gas cutting (OFC) is similar to oxyfuel welding, but the heat source is now used to remove a narrow zone from a metal plate or sheet (Fig. 27.18a). This process is particularly suitable for steels.

The basic reactions with steel are

$$Fe + O \rightarrow FeO + heat, \qquad (27.3)$$

$$3Fe + 2O_2 \rightarrow Fe_3O_4 + heat, \qquad (27.4)$$

and

$$4Fe + 3O_2 \rightarrow 2Fe_2O_3 + heat. \qquad (27.5)$$

The greatest heat is generated by the second reaction, and it can produce a temperature rise to about 870 °C (1600 °F). However, this temperature is not sufficiently high to cut steels, so the workpiece is *preheated* with fuel gas, and oxygen is introduced later (see nozzle cross-section in Fig. 27.18a). The higher the carbon content of the steel is, the higher the preheating temperature must be.

Cutting occurs mainly by the oxidation (burning) of the steel; some melting also takes place. Cast irons and steel castings can also be cut by this method. The process generates a **kerf**, similar to that produced by sawing with a saw blade (Section 23.6) or wire EDM (see Fig. 26.13).

Process Capabilities. The maximum thickness that can be cut by OFC depends mainly on the gases used. With oxyacetylene gas, the maximum thickness is about 300 to 350 mm (12 to 14 in.); with oxyhydrogen, about 600 mm (24 in.). Kerf widths range from about 1.5 mm to 10 mm (0.06 to 0.4 in.), with reasonably good control of tolerances. The flame leaves **drag lines** on the cut surface (Fig. 27.18b), which ends up rougher than sur-

FIGURE 27.18   (a) Flame cutting of steel plate with an oxyacetylene torch, and a cross-section of the torch nozzle. (b) Cross-section of a flame-cut plate showing drag lines.

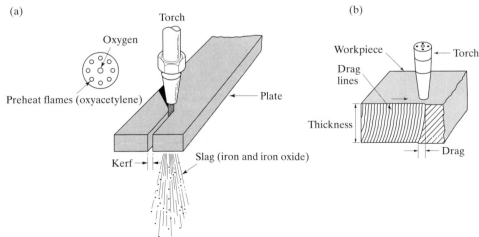

faces produced by sawing, by blanking, or by other operations using mechanical cutting tools. Distortion caused by uneven temperature distribution can be a problem in OFC.

Although long used for salvage and repair work, oxyfuel gas cutting can be used in manufacturing. Torches may be guided along various paths manually, mechanically, or by automatic machines using programmable controllers and robots. *Underwater cutting* is done with specially designed torches that produce a blanket of compressed air between the flame and the surrounding water.

27.9.2 Arc Cutting

Arc-cutting processes are based on the same principles as arc-welding processes. A variety of materials can be cut at high speeds by arc cutting. As in welding, arc-cutting processes also leave a heat-affected zone which needs to be taken into account, particularly in critical applications.

In **air carbon-arc cutting** (CAC-A), a carbon electrode is used, and the molten metal is blown away by a high-velocity air jet. Thus the metal being cut doesn't have to oxidize. This process is used especially for gouging and scarfing (removal of metal from a surface). However, the process is noisy, and the molten metal can be blown substantial distances and so cause safety hazards.

Plasma-arc cutting (PAC) produces the highest temperatures. It is used for rapid cutting of nonferrous and stainless-steel plates. The cutting productivity of this process is higher than that of oxyfuel gas methods. It produces good surface finish and narrow kerfs, and it is the most popular cutting process utilizing programmable controllers that is employed in manufacturing today.

Lasers and **electron beams** are used for very accurately cutting a wide variety of metals, as was described in Sections 26.7 and 26.8. Surface finish is better than that from other thermal cutting processes, and the kerf is narrower. Proper safety precautions are important.

27.10 WELDING SAFETY

There are certain hazards in welding and cutting, (as there are in all manufacturing operations). Although safety considerations are mentioned throughout Chapters 27 and 28, this section summarizes the major hazards that are present where welding is done and the safe welding practices used to counteract them. Some of the hazards are related to the machinery and equipment involved; others are related to the welding processes themselves. (See also Section 37.3.)

Surroundings.   Because of the heat sources, such as open flames, arcs, sparks, and hot metal, used in welding and related operations, fire and explosion hazards are always present in the work area. Thus, welding processes should be carried out away from all combustible materials, including flammable fluids, vapors, gases, fuel, wood, and textiles. Floors, partitions, platforms, and ceilings may also have been made of flammable materials and thus may present potential safety hazards.

Personal Danger.   Fires and explosions can cause serious injury and even fatality. Protection of the operator's eyes, face, and body against sparks, spatter, and infrared and ultraviolet radiation is essential. Several types of safety equipment and protective clothing are available; they should be used.

Noise and Shock.   Excessive and prolonged noise generated by welding or cutting operations can cause temporary or permanent hearing loss. Ear protection devices should be used. Welding and related methods and machinery that use electricity as a source of energy also present hazards. Proper installation and maintenance of equipment and training of personnel are essential.

Fumes.   Various shielding gases are used during welding operations; many other welding processes emit fumes and gases. Some of these gases are toxic and can be hazardous to health. Consequently, *environmental issues* are involved in the use of welding processes. Some important factors to be considered follow: the nature of the fumes and the gases evolved during welding; the proper disposal of used electrodes, fluxes, and slag; and the proper handling and disposal of some of the highly toxic chemicals used in surface preparation prior to welding.

SUMMARY

- Oxyfuel gas, arc, and high-energy-beam welding are among the most commonly used joining operations. Gas welding uses chemical energy; to supply the necessary heat, arc and high-energy-beam welding use electrical energy instead.
- In all these processes, heat is used to bring the joint being welded to a liquid state. Shielding gases are used to protect the molten weld pool and the weld area against oxidation. Filler rods may or may not be used in oxyfuel gas and arc welding to fill the weld area.
- The selection of a welding process for a particular operation depends on the workpiece material, on its thickness and size, on its shape complexity, on the type of joint, on the strength required, and on the change in product appearance caused by welding.
- A variety of welding equipment is available, much of which is now computer controlled with programmable features.
- The cutting of metals also can be done by processes, the principles of which are based on oxyfuel gas and arc welding. The cutting of steels occurs mainly through oxidation (burning). The highest temperatures for cutting are obtained by plasma-arc cutting.

TRENDS

- A major trend in welding is the automatation of welding processes, done in order to control process variables accurately and repeatedly and to reduce the need for skilled labor.
- Computer controls and programmable robots are being used extensively for many welding operations. These developments are being further enhanced by the use of appropriate sensors (particularly infrared) to track the weld joint. They monitor the conditions during welding and, with feedback controls, make the adjustments necessary to maintain weld quality and integrity.
- The flux-cored arc-welding process has advanced far beyond gas metal-arc welding in replacing shielded-metal-arc welding.
- Pulsed-arc gas metal-arc welding is gaining wide usage for thin ferrous and nonferrous metals.
- Laser-beam welding of flat sheet metal for automotive bodies (butt welding), prior to stamping, is now in production.
- The thickness capability of laser-beam welding is being increased by the use of filler metals; this practice extends its applications to heavy steel fabrication, pipelines, shipbuilding, and nuclear reactor components.

KEY TERMS

Arc cutting

Arc welding

Atomic-hydrogen welding

Carburizing flame

Coated electrode

Consumable electrode

Drag lines

Electrode

Electrogas welding

Electron-beam welding

Electroslag welding

Filler metal

Flux

Flux-cored arc welding

Fusion welding

Gas metal-arc welding

Gas tungsten-arc welding

Joining

Kerf

Keyhole technique

Laser-beam welding

Neutral flame

Nonconsumable electrode

Oxidizing flame

Oxyfuel gas cutting

Oxyfuel gas welding

Plasma-arc welding

Polarity

Reducing flame

Shielded metal-arc welding

Slag

Stick welding

Submerged arc welding

Thermit welding

Welding gun

Welding torch

BIBLIOGRAPHY

ASM Handbook, Vol. 6: *Welding, Brazing, and Soldering.* ASM International, 1993.

Bowditch, W.A., and K.E. Bowditch, *Welding Technology Fundamentals.* Goodheart–Willcox, 1997.

Cary, H.B., *Modern Welding Technology* (4th ed.). Prentice Hall, 1997.

Davies, A.C., *The Science and Practice of Welding* (10th ed.), 2 vols. Cambridge University Press, 1993.

Galyen, J., G. Sear, and C. Tuttle, *Welding: Fundamentals and Procedures.* Wiley, 1984.

Jeffus, L.F., *Welding: Principles and Applications* (4th ed.). Delmar Publishers, 1997.

Jellison, R., *Welding Fundamentals.* Prentice Hall, 1995.

Messler, R.W., Jr., *Joining of Advanced Materials.* Butterworth-Heinemann, 1993.

———, *Gas Tungsten Arc Welding Handbook*, 1995.

———, *Flux Cored Arc Welding Handbook*, 1998.

Minnick, W.H., *Gas Metal Arc Welding Handbook.* Goodheart–Willcox, 1999.

Powell, J., *CO_2 Laser Cutting.* Springer, 1992.

Steen, W.M., *Laser Material Processing* (2d ed.), Springer, 1998.

Tool and Manufacturing Engineers Handbook, Vol. 4: *Quality Control and Assembly.* Society of Manufacturing Engineers, 1986.

Welding Handbook (8th ed.), 3 vols. American Welding Society, 1987.

REVIEW QUESTIONS

27.1 Explain fusion as it relates to welding operations.

27.2 Describe the reactions that take place in an oxyfuel gas torch. What is the level of temperatures generated?

27.3 Explain the features of neutral, reducing, and oxidizing flames. Why is a reducing flame so called?

27.4 Why is an oxidizing flame desirable in welding copper alloys?

27.5 Describe the procedure to be followed in an oxyfuel gas welding operation.

27.6 Explain the basic principles of arc-welding processes.

27.7 Why is shielded metal-arc welding a commonly used process? Why is it also called stick welding?

27.8 Why is the quality of submerged arc welding very good?

27.9 Describe the features of three types of arcs in gas metal-arc welding. Why has it been called MIG welding?

27.10 Describe the functions and characteristics of electrodes. What functions do coatings have? How are electrodes classified?

27.11 What are the similarities and differences between consumable and nonconsumable electrodes?

27.12 Explain how cutting takes place when an oxyfuel gas torch is used. How is underwater cutting done?

27.13 What is the purpose of flux?

27.14 Why is tungsten the preferred material for nonconsumable electrodes?

27.15 What is thermit welding?

27.16 What is the advantage of electron-beam and laser-beam welding, as compared to arc welding?

27.17 Which of the processes described in this chapter are portable?

27.18 Why is flux not needed in gas tungsten-arc welding?

QUALITATIVE PROBLEMS

27.19 Explain why so many different welding processes have been developed.

27.20 What is the effect of the thermal conductivity of the workpiece on kerf width in oxyfuel-gas cutting?

27.21 Describe the differences between oxyfuel-gas cutting of ferrous and of nonferrous alloys.

27.22 Could you use oxyfuel-gas cutting for a stack of sheet metals (stack cutting; see Fig. 23.27e)? Explain.

27.23 Discuss the need and role of fixtures for the holding of workpieces in the welding operations described in this chapter.

27.24 Could plasma-arc cutting be used for nonmetallic materials? If so, would you select a transferred or a nontransferred type of arc? Explain.

27.25 What factors influence the size of the two weld beads in Fig. 27.16?

27.26 Describe your observations concerning the contents of Table 27.1.

27.27 How close would you hold an oxyacetylene flame to the surfaces to be welded? Explain.

27.28 Comment on your observations regarding Fig. 27.6.

27.29 What determines whether a certain welding process can be used for workpieces in horizontal, in vertical, or in upside down positions (or any)? Explain your answer, and give appropriate examples.

27.30 Explain the factors involved in electrode selection in arc-welding processes.

27.31 In Table 27.1, there is a column on the distortion of welded components, ordered from lowest distortion to highest. Explain why the degree of distortion varies between different welding processes.

27.32 In arc welding, there is obviously a great deal of electrical energy involved. Discuss the safety aspects in such an operation.

27.33 What are the workpiece material requirements for arc welding?

27.34 Why is oxyacetylene welding limited to rather thin sections?

27.35 Rank the processes in this chapter in terms of (a) cost, (b) weld quality.

27.36 What are the sources of weld spatter? How can spatter be controlled?

QUANTITATIVE PROBLEMS

27.37 A welding operation takes place on an aluminum alloy plate. A pipe 2.5 in. in diameter, with a 0.20-in. wall thickness and a 2-in. length, is butt-welded onto a section of 6 in. by 6 in. by 0.25 in. angle iron. The angle iron is of an L-shape and has a length of one foot. If the weld zone in a gas-tungsten arc welding process is approximately one-half inch wide, what would be the temperature increase of the entire structure due to the heat input from welding only? What if the process were an electron-beam welding operation with a bead width of 0.08 in.? Assume that the electrode requires 1500 J and the aluminum alloy requires 1200 J to melt one gram.

27.38 A welding operation will take place on carbon steel. The desired welding speed is around 1 in./s. If an arc-welding power supply is used with a voltage of 10 V, what current is needed if the weld width is to be 0.25 in.?

27.39 In oxyacetylene, arc, and laser-beam cutting, the process basically involves melting of the workpiece. If a 100-mm. diameter hole is to be cut from a 200-mm. diameter, 10-mm. thick plate, plot the mean temperature rise in the blank as a function of kerf. Assume that one-half of the energy goes into the blank.

SYNTHESIS AND DESIGN

27.40 Comment on workpiece size and shape limitations, if any, for each of the processes described in this chapter.

27.41 Make a summary table outlining the principles of the processes described in this chapter, together with examples of their applications.

27.42 Prepare a table of the processes described in this chapter, and give the range of welding speeds as a function of workpiece material and thicknesses.

27.43 Make a table comparing the quality of the cuts made by the processes described in this chapter to that of those made by other processes (described in Part IV).

27.44 Section 27.10 describes the general guidelines for safety in welding operations. For each of the operations described in this chapter, prepare a poster which effectively and concisely gives specific instructions for safe practices in welding (or cutting). Consult the references at the end of Chapter 37 and the various publications of the National Safety Council.

27.45 Hydrogen embrittlement of steels is a serious problem for structural components. Recognizing this, investigate the sources of argon and helium gases, and make a recommendation about which is preferable as a shielding gas for welding steels.

27.46 In the building of large ships, there is a need to weld large sections of steel together to form a hull. For this application, consider each of the welding operations discussed in this chapter, and list the benefits and drawbacks of that operation for this product. Which welding process would you select? Why?

27.47 Perform an Internet and/or literature search on the relative advantages of CO_2 and Nd : YAG lasers.

28

Solid-State Welding Processes

28.1   INTRODUCTION

This chapter describes processes in which joining takes place without fusion (melting) of the workpieces. Unlike in the fusion-welding processes described in Chapter 27, no liquid (molten) phase is present in the joint. The principle of **solid-state welding** is best demonstrated with the following example. If two clean surfaces are brought into atomic contact with each other under sufficient pressure (and in the absence of oxide films and other contaminants), they form bonds and produce a strong joint (see Section 31.2).

Applying external heat improves the bond by **diffusion**. Small interfacial movements on the contacting surfaces of the two pieces to be joined (the **faying surfaces**) disturb the surfaces, break up any oxide films, and generate new, clean surfaces; this mechanism improves the strength of the bond. Heat may be generated by *friction*, as well, an effect utilized in *friction welding*. Electric-resistance heating is utilized extensively in *resistance-welding* processes. In *explosion welding*, very high contact pressures are developed, to cause welding of the interface.

28.2   COLD WELDING

In *cold welding* (CW), pressure is applied to the workpieces, through either dies or rolls. Because of the **plastic deformation** involved, it is necessary that at least one, but preferably both, of the mating parts be ductile. Prior to welding, the interface is degreased, wire-

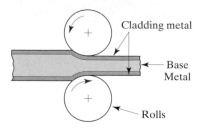

FIGURE 28.1   Schematic illustration of the roll bonding, or cladding, process.

brushed, and wiped to remove oxide smudge. Cold welding can be used to join small workpieces made of soft, ductile metals.

During the joining of two *dissimilar* metals that are mutually soluble, brittle *intermetallic compounds* may form (Section 4.2.2); these will produce a weak and brittle joint. An example occurs in the bonding of aluminum and steel, where a brittle intermetallic compound is formed at the interface. The best bond strength is obtained with two similar materials.

Roll Bonding.   The pressure required for cold welding can be applied through a pair of rolls (Fig. 28.1); hence, the process is called *roll bonding*. Developed in the 1960s, roll bonding is used for manufacturing some U.S. coins. (See the Example below.) The process can be carried out at elevated temperatures (*hot roll bonding*). Typical examples are the cladding of pure aluminum over aluminum-alloy sheet (Alclad) and of stainless steel over mild steel, for corrosion resistance.

Example: Roll Bonding of the U.S. Quarter

The technique used for manufacturing composite U.S. quarters is the roll bonding of two outer layers of 75% copper–25% nickel (cupronickel), each 1.2 mm (0.048 in.) thick, with an inner layer of pure copper 5.1 mm (0.20 in.) thick. To obtain good bond strength, the faying surfaces are chemically cleaned and wire-brushed. The strips are first rolled to a thickness of 2.29 mm (0.090 in.); a second rolling operation reduces the thickness to 1.36 mm (0.0535 in.). The strips thus undergo a total reduction in thickness of 82%.

Because volume constancy is maintained in plastic deformation, there is a major increase in the surface area between the layers, and it causes the generation of clean interfacial surfaces. This extension in surface area under the high pressure of the rolls, combined with the solid solubility of nickel in copper (see Section 4.2.1), produces a strong bond.

28.3 ULTRASONIC WELDING

In *ultrasonic welding* (USW), the faying surfaces of the two components are subjected to a static normal force and oscillating shearing (tangential) stresses. The shearing stresses are applied by the tip of a **transducer** (Fig. 28.2a), similar to that used for ultrasonic machining. (See Fig. 25.24a.) The frequency of oscillation is generally in the range of 10 kHz to 75 kHz, although an even lower or higher frequency can be employed. Proper coupling between the transducer and the tip (called a *sonotrode*, from the word *sonic*, by analogy with *electrode*) is important for efficient operation.

The shearing stresses cause plastic deformation at the interface of the two components, breaking up oxide films and contaminants and thus allowing good contact and producing a strong solid-state bond. The temperature generated in the weld zone is usually in the range from one-third to one-half of the melting point (absolute scale) of the metals joined; consequently, neither melting nor fusion takes place.

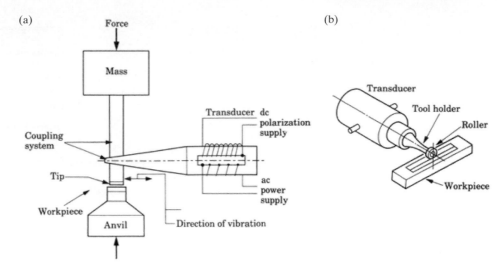

FIGURE 28.2   (a) Components of an ultrasonic welding machine for lap welds. The lateral vibrations of the tool tip cause plastic deformation and bonding at the interface of the workpieces. (b) Ultrasonic seam welding using a roller.

In certain situations, however, the temperature generated can be sufficiently high to cause metallurgical changes in the weld zone (see Section 29.2). The mechanism responsible for the joining of *thermoplastics* by ultrasonic welding is different from that for metals, and melting does take place at the interface, because plastics have much lower melting temperatures. (See Table 7.2.)

The ultrasonic welding process is versatile and reliable. It can be used with a wide variety of metallic and nonmetallic materials, including dissimilar metals (*bimetallic strips*). It is used extensively for the joining of plastics, in packaging with foils, and (in the automotive and consumer electronics industries) for the lap welding of sheet, foil, and thin wire. The welding tip can be replaced with *rotating disks* (Fig. 28.2b) for the seam-welding of structures in which one component is sheet or foil (a process similar *to resistance seam welding*, Section 28.5.2). Moderate skill is required to operate the equipment.

28.4 FRICTION WELDING

In the joining processes described thus far, the energy required for welding (typically, chemical, electrical, or ultrasonic) is supplied from external sources. In *friction welding* (FRW), the heat required for welding is generated through, as the name implies, *friction* at the interface of the two components being joined. You can demonstrate the significant rise in temperature caused by friction by rubbing your hands together or by sliding down a rope rapidly.

In friction welding, developed in the 1940s, one of the components remains stationary while the other is placed in a chuck or collet and rotated at a high constant speed. The two members to be joined are then brought into contact under an axial force (Fig. 28.3a). After sufficient contact is established, the rotating member is brought to a quick stop (so that the weld is not destroyed by shearing), while the axial force is increased. Oxides and other contaminants at the interface are removed by the radially outward movement of the hot metal at the interface (Fig. 28.3d).

The rotating member must be clamped securely to the chuck or collet, to resist both torque and axial forces without slipping. The pressure at the interface and the resulting friction produce sufficient heat for a strong joint to form.

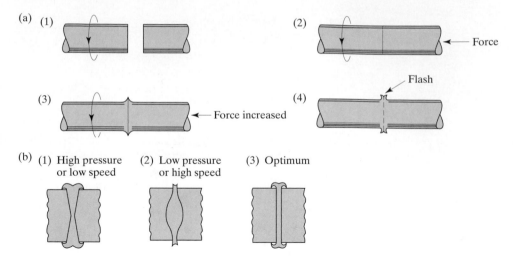

FIGURE 28.3   (a) Sequence of operations in the friction welding process: (1) Left-hand component is rotated at high speed. (2) Right-hand component is brought into contact under an axial force. (3) Axial force is increased; flash begins to form. (4) Left-hand component stops rotating; weld is completed. The flash can subsequently be removed by machining or grinding. (b) Shape of fusion zone in friction welding, as a function of the force applied and the rotational speed.

The weld zone is usually confined to a narrow region whose size depends on the following parameters:

1. the amount of heat generated;
2. the thermal conductivity of the materials; and
3. the mechanical properties of the materials at elevated temperatures.

The shape of the welded joint depends on the rotational speed and on the axial pressure applied (Fig. 28.4). These factors must be controlled to obtain a uniformly strong joint.

28.4.1 Process Capabilities

Friction welding can be used to join a wide variety of materials, provided that one of the components has some rotational symmetry. Solid or tubular parts can be joined by this method, with good joint strength. Solid steel bars up to 100 mm (4 in.) in diameter and pipes up to 250 mm (10 in.) in outside diameter have been welded successfully by this process.

The surface speed of the rotating member may be as high as 900 m/min (3000 ft/min). Because of the combined heat and pressure, the interface in FRW develops a flash by plastic deformation (upsetting) of the heated zone. This flash, if objectionable, can easily be removed by machining or grinding.

Friction welding machines are fully automated, and the operator skill required is minimal, if individual cycle times for the complete process are set properly. The cost is generally between $75,000 and $300,000, depending on size and capacity.

28.4.2 Inertia Friction Welding

Inertia friction welding is a modification of FRW, although the term has been used interchangeably with friction welding. The energy required for frictional heating in inertia friction welding is supplied by the kinetic energy of a flywheel. The flywheel is accelerated to the proper speed, the two members are brought into contact, and an axial force is applied. As friction

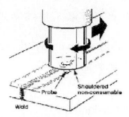

FIGURE 28.4   The principle of the friction stir welding process. Alluminum-alloy plates up to 75 mm (3 in.) thick have been welded by this process. *Source*: TWI, Cambridge, U.K.

at the interface slows the flywheel, the axial force is increased. The weld is completed when the flywheel has come to a stop. The timing of this sequence is important for good weld quality.

The rotating mass in inertia friction welding machines can be adjusted for applications requiring different levels of energy (these levels depend on workpiece size and properties). In one application of inertia friction welding, 10-mm- (0.4-in.)-diameter shafts are welded to automotive turbocharger impellers at a rate of one joint every 15 seconds.

28.4.3 Linear Friction Welding

In further development of friction welding, the interface of the two components to be joined is subjected to a *linear* reciprocating motion, as opposed to a rotary motion. In *linear friction welding*, the components do not have to be circular or tubular in cross-section. The process is capable of welding square or rectangular components, as well as round parts, made of metals or plastics. In this process, one part is moved across the face of the other part using a balanced reciprocating mechanism.

In one application, a rectangular titanium-alloy part was friction-welded at a linear frequency of 25 Hz, with an amplitude of ±2 mm (0.08 in.), under a pressure of 100 MPa (15,000 psi) acting on a 240 mm^2 (0.38 in.^{2}) interface. Various other metal parts have been welded successfully, with rectangular cross-sections as large as 50 mm × 20 mm (2 in. × 0.8 in.).

28.4.4 Friction Stir Welding (FSW)

This is a new process originally intended for welding of aerospace alloys, espccially aluminum extrusions, although current research is being directed at extending this process towards polymers and composite materials.

Whereas in conventional friction welding, heating of interfaces is achieved through friction by rubbing two contacting surfaces, in the FSW process, a third body is rubbed against the two surfaces to be joined in the form of a small (5 to 6 mm diameter, 5 mm height) rotating nonconsumable tool that is plunged into the joint (Fig. 28.4). The contact pressures cause frictional heating, raising the temperature to the range of 230 °C to 260 °C (450 °F to 500 °F). The probe at the tip of the rotating tool forces heating and mixing or stirring of the material in the joint.

The welding equipment can be a conventional, vertical-spindle milling machine (Fig. 23.16a) and the process is relatively easy to implement. The thickness of the welded material can be as little as 1 mm and as much as 30 mm or so. FSW welds are of high quality, with minimal pores and with uniform material structure. The welds are produced with low heat input and, therefore, low distortion and little microstructural changes. Furthermore, there are no fumes or spatter produced and the process is suitable for automation.

28.5 RESISTANCE WELDING

The category *resistance welding* (RW) covers a number of processes in which the heat required for welding is produced by means of **electrical resistance** across the two components to be joined. These processes have major advantages, such as not requiring consumable electrodes, shielding gases, or flux.

The heat generated in resistance welding is given by the general expression

$$H = I^2 Rt, \tag{28.1}$$

where

H = heat generated (in joules (watt-seconds)),
I = current (in amperes),
R = resistance (in ohms), and
t = time of current flow (in seconds).

Equation (28.1) is often modified so that it represents the actual heat energy available in the weld, by including a factor K which represents the energy losses through radiation and conduction. The equation then becomes $H = I^2 RtK$, where the value of K is less than unity.

The *total resistance* in these processes—for example, in the resistance spot welding shown in Fig. 28.5—is the sum of the following properties:

a. the resistances of the electrodes;
b. the electrode–workpiece contact resistance;
c. the resistances of the individual parts to be welded;
d. the workpiece–workpiece contact resistance (between the *faying surfaces*).

The actual temperature rise at the joint depends on the specific heat and on the thermal conductivity of the metals to be joined. For example, metals such as aluminum and copper have high thermal conductivity, and so they require high heat concentrations. Similar or dissimilar metals can be joined by resistance welding. The magnitude of the current in resistance welding operations may be as high as 100,000 A, although the voltage is typically only 0.5 V–10 V.

FIGURE 28.5 (a) Sequence in resistance spot welding. (b) Cross-section of a spot weld, showing the weld nugget and the indentation of the electrode on the sheet surfaces. This is one of the most commonly used processes in sheet-metal fabrication and in automotive-body assembly.

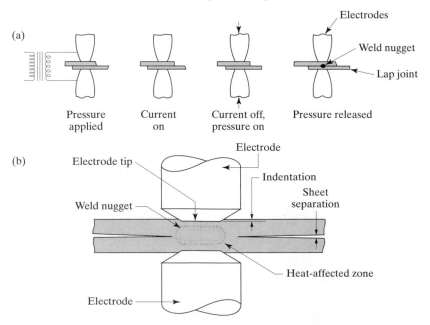

Developed in the early 1900s, resistance welding processes require specialized machinery. Much of it is now operated by programmable computer control. The machinery is generally not portable, and the process is suitable primarily for use in manufacturing plants and machine shops. The operator skill required is minimal, particularly with modern machinery. Safety precautions are similar to those for other welding operations. Cost of the total system typically ranges from $20,000 to more than $50,000.

28.5.1 Resistance Spot Welding

In *resistance spot welding* (RSW), the tips of two opposing solid cylindrical electrodes touch a lap joint of two sheet metals, and resistance heating produces a spot weld (Fig. 28.5a). In order to obtain a strong bond in the **weld nugget**, pressure is applied until the current is turned off. Accurate control and timing of the electric current and of the pressure are essential in resistance welding.

The strength of the bond depends on surface roughness and on the cleanness of the mating surfaces. Oil, paint, and thick oxide layers should, therefore, be removed before welding. The presence of uniform, thin layers of oxide and of other contaminants is not critical.

The weld nugget (Fig. 28.5b) is generally 6 to 10 mm (0.25 to 0375 in.) in diameter. The surface of the weld spot has a slightly discolored indentation. Currents range from 3000 A to 40,000 A; the level depends on the materials being welded and on their thicknesses.

Process Capabilities. Spot welding is the simplest and the most commonly used resistance-welding process. Welding may be performed by means of single (most common) or multiple pairs of electrodes, and the required pressure is supplied through mechanical or pneumatic means. **Rocker-arm type** spot-welding machines (Fig. 28.6a) are normally used for smaller parts; **press type** machines are used for larger workpieces. The shape and surface condition of the electrode tip and the accessibility of the site are important factors in spot welding. A variety of electrode shapes are used to spot-weld areas that are difficult to reach (Figs. 28.6b and c).

Spot welding is widely used for fabricating sheet metal parts. Examples range from the attaching of handles to stainless-steel cookware (Fig. 28.7a) to the spot welding of mufflers (Fig. 28.7b). Modern spot-welding equipment is computer controlled for optimum timing of current and pressure; its spot-welding guns are manipulated by programmable robots (Fig. 28.7c). Automobile bodies can have as many as 10,000 spot welds; they are welded at high rates by the use of multiple electrodes (Fig. 28.8).

Example: Heat Generated in Spot Welding

Assume that two steel sheets 1-mm (0.04-in.) thick are being spot-welded at a current of 5000 A and over a current flow time of 0.1 second, by means of electrodes 5 mm (0.2 in.) in diameter. Estimate the heat generated and its distribution in the weld zone.

Solution: Let's assume that the effective resistance in this operation is 200 $\mu\Omega$. Then, according to Eq. (28.1),

$$\text{Heat} = (5000)^2 (0.0002) (0.1) = 500 \text{ J.}$$

From the information given, we estimate the weld nugget volume to be 30 mm³ (0.0018 in³). Assume that the density for steel (Table 3.1) is 8000 kg/m³ (0.008 g/mm³); then the weld nugget has a mass of 0.24 g. The heat required to melt 1 g of steel is about 1400 J, so the heat required to melt the weld nugget is (1400) (0.24) = 336 J. The remaining heat (164 J) is dissipated into the metal surrounding the nugget.

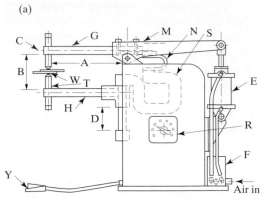

(a)

A - Throat depth
B - Horn spacing
C - Centerline of rocker arm
D - Lower arm adjustment
E - Air cylinder
F - Air valve
G - Upper horn

H - Lower horn
M - Rocker arm
N - Secondary flexible conductor
R - Current regulator (tap switch)
S - Transformer secondary
T - Electrode holder
W - Electrode
Y - Foot control

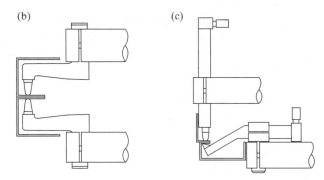

FIGURE 28.6   (a) Schematic illustration of an air-operated rocker-arm spot-welding machine. *Source*: American Welding Society. (b) and (c) Electrode designs for easy access into components to be welded.

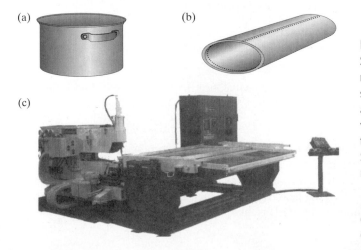

FIGURE 28.7   (a) and (b) Spot-welded cookware and muffler. (c) An automated spot-welding machine with a programmable robot; the welding tip can move in three principal directions. Sheets as large as 2.2 m × 0.55 m (88 in. × 22 in.) can be accommodated in this machine. *Source*: Courtesy of Taylor–Winfield Corporation.

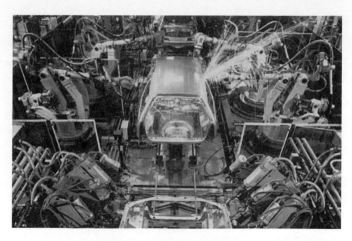

FIGURE 28.8   Robots equipped with spot-welding guns and operated by computer controls, in a mass-production line for automotive bodies. *Source*: Courtesy of Cincinnati Milacron, Inc.

28.5.2 Resistance Seam Welding

Resistance seam welding (RSEW) is a modification of spot welding wherein the electrodes are replaced by rotating wheels or rollers (Fig. 28.9a). Using a continuous AC power supply, the electrically conducting rollers produce a spot weld whenever the current reaches a sufficiently high level in the AC cycle. These spot welds actually overlap into a continuous

FIGURE 28.9   (a) Seam-welding process in which rotating rolls act as electrodes. (b) Overlapping spots in a seam weld. (c) Roll spot welds. (d) Resistance-welded gasoline tank.

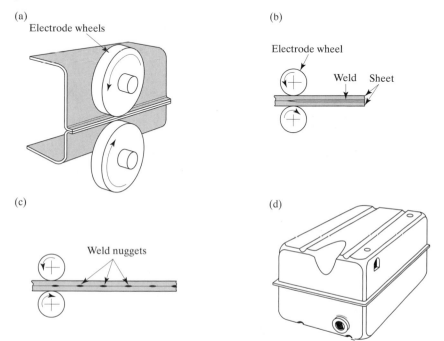

(a)   (b)

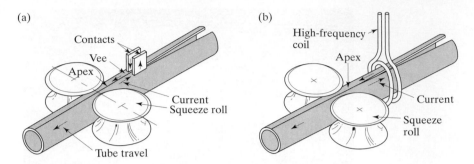

FIGURE 28.10   Two methods of high-frequency butt welding of tubes.

seam and produce a joint that is liquid-tight and gas-tight (Fig. 28.9b). With only intermittent application of current to the rollers, a series of spot welds at specified intervals can be made along the length of the seam (Fig. 28.9c); this procedure is called **roll spot welding**.

The RSEW process is used to make the longitudinal (side) seam of cans for household products, mufflers, gasoline tanks (Fig. 28.9d), and other containers. The typical welding speed is 1.5 m/min (60 in./min) for thin sheet.

28.5.3 High-Frequency Resistance Welding

High-frequency resistance welding (HFRW) is similar to seam welding, except that high-frequency current (up to 450 kHz) is employed. A typical application is the production of butt-welded tubing where the current is conducted through two sliding contacts (Fig. 28.10a) to the edges of roll-formed tubes. The heated edges are then pressed together by passing the tube through a pair of squeeze rolls.

In another method, the roll-formed tube is subjected to high-frequency induction heating (Fig. 28.10b). Structural sections such as I-beams can also be fabricated by HFRW, by welding the webs and flanges made from long flat pieces. Spiral pipe and tubing, as well as finned tubes (for heat exchangers), may be made by these techniques.

28.5.4 Resistance Projection Welding

In *resistance projection welding* (RPW), high electrical resistance at the joint is developed by embossing one or more projections (dimples—see Fig. 16.37) on one of the surfaces to be welded (Figs. 28.11a and b). The projections may have different shapes for design or strength purposes.

High localized temperatures are generated at the projections, which are in contact with the flat mating part. The electrodes, made of copper-based alloys, and water-cooled to keep their temperature low, are large and flat. Weld nuggets similar to those in spot welding are formed as the electrodes exert pressure to compress the projections.

Process Capabilities.   Spot-welding equipment can be used for RPW by modifying the electrodes. Although the embossing of the workpieces adds expense, this process produces a number of welds in one pass, extends electrode life, and is capable of welding metals of different thicknesses.

Nuts and bolts can be welded to sheet and plate by this process (Figs. 28.11c and d), with projections that are produced by machining or forging. Joining a network of wires (such as the ones making up metal baskets, grills, oven racks, and shopping carts) is also considered resistance projection welding, because of the many small contact areas at the grid intersections (illustrated in Fig. 28.11e).

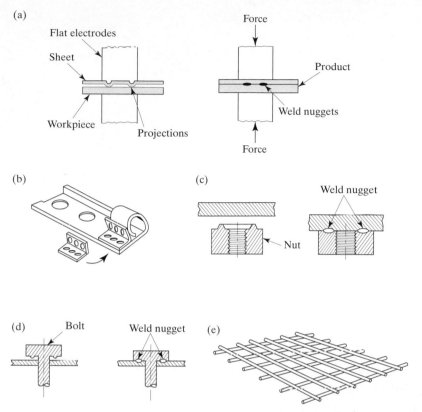

FIGURE 28.11   (a) Schematic illustration of resistance projection welding. (b) A welded bracket. (c) and (d) Projection welding of nuts or threaded bosses and studs. *Source*: American Welding Society. (e) Resistance-projection-welded grills.

28.5.5 Flash Welding

In *flash welding* (FW), also called **flash butt welding**, heat is generated from the arc as the ends of the two members begin to make contact and develop an electrical resistance at the joint (Fig. 28.12a). After the proper temperature is reached and the interface begins to soften, an axial force is applied at a controlled rate, and a weld is formed by plastic deformation (upsetting) of the joint. Some metal (flash) is expelled from the joint as a shower of sparks during the process. (Because of the presence of an arc, this process can also be classified as arc welding.)

Impurities and contaminants are squeezed out during this operation, so the quality of the weld is good. A significant amount of material may, however, be burned off during the welding process. The joint may later be machined to improve its appearance. The machines for FW are usually automated and large, with a variety of power supplies ranging from 10 kVA to 1500 kVA.

Process Capabilities.   The flash-welding process is suitable for end-to-end or edge-to-edge joining of sheets of similar or dissimilar metals 0.2 mm-25 mm (0.01 in.-1 in.) thick and for end joining of bars 1 mm-75 mm (0.05 in.-3 in.) in diameter. Thinner sections have a tendency to buckle under the axial force applied during welding. Rings made by forming processes, such as those shown in Fig. 16.22b and c, can also be flash butt welded (Figs. 28.12b and c). This process is also used to repair broken band-saw blades, with the use of fixtures that are mounted on the band-saw frame.

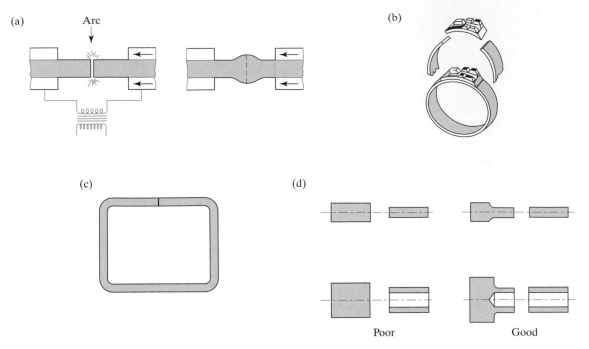

FIGURE 28.12   (a) Flash-welding process for end-to-end welding of solid rods or tubular parts. (b) and (c) Typical parts made by flash welding. (d) Design guidelines for flash welding.

The flash-welding process can be automated for reproducible welding operations. Typical applications are the joining of pipe and of tubular shapes for metal furniture and windows. It is also used for welding the ends of coils of sheet or wire in continuously operating rolling mills (Chapter 13) and in the feeding of wire-drawing equipment (Chapter 15). Once the appropriate process parameters are established, the required operator skill is minimal. Prices of FW machines range from about $5000 to as much as $1 million (for the large machines used in steel mills).

Design guidelines for mating surfaces in flash welding are shown in Fig. 28.12d. Note the importance of uniform cross-sections at the joint.

28.5.6 Stud Welding

Stud welding (SW), also called *stud arc welding*, is similar to flash welding. The stud, which may be a small part or a threaded rod or hanger, serves as one of the electrodes while being joined to another component, which is usually a flat plate (Fig. 28.13).

In order to concentrate the heat generated, prevent oxidation, and retain the molten metal in the weld zone, a disposable ceramic ring (*ferrule*) is placed around the joint. The equipment for stud welding can be automated, with various controls for arcing and for applying pressure. Portable stud-welding equipment is also available.

In **capacitor-discharge stud welding**, a direct-current arc is produced from a capacitor bank. No ferrule or flux is required because the welding time is very short, on the order of 1 to 6 milliseconds. The choice between this process and stud arc welding depends on such factors as the types of metals to be joined, the workpiece thickness, the stud diameter, and the shape of the joint.

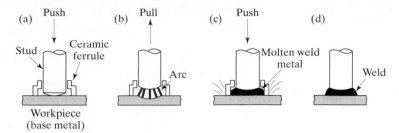

FIGURE 28.13   The sequence of operations in stud welding, which is used for welding bars, threaded rods, and various fasteners onto metal plates.

28.5.7 Percussion Welding

The resistance-welding processes already described usually employ an electrical transformer to meet the power requirements; alternatively, however, the electrical energy for welding may be stored in a capacitor. *Percussion welding* (PEW) utilizes this latter technique, in which the power is discharged within 1 to 10 milliseconds to develop localized high heat at the joint. This process is useful where heating of the components adjacent to the joint is to be avoided, such as in electronic assemblies.

Example: Resistance Welding vs. Laser-Beam Welding in the Can-Making Industry

The cylindrical bodies of cans for food and for household products have for many years been resistance seam welded (a lap joint up the side of the can). Beginning in about 1987, the laser-beam welding technology was introduced into the can-making industry. The joints are welded by lasers, with the same productivity as, but with the following advantages over, resistance welding:

1. As opposed to the lap joints suitable for resistance welding, laser welding utilizes butt joints; thus, some material is saved, an amount which, multiplied by the billions of cans made each year, becomes a very significant savings.
2. Because laser welds produce a very narrow heat-affected zone (Fig. 28.14; also Fig. 27.16), the unprinted area on the can surface (printing margin) is greatly reduced; as a result, the can's appearance and its customer acceptance are improved.
3. The resistance lap-welded joint can be subject to corrosion by the contents of the can (tomato juice, for example); this effect may change taste and cause potential liability risk. A butt joint made by laser eliminates this problem. *Source*: G. F. Benedict.

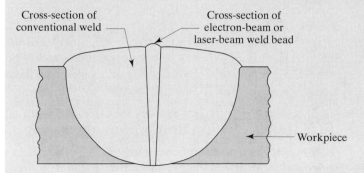

FIGURE 28.14   The relative sizes of the weld beads obtained by conventional (tungsten arc) and by electron-beam or laser-beam welding.

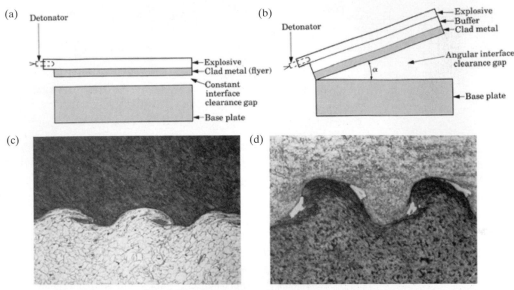

FIGURE 28.15   Schematic illustration of the explosion welding process: (a) constant interface clearance gap and (b) angular interface clearance gap. (c) Titanium over low-carbon steel, (d) incoloy 800 over low-carbon steel.

28.6 EXPLOSION WELDING

In *explosion welding* (EXW), pressure is applied by detonating a layer of explosive that has been placed over one of the components being joined, (called the *flyer plate*, Figs. 28.15a and b). The contact pressures developed are extremely high, and the kinetic energy of the plate striking the mating component causes a wavy interface.

This impact mechanically interlocks the two surfaces (Figs. 28.15c and d). Cold pressure welding by plastic deformation also takes place (see Section 28.2). The flyer plate is placed at an angle, and any oxide films present at the interface are broken up and propelled out of the interface. As a result, the bond strength from explosion welding is very high.

The explosive may be flexible plastic sheet, cord, granulated, or liquid, which is cast or pressed onto the flyer plate. Detonation speed is usually in the range of from 2400 to 3600 m/s (8000 to 12,000 ft/s); it depends on the type of explosive, the thickness of the explosive layer, and its packing density. There is a minimum denotation speed necessary for welding to occur in this process. Detonation is carried out using a standard commercial blasting cap.

Process Capabilities.   This process was developed in the 1940s. It is particularly suitable for cladding a plate or a slab with a dissimilar metal. Plates as large as 6 m × 2 m (20 ft × 7 ft) have been explosively clad. These plates may then be rolled into thinner sections. Tube and pipe can be joined to the holes in the head plates of boilers and heat exchangers by placing the explosive inside the tube; the explosion expands the tube. Explosion welding is inherently dangerous, so it requires safe handling by well-trained and experienced personnel.

28.7 DIFFUSION BONDING (WELDING)

Diffusion bonding, or **diffusion welding** (DFW), is a process in which the strength of the joint results primarily from diffusion (movement of atoms across the interface) and secondarily from plastic deformation of the faying surfaces. This process requires temperatures of about $0.5T_m$ (where T_m is the melting point of the metal on the absolute scale) in order to have a sufficiently high diffusion rate between the parts being joined.

The bonded interface in DFW has essentially the same physical and mechanical properties as the base metal. Its strength depends on (a) pressure, (b) temperature, (c) time of contact, and (d) the cleanness of the faying surfaces. These requirements can be relaxed by using a filler metal at the interface.

In diffusion bonding, pressure may be applied by dead weights, by a press, by differential gas pressure, or by the thermal expansion of the parts to be joined. The parts are usually heated in a furnace or by electrical resistance. High-pressure autoclaves are also used for bonding complex parts.

Although this process was developed in the 1970s as a modern welding technology, the principle of diffusion bonding dates back centuries, to when goldsmiths bonded gold over copper to create a product called **filled gold**. First, a thin layer of gold foil is produced by hammering; then, the gold is placed over copper, and a weight is placed on top of it. Finally, assembly is placed in a furnace and left until a strong bond is obtained.

Process Capabilities.   Diffusion bonding is generally most suitable for joining dissimilar metals; it is also used for reactive metals, such as titanium, beryllium, zirconium, and refractory metal alloys, and for composite materials. Because diffusion involves migration of the atoms across the joint, this process is slower than other welding processes. Although DFW is used for fabricating complex parts in low quantities for the aerospace, nuclear, and electronics industries, it has been automated to make it suitable and economical for moderate-volume production.

Unless the process is highly automated, considerable operator training and skill is required. Equipment cost is related approximately to the diffusion-bonded area and is in the range of $3/mm^2 to $6/mm^2 ($2000/in.^{2} to $4000/in.^{2}).

Example: Diffusion-Bonding Applications

Diffusion bonding is especially suitable for such metals as titanium and the superalloys used in military aircraft. Design possibilities allow the conservation of expensive strategic materials and the reduction of manufacturing costs. The military aircraft illustrated in Fig. 28.16 has more than 100 diffusion-bonded parts, some of which are shown in the figure.

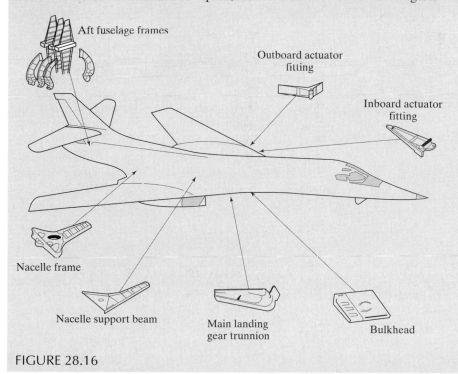

FIGURE 28.16

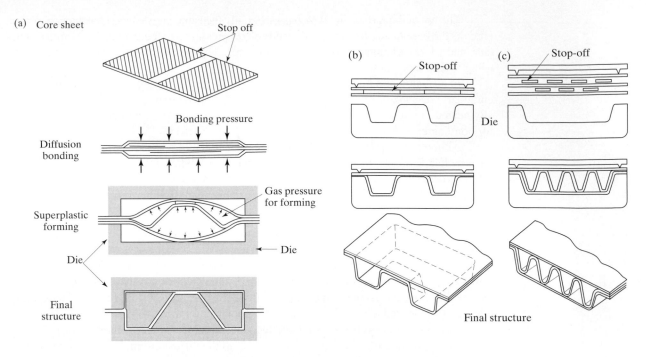

FIGURE 28.17   The sequence of operations in the fabrication of various structures by diffusion bonding and then superplastic forming of (originally) flat sheets. *Sources*: (a) After D. Stephen and S.J. Swadling. (b) and (c) Rockwell International Corp.

28.8 DIFFUSION BONDING/SUPERPLASTIC FORMING

An important development is the ability to fabricate sheet-metal structures by combining *diffusion bonding* with *superplastic forming*. (See also Section 16.12). Typical structures in which flat sheets (usually) are diffusion bonded and formed are shown in Fig. 28.17. After the diffusion bonding of selected locations of the sheets, the unbonded (*stop-off*) regions are expanded in a mold by air pressure. These structures are thin and have high stiffness-to-weight ratios, so they are particularly useful in aircraft and aerospace applications.

This process improves productivity by eliminating mechanical fasteners, and it produces parts with good dimensional accuracy and low residual stresses. The technology is now well advanced for titanium structures (typically Ti-6Al-4V alloy) for aerospace applications. Structures made of 7475-T6 aluminum alloy and other alloys are also being developed using this technique.

SUMMARY

- In addition to the traditional joining processes of oxyfuel gas and arc welding, a number of other joining processes that are based on producing a strong joint under pressure and/or heat are available.

- Surface preparation and cleanliness are important in some of these processes. Pressure is applied mechanically or by explosives. Heat may be supplied externally, or it may be generated internally (as in friction welding).

- Among important developments is the combining of the diffusion-bonding and superplastic-forming processes. Productivity is improved, as is the capability to make complex parts economically.

- As in all manufacturing operations, certain hazards are inherent in welding operations. Some relate to the machinery and equipment used, others to the nature of the process. Proper safety precautions must always be taken in work areas where welding is done.

TRENDS

- As in other joining processes, the trend in the processes described in this chapter is toward automation that utilizes computer controls and programmable robots even more extensively.

- Diffusion bonding combined with superplastic forming is becoming an important manufacturing process, particularly in the aerospace industry.

KEY TERMS

Cold welding	Friction welding	Roll bonding
Diffusion bonding (welding)	High-frequency resistance welding	Roll spot welding
Explosion welding	Inertia friction welding	Solid-state welding
Faying surfaces	Linear friction welding	Stud welding
Ferrule	Percussion welding	Superplastic forming
Filled gold	Resistance projection welding	Ultrasonic welding
Flash welding	Resistance seam welding	Weld nugget
Flyer plate	Resistance spot welding	
Friction stir welding	Resistance welding	

BIBLIOGRAPHY

ASM Handbook, Vol. 6: *Welding, Brazing, and Soldering.* ASM International, 1993.

Bowditch, W.A., and K.E. Bowditch, *Welding Technology Fundamentals.* Goodheart–Willcox, 1997.

Cary, H.B., *Modern Welding Technology* (4th ed.). Prentice Hall, 1997.

Davies, A.C., *The Science and Practice of Welding* (10th ed.), 2 vols. Cambridge University Press, 1993.

Jeffus, L.F., *Welding: Principles and Applications* (4th ed.). Delmar Publishers, 1997.

Jellison, R., *Welding Fundamentals.* Prentice Hall, 1995.

Messler, R.W., Jr., *Joining of Advanced Materials.* Butterworth–Heinemann, 1993.

Nicholas, M.G., *Joining Processes: Introduction to Brazing and Diffusion Bonding.* Chapman & Hall, 1998.

Tool and Manufacturing Engineers Handbook, Vol. 4: *Quality Control and Assembly.* Society of Manufacturing Engineers, 1986.

Welding Handbook (8th ed.), 3 vols. American Welding Society, 1987.

REVIEW QUESTIONS

28.1 Explain what is meant by solid-state welding.

28.2 What is cold welding?

28.3 What are faying surfaces in solid-state welding processes?

28.4 Describe the principle of ultrasonic welding.

28.5 What advantages does friction welding have over other methods described in this chapter?

28.6 Explain the difference between friction welding and inertia friction welding.

28.7 Describe the advantages and limitations of explosion welding.

28.8 Can roll bonding be applied to a variety of part configurations? Explain.

28.9 Describe the mechanism of diffusion bonding.

28.10 Why is diffusion bonding, when combined with superplastic forming of sheet metals, an attractive fabrication process? Does it have any limitations?

28.11 Describe the principle behind resistance-welding processes.

28.12 What kind of items are suitable for stud welding? Why?

28.13 What is the advantage of linear friction welding over inertia friction welding?

QUALITATIVE PROBLEMS

28.14 Explain the similarities and differences between the joining processes described in this chapter and those described in Chapter 27.

28.15 Why were the processes described in this chapter developed?

28.16 Describe what you observe in Fig. 28.15.

28.17 Make a list of the safety precautions necessary in applying the joining processes described in this chapter.

28.18 Discuss the factors that influence the strength of (a) a diffusion-bonded and (b) a cold-welded component.

28.19 Explain the sources of heat for the processes described in this chapter.

28.20 Give some applications for ultrasonic seam welding, which is shown in Fig. 28.2b.

28.21 Describe the difficulties you might encounter in applying explosion welding in a factory environment.

28.22 Inspect the edges of a U.S. quarter and comment on your observations. Is the cross-section symmetrical? Explain your comments and response.

28.23 What advantages do resistance-welding processes have over the others described in this chapter?

28.24 Describe the features of a weld nugget. What does its strength depend on?

28.25 Make a list of some products that can be fabricated by resistance-welding processes.

28.26 Give some applications for flash welding, some for stud welding, and some for percussion welding.

28.27 Give some of the reasons that spot welding is commonly used in automotive bodies and in home appliances.

28.28 Explain the significance of the magnitude of the pressure applied through the electrodes during resistance-welding operations.

28.29 Discuss the need and role of fixtures in the holding of the workpieces in the welding operations described in this chapter.

28.30 Inspect Fig. 28.3b, and explain why those particular fusion-zone shapes are developed (as a function of pressure and speed). Comment on the influence of the material's properties.

28.31 Discuss your observations concerning the welding design guidelines illustrated in Fig. 28.12d.

28.32 Could the process shown in Fig. 28.10 also be applicable to part shapes other than tubular? Explain your answer, and give specific examples.

28.33 What applications could be suitable for the roll-spot-welding process shown in Fig. 28.9?

28.34 Survey the available technical literature on friction welding, and prepare a table of the similar and dissimilar metals and nonmetallic materials that can be friction-welded. Comment on the respective strengths obtained.

28.35 Could the projection-welded parts shown in Fig. 28.12b and c be made by any of the processes described in other chapters in this text? Explain.

28.36 Explain the difference between resistance seam welding and resistance spot welding.

28.37 Could you use any of the processes described in Chapters 27 and 28 to make a large bolt by welding the head to the shank? (See Fig. 14.11b.) Explain the advantages and limitations of this approach.

28.38 The energy required in ultrasonic welding is known to be related to the product of the thickness and the hardness of the workpiece. Explain why this relationship exists.

QUANTITATIVE PROBLEMS

28.39 Two flat copper sheets, each 1.0 mm thick, are being spot-welded by the use of a current of 5000 A and a current flow time of 0.25 s. The electrodes are 5 mm in diameter. Estimate the heat generated in the weld zone. Assume that the resistance is 100 $\mu\Omega$.

28.40 Calculate the temperature rise in Problem 28.39, assuming that the heat generated is confined to the volume of material directly between the two round electrodes and the temperature is distributed uniformly.

28.41 Calculate the range of allowable currents for Problem 28.39, if the temperature should be between 0.7 and 0.85 times the melting temperature of copper. Repeat this problem for carbon steel.

28.42 The energy applied in friction welding is given by the formula $E = IS^2/C$, where I is the moment of inertia of the flywheel, S is the spindle speed in rpm, and C is a constant of proportionality (5873, when the moment of inertia is given in lb-ft^2). For a spindle speed of 600 rpm and an operation in which a steel tube (3.5 in. OD, 0.25 in. wall thickness) is welded to a flat frame, what is the required moment of inertia of the flywheel if all of the energy is used to heat the weld zone, approximated as the material $\frac{1}{4}$ in. deep and directly below the tube? Assume that 1.4 ft-lbm is needed to melt the electrode.

SYNTHESIS AND DESIGN

28.43 Explain how you would fabricate the structures shown in Fig. 28.17 by means of methods other than diffusion bonding and superplastic forming.

28.44 Comment on workpiece size and shape limitations, if any, for each of the processes described in this chapter.

28.45 Describe part shapes that cannot be joined by the processes described in this chapter. Gives specific examples.

28.46 Prepare a table giving the welding speeds, as a function of the relevant parameters, for the processes described in Chapters 27 and 28. Comment on your observations.

28.47 Make a comprehensive outline of this Chapter; include sketches of possible welded-joint designs and of their engineering applications. Give specific examples for each type of joint.

28.48 Section 27.10 described the general guidelines for safety in welding operations. For each of the operations described in this chapter, prepare a poster which effectively and concisely gives specific instructions for safe practices in welding. Consult the references at the end of Chapter 37 and the various publications of the National Safety Council.

28.49 Make a survey of metal containers for household products and for foods and beverages. Identify those that have utilized any of the processes described in Chapters 27 and 28. Describe your observations.

28.50 Discuss various other processes that can be used in attaching tubes to head plates.

28.51 Describe designs that cannot be joined by friction-welding processes.

28.52 Design a machine that can perform friction welding of two cylindrical pieces and will remove the flash from the welded joint. (See Fig. 28.3.)

28.53 How would you modify your design in Problem 28.52 if one of the pieces to be welded is noncircular?

28.54 Alclad stock is made from 5182 aluminum alloy and has both sides coated with a layer of pure aluminum. The 5182 provides high strength, while the outside layers of pure aluminum provide good corrosion resistance (because of their stable oxide film); Alclad is, therefore, commonly used in aerospace structural applications. Investigate other common roll-bonded materials and their uses, and prepare a summary table.

28.55 Perform an Internet survey of available spot-welding machines, their capabilities, and their costs.

29

The Metallurgy of Welding; Welding Design and Process Selection

29.1 INTRODUCTION

The basic principles of the welding processes that utilize chemical, electrical, thermal, or mechanical sources of energy were described in Chapters 27 and 28. It is apparent that heating the components to be welded to a temperature sufficiently high to produce a weld involves important metallurgical and physical changes in the materials.

As will be described in this chapter, the strength, ductility, and toughness of a welded joint depend on several factors. For example, the rate of heat application and the thermal properties of metals are important, in that they control the magnitude and the distribution of temperatures in the joint. The microstructure and grain size of the welded joint depend on the amount of heat applied and the consequent temperature rise, on the degree of prior cold work of the metals, and on the rate of cooling after the weld is produced.

Weld quality depends on many factors, among them the geometry of the weld bead and the presence of cracks, residual stresses, inclusions, and oxide films. Control of such factors is essential to the creation of reliable welds that have acceptable mechanical properties. This chapter concludes with general guidelines for proper weld design and with a survey of the factors involved in selecting the appropriate welding process for a specific application.

819

29.2 THE WELDED JOINT

Three distinct zones can be identified in a typical fusion-weld joint (as shown in Fig. 29.1):

1. **base metal**;
2. **heat-affected zone**;
3. **weld metal**.

The metallurgy and properties of the second and third zones depend strongly on the metals joined, on the welding process, on the filler metals used, if any, and on process variables. A joint produced without a filler metal is called *autogenous*, and its weld zone is composed of the *resolidified base metal*. A joint made with a filler metal has a central zone called the *weld metal*, composed of a mixture of the base and the filler metals.

29.2.1 Solidification of the Weld Metal

After the application of heat and the introduction of filler metal (if any) into the weld area, the molten weld joint is allowed to cool to ambient temperature. The *solidification* process is similar to that in casting and begins with the formation of columnar (dendritic) grains. (See Fig. 10.2.)

These grains are relatively long and form parallel to the heat flow. Because metals are much better heat conductors than the surrounding air, the grains lie parallel to the plane of the two components being welded (Fig. 29.2a). The grains in a shallow weld are shown in Figs. 29.2b and 29.3.

Grain structure and size depend on the specific alloy, the specific welding process employed, and the specific filler metal. In comparison with weld beads produced by traditional welding methods, the size of a weld bead made by the electron-beam or the laser-beam process is much narrower. (See Figs. 27.16 and 28.14.)

The weld metal has, basically, a *cast structure* and, because it has cooled slowly, it has coarse grains. Consequently, this structure has generally low strength, toughness, and ductility. However, the proper selection of filler-metal composition or of heat treatments following welding can improve the mechanical properties of the joint.

The results depend on the particular alloy, on its composition, and on the thermal cycling to which the joint is subjected. Cooling rates may, for example, be controlled (and reduced) by a preheating of the general weld area prior to the welding. Preheating is particularly

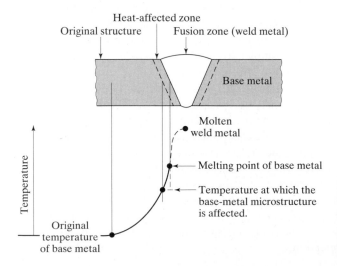

FIGURE 29.1
Characteristics of a typical fusion weld zone in oxyfuel gas and arc welding. See also Figs. 27.16 and 28.14.

(a)   (b)

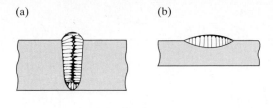

FIGURE 29.2   Grain structure in (a) a deep weld (b) a shallow weld. Note that the grains in the solidified weld metal are perpendicular to the surface of the base metal. In a good weld, the solidification line at the center in the deep weld shown in (a) has grain migration, which develops uniform strength in the weld bead.

(a)   (b)

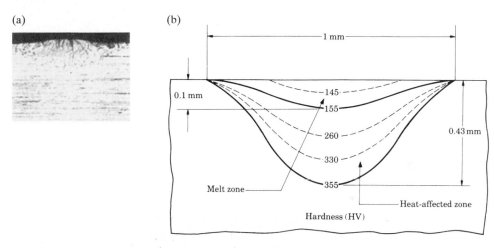

FIGURE 29.3   (a) Weld bead (on a cold-rolled nickel strip) produced by a laser beam. (b) Microhardness profile across the weld bead. Note the lower hardness of the weld bead compared to the base metal. *Source*: IIT Research Institute.

important for metals having high thermal conductivity, such as aluminum and copper; without it, the heat produced during welding dissipates rapidly.

29.2.2 Heat-Affected Zone

The *heat-affected zone* (HAZ) is within the base metal itself. It has a microstructure different from that of the base metal prior to welding, because it has been subjected to elevated temperatures for a period of time during welding. The portions of the base metal that are far enough away from the heat source do not undergo any structural changes during welding.

The properties and microstructure of the HAZ depend on (1) the rate of heat input and cooling, and (2) the temperature to which this zone was raised. The HAZ (and the corresponding phase diagram) for 0.3% carbon steel are shown in Fig. 29.4. In addition to metallurgical factors (such as original grain size, grain orientation, and degree of prior cold work), physical properties (such as the specific heat and thermal conductivity of the metals) influence the size and characteristics of this zone.

The strength and hardness of the heat-affected zone depend partly on how the original strength and hardness of the base metal was developed prior to the welding. As was described in Chapters 2 and 4, they may have been developed (a) by cold working, (b) by solid-solution strengthening, (c) by precipitation hardening, or (d) by various heat treatments.

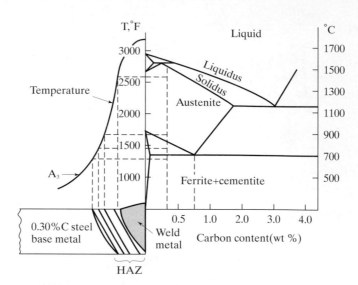

FIGURE 29.4   Schematic illustration of various regions in a fusion weld zone (and the corresponding phase diagram) for 0.30% carbon steel. *Source*: American Welding Society.

The effects of these strengthening methods are complex, and the simplest to analyze are those in the base metal that has been cold-worked—say, by cold rolling or by forging.

The heat applied during welding *recrystallizes* the elongated grains of the cold-worked base metal (changes their preferred orientation). Grains that are away from the weld metal will recrystallize into fine equiaxed grains. Grains close to the weld metal, on the other hand, have been subjected to elevated temperatures for a longer period of time; consequently, they will grow. This growth will cause their region to be softer and to have less strength.

Such a joint will be weakest in its heat-affected zone. The grain structure of such a weld that is exposed to corrosion by chemical reaction is shown in Fig. 29.5; the vertical center line is where the two pieces meet.

The effects of heat on the HAZ for joints made from dissimilar metals, and for alloys strengthened by other methods, are so complex as to be beyond the scope of this text. Details can be found in the more advanced texts listed in the bibliography at the end of this chapter.

FIGURE 29.5   Intergranular corrosion of a 310-stainless-steel welded tube after exposure to a caustic solution. The weld line is at the center of the photograph. Scanning electron micrograph at 20×. *Source*: Courtesy of B. R. Jack, Allegheny Ludlum Steel Corp.

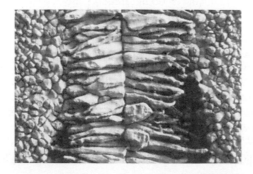

29.3 WELD QUALITY

As a result of a history of thermal cycling and its attendant microstructural changes, a welded joint may develop various **discontinuities**. Welding discontinuities can also be caused by inadequate or careless application of established welding technologies or by substandard operator training. The major discontinuities that affect weld quality are described below.

29.3.1 Porosity

Porosity in welds is caused (a) by gases released during melting of the weld area but trapped during solidification, (b) by chemical reactions during welding, or (c) by contaminants. Most welded joints contain some porosity, which is generally in the shape of spheres or of elongated pockets. (See also Section 10.3.6.) The distribution of porosity in the weld zone may be random, or the porosity may be concentrated in a certain region.

Porosity in welds can be reduced by the following practices:

   a. proper selection of electrodes and filler metals;
   b. improved welding techniques, such as preheating of the weld area or an increase in the rate of heat input;
   c. proper cleaning, and the prevention of contaminants from entering the weld zone;
   d. reduced welding speeds, to allow time for gas to escape.

29.3.2 Slag Inclusions

Slag inclusions are compounds such as oxides, fluxes, and electrode-coating materials that are trapped in the weld zone. If shielding gases are not effective during welding, contamination from the environment may also contribute to such inclusions. Welding conditions are important; with proper techniques, the molten slag will float to the surface of the molten weld metal and will not become entrapped.

Slag inclusions can be prevented by the following practices:

   a. cleaning the weld-bead surface before the next layer is deposited, by means of a wire brush (hand or power);
   b. providing enough shielding gas;
   c. redesigning the joint so as to permit sufficient space for proper manipulation of the puddle of molten weld metal.

29.3.3 Incomplete Fusion and Penetration

Incomplete fusion (lack of fusion) produces poor weld beads, such as those shown in Fig. 29.6. A better weld can be obtained by the use of the following practices:

   a. raising the temperature of the base metal;
   b. cleaning the weld area, prior to the welding;
   c. changing the joint design and the type of electrode;
   d. providing enough shielding gas.

Incomplete penetration occurs when the depth of the welded joint is insufficient. Penetration can be improved by the following practices:

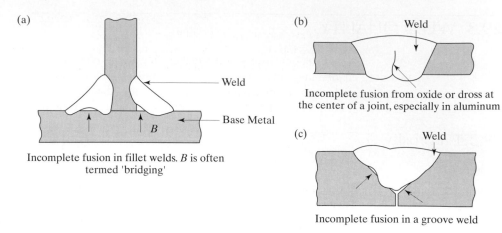

FIGURE 29.6   Low-quality weld beads, the result of incomplete fusion. *Source*: American Welding Society.

    a. increasing the heat input;
    b. reducing the travel speed during the welding;
    c. changing the joint design;
    d. ensuring that the surfaces to be joined fit properly.

29.3.4 Weld Profile

Weld profile is important not only because of its effects on the strength and appearance of the weld, but also because it can signal incomplete fusion or the presence of slag inclusions in multiple-layer welds.

    Underfilling results when the joint is not filled with the proper amount of weld metal (Fig. 29.7a).

    Undercutting (Fig. 29.7b) results from the melting away of the base metal and the consequent generation of a groove in the shape of a sharp recess or notch. If it is deep or sharp,

FIGURE 29.7   Schematic illustration of various discontinuities in fusion welds. *Source*: American Welding Society.

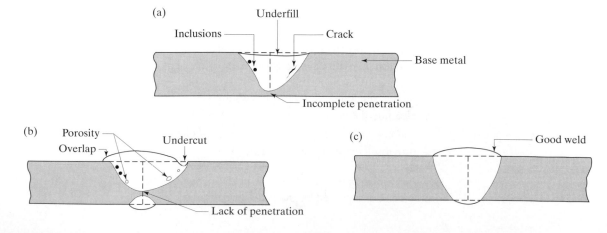

an undercut can act as a stress raiser and can reduce the fatigue strength of the joint; in such cases, it may lead to premature failure.

Overlap (Fig. 29.7b) is a surface discontinuity usually caused by poor welding practice and by the selection of improper materials. A good weld is shown in Fig. 29.7c.

29.3.5 Cracks

Cracks may occur in various locations and directions in the weld area. The typical types of cracks are longitudinal, transverse, crater, underbead, and toe cracks (Fig. 29.8).

These cracks generally result from a combination of the following factors:

a. temperature gradients that cause thermal stresses in the weld zone;

b. variations in the composition of the weld zone that cause different rates of contraction;

c. embrittlement of grain boundaries (Section 1.4.3), caused by the segregation of such elements as sulfur to the grain boundaries as the solid–liquid boundary moves when the weld metal begins to solidify;

d. hydrogen embrittlement (Section 2.10.2);

e. inability of the weld metal to contract during cooling (Fig. 29.9); this is a situation similar to *hot tears* that develop in castings and is related to excessive restraint of the workpiece. (See Fig. 10.11.)

Cracks are classified as *hot* or *cold*. **Hot cracks** occur while the joint is still at elevated temperatures. **Cold cracks** develop after the weld metal has solidified.

The basic crack-prevention measures are the following:

a. Change the joint design, to minimize stresses from shrinkage during cooling;

b. Change the parameters, the procedures, and the sequence of the welding process;

FIGURE 29.8   Types of cracks (in welded joints) caused by thermal stresses that develop during solidification and contraction of the weld bead and the surrounding structure. (a) Crater cracks. (b) Various types of cracks in butt and T joints.

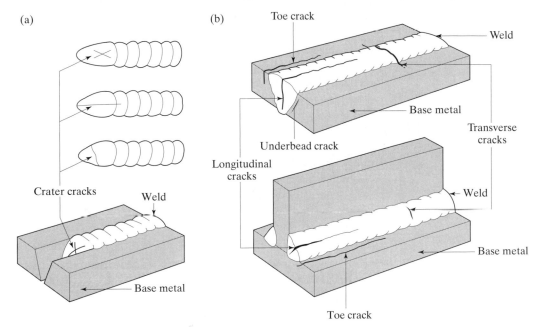

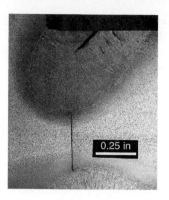

0.25 in

FIGURE 29.9   Crack in a weld bead, due to the fact that the two components were not allowed to contract after the weld was completed. *Source*: S. L. Meiley, Packer Engineering Associates, Inc.

   c. Preheat the components to be welded;

   d. Avoid rapid cooling of the welded components.

29.3.6 Lamellar Tears

In describing the anisotropy of plastically deformed metals (Section 1.5), it was stated that, because of the alignment of nonmetallic impurities and inclusions (stringers), the workpiece is weaker when tested in its thickness direction. This condition is particularly evident in rolled plates and in structural shapes.

In the welding of such components, *lamellar tears* may develop, because of shrinkage of the restrained components in the structure during cooling. Such tears can be avoided by providing for shrinkage of the members or by changing the joint design to make the weld bead penetrate the weaker component more deeply.

29.3.7 Surface Damage

Some of the metal may spatter during welding and be deposited as small droplets on adjacent surfaces. In arc-welding processes, the electrode may inadvertently touch the parts being welded at places other than the weld zone (**arc strikes**). Such surface discontinuities may be objectionable for reasons of appearance or of subsequent use of the welded part.

If severe, these discontinuities may adversely affect the properties of the welded structure, particularly for notch-sensitive metals. Using proper welding techniques and procedures is important in avoiding surface damage.

29.3.8 Residual Stresses

Because of localized heating and cooling during welding, expansion and contraction of the weld area causes *residual stresses* in the workpiece. (See also Section 2.11.) Residual stresses can cause the following defects:

   a. distortion, warping, and buckling of the welded parts (Fig. 29.10);

   b. stress-corrosion cracking;

   c. further distortion, if a portion of the welded structure is subsequently removed (say, by machining or by sawing);

   d. reduced fatigue life.

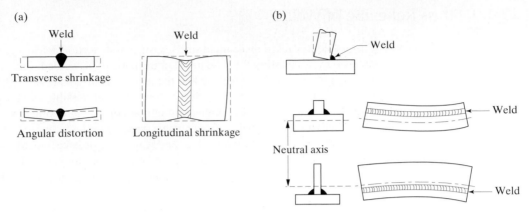

FIGURE 29.10 Distortion of parts after welding: (a) butt joints; (b) fillet welds. Distortion is caused by differential thermal expansion and contraction of different parts of the welded assembly.

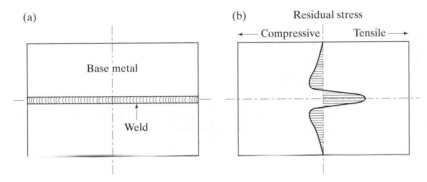

FIGURE 29.11 Residual stresses developed during welding of a butt joint. *Source*: American Welding Society.

The type and distribution of residual stresses in welds is best described by reference to Fig. 29.11a. When two plates are being welded, a long narrow zone is subjected to elevated temperatures, while the plates as a whole are essentially at ambient temperature. After the weld is completed, and as time elapses, the heat from the weld zone dissipates laterally into the plates, while the weld area cools. The plates thus begin to expand longitudinally, while the welded length begins to contract.

These two opposing effects cause residual stresses that are (typically) distributed as shown in Fig. 29.11b. Note that the magnitude of the compressive residual stresses in the plates diminishes to zero at a point far away from the weld area. Because no external forces are acting on the welded plates, the tensile and compressive forces represented by these residual stresses must balance each other.

In complex welded structures, residual stress distributions are three-dimensional and, consequently, difficult to analyze. The preceding example involves two plates that are not restrained from movement; in other words, the plates are not an integral part of a larger structure. If, on the other hand, they are restrained, reaction stresses will be generated, because the plates are not free to expand or contract. This situation arises particularly in structures with high stiffness.

29.3.9 Stress Relieving of Welds

The problems caused by residual stresses, such as distortion, buckling, and cracking, can be reduced by **preheating** the base metal or the parts to be welded. Preheating reduces distortion by reducing the cooling rate and the level of thermal stresses (by reducing the elastic modulus). This technique also reduces shrinkage and possible cracking of the joint.

For optimum results, preheating temperatures and cooling rates must be carefully controlled in order to maintain acceptable strength and toughness in the welded structure. The workpieces may be heated in several ways: in a furnace; electrically (resistively or inductively); or, for thin sections, by radiant lamps or hot-air blast. The temperature and time required for *stress relieving* depend on the type of material and on the magnitude of the residual stresses developed.

Some other methods of stress relieving are peening, hammering, or surface rolling of the weld bead area. (See Section 33.2.) These processes induce compressive residual stresses, which reduce or eliminate tensile residual stresses in the weld. For multilayer welds, the first and last layers should not be peened, in order to protect them against possible peening damage.

Residual stresses can also be relieved or reduced by *plastically deforming* the structure by a small amount. This technique can, for instance, be used in welded pressure vessels by pressurizing the vessels internally (*proof-stressing*). In order to reduce the possibility of sudden fracture under high internal pressure, the weld must be made properly and must be free from notches and discontinuities, which could act as points of stress concentration.

In addition to being preheated for stress relieving, welds may be *heat treated* by various other techniques in order to modify other properties. These techniques include the annealing, normalizing, quenching, and tempering of steels and the solution treatment and aging of various alloys (Chapter 4).

29.4 WELDABILITY

The *weldability* of a metal is usually defined as its capacity to be welded into a specific structure that has certain properties and characteristics and will satisfactorily meet service requirements. Weldability involves a large number of variables, so generalizations are difficult. As we have seen, the material characteristics (such as the alloying elements, the impurities, the inclusions, the grain structure, and the processing history) of the base metal and the filler metal are important.

Because of the effects of melting and solidification and of the consequent microstructural changes, a thorough knowledge of the phase diagram and of the response of the metal or alloy to elevated temperatures over a period of time is essential. Also influencing weldability are mechanical and physical properties: strength, toughness, ductility, notch sensitivity, elastic modulus, specific heat, melting point, thermal expansion, surface-tension characteristics of the molten metal, and corrosion resistance.

Preparation of surfaces for welding is important; so are the nature and properties of surface oxide films and of adsorbed gases. The particular welding process employed significantly affects the temperatures developed and their distribution in the weld zone. Other factors are shielding gases, fluxes, the moisture content of the coatings on electrodes, welding speed, welding position, cooling rate, and preheating, as well as such post-welding techniques as stress relieving and heat treating.

An overview of the weldability of various metals and alloys and of recommended joining processes and part thickness ranges is given in Table 29.1. Here is a brief summary of the general weldability characteristics of metals and alloys:

a. *Plain-carbon steels:* Weldability is excellent for low-carbon steels, fair to good for medium-carbon steels, poor for high-carbon steels.

b. *Low-alloy steels:* Weldability is similar to that of medium-carbon steels.

c. *High-alloy steels:* Weldability is generally good under well-controlled conditions.

d. *Stainless steels:* These are weldable by various processes.

e. *Aluminum alloys:* These are weldable at a high rate of heat input. Aluminum alloys containing zinc or copper generally are considered unweldable. (See Section 6.2.)

f. *Copper alloys:* Weldability is similar to that of aluminum alloys.

g. *Magnesium alloys:* These are weldable with the use of protective shielding gas and fluxes.

h. *Nickel alloys:* Weldability is similar to that of stainless steels.

i. *Titanium alloys:* These are weldable with the proper use of shielding gases.

j. *Tantalum:* Weldability is similar to that of titanium.

k. *Tungsten:* This is weldable under well-controlled conditions.

l. *Molybdenum:* Weldability is similar to that of tungsten.

m. *Niobium (columbium):* Weldability is good.

TABLE 29.1   Overview of Commercial Joining Processes*

The last seven columns (TB, FB, IB, RB, DB, IRB, DFB) are Brazing processes.

Material	Thickness	SMAW	SAW	GMAW	FCAW	GTAW	PAW	ESW	EGW	RW	FW	OFW	DFW	FRW	EBW	LBW	TB	FB	IB	RB	DB	IRB	DFB
Carbon steel	S	x	x	x		x				x	x	x			x	x	x	x	x	x	x	x	x
	I	x	x	x	x	x				x	x	x		x	x	x	x	x	x	x	x		x
	M	x	x	x	x					x	x	x		x	x	x	x	x	x				x
	T	x	x	x	x			x	x	x	x			x	x			x					x
Low-alloy steel	S	x	x	x		x				x	x	x	x		x	x	x	x	x	x	x	x	x
	I	x	x	x	x	x				x	x		x	x	x	x	x	x	x				x
	M	x	x	x	x					x		x	x	x	x	x	x	x	x				x
	T	x	x	x	x			x		x	x		x	x	x		x					x	
Stainless steel	S	x	x	x		x	x			x	x	x	x		x	x	x	x	x	x	x	x	x
	I	x	x	x	x	x	x			x	x		x	x	x	x	x	x	x				x
	M	x	x	x	x			x	x			x	x	x	x	x	x	x	x				x
	T	x	x	x	x	x						x	x	x			x						x
Cast iron	I	x										x					x	x	x				x
	M	x	x	x	x							x					x	x	x				x
	T	x	x	x	x							x					x						x
Nickel and alloys	S	x		x		x	x			x	x	x			x	x	x	x	x	x	x	x	x
	I	x	x	x		x	x			x	x		x	x	x	x	x	x	x				x
	M	x	x	x			x			x			x	x	x	x	x						x
	T	x		x						x			x	x			x						x

(continued on next page)

TABLE 29.1   *(continued)*   Overview of Commercial Joining Processes*

Material	Thick-ness	SMAW	SAW	GMAW	FCAW	GTAW	PAW	ESW	EGW	RW	FW	OFW	DFW	FRW	EBW	LBW	TB	FB	IB	RB	DB	IRB	DFB	S
Aluminum and alloys	S	x		x		x	x			x	x	x	x	x	x	x	x	x	x	x	x	x	x	x
	I	x		x		x				x	x		x	x	x	x	x	x			x			x
	M	x		x		x					x		x	x	x		x	x			x			x
	T	x		x				x	x		x				x	x	x							x
Titanium and alloys	S			x		x	x			x	x		x		x	x		x	x			x		x
	I			x		x	x				x	x	x	x		x								x
	M			x		x	x				x	x	x	x		x								x
	T			x							x		x			x	x	x						x
Copper and alloys	S			x		x	x				x		x			x	x	x	x				x	x
	I			x			x				x	x	x			x	x		x			x	x	
	M			x						x	x				x	x						x		
	T			x							x		x			x							x	
Magnesium and alloys	S			x		x				x		x	x	x	x					x		x		
	I			x		x				x	x		x	x	x	x	x			x		x		
	M			x							x		x	x	x		x						x	
	T			x							x				x									
Refractory alloys	S			x		x	x			x	x		x			x	x	x	x			x		x
	I			x			x				x		x			x	x						x	
	M									x	x													
	T																							

*This table is presented as a general survey only. In selecting processes to be used with specific alloys, the reader should refer to other appropriate sources of information.

Source: Courtesy of the American Welding Society.

Legend

Process code		Thickness
SMAW—Shielded Metal-Arc Welding	FRW—Friction Welding	S—Sheet: up to 3 mm $\left(\frac{1}{8} \text{ in.}\right)$
SAW—Submerged Arc Welding	EBW—Electron Beam Welding	I—Intermediate: 3 to 6 mm $\left(\frac{1}{8} \text{ to } \frac{1}{4} \text{ in.}\right)$
GMAW—Gas Metal-Arc Welding	LBW—Laser Beam Welding	M—Medium: 6 to 19 mm $\left(\frac{1}{4} \text{ to } \frac{3}{4} \text{ in.}\right)$
FCAW—Flux-Cored Arc Welding	TB—Torch Brazing	T—Thick: 19 mm $\left(\frac{3}{4} \text{ in.}\right)$ and up
GTAW—Gas Tungsten-Arc Welding	FB—Furnace Brazing	
PAW—Plasma Arc Welding	IB—Induction Brazing	
ESW—Electroslag Welding	RB—Resistance Brazing	
EGW—Electrogas Welding	DB—Dip Brazing	
RW—Resistance Welding	IRB—Infrared Brazing	
FW—Flash Welding	DFB—Diffusion Brazing	
OFW—Oxyfuel Gas Welding	S—Soldering	
DFW—Diffusion Welding		

29.5 TESTING WELDED JOINTS

As in all manufacturing processes, the *quality* of a welded joint is established by testing. Several standardized tests and test procedures have been established; they are available from many organizations, such as the American Society for Testing and Materials (ASTM), the American Welding Society (AWS), the American Society of Mechanical Engineers (ASME), the American Society of Civil Engineers (ASCE), and various federal agencies.

Welded joints may be tested either destructively or nondestructively. (See also Sections 36.9 and 36.10.) Each technique has certain capabilities and limitations and sensitivity reliability, and requirement for special equipment and operator skill.

29.5.1 Destructive Techniques

The common methods of testing welded joints destructively are reviewed in this section.

Tension Test. Longitudinal and transverse tension tests are performed, on specimens removed from actual welded joints and from the weld-metal area. Stress–strain curves are then obtained by the procedures described in Section 2.2. These curves indicate the yield strength (Y), ultimate tensile strength (UTS), and ductility of the welded joint (elongation and reduction of area) in different locations and directions.

Tension-Shear Test. The specimens in the tension-shear test (Figs. 29.12a and b) are specially prepared to simulate actual welded joints and procedures. The specimens are subjected to tension, and the shear strength of the weld metal and the location of fracture are determined.

Bend Test. Several bend tests have been developed to determine the ductility and strength of welded joints. In one test, the welded specimen is bent around a fixture (*wraparound* bend test; Fig. 29.13a). In another test, the specimens are tested in *three-point transverse bending* (Fig. 29.13b; also Fig. 2.11a). These tests help to determine the relative ductility and strength of welded joints.

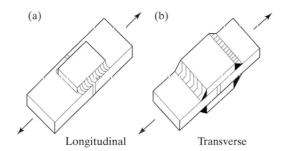

(a) Longitudinal   (b) Transverse

FIGURE 29.12   Two types of specimens for tension-shear testing of welded joints.

FIGURE 29.13   (a) Wrap-around bend test method. (b) Three-point bending of welded specimens—see also Fig. 2.11.

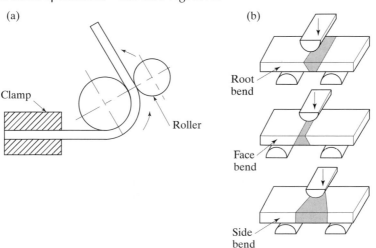

(a) Clamp   Roller

(b) Root bend   Face bend   Side bend

Fracture Toughness Test.   Fracture toughness tests commonly utilize the impact testing techniques, described in Section 2.9. *Charpy V-notch* specimens are first prepared and then tested for toughness. Another toughness test is the *drop-weight test*, in which the energy is supplied by a falling weight.

Corrosion and Creep Tests.   In addition to mechanical tests, welded joints may be tested for resistance to corrosion and creep. Because of the difference in the composition and microstructure of the materials in the weld zone, *preferential corrosion* may take place in it. (See Fig. 29.5.) Creep tests are important in determining the behavior of welded joints at elevated temperatures.

Testing of Spot Welds.   Spot-welded joints may be tested for weld-nugget strength using the following tests (Fig. 29.14):

1. **tension-shear**;
2. **cross-tension**;
3. **twist**;
4. **peel**. (See also Fig. 30.8.)

Because they are easy to perform and inexpensive, tension-shear tests are commonly used in fabricating facilities. The cross-tension and twist tests are capable of revealing flaws, cracks, and porosity in the weld area. The peel test is commonly used for thin sheets; after the bending and peeling of the joint, the shape and size of the torn-out weld nugget is observed.

FIGURE 29.14   (a) Tension-shear test for spot welds. (b) Cross-tension test. (c) Twist test. (d) Peel test; see also Fig. 30.8.

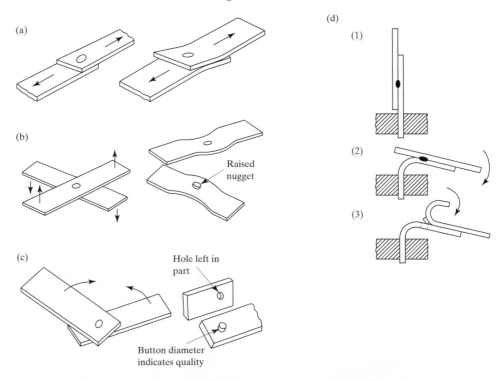

29.5.2 Nondestructive Techniques

Welded structures often have to be tested nondestructively, particularly for critical applications where weld failure can be catastrophic, such as pressure vessels, load-bearing structural members, and power plants. Nondestructive testing techniques for welded joints usually consist of (a) **visual**, (b) **radiographic**, (c) **magnetic-particle**, (d) **liquid-penetrant**, and (e) **ultrasonic** testing methods.

The details of these tests are described in Section 36.9. Testing for *hardness* distribution in the weld zone may also be a useful indicator of weld strength and microstructural changes.

29.6 WELD DESIGN AND PROCESS SELECTION

In addition to the material characteristics described thus far, the selection of a weld joint and of a welding process involves the following considerations:

- the configuration of the components or structure to be welded, and their thickness and size;
- the methods used to manufacture the components;
- the service requirements, such as the type of loading and the stresses generated;
- the location, accessibility, and ease of welding;
- the effects of distortion and discoloration;
- the appearance;
- the costs involved in the edge preparation, the welding, and the post-processing of the weld, including those from machining and finishing operations.

As in all manufacturing processes, the optimum choice is the one that meets all design and service requirements at minimum cost. Some examples of weld characteristics are shown in Fig. 29.15; they emphasize the need for careful consideration of the factors just identified.

FIGURE 29.15 Design guidelines for welding. *Source*: J. G. Bralla (ed.), *Handbook of Product Design for Manufacturing.* Copyright © 1986, McGraw-Hill Publishing Company. Used with permission.

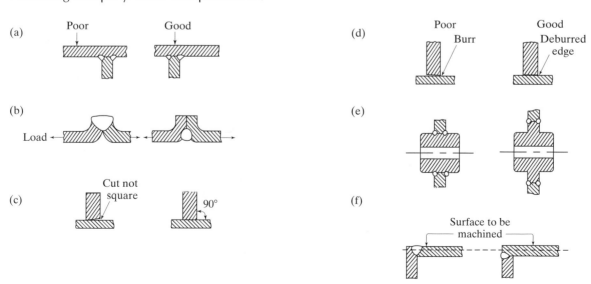

Basic arc and gas weld symbols							
Bead	Fillet	Plug or slot	Groove				
			Square	V	Bevel	U	J
⌒	◺	⏌⎽⏌	‖	⋁	⋁	⋃	⋃

Basic resistance weld symbols			
Spot	Projection	Seam	Flash or upset
✕	✕	✕✕✕	❘

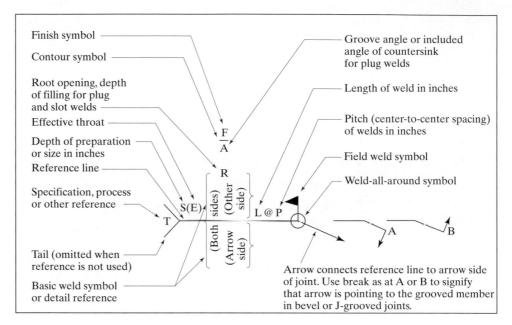

FIGURE 29.16   Standard identification and symbols for welds.

General design guidelines may be summarized as follows:

a. Product design should minimize the number of welds, because welding can be costly unless automated. Weld location should be selected so as to avoid excessive stresses or stress concentrations in the welded structure, and secondarily for appearance.

b. Components should fit properly before welding. The method used to prepare edges (such as sawing, machining, or shearing) can affect weld quality.

c. Some designs can avoid or minimize the need for edge preparation.

d. Weld-bead size should be kept to a minimum, to conserve weld metal.

e. Weld location should be selected so as not to interfere with further processing of the part or with its intended use and appearance.

Weld Symbols.   Standardized symbols commonly used in engineering drawings to describe the type of weld and its characteristics are shown in Fig. 29.16. These symbols identify the type of weld, the groove design, the weld size and length, the welding process, the sequence of operations, and various other information. Further details about these symbols can be found in the references cited at the end of this chapter.

Example: Weld Design Selection

Three different types of weld design are shown in Fig. 29.17. In illustration (a), the two vertical joints can be welded either externally or internally. Note that full-length external welding will take considerable time and will require more weld material than the alternative design, which consists of intermittent internal welds. Moreover, by the alternative method, the appearance of the structure is improved and distortion is reduced.

In illustration (b), it can be shown that the design on the right can carry three times the moment M of the one on the left. Note that both designs require the same amount of weld metal and welding time.

In illustration (c), the weld on the left requires about twice the amount of weld material than does the design on the right. Note, also, that, because more material must be machined, the design on the left will require more time for edge preparation, and more base metal will be wasted.

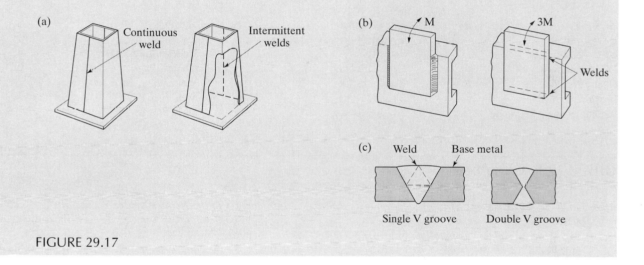

FIGURE 29.17

SUMMARY

- The metallurgy of the welded joint is an important aspect of all welding processes, because it determines the strength and toughness of the joint. The welded joint consists of solidified metal and a heat-affected zone; each has a wide variation in microstructure and properties, depending on the metals joined and on the filler metals.

- Because of severe thermal gradients in the weld zone, distortion, residual stresses, and cracking can be a significant problem.

- Metals and alloys can be welded and joined by a variety of processes. Their weldability depends greatly on their composition, on the type of welding operation involved, and on the control of welding parameters. Important considerations include the joint design, the surface preparation, the protective atmosphere(s), the appearance and quality of the weld, and the subsequent testing of welded joints for safety and reliability.

- General guidelines are available to help in the initial selection of suitable and economical welding methods for a particular application.

TRENDS

- The characteristics and properties of the welded joint for newly developed high-strength alloys are under continued study.
- Quality assurance and joint reliability continue to be important topics in welding processes and their development.
- Welding techniques for aluminum aerospace structures and for newly developed alloys are under continued development.
- Methods for nondestructive evaluation of welded joints continue to be an important area of research. Especially important is the reinspection of existing welded structures that may have been subjected to stress corrosion and/or fatigue, such as aging aircraft.

KEY TERMS

Arc strikes	Lamellar tears	Tension-shear test
Base metal	Overlap	Twist test
Cross-tension test	Porosity	Undercutting
Discontinuities	Proof-stressing	Underfilling
Heat-affected zone	Residual stresses	Weldability
Incomplete fusion	Slag inclusions	Weld metal
Incomplete penetration	Stress relieving	Weld profile

BIBLIOGRAPHY

ASM Handbook, Vol. 6: *Welding, Brazing, and Soldering.* ASM International, 1993.

Cary, H.B., *Modern Welding Technology* (4th ed.). Prentice Hall, 1997.

Croft, D., *Heat Treatment of Welded Steel Structures.* Woodhead Publishing Ltd., 1996.

Davies, A.C., *The Science and Practice of Welding* (10th ed.), 2 vols. Cambridge University Press, 1993.

Evans, G.M., and N. Bailey, *Metallurgy of Basic Weld Metal.* Woodhead Publishing Ltd., 1997.

Galyen, J., G. Sear, and C. Tuttle, *Welding: Fundamentals and Procedures.* Wiley, 1985.

Granjon, H., *Fundamentals of Welding Metallurgy.* Woodhead Publishing, 1991.

Introduction to the Nondestructive Testing of Welded Joints (2d ed.). American Society of Mechanical Engineers, 1996.

Jeffus, L.F., *Welding: Principles and Applications* (4th ed.). Delmar Publishers, 1997.

Jellison, R., *Welding Fundamentals.* Prentice Hall, 1995.

Kou, S., *Welding Metallurgy.* Wiley, 1987.

Lancaster, J.F., *Metallurgy of Welding.* Chapman & Hall, 1993.

Mouser, J.D., *Welding Codes, Standards, and Specifications.* McGraw-Hill, 1997.

Stout, R.D., *Weldability of Steels.* Welding Research Council, 1987.

Welding Handbook (8th ed.), 3 vols. American Welding Society, 1987.

Welding Inspection. American Welding Society, 1980.

REVIEW QUESTIONS

29.1 Describe the features of a fusion weld, and identify the different regions.

29.2 What are the characteristics of the heat-affected zone?

29.3 What is meant by weld quality? Discuss the factors that influence it.

29.4 Describe the common types of discontinuities in welds.

29.5 Why are residual stresses important in welded components? Describe the methods used for relieving or reducing residual stresses in welds.

29.6 What is weldability?

29.7 Explain why some joints may have to be preheated prior to welding.

29.8 List the rules that must be followed to avoid cracking in welded joints.

29.9 How can underbead cracks be detected?

29.10 How can slag inclusions in welding be avoided?

29.11 Explain the reasons for incomplete fusion.

29.12 What should one do if a weld is underfilled?

29.13 Describe the drawback of (a) underfill, and (b) overfill.

QUALITATIVE PROBLEMS

29.14 What are the similarities and differences between the casting of metals (Chapters 10 and 11) and fusion welds?

29.15 Explain the effect of the stiffness of the various components to be welded on weld defects.

29.16 Discuss the weldability of several metals, and explain why some metals are easier to weld than others. Cast iron is generally difficult to weld. Why?

29.17 Must the filler metal be of the same composition as the base metal to be welded? Explain your response.

29.18 Explain the factors that contribute to any differences in properties across a welded joint.

29.19 Comment on your observations concerning Fig. 29.14.

29.20 Describe the factors that contribute to the cost of welding. Which costs are difficult to minimize?

29.21 Describe your observations concerning Figs. 29.3 and 29.4.

29.22 How does the weldability of steel change as its carbon content increases? Why?

29.23 Describe your observations concerning the welding design guidelines illustrated in Fig. 29.15.

29.24 In Fig. 29.11, assume that most of the top portion of the top piece is cut horizontally with a sharp saw. The residual stresses will now be disturbed and, as was described in Section 2.11, the part will undergo shape change. For this case, how do you think the part will distort: curved downward or upward? Explain your response (See also Problem 2.42 and Fig. 2.29d).

29.25 It was stated in the text that incomplete fusion can be avoided by providing enough shielding gas. Explain how shielding gases affect fusion.

29.26 Why does preheating the parts to be welded reduce the likelihood of cracking?

29.27 If much welding has to be done on a part, should all of it be done at once or should it be done a little at a time, with sufficient time allowed for cooling between weld beads?

29.28 Describe the reasons that fatigue failures generally occur in the heat-affected zones of welds instead of through the weld bead itself.

29.29 If the materials to be welded are preheated, is the likelihood for porosity increased or decreased? Explain your response.

29.30 In the spot-weld tests shown in Figure 29.14, what would be the reasons for weld failures to occur at the interface of the two components, instead of forming a raised nugget as in sketch (d)(3)?

QUANTITATIVE PROBLEMS

29.31 Review the two weld designs in Fig. 29.17b. On the basis of what you learned in courses on *Strength of Materials*, show that the design on the right is capable of supporting a larger external moment, as shown in the figure.

29.32 Plot the hardness in Fig. 29.3b as a function of the distance from the top surface, and discuss your observations.

SYNTHESIS AND DESIGN

29.33 Are there common factors affecting the weldability, the castability, the formability, and the machinability of metals? Explain with appropriate examples.

29.34 In Fig. 29.17, three different weld designs are illustrated. Survey the literature on weld designs, and give several other examples where such choices have to be made for various reasons.

29.35 Assume that you are asked to inspect a weld for a critical application. Describe the procedure that you would follow during your inspection. Would the size of the part or structure you are inspecting have an influence on your methodology? Explain.

29.36 If you find a flaw in a welded joint during inspection, how would you go about determining whether the flaw is important?

29.37 Lattice booms for cranes are constructed from extruded cross sections that are welded together. Any warpage which causes such a boom to deviate from straightness severely reduces its lifting capacity. Perform a literature search on the approaches used to minimize distortion due to welding and to correct for it, in the construction of lattice booms.

29.38 A common practice for repairing expensive broken or worn parts, such as may occur when, for example, a fragment is broken from a forging, is to fill the area with layers of weld bead and then to machine the part back to its original dimensions. Make a list of the precautions that you would suggest to someone who uses this approach.

29.39 A welded frame needs first to be disassembled and then to be repaired (by rewelding the members). What procedures would you recommend for disassembly and for preparation for welding?

30

Brazing, Soldering, Adhesive-Bonding, and Mechanical-Fastening Processes

30.1 INTRODUCTION

In almost all the joining processes described in Chapters 27 through 29, the metals to be joined were heated to elevated temperatures by various means to cause fusion or bonding at the joint. What if we want to join materials that cannot withstand high temperatures, such as electronic components? What if the parts to be joined are delicate or intricate, or are made of two or more materials with very different characteristics, properties, thicknesses, and cross-sections?

This chapter first describes two joining processes (brazing and soldering) which permit lower temperatures than those required for welding. Filler metals are first placed in or supplied to the joint; they are then melted using an external source of heat. Upon solidification, a strong joint is obtained. Brazing and soldering are arbitrarily distinguished by temperature. Temperatures for soldering are lower than those for brazing, and the strength of a soldered joint is much lower.

This chapter also describes adhesive-bonding techniques. The ancient method of joining parts with animal-derived glues, which is employed in labeling, packaging, and bookbinding, has now been developed into an important technology, with wide applications in aerospace and various other industries.

All the joints described so far are of a permanent nature. In many applications, there are situations where joined parts have to be taken apart for replacement, maintenance, repair, or adjustment. How do we take apart a product without destroying the joint? If we need joints that are truly nonpermanent, but are as strong as welded joints, the solution obviously is to use mechanical means, such as bolts, screws, nuts, and a variety of similar fasteners.

This chapter also describes the advantages and limitations of mechanical fastening techniques. With this chapter, our description of all commonly used methods of joining is concluded.

30.2 BRAZING

Brazing is a joining process in which a filler metal is placed at or between the faying surfaces to be joined, and the temperature is raised enough to melt the filler metal but not the workpieces (Fig. 30.1a). The molten metal fills the closely fitting space by *capillary* action. Upon cooling and solidification of the filler metal, a strong joint is obtained. Brazing comes from the word *brass*, an archaic word meaning to harden, and was first used as far back as 3000–2000 B.C.

There are two main types of brazing processes: (a) Ordinary **brazing**, which we have already described, and (b) **braze welding** (Fig. 30.1b), in which the filler metal is deposited at the joint with a technique similar to oxyfuel gas welding.

Filler metals used for brazing melt above 450 °C (840 °F). The temperatures employed in brazing are below the melting point (solidus temperature) of the metals to be joined. The strength of the brazed joint depends on (a) joint design and (b) the adhesion at the interfaces between the workpieces and the filler metal. Consequently, the surfaces to be brazed should be chemically or mechanically cleaned to ensure full capillary action; the use of a flux is therefore important.

30.2.1 Filler Metals

Several *filler metals (braze metals)* are available, with a range of brazing temperatures (Table 30.1). They come in a variety of shapes, such as wire, rings, shims, and filings. The choice of the filler metal and of its composition are important, in order to avoid embrittlement of the joint (by grain boundary penetration of liquid metal), formation of brittle

FIGURE 30.1   (a) Brazing and (b) braze welding operations.

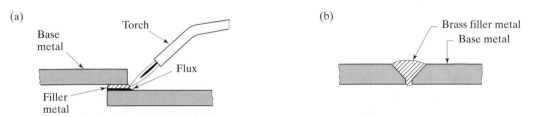

TABLE 30.1   Typical Filler Metals for Brazing Various Metals and Alloys

Base metal	Filler metal	Brazing temperature, (°C)
Aluminum and its alloys	Aluminum-silicon	570–620
Magnesium alloys	Magnesium-aluminum	580–625
Copper and its alloys	Copper-phosphorus	700–925
Ferrous and nonferrous (except aluminum and magnesium)	Silver and copper alloys, copper- phosphorus	620–1150
Iron-, nickel-, and cobalt-base alloys	Gold	900–1100
Stainless steels, nickel- and cobalt-base alloys	Nickel-silver	925–1200

intermetallic compounds at the joint (Section 4.2.2), and galvanic corrosion in the joint. Note that filler metals for brazing, unlike those for other welding operations, generally have a composition significantly different from the metal(s) to be joined.

Because of diffusion between the filler metal and the base metal, the mechanical and metallurgical properties of a joint can change in subsequent processing or during the service life of a brazed component. For example, when titanium is brazed with pure tin as the filler metal, it is possible for the tin to diffuse completely into the titanium base metal, by subsequent aging or by heat treatment; when that happens, the joint no longer exists.

30.2.2 Fluxes

The use of a *flux* is essential in brazing, in order to prevent oxidation and to remove oxide films from workpiece surfaces. Brazing fluxes are generally made of borax, boric acid, borates, fluorides, and chlorides. *Wetting agents* may also be added, to improve both the wetting characteristics of the molten filler metal and the capillary action.

Surfaces to be brazed must be clean of and free from rust, oil, and other contaminants. Clean surfaces are essential, in order to obtain proper wetting and spreading characteristics of the molten filler metal in the joint and to develop maximum bond strength. Sand blasting may also be used to improve the surface finish of faying surfaces. Because they are corrosive, fluxes should be removed after brazing (usually by washing with hot water).

30.2.3 Brazing Methods

The heating methods used also identify the various brazing processes as described below.

Torch Brazing.   The heat source in *torch brazing* (TB) is oxyfuel gas with a carburizing flame (Fig. 27.1c). Brazing is performed by first heating the joint with the torch, then depositing the brazing rod or wire in the joint. Suitable part thicknesses are usually in the range of from 0.25 to 6 mm (from 0.01 to 0.25 in.). More than one torch may be used in this process.

Although it can be automated as a production process, torch brazing is difficult to control and requires skilled labor. This process can also be used for repair work. The basic equipment for manual brazing costs about $300, but the cost can run more than $50,000 for automated systems.

Furnace Brazing.   The parts in *furnace brazing* (FB) are first precleaned, and then preloaded with brazing metal in appropriate configurations (Fig. 30.2), before being placed in a furnace. Furnaces may be batch-type, for complex shapes, or continuous-type, for high

FIGURE 30.2   An example of furnace brazing: (a) before, (b) after. Note that the filler metal is a shaped wire.

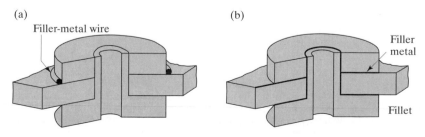

(a)

Filler-metal wire

(b)

Filler metal

Fillet

production runs—especially for small parts with simple joint designs. Vacuum furnaces or neutral atmospheres are used for metals that react with the environment.

Skilled labor is not required, and complex shapes can be brazed, because the whole assembly is heated uniformly in the furnace. The costs of the furnaces vary widely, ranging from about $2,000 for simple batch furnaces to more than $300,000 for continuous vacuum furnaces.

Induction Brazing.   The source of heat in *induction brazing* (IB) is induction heating by high-frequency AC current. (See Section 4.12.5.) Parts are preloaded with filler metal and are placed near the induction coils for rapid heating. Unless a protective atmosphere is utilized, fluxes are generally used. Part thicknesses are usually less than 3 mm (0.125 in.). Induction brazing is particularly suitable for brazing parts continuously (Fig. 30.3). The cost for small units is about $10,000.

Resistance Brazing.   In *resistance brazing* (RB), the source of heat is the electrical resistance of the components to be brazed. Electrodes are utilized for this method, much as they are in resistance welding. Either parts are preloaded with filler metal, or it is supplied externally during brazing. Parts that are brazed by this process commonly have thicknesses of 0.1 mm–12 mm (0.004 in.–0.5 in.).

As in induction brazing, the process is rapid, heating zones can be confined to very small areas, and the process can be automated to produce uniform quality. Equipment costs range from $1,000 for simple units to more than $10,000 for larger, more complex units.

Dip Brazing.   *Dip brazing* (DB) is carried out by dipping the assemblies to be brazed into either a molten filler-metal bath or a molten salt bath (Section 4.12.3), at a temperature just above the melting point of the filler metal. All workpiece surfaces are thus coated with the filler metal. Consequently, dip brazing in metal baths is used only for small parts, such as sheet, wire, and fittings, usually of less than 5 mm (0.2 in.) in thickness or diameter. Molten salt baths, which also act as fluxes, are used for complex assemblies of various thicknesses.

Depending on the size of the parts and the size of the bath, as many as 1000 joints can be made at one time by dip brazing. The cost of equipment varies widely, from about $2,000 to more than $200,000; the more expensive equipment includes various computer-control features.

Infrared Brazing.   The heat source in *infrared brazing* (IRB) is a high-intensity quartz lamp. This process is particularly suitable for brazing very thin components, usual-

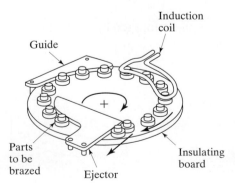

FIGURE 30.3   Schematic illustration of a continuous induction-brazing setup, for increased productivity. *Source*: ASM International.

ly less than 1 mm (0.04 in.) thick, including honeycomb structures (Section 16.14). The radiant energy is focused on the joint, and the process can be carried out in a vacuum. Equipment cost ranges from $500 to $30,000.

Diffusion Brazing. *Diffusion brazing* (DFB) is carried out in a furnace where, with proper control of temperature and time, the filler metal diffuses into the faying surfaces of the components to be joined. The brazing time required may range from 30 minutes to 24 hours. Diffusion brazing is used for strong lap or butt joints and for difficult joining operations. Because the rate of diffusion at the interface does not depend on the thickness of the components, part thicknesses may range from foil to as much as 50 mm (2 in.). The cost of equipment ranges from about $50,000 to $300,000.

30.2.4 Braze Welding

The joint in *braze welding* is prepared as it is in fusion welding (see Chapter 27). While an oxyacetylene torch with an oxidizing flame is used, filler metal is deposited at the joint (see Fig. 30.1b), rather than by capillary action (as in ordinary brazing). As a result, considerably more filler metal is used than in brazing. However, temperatures in braze welding are generally lower than in fusion welding, and part distortion is minimal.

The use of a flux is essential in this process. The principal use of braze welding is for maintenance and repair work, such as on ferrous castings and on steel components.

30.2.5 Brazing Process Capabilities

Typical brazed joints are illustrated in Fig. 30.4. In general, dissimilar metals can be assembled with good joint strength; typical products are carbide drill bits and carbide inserts on steel shanks. (See Fig. 22.23f.) The shear strength of brazed joints can reach 800 MPa (120 ksi) by the use of brazing alloys containing silver (silver solder). Intricate, lightweight shapes can be joined rapidly and with little distortion. Brazing can be automated and used for mass production.

FIGURE 30.4   Joint designs commonly used in brazing operations. The clearance between the two parts being brazed is an important factor in joint strength. If the clearance is too small, the molten braze metal will not fully penetrate the interface. If it is too large, there will be insufficient capillary action for the molten metal to fill the interface.

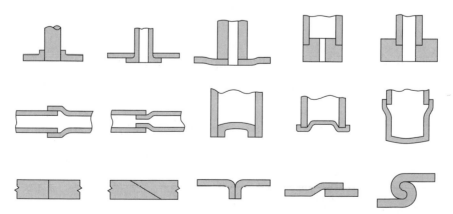

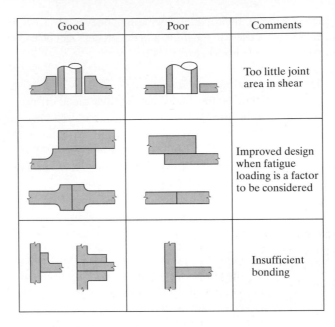

Good	Poor	Comments
		Too little joint area in shear
		Improved design when fatigue loading is a factor to be considered
		Insufficient bonding

FIGURE 30.5   Examples of good and poor design for brazing. *Source:* American Welding Society.

30.2.6 Design for Brazing

As in all joining processes, joint design is important in brazing. Some design guidelines are given in Fig. 30.5. Strong joints require a larger contact area for brazing than for welding. The typical joint clearance in brazing ranges from 0.025 mm to 0.2 mm (0.001 in. to 0.008 in.). The clearances must fit within a very small dimensional tolerance range, because larger clearances reduce the strength of the brazed joint. A variety of special fixtures may be required to hold the parts together during brazing; some will have provision for thermal expansion and contraction.

30.3 SOLDERING

In *soldering*, the filler metal, called **solder**, melts at a relatively low temperature. As in brazing, the solder fills the joint by capillary action between closely fitting or closely placed components. Thus, important characteristics for solders are high wetting capability and low surface tension. Heat sources for soldering are usually soldering irons, torches, or ovens. Soldering with copper–gold and tin–lead alloys was first practiced as far back as 4000–3000 B.C.

Some soldering techniques are similar to brazing methods. (See Section 30.2.3.) Among them are the following:

a. **torch soldering** (TS);
b. **furnace soldering** (FS);
c. **iron soldering** (INS), with the use of a soldering iron;
d. **induction soldering** (IS);
e. **resistance soldering** (RS);
f. **dip soldering** (DS);
g. **infrared soldering** (IRS).

Other techniques are the following:

h. ultrasonic soldering, in which a transducer subjects the molten solder to ultrasonic cavitation and thereby removes the oxide films from the surfaces to be joined and so eliminates the need for a flux;

i. reflow (paste) soldering (also RS);

j. wave soldering (WS).

The last two soldering techniques, which are significantly different from other soldering methods, are described in more detail in the following sections below.

30.3.1 Reflow (Paste) Soldering

Solder pastes are solder-metal particles held together by flux and by binding and wetting agents. The pastes are semi-solid in consistency. They have high viscosity but are able to maintain a solid shape for relatively long periods of time—in this property they are similar to greases and cake frostings.

The paste is placed directly onto the joint, or on flat objects for finer detail, and it can be applied via a screening or stenciling process, as shown in Fig. 30.6a. Stenciling is very commonly used during the attaching of electrical components to printed circuit boards. An additional benefit of this method is that the surface tension of the paste helps keep surface-mount packages aligned on their pads; this feature improves the reliability of these solder joints.

Once the paste has been placed and the joint assembled, the paste is heated in a furnace, and reflow soldering takes place. In reflow soldering, the product is heated in a controlled manner, so that the following sequence of events occurs:

1. Solvents present in the paste are evaporated.

2. The flux in the paste is activated, and fluxing action occurs.

3. The components are carefully preheated.

4. The solder particles are melted and wet the joint.

5. The assembly is cooled at a low rate to prevent thermal shock to and fracture of the solder joint.

While this process appears to be straightforward, there are many process variables for each stage, and good control over temperatures and exposures must be maintained at each stage, to ensure proper joint strength.

30.3.2 Wave Soldering

Wave soldering is a very popular approach for attaching circuit components to their boards. To understand wave soldering, it is imperative to appreciate that molten solder does not wet all surfaces; indeed, solder will not stick to most polymer surfaces, and it is easy to remove while molten. Also, as can be shown with a simple hand soldering iron, the solder only wets metal surfaces and forms a good bond when the metal is preheated to a certain temperature. Therefore, wave soldering requires separate fluxing and preheating operations before it can be successfully completed.

A typical wave-soldering operation is shown in Figure 30.6b. A standing laminar wave of molten solder is generated by a pump. Preheated and prefluxed circuit boards are conveyed over the wave; the solder wets the exposed metal surfaces, but it does not stay attached to the polymer package for the integrated circuits and it does not stick to the

(a)

(1)

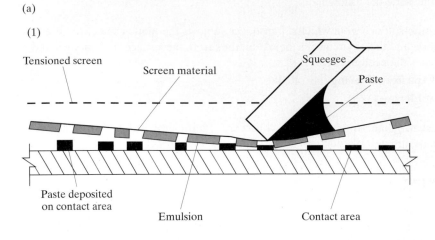

(2)

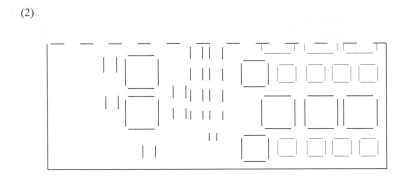

(b)

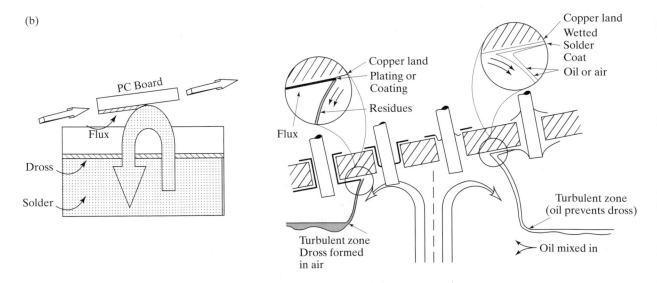

FIGURE 30.6   (a) Screening or stenciling paste onto a printed circuit board: 1. schematic illustration of the stenciling process; 2. a section of a typical stencil pattern. (b) Schematic illustration of the wave soldering process. *(continued)*

(c)
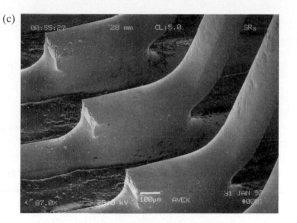

polymer-coated circuit boards. An air knife (basically a high velocity jet of hot air) blows excess solder from the joint, to prevent bridging between adjacent leads.

When surface-mount packages are to be wave soldered, they must be adhesively bonded to the circuit board before the soldering can commence. This bonding is usually accomplished by screening or stenciling epoxy onto the boards, placing the components in their proper locations, curing the epoxy, inverting the board and then performing wave soldering. An SEM photograph of a typical surface-mount joint is shown in Figure 30.6c.

Example: Soldering of Components onto a Printed Circuit Board

The computer and consumer electronics industries place extremely high demands on electronic components. It is expected that the integrated circuits and other electronic devices will function reliably for extended periods of time, during which they can be subjected to significant temperature variation and to vibration. In recognition of this requirement, it is essential that the solder joints used to attach such devices to circuit boards be sufficiently strong and reliable and also that the solder joints be applied extremely rapidly with automated equipment.

A continuing trend in the computer industry and in the consumer electronics industry is toward continual reduction of chip sizes and increasing compactness of circuit boards. Further space savings are achieved by mounting integrated circuits into surface-mount packages, which allow tighter packing on a circuit board and, more importantly, the mounting of components on both sides of a circuit board. (See Figure 34.12.)

A challenging problem arises when a printed circuit board has both surface-mount and in-line circuits on the same board, and it is desired to solder all the joints via a reliable automated process. A subtle point should be recognized: all of the in-line circuits should be restricted to insertion from one side of the board. Indeed, there is no performance requirement which would dictate otherwise, and this restriction greatly simplifies manufacturing.

The basic steps in soldering the connections on such a board are as follows (Fig. 30.6):

1. Apply solder paste to one side.
2. Place the surface-mount packages onto the board; also, insert in-line packages through the primary side of the board.
3. Reflow the solder.
4. Apply adhesive to the secondary side of the board.
5. Attach the surface mount devices on the secondary side using the adhesive.
6. Cure the adhesive.

7. Perform a wave soldering operation on the secondary side, to produce electrical attachment of the surface mounts and the in-line circuits to the board.

Applying solder paste is done with chemically etched stencils or screens, so that the paste is placed only onto the designated areas of a circuit board. (Stencils are more widely used for fine-pitch devices and produce a more uniform thickness of paste.) Surface-mount circuit components are then placed on the board, and the board is heated in a furnace to around 200 °C (400 °F), to reflow the solder and thus to form strong connections between the surface mount and the circuit board.

At this point, the leaded components are inserted into the primary side of the board, their leads are crimped, and then the board is flipped over. An adhesive pattern is printed onto the board, using a dot of epoxy at the center of a surface-mount component location. The surface-mount packages are then placed onto the adhesive, usually by high speed automated computer-controlled systems. The adhesive is then cured, the board is flipped and wave soldering is done.

The wave soldering operation simultaneously joins the surface-mount components to the secondary side and solders the leads of the in-line components from the board's primary side. The board is then cleaned and inspected before electronic quality checks are performed.

30.3.3 Types of Solders and Fluxes

Solders, from the Latin *solidare*, meaning to make solid, melt at a temperature that is the eutectic point of the solder alloy. (See also Fig. 4.7.) Solders have traditionally been tin–lead alloys, in various proportions. For example, a solder of 61.9% Sn–38.1% Pb melts at 370° F, whereas tin melts at 232° C (450° F) and lead at 327° C (621° F). For special applications and higher joint strength, especially at elevated temperatures, other solder compositions that can be used are tin–zinc, lead–silver, cadmium–silver, and zinc–aluminum alloys (Table 30.2).

Because of the toxicity of lead and its adverse effects on the environment, **lead-free solders** are being developed and are now coming into wider use. Among various materials under consideration are silver, indium, and bismuth eutectic alloys, in combination with tin. Three typical compositions are 96.5% Sn–3.5% Ag, 42% Sn–58% Bi, and 48% Sn–52% In. However, none of these combinations appears to meet all desirable requirements.

Fluxes.   In soldering, *fluxes* are used, as they are in welding and brazing, and for the same purposes. (See Section 30.2.2.) Fluxes are generally of two types:

1. *inorganic acids* or *salts*, such as zinc ammonium chloride solutions, which clean the surface rapidly. After the soldering, the flux residues should be removed by washing the joint thoroughly with water, to avoid corrosion.

2. noncorrosive *resin-based fluxes*, used in electrical applications.

TABLE 30.2   Types of Solders and their Applications

Tin-lead	General purpose
Tin-zinc	Aluminum
Lead-silver	Strength at higher than room temperature
Cadmium-silver	Strength at high temperatures
Zinc-aluminum	Aluminum; corrosion resistance
Tin-silver	Electronics
Tin-bismuth	Electronics

30.3.4 Soldering Process Capabilities

Soldering is used extensively in the electronics industry. Unlike brazing, soldering temperatures are relatively low, so a soldered joint has very limited use at elevated temperatures. Moreover, because solders do not generally have much strength, they are not used for load-bearing (structural) members. Because of the small faying surfaces, butt joints are rarely made with solders. In other situations, joint strength is improved by *mechanical interlocking* of the joint (Fig. 30.7).

Soldering can be used to join various metals and thicknesses. Copper and such precious metals as silver and gold are easy to solder. Aluminum and stainless steels are difficult to solder, because of their strong, thin oxide film. (See Section 31.2.) However, these and other metals can be soldered with the aid of special fluxes that modify surfaces.

Although manual operations require skill and are time-consuming, soldering speeds can be high with automated equipment. The cost of soldering equipment depends on its complexity and on the level of automation. It ranges from less than $100, for industrial soldering irons, to more than $50,000, for automated equipment.

Design guidelines for soldering are similar to those for brazing. Some frequently used joint designs are shown in Fig. 30.7. Note again the importance of large contact surfaces for developing sufficient joint strength in soldered products.

FIGURE 30.7 Joint designs commonly used for soldering. Note that examples (e), (g), (i), and (j) are mechanically joined prior to being soldered, for improved strength. *Source*: American Welding Society and M.P. Groover. *Fundamentals of Modern Manufacturing: Materials, Processes and Systems.* ©1996. Reprinted by permission of John Wiley and Sons.

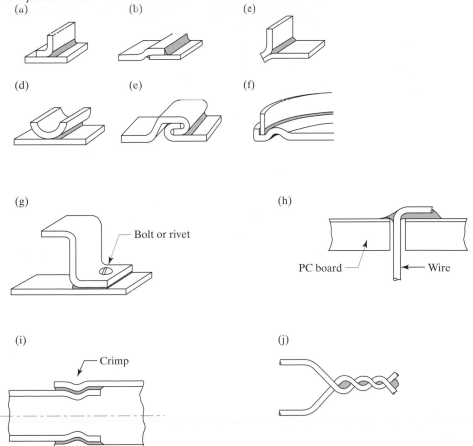

30.4 ADHESIVE BONDING

Many components and products can be joined and assembled by the use of an **adhesive**, rather than by one of the joining methods described thus far. *Adhesive bonding* has been a common method of joining and assembly in such applications as labeling, packaging, bookbinding, home furnishings, and footware.

Plywood, developed in 1905, is a typical example of the adhesive bonding of several layers of wood with glue. Adhesive bonding has been gaining increased acceptance in manufacturing ever since its first use on a large scale: the assembly of load-bearing components in aircraft during World War II (1939–1945).

Adhesives are available in several forms: liquid, paste, solution, emulsion, powder, tape, and film. When applied, adhesives generally are about 0.1 mm (0.004 in.) thick.

To meet the requirements of a particular application, an adhesive may need one or more of the following properties (Table 30.3):

- strength (shear and peel);
- toughness;
- resistance to various fluids and chemicals;
- resistance to environmental degradation, including heat and moisture; and
- ability to wet the surfaces to be bonded.

30.4.1 Types of Adhesives, and Adhesive Systems

Several types of adhesives are available (and they continue to be developed) that provide adequate joint strength, including fatigue strength (Table 30.4). The three basic types of adhesives are the following:

1. **natural adhesives**, such as starch, dextrin (a gummy substance obtained from starch), soya flour, and animal products;

TABLE 30.3   Typical Properties and Characteristics of Chemically Reactive Structural Adhesives

	Epoxy	Polyurethane	Modified acrylic	Cyanoacrylate	Anaerobic
Impact resistance	Poor	Excellent	Good	Poor	Fair
Tension-shear strength, MPa (10^3 psi)	15.4 (2.2)	15.4 (2.2)	25.9 (3.7)	18.9 (2.7)	17.5 (2.5)
Peel strength, N/m (lbf/in.)	<525 (3)	14,000 (80)	5250 (30)	<525 (3)	1750 (10)
Substrates bonded	Most materials	Most smooth, nonporous	Most smooth, nonporous	Most nonporous metals or plastics	Metals, glass, thermosets
Service temperature range, °C (°F)	−55 to 120 (−70 to 250)	−160 to 80 (−250 to 175)	70 to 120 (−100 to 250)	−55 to 80 (−70 to 175)	−55 to 150 (−70 to 300)
Heat cure or mixing required	Yes	Yes	No	No	No
Solvent resistance	Excellent	Good	Good	Good	Excellent
Moisture resistance	Excellent	Fair	Good	Poor	Good
Gap limitation, mm (in.)	None	None	0.75 (0.03)	0.25 (0.01)	0.60 (0.025)
Odor	Mild	Mild	Strong	Moderate	Mild
Toxicity	Moderate	Moderate	Moderate	Low	Low
Flammability	Low	Low	High	Low	Low

Source: Advanced Materials & Processes, July 1990, ASM International.

TABLE 30.4   General Properties of Adhesives

Type	Comments	Applications
Acrylic	Thermoplastic; quick setting; tough bond at room temperature; two component; good solvent chemical and impact resistance; short work life; odorous; ventilation required	Fiberglass and steel sandwich bonds, tennis racquets, metal parts, plastics.
Anaearobic	Thermoset; easy to use; slow curing; bonds at room temperature; curing occurs in absence of air, will not cure where air contacts adherents; one component; not good on permeable surfaces	Close fitting machine parts such as shafts and pulleys, nuts and bolts, bushings and pins.
Epoxy	Thermoset; one or two component; tough bond; strongest of engineering adhesives; high tensile and low peel strengths; resists moisture and high temperature; difficult to use	Metal, ceramic and rigid plastic parts.
Cyanoacrylate	Thermoplastic; quick setting; tough bond at room temperature; easy to use; colorless.	"Crazy glue."™
Hot melt	Thermoplastic; quick setting, rigid or flexible bonds; easy to apply; brittle at low temperatures; based on ethylene vinyl acetate, polyolefins, polyamides and polyesters	Bonds most materials. Packaging, book binding, metal can joints.
Pressure sensitive	Thermoplastic; variable strength bonds. Primer anchors adhesive to roll tape backing material, a release agent on the back of web permits unwinding. Made of polyacrylate esters and various natural and synthetic rubber	Tapes, labels, stickers.
Phenolic	Thermoset; oven cured, strong bond; High tensile and low impact strength; brittle, easy to use; cures by solvent evaporation.	Acoustical padding, brake lining and clutch pads, abrasive grain bonding, honeycomb structures.
Silicone	Thermoset; slow curing, flexible; bonds at room temperature; high impact and peel strength; rubber-like	Gaskets, sealants.
Formaldehyde: -urea -melamine -phenol -resorcinol	Thermoset; strong with wood bonds; urea is inexpensive, available as powder or liquid and requires a catalyst; melamine is more expensive, cures with heat, bond is waterproof; resorcinol forms waterproof bond at room temperature. Types can be combined	Wood joints, plywood, bonding.
Urethane	Thermoset; bonds at room temperature or oven cure; good gap filling qualities	Fiberglass body parts, rubber, fabric.
Water-base -animal -vegetable -rubbers	Inexpensive, nontoxic, nonflammable.	Wood, paper, fabric, leather, dry seal envelopes.

2. **inorganic adhesives**, such as sodium silicate and magnesium oxychloride;
3. **synthetic organic adhesives**, which may be thermoplastics (used for non-structural and some structural bonding) or thermosetting polymers (used primarily for structural bonding).

Because of their strength, synthetic organic adhesives are the most important in manufacturing processes, particularly for load-bearing applications. They are classified as follows.

a. **Chemically reactive**: polyurethanes, silicones, epoxies, cyanoacrylates, modified acrylics, phenolics, polyimides, and anaerobics are examples.

b. **Pressure sensitive**: examples are natural rubber, styrene–butadiene rubber, butyl rubber, nitrile rubber, and polyacrylates.

c. **Reactive hot melt**: examples are thermoplastics (such as ethylene–vinyl acetate copolymers, polyolefins, polyamides, and polyester) and thermoplastic elastomers.

d. **Evaporative** or **diffusion**: these include vinyls, acrylics, phenolics, polyurethanes, synthetic rubbers, and natural rubbers.

e. **Film** and **tape**: examples are nylon–epoxies, elastomer–epoxies, nitrile–phenolics, vinyl–phenolics, and polyimides.

f. **Delayed tack**: examples are styrene–butadiene copolymers, polyvinyl acetates, polystyrenes, and polyamides.

g. **Electrically** and **thermally conductive**: this class includes epoxies, polyurethanes, silicones, and polyimides. Electrical conductivity is obtained by the addition of fillers, such as silver (used most commonly), copper, aluminum, and gold. Fillers that improve the electrical conductivity of adhesives generally also improve their thermal conductivity. (See also Section 7.3.)

Likewise, **adhesive systems** may be classified on the basis of their specific chemistries.

a. **Epoxy-based systems**: These have high strength and high-temperature properties, up to as high as 200 °C (400 °F), with typical applications being in automotive brake linings and as a bonding agent for sand molds for casting (Section 11.3).

b. **Acrylics**: These are suitable for applications with substrates that are not clean.

c. **Anaerobic systems**: The curing of these adhesives is done under oxygen deprivation, and the bond is usually hard and brittle. Curing times can be reduced by external heat or by ultraviolet (UV) radiation.

d. **Cyanoacrylate**: The bond lines are thin and the bond sets within from 5 to 40 s.

e. **Urethanes**: These have high toughness and flexibility at room temperature, and they are widely used as sealants.

f. **Silicones**: Highly resistant to moisture and solvents, these have high impact and peel strength; however, curing times are typically in the range of 1 to 5 days.

Many of these adhesives can be combined to optimize their properties, such as *epoxy-silicon*, *nitrile-phenolic*, and *epoxy-phenolic*.

The least expensive adhesives are epoxies and phenolics, which are followed in affordability by polyurethanes, acrylics, silicones, and cyanoacrylates. Adhesives for high-temperature applications in a range up to about 260 °C (500 °F), such as polyimides and polybenzimidazoles, are generally the most expensive.

30.4.2 Electrically Conducting Adhesives

Although the majority of the usage of adhesive bonding is for mechanical strength, a relatively recent advance is the development and application of electrically-conducting adhesives, to replace lead-based solder alloys, particularly in the electronics industry. They also require curing or setting temperatures that are lower than those required for soldering.

In these adhesives, the polymer is the matrix, containing conducting metals (fillers) in forms such as flakes and particles. (See also Section 10.7.2 on *conducting polymers*.) There is a minimum proportion (by volume) of fillers necessary in order to make the adhesive electrically conducting; typically it is in the range of 40-70 percent. They are available as film or as paste.

The size, shape, and distribution of the metallic particles, the heat and pressure application method, and the individual conducting particle contact geometry can be controlled so as to impart isotropic or anisotropic electrical conductivity to the adhesive. Typical fillers are silver, carbon, nickel, copper, and gold. New developments in fillers include the use of polymeric particles, such as polystyrene, coated with thin films of silver or gold. Matrix materials are generally epoxies, although thermoplastics are also used.

Applications of electrically-conducting adhesives include calculators, remote controls, and control panels, and there are high-density uses in electronic assemblies, liquid-crystal displays, electronic games, and pocket TVs.

30.4.3 Surface Preparation and Application

Surface preparation is very important in adhesive bonding. Joint strength depends greatly on the absence of dirt, dust, oil, and various other contaminants; this dependence can be observed when one is attempting to apply an adhesive tape over a dusty or oily surface. Contaminants also affect the wetting ability of the adhesive and prevent spreading of the adhesive evenly over the interface.

Thick, weak, or loose oxide films on workpiece surfaces are detrimental to adhesive bonding. On the other hand, a porous (or thin) strong oxide film may be desirable, particularly one with some surface roughness to improve adhesion. Various compounds and primers are available which modify surfaces to improve adhesive-bond strength. Liquid adhesives may be applied by brushes, sprayers, and rollers.

30.4.4 Process Capabilities

Adhesives can be used for bonding a wide variety of similar and dissimilar metallic and non-metallic materials and components with different shapes, sizes, and thicknesses. Adhesive bonding can also be combined with mechanical joining methods (Section 30.5) to improve the strength of the bond. Joint design and bonding methods require care and skill. Special equipment, such as fixtures, presses, tooling, and autoclaves and ovens for curing, is usually required.

Adhesive joints are designed to withstand shear, compressive, and tensile forces, but they should not be subjected to peeling forces (Fig. 30.8). Note, for example, how easily you can peel adhesive tape from a surface, yet be unable to slide it along the surface. During

FIGURE 30.8   Characteristic behavior of (a) brittle and (b) tough adhesives in a peeling test. This test is similar to the peeling of adhesive tape from a solid surface.

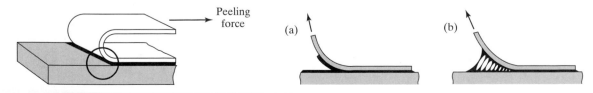

peeling the behavior of an adhesive may be brittle, or it may be ductile and tough, requiring high forces to peel it.

Major industries that use adhesive bonding extensively are aerospace, automotive, appliances, and building products. Applications include: the attachment of rear-view mirrors to windshields, automotive brake-lining assemblies, laminated windshield glass, appliances, helicopter blades, honeycomb structures, and aircraft bodies and control surfaces.

An important consideration in the use of adhesives in production is *curing time*, which can range from a few seconds (at high temperatures) to several hours (at room temperature), particularly for thermosetting adhesives. Thus, production rates can be low, compared to those of other joining processes. Furthermore, adhesive bonds for structural applications are rarely suitable for service above 250 °C (500 °F).

Nondestructive inspection of the quality and strength of adhesively bonded components can be difficult. Some of the techniques described in Section 36.9, such as acoustic impact (tapping), holography, infrared detection, and ultrasonic testing, are effective nondestructive testing methods.

The major advantages of adhesive bonding are outlined below.

a. It provides a bond at the interface, either for structural strength or for such nonstructural applications as sealing, insulation, the prevention of electrochemical corrosion between dissimilar metals, and the reduction of vibration and of noise (by means of internal damping at the joints).

b. It distributes the load at an interface and thereby eliminates localized stresses that usually result from joining the components with mechanical fasteners, such as bolts and screws. Moreover, structural integrity of the sections is maintained, because no holes are required, and the appearance of the components is generally improved.

c. Very thin and fragile components can be bonded without significant increase in their weight.

d. Porous materials and materials of very different properties and sizes can be joined.

e. Because it is usually carried out at a temperature between room temperature and about 200 °C (400 °F), there is no significant distortion of the components or change in their original properties. This avoidance of distortion is particularly important for materials that are heat-sensitive.

The major limitations of adhesive bonding are the following:

a. a limited range of service temperatures;

b. possibly, a long bonding (curing) time;

c. the need for great care in surface preparation;

d. the difficulty of testing bonded joints nondestructively, particularly for large structures; and

e. the limited reliability of adhesively bonded structures during their service life.

The cost of adhesive bonding depends on the particular operation. In many cases, however, the overall economics of the process make adhesive bonding an attractive joining process. Sometimes it is the only one that is feasible or practical. The cost of equipment varies greatly, depending on the size and type of operation.

30.4.5 Design for Adhesive Bonding

a. Designs for adhesive bonding should ensure that joints are subjected only to compressive, tensile, and shear forces and not to peeling or cleavage. (See Fig. 30.8.)

b. Several joint designs for adhesive bonding are shown in Figs. 30.9 and 30.10. They vary considerably in strength; hence, selection of the appropriate design is important and should include considerations such as the type of loading and the environment.

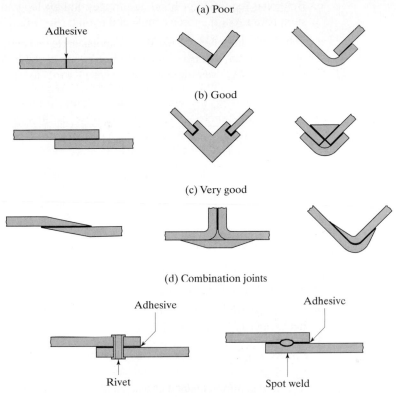

FIGURE 30.9   Various joint designs in adhesive bonding. Note that good designs require large contact areas between the members to be joined.

FIGURE 30.10   Various configurations for adhesively bonded joints: (a) single lap, (b) double lap, (c) scarf, (d) strap.

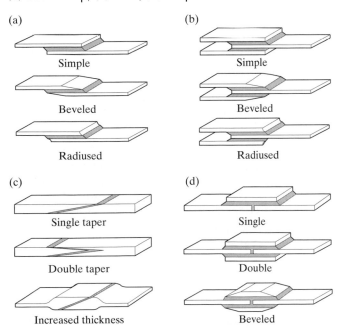

c. Butt joints require large bonding surfaces. Simple lap joints tend to distort under tension, because of the force couple at the joint. (See Fig. 29.14a.)

d. The coefficients of expansion of the components to be bonded should preferably be close, in order to avoid internal stresses during adhesive bonding. Also, situations in which thermal cycling can cause differential movement across the joint should be avoided.

30.5 MECHANICAL FASTENING

Numerous objects, including mechanical pencils, caps, and lids on containers and mechanical watches, engines, and bicycles have components that are fastened mechanically. *Mechanical fastening* may be preferred over other methods for the following reasons:

- ease of manufacturing;
- ease of assembly and transportation;
- ease of disassembly, maintenance, parts replacement, or repair;
- ease in creating designs that require movable joints, such as hinges, sliding mechanisms, and adjustable components and fixtures;
- lower overall cost of manufacturing the product.

The most common method of mechanical fastening is by the use of bolts, nuts, screws, pins, and a variety of other **fasteners**. These processes are known also as mechanical assembly. Mechanical fastening generally requires that the components have *holes* through which fasteners are inserted. These joints may be subjected to both shear and tensile stresses and should be designed to resist these forces.

30.5.1 Hole Preparation

Hole preparation is an important aspect of mechanical fastening. As described in Chapters 16, 22, and 26, a hole in a solid body can be produced by several processes, such as punching, drilling, chemical and electrical means, and high-energy beams—the choice depends on the type of material, its properties, and its thickness.

Recall, from Parts II and III, that holes also may be produced integrally in the product during casting, forging, extrusion, and powder metallurgy. For the sake of improved accuracy and surface finish, many of these holemaking operations may be followed by finishing operations, such as shaving, deburring, reaming, and honing, as was described in various sections in Part IV.

Because of the fundamental differences in their characteristics, the several holemaking operations produce holes with different surface finishes, surface properties, and dimensional tolerances. The most significant influence of a hole in a solid body is its tendency to reduce the component's fatigue life (by stress concentration).

Fatigue life can best be improved by inducing compressive residual stresses on the cylindrical surface of the hole. These stresses are usually developed by pushing a round rod (*drift pin*) through the hole and expanding it by a very small amount. This operation plastically deforms the surface layers of the hole, in a manner similar to that seen in shot peening or in roller burnishing (Section 33.2).

30.5.2 Threaded Fasteners

Bolts, screws, and nuts are among the most commonly used *threaded fasteners*. Numerous standards and specifications, including thread dimensions, tolerances, pitch, strength, and the quality of the materials used to make these fasteners, are described in the references at the end of this chapter. (See also Section 22.5.1.)

Bolts and screws may be secured with nuts (carriage bolts, machine screws), or they may be *self-tapping*: the screw either cuts or forms the thread into the part to be fastened. The self-tapping method is particularly effective and economical in plastic products, where fastening does not require a tapped hole or a nut.

If the joint is to be subjected to vibration, such as ones in aircraft and various types of engines and high-speed machinery, several specially designed nuts and lock washers are available. They increase the frictional resistance in the torsional direction and so inhibit vibrational loosening of the fasteners.

30.5.3 Rivets

The most common method of permanent or semipermanent mechanical joining is by *riveting* (Fig. 30.11); hundreds of thousands of rivets may be used in the construction and assembly of one large commercial aircraft. Installing a rivet takes two steps: placing the rivet in the hole, and deforming the end of its shank by upsetting (heading—Fig. 14.11).

Riveting may be done either at room or at elevated temperature. Explosives can be placed within the rivet cavity and detonated to expand the end of the rivet. Some design guidelines for riveting are illustrated in Fig. 30.12.

FIGURE 30.11   Examples of rivets: (a) solid, (b) tubular, (c) split (or bifurcated), (d) compression.

(a)   (b)   (c)   (d)

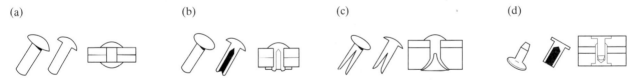

FIGURE 30.12   Design guidelines for riveting. (a) Exposed shank is too long; the result is buckling instead of upsetting. (b) Rivets should be placed sufficiently far from edges to avoid stress concentrations. (c) Joined sections should allow ample clearance for the riveting tools. (d) Section curvature should not interfere with the riveting process. *Source*: J. G. Bralla.

(a)   (c)

(b)   (d)

Poor   Good

30.5.4 Design for Mechanical Fastening

The design of mechanical joints requires consideration of the type of loading—for example shear or tension—to which the structure will be subjected and of the size and spacing of holes.

Compatibility of the fastener material with that of the components to be joined is important. Incompatibility may lead to *galvanic corrosion*, also known as *crevice corrosion* (Section 3.8). In a system where, for example, a steel bolt or rivet is used to fasten copper sheets, the bolt is anodic and the copper plate cathodic; this combination causes rapid corrosion and loss of joint strength. Aluminum or zinc fasteners on copper products react in a similar manner.

Other general design guidelines for mechanical joining include the following (see also Section 38.10, on *Design for Assembly, Disassembly, and Service*):

a. Using fewer but larger fasteners is generally less costly than using a large number of small ones.

b. Part assembly should be accomplished with a minimum number of fasteners.

c. The fit between parts to be joined should be as loose as possible, to reduce costs and to facilitate the assembly process.

d. Fasteners of standard size should be used whenever possible.

e. Holes should be far from edges or corners, to avoid tearing of the material when it is subjected to external forces.

30.5.5 Other Fastening Methods

Many types of fasteners are used in numerous joining and assembly applications. The most common types are described below.

Metal Stitching or Stapling.   The process of *metal stitching* or *stapling* (Fig. 30.13) is much like that of ordinary stapling of papers. This operation is fast, and it is particularly suitable for joining thin metallic and nonmetallic materials. A common example is the stapling of cardboard containers.

Seaming.   *Seaming* is based on the simple principle of folding two thin pieces of material together. It is a process much like the joining of two pieces of paper (when a paper clip is not available) by folding them at the corner. Common examples of seaming (Fig. 30.14) are at the tops of beverage cans (see Fig. 16.31), in containers for food and household products, and in heating and air-conditioning ducts.

FIGURE 30.13   Various examples of metal stitching.

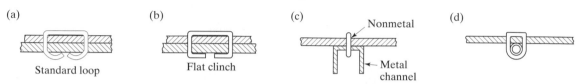

FIGURE 30.14   Stages in forming a double-lock seam.

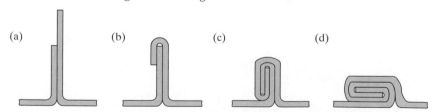

(a)   (b)

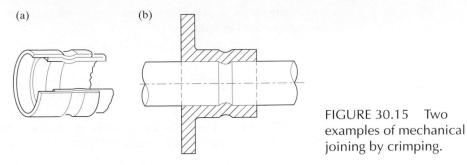

FIGURE 30.15   Two examples of mechanical joining by crimping.

In seaming, the materials should be capable of undergoing bending and folding at very small radii (see Section 16.5.1); otherwise, they will crack. The performance and reliability of seams may be improved by the addition of adhesives, coatings, or seals or by soldering.

Crimping.   The *crimping* process is a method of joining without using fasteners. It can be done with beads or dimples (Fig. 30.15), which can be produced by shrinking or swaging operations (see Figs. 14.16 and 14.17). Crimping can be done on both tubular and flat parts, provided that the materials are sufficiently thin and ductile to withstand the large localized deformations. Caps are fastened to bottles by crimping, just as some connectors are to electrical wiring.

Snap-In Fasteners.   Several types of spring or snap-in fastener are shown in Fig. 30.16. Such fasteners are widely used in automotive bodies and household appliances. They are economical, and they permit easy and rapid component assembly.

Shrink and Press Fits.   Components may also be assembled by shrink fitting and press fitting. **Shrink fitting** is based on a difference between the thermal contractions of two components. Typical applications are the assembly of die components and mounting gears

FIGURE 30.16   Examples of spring and snap-in fasteners used to facilitate assembly.

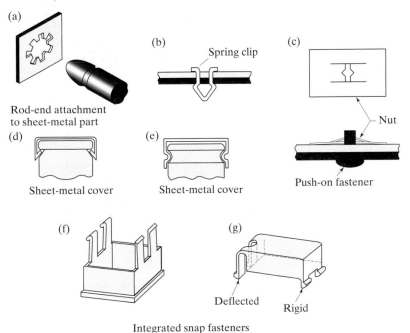

and cams onto shafts. In **press fitting**, one component is forced over another; this process results in high joint strength.

30.6 JOINING PLASTICS

Plastics can be joined by many of the methods already described for joining metals and nonmetallic materials, especially heat and mechanical fastening.

30.6.1 Joining Thermoplastics

As was described in Chapter 7, thermoplastics soften and melt as temperature increases; consequently, they can be joined by means whereby heat (from an external or internal source) is generated at the interface (see below). The heat softens the thermoplastic at the interface to a viscous or molten state and, with the application of pressure to ensure a good bond, allows **fusion** to take place. Filler materials of the same type of polymer may also be used.

External heat sources may be from among the following; the choice depends on the compatibility of the polymers to be joined:

   a. *Hot air* or *gases*, or *infrared radiation* using high-intensity quartz heat lamps.
   b. Heated tools and dies (in a process known as *hot-plate welding*), which press against and heat surfaces which are to be joined by interdiffusion of molecular chains. This process is commonly used to butt-weld pipe and tubing (end-to-end).
   c. *Radio-frequency* or *dielectric heating*, which is particularly useful for thin films.
   d. *Electrical-resistance* wire or braids, or carbon-based tapes, sheet, and ropes, which are placed at the interface to create heat by the passing of electrical current. This process is known as *resistive-implant welding*. Alternatively, the elements at the interface may be subjected to a radio-frequency field (*induction welding*). In both cases, the elements at the interface must be compatible with the use of the joined product, because they are left in the weld zone.
   e. *Lasers* emitting defocused beams at low power, to prevent degradation of the polymer.

Internal heat sources are developed by the following means:

   a. *Ultrasonic welding* is the most commonly used process for thermoplastics, particularly amorphous polymers such as ABS and high-impact polystyrene.
   b. *Friction welding* (called *spin welding* for polymers) includes linear friction welding (also called *vibration welding*). This last process is particularly useful for joining polymers with a high degree of crystallinity (Section 10.2.2), such as acetal, polyethylene, nylons, and polypropylene.
   c. *Orbital welding* is similar to friction welding, but the rotary motion of one component is in an orbital path. (See also Fig. 14.15.)

Applications.   The fusion method is particularly effective with plastics that cannot be bonded easily by means of adhesives. Plastics such as polyvinyl chloride, polyethylene, polypropylene, acrylics, and acrylonitrile butadiene styrene (ABS) can be joined in this manner. For example, specially designed portable fusion-sealing systems have been developed to allow in-the-field joining of plastic pipe (usually made of polyethylene and used for natural-gas delivery).

Coextruded multiple food wrappings consist of different types of films, which are bonded by heat during extrusion (Section 18.2). Each film has a different function—for example, one may keep out moisture, one may keep out oxygen, and a third may facilitate heat sealing during the packaging process. Some wrappings have as many as seven layers, all bonded together during production of the film.

Oxidation can occur during the joining of some polymers, such as polyethylene, and it can cause degradation. In such cases, an inert shielding gas such as nitrogen is used to prevent oxidation. Because of the low thermal conductivity of thermoplastics, the heat source may burn or char the surfaces of the components if the heat is applied at a high rate; this effect can cause difficulties in obtaining sufficiently deep fusion.

Adhesive bonding of plastics is best illustrated in the joining of sections of polyvinyl chloride pipe (used extensively in home plumbing systems) and ABS pipe (used in drain, waste, and vent systems). The adhesive is applied to the connecting sleeve and pipe surfaces, using a primer to improve adhesion (a step much like that using primers in painting), and the pieces are pushed together.

Adhesive bonding of polyethylene, polypropylene, and polytetrafluoro-ethylene (Teflon) can be difficult, because adhesives do not bond readily to them. The surfaces of parts made of these materials usually have to be treated chemically to improve bonding. The use of adhesive primers or double-sided adhesive tapes is also effective.

In other methods of joining plastics, **integrated snap fasteners** are gaining acceptance as a tool for simplifying assembly operations. Examples of such fastener geometries are shown in Figure 30.16f. Because the fastener can be directly molded at the same time as the plastic, it adds very little to the cost of the assembly, so this technique is very cost-effective, because it reduces assembly time and minimizes the number of parts needed.

Mechanical fastening is particularly effective with most plastics, because of their inherent toughness and resilience. The use of self-tapping screws is a common practice.

30.6.2 Joining Thermosets

Because they do not soften or melt with increasing temperature, thermosetting plastics, such as epoxy and phenolics, are usually joined by using the following techniques:

1. threaded or other molded-in inserts;
2. mechanical fasteners, particularly self-tapping screws and integrated snap fasteners;
3. solvent bonding.

The basic process of thermoset bonding with solvents consists of the following sequence of steps:

a. roughening the surfaces with an abrasive;
b. wiping and cleaning the surfaces with a solvent;
c. pressing the surfaces together and then holding them until sufficient bond strength is developed.

SUMMARY

- Joining processes that do not rely on fusion or pressure at the interfaces include brazing and soldering. These processes instead utilize filler material that requires some temperature rise in the joint. They can be used to join dissimilar metals of intricate shapes and various thicknesses.

- Adhesive bonding has gained increased acceptance in major industries, such as aerospace and automotive. In addition to good bond strength, adhesives have other favorable characteristics, such as the ability to seal, to insulate, to prevent electrochemical corrosion between dissimilar metals, and to reduce vibration and noise by means of internal damping in the bond.

- Surface preparation and joint design are important factors in adhesive bonding.

- Mechanical fastening is one of the oldest and most common joining methods. Bolts, screws, and nuts are common fasteners for machine components and structures, which are likely to be taken apart for maintenance, for ease of transportation, or for various other reasons.

- Rivets are semipermanent or permanent fasteners used in buildings, bridges, and transportation equipment. A wide variety of other fasteners and fastening techniques is available for numerous permanent or semipermanent applications.

- Thermoplastics can be joined by fusion-welding techniques, by adhesive bonding, or by mechanical fastening. Thermosets are usually joined by mechanical means, such as molded-in inserts and fasteners, or by solvent bonding.

TRENDS

- Automation, and a consequent reduction in the labor requirements for many of the joining processes described, is continuing.

- Adhesive bond strength and reliability under various environmental conditions are under constant investigation.

- Lead-free solders are being developed with properties somewhat similar to those of traditional solders.

- A wide variety of metallic and nonmetallic snap-in fasteners is being developed, primarily for automated and economical assembly of parts manufactured in computer-integrated manufacturing systems.

KEY TERMS

Adhesive bonding	Integrated snap fastener	Shrink fitting
Braze welding	Hole preparation	Snap-in fastener
Brazing	Head-free solders	Soldering
Crimping	Mechanical fastening	Solvent bonding
Electrically conducting adhesives	Press fitting	Stapling
Fasteners	Reflow soldering	Stitching
Filler metal	Rivet	Threaded fasteners
Flux	Seaming	Wave soldering

BIBLIOGRAPHY

Adams, R.D., J. Comyn, and W.C. Wake, *Structural Adhesive Joints in Engineering*. Chapman & Hall, 1997.

ASM Handbook, Vol. 6: *Welding, Brazing, and Soldering*. ASM International, 1993.

Bickford, J.H., and S. Nassar (eds.), *Handbook of Bolts and Bolted Joints*. Marcel Dekker, 1998.

Brazing Handbook (4th ed.). American Welding Society, 1991.

Engineered Materials Handbook, Vol. 3: *Adhesives and Sealants*. ASM International, 1991.

Hamrock, B.J., Jacobson, B., and S.R. Schmid, *Fundamentals of Machine Elements*. McGraw-Hill, 1998.

Handbook of Plastics Joining: A Practical Guide. William Andrew Inc., 1996.

Humpston, G., and D.M. Jacobson, *Principles of Soldering and Brazing*. ASM International, 1993.

Hwang, J.S., *Modern Solder Technology for Competitive Electronics Manufacturing*. McGraw-Hill, 1996.

Lee, L.-H., *Adhesive Bonding*. Plenum, 1991.

Manko, H.H., *Soldering Handbook for Printed Circuits and Surface Mounting*. Van Nostrand Reinhold, 1995.

Messler, R.W., Jr., *Joining of Advanced Materials*. Butterworth–Heinemann, 1993.

Nicholas, M.G., *Joining Processes: Introduction to Brazing and Diffusion Bonding*, Chapman & Hall, 1998.

Parmley, R.O. (ed.), *Standard Handbook of Fastening and Joining* (3d ed.). McGraw-Hill, 1997.

Pecht, M.G., *Soldering Processes and Equipment*. Wiley, 1993.

Rahn, A., *The Basics of Soldering*. Wiley Interscience, 1993.

Sadek, M.M., *Industrial Applications of Adhesive Bonding*. Elsevier, 1987.

Satas, D. (ed.), *Handbook of Pressure Sensitive Adhesive Technology* (3d ed.). Satas & Associates, 1999.

Schwartz, M.M., *Brazing: For the Engineering Technologist*. Chapman & Hall, 1995.

———, *Ceramic Joining*. ASM International, 1990.

———, *Joining of Composite-Matrix Materials*. ASM International, 1994.

Shields, J., *Adhesives Handbook* (3d ed.). Butterworths, 1984.

Skeist, I., *Handbook of Adhesives* (3d ed.). Van Nostrand Reinhold, 1990.

Speck, J.A., *Mechanical Fastening, Joining, and Assembly*. Marcel Dekker, 1997.

Welding Handbook (8th ed.), 3 vols. American Welding Society, 1987.

Woodgate, R.W., *Handbook of Machine Soldering*. Wiley, 1996.

REVIEW QUESTIONS

30.1 Explain the principle underlying brazing.

30.2 What is the difference between brazing and braze welding?

30.3 What are the relative advantages of braze welding and fusion welding?

30.4 Are fluxes necessary in brazing? If so, why?

30.5 Do you think that it is acceptable to differentiate brazing from soldering arbitrarily, by temperature of application? Comment.

30.6 Describe the types of fluxes used in soldering and their applications.

30.7 Why is surface preparation important in adhesive bonding?

30.8 Why have mechanical joining methods been developed? Give several specific examples of their applications.

30.9 Explain why hole preparation may be important in mechanical joining.

30.10 Describe the similarities and differences between the functions of a bolt and those of a rivet.

30.11 What precautions should be taken in the mechanical joining of dissimilar metals?

30.12 Explain the principles of various types of mechanical joining and fastening methods.

30.13 What difficulties are involved in joining plastics? Why?

30.14 What is wave soldering?

30.15 Describe the difference between brazing and soldering.

30.16 What is a peel test? Why is it useful?

30.17 How is the filler metal applied in furnace brazing?

30.18 Why is welding not used in attaching electrical components to circuit boards?

30.19 Describe some applications in manufacturing for single-sided and some for double-sided tapes.

QUALITATIVE PROBLEMS

30.20 Comment on your observations concerning the joints shown in Figs. 30.4 and 30.10.

30.21 How different is adhesive bonding from other joining methods? What limitations does it have?

30.22 Discuss the need for fixtures for holding workpieces in the processes described in this chapter.

30.23 Soldering is generally applied to thinner components. Explain why.

30.24 Do you think that the strength of an adhesively bonded joint is as high as that of one created by diffusion bonding? Explain your response.

30.25 Explain why adhesively bonded joints tend to be weak in peeling.

30.26 Write brief paragraphs about the soldering processes listed in Section 30.3, giving an application for each.

30.27 It is common practice to tin plate electrical terminals to ease soldering. Why is it tin that is used?

30.28 How important is a close fit for two parts that are to be brazed?

30.29 If you are designing a joint that will be subjected to high stresses and a cyclic (fatigue) loading, what kind of joint would you use? Explain.

30.30 If you are designing a joint that needs to be strong and yet needs to be disassembled a few times during the product life, what kind of joint would you use? Explain.

30.31 Loctite™ is an adhesive used to keep bolts from vibrating loose; it basically glues the bolt to the nut and threaded hole. Explain how it works.

SYNTHESIS AND DESIGN

30.32 Examine various household products, and describe how they are joined and assembled. Explain why those particular processes were used.

30.33 Name several products that have been assembled by (a) seaming, (b) stitching, (c) soldering.

30.34 Suggest methods of attaching a round bar (made of a thermosetting plastic) perpendicularly to a flat metal plate.

30.35 Describe the tooling and equipment that are necessary to perform the double-lock seaming operation shown in Fig. 30.14, starting with flat sheet.

30.36 Prepare a list of design guidelines for joining by the processes described in this chapter. Would these guidelines be common to most processes? Explain.

30.37 Examine your automobile, and identify various components that have been joined by the processes described in this chapter.

30.38 In your inspection in Problem 30.37, would you join these components by different methods, and, if so, what would be the advantages?

30.39 What joining methods would be suitable for assembling a thermoplastic cover over a metal frame? Assume that the cover is removed periodically, such as the top of a coffee or shortening can.

30.40 Solve the same as Problem 30.39, but for a cover made of (a) a thermoset, (b) a metal, (c) a ceramic. Describe the factors involved in your selection of methods.

30.41 Describe the various costs involved in using the joining processes described in Part V. Identify those costs that are likely to be the highest in each group and those that are likely to be the lowest.

30.42 Comment on workpiece size and shape limitations, if any, for each of the processes described in this chapter.

30.43 Describe part shapes that cannot be joined by the processes explained in this chapter. Give specific examples.

30.44 Make a comprehensive outline of joint designs classified by the processes described in this chapter. Give specific examples of engineering applications for each type of joint.

30.45 Section 27.10 describes the general guidelines for safety in welding operations. For each of the operations described in this chapter, prepare a poster which effectively and concisely gives specific instructions for safe practices. Consult the references at the end of Chapter 37 and the various publications of the National Safety Council.

30.46 Make a survey of metallic and nonmetallic containers for household products and for food and beverage items. Identify those that have utilized any of the processes described in this chapter. Describe your observations.

30.47 Give several applications for fasteners in various products, and explain why other joining methods were not used.

30.48 In Fig. 30.12, why are the designs on the left labeled poor and the ones on the right good?

30.49 Describe the similarities and differences between the processes described in this chapter and those described in Chapters 27 and 28.

30.50 What types of materials and part configurations would be difficult to join by brazing?

30.51 Give examples of products in which rivets in a structure or assembly might have to be removed and later replaced by new rivets.

30.52 A major cause of erratic behavior (hardware bugs) and failures of computer equipment is fatigue failure of the solder joints, especially in surface mount devices and those with bond wires. (See Figure 34.11.) Perform a literature search surveying this problem, and describe current research being conducted on the prevention of these failures.

30.53 Using the Internet, investigate the geometry of the heads of screws that are permanent fasteners— that is, ones that can be screwed in but not out.

30.54 Under the supervision of your instructor, obtain a soldering iron and attempt to solder two wires together. First, try to apply the solder at the same time as you first put the soldering iron tip to the wires. Second, preheat the wires before applying the solder. Repeat the same procedure for a cool flat surface and a heated flat surface. Record your results and explain your findings.

30.55 Perform a literature search to determine the properties and types of adhesives used to affix artificial hips onto the human femur.

30.56 Using two strips of steel 1 in. wide and 8 in. long, design and fabricate a joint which gives the highest strength in a tension test in the longitudinal direction.

Part VI
Surface Technology

INTRODUCTION

Our first visual or tactile contact with objects around us is through their **surfaces**. We can see or feel surface roughness, texture, waviness, color, reflectivity, and other features like scratches and nicks. The preceding chapters described the *properties* of materials and manufactured components basically in terms of their *bulk* characteristics, such as strength, ductility, hardness, and toughness. Also included were some descriptions of the influences of surfaces on these properties, influences such as the effect of surface preparation on fatigue life and the sensitivity of brittle materials to surface scratches.

Machinery and accessories have many members that slide against each other: pistons and cylinders, slideways, bearings, and tools and dies for cutting and forming. Close examination reveals that (a) some of these surfaces are smooth while others are rough, (b) some are lubricated while others are dry, (c) some are subjected to heavy loads while others support light loads, (d) some are subjected to elevated temperatures (hot-working dies) while others are at room temperature, and (e) some surfaces slide against each other at high relative speeds (high cutting speeds) while others move slowly (such as the saddle or carriage on a machine-tool bed, Fig. 22.2).

In addition to its geometric features, a surface constitutes a thin layer on the bulk material. A surface's physical, chemical, metallurgical, and mechanical properties depend not only on the material and its processing history, but also on the environment to which the surface is exposed. The term **surface integrity** is used to describe its physical, chemical, and mechanical characteristics.

Because of the various mechanical, physical, thermal, and chemical effects which result from its processing history, the surface of a manufactured part generally possesses properties and behavior that are significantly different from those of its bulk. Although the bulk material generally determines the component's overall mechanical properties, the component's surfaces directly influence the part performance in the following areas (Fig. VI.1):

FIGURE VI.1   Components in a typical automobile that are related to the topics described in Part VI.

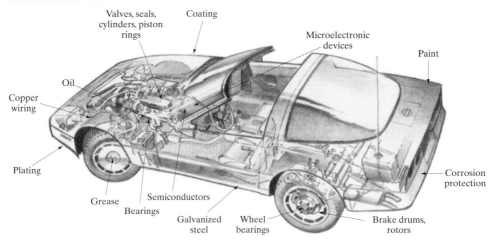

- Friction and wear of tools and dies and the products made.
- Effectiveness of lubricants during manufacturing processes and throughout the part's service life.
- Appearance and geometric features of the part, and their role in subsequent operations such as welding, soldering, adhesive bonding, painting, and coating, as well as resistance to corrosion.
- Initiation of cracks as a result of surface defects like roughness, scratches, seams, and heat-affected zones, which can lead to weakening and premature failure of the part, such as through fatigue.
- Thermal and electrical conductivity of contacting bodies. Rough surfaces, for example, have higher thermal and electrical resistances than do smooth surfaces.

Following the outline shown in Fig. VI.2, this part of the text will present surface characteristics in terms of their structure and topography. The material and process variables that influence friction and wear of materials will then be described. We will also cover several mechanical, thermal, electrical, and chemical methods that can be used to modify surfaces for improved frictional behavior, effectiveness of lubricants, resistance to wear and corrosion, and surface finish and appearance.

The manufacturing of microelectronic devices is covered in Chapter 34. We will describe the sequence of operations involved in manufacturing semiconductors, which have been a critical element in integrated-circuit technology and in computers and computer-integrated manufacturing operations.

FIGURE VI.2   An outline of topics covered in Part VI.

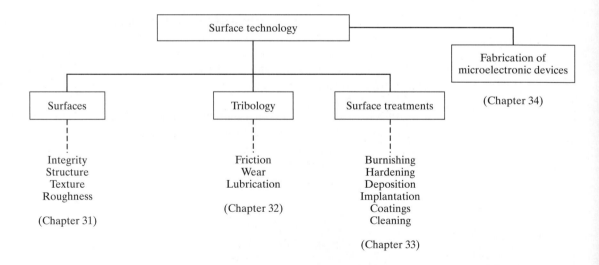

31

Surfaces: Their Nature, Roughness, and Measurement

31.1 INTRODUCTION

This chapter begins with a description of the nature of surfaces and their structures, which are distinct entities and have properties different from those of the bulk, particularly because of the presence of various surface oxide layers. Several defects can exist on a surface, according to the manner in which the surface was generated. These defects, as well as various surface textures, can have a major influence on the surface integrity of workpieces, tools, and dies during production and during their service life.

We then describe two common methods of surface roughness measurement in engineering practice, and the instrumentation involved. Because of their increasing importance in precision manufacturing and nanofabrication, three-dimensional surface measurements are also discussed and illustrated. The chapter ends with a brief description of surface roughness requirements in engineering practices.

31.2 SURFACE STRUCTURE AND PROPERTIES

Upon close examination of the surface of a piece of metal, we find that it generally consists of several layers (Fig. 31.1). The characteristics of these layers are outlined briefly here:

1. The *bulk* metal, also known as the metal **substrate**, has a structure that depends on the composition and processing history of the metal.

2. Above this bulk metal is a layer that usually has been plastically deformed and work-hardened to a greater extent during the manufacturing process. The depth and prop-

869

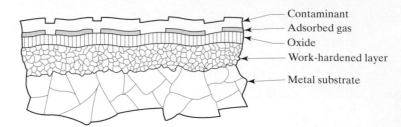

FIGURE 31.1   Schematic illustration of a cross-section of the surface structure of metals. The thickness of the individual layers is dependent on processing conditions and processing environment.

erties of the work-hardened layer (the **surface structure**) depend on such factors as the processing method used and how much frictional sliding the surface undergoes.

The use of sharp tools and the selection of appropriate processing parameters result in surfaces with little or no disturbance. For example, if the surface is produced by machining using a dull and worn tool, or which takes place under poor cutting conditions, or if the surface is ground with a dull grinding wheel, the surface structure layer will be relatively thick. Also, nonuniform surface deformation or severe temperature gradients during manufacturing operations usually cause residual stresses in the work-hardened layer.

3. Unless the metal is processed and kept in an inert (oxygen-free) environment, or is a noble metal such as gold or platinum, an **oxide layer** forms over the work-hardened layer. For example,

    a. *Iron* has an oxide structure with FeO adjacent to the bulk metal, followed by a layer of Fe_3O_4 and then a layer of Fe_2O_3, which is exposed to the environment.
    b. *Aluminum* has a dense, amorphous (without crystalline structure) layer of Al_2O_3, with a thick, porous hydrated aluminum-oxide layer over it.
    c. *Copper* has a bright, shiny surface when freshly scratched or machined. Soon after, however, it develops a Cu_2O layer, which is then covered with a layer of CuO. This gives copper its somewhat dull color.
    d. *Stainless steels* are "stainless" because they develop a protective layer of chromium oxide (**passivation**), as described in Section 3.8.

4. Under normal environmental conditions, surface oxide layers are generally covered with *adsorbed* layers of gas and moisture. Finally, the outermost surface of the metal may be covered with *contaminants* such as dirt, dust, grease, lubricant residues, cleaning-compound residues, and pollutants from the environment.

Thus, surfaces have properties that generally are very different from those of the substrate. The oxide on a metal surface is generally much harder than the base metal. The *hardness ratios of oxide-to-base metals*, for example, are as follows:

Tin	90
Aluminum	70
Lead	20
Nickel	2
Copper	1.6
Tantalum	0.6
Molybdenum	0.3

Consequently, oxides tend to be brittle and abrasive (see Section 32.6). This surface characteristic has several important effects on friction, wear, and lubrication in materials processing, and on products.

The factors which pertain to the surface structures of the metals just described are also factors, to a large extent, in the surface structure of plastics and ceramics. The surface texture of these materials depends, as with metals, on the method of production. (See Chapters 7, 8, and 18.)

31.3 SURFACE INTEGRITY

Surface integrity describes not only the topological (geometric) features of surfaces and their physical and chemical properties, but their mechanical and metallurgical properties and characteristics as well. Surface integrity is an important consideration in manufacturing operations because it influences properties, such as fatigue strength, resistance to corrosion, and service life. The detrimental effect of improper (abusive) grinding on the fatigue life of an alloy steel, for example, is shown in Fig. 31.2. (See also Fig. 2.28.)

Surface Defects.   Several *defects* caused by and produced during component manufacturing can be responsible for inadequate surface integrity. These defects are usually caused by a combination of factors, such as (a) defects in the original material, caused by a casting or metalworking process, (b) the method by which the surface is produced, and (c) lack of proper control of process parameters, which can result in excessive stresses, excessive temperatures, or surface deformation.

The following are general definitions of the major surface defects (listed in alphabetical order) found in practice:

1. **Cracks** are external or internal separations with sharp outlines; cracks that require a magnification of 10X or higher to be seen by the naked eye are called **microcracks**.
2. **Craters** are shallow depressions.
3. **Folds** are the same as seams. (See below.)
4. **Heat-affected zone** is the portion of a metal which is subjected to thermal cycling without melting. (See Fig. 29.1.)
5. **Inclusions** are small, nonmetallic elements or compounds in the metal. (See Section 2.23.)

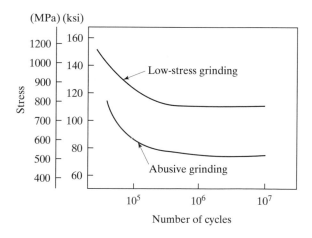

FIGURE 31.2   Fatigue curve for surface-ground 4340 steel, quenched and tempered, 51 HRC. Note the severe reduction in fatigue strength under abusive grinding conditions. (See also Fig. 2.28.)

6. **Intergranular attack** is the weakening of grain boundaries through liquid-metal embrittlement and corrosion. (See Section 1.4.2.)

7. **Laps** are the same as *seams*.

8. **Metallurgical transformation** involves microstructural changes caused by temperature cycling (Chapter 4). These changes may consist of phase transformations, recrystallization, alloy depletion, decarburization, and molten and recast, resolidified, or redeposited material, as in electrical-discharge machining.

9. **Pits** are shallow surface depressions, usually the result of chemical or physical attack.

10. **Plastic deformation** is a severe *surface deformation* caused by high stresses due to friction, tool and die geometry, worn tools, and processing method.

11. **Residual stresses** (tension or compression) on the surface are caused by nonuniform deformation and nonuniform temperature distribution. (See also Section 2.11.)

12. **Seams** are surface defects which result from overlapping of the material during processing.

13. **Splatter** is when small resolidified molten metal particles are deposited on a surface, such as during welding.

Techniques for Testing Surface Structure. One of the most commonly used techniques for testing surface integrity is *metallography*. Samples from the workpiece are removed (**destructive testing**; see Section 36.10), polished, etched, and observed under an optical or electron microscope. The test samples are usually much smaller than the part or component being analyzed, so they must be taken from appropriate locations in the workpiece. Several **nondestructive** techniques that are commonly used to observe and test surfaces are described in Section 36.9.

31.4 SURFACE TEXTURE

Regardless of the method of production, all surfaces have their own characteristics, which are collectively referred to as **surface texture**. The description of surface texture as a geometrical property is complex. However, certain guidelines have been established for identifying surface texture in terms of well-defined and measurable quantities (Fig. 31.3). For example,

1. **Flaws**, or *defects*, are random irregularities, such as scratches, cracks, holes, depressions, seams, tears, or inclusions (Section 31.3).

2. **Lay**, or *directionality*, is the direction of the predominant surface pattern and is usually visible to the naked eye.

3. **Roughness** is defined as closely spaced, irregular deviations on a scale smaller than that of waviness. Roughness may be superimposed on waviness. Roughness is expressed in terms of its height, its width, and its distance on the surface along which it is measured.

4. **Waviness** is a recurrent deviation from a flat surface, much like waves on the surface of water. It is measured and described in terms of the space between adjacent crests of the waves (*waviness width*) and height between the crests and valleys of the waves (*waviness height*). Waviness can be caused by (a) deflections of tools, dies, or the workpiece, (b) forces or temperature sufficient to cause warping, (c) uneven lubrication, (d) vibration, or (e) any periodic mechanical or thermal variations in the system during manufacturing operations.

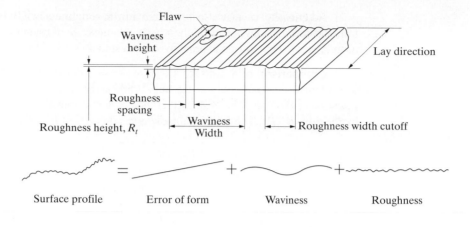

FIGURE 31.3   Standard terminology and symbols to describe surface finish. The quantities are given in μin.

31.5 SURFACE ROUGHNESS

Surface roughness is generally described using two methods: arithmetic mean value and root mean square average.

The **arithmetic mean value** (R_a, formerly identified as *AA* for *arithmetic average* or *CLA* for *center-line average*) is based on the schematic illustration of a rough surface, which is shown in Fig. 31.4. The arithmetic mean value, R_a, is defined as

$$R_a = \frac{a + b + c + d + \cdots}{n}, \tag{31.1}$$

where all ordinates, $a, b, c, \ldots$, are absolute values, and n is the number of readings.

The **root-mean-square average** (R_q, formerly identified as *RMS*) is defined as

$$R_q = \sqrt{\frac{a^2 + b^2 + c^2 + d^2 + \cdots}{n}}. \tag{31.2}$$

The datum line *AB* in Fig. 31.4 is located so that the sum of the areas above the line is equal to the sum of the areas below the line. The units generally used for surface roughness are μm (micrometer, or micron) or μin. (microinch). Note, for example, that $1\ \mu\text{m} = 40\ \mu\text{in}$. and $1\ \mu\text{in}. = 0.025\ \mu\text{m}$.

FIGURE 31.4   Coordinates used for surface-roughness measurement, using Eqs. (31.1) and (31.2).

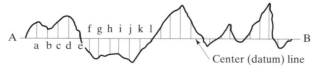

Additionally, we may also use the **maximum roughness height** (R_t), defined as the height from the deepest trough to the highest peak, as a measure of roughness. It indicates how much material has to be removed in order to obtain a smooth surface by polishing or other means.

Comparison of R_a and R_q. Because of its simplicity, the arithmetic mean value (R_a) was adopted internationally in the mid-1950s and is used widely in engineering practice. Equations (31.1) and (31.2) show that there is a relationship between R_q and R_a, as shown by the ratio R_q/R_a. The following table gives this ratio for various surfaces:

Surface	R_q/R_a
Sine curve	1.1
Machining by cutting	1.1
Grinding	1.2
Lapping and honing	1.4

In general, a surface cannot be described by its R_a or R_q value alone, since these values are averages. Two surfaces may have the same roughness value but have actual topography which is very different. A few deep troughs on an otherwise smooth surface, for example, do not affect the roughness values significantly. However, the type of surface profile can be significant in terms of friction, wear, and fatigue characteristics of a manufactured product.

It is, therefore, important to analyze the surface in great detail, particularly for parts used in critical applications. Some 130 parameters have been identified thus far for measuring surface roughness.

31.5.1 Symbols for Surface Roughness

Acceptable limits for surface roughness are specified on technical drawings by symbols (these symbols are shown around the check mark in the lower portion of Fig. 31.3), and the values of these limits are placed to the left of the check mark. The symbols, and their meanings concerning lay, are given in Fig. 31.5. Note that the symbol for lay is placed at the lower right of the check mark.

Symbols used to describe a surface specify only its roughness, waviness, and lay; they do not include flaws. Therefore, whenever necessary, a special note is included in technical drawings to describe the method which should be used to inspect for surface flaws.

31.5.2 Measuring Surface Roughness

Several commercially available instruments, called **surface profilometers**, are used to measure and record surface roughness. The most commonly used instruments feature a *diamond stylus* which travels along a straight line over the surface (Fig. 31.6a).

The distance that the stylus travels is called the **cutoff** (see Fig. 31.3); it generally ranges from 0.08 mm to 25 mm (0.003 in. to 1 in.); 0.8 mm (0.03 in.) is typical for most applications. The rule of thumb is that the cutoff must be large enough to include 10 to 15 roughness irregularities as well as all surface waviness.

In order to highlight the roughness, profilometer traces are recorded on an exaggerated vertical scale (a few orders of magnitude larger than the horizontal scale; see Fig. 31.7); the magnitude of the scale is called **gain** on the recording instrument. Thus, the recorded profile is significantly distorted, and the surface appears to be much rougher than it actually is. The recording instrument compensates for any surface waviness; it indicates only roughness. A record of the surface profile is made using mechanical and electronic instruments (Fig. 31.6b).

Because of the finite radius of the diamond stylus tip, the path of the stylus is less rough than the actual surface (note the path with the broken line in Fig. 31.6c). The most commonly

Lay symbol	Interpretation	Examples
—	Lay parallel to the line representing the surface to which the symbol is applied	$\sqrt{=}$
⊥	Lay perpendicular to the line representing the surface to which the symbol is applied	$\sqrt{\perp}$
X	Lay angular in both directions to line representing the surface to which symbol is applied	$\sqrt{X}$
M	Lay multidirectional	$\sqrt{M}$

Lay symbol	Interpretation	Examples
C	Lay approximately circular relative to the center of the surface to which the symbol is applied	$\sqrt{C}$
R	Lay approximately radial relative to the center of the surface to which the symbol is applied	$\sqrt{R}$
P	Pitted, protuberant, porous, or particulate nondirectional lay	$\sqrt{P}$

FIGURE 31.5   Standard lay symbols for engineering surfaces.

FIGURE 31.6   (a) Measuring surface roughness with a stylus. The rider supports the stylus and guards against damage. (b) Surface measuring instrument.*Source*: Sheffield Measurement Division of Warner & Swasey Co. (c) Path of stylus in surface roughness measurements (broken line) compared to actual roughness profile. Note that the profile of the stylus path is smoother than that of the actual surface. *Source*: D. H. Buckley.

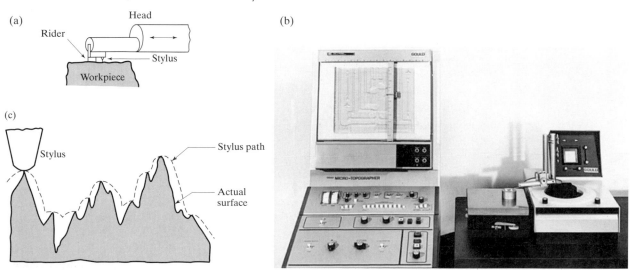

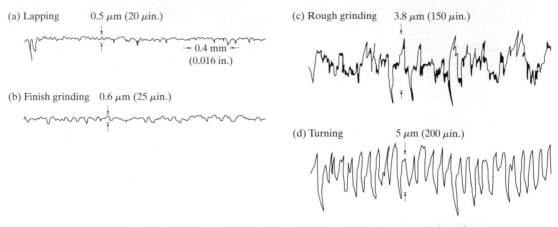

(a) Lapping   0.5 μm (20 μin.)

→ 0.4 mm ←
(0.016 in.)

(b) Finish grinding   0.6 μm (25 μin.)

(c) Rough grinding   3.8 μm (150 μin.)

(d) Turning   5 μm (200 μin.)

FIGURE 31.7   Typical surface profiles produced by various machining and surface-finishing processes. Note the difference between the vertical and horizontal scales. See also Fig. 32.4. *Source*: D. B. Dallas (ed.), *Tool and Manufacturing Engineers Handbook*, 3d ed. Copyright © 1976, McGraw-Hill Publishing Company. Used with permission.

used stylus tip diameter is 10 μm (400 μin.). The smaller the stylus diameter and the smoother the surface, the closer the path of the stylus to the actual surface profile.

Surface roughness can be directly observed through an *optical* or *scanning electron microscope*. Stereoscopic photographs are particularly useful for three-dimensional views of surfaces, and can also be used to measure surface roughness.

31.5.3 Three-Dimensional Surface Measurement

Because surface properties can vary depending on the direction in which a profilometer trace is taken, there is often a need to measure three-dimensional surface profiles. In the simplest case, this can be done with a surface profilometer that has a capability of indexing a short distance between traces. A number of alternatives have been developed (two of which, optical interferometers and atomic force microscopes, are described below).

Optical interference microscopes shine a light against a reflective surface and record the interference fringes that result from the incident and its reflected waves. This technique allows for a direct measurement of the slope of the surface over the area of interest. As the vertical distance between the sample and interference objective is changed, the fringe patterns also change, and thus allow for a surface height measurement. A typical measurement on a rolled aluminum surface is shown in Fig. 31.8.

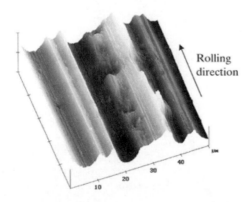

Rolling direction

FIGURE 31.8   Surface of rolled aluminum.

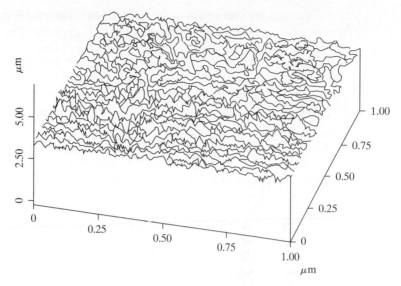

FIGURE 31.9   A highly polished silicon surface measured in an atomic force microscope. The surface roughness is $R_q = 0.134$ nm.

Atomic force microscopes (AFMs) are used to measure extremely smooth surfaces, and have the capability of distinguishing atomic scales on atomically smooth surfaces. As described in Section 26.11 (*nanofabrication*) and illustrated in Fig. 26.18, the specimen is placed into a holder and is brought in contact with a cantilever that contains a sharp imaging tip.

A laser is reflected from a mirror on the tip of the cantilever to a panel of four photosensors which record the lateral and vertical deflections of the cantilever. The specimen is then rastered back and forth by the piezo elements, and the cantilever deflections are recorded by photosensors. The surface profile can therefore be measured with high accuracy.

In principle, an AFM is merely a very fine surface profilometer with a laser that is used to measure heights. With the proper cantilevers, vertical resolution is on the atomic scale, and scan areas can be on the order of 100 μm square, although smaller areas are more common.

AFMs are often used in the tapping mode, which is when the cantilever is vibrated near its resonant frequency and taps against the surface. Etched silicon cantilevers, often with a diamond coating, are used in this test because they give extremely fine resolutions of surface details. For example, Fig. 31.9 shows a highly polished silicon surface that will be used in chip manufacture; its surface roughness, R_q, $= 0.134$ nm. AFMs are useful for this particular range of roughness, but have difficulty with very rough surfaces.

31.5.4 Surface Roughness in Engineering Practice

Requirements for surface roughness design in typical engineering applications vary by as much as two orders of magnitude. Some examples are as follows:

Clutch-disk faces	3.2 μm	(125 μin.)
Brake drums	1.6	(63)
Crankshaft bearings	0.32	(13)
Bearing balls	0.025	(1)

Furthermore, because of the many material and process variables involved, the range of roughness produced even within a particular manufacturing process can be significantly large, as is clear in Figs. 11.12, 20.23, 22.14, and 26.4.

The reasons and considerations for the large differences in surface roughness design requirements include the following:

1. The **precision** that is required on mating surfaces, such as seals, fittings, gaskets, tools, and dies. For example, ball bearings and gages require very smooth surfaces, whereas surfaces for gaskets and brake drums can be quite rough.

2. **Frictional considerations**, that is, the effect of roughness on friction, wear, and lubrication.

3. **Fatigue and notch sensitivity**, because the rougher the surface, the shorter the fatigue life (see Fig. 2.28).

4. **Electrical and thermal contact resistance**, because the rougher the surface, the higher the resistance will be.

5. **Corrosion resistance**, because the rougher the surface, the greater the possibility of entrapped corrosive media.

6. **Subsequent processing** that may be performed, such as painting and coating, in which a certain roughness can result in improved bonding.

7. **Appearance**.

8. **Cost**, because the finer the finish, the higher the cost (see Fig. 25.33).

All these factors should be considered prior to making a decision about the specifications on surface roughness for a particular part. As in all manufacturing processes, the cost involved in the selection should also be a major consideration.

SUMMARY

- Surfaces and their properties are as important as the bulk properties of the materials. A surface has not only a particular shape, roughness, and appearance, but it has properties that differ significantly from those of the bulk material as well.

- Surfaces are exposed to the environment and thus are subject to environmental attack. They may also come into contact with tools and dies (during processing) or with other components (during their service life).

- The geometric and material properties of surfaces can significantly affect their friction, wear, fatigue, corrosion, and electrical and thermal conductivity.

- The measurement and description of surface features, including their characteristics, are among important aspects of manufacturing. The most common surface roughness measurement is the arithmetic mean value. The instrument usually used to measure surface roughness is a profilometer.

TRENDS

- Efforts are continually being made, and methods refined, to accurately define and describe surfaces and their characteristics.

- In-process measurement of surface roughness (measurement as parts are being produced) is an important and growing trend in quality control.

- Measuring instruments with higher sensitivity and accuracy are being developed for computer-integrated manufacturing systems.

- Instruments which accurately measure surfaces with atomic-scale roughness are under development. Such extremely smooth surfaces are increasingly being encountered in microelectronics applications.

KEY TERMS

Arithmetic mean value	Oxide layer	Surface integrity
Atomic force microscope	Pit	Surface profilometer
Cutoff	Root-mean-square average	Surface roughness
Flaw	Substrate	Surface structure
Lay	Surface defects	Surface texture
Maximum roughness height	Surface finish	Waviness

BIBLIOGRAPHY

ASM Handbook, Vol. 18: *Friction, Lubrication, and Wear Technology.* ASM International, 1992.

ASM Handbook, Vol. 10: *Materials Characterization,* ASM International, 1986.

_____, Vol. 8: *Mechanical Testing.* ASM International, 1985.

Bhushan, B., (ed.), *Handbook of Micro/Nanotribology.* CRC Press, 1995.

Bhushan, B., *Principles and Applications of Tribology.* Wiley, 1999.

Blau, P.J., *Friction Science and Technology.* Marcel Dekker, 1995.

Booser, E.R. (ed.), *Tribology Data Handbook.* CRC Press, 1997.

Hutchins, I.M., *Tribology: Friction and Wear of Engineering Materials.* CRC Press, 1992.

Ludema, K.C., *Friction, Wear, Lubrication : A Textbook in Tribology.* CRC Press, 1996.

Machining Data Handbook (3d ed.), 2 vols. Machinability Data Center, 1980.

Neele, M.J. (ed.), *The Tribology Handbook,* (2nd ed.). Butterworth-Heinemann, 1995.

Peterson, M.R., and W.O. Winer (eds.), *Wear Control Handbook.* American Society of Mechanical Engineers, 1980.

Schey, J.A., *Tribology in Metalworking—Friction, Lubrication and Wear.* ASM International, 1983.

REVIEW QUESTIONS

31.1 What is meant by "surface integrity"? "Surface texture"?

31.2 List and explain the types of defects found on surfaces.

31.3 Explain the terms (a) roughness, (b) waviness, and (c) lay.

31.4 How is surface roughness generally measured?

31.5 What is "cutoff"? What is its significance?

31.6 What is an atomic force microscope?

31.7 Why are the results from a profilometer not a true depiction of the actual surface?

31.8 What do R_a, R_q, and R_t stand for?

31.9 Sketch the features which exist at and just below a metal surface.

QUALITATIVE PROBLEMS

31.10 What is the significance of the fact that hardness of metal oxides is generally much higher than the base metals themselves?

31.11 Describe the effects that various surface defects have on the performance of products in service.

31.12 What factors would you consider in specifying the lay of a surface for a part?

31.13 Explain why identical surface-roughness values do not necessarily represent the same type of surface.

31.14 In using a surface-roughness-measuring instrument, how would you go about determining the cutoff value?

31.15 Comment on the surface roughness of various parts and components with which you are familiar.

31.16 What is the significance of the fact that the path of the stylus and the actual profile of the surface are not necessarily the same?

31.17 What processes could be used to produce the surfaces shown in Fig. 31.5? What would be the effect of these processes on finishing costs?

31.18 Give two examples for each category in which surface waviness would be (a) desirable and (b) undesirable.

31.19 Same as Problem 31.18, but for surface roughness.

31.20 Explain the importance of studying workpiece, tool, and die surfaces.

31.21 Using Fig. 31.1, discuss the factors that contribute to the thickness of the work-hardened layer on the metal substrate.

31.22 For each of the surface lays shown in Fig. 31.5, give an example of a manufacturing process which will produce that lay.

31.23 Among the measuring devices described in this chapter, which would be suitable and which not suitable for the measurement of surface profiles in the following applications? (a) Rolling element bearing, (b) graphite EDM electrode, (c) silicon wafer, (d) mirror, (e) rough turned shaft, (f) eyeglass lens, and (g) powder-metallurgy connecting rod. Explain your answers.

31.24 Why does cost increase with finer finishes? What is the significance of this relationship?

31.25 Review the individually-labeled items in Fig. VI.1 and explain which of these are relevant to the contents of this chapter.

QUANTITATIVE PROBLEMS

31.26 Survey the available technical literature on the hardness of ferrous and nonferrous metals and their oxides, then prepare a table of metals vs. the ratio of oxide hardness/base metal hardness. Comment on your observations.

31.27 Figure 31.1 shows various layers in the surface structure of metals. Review the references given at the end of this chapter, obtain data on the range of thicknesses for each of these layers, and comment on your observations.

31.28 Refer to the profile in Fig. 31.4 and give some numerical values for the vertical distances from the center line. Calculate the R_a and R_q values. Then give another set of values for the same general profile, and calculate the same two quantities. Comment on your observations.

31.29 Obtain several different parts made of various materials, inspect their surfaces under an optical microscope at different magnifications, and make an educated guess as to what manufacturing process or finishing process was used to produce each of these parts. Explain your reasoning.

31.30 Refer to Fig. 31.5 and give reasons for selecting a particular lay for the surface of an engineering component. Give specific examples. Also describe your thoughts about possible optical or aesthetic uses for the component.

31.31 Consider two surfaces, a square wave and a sine wave. If their R_a values are equal what is the ratio of their R_t?

31.32 Consider a turning operation in which the tool nose is approximated as triangular and has an included angle of 90°. If the feed is 0.002 in./rev, and it is a roughing cut, what is the resultant surface roughness in the feed direction?

31.33 Write a computer program to calculate the R_a roughness of a sine wave. Be sure to consider the cases in which the sample length is (a) equal to the sine wave wavelength, (b) one-half the wavelength, and (c) one-tenth the wavelength. Use one thousand, evenly spaced points for each case.

SYNTHESIS AND DESIGN

31.34 Would it be desirable to integrate the surface-measuring instruments described in this chapter into the machine tools described in Parts III and IV? How would you go about doing so, taking into consideration the factory environment in which they are to be used? Make some preliminary sketches.

31.35 Section 31.3 listed major surface defects. How would you go about determining whether or not each of these defects is a big factor in a particular application?

31.36 Why are the requirements for surface roughness design in engineering applications so broad? Explain with specific examples.

31.37 Design an experimental rig which allows a conventional profilometer to be indexed across a surface and thereby measure the surface in three dimensions.

31.38 Perform an Internet search and a literature search on the variety of cantilevers that are used with atomic force microscopes.

31.39 This chapter did not present all of the surface roughness measurement methods available. Perform a literature search and then summarize the various other methods available for surface measurement.

32

Tribology: Friction, Wear, and Lubrication

32.1 INTRODUCTION

In the preceding chapters we have described the general effects of friction, lubrication, and wear on manufacturing processes and operations, such as forces, power, temperature, surface finish and integrity, dimensional accuracy, and product quality. However, we have not yet described their fundamental mechanisms, particularly with regard to the interaction of workpieces, tools, and dies under actual processing conditions.

Tribology is the science and technology of *friction*, *wear*, and *lubrication*. This chapter describes those aspects of tribology that are relevant to manufacturing processes and operations and to the service life of products. We will first describe friction and wear, and how they are influenced by various material and process variables, such as types of materials involved, surface conditions, contact stresses, speeds, and temperatures.

An understanding of these relationships is necessary for the proper selection of tool and die materials, as well as metalworking fluids for a particular operation. The economic impact of wear is clear when one looks at the estimate that in the United States alone, the total cost of replacing worn parts is more than $100 billion per year.

This chapter will then describe the fundamentals of metalworking fluids, including the types, characteristics, and application of commonly used liquid and solid lubricants, and lubrication practices. It will also highlight the importance of biological and environmental considerations in the use, application, recycling, and ultimate disposal of metalworking fluids.

32.2 FRICTION IN METALS

Friction is defined as the resistance to relative motion between two bodies in contact, under a normal load. Friction plays an important role in metalworking and manufacturing processes because of the relative motion and forces that are always present on tools, dies, and workpieces.

Friction dissipates energy, thus generating heat, which can have detrimental effects on an operation. Furthermore, because friction impedes free movement at interfaces, it can significantly affect the flow and deformation of materials in metalworking processes. On the other hand, friction is not always undesirable; without friction, for example, it would be impossible to roll metals, clamp workpieces on machines, or hold drill bits in chucks.

A commonly accepted theory of friction is the **adhesion theory**, developed by F.P. Bowden (1903–1968) and D. Tabor (1913–). The theory is based on the observation that two clean and dry surfaces, regardless of how smooth they are, contact each other (*junction*) at only a fraction of their apparent area of contact (Fig. 32.1). The maximum slope of the hills on these surfaces ranges typically between 5° and 15°.

In such a situation, the normal (contact) load, N, is supported by the minute **asperities** (small projections from the surface) that are in contact with each other. The normal stresses at these asperities are, therefore, high; this causes *plastic deformation* at the junctions. Their contact creates an *adhesive bond*: the asperities form **microwelds**. Cold pressure welding (see Section 28.2) is based on this principle.

Sliding motion between two bodies which have such an interface is possible only if a *tangential force* is applied. This tangential force is the force required to *shear* the junctions; it is called the **friction force**, F. The ratio of F to N (see Fig. 32.1) is the **coefficient of friction**, μ.

In addition to the force required to break these junctions by shearing, a *plowing* (or ploughing) *force* can also be present if one surface scratches the other (abrasive action; see Section 32.6.2). This force can contribute significantly to friction at the interface. Plowing may (a) cause displacement of the material and/or (b) produce small chips or slivers, as in cutting and abrasive processes (see Fig. 25.11). Depending on materials and processes involved, coefficients of friction in manufacturing vary significantly, as is obvious in Table 32.1.

Almost all of the energy dissipated in overcoming friction is converted into heat (a small fraction becomes stored energy in the plastically deformed regions; see Section 1.6), raising the interface temperature. The temperature increases with friction, sliding speed,

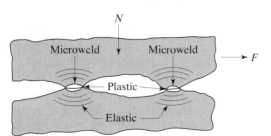

FIGURE 32.1   Schematic illustration of the interface of two bodies in contact, showing real areas of contact at the asperities. In engineering surfaces, the ratio of the apparent to real areas of contact can be as high as 4–5 orders of magnitude.

TABLE 32.1   Range of Coefficients of Friction
in Metalworking Processes

Process	Coefficient of friction (μ)	
	Cold	Hot
Rolling	0.05–0.1	0.2–0.7
Forging	0.05–0.1	0.1–0.2
Drawing	0.03–0.1	—
Sheet-metal forming	0.05–0.1	0.1–0.2
Machining	0.5–2	—

decreasing thermal conductivity, and decreasing specific heat of the sliding materials. The interface temperature may be high enough to soften and even melt the surfaces, and sometimes to cause microstructural changes.

Temperature also affects the viscosity and other properties of lubricants, causing their breakdown. Note, for example, how butter and oil burn and are degraded when temperatures are excessive. These results, in turn, adversely affect the operations involved, and cause surface damage to the object.

32.3 FRICTION IN PLASTICS AND CERAMICS

Although their strength is low compared to that of metals (see Tables 2.2 and 7.1), *plastics* generally possess low frictional characteristics. This property makes plastics, or polymers, better than metals for bearings, gears, seals, prosthetic joints, and general friction-reducing applications. In fact, polymers are sometimes described as **self-lubricating**.

The factors involved in friction and wear of metals are also generally applicable to polymers. In sliding, the plowing component of friction in thermoplastics and elastomers is a significant factor because of their viscoelastic behavior (they exhibit both viscous and elastic behavior) and subsequent loss of hysteresis (see Fig. 7.12). We can simulate this condition by dragging a dull nail across the surface of a rubber tire and observing how the tire surface quickly recovers its shape.

An important factor in plastics applications is the effect of temperature rise at the sliding interfaces caused by friction. As described in Section 7.3, thermoplastics lose their strength and become soft as temperature increases. Their low thermal conductivity and low melting points are significant, considering the heat generated by friction. If the temperature rise is not controlled, sliding surfaces can undergo permanent deformation and thermal degradation.

The frictional behavior of various polymers on metals is similar to that of metals on metals. The well-known low friction of PTFE (Teflon) is attributed to its molecular structure, which has no reaction to metals. Thus, its adhesion is poor and its friction is low.

The frictional behavior of *ceramics* is now being studied extensively, and investigations indicate that the origin of friction in ceramics is similar to that in metals. Thus, adhesion and plowing at interfaces contribute to the friction force in ceramics as well.

32.4 REDUCING FRICTION

Friction can be reduced through the selection of materials that have low adhesion, such as carbides and ceramics, and through the use of surface films and coatings. (See various sections in Chapters 32 and 33.)

chined to make gears, pulleys, sprockets, and similar mechanical components. Because plastics can be made with a wide variety of compositions, they can also be blended with internal lubricants, such as PTFE (teflon), silicon, graphite, and molybdenum disulfide, and with rubber particles that are interspersed within the polymer matrix (Section 7.5).

Wear of Reinforced Plastics.   The wear resistance of reinforced plastics depends on the type, amount, and direction of reinforcement in the polymer matrix (Chapter 9). Carbon, glass, and aramid fibers all improve wear resistance. Wear takes place when fibers are pulled out of the matrix (fiber pullout).

Wear is greatest when the sliding direction is parallel to the fibers, because they can be pulled out more easily in this case. Long fibers increase the wear resistance of composites because they are more difficult to pull out, and they prevent cracks in the matrix from propagating to the surface as easily. (See Fig. 9.6).

Wear of Ceramics.   When ceramics slide against metals, wear is caused by (a) small-scale plastic deformation and brittle surface fracture, (b) surface chemical reactions, (c) plowing, and (d) possible fatigue. Metals can be transferred to the oxide-type ceramic surfaces, forming metal oxides; thus, sliding actually takes place between the metal and the metal-oxide surface. Conventional lubricants do not appear to significantly influence the wear rate of ceramics.

32.8 WEAR MEASUREMENT

Several methods can be used to observe and measure wear. The choice of a particular method depends on the accuracy desired and the physical constraints of the system (such as specimen or part size, or difficulty of the disassembly required to observe worn surfaces).

Although not quantitative, the simplest methods are visual and tactile (touching) inspection. Measuring dimensional changes, gaging the worn component, using profilometry, and weighing are more accurate than are visual and tactile inspections. However, for large workpieces or tools and dies, the weighing method is not accurate because the amount of wear is usually very small compared to the overall weight of the components involved. Performance and noise level can also be monitored; worn machinery components emit more noise than new ones.

Radiography is a method in which wear particles from an irradiated surface are transferred to the mating surface, which is then measured for its amount of radiation. (An example is the transfer of wear particles from irradiated cutting tools to the back side of chips.) In other situations, the lubricant can be analyzed for wear particles (this method is called *spectroscopy*). This is a precision method and is used widely for applications like checking jet-engine component wear.

32.9 LUBRICATION

We have noted that the surfaces of tools, dies, and workpieces are subjected to (a) forces and contact pressures, which range from very low values to multiples of the yield stress of the workpiece material, (b) relative speeds, from very low to very high, and (c) temperatures, which range from ambient to melting.

In addition to selecting appropriate materials and controlling process parameters, we can also apply **metalworking fluids** to effectively reduce friction and wear. **Lubrication**, the process of applying these fluids, is used extensively to reduce friction and wear.

32.9.1 Types of Lubrication

There are four types of lubrication that are generally of interest in manufacturing operations (Fig. 32.8):

a. In **thick-film lubrication**, the surfaces are completely separated, and lubricant viscosity is the important factor. Such films can develop in some regions of the workpiece in high-speed operations, and can also develop from high-viscosity lubricants that become trapped at die-workpiece interfaces.

   A thick lubricant film results in a dull, grainy surface appearance on the workpiece, whereby the degree of roughness depends on grain size (Fig. 32.9). In opera-

FIGURE 32.8   Types of lubrication generally occurring in metalworking operations. *Source*: After W.R.D. Wilson.

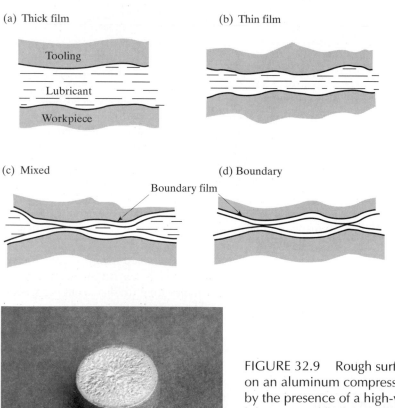

(a) Thick film

Tooling

— Lubricant — —

Workpiece

(b) Thin film

(c) Mixed

Boundary film

(d) Boundary

FIGURE 32.9   Rough surface developed on an aluminum compression specimen by the presence of a high-viscosity lubricant and high compression speed. The coarser the grain size, the rougher the surface. *Source*: A. Mulc and S. Kalpakjian.

tions such as coining and precision forging (Chapter 14), trapped lubricants are un-desirable because they prevent accurate shape generation.

b. As the load between the die and workpiece increases or as the speed and viscosity of the metalworking fluid decrease, the lubricant film becomes thinner (**thin-film lubrication**). This condition raises the friction at the sliding interfaces and results in slight wear.

c. In **mixed lubrication**, a significant portion of the load is carried by the physical contact of the two surfaces. The rest is carried by the fluid film trapped in pockets, such as the valleys of asperities.

d. In **boundary lubrication**, the load is supported by contacting surfaces covered with a *boundary film* of lubricant (Fig. 32.8d). This is a thin (molecular) lubricant layer that is physically attracted to the metal surfaces, thus preventing direct metal-to-metal contact of the two bodies and hence reducing wear. Boundary lubricants are typically natural oils, fats, fatty acids, esters, or soaps. Boundary films can, however, *break down* as a result of (a) desorption caused by high temperatures at the sliding interfaces or (b) being rubbed off during sliding. Deprived of this protective film, the sliding metal surfaces may then wear and score severely.

32.9.2 Other Considerations

The valleys in the surface roughnesses of the contacting bodies can serve as local reservoirs or pockets for lubricants, thereby supporting a substantial portion of the load. The workpiece, not the die, should have the rougher surface; otherwise, the rougher and harder die surface, acting as a file, may damage the workpiece surface. The recommended surface roughness on most dies is about 0.4 μm (15 μin.).

The overall **geometry** of the interacting bodies is also an important consideration in ensuring proper lubrication. The movement of the workpiece into the deformation zone, as during wire drawing, extrusion, and rolling, should allow a supply of lubricant to be carried into the die–workpiece interface. With proper selection of process parameters, a relatively thick lubricant film can be entrained and maintained.

32.10 METALWORKING FLUIDS

The functions of a *metalworking fluid* are to:

a. reduce friction, thus reducing force and energy requirements, and temperature rise.

b. reduce wear, seizure, and galling.

c. improve material flow in tools, dies, and molds.

d. act as a **thermal barrier** between the workpiece and tool and die surfaces, thus preventing workpiece cooling in hot-working processes.

e. act as a **release** or **parting agent**, a substance which helps in the removal or ejection of parts from dies and molds.

Several types of metalworking fluids are now available which fulfill these requirements and which have diverse chemistries, properties, and characteristics (see also Section 21.13). This section describes the general properties of the most commonly used lubricants.

32.10.1 Oils

Oils maintain high film strength on the surface of a metal, as we can observe when trying to clean an oily surface. Although they are very effective in the reduction of friction and wear, oils have low thermal conductivity and low specific heat. Consequently, they do not effectively conduct away the heat generated by friction and plastic deformation. In addition, it is difficult and costly to remove oils from component surfaces that are to be painted or welded, and it is difficult to dispose of them. (See also Section 33.16).

The sources of oils can be **mineral** (petroleum), **animal**, **vegetable**, or **fish**. Oils may be **compounded** with any number of additives or with other oils; this process is used to change such properties as viscosity-temperature behavior and surface tension, heat resistance, and boundary layer characteristics. Mineral (hydrocarbon) oils with or without additives, used undiluted, are known as **neat oils**.

Oils can be contaminated by the lubricants used for the slideways and various components of the machine tools and metalworking machinery. These oils have different characteristics than those used for the process itself, and thus can have adverse effects. When present in the metalworking fluid itself, these oils are known as **tramp oil**.

32.10.2 Emulsions

An *emulsion* is a mixture of two immiscible liquids, usually of oil and water in various proportions, along with additives. *Emulsifiers* are substances that prevent the dispersed droplets in a mixture from joining together (hence the term immiscible).

Milky in appearance, emulsions are also known as **water-soluble oils** or **water-base coolants**, and are of two types: direct and indirect. In a *direct emulsion*, mineral oil is dispersed in water in the form of very small droplets. In an *indirect emulsion*, water droplets are dispersed in the oil.

Direct emulsions are important fluids because the presence of water gives them high cooling capacity. They are particularly effective in high-speed machining (Section 22.4) where temperature rise has detrimental effects on tool life, the surface integrity of workpieces, and the dimensional accuracy of parts.

32.10.3 Synthetic and Semisynthetic Solutions

Synthetic solutions are chemical fluids that contain inorganic and other chemicals dissolved in water; they do not contain any mineral oils. Various chemical agents are added to a particular solution to impart different properties. *Semisynthetic* solutions are basically synthetic solutions to which small amounts of emulsifiable oils have been added.

32.10.4 Soaps, Greases, and Waxes

Soaps are typically reaction products of sodium or potassium salts with fatty acids. Alkali soaps are soluble in water, but other metal soaps are generally insoluble. Soaps are effective *boundary lubricants* and can also form thick film layers at die–workpiece interfaces, particularly when applied on conversion coatings for cold metalworking applications (Section 32.12).

Greases are solid or semisolid lubricants and generally consist of soaps, mineral oil, and various additives. They are highly viscous and adhere well to metal surfaces. Although used extensively in machinery, greases are of limited use in manufacturing processes.

Waxes may be of animal or plant (*paraffin*) origin; compared to greases, they are less "greasy" and are more brittle. Waxes are of limited use in metalworking operations, except as lubricants for copper and, as chlorinated paraffin, as lubricants for stainless steels and high-temperature alloys.

32.10.5 Additives

Metalworking fluids are usually blended with various additives, such as the following:

- **a.** oxidation inhibitors.
- **b.** rust-preventing agents.
- **c.** foam inhibitors.
- **d.** wetting agents.
- **e.** odor-controlling agents.
- **f.** antiseptics.

Sulfur, chlorine, and phosphorus are important oil additives. Known as **extreme-pressure (EP) additives** and used singly or in combination, they react chemically with metal surfaces and form adherent surface films of metallic sulfides and chlorides.

These films have low shear strength and good anti-weld properties and, thus, effectively reduce friction and wear. On the other hand, they may preferentially attack the cobalt binder in tungsten carbide tools and dies (**selective leaching**), causing changes in the surface roughness and integrity of tools. (See Section 3.8)

32.11 SOLID LUBRICANTS

Because of their unique properties and characteristics, several solid materials are used as lubricants in manufacturing operations. Described below are four of the most commonly used *solid lubricants*.

32.11.1 Graphite

The general properties of graphite are described in Section 8.6. Graphite is weak in shear along its basal planes (see Fig. 1.4) and thus has a low coefficient of friction in that direction. It can be an effective solid lubricant, particularly at elevated temperatures.

However, friction is low only in the presence of air or moisture. In a vacuum or an inert gas atmosphere, friction is very high; in fact, graphite can be abrasive in these situations. We can apply graphite either by rubbing it on surfaces or by making it part of a **colloidal** (dispersion of small particles) suspension in a liquid carrier such as water, oil, or an alcohol.

As described in Section 8.6, there is a more recent development in carbon called **fullerenes** or **Buckyballs**. These are carbon molecules in the shape of soccer balls. When placed between sliding surfaces, these molecules act like tiny ball bearings. They perform well as solid lubricants, and are particularly effective in aerospace applications as bearings.

32.11.2 Molybdenum Disulfide

This is a widely used lamellar solid lubricant; it is somewhat similar in appearance to graphite. However, unlike graphite, it has a high friction coefficient in ambient environment. Oils are commonly used as carriers for molybdenum disulfide (MoS_2) and are used as a lubricant at room temperature. Molybdenum disulfide can be rubbed onto the surfaces of a workpiece.

32.11.3 Metallic and Polymeric Films

Because of their low strength, thin layers of soft metals and polymer coatings are also used as solid lubricants. Suitable metals include lead, indium, cadmium, tin, silver, polymers such as PTFE (Teflon) polyethylene, and methacrylates. However, these coatings have limited applications because of their lack of strength under high contact stresses and at elevated temperatures.

Soft metals are also used to coat high-strength metals such as steels, stainless steels, and high-temperature alloys. Copper or tin, for example, is chemically deposited on the surface of the metal before it is processed. If the oxide of a particular metal has low friction and is sufficiently thin, the oxide layer can serve as a solid lubricant, particularly at elevated temperatures.

32.11.4 Glasses

Although it is a solid material, glass becomes viscous at elevated temperatures and, hence, can serve as a liquid lubricant. Viscosity is a function of temperature, but not of pressure, and depends on the type of glass. Poor thermal conductivity also makes glass attractive, since it acts as a thermal barrier between hot workpieces and relatively cool dies. Glass lubrication is typically used in such applications as hot extrusion and forging (Chapters 15 and 14, respectively).

32.12 CONVERSION COATINGS

Lubricants may not always adhere properly to workpiece surfaces, particularly under high normal and shearing stresses. This property has the greatest effects in forging, extrusion, and wire drawing of steels, stainless steels, and high-temperature alloys.

For these applications, the workpiece surfaces are first transformed through chemical reaction with acids (hence the term *conversion*). The reaction leaves a somewhat rough and spongy surface, which acts as a carrier for the lubricant. After treatment, any excess acid from the surface is removed using borax or lime. A liquid lubricant, such as a soap, is then applied to the surface. The lubricant film adheres to the surface and cannot be scraped off easily.

Zinc phosphate conversion coatings are often used on carbon and low-alloy steels. **Oxalate** coatings are used for stainless steels and high-temperature alloys.

32.13 SELECTION OF METALWORKING FLUIDS

Selecting a metalworking fluid for a particular application and workpiece material involves consideration of several factors:

1. Specific manufacturing process.
2. Workpiece material.
3. Tool or die material.
4. Processing parameters.

5. Compatibility of the fluid with the tool and die materials and workpiece.

6. Required surface preparation.

7. Method of fluid application.

8. Removal of the fluid and cleaning of the workpiece after processing.

9. Contamination of the fluid by other lubricants, such as those used to lubricate machinery.

10. Storage and maintenance of fluids.

11. Treatment of waste lubricant.

12. Biological and environmental considerations.

13. Costs involved in all aspects listed above.

When selecting an oil as a lubricant, it is necessary to investigate its viscosity-temperature-pressure characteristics. Low viscosity can have a significantly detrimental effect and cause high friction and wear. The specific function of a metalworking fluid (whether primarily a *lubricant* or a *coolant*) must also be taken into account. Water-base fluids are very effective coolants, but, as lubricants, they are not as effective as oils. It is estimated that water-base fluids are used in 80% to 90% of all machining applications.

Metalworking fluids should:

a. not leave any harmful residues that could interfere with machinery operations.

b. not stain or corrode the workpiece or equipment.

c. be checked periodically for deterioration caused by bacterial growth, accumulation of oxides, chips, and wear debris, and general degradation and breakdown due to temperature and time. The presence of wear particles is particularly important, because they cause damage to the system; proper inspection and filtering are therefore essential.

After the completion of manufacturing operations, workpiece surfaces usually have lubricant residues; these should be removed prior to further processing, such as welding or painting. Oil-base lubricants are more difficult and expensive to remove than water-base fluids. Various cleaning solutions and techniques used for this purpose are described in Section 33.16.

Biological and Environmental Considerations.   As stated in the General Introduction and discussed further in Section 37.4, environmental and biological considerations are important factors in metalworking fluid selection, use, recycling, and ultimate disposal. Potential hazards (such as *dermatitis*, inflammation of the skin) may be involved in contacting or inhaling some of these fluids, including long-term exposure to *carcinogens*.

The improper disposal of metalworking fluids may cause adverse effects on the environment as well. To prevent or restrict the growth of microorganisms such as bacteria, yeasts, molds, algae, and viruses, chemicals (*biocides*) are added to metalworking fluids.

Much progress is being made in developing environmentally-safe fluids and in developing the technology and equipment for their proper treatment, recycling, and disposal. The recycling and disposal of waste metalworking fluids and the costs involved are important factors to be considered.

Laws and regulations concerning the manufacture, transportation, use, and disposal of metalworking fluids are promulgated by the Occupational Safety and Health Administration (OSHA), the National Institute for Occupational Safety and Health (NIOSH), and the Environmental Protection Agency (EPA) of the United States.

SUMMARY

- Friction and wear are among the most significant factors in processing materials. Much progress has been made in understanding these phenomena and identifying the factors that govern them.
- Among important factors are the affinity and solid solubility of the two materials in contact, the nature of surface films, the presence of contaminants, and process parameters such as load, speed, and temperature.
- A wide variety of metalworking fluids is available for specific applications, including oils, emulsions, synthetic solutions, and solid lubricants.
- The selection and use of lubricants require careful consideration of many factors regarding workpiece and die materials and the particular manufacturing process.
- These fluids have various lubricating and cooling characteristics. Biological and environmental considerations are also important factors.

TRENDS

- Because of its major economic impact, tribology continues to be investigated, particularly for new metal alloys, ceramics, and composite materials.
- Biological and environmental aspects of lubricants and lubrication practices are being studied extensively. Ecologically acceptable metalworking fluids are under constant development.
- Studies are continuing on the development of test methods to determine friction and wear characteristics under various and more realistic processing conditions.
- Surface modifications and development of various synthetic solutions as metalworking fluids are under continuing investigation.
- Improvements in the wear resistance of ceramics continue to be made through the control of their grain size, porosity, and phase structure; and for polymers, through the reinforcement of fibers and the lubrication of additives.
- Various coatings are being developed to improve tribological properties of surfaces.

KEY TERMS

Abrasive wear	Asperities	Compounded oils
Additives	Boundary lubrication	Conversion coatings
Adhesion	Buckyballs	Coolant
Adhesive wear	Coefficient of friction	Corrosive wear

Emulsion	Metalworking fluids	Severe wear
Erosion	Microwelds	Soaps
Extreme-pressure additives	Mild wear	Solid lubricants
Fatigue wear	Mixed lubrication	Thick-film lubrication
Fretting corrosion	Neat oils	Thin-film lubrication
Friction force	Oils	Tribology
Fullerenes	Plowing	Ultrasonic vibrations
Greases	Ring-compression test	Water-soluble oils
Impact wear	Running-in	Waxes
Lubricant	Selective leaching	Wear coefficient
Lubrication	Self-lubricating	Wear parts

BIBLIOGRAPHY

Arnell, R.D., P.B. Davies, J. Halling, and T.L. Whomes, *Tribology: Principles and Design Applications.* Springer, 1991.

ASM Handbook, Vol. 18: *Friction, Lubrication, and Wear Technology.* ASM International, 1992.

Bayer, R.G., *Mechanical Wear Prediction and Prevention.* Marcel Dekker, 1994.

Bhushan, B., (ed.), *Handbook of Micro/Nanotribology* (2d ed.). CRC Press, 1998.

Bhushan, B., *Principles and Applications of Tribology.* Wiley, 1999.

Blau, P.J., *Friction Science and Technology.* Marcel Dekker, 1995.

Booser, E.R. (ed.), *Tribology Data Handbook.* CRC Press, 1998.

Byers, J.P. (ed.), *Metalworking Fluids.* Marcel Dekker, 1994.

Dowson, D., *History of Tribology.* Institution of Mechanical Engineers, 1997.

Friction and Wear Devices (2d ed.). American Society of Lubrication Engineers, 1976.

Glasser, W.A., *Materials for Tribology.* Elsevier, 1992.

Hutchings, I.M., *Tribology: Friction and Wear of Engineering Materials.* Arnold, 1992.

Lansdown, A.R., and A. L. Price, *Materials to Resist Wear: A Guide to Their Selection and Use.* Pergamon Press, 1986.

Ludema, K.C., *Friction, Wear, Lubrication: A Textbook in Tribology.* CRC Press, 1996.

Miller, R.W., *Lubricants and Their Applications.* McGraw-Hill, 1993.

Nachtman, E.S., and S. Kalpakjian, *Lubricants and Lubrication in Metalworking Operations.* Marcel Dekker, 1985.

Neele, M.J. (ed.), *The Tribology Handbook* (2d ed.). *Butterworth-Heinemann, 1995.*

Peterson, M.B., and W.O. Winer (eds.), *Wear Control Handbook.* New York: American Society of Mechanical Engineers, 1980.

Rabinowicz, E., *Friction and Wear of Materials* (2d ed.). Wiley, 1995.

Schey, J.A., *Tribology in Metalworking—Friction, Lubrication and Wear.* ASM International, 1983.

Seireg, A.A., *Friction and Lubrication in Mechanical Design.* Marcel Dekker, 1998.

Williams, J.A., *Engineering Tribology.* Oxford University Press, 1995.

REVIEW QUESTIONS

32.1 Give several examples that show the importance of friction in manufacturing processes.

32.2 What is the nature of the friction force? What is the plowing (ploughing) force?

32.3 What is the significance of a rise in surface temperature resulting from friction?

32.4 Describe the features of the ring compression test. Does it require the measurement of forces?

32.5 List the types of wear generally observed in engineering practice.

32.6 How can adhesive wear be reduced? Abrasive wear?

32.7 What functions should a lubricant perform in manufacturing processes?

32.8 List the different types of fluid and solid lubricants used in metalworking operations.

32.9 What are conversion coatings used for?

32.10 Describe the factors involved in lubricant selection.

32.11 How can fatigue wear be reduced?

32.12 How do wear mechanisms affect mold and tooling design?

32.13 What is the Archard wear law?

32.14 Why do plastics have low friction?

32.15 What are wear plates?

QUALITATIVE PROBLEMS

32.16 Explain why the bearings of skateboard wheels (if not sealed) should not be lubricated.

32.17 Give several reasons why an originally round specimen in a ring compression test may become oval after it is upset.

32.18 Can the rise in temperature at a sliding interface exceed the melting point of the metals? Explain.

32.19 Explain how a shoe horn (metal or plastic) facilitates the process of putting on shoes.

32.20 Describe what happens in the running-in process.

32.21 It has been stated that as the normal load decreases, abrasive wear is reduced. Explain why this is so.

32.22 Why is the abrasive wear resistance of a material a function of its hardness?

32.23 Explain the similarities and differences between the friction of metals and polymers.

32.24 Would ceramics be suitable for sliding at high speeds? Explain.

32.25 How are ultrasonic vibrations effective in reducing friction?

32.26 Explain the similarities and differences between wear of metals and that of polymers.

32.27 As stated in Section 32.2, in the plowing process it is possible that material is removed from the surface in the shape of slivers or chips. Describe the conditions under which this happens.

32.28 Make an extensive list of parts and components in consumer and industrial products that have to be replaced because of wear.

32.29 Survey the available literature and write a brief paper on why Teflon has such a low friction coefficient.

32.30 List manufacturing operations where high friction is desirable, and those where low friction is desirable.

32.31 From your understanding of surface geometry in Chapter 31, are sharp asperities or dull asperities likely to lead to low friction if adhesive friction is the dominant mechanism? What if abrasive friction is also present?

32.32 It was stated that wear coefficient is a function of the lubricant and process parameters. Which process parameters do you think are important? Explain.

32.33 Give examples of manufacturing operations where wear is undesirable. Give examples where wear is necessary.

32.34 Is there any reason to use solid lubricants other than for elevated-temperature applications?

32.35 Explain how a pencil and an eraser function.

QUANTITATIVE PROBLEMS

32.36 Refer to Fig. 32.2b and make measurements of the external and internal diameters (in the horizontal direction in the photograph) of the four specimens shown. Remembering that the volume of the rings remains constant in plastic deformation, calculate (a) the reduction in height and (b) the coefficient of friction for each of the three compressed specimens.

32.37 Using Fig. 32.3, make a plot of the coefficient of friction versus the change in internal diameter for a constant reduction in height of 40%.

32.38 Assume that in the example problem in Section 32.5 the coefficient of friction is 0.15. If all other parameters remain the same, what is the new internal diameter of the specimen?

32.39 Estimate the wear coefficient for pencil on paper, based on your observations while writing with a standard pencil.

SYNTHESIS AND DESIGN

32.40 How does the processing history of a part affect wear? For example, if a cam is forged, cast, machined or made from EDM, how would you expect its wear behavior to change?

32.41 Explain why gym shoes create higher friction on dry floor surfaces than do leather-soled dress shoes.

32.42 Describe the tribological differences between ordinary machine elements (such as gears and bearings) and metalworking processes. Consider such factors as load, speed, and temperature.

32.43 Describe the applicability of simulated friction and wear tests to actual manufacturing operations.

32.44 Explain why the types of wear in Fig. 32.7 occur in those particular locations in the forging die.

32.45 Wear can have detrimental effects in manufacturing operations. Can you visualize situations in which wear could be beneficial? Give examples.

32.46 On the basis of the topics described in this chapter, do you think there is a direct correlation between friction and wear of materials? Explain.

32.47 You have undoubtedly replaced parts in various appliances and automobiles because they were worn. Describe the methodology you would follow in determining the type(s) of wear these components have undergone.

32.48 Following your observations and opinions regarding Problem 32.48, state how you would go about changing materials or designs to reduce the wear of these components.

32.49 The Archard wear law is only one of many wear equations that been put forth. Perform a literature search and compile a list of other wear rules.

33

Surface Treatment, Coating, and Cleaning

33.1 INTRODUCTION

After a part is manufactured, some of its surfaces may have to be processed further in order to ensure certain properties and characteristics. It may be necessary to perform **surface treatments** in order to

- Improve resistance to wear, erosion, and indentation (in machine-tool ways, wear surfaces of machinery, and shafts, rolls, cams, and gears).
- Control friction (on the sliding surfaces of tools, dies, bearings, and machine ways).
- Reduce adhesion (electrical contacts).
- Improve lubrication (surface modification to retain lubricants).
- Improve resistance to corrosion and oxidation (on sheet metals for automobiles, gas turbine components, and medical devices).

902

TABLE 33.1   Surface Treatments for Various Metals

Metal	Treatment
Aluminum	Chrome plate; anodic coating, phosphate; chromate conversion coating
Beryllium	Anodic coating; chromate conversion coating
Cadmium	Phosphate; chromate conversion coating
Die steels	Boronizing; ion nitriding; liquid nitriding
High-temperature steels	Diffusion
Magnesium	Anodic coating; chromate conversion coating
Mild steel	Boronizing; phosphate; carburizing; liquid nitriding; carbonitriding; cyaniding
Molybdenum	Chrome plate
Nickel- and cobalt-base alloys	Boronizing; diffusion
Refractory metals	Boronizing
Stainless steel	Vapor deposition; ion nitriding; diffusion; liquid nitriding; nitriding
Steel	Vapor deposition; chrome plate; phosphate; ion nitriding; induction hardening; flame hardening; liquid nitriding
Titanium	Chrome plate; anodic coating; ion nitriding
Tool steel	Boronizing; ion nitriding; diffusion; nitriding; liquid nitriding
Zinc	Vapor deposition; anodic coating; phosphate; chromate chemical conversion coating

Source: After M. K. Gabel and D. M. Doorman in *Wear Control Handbook*, New York, ASME, 1980 p. 248.

- Improve fatigue resistance (bearings and shafts with fillets).
- Rebuild surfaces on worn components (worn tools, dies, and machine components).
- Modify surface texture (appearance, dimensional accuracy, and frictional characteristics).
- Impart decorative features (color).

Several techniques are used to impart these characteristics to various types of materials, as shown in Table 33.1. This chapter describes the methods used to modify the surface's structure, properties, textures in order to impart desirable characteristics. We begin with surface hardening techniques, which involve mechanical or thermal means, and continue with descriptions of different types of coatings that are applied to surfaces using various means. Some of these techniques are also used in the manufacture of semiconductor devices (Chapter 34).

Finally, we describe techniques used to clean manufactured surfaces before the components are processed further and are assembled, and before the product is placed in service. Environmental considerations regarding the fluids used and the waste material from various surface treatment processes are one of the important factors we will also consider.

33.2 MECHANICAL SURFACE TREATMENT AND COATING

Several techniques are used to mechanically improve the surface properties of finished components. The more common methods are described next.

33.2.1 Shot Peening

In *shot peening*, the workpiece surface is hit repeatedly with a large number of cast steel, glass, or ceramic shot (small balls), which make overlapping indentations on the surface. This action causes plastic surface deformation, at depths up to 1.25 mm (0.05 in.), using shot sizes that range from 0.125 mm to 5 mm (0.005 in. to 0.2 in.) in diameter.

Because the plastic deformation is not uniform throughout the part's thickness, shot peening causes compressive residual stresses on the surface, thus improving the fatigue life of the component. This process is used extensively on shafts, gears, springs, oil-well drilling equipment, and jet-engine parts (such as turbine and compressor blades).

33.2.2 Water-Jet Peening

In this relatively new process, a water jet at pressures as high as 400 MPa (60,000 psi) impinges on the surface of the workpiece, inducing compressive residual stresses and surface and subsurface hardening at the same level as in shot peening. The water-jet peening process has been used successfully on steels and aluminum alloys. The control of process variables (jet pressure, jet velocity, and the design of the nozzle and its distance from the surface) is important in order to avoid excessive surface roughness and surface damage.

33.2.3 Laser Peening

In *laser peening*, which was developed in the early 1990s, the workpiece surface is subjected to laser shocks from high-powered lasers. This surface-treatment process produces compressive residual stress layers that are typically 1 mm (0.04 in.) deep. *Laser peening* has been applied successfully to jet-engine fan blades and materials such as titanium and nickel alloys.

Laser intensities necessary for this process are on the order of 100 to 300 J/cm^2, and have a pulse duration of about 30 nanoseconds. Currently, the basic limitation of this process for industrial, cost-effective applications is the expense of high-power lasers (up to 1 kW) that must operate at energy levels of 100 J/pulse.

33.2.4 Roller Burnishing

In *roller burnishing*, also called **surface rolling**, the surface of the component is cold-worked by a hard and highly polished roller or rollers. This process is used on various flat, cylindrical or conical surfaces (Figs. 33.1 and 33.2). Roller burnishing improves surface finish by removing scratches, tool marks, and pits. Consequently, corrosion resistance is also improved, since corrosive products and residues cannot be entrapped.

Internal cylindrical surfaces are burnished by a similar process, called **ballizing** or **ball burnishing**. A smooth ball, slightly larger than the bore diameter, is pushed through the length of the hole.

Roller burnishing is used to improve the mechanical properties of surfaces, as well as their surface finish. It can be used either by itself or in combination with other finishing processes, such as grinding, honing, and lapping. All types of metals, soft or hard, can be roller-burnished. Roller burnishing is typically used on hydraulic-system components, seals, valves, spindles, and fillets on shafts.

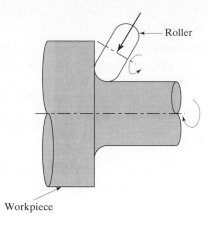

FIGURE 33.1   Roller burnishing of the fillet of a stepped shaft to induce compressive surface residual stresses for improved fatigue life.

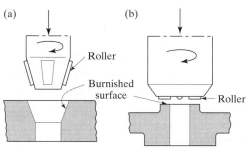

FIGURE 33.2   Examples of roller burnishing of (a) a conical surface and (b) a flat surface and the burnishing tools used. *Source*: Sandvik, Inc.

33.2.5 Explosive Hardening

In *explosive hardening*, the surfaces are subjected to high transient pressures through the placement and detonation of a layer of explosive sheet directly on the workpiece surface. The contact pressures that develop as a result can be as high as 35 GPa (5×10^6 psi), and can last about 2–3 μs. Major increases in surface hardness can be effected using this method, with very little change (less than 5%) in the shape of the component. Railroad rail surfaces can be hardened by this method.

33.2.6 Cladding (Clad Bonding)

In the process of *cladding*, metals are bonded with a thin layer of corrosion-resistant metal through the application of pressure, using rolls or other means. A typical application is cladding of aluminum (*Alclad*), in which a corrosion-resistant layer of aluminum alloy is clad over aluminum-alloy body (core), usually in sheet or tubular form. The cladding layer is anodic to the core and usually has a thickness which is less than 10% of the total thickness; examples are as follows (see also Section 6.4):

a. 2024 aluminum clad with 1230 aluminum.
b. 3003, 6061, and 7178 aluminum clad with 7072 aluminum.

Other applications are steels clad with stainless steel or nickel alloys. The cladding material may also be applied using dies (as in cladding steel wire with copper) or explosives. Multiple-layer cladding is also utilized in special applications (See also Fig. 28.1.)

33.2.7 Mechanical Plating

In the process of *mechanical plating* (also called *mechanical coating*, *impact plating*, or *peen plating*), fine metal particles are compacted over the workpiece surfaces by glass, ceramic, or porcelain beads that are propelled by rotary means. The process is used typically for hardened steel parts for automobiles, with plating thickness usually less than 0.025 mm (0.001 in.).

33.3 CASE HARDENING AND HARD FACING

Surfaces may be hardened by thermal means in order to improve their frictional and wear properties, as well as their resistance to indentation, erosion, abrasion, and corrosion. The most common methods are described next.

33.3.1 Case Hardening

Traditional methods of *case hardening* (*carburizing*, *carbonitriding*, *cyaniding*, *nitriding*, *flame hardening*, and *induction hardening*) were described in Section 4.10 and were summarized in Table 4.1. In addition to common heat sources (gas and electricity), a laser beam can be used as a heat source in surface hardening of both metals and ceramics.

Case hardening, as well as some of the other surface-treatment processes described in this chapter, induces residual stresses on surfaces. The formation of martensite during case hardening causes compressive residual stresses on surfaces. Such stresses are desirable, because they improve the fatigue life of components by delaying the initiation of fatigue cracks.

33.3.2 Hard Facing

In *hard facing*, a relatively thick layer, edge, or point of wear-resistant hard metal is deposited on the surface using any of the welding techniques described in Chapters 27 and 28. Numerous layers are usually deposited (**weld overlay**). Hard coatings of tungsten carbide, or chromium and molybdenum carbides, can also be deposited using an electric arc (**spark hardening**).

Hard-facing alloys can be used as electrodes, rod, wire, or powder. Typical applications for these alloys are valve seats, oil-well drilling tools, and dies for hot metalworking. Worn parts are also hard-faced for extended use.

33.4 THERMAL SPRAYING

In *thermal spraying* processes, coatings (various metals and alloys, carbides, and ceramics) are applied to metal surfaces by a spray gun with a stream of oxyfuel flame, electric arc, or plasma arc. The coating material can be in the form of wire, rod, or powder, and the droplets or particles impact the surfaces at speeds in the range of 100 to 1200 m/s (325 to 3900 ft/s).

The surfaces to be sprayed are first cleaned and roughened to improve bond strength (which depends on the particular process and techniques used). The coating has a layered structure of deposited material, and may have porosity (as high as 20%) due to entrapped air and oxide particles because of the high temperatures involved.

The earliest applications of thermal spraying (in the 1910s) involved metals; hence, the term **metallizing** has also been used. Typical applications include aircraft engine components (such as in rebuilding worn parts), structures, storage tanks, tank cars, rocket motor nozzles, and components which require resistance to wear and corrosion.

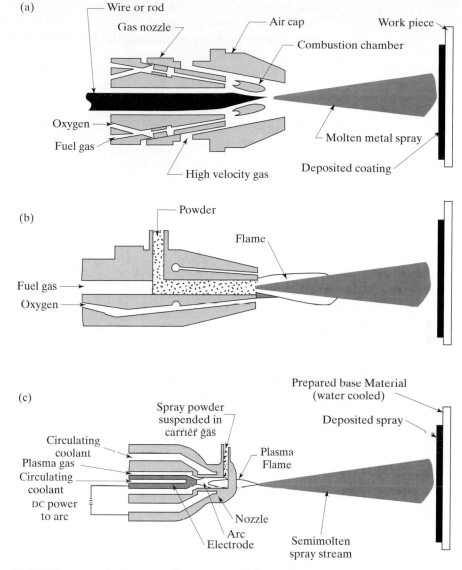

FIGURE 33.3   Schematic illustrations of thermal spray operations. (a) Thermal wire spray. (b) Thermal metal-powder spray. (c) Plasma spray.

There are several types of thermal spraying processes:

a. Thermal wire spraying (Fig. 33.3a), in which the oxyfuel flame melts the wire and deposits it on the surface. Its bond is of medium strength, but the process is relatively inexpensive.

b. Thermal metal-powder spraying (Fig. 33.3b), similar to (a) but using metal powder instead of the wire. (see also Section 17.2).

c. Plasma, either conventional, high-energy, or vacuum (Fig. 33.3c). It produces temperatures on the order of 8300 °C (15,000 °F), and results in very good bond strength with very low oxide content.

d. **Detonation gun**, in which a controlled explosion takes place using an oxyfuel gas mixture. The detonation gun has a performance similar to that of plasma.

e. **High-velocity oxyfuel gas spraying** (HVOF), which produces a similarly high performance as the detonation gun, but is less expensive.

f. **Wire arc**, in which an arc is formed between two consumable wire electrodes. The bond has bond strength and the process is the least expensive.

Example: Repair of a Worn Turbine-Engine Shaft by Thermal Spraying

The shaft of the helical-gear for a GE T-38 gas turbine engine had two worn regions on its nitrided surfaces. The case-hardened depth was 0.3 mm (0.012 in.). Even though the helical gears were in good condition, the part was considered scrap because there was no approved method of repair.

The worn regions were first machined undersize, grit blasted, and coated with tungsten carbide (12% cobalt content; see Section 21.5) using the high-velocity oxyfuel (HVOF) thermal spraying technique. The part was then finish-machined to the dimensions of the original new shaft. The total cost of repair was a fraction of the projected cost of replacing the part. *Source*: Plasma Technology, Inc.

33.5 VAPOR DEPOSITION

Vapor deposition is a process in which the substrate (workpiece surface) is subjected to chemical reactions by gases that contain chemical compounds of the material to be deposited. The coating thickness is usually a few μm, which is much less than the thicknesses that result from the techniques described in Sections 33.2 and 33.3.

The deposited materials can consist of metals, alloys, carbides, nitrides, borides, ceramics, or oxides. Control of coating composition, thickness, and porosity are important. The substrate may be metal, plastic, glass, or paper. Typical applications for vapor deposition are the coating of cutting tools (see Fig. 21.8), drills, reamers, milling cutters, punches, dies, and wear surfaces.

There are two major vapor deposition processes: physical vapor deposition and chemical vapor deposition.

33.5.1 Physical Vapor Deposition

The three basic types of *physical vapor deposition* (PVD) processes are (a) vacuum or arc evaporation, (b) sputtering, and (c) ion plating. These processes are carried out in a high vacuum and at temperatures in the range of 200 °C-500 °C (400 °F-900 °F). In physical vapor deposition, the particles to be deposited are carried physically to the workpiece, rather than carried by chemical reactions, as in chemical vapor deposition.

a. **Vacuum evaporation.** In *vacuum evaporation*, the metal to be deposited is evaporated at a high temperature in a vacuum and is deposited on the substrate, which is usually at room temperature or slightly higher. Coatings of uniform thickness can be deposited, even on complex shapes.

In **arc evaporation** (PV/ARC), the coating material (cathode) is evaporated by several arc evaporators (three are shown in Fig. 33.4), using highly localized electric arcs. The arcs produce a highly reactive plasma which consists of ionized vapor of the coating material. The vapor condenses on the substrate (anode) and coats it.

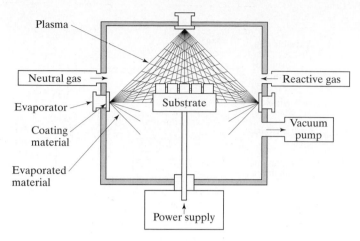

FIGURE 33.4   Schematic illustration of the physical deposition process. *Source*: Cutting Tool Engineering.

Applications for this process are both functional (oxidation-resistant coatings for high temperature applications, electronics, and optics) and decorative (hardware, appliances, and jewelry).

b. Sputtering. In *sputtering*, an electric field ionizes an inert gas (usually argon). The positive ions bombard the coating material (cathode) and cause sputtering (ejecting) of its atoms. These atoms then condense on the workpiece, which is heated to improve bonding (Fig. 33.5).

   In **reactive sputtering**, the inert gas is replaced by a reactive gas, such as oxygen, in which case the atoms are oxidized and the oxides are deposited. Carbides and nitrides are also deposited by reactive sputtering. Very thin polymer coatings can be deposited on metal and polymeric substrates with a reactive gas, causing polymerization of the plasma.

   Radio-frequency (RF) sputtering is used for nonconductive materials such as electrical insulators and semiconductor devices.

FIGURE 33.5   Schematic illustration of the sputtering process. *Source*: ASM International.

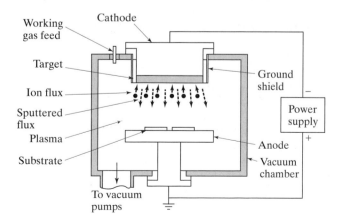

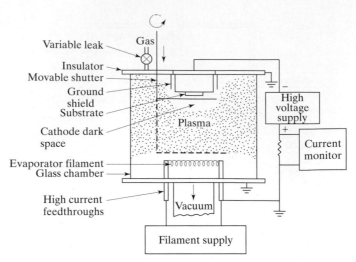

FIGURE 33.6   Schematic illustration of an ion-plating apparatus.
Source: ASM International.

    c. Ion plating. *Ion plating* is a generic term that describes the combined processes of sputtering and vacuum evaporation. An electric field causes a glow discharge, generating a plasma (Fig. 33.6). The vaporized atoms in this process are only partially ionized.

    d. Dual ion-beam assisted deposition is a recently-developed hybrid coating technique that combines physical vapor deposition with simultaneous ion-beam bombardment. This technique results in good adhesion on metals, ceramics, and polymers. Ceramic bearings and dental instruments are examples of its applications.

33.5.2 Chemical Vapor Deposition

Chemical vapor deposition (CVD) is a thermochemical process (Fig. 33.7). In a typical application, such as coating cutting tools with titanium nitride (TiN), the tools are placed on a graphite tray and heated to 950 °C-1050 °C (1740 °F-1920 °F) at atmospheric pressure in an inert atmosphere. Titanium tetrachloride (a vapor), hydrogen, and nitrogen are then introduced into the chamber. The chemical reactions form titanium nitride on the tool surfaces. For a coating of titanium carbide, methane is substituted for the gases.

    Deposited coatings are usually thicker than those obtained using PVD. A typical cycle for CVD is long, consisting of (a) three hours of heating, (b) four hours of coating, and (c) six to eight hours of cooling to room temperature. The thickness of the coating depends on the flow rates of the gases used, the time, and the temperature.

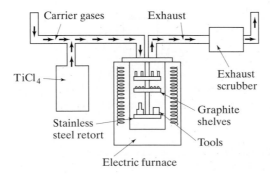

FIGURE 33.7   Schematic illustration of the chemical vapor deposition process.

The types of coatings and workpiece materials allowable are fairly unrestricted in CVD. Almost any material can be coated and any material can serve as a substrate, although bond strength may vary. The CVD process is also used to produce diamond coatings (Section 33.13) without using binders, unlike polycrystalline diamond films, which use 1% to 10% binder materials.

A recent development in chemical vapor deposition is **medium-temperature CVD** (MTCVD). This technique results in a higher resistance to crack propagation than CVD coatings. (See Section 21.6.1.)

33.6 ION IMPLANTATION

In *ion implantation*, ions (charged atoms) are introduced into the surface of the workpiece material. The ions are accelerated in a vacuum to such an extent that they penetrate the substrate to a depth of a few μm. Ion implantation (not to be confused with ion plating) modifies surface properties by increasing surface hardness and improving resistance to friction, wear, and corrosion. This process can be accurately controlled, and the surface can be masked to prevent ion implantation in unwanted locations.

Ion implantation is particularly effective on materials such as aluminum, titanium, stainless steels, tool and die steels, carbides, and chromium coatings. This process is typically used on cutting and forming tools, dies and molds, and metal prostheses such as artificial hips and knees. When used in specific applications, such as semiconductors (Chapter 34), this process is called **doping**, meaning alloying with small amounts of various elements.

33.7 DIFFUSION COATING

Diffusion coating is a process in which an alloying element is diffused into the surface of the substrate, thus altering its properties. The alloying elements can be supplied in solid, liquid, or gaseous states. This process has different names, depending on the diffused element (as can be seen in Table 4.1, which describes the diffusion processes of carburizing, nitriding, and boronizing).

33.8 ELECTROPLATING, ELECTROLESS PLATING, AND ELECTROFORMING

Plating, as with other coating processes, imparts the properties of resistance to wear and corrosion, high electrical conductivity, and better appearance and reflectivity, as well as similar desirable properties.

33.8.1 Electroplating

In *electroplating*, the workpiece (cathode) is plated with a different metal (anode), while both are suspended in a bath containing a water-base electrolyte solution (Fig. 33.8). Although the plating process involves a number of reactions, basically the process consists of the following:

1. The metal ions from the anode are discharged using the potential energy from the external source of electricity,

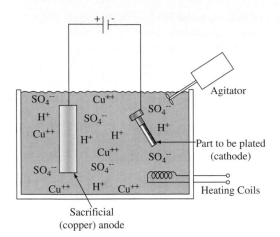

FIGURE 33.8   Schematic illustration of the electroplating process.

2. The metal ions combine with the ions in the solution, and

3. They are deposited on the cathode.

Chemical cleaning and degreasing and thorough rinsing of the workpiece prior to plating are essential. The parts are placed on racks or in a barrel (bulk plating) and lowered into the plating bath. All metals can be electroplated; electroplate thicknesses range from a few atomic layers to a maximum of about 0.05 mm (0.002 in.). Complex shapes may have varying plating thicknesses. Some design guidelines for electroplating are shown in Fig. 33.9.

Chromium, nickel, cadmium, copper, zinc, and tin are common plating materials. **Chromium plating** is done by plating the metal, first with copper, then with nickel, and finally with chromium. **Hard chromium plating** is done directly on the base metal and results in a hardness of up to 70 HRC. This method is used to improve the resistance to wear and corrosion of tools, valve stems, hydraulic shafts, and diesel- and aircraft-engine cylinder liners—and it is also used to rebuild worn parts.

Electroplating is used in copper-plating aluminum wire and phenolic boards for printed circuits, chrome-plating of hardware, tin-plating copper electrical terminals (for ease of soldering), and components that require resistance to wear and corrosion and a good ap-

FIGURE 33.9   (a) Schematic illustration of nonuniform coatings (exaggerated) in electroplated parts. (b) Design guidelines for electroplating. Note that sharp external and internal corners should be avoided for uniform plating thickness. *Source*: ASM International.

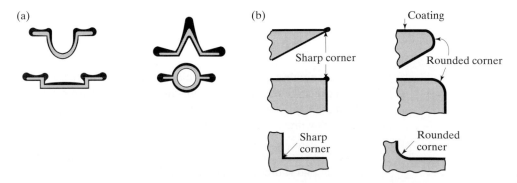

pearance. Metals such as gold, silver, and platinum are important electroplating materials in the electronics and jewelry industries.

Plastics such as ABS, polypropylene, polysulfone, polycarbonate, polyester, and nylon can also be electroplating substrates. Because they are not electrically conductive, plastics must be preplated using such processes as electroless nickel plating (Section 33.8.2; see also Section 7.3). Parts to be coated may be simple or complex, and size is not a limitation.

33.8.2 Electroless Plating

Electroless plating is done by chemical reaction and without the use of an external source of electricity. The most common application utilizes nickel, although copper is also used.

In electroless nickel plating, nickel chloride (a metallic salt) is reduced, using sodium hypophosphite as the reducing agent, to nickel metal, which is then deposited on the workpiece. The hardness of nickel plating ranges between 425 HV and 575 HV, and can subsequently be heat-treated to 1000 HV. The coating has excellent wear and corrosion resistance.

Cavities, recesses, and the inner surfaces of tubes can be plated successfully. This process can also be used with nonconductive materials, like plastics and ceramics. Electroless plating is more expensive than electroplating. However, unlike that of electroplating, the coating thickness of electroless plating is always uniform (see Fig. 33.9).

33.8.3 Electroforming

A variation of electroplating is *electroforming*, which actually is a metal fabricating process. Metal is electrodeposited on a *mandrel* (also called mold or matrix), which is then removed; thus, the coating itself becomes the product. Both simple and complex shapes can be produced by electroforming, with wall thicknesses as small as 0.025 mm (0.001 in.). Parts may weigh from a few grams to as much as 270 kg (600 lb). Production rates can be increased through the use of multiple mandrels.

Mandrels are made from a variety of materials: metallic (zinc or aluminum) or nonmetallic (which can be made electrically conductive with the proper coatings). Mandrels should be able to be physically removed without damaging the electroformed part. They may also be made of low-melting alloys, wax, or plastics, which can be melted away or dissolved with suitable chemicals.

The electroforming process is particularly suitable for low production quantities or intricate parts (such as molds, dies, waveguides, nozzles, and bellows) made of nickel, copper, gold, and silver. It is also suitable for aerospace, electronics, and electrooptics applications.

33.9 ANODIZING

Anodizing is an oxidation process (*anodic oxidation*) in which the workpiece surfaces are converted to a hard and porous oxide layer that provides corrosion resistance and a decorative finish. The workpiece is the anode in an electrolytic cell immersed in an acid bath, which results in chemical adsorption of oxygen from the bath. Organic dyes of various colors (typically black, red, bronze, gold, or gray) can be used to produce stable, durable surface films.

Typical applications for anodizing are aluminum furniture and utensils, architectural shapes, automobile trim, picture frames, keys, and sporting goods. Anodized surfaces also serve as a good base for painting, especially on aluminum, which otherwise is difficult to paint.

33.10 CONVERSION COATING

Conversion coating, also called *chemical reaction priming*, is the process of producing a coating that forms on metal surfaces as a result of chemical or electrochemical reactions. Various metals, particularly steel, aluminum, and zinc, can be conversion-coated. Oxides that naturally form on their surfaces are a form of conversion coating.

Phosphates, *chromates*, and *oxalates* are used to produce these coatings. They are used for purposes such as corrosion protection, prepainting, and decorative finish. An important application is in conversion coating of workpieces to serve as lubricant carriers in cold forming operations. (See Section 32.12.) The two common methods of coating are *immersion* and *spraying*. The equipment required depends on the method of application, the type of product, and quality considerations.

As the name implies, **coloring** involves processes that alter the color of metals, alloys, and ceramics. It is caused by the conversion of surfaces (by chemical, electrochemical, or thermal processes) into chemical compounds such as oxides, chromates, and phosphates. An example is **blackening** of iron and steels, a process that utilizes solutions of hot caustic soda and results in chemical reactions that produce a lustrous, black oxide film on surfaces.

33.11 HOT DIPPING

In *hot dipping*, the workpiece (usually steel or iron) is dipped into a bath of molten metal, such as zinc (for galvanized-steel sheet and plumbing supplies), tin (for tinplate and tin cans for food containers), aluminum (aluminizing), and terne (lead alloyed with 10% to 20% tin). Hot-dipped coatings on discrete parts provide long-term corrosion resistance to galvanized pipe, plumbing supplies, and many other products.

A typical continuous hot-dipped galvanizing line for steel sheet is shown in Fig. 33.10. The rolled sheet is first cleaned electrolytically and scrubbed by brushing. The sheet is then

FIGURE 33.10   Flowline for continuous hot-dip galvanizing of sheet steel. The welder (upper left) is used to weld the ends of coils to maintain continuous material flow. *Source*: American Iron and Steel Institute.

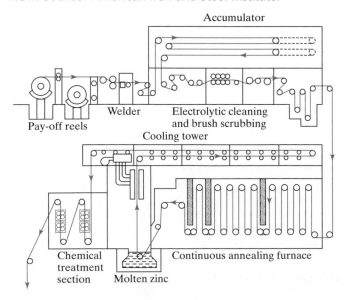

annealed in a continuous furnace with controlled atmosphere and temperature and dipped in molten zinc at about 450 °C (840 °F). The thickness of the zinc coating is controlled by a wiping action from a stream of air or steam, called an *air knife* (similar to air-drying in car washes). Proper draining, for the removal of excess coating materials, is important.

The coating thickness is usually given in terms of coating weight per unit surface area of the sheet, typically 150 to 900 g/m^2 (0.5 to 3 oz/ft^2). Service life depends on the thickness of the zinc coating and the environment to which it is exposed. Various **precoated** sheet steels are used extensively in automobile bodies.

33.12 PORCELAIN ENAMELING, CERAMIC COATING, AND ORGANIC COATINGS

Metals can be coated with a variety of glassy (vitreous) coatings to provide corrosion and electrical resistance, and to provide protection at elevated temperatures. These coatings are usually classified as **porcelain enamels**, and generally include enamels and ceramics. (The word *enamel* is also used for glossy paints, indicating a smooth, hard coating.)

Porcelain enamels are glassy inorganic coatings that consist of various metal oxides. **Enameling**, which was a fully developed art by the Middle Ages, involves fusing the coating material to the substrate by heating them both to 425 °C-1000 °C (800 °F-1800 °F) to liquefy the oxides. The coating may be applied by dipping, spraying, or electrodeposition, and thicknesses are usually 0.05 mm-0.6 mm (0.002 in.-0.025 in.). Depending on their composition, enamels have varying resistances to alkali, acids, detergents, cleansers, and water; they are also available in various colors.

Typical applications for porcelain enameling are for household appliances, plumbing fixtures, chemical processing equipment, signs, cookware, and jewelry. Porcelain enamels are also used as protective coatings on jet engine components. Metals coated are typically steels, cast iron, and aluminum. Glasses are used as a lining, for chemical resistance, and the thickness is much greater than that of enameling. **Glazing** is the application of glassy coatings on ceramic wares to give them decorative finishes and to make them impervious to moisture.

Ceramic coatings, such as aluminum oxide or zirconium oxide, are applied at room temperature, using binders, to the substrate. Such coatings act as thermal barriers, and have been applied (usually by thermal spraying techniques) to hot extrusion dies, turbine blades, and diesel-engine components, to extend life of these parts.

Metal surfaces can be coated or precoated with a variety of **organic coatings**, films, and laminates to improve appearance, eye appeal, and corrosion resistance. Coatings are applied to the coil stock on continuous lines, with thicknesses generally of 0.0025 mm-0.2 mm (0.0001 in.-0.008 in.).

Such coatings have a wide range of properties: flexibility, durability, hardness, resistance to abrasion and chemicals, color, texture, and gloss. Coated sheet metal is subsequently formed into various products, such as TV cabinets, appliance housings, paneling, shelving, residential building siding, gutters, and metal furniture.

More critical applications involve, for example, naval aircraft, which are subjected to high humidity, rain, sea water, pollutants (such as from ship exhaust stacks), aviation fuel, deicing fluids, and battery acid, and which are also impacted by particles such as dust, gravel, stones, and deicing salts.

For aluminum structures, organic coatings consist typically of an epoxy primer and a polyurethane topcoat, with a lifetime of four to six years. Primer performance is an important factor in the durability of the coating; consequently, a lot of research is being conducted to develop improved coating materials.

> ### Example: Ceramic Coatings for High Temperature Applications
>
> Certain product characteristics, such as wear resistance and thermal and electrical insulation (particularly at elevated temperatures), can be imparted through ceramic coatings rather than imparting these properties to the base metals or materials themselves. Selecting materials with such bulk properties can be expensive and may not meet the structural strength requirements in a particular application.
>
> For example, a wear-resistance component does not have to be made completely from a wear-resistant material, since the properties of only a thin layer on its surface are relevant to wear. Consequently, coatings have important applications. Table 33.2 shows various ceramic coatings and their typical applications at elevated temperatures. These coatings may be applied either singly or in layers, as is done in multiple-layer coated cutting tools; (See Section 21.6.)
>
> TABLE 33.2
>
> | Property | Type of ceramic | Application |
> | --- | --- | --- |
> | Wear resistance | Chromium oxide
Aluminum oxide
Aluminum titania | Pumps, turbine shafts, seals, compressor rods for the petroleum industry; plastics extruder barrels; extrusion dies |
> | Thermal insulation | Zirconium oxide
(yttria stabilized)
Zirconium oxide
(calcia stabilized)
Magnesium zirconate | Fan blades, compressor blades, and seals for gas turbines; valves, pistons, and combustion heads for automotive engines |
> | Electrical insulation | Magnesium aluminate
Aluminum oxide | Induction coils, brazing fixtures, general electrical applications |

33.13 DIAMOND COATING

The properties of *diamond* that are relevant to manufacturing engineering are described in Section 8.7. Important advances have been made in the diamond coating of metals, glass, ceramics, and plastics, using various techniques, such as chemical vapor deposition (CVD), plasma-assisted vapor deposition, and ion-beam-enhanced deposition.

Examples of diamond-coated products are: scratchproof windows (such as those used in aircraft and missile sensors for protection against sandstorms); sunglasses; cutting tools (such as inserts, drills, and end mills); wear faces of micrometers and calipers; surgical knives; razors; electronic and infrared heat seekers and sensors; light-emitting diodes; diamond-coated speakers for stereo systems; turbine blades; and fuel-injection nozzles.

Techniques have also been developed to produce **free-standing diamond films** on the order of 1 mm (0.040 in.) thick and up to 125 mm (5 in.) in diameter; these include smooth, optically clear diamond film, unlike the hazy gray diamond film formerly produced. The film is then laser cut to desired shapes and brazed onto, for example, cutting tools.

The development of these techniques, combined with the important properties of diamond (hardness, wear resistance, high thermal conductivity, and transparency to ultraviolet light and microwave frequencies), have enabled the production of various aerospace and electronic parts and components.

Studies are also continuing into the growth of diamond films on crystalline copper substrate by the implantation of carbon ions. An important application is in making computer chips (Chapter 34). Diamond can be doped to form *p*- and *n*-type ends on semiconductors to make transistors, and its high thermal conductivity allows closer packing of chips than would be possible with silicon or gallium–arsenide chips, significantly increasing the speed of computers.

Diamond-Like Carbon.   A more recent development is *diamond-like carbon* (DLC) coatings, a few nanometers in thickness, which use a low-temperature, ion-beam-assisted deposition process. Less expensive than diamond films but with similar properties (such as low friction, high hardness, and chemical inertness, as well as a smooth surface), DLC has applications in such areas as engine components, tools and dies, gears, bearings, micro-electromechanical systems, and microscale probes.

33.14 PAINTING

Because of its decorative and functional properties (such as environmental protection, low cost, relative ease of application, and the range of available colors), **paint** is widely used as a surface coating. The engineering applications of painting range from machinery to automobile bodies.

Paints are classified as (a) **enamels**, which produce a smooth coat and dry with a glossy or semiglossy appearance; (b) **lacquers**, which form a film by evaporation of a solvent; and (c) **water-based paints**, which are easily applied but have a porous surface and absorb water, making them more difficult to clean than the first two.

Paints are now available with good resistance to abrasion, fading, and temperature extremes; they are easy to apply and dry quickly. Selection of a particular paint depends on specific requirements. Among these are resistance to mechanical actions (abrasion, marring, impact, and flexing) or to chemical actions (acids, solvents, detergents, alkalis, fuels, staining, and general environmental attack).

Common methods of applying paint are dipping, brushing, and spraying (Fig. 33.11). In **electrocoating** or **electrostatic spraying**, paint particles are charged *electrostatically* and are attracted to surfaces, producing a uniformly adherent coating. Unlike conventional spraying, in which as much as 70% of the paint may be lost, the loss can be as little as 10% in electrostatic spraying. However, deep recesses and corners are difficult to coat with this method.

FIGURE 33.11   Methods of paint application: (a) dip coating, (b) flow coating, and (c) electrostatic spraying. *Source*: Society of Manufacturing Engineers.

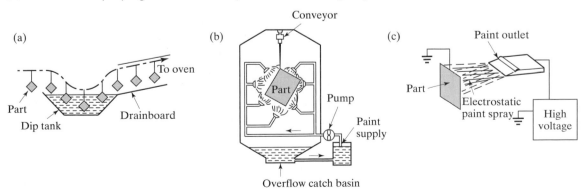

33.15 SURFACE TEXTURING

As seen throughout the preceding chapters, each manufacturing process (such as casting, forging, powder metallurgy, injection molding, machining, grinding, polishing, electrical-discharge machining, grit blasting, and wire brushing), produces a certain surface texture and appearance. Obviously, some of these processes can be used to modify the surface produced by a previous process; for example, grinding some surfaces of a cast part. However, manufactured surfaces can further be modified by secondary operations for technical, functional, optical, or aesthetic reasons.

Called *surface texturing*, these additional processes generally consist of the following:

a. **Etching**, using chemicals or sputtering techniques,
b. **Electric arcs** and **laser pulses**, and
c. **Atomic oxygen**, which reacts with surfaces and produces fine, conelike surface textures.

The possible adverse effects of these processes on material properties and performance should be considered.

33.16 CLEANING SURFACES

We have stressed the importance of surfaces and the influence of deposited or adsorbed layers of various elements and contaminants on surfaces. A clean surface can have both beneficial and detrimental effects. Although a surface that is not clean may reduce the tendency for adhesion and galling, cleanliness is generally essential for more effective application of coating, painting, adhesive bonding, welding, brazing, and soldering, as well as for the reliable functioning of manufactured parts in machinery, assembly operations, and of course food and beverage containers.

Cleaning involves the removal of solid, semisolid, or liquid contaminants from a surface, and it is an important part of manufacturing operations and the economics of production. The word **clean**, or the degree of cleanliness of a surface, is somewhat difficult to define. Two simple and common tests are as follows:

1. Wiping with a clean cloth and observing any residues on the cloth.
2. Observing whether water continuously coats the surface. If water collects as individual droplets, the surface is not clean (**waterbreak test**). Test this phenomenon yourself by wetting dinner plates that have been cleaned to different degrees.

   The type of cleaning process required depends on the type of *metalworking fluid residues* and *contaminants* to be removed. For example, water-based fluids are easier and less expensive to remove than oil-based fluids. Contaminants, also called *soils*, may consist of rust, scale, chips (and other metallic and nonmetallic debris), metalworking fluids, solid lubricants, pigments, polishing and lapping compounds, and general environmental elements.

Cleaning Processes.   Basically, there are two types of cleaning methods: mechanical and chemical.

Mechanical cleaning consists of physically disturbing the contaminants, often with wire or fiber brushing, abrasive blasting, tumbling, or steam jets. Many of these processes are particularly effective in removing rust, scale, and other solid contaminants. **Ultrasonic** cleaning is also placed in this category.

Chemical cleaning usually involves the removal of oil and grease from surfaces. It consists of one or more of the following processes:

a. **Solution.** The soil dissolves in the cleaning solution.

b. **Saponification.** A chemical reaction that converts animal or vegetable oils into a soap that is soluble in water.

c. **Emulsification.** The cleaning solution reacts with the soil or lubricant deposits and forms an emulsion; the soil and the emulsifier then become suspended in the emulsion.

d. **Dispersion.** The concentration of soil on the surface is decreased by surface-active elements in the cleaning solution.

e. **Aggregation.** Lubricants are removed from the surface by various agents in the cleaner and are collected as large dirt particles.

Common **cleaning fluids** used in conjunction with electrochemical processes for more effective cleaning include the following:

a. **Alkaline solutions**, which are a complex combination of water-soluble chemicals. They are the least expensive and most widely used in manufacturing operations. Small parts may be cleaned in rotating drums or barrels. Most parts are cleaned on continuous conveyors by spraying them with the solution and rinsing them with water.

b. **Emulsions**, which generally consist of kerosene and oil in water and various types of emulsifiers.

c. **Solvents**, which are typically petroleum solvents, chlorinated hydrocarbons, and mineral spirits. They are generally used for short runs; fire and toxicity are major hazards.

d. **Hot vapors** of chlorinated solvents, which can be used to remove oil, grease, and wax. The solvent is boiled in a container and then condensed. The process is simple and the cleaned parts are dry.

e. Various **acids**, **salts**, and **organic compound mixtures**, which are effective in cleaning parts covered with heavy paste or oily deposits and rust.

Cleaning discrete parts with complex shapes can be difficult. Some *design guidelines* are as follows:

a. Avoid deep blind holes.

b. Make several smaller components instead of one large component, which may be difficult to clean.

c. Provide appropriate drain holes in the parts to be cleaned.

The *treatment* and *disposal* of cleaning fluids, as well as of various fluids and waste materials from the processes described in this chapter, are among the most important considerations for environmentally safe manufacturing operations. These factors are described in greater detail in Section 37.4.

SUMMARY

- Surface treatment is an important aspect of all manufacturing processes. It is used to impart specific physical and mechanical properties, such as appearance, and corrosion, friction, wear, and fatigue resistance. Several techniques are available for modifying surfaces.
- The processes used include mechanical working and coating of surfaces, heat treatment, deposition, plating, and coatings, such as enamels, nonmetallic materials, and paints.
- Clean surfaces can be important in further processing and use of the product (e.g., coating, painting, or welding). Cleaning can have a significant economic impact on manufacturing operations. Various mechanical and chemical cleaning methods may be utilized.

TRENDS

- The structure and properties of coatings, bonding to the substrate, surface preparation and modification, porosity and coating densification, and coating integrity are major areas of study.
- Techniques are being developed to coat various metallic and nonmetallic materials with diamond, as well as to prepare diamond film.
- Spalling or delamination of diamond films and limitations to their thickness are also important areas of study.
- Chemical vapor deposition is being modified to incorporate a fluidized bed, using powder; parts with various shapes and with close dimensional control are being fabricated by this method.
- Surface texturing is an area of increased interest for the optimization of tool and die surfaces with respect to friction and wear.
- Water-based paints, especially for automotive applications, are gaining increased use because of environmental considerations.
- Strict government regulations are forcing tighter control of the use and disposal of chemicals used in surface treatments, coatings, and cleaning

KEY TERMS

Anodizing
Ballizing
Blackening
Case hardening
Chemical cleaning
Chemical vapor deposition
Cladding
Cleaning fluids
Coloring
Conversion coating
Diamond coating
Diamond-like carbon
Diffusion coating
Electroforming

Electroless plating
Electroplating
Enamel
Explosive hardening
Free-standing diamond film
Glazing
Hard chromium plating
Hard facing
Hot dipping
Ion implantation
Ion plating
Laser peening
Mechanical plating
Metallizing

Painting
Physical vapor deposition
Porcelain enamel
Roller burnishing
Shot peening
Spraying
Sputtering
Surface texturing
Thermal spraying
Vacuum evaporation
Vapor deposition
Waterbreak test
Water-jet peening

BIBLIOGRAPHY

ASM Handbook, Vol. 5: *Surface Engineering*. ASM International, 1994.

Bhushan, B., and B.K. Gupta, *Handbook of Tribology: Materials, Coatings, and Surface Treatments*. McGraw-Hill, 1991.

Burakowski, T., and T. Wierschon, *Surface Engineering of Metals: Principles, Equipment, Technologies*. CRC Press, 1998.

Handbook of Industrial Diamonds and Diamond Films. Marcel Dekker, 1997.

Holmberg, K., and A. Matthews, *Coating Tribology: Properties, Techniques, and Applications*. Elsevier, 1994.

Dennis, J.K., and T.E. Such, *Nickel and Chromium Plating* (3d ed.). ASM International, 1993.

Inagaki, N., *Plasma Surface Modification and Plasma Polymerization*. Technomic, 1996.

Nachtman, E.S., and S. Kalpakjian, *Lubricants and Lubrication in Metalworking Operations*. Marcel Dekker, 1985.

Peterson, M.B., and W.O. Winer (eds.), *Wear Control Handbook*. American Society of Mechanical Engineers, 1980.

Prelas, M.A., G. Popovichi, and L.K. Bigelow (eds.), *Handbook of Industrial Diamonds and Diamond Films*. Marcel Dekker, 1998.

Schey, J.A., *Tribology in Metalworking—Friction, Lubrication and Wear*. ASM International, 1983.

Stern, K.H. (ed.), *Metallurgical and Ceramic Protective Coatings*. Chapman & Hall, 1997.

Sudarshan, T.S. (ed.), *Surface Modification Technologies*. ASM International, 1998.

Tool and Manufacturing Engineers Handbook (4th ed.), Vol. 3: *Materials, Finishing and Coating*. Society of Manufacturing Engineers, 1985.

van Ooij, W.J., G.P. Bierwagen, B.S. Skerry, and D. Mills, *Corrosion Control of Metals by Organic Coatings*. CRC Press, 1999.

REVIEW QUESTIONS

33.1 Explain why the surface treatment of manufactured products may be necessary.

33.2 Explain the advantages of roller burnishing.

33.3 Explain the difference between case hardening and hard facing.

33.4 State why you might want to coat parts with ceramics.

33.5 Explain the principles of physical and chemical vapor deposition. What applications do they have?

33.6 What is doping? Why is it used?

33.7 What is the principle of electroforming? What are its advantages?

33.8 Explain the difference between electroplating and electroless plating.

33.9 How is hot dipping performed?

33.10 What is an air knife?

33.11 What tests are there to determine the cleanliness of surfaces?

33.12 Explain the common methods of cleaning and the solutions used for manufactured products.

33.13 Describe the common painting systems in use in industry.

33.14 What is a conversion coating?

33.15 What are the similarities and differences between electroplating and anodizing?

33.16 Describe the difference between thermal spray and plasma spray.

33.17 What are the advantages of cladding?

QUALITATIVE PROBLEMS

33.18 Explain how roller burnishing processes induce residual stresses on the surfaces of parts.

33.19 Explain the principles involved in various techniques for applying paints.

33.20 Give examples of part designs that are suitable for hot-dip galvanizing.

33.21 Repeat Question 33.20, but for cleaning.

33.22 Refer to Table 33.1 and name the two surface-treatment processes that are the most common. Why are they common?

33.23 Give some applications of mechanical surface treatment.

33.24 It has been observed in practice that a thin layer of chrome plating, such as that on older-model automobile bumpers, is better than a thick layer. Explain why, considering the effect of thickness on cracking tendency.

33.25 As we know, coatings may be removed or depleted during the service life of components, particularly at elevated temperatures. Describe the factors involved in the strength of coatings and their durability.

33.26 Because they evaporate, solvents and similar cleaning solutions have adverse environmental effects. Describe your thoughts on what modifications could be made to render cleaning solutions more environmentally friendly.

33.27 Roller burnishing is usually applied to steels. Why is this so?

33.28 A roller burnishing operation is performed on a shaft shoulder to increase fatigue life. It is noted that the resultant surface finish is poor, and a proposal is made to machine the surface layer to further improve fatigue life. Will this work? Explain.

33.29 Make a list of the coating processes described in this chapter and classify them as providing "thick" or "thin" films.

33.30 Which of the processes described in this chapter are used only for small parts? Why is this the case?

33.31 Metallic balloons are commonly made with printed patterns which are produced by printing screens and then plating the balloons. How can metallic coatings be plated onto a rubber sheet?

33.32 When a specimen which is electrically insulating is to be placed in a scanning electron microscope, a thin layer of gold is placed onto the specimen. How would you produce this layer of gold?

33.33 Why is galvanizing important for automotive body sheet?

33.34 It is known that a mirror-like surface finish is possible when plating workpieces that are ground; that is, the surface roughness is low. Explain how this occurs.

QUANTITATIVE PROBLEMS

33.35 You can simulate the shot peening process by using a ball-peen hammer (in which one of the heads is round). Using such a hammer, make numerous indentations on the surface of a piece of aluminum sheet (a) 2-mm and (b) 10-mm thick, respectively, placed on a hard flat surface. You will note that both pieces will develop curvatures, but in different directions, i.e., concave and convex. Describe your observations and explain the results.

33.36 How would you go about estimating the forces required for roller burnishing? Give a specific numerical example.

SYNTHESIS AND DESIGN

33.37 An artificial implant has a porous surface area where it is expected that the bone will attach and grow into the implant. Give your recommendations for producing a porous surface and then review the literature to determine the actual approaches used.

33.38 If one is interested in obtaining a textured surface on a coated cutting tool, should one apply a coating first or apply the texture first?

33.39 Which surface treatments are functional and which are decorative? Are there any that serve both functions? Explain.

33.40 List several applications of coated sheet metal.

33.41 Outline the reasons why the topics described in this chapter are important in manufacturing processes and operations.

33.42 List several products or components that could not be made properly, or function effectively in service, without implementing the knowledge involved in this chapter.

33.43 Write a brief paper on which processes described in this chapter are used to improve the corrosion resistance of an automobile.

33.44 Solar energy has been used as an energy source for surface hardening and the post-treatment of coatings and films. Make a sketch of an installation that could use solar energy for this purpose.

33.45 Based on the information given in this chapter, make a comprehensive table summarizing the characteristics and applications of surface treatment and coating techniques.

33.46 Obtain several metal pieces, parts, or components, and perform the waterbreak test on them (as described in Section 33.16). Then clean the surfaces using various cleaning fluids and repeat the test. Describe your observations.

33.47 Survey the available literature and prepare a brief report on the environmental considerations regarding the application of the processes described in this chapter.

33.48 Given your knowledge of cleaning and plating, lay out a series of process tanks to plate gold onto metal jewelry. Make sure that oxides are removed from the surface prior to plating, and recover residue gold from the pieces.

33.49 Write a brief paper on the hazards and safety requirements for electroplating.

33.50 As you know, vandalism of public places (such as graffiti, scratching, spray painting, etc.) is a serious problem. Based on the contents of Chapters 32 and 33, make a list of possible methods of minimizing such damage, and explain how effective they would be.

34

Fabrication of Microelectronic Devices*

34.1 INTRODUCTION

Although semiconducting materials have been used in electronics since the early decades of this century, it was the invention of the *transistor* in 1948 that set the stage for what would become one of the greatest technological advancements in all of history. *Microelectronics* have played an ever-increasing role in our lives since **integrated circuit (IC)** technology became the foundation for calculators, wrist watches, home appliances control, information systems, telecommunications, automotive controls, robotics, space travel, military weaponry, and personal computers.

The major advantages of today's ICs are their small size and cost. As fabrication technology becomes more advanced, the size of devices decreases; consequently, more components can be put onto a **chip** (a small piece of semiconducting material on which the circuit is fabricated). In addition, mass processing and process automation have helped to reduce the cost of each completed circuit. The components fabricated include transistors, diodes, resistors, and capacitors.

*By Kent M. Kalpakjian.

924

FIGURE 34.1   A collection of printed circuit boards. *Source*: Phoenix Technologies, Inc.

Typical chips produced today have sizes that range from 3 mm $\times$ 3 mm to more than 50 mm $\times$ 50 mm. In the past, no more than 100 devices could be fabricated on a single chip; new technology, however, allows densities the range of 10 million devices per chip (Fig. 34.1). This magnitude of integration has been termed **very large scale integration (VLSI)**. Some of the most advanced ICs may contain more than 100 million devices.

Because of the minute scale of microelectronic devices, all fabrication must take place in an extremely clean environment. Clean rooms are used for this purpose and are allowed to have a maximum number of 0.5-μm particles per cubic foot. Most modern clean rooms are class 1 (one particle per cubic foot) to class 10 (ten particles per cubic foot) facilities. In comparison, the contamination level in modern hospitals is on the order of 10,000 particles per cubic foot.

This chapter describes the current processes used in the fabrication of microelectronic devices and integrated circuits, and follows the outline shown in Fig. 34.2. The major steps in fabricating a **metal-oxide-semiconductor field effect transistor (MOSFET)**, which is one of the dominant devices used in modern IC technology, are shown in Fig. 34.3.

This chapter will first introduce the basic properties of semiconductors and the material properties of silicon, and then discuss each of the major fabrication steps. Finally, we will describe trends and expectations in the microelectronics industry.

34.2 SEMICONDUCTORS AND SILICON

As the name suggests, **semiconductor materials** have electrical properties that lie between those of conductors and insulators, and exhibit resistivities between 10^{-3} Ω-cm and 10^8 Ω-cm. Semiconductors have become the foundation for electronic devices because their electrical properties can be altered when controlled amounts of selected impurity atoms are added to their crystal structures. These impurity atoms, also known as **dopants**, have either one more valence electron (*n*-type or negative dopant) or one less valence electron (*p*-type or positive dopant) than the atoms in the semiconductor lattice.

For silicon, which is a group IV element, typical *n*-type and *p*-type dopants include phosphorus (group V) and boron (group III), respectively. The electrical operation of semiconductor devices can be controlled through the creation of regions of different doping types and concentrations.

Although the earliest electronic devices were fabricated on germanium, **silicon** has become the industry standard. The abundance of alternative forms of silicon is second only to that of oxygen, making it economically attractive. Silicon's main advantage over germani-

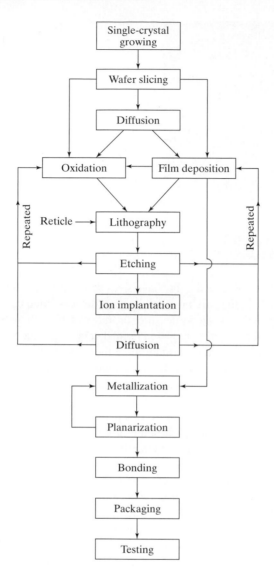

FIGURE 34.2   General fabrication sequence for integrated circuits.

um is its large energy gap (1.1 eV) compared to that of germanium (0.66 eV). This energy gap allows silicon-based devices to operate at temperatures about 150 °C (270 °F) higher than devices fabricated on germanium (about 100 °C; 180 °F).

Silicon's important processing advantage is that its oxide (silicon dioxide) is an excellent insulator and can be used for both isolation and passivation purposes. Conversely, germanium oxide is water soluble and unsuitable for electronic devices.

However, silicon has some limitations, which have encouraged the development of compound semiconductors, specifically **gallium arsenide**. Its major advantage over silicon is its ability to emit light, allowing fabrication of devices such as lasers and light-emitting diodes (LEDs). It also has a larger energy gap (1.43 eV) and therefore a higher maximum operating temperature (about 200 °C; 400 °F).

Devices fabricated on gallium arsenide also have much higher operating speeds than those fabricated on silicon. Some of gallium arsenide's disadvantages include its considerably higher cost, greater processing complications, and the difficulty of growing high-quality oxide layers (the need for which is emphasized throughout this chapter).

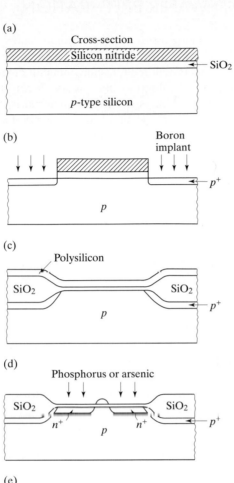

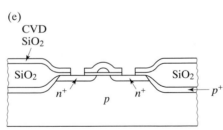

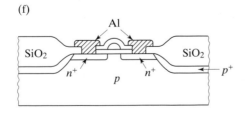

FIGURE 34.3   Cross-sectional views of the fabrication of a MOS transistor. *Source*: R. C. Jaeger.

34.3   CRYSTAL GROWING AND WAFER PREPARATION

Silicon occurs naturally in the forms of silicon dioxide and various silicates. It must undergo a series of purification steps in order to become the high-quality, defect-free, single-crystal material that is required for semiconductor device fabrication. The process begins by heating silica and carbon together in an electric furnace, which results in a 95% to 98% pure polycrystalline silicon. This material is converted to an alternative form, commonly trichlorosilane, which in turn is purified and decomposed in a high-temperature hydrogen atmosphere. The result is extremely high-quality electronic-grade silicon (EGS).

Single-crystal silicon is usually obtained through the **Czochralski process** (see Fig. 11.32a). This process utilizes a seed crystal that is dipped into a silicon melt and then slowly pulled out while being rotated. At this point, controlled amounts of impurities can be added to the system to obtain the result of a uniformly doped crystal. Typical pull rates are on the order of 10 μm/s.

The result of this growing technique is a cylindrical single-crystal ingot, typically 150 mm–300 mm (6–12 in.) in diameter and over 1 m (40 in.) in length. Unfortunately, this technique does not allow for exact control of the ingot diameter. Therefore, ingots are commonly grown a few millimeters larger than required and then ground to a precise diameter.

Next, the crystal is sliced into individual **wafers** by using an inner diameter blade. In this method a rotating blade with its cutting edge on the inner ring is utilized. While the substrate depth needed for most electronic devices is no more than several microns, wafers are typically cut to a thickness of about 0.5 mm (0.02 in.). This thickness provides the necessary physical support for the absorption of temperature variations, and the mechanical support needed during subsequent fabrication. Finally, the wafers must be polished and cleaned to remove surface damage caused by the sawing process.

Fabrication takes place over the entire wafer surface, and many identical circuits are generated at the same time. Because of decreasing device sizes and larger wafer diameters, thousands of individual circuits can be put on one wafer. Once processing is finished, the wafer is sliced into individual **chips**, each containing one complete integrated circuit.

34.4   FILM DEPOSITS

Films of many different types, particularly insulating and conducting films, are used extensively in microelectronic device processing. Common depositing films include polysilicon, silicon nitride, silicon dioxide, tungsten, titanium, and aluminum. In some instances, the wafers serve merely as a mechanical support on which custom *epitaxial layers* are grown (see below). **Epitaxy** is defined as the growth of a vapor deposit or electrodeposit in which the crystal orientation of the deposit is directly related to the crystal orientation in the underlying crystalline substrate. The advantages of processing on these deposited films, instead of on the actual wafer surface, include fewer impurities (notably carbon and oxygen), improved device performance, and the tailoring of material properties, which cannot be done on the wafers themselves.

Some of the major functions of deposited films are **masking**, for diffusion or implants, and protection of the semiconductor surface. In masking applications, the film must effectively inhibit the passage of dopants and concurrently display an ability to be etched into patterns of high resolution. Upon completion of device fabrication, films are applied to protect the underlying circuitry. Films used for masking and protection include silicon dioxide, phosphosilicate glass (PSG), and silicon nitride. Each of these materials has distinct advantages, and they are often used in combination.

Other films contain dopant impurities and are used as doping sources for the underlying substrate. Conductive films are used primarily for device interconnection. These films must have a low resistivity, be capable of carrying large currents, and be suitable for connection to terminal packaging leads with wire bonds. Generally, aluminum and copper are used for this purpose. Increasing circuit complexity has required up to six levels of conductive layers, which must all be separated by insulating films.

Films may be deposited using a number of techniques, which involve a variety of pressures, temperatures, and vacuum systems, as described here:

a. One of the simplest and oldest methods is **evaporation**, which is used primarily for depositing metal films. In this process the metal is heated to its point of vaporization in a vacuum. Upon evaporation, the metal forms a thin layer on the substrate surface. The heat for evaporation is usually generated by a heating filament or electron beam.

b. Another method of metal deposition is **sputtering** and entails bombarding a target with high-energy ions, usually argon (Ar^+), in a vacuum (see Section 33.5). Sputtering systems usually include a dc power source to obtain the energized ions. As the ions impinge on the target, atoms are knocked off and subsequently deposited on wafers mounted within the system. Although some argon may be trapped within the film, this technique results in very uniform coverage. Advances in this field include using a radio-frequency power source **(RF sputtering)** and introducing magnetic fields **(magnetron sputtering)**.

c. In one of the most common techniques, **chemical vapor deposition (CVD)**, film depositing is achieved by way of the reaction and/or decomposition of gaseous compounds (see Section 33.5). Using this technique, silicon dioxide is routinely deposited by the oxidation of silane or a chlorosilane. Figure 34.4a shows a continuous CVD reactor that operates at atmospheric pressure.

A similar method that operates at lower pressures, referred to as **low-pressure chemical vapor deposition (LPCVD)**, is shown in Fig. 34.4b. Capable of coating hundreds of wafers at a time, this method results in a much higher production rate than that of atmospheric-pressure CVD, and provides superior film uniformity with less consumption of carrier gases. This technique is commonly used for depositing polysilicon, silicon nitride, and silicon dioxide.

FIGURE 34.4   Schematic diagrams of (a) continuous, atmospheric-pressure CVD reactor and (b) low-pressure CVD. *Source*: S. M. Sze.

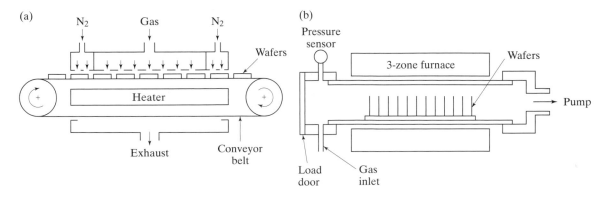

d. **Plasma-enhanced chemical vapor deposition (PECVD)** involves the process of wafers in an RF plasma containing the source gases. This method has the advantage of maintaining low wafer temperature during deposition.

Silicon **epitaxy** layers, in which the crystalline layer is formed using the substrate as a seed crystal can be grown using a variety of methods. If the silicon is deposited from the gaseous phase, the process is known as **vapor-phase epitaxy (VPE)**. In another variation, the heated substrate is brought into contact with a liquid solution containing the material to be deposited (**liquid-phase epitaxy**, or LPE).

Another high-vacuum process utilizes evaporation to produce a thermal beam of molecules that are deposited on the heated substrate. This process, called **molecular beam epitaxy (MBE)**, results in a very high degree of purity. In addition, since the films are grown one atomic layer at a time, it is possible to have excellent control over doping profiles. This level of control is especially important in gallium arsenide technology. Unfortunately, MBE suffers from relatively low growth rates compared to other conventional film-deposition techniques.

34.5 OXIDATION

Recall that the term *oxidation* refers to the growth of an oxide layer as a result of the reaction of oxygen with the substrate material. Oxide films can also be formed using the previously described deposition techniques. The thermally grown oxides described in this section display a higher level of purity than deposited oxides because they are grown directly from the high-quality substrate. However, deposition methods must be used if the composition of the desired film is different from that of the substrate material.

Silicon dioxide is the most widely used oxide in IC technology today, and its excellent characteristics are one of the major reasons for the widespread use of silicon. Aside from its effectiveness in dopant masking and device isolation, silicon dioxide's most critical role is that of the "gate oxide" material.

Silicon surfaces have an extremely high affinity for oxygen, and a freshly sawed slice of silicon will quickly grow a native oxide of 30 Å–40 Å. Modern IC technology requires oxide thicknesses from the tens to the thousands of angstroms.

a. **Dry oxidation** is a relatively simple process and is accomplished by elevating the substrate temperature typically to 750 °C–1100 °C (1380 °F–2020 °F), in an oxygen-rich environment.

As a layer of oxide forms, the oxidizing agents must be able to pass through the oxide and reach the silicon surface where the actual reaction takes place. Thus, an oxide layer does not continue to grow on top of itself, but rather it grows from the silicon surface outward. Some of the silicon substrate is consumed in the oxidation process (Fig. 34.5).

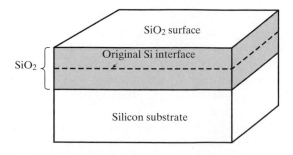

FIGURE 34.5 Growth of silicon dioxide, showing consumption of silicon. *Source*: S. M. Sze.

The ratio of oxide thickness to amount of silicon consumed is found to be 1:0.44. Therefore, to obtain an oxide layer 1000 Å thick, roughly 440 Å of silicon will be consumed. This does not present a problem, as substrates are always grown sufficiently thick.

One important effect of this consumption of silicon is the rearrangement of dopants in the substrate near the interface. As different impurities have different segregation coefficients in silicon dioxide, some dopants deplete away from the oxide interface while others pile up. Hence, processing parameters must be adjusted to compensate for this effect.

b. Another oxidizing technique utilizes a water-vapor atmosphere as the agent and is called, appropriately, **wet oxidation**. This method effects a considerably higher growth rate than that of dry oxidation, but it suffers from a lower oxide density and therefore a lower dielectric strength. Common practice is to combine both dry and wet oxidation methods, growing an oxide in a three-part layer: dry, wet, dry. This approach combines the advantages of wet oxidation's much higher growth rate and dry oxidation's high quality.

c. These oxidation methods are useful primarily for coating the entire silicon surface with oxide, but it can also be necessary to oxidize only certain portions of the substrate surface. The procedure of oxidizing only certain areas is termed **selective oxidation** and uses silicon nitride, which inhibits the passage of oxygen and water vapor. Thus, through the masking of certain areas with silicon nitride, the silicon under these areas remains unaffected but the uncovered areas are oxidized.

34.6 LITHOGRAPHY

Lithography is the process by which the geometric patterns that define devices are transferred from a **reticle** to the substrate surface. In current practice, the *lithographic* process is applied to each microelectronic circuit many times, each time using a different reticle to define the different areas of the working devices. Typically designed at several thousand times their final size, reticle patterns go through a series of reductions before being applied permanently to a defect-free quartz plate.

Computer-aided design (CAD) has had a major impact on reticle design and generation. Cleanliness is especially important in lithography, and many manufacturers are now using robotics and specialized wafer-handling apparatus in order to minimize dust and dirt contamination.

Once the film deposition process is completed and the desired reticle patterns have been generated, the wafer is cleaned and coated with an organic **photoresist (PR)**, which is sensitive to ultraviolet (UV) light. Photoresist layers of 0.5 μm–2.5 μm (20 μin.–100 μin.) thick are obtained by applying the PR to the substrate in liquid form and then spinning it at several thousand rpm for 30 or 60 seconds to give uniform coverage.

The next step in lithography is **prebaking** the wafer to remove the solvent from the PR and harden it. This step is carried out on a hot plate that has been heated to around 100 °C. The wafer is then aligned under the desired reticle in a "stepper". In this crucial step, called **registration**, the reticle must be aligned correctly with the previous layer on the wafer. Once the reticle is aligned, it is stepped across the wafer and subjected to UV radiation. Upon development and removal of the exposed PR, a duplicate of the reticle pattern will appear in the PR layer.

As can be seen in Fig. 34.6, the reticle can be a negative or a positive image of the desired pattern. A positive reticle uses the UV radiation to break down the chains in the organic

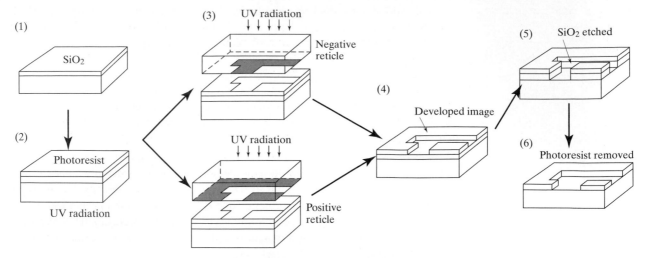

FIGURE 34.6 Pattern transfer by lithography. Note that the mask in step three can be a positive or negative image of the pattern. *Source*: After W. C. Till and J. T. Luxon.

film, so that these films are preferentially removed by the developer. Positive masking has become dominant because it complements dry etching (see below).

Following the exposure and development sequence, the wafer is **postbaked** to toughen and improve the adhesion of the remaining resist. In addition, a deep UV treatment (baking the wafer to 150 °C–200 °C in ultraviolet light) can be used to further strengthen the resist against high-energy implants and dry etches. The underlying film not covered by the PR is then etched away (Section 34.7) or implanted (Section 34.8). Finally, the PR is stripped, by exposure to oxygen plasma (Fig. 34.6). The lithography process is sometimes repeated as many as 25 times in the fabrication of the most advanced ICs.

One of the major issues in the area of lithography is **linewidth**, which refers to the width of the smallest feature imprintable on the silicon surface. As circuit densities have escalated over the years, device sizes and features have become smaller and smaller. Today, minimum commercially feasible linewidths are between 0.15 μm and 0.25 μm (6 μin. and 10 μin.), with considerable research being done in regard to smaller linewidths of 0.12 μm.

As pattern resolution and device miniaturization have been limited by the wavelength of the radiation source used, the need has arisen to move to wavelengths shorter than those in the ultraviolet range, such as "deep" UV wavelengths, electron beams, and x-rays. In these technologies, the photoresist is replaced by a similar resist that is sensitive to a specific range of shorter wavelengths.

34.7 ETCHING

Etching is the process by which entire films or particular sections of films are removed, and it plays an important role in the fabrication sequence. One of the most important criteria in this process is **selectivity**, which refers to the ability to etch one material without etching another.

In silicon technology, an etching process must effectively etch the silicon dioxide layer with minimal removal of the underlying silicon or the resist material. In addition, polysilicon and metals must be etched into high-resolution lines with vertical wall profiles and with minimal removal of the underlying insulating film or photoresist. Typical etch

(a)   (b)

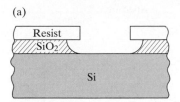 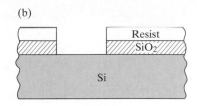

FIGURE 34.7   Etching profiles resulting from (a) isotropic wet etching and
(b) anisotropic dry etching. *Source*: R. C. Jaeger.

rates range from hundreds to several thousands of angstroms per minute, and selectivities
(defined as the ratio of the etch rates of the two films) can range from 1:1 to 100:1.

An older etching method requires the wafers to be immersed in a liquid solution (**wet
etching**). If silicon dioxide is to be etched, this solution usually contains hydrofluoric acid,
which etches silicon very slowly. The main drawback of this etching technique is that it is
isotropic, meaning that the etch occurs equally in all directions. This condition leads to
undercutting (Fig. 34.7a), which in turn prohibits the transfer of very high resolution patterns.

Modern ICs are processed using, exclusively, **dry etching** which involves the use of
chemical reactants in a low-pressure system. In contrast to the wet process, dry etching
allows for a high degree of directionality, resulting in highly anisotropic etch profiles
(Fig. 34.7b). Also, the dry process requires only small amounts of reactant gases, whereas
the aqueous solutions used in the wet process need to be refreshed periodically.

The most widely used dry-etching techniques include (a) **sputter etching**, which removes material by bombarding it with noble gas ions, usually Ar^+, and (b) **plasma etching**,
which utilizes a gaseous plasma of chlorine or fluorine ions generated by RF excitation.
Reactive ion etching combines these two processes, using both momentum transfer and
chemical reaction to remove material.

34.8 DIFFUSION AND ION IMPLANTATION

We should mention again that the electrical operation of microelectronic devices depends
on regions that have different doping types and concentrations. The electrical character of
these regions is altered through the introduction of dopants into the substrate, which is accomplished by the *diffusion* and *ion implantation* processes. This step in the fabrication sequence is repeated several times, since many different regions of microelectronic devices
must be defined.

In the *diffusion* process, the movement of atoms is a result of thermal excitation.
Dopants can be introduced to the substrate surface in the form of a deposited film, or the substrate can be placed in a vapor containing the dopant source. The process takes place at elevated temperatures, usually 800 °C–1200 °C (1500 °F–2200 °F). Dopant movement within
the substrate is strictly a function of temperature, time, and the diffusion coefficient (or dif-
fusivity) of the dopant species, as well as the type and quality of the substrate material.

Because of the nature of diffusion, the dopant concentration is very high at the substrate surface and, away from the surface, drops off sharply. To obtain a more uniform concentration within the substrate, the wafer is heated further to drive in the dopants in a process
called **drive-in diffusion**. Diffusion, desired or undesired, will always occur at high temperatures; this fact is always taken into account during subsequent processing steps. Although the diffusion process is relatively inexpensive, it is highly isotropic.

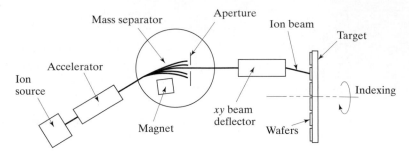

FIGURE 34.8   Apparatus for ion implantation.

Ion implantation is a much more extensive process and requires specialized equipment (Fig. 34.8; see also Section 33.6). Implantation is accomplished by accelerating the ions through a high-voltage field of as much as one million electron-volts and then choosing the desired dopant by means of a mass separator. In a manner similar to that of cathode-ray tubes, the beam is swept across the wafer by sets of deflection plates, thus ensuring uniform coverage of the substrate. The complete implantation system must be operated in a vacuum.

The high-velocity impact of ions on the silicon surface damages the lattice structure and results in lower electron mobilities. This condition is undesirable, but the damage can be repaired by an annealing step, which involves heating the substrate to relatively low temperatures, usually 400 °C–800 °C (750 °F–1500 °F), for 15–30 min. This provides the energy that the silicon lattice needs to rearrange and mend itself.

Another important function of annealing is driving in the implanted dopants. Implantation alone imbeds the dopants less than half a micron below the silicon surface; the annealing step enables the dopants to diffuse to a more desirable depth of a few microns.

34.9 METALLIZATION AND TESTING

The preceding sections focused only on device fabrication. However, generating a complete and functional integrated circuit requires these devices to be interconnected. **Interconnections** are made by metals that exhibit low electrical resistance and good adhesion to dielectric insulator surfaces. Aluminum and aluminum-copper alloys remain the most commonly used materials for this purpose in VLSI technology today.

However, as device dimensions continue to shrink, electromigration has become more of a concern with aluminum interconnects. **Electromigration** is the process by which aluminum atoms are physically moved by the impact of drifting electrons under high current conditions. In extreme cases, this can lead to severed and/or shorted metal lines. Solutions to the electromigration problem include (a) the addition of sandwiched metal layers such as tungsten and titanium, and more recently, (b) the usage of pure copper, which displays lower resistivity and significantly better electromigration performance than aluminum.

Metals are deposited using standard deposition techniques, and interconnection patterns are generated through lithographic and etching processes as previously described. Modern ICs typically have one to six layers of metallization, in which case each layer of metal is insulated by a dielectric.

Planarization (producing a planar surface) of these inter-layer dielectrics is critical in the reduction of metal shorts and of the linewidth variation of the interconnect. A common method used to achieve a planar surface is a uniform oxide etch process that smoothens out the "peaks" and "valleys" of the dielectric layer.

Example: Processing of a *p*-Type Region in *n*-Type Silicon.

Assume that we wish to create a *p*-type region within a sample of *n*-type silicon. Draw cross-sections of the sample at each processing step in order to accomplish this. (See Fig. 34.9.)

Solution: This simple device is known as a *pn junction diode*, and the physics of its operation are the foundation for most semiconductor devices.

SOLUTION

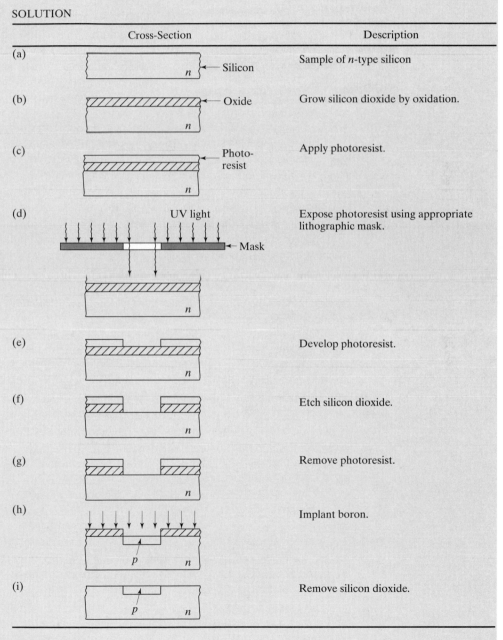

	Cross-Section	Description
(a)		Sample of *n*-type silicon
(b)		Grow silicon dioxide by oxidation.
(c)		Apply photoresist.
(d)		Expose photoresist using appropriate lithographic mask.
(e)		Develop photoresist.
(f)		Etch silicon dioxide.
(g)		Remove photoresist.
(h)		Implant boron.
(i)		Remove silicon dioxide.

FIGURE 34.9

(a)

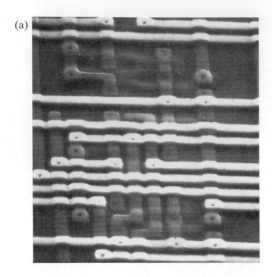

(b)

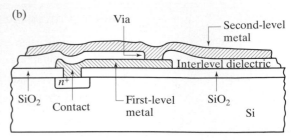

FIGURE 34.10 (a) Scanning electron microscope photograph of a two-level metal interconnect. Note the varying surface topography. *Source:* National Semiconductor Corporation. (b) Schematic drawing of a two-level metal interconnect structure. *Source:* R. C. Jaeger.

However, today's standard for planarizing high density interconnects and has quickly become *chemical mechanical polishing* (CMP; see Section 25.10.6). This process entails physically polishing the wafer surface in as manner similar to that by which a disc or belt sander flattens the ridges in a piece of wood. A typical CMP process combines an abrasive medium with a polishing compound, or slurry, and can polish a wafer to within 300 angstroms (1.2×10^{-6} in.) of being perfectly flat.

Layers of metal are connected together by **vias**; access to the devices on the substrate is achieved through **contacts** (Fig. 34.10). In recent years, as devices have become smaller and faster, the size and speed of some chips have become limited by the metallization itself.

Wafer processing is complete upon application of a *passivation layer*, usually silicon nitride (Si_3N_4). The silicon nitride acts as an ion barrier for sodium ions and also provides excellent scratch resistance.

The next step is to test each of the individual circuits on the wafer. Each chip, also known as a **die**, is tested by a computer-controlled probe platform that contains needlelike probes which access the bonding pads on the die. The platform steps across the wafer, and tests whether each circuit functions properly with computer-generated timing waveforms. If a defective chip is encountered, it is marked with a drop of ink.

After this wafer-level testing is complete, each die is separated from the wafer. *Diamond sawing* is a commonly-used separation technique and results in very straight edges, with minimal chipping and cracking damage. The chips are then sorted; the functional dies are sent on for packaging, and the inked dies are discarded.

34.10 BONDING AND PACKAGING

The working dice must be attached to a more rugged foundation to ensure reliability. One simple method is to fasten a die to its packaging material with an epoxy cement. Another method makes use of a eutectic bond, which is made by heating metal-alloy systems (see Sections 4.3 and 4.4). One widely used mixture is 96.4% gold and 3.6% silicon, and has a eutectic point at 370 °C (700 °F).

Once the chip has been attached to its substrate, it must be electrically connected to the package leads. This is accomplished by **wire-bonding** very thin (25 μm diameter; 0.001 μin.) gold wires from the package leads to bonding pads located around the perimeter or down the center of the die (Fig. 34.11a). The bonding pads on the die are typically

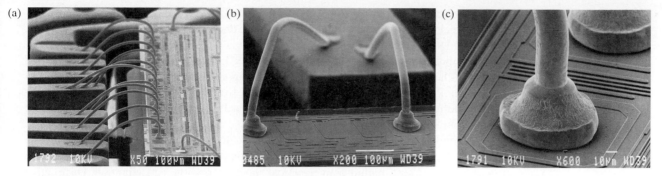

FIGURE 34.11   (a) SEM photograph of wire bonds connecting package leads (left-hand side) to die bonding pads. (b) and (c) Detailed views of (a). *Source*: Courtesy of Micron Technology, Inc.

drawn at 75 μm–100 μm (0.003 in.–0.004 in.) per side, and the bond wires are attached using thermocompression, ultrasonic, or thermosonic techniques (Figs 31.11b and c).

The connected circuit is now ready for final packaging. The *packaging* process largely determines the overall cost of each completed IC, since the circuits are mass produced on the wafer but then packaged individually. Packages are available in a variety of styles; the appropriate one must reflect operating requirements.

Consideration of a circuit's package includes chip size, number of external leads, operating environment, heat dissipation, and power requirements. For example, ICs that are used for military and industrial applications require packages of particularly high strength, toughness, and temperature resistance.

An older style of packaging is the **dual-in-line package (DIP)**, shown schematically in Fig. 34.12a. Characterized by low cost and ease of handling, DIP packages are made of *thermoplastic*, epoxy, or ceramic and can have from 2 to 500 external leads. *Ceramic* packages are designed for use over a broader temperature range and in high-reliability and military applications, thus costing considerably more than plastic packages.

Figure 34.12b shows a flat ceramic package in which the package and all the leads are in the same plane. This package style does not offer the ease of handling or the modular design of the DIP package. For this reason, it is usually permanently affixed to a multiple-level circuit board in which the low profile of the flat pack is necessary.

FIGURE 34.12   Schematic illustrations of different IC packages: (a) dual-in-line (DIP), and (b) ceramic flat pack, and (c) common surface mount configuration. *Sources*: R. C. Jaeger and A. B. Glaser; G. E. Subak-Sharpe.

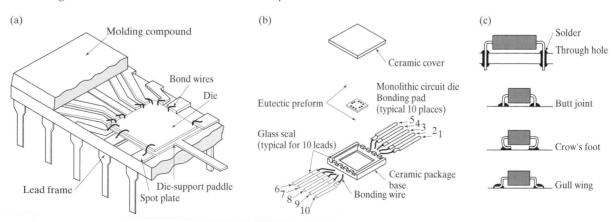

Surface mount packages have become the standard for today's integrated circuits. As can be seen in Fig. 34.12, the main difference in the designs is in the shape of the connectors.

The DIP connection to the surface board is via prongs which are inserted into corresponding holes, while a surface mount is soldered onto specially fabricated pad or *land designs*. A land is a raised solder platform for component interconnections in a printed circuit board. Package size and layouts are selected from standard patterns, and usually require adhesive bonding of the package to the board, followed by **wave soldering** of the connections. (See Section 30.3.2.)

After the chip has been sealed in the package, it undergoes final testing. Because one of the main purposes of packaging is isolation from the environment, testing at this stage usually involves heat, humidity, mechanical shock, corrosion, and vibration. Destructive tests are also performed to investigate the effectiveness of sealing.

34.11 YIELD AND RELIABILITY

Yield is defined as the ratio of functional chips to the total number of chips produced. The overall yield of the total IC manufacturing process is the product of the wafer yield, bonding yield, packaging yield, and test yield. This can range from only a few percent for new processes to more that 90% for mature manufacturing lines.

Most yield loss occurs during wafer processing, due to the more complex nature of this type of processing, and wafers are commonly separated into regions of good and bad chips. Failures at this stage can arise from point defects (such as oxide pinholes), film contamination, or metal particles, and also from area defects such as uneven film deposition or etch nonuniformity.

A major concern about completed ICs is their **reliability** and **failure rate**. Since no device has an infinite lifetime, statistical methods are used to characterize the expected lifetimes and failure rates of microelectronic devices. The unit for failure rate is the FIT, defined as one failure per 1 billion device-hours. However, complete systems may have millions of devices, so the overall failure rate in entire systems is correspondingly higher.

Equally important in failure analysis is determining the *failure mechanism*, that is, the actual process that causes the device to fail. Common failures due to processing involve the following:

  a. diffusion regions (nonuniform current flow and junction breakdown),
  b. oxide layers (dielectric breakdown and accumulation of surface charge),
  c. lithography (uneven definition of features and mask misalignment), and
  d. metal layers (poor contact and electromigration resulting from high current densities).

Other failures can originate in improper chip mounting, poorly formed wire bonds, and loss of package hermeticity.

Because device lifetimes are very long, it is impractical to study device failure under normal operating conditions. One method of studying failures efficiently is called **accelerated life testing**, and involves accelerating the conditions whose effects cause device breakdown. Cyclic variations in temperature, humidity, voltage, and current are used to stress the components. Chip mounting and packaging are strained by cyclical temperature variations. Statistical data taken from these tests are then used to predict device failure modes and device life under normal operating conditions.

In addition to the metal-oxide semiconductor structure introduced at the beginning of this chapter, the **bipolar junction transistor (BJT)** is used, but to a lesser extent. While this device's actual fabrication steps are very similar to those of both the MOSFET and BJT technologies, their circuit applications are different.

Memory circuits, such as RAMs and ROMs, and microprocessors consist primarily of MOS devices, whereas linear circuits, such as amplifiers and filters, contain mostly bipolar transistors. Other differences between these two devices include the faster operating speeds of the BJT and the smaller size (and therefore greater circuit density) and lower current of the MOSFET.

34.12 PRINTED CIRCUIT BOARDS

Packaged ICs are seldom used alone. Rather, they are usually combined with other ICs to serve as building blocks for a yet larger circuit. A **printed circuit board** is the foundation for the final interconnections among all the completed circuits, and serves as the communication link between the outside world and the microelectronic circuitry within each packaged IC.

In addition to the ICs, circuit boards also usually contain discrete circuit components, such as resistors and capacitors, which take up too much "real estate" on the limited silicon surface or have special power dissipation requirements. Other common discrete components are inductors, which cannot be integrated onto the silicon surface, and high-performance transistors.

A printed circuit board is basically an epoxy-glass composite material (see Chapter 9) that contains several layers of copper foil. The conductive patterns on circuit boards are defined through lithography and selective etching of the copper. The ICs and other discrete components are then fastened to the board by soldering, or adhesive bonding and then soldering, of surface mount packages. Such circuit boards are the brains behind today's computers and large electronic systems.

SUMMARY

- The microelectronics industry is developing rapidly. The possibilities for new device concepts and circuit designs appear to be endless. The fabrication of microelectronic devices and integrated circuits involves many different types of processes, most of which have been adapted from those of other fields of manufacturing.
- After bare wafers have been prepared, they undergo repeated oxidation or film deposition, lithographic, and etching steps to open windows in the oxide layer in order to access the silicon substrate.
- After each of these processing cycles is complete, dopants are introduced into various regions of the silicon structure through diffusion and ion implantation.
- After all the doping regions have been established, devices are interconnected by multiple metal layers, and the completed circuit is packaged and made accessible through electrical connections.
- Finally, the packaged circuit and other discrete devices are soldered to a printed circuit board for final installation.

TRENDS

- Progress is being made in the miniaturization of devices to below 0.10-μm linewidths and the integration of scales exceeding hundreds of millions of components per chip.
- Stacked and three-dimensional device and circuit structures are being developed.
- Gallium arsenide layers are being grown on silicon substrates to combine the optical capabilities of gallium arsenide with the established electrical properties and superior strength and heat dissipation of silicon.
- Research is being conducted on optical integration of devices (transmission by light pulses, not electrical signals) to yield faster operating speeds.
- The "Quantum Transistor," in which a single electron determines the state (ON or OFF) of the device, is being actively developed and could eventually replace today's conventional transistor structure.

KEY TERMS

Accelerated life testing
Bipolar junction transistor
Bonding
Chemical vapor deposition
Chemical mechanical polishing
Chip
Contacts
Czochralski process
Die
Diffusion
Dopants
Dry etching
Dry oxidation
Dual-in-line package
Electromigration
Epitaxy
Etching
Evaporation

Failure rate
Film deposition
Gallium arsenide
Integrated circuit
Ion implantation
Linewidth
Lithography
Masking
Metal-oxide-semiconductor field effect
    transistor
Metallization
Oxidation
Packaging
Photoresist
Planarization
Postbaking
Prebaking
Printed circuit board

Registration
Reliability
Reticle
Selective oxidation
Selectivity
Semiconductor
Silicon
Sputtering
Surface mount package
Very large scale integration
Vias
Yield
Wafer
Wet etching
Wet oxidation
Wire bonding
Yield

BIBLIOGRAPHY

Bakoglu, H.B., *Circuits, Interconnections, and Packaging for VLSI*. Addison–Wesley, 1990.

Berger, L.I., *Semiconductor Materials*. CRC Press, 1997.

Brar, A.S., and P.B. Narayan, *Materials and Processing Failures in the Electronics and Computer Industries: Analysis and Prevention*. ASM International, 1993.

Campbell, S.A., *The Science and Engineering of Microelectronic Fabrication*. Oxford University Press, 1996.

Chandrakasan, A., and R. Brodersen (eds.), *Low Power CMOS Design*. IEEE, 1998.

Chandrakasan, A., and R. Brodersen, *Low Power Digital CMOS Design*. Kluwer Academic Pub., 1995.

Ghandhi, S.K., *VLSI Fabrication Principles Silicon and Gallium Arsenide* (2d ed.). Wiley, 1993.

Electronic Materials Handbook, Vol. 1: *Packaging*. ASM International, 1989.

Harper, C.A. (ed.), *Electronic Packaging and Interconnection Handbook* (2d ed.). McGraw–Hill, 1996.

Hwang, J.S., *Modern Solder Technology for Competitive Electronics Manufacturing*. McGraw–Hill, 1996.

Judd, M., and K. Brindley, *Soldering in Electronics Assembly* (2d ed.). Newnes, 1999.

Lau, J.H. (ed.), *Electronic Packaging: Design, Materials, Process, and Reliability*. McGraw–Hill, 1998.

Madou, M.J., *Fundamentals of Microfabrication*. CRC Press, 1997.

Mahajan, S., and K.S.S. Harsha, *Principles of Growth and Processing of Semiconductors*. McGraw-Hill, 1998.

Manko, H.H., *Soldering Handbook for Printed Circuits and Surface Mounting*. Van Nostrand Reinhold, 1995.

Matisoff, B.S., *Handbook of Electronics Manufacturing*, (3d ed.). Chapman & Hall, 1996.

Mroczkowski, R.S., *Electronic Connector Handbook: Theory and Applications*. McGraw–Hill, 1997.

Pecht, M. (ed.), *Electronic Packaging Materials and Their Properties*. CRC Press, 1998.

Runyan, W.R., and T.J. Shaffner, *Semiconductor Measurements and Instrumentation* (2d ed.). McGraw–Hill, 1998.

Schroder, D.K., *Semiconductor Material and Device Characterization* (2d ed.). Wiley-Interscience, 1998.

Taur, Y., and T.H. Ning, *Fundamentals of Modern VLSI Devices*. Cambridge, 1998.

Tummala, R., E.J. Rymaszewski and A.G. Klopfenstein, *Microelectronics Packaging Fundamentals*. Chapman & Hall, 1999.

Wolf, W.H., Modern VLSI Design: Systems on Silicon (2d ed.). Prentice Hall, 1998

Sze, S.M. (ed.), *High Speed Semiconductor Devices*. Wiley, 1993.

————, Modern Semiconductor Device Physics. Wiley, 1997.

Wolf, S., and R.N. Tauber, *Silicon Processing for the VLSI Era*, Vol. 1: *Process Technology*, 1986; Vol. 2: *Process Integration*, 1990. Lattice Press.

Yeap, G., *Practical Low Power Digital VLSI Design*. Kluwer Academic Pub., 1997.

REVIEW QUESTIONS

34.1 Define "wafer", "chip", "device", and "integrated circuit".

34.2 Why is silicon the semiconductor most used in IC technology?

34.3 What do VLSI, IC, CVD, CMP, and DIP stand for?

34.4 How do *n*-type and *p*-type dopants differ?

34.5 How is epitaxy different from other techniques used for depositing?

34.6 Compare wet and dry oxidation.

34.7 How is silicon nitride used in oxidation?

34.8 What are the purposes of prebaking and postbaking in lithography?

34.9 Define selectivity and isotropy and their importance in relation to etching.

34.10 What do the terms "linewidth" and "registration" refer to?

34.11 Compare diffusion and ion implantation.

34.12 What is the difference between evaporation and sputtering?

34.13 What is the definition of "yield"?

34.14 What is accelerated life testing?

34.15 What do BJT and MOSFET stand for?

QUALITATIVE PROBLEMS

34.16 In a horizontal epitaxial reactor (see the accompanying figure), the wafers are placed on a stage (susceptor) that is tilted by a small amount, usually 1°–3°. Why is this done?

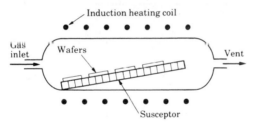

34.17 The table below describes three wafer manufacturing changes: increasing the wafer diameter, reducing the chip size, and increasing the process complexity. Complete the table by filling in "increase," "decrease," or "no change," indicating the effect that each change would have on the wafer yield and on the overall number of functional chips.

Effects of Manufacturing Changes

Change	Wafer Yield	of Functional Chips
Increase wafer diameter		
Reduce chip size		
Increase process complexity		

34.18 The speed of a transistor is directly proportional to the width of its polysilicon gate; a narrower gate results in a faster transistor, and a wider gate results in a slower transistor. Knowing that the manufacturing process has a certain variation for the gate width, say ±0.1 microns, how might a designer alter the gate sizing of a critical circuit in order to minimize its speed variation? Are there any negative effects of this change?

34.19 A common problem in ion implantation is channeling, in which the high velocity ions travel deep into the material via channels along the crystallographic planes before finally being stopped. What is one simple way to stop this effect?

QUANTITATIVE PROBLEMS

34.20 A certain wafer manufacturer produces two equal-sized wafers, one containing 500 chips and the other containing 300 chips. After testing, it is observed that 50 chips on each wafer are defective. What are the yields of these two wafers? Can any relationship be drawn between chip size and yield?

34.21 A chlorine-based polysilicon etch process displays a polysilicon:resist selectivity of 4:1 and a polysilicon:oxide selectivity of 50:1. How much resist and exposed oxide will be consumed in etching 3500 Å of polysilicon? What would the polysilicon:oxide selectivity have to be in order to reduce the loss to only 40 Å of exposed oxide?

34.22 During a processing sequence, three silicon dioxide layers are grown by oxidation: 2500 Å, 4000 Å, and 1500 Å. How much of the silicon substrate is consumed?

34.23 A certain design rule calls for metal lines to be no less than 2 microns wide. If a 1-micron-thick metal layer is to be wet-etched, what is the minimum photoresist width allowed (assuming that the wet etch is perfectly isotropic)? What would be the minimum photoresist width if a perfectly anisotropic dry-etch process is used?

SYNTHESIS AND DESIGN

34.24 The figure below shows the cross-section of a simple *npn* bipolar transistor. Using the cross-sections in the example in Section 34.8 as a guide, develop a process flowchart to fabricate this device.

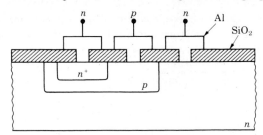

34.25 Referring to the MOS transistor cross-section and the given table of design below, what is the smallest obtainable transistor size W? Which design rules, if any, have no impact on W?

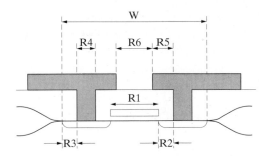

Design Rule Table

Rule #	Rule Name	Value (μm)
R1	Minimum polysilicon width	0.50
R2	Minimum poly-to-contact spacing	0.15
R3	Minimum enclosure of contact by diffusion	0.10
R4	Minimum contact width	0.60
R5	Minimum enclosure of contact by metal	0.10
R6	Minimum metal-to-metal spacing	0.80

PART VII
Common Aspects of Manufacturing

Thus far we have described basic manufacturing processes used for a wide variety of industrial and consumer products. Previous chapters have presented the techniques used to modify surfaces of components and products to obtain certain desirable properties, and we have discussed the advantages and limitations of each technique. Although dimensional accuracies obtained in individual manufacturing processes were described, we have not yet explained how parts are measured and inspected before they are assembled.

Why must we accurately measure and inspect parts? Dimensions and other surface features of a part are measured to ensure that it is manufactured consistently and within the specified range of dimensional accuracy. The majority of manufactured parts are components or a subassembly of a product, and they must fit and be assembled properly so that the product performs its intended function during its service life.

For example, (a) a piston should fit into a cylinder within specified tolerances; (b) a turbine blade should fit properly into its slot on a turbine disk; and (c) the slideways of a machine tool must be produced with a certain accuracy so that the parts produced on the machine are, in turn, accurate within specified dimensional tolerances.

Measurement of the relevant dimensions and features of parts is an integral aspect of **interchangeable manufacture**, the basic concept of standardization and mass production. For example, if a ball bearing in a machine is worn and has to be replaced, all one has to do is purchase a similar one with the same specification or part number. The same can be done with products such as bolts, faucets, tires, and spark plugs.

In this part of the text, we describe the principles involved in, and the various instruments and machines used for, measuring dimensional features such as length, angle, flatness, and roundness. Testing and inspection of parts are important aspects of manufacturing operations, so we will also describe the methods used for nondestructive and destructive testing of parts.

One of the most important aspects of manufacturing is **product quality**. We explain the technological and economic importance of *building quality into a product*, rather than inspecting the product after it is made. The significance of this concept should be clear in view of the strong and sustained trend of manufactured parts in the global economy and international trade.

The final chapter describes those aspects of human-factors engineering that are particularly relevant to manufacturing equipment and operations. These include ergonomics, workstations, noise, environmental considerations, and safety hazards, as well as the legal aspects of product liability.

35

Engineering Metrology and Instrumentation

35.1 INTRODUCTION

This chapter presents the principles, methods, and characteristics of the instruments used for various dimensional measurements. **Engineering metrology** is defined as the measurement of dimensions: length, thickness, diameter, taper, angle, flatness, profiles, and others. For example, consider the slideways for machine tools (Fig. 35.1); these components must have specific dimensions, angles, and flatness in order for the machine to function properly and function with the desired dimensional accuracy.

Traditionally, measurements have been made *after* the part has been produced; this is known as **post-process inspection**. Here, the term "inspection" means checking the dimensions of what has been produced or is being produced, and determining whether it complies with the specified dimensional accuracy. The trend now is to make measurements while the part is being produced on the machine; this is known as **in-process**, *on-line*, or *real-time* **inspection**. Much progress has been made in developing new, automated instruments that are highly sensitive to small variations.

An important aspect of metrology in manufacturing processes is **dimensional tolerance**, that is, the permissible variation in the dimensions of a part. Tolerances are important because of their impact on not only the proper functioning of a product, but the manufacturing costs as well; generally, the smaller the tolerance, the higher the production costs.

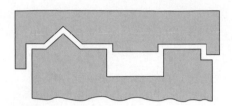

FIGURE 35.1   Cross-section of a machine tool slideway. The width, depth, angles, and other dimensions must be produced and measured accurately for the machine tool to function as expected.

35.2 MEASUREMENT STANDARDS

One's earliest experience with measurement is usually with a simple *ruler* to measure lengths (linear dimensions). A ruler is inscribed with lines that are a certain distance apart, typically 1 mm (0.040 in.). Thus, we use the ruler as a *standard* against which dimensions are measured. Traditionally, in English-speaking countries the units of *inch* and *foot* (which were originally based on parts of the human body) have been used. Consequently, it was not unusual to find significant variations in the length of one foot.

In most of the world, however, the *meter* (and metric system) has been used as a standard. Originally, one meter was defined as one ten-millionth of the distance between the North Pole and the equator. The original meter length was then standardized as the distance between two scratches on a platinum-iridium bar that is kept, under controlled conditions, in a building outside Paris.

In 1960 the meter was officially defined as 1,650,763.73 wavelengths, in a vacuum, of the orange light given off by electrically excited krypton 86 (a rare gas). The precision of this measurement was set as 1 part in 10^9. The meter is now a Système International d'Unites, or SI, unit of length, and is the international standard. The smallest dimensions are measured in nanometers (1 nm $= 10^{-9}$ m).

Numerous measuring instruments and devices are used in engineering metrology, each of which has its own application, sensitivity, and precision (Table 35.1). Let's define two terms that are commonly used to describe the type and quality of an instrument (see Section 35.10):

a. Sensitivity, also called **resolution**, is the smallest difference in dimensions that the instrument can detect or distinguish. A wooden yardstick, for example, has far less sensitivity than a finely graduated steel rule.

b. Precision, sometimes incorrectly called accuracy, is the degree to which the instrument gives repeated measurements of the same standard. A common wooden or aluminum ruler, for example, will expand or contract, depending on the environmental temperature, thus giving different (and hence unreliable) measurements.

In engineering metrology, the words **instrument** and **gage** are often used interchangeably; however, a category specific to gages is discussed in Section 35.7. In this category, temperature control is important, particularly for making fine measurements with precision instruments. The standard measuring temperature is 20 °C (68 °F), and all gages are calibrated at this temperature. Therefore, in the interest of accuracy, measurements should be taken in controlled environments, maintaining this temperature usually within ±0.3 °C (0.5 °F).

Example: Length Measurements Throughout History

Many standards for length measurement have been developed during the past 6000 years. A common standard in Egypt around 4000 B.C. was the King's Elbow, which was equivalent to 0.4633 m. One *elbow* was equal to 1.5 feet (or 2 hand-spans, 6 hand-widths, or 24 finger-thicknesses). In A.D. 1101, King Henry I declared a new standard, called the *yard* (0.9144 m), which was the distance from his nose to the tip of his thumb.

During the Middle Ages almost every kingdom and city established its own length standard, some with identical names. In 1528, French physician J. Fernel proposed, as a general length reference, the distance between Paris and Amiens (a city 120 km north of Paris). During the 17th century, some scientists suggested that the length of a certain pendulum be used as a standard. In 1661, British architect Sir Christopher Wren suggested a pendulum with a period of 1/2 second be used. Dutch mathematician C. Huygens proposed a pendulum which had a length one-third of Wren's and which had a period of 1 second.

To put an end to the confusion of length measurement, a definitive length standard began to be developed in 1790 in France with the concept of a *métre*, from the Greek word *metron*, meaning measure. A gage block one meter long was made of pure platinum with a rectangular cross-section and was placed in the National Archives in Paris in 1799. Copies of this gage were made for other countries over the years.

During the three years 1870–1872, international committees met and decided on an international meter standard. The new bar was made of 90% platinum/10% iridium, with an X-shaped cross-section and overall dimensions of 20 mm × 20 mm. Three marks were engraved at each end of the bar. The standard meter is the distance between the central marks at each end, measured at 0 °C. Extremely accurate measurement is now based on the speed of light in a vacuum, calculated by multiplying the wavelength of the standardized infrared beam of a laser by its frequency.

TABLE 35.1   Types of Measurement and Instruments Used

Measurement	Instrument	Sensitivity	
		μm	μin.
Linear	Steel rule	0.5 mm	$\frac{1}{64}$ in.
	Vernier caliper	25	1000
	Micrometer, with vernier	2.5	100
	Diffraction grating	1	40
Angle	Bevel protractor, with vernier	5 min	
	Sine bar		
Comparative length	Dial indicator	1	40
	Electronic gage	0.1	4
	Gage blocks	0.05	2
Straightness	Autocollimator	2.5	100
	Transit	0.2 mm/m	0.002 in./ft
	Laser beam	2.5	100
Flatness	Interferometry	0.03	1
Roundness	Dial indicator		
	Circular tracing	0.03	1
Profile	Radius or fillet gage		
	Dial indicator	1	40
	Optical comparator	125	5000
	Coordinate measuring machines	0.25	10
GO-NOT GO	Plug gage		
	Ring gage		
	Snap gage		
Microscopes	Toolmaker's	2.5	100
	Light section	1	40
	Scanning electron	0.001	0.04
	Laser scan	0.1	5

35.3 LINE-GRADUATED INSTRUMENTS

Line-graduated instruments are used for measuring length (linear measurements) or angles (angular measurements). *Graduated* means marked to indicate a certain quantity.

35.3.1 Linear Measurements (Direct Reading)

Several commonly used linear-measurement instruments can be used to read dimensions directly:

a. Rules. The simplest and most commonly used instrument for making linear measurements is a steel rule (*machinist's rule*), bar, or tape, with fractional or decimal graduations. Lengths are measured directly to an accuracy that is limited to the nearest division, usually 1 mm or 0.040 in. Rules can be rigid or flexible, and are sometimes equipped with a hook at one end to ease measuring from an edge. *Rule depth gages* are similar to rules, but slide along a special head.

b. Vernier calipers. Named for P. Vernier, who lived in the 1600s, *vernier calipers* have a graduated beam and a sliding jaw with a *vernier*. These instruments are also called **caliper gages** (Fig. 35.2a). The two jaws of the caliper contact the part being measured, and the dimension is read at the matching graduated lines (Fig. 35.2b). Vernier calipers

FIGURE 35.2   (a) A caliper gage with a vernier. (b) A vernier, reading $27.00 + 0.42 = = 27.42$ mm, or $1.000 + 0.050 + 0.029 = 1.079$ in. We arrive at the last measurement as follows: First note that the two lowest scales pertain to the inch units. We next note that the 0 (zero) mark on the lower scale has passed the 1-in. mark on the upper scale. Thus, we first record a distance of 1.000 in. Next we note that the 0 mark has also passed the first (shorter) mark on the upper scale. Noting that the 1-in. distance on the upper scale is divided into 20 segments, we have passed a distance of 0.050 in. Finally, note that the marks on the two scales coincide at the number 29. Each of the 50 graduations on the lower scale indicates 0.001 in., so we also have 0.029 in. Thus the total dimension is 1.000 in. + 0.050 in. + 0.029 in. = 1.079 in.

(a)

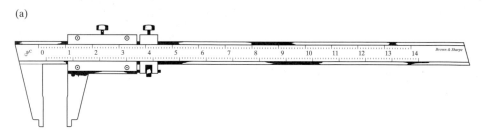

(b)

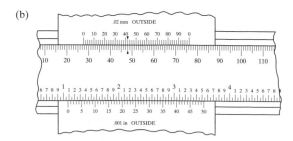

(a) (b) (c)

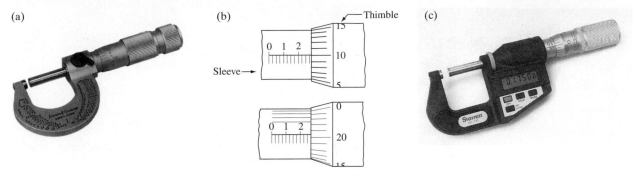

FIGURE 35.3   (a) A micrometer being used to measure the diameter of round rods. *Source*: L. S. Starrett Co. (b) Vernier on the sleeve and thimble of a micrometer. Upper one reads $0.200 + 0.075 + 0.010 = 0.285$ in.; lower one reads $0.200 + 0.050 + 0.020 + 0.0003 = 0.2703$ in. These dimensions are read in a manner similar to that described in the caption for Fig. 35.2. (c) A digital micrometer with a range of 0–1 in. (0–25 mm) and a resolution of 0.00005 in. (0.001 mm). Note how much easier it is to read dimensions on this instrument than on the analog micrometer shown in (a). However, such instruments should be handled carefully. *Source*: Mitutoyo Corp.

can be used to measure inside or outside lengths. The vernier improves the sensitivity of a simple rule by indicating fractions of the smallest division on the graduated beam, usually to 25 μm (0.001 in.).

Vernier calipers are also available with *digital readouts* (English or metric). These electronic devices (see Section 35.4.2) are easier to read and less subject to human error than analog verniers. An important feature of digital verniers is that they can be equipped with printers for data acquisition and with microprocessors. They also have statistical process and quality control capabilities. (See Chapter 36).

c. **Micrometers.** Commonly used for measuring the thickness and inside or outside dimensions of parts (Fig. 35.3a), the **micrometer** has a threaded spindle and a graduated thimble and sleeve (Fig. 35.3b). Circumferential vernier readings to a sensitivity of 2.5 μm (0.0001 in.) can be obtained with a micrometer. Micrometers are also available for measuring depths (*micrometer depth gage*) and internal diameters (*inside micrometer*) with the same sensitivity.

The anvils on micrometers can be equipped with conical or ball contacts. They are used to measure inside recesses, threaded rod diameters, and wall thickness of tubes and curved sheets. *Digital micrometers* are also available, and are equipped with digital readouts in English or metric units (Fig. 35.3c); these, too, can be integrated with microprocessors for statistical process and quality control. (See Section 36.6).

d. **Diffraction gratings.** *Diffraction gratings* consist of two flat optical glasses of different lengths with closely spaced parallel lines scribed on their surfaces. The grating on the shorter glass is slightly inclined. As a result, interference fringes develop when it is viewed over the longer glass.

The position of these fringes depends on the relative position of the two sets of glasses. With modern equipment and using electronic counters and photoelectric sensors, sensitivities of 2.5 μm (0.0001 in.) can be obtained with gratings having 40 lines/mm (1000 lines/in.).

(a)   (b)

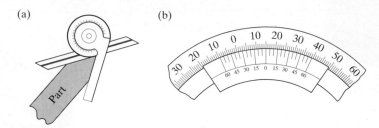

FIGURE 35.4   (a) Schematic illustration of a bevel protractor for measuring angles. (b) Vernier for angular measurement, indicating 14° 30′.

35.3.2 Linear Measurements (Indirect Reading)

Indirect-reading instruments are typically **calipers** and **dividers** without any graduated scales. They are used to transfer the measured size to a direct-reading instrument, such as a rule. After adjusting the legs to contact the part at the desired location, the instrument is held against a graduated rule, and the dimension is read.

Because of the experience required to use them and their dependence on graduated scales, the accuracy of indirect measurement tools is limited. *Telescoping gages* can be used for indirect measurement of holes or cavities.

35.3.3 Angle-Measuring Instruments

Angles are measured using the methods described next, either in degrees or radians. Because of the geometry involved, it is usually more difficult to measure angles than linear dimensions.

a. Bevel protractor. A *bevel protractor* is a direct-reading instrument similar to a common protractor, except that it has a movable element (Fig. 35.4a). The two blades of the protractor are placed in contact with the part being measured, and the angle is read directly on the vernier scale. The sensitivity of the instrument depends on the graduations of the vernier (Fig. 35.4b). Another type of bevel protractor is the **combination square**, which is a steel rule equipped with devices for measuring 45 ° and 90 ° angles.

b. Sine bar. Measuring with a *sine bar* involves placing the part on an inclined bar or plate and adjusting the angle by placing gage blocks on a surface plate (Fig. 35.5). After the part is placed on the sine bar, a dial indicator (Section 35.4.1) is used to scan the top surface of the part.

Gage blocks (Section 35.7.1) are added or removed as necessary until the top surface is parallel to the surface plate. The angle on the part is then calculated using trigonometric relationships; these calculations are often further simplified by using a 10-in. spacing between cylinders so that the sine of the bar's angle is easy to calculate (hence the term sine bar).

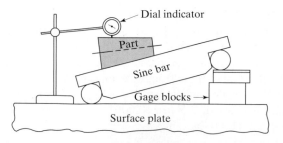

Dial indicator

Part

Sine bar

Gage blocks →

Surface plate

FIGURE 35.5   Setup showing the use of a sine bar for precision measurement of workpiece angles.

   c. **Surface plates.** These are made of cast iron or natural stones, such as granite, and are used extensively in engineering metrology. Granite surface plates have the desirable properties of being resistant to corrosion, being nonmagnetic, and having low thermal expansion.

   d. **Other methods.** Angles can also be measured using **angle gage blocks**. These are blocks with different *tapers* that can be assembled in various combinations and used in a manner similar to that used with sine bars. Angles on small parts can be measured through microscopes with graduated eyepieces, or with optical projectors (Section 35.5.6). Inclination angles can also be measured with a digital electronic instrument.

35.4 COMPARATIVE LENGTH-MEASURING INSTRUMENTS

Unlike the instruments just described, instruments used for measuring comparative lengths, also called *deviation-type* instruments, amplify and measure variations or deviations in the distance between two or more surfaces. These instruments compare dimensions, hence the word *comparative*. Described below are common types of instruments used for making comparative measurements.

35.4.1 Dial Indicators

Dial indicators are simple mechanical devices that convert linear displacements of a pointer to the amount of rotation of an indicator on a circular dial (Fig. 35.6). The indicator is set to zero at a certain reference surface, and the instrument or the surface to be measured (either external or internal) is brought into contact with the pointer. The movement of the indicator is read directly on the circular dial (either plus or minus) to accuracies as high as 1 μm (40 μin.).

Dial indicators of several designs are available for use as portable or benchtop units. The basic design consists of a rack-and-pinion and a gear-train mechanism that, together, convert linear motion to rotary motion, with large amplifications. These instruments are also used for multiple-dimension gaging of parts (Fig. 35.6c). Instruments with electrical and fluidic amplification mechanisms and with digital readout are also available.

35.4.2 Electronic Gages

Unlike mechanical systems, *electronic gages* sense the movement of the contacting pointer through changes in the electrical resistance of a strain gage or through inductance or capacitance. The electrical signals are then converted and displayed digitally as linear dimensions (*digital readout*). A digital micrometer is shown in Fig. 35.3c.

A hand-held electronic gage for measuring bore diameters is shown in Fig. 35.7. When its handle is squeezed slightly, the tool can be inserted into the bore, and the bore diameter is read directly (shown in millimeters in Fig. 35.7). A microprocessor-assisted electronic gage for measuring vertical length is shown in Fig. 35.8. A commonly used electronic gage

FIGURE 35.6   Three uses for dial indicators: (a) roundness, (b) depth, and (c) multiple-dimension gaging of a part.

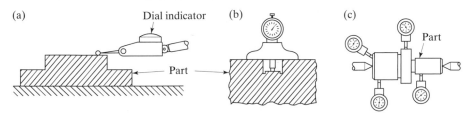

FIGURE 35.7 An electronic gage for measuring bore diameters. The measuring head is equipped with three carbide-tipped steel pins for wear resistance. The LED display reads 29.158 mm. *Courtesy of* TESA SA.

FIGURE 35.8 An electronic vertical length measuring instrument, with a sensitivity of 1 μm (40 μin.). *Courtesy of* TESA SA.

is the **linear variable differential transformer (LVDT)**, used extensively for measuring small displacements.

Although they are more expensive than other types, electronic gages have advantages: ease of operation, rapid response, digital readout, less possibility of human error, versatility, flexibility, and the capability to be integrated into automated systems through microprocessors and computers (Section 36.11).

However, because they are more fragile, electronic gages and instruments should be handled carefully and their calibration checked frequently. Electronic caliper gages with diamond-coated edges are now available. The chemical vapor deposition (CVD) coating (see Section 33.5.2) on these gages has wear resistance superior to that of steel or tungsten carbide edges; it also resists chemicals.

35.4.3 Laser Scan Micrometers

A more recent development is the use of laser beams for *noncontact* measurements (Fig. 35.9). In this particular instrument, the laser beam scans the workpiece at a speed of 350 times per second. Such micrometers are capable of resolutions as high as 0.125 μm (5 μin.), and are suitable for on-line measuring of stationary, rotating, or vibrating parts, as well as parts that are at elevated temperature or are too elastic or brittle.

(a) Direct measurement of diameter D

(b) Runout of shaft in rotation

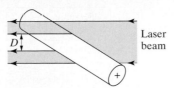

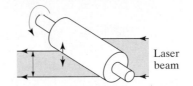

FIGURE 35.9   Two types of measurement made with a laser scan micrometer. *Source*: Mitutoyo Corp.

35.5 GEOMETRIC FEATURES: MEASURING STRAIGHTNESS, FLATNESS, ROUNDNESS, AND PROFILE

Geometric features (straightness, flatness, roundness, and profile) are important aspects of engineering design and manufacturing. For example, piston rods, instrument components, and machine-tool slideways should all meet certain requirements with regard to these characteristics in order to function properly. For this reason, their accurate measurement is essential.

35.5.1 Straightness

Straightness can be checked using a straightedge or a dial indicator (Figs. 35.10a and b). An **autocollimator**, which resembles a telescope with a light beam that bounces back from the object, is used to accurately measure small angular deviations on a flat surface. Optical means such as *transits* and *laser beams* are used to align individual machine elements in the assembly of machine components.

35.5.2 Flatness

Flatness can be measured by mechanical means using a surface plate and a dial indicator. This method can also be used to measure perpendicularity, which can also be measured using precision steel squares. The instrument shown in Fig. 35.8 can also be used to measure perpendicularity.

Interferometry.   Another method for measuring flatness is interferometry, using an **optical flat**. The device, a glass disk or fused quartz disk with parallel flat surfaces, is placed on the surface of the workpiece (Fig. 35.11a). When a *monochromatic* light beam (a light

FIGURE 35.10   Measuring straightness with (a) a knife-edge rule and (b) a dial indicator attached to a movable stand resting on a surface plate. *Source*: F.T. Farago.

(a)

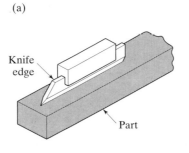

Knife edge

Part

(b)

Dial indicator

Part

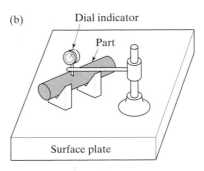

Surface plate

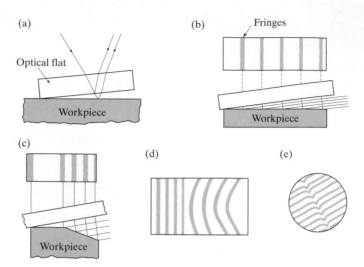

FIGURE 35.11 (a) Interferometry method for measuring flatness using an optical flat. (b) Fringes on a flat inclined surface. An optical flat resting on a perfectly flat workpiece surface will not split the light beam, and no fringes will be present. (c) Fringes on a surface with two inclinations. *Note*: the greater the incline, the closer the fringes. (d) Curved fringe patterns indicate curvatures on the workpiece surface. (e) Fringe pattern indicating a scratch on the surface.

beam with one wavelength) is aimed at the surface at an angle, the optical flat splits the light beam into two beams, appearing as light and dark bands to the naked eye (Fig. 35.11b).

The number of fringes that appear is related to the distance between the surface of the part and the bottom surface of the optical flat (Fig. 35.11c). Consequently, a truly flat work-piece surface (that is, one in which the angle between the two surfaces in Fig. 35.11a is zero) will not split the light beam and fringes will not appear. When surfaces are not flat, the fringes are curved (Fig. 35.11d). The interferometry method is also used for observing surface textures and scratches (Fig. 35.11e).

Laser interferometry is used to check and calibrate machine tools (see Part IV) for various geometric features during assembly; this method has better accuracies than gages or indicators. Laser interferometers are also used to automatically compensate for positioning errors in coordinate measuring machines (Section 35.6) and computer-numerical control machines (Section 38.3).

35.5.3 Roundness

Roundness is usually described as a deviation from true roundness (which, mathematically, is manifested in a circle). The term **out of roundness** (ovality) is actually more descriptive of the shape of the part (Fig. 35.12a) than "roundness". True roundness is essential to the proper functioning of rotating shafts, bearing races, pistons and cylinders, and steel balls in bearings.

Methods of measuring roundness generally fall into two categories. In the first, the round part is placed on a V-block or between centers (Figs. 35.12b and c, respectively) and is rotated, while the point of a dial indicator is in contact with the surface. After a full rotation of the workpiece, the difference between the maximum and minimum readings on the dial is noted. This difference is called the **total indicator reading** (TIR) or *full indicator movement*. This method is also used to measure the straightness (squareness) of end faces of shafts.

In the second method, called *circular tracing*, the part is placed on a platform and its roundness is measured by rotating the platform (Fig. 35.12d). Conversely, the probe can be rotated around a stationary part to take the measurement.

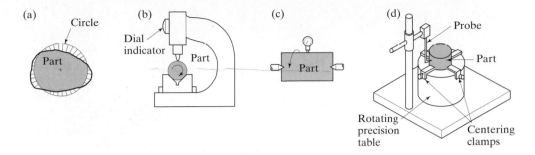

FIGURE 35.12   (a) Schematic illustration of "out of roundness" (exaggerated). Measuring roundness using (b) V-block and dial indicator, (c) part supported on centers and rotated, and (d) circular tracing, with part being rotated on a vertical axis. *Source*: After F.T. Farago.

35.5.4 Profile

Profile may be measured by several methods. In one method, a surface is compared with a template or profile gage to check shape conformity. Radii or fillets can be measured using this method (Fig. 35.13a). Profile can also be measured with a number of dial indicators or similar instruments (Fig. 35.13b), or by the machines described in Section 35.6.

35.5.5 Measuring Screw Threads and Gear Teeth

Threads and *gear teeth* have several features with specific dimensions and tolerances. These dimensions must be produced accurately for (a) smooth operation of gears, (b) the reduction of wear and noise level, and (c) interchangeability of parts.

These features are measured basically by means of **thread gages** of various designs that compare the produced thread against a standard thread. Some of the gages used are **threaded plug gages**, **screw-pitch gages** (similar to radius gages; see Fig. 35.13a), micrometers with cone-shaped points, and **snap gages** (Section 35.7) with anvils in the shape of threads.

Gear teeth are measured using (a) instruments that are similar to dial indicators, (b) calipers (Fig. 35.14a), and (c) micrometers using pins or balls of various diameters (Fig. 35.14b). Special profile-measuring equipment is also available, including optical projectors and coordinate measuring machines.

35.5.6 Optical Contour Projectors

Optical contour projectors, also called **optical comparators**, were first developed in the 1940s to check the geometry of cutting tools for machining screw threads, but they are now used for checking all profiles (Fig. 35.15). The part is mounted on a table or between centers, and the image is projected onto a screen, at magnifications of $100 \times$ or higher.

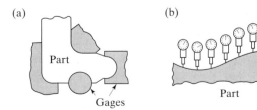

FIGURE 35.13   Measuring profiles with (a) radius gages and (b) dial indicators.

(a)   (b)

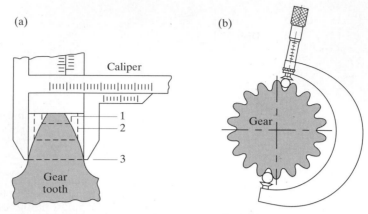

FIGURE 35.14   Measuring gear-tooth thickness and profile with (a) a gear-tooth caliper and (b) pins or balls and a micrometer. *Source*: American Gear Manufacturers Association.

FIGURE 35.15   A bench model horizontal-beam contour projector with a 16 in.-diameter screen with 150-W tungsten halogen illumination. *Courtesy of* L. S. Starrett Company, Precision Optical Division.

Linear and angular measurements are made directly on the screen, which is marked with reference lines and circles. The screen can be rotated to allow angular measurements as small as 1 min, using verniers such as that shown in Fig. 35.4b.

35.6 COORDINATE-MEASURING AND LAYOUT MACHINES

Coordinate-measuring and layout machines are important developments in measurement technology. Basically, each consists of a platform on which the workpiece being measured is placed and then moved linearly or rotated. A probe, attached to a head capable of lateral and vertical movements, records all measurements (Fig. 35.16). *Coordinate measuring machines (CMM)*,

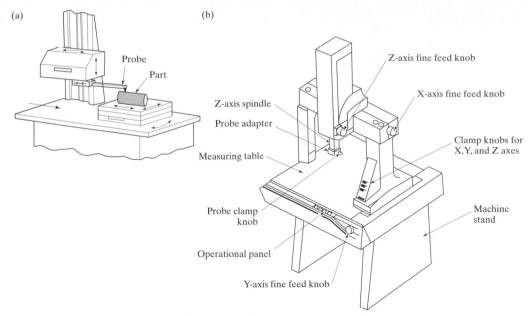

(a)

Probe
Part

(b)

Z-axis fine feed knob

X-axis fine feed knob

Z-axis spindle
Probe adapter

Clamp knobs for
X,Y, and Z axes

Measuring table

Probe clamp
knob

Machine
stand

Operational panel

Y-axis fine feed knob

FIGURE 35.16   (a) Schematic illustration of one type of coordinate measuring machine.
(b) Components of another type of coordinate measuring machine. These machines are
available in various sizes and levels of automation and with a variety of probes (attached to the
probe adapter), and are capable of measuring several features of a part. *Source*: Mitutoyo Corp.

FIGURE 35.17   A
coordinate measuring
machine. Brown & Sharpe
Manufacturing Co.

also called **measuring machines**, are very versatile; they are capable of recording measurements
of complex profiles with high sensitivity (0.25 μm; 10 μin.) and with high speed.

These machines are built rigidly and are very precise. They are equipped with digital
readout and can also be linked to computers for on-line inspection of parts (Section 35.9).
These machines can be placed close to machine tools for efficient inspection and rapid feedback; this way, processing parameters are corrected before the next part is made.

Measuring machines are being made more rugged to resist environmental effects in
manufacturing plants, such as temperature variations, vibration, and dirt. A coordinate measuring machine for inspection of an engine block is shown in Fig. 35.17.

Dimensions of large parts and workpieces are measured using **layout machines**, which
feature digital readout. These machines are equipped with scribing tools for marking dimensions on large parts, with a sensitivity of $\pm$0.04 mm (0.0016 in.).

35.7 GAGES

Thus far we have used the word **gage** to describe several types of measuring instruments such as a caliper gage, depth gage, telescoping gage, electronic gage, and radius gage. The words *instrument* and *gage* (also spelled *gauge*) have traditionally been used interchangeably.

As we have seen, the word gage has a variety of meanings: pressure gage, gage length of a tension-test specimen, strain gage, or a gages for sheet metal, wire, railroad rail, and the bore of shotguns. This section describes several common gages that have simple solid shapes and cannot be classified as instruments.

35.7.1 Gage Blocks

Gage blocks, first developed by C.E. Johansson in the early 1900s and also called *Johansson blocks*, are individual square, rectangular, or round metal blocks of various sizes (see the gage blocks in Fig. 35.5), made very precisely from heat-treated and stress-relieved alloy steels or carbides. Their surfaces are lapped and are flat and parallel within a range of 0.02 to 0.12 μm (1 to 5 μin.). *Zirconia* ceramic gage blocks are now also available.

Gage blocks are available in sets of various sizes, some sets containing almost a hundred blocks. The blocks can be assembled in many different combinations to reach desired lengths. Dimensional accuracy can be as high as 0.05 μm (2 μin.). Environmental temperature control is important when gages are used for high-precision measurements.

The individual gage blocks are assembled by *wringing,* which is a sliding and twisting motion. The adsorbed films of moisture and oil between the gage blocks develop negative pressure at the interface, thus forcing the blocks to adhere to each other. This phenomenon is similar to the tendency of papers to stick together in a humid environment.

Although their use requires some skill, gage-block assemblies are commonly utilized in industry as accurate reference lengths. Worn or damaged gage blocks should not be used when highly accurate measurements are required, although they may still be viable when less accuracy is needed. *Angle blocks* are made the same way and are used for angular gaging.

The four basic grades of gage blocks, in decreasing order of accuracy, are as follows:

- Grade 0.5 (formerly AAA): reference gages, for very high precision work.
- Grade 1 (AA): laboratory grade, for calibration of instruments and other gages.
- Grade 2 (A+): precision grade, for toolrooms and inspection.
- Grade 3 (A and B): working grade, for use in production.

35.7.2 Fixed Gages

Fixed gages are replicas of the shapes of the parts to be measured. Although fixed gages are easy to use and inexpensive, they only indicate whether a part is too small or too large, compared to an established standard. They do not measure actual dimensions.

a. **Plug gages** are commonly used for holes (Figs. 35.18a and b). The *GO gage* is smaller than the *NOT GO* (or *NO GO*) *gage* and slides into any hole which has a dimension smaller than the diameter of the gage. The *NOT GO* gage must not go into the hole.

Two gages are required for such measurements, although both may be on the same device, either at opposite ends or in two steps at one end (*step-type gage*). Plug gages are also available for measuring internal tapers (in which deviations between the gage and the part are indicated by the looseness of the gage), splines, and threads (in which the *GO* gage must screw into the threaded hole).

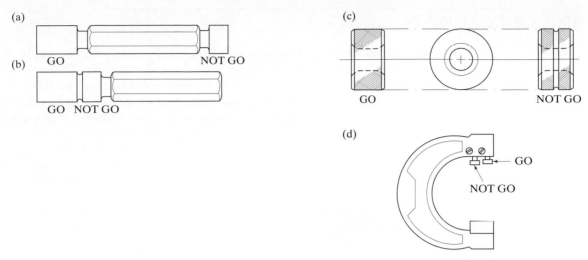

FIGURE 35.18   (a) Plug gage for holes, with GO–NOT GO on opposite ends. (b) Plug gage with GO–NOT GO on one end. (c) Plain ring gages for gaging round rods. Note the difference in knurled surfaces to identify the two gages. (d) Snap gage with adjustable anvils.

b. Ring gages (Fig. 35.18c) are used to measure shafts and similar round parts. Ring thread gages are used to measure external threads. The *GO* and *NOT GO* features on these gages are identified by the type of knurling on the outside diameters of the rings, as shown in the figure.

c. Snap gages (Fig. 35.18d) are commonly used to measure external dimensions. They are made with adjustable gaging surfaces for use with parts which have different dimensions. One of the gaging surfaces can be set at a different gap from the other, thus making it a one-unit *GO–NOT GO* gage.

35.7.3 Pneumatic Gages

Although there are several types of *pneumatic gages*, also called **air gages**, their basic operation is shown in Fig. 35.19. The gage head has holes through which pressurized air, supplied by a constant-pressure line, escapes. The smaller the gap between the gage and the hole, the more difficult it is for the air to escape, and the higher the back pressure.

The back pressure, which is sensed and indicated by a pressure gage, is calibrated to measure dimensional variations of holes. The principle of air gages can be observed when one blows air through a soda straw while holding it vertically over a flat surface, and then at different distances from the surface.

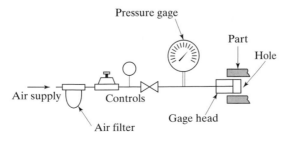

FIGURE 35.19   Schematic illustration of one type of pneumatic gage.

35.8 OPTICAL INSTRUMENTS

Microscopes are optical instruments used to view and measure very fine details, shapes, and dimensions on small and medium-sized tools, dies, and workpieces. The most common and versatile microscope used in tool rooms is the **toolmaker's microscope**. It is equipped with a *stage* that is movable in two principal directions and can be read to 2.5 μm (0.0001 in.). Several models of microscopes are available, with various features for specialized inspection, including digital readout.

Optical inspection and measuring systems are being developed further so that objects or surfaces that are too, far from the instrument, delicate, or difficult to illuminate for a normal microscope can still be visually inspected. Among the instruments which can do this are **fiberscopes** (flexible fiber-optic probes, as long as 6 m and as small as 0.6 mm in diameter, that can be snaked through passages), and **borescopes** (as small as 1.2 mm in diameter, for viewing small and deep internal surfaces). These devices are used in conjunction with a variety of video and computer-based enhancement equipment with software for data storage and analysis capabilities.

Light Section Microscope. The *light section microscope* is used to measure (a) small surface details such as scratches, and (b) the thickness of deposited films and coatings. A thin light band is applied obliquely to the surface and the reflection is viewed at 90°, showing surface roughness, contours, and other features.

Scanning Electron Microscope. Unlike ordinary optical microscopes, the *scanning electron microscope* (SEM) has excellent depth of field, even at magnifications higher than 100,000X. As a result, all regions of a complex part are in focus and can be viewed and photographed to show extremely fine detail. Although it cannot be used for metrology, this type of microscope is particularly useful for studying surface textures and fracture patterns.

35.9 AUTOMATED MEASUREMENT

As automation increases in all aspects of manufacturing processes and operations, the need for *automated measurement* (also called *automated inspection*; Section 36.11) has become obvious. Flexible manufacturing systems and manufacturing cells (Chapter 39) have led to the adoption of advanced measuring techniques and systems. In fact, installation and utilization of these systems is now necessary and essential in manufacturing.

In the past, a batch of parts was manufactured and sent to be measured in a separate quality-control room; if this batch passed measurement inspection, it was put into inventory. Automated inspection, however, is based on various **on-line sensor systems** that monitor the dimensions of parts while they are being made, and if necessary, use these measurements as input to correct the process. (See Section 38.8.)

To appreciate the importance of on-line monitoring of dimensions, let's consider the following question: If a machine has been producing a certain part with acceptable dimensions, what factors contribute to subsequent deviation in the dimensions of the same part produced by the same machine? There are several technical as well as human factors involved:

a. Static and dynamic deflections of the machine because of vibrations and fluctuating forces, caused by machine characteristics and variations in the properties and dimensions of the incoming material.

b. Distortion of the machine because of thermal effects, such as changes in temperature of the environment, metalworking fluids, and machine bearings and various components.

c. Wear of tools, dies, and molds, which, in turn, affects the dimensional accuracy of the parts produced.

d. Human errors and miscalculations.

As a result of these factors, the dimensions of parts will vary, making continuous monitoring during production necessary.

35.10 GENERAL CHARACTERISTICS AND SELECTION OF MEASURING INSTRUMENTS

The characteristics and quality of measuring instruments are generally described by various specific terms, defined as follows:

1. **Accuracy.** The degree of agreement of the measured dimension with its true magnitude.
2. **Amplification.** See Magnification.
3. **Calibration.** Adjusting or setting an instrument to give readings that are accurate within a reference standard.
4. **Drift**. See Stability.
5. **Linearity.** The accuracy of the readings of an instrument over its full working range.
6. **Magnification.** The ratio of instrument output to the input dimension.
7. **Precision.** Degree to which an instrument gives repeated measurement of the same standard.
8. **Repeat accuracy**. Same as accuracy, but repeated many times.
9. **Resolution.** Smallest dimension that can be read on an instrument.
10. **Rule of 10** (*Gage Maker's rule*). An instrument or gage should be 10 times more accurate than the dimensional tolerances of the part being measured. (A factor of 4 is known as the *Mil Standard rule*).
11. **Sensitivity**. Smallest difference in dimension that an instrument can distinguish or detect.
12. **Speed of response.** How rapidly an instrument indicates the measurement, particularly when a number of parts are measured in rapid succession.
13. **Stability.** An instrument's capability to maintain its calibration over a period of time (also called *drift*).

Selection of an appropriate measuring instrument for a particular application also depends on (a) the size and type of parts to be measured, (b) the environment (temperature, humidity, dust, and so on), (c) operator skills required, and (d) cost of equipment.

35.11 GEOMETRIC DIMENSIONING AND TOLERANCING

Individually manufactured parts and components are eventually assembled into products. We take it for granted that when, for example, a thousand lawnmowers are manufactured and assembled, each part of the mower will mate properly with another component. For example, the wheels of the lawnmower will slip easily into their axles, or the pistons will fit properly into the cylinders, being neither too tight nor too loose.

Likewise, when we have to replace a broken or worn bolt on an old machine, we purchase an identical bolt. We are confident that, from similar experiences in the past, the new bolt will fit properly in the machine. The reason we feel confident is that the bolt is manufactured according to certain standards and that the dimensions of all similar bolts vary by only a small, specified amount.

In other words, the bolts are manufactured within a certain range of dimensional tolerance; thus, all similar bolts are *interchangeable*. We also expect that the new bolt will function satisfactorily for a period of time, unless abused or misused. Bolts are periodically subjected to various tests during their production to make sure that their quality is within specifications. (See also Chapter 36.)

Dimensional tolerance is defined as the permissible or acceptable variation in the dimensions (height, width, depth, diameter, angles) of a part. The root of the word tolerance is the Latin *tolerare*, meaning to endure or put up with. Tolerances are unavoidable because it is virtually impossible (and unnecessary) to manufacture two parts that have precisely the same dimensions.

Furthermore, because close dimensional tolerances can significantly increase the product cost, a narrow tolerance range is undesirable economically. However, for some parts, close tolerances are necessary for proper functioning, and are therefore worth the added expense associated with narrow tolerance ranges. Examples are precision measuring instruments and gages, hydraulic pistons, and bearings for aircraft engines.

Measuring dimensional tolerances and features of parts rapidly and reliably can be a challenging task. For example, each of the 6 million parts on a Boeing 747-400 aircraft requires measurement of about 25 features, a total of 150 million measurements.

Recent surveys by the U.S. National Institute of Standards and Technology (NIST) have shown that the dimensional tolerances on state-of-the-art manufactured parts are shrinking by a factor of 3 every 10 years, and that this trend will continue. It is estimated that accuracies of (a) conventional turning and milling machines (Chapters 22 and 23) will soon rise from the present 7.5 μm to 1 μm, (b) diamond-wheel wafer-slicing machines for semiconductor fabrication to 0.25 μm, (c) precision diamond turning machines to 0.01 μm, and (d) ultraprecision ion-beam machining to less than 0.001 μm.

35.11.1 Importance of Dimensional Tolerance Control

Dimensional tolerances become important only when a part is to be assembled or mated with another part. Surfaces that are free and not functional do not need close tolerance control. Thus, for example, the accuracy of the holes and the distance between the holes for a connecting rod are far more critical than the rod's width and thickness at various locations along its length (see Fig. 14.7). By reviewing the figures throughout this text, we can determine which dimensions and features of the parts illustrated are more critical than others.

To appreciate the importance of dimensional tolerances, let's assemble a simple round shaft (axle) and a wheel with a round hole, assuming that we want the axle's diameter to be 1 in. (Fig. 35.20). We go to a hardware store and purchase a 1-in. round rod and a wheel with a 1-in. hole. Will the rod fit into the hole without forcing it or will it be loose in the hole?

The 1-in. dimension is the **nominal size** of the shaft. If we purchase such a rod from different stores, or at different times, or select one randomly from a large lot, the chances are that each rod will have a slightly different diameter. Machines may, with the same setup, produce rods of slightly different diameters, depending on a number of factors such as speed of operation, temperature, lubrication, and variations in the properties of the incoming material. If we now specify a *range* of diameters for both the rod and the hole of the wheel, we can correctly predict the type of fit.

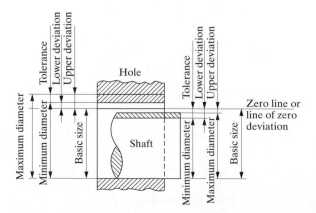

FIGURE 35.20   Basic size, deviation, and tolerance on a shaft, according to the ISO system.

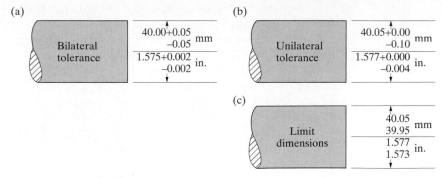

FIGURE 35.21   Various methods of assigning tolerances on a shaft. *Source*: L. E. Doyle.

Certain terminology has been established to clearly define these geometric quantities, such as the ISO (International Organization for Standardization) system shown in Fig. 35.20. Note that both the shaft and the hole have minimum and maximum diameters, respectively, the difference being the tolerance for each member. A proper engineering drawing would specify these parameters with numerical values, as shown in Fig. 35.21.

The range of dimensional tolerances possible in manufacturing processes is given in various figures and tables throughout this text. There is a general relationship between tolerances and part size (Fig. 35.22) and between tolerances and the surface finish of parts

FIGURE 35.22   Tolerances as a function of part size for various manufacturing processes. *Note*: Because many factors are involved, there is a broad range for tolerances.

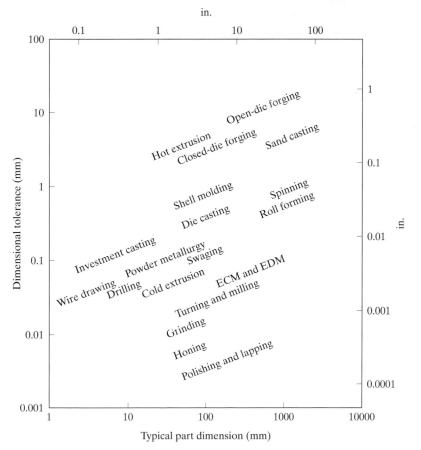

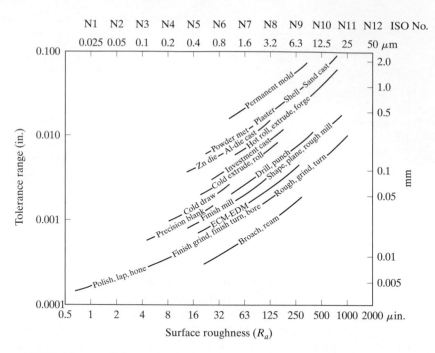

FIGURE 35.23   Tolerances and surface roughness obtained in various manufacturing processes. These tolerances apply to a 25-mm (1-in.) workpiece dimension. *Source*: J. A. Schey.

manufactured by various processes (Fig. 35.23). Note the wide range of tolerances and surface finishes obtained; also, the larger the part, the greater its obtainable tolerance range.

35.11.2 Definitions

Several terms are used to describe features of dimensional relationships between mating parts. Details of these definitions are available in the ANSI B4.2, ANSI Y14.5, and ISO/TC10/SC5 standards. Because of the complex geometric relationships involved between parts to be assembled, the definitions of these terms are inevitably somewhat confusing.

The symbols commonly used to indicate geometric characteristics are shown in Fig. 35.24. The commonly used terms are defined briefly as follows, in alphabetical order:

1. **Allowance.** The specified difference in dimensions between mating parts; also called *functional dimension* or *sum dimension*.

2. **Basic size.** Dimension from which limits of size are derived, using tolerances and allowances.

3. **Bilateral tolerance.** Deviation (plus or minus) from the basic size.

4. **Clearance.** The space between mating parts.

5. **Clearance fit**. Fit that allows for rotation or sliding between mating parts.

6. **Datum.** A theoretically exact axis, point, line, or plane.

(a)

Type of feature	Type of tolerance	Characteristic	Symbol
Individual (no datum reference)	Form	Flatness	▱
		Straightness	—
		Circularity (roundness)	○
		Cylindricity	⌭
Individual or related	Profile	Profile of a line	⌒
		Profile of a surface	⌓
Related (datum reference required)	Orientation	Perpendicularity	⊥
		Angularity	∠
		Parallelism	//
	Location	Position	⊕
		Concentricity	◎
	Runout	Circular runout	↗
		Total runout	⌰

(b)

.605
Basic, or exact, dimension

-A-
Datum feature symbol

Ⓜ
Maximum material condition

Ⓢ
Regardless of feature size

Ⓛ
Least material condition

Ⓟ
Projected tolerance zone

∅
Diametrical (cylindrical) tolerance zone or feature

⊕ ∅.005 Ⓜ A
Feature control frame

A1
Datum target symbol

FIGURE 35.24   Geometric characteristic symbols to be indicated on engineering drawings of parts to be manufactured. *Source*: The American Society of Mechanical Engineers.

7. **Feature.** Physically identifiable portion of a part, such as hole, slot, pin, or chamfer.

8. **Fit.** The range of looseness or tightness that can result from the application of a specific combination of allowance and tolerance in the design of mating part features.

9. **Geometric tolerancing.** Tolerances that involve shape features of the part.

10. **Hole-basis system.** Tolerances based on a zero line on the hole; also called *standard hole practice* or *basic hole system*.

11. **Interference.** Negative clearance.

12. **Interference fit.** A fit having limits of size so prescribed that an interference always results when mating parts are assembled.

13. **International tolerance grade (IT).** A group of tolerances that vary depending on the basic size, but provide the same relative level of accuracy within a grade.

14. **Limit dimensions.** The maximum and minimum dimensions of a part; also called *limits*.

15. **Maximum material condition (MMC).** The condition where a feature of a certain size contains the maximum amount of material within the stated limits of that size.

16. **Nominal size.** An approximate dimension that is used for the purpose of general identification.

17. **Positional tolerancing.** A system of specifying the true position, size, and form of the features of a part, including allowable variations.

18. **Shaft-basis system.** Tolerances based on a zero line on the shaft; also called *standard shaft practice* or *basic shaft system*.

19. **Standard size.** Nominal size in integers and common subdivisions of length.

20. **Transition fit.** Fit with small clearance or interference that allows for accurate location of mating parts.

21. **Unilateral tolerancing.** Deviation in one direction only from the nominal dimension.

22. **Zero line.** Reference line along the basic size from which a range of tolerances and deviations are specified.

Because the dimensions of holes are more difficult to control than those of shafts, the hole-basis system is commonly used for specifying tolerances in shaft and hole assemblies. The symbols commonly used to indicate geometric characteristics are shown in Figs. 35.24a and b.

35.11.3 Limits and Fits

Limits and fits are essential in specifying dimensions for holes and shafts. There are two standards on limits and fits, as described by the American National Standards Institute (see ANSI B4.1, B4.2, and B4.3). One standard is based on the traditional inch unit; the other is based on the metric unit and has been developed in greater detail. In these standards, capital letters always refer to the hole and lowercase letters to the shaft.

In the *inch* units, **fits** are divided into the following general classifications, each of which has limits of clearances with the hole size as the basic size:

- *Running and sliding fits*, which are subdivided into the following classes:
  Class RC1. Close-sliding fits, for accurate location of parts to be assembled without perceptible play.
  Class RC2. Sliding fits, for parts that turn and move easily.
  Class RC3. Precision-running fits, for precision work at low speeds and light pressures.
  Class RC4. Close-running fits, for accurate machinery with moderate speeds and pressures.
  Classes RC5 and RC6. Medium-running fits, for higher speeds and high pressures.
  Class RC7. Free-running fits, where accuracy is not important.
  Classes RC8 and RC9. Loose-running fits.

- *Locational clearance fits*, for stationary parts to be freely assembled and disassembled.

- *Locational transition fits*, where accuracy of location is important.

- *Locational interference fits*, where accuracy of location is very important and for parts requiring rigidity and proper alignment.

- *Force and shrink fits*, which are subdivided into the following classes:

  Class FN1. Light-drive fits, for assembly requiring light pressures.
  Class FN2. Medium-drive fits, for ordinary parts and shrink fits on light sections.
  Class FN3. Heavy-drive fits, for heavier parts and shrink fits on medium sections.
  Classes FN4 and FN5. Force fits, for parts that are to be highly stressed.

In the *metric* system, fits are classified in a similar manner by ISO and are outlined as follows:

	ISO symbol	
	Hole basis	Shaft basis
Clearance fits		
Loose running	H11/c11	C11/h11
Free running	H9/d9	D9/h9
Close running	H8/f7	F8/h7
Sliding	H7/g6	G7/h6
Locational clearance	H7/h6	H7/h6
Transition fits		
Locational transition (accurate)	H7/k6	K7/h6
Locational transition (more accurate)	H7/n6	N7/h6
Interference fits		
Locational interference	H7/p6	P7/h6
Medium drive	H7/s6	S7/h6
Force fits	H7/u6	U7/h6

SUMMARY

- In modern manufacturing technology, many parts are processed using a high degree of precision, and thus require measuring instrumentation with several features and characteristics.
- Many devices are available for inspection, from simple gage blocks to electronic gages with high sensitivity. The selection of any measuring instrument depends on factors such as the type of measurement for which it will be used, the environment in which it will be used, and the accuracy of measurement necessary.
- Gages must be checked periodically against a reliable standard. Humidity, heat, cold, vibration, and dirt can have adverse effects on the accuracy and reliability of gages and their measurements. Skill required of the operator and cost of instrumentation are also important considerations.
- Major advances have been made in automated measurement, linking measuring devices to microprocessors and computers for accurate in-process control of manufacturing operations. Reliable linking, monitoring, display, distribution, and manipulation of data are important factors, as are the significant costs involved in implementing them.
- Dimensional tolerances and their selection are important factors in manufacturing. Tolerances not only affect the accuracy and operation of all types of machinery and equipment, but can also significantly influence product cost.
- The smaller (or tighter) the range of tolerances specified, the higher the cost of production. Tolerances should be as broad as possible, but should also maintain the functional requirements of the product.

TRENDS

- Studies are continually being made regarding the accuracy, reliability, and speed of measuring instruments and coordinate measuring machines, used either individually or as components in computer-integrated manufacturing systems.

- Automated measurement and inspection will continue to be essential parts of all manufacturing operations.

- GO-NOT GO gages are being displaced by gages which produce a numerical measurement in response to quality control and its statistical techniques in manufacturing.

- Dimensional tolerances and their control during manufacturing continue to be important factors in product quality and in reliability of products.

- Electronic measuring instruments, such as digital micrometers and coordinate measuring machines, are now being integrated with various software for statistical process control of manufacturing processes.

KEY TERMS

Autocollimator	Fixed gage	Plug gage
Bevel protractor	Gage	Pneumatic gage
Comparative length-measuring instruments	Gage block	Precision
	Instrument	Resolution
Coordinate measuring machine	Interferometry	Ring gage
Dial indicator	Layout machine	Sensitivity
Diffraction grating	Limits	Sine bar
Digital readout	Line-graduated instruments	Snap gage
Dimensional tolerance	Measurement standards	Tolerance
Electronic gages	Micrometer	Toolmaker's microscope
Engineering metrology	Optical contour projector	Total indicator reading
Fits	Optical flat	Vernier caliper

BIBLIOGRAPHY

Bentley, J.P., *Principles of Measurement Systems* (3d ed.). Addison-Wesley, 1995.

Bjorke, O., *Computer-Aided Tolerancing* (2d ed.). ASME Press, 1992.

Bosch, J.A., *Coordinate Measuring Machines and Systems.* Marcel Dekker, 1995.

Creveling, C.M., *Tolerance Control: A Handbook for Developing Optimal Specifications.* Addison-Wesley, 1996.

Farago, F.T., and M.A. Curtis, *Handbook of Dimensional Measurement* (3d ed.). Industrial Press, 1994.

Gooldy, G., *Geometric Dimensioning and Tolerancing* (Rev. ed.). Prentice Hall, 1995.

Henzold, G., *Handbook of Geometric Tolerancing: Design, Manufacturing and Inspection.* Wiley, 1995.

Kennedy, C.W., E.G. Hoffman, and S.D. Bond, *Inspection and Gaging* (6th ed.). Industrial Press, 1987.

Liggett, J.V., *Dimensional Variation Management Handbook: A Guide for Quality, Design, and Manufacturing Engineers.* Prentice Hall, 1993.

Machinery's Handbook. Industrial Press (revised periodically).

Meadows, J.D., *Geometric Dimensioning and Tolerancing.* Marcel Dekker, 1995.

———, *Measurement of Geometric Tolerances in Manufacturing.* Marcel Dekker, 1998.

Tool and Manufacturing Engineers Handbook (4th ed.), Vol. 4: *Quality Control and Assembly.* Society of Manufacturing Engineers, 1987.

Whitehouse, D.J., *Handbook of Surface Metrology.* IOP Publishing, 1994.

Wilson, B.A., *Design Dimensioning and Tolerancing.* Goodheart–Wilcox, 1996.

———, *Dimensioning and Tolerancing Handbook.* Genium, 1998.

REVIEW QUESTIONS

35.1 Explain what is meant by "standards for measurement."

35.2 Why is it important to control temperature during measurement of dimensions?

35.3 Explain the difference between direct- and indirect-reading linear measurements. Name the instruments used in each category.

35.4 Describe the principle of a vernier.

35.5 Explain how a diffraction grating works.

35.6 What is meant by "comparative length measurement"?

35.7 Describe the characteristics of electronic gages.

35.8 Explain how flatness is measured. What is an optical flat?

35.9 Describe the principle of an optical comparator.

35.10 Why have coordinate measuring machines become important instruments?

35.11 Why are there different grades of gage blocks?

35.12 What is the difference between a plug gage and a ring gage?

35.13 Describe what is meant by "automated inspection."

35.14 List and explain the general characteristics of measuring instruments.

35.15 What are dimensional tolerances? Why is their control important?

35.16 Explain the difference between tolerance and allowance.

35.17 Explain what is meant by "fit of mating parts."

35.18 What is a sine bar? Why does it have this name?

35.19 What is the difference between bilateral and unilateral tolerance?

35.20 How is straightness measured?

35.21 How are indirect length measurements made?

QUALITATIVE PROBLEMS

35.22 Why are the words "accuracy" and "precision" so often incorrectly interchanged?

35.23 Explain why a particular instrument may not have sufficient precision.

35.24 Explain how the presence of moisture and oil between gage blocks develops negative pressure.

35.25 Why do manufacturing processes produce parts with a wide range of tolerances?

35.26 Explain the need for automated inspection.

35.27 Dimensional tolerances for nonmetallic stock are usually wider than for metallic materials. Explain why.

35.28 Comment on your observations regarding Fig. 35.23. Why does dimensional tolerance increase with increasing surface roughness?

35.29 Can the gages shown in Fig. 35.18 be automated for use in a high-production facility? Give examples.

35.30 It was stated in Section 35.7.1 that zirconia ceramic gage blocks are now being made. What are the advantages and limitations of such gages?

35.31 How would you go about specifying dimensional tolerances in a layout machine application concerning an automobile door? What would be the consequences of exceeding these tolerance limits?

35.32 Review Fig. 35.22 and comment on the range of tolerances and part dimensions produced by various manufacturing processes.

35.33 Describe your thoughts on the merits and limitations of digital measuring equipment over analog. Give specific examples.

35.34 A shaft must meet a design requirement of being at least 1.25 in. in diameter, but it can be 0.01 in. oversized. Express the shaft's tolerance as it would appear on an engineering drawing.

35.35 What are the differences between the Gage Maker's Rule and the Mil Standard Rule? What are the implications for measurement devices which must conform to these rules?

35.36 In the game of darts, is it better to be accurate or precise?

35.37 What are the advantages and disadvantages of GO and NOT GO gages?

QUANTITATIVE PROBLEMS

35.38 Assume that a steel rule expands by 0.15% due to an increase in environmental temperature. What will be the indicated diameter of a shaft whose diameter at room temperature was 2.000 in.?

35.39 Sketch a vernier similar to the ones shown in Fig. 35.3b to read 0.106 in. for the upper illustration and 0.3997 in. for the lower illustration.

35.40 Sketch a vernier similar to the one shown in Fig. 35.4b to read (a) 15° 17' and (b) 2° 56'.

35.41 Calculate the included angle of the part being measured in Fig. 35.5 if the height of the gage blocks is 4.2400 in. and the distance between the centers of the round bars under the sine bar is 5.00 in.

35.42 If the same steel rule as in problem 35.38 is used to measure aluminum extrusions, what will be the indicated diameter of a part that was 2.000 in. at room temperature? What is the actual dimension? What if the part were a thermoplastic?

35.43 For a sine bar where the round bars are 10 in. apart, what height of gage blocks leads to a 45° angle from horizontal?

SYNTHESIS AND DESIGN

35.44 Make some simple sketches of various forming and cutting machine tools (see Parts III and IV) and integrate them with the various types of equipment described in this chapter. Comment on the possible difficulties involved.

35.45   Give several engineering examples for the fits described in this chapter. Comment on your selection of fits for a particular application.

35.46 Obtain one or more of the following parts and describe how you would measure as many of the key dimensions as possible; include the type of instruments to be used and the measurement method. (a) An automotive brake pad, (b) A plastic soft-drink bottle, and (c) A compact disc or floppy disk.

36

Quality Assurance, Testing, and Inspection

36.1 INTRODUCTION

Throughout this text we have observed that a manufactured product develops certain external and internal characteristics which result, in part, from the production processes used. External characteristics most commonly involve dimensions and size, and surface finish and integrity issues such as surface damage from cutting tools or friction during processing of the workpiece.

Internal characteristics include various defects, such as porosity, impurities, inclusions, phase transformations, embrittlement, cracks, debonding of laminations, and residual stresses. Some of these defects may exist in the original stock; some are introduced or induced during the manufacturing operation.

Before they are marketed, manufactured parts and products are inspected for several characteristics. This inspection routine is particularly important, to (a) ensure dimensional accuracy so that parts fit properly during assembly and (b) identify products whose failure or malfunction has potentially serious implications, such as bodily injury or fatality.

Typical examples are the fracture or failure of cables, switches, brakes, grinding wheels, railroad wheels, turbine blades, pressure vessels, and welded joints. This chapter identifies and describes the various methods that are commonly used to inspect manufactured products.

Product quality has always been one of the most important aspects of manufacturing operations. In view of the present global economy and competition, **continuous improvement in quality** has become a major priority, particularly for major corporations in the U.S. and other industrialized countries. In Japan, for example, the single term **kaizen** is used; it signifies never-ending improvement.

Prevention of defects in products and on-line inspection are major goals in manufacturing activities. We again emphasize that *quality must be built into a product* and not merely checked after the product has been made. Thus, close cooperation and communication between design and manufacturing engineers and direct involvement and encouragement of the company management are vital.

Major advances in quality engineering and productivity have been made, largely because of the efforts of quality experts such as Deming, Taguchi, and Juran. The importance of quality, reliability, and safety of products in a global economy is now being recognized internationally by the establishment of the ISO 9000 standard and other standards, and in the U.S. by the Malcolm Baldrige National Quality Award.

36.2 PRODUCT QUALITY

We have all used terms like "poor quality" or "high quality" to describe a particular product, a certain store, or the products of a particular company. What is quality? Although we may recognize it when we see or use a product, quality, unlike most technical terms, is difficult to define precisely.

Quality has been defined as:

a. a product's fitness for use, and

b. the totality of features and characteristics that bear on a product's ability to satisfy a given need. More recently, several dimensions of quality have been identified, including the product's performance, features, conformance, durability, reliability, serviceability, aesthetics, and perceived quality.

Quality is a broadbased characteristic or property; its factors consist of not only well-defined technical considerations, but subjective opinions as well. For example: (a) the handle on a kitchen utensil that has been installed crookedly, (b) a product which has walls so thin that it warps when subjected to small forces or temperature variations, (c) a calculator or weighing scale that functions erratically, and (d) a machine tool that cannot maintain the dimensional tolerances of the workpiece because of lack of stiffness or poor construction. These examples all lead us to believe that the product is of low quality.

The public's perception is that a high-quality product is one which performs its functions reliably over a long period of time, without breaking down or requiring repairs. A few examples of this type of product are "good quality" refrigerators, washing machines, automobiles, bicycles, and kitchen knives. If, on the other hand, the stem of a screwdriver bends, its handle discolors or cracks, or its tip chips off or wears out more rapidly than we had expected, we say that this screwdriver is of low quality.

Note that, in describing good- or poor-quality products, this text has not yet stated the lifetimes of products or any of their technical specifications. We have seen that design and manufacturing engineers have the responsibility and freedom to select and specify materials for the products to be made.

Thus, when selecting the metal for a screwdriver stem, we can specify materials that have high strength and high resistance to wear and corrosion. As a result, the screwdriver will perform better and last longer than one made of materials with inferior properties.

It must be noted , however, that materials possessing better properties are generally more expensive and may even be more difficult to process than those with poorer properties. Moreover, because the range of available materials and their properties is so broad, manufacturers have usually set some limit on expected product life.

The following are some examples of typical life expectancies:

Dollar bills: 18 months

Car batteries: 4 years

Hair dryers: 5 years

Water heaters for homes: 10 years

Vacuum cleaners: 10 years

Air conditioning units: 15 years

Nuclear reactors: 40 years

Automobile disk brakes: 65,000 km (40,000 miles)

Mufflers: 50,000 km (30,000 miles)

Tires: 65,000–100,000 km (40,000–60,000 miles)

The level of quality that a manufacturer chooses for its products may depend on the market for which the products are intended. For example, low-cost, low-quality tools have their own market niche. Even this sort of product, however, has its own required quality performance. Quality standards are essentially a balance between several considerations; this balance is also called **return on quality (ROQ)**.

As described in Chapter 40, the total product cost depends on several variables, including the level of automation in the manufacturing plant. Thus, there are many ways for the engineer to review and modify overall product design and manufacturing processes to minimize a product's cost, without affecting its quality.

Contrary to general public perception, quality products do not necessarily cost more. In fact, higher quality can actually result in lower cost; consider the fact that poor-quality products

a. have the significant built-in cost of customer dissatisfaction.

b. make for difficulties in assembling and maintaining components.

c. result in the need for in-field repairs.

36.3 QUALITY ASSURANCE

Quality assurance can be defined as all actions necessary to ensure that quality requirements will be satisfied, whereas *quality control* is the set of operational techniques used to fulfill requirements for quality. Quality assurance is the total effort made by a manufacturer to ensure that its products conform to a detailed set of specifications and standards.

These standards cover several types of parameters, such as dimensions, surface finish, tolerances, composition, and color, as well as mechanical, physical, and chemical properties. In addition, standards are usually written to ensure proper assembly, using interchangeable defect-free components and resulting in a product that performs as originally intended by its designers.

Quality assurance is the responsibility of everyone involved with design and manufacturing. The often-repeated statement that quality must be built into a product reflects this important concept. Although a finished product can be inspected for quality, quality cannot be inspected *into* a finished product.

Increased domestic and global competition has caused quality assurance to become even more important. Every aspect of design and manufacturing operations (such as material selection, production, and assembly) is now being analyzed in detail to ensure that quality is truly built into the final product.

An important aspect of quality assurance is the capability to analyze defects and promptly eliminate them or reduce them to acceptable levels. In an even broader sense, quality assurance involves evaluating the product and customer satisfaction. The sum total of all these activities is referred to as **total quality control (TQC)**, and, in a larger sense, **total quality management**.

It is clear that in order to control quality, we have to be able to

a. measure quantitatively the level of quality, and
b. identify all the material and process variables that can be controlled.

The level of quality built in during production can then be checked by inspecting the product to determine whether it meets the specifications for dimensional tolerances, surface finish, defects, and other characteristics.

36.4 TOTAL QUALITY MANAGEMENT

Total quality management is a management system which emphasizes the idea that quality must be designed and built into a product. **Defect prevention**, rather than *defect detection*, is the major goal. Total quality management is a systems approach in that both management and workers make a concerted effort to consistently manufacture high-quality products.

Leadership and *teamwork* in the organization are essential; they ensure that the goal of **continuous improvement** of manufacturing operations is kept in sight at all times, they reduce product variability, and they improve *customer satisfaction*. The TQM concept also requires us to **control the processes**, *not* the parts produced, so that no defective parts are allowed to continue through the production line.

A related concept is the **quality circle**. This concept consists of regular meetings by groups of workers who discuss how to improve and maintain product quality at all stages of the manufacturing process. Worker involvement and responsibility are emphasized, and comprehensive training is provided so that the worker can become capable of analyzing statistical data, identifying causes of poor quality, and taking immediate action to correct the situation. Putting this concept into practice requires the recognition of quality assurance as a major company-wide management policy which affects all personnel and all aspects of production.

In recognition of the importance of quality in manufacturing in the United States, the *Malcolm Baldrige National Quality Award* was established in 1988. Named after a former U.S. secretary of commerce, the purposes of this award are to:

a. promote awareness and understanding of the importance of quality improvement to the nation's economy,
b. recognize companies for outstanding quality management and achievement, and
c. share nonproprietary information on successful quality strategies.

The award's main criteria concern two key competitiveness thrusts: delivery of ever-improving value to customers, and systematic and continued improvement of a company's overall operational performance.

Quality Engineering as a Philosophy.   Certain experts in quality control have put into larger perspective many of the quality-control concepts and methods described thus far. Notable among these experts are Deming, Juran, and Taguchi, whose philosophies of quality and product cost have had a major impact on modern manufacturing. Their philosophies of quality engineering are outlined below.

36.4.1 Deming Methods

During World War II, W.E. Deming (1900–1993) and several others developed new methods of statistical process control for war-industry manufacturing plants. The methods of statistical control arose from the recognition that there were variations in (a) the performance of machines and people and (b) the quality and dimensions of raw materials. Their efforts involved not only statistical methods of analysis, but also a new way of looking at manufacturing operations: from the perspective of improving quality and lowering costs.

Deming recognized that manufacturing organizations are systems of management, workers, machines, and products. His basic ideas are summarized in the now-famous 14 Points, which are summarized in Table 36.1. These points are not to be seen as a checklist or menu of tasks; they are the characteristics that Deming recognized in companies that produce high quality goods.

Note that Deming placed great emphasis on communication, direct worker involvement, and education in statistics and modern manufacturing technology. His ideas have been widely accepted in Japan since the end of World War II, but only recently have some segments of the U.S. manufacturing community begun to implement them.

TABLE 36.1   Deming's 14 Points

1.	Create constancy of purpose toward improvement of product and service.
2.	Adopt the new philosophy.
3.	Cease dependence on mass inspection to achieve quality.
4.	End the practice of awarding business on the basis of price tag.
5.	Improve constantly and forever the system of production and service, to improve quality and productivity, and thus constantly decrease cost.
6.	Institute training on the job.
7.	Institute leadership (as opposed to supervision).
8.	Drive out fear so that everyone can work effectively.
9.	Break down barriers between departments.
10.	Eliminate slogans, exhortations and targets for zero defects and new levels of productivity.
11.	Eliminate quotas and management by numbers, numerical goals. Substitute leadership.
12.	Remove barriers that rob the hourly worker of pride of workmanship.
13.	Institute a vigorous program of education and self-improvement.
14.	Put everybody in the company to work to accomplish the transformation.

36.4.2 Juran Methods

A contemporary of Deming, J.M. Juran (1904–), emphasizes the following ideas:

a. Recognizing quality at all levels of an organization, including upper management.

b. Fostering a responsive corporate culture.

c. Training all personnel in how to *plan*, *control*, and *improve* quality.

The concern of the top management in an organization is with business and management, whereas those in quality control are concerned with technology. These different worlds have often been at odds, and their conflicts have led to quality problems.

Planners determine who the customers are and what their needs are. An organization's customers may be external (the end users who purchase the product or service), or they may be internal (the different parts of an organization that rely on other segments of the organization to supply them with products and services).

The planners then develop product and process designs to respond to the customer's needs. The plans are then turned over to those in charge of operations, who are responsible for quality control and continued improvement in quality.

36.5 TAGUCHI METHODS

In the G. Taguchi (1924–) methods, high quality and low costs are achieved by combining engineering and statistical methods to optimize product design and manufacturing processes. Loss of quality is defined as the financial loss to society after the product is shipped, with the following results:

a. Poor quality leads to customer dissatisfaction.

b. Costs are incurred in servicing and repairing defective products, some in the field.

c. The manufacturer's credibility in the marketplace is diminished.

d. The manufacturer eventually loses its share of the market.

The Taguchi methods of quality engineering emphasize the importance of

- enhancing **cross-functional team interaction**. In this interaction, design engineers and process or manufacturing engineers communicate with each other in a common language. They quantify the relationships between design requirements and manufacturing process selection. (See also Section 3 in the General Introduction).

- implementing **experimental design**, in which the factors involved in a process or operation and their interactions are studied simultaneously.

In experimental design, the effects of controllable and uncontrollable variables on the product are identified. This approach minimizes variations in product dimensions and properties, and ultimately brings the mean to the desired level.

The methods used for experimental design are complex; they involve the use of **factorial design** and orthogonal arrays, which reduce the number of experiments required. These methods are also capable of identifying the effects of variables that cannot be controlled (called *noise*), such as changes in environmental conditions.

The use of these methods results in (a) rapid identification of the controlling variables (observing *main effects*) and (b) the ability to determine the best method of process control. The control of these variables which takes place next, sometimes requires new equipment or major modifications to existing equipment. For example, variables affecting dimensional tolerances in machining a particular component can be readily identified and, whenever possible, the correct cutting speed, feed, cutting tool, and cutting fluids can be specified.

An important concept introduced by Taguchi is that any deviation from a design objective constitutes a loss in quality. Consider, for example, the tolerancing standards in Fig. 35.24. There is a range of dimensions over which a part is acceptable. The Taguchi philosophy calls for a minimization of deviation about the design objective.

Thus, using Figure 35.24a as an example, a shaft with a diameter of 40.03 mm would normally be considered acceptable and would pass inspections. In the Taguchi approach, however, the part with this diameter represents a deviation from the design objective. Such deviations generally reduce the robustness (see below) and performance of products, especially in complicated systems.

36.5.1 Robustness

Another aspect of quality is a concept, originally suggested by Taguchi, which has continuously grown in importance and is referred to as *robustness*. A robust design, process, or system is one that continues to function within acceptable parameters despite variabilities (often unanticipated variabilities) in its environment. In other words, its outputs, such as its function and performance, have minimal sensitivity to its input variations such as environment, load, and power source. In addition, robustness refers to a product or machine performance being insensitive to tolerance changes, and the performance should not deteriorate significantly over its intended life.

For example, in a robust part design, the part will function sufficiently well even if the loads applied, or their directions, go beyond anticipated values. Likewise, a robust machine or system will undergo minimal degradation in performance even if it experiences unanticipated variations in environmental conditions such as temperature, humidity, and vibrations. Also, a robust machine will have no significant drop in performance over its life, whereas a less robust design will perform less efficiently as time passes.

As a simple illustration of robust design, consider a sheet-metal mounting bracket to be attached to a wall with two bolts (Fig. 36.1a). The positioning of the two mounting holes on the bracket will include some error, due to the manufacturing process involved. This error will then prevent the top edge of the bracket from being perfectly horizontal.

A more robust design is shown in Fig. 36.1b, in which the mounting holes have been moved twice as far apart as in the first design. Even though the precision of hole location remains the same and the manufacturing cost is also the same, the variability in the top edge of the bracket has been reduced by one half. However, if the bracket is subjected to vibration, the bolts may loosen over time. The more robust design approach would be to use an adhesive to hold the threads in place or to use some type of fastener which would not loosen over time.

FIGURE 36.1   A simple example of robust design. (a) Location of two mounting holes on a sheet-metal bracket, where the deviation of the top surface of the bracket from being perfectly horizontal is $\pm\alpha$. (b) New location of holes, whereby the deviation of the top surface of the bracket from being perfectly horizontal is reduced to $\pm\alpha/2$.

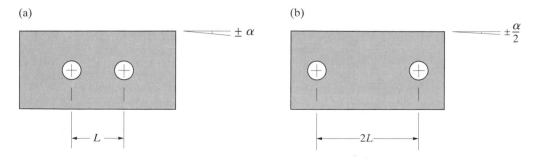

36.5.2 Taguchi Loss Function

Because traditional accounting practices had no real way of calculating losses on parts that met design specifications, the Taguchi loss function was introduced. In the traditional accounting approach, a part is defective and incurs a loss to the company when it exceeds its design tolerances; otherwise, there is no loss to the company.

The Taguchi loss function calculates an increasing loss to the company, the further the component is from the design objective. This function is defined as a parabola, where one point is the cost of replacement (including shipping, scrapping, and handling costs) at an extreme of the tolerances, while a second point corresponds to zero loss at the design objective.

Mathematically, the loss cost can be written as

$$\text{Loss cost} = k\left[(Y - T)^2 + s^2\right], \tag{36.1}$$

where Y is the mean value from manufacturing, T is the target value from design, s is the standard deviation of parts from manufacturing, and k is a constant, defined as

$$k = \frac{\text{Replacement cost}}{(LSL - T)^2}, \tag{36.2}$$

where LSL is the lower specification limit. When the lower (LSL) and upper (USL) specification limits are the same (that is, the tolerances are balanced), either of the limits can be used in this equation.

Example: Production of Polymer Tubing

High-quality polymer tubes are being produced for medical applications, where the target wall thickness is 2.6 mm, with an upper specification limit of 3.2 mm and a lower specification limit of 2.0 mm. If the units are defective, they are replaced at a shipping-included cost of $10.00. The current process produces parts with a mean of 2.6 mm and a standard deviation of 0.2 mm. The current volume is 10,000 sections of tube per month.

An improvement is being considered for the extruder heating system. This improvement will cut the variation in half, but it costs $50,000. Determine the Taguchi loss function and the payback period for both cases.

Solution: We first identify the quantities involved as follows: $USL = 3.2$ mm, $LSL = 2.0$ mm, $T = 2.6$ mm, $s = 0.2$ mm, and $Y = 2.6$ mm.

The quantity k is given by

$$k = \frac{(\$10.00)}{(3.2 - 2.6)^2} = \$27.78 \,.$$

The loss cost is then

$$\text{Loss cost} = (27.78)\left[(2.6 - 2.6)^2 + 0.2^2\right] = \$1.11 \text{ per unit.}$$

After the improvement, the standard deviation is 0.1 mm; thus, the loss cost is

$$\text{Loss cost} = (27.78)\left[(2.6 - 2.6)^2 + 0.1^2\right] = \$0.28 \text{ per unit.}$$

The savings are then $(\$1.11\text{-}\$0.28)(10{,}000) = \$8300$ per month. Hence, the payback period for the investment is $\$50{,}000 / (\$8300/\text{month}) = 6.02$ months.

Example: Manufacture of Televisions by Sony Corp.

Sony Corporation executives found a confusing situation confronting them in the mid-1980s. Televisions produced in Japanese production facilities were better sellers than televisions produced in a San Diego facility, even though the two types were produced from identical designs and blueprints. There were no marks distinguishing the televisions made in Japan from those made in the U.S., so there was no apparent reason for the discrepancy.

However, investigations revealed that the televisions produced in Japan were superior to the American versions; color sharpness was better and hues were more brilliant. Since the televisions were on display in stores, consumers could easily detect and purchase the model that had the best picture.

The difference in quality was clear, but the reasons for this difference were not clear. A further point of confusion was the constant assurance that the San Diego facility had a total quality program in place, and that it was maintaining quality control standards so that no defective parts were produced. The Japanese facility did not have a total quality program, but there was an emphasis on reducing variation from part to part.

Further investigations found a typical pattern in an integrated circuit that was critical in affecting color density. The distribution of parts meeting the color-design objective is shown in Fig. 36.2a; the Taguchi loss function for these parts is shown in Fig. 36.2b.

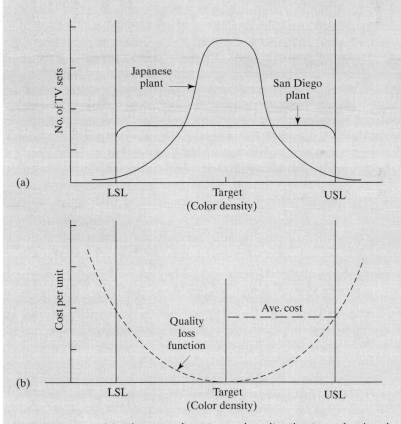

FIGURE 36.2   (a) Objective function value distribution of color density for television sets. (b) Taguchi loss function, showing the average replacement cost per unit to correct quality problems. *Source*: After G. Taguchi.

In the San Diego facility, where the number of defective parts was minimized (zero in this case), a uniform distribution within the specification limits was achieved.

The Japanese facility actually produced parts outside of the design specification, but the standard deviation about the mean was lower. Using the Taguchi loss function approach (see preceding Example), the San Diego facility lost about $1.33 per unit, while the Japanese facility lost $0.44 per unit.

Traditional quality viewpoints would find the uniform distribution without defects to be superior to the distribution where a few defects are produced but the majority of parts are closer to the design target values. However, consumers can readily detect which product is superior, and the marketplace proves that minimizing deviations is a worthwhile quality goal. The Taguchi loss function is a tool for comparing quality, based on minimizing variations *Source*: After D.M. Byrne and S. Taguchi.

Example: Increasing Quality Without Increasing the Cost of a Product

A manufacturer of clay tiles noticed that, because of temperature variations in the kiln used to fire the tiles, excessive scrap was being produced and adversely affecting the company's profits. The first solution which the manufacturer considered was purchasing new kilns with better temperature controls.

This solution, however, would require a major capital investment. A study was then undertaken to determine whether modifications could be made in the composition of the tile so that it would be less sensitive to temperature fluctuations during firing.

Based on factorial experiment design, in which the factors involved in a process and their interactions are studied simultaneously, it was found that increasing the lime content of the tiles made them less sensitive to temperature variations during firing. This modification, which was also the low-cost alternative, was implemented, reducing scrap substantially and improving tile quality.

36.6 THE ISO AND QS STANDARDS

With increasing international trade, global manufacturing, and price-sensitive competition have come a wide choice of industrial and consumer products. Customers are increasingly demanding **high-quality products** and services at low prices, and are looking for suppliers that can respond to this demand consistently and reliably.

This trend has, in turn, created the need for international conformity and consensus regarding the establishment of methods for quality control, reliability, and safety of a product. In addition to these considerations, equally important concerns regarding the environment and quality of life are now being addressed with new international standards. In this section, we describe the standards that are relevant to product quality and environmental issues.

36.6.1 The ISO 9000 Standard

First issued in 1987, and then revised in 1994, the ISO 9000 standard (*Quality Management and Quality Assurance Standards*) is a deliberately generic series of quality-system management standards. The ISO 9000 standard has permanently influenced the way manufacturing companies conduct business in world trade, and has become the world standard for quality.

The ISO 9000 series includes the following standards:

- ISO 9001 — *Quality systems: Model for quality assurance in design/development, production, installation, and servicing.*

- ISO 9002 — *Quality systems: Model for quality assurance in production and installation.*

- ISO 9003 — *Quality systems: Model for quality assurance in final inspection and test.*

- ISO 9004 — *Quality management and quality system elements: Guidelines.*

Companies voluntarily register for these standards and are issued certificates. Registration may be sought generally for ISO 9001 or 9002, and some companies have registration up to ISO 9003. The 9004 standard is simply a guideline and not a model or basis for registration. For certification, a company's plants are visited and audited by accredited and independent third-party teams to certify that the standard's 20 key elements are in place and functioning properly.

Depending on the extent to which a company fails to meet the requirements of the standard, registration may or may not be recommended at that time. The audit team does not advise or consult with the company on how to fix discrepancies, but merely describes the nature of the noncompliance.

Periodic audits are required to maintain certification. The certification process can take from six months to a year or more, and can cost tens of thousands of dollars; cost depends on the company's size, number of plants, and product line.

The ISO 9000 standard is not a product certification, it is a **quality process certification**. Companies establish their own criteria and practices for quality. However, the documented quality system must be in compliance with the ISO 9000 standard; thus, a company cannot write into the system any criterion which opposes the intent of the standard.

Registration symbolizes a company's commitment to conform to consistent practices, as specified by the company's own quality system (such as quality in design, development, production, installation, and servicing), including proper documentation of such practice. In this way, customers, including government agencies, are assured that the supplier of the product or service (which may or may not be within the same country) is following specified practices. In fact, manufacturing companies are themselves assured of such practice regarding their own suppliers who have ISO 9000 registration; they are now demanding that their suppliers also be registered.

36.6.2 The QS 9000 Standard

The QS 9000 was first published in August 1994; Chrysler, Ford, and General Motors jointly developed this standard. Prior to the development of QS 9000, each of the Big Three automotive companies had its own standard for quality system requirements.

Tier I suppliers have been required to obtain third-party registration to QS 9000 before dates established by each of the Big Three companies. Very often, QS 9000 has been described as an "ISO 9000 chassis with a lot of extras." This is a good description, seeing that all of the ISO 9000 clauses serve as the foundation of QS 9000; however, the little "extras" are substantial.

The February 1995 edition of QS 9000 has three sections. Section I contains all 20 of the ISO 9001 clauses, but almost every clause has additional requirements for QS 9000. Section II has three sections: Production Part Approval Process, Continuous Improvement, and Manufacturing Capabilities. Section III is entitled Customer-Specific Requirements, and contains separate sections for Chrysler, General Motors, Ford, and Truck Manufacturers, respectively. Existing QS 9000 registrations are continuously being upgraded to comply with new editions of QS 9000.

36.6.3 The ISO 14000 Standard

ISO 14000 is a family of standards, first published in September 1996, pertaining to international **Environmental Management Systems (EMS)**. It concerns the way an organization's activities affect the environment throughout the life of its products (see also Section 11 in the General Introduction). These activities (a) may be internal or external to the organization, (b) range from production to ultimate disposal of the product after its useful life, and (c) include effects on the environment such as pollution, waste generation and disposal, noise, depletion of natural resources, and energy use.

A rapidly increasing number of companies in many countries (with Japan leading) have been obtaining certification for this standard. The ISO 14000 family of standards has several sections: Guidelines for Environmental Auditing, Environmental Assessment, Environmental Labels and Declarations, and Environmental Management. ISO 14001: *Environmental Management System Requirements* consists of sections on General Requirements, Environmental Policy, Planning, Implementation and Operation, Checking and Corrective Action, and Management Review.

36.7 STATISTICAL METHODS OF QUALITY CONTROL

The study of **statistics** deals with the collection, analysis, interpretation, and presentation of large amounts of numerical data. Because of the large amount of material and number of process variables involved, the use of statistical techniques in modern manufacturing operations is essential. The following are some of the commonly observed variables in manufacturing:

- Cutting tools, dies, and molds are subject to wear; thus, part dimensions and surface characteristics vary over a period of time.
- Machinery performs differently depending on its age, condition, and maintenance. Thus, older machines tend to vibrate, are difficult to adjust, and do not maintain tolerances as well as new machines.
- Metalworking fluids (coolants and lubricants) perform differently as they degrade; thus, tool and die life, surface finish of the workpiece, and forces and energy requirements are affected.
- Environmental conditions, such as temperature, humidity, and air quality in the plant, may change from one hour to the next, affecting machines, workspaces, and employees.
- Different shipments of raw materials may have significantly different dimensions, properties, and surface characteristics.

- Operator skill and attention may vary during the day, from machine to machine or from operator to operator.

In the preceding list, those events that occur randomly, that is, without any particular trend or pattern, are called **chance variations** or **special cause**. Those that can be traced to specific causes are called **assignable variations** or **common cause**.

The existence of *variability* in production operations has been recognized for centuries, but Eli Whitney (1765–1825) first grasped its full significance when he found that interchangeable parts were indispensable to the mass production of firearms. Modern statistical concepts relevant to manufacturing engineering were first developed in the early 1900s, notably through the work of W.A. Shewhart (1891–1967).

36.7.1 Statistical Quality Control

To understand **statistical quality control (SQC)**, let's first review some of the terms that are commonly used:

a. **Sample size.** The number of parts to be inspected in a sample; the properties of the parts in the sample are studied to gain information about the whole population.

b. **Random sampling.** Taking a sample from a population or lot in which each item has an equal chance of being included in the sample. Thus, when taking samples from a large bin, the inspector does not take only those that happen to be within reach.

c. **Population.** The total number of individual parts of the same design from which samples are taken; also called the **universe**.

d. **Lot size.** A subset of population. A lot or several lots can be considered subsets of the population and may be considered as representative of the population.

The sample is inspected for several characteristics and features, such as tolerances, surface finish, and defects, using the instruments and techniques described in Chapter 35 and Sections 36.10 and 36.11. These characteristics fall into two categories: those that can be measured quantitatively (method of variables) and those that are measured qualitatively (method of attributes).

1. The **method of variables** is the *quantitative* measurement of the part's characteristics: dimensions, tolerances, surface finish, or physical or mechanical properties. Such measurements are made for each of the units in the group under consideration, and the results are compared against specifications.

2. The **method of attributes** involves observing the presence or absence of *qualitative* characteristics such as external or internal defects in machined, formed, or welded parts or dents in sheet-metal products, in each of the units in the group under consideration. Sample size for attributes-type data is generally larger than for variables-type data.

During the inspection process, the results of the measurement will vary. For example, assume that you are measuring the diameter of turned shafts as they are produced on a lathe, using a micrometer (Fig. 35.3). You soon note that their diameters vary, even though, ideally, you want all the shafts to be exactly the same size.

Let's now turn to consideration of statistical quality-control techniques, which allow us to evaluate these variations and set limits for the acceptance of parts. If you list the measured diameters of the turned shafts in a given population, you will note that one or more parts have the smallest diameter, and one or more have the largest diameter. The rest of the turned shafts have diameters that lie between these extremes.

If we group these diameters and plot them, the plot consists of a *histogram* (bar graph) representing the number of parts in each diameter group (Fig. 36.3a). The bars show a **distribution**, also called a *spread* or *dispersion*, of the shaft-diameter measurements. The *bell-shaped curve* in Fig. 36.3a is called a **frequency distribution**, or the frequency with which parts of each diameter size are being produced.

Data from manufacturing processes often fit curves represented by a mathematically derived **normal distribution curve** (Fig. 36.3b). This type of curve is also called *Gaussian*, after K. F. Gauss (1777–1855), who developed it on the basis of probability. The bell-shaped Normal distribution curve fitted to the data in Fig. 36.3a has two important features.

First, it shows that most part diameters tend to cluster around an *average* value (**arithmetic mean**). This average is usually designated as $\bar{x}$ and is calculated from the expression

$$\bar{x} = \frac{(x_1 + x_2 + x_3 \dots x_n)}{n},$$

(36.3)

where the numerator is the sum of all measured values (shaft diameters), and n is the number of measurements (number of shafts).

The second feature of this curve is its width, indicating the **dispersion** of the diameters measured; the wider the curve, the greater the dispersion. The difference between the largest value and the smallest value is called the **range**, R:

$$R = x_{\max} - x_{\min}$$

(36.4)

Dispersion is estimated by the **standard deviation**, σ, and is given by the expression

$$\sigma = \frac{\sqrt{(x_1 - \bar{x})^2 + (x_2 - \bar{x})^2 + \dots + (x_n - \bar{x})^2}}{n - 1},$$

(36.5)

where x_i is the measured value for each part.

FIGURE 36.3   (a) A histogram of the number of shafts measured and their respective diameters. This type of curve is called frequency distribution. (b) A Normal distribution curve indicating areas within each range of standard deviation. *Note*: the greater the range, the higher the percentage of parts that fall within it.

(a)

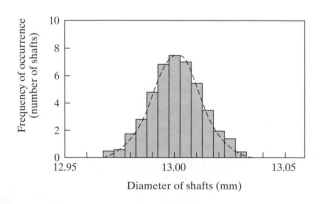

(b)

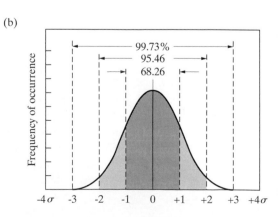

Note from the numerator in Eq. (36.5) that as the curve widens, the standard deviation becomes greater. Also note that σ has the unit of linear dimension. In comparing Eqs. (36.4) and (36.5), it can be seen that the range, R, is a simpler and more convenient measure of dispersion.

Since we know the number of turned parts that fall within each group, we can calculate the percentage of the total population represented by each group. Thus, Fig. 36.3b shows that in the measurement of shaft diameters,

99.73% fall within the range of $\pm 3\sigma$,

95.46% within $\pm 2\sigma$, and

68.26% within $\pm 1\sigma$.

Hence, only 0.27% fall outside $\pm 3\sigma$ range. Note, however, that these quantities are only valid for distributions that are Normal (as shown in Fig. 36.3) and are not skewed.

36.8 STATISTICAL PROCESS CONTROL

If the number of parts that do not meet set standards (defective parts) increases during a production run, we must be able to determine the cause (incoming materials, machine controls, degradation of metalworking fluids, operator boredom, or others) and take appropriate action. Although this statement at first appears to be self-evident, it was only in the early 1950s that a systematic statistical approach was developed to guide operators in manufacturing plants.

This approach advises the operator to take certain measures and actions and tells the operator when to take them in order to avoid producing further defective parts. Known as **statistical process control (SPC)**, this technique consists of several elements:

a. Control charts and control limits,

b. Capabilities of the particular manufacturing process, and

c. Characteristics of the machinery involved.

36.8.1 $\bar{x}$ and R Charts (Shewhart Control Charts)

The frequency distribution curve in Fig. 36.3b shows a range of shaft diameters being produced that may fall beyond the design tolerance range. Figure 36.4 shows the same bell-shaped curve, which now includes the specified tolerances for the diameter of turned shafts.

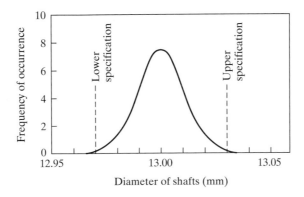

FIGURE 36.4   Frequency distribution curve, showing lower and upper specification limits.

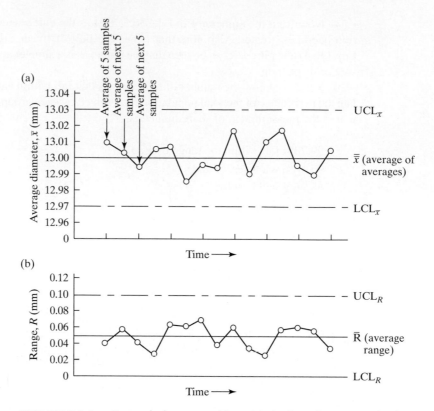

FIGURE 36.5   Control charts used in statistical quality control. The process shown is in statistical control because all points fall within the lower and upper control limits. In this illustration sample size is five and the number of samples is 15.

Control charts graphically represent the variations of a process over a period of time. They consist of data plotted during production. Typically, there are two plots. The quantity $\bar{x}$ (Fig. 36.5a) is the average for each subset of samples taken and inspected, say, a subset consisting of five parts. A sample size of between 2 and 10 parts is sufficiently accurate (although more parts are better), provided that sample size is held constant throughout inspection.

The frequency of sampling depends on the nature of the process. Some processes may require continual sampling, whereas others may require only one sample per day. Quality-control analysts are best qualified to determine this frequency for a particular application. Since the measurements in Fig. 36.5a are made consecutively, the abscissa of these control charts also represents time.

The solid horizontal line in this figure is the **average of averages (grand average)**, denoted as $\bar{\bar{x}}$, and represents the population mean. The upper and lower horizontal broken lines in these control charts indicate the **control limits** for the process.

The control limits are set on these charts according to statistical-control formulas designed to keep actual production within acceptable variation levels. One common approach is to make sure that all parts are within three standard deviations of the mean ($\pm 3\sigma$). The standard deviation can be expressed as a function of range. Thus, for $\bar{x}$, we have

$$\text{Upper control limit } \left(\text{UCL}_{\bar{x}}\right) = \bar{x} + 3\sigma = \bar{\bar{x}} + A_2\bar{R} \qquad (36.6)$$

and

$$\text{Lower control limit } \left(\text{LCL}_{\bar{x}}\right) = \bar{x} - 3\sigma = \bar{\bar{x}} - A_2\bar{R} \qquad (36.7)$$

TABLE 36.2   Constants for Control Charts

Sample size	A_2	D_4	D_3	d_2
2	1.880	3.267	0	1.128
3	1.023	2.575	0	1.693
4	0.729	2.282	0	2.059
5	0.577	2.115	0	2.326
6	0.483	2.004	0	2.534
7	0.419	1.924	0.078	2.704
8	0.373	1.864	0.136	2.847
9	0.337	1.816	0.184	2.970
10	0.308	1.777	0.223	3.078
12	0.266	1.716	0.284	3.258
15	0.223	1.652	0.348	3.472
20	0.180	1.586	0.414	3.735

where A_2 is obtained from Table 36.2, and $\bar{R}$ is the average of R values. The quantities $\bar{\bar{x}}$ and $\bar{R}$ are estimated from the measurements taken.

These control limits are calculated on the basis of the past production capability of the equipment itself; they are not associated with either design tolerance specifications or dimensions. They indicate the limits within which a certain percentage of measured values are normally expected to fall, because of the inherent variations of the process itself, upon which the limits are based.

The major goal of statistical process control is to improve the manufacturing process with the aid of control charts, so as to eliminate assignable causes. The control chart continually indicates progress in this area.

The second control chart (Fig. 36.5b) shows the range, R, in each subset of samples. The solid horizontal line represents the average of R values in the lot, denoted as $\bar{R}$, and is a measure of the variability of the samples. The upper and lower control limits for R are obtained from the equations

$$UCL_R = D_4\bar{R} \tag{36.8}$$

and

$$LCL_R = D_3\bar{R}, \tag{36.9}$$

where the constants D_4 and D_3 take on values given in Table 36.2. This table also includes the constant d_2, which is used to estimate the standard deviation of the process distribution shown in Fig. 36.4 from the equation

$$\sigma = \frac{\bar{R}}{d_2}. \tag{36.10}$$

When the curve of a control chart is like the one shown in Fig. 36.5a, we say that the process is "**in good statistical control**". In other words, (a) there is no discernible trend in the pattern of the curve, (b) the points (measured values) are random with time, and (c) the points do not exceed the control limits.

However, we can see that in curves such as those in Figs. 36.6a, b, and c, there are certain trends. For example, note in the middle of curve (a) that the diameter of the shafts increases with time. The reason for this increase may be a change in one of the process variables, such as wear of the cutting tool.

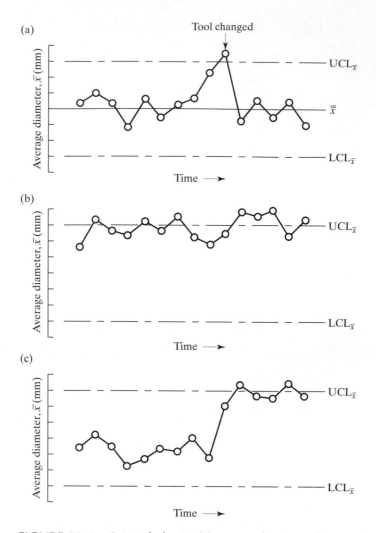

FIGURE 36.6   Control charts. (a) Process begins to become out of control because of such factors as tool wear (*drift*). The tool is changed and the process is then in statistical control. (b) Process parameters are not set properly; thus all parts are around the upper control limit (*shift in mean*). (c) Process becomes out of control because of factors such as a change in the properties of the incoming material (*shift in mean*).

If the trend is of consistently large diameters, as in curve (b), with diameters that hover around the upper control limit, it could mean that the tool settings on the lathe may not be correct, and, as a result, the parts being turned are consistently too large.

Curve (c) shows two distinct trends that may be caused by factors like a change in the properties of the incoming material or a change in the performance of the cutting fluid (for example, its degradation). These situations place the process "**out of control**" *Warning limits* are sometimes set at $\pm 2\sigma$.

Analyzing patterns and trends in control charts requires considerable experience so that one may identify the specific cause(s) of an out-of-control situation. Such causes may be those changes outlined at the beginning of Section 36.7. Overcontrol of the manufacturing process, that is, setting upper and lower control limits too close to each other (hence smaller

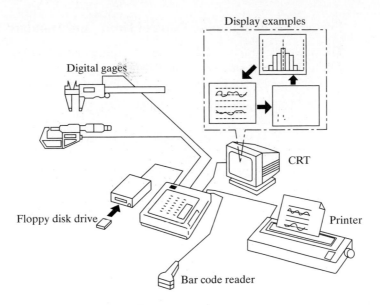

Display examples

Digital gages

CRT

Floppy disk drive

Printer

Bar code reader

FIGURE 36.7   Schematic illustration showing integration of digital gages with microprocessor for real-time data acquisition and SPC/SQC capabilities. Note the examples on the CRT displays, such as frequency distribution (see Fig. 36.3) and control charts (see Fig. 36.4). *Source*: Mitutoyo Corp.

standard deviation range), is a further cause for out-of-control situations. This is the reason that we calculate control limits based on *process variability* rather than on potentially inapplicable criteria.

It is evident that operator training is critical for successful implementation of SPC on the shop floor. Once process control guidelines are established, operators should, in the interest of efficiency of operation, also have some responsibility for making adjustments in processes that are beginning to become out of control. The capabilities of individual operators also should be taken into account so that they are not overloaded with data input and the data's proper interpretation.

This task is being made easier by a variety of software that is being constantly developed. For example, digital readouts on electronic measuring devices are now integrated directly into a computer system for real-time SPC. Figures 36.7a and b show such a multifunctional computer system, in which the output from a digital caliper or micrometer is analyzed by a microprocessor in real time and is displayed in several ways such as frequency distribution curves and control charts.

36.8.2 Process Capability

Process capability is defined as the set of limits within which individual measurement values resulting from a particular manufacturing *process* would normally be expected to fall, when only random variation is present. Thus, process capability tells us that the process can produce parts within certain limits of precision. Since a manufacturing process involves materials, machinery, and operators, each can be analyzed individually to identify a problem when process capabilities do not meet part specifications.

Example: Calculation of Control Limits and Standard Deviation

The data given in Table 36.3 show length measurements (in.) taken on a machined work-piece. The sample size is five, and the number of samples is 10; thus, the total number of parts measured is 50. The quantity $\bar{x}$ is the average of five measurements in each sample.

We first calculate the average of averages, $\bar{\bar{x}}$,

$$\bar{\bar{x}} = \frac{44.296}{10} = 4.430 \text{ in.,}$$

and the average of R values,

$$\bar{R} = \frac{1.03}{10} = 0.103 \text{ in.,}$$

Since the sample size is five, we determine from Table 36.2 the following constants: $A_2 = 0.577$, $D_4 = 2.115$, and $D_3 = 0$. We can now calculate the control limits using Eqs. (36.4)–(36.7). Thus, for averages,

$$\text{UCL}_x = 4.430 + (0.577)(0.103) = 4.489 \text{ in.,}$$

$$\text{LCL}_x = 4.430 - (0.577)(0.103) = 4.371 \text{ in.,}$$

and for ranges,

$$\text{UCL}_R = (2.115)(0.103) = 0.218 \text{ in.,}$$

$$\text{LCL}_R = (0)(0.103) = 0 \text{ in.,}$$

We can now estimate the standard deviation of the process population of individuals using Eq. (36.10) and a value of $d_2 = 2.326$. Thus,

$$\sigma = \frac{0.103}{2.326} = 0.044 \text{ in.}$$

TABLE 36.3

Sample number	x_1	x_2	x_3	x_4	x_5	$\bar{x}$	R
1	4.46	4.40	4.44	4.46	4.43	4.438	0.06
2	4.45	4.43	4.47	4.39	4.40	4.428	0.08
3	4.38	4.48	4.42	4.42	4.35	4.410	0.13
4	4.42	4.44	4.53	4.49	4.35	4.446	0.18
5	4.42	4.45	4.43	4.44	4.41	4.430	0.04
6	4.44	4.45	4.44	4.39	4.40	4.424	0.06
7	4.39	4.41	4.42	4.46	4.47	4.430	0.08
8	4.45	4.41	4.43	4.41	4.50	4.440	0.09
9	4.44	4.46	4.30	4.38	4.49	4.414	0.19
10	4.42	4.43	4.37	4.47	4.49	4.436	0.12

Example: Dimensional Control of Plastic Parts in the Saturn Automobile

The Saturn automobile has some 38 different injection-molded interior plastic parts (poly-carbonate, polypropylene, and ABS; see Chapter 7), such as door panels, air inlet ducts, consoles, and trim, all of which must conform to tight dimensional tolerances so that they fit and snap properly during assembly, without unsightly gaps or buckles.

However, dimensions of these plastic parts change with temperature and humidity, and, because of their flexibility, they also tend to bend and curl. For this reason, measurement and inspection of plastic parts, including the use of coordinate measuring machines (CMM, see Section 35.6), are difficult. Although traditional gages are also used for monitoring process parameters in making these parts so that they are molded properly, a superior inspection system has been developed whereby SPC feedback is received from a direct computer-controlled CMM.

The system compensates for the flexibility of the parts, allows automatic measurement of various part features, and makes measurements of the mold at periodic intervals. The data are analyzed on a regular basis and, when necessary, corrective actions are taken and changes are made in materials, processing cycle, or mold design, so that the parts being molded will maintain good dimensional stability. *Source*: Saturn Corp. and *Manufacturing Engineering*.

36.8.3 Acceptance Sampling and Control

Acceptance sampling consists of taking only a few random samples from a lot and inspecting them to judge whether the entire lot is acceptable or whether it should be rejected or reworked. Developed in the 1920s and used extensively during World War II for military hardware (MIL STD 105), this statistical technique is widely used and valuable.

Acceptance sampling is particularly useful for inspecting high-production-rate parts where 100% inspection would be too costly. There are certain critical devices, however (such as pacemakers, prosthetic devices, and components of the space shuttle), which must be inspected 100%.

A variety of acceptance sampling plans have been prepared for both military and national standards, based on an acceptable, predetermined, and limiting percentage of nonconforming parts in the sample. If this percentage is exceeded, the entire lot is rejected, or it is reworked if economically feasible. Note that the actual number of samples (not percentages of the lot that are in the sample) can be significant in acceptance sampling.

The greater the number of samples taken from a lot, the greater the chance that the sample will contain nonconforming parts, and the lower the probability of the lot's acceptance. **Probability** is defined as the relative occurrence of an event. The probability of acceptance is obtained from various operating characteristics curves, one example of which is shown in Fig. 36.8.

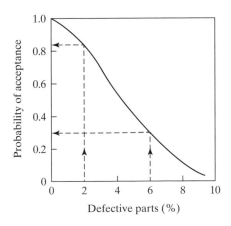

FIGURE 36.8   A typical operating-characteristics curve used in acceptance sampling. The higher the percentage of defective parts, the lower the probability of acceptance by the consumer. There are several methods of obtaining these curves.

The **acceptance quality level (AQL)** is commonly defined as the level at which there is a 95% acceptance probability for the lot. This percentage indicates to the manufacturer that 5% of the parts in the lot may be rejected by the consumer (**producer's risk**). Likewise, the consumer knows that 95% of the parts are acceptable (**consumer's risk**).

The manufacturer can salvage those lots that do not meet the desired quality standards through a secondary rectifying inspection. In this method, a 100% inspection is made of the rejected lot, and the defective parts are removed. This time-consuming and costly process is an incentive for the manufacturer to better control the production process.

Acceptance sampling requires less time and fewer inspections than do other sampling methods. Consequently, inspection of the parts can be more detailed. Automated inspection techniques are now being developed rapidly so that 100% inspection of all parts is indeed possible and can also be economical.

36.9 RELIABILITY

All products eventually fail in some manner or other. For example, automobile tires become worn and smooth, motors burn out, water heaters begin to leak, and machinery stops functioning properly. *Reliability* is defined as the probability that a product will perform its intended function in a given environment and for a specified period of time, without failure.

The more critical the application of a particular product, the higher its reliability should be. Thus, the reliability of an aircraft jet engine or a medical instrument should be much higher than that of a kitchen faucet or a mechanical pencil. From the topics described in this chapter, it can be seen that as the quality of each component of a product increases, so too does the reliability of the final product. Reliability, of course, also depends on whether a product is properly used and maintained.

The expected reliability of a product depends on the nature of the product. For an ordinary steel chain, the reliability of each link in the chain is very important; similarly, the reliability of each gear in a machine's gear train is very important. This condition is known as **series reliability**.

On the other hand, for a steel cable consisting of many individual wires, the reliability of each wire is not as critical. This condition is known as **parallel reliability**. The parallel reliability concept is important in the design of backup systems, which permit a product to continue functioning in the event that one of its components fails. Electrical or hydraulic systems in an aircraft, for example, are backed by mechanical systems, which are called **redundant systems**.

Predicting reliability has become an important science and involves complex mathematical relationships and calculations. The importance of predicting the reliability of the critical components of civilian or military aircraft is obvious. The reliability of an automated and computer-controlled high-speed production line, with all its complex mechanical and electronic components, is also important, as its failure can result in major economic losses to the manufacturer.

36.10 NONDESTRUCTIVE TESTING

Nondestructive testing (NDT) is carried out in such a manner that product integrity and surface texture remain unchanged. These techniques generally require considerable operator skill, and interpreting test results accurately may be difficult because the results can be subjective. However, the use of computer graphics and other enhancement techniques have significantly reduced the likelihood of human error.

Unlike the relatively simple equipment used in the past, many of the instruments used in testing today have become advanced, multicomponent systems equipped with computer systems. Surfaces are enlarged and viewed on color monitors, and the systems have various capabilities for data acquisition and qualitative and quantitative inspection and analysis.

Listed below are the basic principles of the more commonly-used nondestructive testing techniques.

36.10.1 Liquid Penetrants

In the *liquid-penetrants technique*, fluids are applied to the surfaces of the part and allowed to penetrate into surface cracks, seams, and pores (Fig. 36.9). The penetrant can seep into cracks as small as 0.1 μm (4 μin.) in width. Two common types of liquids used for this test are (a) *fluorescent penetrants* with various sensitivities, which fluoresce under ultraviolet light, and (b) *visible penetrants*, using dyes (usually red in color) which appear as bright outlines on the surface.

The surface to be inspected is first thoroughly cleaned and dried. The liquid is brushed or sprayed on the surface which will be inspected, and is allowed to remain long enough to seep into surface openings. Excess penetrant is then wiped off or washed away with water or solvent. A developing agent is applied, to allow the penetrant to seep back to the surface (by capillary action) and to spread to the edges of openings, thus magnifying the size of the defects. The surface is then inspected for defects, either visually (in the case of dye penetrants) or with fluorescent lighting.

This method can be used to detect a variety of surface defects. The equipment is simple and easy to use, can be portable, and is less costly to operate than that of other methods. However, this method can only detect defects that are open to the surface, or external.

36.10.2 Magnetic-Particle Inspection

The *magnetic-particle inspection technique* consists of placing fine ferromagnetic particles on the surface of the part. The particles can be applied either dry or in a liquid carrier such as water or oil. When the part is magnetized with a magnetic field, a discontinuity (defect) on the surface causes the particles to gather visibly around it (Fig. 36.10).

Thus, the defect becomes a magnet due to flux leakages where magnetic-field lines are interrupted by the defect. This, in turn, creates a small-scale *N-S* pole at either side of the defect as field lines exit the surface. The particles generally take the shape and size of the defect.

FIGURE 36.9   Sequence of operations for liquid-penetrant inspection to detect the presence of cracks and other flaws in a workpiece. *Source*: *Metals Handbook, Desk Edition*. Copyright © 1985, ASM International, Metals Park, Ohio. Used with permission.

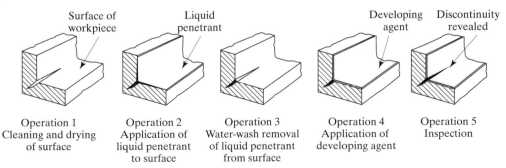

Surface of workpiece	Liquid penetrant		Developing agent	Discontinuity revealed
Operation 1 Cleaning and drying of surface	Operation 2 Application of liquid penetrant to surface	Operation 3 Water-wash removal of liquid penetrant from surface	Operation 4 Application of developing agent	Operation 5 Inspection

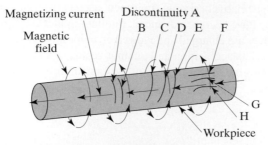

FIGURE 36.10   Schematic illustration of magnetic-particle inspection of a part with a defect in it. Cracks that are in a direction parallel to the magnetic field, such as in A, would not be detected, whereas the others shown would. Cracks F, G, and H are the easiest to detect. *Source*: *Metals Handbook, Desk Edition*. Copyright © 1985, ASM International, Metals Park, Ohio. Used with permission.

Subsurface defects can also be detected by this method, provided they are not deep. The ferromagnetic particles may be colored with pigments for better visibility on metal surfaces. Wet particles are better for detecting fine discontinuities like fatigue cracks.

The magnetic fields can be generated either with direct current or alternating current, using yokes, bars, and coils. Subsurface defects can be detected best with direct current. The magnetic-particle method can be used on ferromagnetic materials only, and parts have to be demagnetized and cleaned after inspection. The equipment may be portable or stationary.

36.10.3 Ultrasonic Inspection

In *ultrasonic inspection*, an ultrasonic beam travels through the part. An internal defect, such as a crack, interrupts the beam and reflects back a portion of the ultrasonic energy. The amplitude of the energy reflected, and the time required for return, indicate the presence and location of any flaws in the workpiece.

The ultrasonic waves are generated by transducers (called search units or probes) of various types and shapes. Transducers operate on the principle of *piezoelectricity* (see Section 3.7), using materials such as quartz, lithium sulfate, or various ceramics. Most inspections are carried out at a frequency range of 1 to 25 MHz. Couplants are used to transmit the ultrasonic waves from the transducer to the test piece; typical couplants are water, oil, glycerin, and grease.

The ultrasonic inspection method has high penetrating power and sensitivity. It can be used from various directions to inspect flaws in large parts, such as railroad wheels, pressure vessels, and die blocks. This method requires experienced personnel to properly conduct the inspection and to correctly interpret the results.

36.10.4 Acoustic Methods

The *acoustic-emission technique* detects signals (high-frequency stress waves) generated by the workpiece itself during plastic deformation, crack initiation and propagation, phase transformation, and abrupt reorientation of grain boundaries. Bubble formation during boiling, and friction and wear of sliding interfaces, are other sources of acoustic signals (see also Section 20.7.5).

Acoustic-emission inspection is typically performed by elastically stressing the part or structure: bending a beam, applying torque to a shaft, or pressurizing a vessel, for example. Sensors consisting of piezoelectric ceramic elements detect acoustic emissions. This method is particularly effective for continuous surveillance of load-bearing structures.

The **acoustic-impact technique** consists of tapping the surface of an object and listening to and analyzing the signals to detect discontinuities and flaws. The principle is basically the same as when one taps walls, desktops, or countertops in various locations with a finger or a hammer and listens to the sound emitted. Vitrified grinding wheels (Section 25.3) are tested in a similar manner (*ring test*) to detect cracks in the wheel that may not be visible to the naked eye.

The acoustic-impact technique is easy to perform and can be instrumented and automated. However, the results depend on the geometry and mass of the part, so a reference standard is necessary for identifying flaws.

36.10.5 Radiography

Radiography uses X-ray inspection to detect internal flaws such as cracks and porosity. The principle involved is difference in density; the metal surrounding the defect is denser and, hence, shows up as lighter than the flaws on an X-ray film. This is similar to the way bones and teeth show up lighter than the rest of the body in X-ray films.

The radiation source is typically an X-ray tube, and a visible permanent image is made on a film or radiographic paper (Fig. 36.11a). Fluoroscopes are used to produce X-ray images very quickly. (This is a real-time radiography technique that shows events as they are occurring.) Radiography does not require film handling and processing; it does, however, necessitate expensive equipment, proper interpretation of results, and a radiation hazard.

a. In **digital radiography**, the film is replaced by a linear array of detectors (Fig. 36.11b). The X-ray beam is collimated into a fan beam (compare Figs. 36.11a and b), and the workpiece is moved vertically. The detectors digitally sample the radiation and the data are stored in computer memory; the monitor then displays the data as a two-dimensional image of the workpiece.

FIGURE 36.11   Three methods of radiographic inspection: (a) conventional radiography, (b) digital radiography, and (c) computed tomography. *Source*: Courtesy of *Advanced Materials and Processes*, November 1990. ASM International.

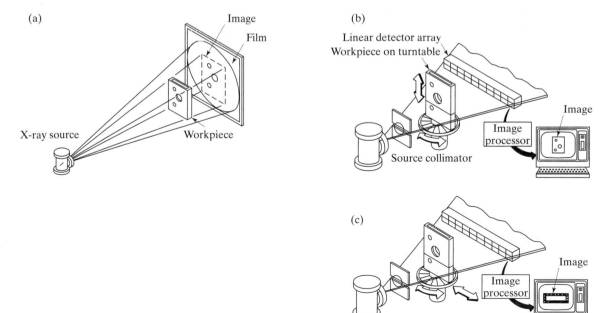

b. In **computed tomography**, the same system as described above is used, except that the workpiece is rotated along a vertical axis as it is being moved vertically (Fig. 36.11c), and the monitor produces X-ray images of thin cross-sections of the workpiece. The translation and rotation of the workpiece provide several angles from which to view the object.

From the data, the computer mathematically reconstructs and displays an image of the cross-section of the workpiece. The size, location, and distribution of flaws can thus be determined more reliably than is possible using ordinary radiography. **Computer-assisted tomography (catscan)**, based on the same principle, is used widely in medical practice and diagnosis.

36.10.6 Eddy-Current Inspection

The *eddy-current inspection method* is based on the principle of electromagnetic induction. The part is placed in, or adjacent to, an electric coil through which alternating current (exciting current) flows at frequencies ranging from 60 Hz to 6 MHz. This current causes eddy currents to flow in the part.

Defects in the part impede and change the direction of eddy currents (Fig. 36.12) and cause changes in the electromagnetic field. These changes affect the exciting coil (inspection coil), the voltage of which is monitored to determine the presence of flaws.

The inspection coils can be made in various sizes and shapes to suit the geometry of the part being inspected. Parts must be electrically conductive, and flaw depths detected are usually limited to 13 mm (0.5 in.). In addition, the technique requires the use of a standard reference sample to set the sensitivity of the tester.

36.10.7 Thermal Inspection

Thermal inspection involves using contact- or noncontact-type heat-sensing devices to detect temperature changes. Defects in the workpiece, such as cracks, debonded regions in laminated structures, and poor joints, cause a change in temperature distribution.

In **thermographic inspection**, materials such as heat-sensitive paints and papers, liquid crystals, and other coatings are applied to the surface. Any changes in their color or appearance indicate defects. The most common method of noncontact thermographic inspection

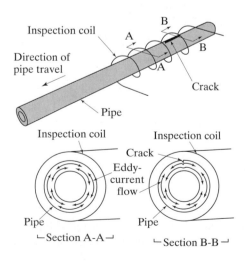

FIGURE 36.12 Changes in eddy-current flow caused by a defect in a workpiece. *Source: Metals Handbook, Desk Edition.* Copyright © 1985, ASM International, Metals Park, Ohio. Used with permission.

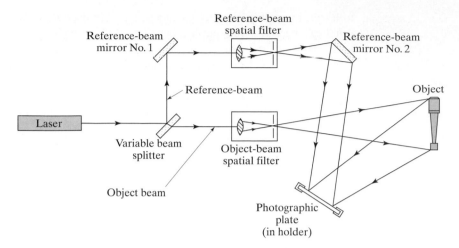

FIGURE 36.13   Schematic illustration of the basic optical system used in holography elements in radiography, for detecting flaws in workpieces. *Source: Metals Handbook, Desk Edition.* Copyright © 1985, ASM International, Metals Park, Ohio. Used with permission.

uses infrared detectors, usually infrared scanning microscopes and cameras, which have high response time and sensitivities of 1°C (2 °F).

Thermometric inspection utilizes devices such as thermocouples, radiometers, pyrometers, and sometimes meltable materials like waxlike crayons.

36.10.8 Holography

The *holography technique* creates a three-dimensional image of the part, utilizing an optical system (Fig. 36.13). Generally used on simple shapes and highly polished surfaces, this technique records the image on a photographic film.

Its use has been extended to **holographic interferometry** for inspection of parts with various shapes and surface conditions. In response to double- and multiple-exposure techniques while the part is being subjected to external forces or time-dependent variations, changes in the images reveal defects in the part.

a. In **acoustic holography**, information on internal defects is obtained directly from the image of the interior of the part. In *liquid-surface acoustical holography*, the workpiece and two ultrasonic transducers (one for the object beam and the other for the reference beam) are immersed in a water-filled tank. The holographic image is then obtained from the ripples in the tank.

b. In **scanning acoustical holography**, only one transducer is used and the hologram is produced by electronic-phase detection. Besides being more sensitive, this system's equipment is usually portable, and it can accommodate very large workpieces by using a water column instead of a tank.

36.11 DESTRUCTIVE TESTING

As the name suggests, the part or product tested using *destructive testing* methods no longer maintains its integrity, original shape, or surface texture. Mechanical test methods (Chapter 2) are all destructive in that a sample or specimen has to be removed from the product in order to test it. In addition to mechanical testing, other destructive tests include speed testing of grinding wheels to determine their bursting speed and high-pressure testing of pressure vessels to determine their bursting pressure.

Hardness tests that leave large indentations (see Figs. 2.12 and 2.13) may be regarded as destructive testing. However, microhardness tests may be regarded as nondestructive because of the very small permanent indentations. This distinction is based on the assumption that the material is not notch-sensitive. Most glasses, highly heat-treated metals, and ceramics are notch-sensitive; that is, the small indentation produced by the indenter will likely lower their strength and toughness.

36.12 AUTOMATED INSPECTION

Traditionally, individual parts and assemblies of parts have been manufactured in batches, sent to inspection in quality-control rooms (**post-process inspection**), and, if approved, put in inventory. If products do not pass the quality inspection, they are either scrapped or kept on the basis of having a certain acceptable deviation from the standard. Obviously, such a system lacks flexibility, requires the maintenance of an inventory, and inevitably results in the approval and passing of some defective parts.

In contrast, one of the trends in modern manufacturing is *automated inspection*. This method uses a variety of sensor systems that monitor the relevant parameters *during* the manufacturing process (**on-line inspection**). Then, using these measurements, the process automatically corrects itself to produce acceptable parts. Thus, further inspection of the part at another location in the plant is unnecessary. Parts may also be inspected immediately after they are produced (**in-process inspection**).

The use of accurate sensors and computer-control systems has integrated automated inspection into manufacturing operations (Chapters 38 and 39). Such a system ensures that no part is moved from one manufacturing process to another (for example, a turning operation followed by cylindrical grinding) unless the part is made correctly and meets the standards of the first operation.

Automated inspection is flexible and responsive to product design changes. Furthermore, because of automated equipment, less operator skill is required, productivity is increased, and parts have higher quality, reliability, and dimensional accuracy.

36.12.1 Sensors for Automated Inspection

Continued advances in **sensor technology** (Section 38.8) are making on-line or real-time monitoring of manufacturing processes feasible. Directly or indirectly, and with the use of various *probes*, sensors can detect dimensions, surface roughness, temperature, force, power, vibration, tool wear, and the presence of external or internal defects.

Sensors may operate on the principles of strain gages, inductance, capacitance, ultrasonics, acoustics, pneumatics, infrared radiation, optics, lasers, and various electronic gages. Sensors may be *tactile* (touching) or *nontactile*.

Sensors can be linked to microprocessors and computers for graphic data display (see also *programmable logic controllers*, Section 38.25). This capability allows rapid on-line adjustment of any processing parameters, which results in the production of parts that are consistently within specified standards of tolerance and quality. Such systems have already been implemented as standard equipment on many metal-cutting machine tools and grinding machines (Part IV).

SUMMARY

- Quality must be built into products. Quality assurance concerns various aspects of production, such as design, manufacturing, and assembly, and especially inspection at each step of production for conformance to specifications.

- Statistical quality control and process control have become indispensable in modern manufacturing. They are particularly important in the production of interchangeable parts and in the reduction of manufacturing costs.

- Although all quality-control approaches have their limits of applicability in the production of certain items, implementation of total quality management and the ISO 9000 standard are among the most important developments in manufacturing quality control.

- Several nondestructive and destructive testing techniques, each of which has its own applications, advantages, and limitations, are available for inspection of completed parts and products.

- The traditional approach has been to inspect the part or product after it is manufactured and to accept a certain number of defective parts. The trend now is strongly towards on-line, 100% inspection of all parts and products being manufactured.

TRENDS

- The importance of quality, reliability, and safety of products in the global economy and trade is now being widely recognized.

- Total quality control will continue to be a crucial manufacturing concept. However, because of the significant costs involved, return on quality is becoming an important consideration in company operations.

- Sensors based on a variety of principles are continuously being developed for on-line inspection for all aspects of quality. Real-time process control of quality is being studied and implemented extensively.

- The trend of on-line automated inspection has become well-established and will continue to be an essential element in manufacturing operations.

- Taguchi methods continue to be applied in many countries to optimize processes and product quality.

- Compliance with ISO 9000 and various other related standards is rapidly becoming a necessity for manufacturers in all industries worldwide.

KEY TERMS

Acceptance quality level
Acceptance sampling
Assignable variations
Automated inspection
Chance variations
Common cause
Consumer's risk
Continuous improvement
Control charts
Control limits

Defect prevention
Deming methods
Destructive testing
Dispersion
Distribution
Environmental management systems
Experimental design
Factorial design
Frequency distribution
Grand average

ISO standards
Juran methods
Kaizen
Lot size
Lower control limit
Method of attributes
Method of variables
Nondestructive testing
Normal distribution curve
Population

Probability	Reliability	Statistical process control
Process capability	Return on quality	Statistical quality control
Producer's risk	Robustness	Statistics
QS standards	Sample size	Taguchi loss function
Quality	Sensors	Taguchi methods
Quality assurance	Shewhart control charts	Total quality control
Quality circle	Special cause	Total quality management
Random sampling	Specification limits	Upper control limit
Range	Standard deviation	Variability

BIBLIOGRAPHY

Aft, L.S., *Fundamentals of Industrial Quality Control* (3d ed.). Addison-Wesley, 1998.

Anderson, D.M., *Design for Manufacturability, Optimizing Cost, Quality, and Time-to-Market.* CIM Press, 1991.

ASM Handbook, Vol. 17: *Nondestructive Evaluation and Quality Control.* ASM International, 1989.

Bentley, J.P., *Introduction to Reliability and Quality Control* (2d ed.). Addison-Wesley, 1999.

Besterfield, D.H., *Quality Control* (5th ed.). Prentice Hall, 1997.

Bothe, D.R., *Measuring Process Capability: Techniques and Calculations for Quality and Manufacturing Engineers.* McGraw-Hill, 1997.

Box, G.E.P., and A. Luceno, *Statistical Control by Monitoring and Feedback Adjustment.* Wiley, 1997.

Bray, D.E., and R.K. Stanley, *Nondestructive Evaluation: A Tool in Design, Manufacturing, and Service* (rev. ed.). CRC Press, 1997.

Breyfogle, III, F.W., *Statistical Methods for Testing, Development, and Manufacturing.* Wiley Interscience, 1992.

Cartz, L., *Nondestructive Testing.* ASM International, 1995.

Clements, R.B., *The Handbook of Statistical Methods in Manufacturing.* Prentice Hall, 1991.

Deming, W.E., *Out of the Crisis.* MIT Press, 1986.

Doty, L.A., *SPC for Short Run Manufacturing,* Hanser Gardner, 1997.

———, *Statistical Process Control* (2d ed.). Industrial Press, 1996.

Elsayed, E.A., *Reliability Engineering.* Addison-Wesley, 1996.

Feigenbaum, A.V., *Total Quality Control* (3d ed., revised). McGraw-Hill, 1991.

Fowlkes, W.Y., and C.M. Creveling, *Engineering Methods for Robust Product Design: Using Taguchi Methods in Technology and Product Development.* Addison-Wesley, 1995.

Grant, E.L., and R.S. Leavenworth, *Statistical Quality Control.* McGraw-Hill, 1997.

Imai, M., *Gemba Kaizen: A Commonsense, Low-Cost Approach to Management.* McGraw-Hill, 1997.

Ireson, W.G., C.F. Coombs, Jr., and R.Y. Moss, *Handbook of Reliability Engineering and Management* (2d ed.). McGraw-Hill, 1996.

Juran, J.M., and A.B. Godfrey (eds.), *Juran's Quality Handbook* (5th ed.). McGraw-Hill, 1999.

Kales, P., *Reliability: For Technology, Engineering, and Management.* Prentice Hall, 1997.

Kane, V.E., *Defect Prevention: Use of Simple Statistical Tools.* Marcel Dekker, 1989.

Kear, F.W., *Statistical Process Control in Manufacturing Practice.* Marcel Dekker, 1997.

Lamprecht, J.L., *Implementing the ISO 9000 Series.* Marcel Dekker, 1993.

Levinson, W.A., and F. Tumbelty, *SPC Essentials and Productivity Improvement: A Manufacturing Approach.* American Society for Quality Control, 1996.

Lewis, E.E., *Introduction to Reliability Engineering* (2d ed.). Wiley, 1995.

Menon, H.G., *TQM in New Product Manufacturing.* McGraw-Hill, 1992.

Montgomery, D.C., *Introduction to Statistical Quality Control* (3d ed.). Wiley, 1996.

Oakland, J.S., *Statistical Process Control* (3d ed.). Butterworth–Heinemann, 1996.

Park, S., *Robust Design and Analysis for Quality Engineering.* Chapman & Hall, 1997.

Quensenberry, C.P., *SPC Methods for Quality Improvement.* Wiley, 1997.

Ross, P.J., *Taguchi Techniques for Quality Engineering* (2d ed.). McGraw-Hill, 1996.

Rothery, B., *ISO 14000 and ISO 9000.* Gower Publishing Co., 1995.

Smith, G.M., *Statistical Process Control and Quality Improvement.* American Society for Quality Control, 1997.

Taguchi, G., *Introduction to Quality Engineering.* UNIPUB/Kraus International, 1986.

———, *Taguchi on Robust Technology Development: Bringing Quality Engineering Upstream.* ASME Press, 1993.

Tool and Manufacturing Engineers Handbook, Vol. 4: *Assembly, Testing, and Quality Control.* Society of Manufacturing Engineers, 1986.

Tool and Manufacturing Engineers Handbook, Vol. 7: *Continuous Improvement.* Society of Manufacturing Engineers, 1993.

Wise, S.A., and D.C. Fair, *Innovative Control Charting.* American Society for Quality Control, 1997.

REVIEW QUESTIONS

36.1 Explain why major efforts are continually being made to build quality into products.

36.2 Name several material and process variables that can influence product quality in metal (a) casting, (b) forming, and (c) machining.

36.3 What are chance variations?

36.4 Define the terms sample size, random sampling, population, and lot size.

36.5 Explain the difference between method of variables and method of attributes.

36.6 Define standard deviation. Why is it important?

36.7 Describe what is meant by "statistical process control."

36.8 Why are control charts made? How are they used?

36.9 What do control limits indicate?

36.10 Define process capability. How is it used?

36.11 What is acceptance sampling? Why was it developed?

36.12 What is the difference between series and parallel reliability?

36.13 Describe the basic features of nondestructive testing techniques that use electrical sources of energy.

36.14 Identify which nondestructive techniques are capable of detecting internal flaws and which ones detect external flaws only.

36.15 If the metal particles in magnetic-particle inspection are the same color as the workpiece itself, how would you go about producing a color contrast to detect flaws?

36.16 How is the depth of a flaw measured in ultrasonic testing?

36.17 What are the limitations of radiographic techniques?

36.18 Give applications of thermal inspection techniques in engineering practice.

36.19 How are large workpieces accommodated in acoustic holography?

36.20 What are the advantages of automated inspection? Why has it become an important part of manufacturing engineering?

36.21 Explain the difference between in-process and post-process inspection of manufactured parts. What trends are there in such inspection?

36.22 What is a Taguchi loss function?

36.23 Describe the important parts of the philosophies of Deming, Juran, and Taguchi.

36.24 What is robustness? What is its significance?

36.25 What is x (double bar on top) in SPC?

36.26 What is meant by three sigma (3σ) quality?

36.27 What is the importance of ISO 9000? ISO 14000?

36.28 What is the difference between probability and reliability?

36.29 What is quality?

QUALITATIVE PROBLEMS

36.30 Comment on the ideas of Deming, Taguchi, and Juran. What aspects of their concepts would be difficult to implement in a typical manufacturing facility? Why?

36.31 What is the consequence of setting lower and upper specifications closer to the peak of the curve in Fig. 36.4?

36.32 Identify several factors that can cause a process to become out of control.

36.33 Should products be designed and built for a certain expected life? Explain.

36.34 Describe situations in which the need for destructive testing techniques is unavoidable.

36.35 Which of the nondestructive inspection techniques are suitable for nonmetallic materials? Why?

36.36 Describe the advantages of the type of system shown in Fig. 36.7.

36.37 Survey the available technical literature and contact various associations, then prepare a comprehensive table concerning the life expectancy of various consumer products.

36.38 Assume that you are in charge of manufacturing operations for a company that has not yet adopted statistical process control techniques. Describe how you would go about developing a plan to do so, including providing for the training of your personnel.

36.39 Give examples that produce curves similar to Figs. 36.6a and b.

36.40 Why is reliability important in manufacturing engineering? Give several examples.

36.41 Would it be desirable to incorporate nondestructive inspection techniques into various metalworking machinery? Give a specific example and make a sketch of such a machine.

36.42 Give examples of the acoustic-impact inspection technique, other than those given in the text.

36.43 Explain how one can simultaneously have a manufacturing process that produces defective parts that also gives superior quality compared to another process with zero defects.

36.44 Is there a relationship between design specifications on blueprints and limits in control charts?

36.45 Explain why Go-Not Go gages are incompatible with the Taguchi philosophy.

36.46 Give examples of products where 100% sampling is not possible or feasible.

36.47 What are the capabilities and limitations of liquid penetrants?

QUANTITATIVE PROBLEMS

36.48 Assume that in the example problem following Section 36.6.2, the number of samples was 7 instead of 10. Using the top half of the data in the table, recalculate control limits and the standard deviation. Compare your observations with the results obtained by using 10 samples.

36.49 Calculate the control limits for averages and ranges for the following: number of samples $= 5$, $\bar{\bar{x}} = 65$, $R = 6$.

36.50 Calculate the control limits for the following: number of samples $= 5$, $\bar{\bar{x}} = 36.5$, $\text{UCL}_R = 4.75$.

36.51 In an inspection with sample size 10 and a sample number of 50, it was found that the average range was 12 and the average of averages was 75. Calculate the control limits for averages and for ranges.

36.52 Determine the control limits for the data shown in the table below.

x_1	x_2	x_3	x_4
0.55	0.60	0.57	0.55
0.59	0.55	0.60	0.58
0.55	0.50	0.55	0.51
0.54	0.57	0.50	0.50
0.58	0.58	0.60	0.56
0.60	0.61	0.55	0.61

36.53 The average of averages of a number of samples of size 8 was determined to be 124. The average range was 17.82 and the standard deviation was 6. The following measurements were taken in a sample: 120, 132, 124, 130, 118, 132, 135, 121, and 127. Is the process in control?

36.54 The trend in the electronics and computer-chip industries is to make products where it is stated that the quality is approaching six sigma (6σ). What would be the reject rate per million parts?

36.55 A manufacturer is ring rolling ball-bearing races (see Fig. 13.14). The inner surface has a surface roughness specification of $0.10 \ \mu\text{m} \pm 0.05 \ \mu\text{m}$. Measurements taken from rolled rings indicate a mean roughness of $0.112 \ \mu\text{m}$ with a standard deviation of $0.02 \ \mu\text{m}$. 30,000 rings per month are manufactured and the cost of discarding a defective ring is $5.00. It is known that by changing lubricants to a special emulsion, the mean roughness could be made essentially equal to the design specification. What additional cost per month can be justified for the lubricant?

36.56 For the data of Quantitative Problem 36.55, assume that the lubricant change can cause the manufacturing process to achieve a roughness of 0.09 μm ± 0.01 μm. What additional cost per month for the lubricant can be justified? What if the lubricant did not add any new cost?

36.57 Beverage can manufacturers try to achieve failure rates of less than one can in ten thousand. If this corresponds to n-sigma quality, find n.

SYNTHESIS AND DESIGN

36.58 Assume that the introduction to this chapter was missing. Write a comprehensive introduction, describing the highlights of the topics described in this chapter.

36.59 This chapter briefly described the concept of experimental design used in identifying the variables that affect product quality. Survey the available technical literature and describe this technique in greater detail, and give a specific example related to manufacturing.

36.60 Review the manufacturing processes described in Parts II through V and identify three different operations in which the systems shown in Fig. 36.7 can be implemented. Describe designs which illustrate these applications.

36.61 Many components have minimal effect on part robustness and quality. For example, the hinges in the glove compartment of an automobile do not really impact the owner's satisfaction, and the glove compartment is opened so few times that a robust design is easy to achieve. Would you advocate using Taguchi methods like the loss function on this type of component?

37

Human-Factors Engineering, Safety, and Product Liability

37.1 INTRODUCTION

Understanding the interaction of human beings with machines and the workplace environment is essential for the proper design and use of machinery, as well as for the development of safe and efficient working conditions in manufacturing plants. Regardless of the level of automation, workers are always involved in one or more aspects of production and in the efficient use, maintenance, and repair of machinery, tooling, and equipment.

Human-factors engineering, also called *human engineering*, concerns all aspects of human–machine interactions. An essentially synonymous term is **ergonomics**, based on the Greek words *ergo*, meaning work, and *nomics*, meaning management. Human-factors engineering has two major goals:

a. to maximize the quality and efficiency of work, and

b. to maximize human values such as operator safety, comfort, and satisfaction and to minimize fatigue and stress.

These goals are occasionally in conflict, thus requiring product engineers to rely on their judgment in developing a reasonably safe machine and workplace.

This chapter describes those aspects of human-factors engineering that are particularly relevant to manufacturing operations. It outlines the basic design considerations for the safe interaction of human beings with machinery and the workplace environment.

Finally, this chapter focuses on the important topic of **product liability**, which concerns the legal responsibilities of the manufacturer and the user of a product in the event of bodily injury or physical and financial losses caused by the malfunction, misuse, or failure of a product (see also Section 12 in the General Introduction).

From the topics described in Chapter 36, it is evident that product quality concepts and philosophies are an integral part of the topics covered in this chapter as well. Product design, engineering, and production processes are part of a continuous improvement system, from the initial concept of a product to its final use by the customer. More recent developments include *quality function deployment*, which is a tool used to identify human factors as well as safety and product liability concerns.

37.2 HUMAN-FACTORS ENGINEERING

The emphasis of *human-factors engineering* is to apply the knowledge gained from the studies of human physiology and psychology, which concern the characteristics and capabilities of the human body and mind. These traits include height, weight, vision, hearing, posture, strength, age, intelligence, educational level, dexterity, and reaction time. Numerous statistical data relating to these characteristics are available.

37.2.1 Workstations

Machinery and related equipment should be designed so that they can be operated with undue strain on the worker (for comfort), and with minimum unnecessary and wasted motion (for efficient operation). Muscle-strain injuries (called **cumulative trauma disorders**) are common in the workplace. Such injuries can be avoided through application of proper lifting procedures and the use of mechanical devices when necessary. Wasted motion can be minimized, for example, by arranging sequential controls in series.

Repetitive motion in the workplace, such as by assembly line workers and data-entry workers, can cause **repetitive stress injuries**. The result is (a) soreness and pain in the arms, neck, shoulders, wrists, or hands; (b) tingling and numbness; (c) loss of strength; and (d) muscle inflammation. One of the most common injuries is a hand and wrist disorder called **carpal tunnel syndrome (CTS)**; this is a condition in which the wrist's median nerve compresses and causes great pain.

Proper training, changes in one's posture and movements, and redesign of the tools, equipment, and machinery used can alleviate CTS. Computer keyboards, for example, are being redesigned to reduce such injuries.

Controls and *displays* should be placed in appropriate locations and should not interfere with each other. They should be identified and marked clearly so that they can be understood and operated without confusion. Local and background *lighting* of machinery should be adequate to minimize eye strain, and glare from improper lighting or reflective surfaces should be minimized as well.

The correct type of *information display* depends on the application. For example, numerical counters are preferable to all other display methods when precise values of static information are desired. However, for rapidly changing information, a pointer moving along a fixed scale is preferable to a counter because of the limited time available for reading values on the scale.

Workstations should be arranged to allow for *efficient movement* of people, parts, and products. Sufficient space should be provided for storage, access, maintenance, and material-handling equipment, when necessary.

37.2.2 Noise

Noise can significantly and adversely affect operator performance and health. Excessive noise interferes with communication and can cause messages to be misunderstood. Noise intensity, measured in decibels (dB) by a sound meter, varies widely depending on the type of equipment involved. Sustained exposure to a noise level above 90 dB can cause hearing loss or permanent deafness.

Although they are somewhat controversial, permissible noise levels have been established by the Occupational Safety and Health Administration (OSHA). In the OSHA guidelines, **noise level** and **operator exposure time** are inversely related. High levels of noise emission by machines may not be objectionable in itself; it is the duration of worker exposure to noise that is important.

Although all machines emit noise, major sources of noise are typically air-actuated mechanisms, gears, material-handling equipment, chutes for conveying goods, impacting-type machinery, hydraulic pumps, motors, fans, and blowers. Noise levels can be reduced through the use of muffling equipment, enclosing machinery totally, lining housings and chutes, and modifying machinery components.

In areas of excessive noise, personal protective equipment such as ear plugs or ear muffs can reduce worker exposure to noise. The regular maintenance and replacement of worn machine components, such as gears and bearings, will effectively reduce noise levels. Vibrations of the machinery or floor not only emit noise but are detrimental to the dimensional accuracy and surface finish of parts produced by nearby machines.

37.3 SAFETY

It is generally recognized that there is no machine or industrial or consumer product that cannot somehow be involved in an accident or injury. *Safety* may be defined as a judgment of the acceptability of danger, where **danger** is the combination of hazard and risk. Thus, the safety of a machine or workplace depends on the hazard and risk involved with machine operation. **Hazard** is defined as an injury producer, while **risk** is defined as the likelihood (probability) that an injury will occur.

The causes of injury are varied, but they include the following factors:

a. Having parts of the body caught in or between machine components.
b. Being struck by an object.
c. Falling from equipment, structures, or ladders.
d. Slipping or tripping on floor surfaces.
e. Explosions and fires.
f. Exposure to dangerous levels of electricity.
g. Burns or exposure to temperature extremes.
h. Exposure to or ingestion of toxic chemicals.
i. Excessive physical strain.

Employers are responsible for providing a *reasonably safe* workplace. Various safety and health standards have been promulgated in the United States, most notably by the *American National Standards Institute*.

These standards have been the basis for many governmental regulations adopted by OSHA. Safety literature is available from the *National Safety Council* (NSC) and similar organizations in both the United States and other industrialized countries.

By their very nature, manufacturing operations involve safety hazards of varying degrees; nevertheless, it is imperative that workers have a reasonably safe working environment. Some hazards and the means of controlling them are obvious, while others are hidden and require additional precautions.

Surveys have indicated that approximately 85% of the accidents involving machinery are caused by the operator, 5% are caused by mechanical failure, and the remainder are caused by other factors. Employers are required to retrofit old machinery with guards.

Manufacturers must include adequate guarding and safety devices on new machinery. Furthermore, employers who emphasize training are much more successful in reducing accidents through hazard-recognition techniques and the development of safer work practices. Experience shows that because literally all machines are now guarded, machine designers and builders cannot influence safety to the extent that machine users can.

Safety professionals and organizations have created the following hierarchy for treating hazards in the workplace:

1. Reduce the danger to a reasonable level through design.
2. Apply safeguarding technology.
3. Use warning signs and labels.
4. Train and instruct the worker.
5. Prescribe personal protective equipment.

There is a tacit understanding in the safety hierarchy that the first steps are the most effective: it is better to *eliminate* hazards or risks of injury through design than to use safeguards, which are in turn more effective than warnings, etc.

Safeguarding Methods.   Several common machinery safeguarding methods have been developed:

1. **Barrier guards.** When properly designed and maintained, *barrier guards* prevent the operator's exposure to nip points and pinch points in machines. These guards may be fixed, adjustable, or self-adjusting. Barrier guards also identify hazardous areas of machinery and, in some cases, prevent projectiles (such as broken pieces of a grinding wheel) from being thrown from the machine.

    Mechanical, electrical, hydraulic, and optical **interlocks** have been applied to prevent machine operation until barrier guards are in place (Fig. 37.1). Unless they are

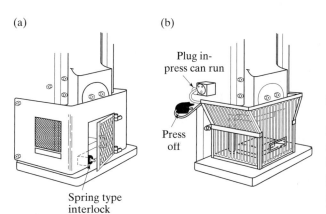

(a)

(b)

Plug in-
press can run

Press
off

Spring type
interlock

FIGURE 37.1   Barrier guards: (a) spring-type interlock shuts off power to machine when guard door is opened; (b) guard can only be removed by removing the plug, which then shuts off power to machine. *Source*: Triodyne, Inc.

(a)   (b)

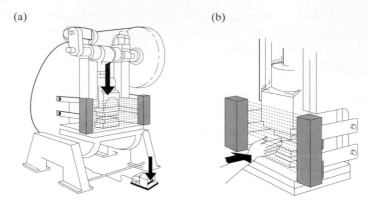

FIGURE 37.2   (a) Presence-sensing device, with light beams forming a curtain across the zone of operation. (b) Breaking the curtain of light beams by operator's hands sets brake on machine and disconnects clutch. *Source*: Triodyne, Inc.

bypassed or are unreliable, interlocks increase the effectiveness of barrier guards in most applications.

2. **Safety devices.** Passive and active safety devices help reduce the risk or severity of injury. These devices include the following:

   a. *Pull-back mechanisms* for the operator's hands.

   b. *Dead-man controls*, a system in which the power is automatically shut off in the event that the operator passes out or dies, as for elevated trains and their conductors.

   c. *Presence-sensing devices* (Fig. 37.2).

3. **Safety during maintenance of machinery.** Various types of servicing, troubleshooting, adjustment, maintenance, and repair must be performed on machines while their guards are temporarily removed or with their safety devices bypassed. Safety devices that are both compatible and critical for safe machine operation can be incompatible when performing maintenance and repair.

   It is the employer's responsibility to ensure that maintenance personnel are competent to interact with the types of hazards expected. It is the employee's responsibility to perform the maintenance in a safe manner.

The person who performs maintenance is required to put the machinery into a **zero mechanical state (ZMS™)** prior to entering the machine or placing any part of the body into the path of a moving part. The ZMS concept includes the following safety features:

   a. Locking out (**lockout**) and tagging main power disconnect switches (**tagout**) as required by law (so that another employee does not unknowingly turn on the equipment while a coworker is engaged in maintenance), and

   b. All potential and kinetic energy sources are to be restrained or controlled so that no unexpected energy release occurs. Examples include (a) releasing compressed air to the atmosphere, (b) isolating pressurized hydraulic fluid, (c) restraining energy stored in springs, and (d) lowering suspended loads.

   Troubleshooting with the power on is often necessary and acceptable, as is removing and bypassing safety devices for setup purposes. For example, if the failure of an electrical interlock is the cause of equipment malfunction, bypassing each interlock is necessary until the problem interlock is isolated and identified. However, the process of defeating safety devices for maintenance purposes must be performed only after ZMS has been achieved. Once the service or maintenance has been completed, all of the safety devices must be restored and their operation verified before the equipment is released back into production.

4. **Warnings.** Posted signs, signals, and instructions warn the worker about hidden hazards, danger-control methods, or non-obvious consequences. Although they can be inconsistent in actual use, the format, size, and color of warnings have been prescribed by industry standards and governmental codes.

5. **Personal protective equipment.** Goggles, face shields, ear plugs, helmets, respirators, and protective clothing (such as gloves and aprons) are types of personal protective equipment that reduce worker exposure to hazards.

37.4 ENVIRONMENTAL CONSIDERATIONS

The possible adverse effects of industrial activities and related operations on the health of individual workers as well as on the environment are by now well recognized by manufacturing industries, the public, and local, state, and federal governments. (See also Section 11 in the General Introduction). Environmental conditions and control of air, water, and land quality are major aspects of all manufacturing activities, as is the conservation of natural resources.

An understanding and appreciation of our **ecological system** should be an integral part of industrial activity. Potential effects include global climate changes, stratospheric ozone depletion, and loss of the earth's biological diversity, as well as less global issues such as oil spills, hazardous waste sites, the spread of pesticides, and leaking underground storage tanks.

Although there are many factors involved in environmental issues, those that are affected primarily by manufacturing activities can be divided into two categories:

a. Pollutants from industrial plants, such as solid and liquid waste, waste water, and discharges from various facilities such as heat-treating plants, and

b. Atmospheric pollutants, such as air pollution from foundries and coolants, lubricants, and various fluids used in manufacturing operations.

The U.S. Congress has enacted several pieces of legislation that regulate a wide variety of industrial practices in the interest of improving the environment. The major federal agencies and the acts relating to them, as they pertain to manufacturing operations, are as follows:

1. **Occupational Safety and Health Act (OSHA)** is concerned with unsafe conditions in the workplace. It encourages both employers and employees to reduce hazards, including exposure to chemical and toxic substances, and to implement existing or new safety and health programs.

    Examples of OSHA regulations directly relevant to manufacturing activities are the Hazard Communication Standard; Right-to-Know; In-Plant Air Quality Standard; Respirator Maintenance Program; Laboratory Safety Plan; Process Safety Management of Highly Hazardous Chemicals Standard; Confined Space Entry Regulations; and Lockout/Tagout Standard.

2. **The National Institute for Occupational Safety and Health (NIOSH)** was established by the OSHA; it conducts research, experiments, and demonstrations to identify toxic materials, determines safe exposure levels, and develops methodology for identifying health hazards.

3. **The Environmental Protection Agency (EPA)** is charged with several responsibilities concerning toxic substances, clean air, water pollution, safe drinking water, and solid waste. The *Toxic Substances Control Act* regulates the manufacture, processing, distribution, use, and disposal of chemicals that present an unreasonable risk to humans or to the environment.

4. The *Clean Air Act* has the responsibility of setting national air-quality standards, through the control of emissions from stationary as well as mobile sources, including, for example, emission of volatile components in lubricants. The *Federal Water Pollution Act*, also known as the *Clean Water Act*, has the responsibility of enforcing the limiting of direct or indirect discharge of pollutants into navigable waters.

5. Solid waste is controlled by two statutes. One is the *Resource Conservation and Recovery Act*, which requires the EPA to establish and periodically revise standards and regulations for hazardous waste generation and its storage, transportation, treatment, and disposal. Wastes are considered hazardous if they exhibit one or more of the following characteristics: (a) ignitability (cause fire or explosion), (b) corrosivity (damage to containers, thus allowing escape of wastes), or (c) toxicity.

   The other statute is the *Comprehensive Environmental Response, Compensation and Liability Act*, which regulates existing hazardous waste sites, including sites of unauthorized discharges and spills. Additional EPA regulations include *Underground Storage Tank Regulation*; *Spill Prevention Control* and *Countermeasure Plan*; and *Used Oil Regulations*.

These regulations require permits for the discharge of pollutants into waterways or into the air. The scope of this program is wide, in that it requires a facility to compile all its air-pollution emissions into a single document. The manufacturing engineer has to work closely with the environmental staff, because a permit may contain certain limits and restrictions that cannot be quickly modified.

Significant costs can be involved in the implementation of such a large number of regulations, mandated by governments on all three levels: local, state, and federal. For example, the average cost for disposal of metalworking fluids (such as a water-base cutting fluid) is about $3 per gallon. In the long run, however, it is in the interest of everyone to ensure a healthy and safe environment.

Example: Environmentally-Conscious Can Manufacturing

The sheet-metal forming operations involved in the manufacture of food and beverage containers is shown in Figure 16.31. What is not shown are non-metal forming operations involved. For example, between the doming and necking operations, a wash/coat operation is performed; it removes residue lubricants from the can to preserve content taste and shelf life, and also applies a base coating to the metal.

After this operation, one or more spray operations are performed where a polymer coating is applied to the can interior. The purpose of the polymer is to provide a barrier between the metal can and the food, yielding a safe food contact surface.

The polymer resin in a spray coat operation is delivered by dissolving the polymer in a carrier such as methyl ethyl ketone or equivalent. The cans are then placed in an oven for curing, where the ketone carrier is also evaporated. In gaseous form, the ketone is a volatile organic compound (VOC) and is a serious environmental hazard. An afterburner is needed to reduce the VOC to carbon dioxide and water vapor.

An alternative manufacturing approach is to coat the metal stock with a polymer through either a powder spray or lamination process. Since the polymer has superior friction properties, it can serve as the lubricant in deep drawing and ironing, thereby eliminating the need for potentially harmful lubricants. Furthermore, the spray coat operations are unnecessary, so that VOC generation is eliminated.

While some environmental hazards are introduced in the lamination or powder spray operation, these are much less severe than the VOC generation. In addition, since one supplier can provide metal for many can manufacturers, the environmental concerns are consolidated in one facility, making management and control of hazards much more plausible.

Source: J.E. Wang, Weirton Steel Corporation

37.5 PRODUCT LIABILITY

In the United States alone, at least 10 million people (about 4% of the population) suffer injuries on the job each year. Thousands of injuries are fatal, and 30% of the injuries are classified as severe. Each year, as a result, millions of workdays are lost, and direct and indirect costs are estimated at more than $30 billion. These injuries, deaths, and expenses are central to the issue of *product liability*.

Assume that you have just purchased a hammer with a wooden handle. After using it for a few months, the handle breaks and the head of the hammer hits you, causing serious injury to your hand and necessitating surgery.

Further assume that the injury leaves your hand permanently deformed, and, as a result, you cannot continue in your job, which provided you with a good income. What recourse should you have to recover for damages to your hand, time lost from work, and the effects on your future employment and livelihood?

Until about one hundred years ago, the prominent legal theory applicable to machinery manufacturers was based on the Roman doctrine of **caveat emptor**, meaning *let the buyer beware*. If an injury resulted from the use of an unreasonably dangerous product, the injured party had virtually no legal possibility of obtaining compensation for the injury. Around 1900, however, the magnitude of the U.S. economy called for a different legal theory to bind manufacturers to their products. Since then, judicial decisions have gradually changed product liability doctrines.

37.5.1 Negligence

Under the legal theory of *negligence*, a party is liable for damages if it failed to act as a reasonable and prudent party would have done under like or similar circumstances. For negligence theory to apply, the injured party, or plaintiff, must demonstrate two conditions:

1. That the standard of care was violated by the accused party, or defendant, and
2. That this violation was the proximate cause of the accident. The plaintiff must also demonstrate no contributory negligence in causing his or her own misfortune.

Several states rely on the concept of **comparative negligence**, or comparative fault, when deciding to what degree each party is responsible for an accident. For example, in comparative negligence, a jury may find that a plaintiff was 50% responsible for the accident and reduce the monetary reward by that amount. The manufacturer as well as the distributor of the product involved may each be held 25% liable and, thus, share equally in the plaintiff's reduced compensation.

In order to cover the expenses and monetary awards involved in product liability litigation, manufacturers add a certain amount to the cost of the product. Thus, every industrial and consumer product has a product liability cost in it. It has been estimated, for example, that $500 of the selling price of a typical car goes to cover potential product liability claims.

37.5.2 Strict Liability

Under the legal theory of *strict liability*, the plaintiff must prove that:

1. the product contained a defect that rendered it unreasonably dangerous (such as a cracked bolt in a lawnmower).
2. the defect existed at the time the product left the defendant's hands (the manufacturer used a cracked bolt).
3. the defect was a proximate cause of the injury (the crack propagated during use of the product by the plaintiff, and the bolt broke, injuring the plaintiff) and, thus, the product was unreasonably dangerous.

Under strict-liability laws, the actions of the plaintiff are irrelevant (the lawnmower was used on rough terrain). Whether the plaintiff acted as a reasonable and prudent party has no bearing on a claim based on strict liability. The emphasis is on the product, and a defense based on the contributory negligence of the plaintiff is invalid in most jurisdictions. Furthermore, manufacturers are required to anticipate reasonably *foreseeable* misuses of that product by the consumer (dropping the lawnmower on the pavement while removing it from the trunk of an automobile).

37.5.3 Defects

The definition of a defect has evolved over time. We may now define a *defect* as a fault, flaw, or irregularity that causes weakness, failure, or inadequacy in the form and function of a product, which results in a risk of injury. A defect may result from product design, material selection, and/or manufacturing or production error.

However, not all products that present risk of injury are defective. A sharp knife is not a defective product, and is not unreasonably dangerous, because the sharpness of the blade is necessary for the intended use of the knife. The risk of injury is outweighed by the usefulness of the knife, which is an effect of its sharpness. Furthermore, the training that each of us receives at an early age in handling a knife helps make this product reasonably safe.

Legal tests of whether a product is defective generally involve the following factors:

a. Usefulness and desirability of the product.
b. Availability of safer alternative products or work methods.
c. Likelihood of injury and its probable seriousness.
d. Obviousness of the hazard.
e. Common knowledge and normal public expectation of the danger involved in the use of the product.
f. Avoidability of injury through the use of ordinary care with the product.
g. Ability to eliminate the hazard without seriously impairing the usefulness of the product.
h. State of the art in the particular industry at the time of product manufacture.
i. Cost of making the product safer.
j. Consumer willingness to pay for a higher-priced but safer product.
k. Bargaining power of the manufacturer as contrasted to that of the consumer.

Warnings and Instructions.   A product can be considered to be defective if *warnings* that would have prevented the accident are not provided on and with the product. Warning theories are complex and not all warnings improve operator safety. Furthermore, warnings are not a substitute for training and instructions.

Relevant instructions for use and maintenance should be presented in a clear and readable manner. Warnings should clearly instruct the user what to do and what not to do in using the product safely. Details should be presented in instruction, operating, and maintenance manuals that accompany the product.

37.5.4 Designing and Manufacturing Safe Products

Over time, and on the basis of accumulated experience, certain guidelines have been established for the design and manufacture of safe products. It is essential that a product's safety be viewed in terms of its design, manufacture, distribution, and ultimate use. Product safety should be the collective responsibility of all parties concerned, including design, materials, and manufacturing engineers, machine operators, supervisors, inspectors, shipping personnel, and management.

Methodologies such as the *Preliminary Hazard Analysis (PHA)* have been developed, and are being used, to identify potential hazards associated with product design and the workplace. Product safety and loss-control programs should be implemented by committees that represent all departments and that have the full support of the company management.

The basic guidelines for designing and manufacturing safe products are as follows:

a. Product design concepts should anticipate obvious and probable dangers in product use and foreseeable misuse, as well as anticipate the injuries that could be caused by the failure of one or more components.

b. All those involved with the design and manufacture of the product should be fully aware of current industry and government standards and regulations concerning that product. The product should meet at least those standards, even though the standards may not fully anticipate all possibilities in the use and misuse of the product. However, complying with these standards does not necessarily protect the manufacturer from product liability lawsuits.

c. All stages of production (raw materials, manufacturing processes, assembly procedures, and inspection techniques) should be monitored carefully and continually to ensure that no defective components pass all the way through the production line. Emphasis should be placed on quality assurance, using statistical sampling methods when 100% inspection of all parts is not practical or economically feasible (see also Chapter 36).

d. Instruction manuals and warning labels that address known hidden hazards should be prepared with great care. Intended use(s) of the product should be addressed in the instruction manual, in addition to reasonably foreseeable misuse, maintenance, and care of the product.

e. It is essential to keep complete records of the design, manufacturing, testing, and quality control of all product components and their assembly, with dates and appropriate identification numbers. For example, if a product is assembled with one lot of defective components or a competitor begins supplying counterfeit substandard parts, the product manufacturer has a means of providing proof of whether the defective component was supplied with the original product. In the event a product recall or retrofitting campaign becomes necessary, good record keeping will help minimize additional costs and maximize the effectiveness of the campaign.

37.6 EXAMPLES OF PRODUCT LIABILITY CLAIMS

Punch Press.   The plaintiff was injured while operating a punch press manufactured by Niagara Machine and Tool Works in 1956 and sold in that year to Hammond Organ Company, the plaintiff's employer. The press was used in primary and secondary operations.

During primary operations, the machine operates automatically while the operator feeds in the raw material. There is no need for the operator to have his hands near the machine's moving components.

During secondary operations, previously prepared parts are finished. The operator places a part in the correct position in the lower die and then activates the ram by pushing a foot lever. It was during a secondary operation that the plaintiff was injured. The punch press, as sold, did not have any safety devices. The machine did have a non-repeat feature to prevent the ram from descending more than once each time the operator pressed the foot lever.

The plaintiff's employer installed a safety device that is attached to an operator and would pull his hands away from the press before the ram descended. At the time of the accident, the pull-back device attached to the plaintiff was broken and inoperable.

The plaintiff claimed that his hand was crushed when the press ram unexpectedly descended a second time. Hammond's fabricating engineer testified that the non-repeat cycle was operating properly when he examined the machine after the accident.

The plaintiff argued that Niagara's failure to equip the machine with a safety device made the machine unreasonably dangerous, and that this failure was sufficient to establish a right to recovery based on strict liability theory.

The claim was rejected by the court. Even though manufacturers must produce reasonably safe products, the press as sold without tooling or dies did not present a hazard. Further, the pull-backs installed by the employer were a proper safety device and eliminated the unreasonably dangerous condition from the machine. Since there is no evidence that causally connects the injury with the original state of the machine, there is no defect. *Source*: Triodyne, Inc. Reference: *Rios v. Niagara Machine & Tool Works.*

Smoke Detector.   The plaintiff claimed that a battery-operated smoke detector was defective because the instructions contained inside the smoke detector did not inform a consumer that the detector required a battery to operate and, also, did not warn of the danger of removing the battery and leaving it out.

The plaintiff admitted that the detector had gone off three or four times when there was smoke in the kitchen, and that at each time she had opened the cover and taken the battery out until the smoke cleared before replacing it. She also admitted that when the battery wore out and the detector began chirping, she took the battery out of the detector and failed to replace it with a new one.

The court found no defect since the danger of removing the battery from the battery-powered smoke detector was obvious to a "reasonable and prudent user of the product" and, additionally, the plaintiff had actual knowledge that this particular detector did not work without a battery. *Source*: Triodyne, Inc. Reference: *Morrison v. Grand Forks Housing Authority.*

Chandelier.   This case involved an action against a distributor of a chandelier that fell while it was being cleaned. A threaded pipe that held the item in a retaining bracket had come unscrewed. The user cleaned the chandelier by rotating it one-half turn on each occasion.

The plaintiff's expert claimed that (a) the item was not a reasonably safe design because there was no anti-rotation locking device, (b) nothing in the design precluded faulty installation, and (c) nothing in the design to the casual observer would indicate that something was wrong. The Idaho Supreme Court ruled in favor of the plaintiff, based on the testimony of the plaintiff's expert. *Source*: Triodyne, Inc. Reference: *Curtis v. DeAtley*.

SUMMARY

- Because technology ultimately serves humanity, the well-being of human beings as operators of machinery and as users of products is an integral consideration in all manufacturing activities.
- Efficient and safe operations can be planned and conducted in the workplace through comprehensive studies of man-machine interactions.
- Proper design of the physical environment, including air quality, lighting, and noise, can increase job performance.
- Safety should be the concern of all who are involved in design and production. Unsafe operation of machinery and products is a major source of worker and user injury and financial loss.
- A variety of safeguarding systems has been developed and should be used.
- Product liability continues to be an important aspect of manufacturing and product use, and has a major impact on the economics of manufacturing operations.

TRENDS

- Human-factors engineering and ergonomics continue to be essential elements in the design and use of manufacturing machinery and equipment, particularly in view of advances that have been made in automation, thus requiring a different role from the employee.
- Safety will continue to be the responsibility of all parties concerned in the manufacture and use of products.
- Product liability will continue to be an important element in design and manufacturing. The upward trend in the number of product liability cases, the high cost of awards by courts, the cost of defending a case, and the cost of product liability insurance have become major concerns.
- Limitations on injury claims and awards and national standardization continue to be considered by state legislatures and the U.S. Congress.

KEY TERMS

Barrier guards
Carpal tunnel syndrome
Caveat emptor (buyer beware)
Comparative negligence
Cumulative trauma disorders
Danger
Defect
Environmental Protection Agency (EPA)
Ergonomics
Hazard

Human-factors engineering
Instructions
Lockout
Negligence
Noise level
Occupational Safety and Health Act (OSHA)
Product liability
Pull-back devices
Repetitive stress injuries

Risk
Safeguarding methods
Safety
Safety devices
Strict liability
Tagout
Warnings
Zero mechanical state

BIBLIOGRAPHY

Abbott, H., and M. Tyler, *Safer by Design: A Guide to the Management and Law of Designing for Product Safety* (2d ed.). Gower Pub. Co., 1997.

Accident Prevention Manual for Industrial Operations. National Safety Council (revised periodically).

Baldwin, S., F.H. Hare, Jr., and F.E. McGovern, *The Preparation of a Product Liability Case* (2d ed.). Aspen Pub., 1998.

Best's Safety Directory, revised periodically.

Brown, S., (ed.), *The Product Liability Handbook: Prevention, Risk, Consequence and Forensics of Product Failure.* Van Nostrand Reinhold, 1991.

Campbell, C. (ed.), *International Product Liability.* Center for International Legal Studies, 1998.

Cattanach, R.E. (ed.), *The Handbook of Environmentally Conscious Manufacturing: From Design and Production to Labeling and Recycling.* Irwin, 1994.

Concurrent Product Design and Environmentally Conscious Manufacturing. American Society of Mechanical Engineers, 1997.

Clark, T.S., and E.N. Corlett, *The Ergonomics of Workspaces and Machines: A Design Manual* (2d ed.). Taylor and Francis, 1995.

Enghagen, L.K., *Fundamentals of Product Liability Law for Engineers.* Industrial Press, 1992.

Hammer, W., *Occupational Safety Management and Engineering* (4th ed.). Prentice Hall, 1989.

Karwowski, W., and W.S. Marras, (eds.), *The Occupational Ergonomics Handbook.* CRC Press, 1999.

Karwowski, W., and G. Salvendy, *Ergonomics in Manufacturing.* Society of Manufacturing Engineers, 1998.

Kolb, J., and S.S. Ross, *Product Safety and Liability: A Desk Reference.* McGraw-Hill, 1988.

Lehto, M.R., and J.M. Miller, *Warnings: Fundamentals, Design, and Evaluation Methodologies.* Fuller Technical Publications, 1986.

Pulat, B.M., *Fundamentals of Industrial Ergonomics* (2d ed.). Waveland Press, 1997.

Roland, H.E., and B. Moriarty, *System Safety Engineering and Management* (2d ed.). Wiley-Interscience, 1990.

Salvendy, G., (ed.), *Handbook of Human Factors and Ergonomics.* Wiley, 1997.

Sanders, M.S., and E.J. McCormick, *Human Factors in Engineering and Design* (7th ed.). McGraw-Hill, 1992.

Wickens, C.D., S.E. Gordon, and Y. Liu, *An Introduction to Human Factors Engineering.* Addison-Wesley, 1997.

Woodson, W.E., *Human Factors Design Handbook* (2d ed.). McGraw-Hill, 1992.

REVIEW QUESTIONS

37.1   Explain your understanding of the elements of human-factors engineering. Why is it important?

37.2   What are the important features of a workstation, as far as the worker is concerned?

37.3   List and explain the environmental conditions that affect the performance of workers.

37.4   Describe your understanding of what safety means.

37.5   Explain what is meant by the terms hazard and risk. Give several examples of each from your own experience.

37.6   List the typical causes of injury to workers. How would you go about avoiding them?

37.7   Describe common methods of safeguarding metalworking machinery.

37.8   What is the basic principle of interlocks? Can they be bypassed? Explain, with examples.

37.9   List some of the equipment used for personal protection of workers. Do they have any disadvantages?

37.10   Why is it that machine builders cannot influence the level of safety to the extent that machine users can?

37.11   Explain the concept of caveat emptor (buyer beware). Why was it commonly accepted until the 1900s?

37.12   What trends in product liability took place after 1900?

37.13   Explain what is meant by negligence. What is comparative negligence?

37.14   List the proofs to be presented by the plaintiff according to strict-liability law.

37.15   What is the legal definition of a defect? What are the legal tests of whether a product is defective?

37.16   List the basic guidelines for designing and manufacturing safe products.

37.17   What is the safety hierarchy?

37.18 How is OSHA related to safety in the workplace?

37.19 What approach must be followed in maintenance operations to prevent injury?

37.20 What is the difference between negligence and comparative fault?

QUALITATIVE PROBLEMS

37.21 Explain why product liability has become such an important factor in manufacturing.

37.22 Can safeguarding devices on machines themselves be dangerous? Give some examples and explain.

37.23 Should monetary awards be limited in product liability cases? What are the pros and cons of such limits? Should they depend on the type of accident?

37.24 The monthly *American Machinist* trade magazine has a page in each issue that gives summaries of court cases on product liability. Make a review of the latest issues of this magazine and describe your observations.

37.25 Describe your own thoughts regarding the environmental considerations described in Section 37.4.

37.26 Section 37.3 outlined certain personal protective equipment. Do you think such equipment can itself present hazards to the worker? Give specific examples.

37.27 How would you go about measuring noise levels in manufacturing plants? Comment on the type and number of machines involved, proximity of the workers to machinery, size of the room, etc.

37.28 When should the cost of a safety device be a factor in whether or not it is provided as standard equipment? Assume the safety device does not cause any additional hazards.

37.29 Is it ever beneficial to have a barrier guard that can be removed from a machine? Explain.

37.30 If a chair designed for people to sit on fails when someone stands on it, is it defective?

37.31 Give examples of situations where the light curtain shown in Fig. 37.2 cannot be used.

37.32 Assume that you are the manufacturer of a product which recycles plastics by chopping them into small granules. The agitator in the machine is recognized as quite hazardous. One of your engineers recommends a warning sign which reads "Danger - stay away from agitator!". Another engineer recommends a large hopper with a lid to safeguard the hazard. Among the two, which is the better suggestion? Why?

SYNTHESIS AND DESIGN

37.33 Inspect some of the measuring instruments with which you are familiar, and explain how you would modify them to make them easier to use and less susceptible to reading errors.

37.34 Describe some unsafe situations or practices in your own home. Why are they unsafe?

37.35 Do you think that a pair of sharp scissors is a defective product? Explain.

37.36 Describe some of the machines that you have seen or used. Explain the features, if any, that make them unsafe. Propose some design changes to make them safer.

37.37 Most modern machines are now built with ergonomic considerations in mind, whereas older machines did not generally have these features. Describe your opinions concerning retrofitting older machines to ensure their safe and comfortable use.

37.38 Assume that you are working as a design and manufacturing engineer in a company. You would like to implement the various topics described in this chapter; however, they are costly and the management is reluctant to approve them to the same extent that you would like to see. How would you go about convincing your supervisors of the merits of your approach?

37.39 There is a trend to limit monetary awards for damages to defendants in product liability cases, particularly in the medical profession. Describe your own thoughts regarding whether there should be a limit to such awards.

37.40 Review the devices shown in Figs. 37.1 and 37.2 and design several other devices for a variety of machines, tools, and equipment described in various sections of this text.

37.41 You should appreciate the fact that one has to have a legal background in order to pass judgment on the examples given in Section 37.6. How do you think you would rule on these cases if you were a manufacturing engineer or technician?

37.42 Pull-backs are a safety device that use a wrist or hand restraint tied through pulleys to a punch-press ram. As the ram descends, the operator's hands are pulled clear of the die area. What are the drawbacks to this device?

37.43 Design a barrier guard that can be used for a punch press where the part size can vary from a silhouette of 1 in, by 4 in, to 1 ft. by 4 ft.

37.44 Consider the case of a rear-seat air bag for automobiles. Debate whether or not such a device should be used.

37.45 What are the drawbacks to automotive seatbelts? If you were a politician, what exceptions would you include in the seat belt law?

PART VIII
Manufacturing in a Competitive Environment

The processes and related operations described in this text thus far constitute the important elements for the design and manufacture of products. Although understanding these processes is fundamental, even more important is to view these technical subjects in the context of the **competitive forces** that control the choice and implementation of various technologies in manufacturing. We have regularly discussed and referred to many of the aspects of these driving forces, especially manufacturing cost, product quality, and the use of automation, as they relate to various manufacturing operations.

Advances in automating manufacturing processes, as described in Chapter 38, have been driven by several competitive forces, such as the continual need to improve productivity and product quality and to decrease manufacturing costs. Beginning with the development of numerical control of machine tools in the early 1950s, automation has become a key factor in several industries, enabling manufacturers to reverse the problems of escalating costs, maintain product quality and, thus, enhance their competitive positions.

Much of the progress in automating manufacturing facilities stems from our ability to view manufacturing operations as a **system**. In implementing a systems approach to manufacturing, we can **integrate** various functions and activities that had previously been separate entities. In this way, we can optimize the entire manufacturing process, rather than having to limit ourselves to considering isolated technical and human elements.

The integration of manufacturing operations and the most promising technologies for accomplishing this integration are described in Chapter 39. Also described are several topics that are now so familiar that they are commonly referred to in terms of acronyms, such as CAD, CAM, NC, FMS, DFMA, and so on.

Each of these technologies has an impact on productivity, product quality, flexibility of operation, and cost of manufacturing. Their total integration into a single system has profound implications for the future of manufacturing.

The final chapter focuses on the following critical aspects of competition: (a) manufacturing economics, emphasizing the costs involved; (b) factors influencing selection of materials for products; and (c) factors influencing selection of manufacturing processes.

The major considerations within these areas are featured by examples that illustrate the key factors involved. This discussion introduces us to the major factors involved in evaluating manufacturing alternatives and helps us develop an ability to identify and assess them.

This book began with a General Introduction, in which we described several goals of manufacturing:

- fully meeting **design** and **service requirements** and product specifications;
- finding the most **economical methods** of environmentally conscious manufacturing;
- building **quality** into the product at each stage of design and manufacturing;
- ensuring that manufacturing processes are sufficiently **flexible** to respond rapidly to changing global market demand, both in product variety and in quantity;
- viewing manufacturing as a **system** in order to integrate its parts and, thus, improve performance; and
- continually striving for higher levels of quality and **productivity**.

A careful review of these goals will provide us with the proper context for studying the topics and examples presented in Part VIII.

38

Automation
of Manufacturing Processes

38.1 INTRODUCTION

Until the early 1950s, most manufacturing operations were carried out on traditional machinery, such as lathes, milling machines, and presses, which lacked flexibility and required considerable skilled labor. Each time a different product was manufactured, the machinery had to be retooled, and the movement of materials had to be rearranged.

The development of new products and of parts with complex shapes required numerous trial-and-error attempts by the operator in order to set the proper processing parameters on the machine. Furthermore, because of the human involvement, making parts that were exactly alike was difficult and time-consuming.

These circumstances meant that processing methods were generally inefficient and that labor costs were a significant portion of the overall production costs. The necessity for reducing the labor share of product cost gradually became apparent, as did the need to improve the efficiency and flexibility of manufacturing operations, particularly because of increased domestic and global competition.

Productivity also became a major concern. Defined as the optimum use of all resources (materials, energy, capital, labor, and technology) or as output per employee per hour, productivity basically measures operating efficiency. With rapid advances in the science and technology of manufacturing, the efficiency of manufacturing operations began to improve, and the percentage of total cost represented by labor costs began to decline.

How can productivity be improved? Mechanization of machinery and operations had, by and large, reached its peak by the 1940s. **Mechanization** runs a process or operation with the use of various mechanical, hydraulic, pneumatic, or electrical devices. Consider, for example, the use of a simple, hand-operated can opener. Opening a thousand cans by hand would take a long time, would require much physical effort, and would be tedious. One would soon lose interest, and one's efficiency would drop. Using an electric can opener takes less time and effort, but the job is still tedious, and efficiency is still likely to drop after a while.

Note that, in mechanized systems, the operator still directly controls the particular process and must check each step of the machine's performance. For example, if a cutting tool breaks during machining, if parts are overheated during heat treatment, if surface finish begins to deteriorate during grinding, or if dimensional tolerances become too large in sheet-metal forming, the operator must intervene and change one or more of the relevant process parameters.

The next step in improving the efficiency of manufacturing operations was **automation** (from the Greek word *automatos*, meaning self-acting). The word automation was coined in the mid-1940s by the U.S. automobile industry to indicate automatic handling and processing of parts in production machines. During the past four decades, major advances and breakthroughs in the types and in the extent of automation have occurred, ones made possible largely through rapid advances in the capacity and sophistication of **computers** and **control systems**.

This chapter follows the outline shown in Fig. 38.1. First, it reviews the history and principles of automation and how they have helped us **integrate** various operations and activities in a manufacturing plant to improve productivity. Then, it introduces the important concept of control of machines and systems through **numerical control** and **adaptive control** techniques.

An essential aspect of manufacturing is material handling—that is, the movement of raw materials and parts in various stages of completion throughout the plant. We describe how material handling has been developed into various systems, particulary ones including the use of **industrial robots** to improve efficiency. The subject of **sensor technology** is

FIGURE 38.1 Outline of topics covered in Chapter 38.

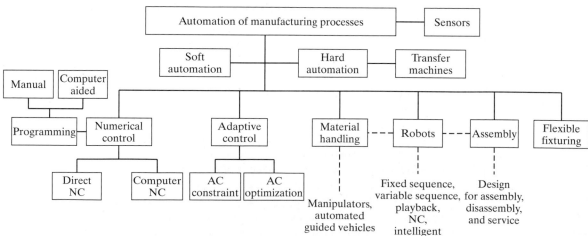

then described; this technology is one that is an essential element in the control and optimization of machinery, processes, and systems.

Among newer developments are **flexible fixturing** and **assembly operations**. These methods enable us to take full advantage of advanced manufacturing technologies, particularly flexible manufacturing systems (Section 39.10), and of major developments in computer-integrated manufacturing systems and their impact on all aspects of manufacturing operations.

38.2 AUTOMATION

Automation is generally defined as the process of having machines follow a predetermined sequence of operations with little or no human labor, using specialized equipment and devices that perform and control manufacturing processes. As described in Section 38.8 and in Chapter 39, automation, in its full potential, is achieved through the use of a variety of devices, sensors, actuators, techniques, and equipment that are capable of observing and controlling all aspects of the manufacturing process, of making decisions concerning the changes that should be made in the operation, and of controlling all aspects of it.

Automation is an *evolutionary* rather than a revolutionary concept. In manufacturing plants it has been implemented successfully in the following basic areas of activity:

- **Manufacturing processes.** Machining, forging, cold extrusion, casting, and grinding operations are typical examples of processes that have been extensively automated.
- **Material handling.** Materials and parts in various stages of completion are moved throughout a plant by computer-controlled equipment, without human guidance.
- **Inspection.** Parts are automatically inspected for quality, dimensional accuracy, and surface finish, either at the time of manufacturing (*in-process inspection*) or after they are made (*postprocess inspection*).
- **Assembly.** Individually manufactured parts are automatically assembled into subassemblies and, finally, into a product.
- **Packaging.** Products are packaged automatically.

38.2.1 Evolution of Automation

Some metalworking processes were developed as early as 4000 B.C. (See Table 1 in the General Introduction.) It was not, however, until the beginning of the Industrial Revolution in the 1750s that automation began to be introduced in the production of goods. Machine tools, such as turret lathes, automatic screw machines, and automatic bottle-making equipment, were developed in the late 1890s and early 1900s. Mass-production techniques and transfer machines were developed in the 1920s.

These machines had *fixed* automatic mechanisms and were designed to produce *specific* products. These developments were best represented in the automobile industry, which produced passenger cars at a high production rate (mass production) and low cost.

The major breakthrough in automation began with numerical control (NC) of machine tools in the early 1950s. Since this historic development, rapid progress has been made in automating most aspects of manufacturing (Table 38.1). These aspects involve the introduction of computers into automation, computerized numerical control (CNC), adaptive control (AC), industrial robots, and computer-integrated manufacturing (CIM) systems, including computer-aided design, engineering, and manufacturing (CAD/CAE/CAM).

TABLE 38.1   Development in the History of Automation
of Manufacturing Processes

Date	Development
1500–1600	Water power for metalworking; rolling mills for coinage strips.
1600–1700	Hand lathe for wood; mechanical calculator.
1700–1800	Boring, turning, and screw cutting lathe, drill press.
1800–1900	Copying lathe, turret lathe, universal milling machine; advanced mechanical calculators.
1808	Sheet-metal cards with punched holes for automatic control of weaving patterns in looms.
1863	Automatic piano player (Pianola).
1900–1920	Geared lathe; automatic screw machine; automatic bottlemaking machine.
1920	First use of the word *robot*.
1920–1940	Transfer machines; mass production.
1940	First electronic computing machine.
1943	First digital electronic computer.
1945	First use of the word *automation*.
1948	Invention of the transistor.
1952	First prototype numerical-control machine tool.
1954	Development of the symbolic language APT (Automatically Programmed Tool); adaptive control.
1957	Commercially available NC machine tools.
1959	Integrated circuits; first use of the term *group technology*.
1960s	Industrial robots.
1965	Large-scale integrated circuits.
1968	Programmable logic controllers.
1970	First integrated manufacturing system; spot welding of automobile bodies with robots.
1970s	Microprocessors; minicomputer-controlled robot; flexible manufacturing systems; group technology.
1980s	Artificial intelligence; intelligent robots; smart sensors; untended manufacturing cells.
1990s	Integrated manufacturing systems; intelligent and sensor-based machines; telecommunications and global manufacturing networks; fuzzy logic devices; artificial neural networks; Internet tools.

38.2.2 Goals of Automation

Automation has the following primary goals:

a. to **integrate** various aspects of manufacturing operations so as to improve product quality and uniformity, minimize cycle times and effort and, thus, reduce labor costs;

b. to **improve productivity** by reducing manufacturing costs through better control of production. Parts are loaded, fed, and unloaded on machines more efficiently, machines are used more effectively, and production is organized more efficiently;

c. to **improve quality** by employing more repeatable processes;

d. to **reduce human involvement**, boredom, and the possibility of human error;

e. to **reduce workpiece damage** caused by manual handling of parts;

f. to **raise the level of safety** for personnel, especially under hazardous working conditions; and

g. to **economize on floor space** in the manufacturing plant by arranging machines, material movement, and auxiliary equipment more efficiently.

Automation and Production Quantity.   Production quantity is crucial in determining the type of machinery and the level of automation required to produce parts economically. Let's first define some basic production terms.

TABLE 38.2   Approximate Annual Volume of Production

Type of production	Number produced	Typical products
Experimental or prototype	1–10	All
Piece or small batch	10–5000	Aircraft, special machinery, dies, jewelry, orthopedic implants, missiles.
Batch or high volume	5000–100,000	Trucks, agricultural machinery, jet engines, diesel engines; computer components, sporting goods.
Mass production	100,000 and over	Automobiles, appliances, fasteners, food and beverage containers.

Total production quantity is defined as the total number of parts to be made. This quantity can be produced in individual batches of various **lot sizes**. Lot size greatly influences the economics of production; this effect will be described in Chapter 39. **Production rate** is defined as the number of parts produced per unit time—for example per day, per month, or per year. The approximate and generally accepted ranges of production volume are shown in Table 38.2 for some typical applications. As you might expect, **experimental** or **prototype** products represent the lowest volume. (See also Chapter 19.)

Small quantities per year (Fig. 38.2) can be manufactured in **job shops**, by the use of various standard general-purpose machine tools (**stand-alone machines**) or machining centers. (See Chapter 24.) These operations have high part variety, meaning that different parts can be produced in a short time without extensive changes in tooling and in production operations. On the other hand, machinery in job shops generally requires skilled labor to operate and production quantity and rate are low; as a result, cost per part can be high (Fig. 38.3). When parts involve a large labor component, their production is called **labor intensive**.

Piece-part production usually involves very small quantities and is suitable for job shops. The majority of piece-part production is in lot sizes of 50 or less. **Small-batch production** quantities typically range from 10 to 100, and general-purpose machines and machining centers with various computer controls are used for them. **Batch production**

FIGURE 38.2   Flexibility and productivity of various manufacturing systems. Note the overlap between the systems; it is due to the various levels of automation and computer control that are possible in each group. See, also, Chapter 39, for details. *Source*: U. Rembold, et al., *Computer Integrated Manufacturing and Engineering.* Addison-Wesley, 1993.

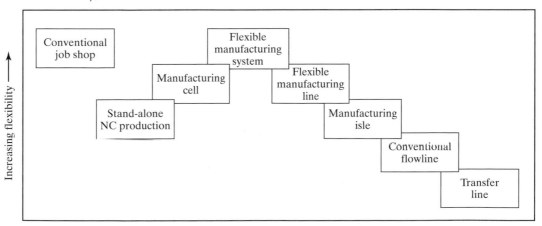

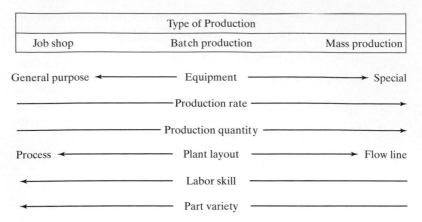

FIGURE 38.3   General characteristics of three types of production methods: job shop, batch, and mass production.

usually involves lot sizes between 100 and 5000; it utilizes machinery similar to that used for small-batch production, but with specially designed fixtures for higher production rates.

Mass production involves quantities often over 100,000; it requires special-purpose machinery (**dedicated machines**) and automated equipment for transferring materials and parts. Although the machinery, equipment, and specialized tooling are expensive, both the labor skills required and the labor costs are relatively low, because of the high level of automation. However, these production systems are organized for a specific type of product and so lack flexibility. Most manufacturing facilities operate with a variety of machines in combination and with various levels of automation and computer controls.

38.2.3 Applications of Automation

Automation can be applied to the manufacturing of all types of goods, from raw materials to finished products, and in all types of production, from job shops to large manufacturing facilities. The decision to automate a new or existing production facility requires taking into account the following additional considerations:

- the type of product manufactured;
- the quantity and the rate of production required;
- the particular phase of the manufacturing operation to be automated;
- the level of skill in the available workforce;
- any reliability and maintenance problems that may be associated with automated systems; and
- economics.

Because automation generally involves high initial cost of equipment and requires a knowledge of the principles of operation and maintenance, a decision about the implementation of even low levels of automation must involve a careful study of the true needs of an organization. It is not unusual for a company to begin the implementation of automation with great enthusiasm and with high across-the-board goals, only to discover that its economic benefits largely were illusory rather than real and that, in the final assessment, automation was not cost-effective. In many situations, **selective automation** (rather than total automation) of a facility is desirable.

Generally, the higher the level of skill available in the workforce, the lower the need for automation, provided that labor costs are justified and that there are sufficient workers available. Conversely, if a manufacturing facility is already automated, the skill level required is lower. As we will see in the rest of Part VIII, there are several important and complex issues involved in the decision-making about the apropriate level of automation.

38.2.4 Hard Automation

In *hard automation* or **fixed-position automation**, the production machines are designed to produce a standardized product, such as an engine block, a valve, a gear, or a spindle. Although product size and processing parameters (such as speed, feed, and depth of cut) can be changed, these machines are specialized, and they lack flexibility. They cannot be modified to any significant extent to accommodate products that have different shapes and dimensions. (See *Group Technology*, Section 39.8). Because these machines are expensive to design and to build, their economical use requires the production of parts in very large quantities.

The machines that are used in hard-automation applications are usually built on the **building-block (modular) principle**. They are generally called **transfer machines**, and they consist of two major components: powerhead production units, and transfer mechanisms.

Powerhead Production Units.   Consisting of a frame or bed, electric drive motors, gearboxes, and tool spindles, **powerhead production units** are self-contained. Their components are commercially available in various standard sizes and capacities; because of this inherent modularity, they can easily be regrouped for producing a different part and thus have some adaptability and flexibility.

Transfer machines consisting of two or more powerhead units can be arranged on the shop floor in linear, circular, or U patterns. The weight and shape of the workpieces influences the arrangement selected. The arrangement is also important for continuity of operation in the event of tool failure or machine breakdown in one or more of the units. **Buffer storage** features are incorporated in these machines to permit continued operation in such an event.

Transfer Mechanisms and Transfer Lines.   *Transfer mechanisms* are used to move the workpiece from one station to another in the machine (or from one machine to another), to enable various operations to be performed on the part. Workpieces are transferred by several methods: (1) rails along which the parts, usually placed on pallets, are pushed or pulled by various mechanisms (Fig. 38.4a); (2) rotary indexing tables (Fig. 38.4b); and (3) overhead conveyors.

FIGURE 38.4   Two types of transfer mechanisms: (a) straight and (b) circular patterns.

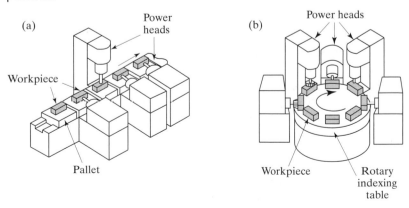

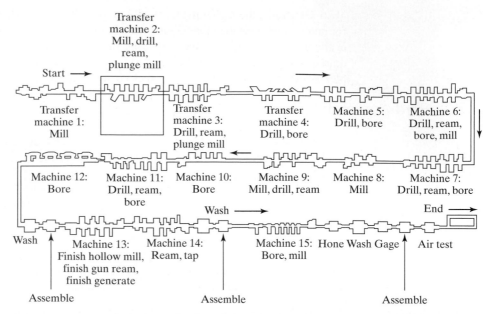

FIGURE 38.5   A large transfer line for producing engine blocks and cylinder heads. *Source*: Ford Motor Company.

Transfer of parts from station to station is usually controlled by sensors and other devices. Tools on transfer machines can be easily changed in toolholders having quick-change features, and these machines can be equipped with various automatic gaging and inspection systems. These systems are utilized between operations, to ensure that the dimensions of a part produced in one station are within acceptable tolerances before that part is transferred to the next station. (As is described in Section 38.10, transfer machines are also used extensively in automatic assembly.)

The **transfer lines** or **flow lines** in a very large system for producing cylinder heads for engine blocks, consisting of a number of transfer machines, are shown in Fig. 38.5. This system is capable of producing 100 cylinder heads per hour. Note the various machining operations performed: milling, drilling, reaming, boring, tapping, honing, washing, and gaging.

38.2.5 Soft Automation

We have seen that hard automation generally involves mass-production machines that lack flexibility. In *soft* (**flexible** or **programmable**) *automation*, greater flexibility is achieved, through the use of computer control of the machine and of its functions by various programs, examples of which are described in detail in Sections 38.3 and 38.4.

Soft automation is an important development, because the machine can be easily and readily reprogrammed to produce a part having a shape or dimensions different from the one produced just before it. Because of this characteristic, soft automation can produce parts having complex shapes. Further advances in flexible automation include the extensive use of modern computers, leading to the development of **flexible manufacturing systems** (Section 39.10), with high levels of efficiency and productivity.

38.2.6 Programmable Controllers

The control of a manufacturing process in the proper sequence, especially one involving groups of machines and material-handling equipment, has traditionally been performed by timers, switches, relays, counters, and similar hardwired devices based on mechanical, electromechanical, and pneumatic principles. Beginning in 1968, **programmable logic controllers (PLC**—also called PC, but not to be confused with personal computer) were introduced to replace these hardwired devices.

The programmable logic controller has been defined by the National Electrical Manufacturers Association (NEMA) as "a digitally operating electronic apparatus which uses a programmable memory for the internal storage of instructions for implementing specific functions such as logic, sequencing, timing, counting, and arithmetic to control, through digital or analog input/output modules, various types of machines or processes." The digital computer, which is used to control the functions of a programmable controller, is considered to be within this scope.

Because PLCs eliminate the need for relay control panels, and because they can be reprogrammed and take less space, they have been widely adopted in manufacturing systems and operations. Their basic functions are on–off, motion, sequential operations, and feedback control. PLCs are also used in system control, with high-speed digital-processing and communication capabilities. These controllers perform reliably in industrial environments and improve the overall efficiency of the operation.

PLCs are becoming less popular in new installations, because of advances in numerical-control machines, but they still represent a very large installation base. There is now a growing trend toward using microcomputers instead of PLCs, because they are less expensive, easier to program, and easy to network. This advance has been made possible by the new breeds of "real time" operating systems such as Windows NT and SCADA (supervisory control and data acquisition software).

38.2.7 Total Productive Maintenance (TPM)

The management and maintenance of a wide variety of machines, equipment, and systems are among the important aspects affecting the productivity of a manufacturing organization. The concepts of *total productive maintenance* and **total productive equipment management (TPEM)** are now being advanced.

These concepts include continued analysis of such factors as equipment breakdown and equipment problems, the monitoring and improving of equipment productivity, the implementation of preventive and predictive maintenance, the reduction of setup time, idle time, and cycle time, the full utilization of machinery and equipment and the improvement of their effectiveness, and the reduction of product defects. Teamwork—for example, as implemented by continuous improvement action teams—is an important component of this activity and involves the full cooperation of the machine operators, the maintenance personnel, the engineers, and the management of the organization. (See, also, **kaizen**, Section 36.1.)

38.3 NUMERICAL CONTROL (NC)

Numerical control is a method of controlling the movements of machine components by directly inserting coded instructions, in the form of numbers and letters, into the system. The system automatically interprets these data and converts them to output signals. These signals, in turn, control various machine components—for example, by turning spindles on and off, changing tools, moving the workpiece or the tools along specific paths, or turning cutting fluids on and off.

In order to appreciate the importance of numerical control of machines, let's briefly review how a process such as machining has traditionally been carried out. After studying the working drawings of a part, the operator sets up the appropriate process parameters (such as cutting speed, feed, depth of cut, cutting fluid, and so on), determines the sequence of the machining operations to be performed, clamps the workpiece in a workholding device (such as a chuck or collet), and proceeds with the making of the part.

Depending on part shape and on the dimensional accuracy specified, this approach usually requires skilled operators. The machining procedure followed may depend on the particular operator; because of the possibilities of human error, even parts produced by the same operator may not all be identical.

Part quality may, therefore, depend on the particular operator or (even with the same operator) on the day of the week or the hour of the day. Because of increased concern with improving product quality and reducing manufacturing costs, such variability (and its effects on product quality) are no longer acceptable. This situation can be eliminated by numerical control of the machining operation.

The importance of numerical control can be further illustrated by the following example. Assume that several holes are to be drilled on a part in the positions shown in Fig. 38.6.

In the traditional manual method of machining this part, the operator positions the drill bit with respect to the workpiece, using reference points given by any of the three methods shown in the figure. The operator then proceeds to drill the holes. Let's first assume that 100 parts, all having exactly the same shape and dimensional accuracy, are to be drilled. Obviously, this operation is going to be tedious, because the operator has to go through the same motions repeatedly. Moreover, the probability is high that, for various reasons, some of the parts machined will be different from others.

Let's now assume that during this production run, the order for these parts is changed, and ten of the parts now require holes in different positions. The machinist now has to reposition the work table; this operation will be time consuming and is subject to error.

Such operations can be performed easily by numerical control machines that are capable of producing parts repeatedly and accurately and of handling different parts (by simply loading different part programs, as will be described later).

In operations under numerical control, data concerning all aspects of the machining operation, such as locations, speeds, feeds, and cutting fluids, can be stored on magnetic media, changing over time from tapes to hard disks. The concept of NC control is that specific information can be relayed from these storage devices to the machine tool's control panel.

FIGURE 38.6   Positions of drilled holes in a workpiece. Three methods of measurements are shown: (a) absolute dimensioning, referenced from one point at the lower left of the part; (b) incremental dimensioning, made sequentially from one hole to another; and (c) mixed dimensioning, a combination of both methods.

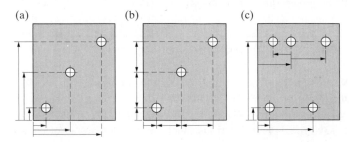

On the basis of input information, relays and other devices (**hard-wired controls**) can be actuated to obtain a desired machine setup. Complex operations (such as turning a part having various contours, or die sinking in a milling machine) can be carried out easily.

Numerical control has had a major impact on all aspects of manufacturing operations. NC machines are now used extensively in small- and medium-quantity production (typically 500 parts or less) of a wide variety of parts, both in small shops and in large manufacturing facilities. Older machines can often be retrofitted with numerical control.

38.3.1 Historical Background

The basic concept behind numerical control apparently was implemented in the early 1800s, when punched holes in sheet-metal cards were used to automatically control the movements of weaving machines. Needles were activated by the sensing of the presence or absence of a hole in the card. This invention was followed by automatic piano players (Pianola), in which the keys were activated by air flowing through holes punched in a perforated roll of paper.

The principle of *numerically* controlling the movements of machine tools was first conceived in the 1940s by J. Parsons (1913–) in his attempt to machine complex helicopter blades. The first prototype NC machine was built in 1952 at the Massachusetts Institute of Technology. It was a vertical-spindle, two-axis copy milling machine retrofitted with servomotors, and the machining operations performed consisted of end milling and face milling (Chapter 23) on a thick aluminum plate.

The numerical data to be punched into the paper tapes were generated by a digital computer, another invention which was being developed at the same time at MIT. In the experiments, parts were machined successfully, accurately, and repeatedly without operator intervention. On the basis of this success, the machine-tool industry began designing, building, and marketing NC machine tools. Later, these machines were equipped with computer numerical controls (CNC) yielding greater flexibility, accuracy, versatility, and ease of operation. The latest developments are **machining centers**, the principles of which were described in Section 24.2.

38.3.2 Computer Numerical Control (CNC)

In the next step in the development of numerical control, the control hardware (mounted on the NC machine) was converted to local computer control by software. Two types of computerized systems were developed: direct numerical control, and computer numerical control.

In **direct numerical control (DNC)**, as originally conceived and developed in the 1960s, several machines are directly controlled, step by step, by a central mainframe computer. In this system, the operator has access to the central computer through a remote terminal. In this way, the handling of tapes and the need for a separate computer on each machine are eliminated. With DNC, the status of all machines in a manufacturing facility can be monitored and assessed from the central computer. However, DNC has a crucial disadvantage: If the computer shuts down, all the machines become inoperative.

A more recent definition of DNC (now meaning **distributed numerical control**) covers the use of a central computer serving as the control system over a number of individual *computer numerical control* machines having onboard microcomputers. This system provides large memory and computational capabilities and offers flexibility while overcoming the disadvantage of direct numerical control.

Computer numerical control is a system in which a control microcomputer is an integral part of a machine or a piece of equipment (*onboard computer*). The part program may be prepared at a remote site by the programmer, and it may incorporate information obtained from drafting software packages and from machining simulations, in order to ensure that the part program is bug free. The machine operator can, however, easily and manually program onboard computers. The operator can modify the programs directly, prepare programs for different parts, and store the programs.

Because of the availability of small computers having a large memory, microprocessor(s), and program-editing capabilities, CNC systems are widely used today. The availability of low-cost programmable controllers also played a major role in the successful implementation of CNC in manufacturing plants.

Some advantages of CNC over conventional NC systems are the following:

- increased *flexibility*—the machine can produce a specific part, followed by other parts with different shapes, and at reduced cost;
- greater *accuracy*—computers have a higher sampling rate and faster operation; and
- more *versatility*—editing and debugging programs, reprogramming, and plotting and printing part shape are simpler.

38.3.3 Principles of NC Machines

The basic elements and operation of a typical NC machine are shown in Fig. 38.7. The functional elements in numerical control and the components involved follow:

a. Data input: The numerical information is read and stored in the tape reader or in computer memory.

b. Data processing: The programs are read into the machine control unit for processing.

c. Data output: This information is translated into commands (typically pulsed commands) to the servomotor (Fig. 38.8). The servomotor then moves the table (on which the workpiece is mounted) to specific positions, through linear or rotary movements, by means of stepping motors, leadscrews, and other similar devices.

Types of Control Circuits.   An NC machine can be controlled through two types of circuits: open-loop and closed-loop. In the **open-loop** system (Fig. 38.8a), the signals

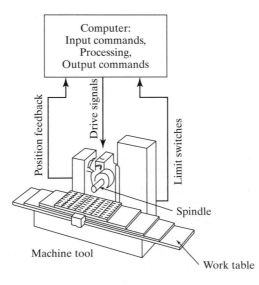

FIGURE 38.7   Schematic illustration of the major components of a numerical-control machine tool.

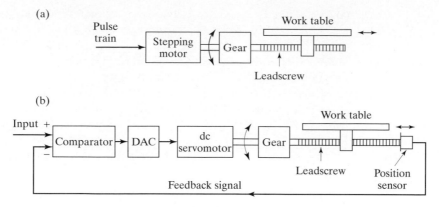

FIGURE 38.8   Schematic illustration of the components of (a) an open-loop and (b) a closed-loop control system for a numerical-control machine. DAC means "digital-to-analog converter."

are sent to the servomotor by the controller, but the movements and final positions of the work table are not checked for accuracy.

The **closed-loop** system (Fig. 38.8b) is equipped with various transducers, sensors, and counters that measure accurately the position of the work table. Through **feedback control**, the position of the work table is compared against the signal. Table movements terminate when the proper coordinates are reached. The closed-loop system is more complicated and more expensive than the open-loop system.

Position measurement in NC machines can be accomplished through direct or indirect methods. In *direct measuring systems*, a sensing device reads a graduated scale on the machine table or slide for linear movement (Fig. 38.9a). This system is the more accurate because the scale is built into the machine, and backlash (the play between two adjacent mating gear teeth) in the mechanisms is not significant.

FIGURE 38.9   (a) Direct measurement of the linear displacement of a machine-tool work table. (b) and (c) Indirect measurement methods.

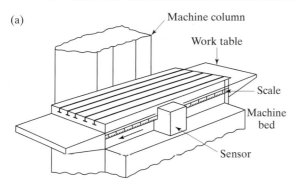

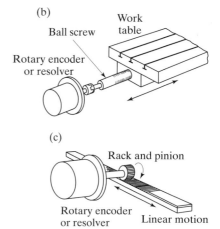

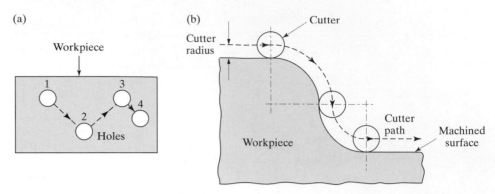

FIGURE 38.10 Movement of tools in numerical-control machining. (a) Point-to-point, in which the drill bit drills a hole at position 1, is retracted and moved to position 2, and so on. (b) Continuous path by a milling cutter. Note that the cutter path is compensated for by the cutter radius. This path can also be compensated for cutter wear.

In *indirect measuring systems*, **rotary encoders** or **resolvers** (Figs. 38.9b and c) convert rotary movement to translation movement. In this system, backlash can significantly affect measurement accuracy. Position feedback mechanisms utilize various sensors that are based mainly on magnetic and photoelectric principles.

38.3.4 Types of Control Systems

There are two basic types of control systems in numerical control: point-to-point and contouring.

a. In a **point-to-point system**, also called **positioning**, each axis of the machine is driven separately by leadscrews and, depending on the type of operation, at different velocities. The machine moves initially at maximum velocity in order to reduce nonproductive time, but decelerates as the tool approaches its numerically defined position. Thus, in an operation such as drilling (or punching a hole), the positioning and cutting take place sequentially (Fig. 38.10a).

After the hole is drilled or punched, the tool retracts upward and moves rapidly to another position, and the operation is repeated. The path followed from one position to another is important in only one respect: It must be chosen to minimize the time of travel, for better efficiency. Point-to-point systems are used mainly in drilling, punching, and straight milling operations.

b. In a **contouring system** (also known as a **continuous path system**), the positioning and the operations are both performed along controlled paths but at different velocities. Because the tool acts as it travels along a prescribed path (Fig. 38.10b), accurate control and synchronization of velocities and movements are important. The contouring system is typically used on lathes, milling machines, grinders, welding machinery, and machining centers.

Interpolation. Movement along the path (*interpolation*) occurs *incrementally* by one of several basic methods (Fig. 38.11). Examples of actual paths in drilling, boring, and milling operations are shown in Fig. 38.12. In all interpolations, the path controlled is that of the *center of rotation* of the tool. Compensation for different types of tools, for different diameters of tools, or for tool wear during machining can be made in the NC program.

a. In **linear interpolation**, the tool moves in a straight line from start to end (Fig. 38.11a), on two or three axes. Theoretically, all types of profiles can be produced by this

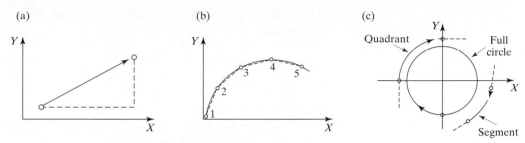

FIGURE 38.11   Types of interpolation in numerical control: (a) linear, (b) continuous path approximated by incremental straight lines, and (c) circular.

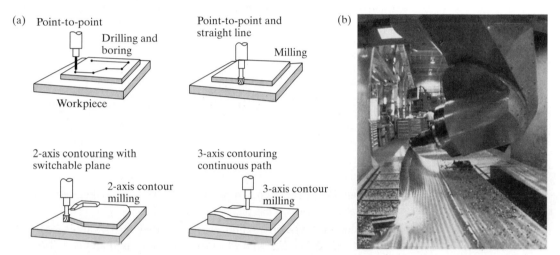

FIGURE 38.12   (a) Schematic illustration of drilling, boring, and milling with various paths. (b) Machining a sculptured surface on a 5-axis numerical control machine. *Source*: The Ingersoll Milling Machine Co.

method, by making the increments between the points small (Fig. 38.11b). However, a large amount of data has to be processed in order to do so.

b. In **circular interpolation** (Fig. 38.11c), the inputs required for the path are the coordinates of the end points, the coordinates of the center of the circle and its radius, and the direction of the tool along the arc.

c. In **parabolic interpolation** and **cubic interpolation**, the path is approximated by curves, using higher-order mathematical equations. This method is effective in 5-axis machines and is particularly useful in die sinking operations for sheet-forming of automotive bodies. These interpolations are also used for the movements of industrial robots, discussed in Section 38.7.

38.3.5 Accuracy in Numerical Control

Positioning accuracy in NC machines is defined by how accurately the machine can be positioned to a certain coordinate system. An NC machine usually has a positioning accuracy of at least ± 3 μm (0.0001 in.). **Repeatability** (the closeness of agreement of repeated position movements under the same operating conditions of the machine) is usually around

± 8 μm (0.0003 in.). **Resolution** (the smallest increment of motion of the machine components) is usually about 2.5 μm (0.0001 in.).

The *stiffness* of the machine tool (see Section 24.4) and the *backlash* in its gear drives and leadscrews are important for dimensional accuracy. Although in older machines backlash has been eliminated with special backlash take-up circuits (whereby the tool always approaches a particular position on the workpiece from the same direction), backlash in modern machines is eliminated by using pre-loaded ball screws. Also, rapid response to command signals requires that friction and inertia be minimized, for example, by reducing the mass of moving components of the machine.

38.3.6 Advantages and Limitations of NC

Numerical control has the following advantages over conventional methods of machine control:

1. Flexibility of operation is improved, as well as the ability to produce complex shapes with good dimensional accuracy, good repeatability, reduced scrap loss, high production rates, high productivity, and high product quality.
2. Tooling costs are reduced, because templates and other fixtures are not required.
3. Machine adjustments are easy to make with microcomputers and digital readouts.
4. More operations can be performed with each setup, and the lead time for setup and machining required is less, as compared to conventional methods. Furthermore, design changes are facilitated, and inventory is reduced.
5. Programs can be prepared rapidly, and they can be recalled at any time, by utilizing microprocessors. Less paperwork is involved.
6. Faster prototype production is possible. (See also Chapter 19.)
7. Operator skill required is less than that for a qualified machinist, and the operator has more time to attend to other tasks in the work area.

The major limitations of NC are the relatively high initial cost of the equipment, the need and cost for programming and computer time, and the special maintenance that requires trained personnel. Because NC machines are complex systems, breakdowns can be costly, so preventive maintenance is essential. However, these limitations are often easily outweighed by the overall economic advantages of NC.

38.4 PROGRAMMING FOR NUMERICAL CONTROL

A program for numerical control consists of a sequence of directions that causes an NC machine to carry out a certain operation, machining being the most common process. **Programming for NC** may be performed by an internal programming department, be done on the shop floor, or be purchased from an outside source.

The program contains instructions and commands. *Geometric instructions* pertain to relative movements between the tool and the workpiece. *Processing instructions* concern spindle speeds, feeds, cutting tools, cutting fluids, and so on. *Travel instructions* pertain to the type of interpolation and to the speed of movement of the tool or the work table. *Switching instructions* concern on/off position for coolant supplies, direction or lack of spindle rotation, tool changes, workpiece feeding, clamping, and so on.

Manual part programming consists first of calculating the dimensional relationships of the tool, workpiece, and work table, on the basis of the engineering drawings of the part (including CAD), the manufacturing operations to be performed, and their sequence. A program sheet is then prepared, detailing the necessary information to carry out the particular operation. The part program is then prepared on the basis of this information.

Manual programming can be done by someone who is knowledgeable about the particular manufacturing process and is able to understand, read, and change part programs. Because they are familiar with machine tools and process capabilities, skilled machinists can (with some training in programming) also do manual programming. However, the work involved is tedious, time-consuming, and uneconomical; consequently, manual programming is used mostly in simple point-to-point applications.

Computer-aided part programming involves special symbolic *programming languages* that determine the coordinate points of corners, edges, and surfaces of the part. A **programming language** is a means of communicating with the computer; it involves the use of symbolic characters. The programmer describes in this language the component to be processed, and the computer converts that description to commands for the NC machine.

Several languages, having various features and applications, are commercially available. The first language that used English-like statements (called **APT**, for *Automatically Programmed Tools*) was developed in the late 1950s. This language, in its various expanded forms, is still the most widely used for both point-to-point and continuous-path programming.

Complex parts are now machined using graphics-based, computer-aided machining programs. A tool path is created in a largely graphic environment that is similar to a CAD program. The machine code (**G-Code**) is created automatically by the program.

Before production begins, the programs should be verified, either by viewing a simulation of the process on a monitor or by making the part from an inexpensive material (such as aluminum, wood, wax, or plastic), rather than from the actual material specified for the finished part.

Computer-aided part programming has the following advantages over manual methods:

a. use of symbolic language (several programs are now available);

b. reduced programming time. Programming is capable of accommodating a large amount of data concerning machine characteristics and process variables, such as power, speeds, feed, tool shape, compensation for tool-shape changes due to tool wear, deflections, and coolant use;

c. reduced possibility of human error, which can occur in manual programming;

d. ability to view a machining sequence on the screen for debugging purposes;

e. capability for simple changeover, either of machining sequence or from one machine to another; and

f. lower cost, because less time is required for programming.

The use of programming languages (**compilers**) not only results in higher part quality but also allows for more rapid development of machining instructions. In addition, simulations can be run on remote computer terminals, to ensure that the program functions as intended. This method prevents unnecessary occupation of expensive machinery for debugging procedures.

Selection of a particular NC programming language depends mainly on the following factors:

a. the level of expertise of the personnel in the manufacturing facility;

b. the complexity of the part;

c. the type of equipment and computers available;

d. the time and costs involved in programming.

38.5 ADAPTIVE CONTROL (AC)

In **adaptive control**, the operating parameters automatically adapt themselves to conform to new circumstances, such as changes in the dynamics of the particular process and any disturbances that may arise. It will readily be appreciated that this approach is basically a feedback system.

You may recognize that human reactions to occurrences in everyday life already contain dynamic feedback control. Driving your car on a smooth road is relatively easy and you need to make few, if any, adjustments. However, on a rough road you may have to steer to avoid potholes by visually and continuously observing the condition of the road. Your body feels the car's rough movements and vibrations; you then react by changing the direction and the speed of the car to minimize the effects of the rough road and to increase the comfort of your ride. The sense in which these responses are adaptive is that the control strategy adapts to changes in the operating conditions.

An **adaptive controller** would check load conditions, adapt an appropriate desired braking profile (for example, antilock brake system and traction control), and then use feedback to implement it. One may contrast dynamic feedback control with adaptive control as follows. Dynamic feedback control has a fixed controller mechanism which adapts or adjusts controller signals in response to measured changes in system behavior. A constant-gain control is a special case of dynamic feedback control, the term **gain** being defined as the ratio of output to input in an amplifier. Adaptive control adjusts not only the controller signals, but also the controller mechanism.

Research in adaptive control began in the early 1950s, and it was concerned with the design of autopilots for high-performance aircraft, which operate over a wide range of altitudes and speeds. During tests, it was observed that constant-gain feedback control systems would work well under some operating conditions but not under others. **Gain scheduling** is perhaps the simplest form of what now is called adaptive control. In gain scheduling, a different gain for the feedback is selected depending on the measured operating conditions. A different gain is assigned to each region of the system's operating space. With advanced adaptive controllers, the gain may vary continuously with changes in operating conditions.

Several adaptive-control systems are now commercially available for applications such as ship steering, chemical-reactor control, rolling mills, and medical technology. In manufacturing engineering, specifically, the purposes of adaptive control are the following:

1. to optimize *production rate;*
2. to optimize *product quality;*
3. to minimize *cost.*

Although adaptive control has, for some time, been used widely in continuous processing in the chemical industry and in oil refineries, its successful application to machining, grinding, forming, and other manufacturing processes is relatively recent. Application of AC in manufacturing is particularly important in situations where workpiece dimensions and quality are not uniform (such as a poor casting or an improperly heat-treated part).

Adaptive control is a logical extension of computer numerical control systems. As described in Section 38.4, the part programmer sets the processing parameters, based on the existing knowledge of the workpiece material and various data on the particular manufacturing process. In CNC machines, these parameters are held constant during a particular process cycle. In AC, on the other hand, the system is capable of automatic adjustments *during* processing, through closed-loop feedback control (Fig. 38.13).

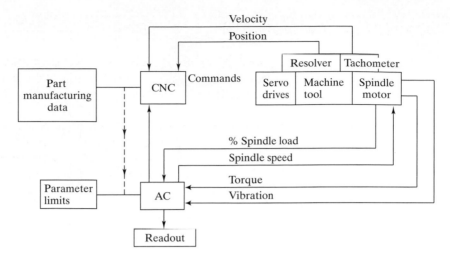

FIGURE 38.13 Schematic illustration of the application of adaptive control (AC) for a turning operation. The system monitors such parameters as cutting force, torque, and vibrations; if they are excessive, it modifies process variables such as feed and depth of cut to bring them back to acceptable levels.

38.5.1 Principles and Applications of Adaptive Control

The basic functions common to adaptive control systems are the following:

1. Determine the operating conditions of the process, including measures of performance. This is typically achieved by using sensors which measure process parameters (such as force, torque, vibration, and temperature).

2. Configure the process control in response to the operating conditions. Large changes in the operating conditions may provoke a decision to make a major switch in control strategy. More modest alterations may be the modification of process parameters (such as changing the speed of operation or of the feed, in machining).

3. Continue to monitor the process, making further changes in the controller when and as needed.

In an operation such as turning on a lathe (Chapter 22), the adaptive control system senses real-time cutting forces, torque, temperature, tool-wear rate, tool chipping or tool fracture, and surface finish of the workpiece. The system then converts this information into commands that modify the process parameters on the machine tool to hold them constant (or within certain limits) or to optimize the cutting operation.

Those systems that place a constraint on a process variable (such as forces, torque, or temperature) are called **adaptive control constraint (ACC)** systems. Thus, if the thrust force and the cutting force (and hence the torque) increase excessively (for example, because of the presence of a hard region in a casting), the adaptive control system changes the speed or the feed to lower the cutting force to an acceptable level (Fig. 38.14).

Without adaptive control (or without the direct intervention of the operator, as is the case in traditional machining operations), high cutting forces may cause the tools to chip or break or cause the workpiece to deflect or distort excessively. As a result, the dimensional accuracy and surface finish deteriorate.

Those systems that optimize an operation are called **adaptive control optimization (ACO)** systems. Optimization may involve maximizing material-removal rate between tool

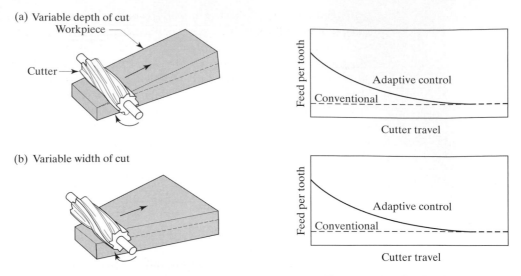

(a) Variable depth of cut

Workpiece

Cutter

Feed per tooth

Adaptive control

Conventional

Cutter travel

(b) Variable width of cut

Feed per tooth

Adaptive control

Conventional

Cutter travel

FIGURE 38.14   An example of adaptive control in milling. As the depth of cut or the width of cut increases, the cutting forces and the torque increase. The system senses this increase and automatically reduces the feed to avoid excessive forces or tool breakage, in order to maintain cutting efficiency. *Source*: Y. Koren.

changes (or resharpening) or improving surface finish. Currently, most systems are based on ACC, because the development and the proper implementation of ACO is complex.

Response time must be short for AC to be effective, particularly in high-speed operations (see Section 22.4). Assume, for example, that a turning operation is being performed on a lathe at a spindle speed of 1000 rpm, and the tool suddenly breaks, adversely affecting the surface finish and dimensional accuracy of the part. In order for the AC system to be effective, the sensing system must respond within a very short time, as otherwise the damage to the workpiece will be extensive.

For adaptive control to be effective in manufacturing operations, *quantitative relationships* must be established and stored in the computer software as mathematical models. For example, if the tool-wear rate in a machining operation is excessive, the computer must be able to decide how much of a change in speed or feed is necessary (and whether to increase it or decrease it) in order to reduce the wear rate to an acceptable level. The system should also be able to compensate for dimensional changes in the workpiece due to such causes as tool wear and temperature rise (Fig. 38.15).

If the operation is, for example, grinding (Chapter 25) the computer software must reflect the desired quantitative relationships among process variables (wheel and work speeds, feed, type of wheel) and such parameters as wheel wear, dulling of abrasive grains, grind-

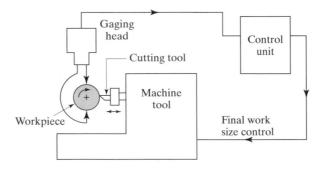

Gaging head

Control unit

Cutting tool

Machine tool

Workpiece

Final work size control

FIGURE 38.15   In-process inspection of workpiece diameter in a turning operation. The system automatically adjusts the radial position of the cutting tool in order to produce the correct diameter.

ing forces, temperature, surface finish, and part deflections. Similarly, for the bending of a sheet in a V-die (Section 16.5), data on the dependence of springback on punch travel and on other material and process variables must be stored in the computer memory.

It is apparent that, because of the many factors involved, mathematical equations for such quantitative relationships in manufacturing processes are difficult to establish. Compared to the other parameters involved, forces and torque in machining have been found to be the easiest to monitor by AC. Various solid-state power controls are now available commercially, in which power is displayed or interfaced with data-acquisition systems. Coupled with CNC, adaptive control is a powerful tool in optimizing manufacturing operations.

38.6 MATERIAL HANDLING AND MOVEMENT

During a typical manufacturing operation, raw materials and parts are moved from storage to machines, from machine to machine, from inspection to assembly and inventory, and finally to shipment. Workpieces are loaded on machines; for example, a forging is mounted on a milling machine bed for further processing, or sheet metal is fed into a press for stamping), parts are removed from one machine and loaded on another (for example, a machined forging is subsequently ground for better surface finish and dimensional accuracy), and finished parts are inspected prior to being assembled into a finished product.

Similarly, tools, molds, dies, and various other equipment and fixtures are also moved in manufacturing plants. Cutting tools are mounted on lathes, dies are placed in presses or hammers, grinding wheels are mounted on spindles, and parts are mounted on special fixtures for dimensional measurement and inspection.

These materials must be moved either manually or by some mechanical means, and time is required to transport them from one location to another. **Material handling** may be defined as the functions and systems associated with the transportation, storage, and control of materials and parts in the total manufacturing cycle of a product. The total time required for manufacturing depends on part size and shape and on the set of operations required. Idle time and the time required for transporting materials can constitute the majority of the time consumed.

Plant layout is an important aspect of the orderly flow of materials and components throughout the manufacturing cycle. The time and distances required for moving raw materials and parts should be *minimized*, and storage areas and service centers should be organized accordingly. For parts requiring multiple operations, equipment should be grouped around the operator or the industrial robot (see *Cellular Manufacturing*, Section 39.9).

Material handling should, therefore, be an integral part of the planning, the implementing, and the controlling of manufacturing operations. Furthermore, material handling should be repeatable and predictable. Consider, for example, what happens if a part or workpiece is loaded improperly into a forging die, a chuck, or the collet on a lathe. The consequences of such action may well be broken dies and tools, improperly made parts, or parts that are out of dimensional tolerance. This action can also present safety hazards and possibly cause injury to the operator and nearby personnel. (See Chapter 37.)

38.6.1 Methods of Material Handling

Several factors have to be considered in selecting a suitable material-handling method for a particular manufacturing operation:

a. the shape, weight, and characteristics of the parts;

b. the types and distances of movements, and the position and orientation of the parts during movement and at their final destination;

   c. the conditions of the path along which the parts are to be transported;

   d. the degree of automation, the level of control desired, and integration with other systems and equipment;

   e. the operator skill required; and

   f. economic considerations.

For small-batch manufacturing operations, raw materials and parts can be handled and transported by hand, but this method is generally costly. Moreover, because it involves human beings, this practice can be unpredictable and unreliable; it can even be unsafe to the operator, because of the weight and shape of the parts to be moved and because of environmental factors (such as heat and smoke in foundries and forging plants). In automated manufacturing plants, computer-controlled material and parts flow is rapidly being implemented. These changes have resulted in improved repeatability and in lower labor costs.

38.6.2 Equipment

Various types of equipment can be used to move materials, such as conveyors, rollers, self-powered monorails, carts, forklift trucks, and various mechanical, electrical, magnetic, pneumatic, and hydraulic devices and manipulators. **Manipulators** can be designed to be controlled directly by the operator, or they can be automated for repeated operations (such as the loading and unloading of parts from machine tools, presses, and furnaces).

Manipulators are capable of gripping and moving heavy parts and of orienting them as required between the manufacturing and assembly operations. Machines are often used in a sequence, so that workpieces are transferred directly from machine to machine. Machinery combinations having the capability of conveying parts without the use of additional material-handling apparatus are called **integral transfer devices**.

Flexible material handling and movement, with real-time control, has become an integral part of modern manufacturing. Industrial robots, specially designed pallets, and **automated guided vehicles (AGVs)** are used extensively in flexible manufacturing systems to move parts and to orient them as required (Fig. 38.16).

Automated guided vehicles, which are the latest development in material movement in plants, operate automatically along pathways with in-floor wiring (or tapes for optical scanning) and without operator intervention. This transport system has high flexibility and is capable of random delivery to different workstations. It optimizes the movement of materials and parts in cases of congestion around workstations, machine breakdown (downtime), or the failure of one section of the system.

The movements of AGVs are planned so that they interface with **automated storage/retrieval systems (AS/RS)**, in order to utilize warehouse space efficiently and to reduce labor costs. Nowadays, however, these systems are considered undesirable, because of the current focus on minimal inventory and on just-in-time production methods. (See Section 39.11.)

Coding systems have been developed to locate and identify parts throughout the manufacturing system and to transfer them to their appropriate stations, as outlined briefly below:

   a. **Bar coding** is the most widely used system and the least costly one. The codes are printed on labels, which are attached to the parts themselves and read by fixed or portable code readers using light pens.

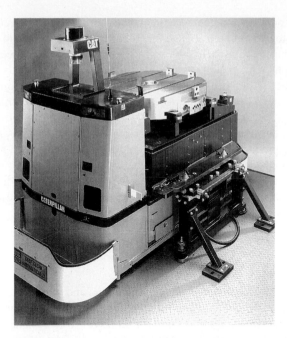

FIGURE 38.16   A self-guided vehicle (Caterpillar Model SGC-M) carrying a machining pallet. The vehicle is aligned next to a stand on the floor. Instead of following a wire or stripe path on the factory floor, this vehicle calculates its own path and automatically corrects for any deviations. *Source*: Courtesy of Caterpillar Industrial, Inc.

h. Magnetic strips (such as those on the back of a credit card) constitute the second most common coding system.

c. The third most popular system uses **RF** (radio frequency) **tags**. Although expensive, they do not need the clear line of sight needed by the previous two systems, they have a long range, and they are rewritable.

Other identification systems are based on acoustic waves, optical character recognition, and machine vision. (See Section 38.8.1.)

38.7 INDUSTRIAL ROBOTS

The word **robot** was coined in 1920 by the Czech author K. Capek in his play *R.U.R.* (Rossum's Universal Robots); it is derived from the Czech word *robota*, meaning "worker." An **industrial robot** has been defined as a reprogrammable multifunctional manipulator, designed to move materials, parts, tools, or other devices by means of variable programmed motions and to perform a variety of other tasks. In a broader context, the term robot also includes manipulators that are activated directly by an operator.

More generally, an industrial robot has been described by the International Organization for Standardization (ISO) as follows: A machine formed by a mechanism including several degrees of freedom, often having the appearance of one or several arms ending in a wrist capable of holding a tool, a workpiece, or an inspection device. In particular, its control unit must use a memorizing device and it may sometimes use sensing or adaptation appliances to take into account environment and circumstances. These multipurpose machines are generally designed to carry out a repetitive function and can be adapted to other operations.

Introduced in the early 1960s, the first industrial robots were used in hazardous operations, such as the handling of toxic and radioactive materials and the loading and unloading of hot workpieces from furnaces and in foundries. Some simple rule-of-thumb applications for robots are the three D's (*dull, dirty, and dangerous, including demeaning but necessary tasks*) and the three H's (*hot, heavy, and hazardous*).

From their early uses for worker protection and safety in manufacturing plants, industrial robots have further been developed and have now become important components in manufacturing processes and systems. They have helped to improve productivity and product quality and to reduce labor costs. Computer-controlled robots were commercialized in the early 1970s; the first robot controlled by a microcomputer appeared in 1974.

38.7.1 Robot Components

To appreciate the functions of robot components and their capabilities, we might simultaneously observe the flexibility and capability of diverse movements of our arm, wrist, hand, and fingers in reaching for and grabbing an object from a shelf, or in using a hand tool, or in operating a car or a machine. Described next are the basic components of an industrial robot (Fig. 38.17a).

FIGURE 38.17   (a) Schematic illustration of a six-axis S-10 GMF robot. The payload at the wrist is 10 kg and repeatability is ±0.2 mm (±0.008 in.). The robot has mechanical brakes on all its axes, which are coupled directly. (b) The work envelope of the robot, as viewed from the side. *Source*: GMFanuc Robotics Corporation.

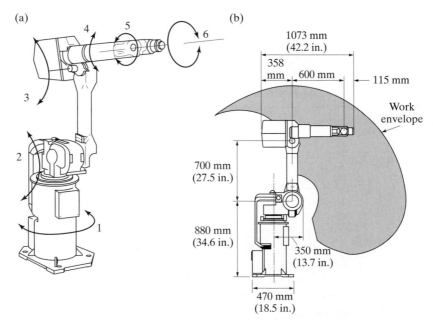

Manipulator.   Also called **arm and wrist**, the **manipulator** is a mechanical unit that provides motions (trajectories) similar to those of a human arm and hand. The end of the wrist can reach a point in space having a specific set of coordinates, in a specific orientation. Most robots have six rotational joints. (See Fig. 38.17a.) There are also four-degrees-of-freedom (d.o.f.) and five-d.o.f. robots, but these kinds, by definition, are not fully dextrous, because being so requires six d.o.f.

Seven-d.o.f. (or "redundant") robots for special applications are also available. Linear-motion robot joints exist, but they are increasingly rare. Manipulation is carried out using mechanical devices, such as linkages, gears, and various joints.

End Effector.   The end of the wrist in a robot is equipped with an **end effector**, also called **end-of-arm tooling**. Depending on the type of operation, conventional end effectors may be equipped with any of the following:

a. grippers, hooks, scoops, electromagnets, vacuum cups, and adhesive fingers, for material handling (Fig. 38.18a);

b. spray guns, for painting;

c. attachments, for spot and arc welding and for arc cutting;

d. power tools, such as drills, nut drivers, and burrs; and

e. measuring instruments, such as dial indicators.

End effectors are generally custom-made to meet special handling requirements. Mechanical grippers are the most commonly used and are equipped with two or more fingers. The selection of an appropriate end effector for a specific application depends on such factors as the payload, environment, reliability, and cost.

Compliant end effectors are used to handle fragile materials or to facilitate assembly. These end effectors can use elastic mechanisms to limit the force which can be applied to the workpiece, or they can be designed with a desired stiffness. For example, the end effector shown in Fig. 38.18b is stiff in the axial direction, but it is very compliant in lateral directions. This arrangement prevents damage to parts in those assembly operations in which slight misalignments can occur, as shown in the figure.

Power Supply.   Each motion of the manipulator (in linear and rotational axes) is controlled and regulated by independent actuators that use an electrical, a pneumatic, or a hydraulic power supply. Each source of energy and each type of motor has its own characteristics, advantages, and limitations.

Control System.   Also known as the **controller**, the **control system** is the communications and information-processing system that gives commands for the movements of the robot. It is the *brain* of the robot; it stores data to initiate and terminate movements of the manipulator. It is also the *nerves* of the robot; it interfaces with computers and other equipment such as manufacturing cells or assembly systems. The manipulators and effectors are the robot's arms and hands.

Feedback devices, such as transducers, are an important part of the control system. Robots with a fixed set of motions have *open-loop control*. In this system commands are given and the robot arm goes through its motions; unlike feedback in *closed-loop systems*, accuracy of the movements is not monitored. Consequently, this system does not have a self-correcting capability.

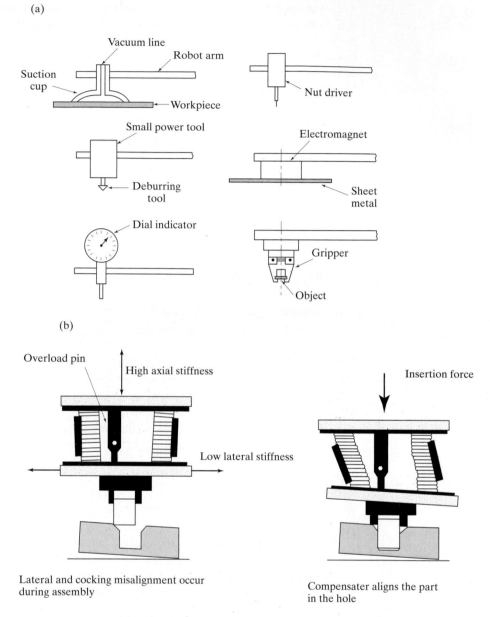

FIGURE 38.18   (a) Various devices and tools attached to end effectors to perform a variety of operations. (b) A system of compensating for misalignment during automated assembly. *Source*: ATI Industrial Automation.

As in numerical control machines, the types of control in industrial robots are point-to-point and continuous-path. (See Section 38.3.4.) Depending on the particular task, the positioning repeatability required may be as small as 0.050 mm (0.002 in.), as in assembly operations for electronic printed circuitry. Specialized robots can reach such accuracy, although most robots are unable to do so. Accuracy and repeatability vary greatly with payload and with position within the work envelope, and as such are very difficult to quantify for most robots.

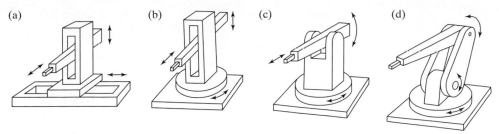

FIGURE 38.19   Four types of industrial robots: (a) cartesian (rectilinear), (b) cylindrical, (c) spherical (polar), (d) articulated (revolute, jointed, or anthropomorphic).

38.7.2 Classification of Robots

Robots may be classified by basic type, as follows:

a. Cartesian or rectilinear.
b. Cylindrical.
c. Spherical or polar.
d. Articulated, or revolute, or jointed, or anthropomorphic (Fig. 38.19).

Robots may be attached permanently to the floor of a manufacturing plant, or they may move along overhead rails (**gantry robots**), or they may be equipped with wheels to move along the factory floor (**mobile robots**). However, a broader classification of robots currently in use is most helpful for our purposes here, as described below.

Fixed- and Variable-Sequence Robots.   The **fixed-sequence robot** (also called a **pick-and-place robot**) is programmed for a specific sequence of operations. Its movements are from point to point, and the cycle is repeated continuously. These robots are simple and relatively inexpensive. The **variable-sequence robot** can be programmed for a specific sequence of operations but can be reprogrammed to perform another sequence of operation.

Playback Robot.   An operator leads or walks the **playback robot** and its end effector through the desired path; in other words, the operator teaches the robot by showing it what to do. The robot memorizes and records the path and sequence of motions and can repeat them continually without any further action or guidance by the operator.

Another type is the **teach pendant**, which utilizes hand-held button boxes that are connected to the control panel; they are used to control and guide the robot and its tooling through the work to be performed. These movements are then registered in the memory of the controller and are automatically reenacted by the robot whenever needed.

Numerically Controlled Robot.   The **numerically controlled robot** is programmed and operated much like a numerically controlled machine. The robot is servocontrolled by digital data, and its sequence of movements can be changed with relative ease. As in NC machines, there are two basic types of controls: point-to-point, and continuous-path.

Point-to-point robots are easy to program and have a higher load-carrying capacity and a larger **work envelope** (also called the **working envelope**—the maximum extent or reach

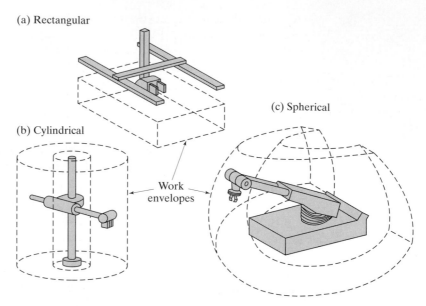

(a) Rectangular

(b) Cylindrical

(c) Spherical

Work envelopes

FIGURE 38.20   Work envelopes for three types of robots. The choice depends on the particular application. See also Fig. 38.17.

of the robot hand or working tool in all directions), (Figs. 38.17b and 38.20). Continuous-path robots have greater accuracy than point-to-point robots, but they have lower load-carrying capacity. More advanced robots have a complex system of path control, enabling high-speed movements with great accuracy.

Intelligent (Sensory) Robot.   The *intelligent robot* is capable of performing some of the functions and tasks carried out by human beings. It is equipped with a variety of sensors with visual (*computer vision*) and tactile (*touching*) capabilities. (See Section 38.8.) Much like humans, the robot observes and evaluates the immediate environment and its proximity to other objects, especially machinery, by perception and pattern recognition. It then makes appropriate decisions for the next movement and proceeds accordingly. Because its operation is very complex, powerful computers are required to control this type of robot.

Significant developments are taking place in intelligent robots so that they will

a. behave more and more like humans, performing tasks such as moving among a variety of machines and equipment on the shop floor and avoiding collisions;

b. recognize, select, and properly grip the correct raw material or workpiece;

c. transport the part to a machine for further processing or inspection; and

d. assemble the components into subassemblies or a final product.

38.7.3 Applications and Selection of Robots

Major applications of industrial robots include the following:

1. Material handling consists of the loading, unloading, and transferring of workpieces in manufacturing facilities. These operations can be performed reliably and repeatedly with robots, thereby improving quality and reducing scrap losses. Here are some examples: (a) casting and molding operations, in which molten metal, raw materials, lubricants, and parts in various stages of completion are handled without operator in-

38.8 SENSOR TECHNOLOGY

A **sensor** is a device which produces a signal in response to its detecting or measuring a property, such as position, force, torque, pressure, temperature, humidity, speed, acceleration, or vibration. Traditionally, sensors, actuators, and switches have been used to set limits on the performance of machines.

Familiar examples of sensors are stops on machine tools to restrict work table movements, pressure and temperature gages with automatic shutoff features, and governors on engines to prevent excessive speed of operation. Sensor technology has become an important aspect of manufacturing processes and systems; it is essential for proper data acquisition and for the monitoring, communication, and computer control of machines and systems (Fig. 38.24).

Because they convert one quantity to another, sensors are also often referred to as **transducers**. **Analog sensors** produce a signal, such as voltage, that is proportional to the measured quantity. **Digital sensors** have numeric or digital outputs that can be transferred to computers directly. **Analog-to-digital converters** (ADC) are available for interfacing analog sensors with computers.

38.8.1 Sensor Classification

Sensors that are of interest in manufacturing may be classified generally as follows.

1. **Mechanical** sensors measure such quantities as position, shape, velocity, force, torque, pressure, vibration, strain, and mass.
2. **Electrical** sensors measure voltage, current, charge, and conductivity.
3. **Magnetic** sensors measure magnetic field, flux, and permeability.
4. **Thermal** sensors measure temperature, flux, conductivity, and specific heat.
5. Other types are acoustic, ultrasonic, chemical, optical, radiation, laser, and fiber-optic.

Depending on its application, a sensor may consist of metallic, nonmetallic, organic, or inorganic materials and fluids, gases, plasmas, or semiconductors. Using the special characteristics of these materials, sensors convert the quantity or property measured to analog or digital output. The operation of an ordinary mercury thermometer, for example, is based on the difference between the thermal expansion of mercury and that of glass.

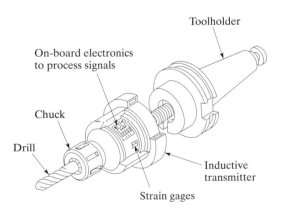

FIGURE 38.24 A toolholder equipped with thrust-force and torque sensors (smart toolholder), capable of continuously monitoring the cutting operation. Such toolholders are necessary for adaptive control of manufacturing operations. (See Section 38.5.) *Source*: Cincinnati Milacron, Inc.

Toolholder
On-board electronics to process signals
Chuck
Drill
Inductive transmitter
Strain gages

FIGURE 38.25 A robot gripper with tactile sensors. In spite of their capabilities, tactile sensors are now being used less frequently, because of their high cost and their low durability in industrial applications. *Source*: Courtesy of Lord Corporation.

Similarly, a machine part or a physical obstruction or barrier in a space can be detected by breaking the beam of light, sensed by a photoelectric cell. (See Fig. 37.2.) A *proximity sensor*, which senses and measures the distance between it and an object or a moving member of a machine, can be based on acoustics, magnetism, capacitance, or optics.

Other actuators physically touch the object and take appropriate action (usually by electromechanical means). Sensors are essential to the control of intelligent robots; they are being developed with capabilities that resemble those of human beings (**smart sensors**).

a. **Tactile sensing.** *Tactile sensing* is the continuous sensing of variable contact forces, commonly by an array of sensors. Such a system is capable of performing within an arbitrary three-dimensional space. Fragile parts (such as glass bottles and electronic devices) can be handled by robots with *compliant (smart) end effectors*.

These effectors can sense the force applied to the object being handled, using piezoelectric devices, strain gages, magnetic induction, ultrasonics, and optical systems of fiber optics and light-emitting diodes. Tactile sensors that are capable of measuring and controlling gripping forces and moments in three axes are available commercially (Fig. 38.25).

The force sensed is monitored and controlled through closed-loop feedback devices. Compliant grippers having force feedback and sensory perception can, however, be complicated and require powerful computers; hence, they can be costly. *Anthropomorphic end effectors* are being designed to simulate the human hand and fingers and to have the capability of sensing touch, force, movement, and pattern. The ideal tactile sensor must also sense *slip*, a capability of human fingers and hand that we tend to take for granted; it can be very important in the use of robots.

b. **Visual sensing (machine vision, computer vision).** In *visual sensing*, cameras optically sense the presence and shape of the object (Fig. 38.26). A microprocessor then processes the image (usually in less than one second), the image is measured, and the measurements are digitized (**image recognition**). There are two basic systems of machine vision: linear array, and matrix array.

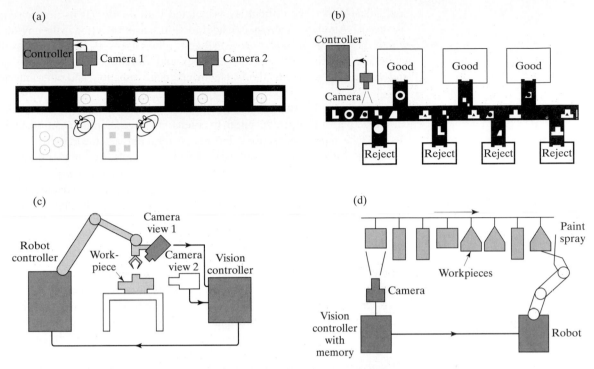

FIGURE 38.26   Examples of machine-vision applications. (a) In-line inspection of parts. (b) Identification of parts with various shapes, and inspection and rejection of defective parts. (c) Use of cameras to provide positional input to a robot relative to the workpiece. (d) Painting parts having different shapes by means of input from a camera. The system's memory allows the robot to identify the particular shape to be painted and to proceed with the correct movements of a paint spray attached to the end effector.

In **linear array**, only one dimension is sensed, such as the presence of an object or some feature on its surface. **Matrix arrays** sense two or even three dimensions and are capable of detecting, for example, a properly inserted component in a printed circuit or a properly made solder joint (assembly verification). When used in automated inspection systems (Section 36.11), these sensors can also detect cracks and flaws.

Machine vision is particularly suitable for inaccessible parts, in hostile manufacturing environments, for measuring a large number of small features, and in situations where physical contact with the part may cause damage. Applications of machine vision include (a) on-line, real-time inspection in sheet-metal stamping lines, and (b) sensors for machine tools that can sense tool offset and tool breakage, verify part placement and fixturing, and monitor surface finish.

Machine vision is capable of in-line identification and inspection of parts and of rejecting defective ones. Several applications of machine vision in manufacturing are shown in Fig. 38.26. With visual sensing capabilities, end effectors are able to pick up parts and grip them in the proper orientation and location.

The *selection* of a sensor for a particular application depends on such factors as (a) the particular quantity to be measured or sensed, (b) the sensor's interaction with other components in the system, (c) its expected service life, (d) its required level of sophistication, (e) the difficulties associated with its use, (f) its power source, and (g) its cost. Another important consideration in sensor selection is the environment in which the sensors are to be used. Rugged (robust) sensors have been developed to withstand extremes of temperature, shock and vibration, humidity, corrosion, dust and various contaminants, fluids, electromagnetic radiation, and other interferences.

Smart Sensors.   Among more recent developments are *smart sensors*, which have the capability to perform a logic function, to conduct two-way communication, and to make decisions and take appropriate actions. The necessary input, and the knowledge required to make a decision, can be built into a smart sensor; for example, a computer chip (see Chapter 34) with sensors can be programmed to turn a machine tool off when a cutting tool fails. Likewise, a smart sensor can stop a mobile robot or a robot arm from accidentally coming in contact with an object (or people) by sensing quantities such as distance, heat, and noise.

38.8.2 Sensor Fusion

Although there is no clear definition of the term *sensor fusion*, it is generally understood that it basically involves the integration of multiple sensors in such a manner that the individual data from each of the sensors (force, vibration, temperature, dimensions, etc.) are combined to provide a higher level of information and reliability. It has been suggested that a common example of sensor fusion occurs when someone drinks from a cup of hot tea or coffee.

Although we take such an everyday event for granted, it can readily be seen that this process involves data input from the person's eyes, hands, lips, and tongue. Through our various senses (sight, hearing, smell, taste, and touch), there is real-time monitoring of relative movements, positions, and temperatures. For example, if the fluid is too hot, the hand movement of the cup toward the lip is controlled accordingly.

The earliest applications of sensor fusion were in robot movement control and in missile flight tracking and similar military applications (primarily because these activities involve movements that mimic human behavior). Another example of sensor fusion is a machining operation in which a set of different but integrated sensors monitors (a) the dimensions and surface finish of the workpiece, (b) cutting-tool forces, vibrations, and wear, (c) the temperatures in various regions of the tool–workpiece system, and (d) the spindle power.

An important aspect in sensor fusion is *sensor validation*: the failure of one particular sensor is detected so that the control system retains high reliability. For this application, the receiving of redundant data from different sensors is essential. It can be seen that the receiving, integrating, and processing of all data from various sensors can be a complex problem.

Although there have been limited applications of sensor fusion in manufacturing operations, much research is being conducted in this area, with a potentially major impact on manufacturing in the near future. With advances in sensor size, quality, and technology, and with new developments in computer-control systems, artificial intelligence, expert systems, and artificial neural networks (see Chapter 39), sensor fusion is becoming practical and available at relatively low cost.

38.9 FLEXIBLE FIXTURING

The preceding chapters have described several workholding devices (such as chucks, collets, mandrels, and various fixtures), many of which are usually operated manually. Other workholding devices are designed and operated at various levels of mechanization and automation (such as power chucks driven by mechanical, hydraulic, or electrical means).

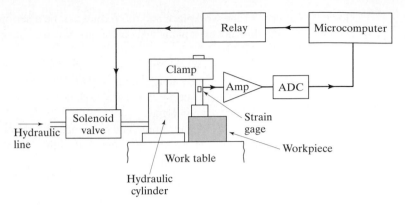

FIGURE 38.27   Schematic illustration of a flexible fixturing setup. The clamping force is sensed by the strain gage, and the system automatically adjusts this force. *Source*: P. K. Wright.

Workholding devices have certain ranges of capacity. For example, (a) a particular collet can accommodate bars within a certain range of diameters; (b) four-jaw chucks can accommodate square or prismatic workpieces having certain dimensions; and (c) various other devices and fixtures are designed and made for specific workpiece shapes and dimensions.

In manufacturing operations, the words clamp, jig, and fixture are often used interchangeably (and sometimes in pairs), as in jigs and fixtures. **Clamps** are simple multifunctional devices; **fixtures** are generally designed for specific purposes; **jigs** have various reference surfaces and points for accurate alignment of parts and tools and are widely used in mass production.

The emergence of flexible manufacturing systems (described in Section 39.10) has necessitated the design and use of workholding devices and fixtures that have built-in flexibility. These devices (**flexible fixturing**) are capable of quickly accommodating a range of part shapes and dimensions without the necessity of changing or extensively adjusting the fixtures or of requiring operator intervention (both of which would adversely affect productivity). A schematic illustration of a flexible fixturing system is shown in Fig. 38.27. The strain gage attached to the clamp senses the magnitude of the clamping force, and the system adjusts this force to keep the workpiece securely clamped on the worktable.

38.9.1 Design Considerations for Flexible Fixturing

The proper design and construction of flexible workholding devices and fixtures is essential to the operation of advanced manufacturing systems. These devices must position the workpiece automatically and accurately and must maintain its location precisely and with sufficient clamping force during the manufacturing operation.

Fixtures should accommodate parts repeatedly in the same position, and they must have sufficient stiffness to resist (without excessive deflection) the normal and shear stresses developed at the workpiece-fixture interfaces. Fixtures and clamps should have low profiles, so as to avoid collision with cutting tools and dies. (Collision avoidance is also an important factor in programming tool paths in machining operations. See Sections 38.3 and 38.4.)

Flexible fixturing must meet additional requirements in order to function properly in flexible manufacturing systems. Because of the increased efficiency of machining centers, machining time is very short. Consequently, the time required to load and unload parts should be minimal in order to reduce cycle times. The presence of loose chips between the locating surfaces of the workpiece and the fixture can be a serious problem. (This type of situation usually does not exist in manual operations, because the operator sees to it that these surfaces are cleaned.)

As with conventional workholding devices, the presence of even a single metal chip or sliver can result in an inaccurately produced part. Chips are most likely to be present in machining operations where cutting fluids are used, because small chips tend to stick to the wet surfaces via surface tension forces.

A flexible fixture should accommodate parts made by various processes (such as casting, forming, or powder metallurgy) and ones with dimensions and surface features that vary from part to part. The clamping force, in turn, must be estimated and applied properly. These considerations are even more important when the workpiece is fragile or made of a brittle material, when it has a relatively soft coating on its surfaces, or when it is a plastic part. (Plastics typically have a low hardness and a low elastic modulus and therefore are very flexible. See Chapter 7.)

38.10 DESIGN FOR ASSEMBLY, DISASSEMBLY, AND SERVICE

The individual parts and components made by various manufacturing processes are **assembled** into finished products by various methods. Some products are simple and have only two or three components to assemble; such an operation can be done with relative ease. (Examples are an ordinary pencil with an eraser, a frying pan with a wooden handle, or an aluminum beverage can.) However, most products consist of many parts (see the table on p. 2 in Section 1 in the General Introduction), and their assembly requires considerable care and planning.

Traditionally, assembly has involved much manual work and so has contributed significantly to product cost. The total assembly operation is usually broken into individual assembly operations (*subassemblies*), with an operator assigned to carry out each step. Assembly costs are typically 25% to 50% of the total cost of manufacturing, with the percentage of workers involved in assembly operations ranging from 20% to 60%. In the electronics industries, some 40% to 60% of total wages are paid to assembly workers.

As production costs and quantities of products to be assembled increase, the necessity for automated assembly become obvious. Beginning with the hand assembly of muskets in the late 1700s (and the early 1800s with interchangeable parts), assembly methods have been vastly improved over the years.

The first application of large-scale modern assembly was the assembly of flywheel magnetos for the Model T Ford; this example eventually led to mass production of the automobile. The choice of an assembly method and system depends on the required production rate, the total quantity to be produced, the product's market life, labor availability, and cost. **Automated assembly** can effectively reduce the overall product cost.

As we have seen, parts are manufactured within certain tolerance ranges. Taking roller bearings as an example, we know that although they all have the same nominal dimensions, some rollers in a lot will be smaller than others by a very small amount. Likewise, some bearing races will be smaller than others in the lot. There are two methods of assembly for such high-volume products: random assembly and selective assembly.

In **random assembly**, parts are put together by selecting them randomly from the lots produced. In **selective assembly**, the rollers and races are segregated by groups of sizes (from smallest to largest). The parts are then selected to mate properly. Thus, the smallest diameter rollers are mated with inner races having the largest outside diameter, and likewise, with outer races having the smallest inside diameters.

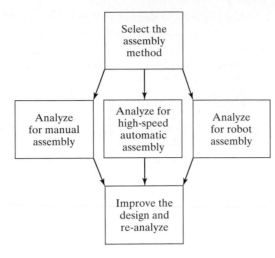

FIGURE 38.28 Stages in the design-for-assembly analysis. *Source*: *Product Design for Assembly*, 1989 edition, by G. Boothroyd and P. Dewhurst. Reproduced with permission.

38.10.1 Assembly Systems

There are three basic methods of assembly: manual, high-speed automatic, and robotic. These methods can be used individually or, as is the case on most applications in practice, in combination. An analysis of the product design should first be made (Fig. 38.28) with regard to the appropriate and economical method of assembly.

a. **Manual assembly** uses relatively simple tools and is economical for small lots. Because of the dexterity of the human hand and fingers, and their capability for feedback through various senses, workers can manually assemble even complex parts without much difficulty. (Recall, however, the potential problem of cumulative trauma disorders, described in Section 37.2.)

In spite of the use of sophisticated mechanisms, robots, and computer controls, the aligning and placing of a simple square peg into a square hole, involving small clearances, can be difficult in automated assembly—yet the human hand is capable of doing this simple operation with relative ease.

b. **High-speed automated assembly** utilizes **transfer mechanisms** designed specially for assembly. Two examples of such assembly are shown in Fig. 38.29, in which

FIGURE 38.29 Transfer systems for automated assembly: (a) rotary indexing machine, (b) in-line indexing machine. *Source*: G. Boothroyd.

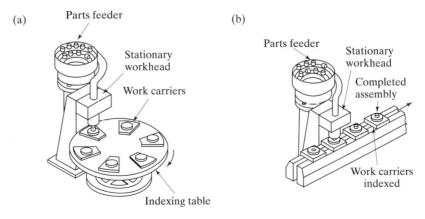

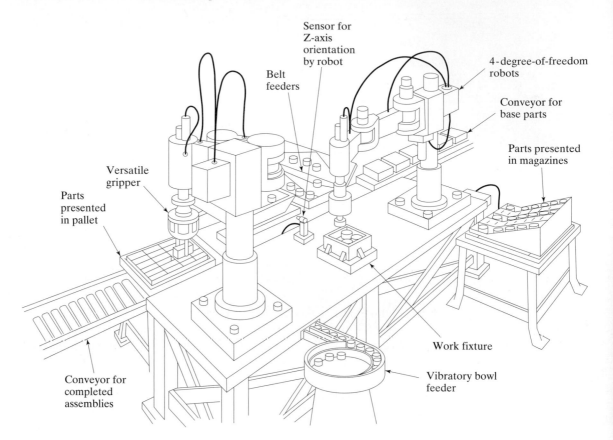

FIGURE 38.30   A two-arm robot assembly station. *Source*: *Product Design for Assembly*, 1989 edition, by G. Boothroyd and P. Dewhurst. Reproduced with permission.

individual assembly is carried out on products that are indexed for proper positioning during assembly. In **robot assembly**, one or two general-purpose robots operate at a single workstation (Fig. 38.30), or the robots operate at a multistation assembly system.

There are three basic types of assembly systems: synchronous, nonsynchronous, and continuous.

a. In **synchronous systems** (also called **indexing**), individual parts and components are supplied and assembled at a constant rate at fixed individual stations. The rate of movement is based on the station that takes the longest time to complete its portion of the assembly. This system is used primarily for high-volume, high-speed assembly of small products.

   Transfer systems move the partial assemblies from workstation to workstation by various mechanical means. Two typical transfer systems (**rotary indexing** and **in-line indexing**) are shown in Fig. 38.29. These systems can operate in either a fully automatic mode or a semiautomatic mode. A breakdown of one station will, however, shut down the whole assembly operation.

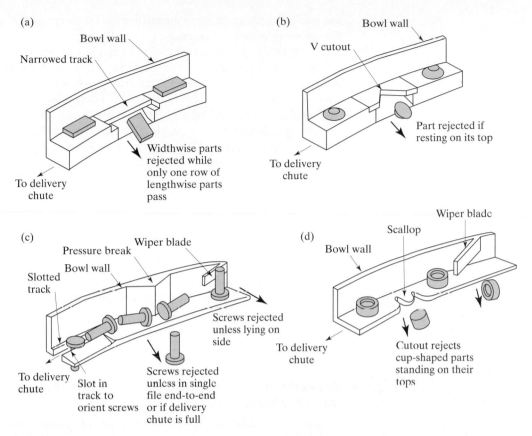

FIGURE 38.31   Various guides that ensure that parts are properly oriented for automated assembly. *Source*: G. Boothroyd.

The part feeders supply the individual parts to be assembled and place them on other components, which are secured on work carriers or fixtures. The feeders move the individual parts (by vibratory or other means) through delivery chutes and ensure their proper orientation by various ingenious means (Fig. 38.31). Orienting parts properly and avoiding jamming are essential in all automated assembly operations.

b. In **nonsynchronous systems**, each station operates independently, and any imbalance is accommodated in storage (**buffer**) between stations. The station continues operating until the next buffer is full or the previous buffer is empty. Furthermore, if one station becomes inoperative for some reason, the assembly line continues to operate until all the parts in the buffer have been used up. Nonsynchronous systems are suitable for large assemblies with many parts to be assembled. For types of assembly in which the times required for individual assembly operations vary widely, the output will be constrained by the slowest station.

c. In **continuous systems**, the product is assembled while moving at a constant speed on pallets (or similar workpiece carriers). The parts to be assembled are brought to the product by various workheads, and their movements are synchronized with the continuous movement of the product. Typical applications of this system are in bottling and packaging plants, although the method has also been used on mass-production lines for automobiles and appliances.

Assembly systems are generally set up for a certain product line; however, they can be modified for increased flexibility, in order to assemble product lines that have a variety of models. Such **flexible assembly systems (FAS)** utilize computer controls, interchangeable and programmable workheads and feeding devices, coded pallets, and automated guiding devices. The General Motors plant for the Saturn subcompact automobile, for example, is designed with a flexible assembly system. The system is capable of assembling up to a dozen different transmission and engine combinations and power steering and air conditioning units.

38.10.2 Guidelines for Design for Assembly, Disassembly, and Service

Although the functions of a product and its design for manufacturing have been matters of considerable interest for some time, only more recently has **design for assembly (DFA)** attracted special attention (particularly design for automated assembly), because of the need to reduce labor costs in assembly operations. Various *guidelines* have been established as an aid in the design of parts for ease of assembly. The general guidelines for **manual assembly** may be summarized as follows:

a. Reduce the number and types of parts in a product so that fewer steps and fixtures are required; this approach lowers assembly costs.

b. Parts to be assembled should have a high degree of symmetry (such as round or square) or a high degree of asymmetry (such as oval or rectangular). They should be designed such that they cannot be installed incorrectly, or such that they do not require locating, aligning, or adjusting.

c. Designs should allow parts to be assembled without obstructions or the lack of a direct line of sight.

Design guidelines for **high-speed automated assembly** include, in addition to some of those for manual assembly, the fact that parts have to be handled not manually but automatically, using various devices. Humans can easily pick parts from bulk (such as from a nearby bin), but automatic handling requires that parts be separated from the bulk and conveyed by hoppers or vibratory feeders (see Fig. 38.30) in the proper orientation for assembly. Consequently, additional guidelines are the following:

a. Part designs should consider such factors as size, shape, weight, flexibility, abrasiveness, and tangling with other parts.

b. Parts should be designed so that they can be inserted from a single direction (preferably vertically to take advantage of gravity); assembly from two or more directions can present problems.

c. Products should be designed (or existing products redesigned) so that there are no physical obstructions to the free movement of the parts during assembly (Fig. 38.32); sharp external and internal corners should be replaced with chamfers, tapers, or radii.

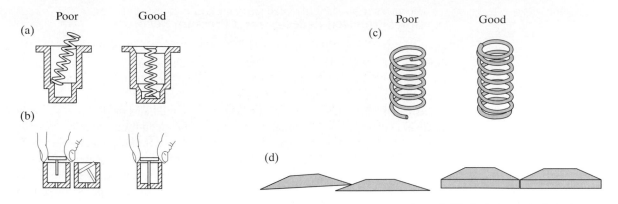

FIGURE 38.32   Redesign of parts to facilitate automated assembly.
Source: G. Boothroyd.

Robotic assembly design guidelines have rules similar to those for manual and high-speed automated assembly, although recent research on compliant end effectors and dexterous manipulators has somewhat relaxed robot inflexibility.

Some distinguishing additional ones are as follows:

a. Parts should be designed so that they can be gripped and manipulated by the same gripper of the robot. (See Fig. 38.18.) Such design avoids the need for different grippers; also, parts should be made available to the gripper in the proper orientation.

b. Assembly that involves threaded fasteners (such as bolts, nuts, and screws) may be difficult for robots. One exception is the use of self-threading screws for sheet metal, plastics, and wooden parts. Robots can, however, handle snap fits, rivets, welds, and adhesives easily.

Design for Disassembly.   The manner and ease with which a product may be taken apart for maintenance or replacement of its parts is another important consideration in product design. Consider, for example, the difficulties one has in removing certain components from under the hood of some automobiles (such as spark plugs or oil filters); similar difficulties exist in the disassembly of several other products. Consequently, **design for disassembly** has become an important factor in the overall design process.

Although there is no established set of guidelines, the general approach to design for disassembly requires the consideration of factors that are similar to those outlined above under design for assembly. Analysis of computer or physical models of products and their components with regard to disassembly should indicate potential problems, such as obstructions, size of passageways, lack of line of sight, and the difficulty of firmly grasping and guiding objects.

Design for Service.   The latest trend in design for assembly and disassembly includes taking into account the ease with which a product can be repaired. Called **design for service**, this approach is based on the concept that the elements that are most likely to need servicing be at the *outer layers* of the product. In this way, individual parts are easier to reach and to service, without the need to remove various other parts.

Example: Proposed Redesign for a Pressure Recorder

The original design for the functional part of an electromechanical pressure recorder is shown in Fig. 38.33a. This design consists of seven subassemblies: pressure regulator, sensor, strap with foam pad, tube assembly, earth lead for grounding, printed circuit board assembly, and knob assembly with set screw.

An analysis of this design, which has 18 parts, indicates the following: (1) the plastic cover need not be of a material different from the metal frame, and the cover does not move relative to the frame; (2) the tube assembly does not move with respect to the pressure regulator body, and it may be made from the same material; (3) the sheet-metal strap (which holds the sensor) does not have to be a separate part; (4) none of the components in this design are self-locating, and there are several redundant parts and a number of alignment and access problems.

A possible redesign, in which the design has been simplified so that the assembly consists of only seven parts, is shown in Fig. 38.33b. It is estimated that the assembly time for the new design is one-quarter of that of the original design. (The reader is encouraged to review these designs and suggest other possibilities.)

Source: Product Design for Assembly, 1989 edition, by G. Boothroyd and P. Dewhurst. Reproduced with permission.

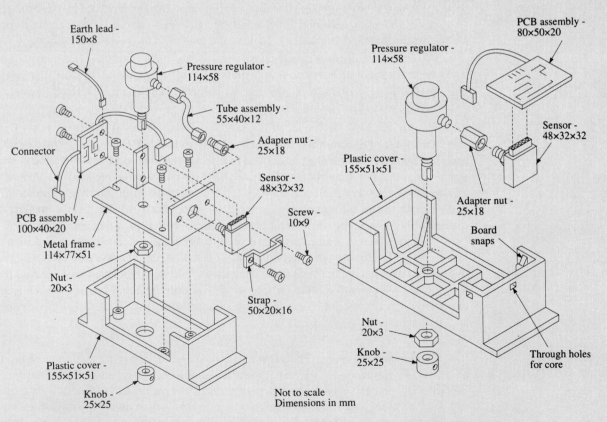

(a) Original design

(b) Proposed design

Not to scale
Dimensions in mm

FIGURE 38.33

SUMMARY

- Automation has been implemented successfully in manufacturing processes, material handling, inspection, assembly, and packaging. There are several levels of automation, ranging from simple automation of machines to untended manufacturing cells (see Section 39.9).
- True automation began with the numerical control of machines, which has the capability of flexibility of operation, lower cost, and ease of making different parts with less operator skill. Production quantity and rate are important factors in determining the economic levels of automation.
- Manufacturing operations are further optimized (both in quality and in cost) by adaptive control techniques, which continuously monitor the operation and make necessary adjustments in the process parameters.
- Major advances have been made in material handling, particularly with the implementation of industrial robots and automated guided vehicles.
- Sensors are essential in the implementation of these modern technologies; a wide variety of sensors based on various principles has been developed and installed.
- Other advances include flexible fixturing and automated assembly techniques that reduce the need for worker intervention and that lower manufacturing costs.
- The efficient and economic implementation of these techniques requires that design for assembly, disassembly, and servicing be recognized as an important factor in the total design and manufacturing process.

TRENDS

- Because of high equipment costs, the economic analysis of various aspects of automation in manufacturing plants and of the use of industrial robots is becoming an important area of study.
- Together with extensive use of computers and rapid advances in sophisticated software, new concepts of manufacturing operations continue to be developed, including adaptive control of manufacturing systems and the use of multiple sensors. Programming of CNC machines is increasingly performed by sophisticated software, without operator assistance.
- There is a growing trend toward using PCs instead of programmable logic controllers, because PCs are less expensive, are easier to program, and are easier to network.
- The trends in sensors include miniaturization, compatibility with logic systems, and a decreased emphasis on electromechanical systems. New developments include sensor fusion and smart sensors, which are capable of microcomputer-based calibration, computation, and decision-making.
- Design for manufacture, assembly, disassembly, and servicing continue to be increasingly important in manufacturing activities.

KEY TERMS

Adaptive control	Buffer	Compliant end effectors
Assembly	Circular interpolation	Computer numerical control
Automated guided vehicle	Closed-loop control	Computer vision
Automation	Compilers	Continuous path

Contouring
Control systems
Cubic interpolation
Dedicated machines
Distributed numerical control
End effector
Feedback
Flexible assembly systems
Flexible fixturing
Flexible manufacturing systems
Gain scheduling
Hard automation
Hard-wired controls
Industrial robot
Intelligent robot
Interpolation

Linear interpolation
Machine vision
Manipulators
Material handling
Mechanization
Numerical control
Open-loop control
Parabolic interpolation
Part programming
Point-to-point system
Positioning
Powerhead production units
Productivity
Programmable controller
Programming language
Random assembly

Repeatability
Resolution
Robot
Selective assembly
Selective automation
Sensor fusion
Sensors
Smart sensors
Soft automation
Stand-alone machines
Tactile sensing
Total productive maintenance
Transfer lines
Visual sensing
Work envelope

BIBLIOGRAPHY

Amic, P.J., *Computer Numerical Control Programming*. Prentice Hall, 1996.

Asfahl, C.R., *Robots and Manufacturing Automation* (2d ed.). Wiley, 1992.

Astrom, K.J., and B. Wittenmark, *Adaptive Control* (2d ed.). Addison-Wesley, 1994.

Bolhouse, V., *Fundamentals of Machine Vision*. Robotic Industries Association, 1997.

Boothroyd, G., *Assembly Automation and Product Design*. Marcel Dekker, 1989.

Boothroyd, G., P. Dewhurst, and W. Knight, *Product Design for Manufacture and Assembly*. Marcel Dekker, 1994.

Brooks, R.R., and S. Iyengar, *Multi-Sensor Fusion: Fundamentals and Applications with Software*. Prentice Hall, 1997.

Burke, M., *Handbook of Machine Vision Engineering*. Chapman & Hall, 1999.

Busch-Vishniac, I., *Electromechanical Sensors and Actuators*. Springer, 1999.

Chow, W., *Assembly Line Design: Methodology and Applications*. Marcel Dekker, 1990.

Fraden, J., *Handbook of Modern Sensors: Physics, Designs, and Applications* (2d ed.). Springer Verlag, 1996.

Galbiati, L.J., *Machine Vision and Digital Image Processing Fundamentals*. Prentice Hall, 1990.

Gibbs, D., and T. Crandell, *CNC: An Introduction to Machining and Part Programming*. Industrial Press, 1991.

Ioannu, P.A., *Robust Adaptive Control*. Prentice Hall, 1995.

Jain, R. (ed.), *Machine Vision*. Prentice Hall, 1995.

Lynch, M., *Computer Numerical Control for Machining*. McGraw-Hill, 1992.

Molloy, O., E.A. Warman and S. Tilley, *Design for Manufacturing and Assembly: Concepts, Architectures and Implementation*. Kluwer, 1998.

Myler, H.R., *Fundamentals of Machine Vision*. Society of Photo-optical Instrumentation Engineers, 1998.

Nanfara, F., T. Uccello, and D. Murphy, *The CNC Workbook: An Introduction to Computer Numerical Controls*. Addison-Wesley, 1995.

Nof, S.Y., W.E. Wilhelm, and H.-J. Warnecke, *Industrial Assembly*. Chapman & Hall, 1998.

Rampersad, H.K., *Integral and Simultaneous Design for Robotic Assembly*. Wiley, 1995.

Rehg, J.A., *Introduction to Robotics in CIM Systems* (3d ed.). Prentice Hall, 1997.

Sandler, B.-Z., *Robotics: Designing the Mechanisms for Automated Machinery* (2d ed.). Prentice Hall, 1999.

Seames, W., *Computer Numerical Control: Concepts and Programming* (3d ed.). Delmar, 1995.

Soloman, S., *Sensors Handbook*. McGraw-Hill, 1997.

Stenerson, J., and K.S. Curran, *Computer Numerical Control: Operation and Programming*. Prentice Hall, 1997.

Tool and Manufacturing Engineers Handbook (4th ed.), Vol. 4: *Assembly, Testing, and Quality Control*. Society of Manufacturing Engineers, 1986.

Tool and Manufacturing Engineers Handbook (4th ed.), Vol. 9: *Material and Part Handling in Manufacturing*. Society of Manufacturing Engineers, 1998.

Valentino, J.V., and J. Goldenberg, *Introduction to Computer Numerical Control*. Regents/Prentice Hall, 1993.

Williams, D.J., *Manufacturing Systems* (2d ed.). Chapman & Hall, 1994.

Zuech, N., *Applying Machine Vision*. Wiley, 1988.

REVIEW QUESTIONS

38.1 Describe the differences between mechanization and automation. Give several specific examples for each.

38.2 Why is automation generally regarded as evolutionary rather than revolutionary?

38.3 Are there activities in manufacturing operations that cannot be automated? Explain.

38.4 Explain the difference between hard and soft automation. Why are they so called?

38.5 Describe the principle of numerical control of machines. What factors led to the need for and development of numerical control? Name typical applications.

38.6 Explain the differences between direct numerical control and computer numerical control. What are their relative advantages?

38.7 Describe open-loop and closed-loop control circuits.

38.8 What are the advantages of computer-aided NC programming?

38.9 Describe the principle and purposes of adaptive control. Give some examples of present applications in manufacturing and others that you think can be implemented.

38.10 What factors have led to the development of automated guided vehicles? Do they have any disadvantages? Explain your answers.

38.11 List and discuss the factors that should be considered in choosing a suitable material-handling system for a particular manufacturing facility.

38.12 Describe the features of an industrial robot. Why are these features necessary?

38.13 Discuss the principles of various types of sensors, and give two applications for each type.

38.14 Describe the concept of design for assembly. Why has it become an important factor in manufacturing?

38.15 Is it possible to have partial automation in assembly? Explain.

38.16 What is adaptive control?

38.17 What are the two kinds of robot joints?

38.18 What are the advantages of flexible fixturing?

38.19 How are robots programmed to follow a certain path?

QUALITATIVE PROBLEMS

38.20 Giving specific examples, discuss your observations concerning Fig. 38.2.

38.21 What are the relative advantages and limitations of the two arrangements for power heads shown in Fig. 38.4?

38.22 Discuss methods of on-line gaging of workpiece diameters in turning operations other than that shown in Fig. 38.15. Explain the relative advantages and limitations.

38.23 Is drilling and punching the only application for the point-to-point system shown in Fig. 38.10a? Explain.

38.24 Describe possible applications for industrial robots not discussed in this chapter.

38.25 What determines the number of robots in an automated assembly line such as that shown in Fig. 38.23?

38.26 Describe situations in which the shape and size of the work envelope of a robot (Fig. 38.20) can be critical.

38.27 Explain the functions of each of the components of the robot shown in Fig. 38.17a.

38.28 Explain the difference between an automated guided vehicle and a self-guided vehicle.

38.29 It has been commonly acknowledged that, at their early stages of development and implementation, the usefulness and cost effectiveness of industrial robots has been overestimated. What reasons can you think of to explain this situation?

38.30 Describe the type of manufacturing operations (see Fig. 38.2) that are likely to make the best use of a machining center (see Chapter 24). Comment on the influence of product quantity and part variety.

38.31 Give two specific examples, one in which an open-loop and one in which a closed-loop control system would be desirable.

38.32 Why should the level of automation in a manufacturing facility depend on production quantity and production rate?

38.33 Explain why sensors have become so essential in the development of automated manufacturing systems.

38.34 Why is there a need for flexible fixturing for holding workpieces? Are there any disadvantages? Explain your answers.

38.35 Describe situations in manufacturing where you would not want to apply numerical control.

38.36 Table 38.2 shows a few examples of typical products for each category. Add several other examples to this list.

38.37 Describe situations where each of the three positioning methods shown in Fig. 38.6 would be desirable.

38.38 Describe applications of machine vision for specific parts, similar to the examples shown in Fig. 38.26.

38.39 Add other examples to those shown in Fig. 38.31.

38.40 Sketch the workspace of each of the robots in Fig. 38.19.

38.41 Name some applications where you would not use a vibratory feeder.

SYNTHESIS AND DESIGN

38.42 Give an example of a forming operation that is suitable for adaptive control similar to that shown in Fig. 38.15.

38.43 Design two different systems of mechanical grippers for widely different applications.

38.44 Give some applications for the systems shown in Fig. 38.26a and c.

38.45 For a system similar to that shown in Fig. 38.27, design a flexible fixturing setup for a lathe chuck.

38.46 Add others to the examples shown in Fig. 38.32.

38.47 Give examples of products that are suitable for the type of production shown in Fig. 38.3.

38.48 Give examples where tactile sensors would not be suitable. Explain why.

38.49 Give examples where machine vision cannot be applied properly and reliably. Explain why.

38.50 Think of a simple product to be made by end milling (Section 23.2) and prepare an NC program for it, similar to that shown in the example in Section 38.4. Explain why you chose those particular cutter paths. If this part is redesigned so that it now includes a threaded hole, how would you machine it? What type of machine would you recommend that still has NC features?

38.51 Choose one machine each from Parts II, III, and IV, and design a system in which sensor fusion can be used effectively. How would you convince a prospective customer of the merits of such a system? Would it be cost-effective?

38.52 Same as Problem 38.52, but for a flexible fixturing system.

38.53 Think of a product, and design a transfer line for it similar to that shown in Fig. 38.5. Specify the types of and the number of machines required.

38.54 Section 38.9 described the basic principles of flexible fixturing and gave an illustration. Considering the wide variety of parts made, prepare design guidelines for flexible fixturing. Make simple sketches illustrating the principle for each type of fixturing, describing its ranges of applications and limitations.

38.55 Describe your thoughts on the usefulness and applications of modular fixturing (consisting of various individual clamps, pins, supports, and attachments mounted on a base plate).

38.56 Inspect several household products, and describe the manner in which they have been assembled. Comment on any changes you would make so that assembly, disassembly, and servicing are simpler and faster.

38.57 Although future trends are difficult to predict with certainty, inspect Table 38.1, and describe your thoughts as to what new developments could possibly be added to the bottom of the list as we move into the early 2000s.

38.58 Design a robot gripper that will pick up and place common eggs without breaking them.

38.59 Obtain an old toaster and disassemble it. Make recommendations on redesign, using the guidelines for manual assembly.

38.60 Design a guide in the same vein as Fig. 38.31, but to align U-shaped parts so that they are inserted with the open end down.

39

Computer-Integrated Manufacturing Systems

39.1 INTRODUCTION

On several occasions, we have described the implementation and benefits of the mechanization, automation, and computer control of various stages of manufacturing operations. This chapter focuses attention on the **integration of manufacturing activities**. (See also Section 7 in the General Introduction.) Integration means that manufacturing processes, operations, and their management are treated as a **system**, one which makes possible total control of the manufacturing facility, thereby increasing productivity, product quality, and reliability and reducing manufacturing costs.

In **computer-integrated manufacturing (CIM)**, the traditionally separate functions of research and development, design, production, assembly, inspection, and quality control are all linked. Consequently, integration requires that quantitative relationships among product design, materials, manufacturing process and equipment capabilities, and related activities be well understood. In this way, changes in, for example, material requirements, product types, or market demand can be accommodated. Also, high quality is far more attainable via the integration of design and manufacturing.

Machines, tooling, and manufacturing operations must have a certain built-in **flexibility**, in order to be able to respond to change and to ensure **on-time delivery** of products to the customer. You can appreciate the significance of on-time product delivery by noting your own dissatisfaction when you do not receive a particular order on its promised date.

Failure of on-time delivery in industry can upset production plans and schedules and, consequently, have a significant economic impact. In a highly competitive global environment, failure of on-time product delivery can cost a company its *competitive edge* because the customer will simply change suppliers.

The importance of product quality was emphasized in Chapter 36, along with the necessity for total commitment of a company's management to total quality control. Recall the statements that *quality must be built into the product*, that high quality does not necessarily mean higher cost, and that marketing poor-quality products can indeed be very costly to the manufacturer.

39.2 MANUFACTURING SYSTEMS

The word *system* is derived from the Greek word *systema*, meaning to combine. It has now come to mean an arrangement of physical entities, one characterized by its identifiable and quantifiable interacting parameters. Manufacturing entails a large number of interdependent activities consisting of distinct entities (such as materials, tools, machines, power, and human beings); it can therefore be regarded as a system.

As we have seen, manufacturing is, in fact, a complex system, because it is composed of many diverse physical and human elements, some of which are difficult to predict and control, such as the supply and cost of raw materials, market changes, and human behavior and performance.

Ideally, we should be able to represent a system by **mathematical and physical models**, which can show us the nature and extent of interdependence of the variables involved. In a manufacturing system, a change or disturbance anywhere in the system requires that it adjust itself system-wide in order to continue functioning efficiently. For example, if the supply of a particular raw material is reduced (for example, by geopolitical maneuvers, wars, or strikes) and, consequently, its cost increases, alternative materials must be selected. This selection should be made only after careful consideration of the effect this change may have on product quality, production rate, and manufacturing costs.

Similarly, the demand for a product may fluctuate randomly and rapidly, on account of its style, size, or capacity. Note, for example, the downsizing of automobiles during the 1980s in response to fuel shortages and the current popularity of sport-utility vehicles. The system must then be able to produce the modified product on a short lead time and, preferably, with a relatively small major capital investment in machinery and tooling. Although the direct labor share of the product cost has been decreasing steadily over the years (in many cases it is now less than 10% of total product cost—see Section 40.7), the system must also be capable of absorbing some of the cost if worker pay escalates.

Modeling such a complex system can be difficult, because of a lack of comprehensive or reliable data on many of the variables involved. Furthermore, it is not always easy to predict correctly, and to control, some of these variables. For example: (a) machine-tool characteristics, their performance, and their response to random external disturbances cannot be modeled precisely, (b) raw-material costs are difficult to predict accurately, and (c) human behavior and performance are difficult to model.

finances, purchasing, sales, marketing, and inventory. This vast array of data is stored in computer memory and recalled or modified as necessary, either by individuals in the organization or by the CIM system itself while it is controlling various aspects of design and production.

A database generally consists of the following items, some of which are classified as technical and others as nontechnical:

a. **product data**, such as part shape, dimensions, and specifications;

b. **data management attributes**, such as owner, revision level, and part number;

c. **production data**, such as the manufacturing processes involved in making parts and products;

d. **operational data**, such as scheduling, lot sizes, and assembly requirements;

e. **resources data**, such as capital, machines, equipment, tooling, and personnel, and their capabilities.

Databases are built by individuals and by the use of various sensors in the machinery and equipment used in production. Data from the latter are collected automatically by a **data acquisition system (DAS)**, which can report, for example, the number of parts being produced per unit of time, their dimensional accuracy, their surface finish, their weight, and so on, at specified rates of sampling.

The components of DAS include microprocessors, transducers, and analog-to-digital converters (ADCs). Data acquisition systems are also capable of analyzing the data and transferring them to other computers for purposes such as statistical analysis, data presentation, and the forecasting of product demand.

Several factors are important in the use and implementation of databases:

a. They should be timely, accurate, easily accessible, easily shared, and user friendly.

b. In the event that something goes wrong with the data, the correct data should be able to be recovered and restored.

c. Because it is used for many purposes and by many people, the database must be flexible and responsive to the needs of different users.

d. CIM systems can be accessed by designers, manufacturing engineers, process planners, financial officers, and the management of the company by using appropriate *access codes*. Companies must protect data against tampering or unauthorized use.

39.4 COMPUTER-AIDED DESIGN (CAD) AND ENGINEERING (CAE)

Computer-aided design involves the use of computers to create design drawings and product models. (See Fig. 6 in the General Introduction.) Computer-aided design is usually associated with **interactive computer graphics** (known as a **CAD system**). Computer-aided design systems are powerful tools and are used in the mechanical design and geometric modeling of products and components.

Computer-aided engineering simplifies the creation of the database, by allowing several applications to share the information in the database. These applications include, for example, (a) finite-element analysis of stresses, strains, deflections, and temperature distribution in structures and load-bearing members, (b) the generation, storage, and retrieval of NC data, and (c) the design of integrated circuits and other electronic devices. (See Chapter 34.)

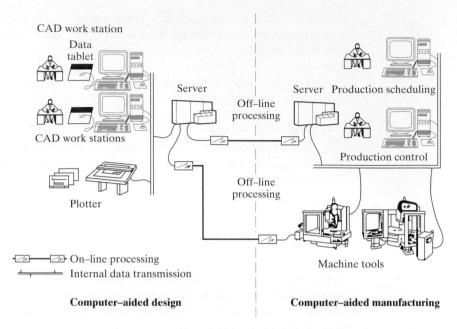

FIGURE 39.2   Information flow chart in CAD/CAM application.

In CAD, the drawing board is replaced by electronic input and output devices, an electronic plotter, and a data tablet (Fig. 39.2), which is divided into sections. Each section represents a mathematically defined geometric function (such as coordinate points, line, plane, circle, or cylinder), called a **menu item**.

The user can generate sections of a drawing from the menu by using a mouse or puck on a digitizer tablet. The design is continuously displayed on the monitor (*graphics screen*). The final drawing is printed or plotted on appropriate hardware connected to the computer.

When using a CAD system, the designer can conceptualize the object to be designed more easily on the graphics screen and can consider alternative designs or modify a particular design quickly to meet the necessary design requirements or changes. The designer can then subject the design to a variety of engineering analyses and can identify potential problems (such as an excessive load or deflection). The speed and accuracy of such analyses far surpass what is available from traditional methods.

The CAD system quickly and accurately produces the definition models for products and their components. One of the outputs of this system is the generation of *working drawings*, which generally have higher quality and better consistency than those produced by traditional manual drafting. The drawings can be reproduced any number of times and at different levels of reduction and enlargement.

In addition to the design's geometric and dimensional features, other information (such as a list of materials, specifications, and manufacturing instructions) is stored in the CAD database. Using such information, the designer can then analyze the economics of alternative designs.

39.4.1 Exchange Specifications

Because of the availability of a wide variety of CAD systems with different characteristics supplied by different vendors, proper communication and exchange of data between these systems has become a significant problem. (See also Section 39.12.) Currently, the need for a single neutral format for better compatibility is filled mainly by the **Initial Graphics Exchange Specification (IGES)**. Vendors need only provide translators for their own systems, to preprocess the data into the neutral format, and to postprocess from the neutral format into their system. IGES is used for translation in two directions (in and out of a system) and is also used widely for translation of 3-D line and surface data.

A more recent development is a solid-model based standard, called **Product Data Exchange Specification (PDES)**, which is based on IGES. Although IGES is adequate for most requirements, PDES requires less memory size and less time for execution, and it is less prone to error. Currently, different standards are used in different countries, but it is expected that these standards will soon be subsumed into an international standard, to be called **Standard for the Exchange of Product Model Data (STEP)**.

39.4.2 Elements of CAD Systems

The design process in a CAD system consists of the four stages described below.

Geometric Modeling. In *geometric modeling*, a physical object (or any of its parts) is described mathematically or analytically. The designer first constructs a geometric model by giving commands that create or modify lines, surfaces, solids, dimensions, and text that, together, are an accurate and complete two- or three-dimensional representation of the object.

The results of these commands are displayed; they can be moved around on the screen, and any section desired can be magnified to view details. These data are digital and are stored in the database contained in computer memory.

The models can be presented in three different ways.

a. In **line representation** (**wire-frame**: Fig. 39.3), all edges of the model are visible as solid lines. This image can be ambiguous, particularly for complex shapes, so various colors are generally used for different parts of the object, to make the object easier to visualize.

The three types of wire-frame representations are 2-D, 2 1/2-D, and 3-D. A 2-D image shows the profile of the object. A 2 1/2-D image can be obtained by translational sweep, that is, by moving the 2-D object along the z axis. For round objects, a 2 1/2-D model can be generated by simply rotating a 2-D model around its axis.

b. In the **surface model**, all visible surfaces are shown in the model.

c. In the **solid model**, all surfaces are shown, but the data describe the interior volume. Solid models can be constructed from "swept volumes" (Figs. 39.3b and c) or by the techniques shown in Fig. 39.4. In **boundary representation (B-rep)**, surfaces are combined to develop a solid model (Fig. 39.4a). In **constructive solid geometry**

FIGURE 39.3   Various types of modeling for CAD.

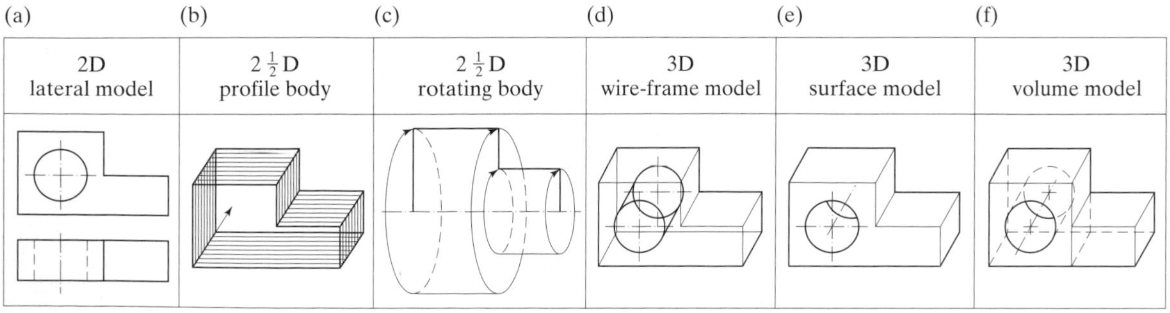

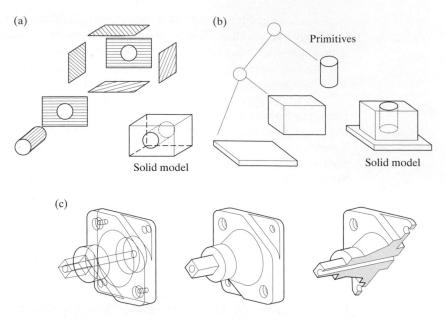

(a)

(b)

Primitives

Solid model

Solid model

(c)

FIGURE 39.4   (a) Boundary representation of solids, showing the enclosing surfaces of the solid model and the generated solid model. (b) A solid model represented as compositions of solid primitives. (c) Three representations of the same part by CAD. *Source*: P. Ranky.

(CSG), simple shapes such as spheres, cubes, blocks, cylinders, and cones (called **primitives of solids**) are combined to develop a solid model (Fig. 39.4b).

Programs are available whereby the user selects any combination of these primitives and their sizes, and combines them into the desired solid model. Although solid models have certain advantages (such as ease of design analysis and ease of preparation for manufacturing the part), they require more computer memory and processing time than the wire-frame and surface models shown in Fig. 39.3.

The **octree representation** of a solid object is shown in Fig. 39.5; it is a three-dimensional analog to pixels on a television screen. Just as any area can be broken

FIGURE 39.5   The octree representation of a solid object. Any volume can be broken down into octants, which are then identified as solid, void, or partially filled. Shown is two-dimensional version, or quadtree, for representation of shapes in a plane.

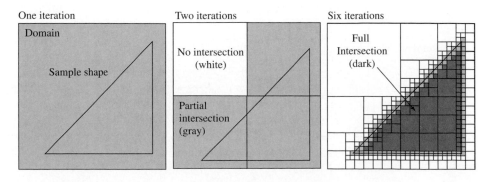

One iteration

Domain

Sample shape

Two iterations

No intersection (white)

Partial intersection (gray)

Six iterations

Full Intersection (dark)

down into quadrants, any volume can be broken down into octants, which are then identified as solid, void, or partially filled. Partially-filled *voxels* (for "volume pixels") are broken into smaller octants and reclassified. With increasing resolution, exceptional part detail is achieved. This process may appear to be somewhat cumbersome, but it allows for accurate description of complex surfaces. It is particularly used in biomedical applications, such as for modeling bone geometries.

Design Analysis and Optimization.   After the geometric features of a particular design have been determined, the design is subjected to an engineering analysis. This phase may consist of analyzing, for example, stresses, strains, deflections, vibrations, heat transfer, temperature distribution, or dimensional tolerances. Various sophisticated software packages are available, having the capabilities to compute these quantities accurately and rapidly.

Because of the relative ease with which such analyses can now be done, designers are increasingly willing to analyze a design more thoroughly before it moves on to production. Experiments and measurements in the field may nonetheless be necessary to determine the actual effects of loads, temperature, and other variables on the designed components.

Design Review and Evaluation.   An important design stage is review and evaluation, to check for any interference between various components. This stage is done in order to avoid difficulties during assembly or use of the part and to determine whether moving members (such as linkages) are going to operate as intended.

Software is available having animation capabilities, to identify potential problems with moving members and other dynamic situations. During the design review and evaluation stage, the part is precisely dimensioned and toleranced, to the full degree required for manufacturing it.

Documentation and Drafting.   After the preceding stages have been completed, the design is reproduced by automated drafting machines, for documentation and reference. At this stage, detail and working drawings are also developed and printed. The CAD system is also capable of developing and drafting sectional views of the part, scaling the drawings, and performing transformations in order to present various views of the part.

Although much of the design process in CAD systems was formerly carried out on workstations connected to a mainframe computer, the trend has changed rapidly to powerful, high-performance, and much less expensive stand-alone desktop 32-bit UNIX workstations. 64-bit processors, having even better performance, are also available.

39.5 COMPUTER-AIDED MANUFACTURING (CAM)

Computer-aided manufacturing involves the use of computers and computer technology to assist in all the phases of manufacturing a product, including process and production planning, machining, scheduling, management, and quality control. CAM encompasses many of the technologies described in Chapter 38 and this chapter. Because of the benefits, computer-aided design and computer-aided manufacturing are often combined into **CAD/CAM systems**.

This combination allows the transfer of information from the design stage into the stage of planning for the manufacture of a product, without the need to reenter the data on part geometry manually. The database developed during CAD is stored; then it is processed further, by CAM, into the necessary data and instructions for operating and controlling production machinery, material-handling equipment, and automated testing and inspection for product quality.

In machining operations, an important feature of CAD/CAM is its capability to describe the tool path for various operations, such as NC turning, milling, and drilling. The instructions (programs) are computer generated, and they can be modified by the programmer to optimize the tool path. The engineer or technician can then display and visually check the tool path for possible tool collisions with clamps, fixtures, or other interferences.

The tool path can be modified at any time, to accommodate other part shapes to be machined. CAD/CAM systems are also capable of coding and classifying parts into groups that have similar shapes, using alphanumeric coding. (See Group Technology, Section 39.8.)

The emergence of CAD/CAM has had a major impact on manufacturing, by standardizing product development and by reducing design effort, tryout, and prototype work; it has made possible significantly reduced costs and improved productivity. The two-engine Boeing 777 passenger airplane, for example, was designed completely by computer (**paperless design**), with 2000 workstations linked to eight computers. The plane is constructed directly from the CAD/CAM software developed (an enhanced CATIA system), and no prototypes or mockups were built, such as were required for previous models. The cost for this development was on the order of $6 billion.

Some typical applications of CAD/CAM are as follows:

- programming for NC, CNC, and industrial robots (Chapter 38);
- design of dies and molds for casting, in which, for example, shrinkage allowances are preprogrammed (Part II);
- dies for metalworking operations, such as complex dies for sheet forming and progressive dies for stamping (Chapter 16);
- design of tools and fixtures and EDM electrodes (Chapter 26);
- quality control and inspection (Chapters 35 and 36)—for instance, coordinate-measuring machines programmed on a CAD/CAM workstation;
- process planning and scheduling (Section 39.6); and
- plant layout.

39.6 COMPUTER-AIDED PROCESS PLANNING (CAPP)

In order for a manufacturing operation to be efficient, all of its diverse activities must be planned. This activity has traditionally been done by process planners. **Process planning** is concerned with selecting methods of production: tooling, fixtures, machinery, sequence of operations, and assembly.

The sequence of processes and operations to be performed, the machines to be used, the standard time for each operation, and similar information are all documented on a **routing sheet** (Fig. 39.6). When done manually, this task is highly labor-intensive and time-consuming and relies heavily on the experience of the process planner. A current trend in routing sheets is to store the relevant data in computers and affix a *bar code* (or other identification) to the part. The production data can then be reviewed at a dedicated monitor.

Computer-aided process planning accomplishes this complex task of process planning by viewing the total operation as an integrated system, so that the individual operations and steps involved in making each part are coordinated with others and are performed efficiently and reliably. Thus, computer-aided process planning is an important adjunct to CAD and CAM.

Although CAPP requires extensive software and good coordination with CAD/CAM (and other aspects of integrated manufacturing systems discussed in the rest of this chapter), it is a powerful tool for efficiently planning and scheduling manufacturing operations. CAPP

ROUTING SHEET

CUSTOMER'S NAME: Midwest Valve Co.   PART NAME: Valve body

QUANTITY: 15   PART NO.: 302

Operation no.	Description of operation	Machine
10	Inspect forging, check hardness	Rockwell tester
20	Rough machine flanges	Lathe No. 5
30	Finish machine flanges	Lathe No. 5
40	Bore and counter bore hole	Boring mill No. 1
50	Turn internal grooves	Boring mill No. 1
60	Drill and tap holes	Drill press No. 2
70	Grind flange end faces	Grinder No. 2
80	Grind bore	Internal grinder No. 1
90	Clean	Vapor degreaser
100	Inspect	Ultrasonic tester

FIGURE 39.6   An example of a simple routing sheet. These *operation sheets* may include additional information on materials, tooling, estimated time for each operation, processing parameters (such as cutting speeds and feeds), and other information. The routing sheet travels with the part from operation to operation. The current trend is to store all relevant data in computers and to affix to the part a bar code that serves as a key into the database of parts information.

is particularly effective in small-volume, high-variety parts production requiring machining, forming, and assembly operations.

39.6.1 Elements of CAPP Systems

There are two types of computer-aided process planning systems: *variant* and *generative* process planning.

a. In the **variant system** (also called the **derivative system**), the computer files contain a standard process plan for the part to be manufactured. The search for a standard plan is made in the database by a code number for the part; the plan is based on its shape and its manufacturing characteristics. See Section 39.8. The standard plan is retrieved, displayed for review, and printed as a routing sheet.

The process plan includes information such as the types of tools and machines to be used, the sequence of manufacturing operations to be performed, the speeds, the feeds, the time required for each sequence, and so on. Minor modifications of an existing process plan (which are usually necessary) can also be made. If the standard plan for a particular part is not in the computer files, a plan that is close to it, with a similar code number and an existing routing sheet, is retrieved. If a routing sheet does not exist, one is made for the new part and stored in computer memory.

b. In the **generative system**, a process plan is automatically generated on the basis of the same logical procedures that would be followed by a traditional process planner in making that particular part. Such a system is complex, however, because it must contain comprehensive and detailed knowledge of the part shape and dimensions, of the process capabilities, about selection of manufacturing methods, machinery, and tools, and of the sequence of operations to be performed. (These capabilities of computers, known as **expert systems**, are discussed in Section 39.13.)

The generative system is capable of creating a new plan instead of having to use and modify an existing plan (as the variant system must). Although currently it is used less commonly than is the variant system, this system has such advantages as (a) flexibility and consistency for process planning for new parts and (b) higher overall planning quality, because of the capability of the decision logic in the system to optimize the planning and to utilize up-to-date manufacturing technology.

The process planning capabilities of computers can be integrated into the planning and control of production systems. These activities are a subsystem of computer-integrated manufacturing, as described in Section 39.3. Several functions can be performed, such as **capacity planning** for plants to meet production schedules, control of *inventory*, *purchasing*, and production *scheduling*.

39.6.2 Advantages of CAPP Systems

The advantages of CAPP systems over traditional process planning methods include the following:

a. The standardization of process plans improves the productivity of process planners, reduces lead times, reduces planning costs, and improves the consistency of product quality and reliability.

b. Process plans can be prepared for parts having similar shapes and features, and they can be retrieved easily to produce new parts.

c. Process plans can be modified to suit specific needs.

d. Routing sheets can be prepared more quickly. Compared to the traditional handwritten routing sheets, computer printouts are neater and much more legible.

e. Other functions, such as cost estimating and work standards, can be incorporated into CAPP.

39.6.3 Material-Requirements Planning (MRP) and Manufacturing Resource Planning (MRP-II)

Computer-based systems for managing inventories and delivery schedules of raw materials and tools are called *material-requirements planning*. This activity (sometimes regarded as a method of *inventory control*) involves the keeping of complete records of inventories of materials, supplies, parts in various stages of production (work in progress), orders, purchasing, and scheduling.

Several files of data are usually involved in a master production schedule. These files pertain to the raw materials required (**bill of materials**), product structure levels (individual items that compose a product, such as components, subassemblies, and assemblies), and scheduling.

A further development is *manufacturing resource planning*, which, through feedback, controls all aspects of manufacturing planning. Although the system is complex, MRP-II is capable of final production scheduling, of monitoring actual results in terms of performance and output, and of comparing those results against the master production schedule.

A more recent step up is **enterprise resource planning (ERP)**, which brings marketing and business issues into the software and the database. ERP software is currently available, but it is still evolving.

39.7 COMPUTER SIMULATION OF MANUFACTURING PROCESSES AND SYSTEMS

With the increasing sophistication of computer hardware and software, one area which has grown rapidly is *computer simulation* of manufacturing processes and systems. Process simulation takes two basic forms: (a) It is a model of a specific operation intended to determine the viability of a process or to optimize or improve its performance. (b) It models multiple processes and their interactions, and it helps process planners and plant designers in the layout of machinery and facilities.

Individual processes have been modeled using various mathematical schemes. Finite-element analysis has been increasingly applied in software packages (**process simulation**) that are commercially available and inexpensive. Typical problems addressed are process viability (such as the formability of sheet metal in a certain die), and **process optimization** (for example, the material flow in forging in a given die, to identify potential defects, or mold design in casting, to eliminate hot spots, to promote uniform cooling, and to minimize defects).

Simulation of an entire manufacturing system involving multiple processes and equipment helps plant engineers to organize machinery and to identify critical machinery elements. In addition, such models can assist manufacturing engineers with scheduling and routing (by **discrete event simulation**). Commercially available software packages are often used for these simulations, but the use of dedicated software programs written for a particular company is not unusual.

39.8 GROUP TECHNOLOGY (GT)

We have seen that many parts produced have certain similarities in their shape and in their method of manufacture. Traditionally, each part has been viewed as a separate entity, and each has been produced in individual batches. *Group technology* is a concept that seeks to take advantage of the **design and processing similarities** among the parts to be produced.

This concept, first developed in Europe in the early 1900s, starts with categorizing the parts and recording them (then, manually, in card files or catalogs). The designs were then retrieved manually as needed. This concept began to evolve further in the 1950s, and the term group technology was first used in 1959. Not, however, until the use of interactive computers became widespread in the 1970s did the use of group technology grow significantly.

The similarity in the characteristics of similar parts (Fig. 39.7) suggests that benefits can be obtained by *classifying* and *coding* these parts into families. Surveys in manufacturing plants have repeatedly indicated the commonness of similarity in parts. Such surveys consist of breaking each product into its components and then identifying the similar parts. One survey, for instance, found that 90% of the 3000 parts made by a company fell into only five major families of parts.

As an example, a pump can be broken into such basic components as the motor, the housing, the shaft, the seals, and the flanges. In spite of the variety of pumps manufactured,

(a)

(b)

(c)

(d)

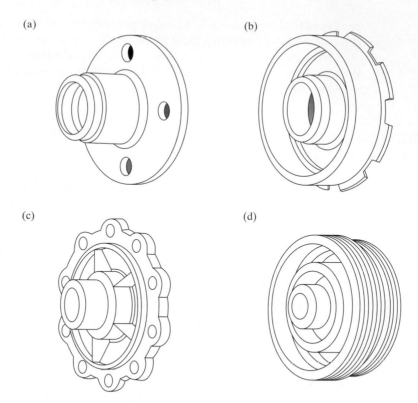

FIGURE 39.7   Grouping parts according to their geometric similarities.

each of these components is basically the same in terms of design and manufacturing methods. Consequently, all shafts, for example, can be placed in one *family* of shafts.

This approach becomes more attractive in view of consumer demand for an ever-greater variety of products, each in smaller quantity. Under these conditions, maintaining high efficiency in batch operations is difficult. Overall manufacturing efficiency is affected adversely, because nearly 75% of manufacturing today is batch production. As a result, questions have been raised about, for example, why a particular part should have so many different sizes of fasteners.

The traditional product flow in a batch manufacturing operation is shown in Fig. 39.8a. Note that machines of the same type are arranged in groups, that is, groups of lathes, of milling machines, of drill presses, and of grinders. In such a layout (**functional layout**), there is usually considerable random movement, as shown by the arrows that indicate movement of materials and parts.

Such an arrangement is not efficient, because it wastes time and effort. The machines in *cellular manufacturing* (Section 39.9) are arranged in a more efficient product flow line (**group layout**; Fig. 39.8b).

39.8.1 Advantages of Group Technology

The major advantages of group technology include the following:

a. It makes possible standardization of part design and minimization of design duplication. New part designs can be developed using similar, yet previous, designs, and

(a)

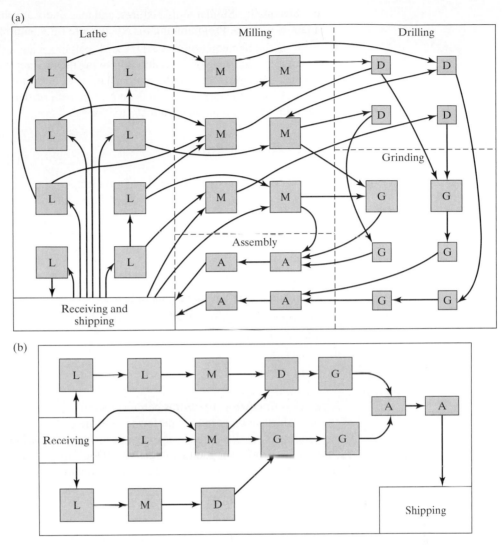

(b)

FIGURE 39.8   (a) Functional layout of machine tools in a traditional plant. Arrows indicate the flow of materials and parts in various stages of completion. (b) Group-technology (cellular) layout. Legend: L = lathe, M = milling machine, D = drilling machine, G = grinding machine, A = assembly. *Source*: M. P. Groover.

in this way a significant amount of time and effort can be saved. The product designer can quickly determine whether data on a similar part already exists in the computer files.

b. Data that reflect the experience of the designer and the manufacturing process planner are stored in the database. Thus, a new and less experienced engineer can quickly benefit from that experience by retrieving any of the previous designs and process plans.

c. Manufacturing costs can be estimated more easily, and the relevant statistics on materials, processes, number of parts produced, and other factors can be more easily obtained.

d. Process plans are standardized and scheduled more efficiently, orders are grouped for more efficient production, and machine utilization is improved. Setup times are reduced, and parts are produced more efficiently and with better and more consistent product quality. Similar tools, fixtures, and machinery are shared in the production of a family of parts. Programming for NC is more fully automated.

e. With the implementation of CAD/CAM, cellular manufacturing, and CIM, group technology is capable of so greatly improving the productivity and reducing the costs in small-batch production as to approach those of mass production. Depending on the level of implementation, potential savings in each of the various design and manufacturing phases can range from 5% to 75%.

39.8.2 Classification and Coding of Parts

In group technology, parts are identified and grouped into families by **classification and coding (C/C) systems**. This process is a critical and complex first step in GT. It is done according to the part's design attributes and manufacturing attributes. (See Fig. 39.7.)

1. Design attributes pertain to similarities in geometric features and consist of the following:

a. external and internal shapes and dimensions;

b. aspect ratios (length-to-width or length-to-diameter);

c. dimensional tolerances;

d. surface finishes;

e. part functions.

2. Manufacturing attributes pertain to similarities in the methods and the sequence of the manufacturing operations performed on the part. As we have seen, selection of a manufacturing process (or processes) depends on many factors, among which are the shape, the dimensions, and other geometric features of the part. Consequently, manufacturing and design attributes are interrelated. The manufacturing attributes of a part consist of the following:

a. the primary processes used;

b. the secondary and finishing processes used;

c. the dimensional tolerances and surface finish;

d. the sequence of operations performed;

e. the tools, dies, fixtures, and machinery used; and

f. the production quantity and production rate.

From these lists, it can be appreciated that the coding can be time-consuming and that it requires considerable experience in the design and manufacture of products. In its simplest form, the coding can be done by viewing the shapes of the parts in a generic way and then classifying the parts accordingly (such as parts having rotational symmetry, parts having rectilinear shape, and parts having large surface-to-thickness ratios). The parts being reviewed and classified should be representative of the company's product lines. A more thorough method is to review all of the data and drawings concerning the design *and* manufacture of all parts.

Parts may also be classified by studying their production flow during the manufacturing cycle; this approach is called **production flow analysis (PFA)**. Recall from Section 39.6 that routing sheets clearly show process plans and the operations to be performed. One drawback to PFA, however, is that a particular routing sheet does not necessarily indicate that the total manufacturing operation is optimized. In fact, depending on the experience of the particular process planner, routing sheets for manufacturing the same part can be quite different. The benefits of computer-aided process planning in avoiding such problems is obvious.

39.8.3 Coding

Coding of parts can be based on a particular company's own system, or it can be based on one of several classification and coding systems that are available commercially. Because of widely varying product lines and organizational needs, none of the C/C systems has been universally adopted. Whether it was developed in-house or it was purchased, the system must be compatible with the company's other systems (such as NC machinery and CAPP systems).

The code structure for part families typically consists of numbers, of letters, or of a combination of the two. Each specific component of a product is assigned a code. This code may pertain to design attributes only (generally less than 12 digits) or to manufacturing attributes only, although most advanced systems include both, using as many as 30 digits.

The three basic **levels of coding** vary in degree of complexity.

1. **Hierarchical coding.** In this code (also called **monocode**), the interpretation of each succeeding digit depends on the value of the preceding digit. Each symbol amplifies the information contained in the preceding digit, so a digit in the code cannot be interpreted alone. The advantage of this system is that a short code can contain a large amount of information. This method is, however, difficult to apply in a computerized system.

2. **Polycodes.** Each digit in this code (also known as **chain type**) has its own interpretation, which does not depend on the preceding digit. This structure tends to be relatively long, but it allows the identification of specific part attributes and is well suited to computer implementation.

3. **Decision-tree coding.** This system (also called **hybrid codes**) is the most advanced, and it combines both design and manufacturing attributes (Fig. 39.9).

FIGURE 39.9   Decision-tree classification for a sheet-metal bracket. *Source*: G. W. Millar.

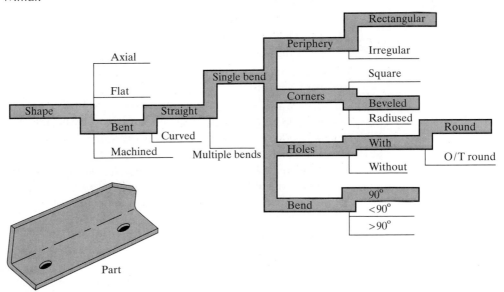

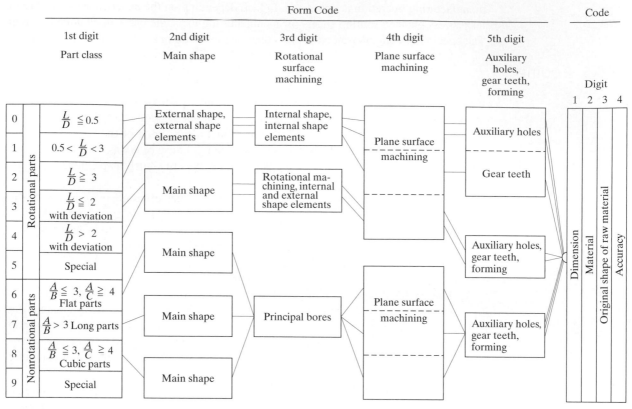

FIGURE 39.10   Classification and coding system according to Opitz, consisting of 5 digits and a supplementary code of 4 digits.

39.8.4 Coding Systems

Three major industrial coding systems are described here:

a. The **Opitz system** was developed in the 1960s in Germany by H. Opitz (1905–1977), and it was the first comprehensive coding system presented. The basic code consists of nine digits (12345 6789) representing design and manufacturing data (Fig. 39.10).

Four additional codes (ABCD) may be used to identify the type and sequence of production operations. This system has two drawbacks: (a) it is possible to have different codes for parts that have similar manufacturing attributes, and (b) a number of parts with different shapes can have the same code.

b. The **MultiClass system** was originally developed under the name MICLASS (for Metal Institute Classification System) by the Netherlands Organization for Applied Scientific Research, and it was marketed in the United States by The Organization for Industrial Research (Fig. 39.11). This system was developed to help automate and standardize several design, production, and management functions. MultiClass involves up to 30 digits; it is used interactively, with a computer that asks the user a number of questions. On the basis of the answers, the computer automatically assigns a code number to the part. The software is available in modules that can be linked; they cost $50,000–$500,000 each, depending on their capabilities.

c. The **KK-3 system** is a general-purpose classification and coding system for parts that are to be machined or ground. Developed by the Japan Society for the Promotion of Machine Industry in the late 1970s, it uses a 21-digit decimal system.

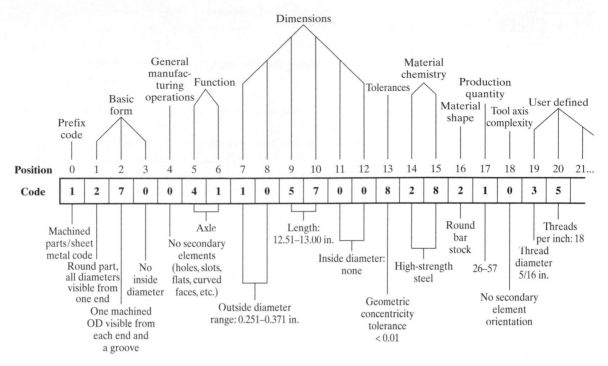

FIGURE 39.11   Typical MultiClass code for a machined part.
Source: Organization for Industrial Research.

This code is much greater in length than the two previous coding systems described, but it classifies dimensions and such dimensional ratios as length-to-diameter of the part. The structure of a KK-3 system for rotational components is shown in Fig. 39.12.

Digit	Items	(Rotational component)
1	Parts	General classification
2	name	Detail classification
3	Materials	General classification
4		Detail classification
5	Major	Length
6	dimensions	Diameter
7	Primary shapes and ratio of major dimensions	
8	External surface	External surface and outer primary shape
9		Concentric screw threaded parts
10		Functional cut-off parts
11		Extraordinary shaped parts
12		Forming
13		Cylindrical surface
14	Internal surface	Internal primary shape
15		Internal curved surface
16		Internal flat surface and cylindrical surface
17	End surface	
18	Nonconcentric holes	Regularly located holes
19		Special holes
20	Noncutting process	
21	Accuracy	

(Shape details and kinds of processes — left vertical label spanning digits 8–21)

FIGURE 39.12   The structure of a KK-3 system for rotational components. *Source*: Japan Society for the Promotion of Machine Industry.

39.9 CELLULAR MANUFACTURING

The concept of group technology can be implemented effectively in *cellular manufacturing*, which consists of one or more manufacturing cells. A **manufacturing cell** is a small unit, of one to several workstations, within a manufacturing system. A workstation usually contains either one machine (a **single machine cell**) or several machines (a **group machine cell**) that each perform a different operation on the part.

The machines can be modified, retooled, and regrouped for different product lines within the same family of parts. Manufacturing cells are particularly effective in producing families of parts that have relatively constant demand.

Cellular manufacturing has been utilized primarily in machining and in sheet-metal forming operations. The machine tools commonly used in manufacturing cells are lathes, milling machines, drills, grinders, electrical-discharge machines, and machining centers. For sheet forming, the equipment consists of shearing, punching, bending, and other forming machines. This equipment may also consist of special-purpose machines or CNC machines.

Cellular manufacturing has some degree of automatic control for the following operations:

- the loading and unloading of raw materials and workpieces at workstations;
- the changing of tools at workstations;
- the transferring of workpieces and tools between workstations;
- the scheduling and controlling of the total operation in the cell.

Central to these activities is a material-handling system, for transferring materials and parts among workstations. In attended (*manned*) machining cells, materials can be moved and transferred manually by the operator (unless the parts are too heavy or the movements are too hazardous) or by an industrial robot located centrally in the cell. Automated inspection and testing equipment can also be a part of this cell.

The important features of cellular manufacturing are the economics of reduced work-in-progress and the fact that product quality problems are detected right away, for improved productivity. Furthermore, because of the variety of the machines and the processes involved, the operator becomes multifunctional and is not subjected to the tedium experienced with always working on the same machine.

The result is increased productivity, an important benefit of attended cells. Another prime benefit is reduced time and labor spent on setup, because all the parts made in the cell have some degree of similarity.

39.9.1 Manufacturing Cell Design

Because of the unique features of manufacturing cells, their design and implementation in traditional plants requires the reorganization of the plant and the rearrangement of existing product flow lines. The machines may be arranged along a line, in a U-shape, in an L-shape, or in a loop. For a group-machine cell (where the materials are handled by the operator), the U-shaped arrangement is convenient and efficient because the operator can easily reach various machines. With mechanized material handling, the linear arrangement and the loop layout are more efficient.

Selecting the best machine and material-handling equipment arrangement also involves taking into account such factors as the production rate, the type of product, and its shape, size, and weight.

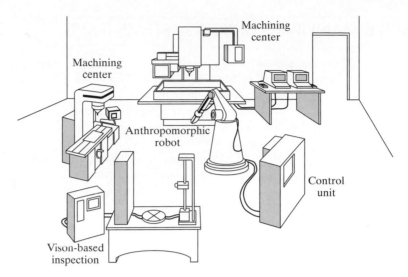

FIGURE 39.13   Schematic view of a flexible manufacturing cell, showing two machine tools, an automated part inspection system, and a central robot serving these machines. *Source*: P. K. Wright.

39.9.2 Flexible Manufacturing Cells (FMC)

In the introduction to this chapter and in Chapter 38, it was stressed that in view of rapid changes in market demand and of the need for more product variety in smaller quantities, **flexibility of manufacturing operations** is highly desirable. Manufacturing cells can be made flexible by using CNC machines and machining centers and by means of industrial robots or other mechanized systems for handling materials. An example of a *flexible manufacturing cell* for machining operations is shown in Fig. 39.13.

Flexible manufacturing cells are usually unattended, so their design and operation are more exacting than those for other cells. The selection of machines and robots, including the types and capacities of end effectors and their control systems, are important to the proper functioning of the FMC. The likelihood of significant change in demand for part families should be considered during design, to ensure that the equipment involved has the proper flexibility and capacity.

As with other flexible manufacturing systems (described in Section 39.10), the cost of flexible cells is high. Cellular manufacturing generally requires more machine tools and thus increases manufacturing cost; however, this disadvantage is outweighed by increased speed of manufacture, flexibility, and controllability. Proper maintenance of the tools and the machinery is essential, as is the implementation of two- or three-shift operations of the cells.

Example: Manufacturing Cells in a Small Machine Shop

The following is an actual example of the application of the manufacturing cell concept in a small shop. Company A has only 10 employees and only 11 milling machines and machining centers. These machines are set up in cells (milling cells and turning cells). The machines in the cells are arranged to allow an operator to machine the part in the most efficient and precise manner. Each cell allows the operator to monitor the performance of the machines in the cell.

Over 1200 different product lots have been produced over the years, with quantities ranging from one part to as many as 35,000 parts of the same design. The parts are inspected as they are produced. Each employee in the shop is involved in the programming and the running of the machines, and in the in-process inspection of parts.

39.10 FLEXIBLE MANUFACTURING SYSTEMS (FMS)

A *flexible manufacturing system* integrates all major elements of manufacturing into a highly automated system. First utilized in the late 1960s, FMS consists of a number of manufacturing cells, each containing an industrial robot (serving several CNC machines) and an automated material-handling system, all interfaced with a central computer. Different computer instructions for the manufacturing process can be downloaded for each successive part passing through the workstation.

This system is highly automated and is capable of optimizing each step of the total manufacturing operation. These steps may involve one or more processes and operations (such as machining, grinding, cutting, forming, powder metallurgy, heat treating, and finishing), as well as handling of raw materials, inspection, and assembly. The most common applications of FMS to date have been in machining and assembly operations. A variety of FMS technology is available from machine-tool manufacturers.

Flexible manufacturing systems represent the highest level of efficiency, sophistication, and productivity that has been achieved in manufacturing plants (Fig. 39.14). The flexibility of FMS is such that it can handle a *variety of part configurations* and produce them *in any order*.

FMS can be regarded as a system which combines the benefits of two other systems: (a) the highly productive but inflexible transfer lines (Section 38.2.3), and (b) job-shop production, which can produce large product variety on stand-alone machines but is inefficient. The relative characteristics of transfer lines and FMS are shown in Table 39.1. Note that in FMS, the time required for changeover to a different part is very short. The quick response to product and market-demand variations is a major attribute of FMS.

39.10.1 Elements of FMS

The basic elements of a flexible manufacturing system are (a) workstations, (b) automated handling and transport of materials and parts, and (c) control systems. The workstations are arranged to yield the greatest efficiency in production, with an orderly flow of materials, parts, and products through the system.

The types of machines in workstations depend on the type of production. For machining operations (Part IV), they usually consist of a variety of three- to five-axis machining centers, CNC lathes, milling machines, drill presses, and grinders. Also included is various other equipment, such as that for automated inspection (including coordinate-measuring machines), assembly, and cleaning.

Other types of operations suitable for FMS include sheet metal forming, punching and shearing, and forging; they incorporate furnaces, forging machines, trimming presses, heat-treating facilities, and cleaning equipment.

Because of the flexibility of FMS, material-handling, storage, and retrieval systems are very important. Material handling is controlled by a central computer and performed by automated guided vehicles, conveyors, and various transfer mechanisms. The system is capable of transporting raw materials, blanks, and parts in various stages of completion to any machine (in random order) and at any time. Prismatic parts are usually moved on specially designed **pallets**. Parts having rotational symmetry (such as those for turning operations) are usually moved by mechanical devices and robots.

The computer control system of FMS is its brains and includes various software and hardware. This sub-system controls the machinery and equipment in workstations and the

FIGURE 39.14   A general view of a flexible manufacturing system, showing several machine tools and an automated guided vehicle. *Source*: Cincinnati Milacron, Inc.

transporting of raw materials, blanks, and parts in various stages of completion from machine to machine. It also stores data and provides communication terminals that display the data visually.

39.10.2 Scheduling

Because FMS involves a major capital investment, efficient machine utilization is essential: machines must not stand idle. Consequently, proper scheduling and process planning are crucial.

Scheduling for FMS is *dynamic*, unlike that in job shops, where a relatively rigid schedule is followed to perform a set of operations. The scheduling system for FMS specifies the types of operations to be performed on each part, and it identifies the machines or

TABLE 39.1   Comparison of the Characteristics of Transfer Lines and Flexible-Manufacturing Systems

Characteristic	Transfer line	FMS
Types of parts made	Generally few	Infinite
Lot size	>100	1–50
Part changing time	$\frac{1}{2}$ to 8 hr	1 min
Tool change	Manual	Automatic
Adaptive control	Difficult	Available
Inventory	High	Low
Production during breakdown	None	Partial
Efficiency	60–70%	85%
Justification for capital expenditure	Simple	Difficult

manufacturing cells to be used. Dynamic scheduling is capable of responding to quick changes in product type and so is responsive to real-time decisions.

Because of the flexibility in FMS, no setup time is wasted in switching between manufacturing operations; the system is capable of performing different operations in different orders and on different machines. However, the characteristics, performance, and reliability of each unit in the system must be checked, to ensure that parts moving from workstation to workstation are of acceptable quality and dimensional accuracy.

39.10.3 Economic Justification of FMS

FMS installations are very capital-intensive, typically starting at well over $1 million. Consequently, a thorough cost-benefit analysis must be conducted before a final decision is made. This analysis should include such factors as the cost of capital, of energy, of materials, and of labor, the expected markets for the products to be manufactured, and any anticipated fluctuations in market demand and product type. An additional factor is the time and effort required for installing and debugging the system.

Typically, an FMS system can take two to five years to install and at least six months to debug. Although FMS requires few, if any, machine operators, the personnel in charge of the total operation must be trained and highly skilled. These personnel include manufacturing engineers, computer programmers, and maintenance engineers.

As is indicated in Fig. 38.2, the most effective FMS applications have been in medium-volume batch production. When a variety of parts is to be produced, FMS is suitable for production volumes of 15,000–35,000 aggregate parts per year. For individual parts of the same configuration, production may reach 100,000 units per year. In contrast, high-volume, low-variety parts production is best obtained from transfer machines (dedicated equipment). Finally, low-volume, high-variety parts production can best be done on conventional standard machinery (with or without NC) or by machining centers.

Compared to conventional manufacturing systems, some benefits of FMS are the following:

- Parts can be produced randomly, in batch sizes as small as one, and at lower unit cost.
- Direct labor and inventories are reduced, to yield major savings over conventional systems.

- The lead times required for product changes are shorter.
- Production is more reliable, because the system is self-correcting, and, so product quality is uniform.
- Work-in-progress inventories are reduced.

Example: Flexible Manufacturing Systems in Large and Small Companies

Because of the advantages of FMS technology, many manufacturers have long considered implementing a large-scale system in their facilities. After detailed review, however, and on the basis of the experience of other companies, most manufacturers have decided on some smaller, simpler, modular, less expensive system that is more cost-effective. These systems include flexible manufacturing cells (the cost of which would be on the order of a few hundred thousand dollars) and even stand-alone machining centers and various CNC machine tools that are easier to control than an FMS.

There is a general feeling that, when FMS became an established alternative, the expectations were high. In some cases, extensive computerization has led to much confusion and inefficiency in company operations. Particularly for smaller companies, important considerations include not only the fact that large capital investment and major hardware and software acquisitions are necessary, but also that the efficient operation of a large FMS requires extensive training of personnel.

In contrast to the experience of small companies, there are several examples of the successful and economically viable implementation of an FMS in a large company. The results of a survey of 20 such operating systems in the United States have indicated improvements gained over prior methods. Some systems are now capable of economically producing lot sizes of one part. In spite of the large cost, the system has paid for itself in a number of companies.

39.11 JUST-IN-TIME (JIT) PRODUCTION

The *just-in-time production* concept was implemented in Japan to eliminate waste of materials, machines, capital, manpower, and inventory throughout the manufacturing system. The JIT concept has the following goals:

- Receive supplies just in time to be used.
- Produce parts just in time to be made into subassemblies.
- Produce subassemblies just in time to be assembled into finished products.
- Produce and deliver finished products just in time to be sold.

In traditional manufacturing, the parts are made in batches, placed in inventory, and used whenever necessary. This approach is known as a **push system**, meaning that parts are made according to a schedule and are in inventory to be used if and when they are needed. In contrast, just-in-time is a **pull system**, meaning that parts are produced to order, and the production is matched with demand for the final assembly of products.

There are no stockpiles, with the ideal production quantity being one (**zero inventory, stockless production, demand scheduling**). Moreover, parts are inspected by the worker as they are manufactured and are used within a short period of time.

In this way, the worker maintains continuous production control, immediately identifying defective parts, and reducing process variation to produce quality products. The worker takes pride in good product quality. Also, the extra motions involved in stockpiling parts and then retrieving them from storage are eliminated.

Implementation of the JIT concept requires that all aspects of manufacturing operations be reviewed and monitored, so that all those operations and all the use of resources that do not add value are eliminated. This approach emphasizes pride and dedication in producing high-quality products, the elimination of idle resources, and teamwork among workers, engineers, and management to quickly solve any problems that arise during production or assembly.

The ability to detect production problems during the making of parts has been likened to the level of water (representing the inventory levels) in a lake covering a bed of boulders (representing production problems). When the water level is high (the high inventories associated with *push* production), the boulders are not exposed. By contrast, when the level is low (the low inventories associated with *pull* production), the boulders are exposed; consequently, they can be identified and removed. This analogy indicates that high inventory levels can mask quality and production problems involving parts that are already stockpiled.

The JIT concept includes as all-important the timely delivery of supplies and parts from outside sources and from other divisions of a company, so it significantly reduces in-plant inventory. As a result, major reductions in storage facilities have already been taking place, and storage space has been reclaimed for productive purposes; in fact, the concept of building large warehouses for parts has become obsolete. Suppliers are expected to deliver, often on a daily basis, pre-inspected goods as they are needed for production. This approach requires reliable suppliers, close cooperation and trust between the company and its vendors, and a reliable system of transportation. Also important for smoother operation is the reduction of the number of suppliers. In one example, an Apple Computer plant cut the number of suppliers from 300 to 70.

The JIT concept of purchasing and delivery is a significant departure from the traditional purchasing of supplies from one or more vendors, whereby deliveries are made (with lead times of weeks or months) in larger quantities and are stored in the inventory. Although a buffer is built into the traditional system, it tends to create large inventory levels and to make controlling the quality of incoming supplies difficult.

39.11.1 Kanban

Although the basic concept of JIT originated in the United States decades ago, it was first demonstrated on a large scale in 1953 at the Toyota Motor Company, under the name *kanban*, meaning visible record. These records usually consist of two types of cards (kanbans): (a) the **production card**, which authorizes the production of one container or cart of identical, specified parts at a workstation, and (b) the **conveyance card** or **move card**, which authorizes the transfer of one container or cart of parts from that particular workstation to the workstation where the parts will be used.

The cards contain information about the type of the part, the place of issue, the part number, and the number of items in the container. These cards have now been replaced by barcoded plastic tags and other devices. The number of containers in circulation at any time is completely controlled and can be scheduled as desired for maximum production efficiency.

39.11.2 Advantages of JIT

The advantages of JIT are as follows:

- low inventory carrying costs;
- fast detection of defects in the production or the delivery of supplies, and, hence, low scrap loss;

- reduced inspection and rework of parts;
- high-quality parts produced at low cost.

Although there can be significant variations, implementation of just-in-time production has resulted in reductions—of 20% to 40% in product cost; of 60% to 80% in inventory; of up to 90% in rejection rates; of 90% in lead times; and of 50% in scrap, rework, and warranty costs—and in increases of 30% to 50% in direct labor productivity and of 60% in indirect labor productivity.

Example: Applications of JIT in the U.S. Automotive Industry

In one application, automotive seats are made in the supplier's plant just two hours before they are needed at the assembly plant, which is 120 km (75 miles) away. The seats are unloaded at the assembly plant and quickly transferred in the proper sequence of style and color (each seat being marked beforehand for a specific car moving down an assembly line). Each seat arrives on the assembly line just in time for installation.

Because the system operates efficiently, there have been trends by the major U.S. automakers to get suppliers of various components to relocate plants closer to assembly lines. However, this is a costly and capital-intensive undertaking on the part of suppliers. An alternative is to have a dependable delivery system of transportation by truck and rail for reliable and timely delivery of supplies.

39.12 COMMUNICATIONS NETWORKS IN MANUFACTURING

In order to maintain a high level of coordination and efficiency of operation in integrated manufacturing, an extensive, high-speed, and interactive **communications network** is required. A major advance in communications technology is the **local area network (LAN)**. In this hardware-and-software system, logically related groups of machines and equipment (such as those in a manufacturing cell) communicate with each other. A local area network links these groups to each other, bringing different phases of manufacturing into a unified operation.

A local area network can be very large and complex, linking hundreds or even thousands of machines and devices in several buildings. Various network layouts (Fig. 39.15) of fiber optics or copper cables are used, over distances ranging from a few meters to as much as 32 km (20 mi). For larger distances, **wide area networks (WAN)** are used.

Different types of networks can be linked (or integrated) through "gateways" and "bridges." Access control to the network is important, otherwise collisions can occur when several workstations transmit simultaneously. Continuous scanning of the transmitting medium is essential.

In the 1970s, a *carrier sense multiple access with collision detection* (CSMA/CD) *system* was developed and implemented in **Ethernet**. Now used by a majority of workstations and minicomputers, Ethernet has become the industry standard. Other access control methods are **token ring** and **token bus**, in which a "token" (special message) is passed from device to device; only the device that has the token is allowed to transmit, while all the other devices receive only.

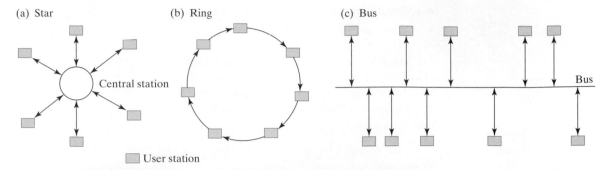

FIGURE 39.15   Three basic types of topology for a local area network (LAN) (a) The *star* topology is suitable for situations that are not subject to frequent configuration changes. All messages pass through a central station. Telephone systems in office buildings usually have this type of topology. (b) In the *ring* topology all individual user stations are connected in a continuous ring. The message is forwarded from one station to the next until it reaches its assigned destination. Although the wiring is relatively simple, the failure of one station shuts down the entire network. (c) In the *bus* topology all stations have independent access to the bus. This system is reliable and is easier than the other two to service. Because its arrangement is similar to the layout of the machines in the factory, its installation is relatively easy, and it can be rearranged when the machines are rearranged.

39.12.1 Communications Standards

Typically, one manufacturing cell is built with machines and equipment purchased from one vendor, another cell with machines purchased from another vendor, a third purchased from yet a third vendor. As a result, a variety of programmable devices are involved, driven by several computers and microprocessors purchased at various times from different vendors and having various capacities and levels of sophistication.

Each cell's computers have their own specifications and proprietary standards, and they cannot communicate beyond the cell with others unless equipped with custom-built interfaces. This situation created "islands of automation," and in some cases up to 50% of the cost of automation used to be related to overcoming difficulties in the communications between individual manufacturing cells and other parts of the organization.

The existence of automated cells that could function independently from each other only, and without a common base for information transfer, led to the need for a *communications standard* to improve communications and the efficiency of computer-integrated manufacturing. The first step toward standardization began in 1980. After considerable effort, and on the basis of existing national and international standards, a set of communications standards known as **manufacturing automation protocol (MAP)** was developed.

The capabilities and effectiveness of MAP were demonstrated in 1984, with the successful interconnection of devices from a number of vendors. As a result, the importance of a worldwide communications standard was fully recognized, and vendors now design their products in compliance with these standards.

The International Organization for Standardization (ISO)/Open System Interconnect (OSI) reference model is accepted worldwide. The ISO/OSI model has a hierarchical structure, in which communication between two users is divided into seven layers (Fig. 39.16).

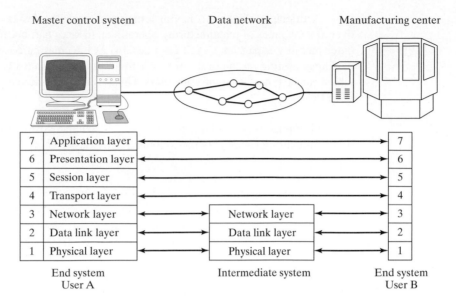

Master control system   Data network   Manufacturing center

7	Application layer		7
6	Presentation layer		6
5	Session layer		5
4	Transport layer		4
3	Network layer	Network layer	3
2	Data link layer	Data link layer	2
1	Physical layer	Physical layer	1

End system   Intermediate system   End system
User A   User B

FIGURE 39.16   The ISO/OSI reference model for open communication. *Source*: U. Rembold, et al. *Computer Integrated Manufacturing and Engineering*. Addison-Wesley, 1993.

Each layer has a special task: (a) mechanical and electronic means of data transmission, (b) error detection and correction, (c) correct transmission of the message, (d) control of the dialog between users, (e) translation of the message into a common syntax, (f) verification that the data transferred has been understood.

The operation of this system is complex. Basically, each standard-sized chunk of message or data from user A to be transmitted to user B moves sequentially through the successive layers at A's end, from layer 7 to layer 1. More information is added to the original message as it travels through each layer. The complete *packet* is transmitted through the physical communications medium to user B, then moves through the layers from 1 to 7 at B's end. The transmission takes place through coaxial cable, fiber-optic cable, microwave, and similar devices.

Communication protocols have been extended to office automation as well, with the development of **technical and office protocol (TOP)** which is based on the ISO/OSI reference model. In this way, total communication (MAP/TOP) is being established among the factory floor and offices at all levels of an organization. A major trend is the use of **Internet tools** (hardware, software, and protocols) within a company to link all departments and functions into a self-contained and fully compatible **Intranet**. Several tools for implementing this linking are available commercially; they are inexpensive, and they are easy to install, integrate, and use.

39.13 ARTIFICIAL INTELLIGENCE (AI)

Artificial intelligence is that part of computer science concerned with systems that exhibit some characteristics usually associated with intelligence in human behavior (such as learning, reasoning, problem-solving, and the understanding of language). The goal of AI is to *simulate* such human behaviors on the computer. The art of bringing relevant principles and tools of AI to bear on difficult application problems is known as **knowledge engineering**.

Artificial intelligence is having a major effect on the design, the automation, and the overall economics of manufacturing operations, in large part because of advances in computer memory expansion (VLSI chip design) and decreasing costs. Artificial intelligence packages costing on the order of a few thousand dollars have been developed, many of which can be run on personal computers. Thus, AI has become accessible to office desks and shop floors.

Elements of Artificial Intelligence.   In general, artificial-intelligence applications in manufacturing encompass the following activities:

   a. expert systems;
   b. natural language;
   c. machine (computer) vision;
   d. artificial neural networks;
   e. fuzzy logic.

39.13.1 Expert Systems (ES)

An **expert system** (also called a **knowledge-based system**) is, generally, defined as an intelligent computer program that has the capability to solve difficult real-life problems by the use of **knowledge base** and **inference** procedures (Fig. 39.17). The goal of an expert system is the capability to conduct an intellectually demanding task in the way that a human expert would.

The field of knowledge required to perform this task is called the **domain** of the expert system. Expert systems utilize a knowledge base containing facts, data, definitions, and assumptions. They also have the capacity for a **heuristic** approach, that is, making good

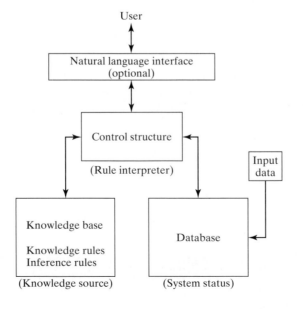

FIGURE 39.17   Basic structure of an expert system. The knowledge base consists of knowledge rules (general information about the problem) and the inference rules (the way conclusions are reached). The results may be communicated to the user through the natural-language interface. *Source*: K. W. Goff, *Mechanical Engineering*, October 1985.

judgments on the basis of discovery and revelation, and making high-probability guesses, just as a human expert would.

The knowledge base is expressed in computer codes (usually in the form of **if-then rules**) and can generate a series of questions. The mechanism for using these rules to solve problems is called an **inference engine**. Expert systems can also communicate with other computer software packages.

To construct expert systems for solving the complex design and manufacturing problems encountered, one needs (a) a great deal of knowledge and (b) a mechanism for manipulating this knowledge to create solutions. Because of the difficulty involved in accurately modeling the many years of experience of an expert (or a team of experts), and the complex inductive reasoning and decision-making capabilities of humans (including the capacity to learn from mistakes), developing knowledge-based systems requires considerable time and effort.

Expert systems operate on a real-time basis, and their short reaction times provide rapid responses to problems. The programming languages most commonly used for this application are C++, LISP, and PROLOG; other languages can also be used. An important development is expert system software **shells** or **environments** (also called **framework systems**). These software packages are essentially expert-system outlines that allow a person to write specific applications to suit special needs. Writing these programs requires considerable experience and time.

Several expert systems have been developed and used since the early 1970s, ones utilizing computers with various capacities, for such specialized applications as the following:

- problem diagnosis in various types of machines and equipment, and determination of corrective actions;
- modeling and simulation of production facilities;
- computer-aided design, process planning, and production scheduling;
- management of a company's manufacturing strategy.

39.13.2 Natural-Language Processing

Traditionally, obtaining information from a database in the computer memory has required the utilization of computer programmers to translate questions in natural language into "queries" in some machine language. Natural-language interfaces with database systems are in various stages of development. These systems allow a user to obtain information by entering English-language commands in the form of simple, typed questions.

Software shells are available, and they are used in such applications as the scheduling of material flow in manufacturing and the analyzing of information in databases. Significant progress is being made on computer software that will have speech synthesis and recognition (**voice recognition**) capabilities, to eliminate the need to type commands on keyboards.

39.13.3 Machine Vision

The basic features of machine vision are described in Section 38.8. Computers and software implementing artificial intelligence are combined with cameras and other optical sensors. These machines then perform such operations as inspecting, identifying, sorting of parts, and guiding of robots (*intelligent robots*—Fig. 39.18), operations that would otherwise require human intervention.

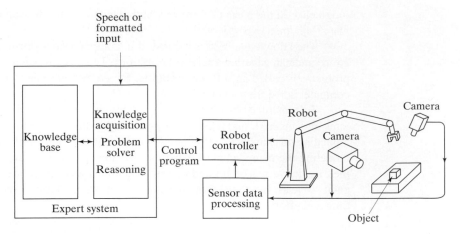

FIGURE 39.18   Expert system, as applied to an industrial robot guided by machine vision.

39.13.4 Artificial Neural Networks (ANN)

Although computers are much faster than the human brain at sequential tasks, humans are much better at pattern-based tasks that can be attacked with parallel processing, such as recognizing features (in faces and voices, even under noisy conditions), assessing situations quickly, and adjusting to new and dynamic conditions. These advantages are also partly due to the ability of humans to use several senses (sight, hearing, smell, taste, and touch) simultaneously (*data fusion*) and in real time. The branch of Artificial Intelligence called **artificial neural networks** attempts to gain some of these capabilities through computer imitation of the way that data is processed by the human brain.

The human brain has about 100 billion linked **neurons** (cells that are the fundamental functional units of nervous tissue) and more than a thousand times that many connections. Each neuron performs only one, simple task: it receives input signals from a fixed set of neurons and, when those input signals are related in a certain way (specific to that particular neuron), it generates an electrochemical output signal which goes to a fixed set of neurons. It is now believed that human learning is accomplished by changes in the strengths of these signal connections between neurons.

A fully developed, feed-forward network is the most common type of ANN, and it is built according to this principle from several layers of processing elements (simulating neurons). The elements in the first (input) layer are fed with input data—for example, forces, velocities, voltages. Each element sums up all its inputs: one per element in the input layer, many per element in succeeding layers. Each element in a layer then transfers the data (according to a transfer function) to all the elements in the next layer. Each element in that next layer, however, receives a different signal, because of the different connection weights between the elements.

The last layer is the output layer, within which each element is compared to the desired output—that of the process being simulated. The difference between the desired output and the calculated one (the error) is fed back to the network by changing the weights of the connections in a way that reduces this error. After this procedure has been repeated several times, the network has been "trained," and it can now be used on input data not previously presented to the system.

Other kinds of ANN are (a) associative memories, (b) self-organizing ANN, and (c) adaptive-resonance ANN. The feature common to these neural networks is that they must be trained with concrete exemplars. It is, therefore, very difficult to formulate input-output relations mathematically and to predict an ANN's behavior with untrained inputs.

Artificial neural networks are being used in such applications as noise reduction (in telephones), speech recognition, and process control. For example, they can be used for predicting the surface finish of a workpiece obtained by end milling, on the basis of input parameters such as cutting force, torque, acoustic emission, and spindle acceleration. Although still controversial, the opinion of many is that true artificial intelligence will evolve only through advances in ANN.

39.13.5 Fuzzy Logic

An element of artificial intelligence having important applications in control systems and pattern recognition is *fuzzy logic* (**fuzzy models**). Introduced in 1965, and based on the observation that people can make good decisions on the basis of imprecise and nonnumerical information, fuzzy models are mathematical means of representing vagueness and imprecise information (hence, the term "fuzzy").

These models have the ability to recognize, represent, manipulate, interpret, and utilize data and information that are vague or lack precision. These methods deal with reasoning and decision-making at a level higher than do neural networks. Typical linguistic examples are the following: few, very, more or less, small, medium, extremely, and almost all.

Fuzzy technologies and devices have been developed (and successfully applied) in areas such as robotics and motion control, image processing and machine vision, machine learning, and the design of intelligent systems. Some applications are in (a) the automatic transmission of the Lexus automobile; (b) a washing machine that automatically adjusts the washing cycle for load size, fabric type, and amount of dirt; and (c) a helicopter that obeys vocal commands to go forward, up, left, and right, to hover, and to land.

39.14 THE FACTORY OF THE FUTURE

On the basis of the advances made in all aspects of manufacturing technology and computer integration, we may envision *the factory of the future* as a fully automated facility in which human beings will not be directly involved with production on the shop floor (hence, the term **untended factories**). All manufacturing, material-handling, assembly, and inspection will be done by computer-controlled machinery and equipment.

Similarly, activities such as the processing of incoming orders, production planning and scheduling, cost accounting, and various decision-making processes (usually performed by management) will also be done automatically by computers. The role of human beings will be confined to activities such as overall supervision, maintenance (especially preventive maintenance), and the upgrading of machines and equipment; the shipping and receiving of supplies and finished products; the provision security for the plant facilities; the programming, upgrading, and monitoring of computer programs; and the monitoring, maintenance, and upgrading of computer hardware.

Some businesses in the food, petroleum, and chemical industries already operate automatically with little human intervention. These industries involve continuous processes that are easier to automate fully than is piece-part manufacturing. Even so, the direct involvement of fewer people in the manufacturing of products is already apparent: Surveys of modern manufacturing facilities show that only 10% to 15% of the workforce is directly involved in production; the majority is involved in the gathering and processing of information.

Virtually untended manufacturing cells already make products such as engine blocks, axles, and housings for clutches and air compressors. For large-scale flexible manufacturing systems, however, highly trained and skilled personnel will always be needed in order to plan, maintain, and oversee operations.

The reliability of machines, equipment, control systems, power supply, and communications networks is crucial to full factory automation. Without rapid human intervention, a local or general breakdown in even one of these components can cripple production. The computer-integrated factory of the future must be capable of automatically rerouting materials and production flows to other machines and to the control of other computers in the case of such emergencies.

In the implementation of advanced concepts of manufacturing (with their attendant impact on the operation of the factory of the future), certain developments and improvements are bound to continue at a rapid pace:

a. common communications networks, software, and standards for every aspect of manufacturing technology, from product design to manufacturing;

b. reduction in the size and increase in the efficiency of knowledge-rich controllers, and their integration into machines instead of their functioning as separate units;

c. increasing availability of off-the-shelf control hardware;

d. increase in the reliability of voice-recognition capabilities, so that machines can understand and implement spoken messages;

e. tighter sensor fusion, employing more rugged sensors, and improving feedback methods for monitoring and diagnosing all aspects of manufacturing operations—both developments augmented by advances in artificial intelligence technology;

f. cost-effective system integration at all levels of an organization.

39.14.1 Concerns and Opportunities

An important consideration in a fully automated factory is the nature and extent of its *impact on employment*, including all the social and political ramifications. Although projections indicate that there will be a decline in the number of machine tool operators and tool-and-die workers, there will be major increases in service occupations (such as computer service technicians and maintenance electricians).

Thus, the generally low-skilled, manual-effort labor force traditionally required in manufacturing will evolve into a knowledge-effort labor force, one having the specialized training or retraining required in such activities as computer programming, information processing, CAD/CAM, information science and technology, and other high-technology tasks. The development of more user-friendly computer software is making retraining of the workforce much easier.

There are many widely divergent opinions about the impact of untended factories. Consequently, predicting the nature of future manufacturing strategies with any certainty is difficult. Although economic considerations and trade-offs are crucial, companies that do not install computer-integrated operations where they will be cost-effective are in obvious jeopardy. It is now recognized that, in a highly competitive global marketplace, rapid adaptability is crucial to the survival of a manufacturing organization.

The continuous advances in all aspects of the science, the engineering, and the technology of manufacturing are constantly being analyzed by corporate management, with a view to the near-term and long-term economic impact on their operations. Over the past few years, much has been written, discussed, and debated concerning the relative manufacturing technologies and industrial strengths among many industrialized nations.

There are various complex issues stemming from the following considerations:

a. the characteristics of each industrialized nation— in particular, its history, its social and demographic structure, and its standard of living;

b. the nature, educational level, and loyalty of its workforce;

c. the relationships among management, labor, and government;

d. interactions among companies, research universities, and social organizations;

e. productivity, and the effective utilization of capital equipment;

f. the missions and the operational philosophies of the management of industrial and business organizations;

g. stockholder attitudes.

The term **world class** is now frequently used to describe a certain quality and level of manufacturing activities, signifying the fact that products must meet international standards and be acceptable worldwide. It should also be recognized that world class (like quality) is not a fixed target for a manufacturing company or a country to reach, but a *moving target*, rising to higher and higher levels as time passes. Manufacturing organizations must be aware of this moving target and plan and execute their programs accordingly.

SUMMARY

- Integrated manufacturing systems are being implemented to various degrees to optimize operations, reduce costs, and improve product quality.
- Computer-integrated manufacturing has become the most important means of improving productivity, of responding to changing market demands, and of better controlling manufacturing and management functions. With extensive use of computers and of the rapid developments in sophisticated software, product designs (and their analysis and simulation) are now more detailed and thorough.
- New developments in manufacturing operations, such as group technology, cellular manufacturing, and flexible manufacturing systems, are contributing significantly to improved productivity.
- Artificial intelligence is likely to create new opportunities in all aspects of manufacturing science, engineering, and technology.

TRENDS

- The trend in manufacturing is toward greater product variety, shorter product life cycles, and increased and continuing emphasis on high product quality at low cost.
- Utilization of computers in all phases of manufacturing will continue to grow. An increasing trend is the use of networking tools (hardware, software, and protocols) within a company to link all departments and functions into a self-contained, fully compatible network.
- Material-requirements planning activities are incorporating marketing and business issues directly into the database, in an activity referred to as Enterprise Resource Planning (ERP).

- The support of the management and of all others in an organization will continue to be an essential element in the successful adoption of new technologies.
- Because of the high costs involved, a thorough analysis of costs and benefits as they relate to implementation of various aspects of computer-integrated manufacturing systems will continue to be important.
- Operators in the factory of the future are likely to perform tasks such as supervision, the upgrading of computers and computer programs, equipment maintenance, plant security, and the shipping and receiving of supplies and finished products.

KEY TERMS

Artificial intelligence
Artificial neural networks
Cellular manufacturing
Classification and coding systems
Coding
Communications network
Communications standard
Computer-aided design and engineering
Computer-aided manufacturing
Computer-aided process planning
Computer-integrated manufacturing
Data acquisition system
Database
Demand scheduling
Design attributes
Enterprise resource planning
Environments
Ethernet
Exchange specifications
Expert systems
Factory of the future

Flexible manufacturing cell
Flexible manufacturing system
Framework systems
Functional layout
Fuzzy logic
Group layout
Group technology
If-then rules
Inference engine
Integration
Internet tools
Islands of automation
Just-in-time production
Kanban
Knowledge engineering
Knowledge-based system
Local area network
Machine vision
Manufacturing attributes
Manufacturing automation protocol
Manufacturing cell

Manufacturing resource planning
Material-requirements planning
Menu item
Modeling
Natural-language processing
Octree representation
Pallet
Paperless design
Production flow analysis
Pull system
Push system
Routing sheet
Scheduling
Shells
Technical and office protocol
Untended factories
Wide area network
World class
Zero inventory

BIBLIOGRAPHY

Amirouche, F.M.L., *Computer-Aided Design and Manufacturing*. Prentice Hall, 1993.

Askin, R.G., and C.R. Standridge, *Modeling and Analysis of Manufacturing Systems*. Wiley, 1993.

Badiru, A.B., *Expert Systems Applications in Engineering and Manufacturing*. Prentice Hall, 1992.

Bedworth, D.D., M.R. Henderson, and P.M. Wolf, *Computer-Integrated Design and Manufacturing*. McGraw-Hill, 1991.

Burbidge, J.L., *Production Flow Analysis for Planning Group Technology*. Oxford, 1997.

Chang, T.-C., R.A. Wysk, and H.P. Wang, *Computer-Aided Manufacturing* (2d ed.). Prentice Hall, 1997.

Cheng, T.C.E., and S. Podolsky, *Just-in-Time Manufacturing: An Introduction* (2d ed.). Chapman & Hall, 1996.

Chorafas, D., *Expert Systems in Manufacturing*. Van Nostrand Reinhold, 1992.

Corbett, J., M. Dooner, J. Meleka, and C. Pym, *Design for Manufacture: Strategies, Principles and Techniques*. Addison-Wesley, 1991.

Driankov, D., H. Hellendoorn, and M. Reinfrank, *Introduction to Fuzzy Control* (2nd ed.). Springer-Verlag, 1996.

Famili, A., D.S. Nau, and S.H. Kim, *Artificial Intelligence Applications in Manufacturing*. American Association for Artificial Intelligence, 1992.

Foston, A.L., C.L. Smith, and T. Au, *Fundamentals of Computer-Integrated Manufacturing*. Prentice Hall, 1991.

Goldratt, E.M., *Theory of Constraints*. North River Press, 1990.

Gu, P., and D.H. Norrie, *Intelligent Manufacturing Planning*. Chapman & Hall, 1995.

Hannam, R., *CIM: From Concept to Realisation*. Addison-Wesley, 1998.

Higgins, P., L.R. Roy, and L. Tierney, *Manufacturing Planning and Control: Beyond MRP II.* Chapman & Hall, 1996.

Hitomi, K., *Manufacturing Systems Engineering* (2d ed.). Taylor & Francis, 1996.

Irani, S. (ed.), *Handbook of Cellular Manufacturing Systems.* Wiley, 1999.

Kasabov, N.K., *Foundations of Neural Networks, Fuzzy Systems, and Knowledge Engineering.* The MIT Press, 1996.

Krishnamoorty, C.S., and S. Rajeev, *Artificial Intelligence and Expert Systems for Engineers.* CRC Press, 1996.

Kusiak, A., *Concurrent Engineering: Automation, Tools, and Techniques.* Wiley, 1993.

———, *Intelligent Design and Manufacturing.* Wiley, 1992.

———, *Intelligent Manufacturing Systems.* Prentice Hall, 1990.

Leondes, C.T. (ed.), *Fuzzy Logic and Expert Systems Applications.* Academic Press, 1998.

Liebowitz, J. (ed.), *The Handbook of Applied Expert Systems.* CRC Press, 1997.

Louis, R.S., *Integrating Kanban with MRP II: Automating a Pull System for Enhanced JIT Inventory Management.* Productivity Press, 1997.

Luggen, W. W., *Flexible Manufacturing Cells and Systems.* Prentice Hall, 1991.

Maus, R., and J. Keyes (eds.), *Handbook of Expert Systems in Manufacturing.* McGraw-Hill, 1991.

McMahon, C., and J. Browne, *CADCAM—From Principles to Practice.* Addison-Wesley, 1993.

Mitchell, F. H., Jr., *CIM Systems: An Introduction to Computer-Integrated Manufacturing.* Prentice Hall, 1991.

Monden, Y., *Toyota Production System: An Integrated Approach to Just-in-Time* (3d ed.). Institute of Industrial Engineers, 1998.

Nee, A.Y.C., K. Whybrew, and A.S. Kumar, *Advanced Fixture Design for FMS.* Springer, 1994.

Popovic, D., and V. Bhatkar, *Methods and Tools for Applied Artificial Intelligence.* Marcel Dekker, 1994.

Rehg, J.A., *Computer-Integrated Manufacturing.* Prentice Hall, 1994.

———, *Introduction to Robotics in CIM Systems* (3d ed.). Prentice Hall, 1997.

Rembold, U., B.O. Nnaji, and A. Storr, *Computer Integrated Manufacturing and Engineering.* Addison-Wesley, 1993.

Sandras, W.W., *Just-in Time: Making It Happen.* Wiley, 1997.

Singh, N., *Systems Approach to Computer-Integrated Design and Manufacturing.* Wiley, 1995.

Singh, N., and D. Rajamani, *Cellular Manufacturing Systems: Design, Planning and Control.* Chapman & Hall, 1996.

Tool and Manufacturing Engineers Handbook (4th ed.), Vol. 5: *Manufacturing Management.* Society of Manufacturing Engineers, 1988.

Tool and Manufacturing Engineers Handbook (4th ed.), Vol. 7. *Continuous Improvement.* Society of Manufacturing Engineers, 1993.

Vajpayee, S.K., *Principles of Computer-Integrated Manufacturing.* Prentice Hall, 1995.

Williams, D.J., *Manufacturing Systems* (2d ed.). Chapman & Hall, 1994.

Wu, J.-K., *Neural Networks and Simulation Methods.* Marcel Dekker, 1994.

REVIEW QUESTIONS

39.1 In what ways have computers had an impact on manufacturing?

39.2 What advantages are there in viewing manufacturing as a system? What are the components of a manufacturing system?

39.3 Discuss the benefits of computer-integrated manufacturing operations.

39.4 What is a database? Why is it necessary? Why should the management of a company have access to databases?

39.5 Explain how a CAD system operates.

39.6 What are the advantages of CAD systems over traditional methods of design? Are there any limitations?

39.7 Describe the purposes of process planning. How are computers used in such planning?

39.8 Explain the features of two types of CAPP systems.

39.9 Describe the features of a routing sheet. Why is it necessary?

39.10 What is group technology? Why was it developed? Explain its advantages.

39.11 What is a manufacturing cell? Why was it developed?

39.12 Describe the principle of flexible manufacturing systems. Why do they require major capital investment?

39.13 Why is a flexible manufacturing system capable of producing a wide range of lot sizes?

39.14 What are the benefits of just-in-time production? Why is it called a pull system?

39.15 Explain the function of a local area network.

39.16 What are the advantages of a communications standard?

39.17 What is meant by the term "Factory of the Future"?

39.18 What are the differences between ring and star networks?

39.19 What is Kanban?

39.20 What is an FMC and what is an FMS? What are the differences?

QUALITATIVE PROBLEMS

39.21 Describe the elements of artificial intelligence. Why is machine vision a part of it?

39.22 Explain why humans will still be needed in the factory of the future.

39.23 How would you describe the principle of computer-aided manufacturing to an older worker in a manufacturing facility who is not familiar with computers?

39.24 Give examples of primitives of solids other than those shown in Figs. 39.4a and b.

39.25 Explain the logic behind the arrangements shown in Fig. 39.8b.

39.26 Describe your observations regarding Fig. 39.14.

39.27 What should be the characteristics of an effective guidance system for an automated guided vehicle?

39.28 Give examples in manufacturing in which artificial intelligence could be effective.

39.29 Describe your opinions concerning the voice-recognition capabilities of future machines and controls.

39.30 Would machining centers be suitable for just-in-time production? Explain.

39.31 Give an example of a push system and of a pull system, to clarify the fundamental difference between the two methods.

39.32 Give a specific example in which the variant system of CAPP is desirable, and one in which the generative system is desirable.

39.33 Artificial neural networks are particularly useful where the problems are ill-defined and the data are fuzzy. Give examples in manufacturing where this is the case.

39.34 Is there a minimum to the number of machines in a manufacturing cell? Explain.

39.35 List many three-letter acronyms (such as CNC) and give a brief definition of each, for your future reference.

39.36 What are the disadvantages of zero inventory?

39.37 Why are robots a major component of a FMC?

39.38 Is it possible to exercise JIT in global companies?

39.39 A term sometimes used to describe factories of the future is "untended factories." Can a factory ever be completely untended? Explain your answer.

39.40 What are the advantages of hierarchical coding?

SYNTHESIS AND DESIGN

39.41 Review various manufactured parts described in this text, and group them in a manner similar to those shown in Fig. 39.7.

39.42 Think of a product, and make a decision-tree chart similar to that shown in Fig. 39.9.

39.43 Think of a commonly used product line, and design a manufacturing cell for making it, describing the features of the machines and equipment involved.

39.44 Surveys have indicated that 95% of all the different parts made in the United States are produced in lots of 50 or less. Comment on this observation, and describe your thoughts regarding the implementation of the technologies outlined in Chapters 38 and 39.

39.45 Assume that you are asked to rewrite Section 39.14 on the Factory of the Future. Briefly outline your thoughts regarding this topic.

39.46 Assume that you own a manufacturing company, and that you are aware that you have not taken full advantage of the technological advances in manufacturing—but that now you would like to do so, and you have the necessary capital. Describe how you would go about analyzing your company's needs and how you would plan to implement these technologies. Consider technical as well as human aspects.

39.47 Think of a simple product and make a routing sheet, similar to that shown in Fig. 39.6. If the same part is given to another person, what is the likelihood that the routing sheet developed will be the same? Explain.

39.48 With specific examples, describe your thoughts concerning the state of manufacturing in the United States as compared to its state in other industrialized countries.

39.49 Describe the trends in product characteristics that have had a major impact on manufacturing.

39.50 It has been suggested by some that artificial intelligence systems will ultimately be able to replace the human brain. Do you agree? Explain your response.

39.51 See Fig. 39.6, then suggest a routing sheet for one of the following: (a) an automotive connecting rod, (b) a compressor blade, (c) a glass bottle, (d) injection-molding die, or (e) a bevel gear.

39.52 A well-known problem is that of the traveling salesman: If a salesperson needs to visit fifty cities across the United States, what route should he or she take in order to travel the minimum distance? Perform a literature search and describe how artificial neural networks have advantages in obtaining solutions, as compared to traditional computer architectures.

40

Competitive Aspects of Manufacturing

40.1 INTRODUCTION

Manufacturing high-quality products at the lowest possible cost requires an understanding of the often complex relationships among many factors. We have seen that product design, selection of materials, and selection of manufacturing processes are all interrelated. Product designs are periodically modified to improve product performance, to take advantage of the characteristics of new materials, to make the products easier to manufacture and assemble, and to strive for zero-based rejection and waste.

Because of the very wide variety of materials and manufacturing processes available today, the task of producing a high-quality product by selecting the best materials and the best processes, while minimizing costs, has become a major challenge as well as an opportunity. The cost of a product often determines its marketability and its customer acceptance. Meeting this challenge requires not only a thorough knowledge of the characteristics of materials and processes, but also innovative and creative approaches to product design and to manufacturing technology.

Although the economics of various manufacturing processes have been described at the end of individual chapters, this chapter takes a broader view and summarizes the important overall manufacturing cost factors. We will investigate cost-reduction methods—in particular, **value engineering**, a powerful tool that can be used to evaluate the cost of each manufacturing step relative to its contribution to the value of the product.

40.2 SELECTION OF MATERIALS

In selecting materials for a product, we must have a clear understanding of the **functional requirements** for each of its individual components. Although the general criteria for selecting materials were described in Section 5 of the General Introduction, this chapter will discuss them in further detail.

40.2.1 Mechanical, Physical, and Chemical Properties

As we saw in Chapter 2, *mechanical properties* include strength, toughness, ductility, stiffness, hardness, and resistance to fatigue, creep, and impact. *Physical properties* (Chapter 3) include density, melting point, specific heat, thermal and electrical conductivity, thermal expansion, and magnetic properties. *Chemical properties* (Chapter 3) that are of primary concern in manufacturing are susceptibility to oxidation and corrosion. The relevance of these properties to product design and manufacturing are described in various chapters in Part I.

Selection of materials is now easier and faster because of the availability of computerized and extensive databases, providing greater accessibility. However, to facilitate the selection of materials and other parameters described below, expert-system software (**smart databases**) has been developed. With a proper input of product design and functional requirements, these systems are capable of identifying appropriate materials for a particular application just as an expert or a team of experts would.

40.2.2 Shapes of Commercially Available Materials

After selecting materials, we need to know the shapes and the sizes in which these materials are commercially available (Table 40.1). They can be obtained in various forms: castings, extrusions, forgings, bar, plate, sheet, foil, rod, wire, and metal powders.

TABLE 40.1   Commercially Available Forms of Materials

Material	Available as
Aluminum	P, F, B, T, W, S, I
Copper and brass	P, f, B, T, W, s, I
Magnesium	P, B, T, w, S, I
Steels and stainless steels	P, B, T, W, S, I
Precious metals	P, F, B, t, W, I
Zinc	P, F, D, W, I
Plastics	P, f, B, T, w
Elastomers	P, b, T
Ceramics (alumina)	p, B, T, s
Glass	P, B, T, W, s
Graphite	P, B, T, W, s

Note: P, plate or sheet; F, foil; B, bar; T, tubing; W, wire; S, structural shapes; I, ingots for casting. Lowercase letter indicates limited availability. Most of these materials are also available in powder form.

Purchasing materials in shapes that require the least additional processing is an important consideration. However, such characteristics as the surface quality, the dimensional tolerances, and the straightness of these raw materials must also be taken into account. Obviously, the better and the more consistent these characteristics are, the less additional processing is required.

For example, if we want to produce simple shafts having good dimensional accuracy, roundness, straightness, and surface finish, we could purchase round bars that are turned and centerless-ground to the dimensions specified. Unless our facilities are capable of producing round bars economically, it is cheaper to purchase them.

On the other hand, if we need to make a stepped shaft (one having different diameters along its length), we could purchase a round bar (having a diameter at least equal to the largest diameter of the final stepped shaft) and turn it on a lathe, or process it by some other means, to reduce the diameter. If the stock has broad dimensional tolerances, or is warped or out of round, we must order a larger size to ensure proper dimensional control of the final shaft.

As we have seen, each manufacturing step produces parts having specific shapes, surface finishes, and dimensional tolerances. For example, (a) hot-rolled or hot-drawn products have a rougher surface finish and greater dimensional tolerances than cold-rolled or cold-drawn products; (b) round bars turned on a lathe have rougher surface finish than bars that are ground on cylindrical grinding machines; (c) the wall thickness of welded tubing is generally more uniform than that of seamless tubing; (d) extrusions have smaller cross-sectional tolerances than parts made by roll forming. Information on these characteristics can be readily found in catalogs available from suppliers of raw materials (incoming stock).

40.2.3 Manufacturing Properties

Manufacturing properties of materials typically include castability, workability, formability, machinability, weldability, and hardenability by heat treatment. Because raw materials have to be formed, shaped, machined, ground, fabricated, or heat treated into individual components having specific shapes and dimensions, these properties are crucial to the proper selection of materials.

Recall also that the quality of a raw material can greatly influence its manufacturing properties. The following are some examples:

a. A rod or bar with a longitudinal seam (lap) will develop cracks during simple upsetting and heading operations.

b. Bars with internal defects and inclusions will crack during seamless-tube production.

c. Porous castings will produce poor surface finish when machined.

d. Blanks that are heat treated nonuniformly, and bars that are not stress-relieved, will distort during subsequent operations.

e. Incoming stock that has variations in composition and microstructure cannot be heat treated or machined consistently.

f. Sheet-metal stock having variations in its cold-worked conditions will exhibit springback during bending and other forming operations, because of differences in yield stress.

g. If prelubricated sheet-metal blanks are supplied with nonuniform lubricant distribution and thickness, their formability, surface finish, and overall quality will be adversely affected.

40.2.4 Reliability of Material Supply

The General Introduction pointed out geopolitical factors that can affect the supply of strategic materials. Other factors (such as strikes, shortages, and the reluctance of suppliers to produce materials in a particular shape, quality, or quantity) also affect reliability of supply. Even though availability of materials may not be a problem throughout the country as a whole, it can be a problem for a certain business because of the location of a particular manufacturing plant.

40.2.5 Cost of Materials and Processing

Because of its processing history, the unit cost of a raw material (cost per unit weight or volume) depends not only on the material itself, but also on its shape, size, and condition. (See Table 6.1.) For example, because more operations are involved in the production of thin wire than in that of round rod, the unit cost of the wire is higher.

Similarly, powder metals are more expensive than bulk metals. Furthermore, the cost of materials generally decreases as the purchase quantity increases (such as packaged food products and bottled beverages in supermarkets). Likewise, certain segments of industry (such as automotive companies) purchase materials in very large quantities; the larger the quantity the lower the cost per unit weight (*bulk discount*).

The cost of a particular material is subject to fluctuations caused by factors as simple as supply and demand or as complex as geopolitics. If a product is no longer cost-competitive, alternative and less costly materials can be selected. For example, the copper shortage in the 1940s led the U.S. government to mint pennies from zinc-plated steel. (See Section 5.3 in the General Introduction.) Similarly, when the price of copper increased substantially during the 1960s, the electrical wiring being installed in homes was, for a time, made of aluminum. (See the example in Section 3.7.)

When *scrap* is produced during manufacturing (as in sheet-metal fabricating, forging, and machining), the value of the scrap is deducted from the material's cost, in order to obtain *net material cost*. As expected, the value of the scrap depends on the type of metal and on the demand for it; typically, it is between 10% to 40% of the original cost of the material. The scrap produced in selected manufacturing processes is given in Table 40.2. Note that, in machining, scrap can be very high, whereas rolling, ring-rolling, and powder metallurgy (all net- or near-net-shape processes) produce the least scrap.

TABLE 40.2 Approximate Amount of Scrap Produced in Various Manufacturing Processes

Process	Scrap (%)	Process	Scrap (%)
Machining	10–60	Cold or hot extrusion, forging	15
Hot closed-die forging	20–25	Permanent-mold casting	10
Sheet-metal forming	10–25	Powder metallurgy	5
Rolling, ring rolling	<1		

Example: Effect of Workpiece Hardness on Cost in Drilling

Gear blanks, forged from 8617 alloy steel and having a hardness range of from 149 HB to 156 HB, required the drilling of a hole 75 mm (3 in.) in diameter in the hub. The blanks were drilled with a standard helix drill. After only 10 pieces, however, the drill began to gall, temperatures increased excessively, the drill became dull, and the drilled holes had a rough internal surface finish.

In order to improve machinability and reduce galling, the hardness of the gear blanks was increased to the range from 217 HB to 241 HB, by heating them to 840 °C (1540 °F) and then quenching them in oil. When blanks at this hardness level were drilled, galling was reduced, the surface finish was improved, the drill life increased to 50 pieces, and the cost of drilling was reduced by 80%. *Source*: ASM International.

40.3 PRODUCT DESIGN AND QUANTITY OF MATERIALS

With high production rates and reduced labor, the cost of materials becomes a significant portion of product cost. Although the material cost cannot be reduced below the market level, reductions can be made in the *amount* of material used in those components that are to be mass produced. Because the overall shape of the part is usually optimized during the design and prototype stages, further reductions in the amount of material used can be achieved only by reducing the thickness of the component.

This approach requires the selection of materials having high strength-to-weight or stiffness-to-weight ratios. (See Section 3.2.) Note that higher ratios can also be obtained by improving the product's design and by selecting better cross-sections, such as ones having a high moment of inertia (as in I-beams), or by using tubular or hollow components instead of solid ones. Techniques such as finite-element analysis, minimum-weight design, design optimization, and computer-aided design and manufacturing have greatly facilitated design analysis, material usage and optimization.

Implementing design changes and minimizing the amount of materials utilized can, however, present significant problems in manufacturing, as is outlined in the following examples:

a. Forging of thin parts requires high forces that are due to causes such as friction and chilling of thin sections. (See Eq. 14.1)

b. Welding of thin sheets or structures can cause distortion due to thermal gradients.

c. Casting of thin sections can present difficulties in mold-cavity filling (due to chilling) and in maintaining dimensional accuracy and good surface finish.

d. Formability (in sheet-metal forming) may be reduced as sheet thickness decreases, and, this reduction can lead to buckling (during forming) due to compressive stresses in the plane of the sheet. (See Section 16.4.)

Conversely, utilizing parts with thick cross-sections can slow production in processes such as in casting and injection molding, for instance, because of the increased length of time required for cooling and for removing the part from the mold. Furthermore, the bendability of sheet metals decreases as their thickness increases (Section 16.5).

40.4 SUBSTITUTION OF MATERIALS

There is hardly a product on the market today for which substitution of materials has not played a major role in helping companies maintain their competitive positions. Automobile and aircraft manufacturing are examples of major industries in which *substitution of materials* is an important and ongoing activity. A similar trend is evident in sporting goods and in various other consumer products.

Although new products continually appear on the market, the majority of the design and manufacturing effort is concerned with improving existing products. Major product improvements can result from substitution of materials, from implementing new or improved processing techniques, from better control of the processing parameters, and from increased plant automation.

There are several reasons for substituting materials in existing products:

1. to reduce the costs of materials and processing;
2. to improve manufacturing and assembly, installation, and conversion to automated assembly;
3. to improve the performance of products—for example, by reducing weight and by improving resistance to wear, fatigue, and corrosion;
4. to increase stiffness-to-weight and strength-to-weight ratios;
5. to reduce the need for maintenance and repair;
6. to reduce vulnerability to the unreliability of domestic and overseas supply of materials;
7. to improve compliance with legislation and regulations prohibiting the use of certain materials, for environmental reasons.
8. to reduce performance variations or environmental sensitivity in the product, i.e., to improve robustness.

Substitution of Materials in the Automobile Industry.   The automobile is a good example of the effective substitution of materials in order to achieve one or more of the objectives listed above. Some examples are as follows:

- Certain parts of the metal body have been replaced with plastic or reinforced-plastic parts.
- Metal bumpers, gears, pumps, fuel tanks, housings, covers, clamps, and various other components have been replaced with plastic substitutes.
- Engine components have been replaced with ceramic and reinforced-plastic parts.
- All-metal driveshafts have been replaced with composite-material driveshafts
- Cast-iron engine blocks have been changed to cast-aluminum blocks, forged crankshafts to cast crankshafts, and forged connecting rods to cast or powder-metallurgy or composite-material connecting rods.

Because the automobile industry is a major consumer of both metallic and nonmetallic materials, there is constant competition among suppliers, particularly in the steel, aluminum, and plastics industries. Industry engineers and management are continually investigating the relative advantages and limitations of these principal materials in their applications, recycling and other environmental considerations, and, in particular, their relative costs and benefits.

Substitution of Materials in the Aircraft Industry.   In the aircraft and aerospace industries, conventional aluminum alloys (2000 and 7000 series) are being replaced with aluminum–lithium alloys and titanium alloys (because of their higher strength-to-weight ratios). Forged parts are being replaced with powder-metallurgy parts that are manufactured with better control of impurities and microstructure; the powder-metallurgy parts also require less machining and produce less scrap of expensive materials. Furthermore, advanced composite materials and honeycomb structures are replacing traditional aluminum airframe components (Fig. 40.1), and metal-matrix composites are replacing some of the aluminum and titanium in structural components.

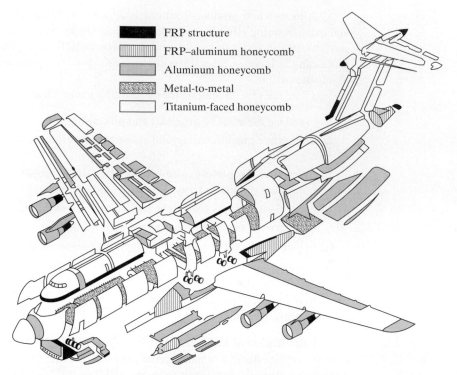

FIGURE 40.1   Advanced materials used on the Lockheed C-5A transport aircraft. (FRP: fiber-reinforced plastic)

Example: Material Changes Between C-5A and C-5B Military Cargo Aircraft

Table 40.3 shows the changes made in materials for various components of the two aircraft and the reasons for the changes. *Source*: H. B. Allison, Lockheed-Georgia.

TABLE 40.3   Material Changes From C-5A to C-5B Military Cargo Aircraft

Item	C-5A Material	C-5B Material	Reason for change
Wing panels	7075–T6511	7175–T73511	Durability
Main frame			
Forgings	7075–F	7049–01	Stress corrosion resistance
Machined frames	7075–T6	7049–T73	
Frame straps	7075–T6 plate	7050–T7651 plate	
Fuselage skin	7079–T6	7475–T61	Material availability
Fuselage underfloor end fittings	7075–T6 forging	7049–T73 forging	Stress corrosion resistance
Wing/pylon attach fitting	4340 alloy steel	PH13–8Mo	Corrosion prevention
Aft ramp lock hooks	D6–AC	PH13–8Mo	Corrosion prevention
Hydraulic lines	AM350 stainless steel	21–6–9 stainless steel	Improved field repair
Fuselage failsafe straps	6Al–4V titanium	7475–T61 aluminum	Titanium strap debond

40.5 SELECTION OF MANUFACTURING PROCESSES

This section describes the importance of proper *selection of manufacturing processes and machinery*, and how the selection process relates to the characteristics of materials, the dimensional tolerances and surface finish obtained, and manufacturing cost. As we have seen, most manufacturing processes have been automated, and are increasingly computer controlled, in order to optimize all aspects of operations. Computerization is also effectively increasing product reliability and product quality and reducing labor costs.

The choice of a manufacturing process is dictated by various considerations, some of which follow:

- the characteristics and properties of the workpiece material (Table 40.4);
- the shape, size, and thickness of the part;
- the dimensional-tolerance and surface-finish requirements;
- the functional requirements of the part;
- the production volume (quantity);
- the level of automation required to meet production volume and production rate;
- the costs involved in individual and combined aspects of the manufacturing operation.

We have seen that some materials can be processed at room temperature, whereas others require elevated temperatures (and thus the need for furnaces and appropriate tooling). Some materials are easy to work because they are soft and ductile; others, being hard, brittle, and abrasive, require special processing techniques and tool and die materials.

Different materials have different manufacturing characteristics (such as castability, forgeability, workability, machinability and weldability), and few materials have favorable characteristics in all the relevant categories. For example, a material that is castable or forgeable may later present difficulties in the machining, grinding, or finishing operations that may be required in order to produce a product with acceptable surface finish, dimensional accuracy, and quality.

Example: Process Selection in Making a Part

Assume that you are asked to make the part shown in Fig. 40.2. You should first determine the part's function, the types of load and environment to which it is to be subjected, the dimensional tolerances and surface finish required, and so on. For the sake of discussion, let's assume that the part is round, that it is 125 mm (5 in.) long, and that the large and small diameters are 38 mm and 25 mm (1.5 in. and 1.0 in.), respectively. Let's further assume that, because of functional requirements (such as stiffness, hardness, and resistance to elevated temperatures), this part should be made of metal.

Which manufacturing process would you choose and how would you organize the production facilities to manufacture a cost-competitive, high-quality product? Recall that, as much as possible, parts should be produced at or near their final shape (net- or near-net-shape manufacturing), an approach that largely eliminates much secondary processing (such as machining, grinding, and other finishing operations) and so reduces the total manufacturing time and manufacturing cost.

This part is relatively simple and could be suitably manufactured by different methods: (a) casting or powder metallurgy, (b) upsetting, (c) extrusion, (d) machining, or (e) joining two separate pieces together.

For net-shape processing, the two logical processes are casting and powder metallurgy, each process having its own characteristics, need for specific tooling and labor

TABLE 40.4 Manufacturing Processes for Commonly Used Metals and Alloys

Type of part	Iron	Carbon steel	Alloy steel	Stainless steel	Tool steel	Aluminum alloys	Copper alloys	Magnesium alloys	Nickel alloys	Zinc alloys	Tin alloys	Lead	Titanium	Precious metals
Extrusions	—	○	○	○	—	●	●	●	○	○	○	○	○	—
Metal stampings	—	●	●	○	—	●	●	○	○	○	—	—	—	●
Metal spinnings	—	●	○	●	—	●	●	○	●	○	○	○	—	—
Cold-headed parts	—	●	○	○	—	●	●	—	○	—	—	○	—	—
Impact extrusions	—	●	○	—	—	●	●	●	○	●	●	●	—	—
Swaged and bent tubing	—	●	●	●	—	●	●	○	●	●	○	—	○	—
Roll-formed sections	—	●	●	●	—	●	●	—	—	●	—	—	—	—
Powder-metal parts	●	○	○	○	○	○	●	—	○	—	—	—	○	—
Forgings	—	●	●	●	○	●	●	●	○	—	—	—	○	—
Screw-machine parts	○	●	○	●	—	●	●	●	●	●	—	—	○	—
Electrical-discharge-machined parts	—	○	○	●	●	○	○	—	—	—	—	—	○	—
Electrochemically machined parts	—	○	●	●	●	○	○	—	●	—	—	—	○	—
Chemically machined parts	—	●	○	●	○	●	●	●	○	—	—	—	●	—
Sand-mold castings	●	○	●	●	○	●	●	●	●	○	○	○	○	—
Permanent-mold castings	●	●	—	—	—	●	●	●	○	○	○	○	—	—
Ceramic-mold castings	●	○	—	—	—	●	●	—	●	○	—	—	—	—
Plaster-mold castings	—	●	—	—	●	●	●	○	○	○	○	○	—	—
Centrifugal castings	●	●	●	—	—	●	●	—	○	●	○	—	—	—
Investment castings	—	●	●	●	●	●	●	○	●	●	○	—	—	○
Die castings	—	—	○	○	○	●	○	●	—	●	○	○	—	—

Material

Note: ●, frequently processed with this method; ○, sometimes processed with this method; —, seldom or never processed with this method.

Source: After J. G. Bralla.

skill, and costs. This part can also be made by cold, warm, or hot forming. One method, for example, is the upsetting of a round bar 25 mm (1 in.) in diameter in a suitable die to form the larger end (heading). Another possibility is the partial extrusion of a 38-mm (1.5-in.) diameter bar, to reduce its diameter to 25 mm. Note that each of these processes shapes the material with little or no material waste.

This part can also be made by the machining of a 38-mm diameter bar stock to obtain the 25-mm diameter section. Machining, however, will take a much longer time than forming, and some material will inevitably be wasted as metal chips. On the other hand, machining does not require special tooling (unlike net-shape processes which generally require special dies), and this operation can easily be carried out on a lathe. Note, finally, that this part could be made in two separate pieces later joined by welding, brazing, or adhesive bonding.

Because of the different operations required in producing the raw materials, costs depend not only on the type of material (ingot, powder, drawn rod, extrusion) but also on its size and shape (Table 5.1). Thus, per unit weight, (a) square bars are more expensive than round bars, (b) cold-rolled plate is more expensive than hot-rolled plate or sheet, (c) hot-rolled bars are much less expensive than powders of the same metal.

Process selection also depends on, in addition to technical requirements, factors such as the required production quantity and production rate (as described in Section 40.6). In summary, it appears that if only a few parts are needed, machining this part is the most economical method. As the production quantity increases, however, producing this part by a heading operation or by cold extrusion would be the proper choice. Joining would be the appropriate choice if the top and bottom pieces of this part needed to be made of different metals.

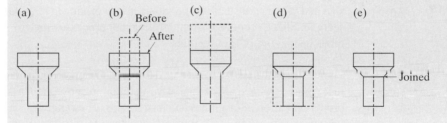

FIGURE 40.2   Various methods of making a simple part: (a) casting or powder metallurgy, (b) forging or upsetting, (c) extrusion, (d) machining, (e) joining two pieces.

40.6 PROCESS CAPABILITIES

Throughout this text, we have seen that each manufacturing process has advantages and limitations. Casting and injection molding, for example, can generally produce more complex shapes than can forging and powder metallurgy (because the molten metal or plastic is capable of filling complex mold and die cavities). On the other hand, forgings can generally be made into complex shapes by subsequent machining and finishing operations, and they have a toughness that is generally superior to that of castings and powder metallurgy products.

Recall that the shape of a product may be such that it can best be fabricated from several parts, by joining them with fasteners or with such techniques as brazing, welding, and adhesive bonding. The reverse may be true for another product: manufacturing it in one

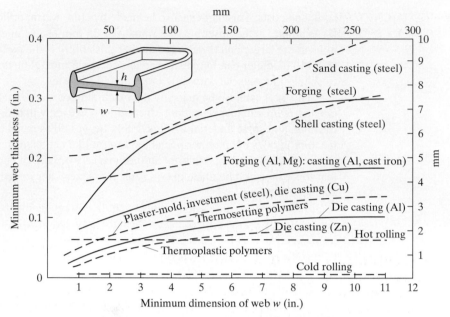

FIGURE 40.3   Manufacturing process capabilities for minimum part dimensions. *Source*: J. A. Schey, *Introduction to Manufacturing Processes* (2d ed.). McGraw–Hill, 1987.

piece may be more economical, because of the significant assembly costs otherwise involved. Other factors that must be considered in process selection are the minimum section size and dimensions that can be satisfactorily produced (Fig. 40.3). For example, very thin sections can be produced by cold rolling, but processes such as sand casting or forging prohibit the making of thin sections.

Dimensional Tolerance and Surface Finish.   The dimensional tolerances and surface finish produced are particularly important in subsequent assembly operations and in the proper operation of machines and instruments. The ranges of surface finish and dimensional tolerance obtained by various manufacturing processes are given throughout the text and are summarized in Figs. 40.4, 35.22, and 35.23. We have seen that in order to obtain finer surface finish and closer tolerances, additional finishing operations, better control of processing parameters, and the use of higher-quality equipment may be required.

The closer the dimensional tolerance required, the higher the cost of manufacturing (Fig. 40.5); also, the finer the surface finish required, the longer the manufacturing time and the higher the product cost (Fig. 40.6). For example, in the machining of aircraft structural members made of titanium alloys, as much as 60% of the cost of machining the part is expended in the final machining pass, in order to maintain proper dimensional tolerances and surface finish.

Unless it is specifically required otherwise by proper technical and economic justification, parts should be made with as rough a surface finish and as wide a tolerance as will be functionally and aesthetically acceptable. In this regard, the importance of continual interaction and communication between the product designer and the manufacturing engineer becomes obvious.

Production Volume.   Depending on the type of product, the *production volume*, or *quantity* (lot size), can vary greatly. For example, paper clips, bolts, washers, spark plugs,

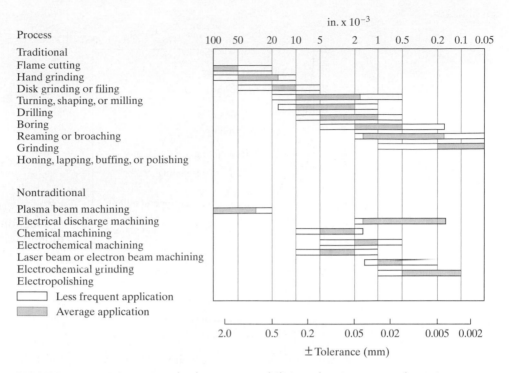

FIGURE 40.4   Dimensional tolerance capabilities of various manufacturing processes.

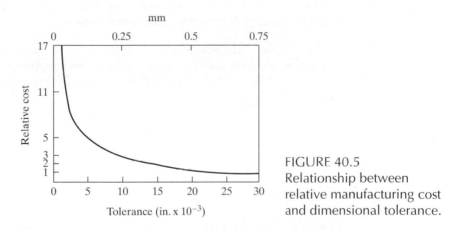

FIGURE 40.5
Relationship between relative manufacturing cost and dimensional tolerance.

bearings, and ball-point pens are produced in very large quantities. On the other hand, jet engines for large commercial aircraft, diesel engines for locomotives, and propellers for cruise ships are manufactured in limited quantities.

Production quantity plays a significant role in process and equipment selection. In fact, an entire manufacturing discipline is devoted to determining mathematically the optimum production quantity, called the **economic order quantity**.

Production Rate.   A significant factor in manufacturing process selection is the *production rate*, defined as the number of pieces to be produced per unit of time (such as per hour, per month, or per year). Such processes as powder metallurgy, die casting, deep

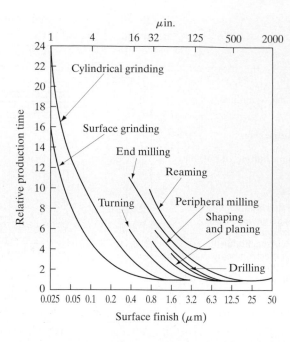

FIGURE 40.6 Relative production time, as a function of surface finish produced by various manufacturing processes. *Source*: American Machinist. See also Fig. 25.33.

drawing, and roll forming are high-production-rate operations. By contrast, sand casting, conventional and electrochemical machining, spinning, superplastic forming, adhesive and diffusion bonding, and the processing of reinforced plastics are relatively slow operations.

These production rates can, of course, be increased by automation or by the use of multiple machines. Note, however, that a lower production rate does not necessarily mean that the manufacturing process is inherently uneconomical.

Lead Time. The selection of a manufacturing process is greatly influenced by the time required to start production, called *lead time*. Such processes as forging, extrusion, die casting, roll forming, and sheet-metal forming typically require extensive (and expensive) dies and tooling.

In contrast, machining and grinding processes generally have a built-in flexibility, and they utilize tooling that can be adapted to most requirements in a relatively short time. Recall also the discussions on machining centers, flexible manufacturing cells, and flexible manufacturing systems, which are capable of responding quickly and effectively to product changes (both in type and in quantity).

Example: Manufacturing a Sheet-Metal Part by Various Methods

We have seen that there is often more than one method of manufacturing a part. Consider, for instance, the following example: forming a simple dish-shaped part from sheet metal (Fig. 40.7). Such a part can be formed by placing a flat piece of sheet metal between a pair of male and female dies, and closing the dies by applying a vertical force in a press (Chapter 16). Parts can be formed at high production rates by this method, generally known as stamping or pressworking.

Assume now that the size of the part is very large, say, 2 m (80 in.) in diameter, and that only 50 parts are required. We now have to reconsider the total operation and ask a number of questions. Is it economical to manufacture a set of dies 2 m in diameter (which are very costly) when the production run (quantity) is so low? Are machines available with sufficient capacity to accommodate such large dies? Does the part have to be made in one piece? What are the alternative methods of manufacturing it?

This part can also be made by welding together smaller pieces of metal formed by other methods (Part V). Note, for example, that ships and municipal water tanks are made by this method. Would a part manufactured by welding be acceptable for its intended purpose? Will it have the required properties and the correct shape after welding, or will it require additional processing?

This part can also be made by explosive forming, as shown in Fig. 40.7b. It will be noted, however, that the deformation of the material in explosive forming takes place at a very high rate. Consequently, several questions have to be asked:

a. Is the material capable of undergoing deformation at high rates without fracture?

b. Does the high rate have any detrimental effect on the final properties of the formed part?

c. Can the dimensional tolerances be held within acceptable limits?

d. Is the life of the die sufficiently long under the high transient pressures generated in this process?

e. Can this operation be performed in a manufacturing plant within a city or should it be carried out in open country?

f. Although explosive forming requires only one die (an obvious advantage), is the overall operation economical?

From this general discussion, it can be appreciated that for each part or component, a similar approach is required to arrive at a conclusion as to which process is the most suitable and economical.

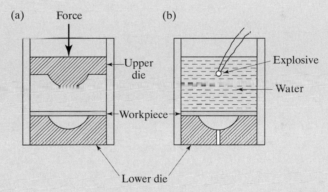

FIGURE 40.7   Two methods of making a dish-shaped sheet-metal part: (a) pressworking, using a male and female die, (b) explosive forming, using one die only.

40.7 MANUFACTURING COSTS

In order for a product to be marketed successfully, its cost must be competitive with that of similar products, particularly in the global marketplace. The total cost of a product consists of several categories, such as material cost, tooling cost, fixed costs, variable costs, direct labor costs, and indirect labor costs.

There are several methods of cost accounting used by manufacturing organizations today. The methodologies of various accounting procedures can be complex (even controversial), and their selection depends on the particular company and its type of operations.

Furthermore, because of the technical and operational factors involved, calculating the individual cost factors is difficult, time consuming, and not always accurate or reliable.

Recent trends in costing systems (**cost justification**) include the following considerations: the intangible benefits of quality improvements and inventory reduction; life-cycle costs; machine usage; the cost of purchasing as compared to that of leasing machinery; the financial risks involved in implementing automation and the new technologies available—all these, and more, must be taken into account.

The costs to a manufacturer that are directly attributable to *product liability* and defense claims have been a matter of concern and discussion among all parties involved. Every modern product has a built-in added cost to cover possible product liability claims. For example, it is estimated that liability suits against car manufacturers in the United States add about $500 to the indirect cost of an automobile, and that 20% of the price of a ladder is attributed to potential product liability costs.

Materials costs are described in Section 40.2, and some cost data are given in various tables throughout this text.

Tooling costs are those involved in making the tools, dies, molds, patterns, and special jigs and fixtures necessary for manufacturing a product. The tooling cost is greatly influenced by the production process selected.

For example, in casting, the tooling cost for die casting is higher than that of sand casting. Similarly, the tooling cost in machining or grinding is much lower than that of powder metallurgy, forging, or extrusion. In machining operations, carbide tools are more expensive than are high-speed steel tools, but their life is longer. If a part is to be manufactured by spinning, the tooling cost for conventional spinning is much lower than that of shear spinning. Tooling for rubber-forming processes is less expensive than that of the die sets (male and female) used for the deep drawing and stamping of sheet metals.

High tooling costs might nonetheless be justified by high volume production of a single item. The expected life of tools and dies and their obsolescence because of product changes are also important considerations.

Fixed costs include the costs of electric power, fuel, taxes on real estate, rent, insurance, and capital (including depreciation and interest). The company must meet these costs regardless of whether or not it made a particular product. Consequently, fixed costs are not sensitive to production volume.

Capital costs represent the investment in buildings, land, machinery, tooling, and equipment; these are major expenses for most manufacturing facilities (Table 40.5). Note the wide range of processes in each category and the fact that some machines cost a million dollars or more. (Coincidentally, the cost per pound of traditional machine tools has historically been approximately equal to that of beef steak; however, this cost can easily double for machinery having computer controls and sophisticated auxiliary equipment.)

As a simple example of capital costs, let's assume that a company has decided to manufacture a variety of valves. A new plant has to be built or an old plant has to be remodeled, and all the necessary machinery, support equipment, and facilities must be purchased. In order to cast and machine the valve bodies, the following items must be purchased: melting furnaces, casting equipment, machine tools, quality control equipment, and related equipment and machinery.

If valve designs are to be modified often or if product lines are likely to vary greatly, the production machinery and equipment must have sufficient flexibility to accommodate these requirements. Machining centers (Chapter 24) and flexible manufacturing cells and systems (Chapter 39) are especially suitable for this purpose.

The equipment and machinery listed are capital cost items, and they require major investment. In view of the generally high equipment costs (see Table 40.5), particularly

TABLE 40.5   Approximate Ranges of Machinery Base Prices

Type of machinery	Price range ($000)	Type of machinery	Price range ($000)
Broaching	10–300	Machining center	50–1000
Drilling	10–100	Mechanical press	20–250
Electrical discharge	30–150	Milling	10–250
Electromagnetic and electrohydraulic	50–150	Ring rolling	500
Fused deposition modeling	60–120		
Gear shaping	100–200		
Grinding		Robots	20–200
Cylindrical	40–150	Roll forming	5–100
Surface	20–100	Rubber forming	50–500
Headers	100–150	Stereolithography	80–200
Injection molding	30–150	Stretch forming	400–>1000
Boring		Transfer machines	100–>1000
Jig	50–150	Welding	
Horizontal boring mill	100–400	Electron beam	200–1000
Flexible manufacturing system	>1000	Spot	10–50
Lathe	10–100	Ultrasonic	50–200
Single- and multi-spindle automatic	30–250		
Vertical turret	100–400		

Note: Prices vary considerably, depending on size, capacity, options, and level of automation and computer controls.

those involving transfer lines and flexible manufacturing cells and systems, high production rates and quantities are necessary to justify such large expenditures and to maintain product costs at or below the all-important competitive level. Lower unit costs can be achieved by continuous production, involving around-the-clock operation, but only as long as demand warrants it. Proper equipment maintenance is essential to ensure high productivity. (See Section 38.2.7.) Any *breakdown of machinery* leading to **downtime** can be very expensive, costing typically from a few hundred dollars per hour to thousands of dollars per hour.

Labor costs are generally divided into direct and indirect costs. The **direct labor cost** is for the labor directly involved in manufacturing the part (*productive labor*). This cost includes all labor, from the time raw materials are first handled to the time when the product is finished. This period is generally referred to as **floor-to-floor time**.

For example, a machine operator picks up a round bar from a bin, machines it into the shape of a threaded rod, and places it into another bin. The direct labor cost is calculated by multiplying the labor rate (hourly wage including benefits) by the time that the worker spends producing the part.

The time required for producing a particular part depends not only on its size, shape, and dimensional accuracy, but also on the workpiece material. For example, in Part IV it was stated that the cutting speeds for high-temperature alloys are lower than those for aluminum or plain-carbon steels. Consequently, the cost of machining aerospace materials is much higher than that for machining the more common alloys, such as those of aluminum and steel.

Indirect labor costs are those that are generated in the servicing of the total manufacturing operation. The total is composed of such activities as supervision, repair, maintenance, quality control, engineering, research, and sales; it also includes the cost of office staff. Because they do not contribute directly to the production of finished parts or they are not chargeable to a specific product, these costs are referred to as **overhead** (**burden rate**) and charged proportionally to all products. The personnel involved in these activities are categorized as **nonproductive labor**.

MANUFACTURING COSTS AND PRODUCTION VOLUME

One of the most significant factors in manufacturing costs is production volume. Obviously, large production volume requires high production rates. High production rates, in turn, require the use of mass-production techniques that involve special machinery (*dedicated machinery*) and employ proportionally less direct labor, as well as of plants that operate on two or three shifts. At the other extreme, small production volume usually means a larger direct labor involvement.

As was described in Section 38.2, *small batch production* is usually done on general-purpose machines, such as lathes, milling machines, and hydraulic presses. The equipment is versatile, and parts with different shapes and sizes can be produced by appropriate changes in the tooling. Direct labor costs are, however, high, because these machines are usually operated by skilled labor.

For larger quantities (*medium-batch production*), these same general-purpose machines can be equipped with various jigs and fixtures or else be computer-controlled. To reduce labor costs further, machining centers and flexible manufacturing systems are important alternatives. Generally, for quantities of 100,000 or more, the machines are designed for specific purposes and they perform a variety of specific operations with very little direct labor.

Cost reduction stems from how the costs described above are interrelated, with **relative costs** depending on many factors. Consequently, the unit cost of the product can vary widely. For example, some parts may be made from expensive materials, but ones that require very little processing (such as minted gold coins). Here, the cost of materials relative to that of direct labor is high.

By contrast, some products may require several complex, expensive production steps to process relatively inexpensive materials (such as carbon steels). For example, an electric motor is made of relatively inexpensive materials, yet many different manufacturing operations are involved in the making of the housing, the rotor, the bearings, the brushes, and other components. In such cases, assembly operations can become a significant portion of the overall cost.

An approximate (but typical) breakdown of costs in manufacturing today is as follows:

Design	5%
Material	50%
Direct Labor	15%
Overhead	30%

In the 1960s, labor accounted for as much as 40% of the production cost; today, it can be as low as 5%, depending on the type of product and the level of automation. Note, in the breakdown above, the very small contribution of the design phase—yet, in the comprehensive sense of *design for manufacture and assembly*, including *concurrent engineering*, the design phase generally has the largest influence on the *quality* and *success* of a product in the marketplace.

Cost reductions can be achieved by a thorough analysis of all the costs incurred in each step in manufacturing a product. The methods employed are described in detail in some of the references in the bibliography at the end of this chapter. We have emphasized the opportunities for cost reduction in various chapters throughout this text. Among these are the following:

a. simplifying part design and the number of subassemblies required;

b. specifying broader dimensional tolerances and allowing rougher surface finish;

c. using less expensive materials;

d. investigating alternative methods of manufacturing;

e. using more efficient machines and equipment.

The introduction of more automation and of up-to-date technology in a manufacturing facility is an obvious means of reducing some types of costs. However, this approach must be undertaken with due care, and only after a thorough **cost-benefit analyses**, with reliable data input and consideration of the technical as well as the human factors involved. Advanced technology implementation (which can be very expensive) should occur only after a complete analysis of the more obvious cost factors, known as **return on investment (ROI)**.

You have undoubtedly noted that, over a period of time, the prices of some products (such as calculators, computers, and digital watches) have decreased, while the prices of other products (such as automobiles, aircraft, houses, and books) have gone up. Such differences generally result from changes in the various component costs over time, including those due to labor, machinery, domestic and international competition, and worldwide economic trends (such as demand, exchange rates, and tariffs), and from the inevitable impact of computers on all aspects of product design and manufacturing.

40.8 VALUE ENGINEERING

There are several areas of activity in manufacturing in which cost reduction is possible. Manufacturing adds **value** to materials as they become discrete products and are then marketed. Because this value is added in individual stages during the creation of the product, utilization of value engineering (*value analysis*, *value control*, and *value management*) is important.

Value engineering is a system that evaluates each step in design, materials, processes, and operations so as to manufacture a product that performs all its intended functions and does so at the lowest possible cost. A monetary value is established for each of two product attributes: (a) **use value**, reflecting the functions of the product and (b) **esteem value** or **prestige value**, reflecting the attractiveness of the product that makes its ownership desirable.

The *value of a product* is then defined as the ratio of product function and performance to the cost of the product. Thus, the goal of value engineering is to obtain maximum performance per unit cost. Value analysis generally consists of the following six phases:

a. the **information** phase, to gather data and determine costs;

b. the **analysis** phase, to define functions and identify problem areas and opportunities;

c. the **creativity** phase, to seek ideas to respond to problems and opportunities, without judging the value of each of these ideas;

d. the **evaluation** phase, to select the ideas to be developed and to identify the costs involved;

    e. the **implementation** phase, to present facts, costs, and values to the company management; to develop a plan; and to motivate positive action, all in order to obtain a commitment of the resources necessary to accomplish the task;

    f. the **review** of the overall value-analysis process and of any adjustments that need to be made.

    Value engineering is an important and all-encompassing interdisciplinary activity. It is usually coordinated by a value engineer and is conducted jointly: by designers; by engineers; by quality control, purchasing, and marketing personnel; and by managers. In order for value engineering to be effective, it must have the full support of a company's top management.

    Implementation of value engineering in manufacturing results in such benefits as significant cost reduction, reduced lead times, better product quality and product performance, reduced product weight and size, and reduced manufacturing times. To properly assess the value of each step in manufacturing a product, several groups of questions have to be asked:

PRODUCT DESIGN

1. Can the product design be simplified without adversely affecting its intended functions? Have all alternative designs been investigated? Can unnecessary features (or some of its components) be eliminated or combined with others? Can the design be made smaller and lighter?

2. Are the dimensional tolerances and surface finish specified necessary? Can they be relaxed?

3. Will the product be difficult to assemble and disassemble for maintenance, repair, or recycling? Is the use of fasteners minimized?

4. Does each component of the product have to be manufactured in the plant? Are some of its parts commercially available as standard items from outside sources?

MATERIALS

5. Do the materials selected have properties that unnecessarily exceed minimum requirements and specifications?

6. Can some materials be replaced by others that are cheaper?

7. Do the materials selected have the proper manufacturing characteristics?

8. Are the raw materials (stock) to be ordered available in standard sizes, dimensions, surface finish, and dimensional tolerances?

9. Is the material supply reliable? Are there likely to be significant price fluctuations?

MANUFACTURING PROCESSES

10. Have all alternative manufacturing processes been investigated?

11. Are the methods chosen economical for the type of material, the shape to be produced, and the required production rate? Can the requirements for dimensional tolerances, surface finish, and product quality be met consistently?

12. Can the part be formed and shaped to final dimensions without requiring the use of material-removal processes? Are machining, secondary processes, and finishing operations necessary?

13. Is the tooling required available in the plant? Can it be purchased as a standard item?

14. Is scrap produced? If so, what is the value of the scrap?

15. Are processing parameters optimized? Have all the automation and computer-control possibilities been explored for all phases of the manufacturing operation? Can group technology be implemented for parts with similar geometric and manufacturing attributes?

16. Are inspection techniques and quality control being implemented properly?

Example: Concurrent Engineering for Intravenous Solution Containers

Baxter Healthcare manufactures over one million intravenous (IV) solution containers every day in the United States, providing critical therapies within the health care industry. Recognizing that patients' lives depend upon the safe delivery of medical solutions, the introduction of new or improved products is highly regulated by internal company standards and external government agencies.

A well-defined product development process provides the framework to meet consistently the regulated quality, reliability, and manufacturing design requirements. More importantly, a concurrent engineering environment catalyzes the development process to minimize development cost and time to market.

In the 1990s, the company focused development efforts on a new set of materials for flexible IV containers. The container system being developed was expected to be more environmentally friendly, compatible with a larger variety of new critical-care drugs, exceed all quality requirements, and remain cost effective. Some of the key design issues shown in the table would allow the product to be safe for patients and maintain economic viability.

Container Product Requirements	Container Processing Requirements
• Provide physical and chemical shelf-life of up to several years without compromising the solution.	• Implement the new product with existing equipment and plant personnel.
• Allow for addition and mixing of various drug solutions in the hospital or alternate site pharmacy.	• Allow product manufacturing at rates up to one million per day without additional production cells.
• Provide a surface for printing of fade, flake, and smear proof labeling.	• Maintain fabrication throughput at over 60 containers per minute per machine.
• Provide a surface for adherence of various pressure-sensitive adhesive labels at room, refrigerated, and elevated temperatures.	• Maintain printing and filling speeds over 120 per minute.
• Withstand pressurization when an infusion device (cuff) is placed on the container for controlled solution delivery to the patient.	• Withstand steam sterilization temperatures, pressures, and times. • Allow packing in cartons that provide fullest density of pallet loading.
• Maintain compatibility with available administration set devices.	• Withstand air and ground shipping and handling through areas as diverse as Arizona and Alaska.

The Matrixed Team.   Given the extensive requirements, Baxter formed a multifunctional team of over 25 individuals. As the requirements and goals indicated, marketing, manufacturing, and development team members worked side by side with specialists in materials science, regulatory affairs, clinical affairs, toxicology, chemical stability, and sterility assurance. The product team members each recognized their responsibility for the success or failure of the product design effort.

The Active Team.   All team members contributed to the master requirements definition during the product conceptualization phase. All team members led and communicated the test and development activities within their respective fields to the team at large during the development phase. All disciplines offered and accepted peer-review criticism of product or process designs at major development steps. All team members assured that the product designs, quality assessment methods, and fabrication techniques were transferred efficiently to the designated plants during the implementation phase. The product team avoided costly design iterations and revisions and minimized duplicative efforts by maintaining a matrixed, active team throughout the process.

The Virtual Team.   Many team members were located at manufacturing plants or development centers throughout northern Illinois and the greater United States. By necessity, team meetings leveraged teleconference and videoconference capabilities, which also minimized travel expense. Electronic mail access provided rapid and broad communication of impending issues and resolutions. A company-wide intranet site was developed to share documents and design prints, which assured that all locations were utilizing the most recent project advancements. The team customized emerging communication technologies to enhance the concurrent development of new materials, processing, and fabrication technologies.

Finished Goods.   The engineering effort of the matrixed, active, and virtual team resulted in a product introduction within three years. New materials and components were developed which met all product and process requirements and ultimately satisfied patient needs. The new product was transparent and patient-care professionals continued to use their existing training and well-practiced techniques. Disposal of the product was streamlined; the new materials can be safely disposed of or recycled. Reliability and user satisfaction remained high. The new materials were compatible with an extended array of solution format drugs packaged in IV containers. Indeed, team success will be measured by the number of additional products introduced in the following years.

Source: Keith Anderson, Baxter Healthcare Corporation, and Shelly Petronis, formerly Baxter Healthcare Corporation, currently Zimmer Inc., a Bristol-Myers Squibb Company.

SUMMARY

- Competitive aspects of production and costs are among the most significant considerations in manufacturing. Regardless of how well a product meets design specifications and quality standards, it must also meet economic criteria in order to be competitive in the domestic and global marketplace.

- The total cost of a product includes several elements, such as cost of materials, of tooling, of capital, of labor, and of overhead. Materials costs can be reduced through careful selection, so that the least expensive material can be identified and used, without compromising design and service requirements, functions, specifications, and standards for good product quality.

- Substitution of materials, modification of product design, and relaxing of dimensional tolerance and surface finish requirements are important methods of cost reduction.

- Guidelines for designing products for economic production have been established. Although labor costs are continually becoming an increasingly smaller percentage of production costs, they can be reduced further through the use of automated and computer-controlled machinery.

- Automation requires major capital expenditures; however, a well-planned production facility can significantly improve productivity.

TRENDS

- The highly competitive nature of domestic and global markets will continue to challenge manufacturing engineers to reduce product costs. Recent studies show major potential for cost reduction in materials and in overhead; one opportunity lies in company organization changes.
- There is an increased need to reduce the time required for product development and market introduction.
- Material substitution and product design modifications are subjects that continue to be studied closely and to be implemented at increasingly higher rates. Various software packages are now available to assist in the selection process and in the optimization of manufacturing operations.
- Value engineering continues to be a powerful tool in reducing costs while improving product function and performance.
- Concurrent engineering; design for manufacture, assembly, disassembly, and recycling; and environmentally conscious manufacturing: all these will continue to be highly important aspects of a company's activities.

KEY TERMS

Burden rate

Capital costs

Cost-benefit analysis

Cost justification

Cost reduction

Dedicated machines

Direct labor

Downtime

Economic order quantity

Fixed costs

Floor-to-floor time

Indirect labor

Lead time

Nonproductive labor

Overhead

Process capabilities

Production rate

Production volume

Relative costs

Return on investment

Scrap

Smart databases

Value

Value Engineering

BIBLIOGRAPHY

Anderson, D.M., *Design for Manufacturability, Optimizing Cost, Quality, and Time-to-Market*. CIM Press, 1991.

ASM Handbook, Vol. 20: *Materials Selection and Design*. ASM International, 1997.

Baxter, M., *Product Design: A Practical Guide to Systematic Methods of New Product Development*. Chapman & Hall, 1995.

Billatos, S., and N. Basaly, *Green Technology and Design for the Environment*. Taylor & Francis, 1997.

Bleach, R., *Product Design and Corporate Strategy: Managing the Connection for Competitive Advantage*. McGraw–Hill, 1993.

Boothroyd, G., P. Dewhurst, and W. Knight, *Product Design for Manufacture and Assembly*. Marcel Dekker, 1994.

Bralla, J.G., *Design for Manufacturability Handbook*. McGraw–Hill, 1999.

Cattanach, R.E. (ed.), *The Handbook of Environmentally Conscious Manufacturing*. Irwin, 1994.

Corbett, J., M. Donner, J. Maleka, and C. Pym, *Design for Manufacture: Strategies, Principles and Techniques*. Addison–Wesley, 1991.

Demaid, A., and J.H.W. DeWit (eds.), *Case Studies in Manufacturing With Advanced Materials*. North–Holland, 1995.

Dettmer, W.H., *Breaking the Constraints to World-Class Performance*. ASQ Quality Press, 1998.

Erhorn, C., and J. Stark, *Competing by Design: Creating Value and Market Advantage in New Product Development*. Wiley, 1995.

Farag, M.M., *Materials Selection for Engineering Design*. Prentice Hall, 1997.

Fleischer, M., and J.K. Liker, *Concurrent Engineering Effectiveness: Integrating Product Development Across Organizations*. Hanser Gardner, 1997.

Ghosh, A., Y. Miyamoto, I. Reimanis, and J.J. Lannutti, *Functionally Graded Materials: Manufacture, Properties, and Applications*. American Ceramic Society, 1997.

Graedel, T.E., and B.R. Allenby, *Design for Environment*. Prentice Hall, 1997.

Halevi, G., *Restructuring the Manufacturing Process: Applying the Matrix Method*. St. Lucie Press, 1998.

Hartley, J.R., and S. Okamoto, *Concurrent Engineering: Shortening Lead Times, Raising Quality, and Lowering Costs*. Productivity Press, 1998.

Kmetovicz, R.E., *New Product Development: Design and Analysis*. Wiley, 1992.

Kusiak, A., (ed.), *Concurrent Engineering: Automation, Tools and Techniques*. Wiley, 1993.

Lesco, J., *Industrial Design: Guide to Materials and Manufacturing*. Van Nostrand Reinhold, 1998.

Magrab, E.B., *Integrated Product and Process Design and Development: The Product Realization Process*. CRC Press, 1997.

Mather, H., *Competitive Manufacturing* (2d ed.), CRC Press, 1998.

Paashuis, V., *The Organization of Integrated Product Development*. Springer, 1997.

Park, R.J., *Value Engineering: A Plan for Invention*. St. Lucie Press, 1999.

Park, S., *Robust Design and Analysis for Quality Engineering*. Chapman & Hall, 1997.

Prasad, B., *Concurrent Engineering Fundamentals* (2 vols.). Prentice Hall, 1995.

Pugh, S., D. Clausing, and R. Andrade (eds.), *Creating Innovative Products Using Total Design*. Addison–Wesley, 1996.

Pugh, S., *Total Design: Integrated Methods for Successful Product Engineering*. Addison–Wesley, 1991.

Ranky, P.G., *An Introduction to Concurrent/Simultaneous Engineering: Methods, Tools, and Case Studies*. CIMWare USA, 1997.

Rhyder, R.F., *Manufacturing Process Design and Optimization*. Marcel Dekker, 1997.

Roozenburg, N.F.M., and J. Eekels, *Product Design: Fundamentals and Methods*. Wiley, 1995.

Schey, J.A., *Introduction to Manufacturing Processes* (3d ed.). McGraw–Hill, 1999.

Shina, S.G. (ed.), *Successful Implementation of Concurrent Engineering Products and Processes*. Wiley, 1997.

Sims, E.R., Jr., *Precision Manufacturing Costing*. Marcel Dekker, 1995.

Stoll, H.W., *Product Design Methods and Practices*. Marcel Dekker, 1999.

Swift, K.G., and J.D. Booker, *Process Selection: From Design to Manufacture*. Wiley, 1997.

Tool and Manufacturing Engineers Handbook (4th ed.), Vol. 7: *Continuous Improvement*. Society of Manufacturing Engineers, 1993.

Tool and Manufacturing Engineers Handbook (4th ed.), Vol. 6: *Design for Manufacturability*. Society of Manufacturing Engineers, 1992.

Tool and Manufacturing Engineers Handbook (4th ed.), Vol 5: *Manufacturing Engineering Management*. Society of Manufacturing Engineers, 1988.

Ulrich, K.T., and S.D. Eppinger, *Product Design and Development*. McGraw–Hill, 1995.

Walker, J.M. (ed.), *Handbook of Manufacturing Engineering*. Marcel Dekker, 1996.

Wang, B., *Integrated Product, Process, and Enterprise Design*. Chapman & Hall, 1997.

Wenzel, H., M. Hauschild, and L. Alting, *Environmental Assessment of Products*, Vol. 1. Chapman & Hall, 1997.

Wenzel, H., and M. Hauschild, *Environmental Assessment of Products*, Vol. 2. Chapman & Hall, 1997.

Woeppel, M., *The Manufacturer's Guide to Implementing the Theory of Constraints*. St. Lucie Press, 1999.

REVIEW QUESTIONS

40.1 List and describe the major considerations involved in selecting materials for products.

40.2 Why is a knowledge of available shapes of materials important? Give five different examples.

40.3 Describe what is meant by the "manufacturing properties" of materials. Give three examples demonstrating the importance of this information.

40.4 Why is material substitution an important aspect of manufacturing engineering? Give five examples from your own experience or observations.

40.5 Why has material substitution been particularly critical in the automotive and aerospace industries?

40.6 What factors are involved in the selection of manufacturing processes? Explain why they are important.

40.7 What is meant by *process capabilities*? Select four different and specific manufacturing processes, and describe their capabilities.

40.8 Is production volume significant in process selection? Explain your answer.

40.9 Discuss the advantages of long lead times, if any, in production.

40.10 What is meant by *economic order quantity*?

40.11 Describe the costs involved in manufacturing. Explain how you could reduce each of these costs.

40.12 What is value engineering? What are its benefits?

40.13 What is meant by *tradeoff*? Why is it important in manufacturing?

40.14 Explain the difference between direct labor cost and indirect labor cost.

QUALITATIVE PROBLEMS

40.15 Explain why the larger the quantity per package of food products, the lower the cost per unit weight.

40.16 Explain why the value of the scrap produced in a manufacturing process depends on the type of material.

40.17 Comment on the magnitude and range of scrap shown in Table 40.2.

40.18 Present your observations concerning the information given in Table 40.4.

40.19 Other than the size of the machine, what factors are involved in the range of prices in each machine category shown in Table 40.5?

40.20 Explain how the high cost of some of the machinery listed in Table 40.5 can be justified.

40.21 Explain the reasons for the relative positions of the curves shown in Fig. 40.3.

40.22 What factors are involved in the shape of the curve shown in Fig. 40.5?

40.23 Make suggestions as to how to reduce the dependence of production time on surface finish (shown in Fig. 40.6).

40.24 Is it always desirable to purchase stock that is close to the final dimensions of a part to be manufactured? Explain your answer, and give some examples.

40.25 What course of action would you take if the supply of a raw material selected for a product line became unreliable?

40.26 Describe the potential problems involved in reducing the quantity of materials in products.

40.27 Present your thoughts concerning the replacement of aluminum beverage cans with steel ones.

40.28 There is a period, between the time that an employee is hired and the time that the employee finishes with training, during which the employee is paid and receives benefits but produces nothing. Where should such costs be placed among the categories given in this chapter?

40.29 Why is there a strong desire in industry to practice near-net-shape manufacturing?

40.30 Estimate the position of the following processes in Fig. 40.6: (a) centerless grinding, (b) electrochemical machining, (c) chemical milling, (d) extrusion.

40.31 Figure 40.5 gives a relationship between relative cost and tolerance. What properties of manufactured parts could be substituted for dimensional tolerance and still give the same shape of the relative cost curve?

40.32 In Section 40.7 there is a breakdown of costs in today's manufacturing environment, maintaining that design costs contribute only 5% to the total cost. Explain why this claim is reasonable.

SYNTHESIS AND DESIGN

40.33 As you can see, Table 40.4, on manufacturing processes, includes only metals and their alloys. Based on the information given in this book and other sources, prepare a similar table for nonmetallic materials, including ceramics, plastics, reinforced plastics, and metal-matrix and ceramic-matrix composite materials.

40.34 Review Fig. 6 in the General Introduction, and present your thoughts concerning the two flow charts. Would you want to make any modifications, and if so, what would they be?

40.35 Over the years, numerous consumer products have become obsolete, or nearly so, such as rotary-dial telephones, analog radio tuners, turntables, and vacuum tubes. In compensation, many new products have entered the market. Make a comprehensive list of obsolete products and one of new products. Comment on the reasons for the changes you observe. Discuss how different manufacturing methods and systems have evolved in order to produce the new products.

40.36 Select three different products, and make a survey of the changes in their prices over the past ten years. Discuss the reasons for the changes.

40.37 Figure 2.1 shows the shape of a typical tensile-test specimen having a round cross-section. Assuming that the starting material (stock) is a round rod, and that only one specimen is needed, discuss the processes and the machinery by which the specimen can be made, including their relative advantages and limitations. Describe how the process you selected can be changed for economical production as the number of specimens required increases.

40.38 Table 40.1 listed several materials and their commercially available shapes. By asking suppliers of materials, extend this list to include the following: (a) titanium, (b) superalloys, (c) lead, (d) tungsten, (e) amorphous metals.

40.39 Select three different products commonly found in homes. State your opinions about (a) what materials were used in each product, and why, and (b) how the products were made, and why those particular manufacturing processes were used.

40.40 Inspect the components under the hood of your automobile. Identify several parts that have been produced to net-shape or near-net-shape condition. Comment on the design and production aspects of these parts and on how the manufacturer achieved the near-net-shape condition.

40.41 Comment on the differences, if any, between the designs, the materials, and the processing and assembly methods used for making such products as hand tools and ladders for professional use and those for consumer use.

40.42 Other than casting, which processes could be used (singly or in combination) in the making of the automotive parts shown in Fig. 11.2? Would they be economical?

40.43 Discuss production and assembly methods that can be used to build the structures for the presses shown in Fig. 16.47.

40.44 The capabilities of some machining processes are shown in Fig. 22.1. Inspect the various shapes produced, and suggest alternative processes. Comment on the properties of materials that would influence your suggestions.

40.45 If the dimensions of the part in Problem 40.48 were (a) ten times larger, (b) one hundred times larger, how different would your answer be? Explain your responses.

40.46 Figure 10 in the General Introduction shows a steel mounting bracket that can be manufactured either by casting or by the stamping of sheet metal. Describe the manufacturing sequence and processes that would be involved in making the part by each of the two methods. Also, comment on the comparative costs involved. Can you suggest other methods of manufacturing this part? Explain your answers.

40.47 Two jet engines are shown, in Fig. 1 in the General Introduction, and in Fig. 6.1. On the basis of the topics covered in this text, select any three individual components of such an engine and describe the materials and processes that you would use in making them in quantities of, say, 1000. Remember that these parts must be manufactured at minimum cost, yet maintain their quality, integrity, and reliability.

40.48 Discuss the tradeoffs involved in selecting between the two materials for each of the applications listed here:

    a. Steel vs. plastic paper clips

    b. Forged vs. cast crankshafts

    c. Forged vs. powder-metallurgy connecting rods

    d. Plastic vs. sheet-metal light-switch plates

    e. Glass vs. metal water pitchers

    f. Sheet metal vs. cast hubcaps

    g. Steel vs. copper nails

    h. Wood vs. metal handle for hammers

    i. Sheet metal vs. reinforced plastic chairs

Also, discuss the typical conditions to which these products are subjected in their normal use.

40.49 Discuss the manufacturing process (or processes) suitable for making the products listed in Problem 40.48. Explain whether they would require additional operations (such as coating, plating, heat treating, and finishing). If so, make recommendations and give the reasons for them.

40.50 Discuss the factors that influence the choice between the following pairs of processes:

    a. sand casting vs. die casting of a fractional electric-motor housing;

    b. machining vs. forming of a large gear;

c.   forging vs. powder-metallurgy production of a gear;

d.   casting vs. stamping a sheet-metal frying pan;

e.   making outdoor furniture from aluminum tubing vs. cast iron;

f.   welding vs. casting of machine-tool structures;

g.   thread-rolling vs. machining of a bolt for a high-strength application;

h.   thermoforming a plastic vs. molding a thermoset to make a fan blade for a household fan.

40.51 The following figure shows a sheet-metal part made of steel. Discuss how this part could be made, and how your selection of a manufacturing process may change (a) as the number of parts required increases from ten, to thousands or (b) as the length of the part increases from 2 m to 20 m.

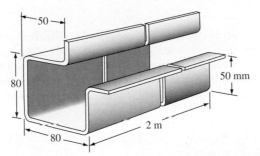

40.52 The part shown in the figure below is a carbon-steel segment (partial) gear. The smaller hole at the bottom is for clamping the part onto a round shaft, using a screw and a nut. Suggest a sequence of processes to make this part, considering such factors as the effect of the number of parts required, of dimensional tolerances, and of surface finish. Discuss such processes as machining from a bar stock, extrusion, forging, and powder metallurgy.

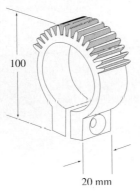

40.53 The part shown below is a cable terminal and is made of 304 stainless steel. The cable is slipped into the hole on the left, and the cylindrical end of the part is swaged over the cable to secure it. Suggest processes to make this part. How else can you attach the cable other than by swaging? Explain your answers.

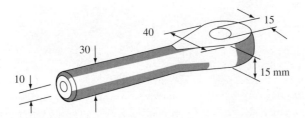

40.54 Several methods can be used to make the part shown in the figure below. List these methods, and, for each one, explain such factors as the machinery and equipment needed, the amount of scrap produced, the strength of the part, etc. Also comment on how different your answers would be if the material were (a) ferrous, (b) nonferrous, (c) thermoplastic, (d) thermoset.

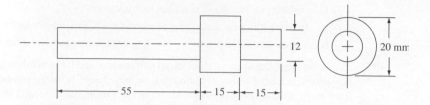

40.55 A common electric outlet box made of sheet metal, is shown in the first following figure, and its thirteen individual components in the second. Inspect such a box, and present your thoughts on the materials and the manufacturing processes used to make this box. Do you have any recommendations for design changes to simplify the manufacture and assembly of this box? Explain your suggestions. Also, inspect such boxes that are instead made of plastics, and present your thoughts.

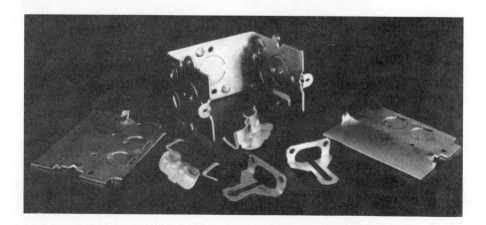

40.56 The following figure shows a cutaway view of a meat grinder. Recommend appropriate materials and manufacturing processes for the labeled components. *Source for illustration*: Triodyne Inc.

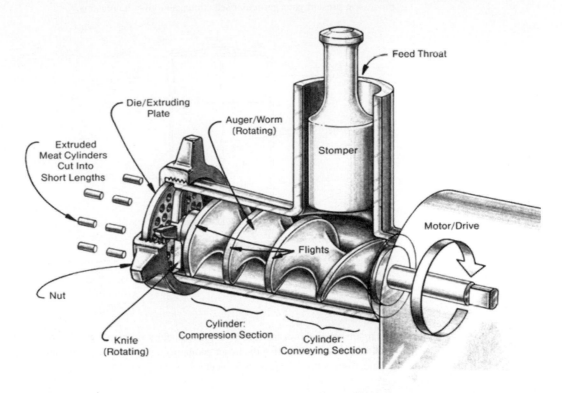

40.57 The following illustration shows various components of a modular artificial knee, which allows surgeons to choose the particular components that best fit an individual patient's needs. Choose any three components, and describe in detail suitable materials and manufacturing processes for producing them. *Source for illustration:* Zimmer, Inc.

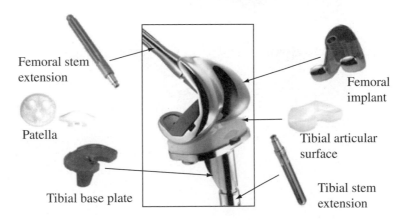

40.58 A schematic illustration of an automatic electric coffee maker follows. For each of its components, suggest a suitable material and a manufacturing process. If there are several candidate materials and processes, present your particular selections, and give the reasons.

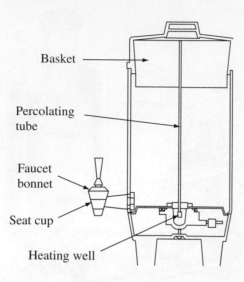

Basket

Percolating tube

Faucet bonnet

Seat cup

Heating well

40.59 The figure below shows an outdoor gas grill with three burners. Describe the materials and processes you would use in manufacturing the major components of this product, including racks, gas tank, burners, and lid. Comment on the reasons for your selections. *Source for illustration*: Weber-Stephen Product Co.

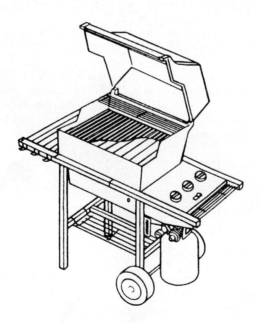

40.60 The components of a staple gun are shown in the figure below. Select five different parts and, for each, suggest materials and processes to make it. *Source for illustration*: Arrow Fastener Co., Inc.

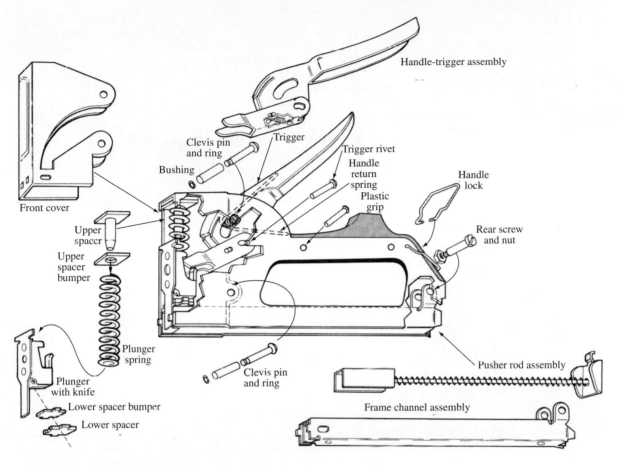

Handle-trigger assembly

Trigger

Clevis pin and ring

Bushing

Front cover

Upper spacer

Upper spacer bumper

Plunger spring

Plunger with knife

Lower spacer bumper

Lower spacer

Trigger rivet

Handle return spring

Plastic grip

Handle lock

Rear screw and nut

Clevis pin and ring

Pusher rod assembly

Frame channel assembly

40.61 The illustration below shows a rotary walk-behind power mower with a gasoline engine. Select five different components of this product, and suggest suitable materials and processes for making them.

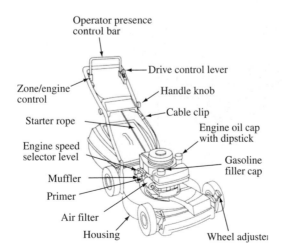

Operator presence control bar

Drive control lever

Zone/engine control

Handle knob

Cable clip

Starter rope

Engine oil cap with dipstick

Engine speed selector level

Gasoline filler cap

Muffler

Primer

Air filter

Housing

Wheel adjuster

40.62 The below figure shows the components of an electric hand drill. Select five components in this product, and explain in detail (a) suitable materials and (b) the processes by which these components can be made economically.

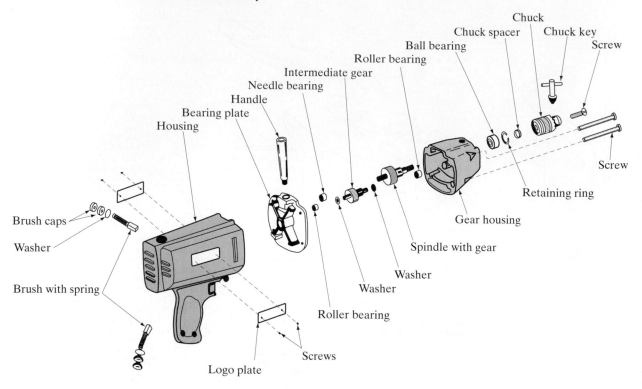

40.63 The following illustration shows a dog sled used in competitive racing. Choose any three components, and describe their manufacture and their assembly into the sled. Choose suitable materials for these parts, considering that they will be exposed to extreme cold. Illustration courtesy of Alyeska Sled Dog Products.

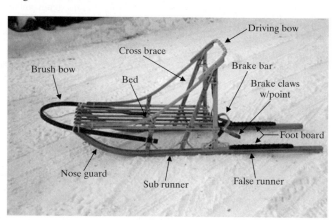

Index

Flexible
 assembly, 1060
 automation, 1028
 fixturing, 1055
 manufacturing cell, 1087
 manufacturing system, 25, 1028, 1088
Flexure. *See* Bending
Flint, 205
Float glass, 467
Floating-zone method, 291
Flood cooling, 587
Floor-to-floor time, 1121
Flow
 lines, 1028
 stress, 344
 turning, 424
Fluid flow, in casting, 246
Fluid forming, 423
Fluidity, 249
 tests, 250
Fluidized bed, 131
Fluid-to-fluid extrusion, 380
Fluorocarbons, 192
Flute, 628
Fluted reamer, 637
Flux, 138, 292, 777, 841, 848
Flux-cored arc welding, 783
Fly cutting, 657
Flyer plate, 812
Foam casting, 495
Foam molding, 495
Foil, 320
Folds, 871
Follow rest, 609
Force fits, 966
Forced vibration, 695
Forces. See individual processes
Forgeability, 355
Forging, 340
 closed-die, 345
 economics, 363
 forces, 344, 347
 impression-die, 344
 isothermal, 350
 machines, 357
 open-die, 342
 orbital, 350
 precision, 346
Form
 block, 416
 grinding, 722
 milling, 656, 672
 tools, 596, 609
Formability. See individual processes
Forming, 318
 tap, 334
 See also individual processes
Forming-limit diagrams, 405
Forward
 extrusion, 371
 spinning, 425
Foundation, 694
Foundries, 294
Four-high mill, 329
Four-jaw chuck, 607
Four-point bending, 68
Four-slide machine, 412
Fourteen points, Deming, 975
Fracture, 76
 of abrasive bonds, 717
 of abrasive grains, 717
 brittle, 78
 of cutting tools, 556
 ductile, 76
 paths, 79
 See also Cracking; Defects
Fracture stress, 58
Fracture surfaces, 77, 79, 228
 in shearing, 405
 See also individual processes

Fracture toughness test, welded joints, 832
Framework systems, 1097
Free bending. See Air bending
Free-cutting wheels, 716
Free-machining steels, 561
Freezing range, 244
Frequency distribution, 984
Fretting corrosion, 890
Friability, 707, 717
Friction, 883
 angle, 538
 in ceramics, 884
 measurement, 885
 in metals, 883
 in metalworking (see individual processes)
 in plastics, 884
 sawing, 402, 670
 stir welding, 803
Friction welding, 801
 inertia, 802
 linear, 803
 stir, 803
Front tension, 324
Fuel gas, 775
Full annealing, 126
Fullerenes, 215, 895
Fullering, 345
Full-mold process, 274
Functional
 dimension, 964
 layout, 1080
Furnace brazing, 841
Furnaces
 atmosphere, 131
 heat treating, 130
 melting, 139, 292
Fused alumina, 707
Fused deposition modeling, 516
Fusion welding processes, 775
 weld joints, 759, 820
Fuzzy logic, 1099
Gage
 blocks, 958
 length, 57
 maker's rule, 961
 numbers, rolling, 328
Gages, 958
Gain, 874, 1038
 scheduling, 1038
Galena, 170
Galling, 888
Gallium arsenide, 926
Galvanic corrosion, 97
Galvanized steel, 914
Galvanizing, 170, 914
Gang drilling, 636
Gantry robot, 1047
Gantry robot-controlled extruder, 516
Gap bed lathe, 606
Garnet, 707
Gas metal-arc welding, 782
Gas tungsten-arc welding, 788
Gases
 in casting, 255
 shielding (see individual processes)
Gate, 247, 266
Gating system, 246
Gaussian, 984
Gear
 honing, 676
 lapping, 676
 rolling, 334, 675
 shaper, 673
Gears
 bevel, 674
 finishing, 675
 form cutting, 672
 generating, 673
 teeth measurement, 955
Generative CAPP system, 1077

Gentle grinding, 716
Geometric
 dimensioning, 961
 modeling, 1073
 tolerancing, 961, 965
Germanium, 925
Giant molecules, 179
Glass
 ceramics, 214
 fibers, 224, 468
 former, 212
 lubrication, 376, 896
 point, 185
 tempered, 471
 wool, 468
Glasses, 212
 as bonding agent, 708
 as lubricants, 376, 896
 processing, 466
 properties, 213
 strengthening, 470
Glass-transition temperature, 184
Glassy behavior, 184
Glaze, 465
Glazing, 465, 915
 of grinding wheels, 718
Global competitiveness, 28, 33
Globular transfer, 783
GO gage, 958
Gold, 171
Grade
 bonded abrasives, 711
 gage blocks, 958
Grain, 45
 abrasive, 707
 boundaries, 43, 45
 columnar, 243
 depth of cut, 713
 flow pattern, 349, 356, 378
 force, 714
 growth, 50
Grain size, 46, 404
Grain boundary
 embrittlement, 47
 sliding, 47, 73
Grain structure, metal casting, 242, 245, 280
Grand average, 986
Granite-epoxy composite, 691
Graphite, 214
 fibers, 224
 lubricant, 895
Graphitization, 113
Gravity
 drop hammer, 359
 effects in casting, 246
 segregation, 246
Gray cast iron, 114, 310
Greases, 894
Green
 ceramics, 462
 compact, 447
 design, 31
 molding sand, 265
 strength, 453
Grindability, 720
Grinding
 economics, 738
 fluids, 729
 forces, 713
 mechanics, 712
 operations, 721
 ratio, 719
 specific energy, 714
 temperature, 715
Grinding wheels, 708
 dressing, 718
 glazing, 718
 loading, 718
 safety, 728
 selection, 720
 See also Bonded abrasives

 wear, 716
Grit, abrasive, 707
Grit blasting, 736
Grooving, 610
Group
 layout, 1080
 machine cell, 1086
 technology, 25, 1079
Guards, 1007
Gun
 drilling, 630
 trepanning, 631
Gutter, 354
Hacksaws, 669
Hafnium nitride, 582
Half nut, 623
Hammers, forging, 359
Hand lay-up, 500
Hard
 automation, 1027
 chromium plating, 912
 facing, 906
 mold casting, 281
 turning, 621
Hard-acting wheel, 719
Hardenability, 120
 bands, 121
Hardeners, 293
Hardening
 case, 124, 906
 explosive, 905
 spark, 906
Hardness, 68
 bonded abrasives, 711
 conversion chart, 72
 hot, 71
 indenters, 69
 scales, 72, 209
 tests, 69
 of various materials, 72
 vs. strength, 71
Hard-wired controls, 1031
Hastelloy, 165, 166
Hazard, 446, 1006. See also individual processes
Head, 661
Headers, 348
Heading, 348
Headstock, 606
Heat, 84
Heat checking, 285, 330, 716
Heat transfer, in casting, 250
Heat treatment, 102
 ferrous alloys, 115
 furnaces, 130
 nonferrous alloys, 122
Heat-affected zone, 821
Heat-affected zone, 871
Heat-resistant alloys. *See* Superalloys
Helicopter blades, 231
Helix angle, 628
Helmets, composite, 232
Hematite, 138
Hemming, 413
Heterogeneous nucleation, 246
Heuristic, 1096
Hexagonal close-packed, 40
Hexapod, 694
Hierarchical coding, 1083
High removal rate machining, 616
High temperature superconductors, 472
High-carbon steel, 146
High-efficiency machining range, 700
High-energy-rate machines, 359
High-frequency resistance welding, 808
High-pressure coolants, 588
High-speed
 automatic assembly, 1057

LIST OF EXAMPLES IN TEXT